SOCIAL SCIENCES

(continued on back cover)

COLLEGE MATHEMATICS

FOR THE MANAGERIAL AND SOCIAL SCIENCES

SOO TANG TAN
Stonehill College

PRINDLE, WEBER & SCHMIDT
Boston, Massachusetts

To Pat, Bill and Michael

PWS PUBLISHERS

Prindle, Weber & Schmidt • Willard Grant Press • Duxbury Press •
Statler Office Building • 20 Providence Street • Boston, Massachusetts 02116

PWS Publishers is a division of Wadsworth, Inc.

87 86 85 84 83 — 10 9 8 7 6 5 4 3 2

ISBN 0-87150-354-9

Library of Congress Cataloging in Publication Data

Tan, Soo Tang.
College mathematics for the managerial and social sciences.

Includes index.
1. Mathematics—1961- 2. Management—Mathematics. 3. Social sciences—Mathematics.
I. Title.
QA37.2.T36 1983 510 82-18036
ISBN 0-87150-354-9

Printed in the United States of America

Cover photograph by Frank Wing/Stock Boston.

Cover and text design by Sara Waller. Typeset by J. W. Arrowsmith Ltd. Artwork by Julie Gecha. Covers printed by New England Book Components, Inc. Text printed and bound by R. R. Donnelley & Sons Co.

CONTENTS

1

SETS AND COORDINATE GEOMETRY

1.1

Sets

The word *set* permeates much of modern mathematics. For our purpose a set is a well defined aggregate or collection of objects. Thus, a set is not just any collection of objects, but it must be well defined in the sense that given any object we should be able to determine whether or not it belongs to the collection.

EXAMPLE 1.1 By our interpretation of the term each of the following are sets:

(a) The set of days in the year 1981.

(b) The set of members of the New York Philharmonic Orchestra.

(c) The set of Ford Pintos produced in the year 1976.

(d) The set of negative integers.*

(e) The set of real numbers.*

The following collections of objects are not well defined and are therefore not sets:

(f) The collection of fine champagne.

(g) The collection of intelligent people.

(h) The collection of hot days this month. ■

element

The objects of a set are called the *elements* or *members* of the set and are usually denoted by lowercase letters a, b, $c, \ldots$, while the sets themselves are

* *See Appendix 1.*

usually denoted by uppercase letters A, B, C, ... The elements of a set may be displayed by listing each element between braces. For example, using the *roster notation*, the set A consisting of the first three letters of the English alphabet is written

roster notation

$$A = \{a, b, c\}$$

The set B of all letters of the alphabet may be written as

$$B = \{a, b, c, \ldots, z\}$$

set-builder notation

Another kind of set notation commonly used is the so-called *set-builder notation*. Here, a rule is given that describes the definite property or properties to be satisfied by an object x to qualify for membership in the set. Using this notation, the set B is written as

$$B = \{x \mid x \text{ is a letter of the English alphabet}\}$$

and read "B is the set of all elements x such that x is a letter of the English alphabet."

EXAMPLE 1.2 List the elements of the set

$$A = \{x \mid x \text{ is a day of the week}\}$$

SOLUTION

$$A = \{\text{Monday, Tuesday, Wednesday, Thursday, Friday, Saturday, Sunday}\}$$ ■

EXAMPLE 1.3 Write the set

$$B = \{5, 6, 7, 8, 9\}$$

in set-builder notation.

SOLUTION

$$B = \{x \mid x \text{ is an integer greater than 4 but less than 10}\}$$ ■

EXAMPLE 1.4 List the elements of the set

$$C = \{x \mid x + 3 = 0;\ x \text{ an integer}\}$$

SOLUTION Only one integer satisfies the condition $x + 3 = 0$, namely, the integer -3. Thus, the set C consists of only the number -3, and $C = \{-3\}$. ■

EXAMPLE 1.5 List the elements of the set of letters in the word *MISSISSIPPI*.

SOLUTION The required set is $\{I, M, P, S\}$. Note that, by convention, an element belonging to a set is listed only once. ■

If a is an element of a set A we write $a \in A$, read "a belongs to A" or "a is an element of A". If, on the other hand, the element a does not belong to the set A then we write $a \notin A$, read "a does not belong to A". For example, if $A = \{1, 2, 3, 4, 5\}$ then $3 \in A$ but $6 \notin A$.

Two sets A and B are *equal*, written $A = B$, if and only if they have exactly the same elements.

EXAMPLE 1.6 Let A, B, and C be the sets

$$A = \{a, e, i, o, u\}$$
$$B = \{a, i, o, e, u\}$$
$$C = \{a, e, i, o\}$$

Then $A = B$ since they both contain exactly the same elements. Note that the order in which the elements are displayed is immaterial. Also, $A \neq C$ since $u \in A$ but $u \notin C$. Similarly, we conclude that $B \neq C$. ■

subset

If every element of a set A is also an element of a set B, then we say A is a *subset* of B and write $A \subseteq B$. In terms of this definition, two sets A and B are equal if and only if (1) $A \subseteq B$ and (2) $B \subseteq A$. This may be verified by the reader (see Exercise set 1.1, problem 14).

EXAMPLE 1.7 Referring to Example 1.6, we find that $C \subseteq B$ since every element of C is also an element of B. Also, if D is the set

$$D = \{a, e, i, o, x\}$$

then D is not a subset of A, written $D \nsubseteq A$, since $x \in D$ but $x \notin A$. Observe that $A \nsubseteq D$ as well since $u \in A$ but $u \notin D$. ■

proper subset

If A and B are sets such that $A \subseteq B$ but $A \neq B$, then we say A is a *proper subset* of B. In other words, a set A is a proper subset of a set B, written $A \subset B$, if (1) $A \subseteq B$ and (2) there exists at least one element in B that is not in A. The latter condition states that the set A is properly "smaller" than the set B.

EXAMPLE 1.8 Let $A = \{1, 2, 3, 4, 5, 6\}$ and $B = \{2, 4, 6\}$. Then B is a proper subset of A since (1) $B \subseteq A$, which is easily verified, and (2) there exists at least one element in A which is not in B—for example, the element 1. ■

empty or null set

In the course of our work we will encounter the set that has no elements in it. Such a set is called the *empty set* or the *null set* and is designated by the symbol

$\varnothing$. Following are examples of the empty set.

(*a*) $\{x \mid x$ is a person who stands over twelve feet tall$\}$

(*b*) $\{x \mid x$ is a horse that flies$\}$

(*c*) $\{x \mid x+2=0;\ x$ is a positive integer$\}$

Observe that the empty set, $\varnothing$, is a subset of every set. To see this, let A be any set. If $\varnothing \not\subseteq A$ then there must exist at least one element in $\varnothing$ which is not in A. But $\varnothing$ is empty! This contradiction establishes the assertion.

EXAMPLE 1.9 List all subsets of the set $A = \{a, b, c\}$.

SOLUTION The subsets are

$$\varnothing, \{a\}, \{b\}, \{c\}, \{a, b\}, \{a, c\}, \{b, c\}, \{a, b, c\}$$ ■

universal set

In contrast with the empty set we have the other extreme, the notion of a *largest* set. The *universal set* is the set of all elements of interest in a particular discussion. It is the largest in the sense that all sets considered in the discussion of the problem are subsets of the universal set. Of course, different universal sets are associated with different problems.

EXAMPLE 1.10 (**a**) If the problem at hand is to determine the ratio of female to male students in a college, then a logical choice of a universal set is the set comprising the whole student-body of the college.

(**b**) If the problem is to determine the ratio of female to male students in the Business Department of the college in part (**a**), then the set of all students in the Business Department may be chosen as the universal set. ■

Observe that the universal set in Example 1.10 (**a**) will serve as a universal set for the problem posed in Example 1.10 (**b**) but not vice-versa. Note also that the set comprising the student-body of another college will not serve as a universal set for the problem in Example 1.10 (**a**), nor can the set of business students in a different college be taken as a universal set for the problem in Example 1.10 (**b**). In practice, the choice of a universal set for a particular problem is usually clear from the context of the problem, and in this case the set need not be mentioned specifically.

Venn diagram

A visual representation of sets is realized through the use of *Venn diagrams.* They are of considerable help in the understanding of the concepts introduced earlier as well as in the solution of problems involving sets. The universal set U is represented by a rectangle and subsets of U are represented by regions lying inside the rectangle.

EXAMPLE 1.11 Use Venn diagrams to illustrate the following statements:

(**a**) The two sets A and B are equal.

(**b**) The set A is a proper subset of the set B.

(**c**) The sets A and B are not subsets of each other.

PREFACE

This book treats the standard topics in finite mathematics and calculus that are normally covered in a two-semester course for students in the managerial and social sciences. Students in other disciplines who do not have a finite mathematics and calculus requirement will also find this book suitable.

Our objective is two-fold. First, to provide the student with the background in the quantitative techniques that are necessary for a better understanding and appreciation of the courses normally taken in his or her undergraduate training. Second, to lay the foundation for more advanced courses such as statistics and operations research. We have hoped to accomplish this by striking a careful balance between theory and applications. However, we took special care to ensure that this does not compromise the mathematical content and accuracy. The applications are drawn from many fields but the greater emphasis is in the areas of business and economics. Every effort was made to make the applications interesting, relevant, and up-to-date. Numerous examples and solved problems are used to motivate each new concept or result, in order to facilitate the student's comprehension of the new material. Each section is accompanied by an extensive set of exercises, which contains an ample set of problems of a routine computational nature that will help the student master new techniques. The routine problems are followed by an extensive set of applications-oriented problems, which test the student's mastery of the topics. The only prerequisite for understanding this book is a year of high school algebra. An algebra review section included in the appendix of the book is provided for any student who wishes to review this material.

Since the book contains more than ample material for the usual year long finite mathematics with calculus course, the instructor may be flexible in choosing the topics most suitable for his or her course. The following chart on chapter dependency is provided to help the instructor design a course that is most suitable for the intended audience.

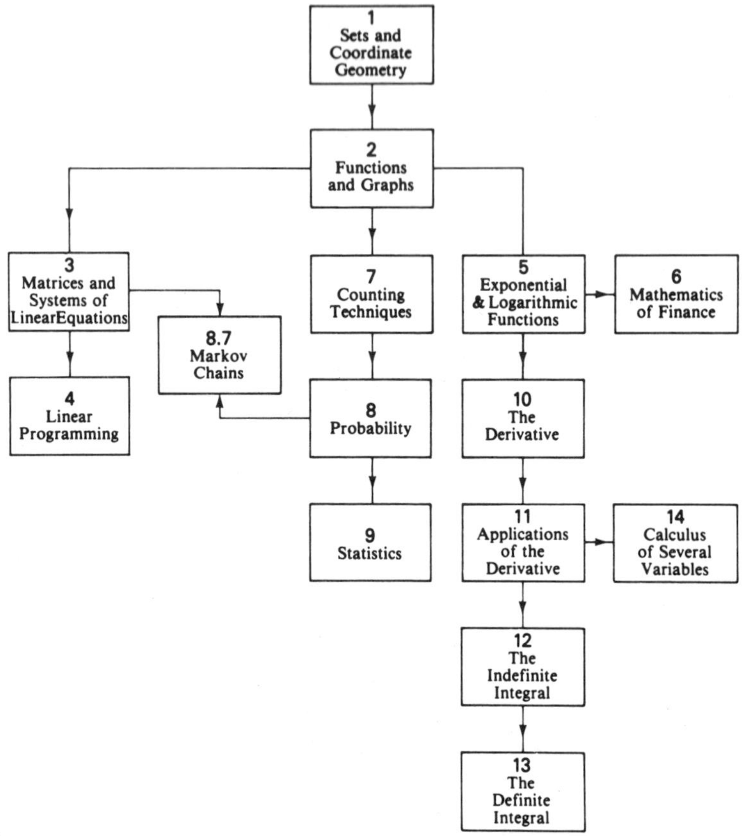

Finally, I wish to express my personal appreciation to each of the following reviewers whose many suggestions helped make a much improved end product: Professors Wilson Banks, Illinois State University; Richard H. Bouldin, University of Georgia; Chris C. Braunschweiger, Marquette University; David H. Carlson, Oregon State University; Duane E. Deal, Ball State University; Joseph W. Fitzpatrick, University of Texas at El Paso; Jimmy R. Hickey, Baylor University; Franz X. Hiergeist, West Virginia University; James R. McKinney, California State Polytechnic University at Pomona; Stephen J. Merrill, Marquette University; W. Kent Moore, Valdosta State College; Robert A. Moreland, Texas Tech. University; Richard D. Porter, Northeastern University; Derald D. Rothman, Moorhead State University; Wesley J. Rozema, Northern Arizona University; Wesley Sanders, Sam Houston State University; and James Wallen, Moorhead State University.

I also wish to thank my colleagues: Professors A. Atmar and W. Norko for reading portions of my manuscript and for their helpful suggestions; Professor L. Hegarty for class testing my manuscript and Dean R. Kruse for his enthusiastic support of this project.

My thanks also go to the editorial and production staff of Prindle, Weber & Schmidt: David Pallai, Mary LeQuesne, and Sara Waller, for their assistance and cooperation in the development and production of this book.

11. List all subsets of the set

$$A = \{\text{IBM, U.S. Steel, Union Carbide, Boeing}\}$$

Which of these are proper subsets of A?

12. Find the *smallest* possible set, (that is, the set with the least number of elements) that contains the given sets as subsets:

(***a***) $\{1, 2\}, \{1, 3, 4\}, \{4, 6, 8, 10\}$

(***b***) $\{1, 2, 4\}, \{a, b\}$

(***c***) {Jill, John, Jack}, {Susan, Sharon}

(***d***) {GM, Ford, Chrysler}, {Daimler-Benz, Volkswagen}, {Toyota, Datsun}

13. Suppose that $A \subset B$ and $B \subset C$, where A and B are any two sets. What conclusion can be drawn regarding the sets A and C?

****14.*** Verify the assertion made in the text: two sets A and B are equal if and only if (1)$A \subseteq B$ and (2) $B \subseteq A$.

15. Use Venn diagrams to represent the following relationships:

(***a***) $A \subset B$ and $B \subset C$.

(***b***) $A \subset U$ and $B \subset U$, where A and B have no elements in common.

(***c***) The sets A, B, and C are equal.

16. Let U denote the set of all students who applied for admission to the freshman class at Faber College for the oncoming academic year and let

$$A = \{x \in U \mid x \text{ is a successful applicant}\}$$
$$B = \{x \in U \mid x \text{ is a female student who enrolled in the freshman class}\}$$
$$C = \{x \in U \mid x \text{ is a male student who enrolled in the freshman class}\}$$

(***a***) Use Venn Diagrams to represent the sets U, A, B, and C.

(***b***) Determine whether the following statements are true or false

(***1***) $A \subseteq B$ (***2***) $B \subset A$ (***3***) $C \subset B$

1.2 Algebra of Sets

Having introduced the concept of a set, our next task is to consider operations on sets; that is, to consider ways in which sets may be combined to yield other sets. The operations to be defined enable us to combine sets in much the same way the operations of addition and multiplication enable us to combine numbers to obtain other numbers. This leads to a mathematical system with a sufficiently rich structure to enable us to solve many problems of practical interest. In what follows all sets are assumed to be subsets of a given universal set U.

union of sets

Let A and B be sets. The *union of A and B*, written $A \cup B$ and read "A union B", is the set of all elements that belong to either A or B or both. In set-builder notation

$$A \cup B = \{x \mid x \in A \text{ or } x \in B \text{ or both}\}$$

The shaded portion of the Venn diagram (Figure 1.2) depicts the set $A \cup B$.

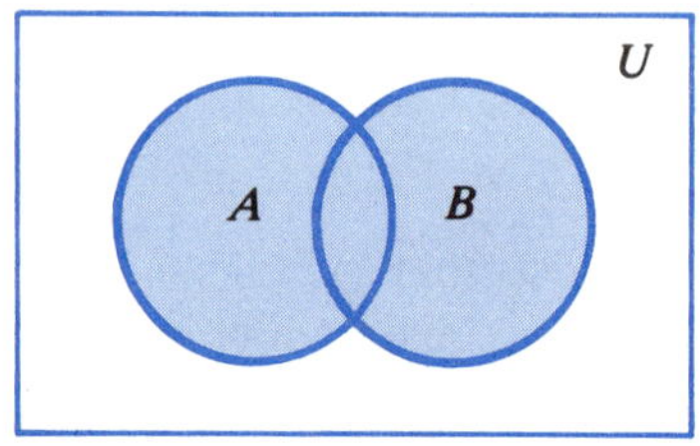

Figure 1.2

EXAMPLE 1.12 If $A = \{a, b, c\}$ and $B = \{a, c, d\}$ then $A \cup B = \{a, b, c, d\}$. ■

intersection of sets

The set of elements in common with the sets A and B, written $A \cap B$ and read "A intersect B," is called the *intersection of A and B*. In short,

$$A \cap B = \{x \mid x \in A \textit{ and } x \in B\}$$

The shaded portion of the Venn diagram (Figure 1.3) depicts the set $A \cap B$.

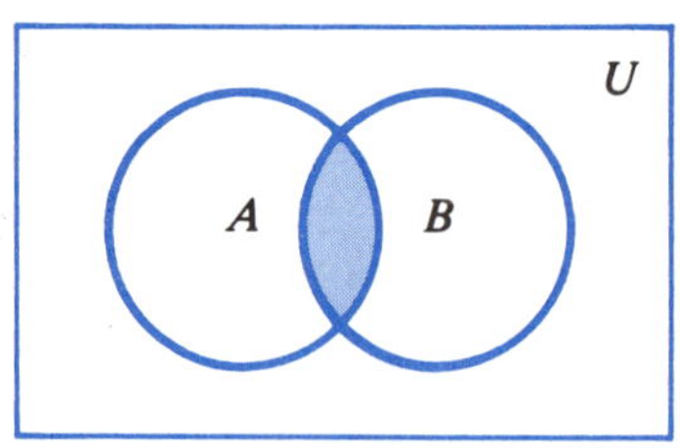

Figure 1.3

EXAMPLE 1.13 Let $A = \{a, b, c\}$ and $B = \{a, c, d\}$. Then $A \cap B = \{a, c\}$. (Compare results with Example 1.12.) ■

EXAMPLE 1.14 Let $A = \{1, 3, 5, 7, 9\}$ and $B = \{2, 4, 6, 8, 10\}$. Then $A \cap B = \varnothing$. ■

disjoint sets

The two sets of Example 1.14 have null intersection. In general, the sets A and B are said to be *disjoint* if they have no elements in common, that is, if $A \cap B = \varnothing$.

EXAMPLE 1.15 If U is the set of all students in the classroom and $M = \{x \in U \mid x \text{ is male}\}$, $F = \{x \in U \mid x \text{ is female}\}$, then $F \cap M = \varnothing$ so that F and M are disjoint. ■

complement of a set Let U be a universal set and suppose A is a subset of U. Then the set of all elements in U that are not in A comprise a set A^c called the *complement of A*. In short,

$$A^c = \{x \mid x \in U, x \notin A\}.$$

The shaded portion of the Venn diagram (Figure 1.4) shows the set A^c.

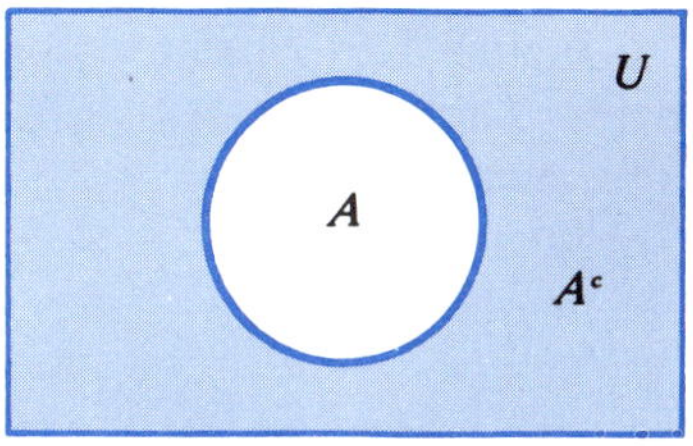

Figure 1.4

EXAMPLE 1.16 Let $U = \{1, 2, 3, 4, 5, 6, 7, 8, 9, 10\}$ and $A = \{2, 4, 6, 8, 10\}$. Then $A^c = \{1, 3, 5, 7, 9\}$. ■

The following rules hold for the operation of complementation. You should have little difficulty verifying them.

$$U^c = \varnothing$$
$$\varnothing^c = U$$
$$A \cup A^c = U$$
$$A \cap A^c = \varnothing$$
$$(A^c)^c = A$$

The following rules govern the operations on sets. Let U be a universal set. If A, B, and C are arbitrary subsets of U, then

$A \cup B = B \cup A$	*Commutative Law for Union*
$A \cap B = B \cap A$	*Commutative Law for Intersection*
$A \cup (B \cup C) = (A \cup B) \cup C$	*Associative Law for Union*
$A \cap (B \cap C) = (A \cap B) \cap C$	*Associative Law for Intersection*
$A \cup (B \cap C) = (A \cup B) \cap (A \cup C)$	*Distributive Law for Union*
$A \cap (B \cup C) = (A \cap B) \cup (A \cap C)$	*Distributive Law for Intersection*

(1.1) $(A \cup B)^c = A^c \cap B^c$

(1.2) $(A \cap B)^c = A^c \cup B^c$

DeMorgan's Laws The last two results are called *DeMorgan's Laws*. Equation (1.1) states that the complement of the union of two sets is equal to the intersection of their complements. Equation (1.2) states that the complement of the intersection of two sets is equal to the union of their complements.

Although all of the above results may be proven rigorously, we shall be content with demonstrating the plausibility of Equation (1.2) through the use of Venn diagrams, as the following example illustrates.

EXAMPLE 1.17 Using Venn diagrams show that

$$(A \cap B)^c = A^c \cup B^c$$

SOLUTION $(A \cap B)^c$ is the set of elements in U but not in $A \cap B$ and is thus the shaded region shown in Figure 1.5. Next, A^c and B^c are shown in Figure 1.6(a) and 1.6(b) respectively. Their union, $A^c \cup B^c$, is easily seen to be equivalent to $(A \cap B)^c$ by referring once again to Figure 1.5.

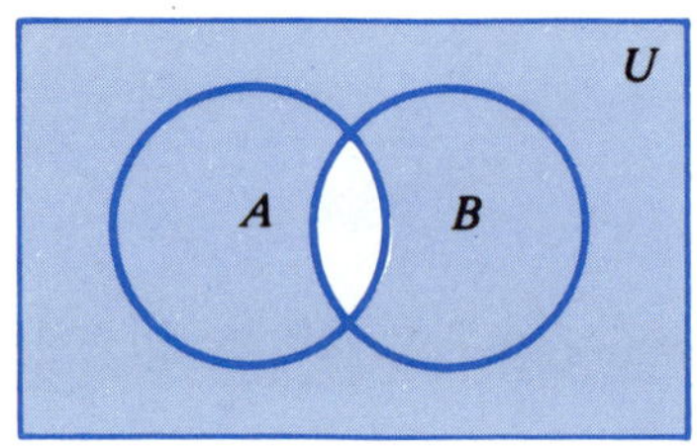

Figure 1.5

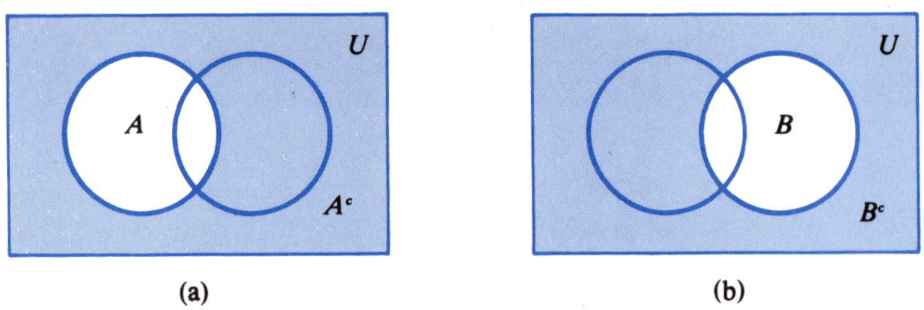

Figure 1.6

EXAMPLE 1.18 Let $U = \{1, 2, 3, 4, 5, 6, 7, 8, 9, 10\}$, $A = \{1, 2, 4, 8, 9\}$, and $B = \{3, 4, 5, 6, 8\}$. Verify by direct computation that $(A \cup B)^c = A^c \cap B^c$.

SOLUTION $A \cup B = \{1, 2, 3, 4, 5, 6, 8, 9\}$ so $(A \cup B)^c = \{7, 10\}$. On the other hand, $A^c = \{3, 5, 6, 7, 10\}$ and $B^c = \{1, 2, 7, 9, 10\}$ so that $A^c \cap B^c = \{7, 10\}$. The required result follows. ■

EXAMPLE 1.19 Let $A = \{1, 3, 4, 5, 8, 10\}$, $B = \{1, 2, 4, 6, 9\}$, and $C = \{2, 4, 6, 8\}$. Verify by direct computation that $A \cap (B \cup C) = (A \cap B) \cup (A \cap C)$.

SOLUTION $B \cup C = \{1, 2, 4, 6, 8, 9\}$, so $A \cap (B \cup C) = \{1, 4, 8\}$. On the other hand, we find $A \cap B = \{1, 4\}$ and $A \cap C = \{4, 8\}$ so that $(A \cap B) \cup (A \cap C) = \{1, 4, 8\}$ and the desired result follows. ■

EXAMPLE 1.20 Let U denote the set of all cars in a car dealer's lot.

Let $A = \{x \in U \mid x \text{ is equipped with automatic transmission}\}$
$B = \{x \in U \mid x \text{ is equipped with factory-installed air conditioning}\}$
$C = \{x \in U \mid x \text{ is equipped with power steering}\}$

Find an expression in terms of A, B, and C for each of the following sets:

(a) The set of cars with at least one of the given options.

(b) The set of cars with exactly one of the given options.

(c) The set of cars with automatic transmission and power steering but no air conditioning.

SOLUTION **(a)** The set of cars with at least one of the given options is $A \cup B \cup C$ (Figure 1.7 part a).

(b) The set of cars with automatic transmission only is given by $A \cap B^c \cap C^c$. Similarly, we find that the set of cars with air conditioning only is given by $B \cap C^c \cap A^c$, whereas the set of cars with power steering only is given by $C \cap A^c \cap B^c$. Thus, the set of cars with exactly one of the given options is $(A \cap B^c \cap C^c) \cup (B \cap C^c \cap A^c) \cup (C \cap A^c \cap B^c)$ (Figure 1.7 part b).

(c) The set of cars with automatic transmission and power steering but no air conditioning is given by $A \cap C \cap B^c$ (Figure 1.7 part c).

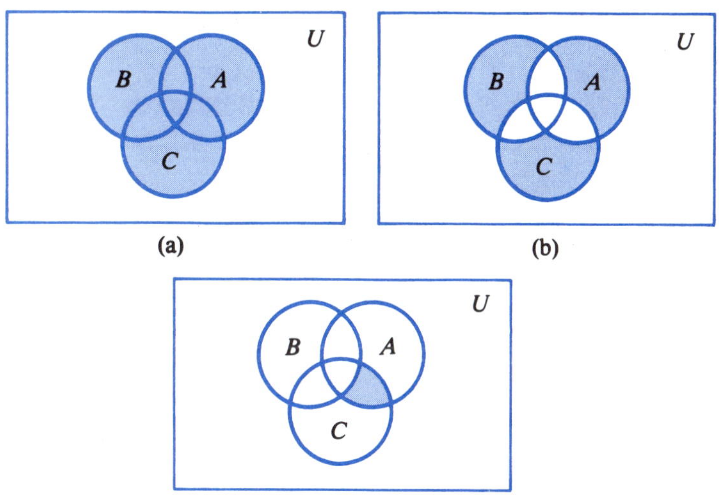

(a) (b) (c)

Figure 1.7 ■

1.2 EXERCISES

1. Shade the portion of the figure shown on p. 12 that represents each of the following sets:

(a) $A \cap B^c$	***(b)*** $A^c \cap B$	***(c)*** $A^c \cap B^c$
(d) $(A \cup B)^c$	***(e)*** $A^c \cup B^c$	***(f)*** $(A \cap B)^c$

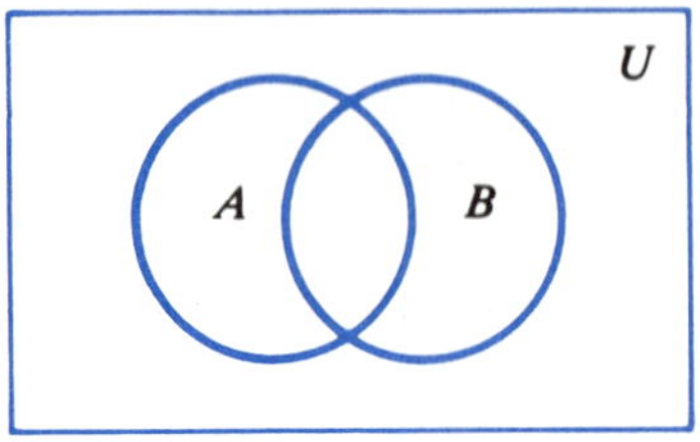

2. Shade the portion of the figure shown below that represents each of the following sets:

(*a*) $A \cup B \cup C$ (*b*) $A \cap B \cap C$ (*c*) $A \cap B \cap C^c$

(*d*) $A^c \cap B \cap C$ (*e*) $A \cap B^c \cap C$ (*f*) $A^c \cap B^c \cap C^c$

(*g*) $(A \cup B)^c \cap C$ (*h*) $A \cup (B \cap C)^c$ (*i*) $(A \cup B \cup C)^c$

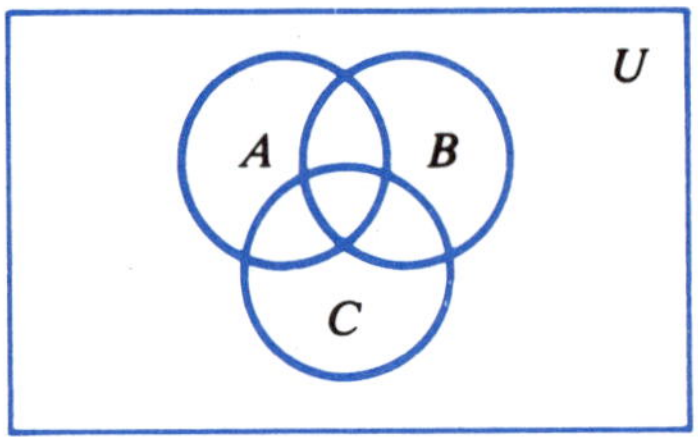

3. Let $U = \{1, 2, 3, 4, 5, 6, 7, 8, 9, 10\}$, $A = \{1, 3, 5, 7, 9\}$, $B = \{2, 4, 6, 8, 10\}$, and $C = \{1, 2, 4, 5, 8, 9\}$. Find the following sets:

(*a*) A^c (*b*) $B \cup C$ (*c*) $C \cup C^c$

(*d*) $C \cap C^c$ (*e*) $A \cup (B \cap C)$ (*f*) $(A \cap C)^c$

(*g*) $(A \cap B) \cup C$ (*h*) $(A \cap B \cap C)^c$ (*i*) $(A \cup B \cup C)^c$

(*j*) $A^c \cap (B \cap C^c)$ (*k*) $(A \cup B^c) \cup (B \cap C^c)$ (*l*) $(A \cup B)^c \cap C^c$

4. Determine if the following pairs of sets are disjoint:

(*a*) $\{1, 2, 3, 4\}, \{4, 5, 6, 7\}$ (*b*) $\{a, c, e, g\}, \{b, d, f\}$

(*c*) $\varnothing, \{1, 3, 5\}$ (*d*) $\{0, 1, 3, 4\}, \{0, 2, 5, 7\}$

(*e*) {Michael, William}, {Jane, Michael, Mary}

5. Let U denote the set of all employees at the Universal Life Insurance Company. Let

$$T = \{x \in U \mid x \text{ drinks tea}\}$$
$$C = \{x \in U \mid x \text{ drinks coffee}\}$$

Describe each of the following sets in words:

(*a*) T^c (*b*) C^c (*c*) $T \cup C$

(*d*) $T \cap C$ (*e*) $T \cap C^c$ (*f*) $T^c \cap C$

(*g*) $T^c \cap C^c$ (*h*) $(T \cup C)^c$ (*i*) $(T \cap C)^c$

6. Refer to Example 1.20. Find an expression in terms of A, B, and C for each of the following sets:

(*a*) The set of cars with all three of the given options.

(*b*) The set of cars with exactly two of the given options.

(*c*) The set of cars with at least two of the given options.

(*d*) The set of cars with automatic transmission and power steering but no air conditioning.

(*e*) The set of cars with none of the three given options.

7. Let U denote the set of all employees in a hospital. Let

$$N = \{x \in U \mid x \text{ is a nurse}\}$$
$$D = \{x \in U \mid x \text{ is a doctor}\}$$
$$A = \{x \in U \mid x \text{ is an administrator}\}$$
$$M = \{x \in U \mid x \text{ is a male}\}$$
$$F = \{x \in U \mid x \text{ is a female}\}$$

Describe each of the following sets in words:

(*a*) D^c (*b*) N^c (*c*) $N \cup D$

(*d*) $D \cap A$ (*e*) $N \cap M$ (*f*) $D \cap M^c$

(*g*) $N \cap F$ (*h*) $D^c \cap F$ (*i*) $(D \cup N)^c$

8. Let U denote the set of all students in the Business College of a certain university and let

$$A = \{x \in U \mid x \text{ had taken a course in accounting}\}$$
$$B = \{x \in U \mid x \text{ had taken a course in economics}\}$$
$$C = \{x \in U \mid x \text{ had taken a course in marketing}\}$$

Write the set that represents each of the following statements:

(*a*) The set of students who have not had a course in economics.

(*b*) The set of students who have had courses in accounting and economics.

(*c*) The set of students who have had courses in accounting and economics but not marketing.

(*d*) The set of students who have had courses in economics but not courses in accounting or marketing.

(*e*) The set of students who have had at least one of the three courses.

(*f*) The set of students who have had all three of the courses.

9. Use Venn diagrams to illustrate each of the following:

(*a*) $A \subset A \cup B$ and $B \subset A \cup B$ (*b*) $A \cap B \subset A$ and $A \cap B \subset B$

10. Using Venn diagrams, show that

(*a*) $A \cup (B \cup C) = (A \cup B) \cup C$ (*b*) $A \cap (B \cap C) = (A \cap B) \cap C$

(*c*) $A \cap (B \cup C) = (A \cap B) \cup (A \cap C)$ (*d*) $(A \cup B)^c = A^c \cap B^c$

11. Let $U=\{1,2,3,4,5,6,7,8,9,10\}$, $A=\{1,3,5,7,9\}$, $B=\{1,2,4,7,8\}$, and $C=\{2,4,6,8\}$. Verify by direct computation each of the equations appearing in problem 10.

12. With reference to the accompanying figure, find the points that belong to each of the following sets.

(***a***) $A\cup B$	(***b***) $A\cap B$	(***c***) $A\cap(B\cup C)$
(***d***) $(B\cup C)^c$	(***e***) A^c	(***f***) $(B\cap C)^c$
(***g***) $(A\cup B\cup C)^c$	(***h***) $(A\cap B)\cap C^c$	(***i***) $(A^c\cap C^c)\cup(B^c\cap C^c)$

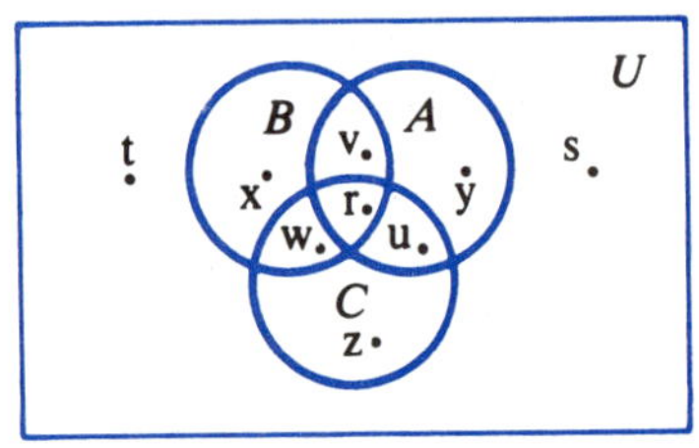

1.3

Real Numbers and Inequalities

The system of real numbers plays a fundamental role throughout this book. This system is made up of the set of real numbers together with the usual operations of addition, subtraction, multiplication and division. We shall assume that you are familiar with the rules governing these algebraic operations (see Appendix I).

number line

It is convenient and fruitful to have a geometrical representation of the set of real numbers. This is realized through using the *number line*, which is constructed as follows: Arbitrarily select a point on a straight line to represent the number 0. This point is called the *origin*. If the line is placed horizontally, then a point at a convenient distance to the right of the origin is chosen to represent the number 1. Points to the right of 0 that are integral multiples of this unit length represent the positive integers while such points to the left of 0 represent the negative integers. Nonintegral numbers are represented by points having distances from 0 that are in the proper proportions.

origin

In this manner a one-to-one correspondence is set up between the set of real numbers and the set of points on the line. All the positive numbers lie to the right of the origin and all the negative numbers lie to the left of the origin (see Figure 1.8).

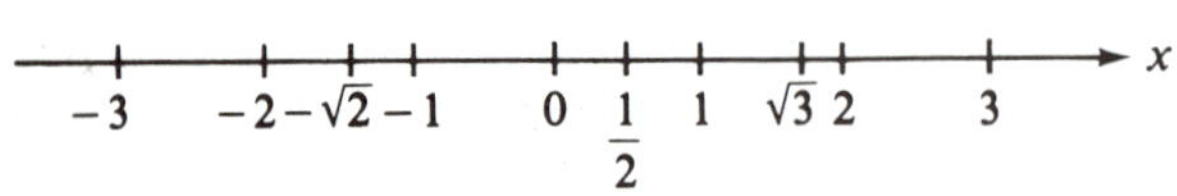

Figure 1.8

In much of our later work, we shall restrict our attention to certain subsets of the set of real numbers. For example, if x denotes the number of cars rolling off an assembly line per day in an automobile assembly plant, then x must be nonnegative, that is, $x \geq 0$. Taking this example one step further, suppose management decides that the daily production of cars in the plant is not to exceed 200, then x must satisfy the inequality $0 \leq x \leq 200$. More generally, we are interested in the following subsets of real numbers.

open, closed, and half-open intervals

A set of real numbers x, satisfying $a < x < b$, where a and b are fixed and distinct numbers, is called an *open interval* (a, b). Thus, the interval (a, b) consists of the set of all numbers lying strictly between a and b. A set of real numbers x, satisfying the inequalities $a \leq x \leq b$ is called a *closed interval* $[a, b]$. (The square brackets indicate that the endpoints a and b belong to the set.) A set of real numbers x, satisfying the inequalities $a \leq x < b$ or $a < x \leq b$ is called a *half-open interval* $[a, b)$ or $(a, b]$. A single term, *interval*, encompasses open, closed, and half-open intervals. Figure 1.9 illustrates the intervals $(-2, 1)$, $[-1, 2]$, $(1/2, 3]$ and $[-1/2, 3)$.

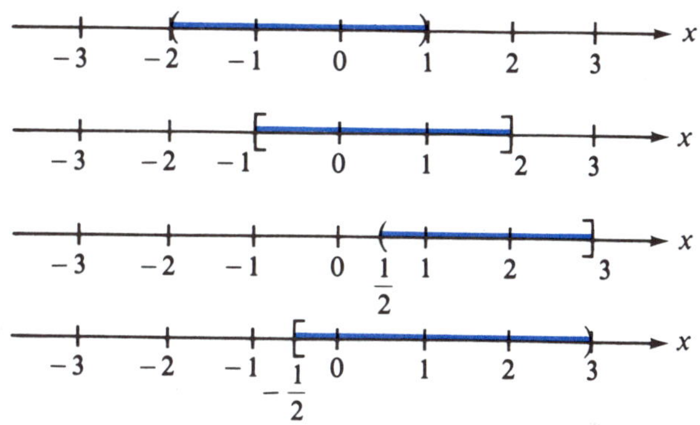

Figure 1.9

finite and infinite intervals

Besides the *finite intervals* defined above we will encounter *infinite intervals*. Examples of infinite intervals are the half-lines (a, ∞), $[a, \infty)$, $(-\infty, a)$, and $(-\infty, a]$ defined by the set of all real numbers satisfying $x > a$, $x \geq a$, $x < a$, and $x \leq a$, respectively. The symbol ∞, called infinity, is not a real number. It is used here only for notational purposes in conjunction with the definition of infinite intervals. The notation $(-\infty, \infty)$ is used for the set of real numbers x since, by definition, the inequalities $-\infty < x < \infty$ hold for any real number x. The infinite intervals $(2, \infty)$ and $(-\infty, 1/2]$ are pictured in Figure 1.10.

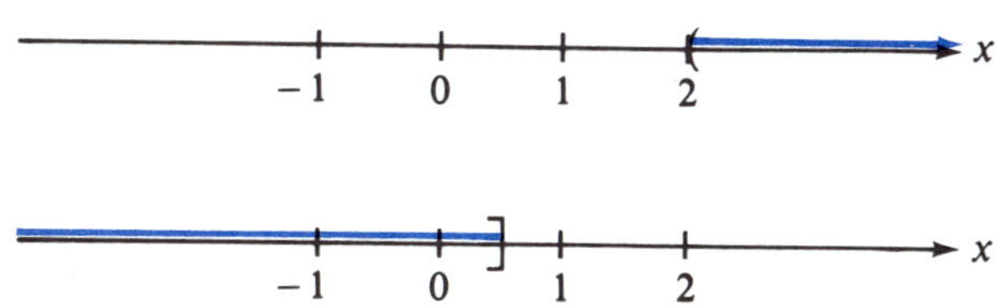

Figure 1.10

In practical applications, the subsets of real numbers are often found by solving one or more inequalities involving a variable x. In such situations, the following properties of inequalities may be used to advantage. Let a, b and c be any real numbers, then

		Example
Property (1.1)	If $a < b$ and $b < c$, then $a < c$	$2 < 3$ and $3 < 8$, so $2 < 8$
Property (1.2)	If $a < b$, then $a + c < b + c$	$-5 < -3$, so $-5 + 2 < -3 + 2$; that is, $-3 < -1$
Property (1.3)	If $a < b$ and $c > 0$, then $ac < bc$	$-5 < -3$, and since $2 > 0$, we have $(2)(-5) < (2)(-3)$; that is, $-10 < -6$
Property (1.4)	If $a < b$ and $c < 0$, then $ac > bc$	$-2 < 4$, and since $-3 < 0$, we have $(-3)(-2) > (-3)(4)$; that is, $6 > -12$

Similar properties hold if each inequality sign "$>$" is replaced by "$\geq$", "$<$" or "$\leq$".

EXAMPLE 1.21 Find the set of real numbers satisfying $-1 \leq 2x - 5 < 7$.

SOLUTION Adding 5 to each member of the given double inequality, we obtain

$$4 \leq 2x < 12$$

Next, multiplying each member of the resulting double inequality by 1/2 yields

$$2 \leq x < 6$$

and the solution is the interval $[2, 6)$. ■

EXAMPLE 1.22 Solve the inequality $x^2 + 2x - 8 < 0$.

SOLUTION Observe that $x^2 + 2x - 8 = (x + 4)(x - 2)$ so that the given inequality is equivalent to the inequality $(x + 4)(x - 2) < 0$. Since the product of two real numbers is negative if and only if the two numbers have opposite signs, we solve the inequality $(x + 4)(x - 2) < 0$ by studying the signs of the two factors $x + 4$ and $x - 2$. Now, $x + 4 > 0$ when $x > -4$, and $x + 4 < 0$ when $x < -4$. Similarly, $x - 2 > 0$ when $x > 2$, and $x - 2 < 0$ when $x < 2$. These results are summarized graphically in Figure 1.11. From Figure 1.11 we see that the two factors $x + 4$ and $x - 2$ have opposite signs when and only when x lies strictly between -4 and 2 so that the required solution is the interval $(-4, 2)$.

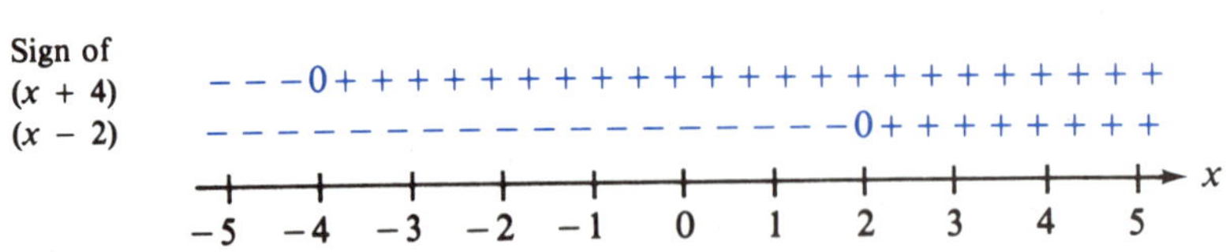

Figure 1.11 ■

EXAMPLE 1.23 Solve the inequality $(x+1)/(x-1) \geq 0$.

SOLUTION The quotient $(x+1)/(x-1)$ is *strictly* positive if and only if both the numerator and the denominator have the same sign. The signs of $x+1$ and $x-1$ are shown in Figure 1.12. From Figure 1.12 we see that both $x+1$ and $x-1$ have the same sign when and only when $x<-1$ or when $x>1$. Next, the quotient $(x+1)/(x-1)$ is equal to zero when and only when $x=-1$. Therefore, the required solution is the set of all x in the interval $(-\infty, -1]$ and the interval $(1, \infty)$.

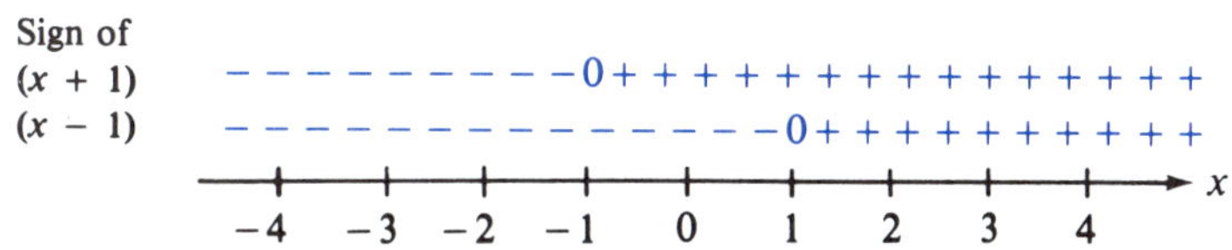

Figure 1.12 ■

absolute value

The *absolute value* of a number a (denoted by $|a|$) is a number satisfying the conditions

$$|a| = \begin{cases} a & \text{if } a \geq 0 \\ -a & \text{if } a < 0 \end{cases}$$

Since $-a$ is a positive number whenever a is negative, it follows that the absolute value of a number is always nonnegative. For example, $|5|=5$ and $|-5|=-(-5)=5$. Geometrically, $|a|$ is the *distance* from the origin to the point on the number line representing the number a (see Figure 1.13).

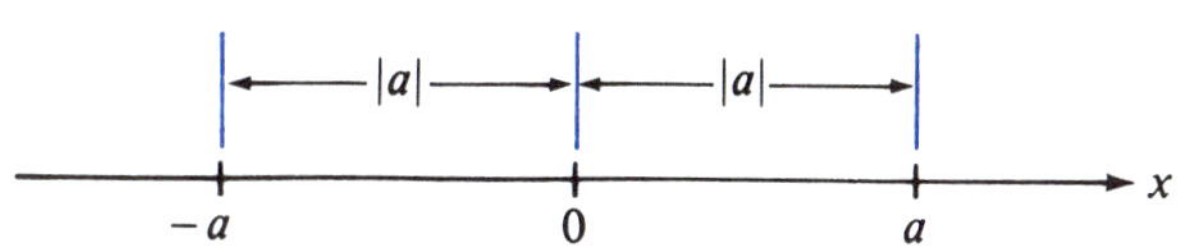

Figure 1.13

The following properties hold for arbitrary numbers a, b, c.

		Example
Property (1.5)	$\lvert -a\rvert = \lvert a\rvert$	$\lvert -3\rvert = -(-3) = 3 = \lvert 3\rvert$
Property (1.6)	$\lvert ab\rvert = \lvert a\rvert \lvert b\rvert$	$\lvert (2)(-3)\rvert = \lvert -6\rvert = 6 = \lvert 2\rvert\,\lvert -3\rvert$
Property (1.7)	$\left\lvert \frac{a}{b} \right\rvert = \frac{\lvert a\rvert}{\lvert b\rvert} \quad (b \neq 0)$	$\left\lvert \frac{(-3)}{(-4)} \right\rvert = \frac{\lvert 3\rvert}{\lvert 4\rvert} = \frac{3}{4} = \frac{\lvert -3\rvert}{\lvert -4\rvert}$
Property (1.8)	$\lvert a+b\rvert \leq \lvert a\rvert + \lvert b\rvert$	$\lvert 8+(-5)\rvert = \lvert 3\rvert = 3 \leq \lvert 8\rvert + \lvert -5\rvert = 13$

The last property is called the *triangle inequality*.

EXAMPLE 1.24 Discuss the inequalities $|x| \leq a$ and $|x| \geq a$, where a is a nonnegative number.

SOLUTION First we consider the inequality $|x| \le a$. If $x \ge 0$, then $|x| = x$ so that $|x| \le a$ implies $x \le a$ in this case. On the other hand, if $x \le 0$ then $|x| = -x$ so that $|x| \le a$ implies $-x \le a$ or $x \ge -a$. Thus, $|x| \le a$ means $-a \le x \le a$ (see Figure 1.14 part a). To obtain an alternative solution, observe that $|x|$ is the distance of the point x from 0 so that the inequality $|x| \le a$ implies immediately that $-a \le x \le a$.

Next, the inequality $|x| \ge a$ states that the distance of x from 0 is greater than or equal to a. This observation yields the result $x \ge a$ or $x \le -a$ (see Figure 1.14 part b).

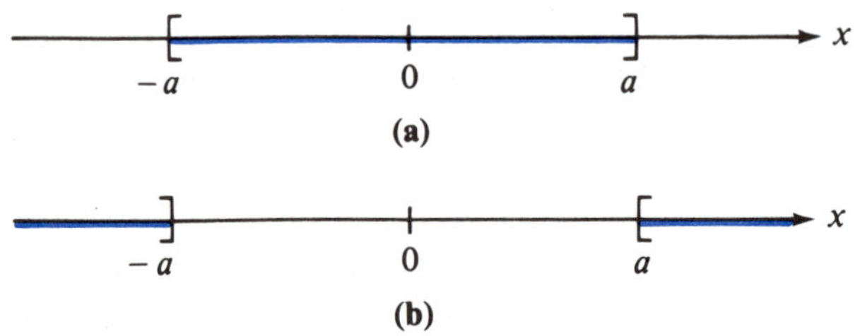

Figure 1.14 ■

EXAMPLE 1.25 Solve the inequality $|2x - 3| \le 1$.

SOLUTION The inequality $|2x - 3| \le 1$ is equivalent to the inequalities $-1 \le 2x - 3 \le 1$ (see Example 1.24), whence $2 \le 2x \le 4$ and $1 \le x \le 2$. The solution is therefore given by the set of all x in the interval $[1, 2]$ (see Figure 1.15).

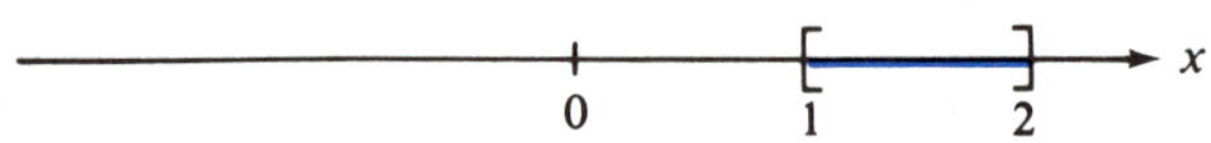

Figure 1.15 ■

1.3 EXERCISES

In problems 1 through 20, find the values of x *satisfying each of the given inequalities.*

1. $2x + 4 < 8$

2. $x + 4 \le 3x - 12$

3. $-4x \ge 20$

4. $-6 < x - 2 < 4$

5. $0 \le x + 1 \le 4$

6. $x + 1 > 4$ or $x + 2 < -1$

7. $x - 2 > 1$ or $x + 3 < 0$

8. $x + 3 > 1$ and $x - 2 < 1$

9. $x - 4 \le 1$ and $x + 3 > 2$

10. $x^2 > 16$

11. $(x + 3)(x - 5) \le 0$

12. $(2x - 4)(x + 2) \ge 0$

13. $2x^2 + 3x - 5 \le 0$

14. $x(x - 1)(x - 2) < 0$

15. $x^2 + 2 < 0$

16. $\dfrac{x + 3}{x - 2} \ge 0$

17. $\dfrac{1}{(x - 4)^2} \le 1$

18. $\dfrac{(x - 1)(x - 2)}{(x - 3)(x - 4)} > 0$

19. $\dfrac{(x-1)(2x-3)}{x^2-1} \le 0$

20. $\dfrac{x^2-3x+2}{x^2-4x+3} > 0$

In problems 21 through 28, find the values of x *that satisfy the given equation.*

21. $|x| = 5$

22. $|x-2| = 4$

23. $|2-3x| = 5$

24. $|x^2-4| = 3$

25. $\left|\dfrac{x-1}{x+1}\right| = 3$

26. $|x| < 4$

27. $|-2x| < 3$

28. $|x-4| \le 7$

29. Suppose that a and b are real numbers other than zero and that $a > b$. State whether the following inequalities are true or false for all such real numbers a and b.

(*a*) $b-a>0$ (*b*) $\dfrac{a}{b}>1$ (*c*) $a^2>b^2$ (*d*) $\dfrac{1}{a}>\dfrac{1}{b}$

(*e*) $a^3>b^3$ (*f*) $-a<-b$ (*g*) $b<\dfrac{a+b}{2}<a$ (*h*) $|a|>|b|$

30. Which of the following statements are true for all real numbers a and b?

(*a*) $|-a| = a$ (*b*) $|b^2| = b^2$ (*c*) $|a-4| = |4-a|$

(*d*) $|a+1| = |a|+1$ (*e*) $|a+b| = |a|+|b|$ (*f*) $|a-b| = |a|-|b|$

31. There are 400 seats in a movie theater. The admission price for the matinee show is \$2.50 for adults and \$1.50 for children. Find the range of the revenue R that can be expected when tickets for the matinee show are "all sold out."

32. An advertisement for a certain car states that the E.P.A. fuel economy for the car is 20 m.p.g. city and 27 m.p.g. highway and that the car's fuel tank capacity rating is 18.1 gallons. Assuming ideal driving conditions determine the driving range for the car from the above data.

33. Find the minimum cost C (in dollars), given that $5(C-25) \ge 1.75 + 2.5C$.

34. Find the maximum profit P (in dollars) given that $6(P-2500) \le 4(P+2400)$.

35. The relationship between Celsius (°C) and Fahrenheit (°F) temperature is given by the formula $C = \frac{5}{9}(F-32)$.

(*a*) If the temperature range for Montreal during the month of January is $-15° < C° < -5°$, find the range in degrees Fahrenheit in Montreal for the same period.

(*b*) If the temperature range for New York City during the month of June is $63° < F° < 80°$, find the range in degrees Celsius in New York City for the same period.

36. The markup on a used car was at least 30% of its current wholesale price. If the car was sold for \$2800 what was the maximum wholesale price?

37. A salesman's monthly commission is 15% on all sales over \$12,000. If his goal is to make a commission of at least \$1000 per month, what are the minimum monthly sales figures that he must aim for?

38. A manufacturer of a certain commodity has estimated that his or her profit in thousands of dollars is given by the expression $-6x^2+30x-10$, where x (in thousands) is the number of units produced. What is the production range that enables the manufacturer to realize a profit of at least \$14,000 on the commodity?

39. Give a geometrical interpretation to Properties 1.1, 1.2, 1.3, and 1.4 of inequalities.

40. Prove Property 1.6 of absolute values: $|ab|=|a||b|$ where a and b are any two real numbers.

1.4

The Cartesian Coordinate System

In Section 1.3 we saw how a one-to-one correspondence between the set of real numbers and the points on a straight line leads to a coordinate system on a line (a one-dimensional space).

Cartesian coordinate system

A similar representation for points in the plane (a two-dimensional space) is realized through the *Cartesian coordinate system*, which is constructed as follows. Take two perpendicular lines, one of which is normally chosen to be horizontal. These lines intersect at a point O called the origin (see Figure 1.16). The horizontal line is called the *axis of abscissas*, or more simply the x-axis. The vertical line is called the *axis of ordinates* or the y-axis. A number scale is set up along the x-axis with the positive numbers lying to the right of the origin and the negative numbers lying to the left of the origin. Similarly, a number scale is set up along the y-axis with the positive numbers lying above the origin and the negative numbers lying below the origin.

axes

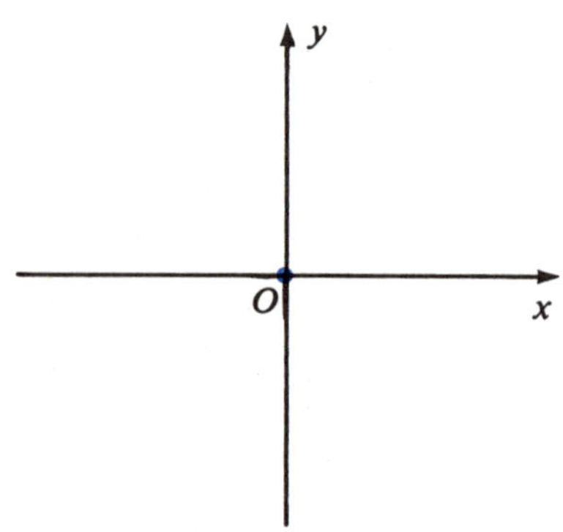

Figure 1.16

Observe that the number scales need not be the same. Indeed, in many applications different quantities are represented by x and y; for example, x may represent the number of units of typewriters sold and y the total revenue resulting from the sales. In such cases it is often desirable to choose different number scales to represent the different quantities. Observe that, by construction, the zeros of both number scales coincide at the origin of the two-dimensional coordinate system.

ordered pair

A point in the plane can now be represented uniquely in this coordinate system by an *ordered pair* of numbers; that is, a pair (x, y) where x is the first number and y the second number. To see this, let P be any point in the plane (see Figure 1.17). Draw perpendiculars from P to the x-axis and y-axis, respectively. Then the number x is precisely the number corresponding to the point on the x-axis at which the perpendicular through P cuts the x-axis. Similarly, y is the number corresponding to the point on the y-axis at which the perpendicular through P crosses the y-axis.

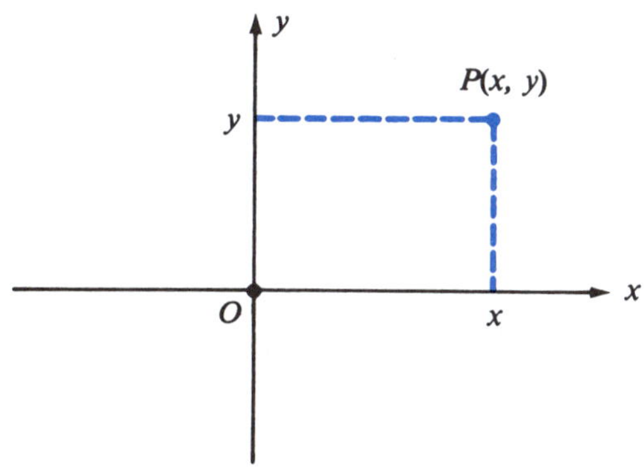

Figure 1.17

Conversely, given an ordered pair (x, y) with x as the first number and y as the second number, a point P in the plane is uniquely determined as follows: locate the point on the x-axis represented by the number x, then draw a line through that point parallel to the y-axis. Next, locate the point on the y-axis represented by the number y and draw a line through that point parallel to the x-axis. The point of intersection of these two lines is the point P (see Figure 1.17).

abscissa

ordinate

In the ordered pair (x, y), x is called the *abscissa* or *x-coordinate*, y is called the *ordinate* or *y-coordinate* and together x and y are referred to as the coordinates of the point P.

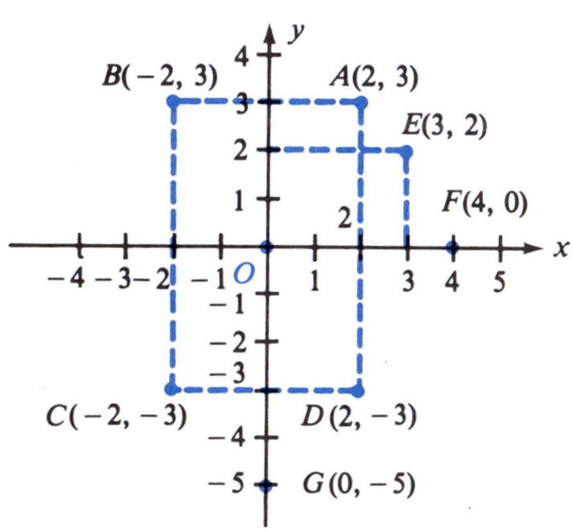

Figure 1.18

The points $A=(2,3)$, $B=(-2,3)$, $C=(-2,-3)$, $D=(2,-3)$, $E=(3,2)$, $F=(4,0)$, and $G=(0,-5)$ are plotted in Figure 1.18. The fact that in general $(x,y)\neq(y,x)$ is clearly illustrated by points A and E in Figure 1.18.

The axes divide the plane into four quadrants. Quadrant I consists of points P with coordinates x and y (denoted by $P(x, y)$) satisfying $x>0$ and $y>0$; Quadrant II, the points $P(x, y)$ where $x<0$ and $y>0$; Quadrant III, the points $P(x, y)$ where $x<0$ and $y<0$; and Quadrant IV, the points $P(x, y)$ where $x>0$ and $y<0$ (see Figure 1.19).

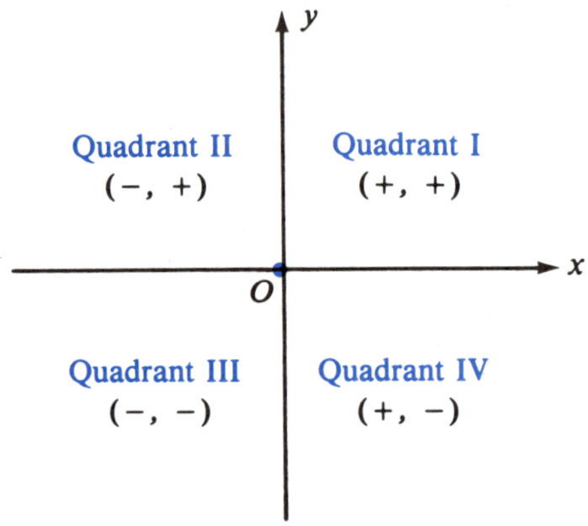

Figure 1.19

One immediate benefit as a result of using the Cartesian coordinate system is that the distance between any two points in the plane may be expressed solely in terms of their coordinates. We begin by looking at the special, and relatively simple case: the two points lie on a horizontal or a vertical line. Then we use these results to help us find the general distance formula, which gives the distance between *any* two points in the plane. To this end, let $P_1(x_1, y_1)$ and $P_2(x_2, y_1)$ be two points lying on a line parallel to the x-axis (see Figure 1.20). Then the distance between P_1 and P_2, denoted by $|P_1P_2|$, is given by

$$|P_1P_2| = |x_2 - x_1| = |x_1 - x_2| = |P_2P_1|$$

As an example, if $P_1=(-3,4)$ and $P_2=(2,4)$, then $|P_1P_2|=|2-(-3)|=5=|-3-2|$.

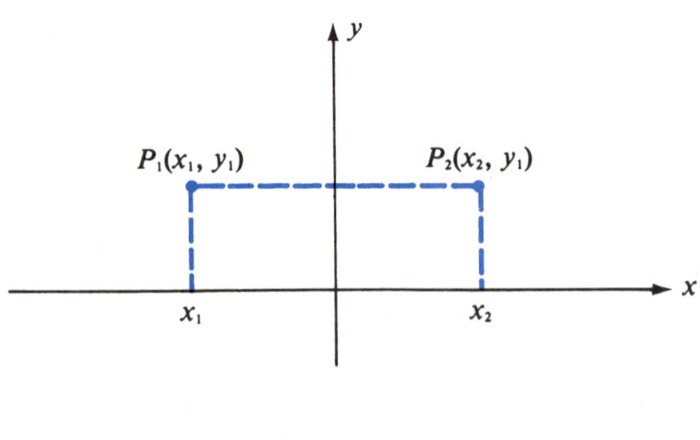

Figure 1.20

Next, if $Q_1(x_1, y_1)$ and $Q_2(x_1, y_2)$ are two points lying on a line parallel to the y-axis, then the distance between Q_1 and Q_2 is given by

$$|Q_1Q_2| = |y_2 - y_1| = |y_1 - y_2| = |Q_2Q_1| \qquad \text{(See Figure 1.21.)}$$

As an example, if $Q_1 = (1, 3)$ and $Q_2 = (1, 7)$, then $|Q_1Q_2| = |7 - 3| = 4$.

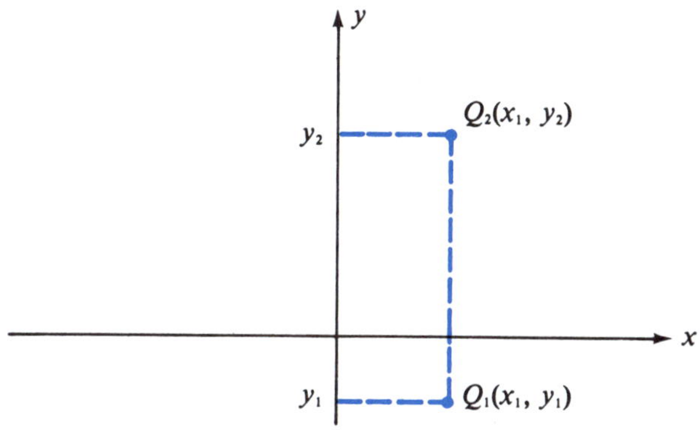

Figure 1.21

distance formula

Using the above results we easily derive a general *formula for the distance* between any two points $P(x_1, y_1)$ and $P(x_2, y_2)$. We have

(1.3)
$$|P_1P_2| = \sqrt{(x_2 - x_1)^2 + (y_2 - y_1)^2}$$

Note that if $P_1(x_1, y_1)$ and $P_2(x_2, y_2)$ are any two points lying on a line parallel to the x-axis or a line parallel to the y-axis, then the formula holds when we compare it with the above results. Keep in mind that $y_1 = y_2$ in the first situation and $x_1 = x_2$ in the second. In the general case, we construct a right triangle P_1QP_2 where the segment P_1P_2 is the hypotenuse and the point $Q(x_2, y_1)$ is the point of intersection of the lines through P_1 and P_2 that are parallel to the x- and y-axis, respectively (see Figure 1.22). From our earlier results, we have $|P_1Q| = |x_2 - x_1|$, $|QP_2| = |y_2 - y_1|$.

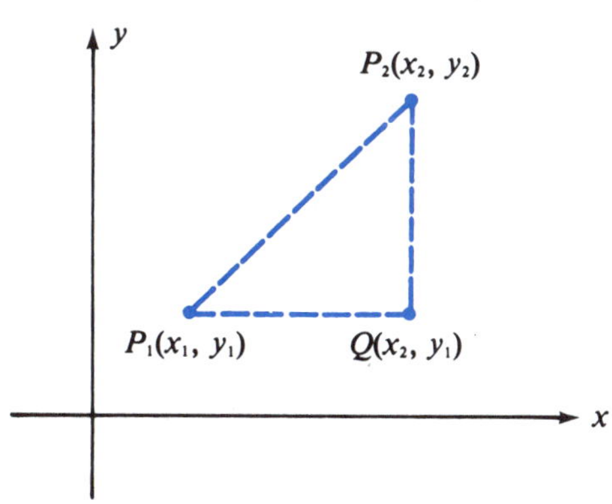

Figure 1.22

By the Theorem of Pythagoras, we have

$$\begin{aligned}|P_1P_2|^2 &= |P_1Q|^2 + |QP_2|^2\\ &= |x_2 - x_1|^2 + |y_2 - y_1|^2\\ &= (x_2 - x_1)^2 + (y_2 - y_1)^2\end{aligned}$$

from which we obtain the desired result by extracting square roots from both sides.

EXAMPLE 1.26 Find the distance between the points $P_1(-4, 3)$ and $P_2(2, 6)$.

SOLUTION We have, by the distance formula (1.3),

$$\begin{aligned}|P_1P_2| &= \sqrt{[2-(-4)]^2 + (6-3)^2}\\ &= \sqrt{6^2 + 3^2} = \sqrt{45}\\ &= 3\sqrt{5}\end{aligned}$$

■

1.4 EXERCISES

1. Sketch a set of coordinate axes and plot the following points:

(***a***) (1, 3) (***b***) (−2, 5) (***c***) (−3, 4) (***d***) (3, −1)
(***e***) (−5/2, 3/2) (***f***) (8, −7/2) (***g***) (1.2, −3.4) (***h***) (4.5, −4.5)

2. Refer to the figure below and determine the coordinates of the following points:

(***a***) *A* (***b***) *B* (***c***) *C*
(***d***) *D* (***e***) *E* (***f***) *F*

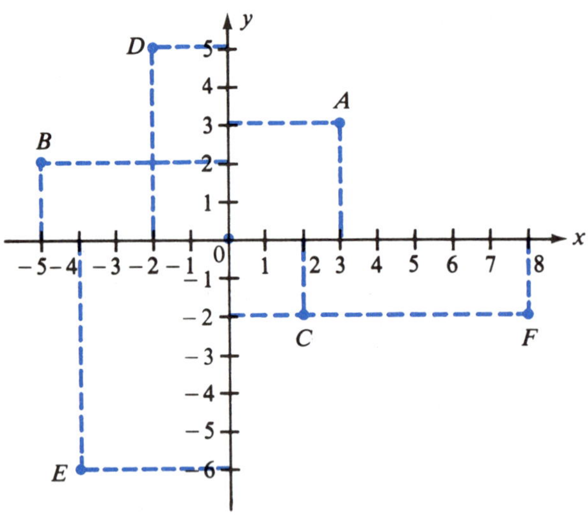

3. Refer to the figure in problem 2 to determine the quadrant in which each of the following points is located.

(*a*) A (*b*) B (*c*) C

(*d*) D (*e*) E (*f*) F

In problems 4 through 10, find the distance between the two given points.

4. (1, 0) and (4, 4) ***5.*** (1, 3) and (4, 7)

6. (6, 1) and (2, 4) ***7.*** (−2, 1) and (10, 6)

8. (−1, 3) and (4, 9) ***9.*** (−3, −4) and (−2, 5)

10. $(-2b, a)$ and $(2b, a)$

11. Find the coordinates of the points that are 5 units away from the origin and have an x-coordinate that is equal to 3.

12. Find the coordinates of the points that are 10 units away from the origin and have a y-coordinate that is equal to −6.

13. Find the distance r between a point (x, y) on a circle and its center (h, k). (See the following figure.)

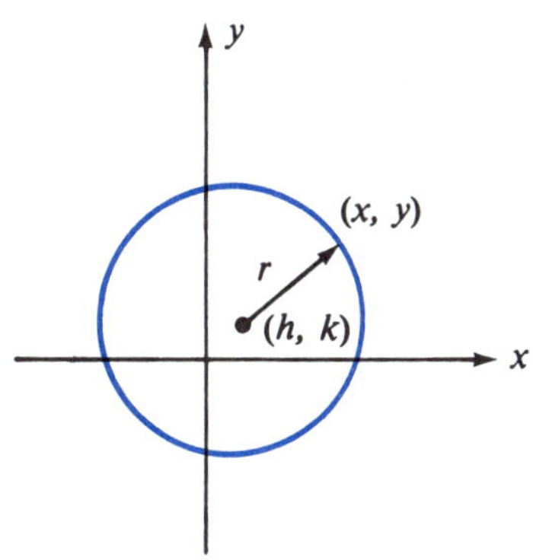

14. Show that the triangle with vertices (−5, 2), (−2, 5) and (5, −2) is a right triangle.

15. Show that the triangle with vertices (−1, 3), (4, −2) and (5, 4) is an isosceles triangle.

16. Show that the points with vertices (3, 4), (−3, 7), (−6, 1) and (0, −2) form the vertices of a square.

17. A furniture store offers free set-up and delivery services to all points within a 25 mile radius of its warehouse distribution center. If you live 20 miles east and 14 miles south of the warehouse, will you incur a delivery charge for furniture purchased from this store? Justify your answer.

18. A grand tour of four cities begins at city A with successive stops at cities B,

C and D before returning to city A. If the cities are located as shown in the figure below, find the total distance covered on the tour.

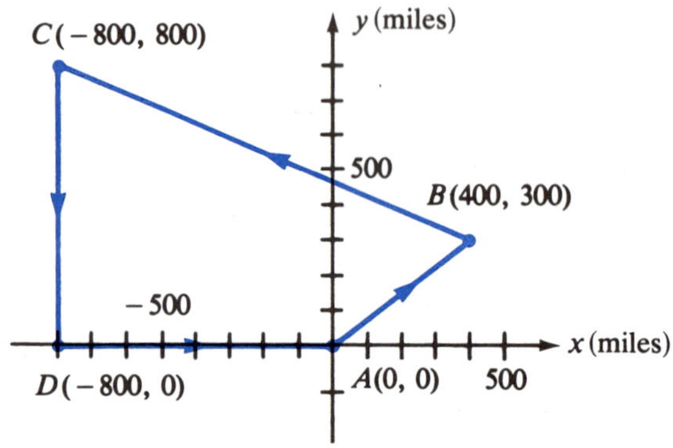

19. Mr. Barclay wishes to determine which antenna he should purchase for his home. The T.V. store has supplied him with the following information:

Range in Miles			
VHF	UHF	Model	Price
30	20	A	\$40.00
45	35	B	\$50.00
60	40	C	\$60.00
75	55	D	\$70.00

He wishes to receive programs from channel 17 (VHF) which is located 25 miles east and 35 miles north of his home and programs from channel 38 (UHF) which is located 20 miles south and 32 miles west of his home. Which model will allow him to receive both channels at the least cost? (Assume there is flat terrain between his home and both broadcasting stations.)

20. Towns A, B, C and D are located as shown in the following figure. There are two highways linking town A to town D; Route 1 runs from town A to town D

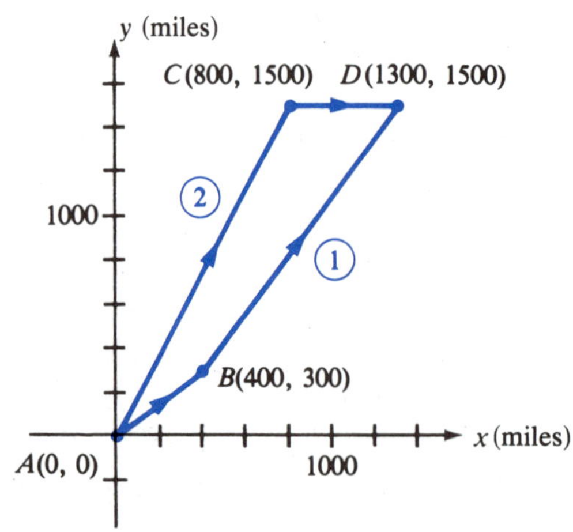

via town B, and Route 2 runs from town A to town D via town C. A salesman wishes to drive from town A to town D. If traffic conditions are such that he could expect to average the same speed on either route, which highway should he take in order to arrive at his destination in the shortest time?

21. Refer to the figure shown in problem 20. Suppose a fleet of 100 cars are to be shipped from an assembly plant located in town A to town D. They may be shipped either by freight train along Route 1 at a cost of 11¢ per mile per car or by truck along Route 2 at a cost of $10\frac{1}{2}$¢ per mile per car. Which means of transport minimizes the shipping cost? What is the net savings?

1.5 Straight Lines

In this section we shall recall the properties of straight lines and show that a straight line in the xy-plane may be represented by a linear equation in x and y.

slope of a line We begin by defining the *slope of a straight line.* Let L denote the unique straight line that passes through the two distinct points $P_1(x_1, y_1)$ and $P_2(x_2, y_2)$. If $x_1 = x_2$ then L is parallel to the y-axis (see Figure 1.23). In this case we say that the

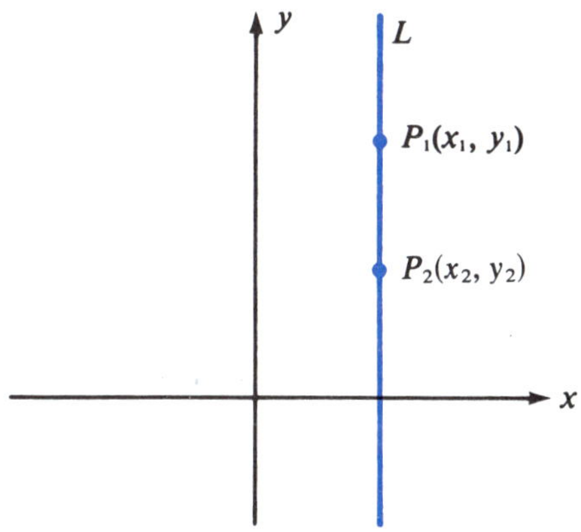

Figure 1.23

slope of L is undefined. In all other cases $x_1 \neq x_2$ and we define the *slope m of L* by the formula

(1.4) $$m = \frac{y_2 - y_1}{x_2 - x_1} \qquad \text{(See Figure 1.24).}$$

Thus, the slope of a straight line is a constant whenever it is defined. Since the number $(y_2 - y_1)$ is a measure of the change in y and $(x_2 - x_1)$ is a measure of the change in x, the slope m of L is a measure of the rate of change of y with respect to x. In other words, the slope m of a straight line L is a measure of the steepness of L with respect to the x-axis. Also, observe that a line with positive slope slants upward from left to right (y increases as x increases) while a line with

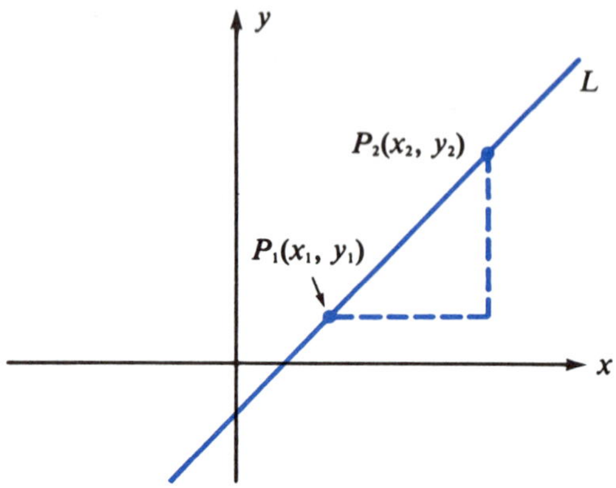

Figure 1.24

negative slope slants downward from left to right (y decreases as x increases). Figure 1.25 shows a family of straight lines passing through the origin with the indicated slopes.

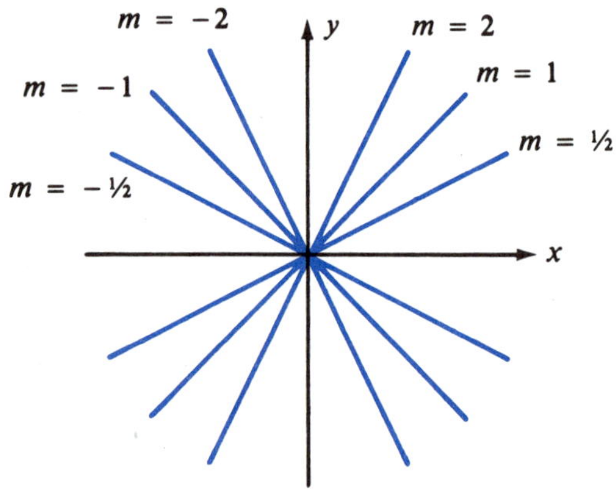

Figure 1.25

EXAMPLE 1.27 Find the slope m of the line passing through the points $(-1, 1)$ and $(5, 3)$.

SOLUTION Choose $P_1(x_1, y_1)$ to be the point $(-1, 1)$ and $P_2(x_2, y_2)$ to be the point $(5, 3)$. Then, with $x_1 = -1$, $y_1 = 1$, $x_2 = 5$, and $y_2 = 3$, we find using Equation (1.4)

$$m = \frac{y_2 - y_1}{x_2 - x_1} = \frac{3-1}{5-(-1)} = \frac{1}{3} \qquad \text{(See Figure 1.26).}$$

Try to verify that the result obtained would have been the same had we chosen the point $(-1, 1)$ to be $P_2(x_2, y_2)$ and the point $(5, 3)$ to be the point $P_1(x_1, y_1)$.

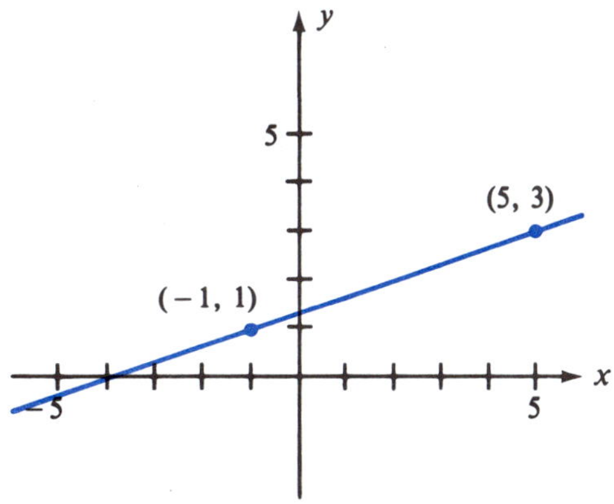

Figure 1.26 ■

EXAMPLE 1.28 Find the slope of the line passing through the points $(-2, 5)$ and $(3, 5)$.

SOLUTION The slope of the required line is given by

$$m = \frac{5-5}{3-(-2)} = \frac{0}{5} = 0 \qquad \text{(See Figure 1.27).}$$

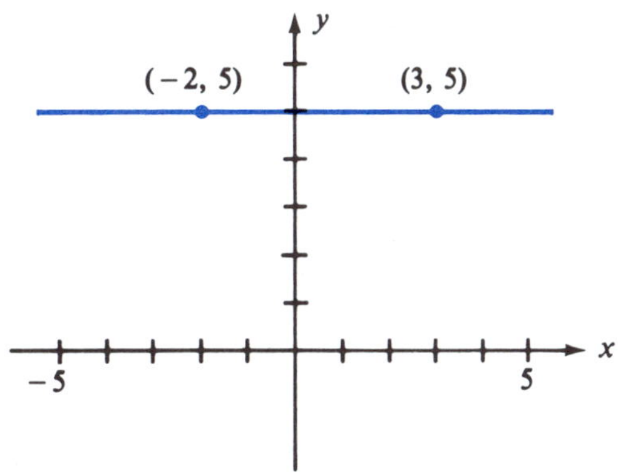

Figure 1.27 ■

In general, the slope of a horizontal line is zero as may be verified by the reader.

parallel and perpendicular lines

Recalling the definition of the slope of a straight line, it is easily seen that two lines are *parallel*, if and only if, they have the same slope or the slope of each line is undefined. A condition also exists for two lines to be *perpendicular* to each other. Suppose first that a line L_1 is vertical (so that its slope is undefined) then another line L_2 is perpendicular to L_1, written $L_2 \perp L_1$, if and only if L_2 is horizontal (so that its slope is zero). Next, suppose that the line L_1 with slope m_1 is neither parallel to the y nor the x-axis. Then the line L_2 with slope m_2 is perpendicular to L_1 if and only if the slopes m_1 and m_2 are negative reciprocals of each other, that is

$$m_2 = -\frac{1}{m_1}$$

or equivalently,

$$m_1 m_2 = -1 \qquad (m_1 \neq 0,\ m_2 \neq 0).$$

We shall not prove this result, however.

EXAMPLE 1.29 Let L_1 be a line that passes through the points $(-2, 9)$ and $(1, 3)$, and let L_2 be the line that passes through the points $(-4, 10)$ and $(3, -4)$. Determine whether L_1 and L_2 are parallel.

SOLUTION The slope m_1 of L_1 is given by

$$m_1 = \frac{3-9}{1-(-2)} = -2$$

The slope m_2 of L_2 is given by

$$m_2 = \frac{-4-10}{3-(-4)} = -2$$

Since $m_1 = m_2$ the lines L_1 and L_2 are in fact parallel (see Figure 1.28).

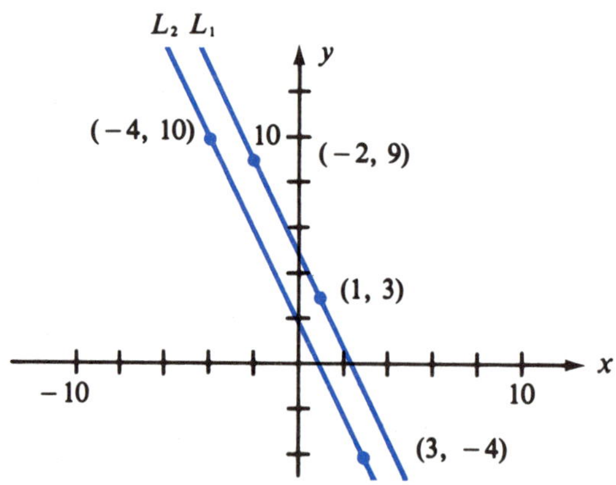

Figure 1.28

We will now show that every straight line lying in the plane may be represented by an equation involving the variables x and y. One immediate benefit of this is that problems involving straight lines may be solved algebraically.

Let L be a straight line that is parallel to the y-axis (perpendicular to the x-axis) (see Figure 1.29). Then L crosses the x-axis at some point $(a, 0)$ with the x-coordinate given by $x = a$, where a is some real number. It is easy to see that every point on such a line is of the form $(a, \bar{y})$ where the number $\bar{y}$ is the appropriate y-coordinate of the point. Thus, the vertical line L is described by the

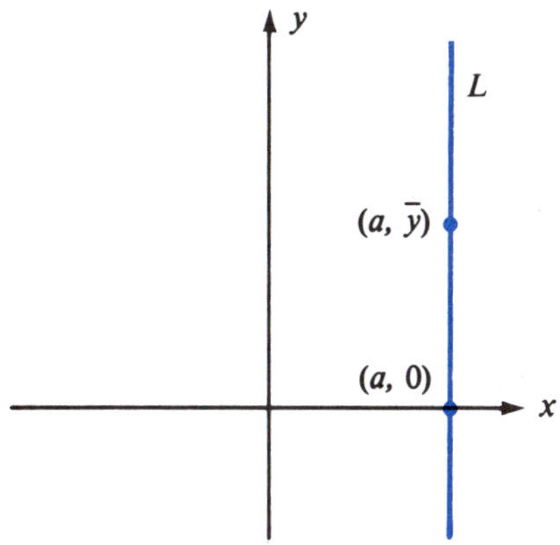

Figure 1.29

sole condition

$$x = a$$

and this is accordingly the equation of L. As an example, the equation $x = -2$ represents a vertical line two units to the left of the y-axis while the equation $x = 3$ represents a vertical line three units to the right of the y-axis (see Figure 1.30).

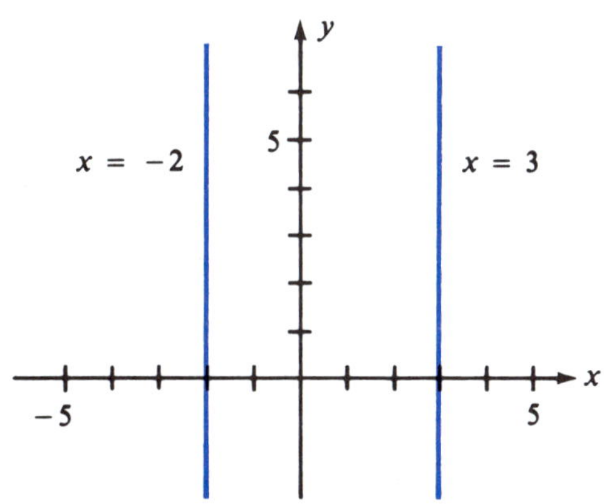

Figure 1.30

Next, suppose L is a nonvertical line so that it has a well-defined slope m. Suppose $P_1(x_1, y_1)$ is a fixed point lying on L and $P(x, y)$ is a variable point on L distinct from $P_1(x_1, y_1)$ (see Figure 1.31). Using Equation (1.4) with $P_1(x_1, y_1)$ and $P_2(x_2, y_2) = P(x, y)$ we find that the slope of L is given by

$$m = \frac{y - y_1}{x - x_1}$$

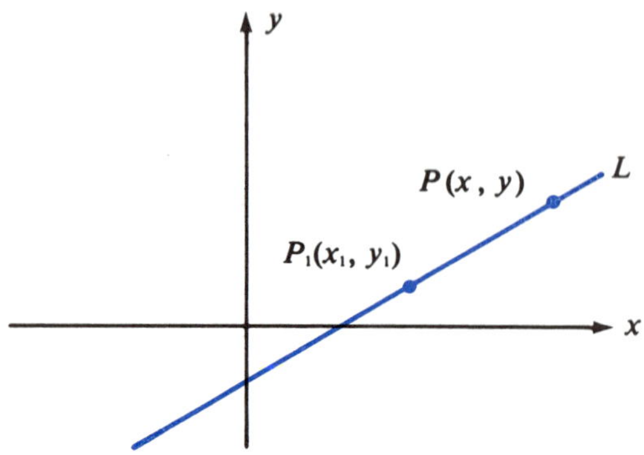

Figure 1.31

Upon multiplying both sides of the equation by $x - x_1$, we obtain the equation

(1.5)
$$y - y_1 = m(x - x_1)$$

point-slope form of the equation of a line

for the line L. Equation (1.5) is called the *point-slope form of the equation of a line* L since it utilizes a given point $P_1(x_1, y_1)$ on the line L and the slope m of L.

EXAMPLE 1.30 Find an equation of a line passing through the point (1, 3) and having slope 2.

SOLUTION Using the point-slope form of the equation of a line with $P_1(1, 3)$ and $m = 2$, we obtain

$$y - 3 = 2(x - 1)$$

which, upon simplification becomes

$$2x - y + 1 = 0 \qquad \text{(See Figure 1.32.)}$$

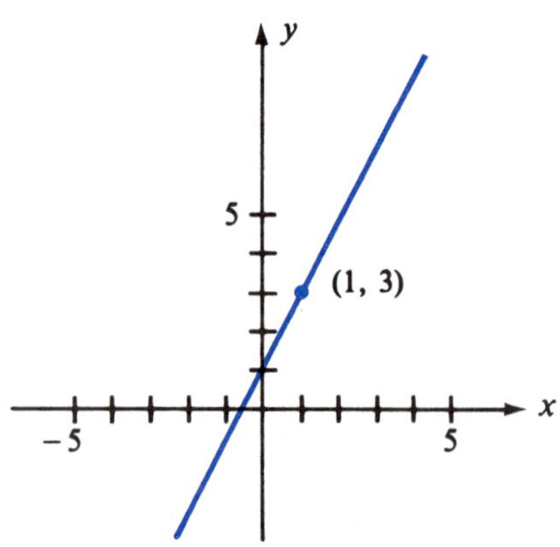

Figure 1.32

■

EXAMPLE 1.31 Find an equation of a line passing through the point (3, 1) and perpendicular to the line of Example 1.30.

SOLUTION Since the slope of the line in Example 1.30 is 2, the slope of the required line is given by $m = -\frac{1}{2}$, the negative reciprocal of 2. Using the point-slope form of the equation of a line, we obtain

$$y - 1 = -\frac{1}{2}(x - 3)$$

$$2y - 2 = -x + 3$$

or $$x + 2y - 5 = 0 \qquad \text{(See Figure 1.33.)}$$

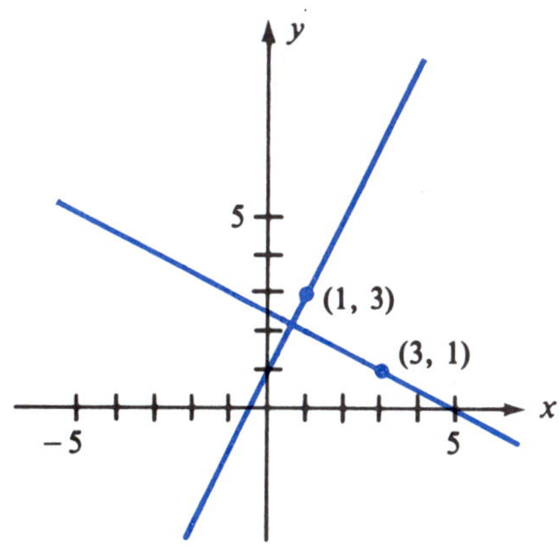

Figure 1.33

EXAMPLE 1.32 Find an equation of a line passing through the points $(-3, 2)$ and $(4, -1)$.

SOLUTION The slope of the line is given by

$$m = \frac{-1-2}{4-(-3)} = -\frac{3}{7}$$

Using the point-slope form of the equation of a line with the point $(4, -1)$ and the slope $m = -\frac{3}{7}$, we have

$$y + 1 = -\frac{3}{7}(x - 4)$$

$$7y + 7 = -3x + 12$$

or $$3x + 7y - 5 = 0 \qquad \text{(See Figure 1.34.)}$$

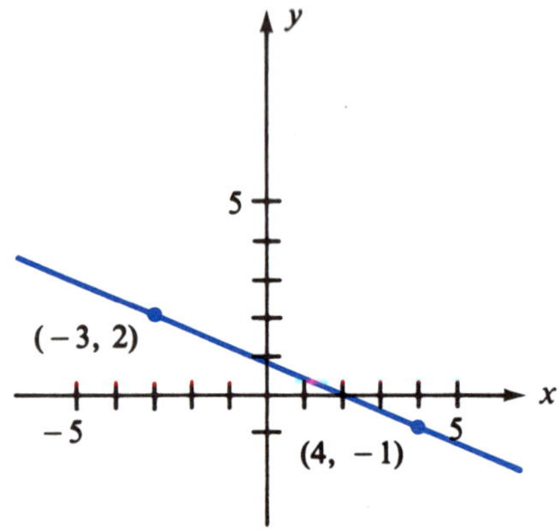

Figure 1.34

EXAMPLE 1.33 The sales manager of a local sporting goods store plotted the sales versus time for the last five years and found the points to lie approximately along a straight line (see Figure 1.35). By using the points corresponding to the first and fifth years find the equation of the trend line. What sales figure may we predict for the sixth year?

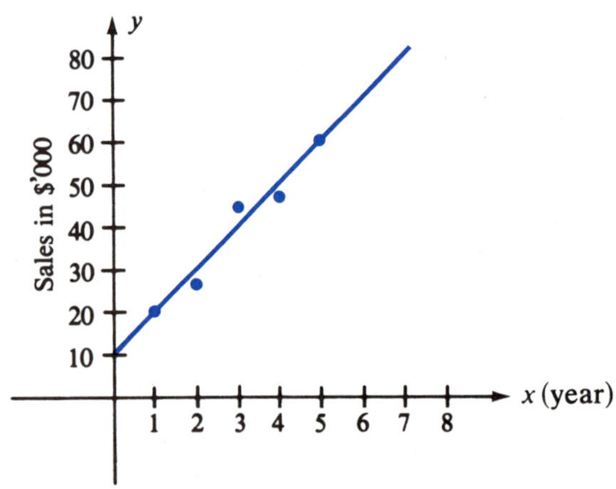

Figure 1.35

SOLUTION Using Equation (1.4) with the two points (1, 20) and (5, 60) we find that the slope of the required line is given by

$$m = \frac{60-20}{5-1} = 10$$

Next, using the point-slope form of the equation of a line with the point (1, 20) and $m = 10$, we obtain

$$y - 20 = 10(x - 1)$$

or

$$y = 10x + 10$$

as the required equation.

The sales figure for the sixth year is obtained by letting $x = 6$ in the above equation giving

$$y = 70$$

or \$70,000. ■

x- and y-intercepts

In general, a straight line L cuts both the x- and the y-axis at, say, the points $(a, 0)$ and $(0, b)$, respectively (see Figure 1.36). The numbers a and b are called the *x-intercept* and *y-intercept*, respectively, of L. Now, let L be a line with slope m and y-intercept b. Using the point-slope form of the equation of a line, Equation (1.5), with the point given by $(0, b)$ and the slope given by m, we have

$$y - b = m(x - 0)$$

(1.6) or

$$y = mx + b$$

slope-intercept form of the equation of a line

the *slope-intercept form of the equation of the line L.*

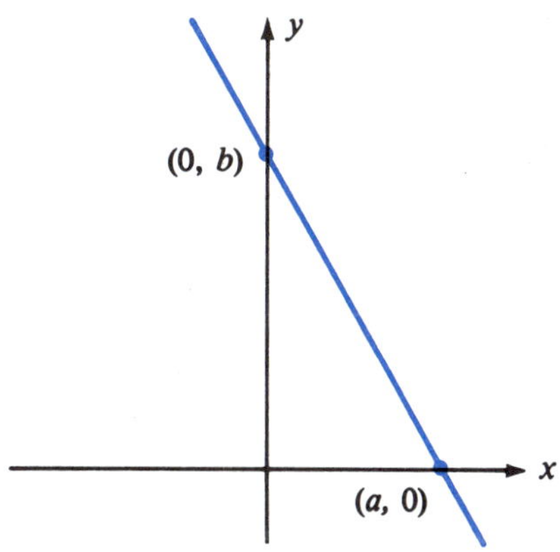

Figure 1.36

EXAMPLE 1.34 Find the equation of the line with slope 3 and y-intercept -4.

SOLUTION Using Equation (1.6) with $m = 3$ and $b = -4$, we obtain

$$y = 3x - 4$$

as the required equation. ■

EXAMPLE 1.35 Suppose an art object purchased at a price of \$50,000 is expected to appreciate in value at a constant rate of \$5,000 per year for the next five years. Use Equation (1.6) to write an equation to predict its value in the next several years. What will its value be three years from the date of purchase?

SOLUTION Let x (in years) denote the time elapsed since the date of purchase of the object and let y (in dollars) denote its value. Then $y = 50{,}000$ when $x = 0$. Furthermore, the slope of the required equation is given by $m = 5000$ since each unit increase in x (one year) implies an increase of 5000 units (dollars) in y. Using Equation (1.6) with $m = 5000$ and $b = 50{,}000$, we obtain

$$y = 5000x + 50{,}000$$

Three years from the date of purchase, the value of the object will be given by

$$y = 5000(3) + 50{,}000$$

or \$65,000. ■

EXAMPLE 1.36 Determine the slope and y-intercept of the line with the equation $3x - 4y = 8$.

SOLUTION Rewrite the given equation in the slope-intercept form obtaining

$$y = \frac{3}{4}x - 2$$

Comparing this result with Equation (1.6), we find $m = 3/4$ and $b = -2$, and conclude that the slope and y-intercept of the given line are $3/4$ and -2, respectively. ■

We have considered several forms of the equation of a straight line in the plane. These different forms of the equation are equivalent to each other. In fact, as will be demonstrated below, each is a special case of the general equation

(1.7) $$Ax + By + C = 0$$

where A, B, and C are constants and A and B are not both zero. Equation (1.7) is referred to as the general form of a *linear equation* in the variables x and y.

linear equation

We now prove an important result concerning the algebraic representation of straight lines in the plane: *The equation of a straight line L is a linear equation*; conversely, *every linear equation represents a straight line.* Observe that if L is a straight line, then the equation of L is either of the form $x = a$ for some number a (in this case L is a vertical line) or is of the form $y = mx + b$. By taking $A = 1$, $B = 0$, and $C = -a$, in the first case, and $A = m$, $B = -1$, and $C = b$, in the second case, we see that each equation is of the form of Equation (1.7) and is thus linear.

Conversely, let $Ax + By + C = 0$ be a linear equation where A and B are not both zero. If $B = 0$, then $A \neq 0$ by assumption and, upon dividing through by A, the equation reduces to $x = -C/A$ which is the equation of a line parallel to the

y-axis. If $B \neq 0$ then $Ax + By + C = 0$ may be cast in the form

$$y = -\frac{A}{B}x - \frac{C}{B}$$

which is easily seen to be the slope-intercept form of the equation of a line with slope $m = -A/B$ and intercept $b = -C/B$. The above results justify the use of the adjective *linear* in describing Equation (1.7).

EXAMPLE 1.37 Sketch the straight line represented by the equation

$$3x - 4y - 12 = 0$$

SOLUTION Since every straight line is uniquely determined by two distinct points we need only find two such points through which the line passes in order to sketch it. For convenience let us compute the points at which the line crosses the x and y axes. Setting $y = 0$ we find $x = 4$, so that the line crosses the x-axis at the point (4, 0). Setting $x = 0$ gives $y = -3$ so that the line crosses the y-axis at the point (0, −3). A sketch of the line appears in Figure 1.37.

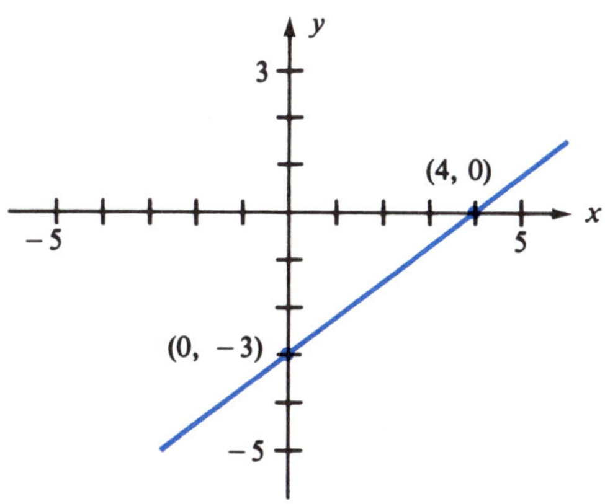

Figure 1.37 ■

In the next chapter, we shall continue our study of linear equations and consider some of their many applications.

1.5 EXERCISES

In problems 1 through 6 find the slope of the line passing through the given pair of points.

1. (4, 3) and (5, 8)
2. (4, 5) and (3, 8)
3. (−2, 3) and (4, 8)
4. (−2, −2) and (4, −4)
5. (a, b) and (c, d)
6. $(-a+1, b-1)$ and $(a+1, -b)$

In problems 7 through 9, determine whether or not the lines through the given pairs of points are parallel to each other.

7. $A(1,-2)$, $B(-3,-10)$ and $C(1,5)$, $D(-1,1)$

8. $A(2,3)$, $B(2,-2)$ and $C(-2,4)$, $D(-2,5)$

9. $A(-2,4)$, $B(2,4)$ and $C(1,-2)$, $D(3,-2)$

In problems 10 and 11, determine whether or not the lines through the given pairs of points are perpendicular to each other.

10. $A(-2,5)$, $B(4,2)$ and $C(-1,-2)$, $D(3,6)$

11. $A(2,0)$, $B(1,-2)$ and $C(4,2)$, $D(-8,4)$.

12. If the line passing through the point $(1, a)$ and $(4,-2)$ is parallel to the line passing through the points $(2,8)$ and $(-7, a+4)$, what must the value of a be?

13. Show that the triangle with vertices $A(-2,-8)$, $B(2,2)$ and $C(-3,4)$ is a right triangle.

In problems 14 and 15, determine whether or not the given set of points lie on a straight line.

14. $A(-2,1)$, $B(1,7)$, and $C(4,13)$

15. $A(-1,7)$, $B(2,-2)$, and $C(5,-9)$

16. Find an equation of the line perpendicular to the x-axis and passing through the point

(***a***) $(0,2)$ (***b***) $(2,2)$ (***c***) $(-3,6)$ (***d***) $(-3,2)$

17. Find an equation of the line passing through the given point $P(x_1, y_1)$ and having the given slope m:

(***a***) $(3,-4)$; $m=2$ (***b***) $(2,4)$; $m=-1$ (***c***) $(-3,2)$; $m=0$

18. Find an equation of the line passing through the two given points:

(***a***) $(2,4)$ and $(3,7)$ (***b***) $(1,2)$ and $(-3,-2)$ (***c***) $(-1,-2)$ and $(3,-4)$
(***d***) $(2,1)$ and $(2,5)$ (***e***) $(3,4)$ and $(5,4)$

19. Find an equation of the line having the slope m and y-intercept b:

(***a***) $m=3$; $b=4$ (***b***) $m=-2$; $b=-1$ (***c***) $m=0$; $b=5$

20. Write each of the following equations in the slope-intercept form and then find the slope and y-intercept of the corresponding lines:

(***a***) $2x-3y-9=0$ (***b***) $3x-4y+8=0$
(***c***) $2x+4y=14$ (***d***) $5x+8y-24=0$
(***e***) $x-2y=0$ (***f***) $y-2=0$

21. Find an equation of the line passing through the point $(-2,2)$ that is parallel to the line $2x-4y-8=0$.

22. Find an equation of the line passing through the point $(2,4)$ that is perpendicular to the line with equation $3x+4y-22=0$.

23. Find an equation of the line satisfying the given conditions.

(***a***) The line parallel to the x-axis and six units below it.

(***b***) The line passing through the origin and parallel to the line joining the points (2, 4) and (4, 7).

(***c***) The line passing through the point (a, b) with slope equal to zero.

24. Find an equation of the line satisfying the given conditions.

(***a***) The line that contains the x-axis.

(***b***) The line passing through $(-3, 4)$ and parallel to the x-axis.

(***c***) The line passing through $(-5, -4)$ and parallel to the line joining $(-3, 2)$ and $(6, 8)$.

(***d***) The line passing through (a, b) with undefined slope.

25. Given that the point $P(-3, 5)$ lies on the line $kx+3y+9=0$, find k.

****26.*** Show that an equation of a line through the points $(a, 0)$ and $(0, b)$ with $a \neq 0$ and $b \neq 0$ can be written in the form

$$\frac{x}{a}+\frac{y}{b}=1$$

(Recall that the numbers a and b are the x- and y-intercepts, respectively, of the line. Accordingly, this form of an equation of a line is called the *intercept form.*)

27. Find an equation of the line whose x- and y-intercepts are:

(***a***) $3; 4$ (***b***) $-2; -4$ (***c***) $-1/2; 3/4$ (***d***) $4; -1/2$

(*Hint*: See Problem 26.)

28. Which of the following are linear equations?

(***a***) $3x+2y^2=4$ (***b***) $3(x+2)+4(y-3)=4$

(***c***) $x(2-y)+3(x-1)=0$ (***d***) $xy=4$

(***e***) $y=0$ (***f***) $\dfrac{3-x}{2}=\dfrac{y-x}{4}$

29. For each of the following sketch the straight line defined by the given linear equations by finding the x- and y-intercepts. (*Hint*: See Example 1.37.)

(***a***) $3x-2y+6=0$ (***b***) $2x-5y+10=0$

(***c***) $x+2y-4=0$ (***d***) $2x+3y-15=0$

(***e***) $y+5=0$ (***f***) $-2x-8y+24=0$

30. Show that the two lines with equation $a_1x+b_1y+c_1=0$ and $a_2x+b_2y+c_2=0$, respectively, are parallel if and only if $a_1b_2-b_1a_2=0$. (*Hint*: Write each equation in the point-slope form and compare.)

*An * indicates the exercise problem is more difficult.*

31. A manufacturer obtained the following data relating the cost, y, in dollars to the number of units, x, of a commodity produced:

Number of units produced (x)	0	20	40	60	80	100
Cost in dollars (y)	200	208	222	230	242	250

(***a***) Plot the cost (y) versus the quantity produced (x).

(***b***) Draw the straight line through the points (0, 200) and (100, 250).

(***c***) Derive an equation of the straight line of part (b).

(***d***) Taking this equation to be an approximation of the relationship between the cost and the level of production, estimate the cost of producing 54 units of the commodity.

32. The annual sales (in millions of dollars) of the Metro Department Store during the past five years were:

Annual sales	5.8	6.2	7.2	8.4	9.0
Year	1	2	3	4	5

(***a***) Plot the annual sales (y) versus the year (x).

(***b***) Draw a straight line L through the points corresponding to the first and fifth year.

(***c***) Derive an equation of the line L.

(***d***) Using this equation estimate the annual sales for the Metro Department Store four years from now.

1

Chapter Review

EXERCISES

1. List the elements of the following sets in roster notation.

(***a***) $\{x|3x-2=7;\ x, \text{ an integer}\}$

(***b***) $\{x|x$ is a letter of the word *TALLAHASSEE*$\}$

(***c***) The set having elements that are the even numbers between 3 and 11.

(***d***) $\{x|(x-3)(x+4)=0;\ x, \text{ a negative integer}\}$

2. Let $A=\{a, c, e, r\}$. Which of the following sets are equal to A?

(***a***) $\{r, e, c, a\}$

(***b***) $\{x|x$ is a letter of the word *career*$\}$

(***c***) $\{x|x$ is a letter of the alphabet$\}$

(***d***) $\{x|x$ is a letter of the word *cares*$\}$

3. List all subsets of the set $A=\{e, f, g\}$. Indicate which of the subsets are proper.

4. Shade the portion of the figure shown below that represents each of the following sets.

(***a***) $A\cup(B\cap C)$ (***b***) $(A\cap B\cap C)^c$ (***c***) $A^c\cap B^c\cap C^c$

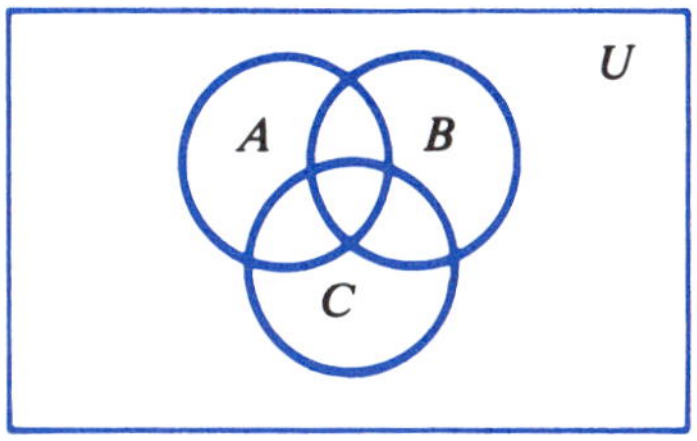

5. Let U denote the set of all undergraduate students at a certain university. Let

$A=\{x\in U|x$ has taken a course in BASIC computer programming$\}$
$B=\{x\in U|x$ has taken a course in COBOL computer programming$\}$
$C=\{x\in U|x$ has taken a course in FORTRAN computer programming$\}$

Find an expression in terms of A, B and C for each of the following:

(***a***) The set of students who have not taken a course in one of the three given computer programming languages.

(***b***) The set of students who have taken a course in BASIC and COBOL.

(***c***) The set of students who have taken a course in BASIC and COBOL but not FORTRAN.

6. Let $U=\{a, b, c, d, e\}$, $A=\{a, b\}$, $B=\{b, c, d\}$ and $C=\{a, d, e\}$.
Verify each of the following equations by direct computation.

(***a***) $A\cup(B\cup C)=(A\cup B)\cup C$ (***b***) $A\cap(B\cap C)=(A\cap B)\cap C$
(***c***) $A\cap(B\cup C)=(A\cap B)\cup(A\cap C)$ (***d***) $A\cup(B\cap C)=(A\cup B)\cap(A\cup C)$

7. Find the distance between the two given points.

(***a***) $(-2, -3)$ and $(1, -7)$ (***b***) $(1/2, \sqrt{3})$ and $(-1/2, 2\sqrt{3})$

In problems 8 through 11, find the value(s) of x *satisfying each of the given expressions.*

8. $2x^2+3x-2\leq 0$ ***9.*** $|2x-3|<5$

10. $\dfrac{1}{x-2}>2$ ***11.*** $\left|\dfrac{x+1}{x-1}\right|=5$

12. Find the equation of the straight line passing through the point $(2, 3)$ and parallel to the line with equation $3x+4y-8=0$.

13. Find the equation of the straight line passing through the point $(-3, -4)$ and parallel to the line joining the points $(-3, 4)$ and $(2, 1)$.

14. Find the equation of the straight line passing through the point $(-2, -4)$ that is perpendicular to the line with equation $2x - 3y - 24 = 0$.

15. Sketch the graph of the equation $3x - 4y = 24$.

2 FUNCTIONS AND GRAPHS

2.1 Functions and their Graphs

In many mathematical applications we are concerned with the relationship between two quantities. The concept of a *function* conveniently describes this relationship.

function For our purpose, a *function* f of a variable x is a rule that assigns to each value of x **one and only one** value y. The number y is normally denoted by $f(x)$ (read "f of x") emphasizing the dependency of y upon x. An example of a function may be taken from the familiar relationship between the area of a circle and its radius. Letting x and y denote the radius and area of a circle, respectively, we have, from elementary geometry,

(2.1) $$y = \pi x^2$$

Equation (2.1) defines y as a function of x since for each admissible value of x (that is, a nonnegative number representing the radius of a certain circle) there corresponds precisely one number $y = \pi x^2$, which gives the area of the circle. This *area function* may be written as

(2.2) $$f(x) = \pi x^2$$

For example to compute the area of a circle of radius 5 inches, we simply replace x in Equation (2.2) by the number 5. Thus, the area of the circle is

$$f(5) = \pi 5^2 = 25\pi$$

or 25π square inches.

EXAMPLE 2.1 Let the function f be defined by the rule $f(x)=2x^2-x+1$. Compute $f(1)$, $f(1/2)$, $f(-2)$ and $f(h)$ where h stands for a real number.

SOLUTION To compute $f(1)$ we replace x in the function $f(x)$ by 1, obtaining

$$f(1)=2(1)^2-1+1=2$$

Similarly, we find

$$f\left(\frac{1}{2}\right)=2\left(\frac{1}{2}\right)^2-\frac{1}{2}+1=1$$

$$f(-2)=2(-2)^2-(-2)+1=11$$

and

$$f(h)=2(h)^2-h+1=2h^2-h+1$$

■

EXAMPLE 2.2 The Thermo-Master Company manufactures an indoor-outdoor thermometer at its Mexico subsidiary. The management of the company estimates that the profit realizable by the company in the manufacture and sale of x units of thermometers per week is $P(x)=-0.001x^2+8x-5000$ dollars. Find the weekly profit of the company if its level of production is (**a**) 1000 thermometers per week and (**b**) 2000 thermometers per week.

SOLUTION (**a**) The weekly profit realizable by the company when the level of production is 1000 units per week is found by evaluating the profit function $P(x)$ at $x=1000$. Thus,

$$P(1000)=-0.001(1000)^2+8(1000)-5000=2000 \quad \text{or} \quad \$2000.$$

(**b**) When the level of production is 2000 units per week, the weekly profit is given by

$$P(2000)=-0.001(2000)^2+8(2000)-5000=7000 \quad \text{or} \quad \$7000.$$

■

independent and dependent variables

Suppose we are given the function $y=f(x)$.* The variable x is called the *independent variable* while the variable y is called the *dependent variable*. The set of all values that may be assumed by x is called the *domain of the function f*, while the set comprising all the values assumed by $y=f(x)$ as x takes on all possible values in its domain, is called the *range of the function f*. For the *area function* (2.2) the domain of f is the set of all x in the interval $[0, \infty)$ while the range of f is also the interval $[0, \infty)$.

domain and range of a function

The domain of the area function is partly determined by the requirement that the radius of a circle must be nonnegative. In general, if a function is defined by a rule relating x to $f(x)$ without specific mention of its domain, the understanding will be that the domain shall consist of all values of x for which the function is defined.

* *It is customary to refer to a function f* as $f(x)$.

EXAMPLE 2.3 Find the domain of each of the functions defined by the following equations:

(**a**) $f(x)=\sqrt{x^2-1}$

(**b**) $f(x)=\dfrac{1}{x^2-4}$

(**c**) $f(x)=x^2+3$

SOLUTION (**a**) Since the square root of a negative number is undefined, we require that $x^2-1\geq 0$. The inequality is satisfied by the set of real numbers $x\geq 1$ or $x\leq -1$. Thus, in this case the domain of f consists of the intervals $(-\infty, -1]$ and $[1, \infty)$.

(**b**) The only restriction on x is that x^2-4 be different from zero since division by zero is not allowed. But, $(x^2-4)=(x+2)(x-2)=0$ if $x=-2$ or $x=2$. Thus, the domain of f in this case consists of the intervals $(-\infty, -2)$, $(-2, 2)$ and $(2, \infty)$.

(**c**) Here all real numbers are admissible so that the domain of f is the set of all real numbers. ■

If f is a function with domain A, then corresponding to each real number x in A there is precisely one real number $f(x)$, which is the *image* of x under f. We can also express this fact by using *ordered pairs* of real numbers. Write each *pre-image* x in A as the first member of an ordered pair and each image $f(x)$ corresponding to x as the second member of the ordered pair. This gives for each x in A exactly one ordered pair $(x, f(x))$. This observation leads to the following equivalent definition of a function f: A function f with domain A is the set of all ordered pairs $(x, f(x))$ where x belongs to A. Observe that the condition that there be *one and only one* image $f(x)$ corresponding to each x in A translates into the requirement that *no two ordered pairs have the same first number.*

graph of a function

Since ordered pairs of real numbers correspond to points in the plane, we have found a way to exhibit a function graphically. The totality of all such points comprising a function is called the *graph* of the function. We obtain much information about the graph of a function by plotting a few points that lie on its graph.

EXAMPLE 2.4 Sketch the graph of the function defined by the equation $y=x^2+1$.

SOLUTION The domain of the function is the set of all real numbers. Since $x^2\geq 0$ for any real number x we see that $x^2+1\geq 1$ for any x in the domain of the function, and the range of the given function is the interval $[1, \infty)$.

Next, by assigning several values to the variable x and computing the corresponding values of y, we obtain the following solutions to the equation $y=x^2+1$:

x	-3	-2	-1	0	1	2	3
y	10	5	2	1	2	5	10

The graph of the function defined by the equation $y=x^2+1$ is a parabola (see Figure 2.1).

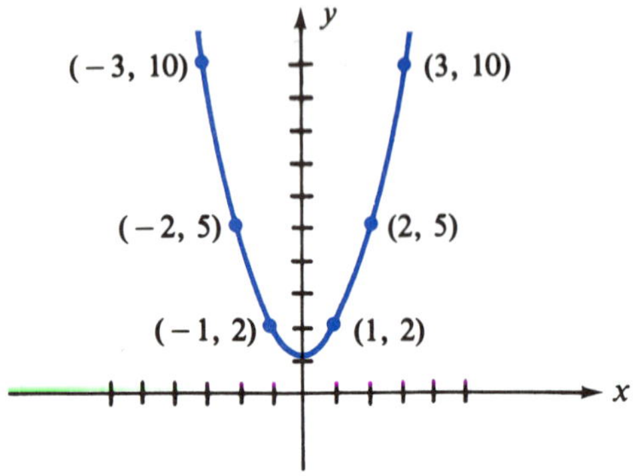

Figure 2.1

■

Some functions are defined in a piecemeal fashion as the following example shows.

EXAMPLE 2.5 Sketch the graph of the function f defined by

$$f(x)=\begin{cases}-x & \text{if } x<0\\ \sqrt{x} & \text{if } x\geq 0\end{cases}$$

SOLUTION The function f is defined in a piecemeal fashion on the set of all real numbers. In the subdomain $(-\infty, 0)$ the rule for f is given by $f(x)=-x$. The equation $y=-x$ is a linear equation in the slope-intercept form (with slope -1 and intercept 0). We see that the graph of f corresponding to the subdomain $(-\infty, 0)$ is the half-line shown in Figure 2.2. Next, in the subdomain $[0, \infty)$, the rule for f is given by $f(x)=\sqrt{x}$. The values of $f(x)$ corresponding to $x=0, 1, 2, 3, 4, 9$ and 16 are tabulated below.

x	0	1	2	3	4	9	16
$f(x)$	0	1	$\sqrt{2}$	$\sqrt{3}$	2	3	4

Using these values we sketch the graph of the function f as follows (Figure 2.2).

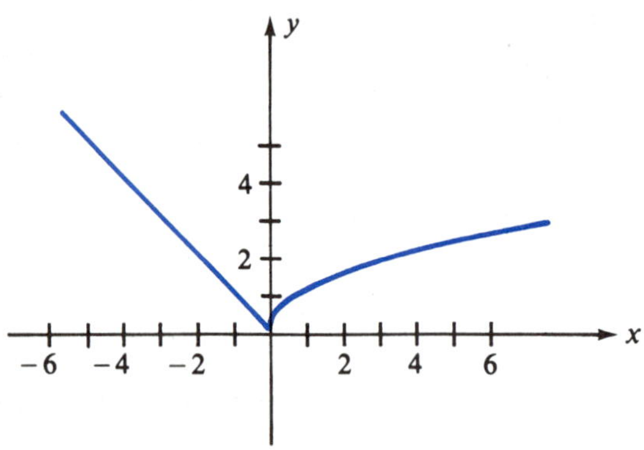

Figure 2.2

■

We close this section by reminding the reader of an important property of a function, namely, corresponding to each pre-image x in the domain of f there is precisely one and only one image $f(x)$. To appreciate the importance of this property, consider a rule that associates with each item (x) in a department store its selling price y. Then corresponding to each such x there should be one and only one y; that is, the rule must be one that satisfies the uniqueness property of a function. In general, any rule that associates each element x in a certain set A with at *least* one element y in a set B is a *relation* from A to B. Thus, a function is a special relation possessing the uniqueness property.

relation

EXAMPLE 2.6 Sketch the graph of the relation defined by $y^2 = x$. Is y a function of x?

SOLUTION Solving for y in terms of x, we find $y = \pm\sqrt{x}$. Since the square root of a negative number is not a real number, we see that the domain of the relation is the set of all nonnegative numbers. To find the values of y corresponding to some sample numbers in the domain of the relation, for example, $x = 0, 3, 4, 9, 16$ and 25, we simply substitute these values of x into the equation and compute the corresponding values of y. The results of the computations are tabulated below.

x	0	3	4	9	16	25
y	0	$\pm\sqrt{3}$	± 2	± 3	± 4	± 5

Thus, for example, the images of the number 9 are the numbers 3 and -3. Note that, in general, each number x is mapped onto two numbers, $+\sqrt{x}$ and $-\sqrt{x}$. As in Example 2.4, we may sketch the graph of this relation by plotting a number of points (x, y), which satisfy the relation $y^2 = x$, and connect them with a "suitable" curve (Figure 2.3).

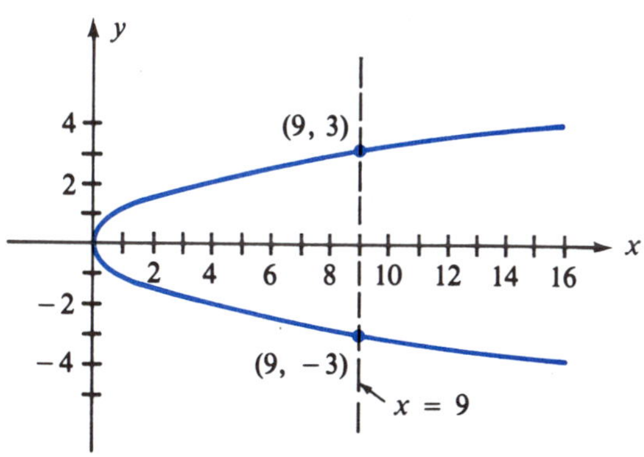

Figure 2.3

Since the ordered pairs $(9, 3)$ and $(9, -3)$ both have the same first number, or equivalently, the pre-image 9 has two images -3 and 3, we conclude that the equation $y^2 = x$ does not define y as a function of x. ■

vertical line test

Observe that the vertical line $x=9$ in Example 2.6 intersects the graph of R at the two points (9, 3) and (9, −3). In general, a relation R is a function if and only if a vertical line intersects the graph of R at no more than one point. This is called the *vertical line test*. It may be used to determine if a given graph is that of a relation or a function.

2.1 EXERCISES

1. Let f be the function defined by $f(x)=5x+6$. Find: $f(3)$, $f(-3)$, $f(a)$, $f(-a)$ and $f(a+3)$.

2. Let g be the function defined by $g(x)=3x^2-6x-3$. Find: $g(0)$, $g(-1)$, $g(a)$, $g(-a)$ and $g(x+1)$.

3. Let h be the function defined by $h(x)=-|x|+1$. Find: $h(-5)$, $h(0)$, $h(a)$, $h(-a)$ and $h(a-1)$.

4. Let s be a function defined by $s(t)=2t/(t^2-1)$. Find: $s(4)$, $s(0)$, $s(a)$, $s(2+a)$ and $s(t+1)$.

5. Let f be a function defined by

$$f(x)=\begin{cases} x^2+1 & \text{if } x\le 0 \\ \sqrt{x} & \text{if } x>0 \end{cases}$$

Find $f(-2)$, $f(0)$ and $f(1)$.

6. Let g be a function defined by

$$g(x)=\begin{cases} -\frac{1}{2}x+1 & \text{if } x<2 \\ \sqrt{x-2} & \text{if } x\ge 2 \end{cases}$$

Find $g(-2)$, $g(0)$, $g(2)$ and $g(4)$.

7. The consumption function in a certain economy is given by the equation

$$C(y)=0.75y+6$$

where $C(y)$ is the personal consumption expenditure in billions of dollars and y is the disposable personal income. Find $C(0)$, $C(50)$, $C(100)$.

8. In a certain state, the sales tax T on the amount of taxable goods is 6% of the value of the goods purchased (x) where both T and x are measured in dollars.

(**a**) Express T as a function of x.

(**b**) Find $f(200)$, $f(5.65)$.

9. The surface area S of a single-celled organism may be found by multiplying 4π times the square of the radius (r) of the cell. Express S as a function of r.

In problems 10 through 19, find the domain of the given function.

10. $f(x)=x^2+3$

11. $f(x)=\dfrac{3x+1}{x^2}$

12. $f(x)=\sqrt{x^2+1}$

13. $f(x)=\sqrt{x^2-25}$

14. $f(x)=\sqrt{25-x^2}$

15. $f(x)=\dfrac{1}{x-2}$

16. $f(x)=\dfrac{x}{x^2-1}$

17. $f(x)=\dfrac{1}{x^2+x-2}$

18. $f(x)=\dfrac{\sqrt{1-x}}{x^2-4}$

19. $f(x)=\sqrt{x^2-2x-3}$

20. Let f be a function defined by the rule $f(x)=x^2-x-6$.

(***a***) Find the domain of f.

(***b***) Compute $f(x)$ for $x=-3, -2, -1, 0, 1/2, 1, 2, 3$.

(***c***) Use the results obtained in parts (***a***) and (***b***) to sketch the graph of f.

(***d***) What is the range of f?

In problems 21 through 27, sketch the graph of the given function.

21. $f(x)=-2x+1$

22. $f(x)=9-x^2$

23. $f(x)=2+\sqrt{x}$

***24.** $f(x)=|x-1|$

***25.** $f(x)=|x|-1$

26. $f(x)=\begin{cases} 4-x & \text{if } x<2 \\ 2x-2 & \text{if } x\geq 2 \end{cases}$

27. $f(x)=\begin{cases} -x-1 & \text{if } x<-1 \\ 0 & \text{if } -1\leq x\leq 1 \\ x+1 & \text{if } x>1 \end{cases}$

28. The postage for first-class mail is 20 cents for the first ounce or fraction thereof, and 17 cents for each additional ounce or fraction thereof. Any parcel not exceeding 12 ounces may be sent by first class mail. Letting x denote the weight of a parcel in ounces and $f(x)$ the postage in cents, complete the following description of the "postage function" f:

$$f(x)=\begin{cases} 20 & \text{if } 0<x\leq 1 \\ 37 & \text{if } 1<x\leq 2 \\ \cdots & \\ ? & \text{if } 11<x\leq 12 \end{cases}$$

(***a***) What is the domain of f?

(***b***) What is the range of f?

(***c***) Sketch the graph of f.

29. The following table gives the rate schedule of a gas company. The quantity, x, is measured in units of hundred cubic feet while the cost is measured in pennies.

	First	Next	Next	Next	Next	Next	Over
Units in '00 cubic feet	1@	9@	30@	60@	200@	200@	500@
Cost in ¢	387.49	52.05	44.07	39.51	32.67	31.53	29.25

(*a*) Complete the following description of the cost function f.

$$f(x)=\begin{cases} 387.49 & \text{if } 0<x\le 1 \\ 387.49+52.05(x-1) & \text{if } 1<x\le 10 \\ 855.94+44.07(x-10) & \text{if } 10<x\le 40 \\ \cdots & \\ ? & \text{if } 500<x \end{cases}$$

(***b***) What is the domain of f?

(***c***) Sketch the graph of f.

(***d***) What is the cost of 9100 cubic feet of gas?

In problems 30 through 33, sketch the graph of the relation defined by the given equation. Is y *a function of* x?

30. $y^2 = 2x$

31. $y^2 = 10x - x^2$

32. $x^2 - y^2 + 2 = 0$

*****33.*** $x = |y+1|$

In problems 34 through 41, use the vertical line test to determine if the given graph represents y *as a function of* x.

34.

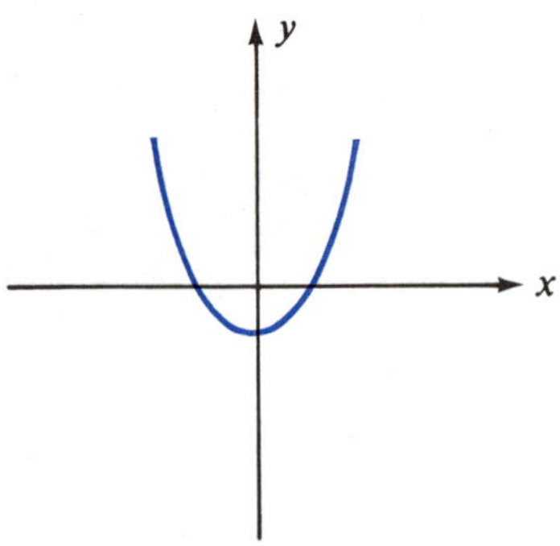

35.

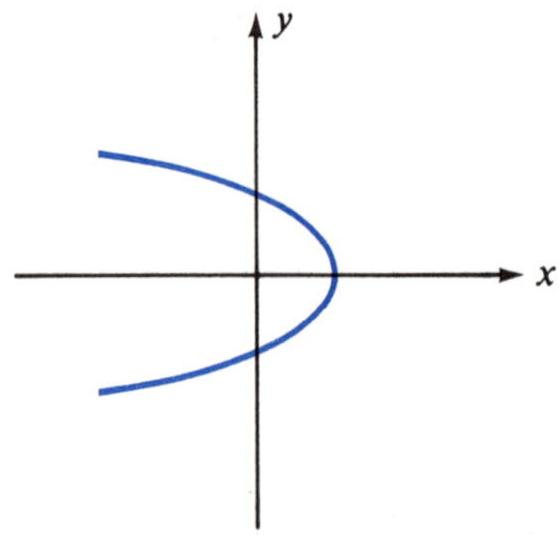

36.

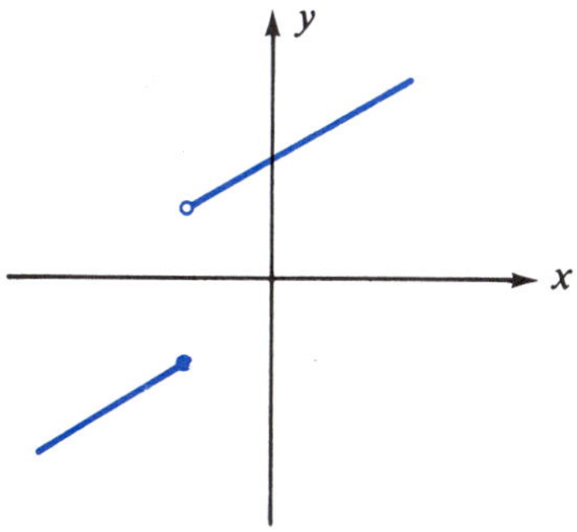

37.

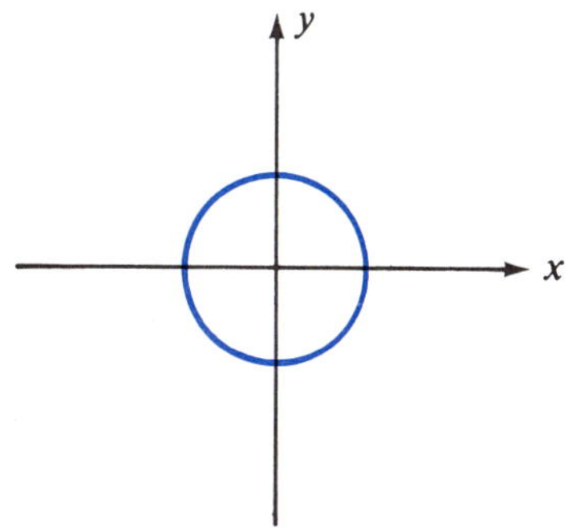

38.

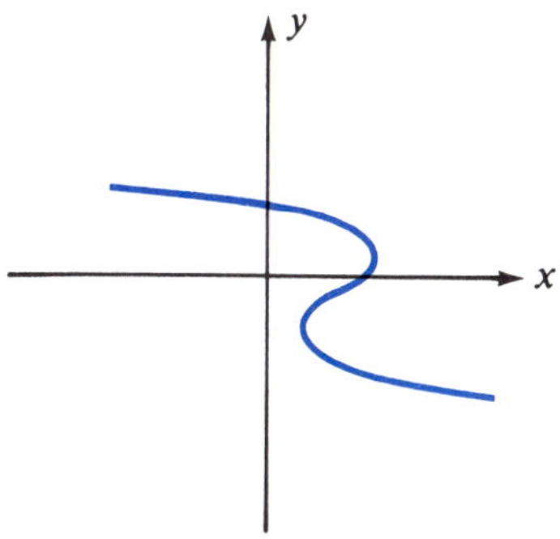

39.

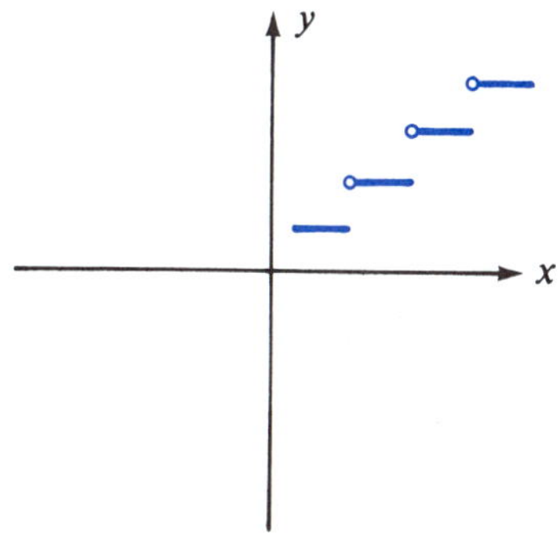

40.

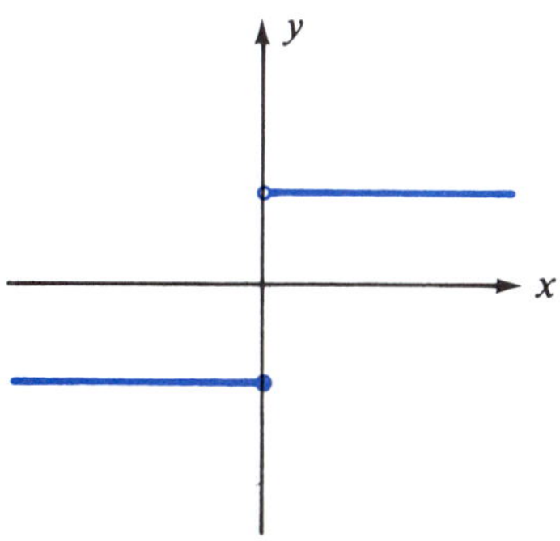

41.

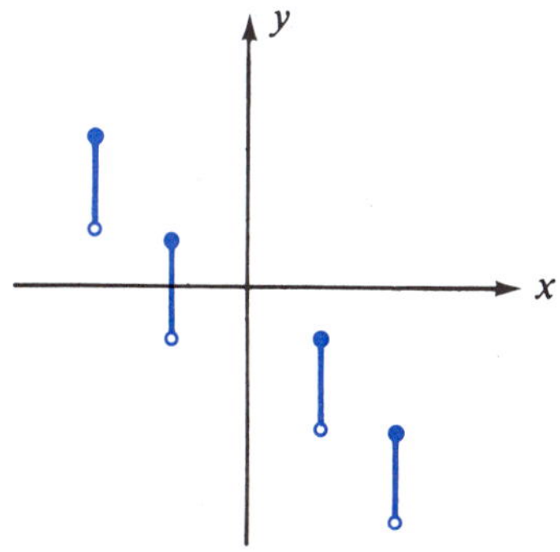

2.2 Linear Functions and their Applications

Recall that a linear equation in x and y is one of the form $Ax+By+C=0$ where A, B, and C are constants and A and B are not both zero. If $B\neq 0$, the equation can always be solved for y in terms of x; in fact, as we have seen in Section 1.5, the equation may be cast in the slope-intercept form

(2.3) $$y=mx+b \qquad (m,\, b \text{ constants})$$

Equation (2.3) defines y as a function of x. The domain (and range) of this function is the set of all real numbers. Furthermore, the graph of the function, as we have seen in Section 1.5, is a straight line in the plane. For this reason, the function f defined by the rule $y = f(x)$ where

(2.4) $$f(x) = mx + b \qquad (m, b \text{ constants})$$

linear function is called a *linear function.*

Linear functions play an important role in the quantitative analysis of business and economic problems. First, many problems arising in these and other fields are *linear* in nature or are *linear* in the intervals of interest and thus can be formulated in terms of linear functions. Second, because linear functions are relatively easy to work with, assumptions involving linearity are often made in the formulation of problems. In many cases these assumptions are justified, and acceptable mathematical models are obtained that approximate real life situations.

Simple Interest

A natural application of linear functions to the business world is found in computations involving *simple interest*—interest that is computed on the original principal only. Thus, if I denotes the interest on a principal P (in dollars) at an interest rate of r per year for n years, then we have

(2.5) $$I = Prn$$

The *accumulated value* A, the sum of the principal and interest after n years is given by

$$A = P + I = P + Prn$$

(2.6) or $$A = P(1 + rn)$$

and is a linear function of n. (See problem 10 in Exercise Set 2.2.) In a business application we are normally interested only in the case when n is positive and so only that part of the line that lies in the first quadrant is of interest to us (Figure 2.4).

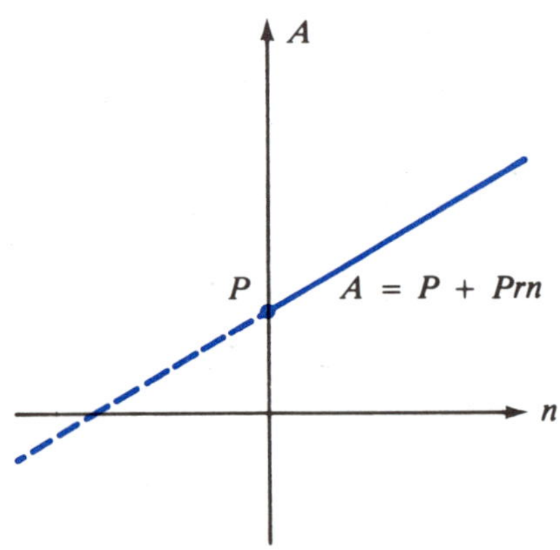

Figure 2.4

EXAMPLE 2.7 A bank pays simple interest at the rate of 8% per year for a certain class of deposits. If a customer deposits \$1000 and makes no withdrawals for 3 years, what is the total amount on deposit at the end of 3 years? What is the interest earned in that period of time?

SOLUTION The total amount on deposit at the end of 3 years is given by

$$\begin{aligned} A &= P(1+rn) \\ &= 1000[1+(0.08)(3)] \\ &= 1240 \end{aligned}$$

or \$1240.

The interest earned over the three year period is given by

$$\begin{aligned} I &= Prn \\ &= 1000(0.08)(3) \\ &= 240 \end{aligned}$$

or \$240. ■

EXAMPLE 2.8 An amount of \$2000 is invested in a ten-year trust fund that pays 6% annual simple interest. What is the total amount of the trust fund at the end of ten years?

SOLUTION The total amount of the trust fund at the end of ten years is given by

$$\begin{aligned} A &= P(1+rn) \\ &= 2000[1+(0.06)(10)] \\ &= 3200 \quad \text{or} \quad \$3200. \end{aligned}$$

■

Simple Discount

For relatively small loans made over relatively short periods of time a *simple discount* procedure is normally employed. The simple discount is also referred to as "Banker's discount" or "interest paid in advance." In this procedure the borrower agrees to pay a certain sum A at a certain date, say in n years time. The lender deducts a certain percentage of this amount and gives the borrower the remainder. The amount deducted, D, is the *amount discounted* and is the (simple) interest on the amount A at the *discount rate* of d(percent) per year for n years. Thus,

$$D = Adn \tag{2.7}$$

If P denotes the amount the borrower receives, called the *present value* of the amount A, then

$$P = A - D = A - Adn$$

(2.8) $$= A(1 - dn)$$

and is a linear function of n (see problem 14, Exercise Set 2.2).

EXAMPLE 2.9 Mr. Brown signs a note at a bank in which he agrees to pay the bank \$1000 in four months. The bank's discount rate is 9%. How much does Mr. Brown receive from the bank?

SOLUTION Mr. Brown receives

$$P = 1000\left[1 - (0.09)\left(\frac{1}{3}\right)\right]$$

$$= 970$$

or \$970. ■

EXAMPLE 2.10 Miss Smith receives \$95.50 from a bank and promises to repay \$100.00 six months later. What is the corresponding discount rate?

SOLUTION We have

$$95.5 = 100\left(1 - \frac{d}{2}\right)$$

$$0.955 = 1 - \frac{d}{2}$$

$$\frac{d}{2} = 1 - 0.955$$

or

$$d = 0.09$$

giving a discount rate of 9% per year. ■

Simple Depreciation

For the purpose of income tax computations, business firms are allowed by law to depreciate certain of their assets such as buildings, machines, furniture, automobiles, etc. over a period of time. The *linear depreciation* or *straight line method* is used widely. For example, to derive an equation describing the book value of an asset being depreciated linearly, let C (in dollars) denote the original cost of the asset and suppose it is depreciated linearly over N years with a scrap value of S dollars. Let V denote the book value of the asset at the end of the nth year. Then the straight line with the required equation passes through the points $(0, C)$ and (N, S). Why? The slope of the required straight line is given by $(S-C)/N$. Using Equation (1.5) with the point (N, S), we see that the required equation is given by

$$V-S=\frac{S-C}{N}(n-N)$$

(2.9) that is

$$V=S+(C-S)\left(1-\frac{n}{N}\right) \qquad (0\leqslant n\leqslant N)$$

EXAMPLE 2.11 A printing machine has an initial value of \$100,000 and is to be depreciated linearly over 5 years with a \$0 scrap value. Determine its book value at the end of the second year.

SOLUTION Using Equation (2.9) with $C=100{,}000$, $S=0$ and $N=5$, we find that its book value at the end of the nth year is given by

$$V=100{,}000\left(1-\frac{n}{5}\right) \qquad (0\leqslant n\leqslant 5)$$

Thus, the book value at the end of the second year is given by

$$V=100{,}000\left(1-\frac{2}{5}\right)=60{,}000$$

or \$60,000. ■

EXAMPLE 2.12 Determine the rate of depreciation of the printing machine in Example 2.11.

SOLUTION Writing Equation (2.9) in the slope-intercept form, we have

$$V=C-\frac{(C-S)}{N}n$$

so that the slope of the corresponding line is given by

$$m=-\frac{(C-S)}{N}$$

But m is the rate of change of V with respect to n so that the rate of depreciation sought is given by $r=-m$. Why? Using the appropriate data from Example 2.11, we find that the required rate of depreciation is given by

$$\begin{aligned} r&=\frac{(100{,}000-0)}{5}\\ &=20{,}000 \end{aligned}$$

or \$20,000 per year. ■

Linear Cost, Revenue, and Profit Functions

The costs incurred in operating a business are usually classified into two categories. Costs that remain more or less constant regardless of the level of activity of the firm are called *fixed costs*. Examples of fixed costs are rental fees and executive salaries. On the other hand, costs that vary with production or sales are called *variable costs*. Examples of variable costs are wages and costs for raw materials.

Suppose a firm has a fixed cost of F dollars, a production cost of c dollars per unit, and a selling price of s dollars per unit. Then the *cost function* $C(x)$, the *revenue function* $R(x)$, and the *profit function* $P(x)$ for the firm are given by

$$C(x) = cx + F$$

$$R(x) = sx$$

and

$$P(x) = R(x) - C(x) \qquad \text{(Revenue minus Cost)}$$

$$= (s - c)x - F$$

where x denotes the number of units of the commodity produced and sold. Each of the functions C, R, and P is a linear function of x.

For the remainder of this section, we shall assume that the cost and the revenue functions are both linear. This not only simplifies the mathematical analysis but gives, in many cases, an acceptable mathematical model which approximates the real situation.

EXAMPLE 2.13 Puritron, a manufacturer of water filters, has a monthly fixed cost of \$20,000, a production cost of \$20 per unit and a selling price of \$30 per unit. Find the cost function, the revenue function, and the profit function for the company.

SOLUTION Let x denote the number of units produced and sold. Then

$$C(x) = 20x + 20{,}000$$

$$R(x) = 30x$$

and

$$P(x) = R(x) - C(x) = 30x - (20x + 20{,}000)$$

$$= 10x - 20{,}000$$

■

The solution of certain practical problems sometimes involves finding the point of intersection of two straight lines. To see how such a problem may be solved algebraically, suppose we are given two straight lines L_1 and L_2 with equations

$$y = m_1x + b_1 \quad \text{and} \quad y = m_2x + b_2,$$

(where m_1, b_1, m_2, and b_2 are constants) which intersect at the point $P(x, y)$ (see Figure 2.5).

The point $P(x, y)$ lies on the line L_1 and therefore satisfies the equation $y = m_1x + b_1$. At the same time, it also lies on the line L_2 and satisfies the equation

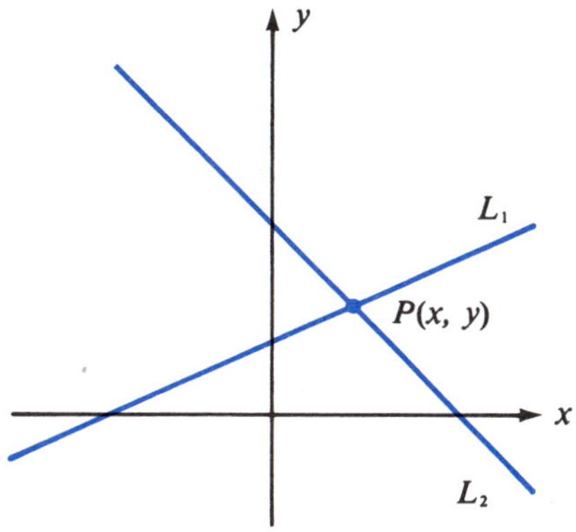

Figure 2.5

$y = m_2x + b_2$. Therefore, to find the point of intersection $P(x, y)$ of the lines L_1 and L_2, we solve the equations

$$y = m_1x + b_1 \quad \text{and} \quad y = m_2x + b_2$$

simultaneously for x and y.

EXAMPLE 2.14 Find the point of intersection of the two straight lines with equations $y = x + 1$ and $y = -2x + 4$.

SOLUTION We solve the given equations simultaneously. Substituting the value y as given in the first equation into the second, we obtain

$$x + 1 = -2x + 4$$
$$3x = 3$$

or

$$x = 1$$

Substituting this value of x into either one of the given equations gives $y = 2$. Therefore, the required point of intersection is $(1, 2)$ (see Figure 2.6).

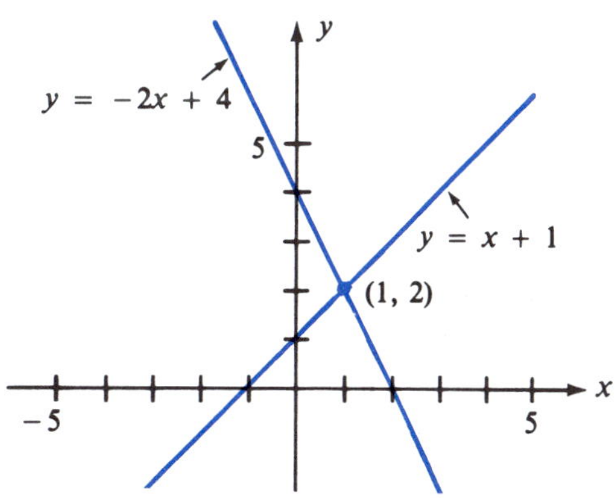

Figure 2.6 ■

We now turn to some applications involving the intersections of pairs of straight lines.

Break-even Analysis

Consider a firm with (linear) cost function $C(x)$, revenue function $R(x)$, and profit function $P(x)$ given by

$$C(x) = cx + F$$

$$R(x) = sx$$

and

$$P(x) = R(x) - C(x) = (s - c)x - F$$

where c denotes the unit cost of production, s denotes the selling price per unit, F denotes the fixed cost incurred by the firm, and x denotes the level of production and sales. The level of production at which the firm neither makes a profit nor sustains a loss is called the *break-even level of operation* and may be determined by solving the equations $p = C(x)$ and $p = R(x)$ simultaneously. For, at this level of production, x_0, the profit is zero so that $P(x_0) = R(x_0) - C(x_0) = 0$ and $R(x_0) = C(x_0)$. The point $P_0(x_0, p_0)$, the solution of the simultaneous equation $p = R(x)$ and $p = C(x)$, is referred to as the *break-even point*; the number x_0 and the number p_0 are called the *break-even quantity* and the *break-even revenue*, respectively.

Geometrically, the break-even point $P_0(x_0, p_0)$ is just the point of intersection of the straight lines representing the cost and revenue functions, respectively. This follows because $P_0(x_0, p_0)$, being the solution of the simultaneous equation $p = R(x)$ and $p = C(x)$, must lie on both these lines simultaneously (Figure 2.7). Note that

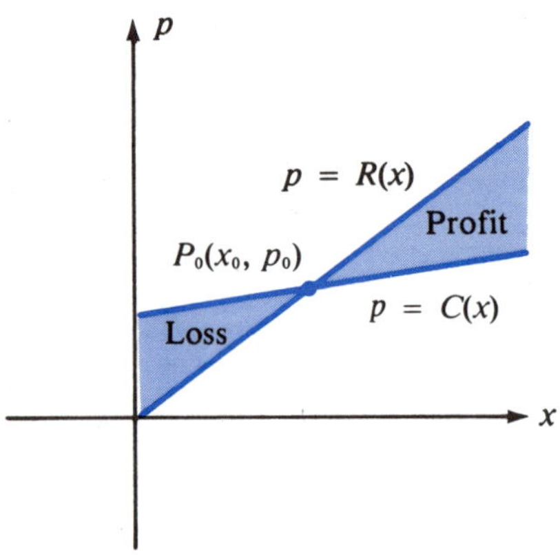

Figure 2.7

if $x < x_0$, then $R(x) < C(x)$ so that $P(x) = R(x) - C(x) < 0$ and thus the firm sustains a loss at this level of production. On the other hand, if $x > x_0$ then $P(x) > 0$ and the firm operates at a profitable level in this case.

EXAMPLE 2.15 Prescott Inc. manufactures its products at a cost of \$4 per unit and sells them for \$10 per unit. If the fixed cost for the firm is \$12,000 per month, determine the break-even point for the firm.

SOLUTION The cost function C and the revenue function R are given by $C(x)=4x+12{,}000$ and $R(x)=10x$, respectively (Figure 2.8). Setting $R(x)=C(x)$, we obtain

$$\begin{aligned} 10x &= 4x+12{,}000 \\ 6x &= 12{,}000 \\ x &= 2000 \end{aligned}$$

Substituting this value of x into $R(x)=10x$ gives $R(10)=(10)(2000)=20{,}000$. So, for a break-even operation, the firm should manufacture 2000 units of its product resulting in a break-even revenue of \$20,000.

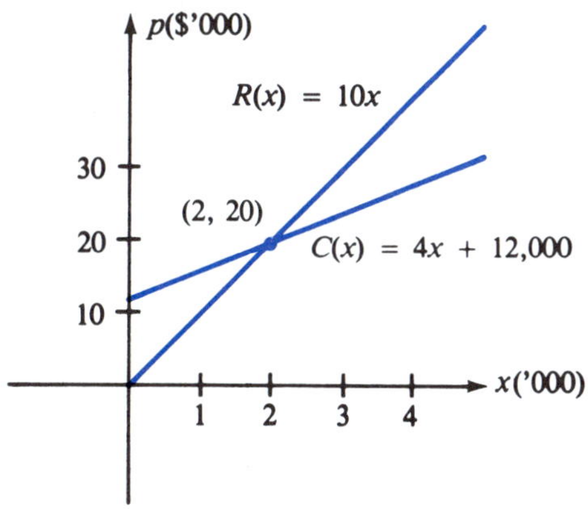

Figure 2.8

■

EXAMPLE 2.16 Using the data supplied in Example 2.15, answer the following questions:

(**a**) What is the loss sustained by the firm if only 1500 units of its products are produced and sold per month?

(**b**) What is the profit if 3000 units are produced and sold per month?

(**c**) What is the number of units the firm should produce in order to realize a minimum monthly profit of \$9000?

SOLUTION The profit function P is given by the rule

$$\begin{aligned} P(x) &= R(x)-C(x) \\ &= 10x-(4x+12{,}000) \\ &= 6x-12{,}000 \end{aligned}$$

(a) If 1500 units are produced and sold per month, we have

$$\begin{aligned} P(1500) &= 6(1500) - 12{,}000 \\ &= -3000 \end{aligned}$$

so that the firm will sustain a loss of \$3000 per month.

(b) If 3000 units are produced and sold per month, we have

$$\begin{aligned} P(3000) &= 6(3000) - 12{,}000 \\ &= 6000 \end{aligned}$$

or a monthly profit of \$6000.

(c) Substituting 9000 for $P(x)$ in the equation $P(x) = 6x - 12{,}000$ we obtain

$$\begin{aligned} 9000 &= 6x - 12{,}000 \\ 6x &= 21{,}000 \\ x &= 3500 \end{aligned}$$

Thus, at least 3500 units should be produced by the firm in order to realize a \$9000 minimum monthly profit. ■

EXAMPLE 2.17 The management of a firm must decide between two manufacturing processes for a certain product. The monthly cost resulting from the use of the first process is given by $C_1(x) = 20x + 10{,}000$ where x is the number of units produced, while the monthly cost resulting from the use of the second process is given by $C_2(x) = 10x + 30{,}000$. Both costs are measured in dollars. If the projected sales are 800 units at a unit price of \$40, which process should the management choose?

SOLUTION The break-even level of operation using the first process is obtained by solving the equation

$$40x = 20x + 10{,}000$$

or

$$20x = 10{,}000$$

whence

$$x = 500$$

giving an output of 500 units. Next, we solve the equation

$$40x = 10x + 30{,}000$$

or

$$30x = 30{,}000$$

whence

$$x = 1000$$

giving an output of 1000 units for a break-even operation using the second process. Since the projected sales are 800 units we conclude that the management should choose the first process which would give the firm a profit. ■

EXAMPLE 2.18 Referring to Example 2.17, what decision should the management make if the projected sales are (**a**) 1500 units and (**b**) 3000 units?

SOLUTION In both cases, the production is past the break-even level. Since the revenue is the same regardless of which process is employed, the decision will be based on the cost involved in using the first or the second process.

(**a**) If $x = 1500$, then

$$C_1(x) = (20)(1500) + 10{,}000 = 40{,}000$$
$$C_2(x) = (10)(1500) + 30{,}000 = 45{,}000$$

Hence, the decision should be made to use the first process.

(**b**) If $x = 3000$, then

$$C_1(x) = (20)(3000) + 10{,}000 = 70{,}000$$
$$C_2(x) = (10)(3000) + 30{,}000 = 60{,}000$$

In this case, the choice should be made to use the second process. ■

2.2 EXERCISES

1. Find the simple interest on a \$500 investment made for 2 years at an interest rate of 8% per annum. What is the accumulated amount?

2. Find the accumulated amount after 180 days on a \$10,000 investment at a simple interest rate of 10% per annum. (Assume 360 days in a year—interest computed under this assumption is called *ordinary simple interest.*)

3. Find the accumulated amount at the end of 9 months on an \$800 deposit with a bank paying simple interest at a rate of 6% per annum.

4. If the accumulated amount is \$1160 at the end of two years and the simple rate of interest is 8% per annum, what is the principal?

5. How many days will it take for a sum of \$1000 to earn \$15 interest if it is deposited with a bank paying ordinary simple interest at the rate of 5% per annum?

6. How much time will it take for a sum of money to double when it earns (simple) interest at the rate of 6% per annum?

7. Mr. Mitchell has been given the option of either paying his \$300 bill now or settling it for \$306 in 30 days time. If he opts for the latter, find the simple interest rate at which he would be charged.

8. A bank deposit paying simple interest at the rate of 5% per annum grew to a sum of \$3100 in 10 months. Find the principal.

9. An automobile including all optional equipment costs \$8400. The trade-in is valued at \$3400. The (simple) interest rate is 8% per annum. Compute the monthly payment on a 3-year contract.

10. Write Equation (2.6) in the slope-intercept form and interpret the meaning of the slope and the A-intercept in terms of r and P.

11. A man receives \$10,000 from a bank and promises to repay \$12,500 two years later. What is the simple discount rate used by the bank?

12. Find the present value of \$3000 due at the end of 2 years if the (simple) discount rate is 8% per annum.

13. What is the present value of a note for \$10,000 due in 60 days if the simple discount rate is 9% per annum? (Use a 360-day year.)

14. Write Equation (2.8) in the slope-intercept form and interpret the meaning of the slope and the P-intercept in terms of d and A. Compare your results with problem 10.

15. An office building worth \$1,000,000 when completed in 1975 is being depreciated linearly over 50 years with a scrap value of \$0. What will the book value of the building be in 1985? in 1990?

16. An automobile purchased for the use of the manager of a firm at a price of \$14,000 is to be depreciated using the straight line method over 5 years. What will the book value of the automobile be at the end of 3 years?

17. The National Textile Company installed a new machine in one of its factories in 1980 at a cost of \$250,000. The machine is depreciated linearly over 10 years with a scrap value of \$10,000.

(***a***) Find an expression for the book value of the machine in the nth year of use ($0 \leq n \leq 10$).

(***b***) Sketch the graph of the function of part (***a***).

(***c***) Find the book value of the machine in 1984.

(***d***) Find the rate at which the machine is being depreciated.

18. A mini-computer purchased at a cost of \$60,000 in 1978 had a residual (scrap) value of \$12,000 at the end of 4 years. If the straight line method of depreciation is used:

(***a***) Find the rate of depreciation.

(***b***) Find the linear equation expressing the book value of the mini-computer at the end of n years.

(***c***) Sketch the graph of the function of part (***b***).

(***d***) Find the book value of the mini-computer at the end of the third year.

19. Write Equation (2.9) in the slope-intercept form and interpret the meaning of the slope, the V-intercept, and the n-intercept in terms of C, S, and N.

In problems 20–25, find the point of intersection of each of the given pairs of straight lines.

20. $y = 3x + 4$
$y = -2x + 14$

21. $y = -4x - 7$
$-y = 5x + 10$

22. $2x - 3y = 6$
$3x + 6y = 16$

23. $2x + 4y = 11$
$-5x + 3y = 5$

24. $y = (1/4)x - 5$
$2x - (3/2)y = 1$

25. $y = (2/3)x - 4$
$x + 3y + 3 = 0$

26. Auto-time, a manufacturer of 24-hour variable timers, has a monthly fixed cost of \$48,000 and a production cost of \$8 for each timer manufactured. The timers sell for \$14 each.

(***a***) What is the cost function?

(***b***) What is the revenue function?

(***c***) What is the profit function?

(***d***) Compute the profit (loss) corresponding to production levels of 4000, 6000, and 10,000 timers, respectively.

27. For the firm in problem 26,

(***a***) Sketch the graphs of the cost function and the revenue function, and hence find the break-even point graphically.

(***b***) Find the break-even point algebraically.

(***c***) Sketch the graph of the profit function.

(***d***) At what point does the graph of the profit function cross the x-axis? Interpret your result.

In problems 28 through 31, find the break-even point for the cost function C and revenue function R. Their rules are given.

28. $C(x) = 5x + 10{,}000, \quad R(x) = 15x$

29. $C(x) = 15x + 12{,}000, \quad R(x) = 21x$

30. $C(x) = 0.2x + 120, \quad R(x) = 0.4x$

31. $C(x) = 150x + 20{,}000, \quad R(x) = 270x$

32. The management of T.M.I. Inc. finds that the monthly fixed costs attributable to the division of the company that produces blank tapes amount to \$12,100 per month. If the cost for producing each reel of tape is \$.60 and each reel of tape sells for \$1.15, find the break-even point for the division.

33. A division of Carter Enterprises produces "Personal Income Tax" diaries. The product sells for \$8. The monthly fixed costs incurred by the division are \$25,000, while the variable cost of producing each diary is \$3.

(***a***) Find the break-even point for the division.

(***b***) What should the level of sales be in order for the division to realize a 15% sales profit? (Discount income tax.)

34. A division of the Gibson Corporation manufactures bicycle pumps. The product sells for \$9, and the variable cost of producing each unit is 40% of the selling price. The monthly fixed costs incurred by the division are \$50,000. What is the break-even point for the division?

35. The Ace Truck Leasing Company leases a certain size truck at \$30.00 a day and \$.15 a mile while the Acme Truck Leasing Company leases the same size trucks at \$25.00 a day and \$.20 a mile.

(***a***) Find the functions describing the daily cost of leasing from each of the companies.

(***b***) Sketch the graphs of the two functions on the same set of axes.

(***c***) Which company should a customer rent a truck from for one day, if he plans to drive at most 70 miles?

(***d***) Solve the two equations of part (***a***) simultaneously and interpret your results.

36. A product may be made using machine I or machine II. The manufacturer estimates that the monthly fixed costs associated with using machine I are \$18,000, while the monthly fixed costs associated with using machine II are \$15,000. The variable costs associated with manufacturing one unit of the product using machine I and machine II are \$15 and \$20, respectively. The product sells for \$50.

(***a***) Obtain expressions for the cost functions associated with using each machine in the manufacturing process.

(***b***) Sketch the graphs of the cost functions of part (***a***) and the revenue function on the same set of axes.

(***c***) Which machine should be chosen by management if the projected sales are 450 units? 550 units? 650 units?

(***d***) What is the profit for each case in part (***c***)?

2.3 Techniques of Graphing

Before sketching the graph of a function f, it is often useful to obtain the following information about the function:

1. **The domain of f** To determine the domain of f one normally studies the restrictions to be placed on the independent variable x so that $f(x)$ is well-defined (see Example 2.3).

2. **The range of f** The range of f may be found by studying the values that $f(x)$ assumes as x runs through all possible values in its domain.

3. **Intercepts** The x-intercept (that is, the point on the x-axis where the graph of $y = f(x)$ crosses it) is found by setting $y = 0$ in the equation $y = f(x)$. Similarly, the y-intercept (the point on the y-axis where the graph of $y = f(x)$ crosses it) is found by setting $x = 0$ in the equation $y = f(x)$.

4. **Symmetry about the y-axis and the origin** To determine if the graph of $y = f(x)$ is symmetric with respect to the y-axis, we replace x by $-x$ in the equation; if the equation remains unchanged then there is symmetry with respect to the y-axis. To see this, we note that a curve is symmetric with respect to the y-axis, if and only if, whenever the point (x, y) is on the curve then the point $(-x, y)$ is also on the curve (Figure 2.9 part a). But the point $(-x, y)$ is on the graph of $y = f(x)$ if and only if it satisfies the equation $y = f(x)$. Next, the graph of $y = f(x)$ is symmetric about the origin if the equation remains unchanged when x and y are replaced by $-x$ and $-y$, respectively, (Figure 2.9 part b).

5. **Behavior of $f(x)$ for large absolute values of x.**

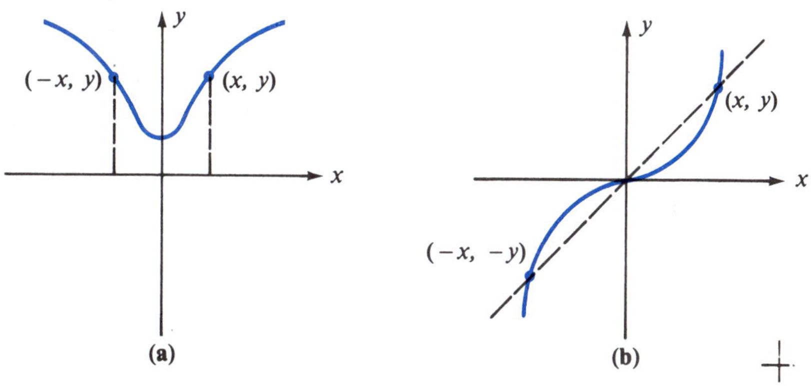

Figure 2.9

EXAMPLE 2.19 Sketch the graph of the function $f(x) = \sqrt{4 - x^2}$.

SOLUTION Since the square root of a negative number is undefined, we require that $4 - x^2 \geq 0$. This inequality is satisfied by the set of real numbers in the interval $[-2, 2]$, the domain of the function f. The range of f is $[0, 2]$. We see this by letting x run through all values in the interval $[-2, 2]$. Next, setting $y = 0$ and $x = 0$, successively, we find $x = \pm 2$ and $y = 2$, giving the x- and y-intercepts, respectively, of f.

There is symmetry with respect to the y-axis since the equation $y = \sqrt{4 - x^2}$ remains unchanged when x is replaced by $-x$. Finally, we determine a few points that lie on the graph of f. It suffices to consider only positive values of x since the graph of f is symmetric with respect to the y-axis. For example, by taking $x = 1$ and $x = \sqrt{2}$, we see that the points $(1, \sqrt{3})$ and $(\sqrt{2}, \sqrt{2})$ both lie on the graph of $f(x) = \sqrt{4 - x^2}$. The graph of f, shown in Figure 2.10, is a semicircle lying in the upper half-plane.

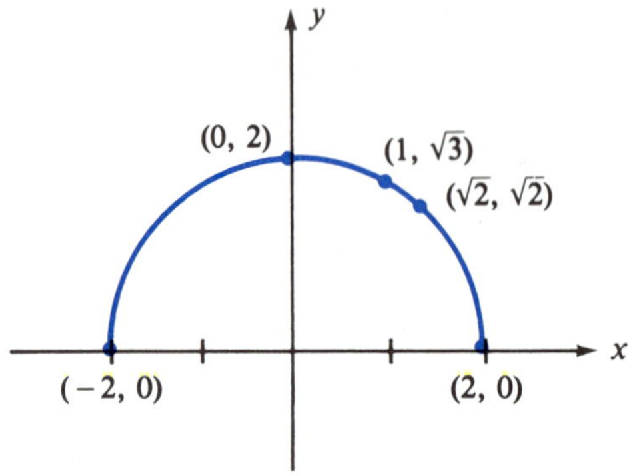

Figure 2.10

EXAMPLE 2.20 Sketch the graph of the function g defined by $g(x)=1/x^2$.

SOLUTION Since division by zero is not permissible, we rule out the possibility that x is zero. Thus, the domain of g is the set of all real numbers except 0. There is no y-intercept since x cannot be set equal to zero. Similarly, there is no x-intercept since upon solving the equation $y=1/x^2$ for x in terms of y, we obtain $x=\pm 1/\sqrt{y}$. We see that y cannot be set equal to zero. There is symmetry with respect to the y-axis since the equation $y=1/x^2$ remains unaltered when x is replaced by $-x$. Next, we note that as x increases without bound, so does x^2, so that $1/x^2$ decreases and approaches zero. A similar statement holds true when x decreases without bound. We easily see that the range of g is the set of all positive numbers. Finally, the following points lie on the graph of g: (1/2, 4), (1, 1), (2, 1/4) and (4, 1/16). Using the information obtained, the graph of g is sketched in Figure 2.11.

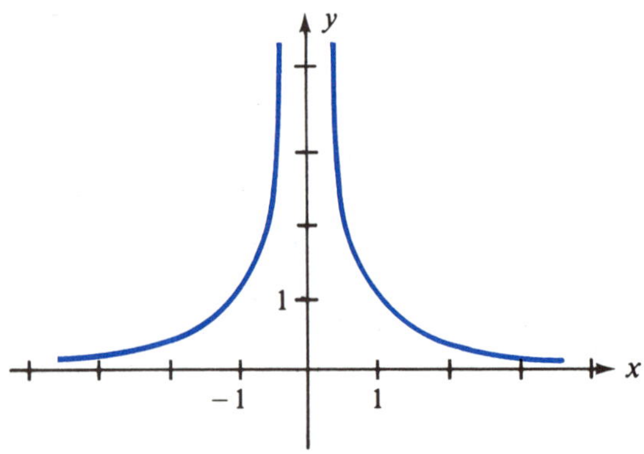

Figure 2.11

EXAMPLE 2.21 Sketch the graph of the function f defined by the rule $f(x)=1/(x^2+1)$.

SOLUTION The denominator of the expression $1/(x^2+1)$ is never equal to zero; therefore, the domain of the function f is the set of all real numbers. Setting $x=0$ gives the number 1 as the y-intercept. Solving the equation $y=1/(x^2+1)$ for x, we obtain the equation $x=\sqrt{(1-y)/y}$. Since y cannot be set equal to zero we conclude that there is no x-intercept. There is symmetry with respect to the y-axis since the equation remains unchanged when x is replaced by $-x$. Next, observe that as x increases (decreases) without bound, $y = 1/(x^2+1)$ decreases and approaches zero. This last observation is also substantiated by the following table of values:

x	1	2	3	4	5	10	100
$f(x)$	$\frac{1}{2}$	$\frac{1}{5}$	$\frac{1}{10}$	$\frac{1}{17}$	$\frac{1}{26}$	$\frac{1}{101}$	$\frac{1}{10001}$

Note that because of the symmetry property mentioned earlier it suffices to consider only positive values of x. Finally, to determine the range of f note that $x^2+1 \geq 1$ for all values of x. This implies that $1/(x^2+1) \leq 1$. Furthermore, $1/(x^2+1) > 0$ for all real numbers x so that the range of f is the interval $(0, 1]$. The function f is sketched in Figure 2.12.

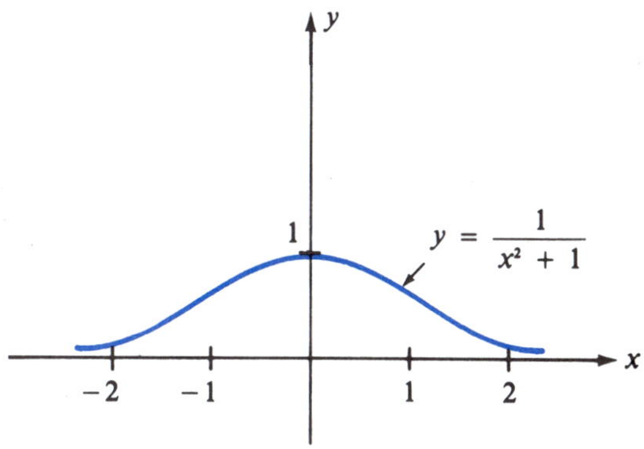

Figure 2.12

2.3 EXERCISES

In problems 1 through 20, obtain the following information concerning the graphs of the functions having the given rules and sketch their graphs:

(a) *The domain of* f.

(b) *The range of* f.

(c) *The* x- *and* y-*intercepts.*

(d) *Symmetry with respect to the* y-*axis and the origin.*

(e) *The behavior of* f(x) *for large absolute values of* x.

1. $f(x) = 2x + 4$

2. $f(x) = x^2 - 2$

3. $f(x) = \frac{|x|}{x}$

4. $f(x) = \frac{x}{|x|}$

5. $f(x) = x^2$

6. $f(x) = x^3$

7. $f(x) = x^4$

8. $f(x) = x^5$

9. $f(x) = x^3 - x$

10. $f(x) = x^4 - x^2$

11. $f(x) = |x|$

12. $f(x) = |x| + 1$

13. $f(x) = |x - 1|$

14. $f(x) = 9 - x^2$

15. $f(x) = \frac{1}{x^2 + 4}$

16. $f(x) = 2 + \frac{1}{x^2 + 1}$

17. $f(x) = \frac{x^2}{x^2 + 2}$

18. $f(x) = \frac{x}{x^2 + 1}$

19. $f(x) = \frac{1}{x - 1}$

20. $f(x) = \frac{1}{(x - 2)^2}$

2.4 Quadratic Functions

quadratic function

In this section we shall apply the graphing techniques introduced in Section 2.3 to help us study the graphs of an important nonlinear function—called the *quadratic function*. Specifically, a quadratic function is one of the form

$$f(x) = ax^2 + bx + c$$

where a, b and c are constants and $a \neq 0$. The function $f(x) = x^2 + 3$ encountered in Example 2.3 is quadratic (put $a = 1$, $b = 0$ and $c = 3$). The graph of the function $f(x) = x^2 + 1$ (see Figure 2.1 in Section 2.1) illustrates the general shape of the graph of a quadratic function, which is a curve called a *parabola*.

parabola

In general, the graph of a quadratic function $f(x) = ax^2 + bx + c$ has the following characteristics:

1. Since $f(x) = ax^2 + bx + c$, which may be computed for any value of x, we see that the domain of the quadratic function is the set of all real numbers.

2. The parabola opens upward if $a > 0$ and opens downward if $a < 0$ (see Figure 2.13). To illustrate this, let us note that for large absolute values of x, x^2 is much

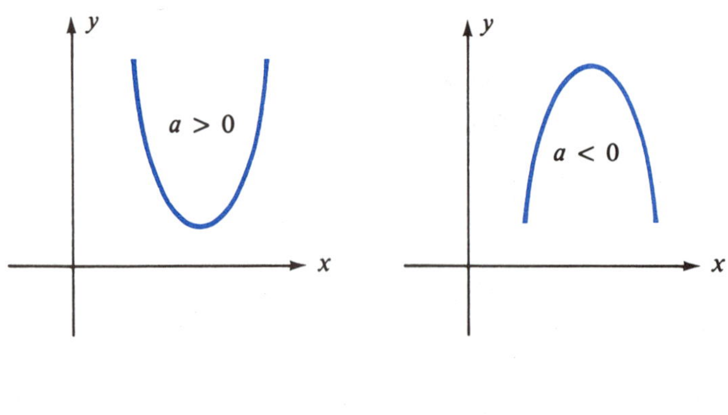

Figure 2.13

larger than $|x|$ so that the dominant term in the expression ax^2+bx+c is ax^2. Thus, for large absolute values of x, $y=f(x)=ax^2+bx+c$ behaves like ax^2 and is therefore positive (the parabola opens upward) or negative (the parabola opens downward) according to whether $a>0$ or $a<0$.

axis of symmetry

3. The parabola has a lowest point in the case when $a>0$ and a highest point in the case when $a<0$. Either point is called the vertex of the parabola and has coordinates given by $(-b/(2a), (4ac-b^2)/(4a))$. The parabola is symmetric with respect to the vertical line passing through its vertex. This line has equation $x=-b/(2a)$, and is called the *axis of symmetry* of the parabola (see Figure 2.14). We remark that these results may be derived using the method of completing the square.

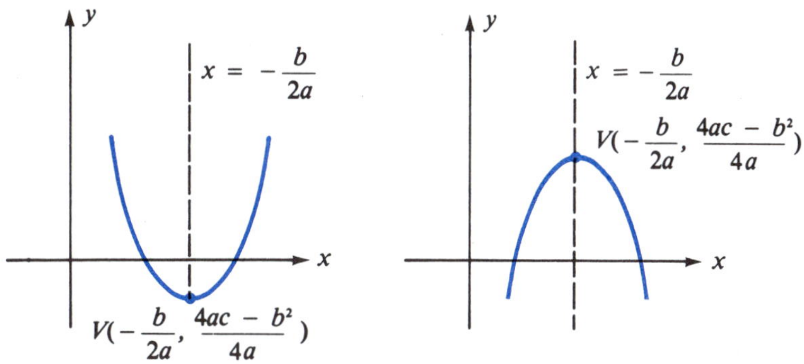

Figure 2.14

quadratic equation

4. The y-intercept is given by $y=c$ (just set $x=0$). To find the x-intercepts, we set $y=0$ obtaining the *quadratic equation*,

$$ax^2+bx+c=0$$

quadratic formula

which is solved using the *quadratic formula*, thus,

$$x=\frac{-b\pm\sqrt{b^2-4ac}}{2a}$$

discriminant

(This formula may be derived using the method of completing the squares but, once again, we omit the proof.) The expression b^2-4ac, under the radical sign, is called the *discriminant* of a quadratic equation. Three cases arise:

roots of an equation

(*a*) If $b^2-4ac>0$, then there are two distinct real solutions to the quadratic equation $ax^2+bx+c=0$ (called *roots of the equation*) corresponding to the two points at which the parabola crosses the x-axis.

(*b*) If $b^2-4ac=0$, then there is one real solution to the quadratic equation $ax^2+bx+c=0$ (called a root of multiplicity two; also called a repeated root of order two) corresponding to the single point at which the vertex of the parabola touches the x-axis.

(*c*) If $b^2-4ac<0$, then there is no real solution to the quadratic equation $ax^2+bx+c=0$. This corresponds to the case when the parabola does not cross the x-axis.

It may be interesting to observe that the three situations just mentioned concerning the x-intercepts of a parabola may be explained using the following visual experiment: Beginning with the parabola sketched in Figure 2.15(a), translate it upward along its axis of symmetry. In the process, the two roots come closer and closer and eventually coalesce, which leads to the case of a repeated root (Figure 2.15 part b). A further translation of the parabola upward then leads to the case shown in Figure 2.15(c) where there is no x-intercept at all.

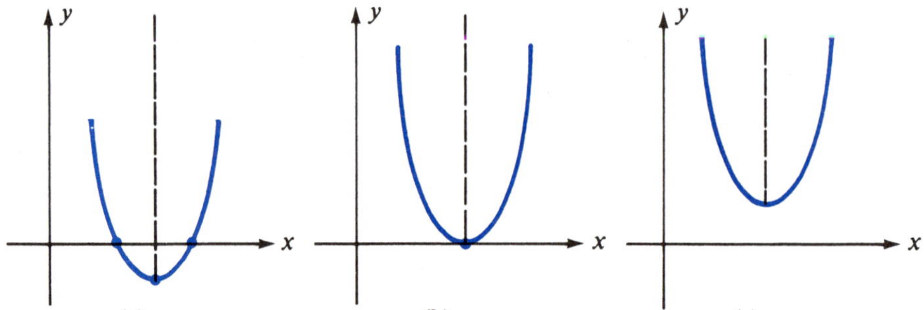

Figure 2.15 (a) Two distinct real roots (b) A repeated real root (c) No real roots

EXAMPLE 2.22 Given the quadratic function

$$f(x) = -2x^2 + 5x - 2$$

(a) Find the vertex of the parabola.

(b) Find the x-intercepts of the parabola, if any.

(c) Sketch the parabola.

SOLUTION (a) Comparing the given equation $f(x) = -2x^2 + 5x - 2$ with the general form of the quadratic equation, we find that $a = -2$, $b = 5$ and $c = -2$. Therefore, the x-coordinate of the vertex of the parabola is given by

$$\begin{aligned} x &= -\frac{b}{2a} \\ &= -\frac{5}{2(-2)} \\ &= \frac{5}{4} \end{aligned}$$

Next, to find the y-coordinate of the vertex, we may use the formula

$$\begin{aligned} y &= \frac{4ac - b^2}{4a} \\ &= \frac{4(-2)(-2) - 5^2}{4(-2)} \\ &= 1\frac{1}{8} \end{aligned}$$

Equivalently, we evaluate $f(x) = -2x^2 + 5x - 2$ at $x = 5/4$ obtaining

$$\begin{aligned} y &= f\left(\frac{5}{4}\right) \\ &= -2\left(\frac{5}{4}\right)^2 + 5\left(\frac{5}{4}\right) - 2 \\ &= -\frac{25}{8} + \frac{25}{4} - 2 \\ &= 1\frac{1}{8} \end{aligned}$$

as before. Thus, the vertex is given by the point (5/4, 9/8).

(**b**) To find the x-intercepts of the parabola, we solve the equation

$$-2x^2 + 5x - 2 = 0$$

using the quadratic formula. We find

$$\begin{aligned} x &= \frac{-5 \pm \sqrt{25 - 4(-2)(-2)}}{2(-2)} \\ &= \frac{-5 \pm \sqrt{9}}{-4} \\ &= \frac{-5 \pm 3}{-4} \\ &= \frac{1}{2} \quad \text{or} \quad 2 \end{aligned}$$

Thus, the x-intercepts of the parabola are $x = 1/2$ and $x = 2$.

(**c**) Since $a = -2 < 0$, the parabola opens downward. The vertex (5/4, 9/8) of the parabola is therefore the highest point on the curve. The parabola crosses the x-axis at the points (1/2, 0) and (2, 0). Setting $x = 0$ gives $y = -2$ as the y-intercept of the curve. Finally, using this information we sketch the parabola shown in Figure 2.16.

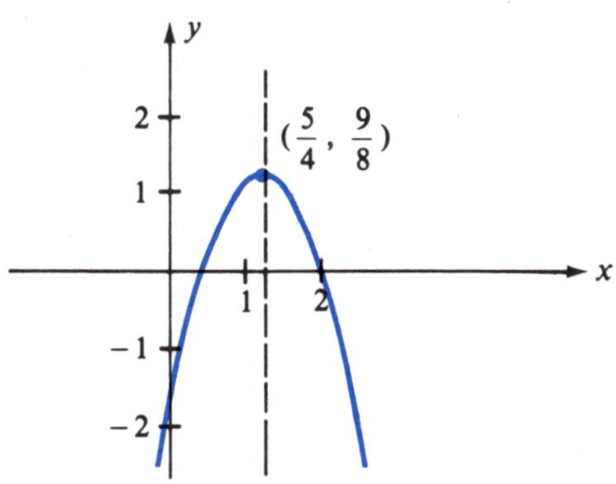

Figure 2.16

■

Applications involving the quadratic function $f(x)=ax^2+bx+c$ appear in the next section and in our work in Calculus. The quadratic function is a special case of the *polynomial function*

polynomial function

$$f(x)=a_0x^n+a_1x^{n-1}+\cdots+a_n$$

where n is a positive integer and $a_0, a_1, \cdots, a_n$ are constants with $a_0 \neq 0$. Polynomial functions and other nonlinear functions are best studied using the tools of the Differential Calculus. We shall return to them later on in our work.

2.4 EXERCISES

In problems 1 through 4, determine whether the given equation is a quadratic equation.

1. $2x+5=3x^2$

2. $\dfrac{x^2+1}{x}=1$

3. $\frac{1}{4}x^2-2x+1=-2$

4. $(x^2-2x+3)x=0$

In problems 5 through 8, determine the nature of the roots of the given quadratic equation. Find all real roots.

5. $x^2+x-12=0$

6. $\frac{1}{4}x^2-x+1=0$

7. $4x^2+4x+4=0$

8. $-6x^2+x+12=0$

In problems 9 through 12, for the given quadratic function (a) find the vertex of the parabola, (b) find the x*-intercepts of the parabola, if any, and (c) sketch the parabola.*

9. $f(x)=-x^2+5x-6$

10. $f(x)=x^2-8x+16$

11. $f(x)=3x^2-2x+1$

12. $f(x)=\frac{3}{8}x^2-2x+2$

2.5 Supply and Demand Curves

In a free market economy, the consumer demand for a particular commodity depends on its unit price. A *demand equation* expresses this relationship between the unit price and the quantity demanded. The corresponding graph of the demand equation is called a *demand curve*. In general the quantity demanded of a commodity decreases as its unit price increases, and vice versa. Accordingly, a *demand function* defined by $p=f(x)$, where p measures the unit price and x measures the number of units of the commodity in question, is generally characterized as a decreasing function of x; that is, $p=f(x)$ decreases as x increases.

The simplest demand function is defined by a linear equation in x and p. Its graph is a straight line having a negative slope and both x and p assume only nonnegative values. Thus, the demand curve in this case is that part of the graph of a straight line that lies in the first quadrant (Figure 2.17). The p-intercept, p_0, is the highest price that anyone would pay for the commodity—there is no demand for the commodity at all if the unit price is greater than or equal to p_0. The x-intercept, x_0, is the quantity demanded when the commodity is free—the total demand never exceeds x_0.

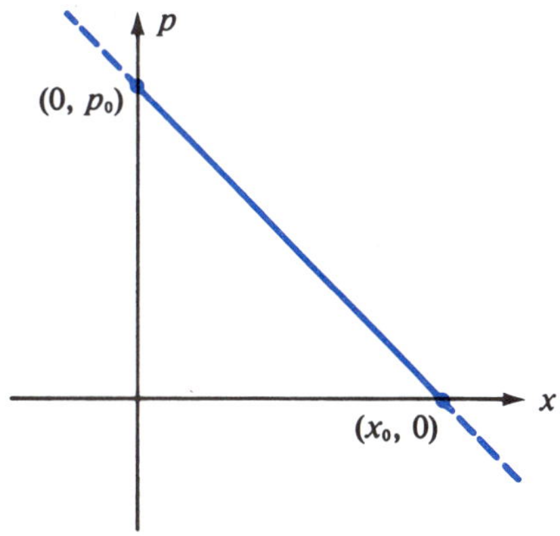

Figure 2.17

EXAMPLE 2.23 A demand equation has the form $4x + 7p - 28 = 0$, $(x \geq 0, p \geq 0)$, where x measures units of the commodity in thousands and p is the unit price in dollars. Draw the demand curve. What is the highest price that the consumer is willing to pay for the commodity? What is the largest quantity of the commodity that will be demanded?

SOLUTION Letting $x = 0$ and $p = 0$ in turn, we find that the p- and x-intercepts are 4 and 7, respectively. A sketch of the demand curve is shown in Figure 2.18. The highest price anyone would pay for a unit of the commodity is \$4, and the largest quantity demanded is 7000 units.

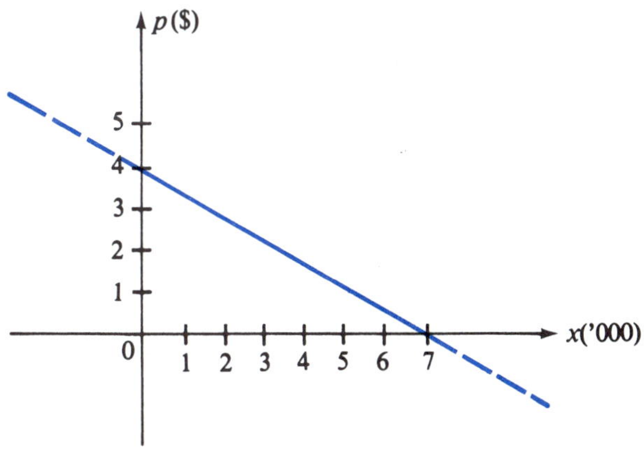

Figure 2.18 ■

EXAMPLE 2.24 The quantity demanded of a certain model of clocks is 48,000 units when the unit price is \$8. At a \$12 unit price, the demand drops to 32,000 units. Given it is linear, find the demand equation. What is the highest price anyone would pay for a clock? What is the maximum quantity demanded?

SOLUTION Let p (in dollars) denote the unit price of a clock and let x (measured in units of a thousand) denote the quantity demanded of the clocks when the unit price is \$$p$. When $p=8$, $x=48$ and the point (48, 8) lies on the demand curve. Similarly, when $p=12$, $x=32$, and the point (32, 12) also lies on the demand curve. Given that the demand equation is linear, its graph is a straight line. The slope of the required line is given by

$$m=\frac{12-8}{32-48}=\frac{4}{-16}=-\frac{1}{4}$$

so that, using the point-slope form of the equation of a line, we find

$$p-8=-\frac{1}{4}(x-48)$$

or

$$p=-\frac{1}{4}x+20$$

as the required equation. The demand curve is shown in Figure 2.19. The highest price anyone would pay for a clock is given by the p-intercept or \$20. The maximum quantity demanded is given by the x-intercept or 80,000 units.

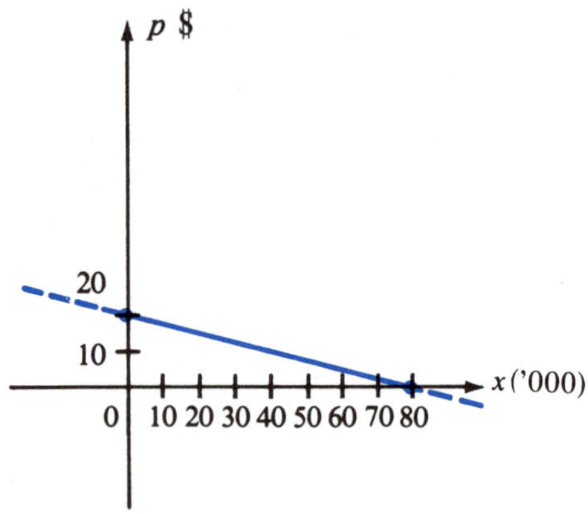

Figure 2.19

■

EXAMPLE 2.25 Sketch the demand curve associated with the demand equation $p=-x^2+9$, where p is measured in dollars and x is measured in units of a thousand. Above what price will there be no demand? What is the maximum quantity demanded?

SOLUTION A sketch of the demand curve appears in Figure 2.20. The p-intercept, which is 9, gives the price above which there will be no demand. We obtain the maximum quantity demanded by setting $p = 0$, which gives $x^2 = 9$ or $x = \pm 3$. Only the positive root is meaningful and the maximum quantity demanded is 3000 units.

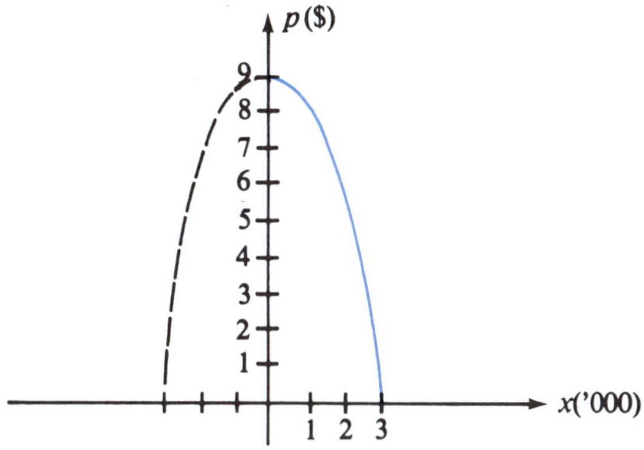

Figure 2.20

In a competitive market, a relationship also exists between the unit price of a commodity and its availability in the market. In general, an increase in the commodity's unit price makes it more conducive for the producer to increase the supply of the commodity. Conversely, a decrease in the unit price generally leads to a drop in the supply. The equation, which expresses this relation between the unit price and the quantity supplied, is called a *supply equation*, and the corresponding graph is called a *supply curve*. A *supply function* defined by $p = f(x)$, is generally characterized by an increasing function of x, that is, $p = f(x)$ increases as x increases.

As in the case of a demand equation, the simplest supply equation is a linear equation in p and x, where p and x have the same meaning as before, but now the line has a positive slope. The supply curve corresponding to a linear supply function is that part of the straight line that lies in the first quadrant (Figure 2.21). The p-intercept, p_0, is the lowest price at which the supplier will offer the commodity.

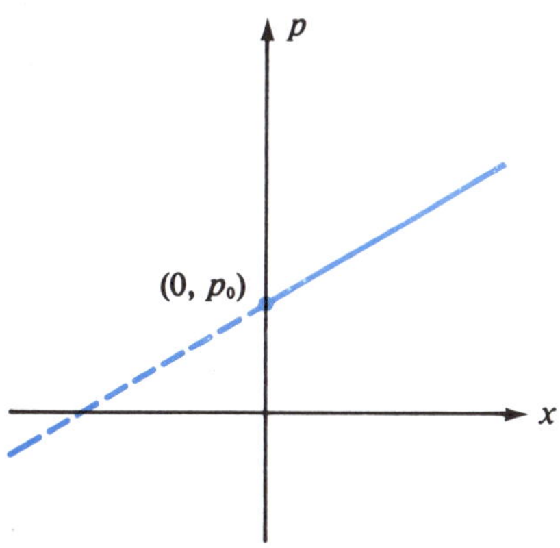

Figure 2.21

EXAMPLE 2.26 The supply equation for a commodity is given by $4p - 5x = 120$ where p is measured in dollars and x is measured in units of a hundred.

(**a**) Sketch the corresponding curve.

(**b**) What is the lowest price at which the supplier will make the commodity available in the market?

(**c**) What is the amount marketed when the unit price is \$55?

SOLUTION (**a**) Setting $x = 0$ and $p = 0$ in turn, we find that the p- and the x-intercepts are 30 and -24, respectively. The supply curve is sketched in Figure 2.22.

(**b**) From the solution to part (**a**) we see that the p-intercept is 30; therefore the lowest price at which the commodity will be made available is \$30.

(**c**) Substituting $p = 55$ in the supply equation we have $4(55) - 5x = 120$ or $x = 20$ so that the amount marketed is 2000 units.

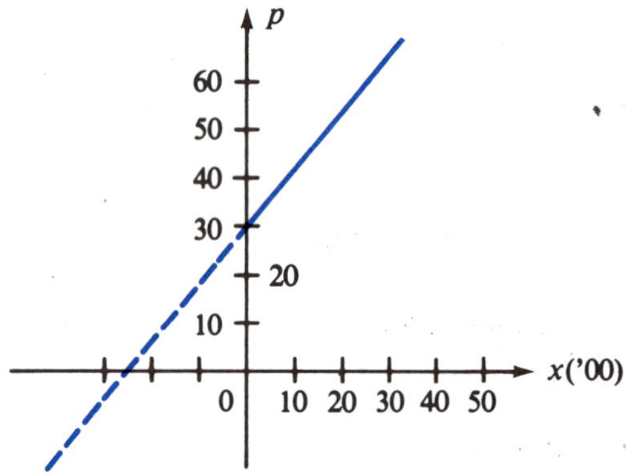

Figure 2.22

Under pure competition, the price of a commodity will eventually settle at a level dictated by the condition that the supply of the commodity be equal to the demand for it. If the price is too high, the consumer will not buy, and if the price is too low, the supplier will not produce. *Market equilibrium* prevails when the quantity produced is equal to the quantity demanded. The quantity produced at market equilibrium is called the *equilibrium quantity* and the corresponding price is called the *equilibrium price*.

market equilibrium

Market equilibrium corresponds to the point at which the demand curve and the supply curve intersect (Figure 2.23). In Figure 2.23, x_0 represents the equilibrium

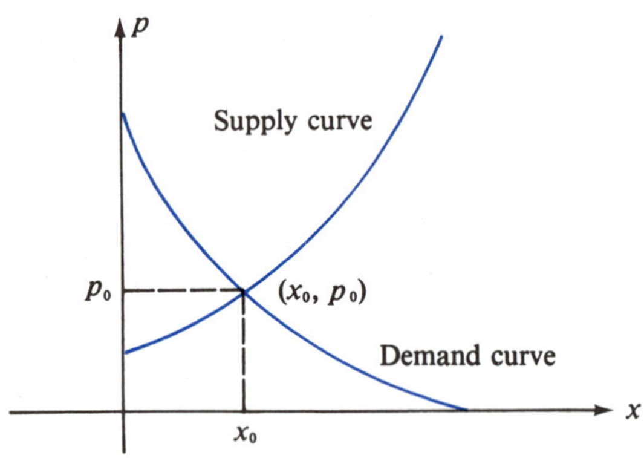

Figure 2.23

quantity and p_0 the equilibrium price. The point (x_0, p_0) lies on the supply curve and therefore satisfies the supply equation. At the same time, it also lies on the demand curve and therefore satisfies the demand equation. Thus, to find the point (x_0, p_0), and hence the equilibrium quantity and price, one solves the demand and supply equations simultaneously for x and p. For meaningful solutions, x and p must both be positive.

EXAMPLE 2.27 Suppose that the supply and demand equations for a certain commodity are given by $3x - 2p + 4 = 0$ and $p = -x^2 + 9$, respectively, where p is expressed in dollars and x in units of a thousand. Find the equilibrium quantity and price.

SOLUTION We solve the following system of equations:

$$3x - 2p + 4 = 0 \qquad (1)$$
$$p = -x^2 + 9 \qquad (2)$$

Solving (1) for p, we obtain $p = (3/2)x + 2$. Substituting this value of p into equation (2) yields

$$\frac{3}{2}x + 2 = -x^2 + 9$$

or

$$2x^2 + 3x - 14 = 0$$

$$(2x + 7)(x - 2) = 0$$

so that $x = -7/2$ or $x = 2$. Because x must be nonnegative, only $x = 2$ may be admitted as a solution. The corresponding value of p is then $p = 5$. Thus, the equilibrium quantity is 2000 and the equilibrium price is \$5. (See Figure 2.24.)

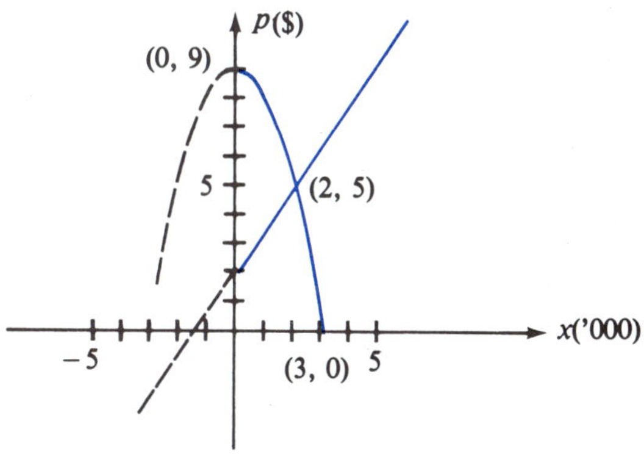

Figure 2.24

EXAMPLE 2.28 There is no demand for a certain model of loudspeakers when the unit price is \$500 or higher. However, at a \$200 unit price the quantity demanded is 10,000 units. The manufacturer of these loudspeakers will not market any if the price is \$100 or lower. On the other hand, for each \$50 increase in the unit price above

\$100 the manufacturer will market an additional 1000 units. Both the demand and the supply equations are known to be linear.

(**a**) Find the demand equation.

(**b**) Find the supply equation.

(**c**) Find the equilibrium quantity and price.

SOLUTION Let p denote the unit price in hundreds of dollars, and let x denote the number of units of loudspeakers in thousands.

(**a**) Since the demand equation is linear, it has the form $p = mx + b$. When $x = 0$, $p = 5$ and when $x = 10$, $p = 2$, leading us to the two equations

$$5 = b$$

and

$$2 = 10m + b$$

Solving the system of equations, we find $b = 5$ and $m = -0.3$. Thus, the demand equation is $p = -0.3x + 5$ (Figure 2.25).

(**b**) Since the supply equation is also linear, it has the form $p = mx + b$. When $x = 0$, $p = 1$ and when $x = 1$, $p = 1.5$, leading us to the two equations

$$1 = b$$

and

$$1.5 = m + b$$

Solving the above system of equations, we find $b = 1$ and $m = 0.5$. Thus, the supply equation is $p = 0.5x + 1$ (Figure 2.25).

(**c**) To find the market equilibrium, we simultaneously solve the system comprising the demand and supply equations obtained in parts (**a**) and (**b**), respectively; that is, the system

$$p = -0.3x + 5$$
$$p = 0.5x + 1$$

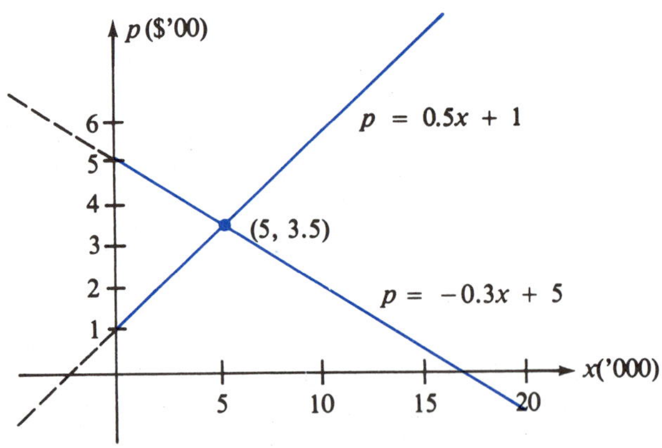

Figure 2.25

Subtracting the first from the second gives

$$0.8x - 4 = 0$$

whence $x = 5$. Substituting this value of x in the second equation gives $p = 3.5$. Thus, the equilibrium quantity is 5,000 units and the equilibrium price is \$350 (Figure 2.25). ■

2.5 EXERCISES

For each of the demand equations in problems 1 through 6, where x *represents the quantity demanded in units of a thousand, and* p *is the unit price in dollars (a) sketch the demand curve, (b) determine the highest price that the consumer is willing to pay for a unit of the commodity and (c) determine the largest amount of the commodity that will be demanded.*

1. $2x + 3p - 18 = 0$

2. $5p + 4x - 80 = 0$

3. $p = -3x + 60$

4. $p = -x^2 + 36$

5. $p = -x^2 + 16$

6. $p = \sqrt{9 - x^2}$

7. At a unit price of \$55, the quantity demanded of a certain commodity is 1000 units. At a unit price of \$85, the demand drops to 600 units. Find the demand equation given that it is linear. Above what price will there be no demand? What is the maximum quantity demanded?

8. There is no demand for a certain commodity when the unit price is \$100 or more. But, for each \$10 decrease in price, the quantity demanded increases by 200 units. Find the demand equation and sketch its graph.

9. Assume the demand equation for a certain commodity has the form $p = -ax^2 + b$ $(a \geq 0,\ b \geq 0)$ where x is the quantity demanded, measured in units of a thousand, and p is the unit price in dollars. Determine the demand equation if the highest price a customer is willing to pay for a unit of the commodity is \$10 and the largest amount of the commodity that will be demanded is 10,000 units. What is the quantity demanded when the unit price is \$7.50?

10. The demand equation for the Sicard wrist watch is given by

$$p = \frac{50}{0.01x^2 + 1} \qquad (0 \leq x \leq 20)$$

where x (measured in units of a thousand) is the quantity demanded per week and p is the unit price in dollars. Sketch the graph of the demand equation. What is the highest price anyone would pay for the watch?

For each of the supply equations in problems 11 through 16, where x *is the quantity supplied in units of a thousand and* p *is the unit price in dollars, (a) sketch the supply curve and (b) determine the lowest price at which the supplier will make the commodity available in the market.*

11. $3x - 4p + 24 = 0$

12. $\frac{1}{2}x - \frac{2}{3}p + 12 = 0$

13. $p = 2x + 10$

14. $p = 2x^2 + 18$

15. $p = x^3 + x + 10$

16. $p = x^2 + 16x + 40$

17. Suppliers of 15″ black and white television sets will not make any available in the market if the unit price is \$40. However, at a unit price of \$50, 20,000 units will be made available in the market. Assuming that the relationship between the unit price and the quantity supplied is linear, derive the supply equation. Sketch the supply curve and determine the quantity available when the unit price is \$70.

18. Producers will make 2000 refrigerators available when the unit price is \$330. At a unit price of \$390, 6000 refrigerators will be marketed. Find the equation, which is known to be linear, that relates the unit price of a refrigerator to the quantity supplied. How many refrigerators will be marketed when the unit price is \$450? What is the lowest price at which a refrigerator will be marketed?

19. Suppliers of transistor radios will market 10,000 units when the unit price is \$20 and 62,500 units when the unit price is \$35. Find the supply equation if it is known to have the form $p = a\sqrt{x} + b$ $(a \geq 0, b \geq 0)$, where x is the quantity supplied and p is the unit price in dollars. Sketch the graph of the supply equation. What is the lowest price at which a radio will be marketed?

For each pair of supply and demand equations in problems 20 through 24, where x *represents the quantity demanded in units of a thousand, and* p *is the unit price in dollars, find the equilibrium quantity and the equilibrium price.*

20. $2x + 7p - 56 = 0$ and $3x - 11p + 45 = 0$

21. $p = -2x + 22$ and $p = 3x + 12$

22. $p = -2x^2 + 80$ and $p = 15x + 30$

23. $11p + 3x - 66 = 0$ and $2p^2 + p - x = 10$

24. $p = 60 - 2x^2$ and $p = x^2 + 9x + 30$

25. There is no demand for video cassette recorders when the unit price is \$2000. However, for each \$300 decrease below \$2000, the quantity demanded increases by 600 units. The suppliers of these recorders will not market any if the unit price is \$600 or lower. At a unit price of \$1050, they are willing to make available 5000 units in the market. Both the demand and supply equations are known to be linear.

(*a*) Find the demand equation.

(*b*) Find the supply equation.

(*c*) Find the equilibrium quantity and price.

2

Chapter Review

EXERCISES

1. A relation is defined by the equation $y^2 = 2x + 1$.

(***a***) Determine the domain and the range of the relation and sketch its graph.

(***b***) Is y a function of x? Why?

(***c***) Is x a function of y? Why?

2. Let f be a function defined by the rule $f(x) = (1/2)x^2 - 2x + 4$.

(***a***) Find the domain of f.

(***b***) Compute $f(x)$ for $x = -2, -1, 0, 1, 2, 3, 4$.

(***c***) Use the results obtained in parts (***a***) and (***b***) to sketch the graph of f.

(***d***) What is the range of f?

3. Sketch the graph of the function defined by

$$f(x) = \begin{cases} x + 1 & \text{if } x < 1 \\ -x^2 + 4x - 1 & \text{if } x \geq 1 \end{cases}$$

4. Find the present value of a \$20,000 note due in 90 days if the simple discount rate is 9% per annum. (Use a 360-day year.)

5. A manufacturer installed a new machine in the factory in 1980 at a cost of \$300,000. The machine is depreciated linearly over 12 years with a scrap value of \$30,000.

(***a***) Find an expression for the book value of the machine in year n $(0 \leq n \leq 12)$.

(***b***) What is the rate of depreciation of the machine per year?

6. The cost function and the revenue function for a certain firm are given by $C(x) = 12x + 20{,}000$ and $R(x) = 20x$, respectively. Find the break-even point for the company.

In problems 7 through 10, obtain the following information concerning the graphs of the given functions and sketch their graphs.

(***a***) *The domain of* f

(***b***) *The range of* f

(***c***) *The* x- *and* y-*intercepts*

(***d***) *Symmetry with respect to the* y-*axis and the origin*

(***e***) *The behavior of* f(x) *for large absolute values of* x

7. $f(x) = x^2 - 4x + 3$

8. $f(x) = \sqrt{x^2 + 1}$

9. $f(x) = x^3 + 1$

10. $f(x) = \dfrac{2}{x^2 + 1}$

11. There is no demand for a certain commodity when the unit price is \$200 or more; but, for each \$10 decrease in price below \$200 the quantity demanded increases by 200 units. Find the demand equation and sketch its graph.

12. Suppliers of bicycles will make 200 bicycles available in the market per month when the unit price is \$50 and 2000 bicycles available per month when the unit price is \$100. Find the supply equation if it is known to be linear. What is the lowest price at which a bicycle will be marketed?

13. Given the demand equation $3x + p - 40 = 0$ and the supply equation $2x - p + 10 = 0$, where p is the unit price in dollars and x represents the quantity in units of a thousand, determine the equilibrium quantitity and the equilibrium price.

3

MATRICES AND SYSTEMS OF LINEAR EQUATIONS

3.1

Matrices

Many problems arising in practical situations are solved by using arithmetic operations on the data associated with the problems. By properly organizing the data associated with such problems into *blocks* of numbers, *matrix theory* may be used to help us in carrying out these arithmetic operations in an orderly and efficient manner. In particular, this systematic approach enables us to utilize the electronic computer to full advantage.

Let us begin by considering how the data describing the monthly output of a manufacturer may be organized. The Acrosonic Company manufactures four different loudspeaker systems in three separate locations. The output of the company for the month of May is summarized in Table 3.1.

Table 3.1

	Model A	Model B	Model C	Model D
Location I	320	280	460	280
Location II	480	360	580	0
Location III	540	420	200	880

Now, if we agree to preserve the location of each of the entries in Table 3.1, the set of data may be summarized further as follows:

$$\begin{bmatrix} 320 & 280 & 460 & 280 \\ 480 & 360 & 580 & 0 \\ 540 & 420 & 200 & 880 \end{bmatrix}$$

matrix

The array of numbers displayed above is an example of a *matrix*. Observe that the numbers in the first row give the output of Models A, B, C and D of Acrosonic loudspeaker systems manufactured in location I; similarly, the numbers in the second and third rows of the matrix give the respective outputs of these loudspeaker systems in locations II and III. The numbers in each column of the matrix give the outputs of a particular model of loudspeaker system manufactured in each of the three manufacturing locations of the company.

More generally, a matrix is an ordered rectangular array of real numbers. For example, each of the following array of numbers is a matrix:

$$A=\begin{bmatrix}3 & 0 & -1\\ 2 & 1 & 4\end{bmatrix}\qquad B=\begin{bmatrix}3 & 2\\ 0 & 1\\ -1 & 4\end{bmatrix}\qquad C=\begin{bmatrix}1\\ 2\\ 4\\ 0\end{bmatrix}\qquad D=[1\ \ 3\ \ 0\ \ 1]$$

elements (entries) of a matrix

The real numbers comprising the array are called the *entries* or *elements of the matrix*. The entries comprising a row in the array are referred to as a *row* of the matrix, while the entries comprising a column in the array are referred to as a *column* of the matrix. For example, matrix A has two rows and three columns, which may be identified as follows:

	Column 1	Column 2	Column 3
Row 1	3	0	−1
Row 2	2	1	4

order of a matrix

The *size* or *order of a matrix* is described in terms of the number of rows and columns of the matrix. For example, matrix A given above has two rows and three columns and is said to have order 2 by 3, denoted by 2×3. In general, a matrix having m rows and n columns is said to have order $m\times n$.

A matrix of order $1\times n$—a matrix having one row and n columns is referred to as a *row matrix* or *row vector* (of dimension n). For example, the matrix D above is a row vector of dimension 4. Similarly, a matrix having m rows and one column is referred to as a *column matrix* or *column vector* (of dimension m). For example, the matrix C above is a column vector of dimension 4. Finally, an $n\times n$ matrix, that is, a matrix having the same number of rows as columns is called a *square matrix*. For example, the matrix

square matrix

$$\begin{bmatrix}-3 & 8 & 6\\ 2 & 1/4 & 4\\ 1 & 3 & 2\end{bmatrix}$$

is a square matrix of order 3×3, or simply of order 3.

EXAMPLE 3.1 Consider the matrix

$$P = \begin{bmatrix} 320 & 280 & 460 & 280 \\ 480 & 360 & 580 & 0 \\ 540 & 420 & 200 & 880 \end{bmatrix}$$

representing the output of loudspeaker systems of the Acrosonic Company discussed earlier (see Table 3.1).

(a) What is the order of the matrix P?

(b) Find a_{24} (the entry in the second row and fourth column of the matrix P) and give an interpretation of this number.

(c) Find the sum of the entries comprising the first row of P and interpret the result.

(d) Find the sum of the entries comprising the fourth column of P and interpret the result.

SOLUTION **(a)** The matrix P has three rows and four columns and hence has order 3×4.

(b) The required entry lies in the second row and fourth column and is the number 0. This means that no Model D loudspeaker system was manufactured in location II in the month of May.

(c) The required sum is given by

$$320 + 280 + 460 + 280 = 1340$$

which gives the total number of loudspeaker systems manufactured in location I in the month of May as 1340 units.

(d) The required sum is given by

$$280 + 0 + 880 = 1160$$

giving the output of Model D loudspeaker systems in the month of May as 1160 units. ■

Two matrices are said to be *equal* if they have the same order and their corresponding entries are equal. For example,

$$\begin{bmatrix} 2 & 3 & 1 \\ 4 & 6 & 2 \end{bmatrix} = \begin{bmatrix} (3-1) & 3 & 1 \\ 4 & (4+2) & 2 \end{bmatrix}$$

but

$$\begin{bmatrix} 1 & 3 & 5 \\ 2 & 4 & 3 \end{bmatrix} \neq \begin{bmatrix} 1 & 2 \\ 3 & 4 \\ 5 & 3 \end{bmatrix}$$

since the matrix on the left has order 2×3 while the matrix on the right has order

3×2, and

$$\begin{bmatrix} 2 & 3 \\ 4 & 6 \end{bmatrix} \neq \begin{bmatrix} 2 & 3 \\ 4 & 7 \end{bmatrix}$$

since the corresponding elements in the second row and second column of the two square matrices are not equal.

EXAMPLE 3.2 Solve the following matrix equation for x, y, and z.

$$\begin{bmatrix} 1 & x & 3 \\ 2 & y-1 & 2 \end{bmatrix} = \begin{bmatrix} 1 & 4 & z \\ 2 & 1 & 2 \end{bmatrix}$$

SOLUTION Since the corresponding elements of the two matrices must be equal, we find that $x = 4$, $z = 3$, and $y - 1 = 1$ or $y = 2$. ■

Two matrices A and B of the *same order* can be added (subtracted) to produce a matrix of the same order. This is done by adding (subtracting) the corresponding entries in the two matrices. For example,

$$\begin{bmatrix} 1 & 3 & 4 \\ -1 & 2 & 0 \end{bmatrix} + \begin{bmatrix} 1 & 4 & 3 \\ 6 & 1 & -2 \end{bmatrix} = \begin{bmatrix} 1+1 & 3+4 & 4+3 \\ -1+6 & 2+1 & 0+(-2) \end{bmatrix} = \begin{bmatrix} 2 & 7 & 7 \\ 5 & 3 & -2 \end{bmatrix}$$

and

$$\begin{bmatrix} 1 & 2 \\ -1 & 3 \\ 4 & 0 \end{bmatrix} - \begin{bmatrix} 2 & -1 \\ 3 & 2 \\ -1 & 0 \end{bmatrix} = \begin{bmatrix} 1-2 & 2-(-1) \\ -1-3 & 3-2 \\ 4-(-1) & 0-0 \end{bmatrix} = \begin{bmatrix} -1 & 3 \\ -4 & 1 \\ 5 & 0 \end{bmatrix}$$

EXAMPLE 3.3 The total output of the Acrosonic Company for the month of June is summarized in Table 3.2.

Table 3.2

	Model A	Model B	Model C	Model D
Location I	210	180	330	180
Location II	400	300	450	40
Location III	420	280	180	740

Find the total output of the company for May and June.

SOLUTION The production matrix for the Acrosonic Company for the month of May (see page 83) is given by

$$A = \begin{bmatrix} 320 & 280 & 460 & 280 \\ 480 & 360 & 580 & 0 \\ 540 & 420 & 200 & 880 \end{bmatrix}$$

Next, from Table 3.2 we see that the production matrix for June is given by

$$B = \begin{bmatrix} 210 & 180 & 330 & 180 \\ 400 & 300 & 450 & 40 \\ 420 & 280 & 180 & 740 \end{bmatrix}$$

Finally, the total output of the Acrosonic Company for the two months in question is given by the matrix

$$A+B = \begin{bmatrix} 320 & 280 & 460 & 280 \\ 480 & 360 & 580 & 0 \\ 540 & 420 & 200 & 880 \end{bmatrix} + \begin{bmatrix} 210 & 180 & 330 & 180 \\ 400 & 300 & 450 & 40 \\ 420 & 280 & 180 & 740 \end{bmatrix}$$

$$= \begin{bmatrix} 530 & 460 & 790 & 460 \\ 880 & 660 & 1030 & 40 \\ 960 & 700 & 380 & 1620 \end{bmatrix}$$

■

The following laws hold for matrix addition. If A, B, and C are matrices of the same order, then

$$A+B=B+A \qquad \text{(Commutative Law for Matrix Addition)}$$

and $$(A+B)+C=A+(B+C)=A+B+C$$
(Associative Law for Matrix Addition)

zero matrix

A *zero matrix* is one in which all of its entries are zero. The zero matrix O has the property that $A+O=O+A=A$ for any matrix A having the same order as that of O. For example, the zero matrix of order 3×2 is the matrix

$$O = \begin{bmatrix} 0 & 0 \\ 0 & 0 \\ 0 & 0 \end{bmatrix}$$

and if A is any 3×2 matrix, then

$$A+O = \begin{bmatrix} a_{11} & a_{12} \\ a_{21} & a_{22} \\ a_{31} & a_{32} \end{bmatrix} + \begin{bmatrix} 0 & 0 \\ 0 & 0 \\ 0 & 0 \end{bmatrix} = \begin{bmatrix} a_{11} & a_{12} \\ a_{21} & a_{22} \\ a_{31} & a_{32} \end{bmatrix} = A$$

where a_{ij} denotes the entry in the ith row and jth column of the matrix A.

transpose of a matrix

If A is an $m \times n$ matrix with elements a_{ij}, then the *transpose* of A, denoted by A^T, is the $n \times m$ matrix A^T with elements a_{ji}. Thus, the matrix A^T is obtained by interchanging the rows and columns of A. For example, if

$$A = \begin{bmatrix} 1 & 2 & 3 \\ 4 & 5 & 6 \\ 7 & 8 & 9 \end{bmatrix}$$

then $$A^T = \begin{bmatrix} 1 & 4 & 7 \\ 2 & 5 & 8 \\ 3 & 6 & 9 \end{bmatrix}$$

scalar product

A matrix A may be multiplied by a real number, called a *scalar* in the context of matrix algebra. The *scalar product*, denoted by cA, is a matrix obtained by multiplying each entry of A by c. For example, the scalar product of the matrix

$$A = \begin{bmatrix} 3 & -1 & 2 \\ 0 & 1 & 4 \end{bmatrix}$$

by the scalar 3 is the matrix

$$3A = 3\begin{bmatrix} 3 & -1 & 2 \\ 0 & 1 & 4 \end{bmatrix} = \begin{bmatrix} 9 & -3 & 6 \\ 0 & 3 & 12 \end{bmatrix}$$

EXAMPLE 3.4 Given

$$A = \begin{bmatrix} 3 & 4 \\ -1 & 2 \end{bmatrix} \quad \text{and} \quad B = \begin{bmatrix} 3 & 2 \\ -1 & 2 \end{bmatrix}$$

find the matrix X satisfying the *matrix equation* $2X + B = 3A$.

SOLUTION From the given equation $2X + B = 3A$ we find that

$$\begin{aligned} 2X &= 3A - B \\ &= 3\begin{bmatrix} 3 & 4 \\ -1 & 2 \end{bmatrix} - \begin{bmatrix} 3 & 2 \\ -1 & 2 \end{bmatrix} \\ &= \begin{bmatrix} 9 & 12 \\ -3 & 6 \end{bmatrix} - \begin{bmatrix} 3 & 2 \\ -1 & 2 \end{bmatrix} = \begin{bmatrix} 6 & 10 \\ -2 & 4 \end{bmatrix} \end{aligned}$$

so that $$X = \frac{1}{2}\begin{bmatrix} 6 & 10 \\ -2 & 4 \end{bmatrix} = \begin{bmatrix} 3 & 5 \\ -1 & 2 \end{bmatrix}$$ ■

EXAMPLE 3.5 The management of the Acrosonic Company has decided to increase its July production of loudspeaker systems by 10% (over its June output). Find a matrix giving the targeted production for the month of July.

SOLUTION From the results of Example 3.3 we see that the total output of the company for the month of June may be represented by the matrix

$$B = \begin{bmatrix} 210 & 180 & 330 & 180 \\ 400 & 300 & 450 & 40 \\ 420 & 280 & 180 & 740 \end{bmatrix}$$

The required matrix is given by

$$(1.1)B = 1.1\begin{bmatrix} 210 & 180 & 330 & 180 \\ 400 & 300 & 450 & 40 \\ 420 & 280 & 180 & 740 \end{bmatrix} = \begin{bmatrix} 231 & 198 & 363 & 198 \\ 440 & 330 & 495 & 44 \\ 462 & 308 & 198 & 814 \end{bmatrix}$$

and is interpreted in the usual manner. ■

3.1 EXERCISES

1. Let

$$A = \begin{bmatrix} 2 & -3 & 9 & -4 \\ -11 & 2 & 6 & 7 \\ 6 & 0 & 2 & 9 \\ 5 & 1 & 5 & -8 \end{bmatrix}$$

(*a*) What is the order of A?

(*b*) Find a_{14}, a_{21}, a_{31}, and a_{43}.

In problems 2 through 4 perform the indicated operations.

2.

$$\begin{bmatrix} 1 & 4 & -5 \\ 3 & -8 & 6 \end{bmatrix} + \begin{bmatrix} 4 & 0 & -2 \\ 3 & 6 & 5 \end{bmatrix} - \begin{bmatrix} 2 & 8 & 9 \\ -11 & 2 & -5 \end{bmatrix}$$

3.

$$3\begin{bmatrix} 1 & 1 & -3 \\ 3 & 2 & 3 \\ 7 & -1 & 6 \end{bmatrix} + 4\begin{bmatrix} -2 & -1 & 8 \\ 4 & 2 & 2 \\ 3 & 6 & 3 \end{bmatrix}$$

4.

$$\frac{1}{2}\begin{bmatrix} 1 & 0 & 0 & -4 \\ 3 & 0 & -1 & 6 \\ -2 & 1 & -4 & 2 \end{bmatrix} + \frac{4}{3}\begin{bmatrix} 3 & 0 & -1 & 4 \\ -2 & 1 & -6 & 2 \\ 8 & 2 & 0 & -2 \end{bmatrix} - \frac{1}{3}\begin{bmatrix} 3 & -9 & -1 & 0 \\ 6 & 2 & 0 & -6 \\ 0 & 1 & -3 & 1 \end{bmatrix}$$

5. Let

$$A = \begin{bmatrix} -1 & 2 \\ 3 & -2 \\ 4 & 0 \end{bmatrix}, \quad B = \begin{bmatrix} 2 & 4 \\ 3 & 1 \\ -2 & 2 \end{bmatrix}, \quad C = \begin{bmatrix} 3 & -1 & 0 \\ 2 & -2 & 3 \\ 4 & 6 & 2 \end{bmatrix}, \quad D = \begin{bmatrix} 2 & -2 & 4 \\ 3 & 6 & 2 \\ -2 & 3 & 1 \end{bmatrix}$$

Compute each of the following:

(*a*) $A+B$ (*b*) $2A-3B$ (*c*) $C-D$ (*d*) $4D-2C$

Solve for u, x, y, *and* z *in each of the following matrix equations:*

6.

$$\begin{bmatrix} 2x-1 & 3 & 2 \\ 2 & 4 & y-2 \\ 2z & -3 & 2 \end{bmatrix} = \begin{bmatrix} 3 & u & 2 \\ 2 & 4 & 5 \\ 4 & -3 & 2 \end{bmatrix}$$

7.

$$\begin{bmatrix} x & -2 \\ 3 & y \end{bmatrix} + \begin{bmatrix} -2 & z \\ -1 & 2 \end{bmatrix} = \begin{bmatrix} 4 & -2 \\ 2u & 4 \end{bmatrix}$$

8.

$$\begin{bmatrix} 1 & x \\ 2y & -3 \end{bmatrix} - 4\begin{bmatrix} 2 & -2 \\ 0 & 3 \end{bmatrix} = \begin{bmatrix} 3z & 10 \\ 4 & -u \end{bmatrix}$$

9.

$$\begin{bmatrix} 1 & 2 \\ 3 & 4 \\ x & -1 \end{bmatrix} - 3\begin{bmatrix} y-1 & 2 \\ 1 & 2 \\ 4 & 2z+1 \end{bmatrix} = 2\begin{bmatrix} -4 & -u \\ 0 & -1 \\ 4 & 4 \end{bmatrix}$$

10. Let

$$A = \begin{bmatrix} 2 & -4 & 3 \\ 4 & 2 & 1 \end{bmatrix}, \quad B = \begin{bmatrix} 4 & -3 & 2 \\ 1 & 0 & 4 \end{bmatrix}, \quad \text{and} \quad C = \begin{bmatrix} 1 & 0 & 2 \\ 3 & -2 & 1 \end{bmatrix}$$

Verify by direct computation the validity of the Commutative Law for matrix addition and the Associative Law for matrix addition for this special case.

11. Let

$$A = \begin{bmatrix} 3 & 1 \\ 2 & 4 \\ -4 & 0 \end{bmatrix} \quad \text{and} \quad B = \begin{bmatrix} 1 & 2 \\ -1 & 0 \\ 3 & 2 \end{bmatrix}$$

Verify by direct computation each of the following equations:

(***a***) $(3+5)A = 3A + 5A$

(***b***) $2(4A) = (2 \cdot 4)A = 8A$

(***c***) $4(A+B) = 4A + 4B$

In problems 12 through 15 find the transpose of the given matrix.

12. $[3 \quad 2 \quad -1 \quad 5]$

13. $\begin{bmatrix} 4 & 2 & 0 & -1 \\ 3 & 4 & -1 & 5 \end{bmatrix}$

14. $\begin{bmatrix} 1 & -1 & 2 \\ 3 & 4 & 2 \\ 0 & 1 & 0 \end{bmatrix}$

15. $\begin{bmatrix} 1 & 2 & 6 & 4 \\ 2 & 3 & 2 & 5 \\ 6 & 2 & 3 & 0 \\ 4 & 5 & 0 & 2 \end{bmatrix}$

16. Mr. Cross, Mr. Jones, and Mr. Smith each suffered from coronary heart disease. As part of their treatment, they were put on special low-cholesterol diets: Mr. Cross on diet I, Mr. Jones on diet II, and Mr. Smith on diet III. Progressive records of each patient's cholesterol level were kept. At the beginning of the first, second, third, and fourth month the cholesterol levels of each patient were:

Mr Cross: 220, 215, 210, and 205

Mr. Jones: 220, 210, 200, and 195

Mr. Smith: 215, 205, 195, and 190

Represent this information in a 3×4 matrix.

17. The Campus Bookstore's inventory of books consists of the following:

Hardcover: Textbooks, 5280; Fiction, 1680; Non-fiction, 2320; Reference, 1890.

Paperback: Fiction, 2810; Non-fiction, 1490; Reference, 2070; Textbooks, 1940.

and the College Bookstore's inventory of books is:

Hardcover: Textbooks, 6340; Fiction, 2220; Non-fiction, 1790; Reference, 1980.

Paperback: Fiction, 3100; Non-fiction, 1720; Reference, 2710; Textbooks, 2050.

(***a***) Represent the inventory of the Campus Bookstore as matrix A.
(***b***) Represent the inventory of the College Bookstore as matrix B.
(***c***) If the two companies decide to merge, write a matrix C which would represent the total inventory of the newly amalgamated company.

18. The number of each type of bank account on January 1 in the Central Bank and its branches is represented by matrix A.

$$A = \begin{array}{r} \text{Main Office} \\ \text{West side branch} \\ \text{East side branch} \end{array} \overset{\begin{array}{ccc} \text{Checking accounts} & \text{Savings accounts} & \text{Fixed deposit accounts} \end{array}}{\begin{bmatrix} 2820 & 1470 & 1120 \\ 1030 & 520 & 480 \\ 1170 & 540 & 460 \end{bmatrix}}$$

The number and types of accounts opened during the first quarter are represented by matrix B while the number and types of accounts closed during the same period are represented by matrix C. Thus,

$$B = \begin{bmatrix} 260 & 120 & 110 \\ 140 & 60 & 50 \\ 120 & 70 & 50 \end{bmatrix}$$

$$C = \begin{bmatrix} 120 & 80 & 80 \\ 70 & 30 & 40 \\ 60 & 20 & 40 \end{bmatrix}$$

(***a***) Find matrix D representing the number of each type of account at the end of the first quarter at each location.

(***b***) Because of the opening of a new manufacturing plant in the immediate area, it is anticipated that there will be an increase of 10% in the number of accounts at each of the three locations during the second quarter. Write a matrix E reflecting this anticipated increase.

3.2

Multiplication of Matrices

In the last section we saw how matrices of the same order may be added or subtracted and how a matrix may be multiplied by a scalar (real number), an operation referred to as scalar multiplication. In this section we shall see how, under certain restrictions, one matrix may be multiplied by another matrix.

In order to define matrix multiplication, let us consider the following problem: On a certain day Al's Service Station sold 800 gallons of premium, 1200 gallons of regular, 1000 gallons of super-unleaded, and 1600 gallons of regular-unleaded gasoline. Suppose the price of gasoline on this day was \$1.80 per gallon for premium, \$1.30 for regular, \$1.60 for super-unleaded, and \$1.50 for regular-unleaded gasoline, find the total revenue realized by Al's Service Station for that day.

The day's sale of gasoline may be represented by the 1×4 (row) matrix

$$A = [800 \quad 1200 \quad 1000 \quad 1600]$$

Next, we let the unit selling price of premium, regular, super-unleaded, and regular-unleaded gasoline be the entries in the 4×1 (column) matrix

$$B = \begin{bmatrix} 1.80 \\ 1.30 \\ 1.60 \\ 1.50 \end{bmatrix}$$

Now, the first entry in matrix A gives the number of gallons of premium gasoline sold while the first entry in matrix B gives the selling price for each gallon of premium gasoline so that their product (800)(1.80) gives the revenue realized from the sale of premium gasoline for the day. A similar interpretation of the second, third, and fourth entries in the two matrices suggests that we multiply the corresponding entries to obtain the respective revenues realized from the sale of regular, super-unleaded, and regular-unleaded gasoline. Finally, the total revenue realized by Al's Service Station from the sale of gasoline is given by adding these products together

$$(800)(1.80) + (1200)(1.30) + (1000)(1.60) + (1600)(1.50) = 7000$$

or \$7000.

The above example suggests that if we have a row matrix

$$A = [a_1 \quad a_2 \quad a_3 \quad \cdots \quad a_n]$$

of order $1 \times n$ and a column matrix

$$B = \begin{bmatrix} b_1 \\ b_2 \\ b_3 \\ \vdots \\ b_n \end{bmatrix}$$

of order $n \times 1$, then we may define the *product* of A and B, written AB, by

$$AB = [a_1 \quad a_2 \quad a_3 \quad \cdots \quad a_n] \begin{bmatrix} b_1 \\ b_2 \\ b_3 \\ \vdots \\ b_n \end{bmatrix} = a_1b_1 + a_2b_2 + a_3b_3 + \cdots + a_nb_n$$

Observe that the number of columns of the row matrix A is *equal* to the number of rows of the column matrix B. Observe further that the product matrix AB has order 1×1 (a real number may be thought of as a 1×1 matrix). Schematically,

order of A — (1×4) order of B — (4×1)

(1×1)

Order of AB

matrix product

More generally, if A is a matrix of order $m \times n$ and B is a matrix of order $n \times p$ (so that the number of columns of A is equal to the number of rows of B) then the *matrix product* of A and B, AB, is defined and is a matrix of order $m \times p$. Schematically,

order of A — $(m \times n)$ order of B — $(n \times p)$

$(m \times p)$

Order of AB

We now illustrate the mechanics of matrix multiplication by computing the product of a 2×3 matrix A and a 3×4 matrix B. Suppose

$$A = \begin{bmatrix} a_{11} & a_{12} & a_{13} \\ a_{21} & a_{22} & a_{23} \end{bmatrix} \quad \text{and} \quad B = \begin{bmatrix} b_{11} & b_{12} & b_{13} & b_{14} \\ b_{21} & b_{22} & b_{23} & b_{24} \\ b_{31} & b_{32} & b_{33} & b_{34} \end{bmatrix}$$

From the schematic

$$\begin{array}{ccc} \text{order of } A & & \text{order of } B \\ (2\times 3) & & (3\times 4) \\ \uparrow & & \uparrow \\ \llcorner\!\!-\!\!-\!\!-\!\!-\!\!-\!\!-\!\!-\!\!-\!\!-\!\!-\!\!- & (2\times 4) & -\!\!-\!\!-\!\!-\!\!-\!\!-\!\!-\!\!-\!\!-\!\!-\!\!-\!\!\lrcorner \end{array}$$

we see that the matrix product $C = AB$ is defined (the number of columns of A equals the number of rows of B, both being equal to three) and has order 2×4. Thus

$$C = \begin{bmatrix} c_{11} & c_{12} & c_{13} & c_{14} \\ c_{21} & c_{22} & c_{23} & c_{24} \end{bmatrix}$$

The entries of C are computed as follows: The entry c_{11} (the entry in the *first* row and *first* column of C) is the product of the row matrix comprising the entries from the *first* row of A and the column matrix comprising the *first* column of B. Thus,

$$c_{11} = [a_{11} \quad a_{12} \quad a_{13}] \begin{bmatrix} b_{11} \\ b_{21} \\ b_{31} \end{bmatrix} = a_{11}b_{11} + a_{12}b_{21} + a_{13}b_{31}$$

The entry c_{12} (the entry in the *first* row and *second* column of C) is the product of the row matrix comprising the *first* row of A and the column matrix comprising the *second* column of B. Thus,

$$c_{12} = [a_{11} \quad a_{12} \quad a_{13}] \begin{bmatrix} b_{12} \\ b_{22} \\ b_{32} \end{bmatrix} = a_{11}b_{12} + a_{12}b_{22} + a_{13}b_{32}$$

The other entries in C are computed in a similar manner.

EXAMPLE 3.6 Let

$$A = \begin{bmatrix} 3 & 1 & 4 \\ -1 & 2 & 3 \end{bmatrix} \quad \text{and} \quad B = \begin{bmatrix} 1 & 3 & -3 \\ 4 & -1 & 2 \\ 2 & 4 & 1 \end{bmatrix}$$

Compute AB.

SOLUTION The order of matrix A is 2×3 while the order of matrix B is 3×3. Since the number of columns of matrix A is equal to the number of rows of matrix B, the matrix product $C = AB$ is defined. Furthermore, the order of matrix C is 2×3. Thus,

$$\begin{bmatrix} 3 & 1 & 4 \\ -1 & 2 & 3 \end{bmatrix} \begin{bmatrix} 1 & 3 & -3 \\ 4 & -1 & 2 \\ 2 & 4 & 1 \end{bmatrix} = \begin{bmatrix} c_{11} & c_{12} & c_{13} \\ c_{21} & c_{22} & c_{23} \end{bmatrix}$$

It remains now to determine the entries c_{11}, c_{12}, c_{13}, c_{21}, c_{22}, and c_{23}. We have

$$c_{11}=\begin{bmatrix}3 & 1 & 4\end{bmatrix}\begin{bmatrix}1\\4\\2\end{bmatrix}=(3)(1)+(1)(4)+(4)(2)=15$$

$$c_{12}=\begin{bmatrix}3 & 1 & 4\end{bmatrix}\begin{bmatrix}3\\-1\\4\end{bmatrix}=(3)(3)+(1)(-1)+(4)(4)=24$$

$$c_{13}=\begin{bmatrix}3 & 1 & 4\end{bmatrix}\begin{bmatrix}-3\\2\\1\end{bmatrix}=(3)(-3)+(1)(2)+(4)(1)=-3$$

$$c_{21}=\begin{bmatrix}-1 & 2 & 3\end{bmatrix}\begin{bmatrix}1\\4\\2\end{bmatrix}=(-1)(1)+(2)(4)+(3)(2)=13$$

$$c_{22}=\begin{bmatrix}-1 & 2 & 3\end{bmatrix}\begin{bmatrix}3\\-1\\4\end{bmatrix}=(-1)(3)+(2)(-1)+(3)(4)=7$$

and

$$c_{23}=\begin{bmatrix}-1 & 2 & 3\end{bmatrix}\begin{bmatrix}-3\\2\\1\end{bmatrix}=(-1)(-3)+(2)(2)+(3)(1)=10$$

so that the required product AB is given by

$$AB=\begin{bmatrix}15 & 24 & -3\\13 & 7 & 10\end{bmatrix}$$ ■

EXAMPLE 3.7 If

$$A=\begin{bmatrix}3 & 2 & 1\\-1 & 2 & 3\\3 & 1 & 4\end{bmatrix},\quad B=\begin{bmatrix}1 & 3 & 4\\2 & 4 & 1\\-1 & 2 & 3\end{bmatrix}$$

then

$$AB=\begin{bmatrix}3\cdot 1+2\cdot 2+1\cdot(-1) & 3\cdot 3+2\cdot 4+1\cdot 2 & 3\cdot 4+2\cdot 1+1\cdot 3\\(-1)\cdot 1+2\cdot 2+3\cdot(-1) & (-1)\cdot 3+2\cdot 4+3\cdot 2 & (-1)\cdot 4+2\cdot 1+3\cdot 3\\3\cdot 1+1\cdot 2+4\cdot(-1) & 3\cdot 3+1\cdot 4+4\cdot 2 & 3\cdot 4+1\cdot 1+4\cdot 3\end{bmatrix}$$

$$=\begin{bmatrix}6 & 19 & 17\\0 & 11 & 7\\1 & 21 & 25\end{bmatrix}$$

$$BA = \begin{bmatrix} 1 \cdot 3 \quad +3 \cdot (-1) + 4 \cdot 3 & 1 \cdot 2 \quad +3 \cdot 2 + 4 \cdot 1 & 1 \cdot 1 \quad +3 \cdot 3 + 4 \cdot 4 \\ 2 \cdot 3 \quad +4 \cdot (-1) + 1 \cdot 3 & 2 \cdot 2 \quad +4 \cdot 2 + 1 \cdot 1 & 2 \cdot 1 \quad +4 \cdot 3 + 1 \cdot 4 \\ (-1) \cdot 3 + 2 \cdot (-1) + 3 \cdot 3 & (-1) \cdot 2 + 2 \cdot 2 + 3 \cdot 1 & (-1) \cdot 1 + 2 \cdot 3 + 3 \cdot 4 \end{bmatrix}$$

$$= \begin{bmatrix} 12 & 12 & 26 \\ 5 & 13 & 18 \\ 4 & 5 & 17 \end{bmatrix}$$

■

As the last example shows, in general $AB \neq BA$ for any two square matrices A and B. However, the following properties are valid for matrix multiplication:

$$A(BC) = (AB)C \qquad \text{(Associative Law for Matrix Multiplication)}$$

and $$A(B+C) = AB + AC \qquad \text{(Distributive Law)}$$

whenever the products are defined.

identity matrix

A square matrix of order n having ones along the main diagonal and zeros elsewhere is called an *identity matrix* of order n. Thus, if I_n denotes the identity matrix of order n, then

$$I_n = \begin{bmatrix} 1 & 0 & \cdot & \cdot & \cdot & 0 \\ 0 & 1 & \cdot & \cdot & \cdot & 0 \\ \cdot & \cdot & & \cdot & & \cdot \\ \cdot & \cdot & & \cdot & & \cdot \\ \cdot & \cdot & & \cdot & & \cdot \\ 0 & 0 & \cdot & \cdot & \cdot & 1 \end{bmatrix}$$

The identity matrix has the property that $I_nA = A$ for any $n \times r$ matrix A, and $BI_n = B$ for any $s \times n$ matrix B. In particular, if A is a square matrix of order n then $I_nA = AI_n = A$.

EXAMPLE 3.8 Let

$$A = \begin{bmatrix} 1 & 3 & 1 \\ -4 & 3 & 2 \\ 1 & 0 & 1 \end{bmatrix}$$

Then

$$I_3A = \begin{bmatrix} 1 & 0 & 0 \\ 0 & 1 & 0 \\ 0 & 0 & 1 \end{bmatrix} \begin{bmatrix} 1 & 3 & 1 \\ -4 & 3 & 2 \\ 1 & 0 & 1 \end{bmatrix} = \begin{bmatrix} 1 & 3 & 1 \\ -4 & 3 & 2 \\ 1 & 0 & 1 \end{bmatrix} = A$$

$$AI_3 = \begin{bmatrix} 1 & 3 & 1 \\ -4 & 3 & 2 \\ 1 & 0 & 1 \end{bmatrix} \begin{bmatrix} 1 & 0 & 0 \\ 0 & 1 & 0 \\ 0 & 0 & 1 \end{bmatrix} = \begin{bmatrix} 1 & 3 & 1 \\ -4 & 3 & 2 \\ 1 & 0 & 1 \end{bmatrix} = A$$

so that $I_3A = AI_3$ confirming the above result for this special case. ■

EXAMPLE 3.9 The Ace Novelty Company received an order from the Magic World Amusement Park for 900 "Giant Pandas", 1200 "Saint Bernards" and 2000 "Big Birds". Management decided that 500 of the Giant Pandas, 800 of the Saint Bernards, and 1300 of the Big Birds could be manufactured in their Los Angeles plant with the balance of the order to be filled from their Seattle plant. Each Giant Panda requires 1.5 square yards of plush, 30 cubic feet of stuffing material, and 5 pieces of trimming; each Saint Bernard requires 2 square yards of plush, 35 cubic feet of stuffing material, and 8 pieces of trimming; and each Big Bird requires 2.5 square yards of plush, 25 cubic feet of stuffing material, and 15 pieces of trimming. The plush costs \$4.50 per square yard, the stuffing material costs \$.10 per cubic foot, and the trimming costs \$.25 per unit.

(*a*) Find the amount of each type of material to be purchased for each of the two plants.

(*b*) What is the total cost of materials incurred by each plant and the total cost of materials incurred by Ace Novelty Company in fulfilling the order?

SOLUTION The quantities of each type of stuffed animal to be produced at each of the two plant locations may be expressed as a 2×3 *production matrix P*. Thus

$$P = \begin{array}{l} \\ \text{L.A.} \\ \text{Seattle} \end{array} \begin{array}{c} \begin{array}{ccc} \text{G. Pandas} & \text{S. Bernards} & \text{B. Birds} \end{array} \\ \begin{bmatrix} 500 & 800 & 1300 \\ 400 & 400 & 700 \end{bmatrix} \end{array}$$

Similarly, we may represent the amount and type of material required to manufacture each type of stuffed animal by a 3×3 *activity matrix A*. Thus

$$A = \begin{array}{l} \\ \text{G. Pandas} \\ \text{S. Bernards} \\ \text{B. Birds} \end{array} \begin{array}{c} \begin{array}{ccc} \text{Plush} & \text{S. Mat.} & \text{Trim} \end{array} \\ \begin{bmatrix} 1.5 & 30 & 5 \\ 2 & 35 & 8 \\ 2.5 & 25 & 15 \end{bmatrix} \end{array}$$

Finally, the unit cost for each type of material may be represented by the 3×1 cost matrix

$$C = \begin{array}{l} \text{Plush} \\ \text{S. Mat.} \\ \text{Trim} \end{array} \begin{bmatrix} 4.50 \\ 0.10 \\ 0.25 \end{bmatrix}$$

(**a**) The amount of each type of material required for each of the two plants is given by the matrix PA. Thus:

$$PA = \begin{bmatrix} 500 & 800 & 1300 \\ 400 & 400 & 700 \end{bmatrix} \begin{bmatrix} 1.5 & 30 & 5 \\ 2 & 35 & 8 \\ 2.5 & 25 & 15 \end{bmatrix}$$

$$= \begin{array}{l} \\ \text{L.A.} \\ \text{Seattle} \end{array} \begin{array}{c} \begin{array}{ccc} \text{Plush} & \text{S. Mat.} & \text{Trim} \end{array} \\ \begin{bmatrix} 5600 & 75{,}500 & 28{,}400 \\ 3150 & 43{,}500 & 15{,}700 \end{bmatrix} \end{array}$$

(b) The total cost of materials to be incurred by each plant is given by the matrix *PAC*

$$PAC = \begin{bmatrix} 5600 & 75{,}500 & 28{,}400 \\ 3150 & 43{,}500 & 15{,}700 \end{bmatrix} \begin{bmatrix} 4.50 \\ 0.10 \\ 0.25 \end{bmatrix}$$

$$= \begin{matrix} \text{L.A.} \\ \text{Seattle} \end{matrix} \begin{bmatrix} 39{,}850 \\ 22{,}450 \end{bmatrix}$$

or \$39,850 for the L.A. plant and \$22,450 for the Seattle plant. The total cost of materials incurred by Ace Novelty Company in fulfilling the order is \$62,300. ■

3.2 EXERCISES

1. For each of the following pairs of matrices whose orders are given, determine the orders of AB and BA whenever they are defined.

(*a*) A is of order 2×3 and B is of order 3×5.

(*b*) A is of order 3×4 and B is of order 4×3.

(*c*) A is of order 1×7 and B is of order 7×1.

(*d*) A is of order 4×4 and B is of order 4×4.

2. Let A be a matrix of order $m \times n$ and B be a matrix of order $s \times t$. Find conditions on m, n, s, and t so that both the matrix products AB and BA are defined.

3. Find condition(s) on the order of a matrix A so that A^2 (that is AA) is defined.

4. Let

$$A = \begin{bmatrix} 2 & 1 & 2 \\ 3 & 2 & 4 \end{bmatrix}, \quad B = \begin{bmatrix} -1 & 2 \\ 4 & 3 \\ 0 & 1 \end{bmatrix}, \quad \text{and} \quad C = \begin{bmatrix} 3 & 2 & 1 \\ -1 & 2 & -1 \\ 4 & 3 & 0 \end{bmatrix}$$

Compute each of the following:

(*a*) AB (*b*) AC (*c*) CB (*d*) BA

In problems 5 through 9 compute the indicated products.

5. $$\begin{bmatrix} 6 & -3 & 0 \\ -2 & 1 & -8 \\ 4 & -4 & 9 \end{bmatrix} \begin{bmatrix} 1 & 0 & 0 \\ 0 & 1 & 0 \\ 0 & 0 & 1 \end{bmatrix}$$

6. $$\begin{bmatrix} 3 & 0 & -2 & 1 \\ 1 & 2 & 0 & -1 \end{bmatrix} \begin{bmatrix} 2 & 1 & -1 \\ -1 & 2 & 0 \\ 0 & 0 & 1 \\ -1 & -2 & 2 \end{bmatrix}$$

7. $4\begin{bmatrix} 1 & -2 & 0 \\ 2 & -1 & 1 \\ 3 & 0 & -1 \end{bmatrix}\begin{bmatrix} 1 & 3 & 1 \\ 1 & 4 & 0 \\ 0 & 1 & -2 \end{bmatrix}$

8. $\begin{bmatrix} 1 & 0 \\ 0 & 1 \end{bmatrix}\begin{bmatrix} 4 & -3 & 2 \\ 7 & 1 & -5 \end{bmatrix}\begin{bmatrix} 1 & 0 & 0 \\ 0 & 1 & 0 \\ 0 & 0 & 1 \end{bmatrix}$

9. $2\begin{bmatrix} 3 & 2 & -1 \\ 0 & 1 & 3 \\ 2 & 0 & 3 \end{bmatrix}\begin{bmatrix} 1 & 0 & 0 \\ 0 & 1 & 0 \\ 0 & 0 & 1 \end{bmatrix}\begin{bmatrix} 1 & 2 & 0 \\ 0 & -1 & -2 \\ 1 & 3 & 1 \end{bmatrix}$

10. Let

$$A = \begin{bmatrix} 1 & 0 & -2 \\ 1 & -3 & 2 \\ -2 & 1 & 1 \end{bmatrix}, \quad B = \begin{bmatrix} 3 & 1 & 0 \\ 2 & 2 & 0 \\ 1 & -3 & -1 \end{bmatrix}, \quad \text{and} \quad C = \begin{bmatrix} 2 & -1 & 0 \\ 1 & -1 & 2 \\ 3 & -2 & 1 \end{bmatrix}$$

Verify the validity of the Associative Law for matrix multiplication and the Distributive Law for matrix multiplication for this special case.

11. Refer to problem 4. Show, by considering the orders of the matrices AB and BA, that $AB \neq BA$ and that matrix multiplication is, in general, not commutative.

12. Let

$$A = \begin{bmatrix} 1 & 2 \\ 3 & 4 \end{bmatrix} \quad \text{and} \quad B = \begin{bmatrix} 2 & 1 \\ 4 & 3 \end{bmatrix}$$

Compute AB, BA and hence deduce that matrix multiplication is, in general, not commutative.

13. Let

$$A = \begin{bmatrix} 0 & 3 & 0 \\ 1 & 0 & 1 \\ 0 & 2 & 0 \end{bmatrix}, \quad B = \begin{bmatrix} 2 & 4 & 5 \\ 3 & -1 & -6 \\ 4 & 3 & 4 \end{bmatrix}, \quad \text{and} \quad C = \begin{bmatrix} 4 & 5 & 6 \\ 3 & -1 & -6 \\ 2 & 2 & 3 \end{bmatrix}$$

(*a*) Compute AB.

(*b*) Compute AC.

(*c*) Using the results of parts (a) and (b) conclude that $AB = AC$ does not imply that $B = C$.

14. Let

$$A = \begin{bmatrix} 3 & 0 \\ 8 & 0 \end{bmatrix} \quad \text{and} \quad B = \begin{bmatrix} 0 & 0 \\ 4 & 5 \end{bmatrix}$$

Show that $AB = O$ thereby demonstrating that for matrix multiplication the equation $AB = O$ does not imply that one or both of the matrices A, B must be the zero matrix.

15. Let

$$A = \begin{bmatrix} 2 & 2 \\ -2 & -2 \end{bmatrix}$$

Show that $A^2 = O$. Compare this with the equation $a^2 = 0$ where a is a real number.

16. Find the matrix A such that

$$A\begin{bmatrix} 1 & 0 \\ -1 & 3 \end{bmatrix} = \begin{bmatrix} -1 & -3 \\ 3 & 6 \end{bmatrix}$$

Hint: Let

$$A = \begin{bmatrix} a & b \\ c & d \end{bmatrix}$$

17. Let

$$A = \begin{bmatrix} 3 & 1 \\ 0 & 2 \end{bmatrix} \quad \text{and} \quad B = \begin{bmatrix} 4 & -2 \\ 2 & 1 \end{bmatrix}$$

(***a***) Compute $(A+B)^2$.

(***b***) Compute $A^2+2AB+B^2$.

(***c***) From the results of parts (***a***) and (***b***) show that in general $(A+B)^2 \neq A^2+2AB+B^2$.

18. If

$$A = \begin{bmatrix} 2 & 4 \\ 5 & -6 \end{bmatrix} \quad \text{and} \quad B = \begin{bmatrix} 4 & 8 \\ -7 & 3 \end{bmatrix}$$

(***a***) Find A^T and show that $(A^T)^T = A$.

(***b***) Show that $(A+B)^T = A^T + B^T$.

(***c***) Show that $(AB)^T = B^T A^T$.

19. The Cinema Center is comprised of four theaters, Cinemas I, II, III, and IV. The admission price for one feature at the Center is \$2.00 for children, \$3.00 for students, and \$4.00 for adults. The attendance for the Sunday matinee is given by the matrix

$$A = \begin{array}{l} \text{Cinema I} \\ \text{Cinema II} \\ \text{Cinema III} \\ \text{Cinema IV} \end{array} \begin{array}{c} \begin{array}{ccc} \text{Children} & \text{Students} & \text{Adults} \end{array} \\ \begin{bmatrix} 225 & 110 & 50 \\ 75 & 180 & 225 \\ 280 & 85 & 110 \\ 0 & 250 & 225 \end{bmatrix} \end{array}$$

Write a column vector B representing the admission prices and compute AB, the column vector showing the gross receipts for each theater. Finally, find the total revenue collected at the Cinema Center for admission charges on that Sunday afternoon.

20. The admissions committee of a university anticipates an enrollment of 8000 students in its freshman class for the next year. For the purpose of satisfying admission quotas, the incoming students have been categorized according to their sex and place of residence prior to enrollment. The number of students in each category is given by the matrix:

$$A = \begin{array}{l} \text{In-state} \\ \text{Out-of-state} \\ \text{Foreign} \end{array} \overset{\begin{array}{cc} \text{Male} & \text{Female} \end{array}}{\begin{bmatrix} 2700 & 3000 \\ 800 & 700 \\ 500 & 300 \end{bmatrix}}$$

By using data accumulated in previous years, the admissions committee has projected that these students will elect to enter the College of Letters and Science, the College of Fine Arts, the School of Business Administration, and the School of Engineering according to the percentages that appear in the matrix

$$B = \begin{array}{l} \text{Male} \\ \text{Female} \end{array} \overset{\begin{array}{cccc} \text{L. \& S.} & \text{Fine Arts} & \text{Bus. Ad.} & \text{Eng.} \end{array}}{\begin{bmatrix} .25 & .20 & .30 & .25 \\ .30 & .35 & .25 & .10 \end{bmatrix}}$$

Find the matrix AB that shows the number of in-state, out-of-state, and foreign students expected to enter each discipline.

21. Refer to Example 3.9. Suppose that the Ace Novelty Company received an order from another amusement park for 1200 Pink Panthers, 1800 Giant Pandas, and 1400 Big Birds. The quantity of each type of stuffed animal to be produced at each plant is shown in the production matrix

$$P = \begin{array}{l} \text{L.A.} \\ \text{Seattle} \end{array} \overset{\begin{array}{ccc} \text{P. Panthers} & \text{G. Pandas} & \text{B. Birds} \end{array}}{\begin{bmatrix} 700 & 1000 & 800 \\ 500 & 800 & 600 \end{bmatrix}}$$

Each Pink Panther requires 1.3 square yards of plush, 20 cubic feet of stuffing material, and 12 pieces of trimming. If the materials required for the production of the other two stuffed animals and the unit cost for each type of material are the same as those given in Example 3.9

(***a***) Find the amount of each type of material to be purchased for each of the two plants.

(***b***) Find the total cost of materials to be incurred at each plant, and (*c*) Find the total cost of materials incurred by Ace Novelty Company in fulfilling the order.

22. The following figure shows the routes of an international airline connecting five cities. A line joining two cities indicates that there is a direct flight between them.

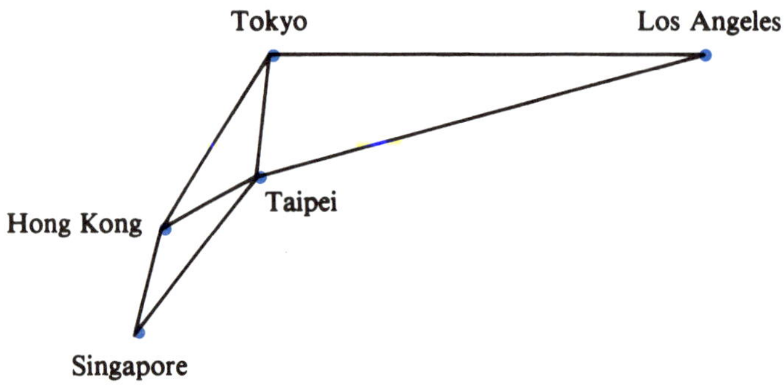

The same information can be represented by the matrix

		Singapore	Hong Kong	Taipei	Tokyo	Los Angeles
	Singapore	0	1	1	0	0
	Hong Kong	1	0	1	1	0
$A =$	Taipei	1	1	0	1	1
	Tokyo	0	1	1	0	1
	L.A.	0	0	1	1	0

where $a_{ij} = 1$ indicates that there is a direct flight between the ith city and the jth city, and $a_{ij} = 0$ indicates that there is no direct flight between the cities.

(*a*) Compute A^2.

(*b*) By referring to the figure, verify that the entry, a_{ij}, of A^2 represents the number of one-stop routes between the ith city and the jth city.

23. The following figure shows the routes of a domestic airline connecting five cities. (Refer to problem 22.)

(*a*) Represent this information by a matrix A.

(*b*) Write the matrix that shows the number of one-stop routes between any two cities.

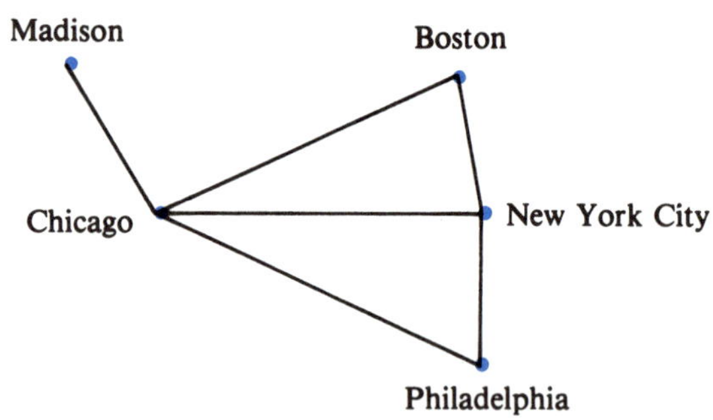

3.3

Systems of Linear Equations: Introduction

We first encountered a system of linear equations in section 2.2 where we were required to solve a system of two linear equations in two variables. Recall that such a system may be written in the general form

(3.1)
$$\begin{cases} ax + by = h \\ cx + dy = k \end{cases}$$

where a, b, c, d, h, and k are real constants and a and b (c and d) are not both zero.

Let us study the nature of the solution of the system (3.1) in more detail. Recall that each of the equations in (3.1) has for its graph a straight line in the plane, so that geometrically the solution to the system is the point(s) of intersection of the two straight lines L_1 and L_2 represented by the first and second equations of the system.

A priori, the two lines L_1 and L_2 may (1) intersect at exactly one point, (2) be parallel and coincident or (3) be parallel and distinct (see Figure 3.1). The reader may convince himself or herself that one and only one of the above cases must occur. In the first case, the system (3.1) has a unique solution corresponding to the single point of intersection of the two lines. In the second case the system (3.1) has infinitely many solutions corresponding to the points lying simultaneously on both lines. Finally, in the third case, the system (3.1) has no solution since the two lines do not intersect each other.

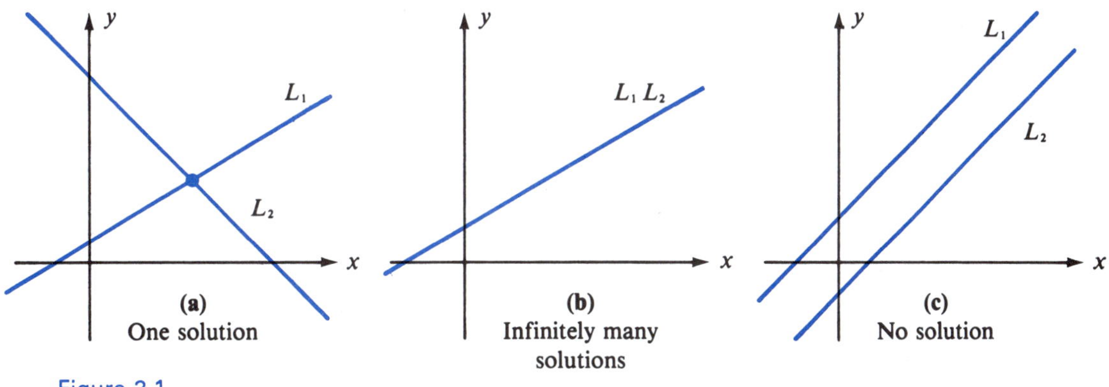

Figure 3.1

The following example illustrates an algebraic approach to the solution of systems of equations involving two linear equations in two variables.

EXAMPLE 3.10 Solve each of the following systems of linear equations and discuss your results geometrically.

(a) $\begin{cases} 2x - y = 1 \\ 3x + 2y = 12 \end{cases}$ (b) $\begin{cases} 2x - y = 1 \\ 6x - 3y = 3 \end{cases}$ (c) $\begin{cases} 2x - y = 1 \\ 6x - 3y = 12 \end{cases}$

SOLUTION (**a**) Solving the first equation for y in terms of x, we obtain the equation $y = 2x - 1$. Substituting this value of y into the second equation gives $3x + 2(2x - 1) = 12$ or $x = 2$. Finally, substituting this value of x into the first equation gives $2(2) - y = 1$ or $y = 3$. Thus, the (unique) solution of the system is given by $x = 2$ and $y = 3$. Geometrically, the two lines represented by the two linear equations comprising the system intersect at the point (2, 3) (see Figure 3.2**a**).

(**b**) Solving the first equation for y in terms of x, we obtain the equation $y = 2x - 1$. Substituting this value of y into the second equation gives $6x - 3(2x - 1) = 3$ or $3 = 3$. This result tells us that the system is equivalent to the single equation $2x - y = 1$. (To see that the second equation is dependent on the first, simply multiply both sides of the first equation by 3.) Thus, any ordered pair of numbers (x, y) satisfying the equation $y = 2x - 1$ constitutes a solution to the system. In particular, by assigning the value t to x where t is any real number we find that $y = 2t - 1$ and so the ordered pair $(t, 2t - 1)$ is a solution of the system. Since t, called a *parameter*, is any real number, there are infinitely many solutions to the system. For example, setting $t = 0$ gives the point $(0, -1)$ as a solution and setting $t = 1$ gives the point $(1, 1)$ as a solution to the system. Geometrically, the two equations represent the same line and all the solutions of the system lie on the line (See Figure 3.2**b**).

parameter

(**c**) Solving the first equation for y in terms of x, we obtain the equation $y = 2x - 1$. Substituting this value of y into the second equation gives $6x - 3(2x - 1) = 12$ or $0 = 9$ which is clearly impossible. Thus, there is no solution to the system of equations. To interpret this situation geometrically, cast both equations in the slope-intercept form getting $y = 2x - 1$ and $y = 2x - 4$. We see at once that the lines represented by these equations are parallel (each having slope 2) and distinct since the first has intercept -1 and the second has intercept -4 (see Figure 3.2**c**). This system is an example of an *inconsistent system of linear equations*.

inconsistent system of linear equations

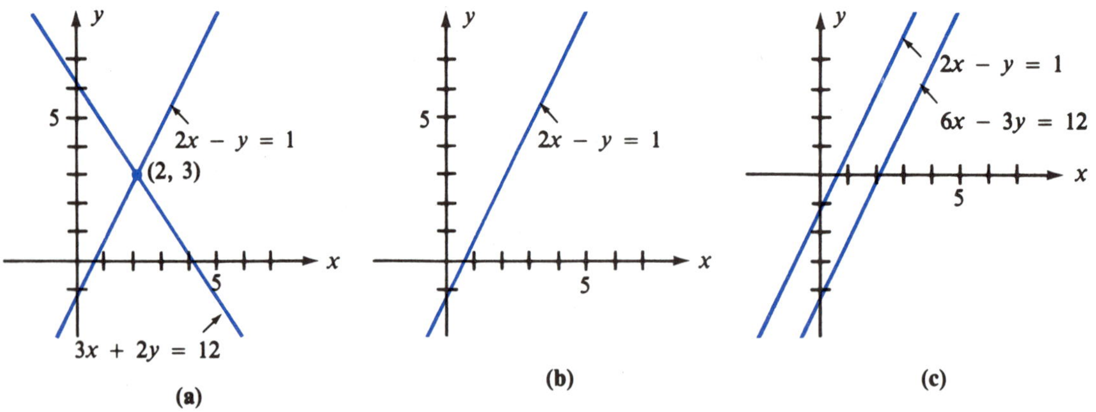

Figure 3.2

■

In general, a linear equation in n variables $x_1, x_2, \ldots, x_n$ is one of the form

$$a_1x_1 + a_2x_2 + \cdots + a_nx_n = c$$

where $a_1, a_2, \ldots, a_n$ (not all zero) and c are constants. For example, t. $3x+2y-4z+6w=8$ is a linear equation in the four variables x, y, z, anc

The following example shows how the mathematical formulation of a pı may result in a system of linear equations.

EXAMPLE 3.11 The Ace Novelty Company wishes to produce three types of souvenirs, types A, B, and C. To manufacture a type A souvenir requires 2 minutes on machine I, 1 minute on machine II, and 2 minutes on machine III. A souvenir of type B requires 1 minute on machine I, 3 minutes on machine II, and 1 minute on machine III. A souvenir of type C requires 1 minute on machine I and 2 minutes on each of machines II and III. There are 3 hours available on machine I, 5 hours available on machine II, and 4 hours available on machine III for processing the order. How many of each type of souvenir should the Ace Novelty Co. make in order to utilize all of the available time? Formulate, but do not solve the problem.

SOLUTION The given information may be tabulated as follows:

	Type A	Type B	Type C	Time available
Machine I	2	1	1	180
Machine II	1	3	2	300
Machine III	2	1	2	240

Let x, y, and z denote the respective numbers of type A, type B, and type C souvenirs to be made. The total amount of time that machine I is utilized is given by $2x+y+z$ minutes and must be equal to 180 minutes. This leads to the equation

$$2x+y+z=180$$

Similar considerations on the utilization of machines II and III lead to the following equations:

$$\begin{aligned} x+3y+2z&=300 \\ 2x+y+2z&=240 \end{aligned}$$

Since the variables x, y, and z must satisfy simultaneously the three conditions represented by the three equations, the solution to the problem is found by solving the following system of linear equations.

$$\begin{aligned} 2x+y+z&=180 \\ x+3y+2z&=300 \\ 2x+y+2z&=240 \end{aligned}$$ ■

We shall complete the solution of the problem posed in Example 3.11 later on (see page 114). For the moment let us look at the geometrical interpretation of a system of linear equations such as the system in Example 3.11 in order to gain some insight into the nature of the solution.

Now, a linear system comprising three linear equations in three variables x, y and z has the general form

$$\begin{aligned} a_1x + b_1y + c_1z &= d_1 \\ a_2x + b_2y + c_2z &= d_2 \\ a_3x + b_3y + c_3z &= d_3 \end{aligned} \tag{3.2}$$

Just as a linear equation in two variables represents a straight line in the plane, it can be shown that a linear equation $ax + by + cz = d$ (a, b, and c not simultaneously equal to zero) in three variables represents a plane in three-dimensional space. Thus, each of the equations in system (3.2) represents a *plane* in three-dimensional space and the *solution(s) of the system* is precisely the point(s) of intersection of the three planes defined by the three linear equations comprising the system. A priori, the system has one and only one solution, infinitely many solutions, or no solution depending on whether and how the planes intersect each other. Figure (3.3) illustrates each of these possibilities.

solution of a system of equations

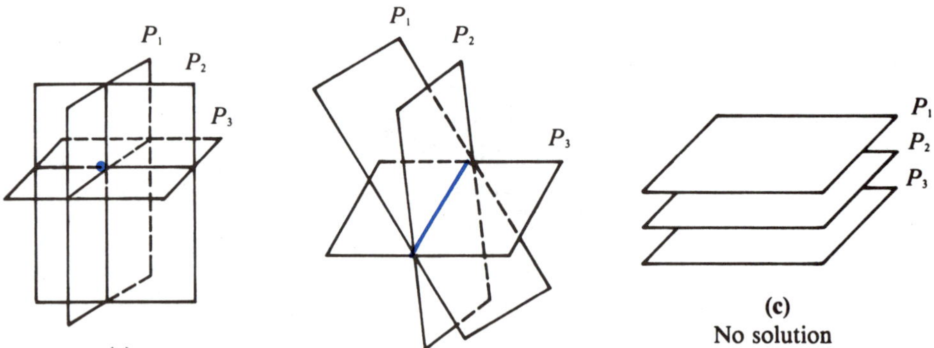

Figure 3.3

(a) One and only one solution

(b) Infinitely many solutions

(c) No solution

In Figure 3.3(**a**) the three planes intersect at a point corresponding to the situation when system (3.2) has a unique solution. Figure 3.3(**b**) depicts the situation where there are infinitely many solutions to the system. Here the three planes intersect along a line and the solutions are represented by the infinitely many points lying on this line. In Figure 3.3(**c**), the three planes are parallel and distinct so that there is no point in common to all three planes and system (3.2) has no solution in this case.

The situations depicted in Figure 3.3 are by no means exhaustive. The reader may consider various other orientations of the three planes that would illustrate the three possible outcomes in solving a system of linear equations involving three variables.

In the case when the number of variables involved in a linear equation exceeds three, we no longer have the geometrical interpretation that we had for the lower-dimensional spaces. Nevertheless, the algebraic concepts of the lower dimensional spaces generalize to higher dimensions. For this reason, a linear equation in n variables $a_1x_1+a_2x_2+\cdots+a_nx_n=c$, where $a_1, a_2, \cdots, a_n$ are not all zero, is referred to as an *n-dimensional hyperplane*. We may interpret the solution(s) to a system comprising a finite number of such linear equations to be the *point(s) of intersection* of the hyperplanes defined by the equations comprising the system. As in the case of systems involving two or three variables, it can be shown that only three possibilities exist regarding the nature of the solution of such a system: (a) *a unique solution*, (b) *infinitely many solutions*, and (c) *no solution*.

3.3 EXERCISES

In problems 1 through 6 determine if each of the given systems of linear equations has (a) one and only one solution, (b) infinitely many solutions, or (c) no solution. Find all solutions whenever they exist.

1. $x-3y=-1$
$4x+3y=11$

2. $x+4y=7$
$(1/2)x+2y=5$

3. $2x-5y=10$
$6x-15y=30$

4. $4x-5y=14$
$2x+3y=-4$

***5.** $x+2y=6$
$3x+y=8$
$2x-3y=2$

***6.** $3x-y=8$
$2x+4y=3$
$x+y=2$

3.4 Solving Systems of Linear Equations

The method of substitution used in the last section is well-suited to solving a system of linear equations when the number of linear equations and the number of variables involved are small. But for large systems, the steps involved in the procedure become difficult to manage.

A technique that is suitable for solving systems of linear equations of any size is the so-called *Gauss-Jordan Elimination Method.* A further advantage of this technique is its adaptability to the electronic computer. This method involves a sequence of operations on the system of linear equations to obtain at each stage an *equivalent system*, in other words, a system having the same solution as the original system. The reduction is completed when the original system has been transformed to one having a certain standard form from which the solution can be easily read off.

The operations referred to above follow:

Type 1 Interchanging any two equations.

Type 2 Replacing any equation by a nonzero multiple of itself.

Type 3 Replacing any equation by the sum of a nonzero multiple of itself and a nonzero multiple of any other equation in the system.

We now illustrate the Gauss-Jordan Elimination Method for solving systems of linear equations by applying it to the solution of the system defined by the following equations:

(3.3)
$$\begin{aligned} x+2y+3z&=1\\ 2x+3y+2z&=2\\ -x+y+2z&=-8 \end{aligned}$$

As a first step, we shall transform the above system into an equivalent one in which the variable x is eliminated from all equations except the first. To accomplish this, we use a Type 3 operation twice as follows. First, replace the second equation of (3.3) by an equation obtained by adding -2 times the first equation to it, getting the equivalent system

(3.4)
$$\begin{aligned} x+2y+3z&=1\\ -y-4z&=0\\ -x+y+2z&=-8 \end{aligned}$$

Second, replace the third equation of (3.4) by an equation obtained by adding the first equation of (3.4) to the third equation of (3.4), giving

(3.5)
$$\begin{aligned} x+2y+3z&=1\\ -y-4z&=0\\ 3y+5z&=-7 \end{aligned}$$

By multiplying the second equation of (3.5) by -1 (a Type 2 operation), we see that (3.5) is equivalent to

(3.6)
$$\begin{aligned} x+2y+3z&=1\\ y+4z&=0\\ 3y+5z&=-7 \end{aligned}$$

We now eliminate the variable y from all equations except the second. Again, this may be accomplished by using Type 3 operations. We replace the first equation in (3.6) by one obtained by adding it to -2 times the second equation of (3.6). This gives,

(3.7)
$$\begin{aligned} x\qquad -5z&=1\\ y+4z&=0\\ 3y+5z&=-7 \end{aligned}$$

Next, we replace the third equation in (3.7) by one obtained by adding −3 times the second equation of (3.7) to it. This leads to the (equivalent) system

(3.8)
$$\begin{aligned} x \quad - 5z &= 1 \\ y + 4z &= 0 \\ -7z &= -7 \end{aligned}$$

Multiplying the third equation of (3.8) by −1/7 gives

(3.9)
$$\begin{aligned} x \quad - 5z &= 1 \\ y + 4z &= 0 \\ z &= 1 \end{aligned}$$

Finally, we eliminate z from the first two equations of (3.9) by (a) replacing the first equation of (3.9) by a sum involving that equation and five times the third equation of (3.9), and (b) replacing the second equation of (3.9) by a sum involving that equation and −4 times the third equation of (3.9). We obtain the equivalent system

(3.10)
$$\begin{aligned} x \quad &= 6 \\ y \quad &= -4 \\ z &= 1 \end{aligned}$$

in standard form, from which we can read off the solution to system (3.3) as $x = 6$, $y = -4$, and $z = 1$ or more concisely the point (6, −4, 1) in three dimensional space.

The reader would have observed from the preceding example that in each step of the reduction process, the variables x, y, and z play no significant role except as a reminder of the position of each of the coefficients in the system of linear equations. With the aid of matrices we can eliminate writing the variables at each step of the reduction and thus save ourselves a great deal of work. To this end, note that the system

(3.11)
$$\begin{aligned} x + 2y + 3z &= 1 \\ 2x + 3y + 2z &= 2 \\ -x + \ y + 2z &= -8 \end{aligned}$$

may be represented in matrix form as follows:

(3.12)
$$\left[\begin{array}{rrr|r} 1 & 2 & 3 & 1 \\ 2 & 3 & 2 & 2 \\ -1 & 1 & 2 & -8 \end{array}\right]$$

matrix of coefficients

where the 3×3 *submatrix* comprising the first three columns of the matrix (3.12) is called the *matrix of coefficients* of the system (3.11). The matrix (3.12) itself is

augmented matrix referred to as the *augmented matrix* of the system (3.11) since it is obtained by joining the matrix of coefficients to the column (matrix) of constants.

The next example shows the reduction in work involved in the computations when this format is used instead of the standard representation of the systems of linear equations.

EXAMPLE 3.12 Write the augmented matrix corresponding to each of the equivalent systems given by (3.3) through (3.10).

SOLUTION The required sequence of augmented matrices is given by:

	Augmented Matrix	Equivalent System
(a)	$\left[\begin{array}{ccc\|c} 1 & 2 & 3 & 1 \\ 2 & 3 & 2 & 2 \\ -1 & 1 & 2 & -8 \end{array}\right]$	$\begin{aligned} x+2y+3z &= 1 \\ 2x+3y+2z &= 2 \\ -x+y+2z &= -8 \end{aligned}$
(b)	$\left[\begin{array}{ccc\|c} 1 & 2 & 3 & 1 \\ 0 & -1 & -4 & 0 \\ -1 & 1 & 2 & -8 \end{array}\right]$	$\begin{aligned} x+2y+3z &= 1 \\ -y-4z &= 0 \\ -x+y+2z &= -8 \end{aligned}$
(c)	$\left[\begin{array}{ccc\|c} 1 & 2 & 3 & 1 \\ 0 & -1 & -4 & 0 \\ 0 & 3 & 5 & -7 \end{array}\right]$	$\begin{aligned} x+2y+3z &= 1 \\ -y-4z &= 0 \\ 3y+5z &= -7 \end{aligned}$
(d)	$\left[\begin{array}{ccc\|c} 1 & 2 & 3 & 1 \\ 0 & 1 & 4 & 0 \\ 0 & 3 & 5 & -7 \end{array}\right]$	$\begin{aligned} x+2y+3z &= 1 \\ y+4z &= 0 \\ 3y+5z &= -7 \end{aligned}$
(e)	$\left[\begin{array}{ccc\|c} 1 & 0 & -5 & 1 \\ 0 & 1 & 4 & 0 \\ 0 & 3 & 5 & -7 \end{array}\right]$	$\begin{aligned} x-5z &= 1 \\ y+4z &= 0 \\ 3y+5z &= -7 \end{aligned}$
(f)	$\left[\begin{array}{ccc\|c} 1 & 0 & -5 & 1 \\ 0 & 1 & 4 & 0 \\ 0 & 0 & -7 & -7 \end{array}\right]$	$\begin{aligned} x-5z &= 1 \\ y+4z &= 0 \\ -7z &= -7 \end{aligned}$
(g)	$\left[\begin{array}{ccc\|c} 1 & 0 & -5 & 1 \\ 0 & 1 & 4 & 0 \\ 0 & 0 & 1 & 1 \end{array}\right]$	$\begin{aligned} x-5z &= 1 \\ y+4z &= 0 \\ z &= 1 \end{aligned}$
(3.13)	$\left[\begin{array}{ccc\|c} 1 & 0 & 0 & 6 \\ 0 & 1 & 0 & -4 \\ 0 & 0 & 1 & 1 \end{array}\right]$	$\begin{aligned} x &= 6 \\ y &= -4 \\ z &= 1 \end{aligned}$

■

The augmented matrix in (3.13) is an example of a matrix in row-reduced form. In general, a $m \times n$ matrix is said to be in row-reduced form if the associated matrix of coefficients has the following properties:

1. The first k rows contain nonzero entries while the remaining $(m-k)$ rows contain zero entries only.

2. The first nonzero entry in each row is a **1** and the column containing such an entry has zeros elsewhere.

3. The first nonzero entry (a **1**) in each nonzero row lies to the right of the first nonzero entry (a **1**) of any row above it.

EXAMPLE 3.13 The following matrices are in row-reduced form

$$\left[\begin{array}{ccc|c} 1 & 0 & 0 & 4 \\ 0 & 1 & 0 & 3 \\ 0 & 0 & 0 & 0 \end{array}\right], \qquad \left[\begin{array}{ccc|c} 1 & 2 & 0 & 3 \\ 0 & 0 & 1 & 2 \\ 0 & 0 & 0 & 3 \end{array}\right]$$

■

The above discussion and examples suggest the following adaptation of the Gauss–Jordan Elimination Method in solving systems of linear equations using the matrix format:

Step 1. Write the augmented matrix corresponding to the given linear system.

row operations

Step 2. Use the following *row operations* to transform the augmented matrix via a sequence of *equivalent augmented matrices* into a matrix in row-reduced form:

Type 1 Interchanging any two rows.

Type 2 Replacing any row by a nonzero multiple of itself.

Type 3 Replacing any row by the sum of a nonzero multiple of itself and a nonzero multiple of any other row of the augmented matrix.

Step 3. Read off the solution(s) to the given system of linear equations by interpreting the row-reduced matrix obtained in Step 2 as a system of equations.

We remark that even though there are many routes one may take in the reduction of the augmented matrix of the original system to the row-reduced form, Step 2 of the above procedure could be made more systematic as follows:

(a) Scan the first column of the augmented matrix to be reduced. If the entry in the a_{11} position is already a **1**, proceed to Step (b), below. Otherwise, use row operations to obtain an equivalent augmented matrix with a **1** in that position. Once this has been accomplished, proceed to obtain an equivalent augmented matrix with zero entries in the rest of the first column using the first row to aid in the elimination procedure.

(b) Repeat the above process, this time working with the second column of the resulting matrix and with the aim of obtaining an equivalent matrix with a **1** in the a_{22} position, if possible, and zeros elsewhere in that column.

(c) Continue until the next to the last column of the (equivalent) augmented matrix, that is, the last column of the coefficient matrix contained in the augmented matrix, is in the required form. We should now have obtained the equivalent matrix in reduced form.

The reader is urged to review Example 3.12 and convince himself or herself that the reduction process performed was done according to the procedure outlined above.

Before proceeding with further examples to illustrate the use of the Gauss–Jordan Elimination Method in solving systems of linear equations, let us introduce the following notations to indicate each of the three types of row operations. Letting R_i denote the ith row of a matrix, we write:

1. $R_i \leftrightarrow R_j$ to mean interchanging row i with row j (a *Type 1* operation).
2. cR_i to mean replacing row i with c times row i (a *Type 2* operation).
3. $aR_i + bR_j$ to mean replacing row i with the sum of a times row i and b times row j (a *Type 3* operation).

EXAMPLE 3.14 Solve the system of linear equations given by

(3.14)
$$\begin{aligned} 3x - 2y + 8z &= 9 \\ -2x + 2y + z &= 3 \\ x + 2y - 3z &= 8 \end{aligned}$$

SOLUTION Using the Gauss–Jordan Elimination Method, we obtain the following sequence of equivalent augmented matrices:

$$\left[\begin{array}{rrr|r} 3 & -2 & 8 & 9 \\ -2 & 2 & 1 & 3 \\ 1 & 2 & -3 & 8 \end{array}\right] \xrightarrow{R_1+R_2} \left[\begin{array}{rrr|r} 1 & 0 & 9 & 12 \\ -2 & 2 & 1 & 3 \\ 1 & 2 & -3 & 8 \end{array}\right] \xrightarrow[R_3-R_1]{R_2+2R_1} \left[\begin{array}{rrr|r} 1 & 0 & 9 & 12 \\ 0 & 2 & 19 & 27 \\ 0 & 2 & -12 & -4 \end{array}\right]$$

$$\xrightarrow{R_2 \leftrightarrow R_3} \left[\begin{array}{rrr|r} 1 & 0 & 9 & 12 \\ 0 & 2 & -12 & -4 \\ 0 & 2 & 19 & 27 \end{array}\right] \xrightarrow{\frac{1}{2}R_2} \left[\begin{array}{rrr|r} 1 & 0 & 9 & 12 \\ 0 & 1 & -6 & -2 \\ 0 & 2 & 19 & 27 \end{array}\right] \xrightarrow{R_3-2R_2}$$

$$\left[\begin{array}{rrr|r} 1 & 0 & 9 & 12 \\ 0 & 1 & -6 & -2 \\ 0 & 0 & 31 & 31 \end{array}\right] \xrightarrow{\frac{1}{31}R_3} \left[\begin{array}{rrr|r} 1 & 0 & 9 & 12 \\ 0 & 1 & -6 & -2 \\ 0 & 0 & 1 & 1 \end{array}\right] \xrightarrow[R_2+6R_3]{R_1-9R_3} \left[\begin{array}{rrr|r} 1 & 0 & 0 & 3 \\ 0 & 1 & 0 & 4 \\ 0 & 0 & 1 & 1 \end{array}\right]$$

The solution to system (3.14) is given by $x = 3$, $y = 4$, and $z = 1$ and may be verified by substitution into system (3.14) as follows:

$$\begin{aligned} 3(3) - 2(4) + 8(1) &= 9 \quad (\checkmark) \\ -2(3) + 2(4) + 1 &= 3 \quad (\checkmark) \\ 3 + 2(4) - 3(1) &= 8 \quad (\checkmark) \end{aligned}$$

■

The following example illustrates the situation when a system of linear equations has infinitely many solutions.

EXAMPLE 3.15 Solve the system of linear equations given by

$$\begin{aligned} x + 2y - 3z &= -2 \\ 3x - y - 2z &= 1 \\ 2x + 3y - 5z &= -3 \end{aligned} \tag{3.15}$$

SOLUTION Using the Gauss–Jordan Elimination Method, we obtain the following sequence of equivalent augmented matrices:

$$\left[\begin{array}{rrr|r} 1 & 2 & -3 & -2 \\ 3 & -1 & -2 & 1 \\ 2 & 3 & -5 & -3 \end{array}\right] \xrightarrow[R_3-2R_1]{R_2-3R_1} \left[\begin{array}{rrr|r} 1 & 2 & -3 & -2 \\ 0 & -7 & 7 & 7 \\ 0 & -1 & 1 & 1 \end{array}\right] \xrightarrow{-\frac{1}{7}R_2} \left[\begin{array}{rrr|r} 1 & 2 & -3 & -2 \\ 0 & 1 & -1 & -1 \\ 0 & -1 & 1 & 1 \end{array}\right]$$

$$\xrightarrow[R_3+R_2]{R_1-2R_2} \left[\begin{array}{rrr|r} 1 & 0 & -1 & 0 \\ 0 & 1 & -1 & -1 \\ 0 & 0 & 0 & 0 \end{array}\right]$$

The last augmented matrix is in row-reduced form. Interpreting it as a system of linear equations gives:

$$\begin{aligned} x \quad - z &= 0 \\ y - z &= -1 \end{aligned}$$

Let us single out one variable, say z, and solve for x and y in terms of it. We obtain

$$\begin{aligned} x &= z \\ y &= z - 1 \end{aligned}$$

If we assign a particular value to z, say $z = 0$, we obtain $x = 0$ and $y = -1$ giving $(0, -1, 0)$ as a solution to system (3.15). By setting $z = 1$ we obtain another solution $(1, 0, 1)$. In general, if we set $z = t$ where t represents some real number, we obtain a solution given by $(t, t-1, t)$. Since t, called a *parameter*, may be any real number, we see that system (3.15) has infinitely many solutions. Geometrically, the solutions of system (3.15) lie on the straight line in three-dimensional space given by the intersection of the three planes determined by the three equations comprising the system. ■

The next example shows what happens in the elimination procedure when the system does not possess a solution.

EXAMPLE 3.16 Solve the system of linear equations given by

$$\begin{aligned} x + y + z &= 1 \\ 3x - y - z &= 4 \\ x + 5y + 5z &= -1 \end{aligned} \tag{3.16}$$

SOLUTION Using the Gauss–Jordan Elimination Method, we obtain the following sequence of equivalent augmented matrices:

$$\left[\begin{array}{ccc|c} 1 & 1 & 1 & 1 \\ 3 & -1 & -1 & 4 \\ 1 & 5 & 5 & -1 \end{array}\right] \xrightarrow[-R_3+R_1]{R_2-3R_1} \left[\begin{array}{ccc|c} 1 & 1 & 1 & 1 \\ 0 & -4 & -4 & 1 \\ 0 & -4 & -4 & 2 \end{array}\right] \xrightarrow{R_3-R_2} \left[\begin{array}{ccc|c} 1 & 1 & 1 & 1 \\ 0 & -4 & -4 & 1 \\ 0 & 0 & 0 & 1 \end{array}\right]$$

Observe that the third row in the last matrix reads $0x+0y+0z=1$, that is, $0=1$! We conclude therefore that system (3.16) is inconsistent and has no solution. Geometrically, we have a situation where two of the planes intersect in a straight line but the third plane is parallel to this line of intersection of the two planes and does not contain it. Consequently, there is no point of intersection of the three planes. ■

Let us now complete the solution of the problem posed in Example 3.11. Recall that the mathematical formulation of the problem led to the following system of linear equations:

$$\begin{aligned} 2x + \ y + \ z &= 180 \\ x + 3y + 2z &= 300 \\ 2x + \ y + 2z &= 240 \end{aligned}$$

where x, y, and z denote the respective numbers of type A, type B, and type C souvenirs to be made.

Solving the above system of linear equations by the Gauss–Jordan Elimination Method we obtain the following sequence of equivalent augmented matrices:

$$\left[\begin{array}{ccc|c} 2 & 1 & 1 & 180 \\ 1 & 3 & 2 & 300 \\ 2 & 1 & 2 & 240 \end{array}\right] \xrightarrow{R_1 \leftrightarrow R_2} \left[\begin{array}{ccc|c} 1 & 3 & 2 & 300 \\ 2 & 1 & 1 & 180 \\ 2 & 1 & 2 & 240 \end{array}\right] \xrightarrow[-R_3+2R_1]{-R_2+2R_1} \left[\begin{array}{ccc|c} 1 & 3 & 2 & 300 \\ 0 & 5 & 3 & 420 \\ 0 & 5 & 2 & 360 \end{array}\right]$$

$$\xrightarrow{\frac{1}{5}R_2} \left[\begin{array}{ccc|c} 1 & 3 & 2 & 300 \\ 0 & 1 & 3/5 & 84 \\ 0 & 5 & 2 & 360 \end{array}\right] \xrightarrow[-R_3+5R_2]{R_1-3R_2} \left[\begin{array}{ccc|c} 1 & 0 & 1/5 & 48 \\ 0 & 1 & 3/5 & 84 \\ 0 & 0 & 1 & 60 \end{array}\right]$$

$$\xrightarrow[R_2-\frac{3}{5}R_3]{R_1-\frac{1}{5}R_3} \left[\begin{array}{ccc|c} 1 & 0 & 0 & 36 \\ 0 & 1 & 0 & 48 \\ 0 & 0 & 1 & 60 \end{array}\right]$$

Thus, $x=36$, $y=48$, and $z=60$, that is to say, the Ace Novelty Co. should make thirty-six type A souvenirs, forty-eight type B souvenirs, and sixty type C souvenirs in order to utilize all the machine time available.

Our final example shows that the formulation of a practical problem may lead to a system of linear equations with infinitely many solutions. This translates into a situation in which there are infinitely many options available for solving the original problem.

EXAMPLE 3.17 Figure 3.4 shows the flow of traffic in a downtown area during the rush hours on a typical weekday. The arrows indicate the direction of the flow of traffic on each of the one-way roads, and the average number of vehicles entering and leaving each of the intersections per hour appears beside the respective roads. Each of the avenues can handle up to 2000 vehicles per hour without causing congestion whereas the maximum capacity of each of the three streets is 1000 vehicles per hour. The flow of traffic is controlled by traffic lights installed at each of the six intersections.

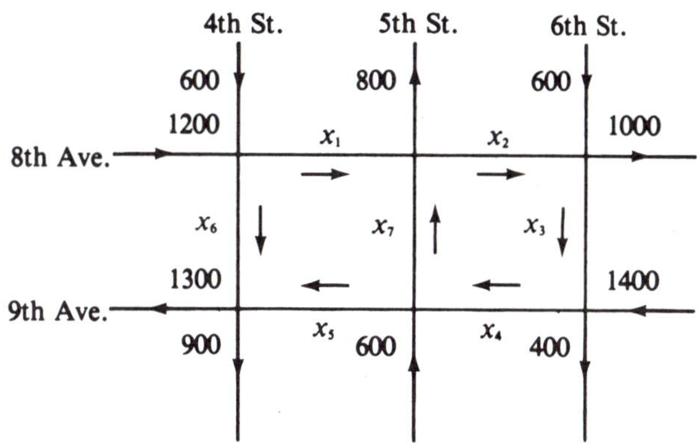

Figure 3.4

(a) Write a general expression involving the rates of flow, $x_1, x_2, \ldots, x_7$ and suggest two possible flow patterns that would ensure that there be no traffic congestion.
(b) Suppose part of 4th Street between 8th Avenue and 9th Avenue is to be resurfaced and that traffic flow between the two junctions has to be slowed down to at most 300 vehicles per hour, find two possible flow patterns that would result in a smooth flow of traffic.

SOLUTION **(a)** If there is to be no congestion, then all traffic entering an intersection must also leave that intersection. Applying this condition to each of the six intersections in a clockwise direction beginning with the 8th Avenue and 4th Street intersection, we obtain the following equations:

$$1800 = x_1 + x_6$$
$$x_1 + x_7 = 800 + x_2$$
$$x_2 + 600 = 1000 + x_3$$
$$x_3 + 1400 = x_4 + 400$$
$$x_4 + 600 = x_5 + x_7$$
$$x_5 + x_6 = 2200$$

This system of six linear equations in the seven variables $x_1, x_2, \ldots, x_7$ may be rewritten in the more standard form as follows:

$$\begin{aligned}
x_1 \qquad\qquad\qquad\qquad + x_6 \qquad &= 1800\\
x_1 - x_2 \qquad\qquad\qquad\qquad + x_7 &= 800\\
x_2 - x_3 \qquad\qquad\qquad\qquad &= 400\\
-x_3 + x_4 \qquad\qquad\qquad &= 1000\\
-x_4 + x_5 \qquad + x_7 &= 600\\
x_5 + x_6 \qquad &= 2200
\end{aligned}$$

Using the Gauss–Jordan Elimination Method to solve the system we obtain

$$\left[\begin{array}{ccccccc|c}
1 & 0 & 0 & 0 & 0 & 1 & 0 & 1800\\
1 & -1 & 0 & 0 & 0 & 0 & 1 & 800\\
0 & 1 & -1 & 0 & 0 & 0 & 0 & 400\\
0 & 0 & -1 & 1 & 0 & 0 & 0 & 1000\\
0 & 0 & 0 & -1 & 1 & 0 & 1 & 600\\
0 & 0 & 0 & 0 & 1 & 1 & 0 & 2200
\end{array}\right]
\xrightarrow{-R_2+R_1}
\left[\begin{array}{ccccccc|c}
1 & 0 & 0 & 0 & 0 & 1 & 0 & 1800\\
0 & 1 & 0 & 0 & 0 & 1 & -1 & 1000\\
0 & 1 & -1 & 0 & 0 & 0 & 0 & 400\\
0 & 0 & -1 & 1 & 0 & 0 & 0 & 1000\\
0 & 0 & 0 & -1 & 1 & 0 & 1 & 600\\
0 & 0 & 0 & 0 & 1 & 1 & 0 & 2200
\end{array}\right]$$

$$\xrightarrow{-R_3+R_2}
\left[\begin{array}{ccccccc|c}
1 & 0 & 0 & 0 & 0 & 1 & 0 & 1800\\
0 & 1 & 0 & 0 & 0 & 1 & -1 & 1000\\
0 & 0 & 1 & 0 & 0 & 1 & -1 & 600\\
0 & 0 & -1 & 1 & 0 & 0 & 0 & 1000\\
0 & 0 & 0 & -1 & 1 & 0 & 1 & 600\\
0 & 0 & 0 & 0 & 1 & 1 & 0 & 2200
\end{array}\right]
\xrightarrow{R_4+R_3}
\left[\begin{array}{ccccccc|c}
1 & 0 & 0 & 0 & 0 & 1 & 0 & 1800\\
0 & 1 & 0 & 0 & 0 & 1 & -1 & 1000\\
0 & 0 & 1 & 0 & 0 & 1 & -1 & 600\\
0 & 0 & 0 & 1 & 0 & 1 & -1 & 1600\\
0 & 0 & 0 & -1 & 1 & 0 & 1 & 600\\
0 & 0 & 0 & 0 & 1 & 1 & 0 & 2200
\end{array}\right]$$

$$\xrightarrow{R_5+R_4}
\left[\begin{array}{ccccccc|c}
1 & 0 & 0 & 0 & 0 & 1 & 0 & 1800\\
0 & 1 & 0 & 0 & 0 & 1 & -1 & 1000\\
0 & 0 & 1 & 0 & 0 & 1 & -1 & 600\\
0 & 0 & 0 & 1 & 0 & 1 & -1 & 1600\\
0 & 0 & 0 & 0 & 1 & 1 & 0 & 2200\\
0 & 0 & 0 & 0 & 1 & 1 & 0 & 2200
\end{array}\right]
\xrightarrow{R_6-R_5}
\left[\begin{array}{ccccccc|c}
1 & 0 & 0 & 0 & 0 & 1 & 0 & 1800\\
0 & 1 & 0 & 0 & 0 & 1 & -1 & 1000\\
0 & 0 & 1 & 0 & 0 & 1 & -1 & 600\\
0 & 0 & 0 & 1 & 0 & 1 & -1 & 1600\\
0 & 0 & 0 & 0 & 1 & 1 & 0 & 2200\\
0 & 0 & 0 & 0 & 0 & 0 & 0 & 0
\end{array}\right]$$

The last augmented matrix is in row-reduced form and is equivalent to a system of five linear equations in the seven variables $x_1, x_2, \ldots, x_7$. Thus, we may express five of the variables in terms of the other two, say x_6 and x_7. Setting $x_6 = s$ and $x_7 = t$ where s and t are real numbers (parameters), we may write the infinitely many solutions to the system as the point

$$(1800 - s, 1000 - s + t, 600 - s + t, 1600 - s + t, 2200 - s, s, t)$$

For example, picking $s = 800$ and $t = 1000$ gives one flow pattern as

$$x_1 = 1000, \quad x_2 = 1200, \quad x_3 = 800, \quad x_4 = 1800,$$
$$x_5 = 1400, \quad x_6 = 800, \quad \text{and} \quad x_7 = 1000$$

Selecting $s = 1000$ and $t = 800$ gives another flow pattern as

$$x_1 = 800, \quad x_2 = 800, \quad x_3 = 400, \quad x_4 = 1400,$$
$$x_5 = 1200, \quad x_6 = 1000, \quad \text{and} \quad x_7 = 800$$

(**b**) In this case x_6 must not exceed 300. Again, using the results of part (**a**) we find upon setting $s = 300$ and $t = 700$ that one possible flow pattern is given by

$$x_1 = 1500, \quad x_2 = 1400, \quad x_3 = 1000, \quad x_4 = 2000,$$
$$x_5 = 1900, \quad x_6 = 300, \quad \text{and} \quad x_7 = 700$$

(Why can't t exceed 700?.) Selecting $s = 200$ and $t = 500$ we have another flow pattern given by

$$x_1 = 1600, \quad x_2 = 1300, \quad x_3 = 900, \quad x_4 = 1900,$$
$$x_5 = 2000, \quad x_6 = 200, \quad \text{and} \quad x_7 = 500$$

■

3.4 EXERCISES

In problems 1 and 2, fill in the missing entries by performing the indicated row operations to obtain the row-reduced matrices.

1.
$$\left[\begin{array}{rrr|r} 1 & 3 & 1 & 3 \\ 3 & 8 & 3 & 7 \\ 2 & -3 & 1 & -10 \end{array}\right] \xrightarrow[R_3-2R_1]{R_2-3R_1} \left[\begin{array}{rrr|r} 1 & 3 & 1 & 3 \\ \cdot & \cdot & \cdot & \cdot \\ \cdot & \cdot & \cdot & \cdot \end{array}\right] \xrightarrow{-R_2} \left[\begin{array}{rrr|r} 1 & 3 & 1 & 3 \\ \cdot & \cdot & \cdot & \cdot \\ 0 & -9 & -1 & -16 \end{array}\right]$$
$$\xrightarrow[R_3+9R_2]{R_1-3R_2} \left[\begin{array}{rrr|r} \cdot & \cdot & \cdot & \cdot \\ 0 & 1 & 0 & 2 \\ \cdot & \cdot & \cdot & \cdot \end{array}\right] \xrightarrow[-R_3]{R_1+R_3} \left[\begin{array}{rrr|r} 1 & 0 & 0 & -1 \\ 0 & 1 & 0 & 2 \\ 0 & 0 & 1 & -2 \end{array}\right]$$

2.
$$\left[\begin{array}{rrr|r} 0 & 1 & 3 & -4 \\ 1 & 2 & 1 & 7 \\ 1 & -2 & 0 & 1 \end{array}\right] \xrightarrow{R_1 \leftrightarrow R_2} \left[\begin{array}{rrr|r} \cdot & \cdot & \cdot & \cdot \\ \cdot & \cdot & \cdot & \cdot \\ 1 & -2 & 0 & 1 \end{array}\right] \xrightarrow{R_3-R_1} \left[\begin{array}{rrr|r} 1 & 2 & 1 & 7 \\ 0 & 1 & 3 & -4 \\ \cdot & \cdot & \cdot & \cdot \end{array}\right]$$
$$\xrightarrow[R_3+4R_2]{R_1+\frac{1}{2}R_3} \left[\begin{array}{rrr|r} \cdot & \cdot & \cdot & \cdot \\ 0 & 1 & 3 & -4 \\ \cdot & \cdot & \cdot & \cdot \end{array}\right] \xrightarrow{\frac{1}{11}R_3} \left[\begin{array}{rrr|r} 1 & 0 & 1/2 & 4 \\ 0 & 1 & 3 & -4 \\ \cdot & \cdot & \cdot & \cdot \end{array}\right] \xrightarrow[R_2-3R_3]{R_1-\frac{1}{2}R_3}$$
$$\left[\begin{array}{rrr|r} 1 & 0 & 0 & 5 \\ 0 & 1 & 0 & 2 \\ 0 & 0 & 1 & -2 \end{array}\right]$$

3. Write a system of linear equations associated with the augmented matrix of problem 1. Using the results of problem 1 determine the solution of the system.

4. Repeat problem 3 for the augmented matrix of problem 2.

In Problems 5 through 14 given that the augmented matrix in row-reduced form is equivalent to the augmented matrix of some system of linear equations (a) *determine whether the system has a solution, and* (b) *find the solution or solutions to the system if they exist.*

5. $\left[\begin{array}{ccc|c} 1 & 0 & 0 & 3 \\ 0 & 1 & 0 & -1 \\ 0 & 0 & 1 & 2 \end{array}\right]$

6. $\left[\begin{array}{ccc|c} 1 & 0 & 0 & 3 \\ 0 & 1 & 0 & 1 \\ 0 & 0 & 0 & 4 \end{array}\right]$

7. $\left[\begin{array}{ccc|c} 1 & 0 & 0 & 1 \\ 0 & 1 & 0 & 2 \\ 0 & 0 & 0 & 0 \end{array}\right]$

8. $\left[\begin{array}{ccc|c} 1 & 0 & 0 & 2 \\ 0 & 0 & 0 & 0 \\ 0 & 0 & 0 & 0 \end{array}\right]$

9. $\left[\begin{array}{cccc|c} 1 & 0 & 0 & 0 & 3 \\ 0 & 1 & 0 & 0 & -2 \\ 0 & 0 & 1 & 0 & 1 \\ 0 & 0 & 0 & 1 & 2 \end{array}\right]$

10. $\left[\begin{array}{cccc|c} 1 & 0 & 0 & 0 & 2 \\ 0 & 1 & 0 & 0 & 1 \\ 0 & 0 & 1 & 0 & 3 \\ 0 & 0 & 0 & 0 & -5 \end{array}\right]$

11. $\left[\begin{array}{cccc|c} 1 & 0 & 0 & 0 & 2 \\ 0 & 1 & 0 & 0 & -1 \\ 0 & 0 & 1 & 1 & 2 \\ 0 & 0 & 0 & 0 & 0 \end{array}\right]$

12. $\left[\begin{array}{cccc|c} 1 & 0 & 0 & 0 & 0 \\ 0 & 1 & 0 & 0 & 1 \\ 0 & 0 & 0 & 0 & 0 \\ 0 & 0 & 0 & 0 & 0 \end{array}\right]$

13. $\left[\begin{array}{cccc|c} 1 & 0 & 0 & 0 & 2 \\ 0 & 0 & 0 & 0 & 0 \\ 0 & 0 & 0 & 0 & 0 \\ 0 & 0 & 0 & 0 & 0 \end{array}\right]$

14. $\left[\begin{array}{cccc|c} 1 & 0 & 0 & 0 & 0 \\ 0 & 1 & 0 & 0 & 0 \\ 0 & 0 & 1 & 0 & 0 \\ 0 & 0 & 0 & 1 & 0 \end{array}\right]$

In problems 15 through 31 solve the system of linear equations using the Gauss–Jordan Elimination Method.

15. $\begin{aligned} x - 2y &= 8 \\ 3x + 4y &= 6 \end{aligned}$

16. $\begin{aligned} 3x + y &= 1 \\ -7x - 2y &= -1 \end{aligned}$

17. $\begin{aligned} x + y + z &= 0 \\ 2x - y + z &= 1 \\ x + y - 2z &= 2 \end{aligned}$

18. $\begin{aligned} 2x + y - 2z &= 4 \\ x + 3y - z &= -3 \\ 3x + 4y - z &= 7 \end{aligned}$

19. $\begin{aligned} 2x_1 + 2x_2 + x_3 &= 9 \\ x_1 \qquad + x_3 &= 4 \\ 4x_2 - 3x_3 &= 17 \end{aligned}$

20. $\begin{aligned} x + 2y + z &= -2 \\ -2x - 3y - z &= 1 \\ 2x + 4y + 2z &= -4 \end{aligned}$

21. $\begin{aligned} 2x + 3y - 2z &= 10 \\ 3x - 2y + 2z &= 0 \\ 4x - y + 3z &= -1 \end{aligned}$

22. $\begin{aligned} 2x_1 - x_2 + x_3 &= -4 \\ 3x_1 - (3/2)x_2 + (3/2)x_3 &= -6 \\ -6x_1 + 3x_2 - 3x_3 &= 12 \end{aligned}$

23. $\begin{aligned} x + y - 2z &= -3 \\ 2x - y + 3z &= 7 \\ x - 2y + 5z &= 0 \end{aligned}$

24. $\begin{aligned} 3x - 2y - z &= 2 \\ x + 3y + 2z &= 1 \\ 5x - 2y - 3z &= -2 \end{aligned}$

25.
$$\begin{aligned} x_1-2x_2+x_3&=-3\\ 2x_1+x_2-2x_3&=2\\ x_1+3x_2-3x_3&=5 \end{aligned}$$

26.
$$\begin{aligned} 2x+3y-z&=4\\ -x+4y-3z&=3\\ 13x-8y+9z&=2 \end{aligned}$$

27.
$$\begin{aligned} 2x_1-x_2+3x_3-2x_4&=-2\\ x_1-2x_2+x_3-3x_4&=2\\ x_1-5x_2+2x_3+3x_4&=-6\\ -3x_1+3x_2-4x_3-4x_4&=9 \end{aligned}$$

28.
$$\begin{aligned} 2x_1+3x_2+2x_3+x_4&=-1\\ x_1-x_2+x_3-2x_4&=-8\\ 5x_1+6x_2-2x_3+2x_4&=11\\ x_1+3x_2+8x_3+x_4&=-14 \end{aligned}$$

29.
$$\begin{aligned} x_1+x_2-x_3-x_4&=-1\\ x_1-x_2+x_3+4x_4&=-6\\ 3x_1+x_2-x_3+2x_4&=-4\\ 5x_1+x_2-3x_3+x_4&=-9 \end{aligned}$$

30.
$$\begin{aligned} 2x_1+x_2+3x_3-x_4&=9\\ -x_1-2x_2\qquad-3x_4&=-1\\ x_1\qquad-3x_3+x_4&=10\\ x_1-x_2-x_3-x_4&=8 \end{aligned}$$

31.
$$\begin{aligned} x_1-2x_2-2x_3+x_4&=1\\ 2x_1-x_2+2x_3+3x_4&=-2\\ -x_1-5x_2+7x_3-2x_4&=3\\ 3x_1-4x_2+3x_3+4x_4&=-4 \end{aligned}$$

32. Cantwell Associates, a real-estate developer, is planning a new apartment complex consisting of 1-bedroom units and 2- and 3-bedroom townhouses. A total of 192 units are planned and the number of family units (2- and 3-bedroom units) will be equal to the number of 1–bedroom units. If the number of 1-bedroom units to be built is three times the number of 3-bedroom units to be built, find the number of each type unit that will be in the complex.

33. The annual return in interest from Mr. Carrington's three investments amounted to \$21,600. The annual yield from his investment in a savings account, in mutual funds, and in money market certificates was 6%, 8%, and 12%, respectively. If the amount of his investment in money market certificates was twice the amount of his investment in the savings account, and the interest earned from his investment in money market certificates was equal to the dividends he received from his investment in mutual funds, find the amount of money that he placed in each type of investment.

34. The management of a private investment club has a fund of \$200,000 earmarked for investment in stocks and bonds. For the purpose of arriving at an overall acceptable risk in the investment, the stocks of the company in which the club may invest have been classified into three categories—high risk, medium risk, and low risk. It is estimated that the stocks of the high risk, medium risk, and low risk categories will yield an investment return of 15%, 10%, and 6%, respectively. The amount invested in stocks of companies in the low risk category is to be twice as large as the sum of the investments in stocks of companies in the other two categories. If the investment goal is to have an average return of 9% on the total investment, determine the amount the club should invest in the companies of each of the three categories.

35. The management of the Hartman Rent-A-Car Agency has allocated \$1 million for purchasing a new fleet of automobiles consisting of compact, intermediate, and full-sized automobiles. The price of a new compact car is \$8000, the price of a new intermediate car is \$12,000, and that of a full-sized car is \$16,000. Given the number of compact cars purchased is to be twice the number of intermediate-sized cars purchased and a total of 100 cars are to be purchased, find the number of each type of car that should be purchased. (Assume that the entire budget is utilized.)

36. A manufacturer of women's blouses makes three types of blouses—sleeveless, short-sleeve, and long-sleeve. The time required by each department of the manufacturing plant to produce a dozen blouses is shown in the table below.

	Sleeveless	Short-sleeve	Long-sleeve
Cutting dept.	9 min.	12 min.	15 min.
Sewing dept.	22 min.	24 min.	28 min.
Packaging dept.	6 min.	8 min.	8 min.

The cutting, sewing, and packaging departments have a maximum of 80, 160, and 48 hours, respectively, available per day. How many dozens of each type of blouse should be produced each day if the plant is operated at full capacity?

*****37.*** The following figure shows the flow of traffic near the Civic Center of a metropolitan area during the rush hours on a typical week day. Each of the roads can handle a maximum of 1000 cars per hour without causing congestion. The flow of traffic is controlled by traffic lights installed at each of the five intersections.

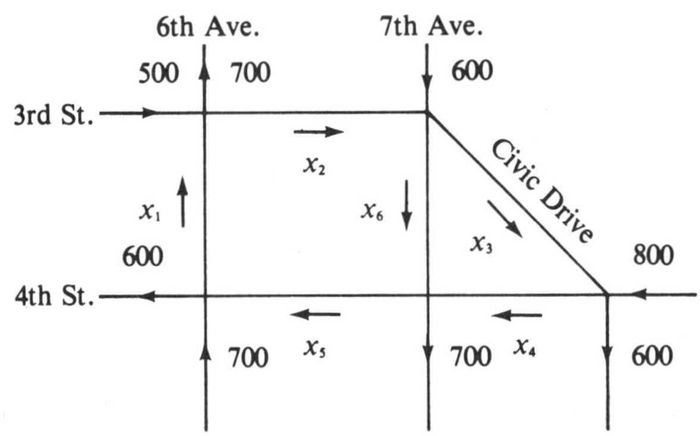

(***a***) Set up a system of linear equations describing the traffic flow.

(***b***) Solve this system of linear equations and suggest two possible traffic flow patterns that would ensure that there is no traffic congestion.

(***c***) Suppose that the road between 3rd and 4th Street along 7th Avenue is soon to be closed for road repairs, find one possible flow pattern that would result in a smooth flow of traffic.

***38.** The following figure shows the flow of traffic in a downtown area during the rush hours on a typical week day. Each of the avenues can handle up to 1500 vehicles per hour without causing congestion whereas the maximum capacity of each of the three roads is 1000 vehicles per hour. The flow of traffic is controlled by traffic lights installed at each of the six intersections.

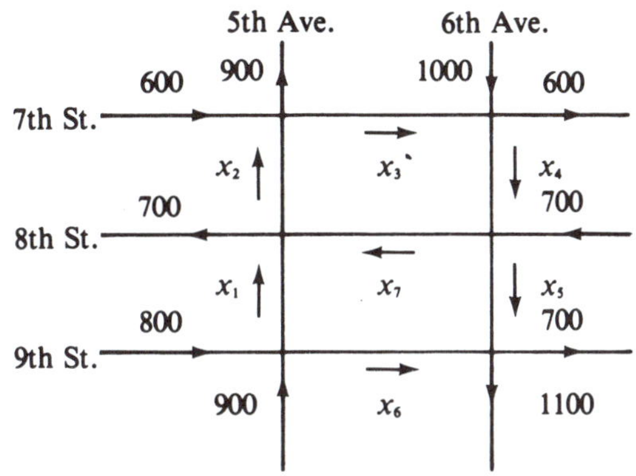

(*a*) Set up a system of linear equations describing the traffic flow.

(*b*) Solve this system of linear equations and suggest two possible traffic flow patterns that would ensure there is no traffic congestion.

(*c*) Suppose that the flow of traffic along 9th Street between 5th Avenue and 6th Avenue, x_6, is restricted due to sewer construction, what is the minimum permissible traffic flow along this road that will not result in traffic congestion?

3.5

Solving Systems of Linear Equations by Inverses

In this section, we shall discuss a procedure for finding the inverse of a matrix and show how the inverse may be used to help us solve a system of linear equations. The inverse of a matrix also plays a central role in the Leontief input–output model to be discussed in Section 3.6.

inverse of a matrix

A square matrix A of order n is said to possess an inverse if there exists a matrix A^{-1} (read "A, *inverse*") of order n with the property that $AA^{-1} = A^{-1}A = I$. Thus, the *inverse of a matrix* plays the same role under the multiplication of matrices that the inverse (reciprocal) of a nonzero real number plays under the multiplication of real numbers. (Compare the above with $aa^{-1} = a^{-1}a = 1$ where a is a nonzero real number). By way of example, the matrix

$$A = \begin{bmatrix} 1 & 2 \\ 3 & 4 \end{bmatrix}$$

has as its inverse

$$A^{-1}=\begin{bmatrix} -2 & 1 \\ 3/2 & -1/2 \end{bmatrix}$$

since

$$AA^{-1}=\begin{bmatrix} 1 & 2 \\ 3 & 4 \end{bmatrix}\begin{bmatrix} -2 & 1 \\ 3/2 & -1/2 \end{bmatrix}=\begin{bmatrix} 1 & 0 \\ 0 & 1 \end{bmatrix}=\begin{bmatrix} -2 & 1 \\ 3/2 & -1/2 \end{bmatrix}\begin{bmatrix} 1 & 2 \\ 3 & 4 \end{bmatrix}=A^{-1}A$$

singular matrix

Not every square matrix has an inverse. A matrix that does not possess an inverse is called *singular*. An example of a singular matrix is given by

$$B=\begin{bmatrix} 0 & 1 \\ 0 & 0 \end{bmatrix}$$

For suppose B has an inverse given by

$$B^{-1}=\begin{bmatrix} a & b \\ c & d \end{bmatrix}$$

where a, b, c, and d are some appropriate numbers. Then, by the very definition of an inverse, we must have $BB^{-1}=I$, that is,

$$\begin{bmatrix} 0 & 1 \\ 0 & 0 \end{bmatrix}\begin{bmatrix} a & b \\ c & d \end{bmatrix}=\begin{bmatrix} 1 & 0 \\ 0 & 1 \end{bmatrix}$$

or

$$\begin{bmatrix} c & d \\ 0 & 0 \end{bmatrix}=\begin{bmatrix} 1 & 0 \\ 0 & 1 \end{bmatrix}$$

which implies that $0=1$!

The methods of the last section can be used to find the inverse of a nonsingular matrix. In order to discover such an algorithm let us find the inverse of the matrix A given by

$$A=\begin{bmatrix} 1 & 2 \\ -1 & 3 \end{bmatrix}$$

Suppose A^{-1} exists and is given by

$$A^{-1}=\begin{bmatrix} a & b \\ c & d \end{bmatrix}$$

where a, b, c, and d are to be determined. By the definition of an inverse, we have $AA^{-1}=I$, or

$$\begin{bmatrix} 1 & 2 \\ -1 & 3 \end{bmatrix}\begin{bmatrix} a & b \\ c & d \end{bmatrix}=\begin{bmatrix} 1 & 0 \\ 0 & 1 \end{bmatrix}$$

which simplifies to

$$\begin{bmatrix} a+2c & b+2d \\ -a+3c & -b+3d \end{bmatrix} = \begin{bmatrix} 1 & 0 \\ 0 & 1 \end{bmatrix}$$

But this matrix equation is equivalent to the following two systems of linear equations:

$$\left.\begin{aligned} a+2c &= 1 \\ -a+3c &= 0 \end{aligned}\right\} \qquad \left.\begin{aligned} b+2d &= 0 \\ -b+3d &= 1 \end{aligned}\right\}$$

with augmented matrices given by

$$\left[\begin{array}{rr|r} 1 & 2 & 1 \\ -1 & 3 & 0 \end{array}\right] \quad \text{and} \quad \left[\begin{array}{rr|r} 1 & 2 & 0 \\ -1 & 3 & 1 \end{array}\right]$$

Note that the matrix of coefficients of the two systems are identical. This suggests that we solve the two systems of linear equations simultaneously by writing the following augmented matrix, which we obtain by joining the two columns of constants and the coefficient matrix.

$$\left[\begin{array}{rr|rr} 1 & 2 & 1 & 0 \\ -1 & 3 & 0 & 1 \end{array}\right]$$

Using the Gauss–Jordan Elimination Method, we obtain the following sequence of equivalent matrices:

$$\left[\begin{array}{rr|rr} 1 & 2 & 1 & 0 \\ -1 & 3 & 0 & 1 \end{array}\right] \xrightarrow{R_2+R_1} \left[\begin{array}{rr|rr} 1 & 2 & 1 & 0 \\ 0 & 5 & 1 & 1 \end{array}\right] \xrightarrow{\frac{1}{5}R_2} \left[\begin{array}{rr|rr} 1 & 2 & 1 & 0 \\ 0 & 1 & 1/5 & 1/5 \end{array}\right]$$

$$\xrightarrow{R_1-2R_2} \left[\begin{array}{rr|rr} 1 & 0 & 3/5 & -2/5 \\ 0 & 1 & 1/5 & 1/5 \end{array}\right]$$

Thus, $a=\frac{3}{5}$, $c=\frac{1}{5}$, $b=-\frac{2}{5}$, and $d=\frac{1}{5}$ giving

$$A^{-1} = \begin{bmatrix} 3/5 & -2/5 \\ 1/5 & 1/5 \end{bmatrix}$$

The following computations verify that A^{-1} is indeed the inverse of A.

$$\begin{bmatrix} 1 & 2 \\ -1 & 3 \end{bmatrix}\begin{bmatrix} 3/5 & -2/5 \\ 1/5 & 1/5 \end{bmatrix} = \begin{bmatrix} 1 & 0 \\ 0 & 1 \end{bmatrix} = \begin{bmatrix} 3/5 & -2/5 \\ 1/5 & 1/5 \end{bmatrix}\begin{bmatrix} 1 & 2 \\ -1 & 3 \end{bmatrix}$$

The preceding example reveals the general algorithm for computing the inverse of a square matrix of order n when it exists. Given the $n \times n$ matrix A, join the $n \times n$ unit matrix I to it to obtain the augmented matrix

(3.17) $$[A \mid I]$$

Use a sequence of row operations to reduce (3.17) to the form

(3.18) $$[I \mid B]$$

if possible. The inverse of A is then given by the matrix B, the square submatrix appearing on the right of the augmented matrix (3.18).

EXAMPLE 3.18 Find the inverse of the matrix

$$A = \begin{bmatrix} 2 & 1 & 1 \\ 3 & 2 & 1 \\ 2 & 1 & 2 \end{bmatrix}$$

SOLUTION We form the augmented matrix

$$\left[\begin{array}{ccc|ccc} 2 & 1 & 1 & 1 & 0 & 0 \\ 3 & 2 & 1 & 0 & 1 & 0 \\ 2 & 1 & 2 & 0 & 0 & 1 \end{array}\right]$$

and use the Gauss–Jordan Elimination Method to reduce it to the form (3.18) as follows:

$$\left[\begin{array}{ccc|ccc} 2 & 1 & 1 & 1 & 0 & 0 \\ 3 & 2 & 1 & 0 & 1 & 0 \\ 2 & 1 & 2 & 0 & 0 & 1 \end{array}\right] \xrightarrow{-R_1+R_2} \left[\begin{array}{ccc|ccc} 1 & 1 & 0 & -1 & 1 & 0 \\ 3 & 2 & 1 & 0 & 1 & 0 \\ 2 & 1 & 2 & 0 & 0 & 1 \end{array}\right] \xrightarrow[-R_3+2R_1]{-R_2+3R_1}$$

$$\left[\begin{array}{ccc|ccc} 1 & 1 & 0 & -1 & 1 & 0 \\ 0 & 1 & -1 & -3 & 2 & 0 \\ 0 & 1 & -2 & -2 & 2 & -1 \end{array}\right] \xrightarrow[-R_3+R_2]{R_1-R_2} \left[\begin{array}{ccc|ccc} 1 & 0 & 1 & 2 & -1 & 0 \\ 0 & 1 & -1 & -3 & 2 & 0 \\ 0 & 0 & 1 & -1 & 0 & 1 \end{array}\right]$$

$$\xrightarrow[R_2+R_3]{R_1-R_3} \left[\begin{array}{ccc|ccc} 1 & 0 & 0 & 3 & -1 & -1 \\ 0 & 1 & 0 & -4 & 2 & 1 \\ 0 & 0 & 1 & -1 & 0 & 1 \end{array}\right]$$

The inverse of A is the matrix

$$A^{-1} = \begin{bmatrix} 3 & -1 & -1 \\ -4 & 2 & 1 \\ -1 & 0 & 1 \end{bmatrix}$$

We leave it to the reader to verify the results. ■

The next example illustrates what happens to the reduction process when a matrix A does not possess an inverse.

EXAMPLE 3.19 Find the inverse of the matrix

$$A=\begin{bmatrix}1&2&3\\2&1&2\\3&3&5\end{bmatrix}$$

SOLUTION We form the augmented matrix

$$\left[\begin{array}{ccc|ccc}1&2&3&1&0&0\\2&1&2&0&1&0\\3&3&5&0&0&1\end{array}\right]$$

and use the Gauss–Jordan Elimination Method as follows:

$$\left[\begin{array}{ccc|ccc}1&2&3&1&0&0\\2&1&2&0&1&0\\3&3&5&0&0&1\end{array}\right]\xrightarrow[-R_3+3R_1]{-R_2+2R_1}\left[\begin{array}{ccc|ccc}1&2&3&1&0&0\\0&3&4&2&-1&0\\0&3&4&3&0&-1\end{array}\right]$$

$$\xrightarrow{R_3-R_2}\left[\begin{array}{ccc|ccc}1&2&3&1&0&0\\0&3&4&2&-1&0\\0&0&0&1&1&-1\end{array}\right]$$

Since all entries in the last row of the 3×3 submatrix comprising the left-hand side of the last augmented matrix obtained above are all equal to zero, the latter cannot be reduced to the form (3.18). Accordingly, we draw the conclusion that A is singular, and does not possess an inverse. ■

We now show how the inverse of a matrix may be used to solve certain systems of linear equations in which the number of equations comprising the system is equal to the number of variables. For simplicity, let us illustrate the process for a system of three linear equations in three variables.

(3.19)
$$\begin{aligned}a_{11}x_1+a_{12}x_2+a_{13}x_3&=c_1\\a_{21}x_1+a_{22}x_2+a_{23}x_3&=c_2\\a_{31}x_1+a_{32}x_2+a_{33}x_3&=c_3\end{aligned}$$

Let us write

$$A=\begin{bmatrix}a_{11}&a_{12}&a_{13}\\a_{21}&a_{22}&a_{23}\\a_{31}&a_{32}&a_{33}\end{bmatrix},\qquad X=\begin{bmatrix}x_1\\x_2\\x_3\end{bmatrix},\quad\text{and}\quad C=\begin{bmatrix}c_1\\c_2\\c_3\end{bmatrix}$$

Then the reader should verify that the system (3.19) of linear equations may be written in the form of the matrix equation

(3.20) $$AX = C$$

Now, if A is nonsingular then the method of this section may be used to compute A^{-1}. Next, multiplying both sides of (3.20) by A^{-1} (on the left), we obtain

$$A^{-1}AX = A^{-1}C \quad \text{or} \quad IX = A^{-1}C \quad \text{or} \quad X = A^{-1}C$$

the desired solution to the problem.

EXAMPLE 3.20 Solve the system of linear equations given by

$$\begin{aligned} 2x + y + z &= 1 \\ 3x + 2y + z &= 2 \\ 2x + y + 2z &= -1 \end{aligned}$$

SOLUTION We may write the given system of equations in the form

$$AX = C$$

where $A = \begin{bmatrix} 2 & 1 & 1 \\ 3 & 2 & 1 \\ 2 & 1 & 2 \end{bmatrix}$, $X = \begin{bmatrix} x \\ y \\ z \end{bmatrix}$, and $C = \begin{bmatrix} 1 \\ 2 \\ -1 \end{bmatrix}$

The matrix A is precisely that given in Example 3.18. Using the results obtained there, we have

$$X = A^{-1}C = \begin{bmatrix} 3 & -1 & -1 \\ -4 & 2 & 1 \\ -1 & 0 & 1 \end{bmatrix} \begin{bmatrix} 1 \\ 2 \\ -1 \end{bmatrix}$$

$$= \begin{bmatrix} 3 \cdot 1 + (-1) \cdot 2 + (-1) \cdot (-1) \\ (-4) \cdot 1 + 2 \cdot 2 + 1 \cdot (-1) \\ (-1) \cdot 1 + 0 \cdot 2 + 1 \cdot (-1) \end{bmatrix} = \begin{bmatrix} 2 \\ -1 \\ -2 \end{bmatrix}$$

or $x = 2$, $y = -1$, and $z = -2$. ■

3.5 EXERCISES

In problems 1 through 4 show that the given matrices are inverses of each other.

1. $\begin{bmatrix} 1 & -3 \\ 1 & -2 \end{bmatrix}$ and $\begin{bmatrix} -2 & 3 \\ -1 & 1 \end{bmatrix}$

2. $\begin{bmatrix} 4 & 5 \\ 2 & 3 \end{bmatrix}$ and $\begin{bmatrix} 3/2 & -5/2 \\ -1 & 2 \end{bmatrix}$

3. $\begin{bmatrix} 3 & 2 & 3 \\ 2 & 2 & 1 \\ 2 & 1 & 1 \end{bmatrix}$ and $\begin{bmatrix} -1/3 & -1/3 & 4/3 \\ 0 & 1 & -1 \\ 2/3 & -1/3 & -2/3 \end{bmatrix}$

4. $\begin{bmatrix} 2 & 4 & -2 \\ -4 & -6 & 1 \\ 3 & 5 & -1 \end{bmatrix}$ and $\begin{bmatrix} 1/2 & -3 & -4 \\ -1/2 & 2 & 3 \\ -1 & 1 & 2 \end{bmatrix}$

In problems 5 through 14 find the inverse (if it exists) of the given matrix. Verify your answer.

5. $\begin{bmatrix} 3 & 4 \\ -2 & 2 \end{bmatrix}$

6. $\begin{bmatrix} 4 & 2 \\ 6 & 3 \end{bmatrix}$

7. $\begin{bmatrix} 2 & -3 & -4 \\ 0 & 0 & -1 \\ 1 & -2 & 1 \end{bmatrix}$

8. $\begin{bmatrix} 1 & -1 & 3 \\ 2 & 1 & 2 \\ -2 & -2 & 1 \end{bmatrix}$

9. $\begin{bmatrix} 4 & 2 & 2 \\ -1 & -3 & 4 \\ 3 & -1 & 6 \end{bmatrix}$

10. $\begin{bmatrix} 1 & 2 & 0 \\ -3 & 4 & -2 \\ -5 & 0 & -2 \end{bmatrix}$

11. $\begin{bmatrix} 1 & 4 & -1 \\ 2 & 3 & -2 \\ -1 & 2 & 3 \end{bmatrix}$

12. $\begin{bmatrix} 3 & -2 & 7 \\ -2 & 1 & 4 \\ 6 & -5 & 8 \end{bmatrix}$

13. $\begin{bmatrix} 1 & 1 & -1 & 1 \\ 2 & 1 & 1 & 0 \\ 2 & 1 & 0 & 1 \\ 2 & -1 & -1 & 3 \end{bmatrix}$

14. $\begin{bmatrix} 1 & 1 & 2 & 3 \\ 2 & 3 & 0 & -1 \\ 0 & 2 & -1 & 1 \\ 1 & 2 & 1 & 1 \end{bmatrix}$

In problems 15 through 22 solve each of the given systems of equations by finding the inverse of the coefficient matrix.

15.
$$\begin{aligned} x+2y &= 14 \\ 2x-y &= 5 \end{aligned}$$

16.
$$\begin{aligned} 3a-2b &= -6 \\ 4a+3b &= 10 \end{aligned}$$

17.
$$\begin{aligned} x+2y+z &= 7 \\ x+y+z &= 4 \\ 3x+y+z &= 2 \end{aligned}$$

18.
$$\begin{aligned} x_1+x_2+x_3 &= 5 \\ x_1-x_2+x_3 &= -3 \\ x_1-2x_2-x_3 &= -1 \end{aligned}$$

19.
$$\begin{aligned} 3x+2y-z &= 2 \\ 2x-3y+z &= -2 \\ x-y-z &= 4 \end{aligned}$$

20.
$$\begin{aligned} 2x_1+x_2+x_3 &= 1 \\ x_1-3x_2+4x_3 &= 4 \\ -x_1+x_3 &= -3 \end{aligned}$$

21.
$$\begin{aligned} x_1+x_2+x_3+x_4 &= 1 \\ x_1-x_2-x_3+x_4 &= -1 \\ x_2+2x_3+2x_4 &= 4 \\ x_1+2x_2+x_3-2x_4 &= 0 \end{aligned}$$

22.
$$\begin{aligned} x_1+x_2+2x_3+x_4 &= 3 \\ 4x_1+5x_2+9x_3+x_4 &= 6 \\ 3x_1+4x_2+7x_3+x_4 &= 5 \\ 2x_1+3x_2+4x_3+2x_4 &= 7 \end{aligned}$$

23. Let

$$A = \begin{bmatrix} 2 & 3 \\ -4 & -5 \end{bmatrix}$$

(*a*) Find A^{-1}.

(*b*) Show that $(A^{-1})^{-1} = A$.

24. Let

$$A = \begin{bmatrix} 6 & -4 \\ -4 & 3 \end{bmatrix} \quad B = \begin{bmatrix} 3 & -5 \\ 4 & -7 \end{bmatrix}$$

(*a*) Find AB, A^{-1}, B^{-1}.

(*b*) Show that $(AB)^{-1} = B^{-1}A^{-1}$.

25. Let

$$A = \begin{bmatrix} 2 & -5 \\ 1 & -3 \end{bmatrix}, \quad B = \begin{bmatrix} 4 & 3 \\ 1 & 1 \end{bmatrix}, \quad C = \begin{bmatrix} 2 & 3 \\ -2 & 1 \end{bmatrix}$$

(*a*) Find ABC, A^{-1}, B^{-1}, C^{-1}.

(*b*) Show that $(ABC)^{-1} = C^{-1}B^{-1}A^{-1}$.

26. Let

$$A = \begin{bmatrix} a & b \\ c & d \end{bmatrix}$$

(*a*) Find A^{-1}.

(*b*) Find the necessary condition for A to be nonsingular.

(*c*) Verify that $AA^{-1} = A^{-1}A = I$.

3.6

Leontief Input-Output Model (Optional)

One of the many important applications of matrix theory to the field of economics is in the study of the relationship between industrial production and consumer demand. At the heart of this analysis is the Leontief input–output model pioneered by Wassily Leontief, who was awarded a Nobel Prize in Economics in 1973 for his contributions to the field.

In order to illustrate this concept, let us consider an over-simplified economy consisting of three sectors—agriculture (A), manufacturing (M), and service (S). In general, part of the output of one sector is absorbed by another sector through inter-industry purchases with the excess available to fulfill consumer demands. The relationship governing both intra-industrial and inter-industrial sales (and purchases) is conveniently represented by means of an *input–output matrix*:

input–output matrix

(3.21)

		Output A	Output M	Output S
Input	A	0.2	0.2	0.1
	M	0.2	0.4	0.1
	S	0.1	0.2	0.3

The first column (read from top to bottom) tells us that the production of 1 unit of agricultural products requires the consumption of 0.2 units of agricultural products, 0.2 units of manufactured goods, and 0.1 units of services. The second column tells us that the production of 1 unit of manufactured products requires the consumption of 0.2 units of agricultural products, 0.4 units of manufactured products, and 0.2 units of services. Finally, the third column tells us that the production of 1 unit of services requires the consumption of 0.1 units each of agricultural goods and manufactured products, and 0.3 units of services.

EXAMPLE 3.21 Refer to the input–output matrix (3.21).

(a) If the units are measured in millions of dollars, determine the amount of agricultural products consumed in the production of \$100 million worth of manufactured goods.

(b) Determine the dollar amount of manufactured products required to produce \$200 million worth of all goods and services in the economy.

SOLUTION **(a)** The production of 1 unit, that is, \$1 million worth of manufactured goods requires the consumption of 0.2 units of agricultural products. Thus, the amount of agricultural products consumed in the production of \$100 million worth of manufactured goods is given by (100)(0.2) or \$20 million.

(b) The amount of manufactured goods required to produce 1 unit of all goods and services in the economy is given by adding the numbers comprising the second row of the input–output matrix; that is, $0.2+0.4+0.1$ or 0.7 units. Therefore, the production of \$200 million worth of all goods and services in the economy requires 200(0.7) or \$140 million worth of manufactured products. ■

Next, suppose the total output of goods of the agriculture and manufacturing sectors and the total output from the service sector of the economy are given by x, y, and z units, respectively. What is the value of agricultural products consumed in the internal process of producing this total output of various goods and services?

To answer this question, we first note, by examining the input–output matrix, that 0.2 units of agricultural products are required to produce 1 unit of agricultural products, so that the amount of agricultural goods required to produce x units of agricultural products is given by $0.2x$ units. Next, again referring to the input–output matrix, we see that 0.2 units of agricultural products are required to produce 1 unit of manufactured products so that the requirement for producing y units of the latter is $0.2y$ units of agricultural products. Finally, we see that 0.1 units of agricultural goods are required to produce 1 unit of services so that the value of agricultural products required to produce z units of services is $0.1z$ units. Thus, the total amount of agricultural products required to produce the total output of goods and services in the economy is

$$0.2x + 0.2y + 0.1z$$

units. In a similar manner, we see that the total amount of manufactured products and the total value of services to produce the total output of goods and services in the economy are given by

$$0.2x + 0.4y + 0.1z$$

and

$$0.1x + 0.2y + 0.3z$$

respectively.

The above results could also be obtained using matrix multiplication. To see this, write the total output of goods and services x, y, and z as a 3×1 matrix

$$X = \begin{bmatrix} x \\ y \\ z \end{bmatrix}$$

The matrix X is called the *gross production matrix*. Then the product

$$AX = \begin{bmatrix} 0.2 & 0.2 & 0.1 \\ 0.2 & 0.4 & 0.1 \\ 0.1 & 0.2 & 0.3 \end{bmatrix} \begin{bmatrix} x \\ y \\ z \end{bmatrix} = \begin{bmatrix} 0.2x + 0.2y + 0.1z \\ 0.2x + 0.4y + 0.1z \\ 0.1x + 0.2y + 0.3z \end{bmatrix}$$

is a 3×1 matrix whose entries represent the respective values of the agricultural products, manufactured products, and services consumed in the internal process of production. The matrix AX is referred to as the *internal consumption matrix*.

Now, since X gives the total production of goods and services in the economy and AX, as we have just seen, gives the amount of products and services consumed in the production of these goods and services, the 3×1 matrix $X - AX$ gives the net output of goods and services that is exactly enough to satisfy consumer demands. Letting matrix D represent these consumer demands, we are led to the following matrix equation:

$$X - AX = D$$

or

$$(I - A)X = D \qquad (I \text{ is the } 3 \times 3 \text{ identity matrix.})$$

Then multiplying both sides of the last equation by $(I - A)^{-1}$ yields

(3.22) $$X = (I - A)^{-1}D$$

Equation (3.22) gives us a means of finding the amount of goods and services to be produced in order to satisfy a given level of consumer demand as illustrated by the following example.

EXAMPLE 3.22 For the three sector economy with input–output matrix given by (3.21), which is reproduced below

$$\begin{bmatrix} 0.2 & 0.2 & 0.1 \\ 0.2 & 0.4 & 0.1 \\ 0.1 & 0.2 & 0.3 \end{bmatrix} \qquad \text{(Each unit equals \$1 million.)}$$

(a) Find the gross output of goods and services needed in order to satisfy a consumer demand of \$100 million worth of agricultural products, \$80 million worth of manufactured products, and \$50 million worth of services.

(b) Find the value of the goods and services consumed in the internal process of production in order to meet this gross output.

SOLUTION **(a)** We are required to determine the gross production matrix

$$X = \begin{bmatrix} x \\ y \\ z \end{bmatrix}$$

where x, y, and z denote the value of the agricultural products, the manufactured products, and services. The matrix representing the consumer demand is given by

$$D = \begin{bmatrix} 100 \\ 80 \\ 50 \end{bmatrix}$$

Next, we compute

$$I - A = \begin{bmatrix} 1 & 0 & 0 \\ 0 & 1 & 0 \\ 0 & 0 & 1 \end{bmatrix} - \begin{bmatrix} 0.2 & 0.2 & 0.1 \\ 0.2 & 0.4 & 0.1 \\ 0.1 & 0.2 & 0.3 \end{bmatrix} = \begin{bmatrix} 0.8 & -0.2 & -0.1 \\ -0.2 & 0.6 & -0.1 \\ -0.1 & -0.2 & 0.7 \end{bmatrix}$$

Using the method of Section 3.5, we find (to two decimal places)

$$(I - A)^{-1} = \begin{bmatrix} 1.43 & 0.57 & 0.29 \\ 0.54 & 1.96 & 0.36 \\ 0.36 & 0.64 & 1.57 \end{bmatrix}$$

Finally, using Equation (3.22), we find

$$X = (I - A)^{-1}D = \begin{bmatrix} 1.43 & 0.57 & 0.29 \\ 0.54 & 1.96 & 0.36 \\ 0.36 & 0.64 & 1.57 \end{bmatrix} \begin{bmatrix} 100 \\ 80 \\ 50 \end{bmatrix} = \begin{bmatrix} 203.1 \\ 228.8 \\ 165.7 \end{bmatrix}$$

that is, to fulfill consumer demands \$203.1 million worth of agricultural products, \$228.8 million worth of manufactured products, and \$165.7 million worth of services should be produced.

(**b**) The amount of goods and services consumed in the internal process of production is given by AX, or equivalently by $X-D$. In this case, it is more convenient to use the latter, which gives the required result of

$$\begin{bmatrix} 203.1 \\ 228.8 \\ 165.7 \end{bmatrix} - \begin{bmatrix} 100 \\ 80 \\ 50 \end{bmatrix} = \begin{bmatrix} 103.1 \\ 148.8 \\ 115.7 \end{bmatrix}$$

or \$103.1 million worth of agricultural products, \$148.8 million worth of manufactured products, and \$115.7 million worth of services. ■

3.6 EXERCISES

1. A simple economy consists of three sectors—agriculture (A), manufacturing (M), and transportation (T). The input–output matrix for this economy is given by

$$\begin{array}{c} \\ A \\ M \\ T \end{array} \begin{array}{c} \begin{array}{ccc} A & M & T \end{array} \\ \begin{bmatrix} .4 & .1 & .1 \\ .1 & .4 & .3 \\ .2 & .2 & .2 \end{bmatrix} \end{array}$$

(*a*) If the units are measured in millions of dollars, determine the amount of agricultural products consumed in the production of \$100 million worth of manufactured goods.

(*b*) Determine the dollar amount of manufactured products required to produce \$200 million worth of all goods in the economy.

(*c*) Which sector consumes the greatest amount of agricultural products in the production of a unit of goods in that sector? the least?

2. The relationship governing the intra-industrial and inter-industrial sales and purchases of four basic industries—agriculture (A), manufacturing (M), transportation (T), and energy (E)—of a certain economy is given by the following input–output matrix:

$$\begin{array}{c} \\ A \\ M \\ T \\ E \end{array} \begin{array}{c} \begin{array}{cccc} A & M & T & E \end{array} \\ \begin{bmatrix} .3 & .2 & 0 & .1 \\ .2 & .3 & .2 & .1 \\ .2 & .2 & .1 & .3 \\ .1 & .2 & .3 & .2 \end{bmatrix} \end{array}$$

(*a*) How many units of energy are required to produce 1 unit of manufactured goods?

(*b*) How many units of energy are required to produce 3 units of all goods in the economy?

(*c*) Which sector of the economy is least dependent on the cost of energy?

(*d*) Which sector of the economy has the smallest intra-industry purchases (sales)?

3. Consider the economy of problem 1 consisting of three sectors—agriculture (A), manufacturing (M), and transportation (T) with input–output matrix given by

$$\begin{array}{c} \\ A \\ M \\ T \end{array} \begin{array}{c} \begin{array}{ccc} A & M & T \end{array} \\ \begin{bmatrix} .4 & .1 & .1 \\ .1 & .4 & .3 \\ .2 & .2 & .2 \end{bmatrix} \end{array}$$

(*a*) Find the gross output of goods needed in order to satisfy a consumer demand for \$200 million worth of agricultural products, \$100 million worth of manufactured products, and \$60 million worth of transportation.

(*b*) Find the value of goods and transportation consumed in the internal process of production in order to meet this gross output.

In problems 4 through 7, matrix A is an input–output matrix associated with an economy, and matrix D (units in millions of dollars) is a demand vector. In each problem find the final inputs of each industry so that the demands of both industry and the open sector are met.

4. $A = \begin{bmatrix} .4 & .2 \\ .3 & .5 \end{bmatrix}, \quad D = \begin{bmatrix} 12 \\ 24 \end{bmatrix}$

5. $A = \begin{bmatrix} .1 & .4 \\ .3 & .2 \end{bmatrix}, \quad D = \begin{bmatrix} 5 \\ 10 \end{bmatrix}$

6. $A = \begin{bmatrix} 1/5 & 2/5 & 1/5 \\ 1/2 & 0 & 1/2 \\ 0 & 1/5 & 0 \end{bmatrix}, \quad D = \begin{bmatrix} 10 \\ 5 \\ 15 \end{bmatrix}$

7. $A = \begin{bmatrix} .2 & .4 & .1 \\ .3 & .2 & .1 \\ .1 & .2 & .2 \end{bmatrix}, \quad D = \begin{bmatrix} 6 \\ 8 \\ 10 \end{bmatrix}$

3

Chapter Review

EXERCISES

In problems 1 through 4 perform each of the given operations, if possible.

1. $\begin{bmatrix} 1 & 2 \\ -1 & 3 \\ 2 & 1 \end{bmatrix} + \begin{bmatrix} 1 & 0 \\ 0 & 1 \\ 1 & 2 \end{bmatrix}$

2. $\begin{bmatrix} -1 & 2 \\ 3 & 4 \end{bmatrix} - \begin{bmatrix} 1 & 2 \\ 5 & -2 \end{bmatrix}$

3. $\begin{bmatrix} -3 & 2 & 1 \end{bmatrix} \begin{bmatrix} 2 & 1 \\ -1 & 0 \\ 2 & 1 \end{bmatrix}$

4. $\begin{bmatrix} 1 & 3 & 2 \\ -1 & 2 & 3 \end{bmatrix} \begin{bmatrix} 1 \\ 4 \\ 2 \end{bmatrix}$

In problems 5 through 12 compute each of the given expressions, if possible, given that

$$A=\begin{bmatrix}1 & 3 & 1\\ -2 & 1 & 3\\ 4 & 0 & 2\end{bmatrix}\qquad B=\begin{bmatrix}2 & 1 & 3\\ -2 & -1 & -1\\ 1 & 4 & 2\end{bmatrix}\qquad C=\begin{bmatrix}3 & -1 & 2\\ 1 & 6 & 4\\ 2 & 1 & 3\end{bmatrix}$$

5. $2A+3B$ ***6.*** $3A-2B$ ***7.*** $2(3A)$

8. $2(3A-4B)$ ***9.*** $A(B-C)$ ***10.*** $AB+AC$

11. $A(BC)$ ***12.*** $(1/2)(CA-CB)$

13. Mr. Spaulding bought 10,000 shares of stock X, 20,000 shares of stock Y, and 30,000 shares of stock Z at a unit price of \$20, \$30, and \$50 per share, respectively. Six months later, the closing price of stock X was \$22 per share, the closing price of stock Y was \$35 per share, and that of stock Z was \$51 per share. No other stock transactions were made by Mr. Spaulding during the period in question. Compare the value of Mr. Spaulding's stock holdings initially and six months later.

14. Mr. Newburg operates three self-service gasoline stations located in different parts of town. On a certain day, Station A sold 600 gallons of premium, 1000 gallons of regular, 800 gallons of super-unleaded, and 1400 gallons of regular-unleaded gasoline; Station B sold 700 gallons of premium, 800 gallons of regular, 600 gallons of super-unleaded, and 1200 gallons of regular-unleaded gasoline; Station C sold 1200 gallons of premium, 800 gallons of regular, 1000 gallons of super-unleaded, and 900 gallons of regular-unleaded gasoline. If the price of gasoline on the day in question was \$1.60 per gallon for premium, \$1.20 per gallon for regular, \$1.50 for super-unleaded, and \$1.30 per gallon for regular-unleaded gasoline, use matrix algebra to find the total revenue at each of the three stations.

In problems 15 through 20, solve the system of linear equations using the Gauss–Jordan Elimination Method.

15.
$$\begin{aligned}2x-3y&=5\\ 3x+4y&=-1\end{aligned}$$

16.
$$\begin{aligned}x-y+2z&=5\\ 3x+2y+z&=10\\ 2x-3y-2z&=-10\end{aligned}$$

17.
$$\begin{aligned}3x-2y+4z&=16\\ 2x+y-2z&=-1\\ x+4y-8z&=-18\end{aligned}$$

18.
$$\begin{aligned}3x-2y+4z&=11\\ 2x-4y+5z&=4\\ x+2y-z&=10\end{aligned}$$

19.
$$\begin{aligned}x-2y+3z+4w&=17\\ 2x+y-2z-3w&=-9\\ 3x-y+2z-4w&=0\\ 4x+2y-3z+w&=-2\end{aligned}$$

20.
$$\begin{aligned}3x-2y+z&=4\\ x+3y-4z&=-3\\ 2x-3y+5z&=7\\ x-8y+9z&=10\end{aligned}$$

In problems 21 through 23, find the inverse (if it exists) of the given matrix.

21. $A = \begin{bmatrix} 2 & 4 \\ 1 & 6 \end{bmatrix}$ **22.** $A = \begin{bmatrix} 1 & 2 & 4 \\ 3 & 1 & 2 \\ 1 & 0 & -6 \end{bmatrix}$ **23.** $A = \begin{bmatrix} 2 & 1 & -3 \\ 1 & 2 & -4 \\ 3 & 1 & -2 \end{bmatrix}$

In problems 24 through 26, write each system of linear equations in the form $AX = C$. *Find* A^{-1} *and use the result to solve the system.*

24. $\begin{aligned} x - 3y &= -1 \\ 2x + 4y &= 8 \end{aligned}$ **25.** $\begin{aligned} 2x - 3y + 4z &= 17 \\ x + 2y - 4z &= -7 \\ 3x - y + 2z &= 14 \end{aligned}$ **26.** $\begin{aligned} x - 2y + 4z &= 13 \\ 2x + 3y - 2z &= 0 \\ x + 4y - 6z &= -15 \end{aligned}$

27. Desmond Jewelry Inc., wishes to produce three types of pendants, type A, type B and type C. To manufacture a type A pendant requires 2 minutes on machines I and II and 3 minutes on machine III. A type B pendant requires 2 minutes on Machine I, 3 minutes on machine II and 4 minutes on machine III. A type C pendant requires 3 minutes on machine I, 4 minutes on machine II and 3 minutes on machine III. There are $3\frac{1}{2}$ hours available on machine I, $4\frac{1}{2}$ hours available on machine II and 5 hours available on machine III. How many of each type should the company make in order to utilize all the available time?

4

LINEAR PROGRAMMING

4.1

Systems of Linear Inequalities

A linear equation in one variable

$$ax + b = 0 \qquad (a \neq 0)$$

half-lines

has the solution $x = -b/a$, which may be represented as a point on the number line. This point divides the number line into two *half-lines* described by the inequalities

$$ax + b < 0$$

and

$$ax + b > 0$$

These half-lines and the point $x = -b/a$ are shown in Figure 4.1.

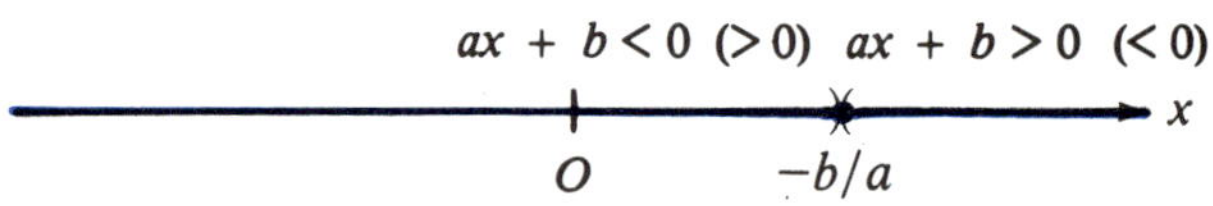

Figure 4.1

EXAMPLE 4.1 Find the graphical solution of the linear inequality $2x - 6 < 0$.

SOLUTION The solution to the given inequality may be found in a straightforward manner using the relevant properties of inequalities. But we prefer to obtain the solution using the following technique. We will find this technique useful when we consider the graphical solution of linear inequalities involving more than one variable.

1. Solve the equation obtained by replacing the given inequality with the corresponding equality. We obtain $2x-6=0$ or $x=3$. The point $x=3$ divides the line into two half-lines described by the linear inequalities $x<3$ and $x>3$. To determine which half-line provides us with the required solution proceed to step 2.

2. Pick a point (called a "test point") lying on one of the half-lines and substitute this value of x into the given inequality. If the inequality is satisfied, then the half-line containing the test point gives the desired solution. Otherwise, the solution is given by the other half-line. For the problem at hand, we find that by using $x=0$ as a test point, the inequality reduces to $2(0)-6<0$ or $-6<0$ which is true. Thus, the required solution is the half-line $x<3$ (Figure 4.2).

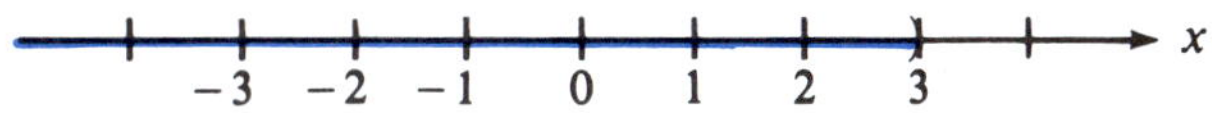

Figure 4.2

■

A linear equation in two variables x and y

$$ax+by+c=0 \qquad (a, b \text{ not both equal to zero})$$

half-planes

has a *solution set* that may be exhibited as points on a line in the plane. This line divides the plane into two *half-planes* described by the inequalities

$$ax+by+c<0$$

and

$$ax+by+c>0 \qquad \text{(Figure 4.3)}$$

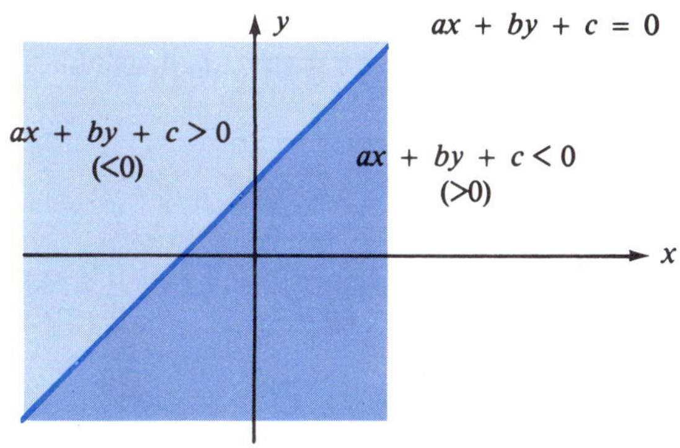

Figure 4.3

The technique used in the graphical solution of the linear inequality in Example 4.1 may also be used to find the graphical solution of linear inequalities in two variables as shown in the following example.

EXAMPLE 4.2 Determine the solution set for the inequality $2x+3y<6$.

SOLUTION Consider the equation $2x+3y=6$ obtained by replacing the inequality "<" with an equality. The graph of this linear equation is shown in Figure 4.4 as a dotted line. Picking the origin for our test point, we have, upon substituting $x=0$ and

$y = 0$ into the inequality, $2(0)+3(0)<6$ or $0<6$. Since the inequality is satisfied we conclude that the half-plane lying below the dotted line is the required solution set to our problem. Note that no point (x, y) on the line constitutes a solution to our problem.

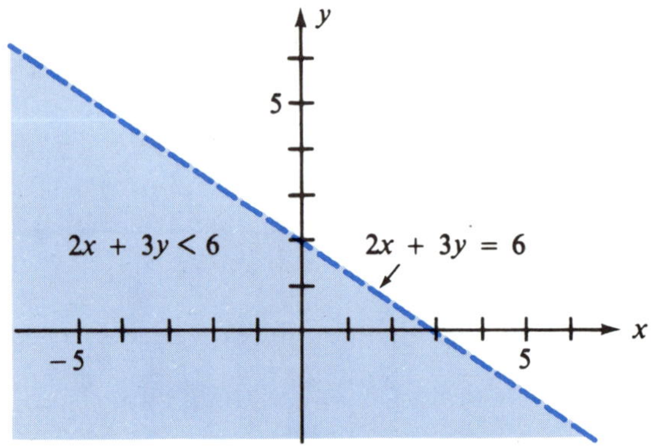

Figure 4.4

EXAMPLE 4.3 Determine the solution set for the inequality $2x+3y \geq 6$.

SOLUTION Replacing the inequality "≥" with an equality, we obtain the equation $2x+3y=6$ whose graph is the straight line shown in Figure 4.5. Instead of a dotted line as in Example 4.2, we use a solid line here to show that all points on the line are also solutions to the problem. Picking the origin as our test point we find $2(0)+3(0) \geq 6$ or $0 \geq 6$, which is impossible. So we conclude that the solution set comprises the half-plane not containing the origin, including in this case the line given by $2x+3y=6$. Compare with Example 4.2.

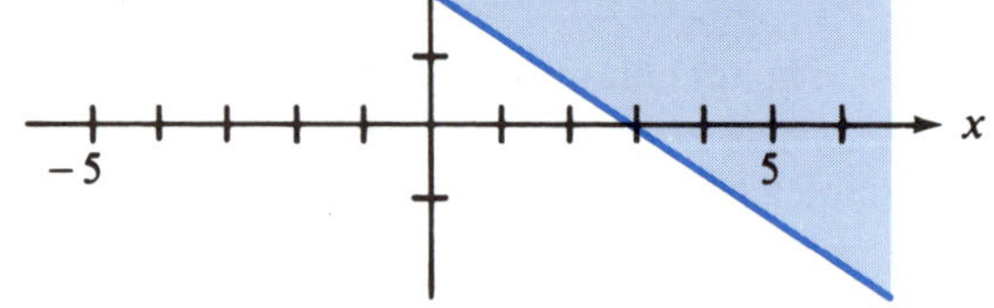

Figure 4.5

solution set of a system of linear inequalities

By the *solution set of a system of linear inequalities* in the two variables x and y, we mean the set of all points (x, y) satisfying each of the inequalities of the system. The graphical solution of such a system may be obtained by graphing the solution set for each inequality independently and then determining the region in common with each solution set.

EXAMPLE 4.4 Determine the solution set for the system

$$4x + 3y \geq 12$$
$$x - y \leq 0$$

SOLUTION Proceeding as in the previous examples, the reader should have no difficulty locating the half-planes determined by each of the linear inequalities comprising the system. These half-planes are shown in Figure 4.6. The intersection of the two half-planes is the shaded region shown. A point in this region is an element of the solution set for the given system. The point P, the intersection of the two straight lines determined by the equations

$$4x + 3y = 12$$
$$x - y = 0$$

is found by solving the equations simultaneously.

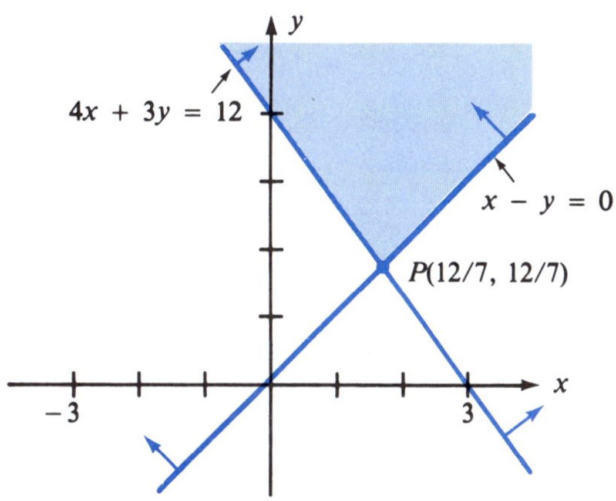

Figure 4.6

EXAMPLE 4.5 Sketch the solution set for the system

$$x \geq 0$$
$$y \geq 0$$
$$x + y - 6 \leq 0$$
$$2x + y - 8 \leq 0$$

SOLUTION The first inequality in the system defines the right half-plane—all points to the right of the y-axis plus all points lying on the y-axis itself. The second inequality in the system defines the upper half-plane including the x-axis. The half-planes defined by the third and fourth inequalities in the system are indicated by arrows in Figure 4.7. Thus the required region, the intersection of the four half-planes defined by the four inequalities comprising the given system of linear inequalities, is the shaded region shown in Figure 4.7. The point P is found by solving the equations $x+y-6=0$ and $2x+y-8=0$ simultaneously.

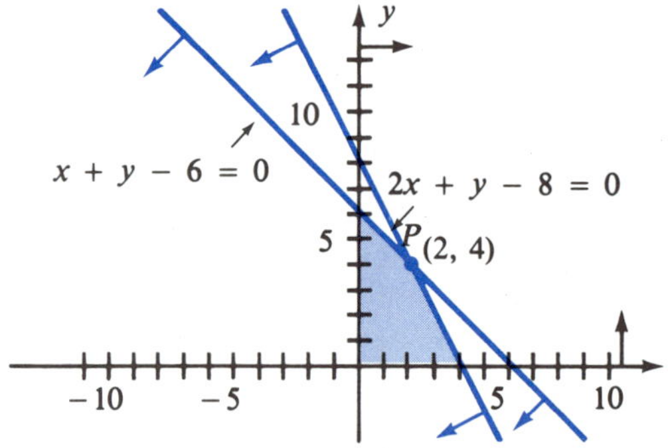

Figure 4.7

EXAMPLE 4.6 Determine the graphical solution set for the following system of linear inequalities:

$$2x+y\geq 50$$
$$x+2y\geq 40$$
$$x\geq 0$$
$$y\geq 0$$

SOLUTION The required solution set is the unbounded region shown in Figure 4.8.

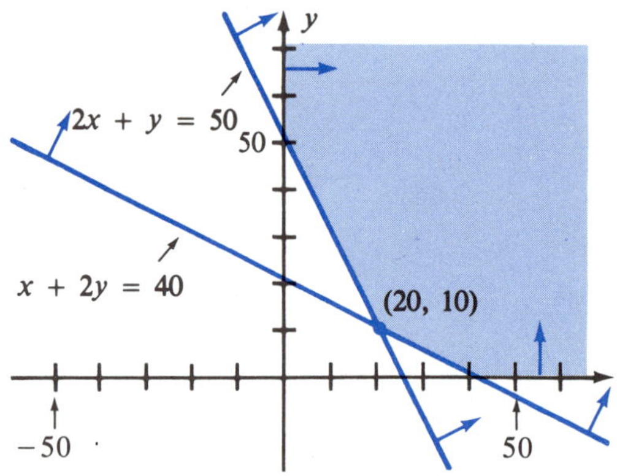

Figure 4.8

4.1 EXERCISES

In problems 1 through 8 find the graphical solution (in the plane) of each of the following inequalities:

1. $4x-8<0$ **2.** $3x+2>0$ **3.** $2x+6\geq x+2$

4. $3x+4\leq 4x-2$ **5.** $2x+y\leq 4$ **6.** $-3x+6y\geq 12$

7. $4x-3y\leq -24$ **8.** $5x-3y\geq 15$

In problems 9 through 25 determine graphically the solution set for each of the following systems of inequalities:

9. $2x+4y>16$, $-x+3y\geq 7$

10. $3x-2y>-13$, $-x+2y>5$

11. $x+2y\geq 3$, $2x+4y\leq -2$

12. $x+y\geq -2$, $3x-y\leq 6$

13. $x-y\leq 0$, $2x+3y\geq 10$

14. $x+y\leq 6$, $0\leq x\leq 3$, $y\geq 0$

15. $3x-6y\leq 12$, $-x+2y\leq 4$, $x\geq 0$, $y\geq 0$

16. $x+y\geq 20$, $x+2y\geq 40$, $x\geq 0$, $y\geq 0$

17. $4x-3y\leq 12$, $5x+2y\leq 10$, $x\geq 0$, $y\geq 0$

18. $3x-7y\geq -24$, $x+3y\geq 8$, $x\geq 0$, $y\geq 0$

19. $x+2y\geq 3$, $5x-4y\leq 16$, $0\leq y\leq 2$, $x\geq 0$

20. $3x+4y\geq 12$, $2x-y\geq -2$, $0\leq y\leq 3$, $x\geq 0$

21. $x+y\leq 4$, $2x+y\leq 6$, $2x-y\geq -1$, $x\geq 0$, $y\geq 0$

22. $6x+5y\geq 30$, $3x+y\leq 6$, $x+y\leq 4$, $x\geq 0$, $y\geq 0$

23. $6x+7y\leq 84$, $12x-11y\leq 18$, $6x-7y\leq 28$, $x\geq 0$, $y\geq 0$

24. $x-y\geq -6$, $x-2y\leq -2$, $x+2y\geq 6$, $x-2y\geq -14$, $x\geq 0$, $y\geq 0$

25. $x-3y\geq -18$, $3x-2y\geq 2$, $x-3y\leq -4$, $3x-2y\leq 16$, $x\geq 0$, $y\geq 0$

4.2 Linear Programming Problems

objective function

In many problems in business and economics we are concerned with optimizing (maximizing or minimizing) a function subject to a system of equalities or inequalities. The function to be optimized is called the *objective function.* (Examples of objective functions are profit functions and cost functions.) The system of equalities or inequalities to which the objective function is subjected reflects the constraints (for example, limitations on resources such as materials and labor) imposed on the solution(s) to the problem. Problems of this nature are called *mathematical programming problems*. In particular, problems where both the objective function and the constraints are expressed as linear equations or inequalities are called *linear programming problems*. As an example of a linear programming problem, let us consider the following simplified version of a production problem involving two variables.

linear programming problems

EXAMPLE 4.7 The Ace Novelty Company wishes to produce two types of souvenirs, type A and type B. It has been determined that each type A souvenir will result in a profit of \$1.00 and each type B souvenir will result in a profit of \$1.20. To manufacture a type A souvenir requires 2 minutes on machine I and 1 minute on machine II. A souvenir of type B requires 1 minute on machine I and 3 minutes on machine II. There are 3 hours available on machine I and 5 hours available on machine II for processing the order. How many of each type of souvenir should the company make in order to maximize profit?

SOLUTION As a first step towards the mathematical formulation of this problem, we tabulate the given information in Table 4.1.

	Type A	Type B	Time available
Machine I	2 min.	1 min.	180 min.
Machine II	1 min.	3 min.	300 min.
Profit per unit	\$1.00	\$1.20	

Table 4.1

Let x be the number of type A souvenirs and y be the number of type B souvenirs to be made. Then the total profit P, in dollars, is given by

$$P = x + 1.2y$$

which is the objective function to be maximized.

The total amount of time that machine I is utilized is given by $2x + y$ minutes and this must not exceed 180 minutes. Thus we have the inequality

$$2x + y \leq 180$$

Similarly, the total amount of time that machine II is used is $x + 3y$ minutes, which cannot exceed 300 minutes, so we are led to the inequality

$$x + 3y \leq 300$$

Finally, neither x nor y can be negative, so

$$x \geq 0$$
$$y \geq 0$$

To summarize, the problem at hand is one of maximizing the objective function

$$P = x + 1.2y$$

subject to the system of inequalities

$$\begin{aligned} 2x + y &\le 180 \\ x + 3y &\le 300 \\ x &\ge 0 \\ y &\ge 0 \end{aligned}$$

The solution to this problem will be completed in Example 4.10. ■

Following are a few more examples of linear programming problems.

EXAMPLE 4.8 A nutritionist advises that an individual who is suffering from an iron and vitamin B deficiency take at least 2400 mg of iron, 2100 mg of vitamin B-1 (Thiamine), and 1500 mg of vitamin B-2 (Riboflavin) over a period of time. Two vitamin pills are suitable, Brand A and Brand B. Each Brand A pill contains 40 mg of iron, 10 mg of vitamin B-1, 5 mg of vitamin B-2, and costs 6¢. Each Brand B pill contains 10 mg of iron, 15 mg each of vitamins B-1 and B-2, and costs 8¢ (see Table 4.2). What combination of pills should the individual purchase in order to meet the minimum iron and vitamin requirements at the lowest cost?

	Brand A	Brand B	Minimum requirement
Iron	40 mg	10 mg	2400 mg
Vitamin B-1	10 mg	15 mg	2100 mg
Vitamin B-2	5 mg	15 mg	1500 mg
Cost per pill	6¢	8¢	

Table 4.2

SOLUTION Let x be the number of Brand A pills and y be the number of Brand B pills to be purchased. The cost C, measured in cents, is given by

$$C = 6x + 8y$$

and is the objective function to be minimized.

The amount of iron contained in x Brand A pills and y Brand B pills is given by $40x + 10y$ mg and this must be greater than or equal to 2400 mg. This translates into the inequality

$$40x + 10y \ge 2400$$

Similar considerations involving the minimum requirements of vitamins B-1 and

B-2 lead to the inequalities

$$10x + 15y \geq 2100$$

and

$$5x + 15y \geq 1500$$

respectively. Thus, the problem here is to minimize the objective function

$$C = 6x + 8y$$

subject to the constraints

$$\begin{aligned} 40x + 10y &\geq 2400 \\ 10x + 15y &\geq 2100 \\ 5x + 15y &\geq 1500 \\ x \geq 0,\ y &\geq 0 \end{aligned}$$

The solution to this problem will be completed in Example 4.11. ■

EXAMPLE 4.9 The Acrosonic Company manufactures its Model F loudspeaker systems in two separate locations, plant I and plant II. The output at plant I is at most 400 per month while the output at plant II is at most 600 per month. These loudspeaker systems are shipped to three warehouses, which serve as distribution centers for the company. In order for the warehouses to meet their orders, the minimum monthly requirements of warehouses A, B, and C are 200, 300, and 400, respectively. Shipping costs from plant I to warehouses A, B, and C are \$20, \$8, and \$10 per loudspeaker system, respectively, while the shipping costs from plant II to each of these warehouses are \$12, \$22, and \$18, respectively. What should the shipping schedule be if the Acrosonic Company wishes to meet the requirements of the distribution centers and at the same time keep its shipping costs to a minimum?

SOLUTION The respective shipping costs per loudspeaker system in dollars may be tabulated as follows (see Table 4.3):

Table 4.3

	Warehouse		
Plant	A	B	C
I	20	8	10
II	12	22	18

Letting x_1 denote the number of loudspeaker systems shipped from plant I to warehouse A, x_2 the number shipped from plant I to warehouse B, and so on, leads to Table 4.4.

Table 4.4

Plant	Warehouse A	Warehouse B	Warehouse C	Max. Prod.
I	x_1	x_2	x_3	400
II	x_4	x_5	x_6	600
Min. Req.	200	300	400	

From Tables 4.3 and 4.4 we see that the cost of shipping x_1 loudspeaker systems from plant I to warehouse A is $\$20x_1$, the cost of shipping x_2 loudspeaker systems from plant I to warehouse B is $\$8x_2$, and so on. Thus the total monthly shipping cost incurred by the Acrosonic Company is given by

$$C = 20x_1 + 8x_2 + 10x_3 + 12x_4 + 22x_5 + 18x_6$$

Next, the production constraints on plants I and II lead to the inequalities

$$x_1 + x_2 + x_3 \leq 400$$

and

$$x_4 + x_5 + x_6 \leq 600$$

(see Table 4.4). Also, the minimum requirements of each of the three warehouses lead to the three inequalities

$$x_1 + x_4 \geq 200$$
$$x_2 + x_5 \geq 300$$

and

$$x_3 + x_6 \geq 400$$

Summarizing, we have the following linear programming problem: Minimize the objective (cost) function

$$C = 20x_1 + 8x_2 + 10x_3 + 12x_4 + 22x_5 + 18x_6$$

subject to the constraints

$$\begin{aligned} x_1 + x_2 + x_3 &\leq 400 \\ x_4 + x_5 + x_6 &\leq 600 \\ x_1 + x_4 &\geq 200 \\ x_2 + x_5 &\geq 300 \\ x_3 + x_6 &\geq 400 \end{aligned}$$

where $x_1 \geq 0, x_2 \geq 0, \ldots, x_6 \geq 0$

The solution to this problem will be completed in Example 4.19 of Section 4.5. ■

4.2 EXERCISES

Formulate, but do not solve, each of the following problems as a linear programming problem.

1. A company manufactures two products, A and B, on two machines I and II. It has been determined that the company will realize a profit of \$3 on each unit of product A and a profit of \$4 on each unit of product B. To manufacture a unit of product A requires 6 minutes on machine I and 5 minutes on machine II. To manufacture a unit of product B requires 9 minutes on machine I and 4 minutes on machine II. There are 5 hours of machine time available on machine I and 3 hours of machine time available on machine II in each work shift. How many units of each product should be produced in each shift to maximize the company's profit?

2. The Kane Manufacturing Company has a division that produces two models of hibachis, Model A and Model B. To produce each Model A hibachi requires 3 pounds of cast iron and 6 minutes of labor. To produce each Model B hibachi requires 4 pounds of cast iron and 3 minutes of labor. The profit for each Model A hibachi is \$2.00 while the profit for each Model B hibachi is \$1.50. If 1000 pounds of cast iron and 20 hours of labor are available for the production of hibachis in a day, how many of each model should the division produce in order to help maximize the company's profits?

3. Refer to problem 2. Because of a backlog of orders in Model A hibachis, the manager of the Kane Manufacturing Company has decided to produce at least 150 of these models a day. Operating under this additional constraint, how many of each model of the hibachis should the company produce to maximize profit?

4. The Madison Finance Company has a total of \$20 million earmarked for home owner and automobile loans. On the average, home owner loans will have a 10% rate of return on the loans given out while automobile loans will yield a 12% rate of return on the loans extended. Management has also stipulated that the total amount of home owner loans should be greater than or equal to four times the total amount of automobile loans. Determine the total amount of loans the company should extend to each of the two categories of customers in order to maximize its returns on the loans extended.

5. A nutritionist attached to the Medical Center has been asked to prepare a special diet for a certain group of patients. He has decided that the meals should contain a minimum of 400 mg of calcium, 10 mg of iron, and 40 mg of vitamin C. He has further decided that the meals are to be prepared from foods A and B. Each ounce of food A contains 30 mg of calcium, 1 mg of iron, 2 mg of vitamin C, and 2 mg of cholesterol; and each ounce of food B contains 25 mg of calcium, 0.5 mg of iron, 5 mg of vitamin C, and 5 mg of cholesterol. Find the number of ounces of each type of food to be used in a meal so that the cholesterol content is minimized and at the same time the minimum requirements in terms of calcium, iron, and vitamin C are met.

6. A farmer has 150 acres of land suitable for the cultivation of crop A and crop B. The cost of cultivating crop A is \$40 per acre while that of crop B is \$60. The farmer has a maximum of \$7400 available for land cultivation. Each acre of crop A requires 20 hours of labor and each acre of crop B requires 25 hours of labor. The farmer has a maximum of 3300 hours of labor available. If the farmer expects to make a profit of \$150 per acre on crop A and \$200 per acre on crop B, how many acres of each crop should he plant in order to maximize his profit?

7. A company manufactures products A, B, and C. Each product is processed in three departments—I, II, and III. The total available man-hours per week for departments I, II, and III are 900, 1080, and 840, respectively. The time requirements (in hours per unit) and profit per unit for each product are as follows:

	Product A	Product B	Product C
Dept. I	2	1	2
Dept. II	3	1	2
Dept. III	2	2	1
Profit	\$18	\$12	\$15

How many units of each product should the company produce in order to maximize its profit?

8. As part of a campaign to promote its Spring Annual Clearance Sale, the Excelsior Company decided to buy television advertising time on Station KAOS. Their television advertising budget was \$102,000. Morning time costs \$3000 per minute, afternoon time costs \$1000 per minute, and evening (prime) time costs \$12,000 per minute. Because of previous commitments, station KAOS could not offer the Excelsior Company more than 6 minutes of prime time and a total of 25 minutes of advertising time over the two weeks in which the commercials were to be run. The station estimated that the commercials run in the morning would be seen by 200,000 people, those run in the afternoon would be seen by 100,000 people, and those run in the evening would be seen by 600,000 people. How much morning, afternoon, and evening advertising time should the Excelsior Company buy to maximize exposure of its commercials?

9. The Custom Office Furniture Company is introducing a new line of executive desks made from a specially selected grade of walnut. Initially three models of different designs, models A, B, and C are to be marketed. Each Model A desk requires $1\frac{1}{4}$ hours for fabrication, 1 hour for assembly, and 1 hour for finishing; each Model B desk requires $1\frac{1}{2}$ hours for fabrication, 1 hour for assembly, and 1 hour for finishing; each Model C desk requires $1\frac{1}{2}$ hours, $\frac{3}{4}$ hour, and $\frac{1}{2}$ hour for fabrication, assembly, and finishing, respectively. The profit on each Model A desk is \$26, the profit on each Model B desk is \$28, and the profit on each Model C desk is \$24. The total time available in the fabrication department, the assembly department, and the finishing department in the first month of production is 310 hours, 205 hours, and 190 hours, respectively. To maximize the company's profit how many of each model of desk should be made in the month?

10. The Acrosonic Company of Example 4.9 also manufactures a Model G loudspeaker system in plant I and plant II. The output at plant I is at most 800 per month while the output at plant II is at most 600 per month. These loudspeaker systems are also shipped to the three warehouses, A, B, and C, whose minimum monthly requirements are 500, 400, and 400, respectively. Shipping costs from plant I to warehouse A, warehouse B, and warehouse C are \$16, \$20, and \$22 per loudspeaker system, respectively, while the shipping costs from plant II to each of these warehouses are \$18, \$16, and \$14, respectively. What shipping schedule will enable the Acrosonic Company to meet the requirements of the warehouses and at the same time keep its shipping costs to a minimum?

11. The Steinwelt Piano Company manufactures uprights and consoles in two plants, plant I and plant II. The output of plant I is at most 300 per month while the output of plant II is at most 250 per month. These pianos are shipped to three warehouses which serve as distribution centers for the company. In order to fulfill current and projected future orders, warehouse A requires a minimum of 200 pianos per month, warehouse B requires at least 150 pianos per month, and warehouse C requires at least 200 pianos per month. The shipping cost of each piano from plant I to warehouse A, warehouse B, and warehouse C is \$60, \$60, and \$80, respectively, while the shipping cost of each piano from plant II to warehouse A, warehouse B, and warehouse C is \$80, \$70, and \$50, respectively. What shipping schedule will enable the Steinwelt Piano Company to meet the requirements of the warehouses while keeping the shipping costs to a minimum?

12. The Boise Lumber Company has decided to enter the lucrative prefabricated housing business. Initially, it plans to offer three models of houses, a standard model, a deluxe model, and a luxury model. Each house is prefabricated and partially assembled in the factory and the final assembly is completed on site. Each standard model house requires \$6000 worth of building material, each deluxe model requires \$8000 worth of building material, and each luxury model requires \$10,000 worth of building material. The amount of labor required for prefabrication and partial assembly of each standard, deluxe, and luxury model house in the factory is estimated to be 240, 220, and 200 man-hours, respectively. The amount of labor required on the site for the erection and final assembly of each standard, deluxe, and luxury model house is estimated to be 180, 210, and 300 man-hours, respectively. The profit from the sale of each standard, deluxe, and luxury model house is expected to be \$3400, \$4000, and \$5000, respectively. For the first year's production, a sum of \$8,200,000 is budgeted for building material; the number of man-hours of labor available for work in the factory (for prefabrication and partial assembly) is not to exceed 218,000 hours; and the amount of labor for work on the site is to be less than or equal to 237,000 man-hours. Determine the number of each type of model house the Boise Lumber Company should produce (market research has confirmed that there should be no problems with sales) to maximize its profit from this new venture.

13. The Bayer Pharmaceutical Company manufactures three kinds of cold formulas, formula I, formula II, and formula III. It takes 2.5 hours to produce 1000 bottles of formula I, 3 hours to produce 1000 bottles of formula II, and 4 hours to produce 1000 bottles of formula III. The profits for each 1000 bottles of formula I, formula II, and formula III are \$180, \$200, and \$300, respectively. Suppose that for a certain production run, there are enough ingredients on hand to make at most 9000 bottles of formula I, 12,000 bottles of formula II, and 6000 bottles of formula III. Furthermore, suppose the time for the production run is limited to a maximum of 70 hours. Find the number of bottles of formula I, formula II, and formula III to be produced in this production run so that the profit is maximized.

4.3 Geometric Solution of Linear Programming Problems

Linear programming problems in two variables have relatively simple geometrical interpretations. For example, the system of linear constraints associated with a two-dimensional linear programming problem, unless it is inconsistent, defines a planar region whose boundary is composed of straight line segments and/or half lines. Such problems are therefore amenable to graphical analysis.

Consider the following two-dimensional linear programming problem: Maximize the objective function

(4.1)
$$P = 3x + 2y$$

subject to the constraints

(4.2)
$$\begin{aligned} 2x + 3y &\le 12 \\ 2x + y &\le 8 \\ x \ge 0,\ y &\ge 0 \end{aligned}$$

feasible solution and set

The system of linear inequalities (4.2) defines the planar region S shown in Figure 4.9. Each point in S is a candidate for the solution of the problem at hand and is referred to as a *feasible solution* and the set S itself is referred to as a *feasible set.* Our goal is to find from among all the points in the set S, the point(s) which optimizes (in this case, maximizes) the objective function P. Such a feasible solution is called an *optimal solution* and constitutes the solution to the linear programming problem under consideration.

optimal solution

As noted earlier, each point $P(x, y)$ in S is a candidate for the (optimal) solution to the problem at hand. For example, the point $(1, 3)$ is easily seen to lie in S and is therefore in the running. The value of the objective function P at the point $(1, 3)$ is given by $P = 3(1) + 2(3) = 9$. Now, if we could compute the value of P corresponding to each point in S, then the point(s) in S, which gave the largest

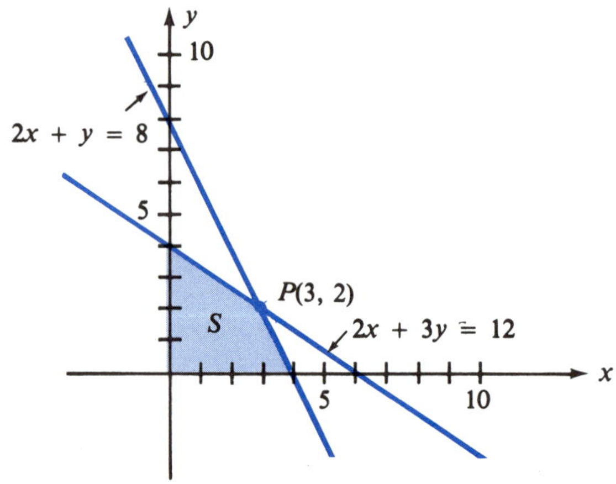

Figure 4.9

value to P, would constitute the solution set sought. Unfortunately, in most problems, the number of candidates is either too large or, as in this problem, the number is infinite. Thus this method is at best unwieldy and at worst impractical.

Let us turn the question around. Instead of asking for the value of the objective function P at a feasible point, let us assign a value to the objective function P and ask if there are feasible points that would correspond to the given value of P. To this end, suppose we assign a value of 6 to P. Then the objective function (4.1) becomes $3x+2y=6$, a linear equation in x and y, and is therefore representable as the graph of a straight line L_1 in the plane. In Figure 4.10 we have drawn the graph of this straight line superimposed on the feasible set S.

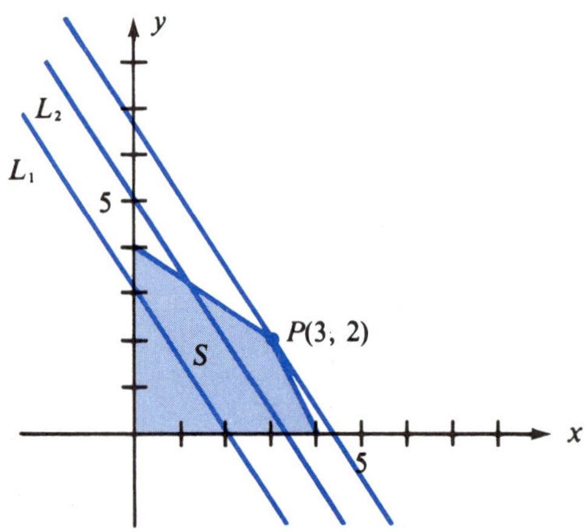

Figure 4.10

It is clear that each point on the straight line segment given by the intersection of the straight line L_1 and the feasible set S corresponds to the given value, 6, of P. Let us repeat the process, this time assigning a value of 10 to P. We obtain the equation $3x+2y=10$ and the line L_2 (see Figure 4.10), which suggests that there are feasible points that correspond to a larger value of P. Observe that the line L_2 is parallel to the line L_1, each with slope equal to $-3/2$ which is easily seen by casting the corresponding equations in the slope-intercept form.

In general, by assigning different values to the objective function, we obtain a family of parallel lines, each with slope equal to $-3/2$. Furthermore, a line corresponding to a larger value of P lies farther away from the origin than one with a smaller value of P. The implication is clear. To obtain the optimal solution(s) to the problem at hand, find the straight line, from this family of straight lines, that is farthest away from the origin and still intersects the feasible set S. The required line is the one that passes through the point $P(3, 2)$ (see Figure 4.10) and so the solution to the problem is given by $x=3$, $y=2$, resulting in a maximum value of $P=3(3)+2(2)=13$.

That the optimal solution to the above problem was found to occur at a vertex of the feasible set S is no accident. In fact, the result is a consequence of the following basic theorem on linear programming, which we state without proof.

THEOREM 4.1 If a unique (optimal) solution exists to a linear programming problem, then it must occur at a vertex or corner point of the feasible set S associated with the problem. Furthermore, if the objective function P is optimized at two adjacent vertices of S, then it is optimized at every point on the line segment joining these vertices, in which case, there are infinitely many solutions to the problem.

Theorem 4.1 tells us that our search for the solution(s) to a linear programming problem may be restricted to the examination of the set of vertices of the feasible set S associated with the problem. Since a feasible set S possesses finitely many vertices, the theorem suggests that the solution(s) to the linear programming problem may be found by inspecting the values of the objective function P at these vertices.

A simple procedure for solving a linear programming problem, based on Theorem 4.1, is:

1. Find all the corner points (vertices) of the feasible set S associated with the linear programming problem.

2. Evaluate the objective function P at each of the corner points of S.

3. Find the vertex that renders P a maximum (minimum). If there is only one such vertex then this vertex constitutes a unique solution to the problem. If P is maximized (minimized) at two adjacent corner points of S, there are infinitely many optimal solutions given by the points on the line segment determined by these two vertices.

EXAMPLE 4.10 We are now in a position to complete the solution to the production problem posed in Example 4.7 of the last section. Recall that the mathematical formulation led to the following linear programming problem.

Maximize

$$P = x + 1.2y$$

subject to the following constraints:

$$\begin{aligned} 2x + y &\leq 180 \\ x + 3y &\leq 300 \\ x &\geq 0 \\ y &\geq 0 \end{aligned}$$

SOLUTION The feasible set S for the problem is shown in Figure 4.11. The vertices of the feasible set are $A(0, 0)$, $B(90, 0)$, $C(48, 84)$, and $D(0, 100)$. The values of P at these vertices may be tabulated as follows:

Vertex	$P = x + 1.2y$
$A(0, 0)$	0
$B(90, 0)$	90
$C(48, 84)$	148.8
$D(0, 100)$	120

From the table one sees that the maximum of $P = x + 1.2y$ occurs at the vertex (48, 84) and has a value of 148.8. Recalling what the symbols x, y, and P represent, we conclude that the Ace Novelty Company would maximize its profit (a figure of \$148.80) by producing 48 type A souvenirs and 84 type B souvenirs.

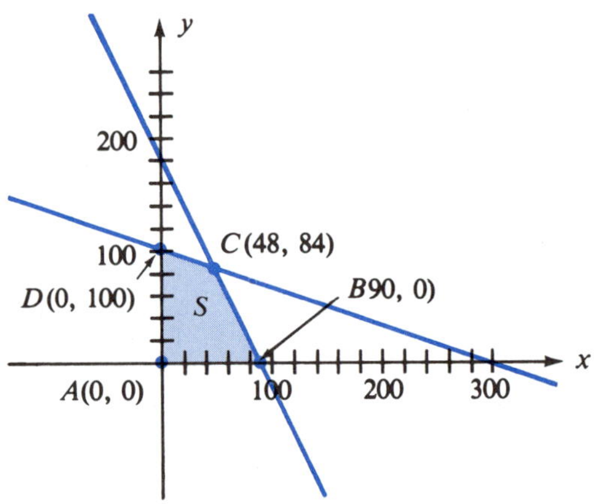

Figure 4.11

EXAMPLE 4.11 Complete the solution of the nutrition problem posed in Example 4.8.

SOLUTION Recall that the mathematical formulation of the problem led to the following linear programming problem in two variables:

Minimize the objective function

$$C = 6x + 8y$$

subject to the constraints

$$\begin{aligned} 40x + 10y &\geq 2400 \\ 10x + 15y &\geq 2100 \\ 5x + 15y &\geq 1500 \\ x \geq 0,\ y &\geq 0 \end{aligned}$$

The feasible set S defined by the system of constraints is shown in Figure 4.12. The vertices of the feasible set S are $A(0, 240)$, $B(30, 120)$, $C(120, 60)$, and $D(300, 0)$. The values of the objective function C at these vertices are given by the following table:

Vertex	$C = 6x + 8y$
$A(0, 240)$	1920
$B(30, 120)$	1140
$C(120, 60)$	1200
$D(300, 0)$	1800

From the table we see that the minimum for the objective function $C = 6x + 8y$ occurs at the vertex $B(30, 120)$ and has a value of 1140. Thus, the individual should purchase 30 Brand A pills and 120 Brand B pills at a (minimum) cost of \$11.40.

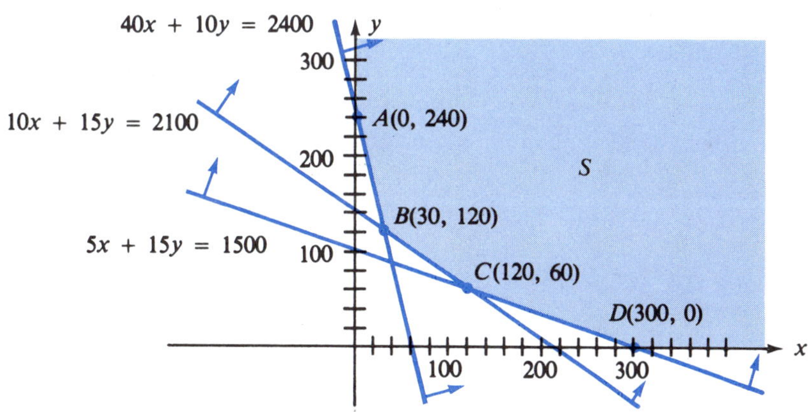

Figure 4.12

EXAMPLE 4.12 Find the maximum and minimum of $P = 2x + 3y$ subject to the following system of linear inequalities:

$$\begin{aligned} 2x+3y &\le 30 \\ y-x &\le 5 \\ x+y &\ge 5 \\ x &\le 10 \\ x &\ge 0 \\ y &\ge 0 \end{aligned}$$

SOLUTION The feasible set S is shown in Figure 4.13. The vertices of the feasible set S are $A(5, 0)$, $B(10, 0)$, $C(10, 10/3)$, $D(3, 8)$, and $E(0, 5)$. The values of the objective function P at these vertices are given by the following table.

Vertex	$P = 2x + 3y$
$A(5, 0)$	10
$B(10, 0)$	20
$C(10, 10/3)$	30
$D(3, 8)$	30
$E(0, 5)$	15

From the table we see that the maximum for the objective function $P = 2x + 3y$ occurs at the vertices $C(10, 10/3)$ and $D(3, 8)$. This tells us that every point on the line segment joining the points $C(10, 10/3)$ and $D(3, 8)$ maximizes P, giving it a value of 30 at each of these points. From the table it is also clear that P is minimized at the point (5, 0) where it attains a value of 10.

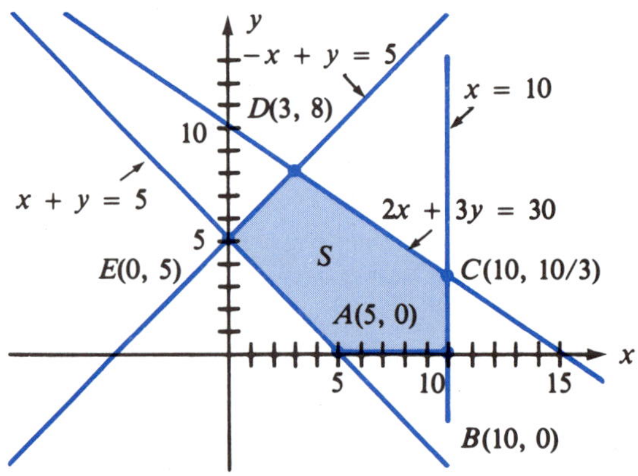

Figure 4.13

The Method of Corners is particularly effective in the solution of two-variable linear programming problems with a small number of constraints, as has been amply demonstrated in the preceding examples. Its effectiveness, however, decreases rapidly as the number of variables and/or constraints increases. For example, it may be shown that a linear programming problem in 3 variables and 5 constraints may have up to 56 feasible corner points. The determination of the feasible corner points calls for the solution of 56 3×3 systems of linear equations and then the verification, by the substitution of each of these solutions into the system of constraints, that it is in fact a feasible point. When the number of variables and constraints goes up to 5 and 10, respectively, (still a very small system from the standpoint of applications in economics) the number of vertices to be found and checked for feasible corner points increases dramatically to 3003 and each of these vertices is found by solving a 5×5 linear system! For this reason, the Method of Corners is seldom used in the solution of linear programming problems; its redeeming value lies in the fact that much insight is gained into the nature of the solutions of linear programming problems through its use in solving two-variable problems.

4.3 EXERCISES

In problems 1 through 15 solve each of the given linear programming problems by the Method of Corners.

1. Maximize $P=2x+3y$ subject to the constraints

$$\begin{aligned} x+y&\le 6\\ x&\le 3\\ x&\ge 0\\ y&\ge 0 \end{aligned}$$

2. Maximize $P=3x+4y$ subject to the constraints

$$\begin{aligned} x+3y&\le 15\\ 4x+\ \ y&\le 16\\ x&\ge 0\\ y&\ge 0 \end{aligned}$$

3. Minimize $C=2x+10y$ subject to the constraints

$$\begin{aligned} 5x+2y&\ge 40\\ x+2y&\ge 20\\ y&\ge 3\\ x&\ge 0 \end{aligned}$$

4. Minimize $C=2x+5y$ subject to the constraints

$$\begin{aligned} 4x+y&\ge 40\\ 2x+y&\ge 30\\ x+3y&\ge 30\\ x&\ge 0\\ y&\ge 0 \end{aligned}$$

5. Minimize $C = 6x + 3y$ subject to the constraints of problem 4.

6. Maximize $P = 2x + 5y$ subject to the constraints

$$\begin{aligned} 2x + y &\le 16 \\ 2x + 3y &\le 24 \\ y &\le 6 \\ x &\ge 0 \\ y &\ge 0 \end{aligned}$$

7. Minimize $C = 10x + 15y$ subject to the constraints

$$\begin{aligned} x + y &\le 10 \\ 3x + y &\ge 12 \\ -2x + 3y &\ge 3 \\ x &\ge 0 \\ y &\ge 0 \end{aligned}$$

8. Maximize $P = 2x + 5y$ subject to the constraints of problem 7.

9. Maximize $P = 3x + 4y$ subject to the constraints

$$\begin{aligned} x + 2y &\le 50 \\ 5x + 4y &\le 145 \\ 2x + y &\ge 25 \\ y &\ge 5 \\ x &\ge 0 \end{aligned}$$

10. Maximize $P = 4x + 3y$ subject to the constraints of problem 9.

11. Maximize $P = 2x + 3y$ subject to the constraints

$$\begin{aligned} x + y &\le 48 \\ x + 3y &\ge 60 \\ 9x + 5y &\le 320 \\ x &\ge 10 \\ y &\ge 0 \end{aligned}$$

12. Minimize $C = 5x + 3y$ subject to the constraints of problem 11.

13. Find the maximum and minimum of $P = 10x + 12y$ subject to the constraints

$$\begin{aligned} 5x + 2y &\ge 63 \\ x + y &\ge 18 \\ 3x + 2y &\le 51 \\ x &\ge 0 \\ y &\ge 0 \end{aligned}$$

14. Find the maximum and minimum of $P = 4x + 3y$ subject to the constraints

$$\begin{aligned} 3x + 5y &\geq 20 \\ 3x + y &\leq 16 \\ -2x + y &\leq 1 \\ x &\geq 0 \\ y &\geq 0 \end{aligned}$$

15. Find the maximum and minimum of $P = 2x + 4y$ subject to the constraints

$$\begin{aligned} x + y &\leq 20 \\ -x + y &\leq 10 \\ x &\leq 10 \\ x + y &\geq 5 \\ y &\geq 5 \\ x &\geq 0 \end{aligned}$$

16. Complete the solution to problem 1 in Exercise set 4.2.

17. Complete the solution to problem 2 in Exercise set 4.2.

18. Complete the solution to problem 3 in Exercise set 4.2.

19. Complete the solution to problem 4 in Exercise set 4.2.

20. Complete the solution to problem 5 in Exercise set 4.2.

21. Complete the solution to problem 6 in Exercise set 4.2.

22. Patricia has \$30,000 to invest in securities in the form of corporate stocks. She has narrowed her choices to two groups of stocks—growth stocks that she assumes will yield a 15% return (dividends and capital appreciation) on her investment within a year and speculative stocks that she assumes will yield a 25% return (mainly due to capital appreciation) on her investment within a year. Determine how much she should invest in each group of stocks in the hope of maximizing the return on her investments within a year if she has decided that her investment in growth stocks should be at least three times as much as her investment in speculative stocks.

23. A veterinarian has been asked to prepare a diet for a group of dogs to be used in a nutrition study at the School of Animal Science. It has been stipulated that each serving should be no larger than 8 ounces and must contain at least 29 units of nutrient I and 20 units of nutrient II. He has decided that the diet may be prepared from two brands of dog food—Brand A and Brand B. Each ounce of Brand A contains 3 units of nutrient I and 4 units of nutrient II. Each ounce of Brand B contains 5 units of nutrient I and 2 units of nutrient II. The cost of Brand A is 3¢ per ounce and that of Brand B is 4¢ per ounce. Determine the number of ounces of each brand of dog food that should be used to meet the given requirements at a minimum cost.

24. The Soundex Company produces two models of clock–radios. Model A requires 15 minutes of work on assembly line I and 10 minutes of work on assembly line II. Model B requires 10 minutes of work on assembly line I and 12 minutes of work on assembly line II. At most, 25 hours of assembly time on line I and 22 hours of assembly time on line II are available per day. It is anticipated that a profit of $12 on Model A and $10 on Model B will be realized by the company. How many of each model should be produced per day in order to maximize the company's profit?

25. The Trendex Corporation, a telephone survey company, has been hired to conduct a television viewing poll among urban and suburban families in the Los Angeles area. The client has stipulated that a maximum of 1500 families are to be interviewed, at least 500 urban families are to be interviewed and at least half of the families interviewed must be from the suburban area. For this service, Trendex will be paid $1500 plus $2.00 for each completed interview. From previous experience the Trendex Corporation has determined that they will incur an expense of $1.10 for each successful interview with an urban family and $1.25 for each successful interview with a suburban family. Find the number of urban and suburban families that the company should interview in order to maximize their profit.

4.4 The Simplex Method: Standard Problems and Maximization

As we mentioned towards the end of the last section, the Method of Corners is not suitable for solving linear programming problems when the number of variables and/or constraints is large. Its major shortcoming is that a knowledge of all the corner points of the feasible set S associated with the problem is required. What we need is a method of solution that is based on a judicious selection of the corner points of the feasible set S thereby reducing the number of points to be inspected. One such technique, called the *simplex method*, was developed in the late 1940s by George Dantzig and is based on the Gauss–Jordan Elimination Method. The simplex method is readily adaptable to the electronic computer, which makes it ideally suitable for solving linear programming problems involving large numbers of variables and constraints.

simplex method

Basically, the simplex method is an iterative procedure; that is, a procedure that is repeated over and over again. Beginning at some initial feasible solution (a corner point of the feasible set S, usually the origin) each iteration brings us to another corner point of S with an improved value for the objective function. The iteration is terminated when the optimal solution (if it exists) is reached.

standard linear programming problem

In this section, we shall describe the simplex method for solving a large class of problems that are referred to as *standard linear programming problems* (non-standard linear programming problems will be dealt with in the next section).

A standard linear programming problem is characterized by the following conditions:

1. The objective function is to be maximized.

2. All the variables involved in the problem are nonnegative.

3. Each linear constraint may be written so that the expression involving the variables is less than or equal to a nonnegative constant.

Example 4.7 is a standard linear programming problem. On the other hand, Example 4.8 is a nonstandard linear programming problem since conditions (1) and (3) are both violated.

Before stating a formal procedure for solving standard linear programming problems based on the simplex method, let us consider the following analysis of a two-variable problem. The ensuing discussions will clarify the general procedure. At the same time they will enhance our understanding of the simplex method by examining the motivation that led to the steps embodied in the procedure.

Consider the standard linear programming problem that we studied at the beginning of Section 4.3.

Maximize the objective function

(4.3) $$P = 3x + 2y$$

subject to the constraints

(4.4)
$$\begin{aligned} 2x + 3y &\le 12 \\ 2x + y &\le 8 \\ \text{where} \quad x \ge 0,\ y &\ge 0 \end{aligned}$$

The feasible set S associated with the above problem is reproduced in Figure 4.14 where we have labeled the four feasible corner points $A(0, 0)$, $B(4, 0)$, $C(3, 2)$, and $D(0, 4)$. Recall that the optimal solution to the problem occurs at the corner point $C(3, 2)$.

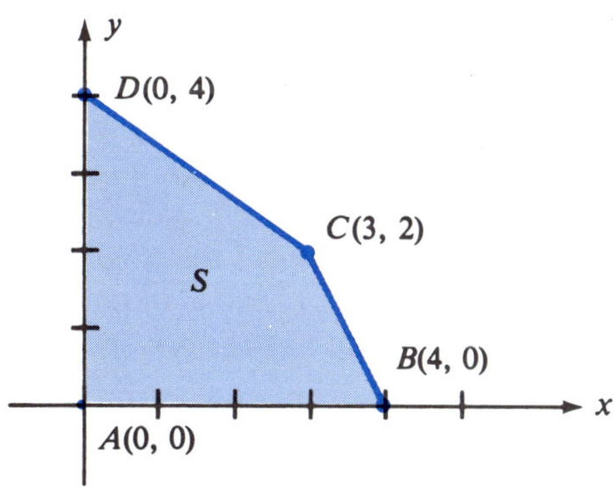

Figure 4.14

As a first step in the solution of the above problem, using the simplex method, we shall replace the system of inequality constraints (4.4) with a system of equality constraints. This may be accomplished through the use of nonnegative variables called *slack variables* whose nomenclature will soon become clear. By adding the slack variable u to the left-hand side of the first inequality in (4.4), $2x+3y \leq 12$, we obtain the equation $2x+3y+u=12$. Note that u takes up the slack between the left-hand side and the right-hand side of the inequality $2x+3y \leq 12$. Similarly, the inequality $2x+y \leq 8$ is converted into the equation $2x+y+v=8$ through the introduction of the slack variable v. The system of linear inequalities (4.4) may now be viewed as the system of linear equations

slack variable

$$\begin{aligned} 2x+3y+u &= 12 \\ 2x+y +v &= 8 \end{aligned}$$

where x, y, u, and v are all nonnegative. Finally, rewriting the objective function (4.3) in the form $-3x-2y+P=0$, where the coefficient of P is $+1$, we are led to the following system of linear equations:

$$\begin{aligned} 2x+3y+u &= 12 \\ 2x+y +v &= 8 \\ -3x-2y +P &= 0 \end{aligned} \tag{4.5}$$

Since the system (4.5) comprises three linear equations in the five variables x, y, u, v, and P, we may solve for three of the variables in terms of the other two. Thus, there are infinitely many solutions to the system (4.5) expressible in terms of two parameters. Our linear programming problem is now seen to be equivalent to the following: From among all the solutions of the system (4.5) for which x, y, u, and v are nonnegative (such solutions are called *feasible* solutions) determine the solution(s) which renders P a maximum.

The augmented matrix associated with system (4.5) is

$$\begin{array}{c} \begin{array}{ccccc} x & y & u & v & P \end{array} \\ \left[\begin{array}{ccccc|c} 2 & 3 & 1 & 0 & 0 & 12 \\ 2 & 1 & 0 & 1 & 0 & 8 \\ -3 & -2 & 0 & 0 & 1 & 0 \end{array}\right] \end{array} \tag{4.6}$$

Observe that each of the u-, v-, and P-columns of the augmented matrix (4.6) is in *unit form*; that is, one of the entries in the column is a 1 while the rest of the entries in the column are equal to zero. The variables associated with columns in unit form are called *basic variables*; all other variables are called *nonbasic variables*. Now, the configuration of the augmented matrix (4.6) suggests that we solve for the basic variables u, v, and P in terms of the nonbasic variables x and y obtaining

basic variable and nonbasic variable

$$\begin{aligned} u &= 12-2x-3y \\ v &= 8-2x-y \\ P &= \phantom{12-{}} 3x+2y \end{aligned} \tag{4.7}$$

Of the infinitely many feasible solutions obtainable by assigning arbitrary nonnegative values to the parameters x and y, a particular solution is obtained by letting $x=0$ and $y=0$. In fact, this solution is given by

$$x=0, \quad y=0, \quad u=12, \quad v=8, \quad \text{and} \quad P=0$$

basic solution

Such a solution, obtained by setting the nonbasic variables equal to zero, is called a *basic solution* of the system. This particular solution corresponds to the corner point $A(0, 0)$ of the feasible set associated with the linear programming problem (see Figure 4.14). Observe that $P=0$ at this point.

Now, if the value of P could not be increased we would have found the optimal solution to the problem at hand. To determine if the value of P could, in fact, be improved let us turn our attention to the objective function in (4.7). Since both the coefficients of x and y are positive, the value of P could be improved by increasing x and/or y; that is, by moving away from the origin. Note that we arrive at the same conclusion by observing that the last row of the augmented matrix (4.6) contains entries that are *negative*. (Compare the original objective function, $P=3x+2y$, with the rewritten objective function, $-3x-2y+P=0$.)

Continuing our quest for an optimal solution, our next task is to determine if it is more profitable to increase the value of x or that of y (increasing x and y simultaneously is more difficult). Since the coefficient of x is greater than that of y, a unit increase in the x-direction would result in a greater increase in the value of the objective function P than a unit increase in the y-direction. Thus, we should increase the value of x while holding y constant. How much can x be increased while holding $y=0$? From system (4.7) we see that, upon setting $y=0$,

(4.8)
$$\begin{aligned} u &= 12-2x \\ v &= 8-2x \end{aligned}$$

Since u must be nonnegative, the first equation of (4.8) implies that x cannot exceed $12/2$ or 6. The second equation of (4.8) and the nonnegativity of v implies that x cannot exceed $8/2$ or 4. Thus, we conclude that x can be increased by at most 4.

Now, if we set $y=0$ and $x=4$ in system (4.7) we obtain the solution

$$x=4, \quad y=0, \quad u=4, \quad v=0, \quad \text{and} \quad P=12$$

which is a basic solution to (4.5), this time with y and v as nonbasic variables (recall that the nonbasic variables are precisely the variables that are set equal to zero).

Let us see how this basic solution may be found by working with the augmented matrix of the system. Since x is to replace v as a basic variable, our aim is to find an augmented matrix that is equivalent to the matrix (4.6) and has a configuration in which the x-column is in the unit form

$$\begin{bmatrix} 0 \\ 1 \\ 0 \end{bmatrix}$$

replacing what is presently the form of the v-column in (4.6). This may be accomplished using elementary row operations as follows:

(4.9) $$\begin{array}{c} \begin{matrix} x & y & u & v & P & \end{matrix} \\ \left[\begin{array}{ccccc|c} 2 & 3 & 1 & 0 & 0 & 12 \\ \textcircled{2} & 1 & 0 & 1 & 0 & 8 \\ -3 & -2 & 0 & 0 & 1 & 0 \end{array}\right] \end{array} \xrightarrow{\frac{1}{2}R_2} \begin{array}{c} \begin{matrix} x & y & u & v & P & \end{matrix} \\ \left[\begin{array}{ccccc|c} 2 & 3 & 1 & 0 & 0 & 12 \\ \textcircled{1} & 1/2 & 0 & 1/2 & 0 & 4 \\ -3 & -2 & 0 & 0 & 1 & 0 \end{array}\right] \end{array}$$

(4.10) $$\xrightarrow[R_3+3R_2]{R_1-2R_2} \begin{array}{c} \begin{matrix} x & y & u & v & P & \end{matrix} \\ \left[\begin{array}{ccccc|c} 0 & 2 & 1 & -1 & 0 & 4 \\ 1 & 1/2 & 0 & 1/2 & 0 & 4 \\ 0 & -1/2 & 0 & 3/2 & 1 & 12 \end{array}\right] \end{array}$$

Using (4.10) we now easily solve for the basic variables x, u, and P in terms of the nonbasic variables y and v, obtaining

$$\begin{aligned} x &= 4-(1/2)y-(1/2)v \\ u &= 4- \quad 2y+ \quad v \\ P &= 12+(1/2)y-(3/2)v \end{aligned}$$

Setting the nonbasic variables y and v equal to zero gives

$$x=4, \quad y=0, \quad u=4, \quad v=0, \quad \text{and} \quad P=12$$

as before.

We have completed one iteration of the simplex procedure and our search has brought us from the feasible corner point $A(0, 0)$ where $P=0$ to the feasible corner point $B(4, 0)$ where P attained a value of 12, which is certainly an improvement!

Before proceeding further, let us introduce the following terminology. The encircled element 2 in the first augmented matrix of (4.9) which was to be converted into a 1, is called a *pivot element.* The column containing the pivot element is called the *pivot column.* The pivot column is associated with the nonbasic variable, which is to be converted to a basic variable. Note that *the last entry in the pivot column is the negative number with the largest absolute value in the last row*—precisely the criterion for choosing the direction of maximum increase in P.

pivot column

pivot row

The row containing the pivot element is called the *pivot row.* The pivot row can also be found by dividing each positive number in the pivot column into the corresponding number in the last column (the column of constants). *The pivot row is the one with the smallest ratio.* In the augmented matrix (4.9), the pivot row is the second row since the ratio 8/2 or 4 is less than the ratio 12/2 or 6. The reader should compare this with the earlier analysis pertaining to the determination of the largest permissible increase in the value of x.

Continuing with the solution to our problem we observe that the last row of the augmented matrix (4.10) contains a negative number, namely, $-1/2$. This indicates that P is not maximized at the feasible corner point $B(4, 0)$ and another iteration is required. Without once again going into a detailed analysis, we proceed immediately to the selection of a pivot element. In accordance with the above rules, we perform the necessary row operations, as follows:

$$\begin{array}{c} \\ \text{pivot row} \rightarrow \\ \\ \\ \end{array}\begin{array}{c} \begin{matrix} x & y & u & v & P & \end{matrix} \\ \left[\begin{array}{ccccc|c} 0 & \textcircled{2} & 1 & -1 & 0 & 4 \\ 1 & 1/2 & 0 & 1/2 & 0 & 4 \\ 0 & -1/2 & 0 & 3/2 & 1 & 12 \end{array}\right] \\ \uparrow \text{ pivot column (y)} \end{array} \quad \begin{array}{c} \text{ratio} \\ 4/2 = 2 \\ \frac{4}{1/2} = 8 \\ \\ \end{array}$$

$$\xrightarrow{\frac{1}{2}R_1} \begin{array}{c} \begin{matrix} x & y & u & v & P & \end{matrix} \\ \left[\begin{array}{ccccc|c} 0 & \textcircled{1} & 1/2 & -1/2 & 0 & 2 \\ 1 & 1/2 & 0 & 1/2 & 0 & 4 \\ 0 & -1/2 & 0 & 3/2 & 1 & 12 \end{array}\right] \end{array}$$

$$\xrightarrow[R_3 + \frac{1}{2}R_1]{R_2 - \frac{1}{2}R_1} \begin{array}{c} \begin{matrix} x & y & u & v & P & \end{matrix} \\ \left[\begin{array}{ccccc|c} 0 & 1 & 1/2 & -1/2 & 0 & 2 \\ 1 & 0 & -1/4 & 3/4 & 0 & 3 \\ 0 & 0 & 1/4 & 5/4 & 1 & 13 \end{array}\right] \end{array}$$

Interpreting the last augmented matrix in the usual fashion we find the basic solution $x = 3$, $y = 2$, and $P = 13$. This solution is optimal since there are no negative entries in the last row indicating that P cannot be increased further. The optimal solution is the feasible corner point $C(3, 2)$ which agrees with the solution to the problem obtained earlier in Section 4.3.

Having seen how the simplex method works, let us now consider an example that highlights the steps involved in the procedure.

EXAMPLE 4.13 Solve the linear programming problem posed in Example 4.7 by the simplex method.

SOLUTION The problem at hand is to maximize the objective (profit) function

$$P = x + 1.2y$$

or, equivalently,

$$P = x + \frac{6}{5}y$$

subject to the following constraints:

$$\begin{aligned} 2x + y &\leq 180 \\ x + 3y &\leq 300 \end{aligned} \qquad (4.11)$$

where $x \geq 0$ and $y \geq 0$.

This is a standard linear programming problem and may be solved by the simplex method as follows:

initial simplex tableau

Step 1 *Set up the initial simplex tableau.*

Since the system (4.11) comprises two linear inequalities we introduce two slack variables u and v to convert it to the system of linear equations

$$\begin{aligned} 2x + \;\; y + u \qquad &= 180 \\ x + 3y \qquad + v &= 300 \end{aligned}$$

Next, by rewriting the objective function in the form

$$-x - \frac{6}{5}y + P = 0$$

where the coefficient of P is $+1$ and placing it below the above system, we obtain the following system of linear equations:

$$\begin{aligned} 2x + \;\; y + u \qquad\qquad &= 180 \\ x + 3y \qquad + v \qquad &= 300 \\ -x - \frac{6}{5}y \qquad\qquad + P &= \;\;\;0 \end{aligned}$$

The initial simplex tableau is just the augmented matrix associated with the above system, that is

(4.12)

x	y	u	v	P	Constant
2	1	1	0	0	180
1	3	0	1	0	300
−1	−6/5	0	0	1	0

Step 2 *Determine if the optimal solution has been reached.*

Since there are negative entries in the last row of the initial simplex tableau, the initial solution is not optimal. We proceed to Step 3.

Step 3 *Perform the following iterations*:

First locate the pivot element:

(a) Since the entry $-6/5$ in the last row of the initial simplex tableau is the negative entry with the larger absolute value, the second column in the tableau is the pivot column.

(b) Divide each positive number of the pivot column into the corresponding entry in the column of constants and compare the ratios thus obtained. We see that the ratio 300/3 is less than the ratio 180/1 so the second row in the tableau is the pivot row.

(*c*) The entry 3 lying in the pivot column and the pivot row is the pivot element.

Next, we convert this pivot element into a 1 by multiplying all the entries in the pivot row by 1/3. Then, using elementary operations we complete the conversion of the pivot column into a unit column.

The details of the iteration are recorded as follows:

	x	y	u	v	P	Constant	ratio
	2	1	1	0	0	180	$180/1 = 180$
pivot row →	1	③	0	1	0	300	$300/3 = 100$
	−1	−6/5	0	0	1	0	
		↑ pivot column					

	x	y	u	v	P	Constant
$\xrightarrow{\frac{1}{3}R_2}$	2	1	1	0	0	180
	1/3	①	0	1/3	0	100
	−1	−6/5	0	0	1	0

(4.13)

	x	y	u	v	P	Constant
$\xrightarrow[R_3+\frac{6}{5}R_2]{R_1-R_2}$	5/3	0	1	−1/3	0	80
	1/3	1	0	1/3	0	100
	−3/5	0	0	2/5	1	120

This completes one iteration. The last row of the simplex tableau contains a negative number so that an optimal solution has not been reached. Therefore, we repeat the iterative step once again as follows:

	x	y	u	v	P	Constant	ratio
pivot row →	(5/3)	0	1	−1/3	0	80	$\frac{80}{5/3} = 48$
	1/3	1	0	1/3	0	100	$\frac{100}{1/3} = 300$
	−3/5	0	0	2/5	1	120	
	↑ pivot column						

	x	y	u	v	P	Constant
$\xrightarrow{\frac{5}{3}R_1}$	①	0	3/5	−1/5	0	48
	1/3	1	0	1/3	0	100
	−3/5	0	0	2/5	1	120

(4.14)

	x	y	u	v	P	Constant
$\xrightarrow[R_3+\frac{3}{5}R_1]{R_2-\frac{1}{3}R_1}$	1	0	3/5	−1/5	0	48
	0	1	−1/5	2/5	0	84
	0	0	9/25	7/25	1	$148\frac{4}{5}$

The last row of the simplex tableau (4.14) contains no negative numbers and we therefore conclude that the optimal solution has been reached.

Step 4 *Determine the optimal solution.*

Locate the basic variables in the final tableau (see Table 4.5). In this case, the basic variables (those heading unit columns) are x, y, and P. The value assigned to the basic variable x is the number 48, which is the entry lying in the column of constants and in the first row (the row which contains the 1).

Table 4.5

x	y	u	v	P	Constant
[1]	0	3/5	−1/5	0	48 ←
0	[1]	−1/5	2/5	0	84 ←
0	0	9/25	7/25	[1]	$148\frac{4}{5}$ ←

Similarly, we conclude that $y=84$ and $P=148.8$. Next, we note that the variables u and v are nonbasic and are accordingly assigned the values $u=0$ and $v=0$. These results agree with those obtained in the last section. ■

How do we interpret the role played by the variables u and v in this production problem? To answer this question, let us recall (see Example 4.10) that the first and second inequalities comprising the system (4.11) are statements pertaining to the time constraints on the use of machines I and II, respectively. Knowing this, it is easy to see that the slack variables u and v stand for the respective amount of machine-time not utilized in a given production run. For the problem at hand, both machines are used to their full capacity, as reflected by the values $u=0$ and $v=0$, in the production run that produces the maximum profit.

It is instructive for you to interpret each of the simplex tableaus (4.12) and (4.13). You should find that the (non-optimal) solutions obtained here correspond to the corner points $A(0, 0)$ and $D(0, 100)$ with the value of P given by 0 and 120, respectively (see Figure 4.11). Thus, beginning at the feasible solution (feasible corner point) $A(0, 0)$, one iteration of the simplex procedure had brought us to the next feasible corner point, $D(0, 100)$ with an improved value for P. The next iteration brought us to the optimal solution, which occurred at the corner point $C(48, 84)$ with $P = 148.8$.

Before looking at further examples, let us summarize the main steps of the Simplex Method used for solving standard problems.

Step 1 *Set up the initial simplex tableau.*

(*a*) Add a slack variable to the left-hand side of each of the linear inequalities comprising the system of constraints to convert the latter to a system of linear equations.

(*b*) Rewrite the objective function $P = c_1x_1 + c_2x_2 + \cdots + c_nx_n$ in the form $-c_1x_1 - c_2x_2 - \cdots - c_nx_n + P = 0$, where the coefficient of P is $+1$ and place it under the system of linear equations obtained in part (*a*).

(*c*) Write the augmented matrix associated with the system of linear equations obtained in part (*a*) with the necessary headings.

Step 2 *Determine if the optimal solution has been reached.*

(*a*) If all the entries in the last row of the simplex tableau are nonnegative, the optimal solution has been reached. Proceed to Step 4 and read off the solution(s) using the interpretation rules there.

(*b*) If there is at least one negative entry in the last row of the simplex tableau, the optimal solution (if any) has not been reached. Proceed to Step 3 and perform the indicated iteration.

Step 3 *Perform the following iteration*:

(*a*) Locate the column in the tableau having the negative entry in the last row with the largest absolute value. If there is more than one such column, choose any one of them. The column thus chosen is the pivot column.

(*b*) Divide each positive number of the pivot column into the corresponding entry in the column of constants. Locate the row with the smallest quotient. If there is a tie, choose any such row. This row is the pivot row. The entry in the pivot row and pivot column is the pivot element.

(*c*) Convert the pivot element into a 1, if necessary, by dividing all the elements in the pivot row by the pivot element. Using row operations, convert the pivot column into a unit column by adding suitable multiples of the pivot row to each of the other rows as required.

This completes one iteration. Proceed to Step 2.

Step 4 *Determine the optimal solution(s).*

(*a*) If a column is in unit form and no two columns are identical, then assign to the variable heading that column, the value given by the entry lying in the column of constants and in the row containing the 1. If a column is not in unit form, then the variable heading that column is assigned the value zero.

(*b*) If two or more unit columns are identical, more than one solution exists. A solution is obtained by assigning to any of the variables heading such a column the entry that lies in the column of constants and in the row containing the 1. All other variables heading identical columns are assigned the value zero. As usual, all other variables heading columns not in unit form are assigned the value zero.

Let us apply the above procedure to the solution of several linear programming problems in standard form.

EXAMPLE 4.14 Maximize the objective function

$$P = 2x + 2y + z$$

subject to the constraints

$$\begin{aligned} 2x + y + 2z &\le 14 \\ 2x + 4y + z &\le 26 \\ x + 2y + 3z &\le 28 \end{aligned}$$

where $x \ge 0$, $y \ge 0$, $z \ge 0$.

SOLUTION Introducing the slack variables u, v, and w, and rewriting the objective function in the standard form gives the following system of linear equations

$$\begin{aligned} 2x + y + 2z + u \qquad\qquad &= 14 \\ 2x + 4y + z \quad + v \qquad &= 26 \\ x + 2y + 3z \qquad + w \quad &= 28 \\ -2x - 2y - z \qquad\qquad + P &= 0 \end{aligned}$$

The initial simplex tableau is given by

x	y	z	u	v	w	P	Constant
2	1	2	1	0	0	0	14
2	4	1	0	1	0	0	26
1	2	3	0	0	1	0	28
−2	−2	−1	0	0	0	1	0

Since there is a tie for the negative entry with the largest absolute value in the last row, we may choose either the x- or the y-column as the pivot column. Choosing the former as the pivot column and proceeding with the first iteration we obtain the following sequence of tableaus:

	x	y	z	u	v	w	P	Constant	ratio
pivot row →	②	1	2	1	0	0	0	14	14/2 = 7
	2	4	1	0	1	0	0	26	26/2 = 13
	1	2	3	0	0	1	0	28	28/1 = 28
	−2	−2	−1	0	0	0	1	0	
	↑ pivot column								

	x	y	z	u	v	w	P	Constant
$\xrightarrow{\frac{1}{2}R_1}$	①	1/2	1	1/2	0	0	0	7
	2	4	1	0	1	0	0	26
	1	2	3	0	0	1	0	28
	−2	−2	−1	0	0	0	1	0

	x	y	z	u	v	w	P	Constant
R_2-2R_1 → R_3-R_1 R_4+2R_1	1	1/2	1	1/2	0	0	0	7
	0	3	−1	−1	1	0	0	12
	0	3/2	2	−1/2	0	1	0	21
	0	−1	1	1	0	0	1	14

Since there is a negative number in the last row of the simplex tableau we perform another iteration as follows:

	x	y	z	u	v	w	P	Constant	ratio
	1	1/2	1	1/2	0	0	0	7	$\frac{7}{1/2} = 14$
pivot row →	0	③	−1	−1	1	0	0	12	12/3 = 4
	0	3/2	2	−1/2	0	1	0	21	$\frac{21}{3/2} = 14$
	0	−1	1	1	0	0	1	14	
		↑ pivot column							

	x	y	z	u	v	w	P	Constant
	1	1/2	1	1/2	0	0	0	7
$\xrightarrow{\frac{1}{3}R_2}$	0	①	−1/3	−1/3	1/3	0	0	4
	0	3/2	2	−1/2	0	1	0	21
	0	−1	1	1	0	0	1	14

	x	y	z	u	v	w	P	Constant
	1	0	7/6	2/3	−1/6	0	0	5
$\xrightarrow[R_3-\frac{3}{2}R_2,\ R_4+R_2]{R_1-\frac{1}{2}R_2}$	0	1	−1/3	−1/3	1/3	0	0	4
	0	0	5/2	0	−1/2	1	0	15
	0	0	2/3	2/3	1/3	0	1	18

All the entries in the last row are nonnegative and we have reached the optimal solution. By the interpretation rule, the solution is given by $x=5$, $y=4$, $z=0$, $u=0$, $v=0$, $w=15$, and $P=18$. ■

EXAMPLE 4.15 Maximize the function

$$P = 2x + 2y - 4z$$

subject to the constraints

$$3x + 3y - 2z \leq 100$$
$$5x + 5y + 3z \leq 150$$

where $x \geq 0$, $y \geq 0$, and $z \geq 0$.

SOLUTION Introducing the slack variables u and v we obtain the following system of linear equations:

$$\begin{aligned} 3x + 3y - 2z + u \quad\quad &= 100 \\ 5x + 5y + 3z \quad + v \quad &= 150 \\ -2x - 2y + 4z \quad\quad + P &= 0 \end{aligned}$$

The initial simplex tableau and the tableaus resulting from the first iteration follow.

	x	y	z	u	v	P	Constant	ratio
	3	3	−2	1	0	0	100	$100/3 = 33\frac{1}{3}$
pivot row →	⑤	5	3	0	1	0	150	$150/5 = 30$
	−2	−2	4	0	0	1	0	
	↑ pivot column							

(We could, of course, have chosen the second column as the pivot column.)

$\xrightarrow{\frac{1}{5}R_2}$

x	y	z	u	v	P	Constant
3	3	−2	1	0	0	100
①	1	3/5	0	1/5	0	30
−2	−2	4	0	0	1	0

$\xrightarrow[R_3+2R_2]{R_1-3R_2}$

x	y	z	u	v	P	Constant
0	0	−19/5	1	−3/5	0	10
1	1	3/5	0	1/5	0	30
0	0	26/5	0	2/5	1	60

All entries in the last row are nonnegative and the tableau is final. By the interpretation rule (*Step 4b* in this instance) we conclude that

$$x = 30,\ y = 0,\ z = 0,\ u = 10,\ v = 0,\ P = 60$$

and

$$x = 0,\ y = 30,\ z = 0,\ u = 10,\ v = 0,\ P = 60$$

are optimal solutions. ■

EXAMPLE 4.16 The Ace Novelty Company has determined that the profits are \$6, \$5, and \$4 for each type A, type B, and type C souvenir that it plans to produce. To manufacture a type A souvenir requires 2 minutes on machine I, 1 minute on machine II and 2 minutes on machine III. A type B souvenir requires 1 minute on machine I, 3 minutes on machine II, and 1 minute on machine III. A type 3 souvenir requires 1 minute on machine I and 2 minutes on each of machines II and III. There are 3 hours available on machine I, 5 hours available on machine II, and 4 hours available on machine III for manufacturing these souvenirs each day. How many of each type should the Ace Novelty Company make per day in order to maximize its profit? (Compare with Example 3.11.)

SOLUTION The given information may be tabulated as follows:

	Machine			
Souvenir type	I	II	III	Profit per unit (\$)
A	2	1	2	6
B	1	3	1	5
C	1	2	2	4
Max. machine-time available (minutes)	180	300	240	

Let x, y, and z denote the respective numbers of type A, type B, and type C souvenirs to be made. The total amount of time that machine I is utilized is given by $2x+y+z$ minutes and must not exceed 180 minutes. Thus, we have the inequality

$$2x+y+z \leq 180$$

Similar considerations on the utilization of machines II and III lead to the following inequalities:

$$\begin{aligned} x+3y+2z &\leq 300 \\ 2x+y+2z &\leq 240 \end{aligned}$$

The profit resulting from the sale of the souvenirs produced is given by

$$P = 6x+5y+4z$$

The mathematical formulation of the problem at hand has led to the following standard linear programming problem:

Maximize the objective (profit) function

$$P = 6x+5y+4z$$

subject to the constraints

$$\begin{aligned} 2x+y+z &\leq 180 \\ x+3y+2z &\leq 300 \\ 2x+y+2z &\leq 240 \end{aligned}$$

where $x \geq 0$, $y \geq 0$, and $z \geq 0$.

Introducing the slack variables u, v, and w gives the following system of linear equations

$$\begin{aligned} 2x+y+z+u &= 180 \\ x+3y+2z+v &= 300 \\ 2x+y+2z+w &= 240 \\ -6x-5y-4z+P &= 0 \end{aligned}$$

The tableaus resulting from the use of the simplex algorithm are as follows:

	x	y	z	u	v	w	P	Constant	ratio
pivot row →	②	1	1	1	0	0	0	180	$180/2=90$
	1	3	2	0	1	0	0	300	$300/1=300$
	2	1	2	0	0	1	0	240	$240/2=120$
	−6	−5	−4	0	0	0	1	0	
	↑ pivot column								

$\xrightarrow{\frac{1}{2}R_1}$

x	y	z	u	v	w	P	Constant
(1)	1/2	1/2	1/2	0	0	0	90
1	3	2	0	1	0	0	300
2	1	2	0	0	1	0	240
−6	−5	−4	0	0	0	1	0

$\xrightarrow[R_3-2R_1 \quad R_4+6R_1]{R_2-R_1}$

	x	y	z	u	v	w	P	Constant	ratio
	1	1/2	1/2	1/2	0	0	0	90	$\frac{90}{1/2}=180$
pivot row →	0	(5/2)	3/2	−1/2	1	0	0	210	$\frac{210}{5/2}=84$
	0	0	1	−1	0	1	0	60	—
	0	−2	−1	3	0	0	1	540	
		↑ pivot column							

$\xrightarrow{\frac{2}{5}R_2}$

x	y	z	u	v	w	P	Constant
1	1/2	1/2	1/2	0	0	0	90
0	(1)	3/5	−1/5	2/5	0	0	84
0	0	1	−1	0	1	0	60
0	−2	−1	3	0	0	1	540

$\xrightarrow[R_4+2R_2]{R_1-\frac{1}{2}R_2}$

x	y	z	u	v	w	P	Constant
1	0	1/5	3/5	−1/5	0	0	48
0	1	3/5	−1/5	2/5	0	0	84
0	0	1	−1	0	1	0	60
0	0	1/5	13/5	4/5	0	1	708

From the final simplex tableau we read off the solution

$$x=48, \quad y=84, \quad z=0, \quad u=0, \quad v=0, \quad w=60, \quad \text{and} \quad P=708$$

Thus, in order to maximize its profit, the Ace Novelty Company should produce 48 type A souvenirs, 84 type B souvenirs and none of the type C souvenirs. The resulting profit is \$708 per day. The value of the slack variable $w=60$ tells us that 1 hour of machine III is left unutilized. ■

It is instructive to compare the results obtained here with those obtained in Example 3.11 (page 105). Recall, that in order to utilize all of the machine-time available on each of the three machines, Ace Novelty had to produce 36 type A, 48 type B, and 60 type C souvenirs. This would have resulted in a profit of \$696. This example shows how, through the optimal use of equipment, a company may boost its profit and at the same time minimize machine wear!

4.4 EXERCISES

Solve each of the following linear programs by the simplex method.

1. Maximize $P = 5x + 3y$ subject to the constraints

$$\begin{aligned} x + y &\le 80 \\ 3x &\le 90 \\ x &\ge 0 \\ y &\ge 0 \end{aligned}$$

2. Maximize $P = 10x + 12y$ subject to the constraints

$$\begin{aligned} x + 2y &\le 12 \\ 3x + 2y &\le 24 \\ x &\ge 0 \\ y &\ge 0 \end{aligned}$$

3. Maximize $P = 5x + 4y$ subject to the constraints

$$\begin{aligned} 3x + 5y &\le 78 \\ 4x + y &\le 36 \\ x &\ge 0 \\ y &\ge 0 \end{aligned}$$

4. Maximize $P = 4x + 6y$ subject to the constraints

$$\begin{aligned} 3x + y &\le 24 \\ 2x + y &\le 18 \\ x + 3y &\le 24 \\ x &\ge 0 \\ y &\ge 0 \end{aligned}$$

5. Maximize $P = 15x + 12y$ subject to the constraints

$$\begin{aligned} x + y &\le 12 \\ 3x + y &\le 30 \\ 10x + 7y &\le 70 \\ x &\ge 0 \\ y &\ge 0 \end{aligned}$$

6. Maximize $P = 3x + 4y + 5z$ subject to the constraints

$$\begin{aligned} x + y + z &\le 8 \\ 3x + 2y + 4z &\le 24 \\ x &\ge 0 \\ y &\ge 0 \\ z &\ge 0 \end{aligned}$$

7. Maximize $P = 3x + 3y + 4z$ subject to the constraints

$$\begin{aligned} x + y + 3z &\le 15 \\ 4x + 4y + 3z &\le 65 \\ x &\ge 0 \\ y &\ge 0 \\ z &\ge 0 \end{aligned}$$

8. Maximize $P = 3x + 4y + z$ subject to the constraints

$$\begin{aligned} 3x + 10y + 5z &\le 120 \\ 5x + 2y + 8z &\le 6 \\ 8x + 10y + 3z &\le 105 \\ x &\ge 0 \\ y &\ge 0 \\ z &\ge 0 \end{aligned}$$

9. Maximize $P = x + 2y - z$ subject to the constraints

$$\begin{aligned} 2x + y + z &\le 14 \\ 4x + 2y + 3z &\le 28 \\ 2x + 5y + 5z &\le 30 \\ x &\ge 0 \\ y &\ge 0 \\ z &\ge 0 \end{aligned}$$

10. Maximize $P = 4x + 6y + 5z$ subject to the constraints

$$\begin{aligned} x + y + z &\le 20 \\ 2x + 4y + 3z &\le 42 \\ 2x \quad + 3z &\le 30 \\ x &\ge 0 \\ y &\ge 0 \\ z &\ge 0 \end{aligned}$$

11. Maximize $P = x + 4y - 2z$ subject to the constraints

$$\begin{aligned} 3x + y - z &\leq 80 \\ 2x + y - z &\leq 40 \\ -x + y + z &\leq 80 \\ x &\geq 0 \\ y &\geq 0 \\ z &\geq 0 \end{aligned}$$

12. Maximize $P = 12x + 10y + 5z$ subject to the constraints

$$\begin{aligned} 2x + y + z &\leq 10 \\ 3x + 5y + z &\leq 45 \\ 2x + 5y + z &\leq 40 \\ x &\geq 0 \\ y &\geq 0 \\ z &\geq 0 \end{aligned}$$

13. Maximize $P = 2x + 6y + 6z$ subject to the constraints

$$\begin{aligned} 2x + y + 3z &\leq 10 \\ 4x + y + 2z &\leq 56 \\ 6x + 4y + 3z &\leq 126 \\ 2x + y + z &\leq 32 \\ x &\geq 0 \\ y &\geq 0 \\ z &\geq 0 \end{aligned}$$

14. Maximize $P = 4x + y + 5z$ subject to the constraints

$$\begin{aligned} x + 2y + 5z &\leq 30 \\ 2x + y + z &\leq 10 \\ 3x + 2y + z &\leq 12 \\ x + y + z &\leq 8 \\ x &\geq 0 \\ y &\geq 0 \\ z &\geq 0 \end{aligned}$$

15. Complete the solution to problem 7 in Exercise set 4.2.

16. Complete the solution to problem 8 in Exercise set 4.2.

17. Complete the solution to problem 9 in Exercise set 4.2.

18. Complete the solution to problem 12 in Exercise set 4.2.

19. Complete the solution to problem 13 in Exercise set 4.2.

4.5

The Simplex Method: Nonstandard Problems and Minimization

In the last section we developed a procedure, called the simplex method, for solving standard linear programming problems. A standard linear programming problem is one, you will recall, in which the following three conditions are satisfied:

1. The objective function is to be maximized.

2. All the variables involved are nonnegative.

3. Each linear constraint may be written so that the expression involving the variables is less than or equal to a nonnegative constant.

nonstandard linear programming problems

Linear programming problems in which at least one of the above conditions does not hold true are called *nonstandard linear programming problems.*

In this section we shall see how, through slight modifications, the simplex method may be adapted to solve certain classes of nonstandard problems. In particular, we shall see how the modified procedure may be utilized to help us solve problems involving the minimization of objective functions.

We begin by considering the class of nonstandard linear programming problems that call for the minimization of the objective functions but otherwise satisfy conditions *(2)* and *(3)* for standard problems. The method of solution for this type of problem is illustrated in the following example.

EXAMPLE 4.17 Minimize the objective function

$$C = -2x - 3y$$

subject to the constraints

$$\begin{aligned} 5x + 4y &\leq 32 \\ x + 2y &\leq 10 \end{aligned}$$

where $x \geq 0$ and $y \geq 0$.

SOLUTION This problem involves the minimization of the objective function and is accordingly a nonstandard linear programming problem. Note, however, that all other conditions for a regular linear programming problem hold true. To solve a problem of this type we observe that minimizing the objective function C is equivalent to maximizing the objective function $P = -C$. Thus, the solution to this problem may be found by solving the following associated standard linear programming problem:

Maximize the objective function

$$P = 2x + 3y$$

subject to the given constraints. Using the simplex method with u and v as slack variables, we obtain the following sequence of simplex tableaus:

	x	y	u	v	P	Constant	ratio
	5	4	1	0	0	32	$32/4 = 8$
pivot row →	1	②	0	1	0	10	$10/2 = 5$
	−2	−3	0	0	1	0	
		↑ pivot column					

	x	y	u	v	P	Constant
	5	4	1	0	0	32
$\xrightarrow{\frac{1}{2}R_2}$	1/2	①	0	1/2	0	5
	−2	−3	0	0	1	0

	x	y	u	v	P	Constant	ratio
pivot row →	③	0	1	−2	0	12	$12/3 = 4$
$\xrightarrow[R_3+3R_2]{R_1-4R_2}$	1/2	1	0	1/2	0	5	$\frac{5}{1/2} = 10$
	−1/2	0	0	3/2	1	15	
	↑ pivot column						

	x	y	u	v	P	Constant
$\xrightarrow{\frac{1}{3}R_1}$	①	0	1/3	−2/3	0	4
	1/2	1	0	1/2	0	5
	−1/2	0	0	3/2	1	15

	x	y	u	v	P	Constant
$\xrightarrow[R_3+\frac{1}{2}R_1]{R_2-\frac{1}{2}R_1}$	1	0	1/3	−2/3	0	4
	0	1	−1/6	5/6	0	3
	0	0	1/6	7/6	1	17

The last tableau is in final form. The solution to the standard linear programming problem associated with the given linear programming problem is $x=4$, $y=3$, and $P=17$ so that the required solution is given by $x=4$, $y=3$, and $C=-17$. You may verify that the solution is correct by using the Method of Corners. ■

Another special class of nonstandard linear programming problems we encounter in practical applications are characterized by the following conditions.

1. The objective function is to be *minimized.*

2. All the variables involved are nonnegative.

3. Each linear constraint may be written so that the expression involving the variables is *greater than* or equal to a constant.

primal and dual problems

A convenient method for solving this type of problem is based on the following observation. Each maximization linear programming problem is associated with a minimization problem and vice-versa. For the purpose of identification, the given problem is called the *primal problem* while the problem related to it is called the *dual problem*. The following example illustrates the technique for constructing the dual of a given linear programming problem.

EXAMPLE 4.18 Write the dual problem associated with the following problem:

Minimize the objective function

$$C=6x+8y$$

subject to the constraints

$$\begin{aligned} 40x+10y &\geq 2400 \\ 10x+15y &\geq 2100 \\ 5x+15y &\geq 1500 \end{aligned}$$

where $x \geq 0$, $y \geq 0$.

SOLUTION We first write down the following tableau for the given (primal) problem:

x	y	Constant
40	10	2400
10	15	2100
5	15	1500
6	8	

Next, we interchange the columns and rows of the above tableau and head the three columns of the resulting array with the three variables u, v, and w, obtaining the tableau

u	v	w	Constant
40	10	5	6
10	15	15	8
2400	2100	1500	

Interpreting the last tableau as if it were part of the initial simplex tableau for a standard linear programming problem, with the exception that the signs of the coefficients pertaining to the objective function are not reversed we construct the required (dual) problem as follows:

Maximize the objective function

$$P = 2400u + 2100v + 1500w$$

subject to the constraints

$$\begin{aligned} 40u + 10v + 5w &\leq 6 \\ 10u + 15v + 15w &\leq 8 \end{aligned}$$

where $u \geq 0$, $v \geq 0$, and $w \geq 0$.

The connection between the solution of the primal problem and that of the dual problem is given by the following theorem. The theorem, attributed to John von Neumann (1903–1957), is stated without proof.

THEOREM 4.2 A primal problem has a solution if and only if the corresponding dual problem has a solution. Furthermore, if a solution exists, then

1. The objective functions of both the primal and the dual problem attain the same optimal value, and

2. The optimal solution to the primal problem appears under the slack variables in the last row of the final simplex tableau associated with the dual problem.

Armed with Theorem 4.2, we proceed to solve the problem posed in Example 4.18. Observe that the dual problem associated with the given (primal) problem is a standard linear programming problem. The solution may thus be found using the simplex algorithm. Introducing the slack variables x and y we obtain the following system of linear equations:

$$\begin{aligned} 40u + 10v + 5w + x &= 6 \\ 10u + 15v + 15w + y &= 8 \\ -2400u - 2100v - 1500w + P &= 0 \end{aligned}$$

Continuing with the simplex algorithm we obtain the following sequence of simplex tableaus:

	u	v	w	x	y	P	Constant	ratio
pivot row →	(40)	10	5	1	0	0	6	$6/40 = 3/20$
	10	15	15	0	1	0	8	$8/10 = 4/5$
	−2400	−2100	−1500	0	0	1	0	
	↑ pivot column							

$\xrightarrow{\frac{1}{40}R_1}$

u	v	w	x	y	P	Constant
(1)	1/4	1/8	1/40	0	0	3/20
10	15	15	0	1	0	8
−2400	−2100	−1500	0	0	1	0

$\xrightarrow[R_3+2400R_1]{R_2-10R_1}$

u	v	w	x	y	P	Constant	ratio
1	1/4	1/8	1/40	0	0	3/20	$\frac{3/20}{1/4} = \frac{3}{5}$
0	(25/2)	55/4	−1/4	1	0	13/2	$\frac{13/2}{25/2} = \frac{13}{25}$
0	−1500	−1200	60	0	1	360	

$\xrightarrow{\frac{2}{25}R_2}$

u	v	w	x	y	P	Constant
1	1/4	1/8	1/40	0	0	3/20
0	(1)	11/10	−1/50	2/25	0	13/25
0	−1500	−1200	60	0	1	360

$\xrightarrow[R_3+1500R_2]{R_1-\frac{1}{4}R_2}$

u	v	w	x	y	P	Constant
1	0	−3/20	3/100	−1/50	0	1/50
0	1	11/10	−1/50	2/25	0	13/25
0	0	450	30	120	1	1140

Solution for the primal problem (30, 120)

The last tableau is final. Theorem 4.2 tells us that the solution to the primal problem is $x = 30$ and $y = 120$ with a minimum value for C of 1140. Observe that the solution to the dual (maximization) problem may be read off from the simplex tableau in the usual manner: $u = 1/50$, $v = 13/25$, $w = 0$ and $P = 1140$. Note that the maximum value of P is equal to the minimum value of C as guaranteed by Theorem 4.2. The solution to the primal problem agrees with the solution of the same problem solved in Example 4.11 using the Method of Corners. ■

Our last example illustrates how the transportation problem posed in Section 4.2 may be solved by duality.

EXAMPLE 4.19 Complete the solution to the transportation problem given in Example 4.9.

(4.15) $$\text{Minimize } C = 20x_1 + 8x_2 + 10x_3 + 12x_4 + 22x_5 + 18x_6$$

subject to the constraints

(4.16)
$$\begin{aligned}
x_1 + x_2 + x_3 \qquad\qquad\qquad &\leq 400 \\
x_4 + x_5 + x_6 &\leq 600 \\
x_1 \qquad\quad + x_4 \qquad\qquad &\geq 200 \\
x_2 \qquad\quad + x_5 \qquad &\geq 300 \\
x_3 \qquad\quad + x_6 &\geq 400
\end{aligned}$$

where $x_1 \geq 0, x_2 \geq 0, \ldots, x_6 \geq 0$.

SOLUTION Upon multiplying each of the first two inequalities of (4.16) by -1, we obtain the following equivalent system of constraints in which each of the expressions involving the variables is greater than or equal to a constant:

$$\begin{aligned}
-x_1 - x_2 - x_3 \qquad\qquad\qquad &\geq -400 \\
-x_4 - x_5 - x_6 &\geq -600 \\
x_1 \qquad\quad + x_4 \qquad\qquad &\geq \ \ 200 \\
x_2 \qquad\quad + x_5 \qquad &\geq \ \ 300 \\
x_3 \qquad\quad x_6 &\geq \ \ 400
\end{aligned}$$

The problem may now be solved by duality. Proceeding we first write the array of numbers

x_1	x_2	x_3	x_4	x_5	x_6	Constant
−1	−1	−1	0	0	0	−400
0	0	0	−1	−1	−1	−600
1	0	0	1	0	0	200
0	1	0	0	1	0	300
0	0	1	0	0	1	400
20	8	10	12	22	18	

Interchanging the rows and columns of the above array of numbers and heading the five columns of the resulting array of numbers by the variables u_1, u_2, u_3, u_4 and u_5 leads to the following:

u_1	u_2	u_3	u_4	u_5	Constant
−1	0	1	0	0	20
−1	0	0	1	0	8
−1	0	0	0	1	10
0	−1	1	0	0	12
0	−1	0	1	0	22
0	−1	0	0	1	18
−400	−600	200	300	400	

from which we construct the associated dual problem:

Maximize the objective function

$$P = -400u_1 - 600u_2 + 200u_3 + 300u_4 + 400u_5$$

subject to the constraints

$$\begin{aligned}
-u_1 \quad + u_3 \qquad\qquad &\le 20\\
-u_1 \qquad\qquad + u_4 \quad &\le 8\\
-u_1 \qquad\qquad\qquad + u_5 &\le 10\\
-u_2 + u_3 \qquad\qquad &\le 12\\
-u_2 + \quad + u_4 \quad &\le 22\\
-u_2 \qquad\qquad + u_5 &\le 18
\end{aligned}$$

where $u_1 \ge 0, u_2 \ge 0, \ldots, u_5 \ge 0$.

Solving the regular linear programming problem by the simplex algorithm, we obtain the following sequence of tableaus ($x_1, x_2, \ldots, x_6$ are slack variables):

	u_1	u_2	u_3	u_4	u_5	x_1	x_2	x_3	x_4	x_5	x_6	P	Constant	ratio
	−1	0	1	0	0	1	0	0	0	0	0	0	20	—
	−1	0	0	1	0	0	1	0	0	0	0	0	8	—
pivot row →	−1	0	0	0	①	0	0	1	0	0	0	0	10	10
	0	−1	1	0	0	0	0	0	1	0	0	0	12	—
	0	−1	0	1	0	0	0	0	0	1	0	0	22	—
	0	−1	0	0	1	0	0	0	0	0	1	0	18	18
	400	600	−200	−300	−400	0	0	0	0	0	0	1	0	
					↑ pivot column									

$\xrightarrow[R_7+400R_3]{R_6-R_3}$

	u_1	u_2	u_3	u_4	u_5	x_1	x_2	x_3	x_4	x_5	x_6	P	Constant	ratio
	−1	0	1	0	0	1	0	0	0	0	0	0	20	—
pivot row →	−1	0	0	①	0	0	1	0	0	0	0	0	8	8
	−1	0	0	0	1	0	0	1	0	0	0	0	10	—
	0	−1	1	0	0	0	0	0	1	0	0	0	12	—
	0	−1	0	1	0	0	0	0	0	1	0	0	22	22
	1	−1	0	0	0	0	0	−1	0	0	1	0	8	—
	0	600	−200	−300	0	0	0	400	0	0	0	1	4000	
				↑ pivot column										

$\xrightarrow[R_7+300R_2]{R_5-R_2}$

	u_1	u_2	u_3	u_4	u_5	x_1	x_2	x_3	x_4	x_5	x_6	P	Constant	ratio
	−1	0	1	0	0	1	0	0	0	0	0	0	20	—
	−1	0	0	1	0	0	1	0	0	0	0	0	8	—
	−1	0	0	0	1	0	0	1	0	0	0	0	10	—
	0	−1	1	0	0	0	0	0	1	0	0	0	12	—
	1	−1	0	0	0	0	−1	0	0	1	0	0	14	14
pivot row →	①	−1	0	0	0	0	0	−1	0	0	1	0	8	8
pivot column →	−300	600	−200	0	0	0	300	400	0	0	0	1	6400	

$\xrightarrow{\substack{R_1+R_6 \\ R_2+R_6}}$ $\substack{R_3+R_6 \\ R_5-R_6 \\ R_7+300R_6}$

	u_1	u_2	u_3	u_4	u_5	x_1	x_2	x_3	x_4	x_5	x_6	P	Constant	ratio
	0	−1	1	0	0	1	0	−1	0	0	1	0	28	28
	0	−1	0	1	0	0	1	−1	0	0	1	0	16	—
	0	−1	0	0	1	0	0	0	0	0	1	0	18	—
pivot row →	0	−1	①	0	0	0	0	0	1	0	0	0	12	12
	0	0	0	0	0	0	−1	1	0	1	−1	0	6	—
	1	−1	0	0	0	0	0	−1	0	0	1	0	8	—
	0	300	−200	0	0	0	300	100	0	0	300	1	8800	
			↑ pivot column											

$\xrightarrow[R_7+200R_4]{R_1-R_4}$

u_1	u_2	u_3	u_4	u_5	x_1	x_2	x_3	x_4	x_5	x_6	P	Constant
0	0	0	0	0	1	0	−1	−1	0	1	0	16
0	−1	0	1	0	0	1	−1	0	0	1	0	16
0	−1	0	0	1	0	0	0	0	0	1	0	18
0	−1	1	0	0	0	0	0	1	0	0	0	12
0	0	0	0	0	0	−1	1	0	1	−1	0	6
1	−1	0	0	0	0	0	−1	0	0	1	0	8
0	100	0	0	0	0	300	100	200	0	300	1	11,200

The last tableau is final and we find that

$$x_1 = 0, \quad x_2 = 300, \quad x_3 = 100, \quad x_4 = 200, \quad x_5 = 0, \quad x_6 = 300,$$
$$\text{and} \quad P = 11{,}200$$

Thus, to minimize shipping costs the Acrosonic Company should ship 300 loudspeaker systems from plant I to warehouse B, 100 systems from plant I to warehouse C, 200 systems from plant II to warehouse A, and 300 systems from plant II to warehouse C at a total cost of \$11,200. ■

In this section we have touched upon two important classes of nonstandard linear programming problems. The solution of other classes of nonstandard linear programming problems may be found in more advanced texts on linear programming.

4.5 EXERCISES

Use the technique developed in this section to solve each of the following nonstandard linear programming problems.

1. Minimize $C = -2x + y$ subject to the constraints

$$\begin{aligned} x + 2y &\le 6 \\ 3x + 2y &\le 12 \end{aligned}$$

where $x \ge 0$ and $y \ge 0$

2. Minimize $C = -2x - 3y$ subject to the constraints

$$\begin{aligned} 3x + 4y &\le 24 \\ 7x - 4y &\le 16 \end{aligned}$$

where $x \ge 0$ and $y \ge 0$

3. Minimize $C = -3x - 2y$ subject to the constraints of problem 2.

4. Minimize $C = x - 2y + z$ subject to the constraints

$$\begin{aligned} x - 2y + 3z &\le 10 \\ 2x + y - 2z &\le 15 \\ 2x + y + 3z &\le 20 \end{aligned}$$

where $x \ge 0$, $y \ge 0$, and $z \ge 0$

5. Minimize $C = 2x - 3y - 4z$ subject to the constraints

$$\begin{aligned} -x + 2y - z &\le 8 \\ x - 2y + 2z &\le 10 \\ 2x + 4y - 3z &\le 12 \end{aligned}$$

where $x \ge 0$, $y \ge 0$, and $z \ge 0$

6. Minimize $C = -3x - 2y - z$ subject to the constraints of problem 5.

In problems 7 through 16 construct the dual problem associated with the given (primal) problem. Solve the (primal) problem.

7. Minimize $C = 2x + 5y$ subject to the constraints

$$x + 2y \geq 4$$
$$3x + 2y \geq 6$$

where $x \geq 0$ and $y \geq 0$

8. Minimize $C = 3x + 2y$ subject to the constraints

$$2x + 3y \geq 90$$
$$3x + 2y \geq 120$$

where $x \geq 0$ and $y \geq 0$

9. Minimize $C = 6x + 4y$ subject to the constraints

$$6x + y \geq 60$$
$$2x + y \geq 40$$
$$x + y \geq 30$$

where $x \geq 0$ and $y \geq 0$

10. Minimize $C = 10x + y$ subject to the constraints

$$4x + y \geq 16$$
$$x + 2y \geq 12$$
$$x \geq 2$$

where $x \geq 0$ and $y \geq 0$

11. Minimize $C = 200x + 150y + 120z$ subject to the constraints

$$20x + 10y + z \geq 10$$
$$x + y + 2z \geq 20$$

where $x \geq 0$, $y \geq 0$ and $z \geq 0$

12. Minimize $C = 40x + 30y + 11z$ subject to the constraints

$$2x + y + z \geq 8$$
$$x + y - z \geq 6$$

where $x \geq 0$, $y \geq 0$ and $z \geq 0$

13. Minimize $C = 6x + 8y + 4z$ subject to the constraints

$$x + 2y + 2z \geq 10$$
$$2x + y + z \geq 24$$
$$x + y + z \geq 16$$

where $x \geq 0$, $y \geq 0$, and $z \geq 0$

14. Minimize $C = 12z + 4y + 8z$ subject to the constraints

$$2x + 4y + z \geq 6$$
$$3x + 2y + 2z \geq 2$$
$$4x + y + z \geq 2$$

where $x \geq 0$, $y \geq 0$, and $z \geq 0$

15. Minimize $C = 30x + 12y + 20z$ subject to the constraints

$$2x + 4y + 3z \geq 6$$
$$6x + z \geq 2$$
$$6y + 2z \geq 4$$

where $x \geq 0$, $y \geq 0$, and $z \geq 0$

16. Minimize $C = 8x + 6y + 4z$ subject to the constraints

$$2x + 3y + z \geq 6$$
$$x + 2y - 2z \geq 4$$
$$x + y + 2z \geq 2$$

where $x \geq 0$, $y \geq 0$, and $z \geq 0$

17. Solve problem 10 of Section 4.2.

18. Solve problem 11 of Section 4.2.

19. The owner of the Health Juice-Bar wishes to prepare a low-calorie fruit juice with a high vitamin A and C content by blending orange juice and pink-grapefruit juice. Each glass of the blended juice is to contain at least 1200 International Units (I.U.) of vitamin A and 200 I.U. of vitamin C. One ounce of orange juice contains 60 I.U. of vitamin A, 16 I.U. of vitamin C, and 14 calories; each ounce of pink-grapefruit juice contains 120 I.U. of vitamin A, 12 I.U. of vitamin C, and 11 calories. How many ounces of each juice should a glass of the blend contain if it is to meet the minimum vitamin requirements and at the same time contain a minimum number of calories?

20. An oil company operates two refineries in a certain city. Refinery I has an output of 200, 100, and 100 barrels of low-, medium-, and high-grade oil per day, respectively. Refinery II has an output of 100, 200, and 600 barrels of low-, medium-, and high-grade oil per day, respectively. The company wishes to produce at least 1000, 1400, and 3000 barrels of low-, medium-, and high-grade oil to fill an order. If it costs \$200 per day to operate refinery I and \$300 per day to operate refinery II, determine the number of days each refinery should be operated to meet the requirements of the order at minimum cost to the oil company.

4

Chapter Review

EXERCISES

1. Maximize $P = 3x + 5y$ subject to the constraints

$$\begin{aligned} 2x + 3y &\leq 12 \\ x + y &\leq 5 \\ x &\geq 0 \\ y &\geq 0 \end{aligned}$$

2. Maximize $P = 2x + 3y$ subject to the constraints

$$\begin{aligned} 2x + y &\leq 12 \\ x - 2y &\leq 1 \\ x &\geq 0 \\ y &\geq 0 \end{aligned}$$

3. Maximize $P = 3x + 2y$ subject to the constraints

$$\begin{aligned} 2x + y &\leq 16 \\ 2x + 3y &\leq 36 \\ 4x + 5y &\geq 28 \\ x &\geq 0 \\ y &\geq 0 \end{aligned}$$

4. Maximize $P = 6x + 2y$ subject to the constraints

$$\begin{aligned} x + 2y &\leq 12 \\ x + y &\leq 8 \\ 2x - 3y &\geq 6 \\ x &\geq 0 \\ y &\geq 0 \end{aligned}$$

5. Minimize $C = 2x + 7y$ subject to the constraints

$$\begin{aligned} 3x + 5y &\geq 45 \\ 3x + 10y &\geq 60 \\ x &\geq 0 \\ y &\geq 0 \end{aligned}$$

6. Minimize $C = 4x + y$ subject to the constraints

$$\begin{aligned} 6x + y &\geq 18 \\ 2x + y &\geq 10 \\ x + 4y &\geq 12 \\ x &\geq 0 \\ y &\geq 0 \end{aligned}$$

7. Find the maximum and minimum of $Q = x + y$ subject to the constraints

$$\begin{aligned} 5x + 2y &\geq 20 \\ x + 2y &\geq 8 \\ x + 4y &\leq 22 \\ x &\geq 0 \\ y &\geq 0 \end{aligned}$$

8. Find the maximum and minimum of $Q = 2x + 5y$ subject to the constraints

$$\begin{aligned} x + y &\geq 4 \\ -x + y &\leq 6 \\ x + 3y &\leq 30 \\ x &\leq 12 \\ x &\geq 0 \\ y &\geq 0 \end{aligned}$$

9. Maximize $P = 2x + 3y + 5z$ subject to the constraints

$$\begin{aligned} &x + 2y + 3z \leq 12 \\ &x - 3y + 2z \leq 10 \\ &x \geq 0,\ y \geq 0,\ z \geq 0 \end{aligned}$$

10. Maximize $P = x + 2y + 3z$ subject to the constraints

$$\begin{aligned} &2x + y + z \leq 14 \\ &3x + 2y + 4z \leq 24 \\ &2x + 5y - 2z \leq 10 \\ &x \geq 0,\ y \geq 0,\ z \geq 0 \end{aligned}$$

11. Minimize $C = 24x + 18y + 24z$ subject to the constraints

$$\begin{aligned} &3x + 2y + z \geq 4 \\ &x + y + 3z \geq 6 \\ &x \geq 0,\ y \geq 0,\ z \geq 0 \end{aligned}$$

12. Minimize $C = 4x + 2y + 6z$ subject to the constraints

$$\begin{aligned} &x + 2y + z \geq 4 \\ &2x + y + 2z \geq 2 \\ &3x + 2y + z \geq 3 \\ &x \geq 0,\ y \geq 0,\ z \geq 0 \end{aligned}$$

13. An investor has decided to commit no more than \$80,000 in the purchase of the common stocks of two companies, Company A and Company B. He has also estimated that there is a chance of a 1% capital loss on his investment in the stocks of Company A and a chance of a 4% loss on his investment in the stocks of Company B and has decided that these losses should not exceed \$2000. On the

other hand, he expects to make a profit of 14% from his investment in the stocks of Company A and 20% from his investment in the stocks of Company B. Determine how much he should invest in the stock of each company in order to maximize his investment returns.

14. A company manufactures three products, A, B, and C, on two machines, I and II. It has been determined that the company will realize a profit of $4 on each unit of product A, $6 on each unit of product B, and $8 on each unit of product C. To manufacture a unit of product A requires 9 minutes on machine I and 6 minutes on machine II; to manufacture a unit of product B requires 12 minutes on machine I and 6 minutes on machine II; and to manufacture a unit of Model C requires 18 minutes on machine I and 10 minutes on machine II. There are 6 hours of machine-time available on machine I and 4 hours of machine-time available on machine II in each work shift. How many units of each product should be produced in each shift in order to maximize the company's profit?

15. Mr. Moody has decided to invest at most $100,000 in securities in the form of corporate stocks. He has classified his options into three groups of stocks—"blue-chip" stocks that he assumes will yield a 10% return (dividends and capital appreciation) on his investment within a year, growth stocks that he assumes will yield a 15% return on his investment within a year, and speculative stocks that he assumes will yield a 20% return (mainly due to capital appreciation) on his investment within a year. Because of the relative risks involved in his investment, Mr. Moody has further decided that no more than 30% of his investment should be in growth and speculative stocks and at least 50% of his investment should be in "blue-chip" and speculative stocks. Determine how much Mr. Moody should invest in each class of stocks in the hope of maximizing the return on his investments.

5

EXPONENTIAL AND LOGARITHMIC FUNCTIONS

5.1 Laws of Exponents

If b is any real number and n is a positive integer, then the expression b^n (read "b to the power n") is defined as the number obtained by multiplying b by itself n times. Thus

$$b^n = \underbrace{b \cdot b \cdot b \ldots b}_{n \text{ factors}}$$

exponent The number b is called the *base* and the superscript n is called the *exponent* of the exponential expression b^n.

EXAMPLE 5.1 (a) $2^5 = 2 \cdot 2 \cdot 2 \cdot 2 \cdot 2 = 32$

(b) $\left(\frac{2}{3}\right)^3 = \left(\frac{2}{3}\right)\left(\frac{2}{3}\right)\left(\frac{2}{3}\right) = \frac{8}{27}$

(c) $(1.2)^2 = (1.2)(1.2) = 1.44$ ■

Computations involving exponents are facilitated by using the *laws of exponents*. These laws are easily verified to be valid for the case when m and n are positive integers, and a and b are real numbers:

(1) $b^m \cdot b^n = b^{m+n}$

(2) $\dfrac{b^m}{b^n} = b^{m-n}$ $(b \neq 0 \text{ and } m > n)$

(3) $(b^m)^n = b^{mn}$

(4) $(ab)^n = a^n \cdot b^n$

(5) $\left(\frac{a}{b}\right)^n = \frac{a^n}{b^n}$ $(b \neq 0)$

EXAMPLE 5.2 **(a)** $3^2 \cdot 3^3 = 3^5 = 243$

(b) $\frac{2^7}{2^3} = 2^{7-3} = 2^4 = 16$

(c) $(2^2)^3 = 2^6 = 64$

(d) $(2 \cdot 3)^3 = 2^3 \cdot 3^3 = 8 \cdot 27 = 216$

(e) $\left(\frac{2}{3}\right)^3 = \frac{2^3}{3^3} = \frac{8}{27}$ (Compare with Example 5.1 part b). ■

Now, if b is any nonzero number and n is any positive integer, then

$$\frac{b^n}{b^n} = \frac{\overbrace{b \cdot b \cdot b \ldots b}^{n \text{ factors}}}{\underbrace{b \cdot b \cdot b \ldots b}_{n \text{ factors}}} = 1$$

Thus, if Law (2) of exponents were required to hold for the case $m = n$ as well, then we would have

$$\frac{b^n}{b^n} = b^{n-n} = b^0 = 1$$

This leads to the following definition of the expression b^0 $(b \neq 0)$; namely,

$$b^0 = 1 \qquad (b\text{, any nonzero number})$$

For example, $2^0 = 1$ and $(-\pi)^0 = 1$ but the expression 0^0 is undefined.

Next, observe that if Law (1) of exponents held for the case of negative integral exponents as well, then we would have

$$b^{-n} \cdot b^n = b^{-n+n} = b^0 = 1$$

and this suggests that we define b^{-n} by

$$b^{-n} = \frac{1}{b^n} \qquad (b \neq 0;\ n\text{, a positive integer})$$

Since the number $(-n)$ is a negative integer whenever n is a positive integer, we have extended our definition of the expression b^n to include all integral exponents. You may easily convince yourself that all the laws of exponents stated earlier are true whenever m and n are whole numbers; in particular, Law (2) holds without the restriction that $m > n$.

EXAMPLE 5.3 (a) $3^{-2} \cdot 3^5 = 3^{-2+5} = 3^3 = 27$

(b) $\dfrac{2^4}{2^6} = 2^{4-6} = 2^{-2} = \dfrac{1}{2^2} = \dfrac{1}{4}$

(c) $(2^{-2})^4 = 2^{-8} = \dfrac{1}{2^8} = \dfrac{1}{256}$

(d) $(3 \cdot 4)^{-2} = 3^{-2} \cdot 4^{-2} = \dfrac{1}{3^2} \cdot \dfrac{1}{4^2} = \left(\dfrac{1}{9}\right)\left(\dfrac{1}{16}\right) = \dfrac{1}{144}$

(e) $\left(\dfrac{2}{3}\right)^{-2} = \dfrac{2^{-2}}{3^{-2}} = \dfrac{3^2}{2^2} = \dfrac{9}{4}$ ■

Next, we will extend our definition of the expression b^n to include all rational numbers n. Observe that if we required Law (3) of exponents above to hold in the case $m = 1/n$ (n, a positive integer), then we must have

$$(b^{1/n})^n = b^{n/n} = b^1 = b$$

nth root of a number

This suggests that we define the expression $b^{1/n}$ as the number which when raised to the nth power is equal to b. Such a number, if it exists, is called the *nth root of* b, also written $\sqrt[n]{b}$. Here a little caution is in order. First, observe that the nth root of a negative number is not defined when n is even. For example, the square root of -2 is not defined since there is no real number b such that $b^2 = -2$. Next, given a number b there might be more than one number satisfying our above definition of the nth root. For example, both 3 and -3 squared equal 9, and each is a square root of 9. To avoid ambiguity, we shall define $b^{1/n}$ to be the *positive* nth root of b whenever it exists. Thus $\sqrt{9} = 9^{1/2} = 3$.

We are now able to define the exponential expression involving a rational exponent. Suppose first that p/q (p, q, positive integers with $q \neq 0$) is a rational number in lowest terms. Then the expression $b^{p/q}$ is defined as the number $(b^{1/q})^p$, or equivalently $\sqrt[q]{b^p}$, whenever it exists. Expressions involving negative rational exponents are taken care of by the definition

$$b^{-p/q} = \frac{1}{b^{p/q}}$$

EXAMPLE 5.4 (a) $\sqrt[4]{-81} = (-81)^{1/4}$ is undefined (that is, it is not a real number)

(b) $\sqrt[4]{81} = 81^{1/4} = 3$

(c) $(-8)^{2/3} = (-8^{1/3})^2 = (-2)^2 = 4$

(d) $16^{3/2} = (16^{1/2})^3 = 4^3 = 64$

(e) $4^{-5/2} = \dfrac{1}{4^{5/2}} = \dfrac{1}{(4^{1/2})^5} = \dfrac{1}{2^5} = \dfrac{1}{32}$ ■

We see that the laws of exponents stated earlier are valid in the case when the exponents are rational numbers. Also, Law (2) holds without the restriction $m > n$.

EXAMPLE 5.5 (a) $16^{7/4} \cdot 16^{-1/2} = 16^{7/4-1/2} = 16^{5/4} = 2^5 = 32$

(b) $\dfrac{8^{5/3}}{8^{-1/3}} = 8^{5/3-(-1/3)} = 8^2 = 64$

(c) $(64^{4/3})^{-1/2} = 64^{(4/3)(-1/2)} = 64^{-2/3} = \dfrac{1}{64^{2/3}} = \dfrac{1}{(64^{1/3})^2} = \dfrac{1}{4^2} = \dfrac{1}{16}$

(d) $(16 \cdot 81)^{-1/4} = 16^{-1/4} \cdot 81^{-1/4} = \dfrac{1}{16^{1/4}} \cdot \dfrac{1}{81^{1/4}} = \dfrac{1}{2} \cdot \dfrac{1}{3} = \dfrac{1}{6}$

(e) $\left\{\dfrac{32}{243}\right\}^{-4/5} = \dfrac{32^{-4/5}}{243^{-4/5}} = \dfrac{243^{4/5}}{32^{4/5}} = \dfrac{(243^{1/5})^4}{(32^{1/5})^4} = \dfrac{3^4}{2^4} = \dfrac{81}{16}$ ■

Finally, let us consider the meaning of the expression b^n when n is an irrational number. First, recall that an irrational number may be approximated by a rational number to any degree of accuracy desired. For example, the irrational number $\sqrt{2}$ may be approximated with increasing accuracy by the sequence of decimals 1, 1.4, 1.41, 1.414, . . . ; this sequence is, of course, a sequence of rational numbers since each term in the sequence has a *terminating* decimal expression. This observation suggests that we interpret b^n when n is irrational as the "limit" (see Section 10.1) of the sequence of numbers

$$b^{r_1}, b^{r_2}, b^{r_3}, \ldots$$

where $r_1, r_2, r_3, \ldots$ is a sequence of rational numbers which *tends* to n. In order to ensure that each of the numbers $b^{r_1}, b^{r_2}, b^{r_3}, \ldots$ is defined, we shall restrict the base b to a positive number. (See problem 31, Exercise set 5.1.) For example, using a pocket calculator with a "y^x" key, we may compute the value of $2^{\sqrt{2}}$. We begin by observing that the irrational number $\sqrt{2}$ is approximated with increasing accuracy by the sequence of rational numbers $r_1 = 1$, $r_2 = 1.4$, $r_3 = 1.41$, $r_4 = 1.414$, $r_5 = 1.4142$, $r_6 = 1.41421, \ldots$. We compute

$$\begin{aligned} 2^{r_1} &= 2^1 = 2 \\ 2^{r_2} &= 2^{1.4} = 2.63902 \\ 2^{r_3} &= 2^{1.41} = 2.65737 \\ 2^{r_4} &= 2^{1.414} = 2.66475 \\ 2^{r_5} &= 2^{1.4142} = 2.66512 \\ 2^{r_6} &= 2^{1.41421} = 2.66514 \end{aligned}$$

and see that $2^{\sqrt{2}} = 2.665$, accurate to 3 decimal places.

The next example illustrates how an equation involving exponentials is solved.

EXAMPLE 5.6 Solve the equation $2^{2x-1} = 4^2$ for x.

SOLUTION We rewrite the given equation in the form

$$2^{2x-1} = (2^2)^2 = 2^4$$

which upon simplification gives

$$2x - 1 = 4 \qquad \text{(since } x^a = x^b \text{ implies } a = b\text{)}$$

or

$$x = \frac{5}{2}$$

■

5.1 EXERCISES

In problems 1 through 10, use the laws of exponents to evaluate the given expressions.

1. (*a*) $4^{-3} \cdot 4^5$ (*b*) $\left(-\frac{3}{8}\right)^2$ (*c*) $\left(\frac{1}{\sqrt{3}}\right)^0$

2. (*a*) $(-3)^2(3)^3$ (*b*) $\frac{5^6}{5^4}$ (*c*) $(2^{-1})^3$

3. (*a*) $(3 \cdot 4)^{-2}$ (*b*) $\frac{(-3)^4}{(-3)^5}$ (*c*) $\left[\left(-\frac{1}{3}\right)^2\right]^{-3}$

4. (*a*) $9(9)^{-1/2}$ (*b*) $\left(\frac{4}{3}\right)^{-3}$ (*c*) $\frac{(2^{-4})(2^6)}{2^{-1}}$

5. (*a*) $81^{3/4}$ (*b*) $(-8)^{5/3}$ (*c*) $\left(\frac{7^{-5} \cdot 7^2}{7^{-2}}\right)^{-1}$

6. (*a*) $\left(\frac{9}{16}\right)^{-1/2}$ (*b*) $\sqrt[3]{2^6}$ (*c*) $(125^{2/3})^{-1/2}$

7. (*a*) $(27 \cdot 64)^{-1/3}$ (*b*) $\sqrt[4]{.0081}$ (*c*) $\frac{16^{5/8}16^{1/2}}{16^{7/8}}$

8. (*a*) $3^{1/4} \cdot (9)^{-5/8}$ (*b*) $\left(\frac{9^{-3} \cdot 9^5}{9^{-2}}\right)^{-1/2}$ (*c*) $\frac{5^{3.3} \cdot 5^{-1.6}}{5^{-0.3}}$

9. (*a*) $(4^{-1/\pi})^{-3\pi}$ (*b*) $\left(\frac{8}{27}\right)^{-1/3}\left(\frac{81}{256}\right)^{-1/4}$ (*c*) $(3^{1-\sqrt{3}})^{1+\sqrt{3}}$

10. (*a*) $(3^{\sqrt{2}})^{\sqrt{8}}$ (*b*) $\left(\frac{\sqrt{2}}{3^{-1}}\right)^2$ (*c*) $10^{1-\sqrt{2}}10^{\sqrt[4]{4}}$

11. State whether the following are true or false. Justify your answer.

(*a*) $x^4 + 2x^4 = 3x^4$ (*b*) $3^2 \cdot 2^2 = 6^2$ (*c*) $x^3 \cdot 2x^2 = 2x^6$

(*d*) $3^3 + 3 = 3^4$ (*e*) $\frac{2^{4x}}{1^{3x}} = 2^{4x-3x}$ (*f*) $(2^2 \cdot 3^2)^2 = 6^4$

12. State whether the following are true or false. Justify your answer.

(*a*) $x^{2/3} \cdot x^{4/3} = x^2$ (*b*) $\frac{1}{4^{-3}} = \frac{1}{64}$ (*c*) $(2x^{2/3})^3 = 2x^2$

(*d*) $\frac{4^{3/2}}{2^4} = \frac{1}{2}$ (*e*) $(1.2^{1/2})^{-1/2} = 1$ (*f*) $5^{2/3} \cdot (25)^{2/3} = 25$

13. Rewrite the following expressions using positive exponents only.

(*a*) $(xy)^{-2}$ (*b*) $3s^{1/3} \cdot s^{-7/3}$ (*c*) $\frac{x^{-1/3}}{x^{1/2}}$

(*d*) $4^{-1}ab^{-2}$ (*e*) $\sqrt{x^{-1}} \cdot \sqrt{9x^{-3}}$ (*f*) $\left(\frac{8x^{-3}y^{1/3}}{64x^{-3}y^{4/3}}\right)^{1/3}$

In problems 14 through 18, simplify the given expression.

14. (*a*) $(64x^9)^{1/3}$ (*b*) $(25x^3y^4)^{1/2}$ (*c*) $\frac{x^{7/3}}{x^{-2}}$

15. (*a*) $(49x^{-2})^{-1/2}$ (*b*) $\sqrt[3]{x^{-2}} \cdot \sqrt{4x^5}$ (*c*) $(x^{r/s})^{s/r}$

16. (*a*) $\frac{x^2 - y^2}{(x-y)^0}$ (*b*) $\sqrt{81x^6y^{-4}}$ (*c*) $\left(\frac{68x^2y}{17x^{-2}y^2}\right)^{-1/2}$

17. (*a*) $\frac{x^{-5}}{(1/x)^2}$ (*b*) $(x^{1+\sqrt{2}})^{1-\sqrt{2}}$ (*c*) $\frac{(a^m \cdot a^{-n})^{-2}}{(a^{m+n})^2}$

18. (*a*) $(e^{ax})^{-x}$ (*b*) $\frac{e^{3x-1}}{e^{2x+1}}$ (*c*) $\frac{a^{2x} - a^x - 2}{a^x + 1}$

19. Given that $2^{1/2} \approx 1.414$ and $3^{1/2} \approx 1.732$, compute the following without using tables.

(*a*) $2^{3/2}$ (*b*) $8^{1/2}$ (*c*) $9^{3/4}$ (*d*) $6^{1/2}$

20. Given that $10^{1/2} \approx 3.162$ and $10^{1/3} \approx 2.153$, compute the following without using tables.

(*a*) $10^{3/2}$ (*b*) $1000^{3/2}$ (*c*) $10^{2.5}$ (*d*) $(0.0001)^{-1/3}$

21. Using the method on page 194, compute the value of $3^{\sqrt{2}}$.

22. Using the method on page 194, compute the value of 5^{π}.

In problems 23 through 30, solve the given equation for x.

23. $3^{3x-4} = 3^5$

24. $10^{2x-1} = 10^{x+3}$

25. $\left(\frac{1}{2}\right)^2 = 2^{x-4}$

26. $3^{2x+4} = 27^{x-4}$

27. $8^x = \left(\frac{1}{32}\right)^{x-2}$

28. $3^{x-x^2} = \frac{1}{9^x}$

29. $3^{2x} - 12 \cdot 3^x + 27 = 0$

30. $(\sqrt{2})^x = 4^{x^2+x}$

***31.** In the definition of b^n when n is any real number (see page 194) we required that b be a positive number. Show that this assumption is necessary. *Hint*: Recall that b^n is defined to be the "limit" of the sequence of numbers

$$b^{r_1}, b^{r_2}, b^{r_3}, \ldots$$

where $r_1, r_2, r_3, \ldots$ is a sequence of rational numbers that "tends" to n. Consider the expression "$(-2)^{\sqrt{2}}$". As before we observe that the sequence 1, 1.4, 1.41, 1.414, . . . tends to $\sqrt{2}$. But $1.41 = 141/100$ so that

$$(-2)^{1.41} = (-2)^{141/100} = [(-2)^{1/100}]^{141}$$

is not defined.

5.2

The Exponential Function

In the last section we saw that whenever b is a positive number and n is any real number, then the expression b^n is a real number. This result enables us to define the function $y = b^x$ where $b > 0$ with domain given by the set of real numbers. Such a function is referred to as an *exponential function*.

The exponential function is the most important function in mathematical analysis. Because of its special characteristics, and as one of the most useful functions, it is found in virtually every field where mathematics is applied. Under ideal conditions the number of bacteria present at any time t in a culture may be described by an exponential function of t; radioactive substances decay over time in accordance with an "exponential" law of decay; money left on fixed or time deposit and earning (compound) interest grows exponentially (see Chapter 6) and some of the most important distribution functions encountered in statistics (see Chapter 9) are exponential, just to mention a few examples.

Let us begin our investigation into the properties of the exponential function by studying its graph.

EXAMPLE 5.7 Sketch the graph of the exponential function $y = 2^x$.

SOLUTION We shall use the techniques of graphing developed in Chapter 2. First, as discussed earlier, the domain of the exponential function $y = f(x) = 2^x$ is the set of real numbers. Next, putting $x = 0$ gives $y = 2^0 = 1$, the y-intercept of f; there is no x-intercept since there is no value of x for which $y = 0$. To find the range of f, consider the following table of values:

x	−5	−4	−3	−2	−1	0	1	2	3	4	5
y	1/32	1/16	1/8	1/4	1/2	1	2	4	8	16	32

We see from the above computations that 2^x decreases and approaches 0 as x decreases without bound and that 2^x increases without bound as x increases without bound. Thus, the range of f is the interval $(0, \infty)$; that is, the set of positive real numbers. Finally, we sketch the graph of $y = f(x) = 2^x$ in Figure 5.1.

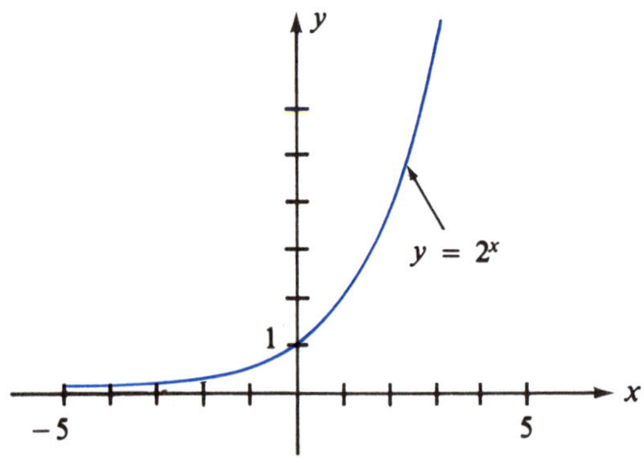

Figure 5.1

EXAMPLE 5.8 Sketch the graph of the exponential function $y = (1/2)^x$.

SOLUTION The domain of the exponential function $y = (1/2)^x$ is, of course, the set of all real numbers. The y-intercept is $(1/2)^0 = 1$; there is no x-intercept since there is no value of x for which $y = 0$. From the following table of values

x	−5	−4	−3	−2	−1	0	1	2	3	4	5
y	32	16	8	4	2	1	1/2	1/4	1/8	1/16	1/32

we deduce that $(1/2)^x = 1/2^x$ increases without bound as x decreases without bound and that $(1/2)^x$ decreases and approaches 0 as x increases without bound. Thus the range of f is the interval $(0, \infty)$. The graph of $y = f(x) = (1/2)^x$ is sketched in Figure 5.2.

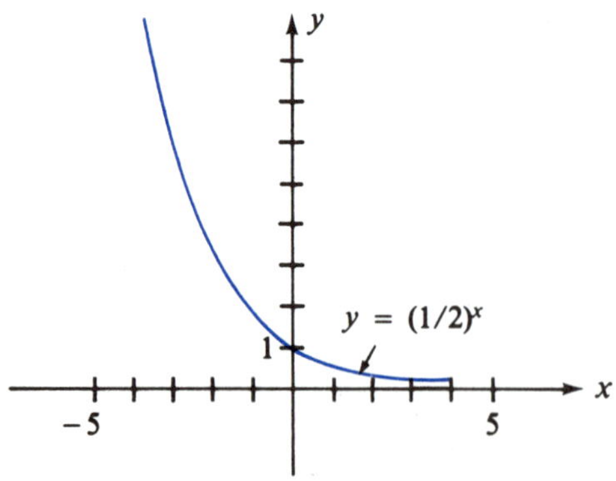

Figure 5.2

The functions $y = 2^x$ and $y = (1/2)^x$ whose graphs were studied in Example 5.7 and Example 5.8 are special cases of the exponential function $y = f(x) = b^x$ obtained by setting $b = 2$ and $b = 1/2$, respectively. However, in general, the exponential function $y = b^x$ with $b > 1$ has a similar graph to $y = 2^x$, while the graph of $y = b^x$ for $0 < b < 1$ is similar to that of $y = (1/2)^x$ (see problems 1 and 2 in Exercise set 5.2). When $b = 1$, the function $y = b^x$ reduces to the constant function $y = 1$. For comparison, the graphs of all three functions are sketched in Figure 5.3.

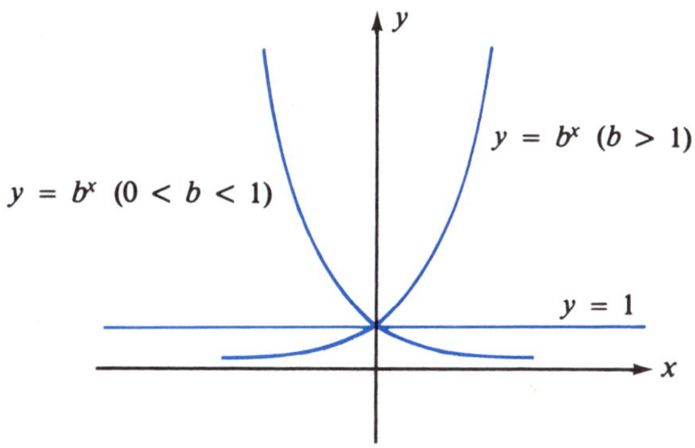

Figure 5.3

Exponential functions to the base e, where e is an irrational number whose value is approximately 2.718 (see problem 12 in Exercise set 10.2), play an important role in both theoretical and applied problems.

EXAMPLE 5.9 Sketch the graph of the function $y = e^x$.

SOLUTION Since $e > 1$ it follows from our previous discussion that the graph of $y = e^x$ is similar to the graph of $y = 2^x$ (Figure 5.1). With the aid of Table I in Appendix II, or by using a pocket calculator we obtain the following table.

x	−3	−2	−1	0	1	2	3
y	0.05	0.14	0.37	1	2.72	7.39	20.09

The graph of $y = e^x$ is sketched in Figure 5.4.

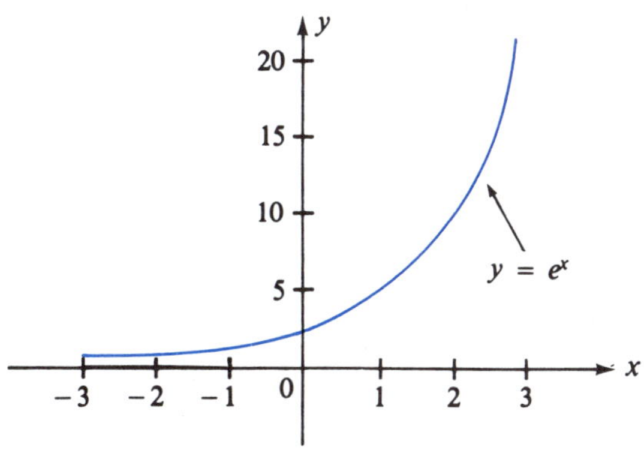

Figure 5.4

■

Next, we will consider another exponential function to the base e, that is closely related to the previous function, and is particularly useful in constructing models that describe "exponential decay".

EXAMPLE 5.10 Using a pocket calculator or Table I in Appendix II, sketch the graph of the function $y = e^{-x}$.

SOLUTION Since $e > 1$, it follows that $0 < 1/e < 1$, so that $f(x) = e^{-x} = 1/e^x = (1/e)^x$ is an exponential function with base less than 1 and therefore has a graph that is similar to that of the exponential function $y = (1/2)^x$. As before, we construct the following table of values of $y = e^{-x}$ for selected values of x.

x	-3	-2	-1	0	1	2	3
y	20.09	7.39	2.72	1	0.37	0.14	0.05

Using this table we sketch the graph of $y = e^{-x}$ in Figure 5.5.

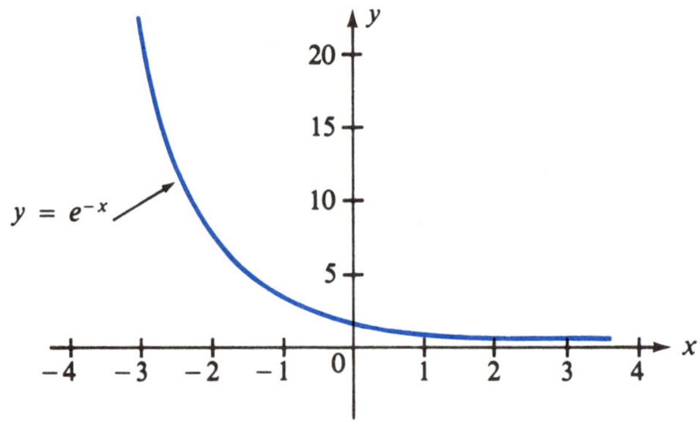

Figure 5.5

Exponential functions with base e have broad application in the fields of probability and statistics. One application involves an exponential function of the form $f(x) = e^{-x^2}$. Its graph, because of its shape, is called the normal or bell-shaped curve (see Figure 5.6).

EXAMPLE 5.11 Using a pocket calculator or Table I in Appendix II, sketch the graph of the function $y = e^{-x^2}$.

SOLUTION The domain of the function $y = e^{-x^2} = 1/e^{x^2}$ is the set of all real numbers. Setting $x = 0$ gives $y = 1$ as the y-intercept. There is no x-intercept since there is no value of x for which $y = 0$. Replacing x by $-x$ leaves the function unchanged indicating that the graph of $y = -e^{-x^2}$ is symmetric with respect to the y-axis. Thus, we may restrict our investigation of the behavior of the function to positive values of x. Since $e > 1$, we see that $e^{-x^2} = 1/e^{x^2}$ approaches 0 as x increases without bound.

Thus, the range of the function is given by the interval (0, 1]. Finally, using the following table, we sketch the required graph (Figure 5.6).

x	0	0.2	0.4	0.6	0.8	1	2
y	1	0.96	0.85	0.70	0.53	0.37	0.018

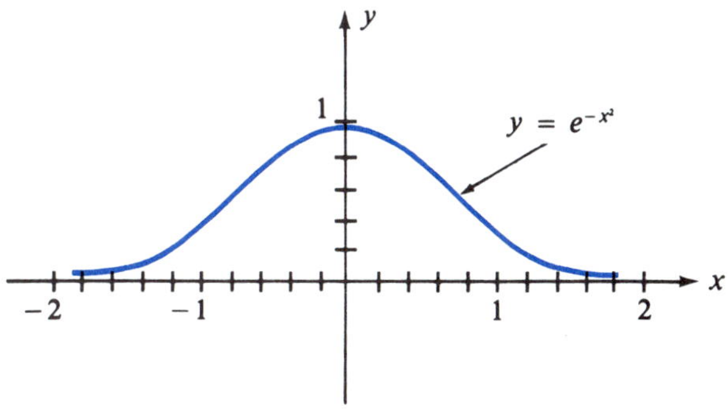

Figure 5.6

5.2 EXERCISES

In problems 1 through 5, sketch the graphs of the given sets of functions on the same set of axes.

1. $y = 2^x, y = 3^x$ and $y = 4^x$

2. $y = \left(\frac{1}{2}\right)^x, y = \left(\frac{1}{3}\right)^x$ and $y = \left(\frac{1}{4}\right)^x$

3. $y = 2^{-x}, y = 3^{-x}$ and $y = 4^{-x}$ (Compare with problem 1.)

4. $y = 4^{0.5x}$ and $y = 4^{-0.5x}$

5. $y = 4^{0.5x}, y = 4^x$ and $y = 4^{2x}$

In problems 6 through 11, sketch the graphs of the given sets of functions on the same set of axes (use Table I in Appendix II).

6. $y = e^x, y = 2e^x$ and $y = 3e^x$

7. $y = e^{0.5x}, y = e^x$ and $y = e^{1.5x}$

8. $y = e^{-0.5x}, y = e^{-x}$ and $y = e^{-1.5x}$

9. $y = 0.5e^{-x}, y = e^{-x}$ and $y = 2e^{-x}$

10. $y = 0.5e^{-x2}, y = e^{-x2}$ and $y = 2e^{-x2}$

11. $y = e^{-x2/2}, y = e^{-x2}$ and $y = e^{-2x2}$

5.3

Laws of Logarithms and the Logarithmic Function

logarithm

In certain instances (see Example 5.19 in Section 5.4) one wishes to solve an equation $b^y = x (b > 0, b \neq 1)$ for y in terms of x. The number y is called the *logarithm* of x to the base b, abbreviated, $y = \log_b x$ and is the exponent to which the base b must be raised to obtain the number x. In short, $y = \log_b x$ if and only if $x = b^y$.

EXAMPLE 5.12

(a) $\log_{10} 100 = 2$ since $10^2 = 100$

(b) $\log_5 125 = 3$ since $5^3 = 125$

(c) $\log_3 \frac{1}{27} = -3$ since $3^{-3} = \frac{1}{3^3} = \frac{1}{27}$

(d) $\log_{20} 20 = 1$ since $20^1 = 20$ ■

EXAMPLE 5.13

Solve for x in each of the following equations:

(a) $\log_3 x = 4$

(b) $\log_{16} 4 = x$

(c) $\log_x 8 = 3$

SOLUTION

(a) By definition, $\log_3 x = 4$ implies $x = 3^4 = 81$.

(b) $\log_{16} 4 = x$ is equivalent to $4 = 16^x = (4^2)^x = 4^{2x}$ from which we easily deduce that $x = 1/2$.

(c) Referring once again to the definition, we see that the equation $\log_x 8 = 3$ is equivalent to the equation $8 = x^3$ and so $x = 2$. ■

common and natural logarithms

The two widely used systems of logarithms are the system of *common logarithms*, which uses the number 10 as the base, and the system of *natural logarithms*, which uses the irrational number $e = 2.71828\ldots$ as the base. Extensive logarithmic tables have been computed using each of these bases. Tables II and III in Appendix II are quite adequate for the computations encountered in this text. Also, it is the standard practice to write *log* for $\log_{10}$ and *ln* for $\log_e$. The system of natural logarithms is widely used in theoretical work. Using natural logarithms often leads to simpler expressions than using logarithms to other bases.

As in the case of computations involving exponents, computations involving logarithms are facilitated by the following laws of logarithms. Their derivations are based on the definition of the logarithm and the corresponding laws of exponents: If m and n are positive numbers, then

$$(1) \quad \log_b mn = \log_b m + \log_b n$$

$$(2) \quad \log_b \frac{m}{n} = \log_b m - \log_b n$$

$$(3) \quad \log_b m^n = n \log_b m$$

(4) $\log_b 1 = 0$

(5) $\log_b b = 1$

Proofs of the above laws are sketched in Exercise set 5.3. The following examples illustrate the properties of logarithms.

EXAMPLE 5.14

(a) $\log 2 \cdot 3 = \log 2 + \log 3$

(b) $\ln \frac{5}{3} = \ln 5 - \ln 3$

(c) $\log \sqrt{7} = \log 7^{1/2} = \frac{1}{2} \log 7$

(d) $\log_5 1 = 0$

(e) $\log_{45} 45 = 1$ ■

EXAMPLE 5.15 Given that $\log 2 \approx 0.3010$, $\log 3 \approx 0.4771$ and $\log 5 \approx 0.6990$, evaluate

(a) $\log 15$

(b) $\log 7.5$

(c) $\log 81$

(d) $\log 50$

SOLUTION **(a)** We note that $15 = 3 \cdot 5$ so that by Rule 1 for logarithms,

$$\begin{aligned} \log 15 &= \log 3 \cdot 5 \\ &= \log 3 + \log 5 \\ &\approx 0.4771 + 0.6990 \\ &= 1.1761 \end{aligned}$$

(b) We first observe that $7.5 = 15/2 = (3 \cdot 5)/2$ and apply Rules 1 and 2 of logarithms, obtaining

$$\begin{aligned} \log 7.5 &= \log \frac{(3)(5)}{2} \\ &= \log 3 + \log 5 - \log 2 \\ &\approx 0.4771 + 0.6990 - 0.3010 \\ &= 0.8751 \end{aligned}$$

(c) Since $81 = 3^4$, we apply Rule 3 of logarithms to obtain

$$\begin{aligned} \log 81 &= \log 3^4 \\ &= 4 \log 3 \\ &\approx 4(0.4771) \\ &= 1.9084 \end{aligned}$$

(**d**) We write $50 = 5 \cdot 10$ and find

$$\begin{aligned} \log 50 &= \log (5)(10) \\ &= \log 5 + \log 10 \\ &\approx 0.6990 + 1 \qquad \text{(using Rule 5)} \\ &= 1.6990 \end{aligned}$$

EXAMPLE 5.16 Solve each of the following equations for x:

(**a**) $\log_4 16 = x$

(**b**) $\log_2 (5x^2 - x - 2) - 2 \log_2 x = 2$

(**c**) $10^{3x} = 125$

SOLUTION (**a**) By the definition of the logarithm, we see that the equation

$$\log_4 16 = x$$

is equivalent to the equation

$$16 = 4^x$$

which may be written as

$$4^x = 4^2$$

or

$$4^{x-2} = 1$$

The last equation is true if and only if

$$x - 2 = 0$$

or

$$x = 2$$

(**b**) We have the following chain of equivalent statements:

$$\begin{aligned} \log_2 (5x^2 - x - 2) - 2 \log_2 x &= 2 \\ \log_2 (5x^2 - x - 2) - \log_2 x^2 &= 2 \\ \log_2 \frac{5x^2 - x - 2}{x^2} &= 2 \\ \frac{5x^2 - x - 2}{x^2} &= 2^2 = 4 \\ 5x^2 - x - 2 &= 4x^2 \\ x^2 - x - 2 &= 0 \\ (x-2)(x+1) &= 0 \end{aligned}$$

or

$$x = -1, 2$$

Since the domain of the logarithmic function must be restricted to the set of positive numbers, we reject the value $x=-1$ and conclude that the required solution to the given equation is $x=2$.

(c) Here, we find

$$\begin{aligned} 10^{3x} &= 125 \\ \log 10^{3x} &= \log 125 \\ \log 10^{3x} &= \log 5^3 \\ 3x \log 10 &= 3 \log 5 \\ 3x &= 3 \log 5 \qquad (\text{since } \log 10 = 1) \\ x &= \log 5 \\ x &\approx 0.6990 \end{aligned}$$

■

EXAMPLE 5.17 Solve the equation $e^{0.08k}=9$ for k.

SOLUTION We have

$$\begin{aligned} \ln e^{0.08k} &= \ln 9 \\ 0.08k &= \ln 9 \\ k &= \frac{\ln 9}{0.08} \\ &\approx \frac{2.1972}{0.08} \\ &= 27.465 \end{aligned}$$

■

logarithmic function

Since the expression $\log_b a$ is a real number whenever $b>0$, $b\neq 1$, we may define a function $y=\log_b x$ with domain given by the set of all *positive* real numbers. This function is referred to as a *logarithmic function*. In particular, the natural logarithmic function is defined to be the logarithmic function to the base e and is normally written $y=\ln x$.

One easy way to obtain the graph of the logarithmic function $y=\log_b x$ is to consult a table of values of the logarithm (base b). However, another method—and a more instructive one—is based on exploiting the intimate relationship between the logarithmic and exponential function. To this end, let us observe that if a point (u, v) lies on the graph of the function $y=\log_b x$, then $v=\log_b u$. But, by definition, the last equation is equivalent to $u=b^v$ so that the point (v, u) is seen to lie on the graph of the function $y=b^x$. We now make the further observation that the two points (u, v) and (v, u) are mirror reflections of each other with respect to the line $y=x$ (see Figure 5.7). Thus, the graph of the function $y=\log_b x$ may be obtained by first drawing the graph of $y=b^x$ and then constructing its mirror reflection with respect to the line $y=x$. Using this technique it is easy to see the general shape of the graph of $y=\log_b x$ for the cases $0<b<1$ and $b>1$ (see Figure 5.8).

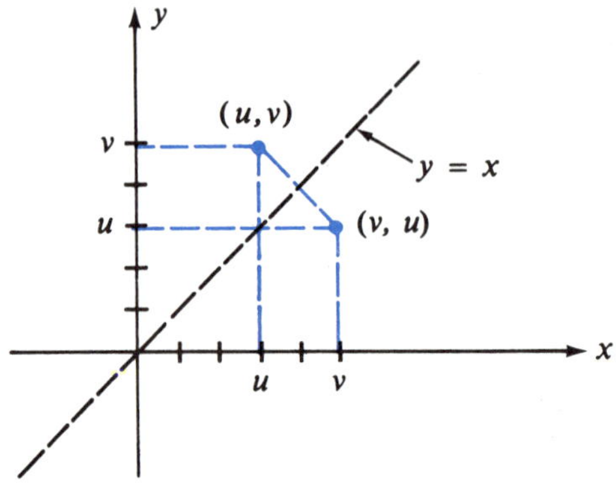

Figure 5.7

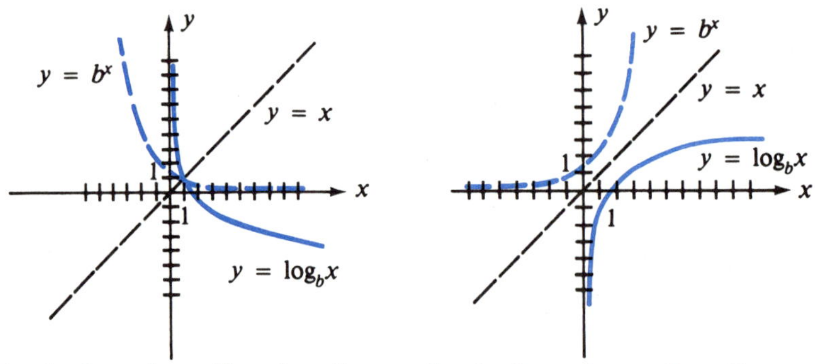

Figure 5.8 Graph of $y = \log_b x$ $(0 < b < 1)$ Graph of $y = \log_b x$ $(b > 1)$

EXAMPLE 5.18 Sketch the graph of the function $y = \ln x$.

SOLUTION We first sketch the graph of $y = e^x$. Then the required graph is obtained by tracing the mirror reflection of the graph of $y = e^x$ with respect to the line $y = x$ (see Figure 5.9).

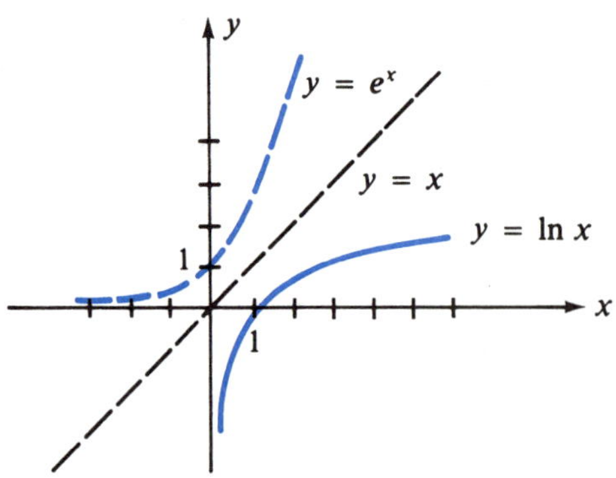

Figure 5.9 ■

5.3 EXERCISES

In problems 1 through 5, express the given equation in logarithmic form.

1. (*a*) $2^6 = 64$ (*b*) $7^0 = 1$

2. (*a*) $3^5 = 243$ (*b*) $3^{-2} = \frac{1}{9}$

3. (*a*) $5^{-3} = \frac{1}{125}$ (*b*) $\left(\frac{1}{3}\right)^1 = \frac{1}{3}$

4. (*a*) $32^{3/5} = 8$ (*b*) $\left(\frac{1}{2}\right)^{-4} = 16$

5. (*a*) $b^{2a} = c$ (*b*) $10^{-3} = 0.001$

In problems 6 through 12, solve the given equation for x.

6. (*a*) $\log_3 x = 3$ (*b*) $\log_{49} 7 = x$

7. (*a*) $\log_4 \frac{1}{256} = x$ (*b*) $\log_8 4 = x$

8. (*a*) $\ln x = -1$ (*b*) $\log_{10} (10)^x = 10$

9. (*a*) $\ln e^x = 3$ (*b*) $\log_x 4 = \frac{2}{3}$

10. (*a*) $\log_3 (243)^4 = x$ (*b*) $\ln (2x) + \ln 3 = \ln 24$

11. (*a*) $\log_2 (4x + 9) = 4$ (*b*) $\log_{10} (3)^{x-1} = 0$

12. (*a*) $\log_8 x^2 = 2$ (*b*) $\log_3 (x^2 + 11) = 3$

13. Given that $\log_b x = 4$ and $\log_b y = 5$, find:

(*a*) $\log_b (xy)$ (*b*) $\log_b \left(\frac{x}{y}\right)$ (*c*) $\log_b \sqrt{x}$

14. Given that $\ln x = -3$, $\ln y = 2$ and $\ln z = 4$, find:

(*a*) $\ln (xyz)$ (*b*) $\ln \left(\frac{yz}{x}\right)$ (*c*) $\ln \left(\frac{x^2 y^3}{yz}\right)^{1/2}$

15. Given that $\log 3 = 0.4771$ and $\log 4 = 0.6021$, find:

(*a*) $\log 12$ (*b*) $\log \frac{3}{4}$ (*c*) $\log 16$

(*d*) $\log \sqrt{3}$ (*e*) $\log 48$ (*f*) $\log \frac{1}{300}$

In problems 16 through 22, use logarithms to solve the given equation for t.

16. $e^{0.4t} = 8$ **17.** $\frac{1}{3} e^{-3t} = 0.9$

18. $4e^{t-1} = 4$

19. $28 - 4e^{5t} = 14$

20. $36 - 3e^{-0.4t} = 9$

21. $A = Be^{-t/2}$

22. $\dfrac{A}{1 + Be^{t/2}} = C$

In problems 23 through 26, sketch the graph of the given equation.

23. $y = \log_3 x$

24. $y = \log_{1/3} x$

25. $y = \ln 2x$

26. $y = \ln \frac{1}{2}x$

In problems 27 and 28 sketch the graph of the two given equations on the same coordinate axes.

27. $y = 2^x$ and $y = \log_2 x$

28. $y = e^{3x}$ and $y = \ln 3x$

29. On the Richter scale, the magnitude R of an earthquake is given by the formula

$$R = \log \frac{I}{I_0}$$

where I is the intensity of the earthquake being measured and I_0 is the standard reference intensity.

(*a*) Express the intensity I of an earthquake of magnitude $R = 5$ in terms of the standard intensity I_0.

(*b*) Express the intensity I of an earthquake of magnitude $R = 8$ in terms of the standard intensity I_0. How many times greater is the intensity of an earthquake of magnitude 8 than the intensity of an earthquake of magnitude 5?

(*c*) In modern times, the greatest loss of life attributable to an earthquake occurred in eastern China in 1976. Known as the Tangshan earthquake, it registered 8.2 on the Richter scale. How does the intensity of this earthquake compare with the intensity of an earthquake of magnitude $R = 5$?

30. The relative loudness of a sound D of intensity I is measured in decibels where

$$D = 10 \log \frac{I}{I_0}$$

and I_0 is the standard threshold of audibility.

(*a*) Express the intensity I of a 30-decibel sound (the sound level of normal conversation) in terms of I_0.

(*b*) Determine how many times greater the intensity of an 80-decibel sound (rock music) is than that of a 30-decibel sound.

(*c*) Prolonged noise above 150 decibels will cause immediate permanent deafness. How does the intensity of a 150-decibel sound compare with the intensity of an 80-decibel sound?

31. (***a***) Given that $2^x = e^{kx}$, find k.

(***b***) Show that, in general, if b is a nonnegative real number, then any exponential function of the form $y = b^x$ may be written in the form $y = e^{kx}$, for some real number k.

32. Use the definition of logarithms to prove

(***a***) $\log_b mn = \log_b m + \log_b n$

(***b***) $\log_b \dfrac{m}{n} = \log_b m - \log_b n$

Hint: Let $\log_b m = p$ and $\log_b n = q$. Then $b^p = m$ and $b^q = n$.

33. Use the definition of logarithms to prove

$$\log_b m^n = n \log_b m$$

34. Use the definition of logarithms to prove:

(***a***) $\log_b 1 = 0$

(***b***) $\log_b b = 1$

5.4 Exponential Functions as Mathematical Models

In Section 5.2 we saw that the exponential function $f(x) = b^x$ is an increasing function when $b > 1$; in particular, the function $f(x) = e^x$ shares this property. From this result and also the results of problems 6 and 7 (Exercise set 5.2) one may deduce that the function $Q(t) = Q_0 e^{kt}$, where Q_0 and k are positive constants, has the following properties:

(i) $Q(0) = Q_0$

(ii) $Q(t)$ increases "rapidly" without bound as t increases without bound (Figure 5.10).

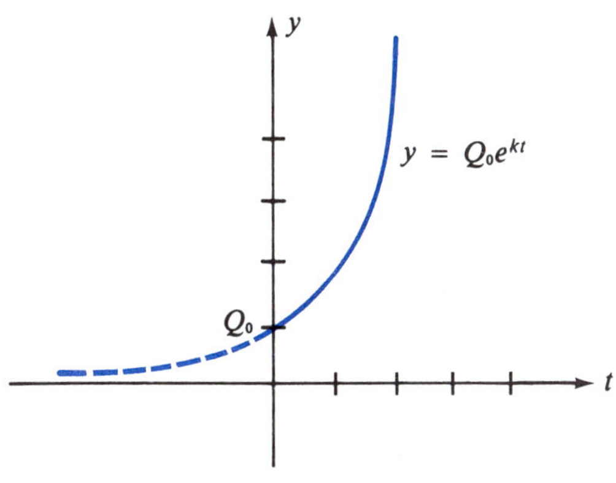

Figure 5.10

Another important property of the exponential function $Q(t) = Q_0 e^{kt}$, which will be demonstrated in Chapter 10 (Example 10.51), is that the rate of increase of $Q(t)$ is directly proportional to $Q(t)$, itself. Thus, the exponential function $Q(t) = Q_0 e^{kt} (t \in [0, \infty))$ provides us with a mathematical model of a quantity $Q(t)$ which is initially present in the amount of $Q(0) = Q_0$ and whose rate of growth at any time t is directly proportional to the amount of the quantity present at time t. Such a quantity is said to exhibit *exponential growth* and the constant k is called the *growth constant*. Interest earned on a fixed deposit when compounded continuously experiences exponential growth (see Section 10.2). Other examples of exponential growth are found in the following examples.

exponential growth

growth constant

EXAMPLE 5.19 Under ideal laboratory conditions, the number of bacteria in a culture grows in accordance with the law $Q(t) = Q_0 e^{kt}$ where Q_0 denotes the number of bacteria initially present in the culture, k is some constant that is determined by the strain of bacteria under consideration, and t is the elapsed time measured in hours. Suppose there are 10,000 bacteria present initially in the culture and 60,000 present 2 hours later. How many bacteria will there be in the culture at the end of 4 hours?

SOLUTION We are given that $Q(0) = Q_0 = 10{,}000$, so that $Q(t) = 10{,}000\, e^{kt}$. Next, the condition that 60,000 bacteria are present 2 hours later translates into $Q(2) = 60{,}000$, or,

$$60{,}000 = 10{,}000\, e^{2k}$$
$$e^{2k} = 6$$

or

$$e^k = (e^{2k})^{1/2} = 6^{1/2}$$

Thus, the number of bacteria present at any time t is given by

$$\begin{aligned} Q(t) &= 10{,}000\, e^{kt} = 10{,}000\, (e^k)^t \\ &= 10{,}000(6^{t/2}) \end{aligned}$$

In particular, the number of bacteria present in the culture at the end of 4 hours is given by

$$\begin{aligned} Q(4) &= 10{,}000(6^{4/2}) \\ &= 360{,}000 \end{aligned}$$

Note that to solve the problem it was not necessary to determine the value of the growth constant, k, specifically. However, if so desired, it could be determined. In fact, from the equation

$$e^{2k} = 6$$

we find that

$$\begin{aligned} \ln e^{2k} &= \ln 6 \\ 2k \ln e &= \ln 6 \\ 2k &= \ln 6 \qquad \text{(since } \ln e = 1\text{)} \\ k &= \frac{1}{2} \ln 6 \\ &\approx 0.8959 \end{aligned}$$

■

exponential decay In contrast to exponential growth, a quantity exhibits *exponential decay* if it decreases at a rate that is directly proportional to its size. Such a quantity may be described by the exponential function $Q(t) = Q_0 e^{-kt} (t \in [0, \infty))$, where the positive constant Q_0 measures the amount present initially $(t = 0)$ and k is some suitable positive number, called the *decay constant*. Its choice is determined by the nature of the substance under consideration. The graph of this function is sketched in Figure 5.11.

decay constant

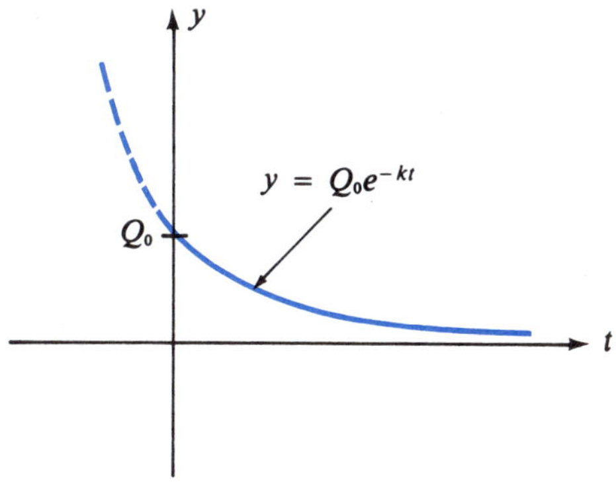

Figure 5.11

EXAMPLE 5.20 Radioactive substances decay exponentially. For example, the amount of radium at any time t obeys the law $Q(t) = Q_0 e^{-kt}$ where Q_0 is the initial amount present and k is a suitable positive constant. The *half-life* of a radioactive substance is the time required for a given amount to be reduced to half that amount. Now, it is known that the half-life of radium is approximately 1600 years. Suppose that initially there are 200 milligrams of pure radium. Find the amount left after t years. What is the amount left after 800 years?

SOLUTION The initial amount of radium present is 200 milligrams, so that $Q(0) = Q_0 = 200$. Thus $Q(t) = 200\, e^{-kt}$. Next, the datum concerning the half-life of radium implies that $Q(1600) = 100$ and this gives

$$100 = 200\, e^{-1600k}$$

$$e^{-1600k} = \frac{1}{2}$$

or

$$e^{-k} = (e^{-1600k})^{1/1600} = \left(\frac{1}{2}\right)^{1/1600}$$

Thus, the amount of radium left after t years is given by

$$\begin{aligned} Q(t) &= 200\, e^{-kt} \\ &= 200\,(e^{-k})^t \\ &= 200\left(\frac{1}{2}\right)^{t/1600} \\ &= 200 \cdot 2^{-(t/1600)} \end{aligned}$$

The amount of radium left after 800 years is given by

$$\begin{aligned} Q(800) &= 200 \cdot 2^{-(800/1600)} \\ &= 200 \cdot 2^{-1/2} \\ &= \frac{200}{\sqrt{2}} \\ &\approx 141 \end{aligned}$$

or 141 milligrams. ■

EXAMPLE 5.21 The radioactive element polonium decays according to the law $Q(t) = Q_0 \cdot 2^{-(t/140)}$, where Q_0 is the initial amount and the time t is measured in days. If the amount of polonium left after 280 days is 20 milligrams, what was the initial amount present?

SOLUTION We have $Q(280) = 20$ so that

$$Q_0 \cdot 2^{-280/140} = 20$$

$$Q_0\left(\frac{1}{4}\right) = 20$$

or

$$Q_0 = 80$$

Thus, the amount of polonium present initially was 80 milligrams. ■

EXAMPLE 5.22 Carbon 14, a radioactive isotope of carbon, has a half-life of 5770 years. What is its decay constant?

SOLUTION We have $Q(t) = Q_0 e^{-kt}$. Since the half-life of the element is 5770 years, half of the substance is left at the end of that period. Therefore,

$$Q(5770) = Q_0 e^{-5770k} = \frac{1}{2} Q_0$$

so that

$$e^{-5770k} = \frac{1}{2}$$

$$-5770k = \ln \frac{1}{2}$$

and

$$k = \frac{\ln 1/2}{-5770}$$

$$\approx 0.00012$$

■

Carbon 14-dating, used by anthropologists, is a well-known method used to establish the age of animal and plant fossils. This method assumes that the proportion of carbon 14 present in the atmosphere has remained constant over the past 50,000 years. Professor Willard Libby, a recipient of a Nobel prize in Chemistry in 1960, proposed this theory.

The amount of C-14 in the tissues of a living plant or animal is constant. However, when an organism dies it stops absorbing new quantities of C-14 and the amount of C-14 in the remains diminishes because of the natural decay of the radioactive substance. Thus, the approximate age of a plant or animal fossil can be determined by measuring the amount of C-14 present in the remains.

EXAMPLE 5.23 A skull recovered from an archeological site has one-tenth the amount of C-14 it originally contained. Determine the approximate age of the skull.

SOLUTION Here

$$Q(t) = Q_0 e^{-kt} = Q_0 e^{-0.00012t}$$

where Q_0 is the amount of C-14 present originally and k, the decay constant, is equal to 0.00012 (see Example 5.22). Putting $Q(t) = (1/10)Q_0$, we have

$$\frac{1}{10}Q_0 = Q_0 e^{-0.00012t}$$

$$\ln\frac{1}{10} = -0.00012t$$

$$t = \frac{\ln 1/10}{-0.00012} \approx 19{,}200$$

or approximately 19,200 years. ■

The next example shows how the exponential function may be applied to describe certain types of learning processes. Consider the function $Q(x) = C - Ae^{-kx}$, where C, A, and k are positive constants. To sketch the graph of the function Q, observe that its y-intercept is given by $Q(0) = C - A$. Also, $Q(x)$ decreases without bound as x decreases without bound, and $Q(x)$ increases and approaches the number C as x increases without bound. The latter follows because, as x increases without bound, Ae^{-kx} decreases and approaches zero. The graph of the function Q is shown in Figure 5.12, where that part of the graph corresponding

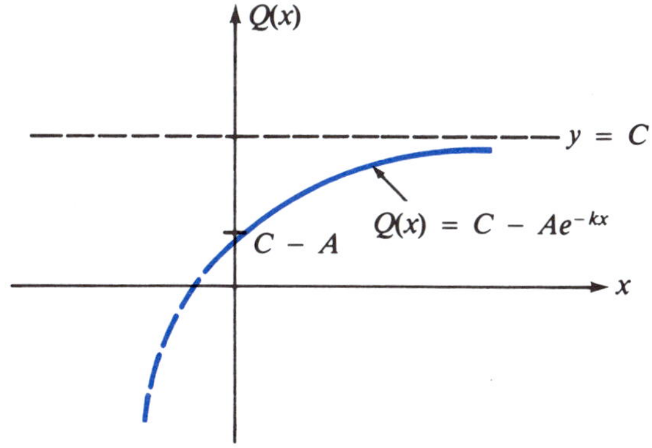

Figure 5.12

to negative values of x is drawn with a dotted line since in practice one normally restricts the domain of the function to the interval $[0, \infty)$.

Observe that $Q(x)$ $(x \geq 0)$ increases rather rapidly initially but the rate of increase slows down considerably after a while. This behavior of the graph of the function Q closely resembles the learning pattern experienced by workers engaged in highly repetitive work. For example, the productivity of an assembly line worker increases very rapidly in the early stages of the training period. The productivity increase is a direct result of the training received and the accumulated experience. But the rate of increase of productivity slows down as time goes by and the worker's productivity level approaches some fixed level imposed by the limitations placed on worker and machine. Because of this characteristic, the graph of the function $Q(x) = C - A e^{-kx}$ is often called a learning curve.

EXAMPLE 5.24 The Camera Division of the Eastman Optical Company produces a 35-mm single lens reflex camera. The company training department determined that a new, previously inexperienced employee, after completing the basic training program, will be able to assemble $Q(t) = 50 - 30 e^{-0.5t}$ Model F cameras per day, t months after he or she starts work on the assembly line.

(a) How many Model F Cameras can a new employee assemble per day after basic training?

(b) How many Model F cameras can an employee with 1 month of experience, 2 months of experience, and 6 months of experience assemble per day?

(c) How many Model F cameras can the average experienced employee assemble per day?

SOLUTION **(a)** The number of Model F cameras a new employee can assemble is given by

$$Q(0) = 50 - 30 = 20$$

(b) The number of Model F cameras that an employee with 1 month of experience, 2 months of experience, and 6 months of experience can assemble per day is given by

$$\begin{aligned} Q(1) &= 50 - 30 e^{-0.5} \approx 31.80 \\ Q(2) &= 50 - 30 e^{-1} \approx 38.96 \\ Q(6) &= 50 - 30 e^{-3} \approx 48.51 \end{aligned}$$

or approximately 32, 39, and 49, respectively.

(c) As t increases without bound, $Q(t)$ approaches 50. Hence, the average experienced employee may ultimately be expected to assemble 50 Model F cameras per day. ■

Other applications of the learning curve are found in models that describe the dissemination of information about a product or the velocity of an object dropped into a viscous medium.

logistic function

Our last example in applying exponential functions to the description of natural phenomena involves the *logistic* (also called the *S-shaped* or *sigmoidal*) *curve*, which is the graph of the function

$$Q(t)=\frac{A}{1+Be^{-kt}}$$

where A, B and k are positive constants. To sketch the graph of the function Q, observe that its y-intercept is given by $Q(0)=A/(1+B)$ and that $Q(t)$ approaches the number A as t increases without bound. The latter follows because, as t increases without bound, Be^{-kt} decreases and approaches zero. The graph of the function Q is shown in Figure 5.13. The part of the graph corresponding to negative values of t is drawn with a dotted line since in applications one normally restricts the domain of the function Q to the interval $[0, \infty)$.

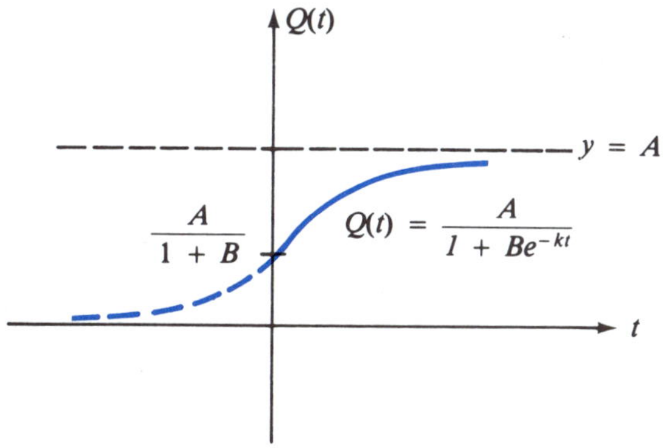

Figure 5.13

Observe that $Q(t)$ increases rather rapidly for small values of t. In fact, for small values of t, the logistic curve resembles an exponential growth curve. However, the rate of growth of $Q(t)$ decreases quite rapidly as t increases. In summary, the logistic curve exhibits both the property of rapidity in growth of the exponential growth curve as well as the "saturation" property of the learning curve. Because of these characteristics the logistic curve serves as a suitable mathematical model for describing many natural phenomena. For example, if a handful of rabbits were introduced to a tiny island in the South Pacific, the rabbit population might be expected to grow very rapidly at first but the growth rate would decrease quickly as overcrowding, scarcity of food, and other environmental factors affected growth. The population would eventually stabilize at a level compatible with the life-support capacity of the environment. Models describing the spread of rumors and epidemics are other examples of the application of the logistic curve (see Example 5.25).

EXAMPLE 5.25 During a flu epidemic, the number of men at Fort MacArthur who contracted influenza after t days is approximated by the exponential model

$$Q(t)=\frac{5000}{1+4999e^{-kt}}$$

If 100 men contracted the flu by the tenth day, find the number of men who contracted the flu by the fifteenth day.

SOLUTION The given information implies that

$$Q(10) = 100$$

Thus,

$$Q(10) = \frac{5000}{1 + 4999\,e^{-10k}} = 100$$

or

$$100(1 + 4999\,e^{-10k}) = 5000$$

$$1 + 4999\,e^{-10k} = \frac{5000}{100} = 50$$

$$e^{-10k} = \frac{49}{4999}$$

$$-10k = \ln \frac{49}{4999}$$

and

$$k = -\frac{\ln(49/4999)}{10} \approx 0.4625$$

Therefore the number of men who contracted the flu after t days is given by

$$Q(t) = \frac{5000}{1 + 4999\,e^{-0.4625t}}$$

In particular, the number of men who contracted the flu by the fifteenth day is given by

$$Q(15) = \frac{5000}{1 + 4999\,e^{-15(0.4625)}}$$

$$\approx 854$$

or approximately 854 men. ■

5.4 EXERCISES

1. Given that a quantity $Q(t)$ is described by the exponential growth function $Q(t) = 400\,e^{0.05t}$, where t is measured in minutes, answer the following questions.

(***a***) What is the growth constant?

(***b***) What quantity is present initially?

(*c*) Using Table I in Appendix II, or a pocket calculator complete the following table of values.

t	0	10	20	100	1000
Q					

(*d*) Determine the length of time required for the quantity Q to double.

2. Given that a quantity $Q(t)$ exhibiting exponential decay is described by the function $Q(t) = 2000\,e^{-0.06t}$, where t is measured in years, answer the following questions.

(*a*) What is the decay constant?

(*b*) What quantity is present initially?

(*c*) Using Table I in Appendix II, or a pocket calculator, complete the following table of values.

t	0	5	10	20	100
Q					

(*d*) Determine the length of time required for a quantity $Q(t)$ to be reduced to half of its value?

3. The growth rate of the bacterium *Escherichia coli*, a common bacterium which is found in the human intestine, is proportional to its size. Under ideal laboratory conditions, when this bacterium is grown in a nutrient broth medium, the number of cells in a culture of this bacterium doubles approximately every twenty minutes. Given that the initial cell population is 100, determine the function $Q(t)$ that expresses the exponential growth of the number of cells of this bacterium as a function of time t (in minutes). How long will it take for a colony of 100 cells to increase to a population of one million? If we were given that the initial cell population was 1000, how would this alter our model?

4. The world population at the beginning of 1980 was 4.5 billion. Assuming that the population continues to grow at its present rate of approximately 2% per year

(*a*) Find the function $Q(t)$ that expresses the world population (in billions) as a function of time t (in years).

(*b*) Using this function complete the following table of values.

Year	1980	1985	1990	1995	2000	2005	2010	2015
World population								

(*c*) Sketch the graph of this function.

5. Refer to problem 4. If the world population continues to grow at its present rate of approximately 2% per year

(*a*) Find the length of time t_0 that would be required for the world population to triple in size.

(*b*) Using the time t_0 found in part (a), what would be the size of the world population if the growth rate were to be reduced to 1.8%?

6. The distribution of income in a certain city can be described by the exponential model $y = (2.8 \cdot 10^{11})(x)^{-1.5}$, where y is the number of families with incomes of x dollars or more.

(*a*) How many families in this city have incomes of \$20,000 or more?

(*b*) How many families in this city have incomes of \$40,000 or more?

(*c*) How many families in this city have incomes of \$100,000 or more?

7. A certain piece of machinery was purchased three years ago by the Garland Mills Company at a cost of \$500,000. Its present resale value is \$320,000. Assuming that the resale value of the machine decreases exponentially, what will be the resale value of the machine four years from now?

8. If the temperature is constant, then the atmospheric pressure P (in pounds per square inch) varies with the altitude above sea level h, in accordance with the law

$$P = p_0 e^{-kh}$$

where p_0 is the atmospheric pressure at sea level and k is a constant. If the atmospheric pressure is 15 pounds per square inch at sea level, and 12.5 pounds per square inch at 4000 feet, find the atmospheric pressure at an altitude of 12,000 feet.

9. Phosphorus-32 has a half-life of 14.2 days. If 100 grams of this substance are present initially, find the amount present after t days. What amount will be left after 7.1 days?

10. Strontium 90, a radioactive isotope of strontium, is present in the fallout resulting from nuclear explosions. It is especially hazardous to animal life (including humans), because upon ingestion of contaminated food it is absorbed into the bone structure. Its half-life is 27 years. If the amount of strontium-90 in a certain area is found to be four times the "safe" level, find the length of time that must elapse before an "acceptable level" will be reached.

11. Wood deposits recovered from an archeological site contain 20% of the carbon-14 they originally contained. How long ago did the tree from which the wood was obtained die?

12. Skeletal remains of the so-called "Pittsburgh Man" unearthed in Pennsylvania lost 82% of the carbon-14 they originally contained. Determine the approximate age of these bones.

13. The American Stenographic Institute finds that the average student taking Advanced Shorthand, an intensive 20-week course, will make progress according to the function

$$Q(t)=120(1-e^{-0.05t})+60$$

where $Q(t)$ measures the number of words (per minute) of dictation that the student can take in shorthand after t weeks in the course. Graph the function for $0 \le t \le 20$ and answer the following questions.

(***a***) What is the beginning shorthand speed for the average student in this course?

(***b***) What shorthand speed does the average student attain half way through the course?

(***c***) How many words per minute can the average student take after completion of this course?

14. The Metro Department Store found that t weeks after the end of a sales promotion the volume of sales was given by a function of the form

$$S(t)=B+A\,e^{-kt} \qquad (0 \le t \le 4)$$

where $B=50{,}000$ and is equal to the average weekly volume of sales before the promotion. The volume of sales at the end of the first week and third week were \$83,515 and \$65,055, respectively. Assume that the sales volume is decreasing exponentially and find

(***a***) the decay constant k.

(***b***) the sales volume at the end of the fourth week.

15. The Universal Instruments Company found that the monthly demand for its new line of Galaxy Home Computers, t months ($t \ge 0$) after placing the line on the market is given by

$$D(t)=2000-1500\,e^{-0.05t}$$

Graph this function and answer the following questions.

(***a***) What is the demand after 1 month? 1 year? 2 years? 5 years?

(***b***) At what level is the demand expected to stabilize?

16. Newton's law of cooling states that the rate at which the temperature of an object changes is proportional to the difference in temperature between the object and that of the surrounding medium. Thus, the temperature $F(t)$ of an object that is greater than that of its surrounding medium is given by

$$F(t)=T+A\,e^{-kt}$$

where t is the time expressed in minutes, T is the temperature of the surrounding medium and A and k are constants. Suppose that a cup of instant coffee is prepared with boiling water (212°F) and left to cool on the counter in a room where the temperature is 72°F. Taking $k = 0.1865$, determine when the coffee will be cool enough (say, 110°F) to drink.

17. During a flu epidemic, the number of children in the Woodbridge Community School System who contracted influenza after t days was given by

$$Q(t) = \frac{1000}{1 + 999\, e^{-0.8t}}$$

(***a***) How many children were stricken by the flu after the first day?

(***b***) How many children had the flu after ten days?

(***c***) How many children eventually contracted the disease?

18. On the basis of data collected during an experiment, a biologist found that the growth of the fruit fly (*Drosophila*) with a limited food supply could be approximated by the exponential model

$$N(t) = \frac{1000}{1 + 24\, e^{-0.02t}}$$

where t denotes the number of days since the beginning of the experiment.

(***a***) What was the initial population of fruit flies in the experiment?

(***b***) What was the maximum population of fruit flies that could be expected under this laboratory condition?

(***c***) What was the population of the colony of fruit flies on the twentieth day?

19. Three hundred students attended the dedication ceremony of a new building on a college campus. The president of the traditionally female college announced a new expansion program, which included plans to make the college a coeducational institution. The number of students who learned of the new program t hours later is given by the function

$$f(t) = \frac{3000}{1 + B\, e^{-kt}}$$

If 600 of the students on campus had heard about the new program two hours after the ceremony, how many students had heard about the policy after four hours?

5 Chapter Review

EXERCISES

1. Perform the indicated operations and simplify.

(***a***) $\dfrac{16^3 - 32^2}{4^6 + 8^5}$ (***b***) $\dfrac{(3^{\sqrt{8}})^{\sqrt{2}}}{(27^{\sqrt{3}})^{\sqrt{3}}}$ (***c***) $\dfrac{(3 \cdot 2^{-3})(4 \cdot 3^5)}{2 \cdot 9^3}$

2. Simplify the given expression

(*a*) $\left(\dfrac{3xy^2}{4x^3y}\right)^{-2}\left(\dfrac{3xy^3}{2x^2}\right)^3$ (*b*) $\sqrt[3]{81x^5y^{10}}\,\sqrt[3]{9xy^2}$ (*c*) $\left(\dfrac{-x^{1/2}y^{2/3}}{x^{1/3}y^{3/4}}\right)^6$

3. Solve the given equation for x.

(*a*) $2^x = 8^{x-2}$ (*b*) $4\,e^x = 16\,e^{x-1}\cdot 8\,e^{1+3x}$

4. Sketch the graphs of the exponential functions defined by the following equations on the same coordinate axes.

(*a*) $y = 2^{-x}$ (*b*) $y = \left(\dfrac{1}{2}\right)^x$

5. Express each equation in logarithmic form:

(*a*) $\left(\dfrac{2}{3}\right)^{-3} = \dfrac{27}{8}$ (*b*) $16^{-1/4} = 0.125$

6. Solve for x in each of the following equations.

(*a*) $\log_4(2x+1) = 2$ (*b*) $\ln(x-1) + \ln 4 = \ln(2x+4) - \ln 2$

7. Given that $\ln 2 = x$, $\ln 3 = y$ and $\ln 5 = z$, find the value of each of the following in terms of x, y and z.

(*a*) $\ln 30$ (*b*) $\ln 3.6$ (*c*) $\ln 75$

8. Solve the given equation for x.

(*a*) $e^{0.03k+1} = 8$ (*b*) $e^{2x} - e^{4x} = -2$

9. A culture of bacteria that initially contained 2000 bacteria has a count of 18,000 bacteria after 2 hours.

(*a*) Determine the function $Q(t)$ that expresses the exponential growth of the number of cells of this bacterium as a function of time (t) in minutes.

(*b*) Find the number of bacteria present after 4 hours.

10. The radioactive element radium has a half-life of 1600 years. What is its decay constant?

11. The V.C.A. Television Company found that the monthly demand for its new line of video-disc players, t months ($t \geq 0$) after placing it on the market is given by

$$D(t) = 4000 - 3000\,e^{-0.06t}$$

Graph this function and answer the following questions.

(*a*) What was the demand after 1 month? 1 year? 2 years?

(*b*) At what level is the demand expected to stabilize?

12. During a flu epidemic, it was found that the number of students at a certain university who contracted influenza after t days could be approximated by the exponential model

$$Q(t) = \frac{3000}{1 + 2999\, e^{-kt}}$$

If 50 students contracted the flu by the tenth day, find the number of students who contracted the flu by the twentieth day.

6

MATHEMATICS OF FINANCE

6.1 Arithmetic and Geometric Progressions

arithmetic progression An *arithmetic progression* is a sequence of numbers in which each term after the first is obtained by adding a constant d to the preceding term. The constant d is called the *common difference*. *common difference* For example, the sequence

$$3, 6, 9, 12, \ldots,$$

is an arithmetic progression with the common difference equal to 3.

Observe that an arithmetic progression is completely determined if the first term and the common difference are known. In fact, if

$$a_1, a_2, a_3, \ldots, a_n, \ldots$$

is an arithmetic progression with the first term given by a and common difference given by d, then by definition,

$$\begin{aligned}
a_1 &= a \\
a_2 &= a_1 + d = a + d \\
a_3 &= a_2 + d = (a + d) + d = a + 2d \\
a_4 &= a_3 + d = (a + 2d) + d = a + 3d \\
&\vdots \\
a_n &= a_{n-1} + d = a + (n-2)d + d = a + (n-1)d
\end{aligned}$$

From the above, we see that the nth term of an arithmetic progression with first term a and common difference d is given by

(6.1) $$a_n = a + (n-1)d$$

EXAMPLE 6.1 Find the twelfth term of the arithmetic progression

$$2, 7, 12, 17, 22, \ldots$$

SOLUTION The first term of the arithmetic progression is $a_1 = a = 2$, the common difference is $d = 5$ so that, upon setting $n = 12$ in Equation (6.1), we find

$$a_{12} = 2 + (12-1)5 = 57$$ ■

EXAMPLE 6.2 Write the first five terms of an arithmetic progression whose 3rd and 11th terms are 21 and 85, respectively.

SOLUTION Using Equation (6.1) we obtain

$$a_3 = a + 2d = 21$$
$$a_{11} = a + 10d = 85$$

Subtracting the first equation from the second gives $8d = 64$ or $d = 8$. Substituting this value of d into the first equation yields $a + 16 = 21$ or $a = 5$. Thus, the required arithmetic progression is given by the sequence

$$5, 13, 21, 29, 37, \ldots,$$ ■

Let S_n denote the sum of the first n terms of an arithmetic progression with first term $a_1 = a$ and common difference d. Then

(6.2) $$S_n = a + (a+d) + (a+2d) + \cdots + [a + (n-1)d]$$

Rewriting the expression for S_n with the terms in reverse order gives

(6.3) $$S_n = [a + (n-1)d] + [a + (n-2)d] + \cdots + (a+d) + a$$

Adding (6.2) and (6.3), we obtain

$$\begin{aligned} 2S_n &= [2a + (n-1)d] + [2a + (n-1)d] + \cdots + [2a + (n-1)d] \\ &= n[2a + (n-1)d] \end{aligned}$$

(6.4) or $$S_n = \frac{n}{2}[2a + (n-1)d]$$

EXAMPLE 6.3 Find the sum of the first twenty terms of the arithmetic progression of Example 6.1.

SOLUTION Putting $a = 2$, $d = 5$, and $n = 20$ in Equation (6.4), we obtain

$$\begin{aligned} S_{20} &= \frac{20}{2}[2 \cdot 2 + 19 \cdot 5] \\ &= 990 \end{aligned}$$

■

EXAMPLE 6.4 The Madison Electric Company had sales of \$200,000 in its first year of operation. If the sales increased by \$30,000 per year thereafter, find the sales of the company in the fifth year and its total sales over the first five years of operation.

SOLUTION The yearly sales of the company follow an arithmetic progression with the first term given by $a = 200{,}000$ and the common difference given by $d = 30{,}000$. The sales in the fifth year are found by using (6.1) with $n = 5$. Thus

$$\begin{aligned} a_5 &= 200{,}000 + (5-1)30{,}000 \\ &= 320{,}000 \end{aligned}$$

or \$320,000.

The total sales of the company over the first five years of operation are found by using (6.4) with $n = 5$. Thus,

$$\begin{aligned} S_5 &= \frac{5}{2}[2(200{,}000) + (5-1)30{,}000] \\ &= 1{,}300{,}000 \end{aligned}$$

or \$1,300,000. ■

geometric progression

common ratio

A *geometric progression* is a sequence of numbers in which each term after the first is obtained by multiplying the preceding term by a constant r. The constant r is called the *common ratio*.

A geometric progression is completely determined if the first term and the common ratio are known. Thus, if

$$a_1, a_2, a_3, \ldots, a_n, \ldots$$

is a geometric progression with the first term given by a and common ratio given by r, then by definition,

$$\begin{aligned} a_1 &= a \\ a_2 &= a_1 r = ar \\ a_3 &= a_2 r = ar^2 \\ a_4 &= a_3 r = ar^3 \\ &\vdots \\ a_n &= a_{n-1} r = ar^{n-1} \end{aligned}$$

From the above, we see that the nth term of a geometric progression with first term a and common ratio r is given by

(6.5) $$a_n = ar^{n-1}$$

EXAMPLE 6.5 Find the eighth term of a geometric progression whose first five terms are 162, 54, 18, 6, 2.

SOLUTION The common ratio is found by taking the ratio of any term other than the first to the preceding term. Taking the ratio of the fourth term to the third term, for example, gives $r = 6/18 = 1/3$. To find the eighth term of the geometric progression, use (6.5) with $a = 162$, $r = 1/3$, and $n = 8$ obtaining

$$a_8 = 162\left(\frac{1}{3}\right)^7$$

$$= \frac{2}{27}$$

■

EXAMPLE 6.6 Find the tenth term of a geometric progression whose third term is 16 and whose seventh term is 1.

SOLUTION Using (6.5) with $n = 3$ and $n = 7$, respectively, yields

$$a_3 = ar^2 = 16$$

and

$$a_7 = ar^6 = 1$$

Dividing a_7 by a_3 gives

$$\frac{ar^6}{ar^2} = \frac{1}{16}$$

from which we obtain $r^4 = 1/16$ or $r = 1/2$. Substituting this value of r into the expression for a_3, we obtain

$$a\left(\frac{1}{2}\right)^2 = 16 \text{ or } a = 64$$

Finally, using (6.5) once again with $a = 64$, $r = 1/2$ and $n = 10$ gives

$$a_{10} = 64\left(\frac{1}{2}\right)^9 = \frac{1}{8}$$

■

To find the sum of the first n terms of a geometric progression with the first term $a_1 = a$ and common ratio r, denote the required sum by S_n. Then

(6.6) $$S_n = a + ar + ar^2 + \cdots + ar^{n-2} + ar^{n-1}$$

Upon multiplying (6.6) by r, we obtain

(6.7) $$rS_n = ar + ar^2 + ar^3 + \cdots + ar^{n-1} + ar^n$$

Subtracting (6.7) from (6.6) gives

$$S_n - rS_n = a - ar^n$$

or

$$(1-r)S_n = a(1-r^n)$$

If $r \neq 1$ we may divide both sides of the last equation by $(1-r)$ obtaining

$$S_n = \frac{a(1-r^n)}{(1-r)}$$

If $r = 1$, then (6.6) gives

$$\begin{aligned} S_n &= a + a + a + \cdots + a \qquad (n \text{ terms}) \\ &= na \end{aligned}$$

Thus,

(6.8) $$S_n = \begin{cases} \dfrac{a(1-r^n)}{1-r} & \text{if } r \neq 1 \\ na & \text{if } r = 1 \end{cases}$$

EXAMPLE 6.7 Find the sum of the first six terms of the geometric series

$$3, 6, 12, 24, \ldots$$

SOLUTION Here $a = 3$ and $r = 6/3 = 2$, so that (6.8) gives

$$S_6 = \frac{3(1-2^6)}{1-2} = 189$$

■

EXAMPLE 6.8 The Michaelson Land Development Company had sales of \$1,000,000 in its first year of operation. If the sales increased by 10% per year thereafter, find the sales of the company in the fifth year and its total sales over the first five years of operation.

SOLUTION The yearly sales of the company follow a geometric progression with the first term given by $a = 1{,}000{,}000$ and the common ratio given by $r = 1.1$. The sales in the fifth year are found by using (6.5) with $n = 5$. Thus,

$$\begin{aligned} a_5 &= 1{,}000{,}000\,(1.1)^4 \\ &= 1{,}464{,}100 \end{aligned}$$

or \$1,464,100.

The total sales of the company over the first five years of operation are found by using (6.8) with $n = 5$. Thus,

$$S_5 = \frac{1{,}000{,}000[1-(1.1)^5]}{1-1.1} = 6{,}105{,}100$$

or \$6,105,100.

6.1 EXERCISES

In problems 1 through 4, find the nth *term of the arithmetic progression which has the given values of* a, d, *and* n.

1. $a = 6$, $d = 3$, $n = 9$

2. $a = -5$, $d = 3$, $n = 7$

3. $a = -15$, $d = 3/2$, $n = 8$

4. $a = 1.2$, $d = 0.4$, $n = 98$

5. Find the first five terms of the arithmetic progression whose 4th term and 11th term are 30 and 107, respectively.

6. Find the first five terms of the arithmetic progression whose 7th term and 23rd term are −5 and −29, respectively.

7. Find the seventh term of the arithmetic progression: $x, x+y, x+2y, \ldots$.

8. Find the eleventh term of the arithmetic progression: $a+b, 2a, 3a-b, \ldots$.

9. Find the sum of the first fifteen terms of the arithmetic progression: 4, 11, 18, ...

10. Find the sum of the first twenty terms of the arithmetic progression: 5, −1, −7, ...

11. Find the sum of all the odd integers between 14 and 58.

12. Find the sum of the even integers between 21 and 99.

13. Find $f(1)+f(2)+f(3)+\cdots+f(20)$, given that $f(x) = 3x - 4$.

14. Find $g(1)+g(2)+g(3)+\cdots+g(50)$, given that $g(x) = 12 - 4x$.

15. Show that Equation (6.4) can be written as $S_n = \frac{n}{2}(a + a_n)$ where a_n represents the last term of an arithmetic progression. Use this formula to find:

(*a*) the sum of the first eleven terms of the arithmetic progression whose first term and last term are 3 and 47, respectively.

(*b*) the sum of the first twenty terms of the arithmetic progression whose first term and last term are 5 and −33, respectively.

16. The Moderne Furniture Company had sales of \$150,000 during its first year of operation. If the sales increased by \$16,000 per year, thereafter, find the sales of the company in the fifth year and its total sales over the first five years of operation.

17. As part of her physical-fitness program, Karen has taken up jogging. If she jogs 1 mile the first day and increases her daily run by 1/2 mile every 4 days, how long will it take her to reach her goal of 10 miles per day?

18. A 100-foot well is to be drilled. The cost of drilling the first foot is \$6.00 and the cost of drilling each additional foot is \$2.50 more than that of the preceding foot. Find the cost of drilling the entire 100 feet.

19. A tourist wishes to go from the airport to his hotel which is 25 miles away. The taxi rate is \$1.00 for the first mile and \$.60 for each additional mile. The airport limousine also goes to his hotel and charges a flat rate of \$7.50. How much money will the tourist save by taking the airport limousine?

20. A recent college graduate received two job offers. Company A offered him an initial salary of \$16,800 with guaranteed annual increases of \$1250 per year for the first five years. Company B offered an initial salary of \$18,000 with guaranteed annual increases of \$900 per year for the first five years.

(***a***) Which company is offering the graduate a higher salary for the fifth year of employment?

(***b***) Which company is offering the graduate more money for the first five years of employment?

21. One of the methods that the Internal Revenue Service allows for computing depreciation of certain business property is the sum-of-the-years-digits method. If a property valued at C dollars has an estimated useful life of N years and a salvage value of S dollars, then the amount of depreciation D_n allowed during the nth year is given by:

$$D_n = (C - S)\frac{N-(n-1)}{S_N} \qquad (0 \le n \le N)$$

where S_N is the sum of the first N positive integers representing the estimated useful life of the property. Thus, $S_N = 1 + 2 + \cdots + N = \dfrac{N(N+1)}{2}$.

(***a***) Verify that the sum of the arithmetic progression $S_n = 1 + 2 + \cdots + N$ is given by

$$\frac{N(N+1)}{2}.$$

(***b***) If office furniture worth \$6000 is to be depreciated by this method over $N = 10$ years, and the salvage value of the furniture is \$500, find the depreciation for the third year by computing D_3.

22. Referring to Example 2.12 in Section 2.2, the amount of depreciation allowed for a printing machine, which has an estimated useful life of 5 years and an initial value of \$100,000 (with no salvage value) was \$20,000 per year using the straight-line method of depreciation. Determine the amount of depreciation that would be allowed for the first year if the printing machine were depreciated using the sum-of-the-years-digits method described in problem 21. Which method would result in a larger depreciation of the asset in its first year of usage?

In problems 23 through 28, determine which of the given sequences are geometric progressions. For each geometric progression, find the seventh term and the sum of the first seven terms.

23. $4, 8, 16, 32, \ldots$

24. $1, -1/2, 1/4, -1/8, \ldots$

25. $1/2, -3/8, 1/4, -9/64, \ldots$

26. $0.004, 0.04, 0.4, 4, \ldots$

27. $243, 81, 27, 9, \ldots$

28. $-1, 1, 3, 5, \ldots$

29. Find the twentieth term and sum of the first twenty terms of the geoı. progression: $-3, 3, -3, 3, \ldots$.

30. Find the twenty-third term in a geometric progression having the fiı term $a = 0.1$ and ratio $r = 2$.

31. It has been projected that the population of a certain city in the Southwest will increase by 8% during each of the next five years. If the current population is 200,000, what is the expected population in five years?

32. The Metro Cable T.V. Company had sales of $2,500,000 in its first year of operation. If the sales increased by 12% of the previous year, thereafter, find the sales of the company in the fifth year and the total sales over the first five years of operation.

33. Suppose that the cost-of-living index had increased by 9% during each of the past six years and that a member of the E.U.W. Union had been guaranteed an annual increase equal to 2% above the cost-of-living index over that period. What would the present salary of a union member be whose salary was $18,000 six years ago?

34. The parents of a 9-year-old boy have agreed to deposit $10 in their son's bank account on his tenth birthday and to double the size of their deposit every year, thereafter, until his 18th birthday.

(***a***) How much will they have to deposit on his 18th birthday?

(***b***) How much will they have deposited by his 18th birthday?

35. Suppose that an employee of the Stenton Printing Company whose current annual salary is $18,000 has an option of taking an annual raise of 8% per year for the next 4 years or a fixed annual raise of $1500 per year. Which option would be more profitable to him considering his total earnings over the 4-year period?

36. A culture of a certain bacteria is known to double in number every 3 hours. If the culture has an initial count of 20, what will the population of the culture be at the end of 24 hours?

37. Ms. Simpson is the recipient of a trust fund which she will receive over a period of 6 years. Under the terms of the trust, she is to receive $10,000 the first year and each succeeding annual payment is to be increased by 15%.

(***a***) How much will she receive during the sixth year?

(***b***) What is the total amount of the 6 payments that she will receive?

6.2

Compound Interest and Compound Depreciation

compound interest

We discussed simple interest in Section 2.2. Recall that in calculating simple interest, the amount of interest is computed on the original principal. Frequently, however, the interest earned is periodically added to the principal and thereafter earns interest itself at the same rate of interest. This is called *compound interest.*

If the original principal is P dollars and if the interest is compounded annually at the rate of r per year, then at the end of the first year the new principal or accumulated value is given by

$$A_1 = P + Pr = P(1+r)$$

The interest earned in the second year is computed on A_1 so that at the end of the second year, the accumulated amount is

$$A_2 = A_1(1+r) = P(1+r)^2$$

and at the end of the third year, the accumulated amount is

$$A_3 = A_2(1+r) = P(1+r)^3$$

Letting A_0 denote the original principal P, we see that the terms A_0, A_1, A_2, $A_3, \ldots,$ form a geometric progression with first term A_0 and common ratio $(1+r)$. It follows, therefore, that the accumulated amount at the end of the nth year (n, a positive integer) is given by

(6.9) $$A_n = A_0(1+r)^n = P(1+r)^n$$

EXAMPLE 6.9 An amount of \$1000 is deposited in a bank that pays 8% per year interest, compounded annually. What is the total amount on deposit at the end of 3 years, assuming no deposits or withdrawals were made during those 3 years? What is the interest earned in that period of time?

SOLUTION Using Equation (6.9) with $P = 1000$, $r = 0.08$, and $n = 3$ we have

$$\begin{aligned} A_3 &= 1000\,(1.08)^3 \\ &= 1259.71 \end{aligned}$$

or \$1259.71. The interest earned over the three-year period is given by

$$1259.71 - 1000 = 259.71$$

or \$259.71. Compare the results with Example 2.7. ■

Using a similar argument to the one used earlier, we can easily derive a formula for the case where interest is compounded more than once a year. To this end, suppose interest at the rate of r per year (called the *stated rate* or *nominal rate*) is compounded m times a year on a principal of P dollars. The interval of time between successive interest calculations is called the *conversion period* and the (simple) interest rate per conversion period is given by $i = r/m$ per period. Therefore, the accumulated amount at the end of the first period is given by

nominal rate

conversion period

$$A_1 = P + Pi = P(1+i)$$

At the end of the second period, the accumulated amount is

$$A_2 = A_1(1+i) = P(1+i)^2$$

at the end of the third period, the accumulated amount is

$$A_3 = A_2(1+i) = P(1+i)^3$$

and, at the end of the nth period, the accumulated amount is

$$A_n = A_{n-1}(1+i) = P(1+i)^n$$

compound interest formula

Thus, we are led to the *compound interest formula*:

If P dollars are invested at a nominal interest rate of r per year, compounded m times a year, then at the end of n conversion periods the accumulated amount is given by

(6.10) $$A_n = P(1+i)^n$$

where $i = r/m$. Normally, the life of a loan is stated in terms of years (say, t years), in which case the number of conversion periods n is given by $n = tm$.

EXAMPLE 6.10 Find the accumulated amount after 3 years if \$1000 is invested at 8% per year compounded (**a**) annually, (**b**) semiannually, (**c**) quarterly, and (**d**) monthly.

SOLUTION (**a**) Here $P = 1000$, $r = 0.08$, and $m = 1$. Thus, $i = r = 0.08$ and $n = 3$ so that (6.10) gives

$$A_3 = 1000\,(1.08)^3$$
$$= 1259.71$$

or \$1259.71*.

* The value for $(1.08)^3$ may be obtained by using a pocket calculator or from Table IV in Appendix II, which gives values of $(1+i)^n$ for selected values of i and n. However, slight differences may occur between the values obtained with a calculator and those found in the table due to the difference in the significant number of digits used.

(b) Here $P = 1000$, $r = 0.08$, and $m = 2$. Thus $i = 0.08/2 = 0.04$ and $n = (3)(2) = 6$ so that (6.10) gives

$$A_6 = 1000\,(1.04)^6 = 1265.32$$

or \$1265.32.

(c) In this case, $P = 1000$, $r = 0.08$, and $m = 4$. Thus $i = 0.08/4 = 0.02$ and $n = (3)(4) = 12$ so that (6.10) gives

$$A_{12} = 1000\,(1.02)^{12} = 1268.24$$

or \$1268.24.

(d) Here $P = 1000$, $r = 0.08$, and $m = 12$. Thus, $i = 0.08/12 = 0.0067$ and $n = (3)(12) = 36$ so that (6.10) gives

$$A_{36} = 1000\,(1.0067)^{36} = 1271.75$$

or \$1271.75. These results are summarized in Table 6.1.

Table 6.1

Nominal rate (r)	Conversion period	Interest rate/ Conversion period	Initial investment	Accumulated amount
8%	Annual ($m = 1$)	8%	\$1000	\$1259.71
8%	Semiannual ($m = 2$)	4%	\$1000	\$1265.32
8%	Quarterly ($m = 4$)	2%	\$1000	\$1268.24
8%	Monthly ($m = 12$)	2/3%	\$1000	\$1271.75

■

effective rate

In the last example, we saw that the interest actually earned on the investment depended on the frequency with which the interest was compounded. Thus, the stated or nominal rate of 8% per year did not reflect the actual rate at which interest was earned. Now, the *effective rate* (also called the *true rate* and the *annual percentage rate*) is the rate, which when compounded annually yields the same accumulated amount as the nominal rate compounded m times a year.

To derive a relationship between the nominal interest rate r per year, compounded m times a year, and its corresponding effective rate R per year, let us suppose that a principal of P dollars is invested for t years and earns interest at the stated rate. Then by definition, the accumulated amount obtained by compounding the interest annually at the effective rate R should be the same as the accumulated amount obtained by compounding the interest m times a year. Thus,

$$P(1+R)^t = P\left(1+\frac{r}{m}\right)^{tm}$$

Dividing both sides of the equation by P and taking the tth root of both sides of the resulting equation yields

$$1+R=\left(1+\frac{r}{m}\right)^m$$

(6.11) or

$$R=\left(1+\frac{r}{m}\right)^m-1 \tag{6.11}$$

EXAMPLE 6.11 Find the effective rate of interest corresponding to a nominal rate of 8% per year compounded (**a**) annually, (**b**) semiannually, (**c**) quarterly, and (**d**) monthly.

SOLUTION (**a**) The effective rate of interest corresponding to a nominal rate of 8% per year compounded annually, is, of course, given by 8% per year. This result is also confirmed by using (6.11) with $r=0.08$ and $m=1$.

Thus,

$$R=(1+0.08)-1=0.08$$

so that the effective rate required is 8% per year.

(**b**) Put $r=0.08$ and $m=2$. Then (6.11) yields

$$\begin{aligned}R&=\left(1+\frac{0.08}{2}\right)^2-1\\&=(1.04)^2-1\\&=0.0816\end{aligned}$$

so that the required effective rate is 8.16% per year.

(**c**) Put $r=0.08$ and $m=4$. Then (6.11) yields

$$\begin{aligned}R&=\left(1+\frac{0.08}{4}\right)^4-1\\&=(1.02)^4-1\\&=0.08243\end{aligned}$$

so that the corresponding effective rate in this case is 8.243% per year.

(**d**) Put $r=0.08$ and $m=12$. Then (6.11) yields

$$\begin{aligned}R&=\left(1+\frac{0.08}{12}\right)^{12}-1\\&=(1.0067)^{12}-1\\&=0.08343\end{aligned}$$

so that the corresponding effective rate in this case is 8.343% per year. ■

Now, if the effective rate of interest R is known, the accumulated amount after n years on an investment of P dollars may be more readily computed by using the formula

$$A_n = (1+R)^n$$

The Truth in Lending Act passed by Congress in 1968 requires that the effective rate of interest be disclosed in all contracts involving interest charges. The passage of this act has benefited the consumer since he or she now has a common basis for comparing the various nominal rates quoted by different financial institutions. Furthermore, the knowledge of the effective rate enables the consumer to compute the actual charges involved in a transaction. Thus, if the effective rates of interest found in the last example were known, the accumulated values of Example 6.10 shown in Table 6.2, could have been readily found.

Nominal rate	Frequency of interest payment	Effective rate	Initial investment	Accumulated amount after 3 years
8%	Annually	8%	\$1000	$1000(1+0.08)^3 = \$1259.71$
8%	Semiannually	8.16%	\$1000	$1000(1+0.0816)^3 = \$1265.32$
8%	Quarterly	8.243%	\$1000	$1000(1+0.08243)^3 = \$1268.23$
8%	Monthly	8.343%	\$1000	$1000(1+0.08343)^3 = \$1271.75$

Table 6.2

Let us return to Equation (6.10) which expresses the accumulated amount at the end of n periods when interest at the rate of r is compounded m times a year. The principal P in (6.10) is often referred to as the *present value* while the accumulated value A_n is called the *future value* since it is realized at a future date. In certain instances, an investor may wish to determine the amount of money that should be invested now, at a fixed rate of interest, so that a certain sum will be realized at some future date. This problem may be solved by expressing P in terms of A_n. Thus, from (6.10) we find

present and future value

$$P = A_n(1+i)^{-n} \tag{6.12}$$

Here, as before, $i = r/m$ where m is the number of conversion periods per year.

EXAMPLE 6.12 Find the sum of money to be deposited in a bank paying interest at the rate of 6% per year compounded monthly, so that at the end of 3 years the accumulated amount will be \$20,000.

SOLUTION Here, $r = 0.06$ and $m = 12$ so that $i = 0.06/12 = 0.005$ and $n = (3)(12) = 36$. Thus, the problem is to determine P given that $A_{36} = 20{,}000$. Using (6.12), we obtain

$$P = 20{,}000\,(1.005)^{-36}$$
$$= 16{,}713$$

or \$16,713. ■

EXAMPLE 6.13 Find the present value of \$49,158.60 due in 5 years at an interest rate of 10% per year compounded quarterly.

SOLUTION Using (6.12) with $r=0.1$ and $m=4$, so that $i=0.1/4=0.025$, $n=(4)(5)=20$, and $A_{20}=49{,}158.6$, we obtain

$$\begin{aligned} P &= (49{,}158.6)(1.025)^{-20} \\ &= 30{,}000 \end{aligned}$$

or \$30,000. ■

double-declining balance method

In Section 2.2 we discussed the straight line method of depreciating an asset. Linear depreciation assumes that the asset depreciates at a constant rate. For certain assets such as machines whose market values drop rapidly in the early years of usage and thereafter less rapidly, another method of depreciation called the *double-declining balance method* is often used. In practice, a business firm normally employs the double-declining balance method for depreciating such assets for a certain number of years and then switches over to the linear method.

To derive an expression for the book value of an asset being depreciated by the double-declining balance method, let C (in dollars) denote the original cost of the asset and suppose it is to be depreciated over N years. Using this method the amount depreciated each year is $2/N$ times the value of the asset at the beginning of that year. Thus, the amount by which the asset is depreciated in its first year of use is given by $2C/N$, so that if $V(1)$ denotes the book value of the asset at the end of the first year, then

$$V(1) = C - \frac{2C}{N} = C\left(1 - \frac{2}{N}\right)$$

Next, if $V(2)$ denotes the book value of the asset at the end of the second year, then a similar argument leads to

$$\begin{aligned} V(2) &= C\left(1-\frac{2}{N}\right) - C\left(1-\frac{2}{N}\right)\frac{2}{N} \\ &= C\left(1-\frac{2}{N}\right)\left(1-\frac{2}{N}\right) \\ &= C\left(1-\frac{2}{N}\right)^2 \end{aligned}$$

Continuing, we find that if $V(n)$ denotes the book value of the asset at the end of n years, then the terms C, $V(1)$, $V(2), \ldots, V(n)$ form a geometric progression with first term C and common ratio $(1-2/N)$. Consequently the nth term $V(n)$ is given by

(6.13) $$V(n) = C\left(1-\frac{2}{N}\right)^n \qquad (1 \le n \le N)$$

Also, if $D(n)$ denotes the amount by which the asset has been depreciated by the end of the nth year, then

(6.14) $$D(n)=C\left[1-\left(1-\frac{2}{N}\right)^n\right]$$

EXAMPLE 6.14 A tractor purchased at a cost of \$60,000 is to be depreciated by the double-declining balance method over 10 years. What is the book value of the tractor at the end of 5 years? By what amount has the tractor been depreciated by the end of the 5th year?

SOLUTION We have $C=60{,}000$ and $N=10$. Thus, using (6.13) with $n=5$ gives the book value of the tractor at the end of 5 years as

$$\begin{aligned} V(5) &= 60{,}000\left(1-\frac{2}{10}\right)^5 \\ &= 60{,}000\left(\frac{4}{5}\right)^5 \\ &= 19{,}660.8 \end{aligned}$$

or \$19,660.80.

The amount by which the tractor has been depreciated by the end of the 5th year is given by

$$60{,}000-19{,}660.8=40{,}339.2$$

or \$40,339.20. You may verify the last result by using (6.14) directly. ■

6.2 EXERCISES

In problems 1 through 10, find the accumulated amount A, *if the principal* P *is invested at the interest rate of* r *per year for* n *years.*

1. $P=\$1000$, $r=7\%$, $n=8$, compounded annually
2. $P=\$1000$, $r=8\frac{1}{2}\%$, $n=6$, compounded annually
3. $P=\$2500$, $r=7\%$, $n=10$, compounded semiannually
4. $P=\$2500$, $r=9\%$, $n=10.5$, compounded semiannually
5. $P=\$12{,}000$, $r=8\%$, $n=10.5$, compounded quarterly
6. $P=\$42{,}000$, $r=7\frac{3}{4}\%$, $n=8$, compounded quarterly
7. $P=\$150{,}000$, $r=14\%$, $n=4$, compounded monthly
8. $P=\$180{,}000$, $r=9\%$, $n=6\frac{1}{4}$, compounded monthly
9. $P=\$150{,}000$, $r=12\%$, $n=3$, compounded daily

10. $P = \$200{,}000$, $r = 8\%$, $n = 4$, compounded daily

In problems 11 through 14, find the effective rate corresponding to the given nominal rate.

11. 10% compounded semiannually

12. 9% compounded quarterly

13. 8% compounded monthly

14. 8% compounded daily

In problems 15–17, find the present value of $40,000 due in 4 years at the given rate of interest.

15. 8% compounded semiannually

16. 8% compounded quarterly

17. 7% compounded monthly

In problems 18 through 20 find the book value of office equipment purchased at a cost C *at the end of the* nth *year if it is to be depreciated by the double-declining balance method over 10 years.*

18. $C = \$20{,}000$, $n = 4$

19. $C = \$150{,}000$, $n = 8$

20. $C = \$80{,}000$, $n = 7$

21. An amount of $25,000 is deposited in a bank that pays interest at the rate of 7% per year, compounded annually. What is the total amount on deposit at the end of 6 years, assuming there are no deposits or withdrawals during those 6 years? What is the interest earned in that period of time?

22. If the cost of a semi-private room in a hospital was $120 per day 5 years ago and hospital costs have risen at the rate of 12% per year since that time, what rate would you expect to pay for a semi-private room today?

23. Today a typical family of four has a $400 monthly expenditure for food. If inflation occurs at the rate of 9% per year over the next 6 years, how much should the typical family of four expect to spend for food 6 years from now?

24. The Brennans are planning to buy a house 4 years from now. Housing experts in their area have estimated that the cost of a home will increase at a rate of 11% per year during that period. If this economic prediction holds true, how much can they expect to pay for a house that currently costs $80,000?

25. A utility company in a metropolitan area in the western region of the U.S. expects the consumption of electricity to increase by 8% per year during the next decade, due mainly to the expected increase in population. If consumption does increase at this rate, find the amount by which the utility company will have to increase its generating capacity to meet the needs of the area at the end of the decade.

26. Find the accumulated amount after 10 years if \$10,000 is invested at 9% per year compounded (*a*) annually. (*b*) semiannually. (*c*) quarterly. (*d*) monthly.

27. The managers of a pension fund have invested \$1.5 million in U.S. government certificates of deposit that pay interest at the rate of 9.5% per year compounded semiannually over a period of 10 years. At the end of this period, how much will the investment be worth?

28. A young man is the beneficiary of a trust fund established for him 21 years ago at his birth. If the original amount placed in trust was \$10,000, how much will he receive if the money has earned interest at the rate of (*a*) 8% compounded annually? (*b*) 8% compounded quarterly? (*c*) 8% compounded monthly?

29. At what annual rate of interest compounded quarterly should an individual invest his money, if he wishes to double his investment within 6 years?

30. What rate of interest compounded quarterly is needed to triple an investment in 10 years?

31. Find the sum of money to be deposited in a bank paying interest at the rate of 8.5% per year compounded quarterly so that at the end of 5 years the accumulated amount will be \$40,000.

32. Find the present value of \$80,000 due in 4 years at an interest rate of 9% per year compounded semiannually.

33. An individual purchased a 4-year \$10,000 promissory note with an interest rate of 8.5% compounded semiannually. How much did he purchase the note for?

34. The parents of a child have just come into a large inheritance and they wish to establish a trust fund for the child's college education. If they estimate that they will need \$60,000 in 13 years, how much should they set aside in trust now, if they can invest the money at $8\frac{1}{2}$% (*a*) compounded annually? (*b*) compounded semi-annually? (*c*) compounded quarterly?

35. Mr. Kaplan invested a sum of money 5 years ago in a savings account, which since that time has paid interest at the rate of 8% compounded quarterly. His investment is now worth \$22,289.22. How much did he originally invest?

36. The proprietors of The Coachmen Inn secured two loans from the Union Bank; one for \$8000 due in 3 years and one for \$15,000 due in 6 years, both at an interest rate of 10% compounded semiannually. The bank has agreed to allow the two loans to be consolidated into one loan payable in 5 years at the same interest rate. What amount will the proprietors be required to pay the bank at the end of 5 years?

37. Find the effective rate of interest corresponding to a nominal rate of 9% per year compounded (*a*) annually. (*b*) semiannually. (*c*) quarterly. (*d*) monthly.

38. Restaurant equipment purchased at a cost of \$150,000 is to be depreciated by the double-declining balance method over 10 years. What is the book value of the equipment at the end of 6 years? By what amount has the equipment been depreciated at the end of the sixth year?

39. Refer to problem 22 in Exercise set 6.1. Recall that a printing machine, which had an estimated useful life of 5 years and an initial value of \$100,000 (with no salvage value) was to be depreciated. At the end of the first year using the straight-line method of depreciation, the amount of depreciation allowed was \$20,000 and when the sum-of-the-digits method was used the depreciation allowed was \$33,333. Determine the amount of depreciation that would be allowed for the first year if the printing machine were depreciated by the double-declining balance method. Which of these three methods would result in the largest depreciation of the asset at the end of its first year of usage?

6.3 Annuities

term of an annuity

An *annuity* is a sequence of payments made at regular time intervals. The time period in which these payments are made is called the *term* of the annuity. Depending upon whether the term is given by a fixed time interval, a time interval that begins at a definite date but extends indefinitely, or one that is not fixed in advance, an annuity is called an *annuity certain*, a *perpetuity*, or a *contingent annuity*, respectively. In general, the payments in an annuity need not be equal but in many important applications they are equal. We shall assume that annuity payments are equal in this section. Examples of annuities are regular deposits to a savings account, monthly home mortgage payments, and monthly insurance payments.

ordinary annuity

Annuities are also classified by payment dates. An annuity in which the payments are made at the end of each payment period is called an *ordinary annuity*, whereas an annuity in which the payments are made at the beginning of each period is called an *annuity due*. Furthermore, an annuity in which the payment period coincides with the interest conversion period is called a *simple annuity*, whereas an annuity in which the payment period differs from the interest conversion period is called a *complex annuity*.

simple and complex annuities

In this section we shall consider ordinary annuities, which are certain and simple. In other words, we shall study annuities that are subject to the following conditions:

1. The terms are given by fixed time intervals.
2. The periodic payments are equal in size.
3. The payments are made at the end of the payment periods.
4. The payment periods coincide with the interest conversion periods.

To find the amount A of an annuity (ordinary, certain and simple), let

P = size of each payment in the annuity

r = interest rate compounded m times per year

i = interest rate per period = r/m

n = number of payment periods

The first payment of P dollars made at the end of the first period earns compound interest at the rate of i over the remaining $(n-1)$ periods and therefore has an accumulated amount of $P(1+i)^{n-1}$ dollars at the end of the term of the annuity (see Figure 6.1). The second payment of P dollars made at the end of the second period earns compound interest at the rate of i over the remaining $(n-2)$ periods and has an accumulated amount of $P(1+i)^{n-2}$ dollars at the end of the term, and so on. The last payment earns no interest since it is due at the end of the term. The amount of the annuity is obtained by adding all the terms in Figure 6.1. Thus,

$$S = P + P(1+i) + P(1+i)^2 + \cdots + P(1+i)^{n-1}$$

The sum on the right is easily seen to be the sum of the first n terms of a geometric progression with first term P and common ratio $(1+i)$ so that we have, by virtue of Formula (6.8),

$$S = \frac{P[1-(1+i)^n]}{1-(1+i)}$$

(6.15) $$= P\left[\frac{(1+i)^n - 1}{i}\right]$$

compound amount factor

The expression inside the brackets is commonly denoted by $s_{\overline{n}|i}$ (read "s angle n at i") and is called the *compound-amount factor.* Extensive tables have been constructed which give values of $s_{\overline{n}|i}$ for different values of i and n (such as Table IV, in Appendix II). In terms of the compound-amount factor,

(6.16) $$S = Ps_{\overline{n}|i}$$

In what follows all annuities are assumed to be ordinary, certain, and simple.

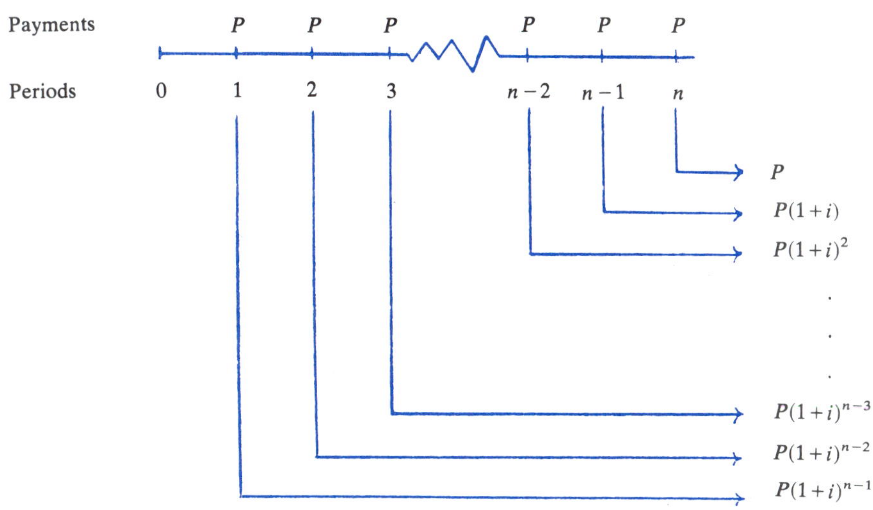

Figure 6.1

EXAMPLE 6.15 Find the amount of an ordinary annuity of 12 payments made monthly of \$100 each which earn interest at 12% per year compounded monthly.

SOLUTION Here $P = 100$, $r = 0.12$, and $m = 12$ so that $i = 0.12/12 = 0.01$, and $n = 12$. Thus, by Formula (6.15) the required amount of the annuity is given by

$$S = \frac{100[(1.01)^{12} - 1]}{0.01}$$
$$= 1268.30 \qquad \text{(using a hand calculator)}$$

or \$1268.30. The same result is obtained by observing that

$$S = 100s_{\overline{12}|0.01}$$
$$= 100(12.6825)$$
$$= 1268.25 \qquad \text{(using Table IV)}$$

■

EXAMPLE 6.16 As a savings program towards their child's college education, the parents of the child decide to deposit \$100 at the end of every month into a time-deposit bank account paying interest at the rate of 6% per year compounded monthly. If the savings program began when the child was 6 years old, how much money would have accumulated by the time the child turned 18?

SOLUTION By the time the child turned 18, the parents would have made 144 deposits into the account. Thus, $n = 144$. Furthermore, we have $P = 100$, $r = 0.06$, and $m = 12$ so that $i = 0.06/12 = 0.005$. Using Formula (6.15), we find that the amount of money that would have accumulated is given by

$$S = \frac{100[(1.005)^{144} - 1]}{0.005}$$
$$= 21{,}015$$

or \$21,015. ■

future value of an annuity

present value of an annuity

The quantity S in Formula (6.15) is realizable at some future date and is accordingly called the *future value of an annuity*. In certain instances, one is interested in determining the amount of money that should be invested now that will provide for a sequence of equal periodic payments over a certain period of time. After each payment is made, the new balance continues to earn interest at some nominal rate. Such an amount is referred to as the *present value of an annuity*. To derive a formula for determining the present value A of an annuity, we appeal to Formula (6.12). Since the future value of the annuity is, by Formula (6.15),

$$S = P\left[\frac{(1+i)^n - 1}{i}\right]$$

we see, by Formula (6.12) that the present value of the annuity A is given by

$$A = S(1+i)^{-n}$$
$$= (1+i)^{-n}P\left[\frac{(1+i)^n - 1}{i}\right]$$

(6.17) or

$$A = P\left[\frac{1-(1+i)^{-n}}{i}\right]$$
$$= Pa_{\overline{n}|i}$$

where the factor $a_{\overline{n}|i}$ (read "a angle n at i") represents the expression inside the brackets. Extensive tables have also been constructed giving values of $a_{\overline{n}|i}$ for different values of i and n (see Table IV, Appendix II).

EXAMPLE 6.17 Find the present value of an ordinary annuity of 24 payments of \$100 each made monthly and earning interest at 12% per year compounded monthly.

SOLUTION Here $P = 100$, $i = r/m = 0.12/12 = 0.01$, and $n = 24$ so that, by Formula (6.17)

$$A = \frac{100[1-(1.01)^{-24}]}{0.01}$$
$$= 2124.34$$

or \$2124.34. The same result may be obtained by using Table IV. Thus,

$$A = 100a_{\overline{24}|0.01}$$
$$= 100(21.2434)$$
$$= 2124.34$$

■

EXAMPLE 6.18 After making a down payment of \$2000 for an automobile, Mr. McMurphy paid \$200 per month for 36 months with interest charged at 12% per year compounded monthly on the unpaid balance. What was the original cost of the car? What portion of Mr. McMurphy's total car payments was for interest charges?

SOLUTION The loan taken up by Mr. McMurphy is given by the present value of the annuity

$$A = \frac{200[1-(1.01)^{-36}]}{0.01} = 200a_{\overline{36}|0.01}$$
$$= 6021.50$$

or \$6021.50. Therefore, the original cost of the automobile is \$8021.50 (\$6021.50 plus the \$2000.00 down payment).

The interest charges paid by Mr. McMurphy are given by

$$\begin{aligned}&(36)(200)-6021.50\\&=1178.50\end{aligned}$$

or $1178.50. ■

6.3 EXERCISES

In problems 1 through 6, find the amount (future value) of each ordinary annuity.

1. $1000 a year for 10 years at 10% per year compounded annually

2. $1500 per semiannual period for 8 years at 9% per year compounded semiannually

3. $1800 per quarter for 6 years at 8% per year compounded quarterly

4. $500 per semiannual period for 12 years at 11% per year compounded semiannually

5. $600 per quarter for 9 years at 12% per year compounded quarterly

6. $150 per month for 15 years at 10% per year compounded monthly

In problems 7 through 12, find the present value of each ordinary annuity.

7. $5000 a year for 8 years at 8% per year compounded annually

8. $1200 per semiannual period for 6 years at 10% per year compounded semiannually

9. $4000 a year for 5 years at 9% per year compounded yearly

10. $3000 per semiannual period for 6 years at 11% per year compounded semiannually

11. $800 per quarter for 7 years at 12% per year compounded quarterly

12. $150 per month for 10 years at 8% per year compounded monthly

13. If a merchant deposits $1500 annually at the end of each tax year in an I.R.A. account paying interest at the rate of 8% per year compounded annually, how much will he have in his account at the end of 25 years?

14. If Mr. Pruitt deposits $100 a month in a savings account earning interest at the rate of 8% per year compounded monthly, how much will he have on deposit in his savings account at the end of 6 years, assuming that he makes no withdrawals during that period?

15. Mrs. Lynde has joined a "Christmas Fund Club" at her bank. At the end of every month, December through October inclusive, she will make a deposit of $40 in her fund. If the money earns interest at the rate of 7% per year compounded monthly, how much will she have in her account on December 1 of the following year?

16. Mr. and Mrs. Betz have leased an apartment for two years at $450 per month payable in advance. If money is worth 9% per year compounded monthly, what is the equivalent cash payment (present value) of this annuity?

17. The Pirerra's are planning to go to Europe three years from now and they have agreed to set aside $150 each month for their trip. If they deposit this money at the end of each month in a savings account paying interest at the rate of 8% per year compounded monthly, how much money will be in their "travel fund" at the end of the third year?

18. Ms. Newburg made a down payment of $2000 towards the purchase of a new car. In order to pay the balance of the purchase price, she has secured a loan from her bank at the rate of 12% per year compounded monthly. Under the terms of her finance agreement, she is required to make payments of $210 per month for 36 months. What is the cash price of the car?

19. A state lottery commission pays the winner of the "Million Dollar" lottery 20 installments of $50,000 per year. Determine the amount of money the commission should have in the bank initially to guarantee the payments assuming that the balance on deposit with the bank earns interest at the rate of 8% per year compounded yearly. (*Hint*: Find the present value of an annuity.)

20. The Johnsons have accumulated a nest egg amounting to $25,000, which they intend to use as a down payment towards the purchase of a new house. Because their present gross income has placed them in a relatively high tax bracket, they have decided to invest a minimum of $800 per month in monthly payments (to take advantage of their tax deductions) towards the purchase of their house. However, because of other financial obligations their monthly payments should not exceed $1000. If local mortgage rates are 14% for a conventional 25-year mortgage, what is the price range of houses that they should consider?

6.4 Amortization and Sinking Funds

The annuity formulas derived in the last section may be used to answer questions involving the amortization of certain types of installment loans. For example, in a typical housing loan, the mortgagee makes periodic payments towards reducing his indebtedness to the lender, who charges interest at a fixed rate on the unpaid portion of the debt. In practice, the borrower is required to repay the lender in periodic installments, usually of the same size and over a fixed term, so that the loan (principal plus interest charges) is amortized at the end of the term.

By thinking of the monthly loan repayments P as the payments in an annuity, we see that the original amount of the loan is given by A, the present value of the annuity. From (6.17), we have

(6.18)
$$A = P\left[\frac{1-(1+i)^{-n}}{i}\right] = Pa_{\overline{n}|i}$$

A question a financier might ask is: What should the size of the monthly installment be so that the loan will be amortized at the end of the term of the loan? To answer this question, we simply solve Formula (6.18) for P in terms of A, obtaining

(6.19)
$$P = \frac{Ai}{1-(1+i)^{-n}} = \frac{A}{a_{\overline{n}|i}}$$

EXAMPLE 6.19 A sum of \$50,000 is to be repaid over a five-year period through equal installments made at the end of each year. If an interest rate of 8% per year is charged on the unpaid balance, and interest calculations are made at the end of each year, determine the size of each installment so that the loan (principal plus interest charges) is amortized at the end of five years. Verify the result by displaying the amortization schedule.

SOLUTION Substituting $A = 50{,}000$, $i = r = 0.08$ (here $m = 1$) and $n = 5$ into Formula (6.19), we obtain

$$P = \frac{(50{,}000)(0.08)}{1-(1.08)^{-5}} = 12{,}522.82$$

giving the required yearly installment as \$12,522.82.

The amortization schedule is presented in Table 6.3.

Table 6.3

End of period	Interest charged	Repayment made	Payment towards principal	Outstanding principal
0				50,000.00
1	4000.00	12,522.82	8522.82	41,477.18
2	3318.17	12,522.82	9204.65	32,272.53
3	2581.80	12,522.82	9941.02	22,331.51
4	1786.52	12,522.82	10,736.30	11,595.21
5	927.62	12,522.82	11,595.20	0.01

The outstanding principal at the end of five years is, of course, zero. (The figure of \$.01 in Table 6.3 is due to round-off errors.) Observe that initially the larger portion of the repayment goes towards payment of interest charges but, as time goes by, the larger portion of the installment goes towards principal repayment. ■

EXAMPLE 6.20 The Blakelys borrowed a sum of \$80,000 from a bank to help finance the purchase of a house. The bank charges interest at a rate of 9% per year on the unpaid balance, with interest computations being done at the end of each month. The Blakelys have agreed to repay the loan in equal monthly installments over 30 years. What should the size of each repayment be if the loan is to be amortized at the end of the term?

SOLUTION Here $A = 80{,}000$, $i = r/m = .09/12 = 0.0075$, and $n = (30)(12) = 360$. Using Formula (6.19), we find that the size of each monthly installment required is given by

$$P = \frac{(80{,}000)(0.0075)}{1-(1.0075)^{-360}}$$
$$= 643.70 \qquad \text{(using a pocket calculator)}$$

or \$643.70. ■

EXAMPLE 6.21 Refer to Example 6.20 and find the amount of equity the Blakelys will have in their home (disregarding the down payment) after the

(**a**) sixtieth payment (5 years)

(**b**) 240th payment (20 years)

SOLUTION (**a**) After sixty payments have been made the outstanding principal is given by the sum of the present values of the remaining installments (that is, $360-60=300$ installments). But this sum is just the present value of an annuity with $n = 300$, $P = 643.70$, and $i = 0.0075$ (see Example 6.20). Using Formula (6.18), we find that

$$A = 643.70\left[\frac{1-(1+0.0075)^{-300}}{0.0075}\right]$$
$$= 76{,}704.32$$

or \$76,704.32. Therefore, we may find the Blakely's equity in their home by subtracting the outstanding principal from the original principal

$$80{,}000 - 76{,}704.32 = 3295.68$$

or \$3295.68.

(**b**) As in part (**a**), we compute the present value of the annuity with $n = 360 - 240 = 120$. Thus,

$$A = 643.70\left[\frac{1-(1+0.0075)^{-120}}{0.0075}\right]$$
$$= 50{,}814.79$$

or \$50,814.79. Therefore, the Blakelys' equity in their home after the 240th payment is

$$80{,}000 - 50{,}814.79 = 29{,}185.21$$

or \$29,185.21. ■

sinking fund

Another important application of the annuity formulas is in the computation of sinking funds. Briefly, a *sinking fund* is a fund that is set up by a party to use for a specific purpose at some future date. For example, an individual might establish a sinking fund for the purpose of discharging a debt at a future date; a corporation might establish a sinking fund in order to accumulate sufficient capital for the purpose of replacing equipment, which is expected to be obsolete at some future date.

By thinking of the amount to be accumulated by a specific date in the future as the future value of an annuity, we can answer questions about a large class of sinking fund problems by invoking Formula (6.15).

EXAMPLE 6.22 The proprietor of the Carson Hardware Store has decided to set up a sinking fund for the purpose of purchasing a computer in two years' time. It is expected that the purchase will involve a sum of \$30,000. If the fund earns 10% per year compounded quarterly, determine the size of each (equal) quarterly installment the proprietor should pay into the fund. Verify the result by displaying the schedule.

SOLUTION The problem at hand is to find the size of each (quarterly) payment P of an annuity, given that its future value is $S = 30{,}000$, the interest earned per conversion period is $i = r/m = 0.1/4 = 0.025$, and that the number of payments is $n = (2)(4) = 8$. The formula for the annuity, from (6.15) is

$$S = P\left[\frac{(1+i)^n - 1}{i}\right]$$

which when solved for P, yields

(6.20) $$P = \frac{iS}{(1+i)^n - 1}$$

or equivalently,

$$P = \frac{S}{s_{\overline{n}|i}}$$

Substituting the appropriate numerical values for i, S, and n into (6.20), we obtain the desired quarterly payment

$$\begin{aligned} P &= \frac{(0.025)(30{,}000)}{(1.025)^8 - 1} \\ &= 3434.07 \end{aligned}$$

or \$3434.07. Table 6.4 shows the required schedule. Once again, the \$.44 in excess of the accumulated amount of \$30,000 is due to round-off errors.

End of period	Deposit made	Interest earned	Addition to fund	Accumulated amount in fund
1	3434.07	0	3434.07	3434.07
2	3434.07	85.85	3519.92	6953.99
3	3434.07	173.85	3607.92	10,561.91
4	3434.07	264.05	3698.12	14,260.03
5	3434.07	356.50	3790.57	18,050.60
6	3434.07	451.27	3885.34	21,935.94
7	3434.07	548.40	3982.47	25,918.41
8	3434.07	647.96	4082.03	30,000.44

Table 6.4 ■

6.4 EXERCISES

1. A sum of \$100,000 is to be repaid over a 10-year period through equal installments made at the end of each year. If an interest rate of 10% per year is charged on the unpaid balance and interest calculations are made at the end of each year, determine the size of each installment so that the loan (principal plus interest charges) is amortized at the end of 10 years.

2. What monthly payment is required to amortize a loan of \$30,000 over 10 years if interest at the rate of 12% per year is charged on the unpaid balance, and interest calculations are made at the end of each month?

3. Complete the following table, which shows the monthly payments on a \$100,000 twenty-five year mortgage at the interest rates shown. Use this information to answer the following questions.

(*a*) What is the difference in monthly payments between a \$100,000 twenty-five year mortgage secured at 10% per year and one secured at 14% per year?

Amount of mortgage	Interest rate	Monthly payment
\$100,000	9%	\$ 839
\$100,000	10%	...
\$100,000	11%	...
\$100,000	12%	...
\$100,000	13%	...
\$100,000	14%	\$1204

(*b*) Use the table to calculate the monthly mortgage payments on a $150,000 mortgage at 12% per year over 25 years and on a $50,000 mortgage at 12% per year over 25 years.

4. The Flemings' secured a loan of $60,000 from a bank to help finance the purchase of a house. The bank charges interest at a rate of 12% per year on the unpaid balance and interest computations are made at the end of each month. They have agreed to repay the loan in equal monthly installments over 25 years. What should the size of each repayment be if the loan is to be amortized at the end of the term?

5. The price of a new car is $8000. If an individual makes a down payment of 25% towards the purchase of the car and secures financing for the balance at the rate of 10% per year compounded monthly

(*a*) what monthly payment will he be required to make if the car is financed over a period of 36 months? over a period of 48 months?

(*b*) what will the interest charges be if he elects the 36-month plan? the 48 month plan?

6. A group of private investors purchased a condominium complex for $2 million. They made an initial down payment of 10% and have obtained financing for the balance. If the loan is to be amortized over 15 years at an interest rate of 12% compounded quarterly, find the required quarterly payment.

7. The Taylors have purchased an $80,000 house. They made an initial down payment of $16,000 and have secured a mortgage with interest charged at the rate of 12% per year on the unpaid balance. Interest computations are made at the end of each month. If the loan is to be amortized over 30 years, what monthly payment will they be required to make? What is their equity after 5 years? after 10 years? after 20 years?

8. A city has $2.5 million worth of school bonds that are due in 20 years and has established a sinking fund to retire this debt. If the fund earns interest at the rate of 7% per year compounded annually, what amount must they deposit annually in this fund?

9. The Lowell Corporation wishes to establish a sinking fund to retire a $200,000 debt which is due in 10 years. If their investment will earn interest at the rate of 9% compounded quarterly, find the amount of the quarterly deposit they must make in order to accumulate the required sum.

10. John Carlson is the beneficiary of a $20,000 trust fund set up for him by his grandparents. Under the terms of the trust, he is to receive the money over a five-year period in equal installments at the end of each year. If the fund earns interest at the rate of 9% per year compounded annually, what amount will he receive each year?

11. The management of the Gibraltar Brokerage Services, Inc. anticipates a capital expenditure of $200,000 in three years time for the purpose of purchasing new Telex machines and has decided to set up a sinking fund to finance this purchase. If the fund earns interest at the rate of 10% per year compounded quarterly, determine the size of each (equal) quarterly installment that should be deposited in the fund.

12. Mr. Berger has deposited \$375 in his I.R.A. account at the end of each quarter for the past 20 years. His investment has earned interest at the rate of 8% per year compounded quarterly over this period. Now, at age 60, he is considering retirement. What quarterly payment will he receive over the next 15 years (assuming that the money is earning interest at the same rate)? If he continues working and makes quarterly payments of the same amount in his I.R.A. account until age 65, what quarterly payment will he receive from his fund upon retirement over the following 10 years?

6 Chapter Review

EXERCISES

1. The third term of an arithmetic progression is -11 and the seventh term is 19.

(***a***) Find the eleventh term.

(***b***) Find the sum of the first fifteen terms.

2. Find the ninth term and the sum of the first ten terms of the geometric progression

$$\frac{1}{4}, -\frac{1}{2}, 1, \ldots$$

3. Find the accumulated amount after 4 years if \$5000 is invested at 10% per year compounded (***a***) annually, (***b***) semiannually, (***c***) quarterly, and (***d***) monthly.

4. Find the effective rate of interest corresponding to a nominal rate of 12% per year compounded (***a***) annually, (***b***) semiannually, (***c***) quarterly, and (***d***) monthly.

5. Find the present value of \$64,540 due in 6 years at an interest rate of 8% per year compounded monthly.

6. What rate of interest compounded quarterly is needed to double an investment in 8 years?

7. Find the amount (future value) of an ordinary annuity of \$150 per quarter for 7 years at 8% per year compounded quarterly.

8. Find the present value of an ordinary annuity of 36 payments of \$250 each made monthly and earning interest at 9% per year compounded monthly.

9. The J.C.N. Media Corporation had sales of \$1,750,000 in the first year of operation. If the sales increased by 14% per year thereafter, find the sales of the company in the fourth year and the total sales over the first four years of operation.

10. A firm bought a word processing machine with a useful life of 10 years at a cost of \$3000. Using the double-declining balance method determine

(***a***) what the book value of the machine is at the end of 6 years?

(***b***) the amount by which the machine has been depreciated at the end of the sixth year?

11. The Blakes have decided to start a monthly savings program in order to provide for their son's college education. How much should they deposit each month in a time-deposit bank account earning interest at the rate of 8% per year compounded monthly, so that at the end of the tenth year the accumulated amount will be \$40,000?

12. Miss Cantwell made a down payment of \$400 towards the purchase of new furniture. In order to pay the balance of the purchase price she has secured a loan from her bank at 12% per year compounded monthly. Under the terms of her finance agreement she is required to make payments of \$75.32 for 24 months. What was the purchase price of the furniture?

13. The Turners have purchased a house for \$120,000. They made an initial down payment of \$24,000 and have secured a mortgage with interest charged at the rate of 12% per year on the unpaid balance. Interest computations are made at the end of each month. If the loan is to be amortized over 25 years

(***a***) what monthly payment will they be required to make?

(***b***) what is the total interest payment?

(***c***) what is their equity after 10 years?

14. The management of a corporation anticipates a capital expenditure of \$500,000 in five years time for the purpose of purchasing replacement machinery. In order to finance this purchase a sinking fund, which earns interest at the rate of 10% per year compounded quarterly, will be set up. Determine the amount of each (equal) quarterly installment that should be deposited in the fund.

7

COUNTING TECHNIQUES

The solution of many problems involving the application of mathematics often centers on determining the number of elements in certain sets. Such is the case in the practical problems we will consider in Chapter 8 on Probability.

In this chapter we shall study some of the elementary techniques used to determine the number of elements in a set. A problem in which we find the number of elements in a set is often called a counting problem and constitutes a field of study known as combinatorics. Our study of combinatorics, however, shall be restricted to the results that will be required for our work in probability later on.

Before proceeding further, we advise the reader to review Sections 1.1 and 1.2 to refamiliarize yourself with the results contained in those sections.

7.1

The Number of Elements in a Finite Set

The number of elements in a finite set is determined by simply counting the elements in the set. If A is a set, then $n(A)$ denotes the number of elements in A. For example, if

$$A=\{1, 2, 3, \ldots, 20\}, \qquad B=\{a, b\}, \qquad C=\{8\}$$

then $n(A)=20$, $n(B)=2$, and $n(C)=1$.

The empty set has no elements in it so that $n(\varnothing)=0$. Another result which is easily seen to be true is the following: If A and B are disjoint sets then

(7.1) $$n(A \cup B)=n(A)+n(B)$$

EXAMPLE 7.1 If $A = \{a, c, d\}$ and $B = \{b, e, f, g\}$, then $n(A) = 3$ and $n(B) = 4$ so that $n(A) + n(B) = 7$. On the other hand, $A \cup B = \{a, b, c, d, e, f, g\}$ and $n(A \cup B) = 7$. Thus, Equation (7.1) holds true in this case. Note that $A \cap B = \varnothing$. ■

In the general case A and B need not be disjoint, which leads us to the general formula

(7.2) $$n(A \cup B) = n(A) + n(B) - n(A \cap B)$$

To see this, we observe that the set $A \cup B$ may be viewed as the union of three mutually disjoint sets with x, y, and z elements, respectively (see Figure 7.1). The figure shows that

$$n(A \cup B) = x + y + z$$

Also, $$n(A) = x + y$$

and $$n(B) = y + z$$

so that
$$\begin{aligned} n(A) + n(B) &= (x + y) + (y + z) \\ &= (x + y + z) + y \\ &= n(A \cup B) + n(A \cap B) \qquad [n(A \cap B) = y] \end{aligned}$$

Thus, solving for $n(A \cup B)$, we obtain

$$n(A \cup B) = n(A) + n(B) - n(A \cap B)$$

the desired result.

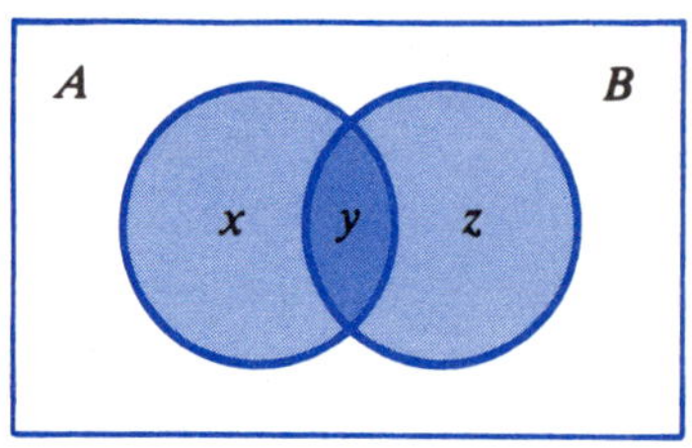

Figure 7.1

EXAMPLE 7.2 Let $A = \{a, b, c, d, e\}$ and $B = \{b, d, f, h\}$. Verify Equation (7.2) directly.

SOLUTION

$$A \cup B = \{a, b, c, d, e, f, h\}, \quad \text{so} \quad n(A \cup B) = 7$$
$$A \cap B = \{b, d\}, \quad \text{so} \quad n(A \cap B) = 2$$

Furthermore, $$n(A) = 5, n(B) = 4$$

so that $$n(A) + n(B) - n(A \cap B) = 5 + 4 - 2 = 7 = n(A \cup B)$$ ■

EXAMPLE 7.3 In a survey of 100 coffee drinkers it was found that 70 take sugar with their coffee, 60 take cream with their coffee, and 50 take both sugar and cream with their coffee. How many coffee drinkers take sugar or cream with their coffee?

SOLUTION Let U denote the set of 100 coffee drinkers surveyed, and let

$$A = \{x \in U \mid x \text{ takes sugar with coffee}\}$$
$$B = \{x \in U \mid x \text{ takes cream with coffee}\}$$

Then $n(A) = 70$, $n(B) = 60$, and $n(A \cap B) = 50$. The set of coffee drinkers who take sugar or cream with their coffee is given by $A \cup B$. Using Equation (7.2) we find

$$\begin{aligned} n(A \cup B) &= n(A) + n(B) - n(A \cap B) \\ &= 70 + 60 - 50 = 80 \end{aligned}$$

So 80 out of the 100 coffee drinkers surveyed take cream or sugar with their coffee. ■

An equation similar to Equation (7.2) may be derived for the case that involves any finite number of finite sets. For example, a relationship involving the number of elements in the sets A, B, and C is given by

(7.3)
$$\begin{aligned} n(A \cup B \cup C) = {} & n(A) + n(B) + n(C) - n(A \cap B) - n(A \cap C) - n(B \cap C) \\ & + n(A \cap B \cap C) \qquad \text{(See problem 15 of Exercise set 7.1.)} \end{aligned}$$

As useful as equations such as (7.3) are, in practice it is often easier to attack a problem directly with the aid of Venn diagrams, as shown by the following example.

EXAMPLE 7.4 A leading manufacturer of cosmetics advertised its products in three magazines: *Cosmopolitan*, *McCalls*, and the *Ladies Home Journal*. A survey of 500 customers by the manufacturer reveals the following information:

180 learned of its products from *Cosmopolitan*
200 learned of its products from *McCalls*
192 learned of its products from the *Ladies Home Journal*
84 learned of its products from *Cosmopolitan* and *McCalls*
52 learned of its products from *Cosmopolitan* and the *Ladies Home Journal*
64 learned of its products from *McCalls* and the *Ladies Home Journal*
38 learned of its products from all three magazines.

How many of the customers saw the manufacturer's advertisement in

(a) at least one magazine?
(b) exactly one magazine?
(c) at least two magazines?
(d) exactly two magazines?

SOLUTION Let U denote the set of all customers surveyed, and let

$$C = \{x \in U \mid x \text{ learned of the products from } \textit{Cosmopolitan}\}$$
$$M = \{x \in U \mid x \text{ learned of the products from } \textit{McCalls}\}$$
$$L = \{x \in U \mid x \text{ learned of the products from the } \textit{Ladies Home Journal}\}$$

The result that 38 customers learned of the products from all three magazines translates into $n(C \cap M \cap L) = 38$ (see Figure 7.2 part a). Next, the result that 64 learned of the products from *McCalls* and the *Ladies Home Journal* translates into $n(M \cap L) = 64$. This leaves

$$64 - 38 = 26$$

who learned of the products from **only** *McCalls* and the *Ladies Home Journal* (Figure 7.2 part b). Similarly, $n(C \cap L) = 52$ so that

$$52 - 38 = 14$$

learned of the product from **only** *Cosmopolitan* and the *Ladies Home Journal*, and $n(C \cap M) = 84$ so that

$$84 - 38 = 46$$

learned of the product from **only** *Cosmopolitan* and *McCalls*. These numbers appear in the appropriate regions in Figure 7.2(b).

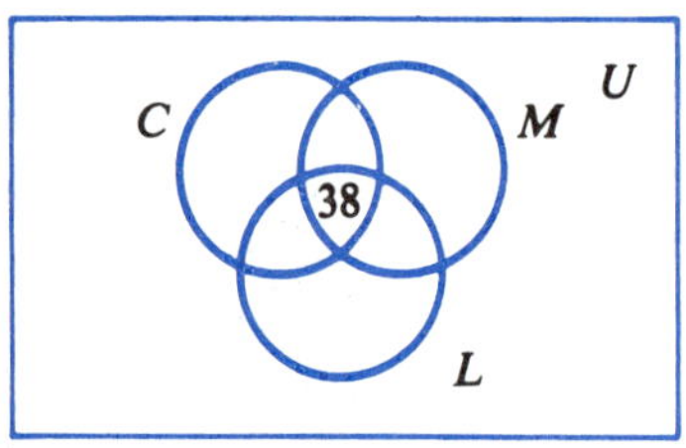

(a)

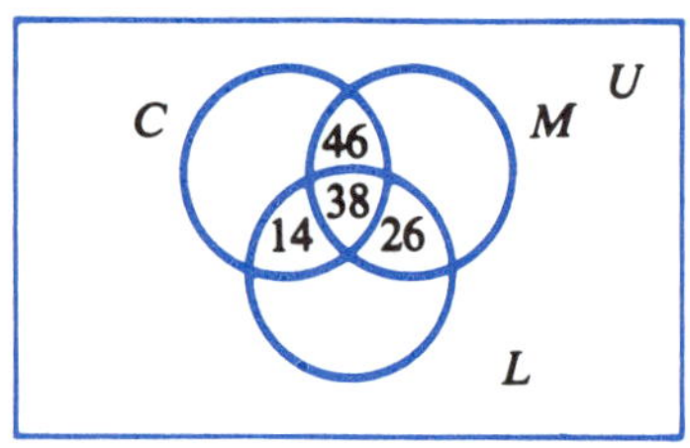

(b)

Figure 7.2

Continuing, we have $n(L) = 192$ so that the number who learned of the products from the *Ladies Home Journal* only is given by

$$192 - 14 - 38 - 26 = 114 \qquad \text{(See Figure 7.3.)}$$

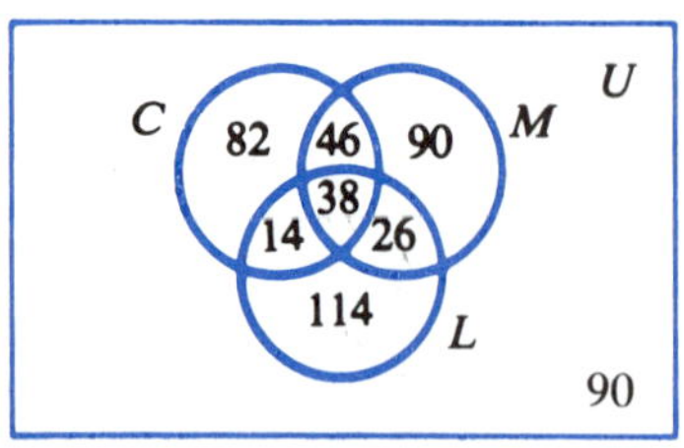

Figure 7.3

Similarly, $n(M) = 200$ so that

$$200 - 46 - 38 - 26 = 90$$

learned of the products from **only** *McCalls*, and $n(C) = 180$ so that

$$180 - 14 - 38 - 46 = 82$$

learned of the products from **only** *Cosmopolitan*. Finally,

$$500 - (90 + 26 + 114 + 14 + 82 + 46 + 38) = 90$$

learned of the products from other sources.

We are now in a position to answer questions (**a**), (**b**), (**c**), and (**d**).

(**a**) Referring to Figure 7.3, we see that the number of customers who learned of the products from at least one magazine is given by

$$n(C \cup M \cup L) = 90 + 26 + 114 + 14 + 82 + 46 + 38 = 410$$

(**b**) The number of customers who learned of the products from exactly one magazine (see Figure 7.4) is given by

$$n(L \cap C^c \cap M^c) + n(M \cap C^c \cap L^c) + n(C \cap L^c \cap M^c) = 90 + 114 + 82 = 286$$

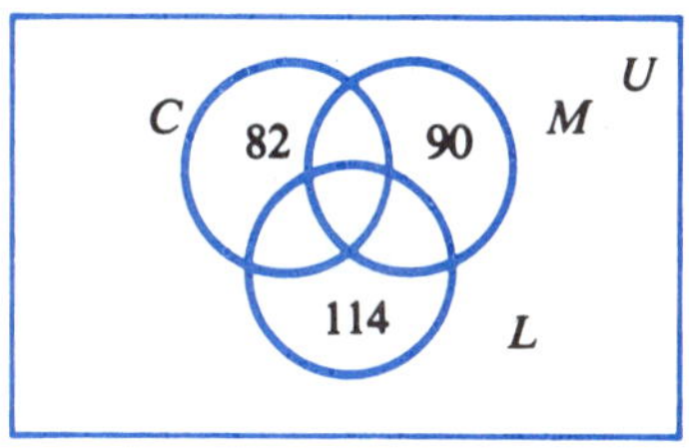

Figure 7.4

(**c**) Referring once again to Figure 7.2, we see that the number of customers who learned of the products from at least two magazines is given by

$$n(L \cap M \cap C^c) + n(C \cap M \cap L^c) + n(C \cap L \cap M^c) + n(C \cap L \cap M)$$
$$= 26 + 46 + 14 + 38 = 124$$

(**d**) The number of customers who learned of the products from exactly two magazines is given by

$$n(L \cap M \cap C^c) + n(C \cap M \cap L^c) + n(C \cap L \cap M^c) = 26 + 46 + 14 = 86$$ ■

7.1 EXERCISES

1. Let $A=\{2,4,6,8\}$ and $B=\{6,7,8,9,10\}$. Compute

(*a*) $n(A)$ (*b*) $n(B)$ (*c*) $n(A\cup B)$ (*d*) $n(A\cap B)$

Verify directly that $n(A\cup B)=n(A)+n(B)-n(A\cap B)$ in this case.

2. Let $A=\{a, e, i, o\ u\}$ and $B=\{b, d, e, o, u\}$. Verify by direct computation that $n(A\cup B)=n(A)+n(B)-n(A\cap B)$.

3. If $n(A)=15$, $n(A\cap B)=5$, and $n(A\cup B)=30$, what is $n(B)$?

4. If $n(A)=10$, $n(A\cup B)=15$, and $n(B)=8$, what is $n(A\cap B)$?

5. Let A and B be subsets of a universal set U and suppose $n(U)=200$, $n(A)=100$, $n(B)=80$, and $n(A\cap B)=40$. Compute each of the following:

(*a*) $n(A\cup B)$ (*b*) $n(A^c)$ (*c*) $n(B^c)$

(*d*) $n(A^c\cap B)$ (*e*) $n(A\cap B^c)$ (*f*) $n(A^c\cap B^c)$

6. A survey of 1000 subscribers to the *Los Angeles Times* revealed that 900 subscribe to the daily morning edition and 500 subscribe to both the daily morning and the Sunday editions. How many subscribe to the Sunday edition? How many subscribe to the Sunday edition only?

7. Of 100 clock-radios sold recently in a department store, 70 had FM circuitry and 90 had AM circuitry. How many of the radios had both FM and AM circuitry? How many could receive FM transmission only? How many could receive AM transmission only?

8. In a recent survey of 200 members of a local sports club, 100 indicated that they plan to attend the next Summer Olympic Games, 60 indicated that they plan to attend the next Winter Olympic Games, and 40 indicated that they plan to attend both the Summer and the Winter Olympic Games. How many members of the club plan to attend

(*a*) at least one of the two Games?

(*b*) exactly one of the Games?

(*c*) the Summer Olympic Games only?

(*d*) none of the Games?

9. In a survey of 120 consumers conducted in a shopping mall, 80 indicated that they buy Brand A of a certain product, 68 buy Brand B, and 42 buy both brands. Determine the number of consumers participating in the survey who buy

(*a*) at least one of these brands.

(*b*) exactly one of these brands.

(*c*) only Brand A.

(*d*) none of these brands.

10. Of 50 employees of a store located in downtown Boston, 18 take the subway to work, 12 take the bus, and 7 take both the subway and the bus. Determine the number of employees who

(***a***) take the subway or the bus to work.

(***b***) take only the bus to work.

(***c***) take either the bus or the subway to work.

(***d***) get to work by some other means.

11. Let A, B, and C be subsets of a universal set U and suppose $n(U) = 100$, $n(A) = 28$, $n(B) = 30$, $n(C) = 34$, $n(A \cap B) = 8$, $n(A \cap C) = 10$, $n(B \cap C) = 15$, and $n(A \cap B \cap C) = 5$. Compute each of the following:

(***a***) $n(A \cup B \cup C)$ (***b***) $n(A^c)$ (***c***) $n(A^c \cap B \cap C)$

(***d***) $n[A \cap (B \cup C)]$ (***e***) $n[A \cup (B \cap C)]$ (***f***) $n(A^c \cap B^c \cap C^c)$

(***g***) $n[A^c \cap (B \cup C)]$ (***h***) $n[A \cap (B \cup C)^c]$ (***i***) $n(A^c \cap B^c \cap C^c)^c$

12. A survey of 100 college students who frequent the reading lounge of a university revealed the following results:

40 read *Time* magazine

30 read *Newsweek*

25 read *U.S. News and World Report*

15 read *Time* magazine and *Newsweek*

12 read *Time* magazine and *U.S. News and World Report*

10 read *Newsweek* and *U.S. News and World Report*

4 read all three magazines.

How many of the students surveyed read

(***a***) at least one magazine? (***b***) exactly one magazine?

(***c***) exactly two magazines? (***d***) none of these magazines?

13. To help plan the number of meals to be prepared in a college cafeteria, a survey was conducted and the following data was obtained:

130 students ate breakfast

180 students ate lunch

275 students ate dinner

68 students ate breakfast and lunch

112 students ate breakfast and dinner

90 students ate lunch and dinner

58 students ate all three meals

How many of the students

(***a***) ate at least one meal in the cafeteria?

(***b***) ate exactly one meal in the cafeteria?

(*c*) ate only dinner in the cafeteria?

(*d*) ate exactly two meals in the cafeteria?

14. The 120 consumers of problem 9 were also asked about their buying preferences concerning another product that is sold in the market under three labels. The results follow:

12 buy only those sold under label A
25 buy only those sold under label B
26 buy only those sold under label C
15 buy only those sold under labels A and B
10 buy only those sold under labels A and C
12 buy only those sold under labels B and C
8 buy the product sold under all three labels

How many of the consumers surveyed buy the product sold under

(*a*) at least one of the three labels? (*b*) labels A and B but not C?

(*c*) label A? (*d*) none of these labels?

****15.*** Derive Equation (7.3). (*Hint*: Equation (7.2) may be written as $n(D \cup E) = n(D) + n(E) - n(D \cap E)$. Now, put $D = A \cup B$ and $E = C$. Repeat the use of Equation (7.2) again if necessary.)

7.2 The Multiplication Principle

A fundamental principle of counting, called the *Multiplication Principle* may be stated as follows: Suppose there are m ways of performing a task T_1 and n ways of performing a task T_2, then there are mn ways of performing the task T_1 followed by the task T_2.

EXAMPLE 7.5 Suppose there are three trunk roads connecting town A and town B and two trunk roads connecting town B and town C.

(a) Use the multiplication principle to find the number of ways a journey from town A to town C via town B may be completed.

(b) Verify the result of part (a) directly by exhibiting all possible routes.

SOLUTION **(a)** Since there are 3 ways of performing the first task (going from town A to town B) followed by 2 ways of performing the second task (going from town B to town C), the multiplication principle says that there are $3 \cdot 2$ or 6 ways to complete a journey from town A to town C via town B.

(b) Label the trunk roads connecting town A and town B by the Roman numerals I, II, and III and the trunk roads connecting town B and town C by the lower-case

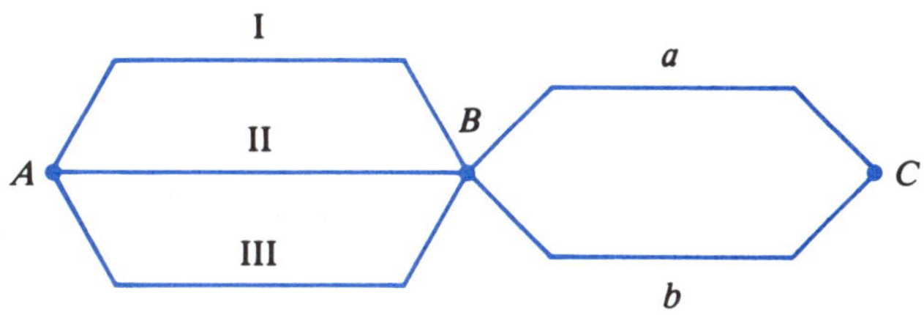

Figure 7.5

letters a and b. A schematic of this is shown in Figure 7.5. Then the routes from town A to town C via town B may be exhibited with the aid of a tree diagram (Figure 7.6). The six routes are represented by the six ordered pairs

$$(\mathrm{I}, a), \quad (\mathrm{I}, b), \quad (\mathrm{II}, a), \quad (\mathrm{II}, b), \quad (\mathrm{III}, a) \quad \text{and} \quad (\mathrm{III}, b)$$

where (I, a) means that the journey from town A to town B is made on trunk road I with the rest of the journey from town B to town C to be completed on trunk road a, and so forth.

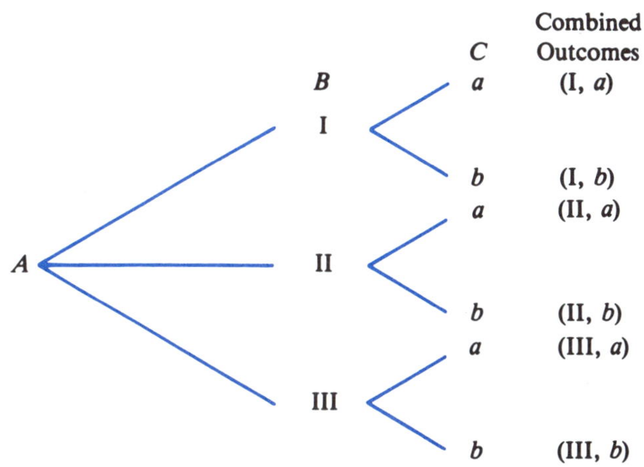

Figure 7.6 ■

EXAMPLE 7.6 Diners at Angelo's Spaghetti Bar may select their entree from 6 varieties of pasta and 28 choices of sauce. How many such combinations are there which consist of one variety of pasta and one kind of sauce?

SOLUTION There are 6 ways of choosing a pasta followed by 28 ways of choosing a sauce so that, by the multiplication principle, there are $6 \cdot 28$ or 168 combinations of this pasta dish. ■

generalized multiplication principle

The multiplication principle may be easily extended, which leads to the *Generalized Multiplication Principle* as follows: Suppose a task T_1 can be performed in N_1 ways, a task T_2 can be performed in N_2 ways, . . . , and finally a task T_n can be performed in N_n ways. Then the number of ways of performing the tasks

$T_1, T_2, \ldots, T_n$ in succession is given by

$$N_1 N_2 \cdots N_n$$

We now illustrate the application of the generalized multiplication principle to several diverse situations.

EXAMPLE 7.7 A coin is tossed three times and the sequence of heads and tails is recorded.

(**a**) Use the generalized multiplication principle to determine the number of outcomes of this activity.

(**b**) Exhibit all the sequences by means of a tree diagram.

SOLUTION (**a**) The coin may land in 2 ways. Therefore, in three tosses the number of outcomes (sequences) is given by $2 \cdot 2 \cdot 2$ or 8.

(**b**) Let H and T denote the outcome "a head" and "a tail", respectively. Then the required sequences may be obtained as shown in Figure 7.7 giving the sequence as HHH, HHT, HTH, HTT, THH, THT, TTH, and TTT.

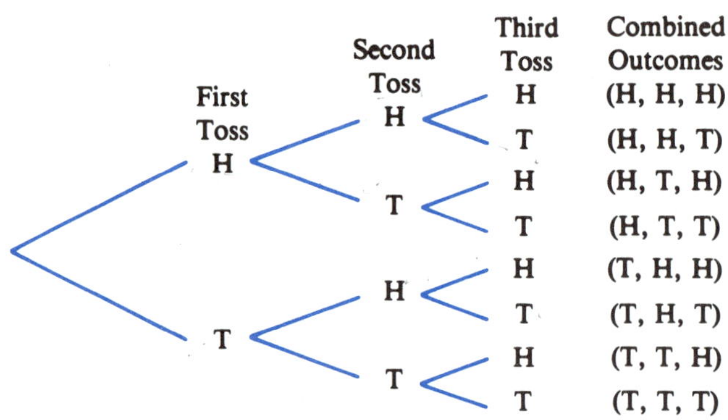

Figure 7.7 ■

EXAMPLE 7.8 A combination lock is unlocked by dialing a sequence of numbers, first to the left, then to the right, and to the left again. If there are 10 digits on the dial, determine the number of possible combinations.

SOLUTION There are 10 choices for the first number followed by 10 for the second, and 10 for the third so that, by the generalized multiplication principle, there are $10 \cdot 10 \cdot 10$ or 1000 possible combinations. ■

EXAMPLE 7.9 An investor has decided to purchase shares in the stocks of a company engaged primarily in aerospace activities, a company involved in energy development, and an electronics company. After some research the account executive of a share brokerage firm has recommended that he or she consider the stocks from a list of 5 aerospace companies, 3 companies engaged in the energy development field, and 4 electronics companies. In how many ways may the investor select the group of three companies from the executive's list for his investment?

SOLUTION He or she has 5 choices for selecting an aerospace company, 3 choices for selecting a company engaged in the energy development field, and 4 choices for selecting an electronics company. Therefore, by the generalized multiplication principle, there are $5 \cdot 3 \cdot 4$ or 60 ways in which a group of three companies, one from each industry group, may be selected for investment by the investor. ■

7.2 EXERCISES

1. Lynbrook West, an apartment complex financed by the State Housing Finance Agency, consists of 1, 2, 3, and 4-bedroom units. The rental rate for each type of unit is determined by the income of the tenant—low, moderate, and market. How many different rates are there?

2. Five different types of monthly commuter passes are offered by the local transit authority in a certain city for three different groups of passengers: youths, adults, and senior citizens. How many different kinds of passes must be printed each month?

3. In the game of "Blackjack", a 2-card hand consisting of an ace and a face card or a ten is called a "blackjack". If a standard 52-card deck is used, determine the number of "blackjack" hands that can be dealt.

4. A coin is tossed 4 times and the sequence of heads and tails is recorded.

(*a*) Use the generalized multiplication principle to determine the number of outcomes of this activity.

(*b*) Exhibit all the sequences by means of a tree diagram.

5. A female executive selecting her fall wardrobe purchased 2 blazers, 4 blouses, and 3 skirts in coordinating colors. How many ensembles consisting of a blazer, a blouse, and a skirt can she create from this collection?

6. There are 4 commuter trains and 3 express buses departing from city A to city B in the morning and 3 commuter trains and 3 express buses operating on the return trip in the evening. In how many ways can a commuter from city A to city B complete a daily round trip via bus and/or train?

7. A psychologist has constructed the maze shown below for use in an experiment. The maze is constructed so that a rat running the maze must pass through

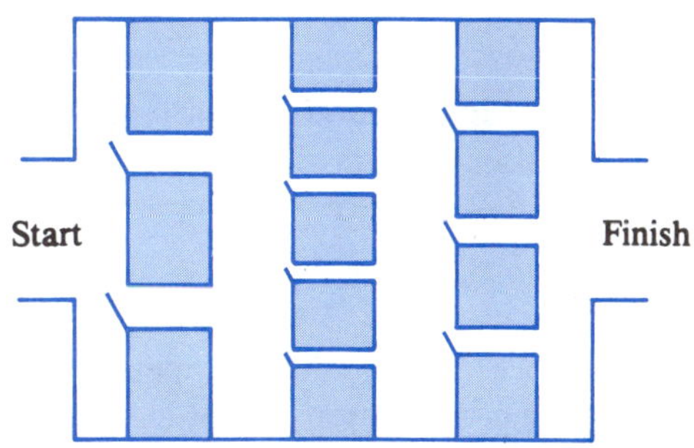

Maze

a series of one-way doors. How many different paths are there from start to finish?

8. Two soups, 5 entrees, and 3 desserts are listed on the "Special" menu at the Neptune Restaurant. How many different selections consisting of 1 soup, 1 entree, and 1 dessert can the clientele choosing their dinner from this menu make?

9. An automobile manufacturer has 3 different subcompact cars in the line. Customers selecting one of these cars have a choice of 3 sizes of engines, 4 body styles, and 3 color schemes. How many different selections can a customer wishing to purchase one of these automobiles make?

10. (***a***) How many positive 3-digit numerals can be formed that are greater than 700?

(***b***) If no digit is repeated within the number, how many 3-digit numbers greater than 700 can be formed?

11. An opinion poll is to be conducted among cable T.V. viewers. Six multiple-choice questions, each with 4 possible answers, will be asked. In how many different ways can a viewer complete the poll, if exactly 1 response is given to each question?

12. An opinion poll was conducted by the Morris Polling Group. Respondents were classified according to their sex (M or F), political affiliation (D, I, R) and the region of the country in which they reside (NW, W, C, S, E, NE).

(***a***) Use the generalized multiplication principle to determine the number of possible classifications.

(***b***) Construct a tree diagram to exhibit all possible classifications.

13. A certain state uses license plates consisting of 3 letters of the alphabet followed by 3 digits. How many different license plate numbers can be formed?

14. An exam consists of 10 true or false questions. Assuming that every question is answered, in how many different ways can a student complete the exam? In how many ways may the exam be completed if a penalty is imposed for each incorrect answer, so that a student may leave some questions unanswered?

15. A warranty identification number for a certain product consists of a letter of the alphabet followed by a 5-digit number. How many possible identification numbers are there if the first digit of the 5-digit number must be nonzero?

16. (***a***) How many 7-digit telephone numbers are possible if the first digit must be nonzero?

(***b***) How many international direct-dialing numbers are possible if each number consists of a 3-digit area code (the first digit of which must be nonzero) and a number of the type described in part (***a***)?

****17.*** A "lucky dollar" is one of the 9 symbols which are printed on each reel of a slot machine with 3 reels. A player receives one of various payouts whenever one or more "lucky dollars" appear in the window of the machine. Find the number of winning combinations for which the machine gives a pay-out. (*Hint*: (a) Compute the number of ways in which the 9 symbols on the 1st, 2nd, and 3rd wheel can appear in the window slot. (b) Compute the number of ways in which the 8 symbols other than the "lucky dollar" can appear in the window slot. (c) The difference $(a-b)$ is the number of ways in which the "lucky dollar" can appear in the window slot. Why?)

7.3 Permutations and Combinations

In this section, we shall apply the generalized multiplication principle to the solution of two types of counting problems. Both these problems involve the determination of the number of ways of arranging the elements of a set and play an important role in the solution of problems in probability.

We begin by considering the permutations of a set. Specifically, given a set of (distinct) objects, a *permutation* of the set is an arrangement of these objects in a definite order.

EXAMPLE 7.10 Let $A = \{a, b, c\}$

(a) Find the number of permutations of A.

(b) List all the permutations of A with the aid of a tree diagram.

SOLUTION **(a)** Each permutation of A consists of a sequence of the 3 letters a, b, c. Therefore we may think of such a sequence as being constructed by filling in each of the three blanks

$$\_\_\_ \quad \_\_\_ \quad \_\_\_$$

with 1 of the 3 letters. Now, there are 3 ways in which we may fill the first blank—we may choose a, b, or c. Having selected a letter for the first blank there are 2 letters left for the second blank. Finally, there is but 1 way left to fill the third blank. Schematically, we have

$$\underline{\;3\;} \quad \underline{\;2\;} \quad \underline{\;1\;}$$

Invoking the generalized multiplication principle we conclude that there are $3 \cdot 2 \cdot 1$ or 6 permutations of the set A.

(b) The tree diagram associated with the problem at hand appears in Figure 7.8 and the 6 permutations of A are *abc*, *acb*, *bac*, *bca*, *cab*, and *cba*.

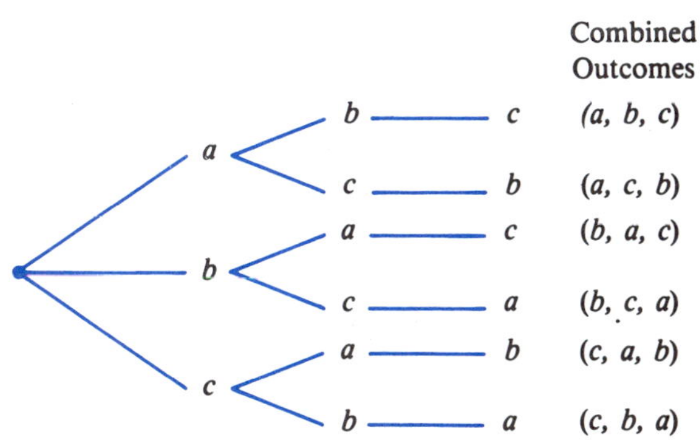

Figure 7.8 ■

EXAMPLE 7.11 Find the number of ways a baseball team consisting of 9 people can arrange themselves in a line for a group picture.

SOLUTION We want to determine the number of permutations of the 9 members of the baseball team. Each permutation in this situation consists of an arrangement of the 9 team members in a line, the 9 positions can be represented by 9 blanks, thus

$$\underset{\text{“1”}}{\overline{\quad}}\ \underset{\text{“2”}}{\overline{\quad}}\ \underset{\text{“3”}}{\overline{\quad}}\ \underset{\text{“4”}}{\overline{\quad}}\ \underset{\text{“5”}}{\overline{\quad}}\ \underset{\text{“6”}}{\overline{\quad}}\ \underset{\text{“7”}}{\overline{\quad}}\ \underset{\text{“8”}}{\overline{\quad}}\ \underset{\text{“9”}}{\overline{\quad}}$$

There are 9 ways to choose from among the 9 players to fill the first position. Next there are 8 players left and this gives us 8 ways to fill the second position. Proceeding in a similar manner, we find that there are 7 ways to fill the third position, and so on. Schematically, we have

$$\underline{\ 9\ }\ \ \underline{\ 8\ }\ \ \underline{\ 7\ }\ \ \underline{\ 6\ }\ \ \underline{\ 5\ }\ \ \underline{\ 4\ }\ \ \underline{\ 3\ }\ \ \underline{\ 2\ }\ \ \underline{\ 1\ }$$

Invoking the generalized multiplication principle, we conclude that there are $9 \cdot 8 \cdot 7 \cdot 6 \cdot 5 \cdot 4 \cdot 3 \cdot 2 \cdot 1$ or 362,880 ways the baseball team can arrange themselves for the picture. ■

Pursuing the same line of argument used in the solution to the problems posed in the last two examples, it is easy to derive an expression for the number of ways of permuting a set A of n distinct objects taken n at a time. In fact each permutation may be viewed as being obtained by filling each of n blanks with one and only one element from the set. There are n ways of filling the first blank, followed by $(n-1)$ ways of filling the second blank and so on, so that, by the generalized multiplication principle, there are

$$n(n-1)(n-2)\cdots 3 \cdot 2 \cdot 1$$

ways of permuting the elements of the set A. Before stating this result formally, let us introduce a notation that will enable us to write many of the expressions that follow in a compact form. Suppose n is a nonnegative integer. Then the expression $n!$ (read "n factorial") is a number defined by

$$n! = n(n-1)(n-2)\cdots 3 \cdot 2 \cdot 1$$

when n is positive and

$$0! = 1$$

For example,

$$\begin{aligned}
1! &= 1\\
2! &= 2 \cdot 1 = 2\\
3! &= 3 \cdot 2 \cdot 1 = 6\\
4! &= 4 \cdot 3 \cdot 2 \cdot 1 = 24\\
5! &= 5 \cdot 4 \cdot 3 \cdot 2 \cdot 1 = 120\\
&\ \ \vdots
\end{aligned}$$

and $$10! = 10 \cdot 9 \cdot 8 \cdot 7 \cdot 6 \cdot 5 \cdot 4 \cdot 3 \cdot 2 \cdot 1 = 3{,}628{,}800$$

Using this notation, we may express *the number of permutations of* n *distinct objects taken* n *at a time*, P(n, n) as

(7.4) $$P(n, n) = n!$$

In many situations one is interested in determining the number of ways of permuting n distinct objects taken r at a time. In the special case when $r = n$ the result is obtained by computing $P(n, n) = n!$ To derive a formula for computing the number of ways of permuting a set consisting of n distinct objects taken r at a time we observe that each such permutation may be viewed as being obtained by filling each of r blanks with precisely one element from the set. Now there are n ways of filling the first blank, followed by $(n-1)$ ways of filling the second blank and so on. Finally, there are $(n-r+1)$ ways of filling the rth blank. We may represent this argument schematically as follows

No. of ways	n	$n-1$	$n-2$	. . .	$n-r+1$
Blank	1st	2nd	3rd		rth

Invoking the generalized multiplication principle we conclude that *the number of ways of permuting* n *distinct objects taken* r *at a time*, P(n, r), *is given by*

$$P(n, r) = n(n-1)(n-2)\cdots(n-r+1)$$

or, since

$$n(n-1)(n-2)\cdots(n-r+1) = \frac{[n(n-1)(n-2)\cdots(n-r+1)][(n-r)(n-r-1)\cdots3\cdot2\cdot1]}{(n-r)(n-r-1)\cdots3\cdot2\cdot1}$$
$$= \frac{n!}{(n-r)!}$$

We have, using the factorial notation,

(7.5) $$P(n, r) = \frac{n!}{(n-r)!}$$

Note that when $n = r$, formula (7.5) reduces to

$$P(n, n) = \frac{n!}{0!} = \frac{n!}{1} = n! \qquad \text{(Note that } 0! = 1\text{)}$$

as expected.

EXAMPLE 7.12 Let $A = \{a, b, c, d\}$

(a) Use formula (7.5) to compute the number of permutations of the set A taken 2 at a time.

(b) Display the permutations of part **(a)** with the aid of a tree diagram.

SOLUTION **(a)** Here $n = 4$ and $r = 2$ so that the required number of permutations is given by

$$P(4, 2) = \frac{4!}{(4-2)!} = \frac{4!}{2!} = \frac{4 \cdot 3 \cdot 2 \cdot 1}{2 \cdot 1} = 4 \cdot 3$$

or 12.

(b) The tree diagram associated with the problem is shown in Figure 7.9 and the permutations of A taken 2 at a time are

$$ab, ac, ad, ba, bc, bd, ca, cb, cd, da, db, \text{ and } dc$$

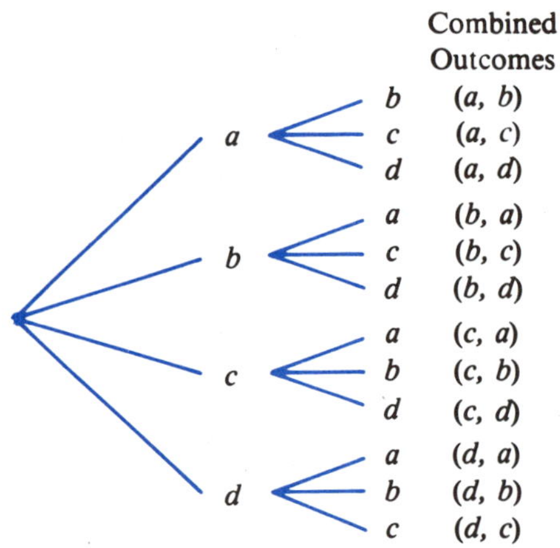

Figure 7.9 ■

EXAMPLE 7.13 Find the number of ways a chairman, a vice-chairman, a secretary, and a treasurer can be chosen from a committee of 8 members.

SOLUTION The problem is equivalent to finding the number of permutations of 8 distinct objects taken 4 at a time. Therefore, the number of ways of choosing the 4 officials from the committee of 8 members is given by

$$P(8, 4) = \frac{8!}{(8-4)!} = \frac{8!}{4!} = 8 \cdot 7 \cdot 6 \cdot 5 = 1680$$

or 1680 ways. ■

EXAMPLE 7.14 In a State Lottery there are 15 finalists eligible for the Big Money Draw. In how many ways can the first, second, and third prizes be awarded if no ticket holder may win more than one prize?

SOLUTION The number of ways the first 3 prizes can be awarded is given by

$$P(15, 3) = \frac{15!}{(15-3)!} = \frac{15!}{12!} = 15 \cdot 14 \cdot 13 = 2730$$

or 2730 ways. ■

The permutations considered thus far have been those of sets of *distinct* objects. In many situations we are interested in finding the number of permutations of a set of objects where not all of the objects are distinct. To derive a formula for use in such a situation, suppose in a set of n objects, n_1 of them are alike and of one kind, n_2 objects are alike and of another kind, . . . , and, finally, n_r objects are alike and of yet another kind (so that $n_1+n_2+\cdots+n_r=n$). Then, the number of permutations of these n objects taken n at a time is given by

(7.6)
$$\frac{n!}{n_1!n_2!\cdots n_r!}$$

To establish Formula (7.6), let us denote the number of such permutations by x. Now, if we *think* of the n_1 objects as being distinct, then they may be permuted in $n_1!$ ways. Similarly, if we *think* of the n_2 objects as being distinct, then they may be permuted in $n_2!$ ways, and so on. Therefore, if we *think* of the n objects as being distinct, then, by the generalized multiplication principle, there are $x\cdot n_1!\cdot n_2!\cdot\ldots\cdot n_r!$ permutations of these objects. But, the number of permutations of a set of n distinct objects taken n at a time is just equal to $n!$. Therefore, we have

$$x(n_1!\cdot n_2!\cdot\ldots\cdot n_r!)=n!$$

from which we deduce that

$$x=\frac{n!}{n_1!n_2!\cdots n_r!}$$

as was to be shown.

EXAMPLE 7.15 Find the number of permutations that can be formed from all of the letters in the word *ATLANTA*.

SOLUTION There are 7 objects (letters) involved so that $n=7$. However, 3 of them are alike and of one kind (the 3a's), 2 of them are alike and of another kind (the 2t's), so that, in this case, $n_1=3$, $n_2=2$, $n_3=1$ and $n_4=1$. Therefore, using formula (7.6), the number of required permutations is given by

$$\frac{7!}{3!2!1!1!}$$

or 420. ■

EXAMPLE 7.16 Weaver and Kline, a stock brokerage firm, has received 9 inquiries regarding new accounts. In how many ways can these inquiries be directed to 3 of the firm's account executives, if each account executive is to handle 3 inquiries?

SOLUTION Here $n = 9$, $n_1 = n_2 = n_3 = 3$, so that the number of ways of assigning the inquiries is given by

$$\frac{9!}{3!3!3!}$$

or 1680 ways. ■

Up to now, we have dealt with permutations of a set; that is, with arrangements of the objects of the set in which the *order* of the elements is taken into consideration. In many situations one is interested in determining the number of ways of arranging, say, r objects from a set of n objects without any regard whatsoever to the order in which the objects are arranged. Such an arrangement is called a *combination*. For example, if one is interested in knowing the number of 5-card poker-hands that can be dealt from a standard deck of 52 cards, then the order in which a poker-hand is dealt is unimportant. In this situation, one is in fact interested in determining the number of combinations of 5 cards (objects) selected from a deck (set) of 52 cards (objects). The solution to this problem will be found later in Example 7.19.

combination

To derive a formula for determining the number of combinations of n objects taken r at a time, written

$$C(n, r) \text{ or } \binom{n}{r}$$

we observe that each of the $C(n, r)$ combinations of r objects (see the schematic in Figure 7.10) can be permuted in $r!$ ways. Thus, by the multiplication principle the product $r!C(n, r)$ gives the number of permutations of n objects taken r at a time; that is,

$$r!C(n, r) = P(n, r)$$

from which we find

$$C(n, r) = \frac{P(n, r)}{r!}$$

or, using Formula (7.5),

(7.7)
$$C(n, r) = \frac{n!}{r!(n-r)!}$$

$$\underbrace{\underline{(r \text{ objects})} \quad \underline{(r \text{ objects})} \cdots \underline{(r \text{ objects})}}_{\longleftarrow C(n,r) \text{ of them} \longrightarrow}$$

Figure 7.10

EXAMPLE 7.17 Compute (**a**) $C(4, 4)$ (**b**) $C(4, 2)$, and interpret the results.

SOLUTION (**a**) $C(4, 4) = \frac{4!}{4!(4-4)!} = \frac{4!}{4!0!} = 1$ (Recall that $0! = 1$.)

This gives 1 as the number of combinations of 4 distinct objects taken 4 at a time.

(**b**) $C(4, 2) = \frac{4!}{2!(4-2)!} = \frac{4!}{2!2!} = \frac{4 \cdot 3}{2} = 6$

This gives 6 as the number of combinations of 4 distinct objects taken 2 at a time ■

EXAMPLE 7.18 A Senate investigation subcommittee of 4 members is to be selected from a Senate committee of 10 members. Determine the number of ways this can be done.

SOLUTION Since the order in which the members of the subcommittee is selected is unimportant, the number of ways of choosing the subcommittee is given by $C(10, 4)$, the number of combinations of 10 objects taken 4 at a time. But

$$C(10, 4) = \frac{10!}{4!(10-4)!} = \frac{10!}{4!6!} = \frac{10 \cdot 9 \cdot 8 \cdot 7}{4 \cdot 3 \cdot 2 \cdot 1} = 210$$

so there are 210 ways of choosing such a subcommittee. ■

EXAMPLE 7.19 Find the number of ways a poker hand of 5 cards can be dealt from a standard deck of 52 cards.

SOLUTION The order in which the 5 cards are dealt is not important and the number of ways of dealing a poker hand of 5 cards from a standard deck of 52 cards is given by $C(52, 5)$, the number of combinations of 52 objects, taken 5 at a time. Now,

$$C(52, 5) = \frac{52!}{5!(52-5)!} = \frac{52!}{5!47!}$$
$$= \frac{52 \cdot 51 \cdot 50 \cdot 49 \cdot 48}{5 \cdot 4 \cdot 3 \cdot 2 \cdot 1} = 2{,}598{,}960$$

so there are 2,598,960 ways of dealing such a poker hand. ■

The next several examples show that solving a counting problem often involves the repeated application of Formula (7.5) and/or Formula (7.7) possibly in conjunction with the multiplication principle.

EXAMPLE 7.20 The members of a string quartet comprising 2 violinists, a violist, and a cellist are to be selected from a group of 6 violinists, 3 violists and 2 cellists, respectively. In how many ways can the string quartet be formed?

SOLUTION The violinist may be selected in $C(6, 2)$ or 15 ways; the violist may be selected in $C(3, 1)$ or 3 ways, while the cellist may be selected in $C(2, 1)$ or 2 ways. By the multiplication principle there are $15 \cdot 3 \cdot 2$ or 90 ways of forming the string quartet. ■

EXAMPLE 7.21 Refer to Example 7.20. In how many ways can the string quartet be formed if one of the violinists is to be designated as the first violinist while the other is to be designated as the second violinist?

SOLUTION The order in which the violinists are selected is important here. Consequently, the number of ways of selecting the violinists is given by $P(6, 2)$ or 30 ways. The number of ways of selecting the violist and the cellist are, of course, 3 and 2, respectively. Therefore, the number of ways in which the string quartet may be formed is given by $30 \cdot 3 \cdot 2$ or 180 ways. ■

EXAMPLE 7.22 Refer to Example 7.9. Suppose the investor had decided to purchase shares in the stocks of 2 aerospace companies, 2 companies involved in energy development, and 2 electronics companies. In how many ways may the investor select the group of 6 companies for the investment from the prepared list?

SOLUTION There are $C(5, 2)$ ways in which the investor may select the aerospace companies, $C(3, 2)$ ways in which he or she may select the companies involved in energy development, and $C(4, 2)$ ways in which he or she may select the electronics companies as investments. By the generalized multiplication principle there are

$$\begin{aligned} C(5, 2)C(3, 2)C(4, 2) &= \frac{5!}{2!3!} \cdot \frac{3!}{2!1!} \cdot \frac{4!}{2!2!} \\ &= \frac{5 \cdot 4}{2} \cdot 3 \cdot \frac{4 \cdot 3}{2} \\ &= 180 \end{aligned}$$

ways of selecting the group of 6 companies for his or her investment. ■

7.3 EXERCISES

1. Evaluate:

(*a*) $P(5, 2)$ (*b*) $P(6, 6)$ (*c*) $P(5, 3)$

2. Evaluate:

(*a*) $P(n, 1)$ (*b*) $P(k, 2)$ (*c*) $P(n, n-2)$

3. Evaluate:

(*a*) $C(7, 4)$ (*b*) $C(8, 8)$ (*c*) $C(5, 0)$

4. Evaluate:

(*a*) $C(9, 3)$ (*b*) $C(9, 6)$ (*c*) $C(n, 2)$ (*d*) $C(7, r)$

5. A group of 5 students studying for a bar exam have formed a study group. Each member of the group will be responsible for preparing a study outline for 1 of 5 courses. In how many different ways can the 5 courses be assigned to the members of the group?

6. In how many ways can a television programming director schedule 6 different commercials in the 6 time slots allocated to commercials during a one hour program?

7. Seven people arrive at the ticket counter of a cinema at the same time. In how many ways can they line up to purchase their tickets?

8. In how many ways can a supermarket chain select 3 out of 12 possible sites for the construction of new supermarkets?

9. A student is given a reading list of 10 books from which he must select 2 books to fulfill an outside reading requirement for a course. In how many ways can he make his selections?

10. In how many ways can a quality control engineer select a sample of 3 transistors for testing from a batch of 100 transistors?

11. Weaver and Kline, a stock brokerage firm, has received 6 inquiries regarding new accounts. In how many ways can these inquiries be directed to its 12 account executives if each executive handles no more than 1 inquiry?

12. A company car, which has a seating capacity of 6, is to be utilized by 6 employees who have formed a car pool. If only 4 of these employees can drive, how many possible seating arrangements are there for the group?

13. At a college library exhibition of faculty publications, 3 mathematics books, 4 social science books, and 3 biology books will be displayed on a shelf.

(*a*) In how many ways can the 10 books be arranged on the shelf?

(*b*) In how many ways can the 10 books be arranged on the shelf if books on the same subject matter are placed together?

14. In how many ways can 4 married couples attending a concert be seated in a row of 8 seats

(*a*) if there are no restrictions?

(*b*) if each married couple is seated together?

(*c*) if the members of each sex are seated together?

15. The Futurists, a rock group, is planning a concert tour with performances to be given in 5 cities—San Francisco, Los Angeles, San Diego, Denver, and Las Vegas. In how many ways can they arrange their itinerary

(*a*) if there are no restrictions?

(*b*) if the 3 performances in California must be given consecutively?

16. Four items from 5 different departments of the Metro Department Store will be featured in a one-page newspaper advertisement as shown in the following diagram

Advertisement

1	2	3	4
5	6	7	8
9	10	11	12
13	14	15	16
17	18	19	20

(*a*) In how many different ways can the 20 featured items be arranged on the page?

(*b*) If items from the same department must be in the same row, how many arrangements are possible?

17. The C & J Realty Company has received 12 inquiries from prospective home-buyers. In how many ways can the inquiries be directed to 4 of the firm's real estate agents, if each agent handles 3 inquiries?

18. In the women's tennis tournament at Wimbledon, 2 finalists, A and B, are competing for the title, which will be awarded to the first player to win 2 sets. In how many different ways can the match be completed?

19. The U.N. Security Council consists of 5 permanent members and 10 nonpermanent members. Decisions made by the council require 9 votes for passage. However, any permanent member may veto a measure and thus block its passage. In how many ways can a measure be passed

(*a*) if all 15 members of the Council vote (no abstentions)?

(*b*) if 2 particular permanent and 2 particular nonpermanent members of the Council abstain from voting?

20. In how many different ways can a panel of 12 jurors and 2 alternate jurors be chosen from a group of 30 prospective jurors?

21. Twelve graduate students have applied for three available teaching assistantships. In how many ways can the assistantships be awarded among these applicants

(*a*) if no preference is given to any student?

(*b*) if 1 particular student must be awarded an assistantship?

(*c*) if the group of applicants includes 7 men and 5 women and it is stipulated that at least 1 woman must be awarded an assistantship?

22. A student taking an examination is required to answer 10 out of 15 questions.

(*a*) In how many ways can the 10 questions be selected?

(*b*) In how many ways can the 10 questions be selected if exactly 2 of the first 3 questions must be answered?

23. The U.B.S. Television Company is considering bids submitted by 7 different firms for 3 different contracts. In how many ways can the contracts be awarded among these firms if no firm is to receive more than 2 contracts?

24. In how many ways can a subcommittee of 4 be chosen from a Senate committee of 5 Democrats and 4 Republicans

(*a*) if all members are eligible?

(*b*) if the subcommittee must consist of 2 Republicans and 2 Democrats?

25. A student planning her curriculum for the oncoming year must select 1 of 5 business courses, 1 of 3 mathematics courses, 2 of 6 elective courses, and either 1 of 4 history courses or 1 of 3 social science courses. How many different curricula are there available for her consideration?

26. The J.C.L. Computer Company has 5 vacancies in its Executive Trainee Program. In how many ways can the company select 5 trainees from a group of 10 female and 10 male qualified applicants

(*a*) if the vacancies may be filled by any combination of men and women?

(*b*) if the vacancies must be filled by 2 men and 3 women?

27. The State Motor Vehicle Department requires learners to pass a written test on the Motor Vehicle Laws of the state. The exam consists of 10 true or false questions of which 8 must be answered correctly to qualify for a permit. In how many different ways may a learner complete the exam and qualify for a permit?

28. The Goodman Tire Company has 32 tires of a particular size and grade in stock, 2 of which are defective. If a set of 4 tires is to be selected,

(*a*) how many different selections can be made?

(*b*) how many different selections can be made that do not include any defective tires?

****29.*** A schematic diagram of the street system in a certain city between the points A and B is shown below. The City Transit Authority is in the process of selecting a route from A to B along which they will provide bus service. If their intention is to keep the route as short as possible, how many routes must they consider?

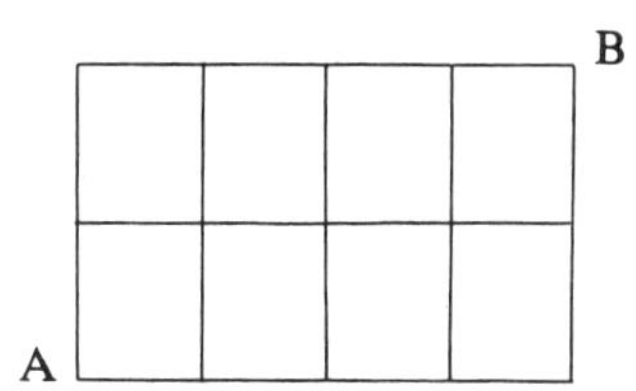

Street system

*30. In the World Series, 1 National League team and 1 American League team compete for baseball's coveted title that is awarded to the first team to win 4 games. In how many different ways can the series of games be completed?

7

Chapter Review

EXERCISES

1. Let A and B be subsets of a universal set U and suppose $n(U)=350$, $n(A)=120$, $n(B)=80$, and $n(A\cap B)=50$. Compute each of the following.

(a) $n(A\cup B)$ (b) $n(A^c)$ (c) $n(B^c)$

(d) $n(A^c\cap B)$ (e) $n(A\cap B^c)$ (f) $n(A^c\cap B^c)$

2. Evaluate:

(a) $C(20, 18)$ (b) $C(n, r)$ (c) $P(9, 7)$

(d) $P(n, n)$ (e) $C(5, 3)\cdot P(4, 2)$

3. How many 3-digit numbers can be formed from the numerals in the set $\{1, 2, 3, 4, 5\}$

(a) if repetition of digits is not allowed?

(b) if repetition of digits is allowed?

4. Find the number of distinguishable permutations that can be formed from the letters of each word.

(a) *CINCINNATI* (b) *HONOLULU*

5. The Department of Foreign Languages of a liberal arts college conducted a survey of its recent graduates to determine the foreign language courses they had taken while undergraduates at the college. Of the 480 graduates

200 had at least one year of Spanish
178 had at least one year of French
140 had at least one year of German
33 had at least one year of Spanish and French
24 had at least one year of Spanish and German
18 had at least one year of French and German
3 had at least one year of all three languages

How many of the graduates had

(a) at least one year of at least one of the three languages?

(b) at least one year of exactly one of the three languages?

(c) less than a year of any of the three languages?

6. In an election being held by the Associated Students Organization there are 6 candidates for President, 4 for Vice-president, 5 for Secretary, and 6 for Treasurer. How many different possible outcomes are there for this election?

7. From a standard 52-card deck, how many 5-card poker hands can be dealt consisting of

(*a*) 5 clubs?

(*b*) 3 kings and a pair?

8. In how many ways can 7 students be assigned seats in a row containing 7 desks

(*a*) if there are no restrictions?

(*b*) if 2 of the students must not be seated next to each other?

9. There are 8 seniors and 6 juniors in the Math Club at Jefferson High School. In how many ways can a math team consisting of 4 seniors and 2 juniors be selected from the members of the Math Club?

10. A sample of 4 balls is to be selected at random from an urn containing 15 balls numbered 1 to 15. If 6 of the balls are green, 5 are white, and 4 are black

(*a*) how many different samples can be selected?

(*b*) how many samples can be selected which contain at least 1 white ball?

11. From a shipment of 60 transistors, 5 of which are defective, a sample of 4 transistors is selected at random.

(*a*) In how many different ways can the sample be selected?

(*b*) How many samples contain 3 defective transistors?

(*c*) How many samples do not contain any defective transistors?

8

PROBABILITY

The systematic study of probability began in the seventeenth century because aristocrats of the time wanted to discover superior strategies to use in the gaming rooms of Europe. Some of the best mathematicians of the period were engaged in this pursuit. Since then, probability has evolved into an important branch of mathematics with widespread applications in virtually every sphere of human endeavor in which an element of uncertainty is present.

We shall give the technical meaning of the term probability in Section 8.2 after we have introduced some of the basic terminology used in the study of the subject. The rest of the chapter will be devoted to the development of techniques for computing the probabilities of the occurrence of certain events.

8.1

Experiments, Sample Spaces, and Events

outcome of an experiment

There are certain specialized terms used in the study of probability. We begin by defining the term experiment. For our purpose, an *experiment* is an activity with observable results. These results are referred to as *outcomes* of the experiment. Examples of some familiar experiments follow

1. Tossing a coin and observing whether it falls "heads" or "tails".

2. Casting a die and observing which of the numbers *one*, *two*, *three*, *four*, *five*, or *six* falls uppermost.

3. Testing a spark-plug from a batch of 1000 spark-plugs manufactured by a firm and observing whether it is defective or nondefective.

sample point and space

An outcome of an experiment is called a *sample point* of the experiment and the set of all possible sample points of an experiment is called the *sample space* of the experiment. A subset of the sample space of an experiment is called an *event* of the experiment. Thus, the sample space of an experiment is a universal set whose elements are precisely the outcomes of the experiment and the events of the experiment are the subsets of the universal set. A sample space associated with an experiment that has a finite number of possible outcomes (sample points) is called a *finite sample space*. This terminology is illustrated in the next several examples.

event

finite sample space

EXAMPLE 8.1 Describe the sample space associated with the experiment of tossing a coin and observing whether it falls "heads" or "tails". What are the events of this experiment?

SOLUTION The two outcomes are "heads" and "tails" and the required sample space is given by $S = \{H, T\}$ where H denotes the outcome "heads" and T denotes the outcome "tails". The events of the experiment, the subsets of S, follow:

$$\varnothing, \{H\}, \{T\}, S$$

■

EXAMPLE 8.2 An experiment consists of tossing a coin three times and observing the resulting sequence of "heads" and "tails".

(**a**) Describe the sample space S of the experiment.

(**b**) Determine the event E that exactly two heads appear.

(**c**) Determine the event F that at least one head appears.

SOLUTION (**a**) The sample points may be obtained with the aid of a tree diagram, (see Figure 8.1). The required sample space S is given by

$$S = \{HHH, HHT, HTH, HTT, THH, THT, TTH, TTT\}$$

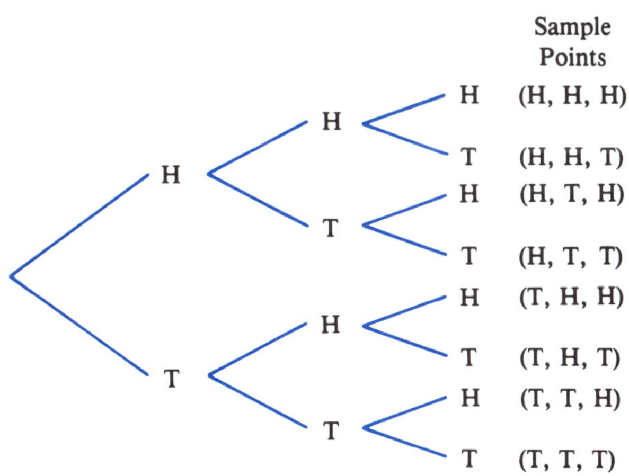

Figure 8.1

(b) By scanning the sample space S obtained in part **(a)**, it is easy to identify the outcomes in which exactly two heads appear and this gives

$$E = \{\text{HHT, HTH, THH}\}$$

(c) Proceeding as in part **(b)**, we find

$$F = \{\text{HHH, HHT, HTH, HTT, THH, THT, TTH}\}$$

■

EXAMPLE 8.3 An experiment consists of casting a pair of dice and observing the number that falls uppermost on each die.

(a) Describe the sample space S of the experiment.

(b) Determine the events $E_2, E_3, E_4, \ldots, E_{12}$ that the sum of the numbers falling uppermost is $2, 3, 4, \ldots, 12$, respectively.

SOLUTION **(a)** We may represent each outcome of the experiment by an ordered pair of numbers, the first representing the number that appears uppermost on the first die and the second representing the number that appears uppermost on the second die. In order to distinguish between the two dice, think of the first die as being red and the second as being green. Since there are 6 possible outcomes for each die, the multiplication principle implies that there are $6 \cdot 6$ or 36 elements in the sample space:

$$\begin{aligned} S = \{&(1, 1), (1, 2), (1, 3), (1, 4), (1, 5), (1, 6),\\ &(2, 1), (2, 2), (2, 3), (2, 4), (2, 5), (2, 6),\\ &(3, 1), (3, 2), (3, 3), (3, 4), (3, 5), (3, 6),\\ &(4, 1), (4, 2), (4, 3), (4, 4), (4, 5), (4, 6),\\ &(5, 1), (5, 2), (5, 3), (5, 4), (5, 5), (5, 6),\\ &(6, 1), (6, 2), (6, 3), (6, 4), (6, 5), (6, 6)\}\end{aligned}$$

(b) With the aid of the results of part **(a)**, we obtain the required results which appear in Table 8.1.

Table 8.1

Sum of uppermost numbers	Event
2	$E_2 = \{(1, 1)\}$
3	$E_3 = \{(1, 2), (2, 1)\}$
4	$E_4 = \{(1, 3), (2, 2), (3, 1)\}$
5	$E_5 = \{(1, 4), (2, 3), (3, 2), (4, 1)\}$
6	$E_6 = \{(1, 5), (2, 4), (3, 3), (4, 2), (5, 1)\}$
7	$E_7 = \{(1, 6), (2, 5), (3, 4), (4, 3), (5, 2), (6, 1)\}$
8	$E_8 = \{(2, 6), (3, 5), (4, 4), (5, 3), (6, 2)\}$
9	$E_9 = \{(3, 6), (4, 5), (5, 4), (6, 3)\}$
10	$E_{10} = \{(4, 6), (5, 5), (6, 4)\}$
11	$E_{11} = \{(5, 6), (6, 5)\}$
12	$E_{12} = \{(6, 6)\}$

■

EXAMPLE 8.4 The manager of a local cinema records the number of patrons attending a first-run movie at the 1:00, 3:00, 5:00, 7:30, and 10:00 P.M. screenings. The theater has a seating capacity of 500.

(a) What is the sample space for this experiment?

(b) Describe the event E that fewer than 50 people attended a screening.

(c) Describe the event F that the theater is filled with greater than half-capacity at a screening.

SOLUTION **(a)** The number of patrons at a particular screening (the outcome) could run from 0 to 500. Therefore, the required sample space S is given by

$$S = \{0, 1, 2, 3, \ldots, 500\}$$

(b) $E = \{0, 1, 2, 3, \ldots, 49\}$

(c) $F = \{251, 252, 253, \ldots, 500\}$ ■

The next example shows that sample spaces may be infinite.

EXAMPLE 8.5 The Ever Brite Battery Company is developing a high-amperage, high-capacity battery as a source for powering electric cars. The battery is tested by installing it in a prototype electric car and running the car with a fully charged battery on a test track at a constant speed of 55 mph until the car runs out of power. The distance covered by the car is then observed.

(a) What is the sample space for this experiment?

(b) Describe the event E that the driving range under test conditions is less than 150 miles.

(c) Describe the event F that the driving range is between 200 and 250 miles inclusive.

SOLUTION **(a)** Since the distance d covered by the car in any run may be given by any nonnegative number, the sample space S is given by

$$S = \{d \mid d \geq 0\}$$

(b) The event E is given by

$$E = \{d \mid d < 150\}$$

(c) The event F is given by

$$F = \{d \mid 200 \leq d \leq 250\}$$ ■

8.1 EXERCISES

1. A bin contains 10 transistors of which 3 are defective. An experiment consists of randomly selecting 3 of the transistors and noting whether they are defective (d) or nondefective (n). What is the sample space for this experiment?

2. An experiment consists of selecting a letter at random from the letters in the word *MASSACHUSETTS* and observing the outcomes.

(*a*) What is the sample space for this experiment?

(*b*) Describe the event "the letter selected is a vowel".

3. An experiment consists of spinning the hand of the numbered disc shown below and observing the region in which the pointer stops. (If the needle stops on a line, the result is discounted and the needle is spun again.)

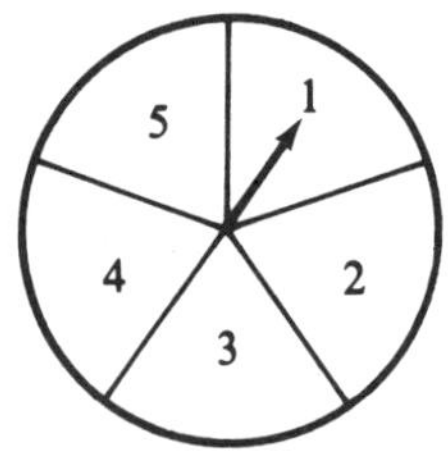

(*a*) What is the sample space for this experiment?

(*b*) Describe the event "the spinner points to the number 2".

(*c*) Describe the event "the spinner points to an odd number".

4. Human blood is classified by the presence or absence of 3 main antigens (A, B, and Rh). When a blood specimen is typed, the presence of the A and/or B antigen is indicated by listing the letter *A* and/or the letter *B*. If neither the A or B antigen is present, the letter *O* is used to represent this case. The presence or absence of the Rh antigen is indicated by the symbols + or −, respectively. Thus, if a blood specimen is classified as AB^+, it contains the A and the B antigens as well as the Rh antigen. Similarly, O^- blood contains none of the 3 antigens. Using this information, determine the sample space corresponding to the different blood groups.

5. An experiment consists of tossing a coin and casting a die and observing the outcomes.

(*a*) Describe the sample space for this experiment.

(*b*) Describe the event "a head is tossed and an even number is cast".

6. In a television game show, the winner is asked to select 3 prizes from 5 different prizes, A, B, C, D, and E.

(*a*) Describe a sample space of possible outcomes.

(*b*) How many points are there in the sample space corresponding to a selection that includes A?

(*c*) How many points are there in the sample space corresponding to a selection that includes A and B?

(*d*) How many points are there in the sample space corresponding to a selection that includes either A or B?

7. Let $S = \{1, 2, 3\}$ be a sample space associated with an experiment.

(***a***) List all events of this experiment.

(***b***) How many subsets of S contain the number 3?

(***c***) How many subsets of S contain either the number 2 or the number 3?

8. The Customer Service Department of the Universal Instruments Company, the manufacturer of the Galaxy Home-computer, conducted a survey among customers who had returned their purchase registration cards. Purchasers of its deluxe model home-computer were asked to report the length of time (t) in days before service was required.

(***a***) Describe a sample space corresponding to this survey.

(***b***) Describe the event E that a home-computer required service before a period of 90 days had elapsed.

(***c***) Describe the event F that a home-computer did not require service before a period of 1 year had elapsed.

9. A time study was conducted by the production manager of the Vista Vision Corporation to determine the length of time in minutes required by an assembly worker to complete a certain task during the assembly of its Pulsar color television sets.

(***a***) Describe a sample space corresponding to this time study.

(***b***) Describe the event E that an assembly worker took 2 minutes or less to complete the task.

(***c***) Describe the event F that an assembly worker took more than 2 minutes to complete the task.

10. An opinion poll is conducted among the electorate in a state to determine the relationship between their income levels and their stands on a proposition aimed at reducing state income taxes. Voters are classified as belonging to either the low-, middle-, or upper-income group. They are asked whether they favor, oppose, or are undecided about the proposition. Let the letters L, M, and U represent the low-, middle-, and upper-income group, respectively, and the letters f, o, and u represent the responses—favor, oppose, and undecided, respectively.

(***a***) Describe the sample space corresponding to this poll.

(***b***) Describe the event E_1 that the respondent favors the proposition.

(***c***) Describe the event E_2 that the respondent opposes the proposition and does not belong to the lower-income group.

(***d***) Describe the event E_3 that the respondent does not favor the proposition and does not belong to the upper-income group.

****11.*** Eight players, A, B, C, D, E, F, G, and H are competing in a series of elimination matches of a tennis tournament, in which the winner of each preliminary match will advance to the semi-finals and the winner of the semi-finals will advance to the finals. An outline of the scheduled matches is given on page 284. Describe a sample space listing the possible participants in the finals.

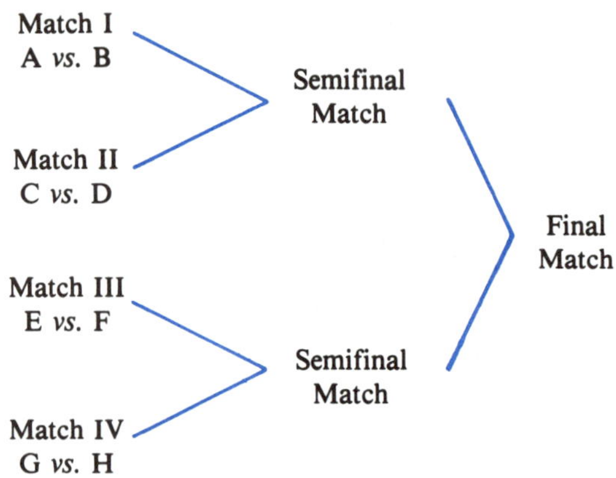

8.2

Definition of Probability

Let us return to the coin-tossing experiment. The sample space of this experiment is given by $S = \{H, T\}$ where the sample points H and T correspond to the experiment's two possible outcomes, a *head* and a *tail.* If the coin is *unbiased*, then there is *1 chance out of 2* of obtaining a head (or a tail) and we say that the *probability* of tossing a head (tail) is $\frac{1}{2}$, abbreviated,

$$P(\mathrm{H}) = \frac{1}{2}, \quad P(\mathrm{T}) = \frac{1}{2}$$

An alternative method of obtaining the values of $P(\mathrm{H})$ and $P(\mathrm{T})$ is based on continued experimentation and does not depend on the assumption that the two outcomes are equally likely. Table 8.2 summarizes the results of such an exercise.

Number of tosses (n)	Number of heads (m)	Relative frequency of heads (m/n)
10	4	0.4000
100	58	0.5800
1000	492	0.4920
10,000	5034	0.5034
20,000	10,024	0.5012
40,000	20,032	0.5008

Table 8.2

Observe that the relative frequencies (column 3) differ considerably when the number of trials are small but, as the number of trials become very large, the relative frequency approaches the number 0.5. This result suggests that we assign to $P(\mathrm{H})$ the value $\frac{1}{2}$, as before.

The second method of arriving at the probability of obtaining a head on one coin-toss provides us with a popular interpretation of the probability of an event. More generally, consider an experiment that may be repeated over and over again under independent and similar conditions. Suppose that in n trials, an event E occurs m times. We call the ratio (m/n) the *relative frequency* of the event E after n repetitions. If this relative frequency approaches some value $P(E)$ as n becomes larger and larger, then $P(E)$ is called the *empirical probability* of E. According to this concept of probability, the probability $P(E)$ of an event occurring is a measure of the proportion of the time that the event E will occur in the long run. Observe that this method of computing the probability of a head occurring is effective even in the case when a biased coin is used in the experiment.

relative frequency

probability of an event

Since the *probability of an event* is a fraction or is obtained by taking the "limit" of fractions that lie between 0 and 1 inclusive, it is itself a number lying between 0 and 1. In general, the larger the probability of an event, the more likely the event will occur. Thus, an event with a probability of 0.8 is more likely to occur than an event with a probability of 0.6. An event with a probability of $\frac{1}{2}$ or 0.5 has a "fifty-fifty" chance of occurring.

Now suppose we are given an experiment and we wish to determine the probabilities associated with certain events of the experiment. This problem could be solved by computing $P(E)$ directly for each event E of interest. However, in practice the number of events that we may be interested in is usually quite large and this approach is not satisfactory.

The following approach is particularly suitable when the sample space of an experiment is finite.* Let S be a finite sample space with n outcomes $s_1, s_2, s_3, \ldots, s_n$; that is

$$S = \{s_1, s_2, s_3, \ldots, s_n\}$$

Then the n singleton sets

$$\{s_1\}, \{s_2\}, \{s_3\}, \ldots, \{s_n\}$$

elementary (basic) events

mutually exclusive events

are called *elementary* or *basic events* of the experiment. The basic events of the experiment are *exhaustive*; that is, one of them must occur. They are also *mutually exclusive*; that is, given any two basic events of the experiment only one can occur. Observe that any (nonempty) event of the experiment may be obtained by taking a finite union of suitable elementary events. The last observation suggests that we assign probabilities to the basic events of the experiment (see Table 8.3).

The numbers $P(s_1), P(s_2), \ldots, P(s_n)$ have the following properties:

1. $0 \leq P(s_i) \leq 1 \qquad (i = 1, 2, \ldots, n)$
2. $P(s_1) + P(s_2) + \cdots + P(s_n) = 1$
3. $P(\{s_i\} \cup \{s_j\}) = P(s_i) + P(s_j) \quad i \neq j \qquad (i = 1, 2, \ldots, n; j = 1, 2, \ldots, n)$

* *For the remainder of the chapter we shall assume that all sample spaces are finite.*

Table 8.3

Elementary event	Probability*
$\{s_1\}$	$P(s_1)$
$\{s_2\}$	$P(s_2)$
$\{s_3\}$	$P(s_3)$
$\vdots$	$\vdots$
$\{s_n\}$	$P(s_n)$

The first property simply states that the probability of an elementary event must be between 0 and 1 inclusive. The second property states that the sum of the probabilities of all elementary events of the sample space is 1. This follows from the fact that the event S is certain to occur. The third property states that the probability of the union of two mutually exclusive events (note that two distinct elementary events are mutually exclusive) is given by the sum of their respective probabilities.

probability distribution

The function P is called a *probability* function and Table 8.3 is called a *probability distribution* for the experiment. As we saw earlier, there is no unique method for assigning probabilities to the elementary events of an experiment or, equivalently, for determining the probability function P. In practice, the methods used to determine the probabilities of the elementary events of an experiment may range from theoretical considerations of the problem on the one extreme to the reliance on "educated guesses" on the other.

uniform sample space

For sample spaces whose outcomes are *equally likely* (such sample spaces are called *uniform sample spaces*) the assignment of probabilities to the elementary events is relatively simple. If there are n sample points comprising such a sample space, say $S = \{s_1, s_2, \ldots, s_n\}$, *then we assign the probabilities*

$$P(s_1) = P(s_2) = \cdots = P(s_n) = \frac{1}{n}$$

to each of the elementary events $s_1, s_2, \ldots, s_n$.

EXAMPLE 8.6 A fair die is cast and the number that falls uppermost is observed. Determine the probability distribution for the experiment.

SOLUTION The sample space for the experiment is $S = \{1, 2, 3, 4, 5, 6\}$ and the elementary events are accordingly given by the sets $\{1\}$, $\{2\}$, $\{3\}$, $\{4\}$, $\{5\}$, and $\{6\}$. Since the die is assumed to be fair, the six outcomes are equally likely. We therefore assign a probability of $\frac{1}{6}$ to each of the elementary events and obtain the following probability

* *For simplicity, we shall use the notation* $P(s_i)$ *instead of the technically more correct* $P(\{s_i\})$.

distribution for the experiment:

Elementary event	Probability
{1}	$\frac{1}{6}$
{2}	$\frac{1}{6}$
{3}	$\frac{1}{6}$
{4}	$\frac{1}{6}$
{5}	$\frac{1}{6}$
{6}	$\frac{1}{6}$

■

The next example shows how the relative frequency interpretation of probability lends itself to the computation of probabilities.

EXAMPLE 8.7 Refer to Example 8.5. The following data was obtained in tests involving 200 test runs. Each run was made with a fully charged battery.

(**a**) Describe the sample space associated with the experiment.

(**b**) Find the probability distribution for the experiment.

Distance covered (x) in miles	Frequency of occurrence
$0 \le x \le 50$	4
$50 < x \le 100$	10
$100 < x \le 150$	30
$150 < x \le 200$	100
$200 < x \le 250$	40
$250 < x$	16

SOLUTION (**a**) Let s_1 denote the outcome that the distance covered by the car does not exceed 50 miles; let s_2 denote the outcome that the distance covered by the car is greater than 50 miles but does not exceed 100 miles, and so on. Finally, let s_6 denote the outcome that the distance covered by the car is greater than 250 miles. Then the required sample space S is given by

$$S = \{s_1, s_2, s_3, s_4, s_5, s_6\}$$

(**b**) To compute the probability distribution for the experiment, we turn to the relative frequency interpretation of probability. Accepting the inaccuracies inherent in a relatively small number of trials (200 runs) we shall take the probability of s_1

occurring as

$$P(s_1) = \frac{\text{number of trials in which } s_1 \text{ occurs}}{\text{total number of trials}}$$

$$= \frac{4}{200}$$

$$= 0.02$$

In a similar manner, we can assign probabilities to the other elementary events, and obtain the following probability distribution for the experiment.

Elementary event	Probability
$\{s_1\}$	0.02
$\{s_2\}$	0.05
$\{s_3\}$	0.15
$\{s_4\}$	0.50
$\{s_5\}$	0.20
$\{s_6\}$	0.08

■

We are now in a position to give a procedure for computing the probability $P(E)$ of an arbitrary event E of an experiment. The steps are:

1. Determine a sample space S associated with the experiment.

2. Assign probabilities to the elementary events of S.

3. *Addition Principle* If E is the empty set $\varnothing$, then $P(E) = 0$. Otherwise, $P(E)$ is given by the sum of the probabilities of the elementary events whose union is E. Thus, if $E = \{s_1, s_2, s_3, \ldots, s_n\}$ where $\{s_1\}$, $\{s_2\}$, $\{s_3\}$, ..., $\{s_n\}$ are elementary events, then $P(E)$ is assigned the value

$$P(E) = P(s_1) + P(s_2) + P(s_3) + \cdots + P(s_n)$$

The addition principle is a consequence of Property *3* of the probability function (page 285).

EXAMPLE 8.8 A pair of fair dice is cast

(a) Calculate the probability that the two dice show the same number.

(b) Calculate the probability that the sum of the numbers of the two dice is six.

SOLUTION From the results of Example 8.3, we see that the sample space S of the experiment consists of 36 outcomes:

$$S = \{(1, 1), (1, 2), \ldots, (6, 5), (6, 6)\}$$

(See Example 8.3 for a complete listing.) Since both dice are fair, each of the 36 outcomes is equally likely. Accordingly, we assign the probability of $\frac{1}{36}$ to each elementary event. We are now in a position to answer the questions posed.

(a) The event that the two dice show the same number is given by

$$E = \{(1, 1), (2, 2), (3, 3), (4, 4), (5, 5), (6, 6)\}$$

Therefore, by the addition principle, the probability that the two dice show the same number is given by

$$\begin{aligned} P(E) &= P[(1, 1)] + P[(2, 2)] + \cdots + P[(6, 6)] \\ &= \frac{1}{36} + \frac{1}{36} + \cdots + \frac{1}{36} \qquad \text{(six terms)} \\ &= \frac{1}{6} \end{aligned}$$

(b) The event that the sum of the numbers of the two dice is six is given by

$$E_6 = \{(1, 5), (2, 4), (3, 3), (4, 2), (5, 1)\} \qquad \text{(See Table 8.1.)}$$

Therefore, the probability that the sum of the numbers on the two dice is six is given by

$$\begin{aligned} P(E_6) &= P[(1, 5)] + P[(2, 4)] + P[(3, 3)] + P[(4, 2)] + P[(5, 1)] \\ &= \frac{1}{36} + \frac{1}{36} + \cdots + \frac{1}{36} \qquad \text{(five terms)} \\ &= \frac{5}{36} \end{aligned}$$

■

EXAMPLE 8.9 Consider the experiment by the Ever Brite Battery Company in Example 8.5. What is the probability that the prototype car will travel more than 150 miles on a fully charged battery?

SOLUTION Using the results of Example 8.7, we see that the event that the car will travel more than 150 miles on a fully charged battery is given by $E = \{s_4, s_5, s_6\}$. Therefore, the probability that the car will travel more than 150 miles on one charge is given by

$$P(E) = P(s_4) + P(s_5) + P(s_6)$$

or using the probability distribution for the experiment obtained in Example 8.7,

$$\begin{aligned} P(E) &= 0.50 + 0.20 + 0.08 \\ &= 0.78 \end{aligned}$$

■

8.2 EXERCISES

1. The grade distribution for a certain class is shown in the table below. Find the probability distribution associated with this data.

Grade	Frequency of occurrence
A	4
B	10
C	18
D	6
F	2

2. The number of cars entering a tunnel leading to an airport in a major city over a period of 200 peak hours was observed and the following data was obtained:

Number of cars (x)	Frequency of occurrence
$0 < x \leq 200$	15
$200 < x \leq 400$	20
$400 < x \leq 600$	35
$600 < x \leq 800$	70
$800 < x \leq 1000$	45
$x > 1000$	15

(*a*) Describe the sample space associated with this experiment.

(*b*) Find the probability distribution for this experiment.

3. The Metro Telephone Company of Belmont compiled the following information during a service-utilization study pertaining to the number of customers using their Dial-the-Time service from 7 A.M. to 9 A.M. on a certain weekday morning. Using this data, find the probability distribution associated with this experiment.

Number of calls received/minute	Frequency of occurrence
10	6
11	15
12	12
13	3
14	12
15	36
16	24
17	0
18	6
19	6

4. The results of a time-study conducted by the production manager of the Ace Novelty Company are shown in the following table, where the number of space action-figures produced each quarter hour during an 8-hour work day have been tabulated. Find the probability distribution associated with this experiment.

Number of figures produced (in dozens)	Frequency of occurrence
30	4
31	0
32	6
33	8
34	6
35	4
36	4

5. If one card is drawn at random from a standard 52-card deck, what is the probability that the card drawn is

(*a*) a diamond?

(*b*) a black card?

(*c*) an ace?

6. One light bulb is selected at random from a lot of 120 light bulbs of which 5% are defective. What is the probability that the light bulb selected is defective?

7. A pair of fair dice is cast, what is the probability that

(*a*) the sum of the numbers shown uppermost is less than five?

(*b*) at least one 6 is cast?

8. If a ball is selected at random from an urn containing 3 red balls, 2 white balls, and 5 blue balls, what is the probability that it will be a white ball?

9. What is the probability of arriving at a traffic light when it is red, if the red signal is flashed for 30 seconds, the yellow signal for 5 seconds, and the green signal for 45 seconds?

10. What is the probability in the game of roulette that the ball will come to rest on an even number other than 0 or 00? (Assume that there are 38 equally likely outcomes consisting of the numbers 1–36, 0 and 00.)

11. Refer to problem 2. What is the probability that more than 600 cars will enter the airport tunnel during a peak hour?

12. Refer to problem 1. What is the probability that a student selected at random from this class received a passing grade (D or better)?

13. One hundred thousand entries have been received in a sweepstakes sponsored by the Gemini Paper Products Company. If 1 grand prize, 5 first prizes, 25 second prizes, and 500 third prizes are to be awarded, what is the probability that

(*a*) a person who has submitted one entry will win the grand prize?

(*b*) a person who has submitted one entry will win a prize?

14. If a coin, which is weighted in such a way that "heads" is 4 times as likely to occur as "tails", is tossed, what is the probability that it will land "heads"?

15. Let $S = \{s_1, s_2, s_3, s_4, s_5, s_6\}$ be the sample space associated with an experiment. Suppose the probability distribution associated with the experiment is as follows:

Outcome	Probability
$\{s_1\}$	$\frac{1}{12}$
$\{s_2\}$	$\frac{1}{4}$
$\{s_3\}$	$\frac{1}{12}$
$\{s_4\}$	$\frac{1}{6}$
$\{s_5\}$	$\frac{1}{3}$
$\{s_6\}$	$\frac{1}{12}$

Find the probability of the event

(*a*) $A = \{s_1, s_3\}$ (*b*) $B = \{s_2, s_4, s_5, s_6\}$ (*c*) S

16. An opinion poll was conducted among a group of registered voters in a certain state concerning a proposition aimed at limiting state and local taxes. Results of the poll indicated that 35% of the voters favored the proposition, 32% were against the proposition, and the remaining group were undecided. If the results of the poll are assumed to be representative of the opinion of the electorate of the state, what is the probability that

(*a*) a registered voter selected at random from the electorate favors the proposition?

(*b*) a registered voter selected at random from the electorate is undecided about the proposition?

8.3 Rules of Probability

In this section we shall examine some of the properties of the probability function and look at the role they play in the solution of certain problems. We begin by looking at the generalization of the three properties of the probability function, which were stated for elementary events in the last section. Let S be a sample space of an experiment and suppose E and F are events of the experiment. Then we have

Property 1 $P(E) \geq 0$ for any E

Property 2 $P(S)=1$

Property 3 If E and F are mutually exclusive (that is, only one of them can occur, or equivalently, $E \cap F = \varnothing$), then

$$P(E \cup F) = P(E) + P(F)$$

Property 3 may be easily extended to the case involving any finite number of mutually exclusive events. Thus, if $E_1, E_2, \ldots, E_n$ are mutually exclusive events, then

$$P(E_1 \cup E_2 \cup \cdots \cup E_n) = P(E_1) + P(E_2) + \cdots + P(E_n)$$

EXAMPLE 8.10 The superintendent of a metropolitan school district has estimated the probabilities associated with the SAT-verbal scores of students from that district. The results are shown in Table 8.4. If a student is selected at random what is the probability that his SAT-verbal score will be

(a) more than 400?

(b) less than or equal to 500?

(c) greater than 400 but less than or equal to 600?

Table 8.4

Score (x)	Probability
$x > 700$	0.01
$600 < x \le 700$	0.07
$500 < x \le 600$	0.19
$400 < x \le 500$	0.23
$300 < x \le 400$	0.31
$x \le 300$	0.19

SOLUTION Let A, B, C, D, E, and F denote, respectively, the event that the score is greater than 700, greater than 600 but less than or equal to 700, greater than 500 but less than or equal to 600, and so forth. Then, these events are mutually exclusive. Therefore

(a) the probability that the student's score will be more than 400 is given by

$$\begin{aligned} P(D \cup C \cup B \cup A) &= P(D) + P(C) + P(B) + P(A) \\ &= 0.23 + 0.19 + 0.07 + 0.01 \\ &= 0.5 \end{aligned}$$

(b) the probability that the student's score will be less than or equal to 500 is given by

$$P(D \cup E \cup F) = P(D) + P(E) + P(F)$$
$$= 0.23 + 0.31 + 0.19$$
$$= 0.73$$

(c) the probability that the student's score will be greater than 400 but less than or equal to 600 is given by

$$P(C \cup D) = P(C) + P(D)$$
$$= 0.19 + 0.23$$
$$= 0.42$$

■

Property 3 holds when and only when E and F are mutually exclusive. In the general case we have

Property 4 If E and F are any two events of an experiment, then

$$P(E \cup F) = P(E) + P(F) - P(E \cap F)$$

Property 4 is a consequence of Formula 7.2, page 254, and its proof is sketched in Exercise set 8.3 problem 20. Observe that when E and F are mutually exclusive, that is, when $E \cap F = \varnothing$, then the equation of Property 4 reduces to that of Property 3.

EXAMPLE 8.11 A card is drawn from a well-shuffled deck of 52 playing cards. What is the probability that it is an ace or a spade?

SOLUTION Let E denote the event that the card drawn is an ace, and let F denote the event that the card drawn is a spade. Then

$$P(E) = \frac{4}{52} \quad \text{and} \quad P(F) = \frac{13}{52}$$

Furthermore, E and F are not mutually exclusive events. In fact $E \cap F$ is the event that the card drawn is an ace of spades. Consequently,

$$P(E \cap F) = \frac{1}{52}$$

The event that a card drawn is an ace or a spade is $E \cup F$ with probability given by

$$P(E \cup F) = P(E) + P(F) - P(E \cap F)$$
$$= \frac{4}{52} + \frac{13}{52} - \frac{1}{52}$$
$$= \frac{4}{13}$$

This result, of course, can be obtained by arguing that 16 of the 52 cards are either spades or aces of other suits. ■

EXAMPLE 8.12 The Quality Control Department of the Vista Vision Corporation, the manufacturer of the Pulsar 19-inch color television sets, has determined from records obtained from the company's service centers that 3% of the sets sold experience video problems, 1% of the sets sold experience audio problems, and 0.1% of the sets sold experience both video as well as audio problems before the expiration of the 90-day warranty. Find the probability that a set purchased by a consumer will experience video or audio problems before the expiration of the warranty.

SOLUTION Let E denote the event that a set purchased will experience video problems within 90 days and let F denote the event that a set purchased will experience audio problems within 90 days. Then

$$P(E)=0.03,\ P(F)=0.01,\ \text{and}\ P(E\cap F)=0.001$$

The event that a set purchased by a consumer will experience video problems or audio problems before the expiration of the warranty is $E\cup F$ and the probability of this event is given by

$$\begin{aligned} P(E\cup F) &= P(E)+P(F)-P(E\cap F) \\ &= 0.03+0.01-0.001 \\ &= 0.039 \end{aligned}$$

■

Another property of the probability function, which is of considerable aid in computations involving probability, follows:

Property 5 If E is an event of an experiment, and E^c denotes the complement of E, then

$$P(E^c)=1-P(E)$$

Property 5 is an immediate consequence of Properties 2 and 3. Indeed, we have $E\cup E^c=S$ and $E\cap E^c=\varnothing$ so that

$$1=P(S)=P(E\cup E^c)=P(E)+P(E^c)$$

whence $$P(E^c)=1-P(E)$$

EXAMPLE 8.13 Refer to Example 8.12. What is the probability that a Pulsar 19-inch color television set bought by a consumer will not experience video or audio difficulties before the expiration of the warranty?

SOLUTION Let E denote the event that a set bought by a consumer will experience video or audio difficulties before expiration of the warranty. Then the event that the set will not experience either problems before expiration of the warranty is given by E^c

with probability

$$\begin{aligned} P(E^c) &= 1 - P(E) \\ &= 1 - 0.039 \\ &= 0.961 \end{aligned}$$

■

We close this section by looking at two further examples illustrating the rules of probability.

EXAMPLE 8.14 Let E and F be two events that are mutually exclusive and suppose $P(E) = 0.1$ and $P(F) = 0.6$. Compute

(a) $P(E \cap F)$

(b) $P(E \cup F)$

(c) $P(E^c)$

(d) $P(E^c \cap F^c)$

(e) $P(E^c \cup F^c)$

SOLUTION **(a)** Since the events E and F are mutually exclusive, that is, $E \cap F = \varnothing$, we have $P(E \cap F) = 0$.

(b)

$$\begin{aligned} P(E \cup F) &= P(E) + P(F) \qquad \text{(since } E \text{ and } F \text{ are mutually exclusive)} \\ &= 0.1 + 0.6 \\ &= 0.7 \end{aligned}$$

(c)

$$\begin{aligned} P(E^c) &= 1 - P(E) \qquad \text{(Property 5)} \\ &= 1 - 0.1 \\ &= 0.9 \end{aligned}$$

(d) Observe that, by DeMorgans's Law, $E^c \cap F^c = (E \cup F)^c$ and so

$$\begin{aligned} P(E^c \cap F^c) &= P[(E \cup F)^c] \\ &= 1 - P(E \cup F) \qquad \text{(Property 5)} \\ &= 1 - 0.7 \qquad \text{(using the result of part } \mathbf{b}\text{)} \\ &= 0.3 \end{aligned}$$

(e) Again, using DeMorgan's Law, we find

$$\begin{aligned} P(E^c \cup F^c) &= P[(E \cap F)^c] \\ &= 1 - P(E \cap F) \\ &= 1 - 0 \qquad \text{(using the result of part } \mathbf{a}\text{)} \\ &= 1 \end{aligned}$$

■

EXAMPLE 8.15 Let E and F bc two events of an experiment with sample space S. Suppose $P(E) = 0.2$, $P(F) = 0.1$, and $P(E \cap F) = 0.05$. Compute

(**a**) $P(E \cup F)$

(**b**) $P(E^c \cap F^c)$

(**c**) $P(E^c \cap F)$ (*Hint*: Draw a Venn diagram.)

SOLUTION (**a**)

$$\begin{aligned} P(E \cup F) &= P(E) + P(F) - P(E \cap F) \qquad \text{(Property 4)} \\ &= 0.2 + 0.1 - 0.05 \\ &= 0.25 \end{aligned}$$

(**b**) Using DeMorgan's Law, we have,

$$\begin{aligned} P(E^c \cap F^c) &= P[(E \cup F)^c] \\ &= 1 - P(E \cup F) \qquad \text{(Property 5)} \\ &= 1 - 0.25 \qquad \text{(using the result of part } \mathbf{a}\text{)} \\ &= 0.75 \end{aligned}$$

(**c**) From the Venn diagram describing the relationship between E, F, and S (Figure 8.2) we have (the shaded subset is the event $E^c \cap F$)

$$P(E^c \cap F) = 0.05$$

This result may also be obtained by using the relationship

$$\begin{aligned} P(E^c \cap F) &= P(F) - P(E \cap F) \\ &= 0.1 - 0.05 \\ &= 0.05 \end{aligned}$$

as before.

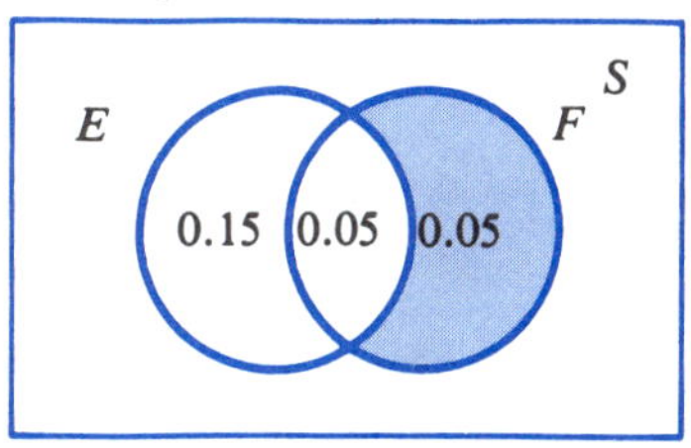

Figure 8.2

8.3 EXERCISES

1. A card is drawn from a well-shuffled deck of 52 playing cards. What is the probability that it is not an ace?

2. Five hundred people have purchased tickets in a lottery. What is the probability that a person holding one ticket will win the first prize? What is the probability that he will not win the first prize?

In Problems 3–9, explain why the given statement is incorrect.

3. The probability that a bus will not arrive on time at the Civic Center is 0.35 and the probability that it will either be on time or late is 0.60.

4. A fair die is cast 3 times. The probability of getting at least 1 six is $\frac{1}{6}+\frac{1}{6}+\frac{1}{6}$.

5. A person participates in a weekly office pool in which he or she has 1 chance in 10 of winning the purse. If he or she participates for 5 weeks in succession, the probability of winning at least one purse is $\frac{5}{10}$.

6. A red die and a green die are tossed. The probability that a 6 will appear uppermost on the red die is $\frac{1}{6}$ and the probability that a 1 will appear uppermost on the green die is $\frac{1}{6}$. Hence, the probability that the red die will show a 6 or the green die will show a 1 is $\frac{1}{6}+\frac{1}{6}$.

7. Joanne, a high school senior, has applied for admission to four colleges, A, B, C, and D. She has estimated that the probability that she will be accepted for admission by A, B, C, and D to be 0.5, 0.3, 0.1, and 0.08, respectively. Thus, the probability that she will be accepted for admission by at least one college is $P(A)+P(B)+P(C)+P(D)=0.5+0.3+0.1+0.08=0.98$.

8. The sample space associated with an experiment is given by $S=\{a, b, c, d, e\}$. The events $E=\{a, b\}$ and $F=\{c, d\}$ are mutually exclusive. Hence, the events E^c and F^c are mutually exclusive.

9. Mr. Owens, an optician, estimates that the probability that a customer coming into his store will purchase one or more pairs of glasses but not contact lenses is 0.40, and the probability that he will purchase one or more pairs of contact lenses but not glasses is 0.25. Hence, he concludes that the probability that a customer coming into his store will purchase neither a pair of glasses nor a pair of contact lenses to be 0.35.

10. An experiment consists of casting a die. What is the probability that the number that appears uppermost will be

(***a***) an odd number greater than 3?

(***b***) an odd number or a number greater than 3?

11. A card is drawn from a well-shuffled deck of 52 playing cards. What is the probability that it is

(***a***) the queen of hearts?

(***b***) a queen or a heart?

(***c***) neither a queen nor a heart?

12. Let E and F be two events which are mutually exclusive and suppose $P(E)=0.2$ and $P(F)=0.5$. Compute

(***a***) $P(E\cap F)$ (***b***) $P(E\cup F)$ (***c***) $P(E^c)$

(***d***) $P(E^c\cap F^c)$ (***e***) $P(E^c\cup F^c)$

13. Let $S=\{s_1, s_2, s_3, s_4\}$ be the sample space associated with an experiment and suppose the probability distribution associated with the experiment is in the list following. If $A = \{s_1, s_2\}$ and $B = \{s_1, s_3\}$, find

(*a*) $P(A), P(B)$ (*b*) $P(A^c), P(B^c)$ (*c*) $P(A \cap B)$

(*d*) $P(A \cup B)$

Outcome	Probability
$\{s_1\}$	$\frac{1}{8}$
$\{s_2\}$	$\frac{3}{8}$
$\{s_3\}$	$\frac{1}{4}$
$\{s_4\}$	$\frac{1}{4}$

14. Let $S = \{s_1, s_2, s_3, s_4, s_5, s_6\}$ be the sample space associated with an experiment and suppose the probability distribution associated with the experiment is in the following list. If $A = \{s_1, s_2\}$ and $B = \{s_1, s_5, s_6\}$, find

(*a*) $P(A), P(B)$ (*b*) $P(A^c), P(B^c)$ (*c*) $P(A \cap B)$

(*d*) $P(A \cup B)$ (*e*) $P(A^c \cap B^c)$ (*f*) $P(A^c \cup B^c)$

Outcome	Probability
$\{s_1\}$	$\frac{1}{3}$
$\{s_2\}$	$\frac{1}{8}$
$\{s_3\}$	$\frac{1}{6}$
$\{s_4\}$	$\frac{1}{6}$
$\{s_5\}$	$\frac{1}{12}$
$\{s_6\}$	$\frac{1}{8}$

15. Let E and F be two events of an experiment with sample space S. Suppose $P(E) = 0.4$, $P(F) = 0.2$, and $P(E \cap F) = 0.1$. Compute

(*a*) $P(E \cup F)$ (*b*) $P(E^c \cap F^c)$ (*c*) $P(E^c \cap F)$

16. Let E and F be two events of an experiment with sample space S. Suppose $P(E) = 0.6$, $P(F) = 0.4$, and $P(E \cap F) = 0.2$. Compute

(*a*) $P(E \cup F)$ (*b*) $P(E^c)$ (*c*) $P(F^c)$

(*d*) $P(E^c \cap F)$ (*e*) $P(E \cap F^c)$ (*f*) $P(E^c \cup F^c)$

17. Among 500 freshmen pursuing a business degree at a university, 320 are enrolled in an economics course, 225 are enrolled in a mathematics course, and 140 are enrolled in both an economics and a mathematics course. What is the probability that a freshman selected at random from this group is enrolled in

(*a*) an economics and/or mathematics course?

(*b*) exactly one of these two courses?

(*c*) neither an economics course nor a mathematics course?

18. A leading manufacturer of kitchen appliances advertised its products in 2 magazines—*Good Housekeeping* and the *Ladies Home Journal.* A survey of 500 customers revealed that 140 learned of its products from *Good Housekeeping*, 130 learned of its products from the *Ladies Home Journal*, and 80 learned of its products from both magazines. What is the probability that a person selected at random from this group saw the manufacturer's advertisment in

(*a*) both magazines?

(*b*) at least one of the 2 magazines?

(*c*) exactly 1 magazine?

19. A time-study was conducted by the production manager of the Universal Instruments Company to determine the length of time required by an assembly worker to complete a certain task during the assembly of its Galaxy Home-computers. Results of the study indicated that 20% of the workers were able to complete the task in less than 3 minutes, 60% of the workers were able to complete the task in 4 minutes or less, and 10% of the workers required more than 5 minutes to complete the task. If an assembly line worker is selected at random from this group, what is the probability that

(*a*) he or she will be able to complete the task in 5 minutes or less?

(*b*) he or she will not be able to complete the task within 4 minutes?

(*c*) the time taken for the worker to complete the task will be between 3 and 4 minutes (inclusive)?

20. Let S be a sample space of an experiment and suppose E and F are events of the experiment. Prove that

$$P(E \cup F) = P(E) + P(F) - P(E \cap F)$$

Hint: Since E and F are subsets of S, Formula 7.2, on page 254, states that $n(E \cup F) = n(E) + n(F) - n(E \cap F)$. Divide both sides of this equation by $n(S)$, assuming the latter is different from zero, and interpret the quotients obtained.

8.4

Use of Counting Techniques in Probability

As we have seen many times before, a problem in which the underlying sample space has a small number of elements may be solved by first determining all such sample points. For problems involving sample spaces with a large number of sample points, however, this approach is neither practical nor desirable.

In this section we shall see how the counting techniques studied in Chapter 7 may be employed to help us solve problems in which the associated sample spaces contain large numbers of sample points. In particular, we shall restrict our attention to the study of uniform sample spaces; that is, sample spaces in which the outcomes are equally likely. For such spaces we have the following result:

Let S be a uniform sample space and let E be any event, then

(8.1) $$P(E) = \frac{\text{number of favorable outcomes in } E}{\text{number of possible outcomes in } S} = \frac{n(E)}{n(S)}$$

EXAMPLE 8.16 An unbiased coin is tossed 6 times.

(a) What is the probability that the coin will land "heads" all 6 times?

(b) What is the probability that the coin will land heads on the first and the last toss?

SOLUTION **(a)** Each outcome of the experiment may be represented as a sequence of heads and tails. Using the generalized multiplication principle, we see that the number of outcomes of this experiment is given by 2^6 or 64 (compare with example 7.7). Let E denote the event that the coin lands "heads" all 6 times. Clearly, there is only one way this can occur, and so the probability of this event is given by

$$P(E)=\frac{n(E)}{n(S)}=\frac{1}{64} \qquad (S\text{, sample space of the experiment})$$

(b) Let F denote the event that the coin lands "heads" on the first and the last toss. Then $n(F)=1\cdot 2\cdot 2\cdot 2\cdot 2\cdot 1=2^4$ and so the probability that this event occurs is

$$P(F)=\frac{2^4}{2^6}$$

$$=\frac{1}{2^2}$$

$$=\frac{1}{4}$$

■

EXAMPLE 8.17 Two cards are selected at random from a well-shuffled pack of 52 playing cards.

(a) What is the probability that they are both aces?

(b) What is the probability that neither of them is an ace?

SOLUTION **(a)** The experiment consists of selecting 2 cards from a pack of 52 playing cards. Since the order in which the cards is selected is immaterial, the sample points are combinations of 52 cards taken 2 at a time. Now, there are $C(52,2)$ ways of selecting 52 cards taken 2 at a time and so the number of elements in the sample space S is given by $C(52,2)$. Next, we observe that there are $C(4,2)$ ways of selecting 2 aces from the 4 in the deck. Therefore, if E denotes the event that the cards selected are both aces, then

$$P(E)=\frac{n(E)}{n(S)}$$

$$=\frac{C(4,2)}{C(52,2)}=\frac{\dfrac{4!}{2!2!}}{\dfrac{52!}{2!50!}}$$

$$=\frac{1}{221}$$

(**b**) Let F denote the event that neither of the 2 cards selected is an ace. Since there are $C(48, 2)$ ways of selecting 2 cards neither of which is an ace, we find that

$$P(F)=\frac{n(F)}{n(S)}=\frac{C(48,2)}{C(52,2)}=\frac{\frac{48!}{2!46!}}{\frac{52!}{2!50!}}=\frac{48\cdot 47}{2}\cdot\frac{2}{52\cdot 51}$$

$$=\frac{188}{221}$$

EXAMPLE 8.18 A bin in the HiFi department of Building 20, a bargain outlet, contains 100 blank cassette tapes of which 10 are known to be defective. If a customer selects 6 of these cassette tapes, determine the probability that:

(**a**) 2 of them are defective.

(**b**) at least 1 of them is defective.

SOLUTION (**a**) There are $C(100, 6)$ ways of selecting a set of 6 cassette tapes from the 100 and this gives $n(S)$, the number of outcomes in the sample space associated with the experiment. Next, we observe that there are $C(10, 2)$ ways of selecting a set of 2 defective cassette tapes from the 10 defective cassette tapes and $C(90, 4)$ ways of selecting a set of 4 nondefective cassette tapes from the 90 nondefective cassette tapes so that, by the multiplication principle, there are $C(10, 2)\cdot C(90, 4)$ ways of selecting 2 defective and 4 nondefective cassette tapes. Thus, the probability of selecting 6 cassette tapes of which 2 are defective is given by

$$\frac{C(10,2)\cdot C(90,4)}{C(100,6)}=\frac{\frac{10!}{2!8!}\,\frac{90!}{4!86!}}{\frac{100!}{6!94!}}$$

$$=\frac{10\cdot 9}{2}\cdot\frac{90\cdot 89\cdot 88\cdot 87}{4\cdot 3\cdot 2\cdot 1}\cdot\frac{6\cdot 5\cdot 4\cdot 3\cdot 2\cdot 1}{100\cdot 99\cdot 98\cdot 97\cdot 96\cdot 95}$$

$$\approx 0.097$$

(**b**) Let E denote the event that none of the cassette tapes selected is defective. Then E^c gives the event that at least 1 of the cassette tapes is defective. But, by Property 5, (see Section 8.3)

$$P(E^c)=1-P(E)$$

To compute $P(E)$, we observe that there are $C(90, 6)$ ways of selecting a set of 6 cassette tapes that are nondefective. Therefore,

$$P(E)=\frac{C(90,6)}{C(100,6)}$$

and
$$P(E^c) = 1 - \frac{C(90,6)}{C(100,6)}$$
$$= 1 - \frac{\dfrac{90!}{6!84!}}{\dfrac{100!}{6!94!}}$$
$$= 1 - \frac{90 \cdot 89 \cdot 88 \cdot 87 \cdot 86 \cdot 85}{6 \cdot 5 \cdot 4 \cdot 3 \cdot 2 \cdot 1} \cdot \frac{6 \cdot 5 \cdot 4 \cdot 3 \cdot 2 \cdot 1}{100 \cdot 99 \cdot 98 \cdot 97 \cdot 96 \cdot 95}$$
$$\approx 0.48$$
■

EXAMPLE 8.19 A group of 5 people is selected at random. What is the probability that at least 2 of the people have the same birthday?

SOLUTION For simplicity we shall assume that none of the 5 people were born on February 29 of a leap year. Since the 5 people were selected at random, we may also assume that each of them is equally likely to have any of the 365 days of a year as his or her birthday. If we let A, B, C, D, and E represent the 5 people, then it is easy to see that an outcome of the experiment may be represented by (a, b, c, d, e), where the numbers a, b, c, d, and e give the birthdays of A, B, C, D and E, respectively. We first observe that since there are 365 possibilities for each of the dates a, b, c, d and e, the multiplication principle implies that there are

$$365 \cdot 365 \cdot 365 \cdot 365 \cdot 365 \quad \text{or} \quad 365^5$$

outcomes of the experiment; that is

$$n(S) = 365^5$$

where S denotes the sample space of the experiment. Next, let E denote the event that 2 or more of the 5 people have the same birthday. It is required to compute $P(E)$. However, a direct computation of $P(E)$ is relatively difficult. It is much easier to compute $P(E^c)$ where E^c is, of course, the event that no 2 of the 5 people have the same birthday and then use the relation

$$P(E) = 1 - P(E^c)$$

To this end, observe that there are 365 ways (corresponding to the 365 dates) on which A's birthday can occur followed by 364 ways on which B's birthday could occur if B were not to have the same birthday as A, and so on, so that, by the generalized multiplication principle

$$n(E^c) = 365 \cdot 364 \cdot 363 \cdot 362 \cdot 361$$

Thus,
$$P(E^c) = \frac{n(E^c)}{n(S)} = \frac{365 \cdot 364 \cdot 363 \cdot 362 \cdot 361}{365^5}$$

and
$$P(E) = 1 - P(E^c) = 1 - \frac{365 \cdot 364 \cdot 363 \cdot 362 \cdot 361}{365^5} \approx 0.027$$

The result obtained in Example 8.19 may be easily extended to the general case involving r people. In fact, if E denotes the event that at least 2 of the r people have the same birthday, an argument similar to that used in Example 8.19 leads to the result

$$P(E) = 1 - \frac{365 \cdot 364 \cdot 363 \cdots (365 - r + 1)}{365^r}$$

By letting r take on the values 5, 10, 15, 20, . . . , 50, in turn, we obtain the probabilities that at least two of 5, 10, 15, 20, . . . , 50 people, respectively, have the same birthday. These results are summarized in Table 8.5. The results show that the chances are greater than 50% that in a group of 23 randomly selected people at least 2 of them will have the same birthday. In a group of 50 people, it is an excellent bet that at least 2 people in the group will have the same birthday.

Table 8.5

r	5	10	15	20	22	23	25	30	40	50
$P(E)$	0.027	0.117	0.253	0.411	0.476	0.507	0.569	0.706	0.891	0.970

8.4 EXERCISES

1. An unbiased coin is tossed 5 times. What is the probability that the coin will land heads

(*a*) all 5 times?

(*b*) exactly once?

(*c*) at least once?

2. Two cards are selected at random from a well-shuffled pack of 52 playing cards. What is the probability that

(*a*) a pair is drawn?

(*b*) a pair is not drawn?

3. Five balls are selected at random without replacement from an urn containing 6 white balls and 9 blue balls. What is the probability that

(*a*) all of the balls are blue?

(*b*) exactly 2 are white?

(*c*) 2 or 3 are white?

4. An exam consists of 10 true or false questions. If a student guesses at every answer, what is the probability that he will answer exactly 6 questions correctly?

5. What is the probability that in a family of 3 children

(*a*) the first 2 are girls? (Assume that the probability of a boy being born is the same as the probability of a girl being born.)

(*b*) 2 are boys and 1 is a girl?

(*c*) at least 1 is a girl?

6. Jacobs & Johnson Inc., an accounting firm, employs 14 accountants of which 8 are C.P.A.'s. If a delegation of 3 accountants are randomly selected from the firm to attend a conference, what is the probability that 3 C.P.A.'s will be selected?

7. Two light bulbs are selected at random from a lot of 24 of which 4 are defective. What is the probability that

(*a*) both of the light bulbs are defective?

(*b*) at least 1 of the light bulbs is defective?

8. A customer at Cavallaro's Fruit Stand picks a sample of 3 oranges at random from a crate containing 60 oranges of which 4 are rotten. What is the probability that the sample contains 1 or more rotten oranges?

9. A shelf in the Metro Department Store contains 80 typewriter cartridge ribbons for a popular portable typewriter. Six of the cartridges are defective. If a customer selects 2 of these cartridges at random from the shelf, determine the probability that

(*a*) both are defective.

(*b*) at least 1 is defective.

10. Electronic baseball games manufactured by Tempco Electronics are shipped in lots of 24. Before shipping a quality control inspector randomly selects a sample of 8 from each lot for testing. If the sample contains any defective games, the entire lot is rejected. What is the probability that a lot containing 2 defective games will still be shipped?

11. The City Transit Authority of a certain city plans to hire 12 new bus drivers. From a group of 100 qualified applicants of which 60 are men and 40 are women, 12 names are to be selected by lot. If Mary and John Lewis are among the 100 qualified applicants,

(*a*) what is the probability that Mary's name will be selected? that both Mary's and John's names will be selected?

(*b*) and it is stipulated that an equal number of men and women are to be selected (6 men from the group of 60 men and 6 women from the group of 40 women), what is the probability that Mary's name will be selected? that Mary's and John's names will be selected?

12. In the game of "Blackjack" a 2-card hand consisting of an ace and a face card or a ten is called a blackjack.

(*a*) If a player is dealt 2 cards from a standard deck of 52 well-shuffled cards, what is the probability that the player will receive a blackjack?

(*b*) If a player is dealt 2 cards from 2 well-shuffled standard decks, what is the probability that the player will receive a blackjack?

13. Refer to problem 17 in Exercise set 7.2, where the "Lucky Dollar" slot machine was described. What is the probability that the 3 "Lucky Dollar" symbols will appear in the window of the slot machine?

14. In 1959 a world record was set for the longest run on an ungaffed (fair) roulette wheel at the El San Juan Hotel in Puerto Rico. The number 10 appeared 6 times in a row. What is the probability of the occurrence of this event? (Assume that there are 38 equally likely outcomes consisting of the numbers 1–36, 0, and "00".)

****15.*** In "The Numbers Game", a state lottery, 4 numbers are drawn with replacement from an urn containing the digits 0–9 inclusive. Prizes are given to ticket holders with the selected numbers in exact order for (a) all 4 digits (b) the first or last 3 digits (c) any 2 digits and (d) any 1 digit. What is the probability of the occurrence of the event (a)? the event (b)? the event (c)? and the event (d)? (A ticket holder may claim only 1 prize for each ticket.)

****16.*** Refer to problem 15. In "The Numbers Game" prizes are also given to ticket holders with the selected numbers in any order for (a) all 4 digits, (b) the first 3 digits, and (c) the last 3 digits. What is the probability of the occurrence of the event (a)?, the event (b)?, and the event (c)? (A ticket holder may claim only 1 prize for each ticket.)

17. If a 5-card poker hand is dealt from a well-shuffled deck of 52 cards (see chart on page 307), what is the probability of being dealt

(*a*) a straight flush? (Note that an ace may be played as either a high or a low card in a straight sequence; that is A, 1, 2, 3, 4 or 10, J, Q, K, A. Hence, there are 10 possible sequences for a straight in one suit.)

(*b*) a straight (but not a straight flush)?

(*c*) a flush (but not a straight flush)?

18. If a 5-card poker hand is dealt from a well-shuffled deck of 52 cards (see chart on page 307), what is the probability of being dealt

(*a*) 4 of a kind?

(*b*) a full house?

(*c*) 2 pairs?

A list of poker hands ranked in order from the highest to the lowest is shown in the following table along with a description and example of each hand. Use this table to answer questions 17 and 18.

Hand	Description	Example
Straight flush	5 cards in sequence in the same suit	A♥ 2♥ 3♥ 4♥ 5♥
Four of a kind	4 cards of the same rank and any other card	K♥ K♦ K♠ K♣ 2♥
Full house	3 of-a-kind and a pair	3♥ 3♦ 3♠ 7♥ 7♦
Flush	5 cards of the same suit that are not all in sequence	5♥ 6♥ 9♥ J♥ K♥
Straight	5 cards in sequence but not all of the same suit	10♥ J♦ Q♣ K♠ A♥
Three-of-a-kind	3 cards of the same rank and 2 unmatched cards	K♥ K♦ K♠ 2♥ 4♦
Two pair	2 cards of the same rank and 2 cards of any other rank with an unmatched card	K♥ K♦ 2♥ 2♠ 4♣
One pair	2 cards of the same rank and 3 unmatched cards	K♥ K♦ 5♥ 2♠ 4♥

19. There are 12 signs of the Zodiac: Aries, Taurus, Gemini, Cancer, Leo, Virgo, Libra, Scorpio, Sagittarius, Capricorn, Aquarius, and Pisces. Each sign corresponds to a different calendar period of approximately one month. Assuming that a person is just as likely to be born under 1 sign as another, what is the probability that in a group of 5 people

(***a***) at least 2 of the people have the same sign?

(***b***) at least 2 of the people were born under the sign of Aries?

20. What is the probability that at least 2 justices of the U.S. Supreme Court have the same birthday?

21. Fifty people are selected at random. What is the probability that none of the people in this group have the same birthday?

****22.*** During an episode of the *Tonight Show*, Johnny Carson related "The Birthday Problem" to the audience—noting that in a group of 50 or more people probabilists have calculated that the probability of at least 2 people having the same birthday is very high. To illustrate this point, he proceeded to conduct his own experiment. A person selected at random from the audience was asked to state his birthday.

Mr. Carson then asked if anyone in the audience had the same birthday. The response was negative. He repeated the experiment. Once again, the response was negative. These results, observed Mr. Carson, were contrary to expectations. In a later episode of the show Mr. Carson explained why this experiment had been improperly conducted. Explain why his experiment failed to illustrate the point that he was trying to make.

8.5

Conditional Probability and Independent Events

The probability of an event is often affected by the occurrence of other events and/or by the knowledge of information relevant to the event. Basically, the injection of conditions into a problem modifies the underlying sample space of the original problem. This in turn leads to a change in the probability of the event.

EXAMPLE 8.20 Two cards are drawn without replacement from a well-shuffled deck of 52 playing cards.

(**a**) What is the probability that the first card drawn is an ace?

(**b**) What is the probability that the second card drawn is an ace given that the first card drawn was not an ace?

(**c**) What is the probability that the second card drawn is an ace given that the first card drawn was an ace?

SOLUTION (**a**) The sample space here consists of 52 equally likely outcomes, 4 of which are aces. Therefore, the probability that the first card drawn is an ace is $\frac{4}{52}$.

(**b**) Having drawn the first card, there are 51 cards left in the deck. In other words, for the second phase of the experiment, we are working in a *reduced* sample space. If the first card drawn was not an ace, then this modified sample space of 51 points contains 4 "favorable" outcomes (the 4 aces), so that the probability that the second card drawn is an ace is given by $\frac{4}{51}$.

(**c**) If the first card drawn was an ace, then there are 3 aces left in the deck of 51 playing cards and so the probability that the second card drawn is an ace is given by $\frac{3}{51}$. ■

Observe that in Example 8.20 the occurrence of the first event reduces the size of the original sample space. The information concerning the first card drawn also leads us to the consideration of modified sample spaces—in part (**b**) the deck contained 4 aces, while in part (**c**), the deck contained 3 aces.

The probability found in part (**b**) or part (**c**) of Example 8.20 is known as a conditional probability, since it is the probability of an event occurring given that another event has already occurred. For example, in part (**b**), we computed the probability of the event that the second card drawn is an ace, given the event that the first card drawn was not an ace. In general, given two events A and B of an experiment, one may, under certain circumstances, compute the probability of the event B given that the event A has already occurred. This probability, denoted by $P(B|A)$, is called the *conditional probability of B given A*.

conditional probability

A formula for computing the conditional probability of B given A may be discovered with the aid of a Venn diagram. Consider an experiment with a uniform sample space S and suppose A and B are two events of the experiment (see Figure 8.3).

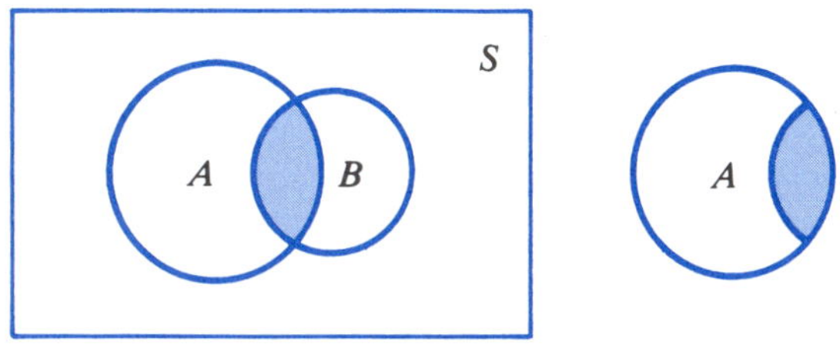

Figure 8.3 Original sample space Reduced sample space

The condition that the event A has occurred tells us that the possible outcomes of the experiment in the second phase are restricted to those outcomes (elements) in the set A. In other words, we may work with the reduced sample space A instead of the original sample space S in the experiment. Next, we observe that, with respect to the reduced sample space A, the outcomes favorable to the event B are precisely those elements in the set $A \cap B$. Consequently, the conditional probability of B given A is

$$P(B|A) = \frac{\text{number of elements in } A \cap B}{\text{number of elements in } A}$$

$$= \frac{n(A \cap B)}{n(A)} \qquad [n(A) \neq 0]$$

Dividing the numerator and the denominator by $n(S)$, the number of elements in S, we have

$$P(B|A) = \frac{\dfrac{n(A \cap B)}{n(S)}}{\dfrac{n(A)}{n(S)}}$$

(8.2) or

$$P(B|A) = \frac{P(A \cap B)}{P(A)} \qquad [P(A) \neq 0]$$

EXAMPLE 8.21 A pair of fair dice is cast. What is the probability that the sum of the numbers falling uppermost is seven if it is known that one of the numbers is a 5?

SOLUTION Let A denote the event that the sum of the numbers falling uppermost is seven and let B denote the event that one of the numbers is a 5. From the results of

Example 8.3, we find that

$$A = \{(6,1),(5,2),(4,3),(3,4),(2,5),(1,6)\}$$

and $$B = \{(5,1),(5,2),(5,3),(5,4),(5,5),(5,6),(1,5),(2,5),(3,5),(4,5),(6,5)\}$$

so that $A \cap B = \{(5,2),(2,5)\}$

Since the dice are fair, each outcome of the experiment is equally likely and therefore

$$P(A \cap B) = \frac{2}{36} \quad \text{and} \quad P(B) = \frac{11}{36} \qquad \text{(Recall that } n(S) = 36.)$$

Therefore, the probability that the sum of the numbers falling uppermost is seven given that one of the numbers is a 5 is, by virtue of formula (8.2),

$$P(A \mid B) = \frac{\frac{2}{36}}{\frac{11}{36}} = \frac{2}{11}$$

■

EXAMPLE 8.22 In a recently conducted test by the U.S. Army, it was found that of 1000 new recruits, 600 men and 400 women, 50 of the men and 4 of the women were red-green colorblind. Given that a recruit selected at random from this group is red-green colorblind, what is the probability that the recruit is a male?

SOLUTION Let C denote the event that a randomly selected subject is red-green colorblind and let M denote the event that the subject is a male recruit. Since 54 out of the 1000 subjects are colorblind, we may take

$$P(C) = \frac{54}{1000} = 0.054$$

Therefore, by formula (8.2), the probability that a subject is male given that he is red-green colorblind is

$$P(M \mid C) = \frac{P(M \cap C)}{P(C)}$$

$$= \frac{0.05}{0.054} = \frac{25}{27}$$

■

In certain problems, the probability of an event B occurring given that A has occurred, written $P(B \mid A)$, is known and we wish to find the probability of A **and** B occurring. The solution to such a problem is facilitated by the use of the formula

(8.3) $$P(A \cap B) = P(A) \cdot P(B \mid A)$$

Product Rule which is obtained from the formula (8.2) by multiplying both sides of the equation by $P(A)$. Formula (8.3) is known as the *Product Rule*. We illustrate its use in the next several examples.

EXAMPLE 8.23 There are 300 seniors in Jefferson High School of which 140 are males. It is known that 80% of the males and 60% of the females have their driver's license. If a student is selected at random from this senior class

(a) What is the probability that he is a male and has a driver's license?

(b) What is the probability that she is a female who does not have a driver's license?

SOLUTION **(a)** Let M denote the event that the student is a male and let D denote the event that the student has a driver's license. Then

$$P(M)=\frac{140}{300} \quad \text{and} \quad P(D|M)=0.8$$

Now, the event that the student selected at random is a male and has a driver's license is $M \cap D$ and, by the product rule, the probability of this event occurring is given by

$$\begin{aligned} P(M \cap D) &= P(M) \cdot P(D|M) \\ &= \left(\frac{140}{300}\right)(0.8)=\frac{28}{75} \end{aligned}$$

(b) Let F denote the event that the student is a female and let D be as before. Then D^c is the event that the student does not have a driver's license. We have

$$P(F)=\frac{160}{300} \quad \text{and} \quad P(D^c|F)=1-0.6=0.4$$

Note that we have used the complement rule in the computation of $P(D^c|F)$ above. Now, the event that the student selected at random is a female and does not have a driver's license is $F \cap D^c$ and, by the product rule, the probability of this event occurring is given by

$$\begin{aligned} P(F \cap D^c) &= P(F) \cdot P(D^c|F) \\ &= \left(\frac{160}{300}\right)(0.4)=\frac{16}{75} \end{aligned}$$

■

EXAMPLE 8.24 Two cards are drawn without replacement from a well-shuffled deck of 52 playing cards. What is the probability that the first card drawn is an ace and the second card drawn is a face card?

SOLUTION Let A denote the event that the first card drawn is an ace and let F denote the event that the second card drawn is a face card. Then $P(A)=\frac{4}{52}$. After drawing the first card there are 51 cards left in the deck of which 12 are face cards. Therefore, the probability of drawing a face card given that the first card drawn was an ace is given by

$$P(F|A)=\frac{12}{51}$$

By the product rule, the probability that the first card drawn is an ace and the second card drawn is a face card is given by

$$\begin{aligned}P(A\cap F)&=P(A)\cdot P(F|A)\\&=\left(\frac{4}{52}\right)\left(\frac{12}{51}\right)=\frac{4}{221}\end{aligned}$$

■

We wish to comment, at this point, that the product rule may be generalized to the case involving any finite number of events. For example, in the case involving the three events E, F, and G, it may be shown that

(8.4) $$P(E\cap F\cap G)=P(E)\cdot P(F|E)\cdot P(G|E\cap F)$$

finite stochastic process

Formula (8.4) and its generalizations may be used to aid us in solving problems that involve *finite stochastic processes*. More specifically, a finite stochastic process is an experiment consisting of a finite number of stages in which the outcomes and associated probabilities of each stage are dependent on the outcomes and associated probabilities of the preceding stages. Experiments involving finite stochastic processes may be described by tree diagrams, the latter also serving as aids to the solution of problems involving such processes. Consider, for example, the experiment consisting of drawing 2 cards without replacement from a well-shuffled deck of 52 playing cards. What is the probability that the second card drawn is a face card?

We may think of this experiment as a stochastic process with two stages. The events associated with the first stage are F, that the card drawn is a face card and F^c, that the card drawn is not a face card. Since there are 12 face cards, we have

$$P(F)=\frac{12}{52}\quad\text{and}\quad P(F^c)=1-\frac{12}{52}=\frac{40}{52}$$

The outcomes of this trial together with the associated probabilities may be represented along two "branches" of a tree diagram as shown in Figure 8.4.

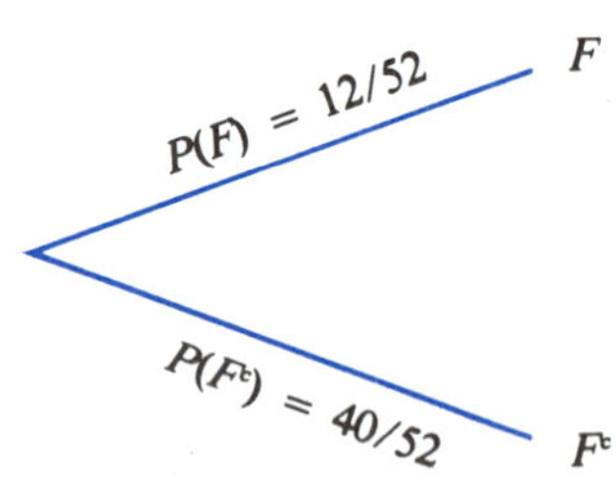

Figure 8.4

In the second trial, we again have two events: G, that the card drawn is a face card and G^c, that the card drawn is not a face card. But the outcome of the second trial is dependent on the outcome of the first trial. For example, if the first card drawn was a face card, then the event G that the second card drawn is a face card has probability given by the *conditional probability* $P(G|F)$. Since the occurrence of a face card in the first draw leaves 11 face cards in a deck of 51 cards for the second draw, we see that

$$P(G|F)=\frac{11}{51}$$

Similarly, the occurrence of a face card in the first draw leaves 40 that are other than face cards in a deck of 51 cards for the second draw. Therefore, the probability of drawing other than a face card in the second draw given that the first card drawn is a face card is

$$P(G^c|F)=\frac{40}{51}$$

The results just obtained allow us to extend the tree diagram of Figure 8.4 by displaying another two branches of the tree growing from its upper branch (see Figure 8.5).

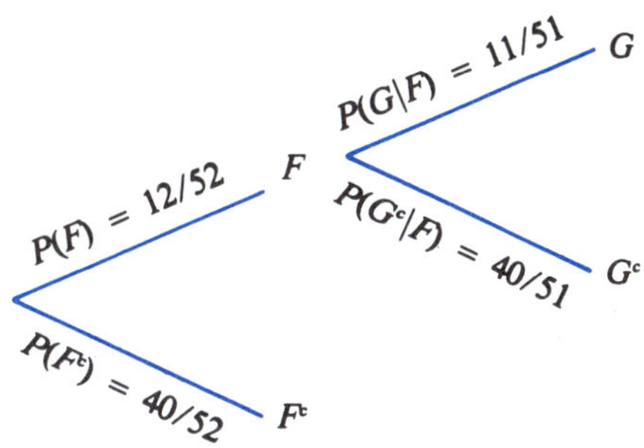

Figure 8.5

To complete the tree diagram we compute $P(G|F^c)$ and $P(G^c|F^c)$, the conditional probabilities that the second card drawn is a face card and other than a face card, respectively, given that the first card drawn is not a face card. We find that

$$P(G|F^c)=\frac{12}{51} \quad \text{and} \quad P(G^c|F^c)=\frac{39}{51}$$

This leads to the completion of the tree diagram shown in Figure 8.6, where the branches of the tree that lead to the two outcomes of interest have been highlighted.

Having constructed the tree diagram associated with the problem, we are now in a position to answer the question posed earlier, namely, what is the probability of the second card being a face card. Observe that Figure 8.6 shows the two ways

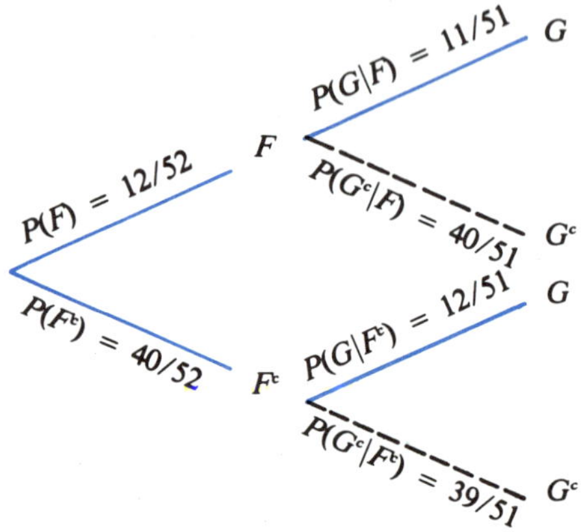

Figure 8.6

in which a face card may result in the second draw, namely the two Gs on the extreme right of the diagram.

Now, by the product rule, the probability that the second card drawn is a face card given that the first card drawn is a face card (this is represented by the upper branch) is

$$P(G \cap F) = P(F) \cdot P(G \mid F)$$

Similarly, the probability that the second card drawn is a face card given that the first card drawn is other than a face card (this corresponds to the other branch) is

$$P(G \cap F^c) = P(F^c) \cdot P(G \mid F^c)$$

Observe that each of these probabilities is obtained by taking the *product of the probabilities appearing on the respective branch.* Since $G \cap F$ and $G \cap F^c$ are mutually exclusive events (why?) the probability that the second card drawn is a face card is given by

$$P(G \cap F) + P(G \cap F^c) = P(F) \cdot P(G \mid F) + P(F^c) \cdot P(G \mid F^c)$$

or, upon replacing the probabilities on the right of the expression by their numerical values,

$$\begin{aligned} P(G \cap F) + P(G \cap F^c) &= \left(\frac{12}{52}\right)\left(\frac{11}{51}\right) + \left(\frac{40}{52}\right)\left(\frac{12}{51}\right) \\ &= \frac{3}{13} \end{aligned}$$

EXAMPLE 8.25 The picture tubes for the Pulsar 19-inch color television sets are manufactured in 3 locations and then shipped to the main plant of the Vista Vision Corporation for final assembly. Plants A, B, and C supply 50%, 30%, and 20%, respectively, of the picture tubes used by the company. The Quality Control Department of the company has determined that 1% of the picture tubes produced by plant A are defective, while 2% of the picture tubes produced by plants B and C are defective. What is the probability that a randomly selected Pulsar 19-inch color television set will have a defective picture tube?

SOLUTION Let A, B, and C denote the events that the set chosen has a picture tube manufactured in plant A, plant B, and plant C, respectively. Also, let D denote the event that a set has a defective picture tube. Using the given information, we draw the tree diagram shown in Figure 8.7. The events that result in a set with a defective picture tube being selected are circled in Figure 8.7. Taking the product of the probabilities along each branch leading to such an event and adding them yields the probability that a set chosen at random has a defective picture tube. Thus, the required probability is given by

$$\begin{aligned}&(0.5)(0.01)+(0.3)(0.02)+(0.2)(0.02)\\&=0.005+0.006+0.004\\&=0.015\end{aligned}$$

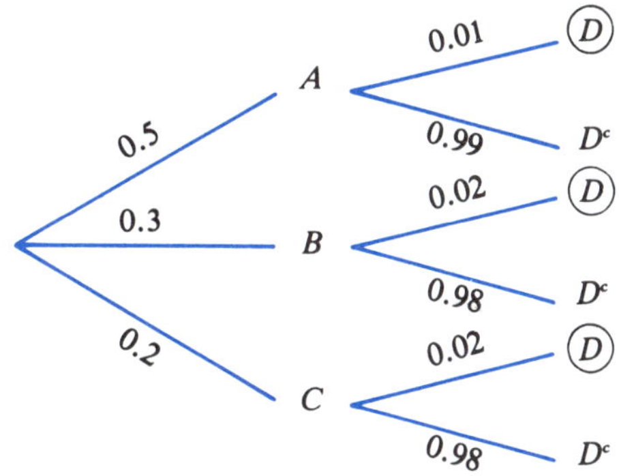

Figure 8.7

EXAMPLE 8.26 A box contains 8 9-volt transistor batteries of which 2 are known to be defective. The batteries are selected 1 at a time without replacement and tested until a nondefective one is found. What is the probability that the number of batteries tested is (a) 1, (b) 2, (c) 3?

SOLUTION We may view this experiment as a multi-stage process with up to three stages. In the first stage, a battery is selected with a probability of $\frac{6}{8}$ of it being nondefective and a probability of $\frac{2}{8}$ of it being defective. If the battery selected is good, the experiment is terminated. Otherwise, a second battery is selected with probabilities of $\frac{6}{7}$ and $\frac{1}{7}$, respectively, of being nondefective and defective. If the second battery selected is good, the experiment is terminated. Otherwise, a third battery is selected with probabilities of 1 and 0, respectively, of being nondefective and defective. The tree diagram associated with this experiment is shown in Figure 8.8, where N denotes the event that the battery selected is nondefective while D denotes the event that the battery selected is defective.

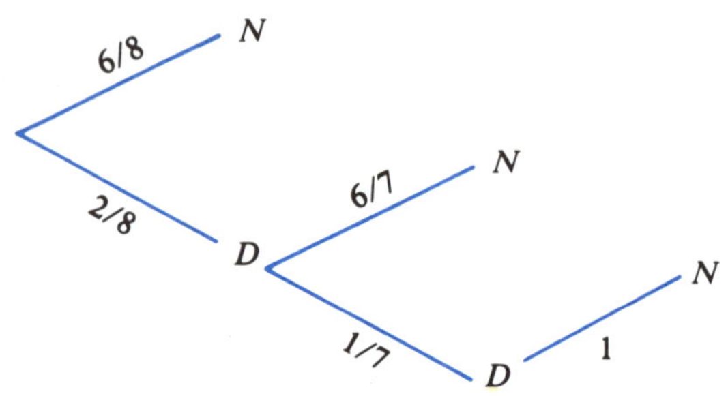

Figure 8.8

With the aid of the tree diagram we see that (a) the probability that only 1 battery is selected is $\frac{6}{8}$, (b) the probability that 2 batteries are selected is $(\frac{2}{8})(\frac{6}{7})$ or $\frac{3}{14}$ and (c) the probability that 3 batteries are selected is $(\frac{2}{8})(\frac{1}{7})(1)=\frac{1}{28}$. ■

Returning to Example 8.24, we see that the event of a face card being drawn was affected by the first outcome—the event of an ace being drawn. In fact, the drawing of the ace reduced the original sample space from 52 elements to one with 51 elements and, in this manner, affected the probability of a face card being drawn next. In certain situations, the occurrence or nonoccurrence of an event is not affected by the occurrence or nonoccurrence of another event. A simple example of such a situation is provided by the experiment of tossing a coin twice and observing the outcomes. It is intuitively clear that the outcome of the second toss is in no way affected by the outcome of the first toss; in this case we say that the two events are independent. In general, two events A and B are *independent* if the outcome of one does not affect the outcome of the other. Symbolically, two events A and B are independent if

independent event

(8.5)
$$P(A|B)=P(A) \quad \text{or} \quad P(B|A)=P(B)$$

In fact, the first equation reads "the probability of A given B is equal to the probability of A" thereby implying the independence of A from B. The second equation has a similar implication.

Using the product rule, it is easy to find a simple test for the independence of two events. Indeed, if A and B are independent, then

$$P(B|A)=P(B)$$

so that, by the product rule, we have

$$P(A\cap B)=P(A)\cdot P(B|A)=P(A)\cdot P(B)$$

Conversely, if the above equation holds, then it may be seen that $P(B|A)=P(B)$, that is, A and B are independent. Accordingly, we have the following *test for the independence of two events*. Two events A and B are independent if and only if

(8.6)
$$P(A\cap B)=P(A)\cdot P(B)$$

EXAMPLE 8.27 Consider the experiment consisting of tossing a fair coin twice and observing the outcomes. Show that the event of "heads" in the first toss and "tails" in the second toss are independent events.

SOLUTION Let A denote the event that the outcome of the first toss is a *head* and let B denote the event that the outcome of the second toss is a *tail*. The sample space of the experiment is

$$S = \{(H, H), (H, T), (T, H), (T, T)\}$$

and
$$A = \{(H, H), (H, T)\}, \qquad B = \{(H, T), (T, T)\}$$

so that
$$A \cap B = \{(H, T)\}$$

Next, we compute

$$P(A \cap B) = \frac{1}{4}, \qquad P(A) = \frac{1}{2}, \quad \text{and} \quad P(B) = \frac{1}{2}$$

and observe that equation (8.6) is satisfied in this case so that A and B are independent events, as we set out to show. ■

EXAMPLE 8.28 A survey conducted by an independent agency for the National Lung Society found that of 2000 women, 680 were "heavy smokers" and 50 had emphysema. Of those who had emphysema, 42 were also heavy smokers. Using the data in this survey determine whether the events "being a heavy smoker" and "having emphysema" are independent events.

SOLUTION Let A denote the event that a woman is a heavy smoker and let B denote the event that a woman has emphysema. Then the probability that a woman is a heavy smoker and has emphysema is given by

$$P(A \cap B) = \frac{42}{2000} = 0.021$$

Next,
$$P(A) = \frac{680}{2000} = 0.34 \quad \text{and} \quad P(B) = \frac{50}{2000} = 0.025$$

so that,
$$P(A) \cdot P(B) = (0.34)(0.025) = 0.0085$$

Since $P(A \cap B) \neq P(A) \cdot P(B)$, we conclude that A and B are not independent events. ■

The solution of many practical problems involves more than two independent events. In such cases it is true that

(8.7)
$$P(E_1 \cap E_2 \cap \cdots \cap E_n) = P(E_1) \cdot P(E_2) \cdot \cdots \cdot P(E_n)$$

where $E_1, E_2, \ldots, E_n$ are known to be independent events. Formula (8.7) states that the probability of the simultaneous occurrence of n independent events is equal to the product of the probabilities of the n events.

It is important to note that the mere requirement that the n events $E_1, E_2, \ldots, E_n$ satisfy formula (8.7) is not sufficient to guarantee that the n events are indeed independent. However, a criteria does exist for determining the independence of n events and may be found in more advanced texts on probability.

EXAMPLE 8.29 It is known that the three events A, B, and C are independent and $P(A)=0.2$, $P(B)=0.4$, and $P(C)=0.5$.

(a) Compute $P(A \cap B)$

(b) Compute $P(A \cap B \cap C)$

SOLUTION Using formula (8.7), we find

(a) $$P(A \cap B) = P(A) \cdot P(B) = (0.2)(0.4) = 0.08$$

(b) $$P(A \cap B \cap C) = P(A) \cdot P(B) \cdot P(C) = (0.2)(0.4)(0.5) = 0.04$$

■

EXAMPLE 8.30 The Acrosonic Model F loudspeaker system has four loudspeaker components—a woofer, a midrange, a tweeter, and an electrical cross-over. The Quality Control manager of the Acrosonic Company has determined that on the average 1% of the woofers, 0.8% of the midranges, and 0.5% of the tweeters are defective while 1.5% of the electrical cross-overs are defective. Determine the probability that an Acrosonic Model F loudspeaker system selected at random coming off the assembly line and before final inspection is not defective. Assume that the defects in the manufacturing of the components are unrelated.

SOLUTION Let A, B, C, and D denote, respectively, the events that the woofer, the midrange, the tweeter, and the electrical cross-over are defective. Then,

$$P(A)=0.01, \quad P(B)=0.008, \quad P(C)=0.005, \quad \text{and} \quad P(D)=0.015$$

and the probabilities of the corresponding complementary events are

$$P(A^c)=0.99, \quad P(B^c)=0.992, \quad P(C^c)=0.995, \quad \text{and} \quad P(D^c)=0.985$$

The event that a loudspeaker system selected at random is not defective is given by $A^c \cap B^c \cap C^c \cap D^c$ and since the events A, B, C, and D (and therefore also A^c, B^c, C^c, and D^c) are assumed to be independent, we find that the required probability is given by

$$\begin{aligned} P(A^c \cap B^c \cap C^c \cap D^c) &= P(A^c) \cdot P(B^c) \cdot P(C^c) \cdot P(D^c) \\ &= (0.99)(0.992)(0.995)(0.985) \\ &\approx 0.96 \end{aligned}$$

■

8.5 EXERCISES

1. Let A and B be events in a sample space S such that $P(A)=0.6$, $P(B)=0.5$, and $P(A\cap B)=0.2$. Find

(***a***) $P(A|B)$ (***b***) $P(B|A)$

2. Let A and B be two events in a sample space S such that $P(A)=0.6$ and $P(B|A)=0.5$. Find $P(A\cap B)$.

3. Let A and B be the events described in problem 1. Find

(***a***) $P(A|B^c)$ (***b***) $P(B|A^c)$ *Hint*: $(A\cap B^c)\cup(A\cap B)=A$

4. In each case determine whether or not the given events A and B are independent.

(***a***) $P(A)=0.6$, $P(B)=0.8$, $P(A\cap B)=0.2$

(***b***) $P(A^c)=0.3$, $P(B^c)=0.4$, $P(A\cap B)=0.42$

(***c***) $P(A)=0.5$, $P(B)=0.7$, $P(A\cup B)=0.85$

5. If A and B are independent events and $P(A)=0.4$ and $P(B)=0.6$, find

(***a***) $P(A\cap B)$ (***b***) $P(A\cup B)$

6. A pair of fair dice is cast. What is the probability that the sum of the numbers falling uppermost is less than nine, if it is known that one of the numbers is a 6?

7. Two cards are drawn without replacement from a well-shuffled deck of 52 playing cards.

(***a***) What is the probability that the first card drawn is a heart?

(***b***) What is the probability that the second card drawn is a heart given that the first card drawn was not a heart?

(***c***) What is the probability that the second card drawn is a heart given that the first card drawn was a heart?

8. Three cards are drawn without replacement from a well-shuffled deck of 52 playing cards. What is the probability that the third card drawn is a diamond?

9. The tree diagram shown below represents an experiment consisting of two trials.

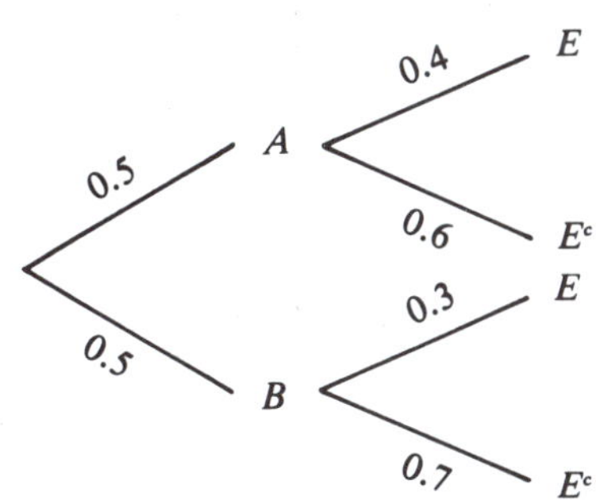

Use the diagram to find

(*a*) $P(A)$ (*b*) $P(E|A)$

(*c*) $P(A \cap E)$ (*d*) $P(E)$

(*e*) Does $P(A \cap E) = P(A) \cdot P(E)$?

(*f*) Are A and E independent events?

10. The tree diagram shown below represents an experiment consisting of two trials. Use the diagram to find

(*a*) $P(A)$ (*b*) $P(E|A)$

(*c*) $P(A \cap E)$ (*d*) $P(E)$

(*e*) Does $P(A \cap E) = P(A) \cdot P(E)$?

(*f*) Are A and E independent events?

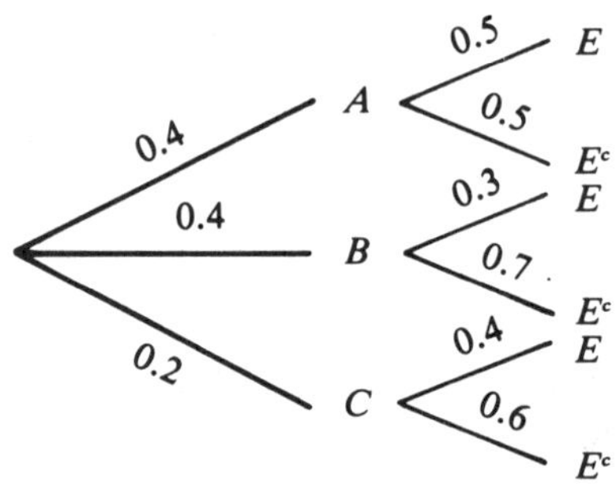

11. Two balls are drawn without replacement from an urn containing 6 white balls and 3 red balls. Find the probability that

(*a*) both are white balls.

(*b*) both are white balls given that the first ball is white.

12. Two cards are drawn without replacement from a well-shuffled deck of 52 cards. Let A be the event that the first card drawn is a heart and let B be the event that the second card drawn is a red card. Show that the events A and B are dependent events.

13. A tax specialist has estimated the probability that a tax-return selected at random will be audited is 0.02. Furthermore, he estimates the probability that an audited return will result in additional assessment being levied upon the taxpayer is 0.6. What is the probability that a tax-return selected at random will result in additional assessments being levied upon the taxpayer?

14. In a 3-child family, what is the probability that all 3 children are girls given that 1 of the children is a girl? (Assume that the probability of a boy being born is the same as the probability of a girl being born.)

15. The probability that a battery will last 10 hours or more is 0.8 and the probability that it will last 15 hours or more is 0.15. Given that a battery has lasted 10 hours, find the probability that it will last 15 hours or more.

16. In a survey of 1000 eligible voters selected at random, it was found that 80 had a college degree. Additionally, it was found that 80% of those who had a college degree voted in the last presidential election, while 55% of the people who did not have a college degree voted in the last presidential election. Assuming that the poll is representative of all eligible voters, find the probability that an eligible voter selected at random

(***a***) had a college degree and voted in the last presidential election.

(***b***) did not have a college degree and did not vote in the last presidential election.

(***c***) voted in the last presidential election.

(***d***) did not vote in the last presidential election.

17. The Personnel Department of the Franklin National Life Insurance Company compiled the following data regarding the income and education of its employees.

	Income \$30,000 or below	Income above \$30,000
Non-College graduate	2040	840
College graduate	400	720

Let A be the event that an employee has a college degree and B the event that an employee's income is more than \$30,000.

(***a***) Find each of the following probabilities.

1 $P(A)$ **2** $P(B)$ **3** $P(A \cap B)$ **4** $P(B|A)$ **5** $P(B|A^c)$

(***b***) Are the events A and B independent events?

18. Suppose that a box contains 2 defective Christmas tree lights that have been inadvertently mixed with 8 nondefective lights. If the lights are selected one at a time without replacement and tested until both defective lights are found, what is the probability that both defective lights will be found after 3 trials?

19. A nationwide survey conducted by the National Cancer Society revealed the following information: Of 10,000 people surveyed, 3200 were "heavy coffee drinkers" and 160 had cancer of the pancreas. Of those who had cancer of the pancreas, 132 were heavy coffee drinkers. Using the data in this survey determine whether the events "being a heavy coffee drinker" and "having cancer of the pancreas" are independent events.

20. The proprietor of Cunningham's Hardware Store has decided to install floodlights on the premises of the store as a further measure against vandalism and theft. If the probability is 0.01 that a certain brand of floodlights will burn out within a year of usage, find the minimum number of floodlights that must be installed to insure the probability that at least one of them will remain functional within the year is at least 0.99999. (Assume the floodlights operate independently of each other.)

21. Copykwik Inc. has 4 photocopy machines, A, B, C, and D. The probability that a given machine will break down on a particular day is as follows:

$$P(A)=\frac{1}{50}, \qquad P(B)=\frac{1}{60}, \qquad P(C)=\frac{1}{75}, \qquad P(D)=\frac{1}{40}$$

Assuming independence, what is the probability on a particular day that

(***a***) all 4 machines will break down?

(***b***) none of the machines will break down?

(***c***) exactly 1 machine will break down?

22. An automobile manufacturer obtains the microprocessors used to regulate fuel consumption in its automobiles from three microelectronic firms, A, B, and C. The Quality Control Department of the company has determined that 1% of the microprocessors produced by Firm A are defective, 2% of those produced by Firm B are defective, and 1.5% of those produced by Firm C are defective. Firms A, B, and C supply 45%, 25%, and 30%, respectively, of the microprocessors used by the company. What is the probability that a randomly selected automobile manufactured by the company will have a defective microprocessor?

23. Before being allowed to enter a maximum security area at a military installation, a person must pass three identification tests—a voice pattern test, a fingerprint test, and a handwriting test. If the reliability of the first test is 97%, the reliability of the second test is 98.5%, and that of the third is 98.5%, what is the probability that this security system will allow an improperly identified person admittance to the maximum security area?

*****24.*** The Office of Admissions of a private university released the following admission data for the preceding academic year: From a pool of 3900 male applicants, 40% were accepted by the university and of these, 40% subsequently enrolled in the university. Additionally, from a pool of 3600 female applicants, 45% were accepted by the university of which 40% subsequently enrolled in the university. Find the probability that

(***a***) a male applicant will be accepted by the university and subsequently will enroll in the university.

(***b***) a student who applies for admission to the university will be accepted by the university.

(***c***) a student who applies for admission to the university will be accepted by the university and subsequently will enroll in the university.

8.6 Bayes' Theorem

In the previous sections we were concerned with the calculation of probabilities that give the likelihood that an event *will* occur. Such probabilities are called *a priori probabilities* since they are calculated *prior* to observing the results of the *a priori and a posteriori probabilities*

experiments. In this section, we shall consider probabilities that are calculated *after* the outcomes of experiments have been observed. Such probabilities are called *a posteriori probabilities*.

Suppose three machines A, B, and C produce similar engine components. Machine A produces 45% of the total components, machine B produces 30%, and machine C, 25%. For the usual production schedule, 6% of the components produced by machine A do not meet established specifications; for machine B and machine C, the corresponding figures are 4% and 3%. One component is selected at random from the total output and is found to be defective. What is the probability that the component selected was produced by machine A?

The answer to this question is found by determining the a posteriori probability for the event that the component selected was produced by machine A. To this end, let A, B, and C denote the event that a component is produced by machine A, machine B, and machine C, respectively. We may represent this experiment with a Venn diagram (Figure 8.9).

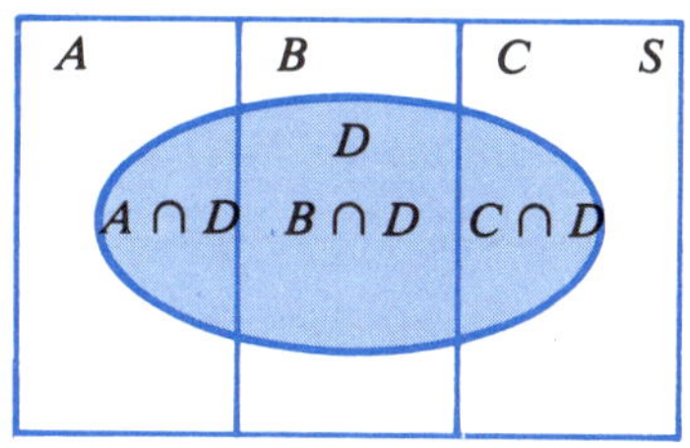

Figure 8.9

partition

The three mutually exclusive events A, B, and C form a *partition* of the sample space S. That is, aside from being mutually exclusive, their union is precisely S. The event D that a component is defective is the area shown shaded. Again referring to Figure 8.9, we see that

1. The event D may be expressed as

$$D = (A \cap D) \cup (B \cap D) \cup (C \cap D)$$

2. The event that a component is defective and is produced by machine A is given by $A \cap D$.

Thus, the posteriori probability that a defective component selected was produced by machine A is given by

$$P(A|D) = \frac{n(A \cap D)}{n(D)}$$

or, upon dividing both the numerator and the denominator by $n(S)$ and observing that the events $A \cap D$, $B \cap D$, and $C \cap D$ are mutually exclusive, we obtain

(8.8)
$$P(A|D) = \frac{P(A \cap D)}{P(D)}$$

$$= \frac{P(A \cap D)}{P(A \cap D) + P(B \cap D) + P(C \cap D)}$$

Next, using the product rule, we may express

$$P(A \cap D) = P(A) \cdot P(D \mid A)$$
$$P(B \cap D) = P(B) \cdot P(D \mid B)$$

and

$$P(C \cap D) = P(C) \cdot P(D \mid C)$$

so that formula (8.8) may be expressed in the form

(8.9) $$P(A \mid D) = \frac{P(A) \cdot P(D \mid A)}{P(A) \cdot P(D \mid A) + P(B) \cdot P(D \mid B) + P(C) \cdot P(D \mid C)}$$

which is a special case of a result known as *Bayes' Theorem*. Observe that the expression on the right of formula (8.9) involves the probabilities $P(A)$, $P(B)$, $P(C)$ and the conditional probabilities $P(D \mid A)$, $P(D \mid B)$, and $P(D \mid C)$, all of which may be calculated in the usual fashion. In fact, by displaying these quantities on a tree diagram associated with the experiment, we obtain Figure 8.10.

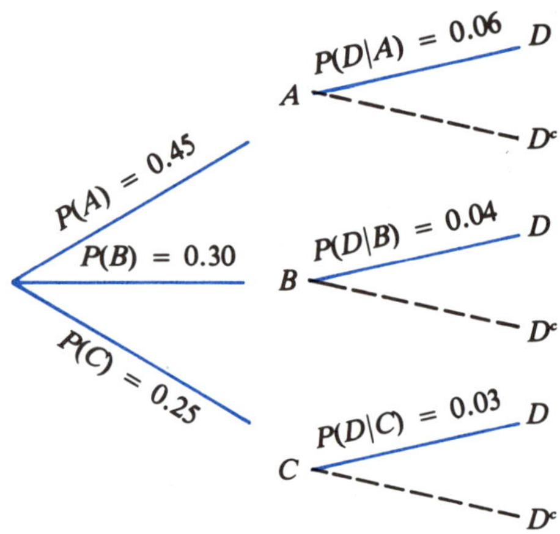

Figure 8.10

We may compute the required probability by substituting the relevant quantities into formula (8.9), or, we may make use of the following device: *the numerator is given by the product of the probabilities along the limb through* A, *while the denominator is just the sum of the products of the probabilities along each limb terminating at* D. In either case, we obtain

$$P(A \mid D) = \frac{(0.45)(0.06)}{(0.45)(0.06) + (0.3)(0.04) + (0.25)(0.03)}$$
$$= 0.58$$

Before looking at any further examples, let us state the general form of Bayes' Theorem.

BAYES' THEOREM

Let $A_1, A_2, \ldots, A_n$ be a partition of a sample space S (that is, $A_1, A_2, \ldots, A_n$ are mutually exclusive events and $S = A_1 \cup A_2 \cup \cdots \cup A_n$)

and let E be an event of the experiment such that $P(E) \neq 0$. Then the a posteriori probability $P(A_i | E)$ $(1 \leq i \leq n)$ is given by

(8.10) $$P(A_i | E) = \frac{P(A_i) \cdot P(E | A_i)}{P(A_1) \cdot P(E | A_1) + P(A_2) \cdot P(E | A_2) + \cdots + P(A_n) \cdot P(E | A_n)}$$

EXAMPLE 8.31 The picture tubes for the Pulsar 19-inch color television sets are manufactured in three locations and then shipped to the main plant of the Vista Vision Corporation for final assembly. Plants A, B, and C supply 50%, 30%, and 20%, respectively, of the picture tubes used by the company. The Quality Control Department of the company has determined that 1% of the picture tubes produced by plant A are defective, while 2% of the picture tubes produced by plants B and C are defective. If a Pulsar 19-inch color television set is selected at random and the picture tube is found to be defective, what is the probability that the picture tube was manufactured in plant C? Compare with Example 8.25, page 314.

SOLUTION Let A, B, and C denote the event that the set chosen has a picture tube manufactured in Plant A, Plant B, and Plant C, respectively. Also, let D denote the event that a set has a defective picture tube. Using the given information we may draw the tree diagram shown in Figure 8.11. Next, using formula (8.10), or otherwise, we find that the required a posteriori probability is given by

$$\begin{aligned} P(C | D) &= \frac{P(C) \cdot P(D | C)}{P(A) \cdot P(D | A) + P(B) \cdot P(D | B) + P(C) \cdot P(D | C)} \\ &= \frac{(0.2)(0.02)}{(0.5)(0.01) + (0.3)(0.02) + (0.2)(0.02)} \\ &\approx 0.27 \end{aligned}$$

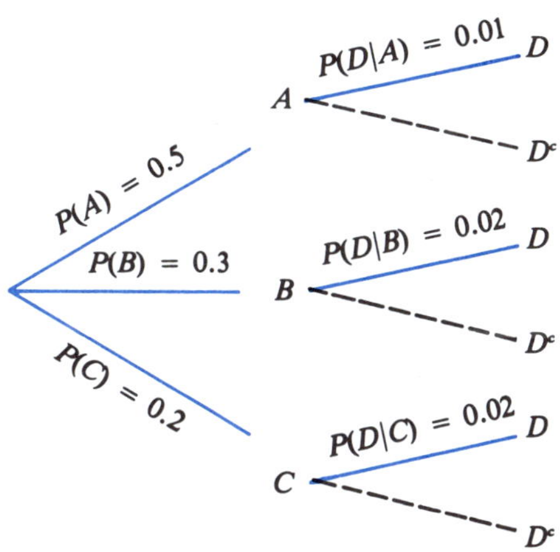

Figure 8.11

EXAMPLE 8.32 A study was conducted in a large metropolitan area to determine the annual incomes of married couples in which the husbands were the sole providers and of those in which the husbands and wives were both employed. Table 8.6 gives the results of this study.

Annual family income ($)	% of Married couples	% of Income group with both spouses working
75,000 & Over	4	65
50,000–74,999	10	73
35,000–49,999	21	68
25,000–34,999	24	63
15,000–24,999	30	43
Under 15,000	11	28

Table 8.6

(**a**) What is the probability that a couple selected at random from this area has two incomes?

(**b**) If a randomly chosen couple has two incomes, what is the probability that the annual income of this couple is over \$75,000?

(**c**) If a randomly chosen couple has two incomes, what is the probability that the annual income of this couple is greater than \$24,999?

SOLUTION Let A, B, C, D, E, and F denote the event, respectively, that the annual income of a couple is \$75,000 and over, between \$50,000 and \$74,999, between \$35,000 and \$49,999, . . . , and under \$15,000. Also, let T denote the event that a couple is a two-income family. Using the information given, we may draw the tree diagram shown in Figure 8.12. We are now in a position to answer the questions posed earlier.

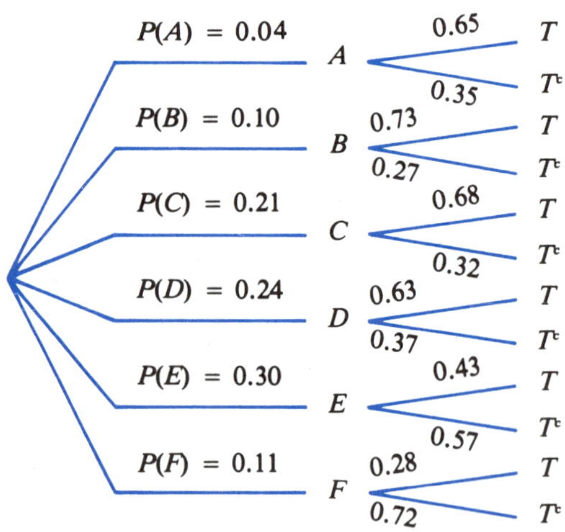

Figure 8.12

(**a**) The probability that a couple selected at random from this group has two incomes is given by

$$
\begin{aligned}
P(T) &= P(A)\cdot P(T|A)+P(B)\cdot P(T|B)+P(C)\cdot P(T|C)+P(D)\cdot P(T|D)\\
&\quad +P(E)\cdot P(T|E)+P(F)\cdot P(T|F)\\
&=(0.04)(0.65)+(0.10)(0.73)+(0.21)(0.68)+(0.24)(0.63)\\
&\quad +(0.30)(0.43)+(0.11)(0.28)\\
&=0.5528
\end{aligned}
$$

(**b**) Using the results of part (**a**) and Bayes' Theorem, we find that the probability that a randomly chosen couple has an annual income over \$75,000 given that both spouses are working is

$$P(A|T)=\frac{P(A)\cdot P(T|A)}{P(T)}=\frac{(0.04)(0.65)}{0.5528}=0.047$$

(**c**) The probability that a randomly chosen couple has an annual income greater than \$24,999 given that both spouses are working is

$$
\begin{aligned}
&P(A|T)+P(B|T)+P(C|T)+P(D|T)\\
&=\frac{P(A)\cdot P(T|A)+P(B)\cdot P(T|B)+P(C)\cdot P(T|C)+P(D)\cdot P(T|D)}{P(T)}\\
&=\frac{(0.04)(0.65)+(0.1)(0.73)+(0.21)(0.68)+(0.24)(0.63)}{0.5528}\\
&=0.711
\end{aligned}
$$

8.6 EXERCISES

1. The tree diagram shown below represents a two-stage experiment. Use the diagram to find

(*a*) $P(A)\cdot P(D|A)$ (*b*) $P(B)\cdot P(D|B)$
(*c*) $P(C)\cdot P(D|C)$ (*d*) $P(A|D)$

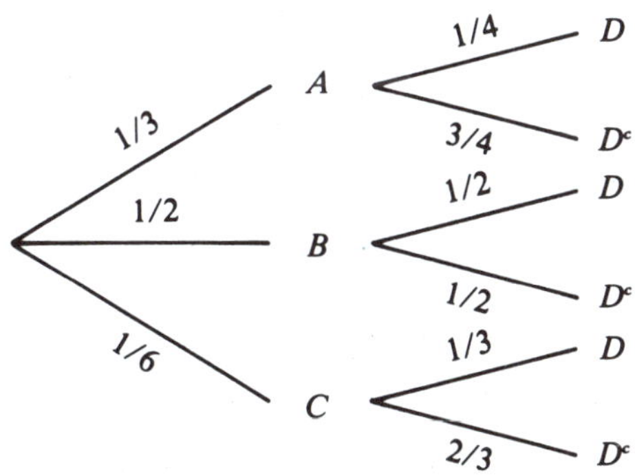

2. The tree diagram shown below represents a two-stage experiment. Use this diagram to find

(*a*) $P(A \cap D)$ (*b*) $P(B \cap D)$ (*c*) $P(C \cap D)$ (*d*) $P(D)$

(*e*) Verify:

$$P(A|D) = \frac{P(A \cap D)}{P(D)} = \frac{P(A) \cdot P(D|A)}{P(A) \cdot P(D|A) + P(B) \cdot P(D|B) + P(C) \cdot P(D|C)}$$

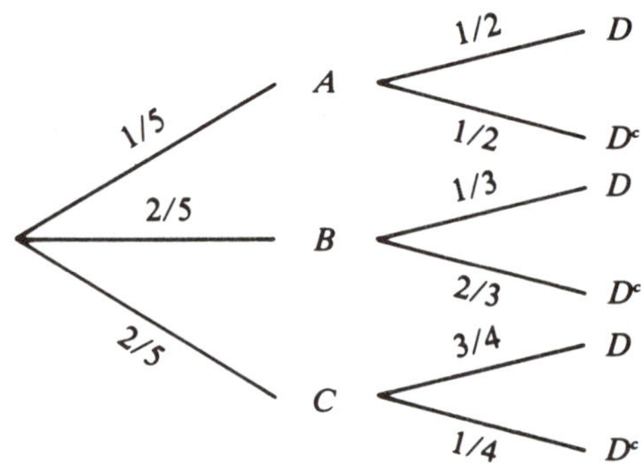

3. The Jansen Electronics Co. has 4 machines that produce an identical component for use in its video cassette players. The proportion of the components produced by each machine and the probability of that component being defective are shown in the following table. What is the probability that

(*a*) a component selected at random is defective?

(*b*) a defective component was produced by machine I?

(*c*) a defective component was produced by machine II?

Machine	Proportion of components produced	Probability of defective component
I	0.15	0.04
II	0.30	0.02
III	0.35	0.02
IV	0.20	0.03

4. An experiment consists of randomly selecting one of three coins, tossing it and observing the outcome—"heads or tails". The first coin is a two-headed coin, the second is a biased coin such that $P(H) = 0.75$ and the third is a fair coin.

(*a*) What is the probability that the coin that is tossed will show "heads"?

(*b*) If the coin selected shows heads, what is the probability that this coin is the fair coin?

5. A medical test has been designed to detect the presence of a certain disease. Among those who have the disease, the probability that the disease will be detected by the test is 0.95. However, the probability that the test will erroneously indicate the presence of the disease in those who do not have the disease is 0.04. It is estimated that 4% of the population who take this test have the disease.

(*a*) If the test administered to an individual is positive, what is the probability that the person actually has the disease?

(*b*) If an individual takes the test twice and both times the test is positive, what is the probability that the person actually has the disease?

6. Refer to problem 5. Suppose that 20% of the people who were referred to a clinic for the test did in fact have the disease. If the test administered to an individual from this group is positive, what is the probability that the person actually has the disease?

7. A desk lamp produced by the Luminar Co. was found to be defective. The company has 3 factories where the lamps are manufactured. The percentage of the total number of desk lamps produced by each factory and the probability that a lamp manufactured by that factory is defective are shown in the following table. What is the probability that the defective lamp was manufactured in factory III?

Factory	Percentage of total production	Probability of defective component
I	0.35	0.015
II	0.35	0.01
III	0.30	0.02

8. An insurance company has compiled the following data relating the age of drivers and the accident rate (the probability of being involved in an accident during a 1-year period) for drivers within that group.

Age group	Percentage of insured drivers	Accident rate
under 25	0.16	0.055
25–44	0.40	0.025
45–64	0.30	0.02
65 & over	0.14	0.04

(*a*) What is the probability that an insured driver will be involved in an accident?

(*b*) What is the probability that an insured driver who is involved in an accident is under 25?

9. The Office of Admissions and Records of a large western university released the following information concerning the contemplated majors of its freshman class.

Major	Percentage of freshmen choosing this major	Percentage of females in this group	Percentage of males in this group
Business	0.24	0.38	0.62
Humanities	0.08	0.60	0.40
Education	0.08	0.66	0.34
Social Science	0.07	0.58	0.42
Natural Sciences	0.09	0.52	0.48
Other majors	0.44	0.48	0.52

(*a*) What is the probability that a student selected at random from the freshman class is a female?

(*b*) What is the probability that a business student selected at random from the freshman class is a male?

(*c*) What is the probability that a female student selected at random from the freshman class is majoring in business?

10. A study was conducted among a certain group of union members whose health insurance policies required second opinions prior to surgery. Of those members who were advised to have surgery by a doctor, 20% were informed by a second doctor that no surgery was needed. Of these, 70% took the second doctor's opinion and did not go through with the surgery. Of the members who were advised to have surgery by both doctors, 95% went through with the surgery. What is the probability that a union member from this group who had surgery was advised to do so by a second doctor?

11. A study conducted by the Metro Housing Agency in a midwestern city revealed the following information concerning the age distribution of renters within the city.

Age	Percentage of adult population	Percentage of group who are renters
21–44	0.51	0.58
45–64	0.31	0.45
65 & over	0.18	0.60

(*a*) What is the probability that an adult selected at random from this population is a renter?

(*b*) If a renter is selected at random, what is the probability that he or she is in the 21–44 age bracket?

(*c*) If a renter is selected at random, what is the probability that he or she is 45 years of age or older?

8.7 Markov Chains (Optional)

Markov process or chain

A finite stochastic process, as we recall, is an experiment consisting of a finite number of stages in which the outcomes and associated probabilities at each stage are dependent on the outcomes and associated probabilities of the preceding stages. In this section we shall be concerned with a special class of stochastic processes, namely, those in which the probabilities associated with the outcomes at any stage of the experiment depend only on the outcomes of the *preceding stage*. Such a process is called a *Markov process* or a *Markov chain*, named after the Russian mathematician A. A. Markov (1856–1922).

current state

The outcome at any stage of the experiment in a Markov process is called the *state* of the experiment. In particular, the outcome at the current stage of the experiment is called the *current state* of the process. Following is a typical problem involving Markov chains. Starting from some state of the process (the current state), determine the probability that the process will be at a particular state some time in the future.

EXAMPLE 8.33 An analyst at Weaver and Kline, a stock brokerage firm, observes that the closing price of the preferred stock of an airline company over a short span of time depends only on its previous closing price. At the end of each trading day he makes a note of the stock's performance for that day by recording the closing price as "higher," "unchanged," or "lower" according to whether the stock closes higher, unchanged, or lower than the previous day's closing price. This sequence of observations may be viewed as a Markov chain. ■

The transition from one state to another in a Markov chain may be studied with the aid of a tree diagram as in the next example.

EXAMPLE 8.34 Refer to Example 8.33. If on a certain day, the closing price of the stock is higher than that of the previous day, then the probability that it closes higher, unchanged, or lower on the next trading day is 0.2, 0.3, and 0.5, respectively. Next, if the closing price of the stock is unchanged from the previous day, then the probability that it closes higher, unchanged, or lower on the next trading day is 0.5, 0.2, and 0.3, respectively. Finally, if the closing price of the stock is lower than that of the previous day, then the probability that it closes higher, unchanged, or lower on the next trading day is 0.4, 0.4, and 0.2, respectively. Describe the transition between states and the probabilities associated with these transitions with the aid of a tree diagram.

SOLUTION The Markov chain being described has three states—"higher," "unchanged," or "lower." Suppose the current state is "higher," then the transition to the other states from this state may be displayed by constructing a tree diagram in which the associated probabilities are shown on the appropriate limbs (see Figure 8.13 part a). Tree diagrams describing the transition from each of the other two possible current states to the other states may be constructed in a similar manner (Figures 8.13 part b and part c).

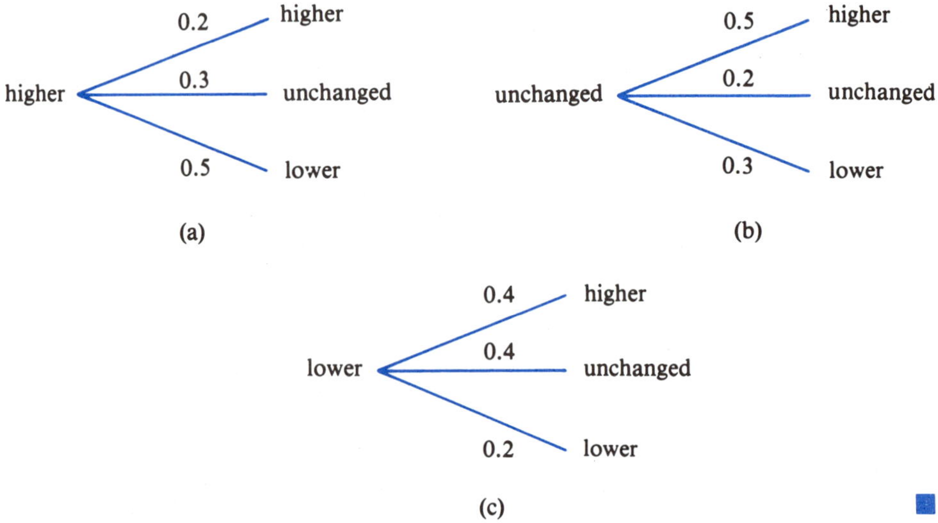

Figure 8.13

transition probabilities

The probabilities encountered in the above example are called *transition probabilities* since they are associated with the transition from one state to the next in the Markov process. These transition probabilities may be conveniently represented in the form of a matrix. Suppose for simplicity that we have a Markov chain with three possible outcomes at each stage of the experiment. Let us refer to these outcomes as state 1, state 2, and state 3. Then the transition probabilities associated with the transition from state 1 to each of the states 1, 2, and 3 in the next phase of the experiment are precisely the respective conditional probabilities that the outcome is state 1, state 2, and state 3 *given* that the outcome state 1 has occurred. In short, the desired transition probabilities are $P(\text{state } 1|\text{state } 1)$, $P(\text{state } 2|\text{state } 1)$, and $P(\text{state } 3|\text{state } 1)$, respectively. Let us write

$$a_{11} = P(\text{state } 1|\text{state } 1)$$
$$a_{12} = P(\text{state } 2|\text{state } 1)$$
and
$$a_{13} = P(\text{state } 3|\text{state } 1)$$

Note that the first subscript in the above notation refers to the current state and the second subscript refers to the state in the next stage of the experiment. In terms of a tree diagram we have the following representation:

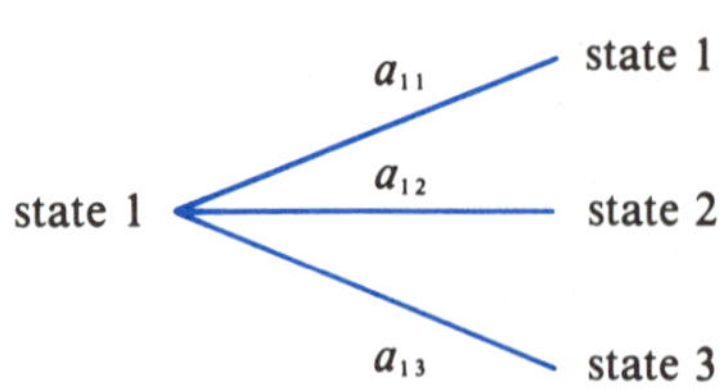

Similarly, the transition probabilities associated with the transition from state 2 and state 3 to each of the states 1, 2, and 3 are

$$\begin{aligned} a_{21} &= P(\text{state } 1 \mid \text{state } 2) \\ a_{22} &= P(\text{state } 2 \mid \text{state } 2) \\ a_{23} &= P(\text{state } 3 \mid \text{state } 2) \end{aligned} \quad \text{and} \quad \begin{aligned} a_{31} &= P(\text{state } 1 \mid \text{state } 3) \\ a_{32} &= P(\text{state } 2 \mid \text{state } 3) \\ a_{33} &= P(\text{state } 3 \mid \text{state } 3) \end{aligned}$$

These observations lead to the following matrix representation of the transition probabilities:

$$\begin{array}{ccc} & & \text{Next state} \\ & & \begin{array}{ccc} \text{state 1} & \text{state 2} & \text{state 3} \end{array} \\ \text{Current state} & \begin{array}{c} \text{state 1} \\ \text{state 2} \\ \text{state 3} \end{array} & \begin{bmatrix} a_{11} & a_{12} & a_{13} \\ a_{21} & a_{22} & a_{23} \\ a_{31} & a_{32} & a_{33} \end{bmatrix} \end{array}$$

EXAMPLE 8.35 Represent the transition probabilities obtained in Example 8.34 in terms of a matrix.

SOLUTION There are three states at each stage of the Markov chain under consideration. Letting state 1, state 2, and state 3 denote the states "higher," "unchanged," and "lower," respectively, we find that

$$a_{11} = 0.2, a_{12} = 0.3, a_{13} = 0.5, \text{ and so on,}$$

so that the required matrix representation is given by

$$T = \begin{bmatrix} .2 & .3 & .5 \\ .5 & .2 & .3 \\ .4 & .4 & .2 \end{bmatrix}$$

■

transition matrix

The matrix obtained above is an example of a *transition matrix* associated with the Markov process. In general, suppose we have a Markov chain with n states, state 1, state 2, . . . , state n, then a transition matrix for this process is an $n \times n$ matrix T with entries a_{ij} $(1 \le i \le n; 1 \le j \le n)$ having the following properties:

1. $a_{ij} \ge 0$ for all i and j.
2. The sum of the entries in each row of T is 1.

Thus,

$$\begin{array}{ccc} & & \text{Next state} \\ & & \begin{array}{cccccc} \text{state 1} & \text{state 2} & \cdots & \text{state } j & \cdots & \text{state } n \end{array} \\ T = \text{Current state} & \begin{array}{c} \text{state 1} \\ \text{state 2} \\ \vdots \\ \text{state } i \\ \vdots \\ \text{state } n \end{array} & \begin{bmatrix} a_{11} & a_{12} & \cdots & a_{1j} & \cdots & a_{1n} \\ a_{21} & a_{22} & \cdots & a_{2j} & \cdots & a_{2n} \\ \vdots & \vdots & & \vdots & & \vdots \\ a_{i1} & a_{i2} & \cdots & a_{ij} & \cdots & a_{in} \\ \vdots & \vdots & & \vdots & & \vdots \\ a_{n1} & a_{n2} & \cdots & a_{nj} & \cdots & a_{nn} \end{bmatrix} \end{array}$$

Since $a_{ij} = P(\text{state } j \mid \text{state } i)$ is the probability of the occurrence of an event, it must be nonnegative, and this is precisely what property 1 implies. Property 2 follows from the fact that the transition from any one of the current states must terminate in one of the n states in the next stage of the experiment. Any square matrix satisfying properties 1 and 2 is referred to as a *stochastic matrix*.

An advantage in representing the transition probabilities in the form of a matrix is that we may use the results from matrix theory to help us solve problems involving Markov processes, a fact that shall be demonstrated repeatedly in the next several examples.

Next, for simplicity, let us consider the following Markov process where each stage of the experiment has precisely two possible states.

EXAMPLE 8.36 Because of the continued successful implementation of an urban renewal program, it is expected that each year 3% of the population currently residing in the city will move to the suburbs, while 6% of the population currently residing in the suburbs, will move into the city. At present, 65% of the total population of the metropolitan area live in the city itself while the remaining 35% live in the suburbs. Assuming that the total population of the metropolitan area remains constant, what will the distribution of the population be like one year hence?

SOLUTION The problem may be solved with the aid of a tree diagram and the techniques of Section 8.5. The required tree diagram describing this process is shown in Figure 8.14. Using the method of Section 8.5, we find the probability that a person selected at random will be a city dweller one year hence is given by

$$(0.65)(0.97) + (0.35)(0.06)$$

or 0.6515. In a similar manner we find that the probability that a person selected at random will reside in the suburbs one year hence is given by

$$(0.65)(0.03) + (0.35)(0.94)$$

or 0.3485. Thus, the population of the area one year later may be expected to be distributed as follows: 65.15% living in the city and 34.85% residing in the suburbs.

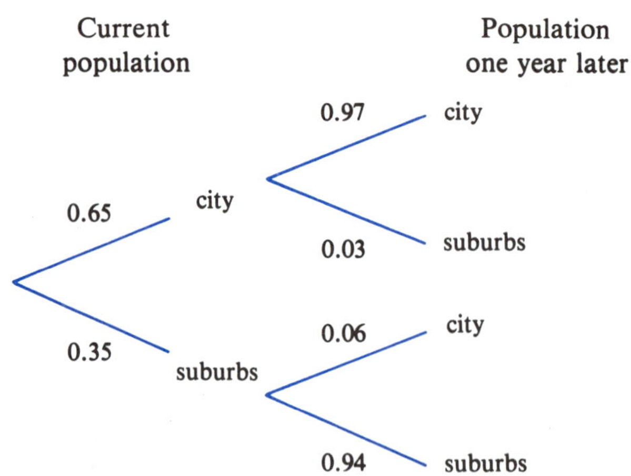

Figure 8.14 ■

Let us re-examine the solution to the above problem. First of all, as noted earlier, the process under consideration may be viewed as a Markov chain with two possible states at each stage of the experiment—"living in the city" (state 1) and "living in the suburbs" (state 2). The transition matrix associated with this Markov chain is

$$T = \begin{array}{c} \\ \text{state 1} \\ \text{state 2} \end{array} \begin{array}{c} \begin{array}{cc} \text{state 1} & \text{state 2} \end{array} \\ \begin{bmatrix} .97 & .03 \\ .06 & .94 \end{bmatrix} \end{array}$$

Next, observe that the initial (current) probability distribution of the population may be summarized in the form of a row vector of dimension 2 (that is, a 1×2 matrix). Thus,

$$X_0 = \begin{array}{cc} \text{state 1} & \text{state 2} \\ [.65 & .35] \end{array}$$

while the population distribution one year later may be written, using the results of Example 8.36, as

$$X_1 = \begin{array}{cc} \text{state 1} & \text{state 2} \\ [.6515 & .3485] \end{array}$$

The reader may now verify that

$$X_0T = [.65 \quad .35]\begin{bmatrix} .97 & .03 \\ .06 & .94 \end{bmatrix}$$

$$= [.6515 \quad .3485] = X_1$$

so this problem may be solved using matrix multiplication.

EXAMPLE 8.37 Refer to Example 8.36. What is the population distribution of the city after 2 years? After 3 years?

SOLUTION Let X_2 be the row vector representing the probability population distribution of the city after 2 years. We may view X_1, the vector representing the probability population distribution of the metropolitan area after 1 year, as representing the "initial" probability distribution in this part of our calculation. Thus,

$$X_2 = X_1T$$

$$= [.6515 \quad .3485]\begin{bmatrix} .97 & .03 \\ .06 & .94 \end{bmatrix}$$

$$= [.6529 \quad .3471]$$

The vector representing the probability distribution of the metropolitan area after

3 years is given by

$$X_3 = X_2T = [.6529 \quad .3471]\begin{bmatrix} .97 & .03 \\ .06 & .94 \end{bmatrix}$$

$$= [.6541 \quad .3459]$$

That is, after 3 years, the population will be distributed as follows: 65.41% live in the city and 34.59% live in the suburbs. ■

Observe that, in the above computations, we have $X_1 = X_0T$, $X_2 = X_1T = X_0T^2$ and $X_3 = X_2T = X_0T^3$. These results are easily generalized. To see this, suppose we have a Markov process where, at each stage of the experiment, there are n possible states. Suppose further that the probability of the system being in state 1, state 2, . . . , state n, initially, is given by $p_1, p_2, \ldots, p_n$, respectively. This distribution may be represented as an n-dimensional vector.

$$X_0 = [p_1, p_2, \ldots, p_n]$$

distribution vector

called a *distribution vector.* If T represents the $n \times n$ transition matrix associated with the Markov process, then the probability distribution of the system after m observations is given by

(8.11) $$X_m = X_0T^m$$

Formula (8.11) may be used to help us investigate the long-term trends of certain Markov processes, as illustrated in the next example.

EXAMPLE 8.38 A survey conducted by the National Commission on the Educational Status of Women reveals that 70% of the daughters of women who have completed two or more years of college have also completed two or more years of college, whereas 20% of the daughters of women who have had less than two years of college have completed two or more years of college. If this trend continues, determine, in the long run, the percentage of women in the population who would have completed at least two years of college given that currently only 20% of the women have completed at least two years of college.

SOLUTION This problem may be viewed as a Markov process with two possible states—"completed two or more years of college" (state 1) and "completed less than two years of college" (state 2). The transition matrix associated with this Markov chain is given by

$$T = \begin{bmatrix} .7 & .3 \\ .2 & .8 \end{bmatrix}$$

The initial distribution vector is given by

$$X_0 = [.2 \quad .8]$$

In order to study the long-term trend pertaining to this particular aspect of the educational status of women, let us compute $X_1, X_2, \ldots$, the distribution vectors associated with the Markov process under consideration. These vectors give the percentage of women with two years or more of college and that of women with less than two years of college after 1 generation, after 2 generations, ... With the aid of Formula (8.11), we find that (to 4 decimal places)

$$X_1 = X_0T = [.2 \quad .8]\begin{bmatrix} .7 & .3 \\ .2 & .8 \end{bmatrix}$$
$$= [.3 \quad .7]$$
$$X_2 = X_1T = [.3 \quad .7]\begin{bmatrix} .7 & .3 \\ .2 & .8 \end{bmatrix}$$
$$= [.35 \quad .65]$$
$$X_3 = X_2T = [.35 \quad .65]\begin{bmatrix} .7 & .3 \\ .2 & .8 \end{bmatrix}$$
$$= [.375 \quad .625]$$

Proceeding further, we obtain the following sequence of vectors:

$$\begin{aligned} X_4 &= [.3875 \quad .6125] \\ X_5 &= [.3938 \quad .6062] \\ X_6 &= [.3969 \quad .6031] \\ X_7 &= [.3985 \quad .6015] \\ X_8 &= [.3993 \quad .6008] \\ X_9 &= [.3997 \quad .6004] \\ X_{10} &= [.3999 \quad .6002] \end{aligned}$$

From the results of the above computation, we see that as m increases, the probability distribution vector X_m approaches the probability distribution vector

$$[.4 \quad .6] \quad \text{or} \quad [2/5 \quad 3/5]$$

steady-state distribution vector

Such a vector is called the *limiting* or *steady-state distribution vector* for the system. The interpretation of the results is as follows: Initially, 20% of the women in the population have completed two or more years of college while 80% of them have completed less than two years of college. After one generation, the former has increased to 30% of the population while the latter has dropped to 70% of the population. The trend continues, and eventually, 40% of all women in future generations would have completed two or more years of college while 60% of them would have completed less than two years of college. ■

In order to explain the above result let us evaluate Formula (8.11) more closely. Now, the initial distribution vector X_0 is a constant; that is, it remains fixed throughout our computation of $X_1, X_2, \ldots$. It appears reasonable, therefore, to conjecture that this phenomenon is due to the behavior of the powers, T^m, of the transition matrix T. Pursuing this line of investigation, we compute

$$T^2=\begin{bmatrix}.7 & .3\\ .2 & .8\end{bmatrix}\begin{bmatrix}.7 & .3\\ .2 & .8\end{bmatrix}=\begin{bmatrix}.55 & .45\\ .3 & .7\end{bmatrix}$$

$$T^3=\begin{bmatrix}.7 & .3\\ .2 & .8\end{bmatrix}\begin{bmatrix}.55 & .45\\ .3 & .7\end{bmatrix}=\begin{bmatrix}.475 & .525\\ .35 & .65\end{bmatrix}$$

Proceeding further, we obtain the following sequence of matrices:

$$T^4=\begin{bmatrix}.4375 & .5625\\ .375 & .625\end{bmatrix}\quad T^5=\begin{bmatrix}.4188 & .5813\\ .3875 & .6125\end{bmatrix}\quad T^6=\begin{bmatrix}.4094 & .5907\\ .3938 & .6063\end{bmatrix}$$

$$T^7=\begin{bmatrix}.4047 & .5954\\ .3969 & .6032\end{bmatrix}\quad T^8=\begin{bmatrix}.4024 & .5977\\ .3985 & .6016\end{bmatrix}\quad T^9=\begin{bmatrix}.4012 & .5988\\ .3993 & .6008\end{bmatrix}$$

$$T^{10}=\begin{bmatrix}.4006 & .5994\\ .3997 & .6004\end{bmatrix}\quad T^{11}=\begin{bmatrix}.4003 & .5997\\ .3999 & .6002\end{bmatrix}$$

The above results show that the powers T^m of the transition matrix T tend toward a fixed matrix as m gets larger and larger. In this case, the "limiting matrix" is the matrix

$$L=\begin{bmatrix}.40 & .60\\ .40 & .60\end{bmatrix}\quad \text{or} \quad \begin{bmatrix}2/5 & 3/5\\ 2/5 & 3/5\end{bmatrix}$$

steady-state matrix

Such a matrix is called the *steady-state matrix* for the system. Thus, as suspected, the long-term behavior of a Markov process such as the one in this example depends on the behavior of the limiting matrix of the powers of the transition matrix—the steady-state matrix for the system. In view of this, the long-term (steady-state) distribution vector for this problem may be found by computing the product

$$X_0L=[.2 \quad .8]\begin{bmatrix}.40 & .60\\ .40 & .60\end{bmatrix}=[.40 \quad .60]$$

which agrees with the result obtained earlier.

Next, since the transition matrix T in this situation seems to have a stabilizing effect over the long-term, we are led to wonder if the steady-state would be reached regardless of the initial state of the system. To answer this question, suppose the initial distribution vector was

$$X_0=[p \quad 1-p]$$

Then, as above, the steady-state distribution vector is given by

$$X_0L = [p \quad 1-p]\begin{bmatrix} .40 & .60 \\ .40 & .60 \end{bmatrix} = [.40 \quad .60]$$

Thus, the steady-state is reached regardless of the initial state of the system!

regular stochastic matrix

regular Markov chain

The transition matrix T of Example 8.38 has several important properties, which we have highlighted in the above discussion. First of all, the sequence T, T^2, $T^3, \ldots$ approaches a steady-state matrix in which the rows of the limiting matrix are all equal. Such a transition matrix is said to be a *regular stochastic matrix*. In general, it can be shown that *a stochastic matrix* T *is regular if some power of* T *has entries, which are all positive*. Second, as in the case of Example 8.38, a Markov chain with a regular transition matrix (called a *regular Markov chain*) has a steady-state distribution vector whose elements coincide with those of a row (since they are all the same) of the steady-state matrix; thus, this steady-state distribution vector is always reached regardless of the initial distribution vector.

We shall return to computations involving regular Markov chains, but, for the moment, let us see how one may determine whether a given matrix is indeed regular.

EXAMPLE 8.39 Determine which of the following matrices are regular:

(**a**) $\begin{bmatrix} .7 & .3 \\ .2 & .8 \end{bmatrix}$ (**b**) $\begin{bmatrix} .4 & .6 \\ 1 & 0 \end{bmatrix}$ (**c**) $\begin{bmatrix} 0 & 1 \\ 1 & 0 \end{bmatrix}$

SOLUTION (**a**) Since all the entries of the matrix are positive, the given matrix is regular. Note that this is the transition matrix of Example 8.38.

(**b**) In this case, one of the entries of the given matrix is equal to zero. Let us compute

$$\begin{bmatrix} .4 & .6 \\ 1 & 0 \end{bmatrix}^2 = \begin{bmatrix} .4 & .6 \\ 1 & 0 \end{bmatrix}\begin{bmatrix} .4 & .6 \\ 1 & 0 \end{bmatrix} = \begin{bmatrix} .76 & .24 \\ .4 & .6 \end{bmatrix}$$

Since the second power of the matrix has entries that are all positive, we conclude that the given matrix is in fact regular.

(**c**) Denote the given matrix by A. Then

$$A = \begin{bmatrix} 0 & 1 \\ 1 & 0 \end{bmatrix}, \qquad A^2 = \begin{bmatrix} 0 & 1 \\ 1 & 0 \end{bmatrix}\begin{bmatrix} 0 & 1 \\ 1 & 0 \end{bmatrix} = \begin{bmatrix} 1 & 0 \\ 0 & 1 \end{bmatrix}$$

$$A^3 = \begin{bmatrix} 0 & 1 \\ 1 & 0 \end{bmatrix}\begin{bmatrix} 1 & 0 \\ 0 & 1 \end{bmatrix} = \begin{bmatrix} 0 & 1 \\ 1 & 0 \end{bmatrix}$$

Observe that $A^3 = A$. It follows, therefore, that $A^4 = A^2$, $A^5 = A$, and so on. In other words, any power of A must coincide with either A or A^2. Since not all the entries of A and A^2 are positive, the same is true of any power of A. We conclude, accordingly, that the given matrix is not regular. ■

We now return to the study of regular Markov chains. In Example 8.38, we found the steady-state distribution vector associated with a regular Markov chain by studying the limiting behavior of a sequence of distribution vectors. Alternatively, as pointed out in the subsequent discussion, the steady-state distribution vector may also be obtained by first determining the steady-state matrix associated with the regular Markov chain, which is obtained by studying the limiting behavior of a sequence of transition matrices associated with the process.

Fortunately, there is a relatively simple procedure for finding the steady-state distribution vector associated with a regular Markov process. It does not involve the rather tedious computations required to obtain the sequences in Example 8.38. The procedure follows:

Let T be a regular stochastic matrix. Then the steady-state distribution vector X may be found by solving the vector equation

$$XT = X$$

together with the condition that the sum of the elements of the vector X be equal to 1.

A justification of the above procedure is given in problem 25 of Exercise set 8.7.

EXAMPLE 8.40 Find the steady-state matrix for the regular Markov chain whose transition matrix is

$$T = \begin{bmatrix} .7 & .3 \\ .2 & .8 \end{bmatrix} \qquad \text{(See Example 8.38.)}$$

SOLUTION Let $X = [x \quad y]$ be the steady-state distribution vector associated with the Markov process, where the numbers x and y are to be determined. The condition $XT = X$ translates into the matrix equation

$$[x \quad y]\begin{bmatrix} .7 & .3 \\ .2 & .8 \end{bmatrix} = [x \quad y]$$

or equivalently, the following system of linear equations

$$0.7x + 0.2y = x$$
$$0.3x + 0.8y = y$$

But each of the equations comprising this system of equations is equivalent to the single equation

$$0.3x - 0.2y = 0$$

Next, the condition that the sum of the elements of X add up to 1 gives

$$x + y = 1$$

Thus, the fulfillment of the two conditions simultaneously implies that x and y be the solutions of the system

$$\begin{aligned} 0.3x - 0.2y &= 0 \\ x + y &= 1 \end{aligned}$$

Solving the first of the above equations for x we obtain

$$x = \frac{2}{3}y$$

which, upon substitution into the second, yields

$$\frac{2}{3}y + y = 1$$

or

$$y = \frac{3}{5}$$

Thus, $x = 2/5$ and the required steady-state matrix is given by $X = [2/5 \quad 3/5]$, which agrees with the result obtained earlier. ■

EXAMPLE 8.41 The Zephyr Cab Company, for the purpose of keeping track of the location of its taxi-cabs, has divided a town into three zones—zone I, zone II and zone III. The management of the company has determined from company records that of the passengers picked up in zone I, 60% are discharged in the same zone, 30% are discharged in zone II, and 10% are discharged in zone III; of those picked up in zone II, 40% are discharged in zone I, 30% are discharged in zone II, and 30% are discharged in zone III; of those picked up in zone III, 30% are discharged in zone I, 30% are discharged in zone II, and 40% are discharged in zone III. Suppose that at the beginning of the day 80% of the taxi-cabs are in zone I, 15% of them are in zone II, and 5% of them are in zone III and that a taxi-cab without a passenger will cruise within the zone it is currently in until a pick-up is made.

(a) Find the transition matrix for the Markov chain that describes the successive locations of a taxi-cab.

(b) Use the results of part **(a)** to determine the long-term distribution of the taxis in the three zones. Compare this with the initial distribution.

SOLUTION **(a)** The required transition matrix is given by

$$T = \begin{bmatrix} 0.6 & 0.3 & 0.1 \\ 0.4 & 0.3 & 0.3 \\ 0.3 & 0.3 & 0.4 \end{bmatrix}$$

(b) Let $X = [x \quad y \quad z]$ be the steady-state distribution vector associated with the Markov process under consideration, where x, y, and z are to be determined. The condition $XT = X$ translates into the matrix equation

$$[x \quad y \quad z]\begin{bmatrix} 0.6 & 0.3 & 0.1 \\ 0.4 & 0.3 & 0.3 \\ 0.3 & 0.3 & 0.4 \end{bmatrix} = [x \quad y \quad z]$$

or, equivalently, the following system of linear equations:

$$\begin{aligned} 0.6x + 0.4y + 0.3z &= x \\ 0.3x + 0.3y + 0.3z &= y \\ 0.1x + 0.3y + 0.4z &= z \end{aligned}$$

This system simplifies into

$$\begin{aligned} 4x - 4y - 3z &= 0 \\ 3x - 7y + 3z &= 0 \\ x + 3y - 6z &= 0 \end{aligned}$$

Since $x + y + z = 1$ as well, we are required to solve the system

$$\begin{aligned} x + \ y + \ z &= 1 \\ 4x - 4y - 3z &= 0 \\ 3x - 7y + 3z &= 0 \\ x + 3y - 6z &= 0 \end{aligned}$$

Using the Gauss-Jordan Elimination Procedure of Chapter 3, we find that

$$x = \frac{33}{70}, \qquad y = \frac{3}{10} \quad \text{and} \quad z = \frac{8}{35}$$

or $x \approx 0.47$, $y = 0.30$, and $z \approx 0.23$. Thus, in the long run 47% of the taxis will be in zone 1, 30% in zone 2, and 23% in zone 3. ■

8.7 EXERCISES

In Problems 1–4, determine which of the given matrices are stochastic:

1. $\begin{bmatrix} .4 & .6 \\ .7 & .3 \end{bmatrix}$

2. $\begin{bmatrix} .8 & .3 \\ .2 & .7 \end{bmatrix}$

3. $\begin{bmatrix} 1/3 & 1/3 & 1/3 \\ 1/4 & 0 & 3/4 \\ 1/2 & -1/2 & 1/2 \end{bmatrix}$

4. $\begin{bmatrix} .1 & .7 & .2 \\ .4 & .2 & .4 \\ .3 & .1 & .6 \end{bmatrix}$

5. The transition matrix for a Markov process is given by

$$T = \text{state}\ \begin{matrix} 1 \\ 2 \end{matrix} \overset{\begin{matrix}\text{state} \\ 1 \quad\ \ 2\end{matrix}}{\begin{bmatrix} .6 & .4 \\ .2 & .8 \end{bmatrix}}$$

and the initial state distribution vector is given by

$$X_0 = \overset{\begin{matrix}\text{state} \\ 1 \quad\ \ 2\end{matrix}}{[.5 \quad .5]}$$

Find X_0T and interpret your result with the aid of a tree diagram.

6. Currently 20% of the commuters within a large metropolitan area utilize the public transportation system, while the remaining 80% commute via automobile. Recently the city has revitalized and expanded its public transportation system. It is expected that 6 months from now 30% of those who are now commuting to work via automobile will switch to public transportation, while 70% will continue to commute via automobile. At the same time, it is expected that 20% of those now using the public transportation system will commute via automobile, while 80% will continue to use the public transportation system.

(***a***) Construct the transition matrix for the Markov chain that describes the change in the mode of transportation used by these commuters.

(***b***) Find the initial distribution vector for this Markov chain.

(***c***) What percentage of the commuters are expected to utilize the public transportation system 6 months from now?

7. The Morris Polling Group conducted a poll 6 months before an election in a state in which a Democrat and a Republican were running for governor and found that 60% of the voters intended to vote for the Democratic candidate and 40% of the voters intended to vote for the Republican candidate. In a poll conducted 3 months later it was found that 70% of those who had earlier stated a preference for the Democratic candidate still maintained that preference, while 30% of these voters now preferred the Republican candidate. Of those who had earlier stated a preference for the Republican candidate, 80% still maintained that preference while 20% now preferred the Democratic candidate.

(***a***) If the election were held at this time who would win?

(***b***) Assuming that this trend continues, which candidate is expected to win the election?

8. Refer to Example 8.36. If the initial probability distribution is

$$X_0 = \overset{\begin{matrix}\text{City} \quad \text{Suburb}\end{matrix}}{[.80 \qquad .20]}$$

what will the population distribution of the city be after 1 year? after 2 years?

9. At a certain university, three bookstores—the University Bookstore, the Campus Bookstore, and the Book-Mart, currently serve the university community. From a survey conducted at the beginning of the fall quarter, it was found that the University Bookstore and the Campus Bookstore each had 40% of the market while the Book-Mart had 20% of the market. Each quarter the University Bookstore retains 80% of its customers, while losing 10% of them to the Campus Bookstore and 10% of them to the Book-Mart. The Campus Bookstore retains 75% of its customers, while losing 10% of them to the University Bookstore and 15% to the Book-Mart. The Book-Mart retains 90% of its customers while losing 5% of them to the University Bookstore and 5% of them to the Campus Bookstore. What percentage of the market will each store have at the beginning of the second quarter? the third quarter?

10. A study conducted by the State Department of Agriculture in a sun-belt state reveals an increasing trend towards urbanization of the farmland within the state. Ten years ago 50% of the land within the state was used for agricultural purposes (A), 15% had been urbanized (U) and the remaining 35% was neither agricultural nor urban (N). Since that time 10% of the agricultural land has been converted to urban land, 5% has been used for other purposes, while the remaining 85% is still agricultural. Ninety-five per cent of the urban land has remained urban, while 5% of it has been used for nonagricultural purposes. Of the land that was neither agricultural or urban, 10% has been converted to agricultural land, 5% has been urbanized, while the remaining 85% remains unchanged.

(***a***) Construct the transition matrix for the Markov chain that describes the shift in land use within the state.

(***b***) Find the probability vector describing the distribution of land within the state 10 years ago.

(***c***) Assuming that this trend continues, find the probability vector describing the distribution of land within the state 10 years from now.

11. A study conducted by the Urban Energy Commission in a large metropolitan area indicates the probabilities that homeowners within the area will use certain heating fuels or solar energy during the next ten years as the major source of heat for their homes. The transition matrix representing the transition probabilities from one state to another is shown below.

$$\begin{array}{l} \\ \text{Electricity} \\ \text{Natural Gas} \\ \text{Fuel Oil} \\ \text{Solar Energy} \end{array} \begin{array}{c} \begin{array}{cccc} \text{Elec.} & \text{Gas.} & \text{Oil} & \text{Solar} \end{array} \\ \begin{bmatrix} .70 & .15 & .05 & .10 \\ 0 & .90 & .02 & .08 \\ 0 & .20 & .75 & .05 \\ 0 & .05 & 0 & .95 \end{bmatrix} \end{array}$$

Among the homeowners within the area, currently 20% are using electricity, 35% are using natural gas, 40% are using oil, and 5% are using solar energy as their major source of heat for their homes. What is the expected distribution of the homeowners that will be using each type of heating fuel or solar energy within the next decade?

In problems 12 through 15, determine which of the given matrices are regular.

12. $\begin{bmatrix} 0 & 1 \\ .3 & .7 \end{bmatrix}$

13. $\begin{bmatrix} 1 & 0 \\ .8 & .2 \end{bmatrix}$

14. $\begin{bmatrix} 1/2 & 1/2 & 0 \\ 3/4 & 0 & 1/4 \\ 0 & 1/2 & 1/2 \end{bmatrix}$

15. $\begin{bmatrix} 1 & 0 & 0 \\ .3 & .4 & .3 \\ .1 & .8 & .1 \end{bmatrix}$

In problems 16 through 19, find the steady-state vector for the given transition matrix.

16. $\begin{bmatrix} .8 & .2 \\ .6 & .4 \end{bmatrix}$

17. $\begin{bmatrix} .9 & .1 \\ 1 & 0 \end{bmatrix}$

18. $\begin{bmatrix} .6 & .4 & 0 \\ .3 & .4 & .3 \\ 0 & .6 & .4 \end{bmatrix}$

19. $\begin{bmatrix} .1 & .1 & .8 \\ .2 & .2 & .6 \\ .3 & .3 & .4 \end{bmatrix}$

20. Refer to problem 6. In the long run what percentage of the commuters will be utilizing the public transportation system?

21. From data compiled over a ten-year period by the State Department of Labor and Commerce in a state-wide study of married couples in which at least one spouse was working, the following transition matrix was constructed. It gives the transitional probabilities for 1 and 2 wage earners among married couples.

		Next state	
		1-Wage Earner	2-Wage Earners
Current state	1-Wage Earner	.72	.28
	2-Wage Earners	.12	.88

At the present time 48% of the married couples (in which at least one spouse is working) have 1-wage earner and 52% have 2-wage earners. Assuming that this trend continues, what will the distribution of 1- and 2-wage earner families be among married couples in this area (***a***) 10 years from now? (***b***) over the long run?

22. Refer to problem 10. In the long run what percentage of the land will be used as farmland?

23. A television poll was conducted among regular viewers of the national news in a certain region where the three national networks share the same time-slot for the evening news. Results of the poll indicate that 30% of the viewers watched the ABC evening news, 40% watched the CBS evening news, and 30% watched the NBC evening news. Furthermore, it was found that of those viewers who watched the ABC evening news during one week, 80% would again watch the ABC evening news during the next week, while 10% of these viewers would watch the CBS news, and 10% would watch the NBC news. Of those viewers who watched the CBS evening news during one week, 85% would again watch the CBS evening news during the next week, while 10% of these viewers would watch the ABC news, and 5% would watch the NBC news. Of those viewers who watched the NBC evening news during one week, 85% would again watch the NBC news during the next week, while 10% of these viewers would watch ABC, and 5% would watch CBS.

(*a*) What share of the audience consisting of regular viewers of the national news will each network command after 2 weeks?

(*b*) In the long run, what share of the audience will each network command?

24. In a certain species of roses, a plant with genotype (genetic makeup) AA has red flowers, a plant with genotype Aa has pink flowers, and a plant with genotype aa has white flowers, where A is the dominant gene and a is the recessive gene for color. If a plant with one genotype is crossed with another plant, then the color of the offspring's flowers is determined by the genotype of the parent plants. If a plant of each genotype is crossed with a pink-flowered plant, then the transition matrix used to determine the color of the offspring's flowers is given by

		Offspring Red	Pink	White
Parent	Red (AA)	1/2	1/2	0
	Pink (Aa) or (aA)	1/4	1/2	1/4
	White (aa)	0	1/2	1/2

If the offspring of each generation are crossed only with pink-flowered plants, in the long run what percentage of the plants will have red flowers? pink flowers? white flowers?

*****25.*** Let T be a regular stochastic matrix. Show that the steady-state distribution vector X may be found by solving the vector equation $XT = X$ together with the condition that the sum of the elements of X be equal to 1. (*Hint*: Take the initial distribution vector to be X, the steady-state distribution vector. Then when n is large, $X \approx XT^n$. Why? Multiply both sides of the last equation by T (on the right) and consider the resulting equation when n is large.)

8

Chapter Review

EXERCISES

1. Let E and F be two events which are mutually exclusive and suppose $P(E) = 0.4$ and $P(F) = 0.2$. Compute

(*a*) $P(E \cap F)$ (*b*) $P(E \cup F)$ (*c*) $P(E^c)$

(*d*) $P(E^c \cap F^c)$ (*e*) $P(E^c \cup F^c)$

2. Let E and F be two events of an experiment with sample space S. Suppose $P(E) = 0.3$, $P(F) = 0.2$, and $P(E \cap F) = 0.15$. Compute

(*a*) $P(E \cup F)$ (*b*) $P(E^c \cap F^c)$ (*c*) $P(E^c \cap F)$

3. Suppose a die is loaded and it was determined that the probability distribution associated with the experiment of casting the die and observing which number falls uppermost is given by

Elementary event	Probability
{1}	0.20
{2}	0.12
{3}	0.16
{4}	0.18
{5}	0.15
{6}	0.19

(*a*) What is the probability of the number being even?

(*b*) What is the probability of the number being either a 1 or a 6?

(*c*) What is the probability of the number being less than 4?

4. An urn contains 6 red, 5 black, and 4 green balls. If two balls are selected at random without replacement from the urn, what is the probability that a red ball and a black ball will be selected?

5. The Quality Control Department of the Starr Communications Company, the manufacturer of video-game cartridges, has determined from records that 1.5% of the cartridges sold have video defects, 0.8% of the cartridges sold have audio defects and 0.4% of the cartridges sold have both audio and video defects. What is the probability that a cartridge purchased by a customer

(*a*) will have a video or audio defect?

(*b*) will not have a video or audio defect?

6. An experiment consists of tossing a fair coin three times and observing the outcomes. Let A be the event that at least one "heads" is thrown and B the event that at most two "tails" are thrown.

(*a*) Find $P(A)$.

(*b*) Find $P(B)$.

(*c*) Are A and B independent events?

7. In a group of 20 ball-point pens on a shelf in the stationery department of the Metro Department Store, 2 are known to be defective. If a customer selects 3 of these pens, what is the probability that

(*a*) at least 1 is defective?

(*b*) no more than 1 is defective?

8. Five people are selected at random. What is the probability that none of the people in this group were born on the same day of the week?

9. A pair of fair dice is cast. What is the probability that the sum of the numbers falling uppermost is 8 if it is known that the two numbers are different.

10. Two cards are drawn at random from a well-shuffled deck of 52 playing cards. What is the probability that the second card is an ace

(***a***) if the first card is replaced before the second card is drawn?

(***b***) if the first card is not replaced before the second card is drawn?

11. Of 320 males and 280 female employees at the home office of the Gibraltar Insurance Company, 160 of the men and 190 of the women are on flex-time (flexible working hours). Given that an employee selected at random from this group is on flex-time, what is the probability that the employee is a male?

12. The tree diagram shown below represents an experiment consisting of two trials. Use the diagram to find

(***a***) $P(A \cap E)$ (***b***) $P(B \cap E)$ (***c***) $P(C \cap E)$
(***d***) $P(E)$ (***e***) $P(A|E)$

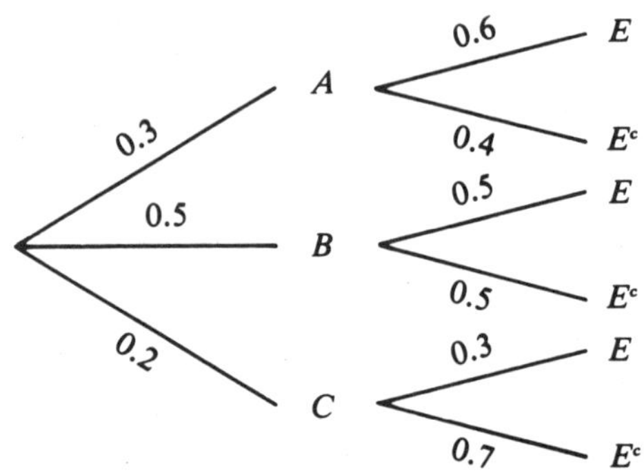

13. In a manufacturing plant, 3 machines, A, B and C produce 40%, 35%, and 25%, respectively, of the total production. The Quality Control Department of the company has determined that 1% of the items produced by Machine A, 1.5% of the items produced by machine B, and 2% of the items produced by machine C are defective. If an item is selected at random and found to be defective, what is the probability that it was produced by machine B?

14. Applicants who wish to be admitted to a certain professional school in a large university are required to take a screening test that was devised by an educational testing service. From past results the testing service has estimated that 70% of all applicants are eligible for admission and that 92% of those who are eligible for admission pass the exam while 12% of those who are ineligible for admission pass the exam. Using these results, find the probability that

(***a***) an applicant for admission who passed the exam was actually ineligible.

(***b***) an application for admission passed the exam.

9

STATISTICS

Statistics is that branch of mathematics concerned with the collection, analysis, and interpretation of data. In the next three sections we shall take a look at descriptive statistics. In these sections our interest is in the description and presentation of data in the form of tables, graphs, and so on. In the rest of the chapter we shall take a glimpse at inductive statistics; here, we shall see how mathematical tools, such as those developed in the last chapter may be used in conjunction with this data to help us draw certain conclusions and to make forecasts.

9.1

Distributions of Random Variables

In many situations, it is desirable to assign numerical values to the outcomes of an experiment. For example, if the experiment consists of casting a die and observing the face that lands uppermost, then it is natural to assign the numbers 1, 2, 3, 4, 5, and 6, respectively, to the outcomes *one*, *two*, *three*, *four*, *five*, and *six* of the experiment. If we let X denote the outcome of the experiment, then X assumes one of the numbers 1, 2, 3, 4, 5, or 6. Because the values assumed by X depend on the outcomes of a chance experiment, the outcome X is referred to as a *random variable*. In general, a random variable is a rule that assigns a number to each outcome of a chance experiment. More precisely, a random variable is a function with domain given by the set of outcomes of a chance experiment and range contained in the set of real numbers.

random variable

EXAMPLE 9.1 A coin is tossed three times. Let the random variable X denote the number of heads that occurs in the three tosses.

(a) List the outcomes of the experiment, that is, find the domain of the function X.

(b) Find the value assigned to each outcome of the experiment by the random variable X.

(c) Find the event comprising the outcomes to which a value of 2 has been assigned by X. This event is written $(X = 2)$ and is the event comprising the outcomes in which 2 heads occur.

SOLUTION **(a)** From the result of Example 8.2 (page 279) we see that the set of outcomes of the experiment is given by the sample space

$$S = \{\text{HHH, HHT, HTH, THH, HTT, THT, TTH, TTT}\}$$

of the experiment.

(b) The outcomes of the experiment are displayed in the first column of Table 9.1. The corresponding value assigned to each such outcome by the random variable X (the number of heads) appears in the second column.

Table 9.1

Outcome	Value of X
HHH	3
HHT	2
HTH	2
THH	2
HTT	1
THT	1
TTH	1
TTT	0

(c) With the aid of Table 9.1, we see that the event $(X = 2)$ is given by the set

$$\{\text{HHT, HTH, THH}\}$$

■

EXAMPLE 9.2 A coin is tossed repeatedly until a head occurs. Let the random variable Y denote the number of tosses of the coin in the experiment. What are the values of Y?

SOLUTION The outcomes of the experiment comprise an infinite set

$$S = \{\text{H, TH, TTH, TTTH, TTTTH}, \ldots\}$$

These outcomes of the experiment are displayed in the first column of Table 9.2.

The corresponding values assumed by the random variable Y (the number of tosses) appear in the second column.

Outcome	Value of Y
H	1
TH	2
TTH	3
TTTH	4
TTTTH	5
⋮	⋮

Table 9.2

■

EXAMPLE 9.3 A disposable flashlight is turned on until its battery runs out. Let the random variable Z denote the length (in hours) of the life of the battery. What values may Z assume?

SOLUTION The values assumed by Z may be any nonnegative real numbers, that is, the possible values of Z comprise the interval $0 \leq Z < \infty$. ■

The advantage of working with random variables rather than working directly with the outcomes of an experiment is that random variables are functions which may be added, subtracted, and multiplied. Because of this, results developed in the field of algebra and other areas of mathematics may be used freely to help us solve problems in the fields of probability and statistics.

finite discrete and infinite discrete random variables

A random variable is classified into three categories depending upon the set of values it assumes. A random variable is called *finite discrete* if it assumes only finitely many values. For example, the random variable X of Example 9.1 is finite discrete since it may assume only values from the finite set $\{0, 1, 2, 3\}$ of numbers. Next, a random variable is said to be *infinite discrete* if it takes on infinitely many values, which may be arranged in a sequence. For example, the random variable Y of Example 9.2 is infinite discrete since it assumes values from the set $\{1, 2, 3, 4, 5, \ldots\}$ which has been arranged in the form of an infinite sequence. Finally, a *random variable* is called *continuous* if the values it may assume comprise an interval of real numbers. For example, the random variable Z of Example 9.3 is continuous since the values it may assume comprise the interval of nonnegative real numbers. For the remainder of this section *all random variables will be assumed to be finite discrete.*

continuous random variable

Now, in Section 8.2, we learned how to construct the probability distribution for an experiment. There, the probability distribution took the form of a table, which gave the probabilities associated with the outcomes of an experiment. Since the random variable associated with an experiment is related to the outcomes of the experiment, it is clear that we should be able to construct a probability distribution associated with the *random variable* rather than one associated with the outcomes of the experiment. Such a distribution is called the *probability distribution of a random variable* and may be given in the form of a formula or displayed

probability distribution of a random variable

in a table, which gives the distinct (numerical) values of the random variable X and the probabilities associated with these values. Thus, if $x_1, x_2, \ldots, x_n$ are the values assumed by the random variable X with associated probabilities $P(X=x_1)$, $P(X=x_2), \ldots, P(X=x_n)$, respectively, then the required probability distribution of the random variable X is given by

x	$P(X=x)$
x_1	p_1
x_2	p_2
x_3	p_3
$\vdots$	$\vdots$
x_n	p_n

The next several examples illustrate the construction of certain probability distributions.

EXAMPLE 9.4 Find the probability distribution of the random variable associated with the experiment of Example 9.1.

SOLUTION From the results of Example 9.1, we see that the values assumed by the random variable X are 0, 1, 2, and 3 corresponding to the events of 0, 1, 2, and 3 heads occurring, respectively. Referring to Table 9.1 once again, we see that the outcome associated with the event $(X=0)$ is given by the set {TTT}. Consequently, the probability associated with the random variable X when it assumes the value 0 is given by

$$P(X=0)=\frac{1}{8} \qquad \text{(Note that } n(S)=8\text{)}$$

Next, observe that the event $(X=1)$ is given by the set {HTT, THT, TTH} and so

$$P(X=1)=\frac{3}{8}$$

In a similar manner we may compute $P(X=2)$ and $P(X=3)$ which gives the following probability distribution (Table 9.3).

Table 9.3

x	$P(X=x)$
0	1/8
1	3/8
2	3/8
3	1/8

■

EXAMPLE 9.5 Let X denote the random variable that gives the sum of the faces that fall upper-most when two fair dice are cast. Find the probability distribution of X.

SOLUTION The values assumed by the random variable X are $2, 3, 4, \ldots, 12$ corresponding to the events $E_2, E_3, E_4, \ldots, E_{12}$ (see Example 8.3 in Section 8.1). Next, the probabilities associated with the random variable X when X assumes the values $2, 3, 4, \ldots, 12$ are precisely the probabilities $P(E_2), P(E_3), \ldots, P(E_{12})$, respectively, and may be computed in much the same way as the solution to Example 8.8 in Section 8.2. Thus,

$$P(X=2)=P(E_2)=\frac{1}{36}, \qquad P(X=3)=P(E_3)=\frac{2}{36}, \quad \text{and so on.}$$

The required probability distribution of X is given by Table 9.4.

x	2	3	4	5	6	7	8	9	10	11	12
$P(X=x)$	$\frac{1}{36}$	$\frac{2}{36}$	$\frac{3}{36}$	$\frac{4}{36}$	$\frac{5}{36}$	$\frac{6}{36}$	$\frac{5}{36}$	$\frac{4}{36}$	$\frac{3}{36}$	$\frac{2}{36}$	$\frac{1}{36}$

Table 9.4 ■

EXAMPLE 9.6 The following data gives the number of cars observed waiting in line at the beginning of every two minutes between 3 and 5 P.M. on a certain Friday at the Drive-in Teller of the Westwood Savings Bank and the corresponding frequency of occurrence. Find the probability distribution of the random variable X, where X denotes the number of cars observed waiting in line.

Number of cars	Frequency of occurrence
0	2
1	9
2	16
3	12
4	8
5	6
6	4
7	2
8	1

SOLUTION Dividing each number on the right of the given table by 60 (the sum of these numbers) gives the respective probabilities (here, we use the relative frequency interpretation of probability) associated with the random variable X when X

assumes the values 0, 1, 2, . . . , 8. For example,

$$P(X=0)=\frac{2}{60}\approx 0.03$$

$$P(X=1)=\frac{9}{60}=0.15 \quad \text{and so on.}$$

The resulting probability distribution is shown in Table 9.5.

x	$P(X=x)$
0	0.03
1	0.15
2	0.27
3	0.20
4	0.13
5	0.10
6	0.07
7	0.03
8	0.02

Table 9.5

■

A probability distribution of a random variable may be exhibited graphically through the use of *histograms*. To construct a histogram of a particular probability distribution, first locate the values of the random variable on the number line. Then, above each such number, erect a rectangle with width 1 and height equal to the probability associated with that value of the random variable. For example, the histogram of the probability distribution appearing in Table 9.3 is shown in Figure 9.1. The histograms of the probability distributions of Examples 9.5 and 9.6 are constructed in a similar manner and displayed in Figures 9.2 and 9.3, respectively.

histogram

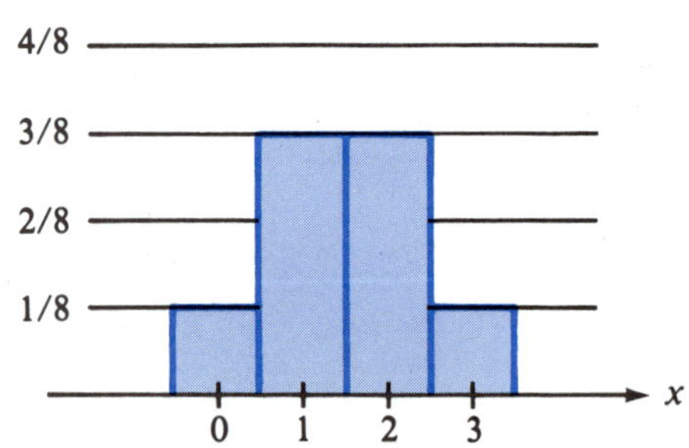

Figure 9.1

Observe that in each of the histograms of probability distributions of random variables, the area of a rectangle associated with a value of a random variable X gives precisely the probability associated with that value of X. This follows because each such rectangle, by construction, has width 1 and height corresponding to the probability associated with the value of the random variable. Another consequence arising from the method of construction of a histogram is that *the probability associated with more than one value of the random variable* X *is given by the sum of the areas of the rectangles associated with those values of* X. For example, in the coin tossing experiment of Example 9.1, the event of obtaining at least two heads (this corresponds to the event $(X=2)$ or $(X=3)$) is given by

$$P(X=2)+P(X=3)$$

and may be obtained from the histogram depicted in Figure 9.1 by adding the areas associated with the values 2 and 3, respectively, of the random variable X. We obtain

$$\begin{aligned} P(X=2)+P(X=3) &= (1)\left(\frac{3}{8}\right)+(1)\left(\frac{1}{8}\right) \\ &= \frac{1}{2} \end{aligned}$$

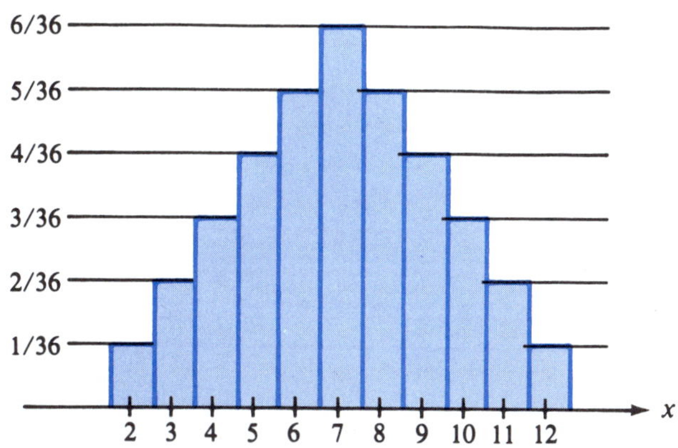

Figure 9.2

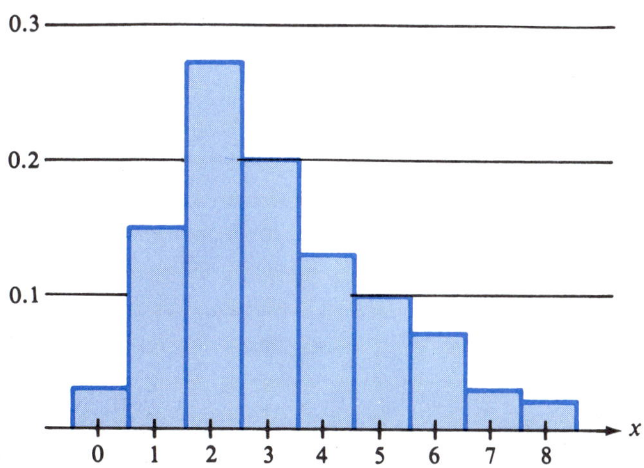

Figure 9.3

This result provides us with a method of computing the probabilities of events associated with an experiment directly from the knowledge of a histogram of the probability distribution of the random variable associated with the experiment.

EXAMPLE 9.7 Suppose that the probability distribution of a random variable X is represented by the histogram shown in Figure 9.4. Identify that part of the histogram whose area gives the probability $P(10 \leq X \leq 20)$. Do not evaluate the result.

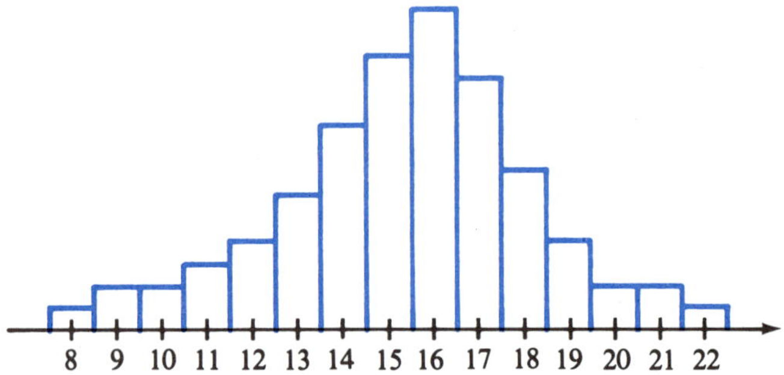

Figure 9.4

SOLUTION The event $(10 \leq X \leq 20)$ is the event comprising outcomes related to the values 10, 11, 12, ..., 20 of the random variable X. The probability of this event $P(10 \leq X \leq 20)$ is therefore given by the shaded area of the histogram in Figure 9.5.

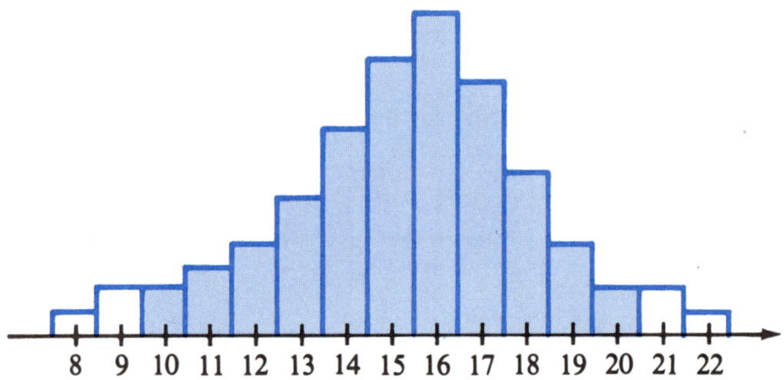

Figure 9.5

9.1 EXERCISES

1. A die is cast repeatedly until a 6 falls uppermost. Let the random variable X denote the number of times the die is cast. What are the values that X may assume?

2. Let X denote the random variable that gives the sum of the faces that fall uppermost when two fair dice are cast. Find $P(X = 7)$.

3. Three balls are selected at random without replacement from an urn containing 4 green balls and 6 red balls. Let the random variable X denote the number of green balls drawn.

(*a*) List the outcomes of the experiment.

(*b*) Find the value assigned to each outcome of the experiment by the random variable X.

(*c*) Find the event comprising the outcomes to which a value of 3 has been assigned by X.

4. Two dice are cast. Let the random variable X denote the number that falls uppermost on the first die and let Y denote the number that falls uppermost on the second die.

(*a*) Find the probability distributions of X and Y.

(*b*) Find the probability distribution of $X+Y$.

In Exercises 5–10, give the range of values that the random variable X *may assume and classify the random variable as finite discrete, infinite discrete, or continuous.*

5. $X =$ the number of times a die is thrown until a 2 appears.

6. $X =$ the number of defective watches in a sample of 8.

7. $X =$ the distance a commuter travels to work.

8. $X =$ the number of hours a child watches television on a given day.

9. $X =$ the number of times an accountant takes the C.P.A. examination before passing.

10. $X =$ the number of boys in a 4-child family.

11. The probability distribution of a random variable X is shown in the following table. Find the following probabilities:

(*a*) $P(X=-10)$ (*b*) $P(X \geq 5)$ (*c*) $P(-5 \leq X \leq 5)$
(*d*) $P(X \leq 20)$

x	$P(X=x)$
−10	0.20
−5	0.15
0	0.05
5	0.10
10	0.25
15	0.10
20	0.15

12. Suppose that a probability distribution of a random variable X is represented by the histogram shown at the top of the next page. Shade that part of the histogram whose area gives the probability $P(17 \leq X \leq 20)$.

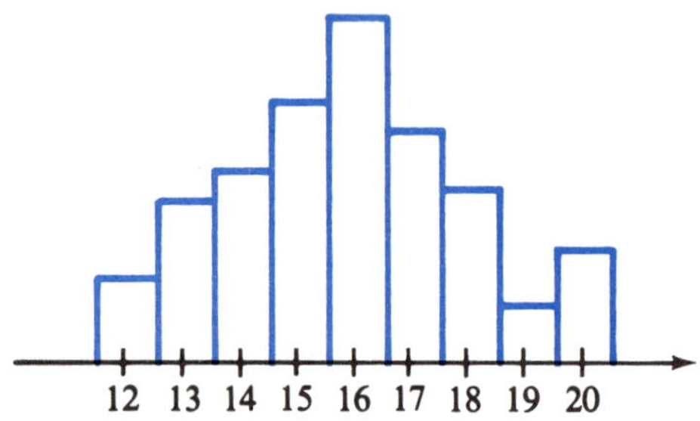

13. An examination consisting of 10 true or false questions was taken by a class of 100 students. The probability distribution of the random variable X, where X denotes the number of questions answered correctly by a student, is represented by the histogram shown below. The rectangle with base centered about the number 8 is missing. What should the height of this rectangle be?

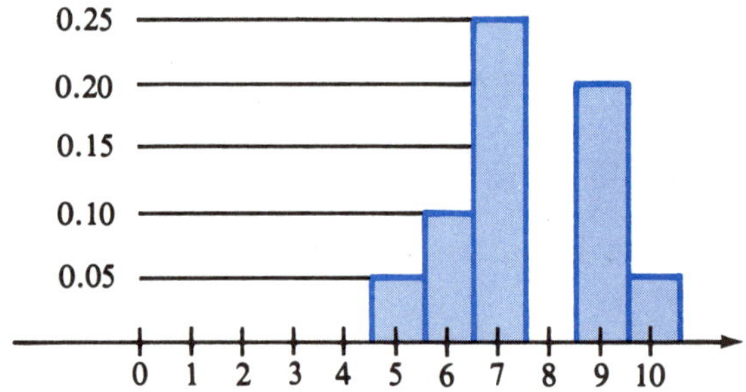

14. The following data was obtained in a study conducted by the manager of the Sav-More Supermarket. In this study the number of customers waiting in line at the express checkout-counter at the beginning of each 3-minute interval between 9 A.M. and 12 noon on Saturday was observed.

Number of customers	Frequency of occurrence
0	1
1	4
2	2
3	7
4	14
5	8
6	10
7	6
8	3
9	4
10	1

(*a*) Find the probability distribution of the random variable X, where X denotes the number of customers observed waiting in line.

(*b*) Draw the histogram representing this probability distribution.

15. A survey was conducted by the Public Housing Authority in a certain community among 1000 families to determine the distribution of families by size. The results are shown below.

Family size	Frequency of occurrence
2	350
3	200
4	245
5	125
6	66
7	10
8	4

(*a*) Find the probability distribution of the random variable X, where X denotes the number of persons in a family.

(*b*) Draw the histogram corresponding to the probability distribution found in part (*a*).

9.2 Expected Value

The average value of a set of numbers is a familiar notion to most people. For example, to compute the average of the four numbers

$$12, 16, 23, 37$$

we simply add these numbers and divide the resulting sum by 4, giving the required average as

$$\frac{12+16+23+37}{4}=\frac{88}{4}$$

average or mean of n numbers

or 22. In general, we define the *average* (also called *mean*) of the *n numbers*

$$x_1, x_2, \ldots, x_n$$

to be the number $\bar{x}$ (read "x bar") where

$$\bar{x}=\frac{x_1+x_2+\cdots+x_n}{n}$$

EXAMPLE 9.8 Refer to Example 9.6. Find the average number of cars waiting in line at the Drive-in-Teller of the bank observed at the beginning of each two minute interval during the period in question.

SOLUTION The number of cars together with its corresponding frequency of occurrence are reproduced in Table 9.6. Observe from the table that the number 0 (of cars) occurs twice, the number 1 occurs 9 times, and so on. There are altogether

$$2+9+16+12+8+6+4+2+1$$

or 60 numbers to be averaged. Therefore, the required average is given by

$$\frac{0\cdot 2+1\cdot 9+2\cdot 16+3\cdot 12+4\cdot 8+5\cdot 6+6\cdot 4+7\cdot 2+8\cdot 1}{60} \approx 3.1 \tag{9.1}$$

or approximately 3.1 cars.

Table 9.6

Number of cars	Frequency of occurrence
0	2
1	9
2	16
3	12
4	8
5	6
6	4
7	2
8	1

■

Let us reconsider the expression (9.1) which gives the average of the frequency distribution shown in Table 9.6. Dividing each term by the denominator, the expression may be cast in the form

$$0\cdot\left(\frac{2}{60}\right)+1\cdot\left(\frac{9}{60}\right)+2\cdot\left(\frac{16}{60}\right)+3\cdot\left(\frac{12}{60}\right)+4\cdot\left(\frac{8}{60}\right)+5\cdot\left(\frac{6}{60}\right)$$
$$+6\cdot\left(\frac{4}{60}\right)+7\cdot\left(\frac{2}{60}\right)+8\cdot\left(\frac{1}{60}\right)$$

Observe that in the above expression, each term in the sum is a product of two factors; the first factor is the value assumed by the random variable X where X denotes the number of cars observed waiting in line, while the second factor is just the probability associated with that value of the random variable (see Example

expected value

9.6). This observation suggests the following general method for calculating the *expected value* (that is, the average or mean) of a random variable X that assumes a finite number of values from the knowledge of its probability distribution: *Let X denote a random variable that assumes the values $x_1, x_2, \ldots, x_n$ with associated probabilities $p_1, p_2, \ldots, p_n$, respectively. Then the expected value of X, E(X), is given by*

$$E(X) = x_1p_1 + x_2p_2 + \cdots + x_np_n \tag{9.2}$$

EXAMPLE 9.9 Resolve Example 9.8 using Table 9.5, the probability distribution associated with the experiment.

SOLUTION Let X denote the number of cars observed waiting in line. Then the average number of cars observed waiting in line is given by the expected value of X, that is, by

$$\begin{aligned} E(X) &= 0 \cdot (0.03) + 1 \cdot (0.15) + 2 \cdot (0.27) + 3 \cdot (0.20) + 4 \cdot (0.13) \\ &\quad + 5 \cdot (0.10) + 6 \cdot (0.07) + 7 \cdot (0.03) + 8 \cdot (0.02) \\ &= 3.1 \end{aligned}$$

or 3.1 cars, which agrees with the result obtained earlier. ■

The expected value of a random variable X is a measure of central tendency of the probability distribution associated with X. In repeated trials of an experiment with random variable X, the observed values of X get closer and closer to the expected value of X as the number of trials gets larger and larger. Geometrically, the expected value of a random variable X has the following simple interpretation: If a laminate is made of the histogram of a probability distribution associated with a random variable X, then the expected value of X corresponds to the point on the base of the laminate at which the latter will balance perfectly when the point is directly over a fulcrum (see Figure 9.6).

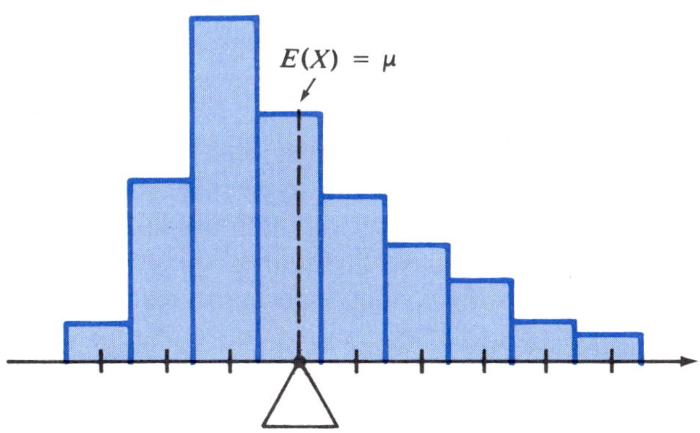

Figure 9.6

EXAMPLE 9.10 Let X denote the random variable that gives the sum of the faces that fall uppermost when two fair dice are cast. Find the expected value, $E(X)$, of X.

SOLUTION The probability distribution of X was found in Example 9.5 and is reproduced below.

x	$P(X=x)$
2	1/36
3	2/36
4	3/36
5	4/36
6	5/36
7	6/36
8	5/36
9	4/36
10	3/36
11	2/36
12	1/36

Using this result we find

$$\begin{aligned} E(X) &= 2\left(\frac{1}{36}\right)+3\left(\frac{2}{36}\right)+4\left(\frac{3}{36}\right)+5\left(\frac{4}{36}\right)+6\left(\frac{5}{36}\right)+7\left(\frac{6}{36}\right)+8\left(\frac{5}{36}\right) \\ &\quad +9\left(\frac{4}{36}\right)+10\left(\frac{3}{36}\right)+11\left(\frac{2}{36}\right)+12\left(\frac{1}{36}\right) \\ &= 7 \end{aligned}$$

Note that, because of the symmetry of the histogram of the probability distribution with respect to the vertical line $x=7$, the result could have been obtained by merely inspecting Figure 9.2. ■

The next example shows how the concept of expected value is used to help us make the best decision in an investment situation.

EXAMPLE 9.11 A group of private investors intends to purchase one of two motels that are currently being offered for sale in a certain city. The terms of sale of the two motels are similar, although the Regina Inn has 52 rooms and is in a slightly better location than the Merlin Motor Lodge, which has 60 rooms. Records obtained for each of the motels reveal that the occupancy rate, with corresponding probabilities, during the May–September tourist season are:

Regina Inn

Occupancy rate	.80	.85	.90	.95	1.00
Probability	.19	.22	.31	.23	.05

Merlin Motor Lodge

Occupancy rate	.75	.80	.85	.90	.95	1.00
Probability	.35	.21	.18	.15	.09	.02

The average profit per day for each occupied room at the Regina Inn is \$10, while the average profit per day for each occupied room at the Merlin Motor Lodge is \$9.

(**a**) Find the average number of rooms occupied per day at each motel.

(**b**) If the objective of the investors is to purchase the motel that generates the higher daily profit, which motel should they purchase? (Compare the expected daily profit of the two motels.)

SOLUTION (**a**) Let X denote the occupancy rate at the Regina Inn. Then the average daily occupancy rate at the Regina Inn is given by the expected value of X, that is, by

$$\begin{aligned}E(X) &= (.80)(.19)+(.85)(.22)+(.90)(.31)+(.95)(.23)+(1.00)(.05)\\ &= .8865\end{aligned}$$

and the average number of rooms occupied per day at the Regina Inn is

$$(.8865)(52) \approx 46.1$$

or 46.1 rooms. Similarly, letting Y denote the occupancy rate at the Merlin Motor Lodge, we have

$$\begin{aligned}E(Y) &= (.75)(.35)+(.80)(.21)+(.85)(.18)+(.90)(.15)\\ &\quad +(.95)(.09)+(1.00)(.02)\\ &= .8240\end{aligned}$$

and the average number of rooms occupied per day at the Merlin Motor Lodge is

$$(.8240)(60) \approx 49.4$$

or 49.4 rooms.

(**b**) The expected daily profit at the Regina Inn is given by

$$46.1(10) = 461$$

or \$461. The expected daily profit at the Merlin Motor Lodge is given by

$$(49.4)(9) = 444.6$$

or \$444.60. From the above results we conclude that the investors should purchase the Regina Inn, which is expected to yield a higher daily profit. ■

EXAMPLE 9.12 The Island Club is holding a fund raising raffle. Ten thousand tickets have been sold for \$2 each. There will be a first prize of \$3000, three second prizes of \$1000 each, five third prizes of \$500 each, and twenty consolation prizes of \$100 each. Letting X denote the net winnings (that is, winnings less the cost of the ticket) associated with the tickets, find $E(X)$. Interpret your results.

SOLUTION The values assumed by X are $(0-2)$, $(100-2)$, $(500-2)$, $(1000-2)$, and $(3000-2)$, that is, -2, 98, 498, 998, and 2998, which correspond, respectively, to the value of a losing ticket, a consolation prize, a third prize, and so on. The probability distribution of X may be calculated in the usual manner and appears in the following table. Using the table, we find

$$\begin{aligned} E(X) &= (-2)(0.9971)+98(0.002)+498(0.0005)+998(0.0003)+2998(0.0001) \\ &= -0.95 \end{aligned}$$

The expected value obtained above gives the long-run average loss (negative gain) of a holder of one ticket; that is, if one participated in such a raffle by purchasing one ticket each time, in the long-run, one may expect to lose, on the average, \$.95 per raffle.

x	$P(X=x)$
−2	0.9971
98	0.0020
498	0.0005
998	0.0003
2998	0.0001

■

EXAMPLE 9.13 In the game of roulette as played in the casinos of Las Vegas, the wheel is divided into 38 compartments numbered 1 through 36, 0, and 00. One-half of the numbers 1 through 36 are red, the other half black, while 0 and 00 are green. Of the many types of bets that may be placed, one involves betting on the outcome of the color of the winning number. For example, one may place a certain sum of money on *red*. If the winning number is red, one wins an amount equal to the bet placed and loses the bet otherwise. Find the expected value of the winnings on a \$1.00 bet placed on *red*.

SOLUTION Let X be a random variable whose values are 1 and -1, which correspond to a win and a loss. The probabilities associated with the values 1 and -1 are $\frac{18}{38}$ and $\frac{20}{38}$, respectively. Therefore, the expected value is given by

$$\begin{aligned} E(X) &= 1\left(\frac{18}{38}\right)+(-1)\left(\frac{20}{38}\right) \\ &= -\frac{2}{38} \\ &\approx -0.053 \end{aligned}$$

Thus, if one places a \$1.00 bet on *red* over and over again, one may expect to lose, on the average, approximately \$.05 per bet in the long-run. ■

The last two examples serve as illustrations of games that are not "fair". Of course, most participants in such games are aware of this fact and participate in them for other reasons. In a fair game, neither party has an advantage, a condition that translates into the condition that $E(X)=0$, where X takes on the values of the winnings of a player.

EXAMPLE 9.14 Mike and Bill play a card game with a standard deck of 52 cards. Mike selects a card from a well-shuffled deck and receives A dollars from Bill if the card selected is a diamond; otherwise, Mike pays Bill a dollar. Determine the value of A if the game is to be fair.

SOLUTION Let X denote a random variable whose values are associated with Mike's winnings. Then X takes on the value A with probability $P(X=A)=\frac{1}{4}$ (since there are 13 diamonds in the deck of cards) if Mike wins and takes on the value -1 with probability $P(X=-1)=\frac{3}{4}$ if Mike loses. Since the game is to be a fair one, the expected value $E(X)$ of Mike's winnings is to be equal to zero, that is,

$$E(X)=A\left(\frac{1}{4}\right)+(-1)\left(\frac{3}{4}\right)=0$$

Solving the above equation for A gives $A=3$. Thus, the card game constructed will be fair if Bill makes a \$3.00 payoff for a winning bet of \$1.00 placed by Mike. ■

In the last example, we saw that the card game could be made fair if Bill agreed to pay Mike \$3.00 for a \$1.00 winning bet placed by Mike. The ratio 3 : 1 is called the *fair odds* for the game. In general, odds of $a:b$ mean that a player who bets \$$b$ and wins will receive a payoff of \$$a$ (in addition to the \$$b$ that was bet). The fair odds for a game may be computed from the knowledge of the probability of winning the bet. To this end, suppose the probability of winning the bet is p. Let X be a random variable associated with the winnings of a player who places a bet of \$$b$ in the game. Then the values taken on by X are a and $-b$ corresponding to a win or a loss with respective probabilities $P(X=a)=p$ and $P(X=-b)=1-p$. Setting $E(X)=0$ for a fair game, we find

fair odds

$$E(X)=ap+(-b)(1-p)=0$$

(9.3) or

$$\frac{a}{b}=\frac{1-p}{p}$$

Observe that Formula (9.3) states that the odds $a:b$ for a fair game is just the ratio of the probability of losing to the probability of winning.

EXAMPLE 9.15 Find the fair odds for a bet on *red* in American roulette.

SOLUTION The probability of winning a bet here—the probability that the ball lands on a red compartment, is given by $p = \frac{18}{38}$. Therefore, the fair odds are

$$\frac{a}{b} = \frac{1 - 18/38}{18/38} = \frac{20}{18} = \frac{10}{9}$$

that is, 10:9. Thus, a player should receive \$10.00 on a winning \$9.00 bet or equivalently \$1.11 on a winning \$1.00 bet. ■

Solving equation (9.3) for p in terms of a and b gives

(9.4) $$p = \frac{b}{a+b}$$

Equation (9.4) enables us to compute the probability of winning a bet given the fair odds for the bet.

EXAMPLE 9.16 The odds for a fair game are known to be 5:4. Find the probability of winning a bet in the game.

SOLUTION The fair odds for the game are $a:b = 5:4$ or, equivalently, $a = 5$ when $b = 4$. Using these values of a and b and Formula (9.4), we find

$$p = \frac{4}{5+4}$$

or approximately 0.44. ■

In concluding this section, we mention that in addition to the mean there are two other measures of central tendency of a set of numerical data. These are the median and the mode of a set of numbers. The *median* is defined as the middle value in a set of data arranged in increasing or decreasing order. (If there is an even number of entries the median is the mean of the two middle numbers.) The *mode* is defined as the value that occurs most frequently in a set of data. (See problems 24 and 25 in Exercise set 9.2.)

9.2 EXERCISES

1. During the first year at a university that uses a 4-point grading system, a freshman took 10 three-credit courses and received 2 As, 3 Bs, 4 Cs, and 1 D.

(***a***) Compute this student's grade-point average.

(*b*) Let the random variable X denote the number of points corresponding to a given letter grade. Find the probability distribution of the random variable X and compute $E(X)$, the expected value of X.

2. Records kept by the chief dietician at the University Cafeteria over a 30-week period show the following weekly consumption of milk (in gallons).

Milk (in gallons)	Number of weeks
200	3
205	4
210	6
215	5
220	4
225	3
230	2
235	2
240	1

(*a*) Find the average number of gallons of milk per week consumed in the cafeteria.

(*b*) Let the random variable X denote the number of gallons of milk consumed in a week at the cafeteria. Find the probability distribution of the random variable X and compute $E(X)$, the expected value of X.

3. Find the expected value of a random variable X having the following probability distribution.

x	$P(X=x)$
−5	0.12
−1	0.16
0	0.28
1	0.22
5	0.12
8	0.10

4. Find the expected value of a random variable X having the following probability distribution.

x	$P(X=x)$
0	1/8
1	1/4
2	3/16
3	1/4
4	1/16
5	1/8

5. The daily earnings X of an employee who works on a commission basis are given by the following probability distribution. Find the employee's expected earnings.

x (in \$)	$P(X = x)$
0	0.07
25	0.12
50	0.17
75	0.14
100	0.28
125	0.18
150	0.04

6. In a 4-child family, what is the expected number of boys? (Assume that the probability of boy being born is the same as the probability of a girl being born.)

7. Based on past experience, the manager of the Video-Rama Store has compiled the following table which gives the probabilities that a customer who enters the Video-Rama Store will buy 0, 1, 2, 3, or 4 videocassettes. How many videocassettes can a customer entering this store be expected to buy?

Number of videocassettes	Probability
0	0.42
1	0.36
2	0.14
3	0.05
4	0.03

8. If a sample of 3 batteries is selected from a lot of 10 of which 2 are defective, what is the expected number of defective batteries?

9. The number of accidents that occur at a certain intersection known as "Five Corners" on a Friday afternoon between the hours of 3:00 and 6:00 P.M. along with the corresponding probabilities are shown in the following table. Find the expected number of accidents during the period in question.

Number of accidents	Probability
0	0.935
1	0.03
2	0.02
3	0.01
4	0.005

10. The owner of a newsstand in a college community estimates the weekly demand for a certain magazine is as follows:

Quantity demanded	10	11	12	13	14	15
Probability	.05	.15	.25	.30	.20	.05

Find the number of issues of the magazine that the owner of the newsstand should expect to sell per week.

11. In a lottery, 5,000 tickets are sold for $1 each. One first prize of $2000, 1 second prize of $500, 3 third prizes of $100, and 10 consolation prizes of $25 are to be awarded. What are the expected net earnings of a person who buys one ticket?

12. A man wishes to purchase a 5-year term life insurance policy that will pay the beneficiary $20,000 in the event that the man's death occurs during the next 5 years. Using life insurance tables, he determines that the probability that he will live another 5 years is 0.96. What is the minimum amount that he can expect to pay for his premium?

13. A woman purchased a $10,000 1-year term life insurance policy for $130. Assuming that the probability that she will live for another year is 0.992, find the company's expected gain.

14. The management of Multi-Vision Inc., a cable T.V. company, intends to submit a bid for the cable television rights in one of two cities, A or B. If the company obtains the rights to city A, the probability of which is 0.2, the estimated profit over the next ten years is $10,000,000; if the company obtains the rights to city B, the probability of which is 0.3, the estimated profit over the next ten years is $7,000,000. The cost of submitting a bid for rights in city A is $250,000 and that for the rights in city B is $200,000. By comparing the expected profits for each venture, determine whether the company should bid for the rights in city A or city B.

15. Mr. Hunt intends to purchase one of two car dealerships, which are currently for sale in a certain city. Records obtained from each of the two dealers reveal that their weekly volume of sales, with corresponding probabilities are as follows:

Dahl Motors

Number of cars sold per week	5	6	7	8	9	10	11	12
Probability	.05	.09	.14	.24	.18	.14	.11	.05

Farthington Auto Sales

Number of cars sold per week	5	6	7	8	9	10
Probability	.08	.21	.31	.24	.10	.06

The average profit per car at Dahl Motors is \$362, while the average profit per car at Farthington Auto Sales is \$436.

(*a*) Find the average number of cars sold per week at each dealership.

(*b*) If Mr. Hunt's objective is to purchase the dealership that generates the higher weekly profit, which dealership should he purchase? (Compare the expected weekly profit for each dealership.)

16. A player casts a fair die and receives a dollar amount equal to the number appearing uppermost on the face of the die. If this is a fair game, determine the amount that the player should be willing to pay to participate in the game.

17. If the probability that it will rain tomorrow is 0.3

(*a*) what are the odds that it will rain tomorrow?

(*b*) what are the odds that it will not rain tomorrow?

18. Find the probabilities corresponding to the given odds in a fair game:

(*a*) 9 to 5 (*b*) 1 to 3 (*c*) 4 to 7

19. If a sports forecaster states that the odds of a certain boxer winning a boxing match are 4 to 3, what is the probability that the boxer will win the match?

20. In American roulette as described in Example 9.13 a player may bet on a split (2 adjacent numbers). In this case if the player bets \$1 and either number comes up, the player wins \$17 and gets his \$1 back. If neither number comes up, he loses his \$1 bet. Find the expected value of the winnings on a \$1 bet placed on a split.

21. If a player placed a \$1 bet on red and a \$1 bet on black in a single play in American roulette, what would the expected value of his winnings be?

22. In European roulette the wheel is divided into 37 compartments numbered 1 through 36 and 0. (In American roulette there are 38 compartments numbered 1 through 36, 0, and 00). Find the expected value of the winnings on a \$1 bet placed on red in European roulette.

23. (*a*) Show that for any number c,

$$E(cX) = cE(X)$$

(*b*) Use this result to find the expected loss if a gambler bets \$300 on red in a single play in American roulette.

24. In an examination given to a class of 20 students the following test scores were obtained:

40, 45, 50, 50, 55, 60, 60, 75, 75, 80, 80, 85, 85, 85, 85, 90, 90, 95, 95, 100

(*a*) Find the mean or average score, the mode, and the median score.

(*b*) Which of these three measures of central tendency do you think is the least representative of the set of scores?

25. The frequency distribution of the hourly wage-rates among blue-collar workers in a certain factory is given below. Find the mean or average wage-rate, the mode, and the median wage-rate of these workers.

Wage rate (in \$)	Frequency
5.70	60
5.80	90
5.90	75
6.00	120
6.10	60
6.20	45

9.3 Variance and Standard Deviation

The mean or expected value of a random variable, introduced in the last section, enables us to express an important property of the probability distribution associated with the random variable in terms of a single number. But the knowledge of the location or central tendency of a probability distribution alone is usually not enough to give a reasonably accurate picture of the probability distribution. Consider, for example, the two probability distributions whose histograms appear in Figure 9.7. Both the distributions have the same expected value or mean $\mu = 4$ (the Greek letter μ is read "mu"). Note that the probability distribution with histogram shown in Figure 9.7 (**a**) is closely concentrated about its mean μ while the one with histogram shown in Figure 9.7 (**b**) is widely dispersed or spread about its mean.

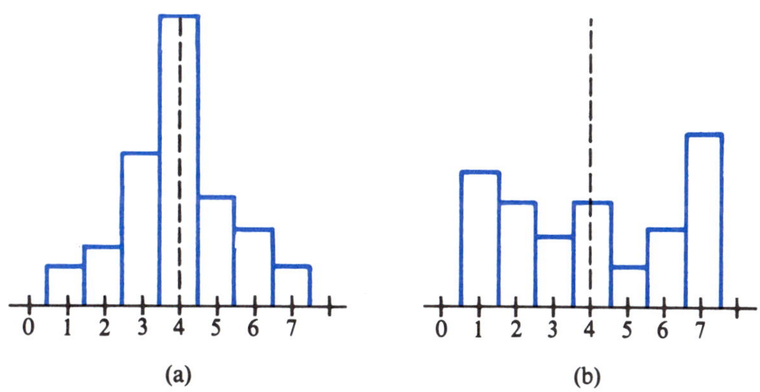

Figure 9.7

As another example, suppose Mr. Alan Horowitz, the host of a popular television show *The Consumer Advocate* decides to demonstrate the accuracy of the weight contents of two popular brands of potato chips. Ten packages of potato chips of each brand are selected at random and weighed carefully. The results are as follows:

Weight in oz

Brand A	16.1	16	15.8	16	15.9	16.1	15.9	16	16	16.2
Brand B	16.3	15.7	15.8	16.2	15.9	16.1	15.7	16.2	16	16.1

It may be readily verified that the mean weights for each of the two brands is 16 ounces (see Example 9.19). However, a cursory examination of the data shows that the weights of the Brand B packages exhibit much greater dispersion about the mean than those of Brand A.

One measure of the degree of dispersion or spread of a probability distribution about its mean is given by the variance of the random variable associated with the probability distribution. A probability distribution with a small spread about its mean will have a small variance, while one with a larger spread will have a larger variance. Thus, the variance of the random variable associated with the probability distribution whose histogram appears in Figure 9.7 (**a**) is smaller than the variance of the random variable associated with the probability distribution whose histogram is shown in Figure 9.7 (**b**) (see Example 9.17). Also, as we shall see later in Example 9.19, the variance of the random variable associated with the weights of the Brand A potato chips is smaller than that of the random variable associated with the weights of the Brand B potato chips. We made this observation earlier.

variance of a random variable

We now define the variance of a random variable. Suppose the random variable X has a probability distribution as shown in Table 9.7 and a mean or expected value given by $E(X)=\mu$. Then the *variance of the random variable* X is defined by

(9.5) $$\text{Var}(X)=p_1(x_1-\mu)^2+p_2(x_2-\mu)^2+\cdots+p_n(x_n-\mu)^2$$

x	$P(X=x)$
x_1	p_1
x_2	p_2
x_3	p_3
$\vdots$	$\vdots$
x_n	p_n

Table 9.7

An explanation of Formula (9.5) is in order. First of all, let us note that the numbers

(9.6) $$x_1-\mu, x_2-\mu, \ldots, x_n-\mu$$

deviation

measure the *deviations* of $x_1, x_2, \ldots, x_n$ from μ, respectively. Thus the numbers

(9.7) $$(x_1-\mu)^2, (x_2-\mu)^2, \ldots, (x_n-\mu)^2$$

measure the squares of the deviations of $x_1, x_2, \ldots, x_n$ from μ, respectively. Next, by multiplying each of the numbers in (9.7) by the respective probability associated with each value of the random variable X, the numbers are weighted accordingly so that their sum is a measure of the variance of X about its mean. We note that an attempt to define the variance of a random variable about its mean in a similar manner using the deviations (9.6) rather than their squares is not fruitful since some of the deviations may be positive while others may be negative and (because of cancellations) the sum does not give a satisfactory measure of the variance of the random variable.

EXAMPLE 9.17 Find the variance of the random variables X and of the random variable Y whose probability distributions follow. These are the probability distributions associated with the histograms shown in Figure 9.7 (**a**) and Figure 9.7 (**b**).

x	$P(X=x)$
1	0.05
2	0.075
3	0.2
4	0.375
5	0.15
6	0.1
7	0.05

y	$P(Y=y)$
1	0.2
2	0.15
3	0.1
4	0.15
5	0.05
6	0.1
7	0.25

SOLUTION The mean of the random variable X is given by

$$\begin{aligned}\mu_x &= (1)(0.05)+(2)(0.075)+(3)(0.2)+(4)(0.375)+(5)(0.15)\\ &\quad +(6)(0.1)+(7)(0.05)\\ &= 4\end{aligned}$$

Therefore, using Formula (9.5) and the data from the probability distribution of X, we find that the variance of X is given by

$$\begin{aligned}\text{Var}(X) &= (0.05)(1-4)^2+(0.075)(2-4)^2+(0.2)(3-4)^2+(0.375)(4-4)^2\\ &\quad +(0.15)(5-4)^2+(0.1)(6-4)^2+(0.05)(7-4)^2\\ &= 1.95\end{aligned}$$

Next, we find that the mean of the random variable Y is given by

$$\begin{aligned}\mu_Y &= (1)(0.2)+(2)(0.15)+(3)(0.1)+(4)(0.15)+(5)(0.05)\\ &\quad +(6)(0.1)+(7)(0.25)\\ &= 4\end{aligned}$$

and so the variance of Y is given by

$$\begin{aligned}\text{Var}(Y) &= (0.2)(1-4)^2+(0.15)(2-4)^2+(0.1)(3-4)^2+(0.15)(4-4)^2\\ &\quad+(0.05)(5-4)^2+(0.1)(6-4)^2+(0.25)(7-4)^2\\ &= 5.2\end{aligned}$$

Note that Var (X) is smaller than Var (Y) which confirms the earlier observations about the spread or dispersion of the probability distribution of X and Y, respectively. ■

standard deviation of a random variable

Because Formula (9.5), which gives the variance of the random variable X, involves the square of the deviations, the unit of measurement of Var (X) is the square of the unit of measurement of the values of X. For example, if the values assumed by the random variable X are measured in units of a gram, then Var (X) will be measured in units involving the *square* of a gram. To remedy this situation one normally works with the square root of Var (X) rather than Var (X) itself. The former is called the standard deviation of X. Thus, the *standard deviation of a random variable X*, written σ_x or just σ (pronounced "sigma") is defined by

(9.8)
$$\begin{aligned}\sigma &= \sqrt{\text{Var}(X)}\\ &= \sqrt{p_1(x_1-\mu)^2+p_2(x_2-\mu)^2+\cdots+p_n(x_n-\mu)^2}\end{aligned}$$

where $x_1, x_2, \ldots, x_n$ denote the values assumed by the random variable X and $p_1=P(X=x_1), p_2=P(X=x_2), \ldots, p_n=P(X=x_n)$

EXAMPLE 9.18 Find the standard deviations of the random variables X and Y of Example 9.17.

SOLUTION From the results of Example 9.17, we have Var (X) = 1.95 and Var (Y) = 5.2. Extracting their respective square roots, we have

$$\begin{aligned}\sigma_X &= \sqrt{1.95}\\ &\approx 1.40\end{aligned}$$

and

$$\begin{aligned}\sigma_Y &= \sqrt{5.2}\\ &\approx 2.28\end{aligned}$$

■

EXAMPLE 9.19 Let X and Y denote the random variables whose values are the weights of the Brand A and Brand B potato chips, respectively (see page 372). Compute the mean and standard deviations of X and Y and interpret your results.

SOLUTION The probability distributions of X and Y may be computed from the given data as follows:

Brand A

x	Relative frequency of occurrence	$P(X=x)$
15.8	1	0.1
15.9	2	0.2
16.0	4	0.4
16.1	2	0.2
16.2	1	0.1

Brand B

y	Relative frequency of occurrence	$P(Y=y)$
15.7	2	0.2
15.8	1	0.1
15.9	1	0.1
16.0	1	0.1
16.1	2	0.2
16.2	2	0.2
16.3	1	0.1

The mean of X and Y are given by

$$\begin{aligned}\mu_X &= (0.1)(15.8)+(0.2)(15.9)+(0.4)(16.0)+(0.2)(16.1)\\ &\quad +(0.1)(16.2)\\ &= 16\end{aligned}$$

$$\begin{aligned}\mu_Y &= (0.2)(15.7)+(0.1)(15.8)+(0.1)(15.9)+(0.1)(16.0)\\ &\quad +(0.2)(16.1)+(0.2)(16.2)+(0.1)(16.3)\\ &= 16\end{aligned}$$

Therefore,

$$\begin{aligned}\text{Var}(X) &= (0.1)(15.8-16)^2+(0.2)(15.9-16)^2+(0.4)(16-16)^2\\ &\quad +(0.2)(16.1-16)^2+(0.1)(16.2-16)^2\\ &= 0.012\end{aligned}$$

and

$$\begin{aligned}\text{Var}(Y) &= (0.2)(15.7-16)^2+(0.1)(15.8-16)^2+(0.1)(15.9-16)^2\\ &\quad +(0.1)(16-16)^2+(0.2)(16.1-16)^2+(0.2)(16.2-16)^2\\ &\quad +(0.1)(16.3-16)^2\\ &= 0.042\end{aligned}$$

so that the required standard deviations are

$$\begin{aligned}\sigma_X &= \sqrt{\text{Var}(X)}\\ &= \sqrt{0.012}\\ &\approx 0.11\end{aligned}$$

and

$$\begin{aligned}\sigma_Y &= \sqrt{\text{Var}(Y)}\\ &= \sqrt{0.042}\\ &\approx 0.21\end{aligned}$$

The mean of X and that of Y are both equal to 16. Therefore, the average weight of a box of cereal of either brand is 16 ounces. However, the standard deviation of Y is greater than that of X. This tells us that the weights of the boxes of Brand B cereal are more widely dispersed about the common mean of 16 than are those of Brand A. ■

The standard deviation of a random variable X may be used in statistical estimations. For example, the following result, due to the Russian mathematician P. L. Chebychev (1821–1894) gives the proportion of the values of X lying within k standard deviations of the expected value of X.

DEFINITION

Chebychev's Inequality
Let X be a random variable with expected value μ and standard deviation σ. Then the probability that a randomly chosen outcome of the experiment lies between $\mu - k\sigma$ and $\mu + k\sigma$ is at least $1-(1/k^2)$, that is,

(9.9) $$P(\mu - k\sigma \le X \le \mu + k\sigma) \ge 1 - \frac{1}{k^2}$$

EXAMPLE 9.20 A probability distribution has a mean of 10 and a standard deviation of 1.5. Use the Chebychev inequality to estimate the probability that an outcome of the experiment lies between 7 and 13.

SOLUTION Here $\mu = 10$ and $\sigma = 1.5$. Next, to determine the value of k, note that $\mu - k\sigma = 7$ and $\mu + k\sigma = 13$. Substituting the appropriate values for μ and σ, we find $k = 2$. Using the Chebychev inequality (9.9), we see that the probability that an outcome of the experiment lies between 7 and 13 is given by

$$P(7 \le X \le 13) \ge 1 - \left(\frac{1}{2^2}\right)$$

$$= \frac{3}{4}$$

that is, at least 75%. ■

EXAMPLE 9.21 The Great Northwest Lumber Company employs 400 workers in its mills. It has been estimated that X, the random variable measuring the number of mill workers meeting with an industrial accident during a one-year period, is normally distributed with a mean of 40 and a standard deviation of 6. Using the Chebychev inequality, estimate the probability that the number of workers who will meet with an industrial accident over a one-year period is between 30 and 50, inclusive.

SOLUTION Here $\mu = 40$ and $\sigma = 6$. We wish to estimate $P(30 \le X \le 50)$. In order to use the Chebychev inequality (9.9), we first determine the value of k from the equation

$$\mu - k\sigma = 30 \quad \text{or} \quad \mu + k\sigma = 50$$

Since $\mu = 40$ and $\sigma = 6$ in this case, we see that k satisfies

$$40 - 6k = 30 \quad \text{and} \quad 40 + 6k = 50$$

from which we deduce that $k = \frac{5}{3}$. Thus, the probability that the number of mill workers who will meet with an industrial accident during a one-year period is between 30 and 50 is given by

$$P(30 \le X \le 50) \ge 1 - \frac{1}{(5/3)^2} = \frac{16}{25}$$

that is, at least 64%. ■

9.3 EXERCISES

In problems 1–4, the probability distribution of a random variable X is given. Compute the mean, variance, and standard deviation of X.

1.

x	$P(X=x)$
1	0.4
2	0.3
3	0.2
4	0.1

2.

x	$P(X=x)$
−4	0.1
−2	0.2
0	0.3
2	0.1
4	0.3

3.

x	$P(X=x)$
−2	1/16
−1	4/16
0	6/16
1	4/16
2	1/16

4.

x	$P(X=x)$
10	1/8
11	2/8
12	1/8
13	2/8
14	1/8
15	1/8

5. The histograms representing the probability distributions of the random variables X and Y are shown at the top of the next page. Determine by inspection which one of the probability distributions has the larger variance.

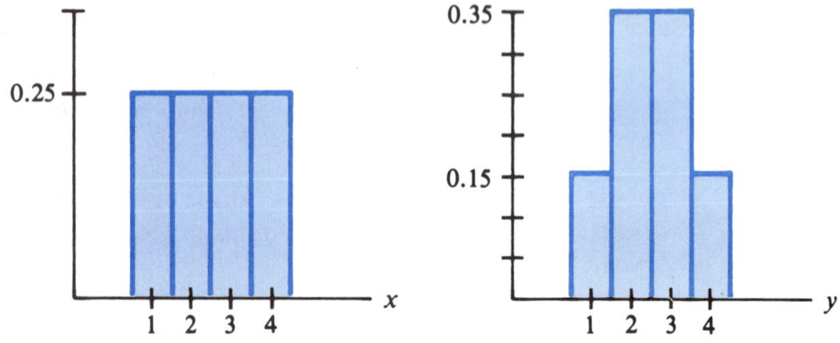

(a) (b)

6. The histograms representing the probability distributions of the random variables X and Y are shown below. Determine by inspection which one of the probability distributions has the larger variance.

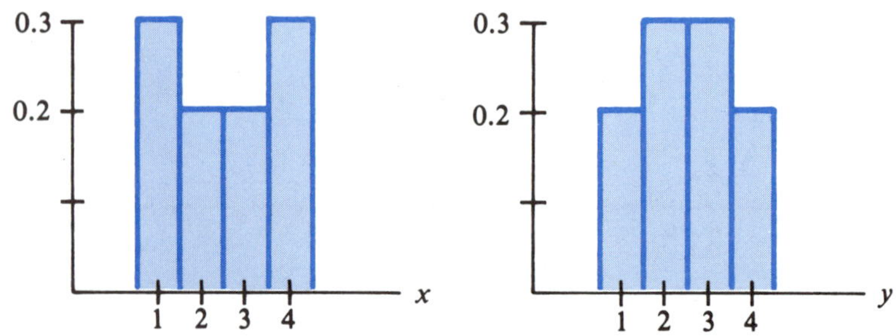

(a) (b)

7. Mr. Hunt is considering two business ventures. The anticipated returns (in thousands of dollars) of each venture is described by the following probability distributions.

Venture A		Venture B	
Earnings	Probability	Earnings	Probability
−20	0.3	−15	0.2
40	0.4	30	0.5
50	0.3	40	0.3

(***a***) Compute the mean and variance for each venture.

(***b***) Which investment would provide Mr. Hunt with the higher expected return (the greater mean)?

(***c***) In which investment would the element of risk be less (that is, which probability distribution has the smaller variance)?

8. The distribution of the number of chocolate chips in a cookie is shown below. Find the mean and the variance of the number of chocolate chips in a cookie.

Number of chocolate chips x	$P(X=x)$
0	0.02
1	0.05
2	0.19
3	0.35
4	0.21
5	0.12
6	0.06

9. Formula 9.5 can also be expressed in the form

$$\text{Var}\,(X)=(p_1x_1^2+p_2x_2^2+\cdots+p_nx_n^2)-\mu^2$$

Find the variance of the distribution of problem 1 using this formula.

10. Find the variance of the distribution of problem 8 using the formula

$$\text{Var}\,(X)=(p_1x_1^2+p_2x_2^2+\cdots+p_nx_n^2)-\mu^2$$

11. A survey was conducted by the market research department of the National Real Estate Company among 500 homeshoppers in a large metropolitan area to determine the maximum price that a prospective homebuyer would be willing to pay for a house. From the data collected the distribution that follows was obtained. Compute the mean, variance, and standard deviation of the maximum price that these homebuyers were willing to pay for a house.

Maximum price considered x (in \$'000.00)	$P(X=x)$
50	10/500
60	20/500
70	75/500
80	85/500
90	70/500
100	90/500
120	90/500
150	55/500
200	5/500

12. A probability distribution has a mean of 20 and a standard deviation of 3. Use the Chebychev inequality to estimate the probability that an outcome of the experiment lies between

(*a*) 15 and 25 (*b*) 10 and 30

13. A probability distribution has a mean of 42 and a standard deviation of 2. Use the Chebychev inequality to estimate the probability that an outcome of the experiment lies between

(*a*) 38 and 46 (*b*) 32 and 52

14. A probability distribution has a mean of 50 and a standard deviation of 1.4. Use the Chebychev inequality to find the value of c, which guarantees that the probability is at least 96% that an outcome of the experiment lies between $50-c$ and $50+c$.

15. Suppose X is a random variable with mean μ and standard deviation σ. If a large number of trials are observed, at least what percentage of these values is expected to lie between $\mu-2\sigma$ and $\mu+2\sigma$?

16. A Christmas tree light has an expected lifetime of 200 hours and a standard deviation of 2 hours.

(*a*) Estimate the probability that one of these Christmas tree lights will last between 190 and 210 hours.

(*b*) Suppose 150,000 of these Christmas tree lights are used by a large city as part of their Christmas decorations. Estimate the number of lights that will require replacement between 180 and 220 hours of usage.

17. The expected lifetime of the deluxe model hair dryer produced by the Roland Electric Company has a mean life of 24 months and a standard deviation of 3 months. Find the probability that one of these hair dryers will last between 20 and 28 months.

18. The mean annual starting salary of a new graduate in a certain profession is $25,000 with a standard deviation of $500. What is the probability that the starting salary of a new graduate in this profession will be between $23,000 and $27,000?

19. Sugar packaged by a certain machine has a mean weight of 5 pounds and a standard deviation of 0.02 pounds. For what value of c can the manufacturer of the machinery claim that the sugar packaged by this machine has a weight between $5-c$ and $5+c$ pounds with probability at least 96%?

9.4

The Binomial Distribution

An important class of experiments that occur are those that have (or may be viewed as having) two outcomes. For example, in a coin-tossing experiment the two outcomes are *heads* and *tails*. In the card game played by Mike and Bill (see Example 9.14) one may view the selection of a diamond as a *win* (for Mike) and the selection of a card of another suit as a *loss* for Mike. For a third example, consider the experiment in which a person is inoculated with a flu vaccine. Here, the vaccine may be classified as being "effective" or "ineffective" with respect to that particular person.

Bernoulli (binomial) trials

In general, experiments with two outcomes such as the examples above are called *Bernoulli trials* or *binomial trials*. It is standard practice to label one of the outcomes of a binomial trial a *success* and the other a *failure*. For example, in a coin-tossing experiment, the outcome *a head* may be called a success in which case the outcome *a tail* will be called a failure. Note that by using the terms success and failure in this way, we depart from their usual connotations.

In a binomial experiment, it is also customary to denote the probability of a success by the letter p and the probability of a failure by the letter q. Because the event of a success and the event of a failure are complementary events, we have the relationship

$$p+q=1$$

or equivalently,

$$q=1-p$$

In the following examples we shall make the assumption that the trials in a binomial experiment are *independent*. The notions introduced above are illustrated in the following example.

EXAMPLE 9.22 A fair die is cast four times. Compute the probability of obtaining exactly one 6 in the four throws.

SOLUTION Each trial of this experiment consists of casting the die once and observing the face that lands uppermost. We may view each trial as an experiment with two outcomes—a success (S) if the face that lands uppermost is a 6 and a failure (F) if it is any of the other five numbers. Letting p and q denote the probability of success and failure, respectively, of a single trial of the experiment, we find that

$$p=\frac{1}{6} \quad \text{and} \quad q=1-\frac{1}{6}=\frac{5}{6}$$

Furthermore, the trials of this experiment may be assumed to be independent. Thus, we have a binomial experiment.

With the aid of the multiplication principle, we see that the experiment has 2^4 or 16 outcomes. We also obtain these outcomes by constructing the tree diagrams associated with the experiment (see Table 9.8 where they are listed according to the number of successes). From Table 9.8, we see that the event of obtaining exactly one success in four trials is given by

$$E=\{\text{SFFF, FSFF, FFSF, FFFS}\}$$

with probability given by

(9.10) $$P(E)=P(\text{SFFF})+P(\text{FSFF})+P(\text{FFSF})+P(\text{FFFS})$$

Table 9.8

0 Success	1 Success	2 Successes	3 Successes	4 Successes
FFFF	SFFF	SSFF	SSSF	SSSS
	FSFF	SFSF	SSFS	
	FFSF	SFFS	SFSS	
	FFFS	FSSF	FSSS	
		FSFS		
		FFSS		

Since the trials (throws) are independent, the terms on the right-hand side of (9.10) may be computed as follows:

$$\begin{aligned}P(\text{SFFF}) &= P(\text{S})P(\text{F})P(\text{F})P(\text{F}) = p \cdot q \cdot q \cdot q = pq^3\\ P(\text{FSFF}) &= P(\text{F})P(\text{S})P(\text{F})P(\text{F}) = q \cdot p \cdot q \cdot q = pq^3\\ P(\text{FFSF}) &= P(\text{F})P(\text{F})P(\text{S})P(\text{F}) = q \cdot q \cdot p \cdot q = pq^3\\ P(\text{FFFS}) &= P(\text{F})P(\text{F})P(\text{F})P(\text{S}) = q \cdot q \cdot q \cdot p = pq^3\end{aligned}$$

Therefore, upon substituting these values in Equation (9.10) we obtain

$$\begin{aligned}P(E) &= pq^3 + pq^3 + pq^3 + pq^3\\ &= 4pq^3\\ &= 4\left(\frac{1}{6}\right)\left(\frac{5}{6}\right)^3\\ &= 0.386\end{aligned}$$

■

Let us re-examine the computation performed in the last example. There it was found that the probability of obtaining exactly one success in a binomial experiment with 4 independent trials with probability of success in a single trial p was given by

(9.11) $$P(E) = 4pq^3 \quad \text{where } q = 1 - p$$

Observe that the coefficient 4 of pq^3 appearing in Equation (9.11) is precisely the number of outcomes of the experiment with exactly one success and three failures, the outcomes being

SFFF, FSFF, FFSF, and FFFS

Another way of obtaining this coefficient is to think of the outcomes as arrangements of the letters S and F. Then, the number of ways of selecting 1 position for S from 4 possibilities is given by

$$\begin{aligned}C(4, 1) &= \frac{4!}{1!(4-1)!}\\ &= 4\end{aligned}$$

Next, observe that, because the trials are independent, each of the four outcomes of the experiment has the same probability given by

$$pq^3$$

where the exponents 1 and 3 of p and q, respectively, correspond to exactly 1 success and 3 failures in the trials comprising each outcome.

As a result of the above discussion, we may write Equation (9.11) as

(9.12) $$P(E) = C(4, 1)pq^3$$

We are also in a position to generalize this result. Suppose that in a binomial experiment, the probability of success in any trial is p. What is the probability of obtaining exactly x successes in n independent trials? We start by counting the number of outcomes of the experiment each of which has exactly x successes. Now, one such outcome involves x successive successes followed by $(n-x)$ failures; that is,

(9.13) $$\underbrace{\text{SS}\cdots\text{S}}_{x}\underbrace{\text{FF}\cdots\text{F}}_{n-x}$$

The other outcomes each of which has exactly x successes are obtained by rearranging the S's (x of them) and F's ($n-x$ of them). But there are $C(n, x)$ ways of arranging these letters. Next, arguing as in Example 9.22, we see that each such outcome has probability given by

$$p^x q^{n-x}$$

For example, for the outcome (9.13), we find

$$\begin{aligned} P(\underbrace{\text{SS}\cdots\text{S}}_{x}\underbrace{\text{FF}\cdots\text{F}}_{(n-x)}) &= \underbrace{P(\text{S})P(\text{S})\cdots P(\text{S})}_{x}\underbrace{P(\text{F})P(\text{F})\cdots P(\text{F})}_{(n-x)} \\ &= \underbrace{pp\cdots p}_{x}\underbrace{qq\cdots q}_{n-x} \\ &= p^x q^{n-x} \end{aligned}$$

Let us state this important result formally:

> In a binomial experiment in which the probability of success in any trial is p, the probability of exactly x successes in n independent trials is given by
>
> $$C(n, x)p^x q^{n-x}$$

binomial random variable

If we let X be the random variable denoting the number of successes in a binomial experiment (such a random variable is called a *binomial random variable*) then the probability of exactly x successes in n independent trials may be written

(9.14) $$P(X = x) = C(n, x)p^x q^{n-x} \qquad (x = 0, 1, 2, \ldots n)$$

The probability distribution of the binomial random variable is called a binomial distribution.

EXAMPLE 9.23 A fair die is cast five times. If a 1 or a 6 lands uppermost in a trial, then the throw is considered a success. Otherwise, the throw is considered a failure.

(**a**) Find the probability of obtaining exactly 0, 1, 2, 3, 4, and 5 successes, respectively, in this experiment.

(**b**) Using the results obtained in the solution to part (a), construct the binomial distribution for this experiment and draw the histogram associated with it.

SOLUTION (**a**) This is a binomial experiment with X, the binomial random variable, taking on each of the values 0, 1, 2, 3, 4, and 5 corresponding to exactly 0, 1, 2, 3, 4, and 5 successes, respectively, in 5 trials. Since the die is fair, the probability of a 1 or a 6 landing uppermost in any trial is given by $p=\frac{2}{6}=\frac{1}{3}$, from which it also follows that $q=1-p=\frac{2}{3}$. Finally, $n=5$ since there are 5 trials (throws of the die) in this experiment. Using Formula (9.14), we find that the required probabilities are

$$P(X=0)=C(5,0)\left(\frac{1}{3}\right)^0\left(\frac{2}{3}\right)^5=\frac{5!}{0!5!}\cdot 1\cdot\frac{32}{243}\approx 0.132$$

$$P(X=1)=C(5,1)\left(\frac{1}{3}\right)^1\left(\frac{2}{3}\right)^4=\frac{5!}{1!4!}\cdot\frac{16}{243}\approx 0.329$$

$$P(X=2)=C(5,2)\left(\frac{1}{3}\right)^2\left(\frac{2}{3}\right)^3=\frac{5!}{2!3!}\cdot\frac{8}{243}\approx 0.329$$

$$P(X=3)=C(5,3)\left(\frac{1}{3}\right)^3\left(\frac{2}{3}\right)^2=\frac{5!}{3!2!}\cdot\frac{4}{243}\approx 0.165$$

$$P(X=4)=C(5,4)\left(\frac{1}{3}\right)^4\left(\frac{2}{3}\right)^1=\frac{5!}{4!1!}\cdot\frac{2}{243}\approx 0.041$$

$$P(X=5)=C(5,5)\left(\frac{1}{3}\right)^5\left(\frac{2}{3}\right)^0=\frac{5!}{5!0!}\cdot\frac{1}{243}\approx 0.004$$

(**b**) Using the results obtained above, we find that the required binomial distribution associated with this experiment is given in Table 9.9. Using Table 9.9, we may construct the histogram associated with the probability distribution (Figure 9.8).

x	$P(X=x)$
0	0.132
1	0.329
2	0.329
3	0.165
4	0.041
5	0.004

Table 9.9

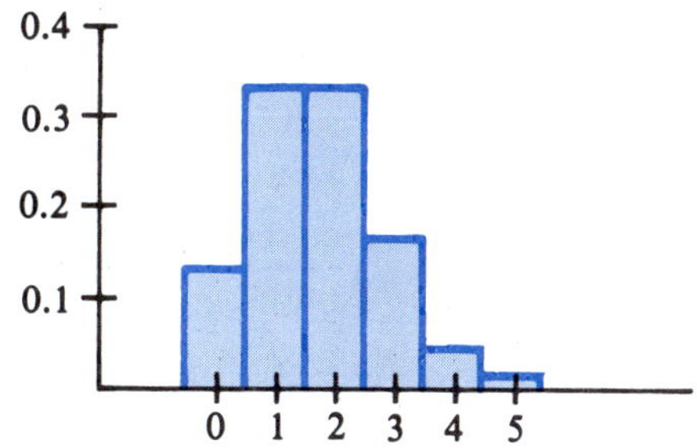

Figure 9.8

EXAMPLE 9.24 A fair die is cast five times. If a 1 or a 6 lands uppermost in a trial, then the throw is considered a success. Use the results from Example 9.23 to answer the following questions:

(**a**) What is the probability of obtaining 0 or 1 success in the experiment?

(**b**) What is the probability of obtaining at least 1 success in the experiment?

SOLUTION Interpreting the probability associated with the random variable X, when X assumes the value $X = a$, as the area of the rectangle centered about $X = a$ (see Figure 9.8), or otherwise, we find that

(**a**) the probability of obtaining 0 or 1 success in the experiment is given by

$$\begin{aligned} P(X=0)+P(X=1) &= 0.132+0.329 \\ &= 0.461 \end{aligned}$$

and

(**b**) the probability of obtaining at least 1 success in the experiment is given by

$$\begin{aligned} &P(X=1)+P(X=2)+P(X=3)+P(X=4)+P(X=5) \\ &\quad = 0.329+0.329+0.165+0.041+0.004 \\ &\quad = 0.868 \end{aligned}$$

Now, suppose X is a (binomial) random variable associated with a binomial experiment. We state without proof that the mean (expected value), the variance, and the standard deviation of X are given by

(9.15) $$\mu = E(X) = np$$

(9.16) $$\text{Var}(X) = npq$$

(9.17) and $$\sigma_X = \sqrt{npq}$$

respectively, where p, q, and n have the usual meanings.

EXAMPLE 9.25 For the experiment in Examples 9.23 and 9.24 compute the mean, the variance, and the standard deviation of X, (**a**) using Formulas 9.15, 9.16, and 9.17, respectively, and (**b**) by direct computation using their respective definitions (see Sections 9.2 and 9.3).

SOLUTION (**a**) We use Formulas 9.15, 9.16, and 9.17 with $p = 1/3$, $q = 2/3$ and $n = 5$ obtaining

$$\begin{aligned}\mu = E(X) &= (5)\left(\frac{1}{3}\right)\\ &= \frac{5}{3}\\ &\approx 1.67\end{aligned}$$

$$\begin{aligned}\text{Var }(X) &= (5)\left(\frac{1}{3}\right)\left(\frac{2}{3}\right)\\ &= \frac{10}{9}\\ &\approx 1.11\end{aligned}$$

and

$$\begin{aligned}\sigma_X &= \sqrt{\text{Var }(X)}\\ &= \sqrt{1.11}\\ &\approx 1.05\end{aligned}$$

We leave it to the reader to interpret the results.

(**b**) Using Equation (9.2) and the values of the probability distribution shown in Table 9.9, we find

$$\begin{aligned}\mu = E(X) &= (0)(0.132) + (1)(0.329) + (2)(0.329)\\ &\quad + (3)(0.165) + (4)(0.041) + (5)(0.004)\\ &\approx 1.67\end{aligned}$$

which agrees with the result obtained in part (**a**). Next, using Equation (9.5) and the knowledge that $\mu = 1.67$, we find

$$\begin{aligned}\text{Var }(X) &= (0.132)(-1.67)^2 + (0.329)(-0.67)^2 + (0.329)(0.33)^2\\ &\quad + (0.165)(1.33)^2 + (0.041)(2.33)^2 + (0.004)(3.33)^2\\ &\approx 1.11\end{aligned}$$

and

$$\begin{aligned}\sigma_X &\approx \sqrt{1.11}\\ &\approx 1.05\end{aligned}$$

which again agrees with the results obtained earlier. ■

We close this section by looking at several examples involving binomial experiments. In what follows, a pocket calculator may be used, or the reader may consult Table V in Appendix II.

EXAMPLE 9.26 A division of the Solaron Corporation manufactures photovoltaic cells to use in the company's solar energy converters. It is estimated that 5% of the cells manufactured are defective. If a random sample of 20 is selected from a large lot of cells manufactured by the company, what is the probability that it will contain at most 2 defective cells?

SOLUTION This is a binomial experiment with $p = 0.05$, $q = 0.95$, and $n = 20$. Letting X denote the number of defective cells, we find that the probability of finding at most 2 defective cells in the sample of 20 is given by

$$\begin{aligned}
&P(X=0)+P(X=1)+P(X=2)\\
&\quad = C(20,0)(0.05)^0(0.95)^{20}+C(20,1)(0.05)^1(0.95)^{19}+C(20,2)(0.05)^2(0.95)^{18}\\
&\quad \approx 0.3585+0.3774+0.1887\\
&\quad = 0.9246
\end{aligned}$$

Thus, for lots of photovoltaic cells manufactured by the company, approximately 93% of the samples will have at most 2 defective cells; equivalently, approximately 7% of the samples will contain more than 2 defective cells. ■

EXAMPLE 9.27 The probability that a heart-transplant operation performed at the Medical Center is successful (that is, the patient survives a year or more after undergoing such an operation) is 0.7. Of 6 patients who have recently undergone such an operation, what is the probability that a year from now

(a) none of the heart recipients will be alive?

(b) exactly 3 will be alive?

(c) at least 3 will be alive?

(d) all will be alive?

SOLUTION Here $n = 6$, $p = 0.7$, and $q = 0.3$. Let X denote the number of successful operations. Then,

(a) the probability that none of the heart recipients will be alive after one year is given by

$$\begin{aligned}
P(X=0) &= C(6,0)(0.7)^0(0.3)^6\\
&= \frac{6!}{0!6!}\cdot 1\cdot (0.3)^6\\
&\approx 0.001
\end{aligned}$$

(b) The probability that exactly 3 will be alive after one year is given by

$$\begin{aligned}
P(X=3) &= C(6,3)(0.7)^3(0.3)^3\\
&= \frac{6!}{3!3!}(0.7)^3(0.3)^3\\
&\approx 0.19
\end{aligned}$$

(**c**) The probability that at least 3 will be alive after one year is given by

$$\begin{aligned}
P(X=3)&+P(X=4)+P(X=5)+P(X=6)\\
&=C(6,3)(0.7)^3(0.3)^3+C(6,4)(0.7)^4(0.3)^2\\
&\quad +C(6,5)(0.7)^5(0.3)^1+C(6,6)(0.7)^6(0.3)^0\\
&=\frac{6!}{3!3!}(0.7)^3(0.3)^3+\frac{6!}{4!2!}(0.7)^4(0.3)^2+\frac{6!}{5!1!}(0.7)^5(0.3)^1\\
&\quad +\frac{6!}{6!0!}(0.7)^6\cdot 1\\
&\approx 0.93
\end{aligned}$$

(**d**) The probability that all will be alive after one year is given by

$$\begin{aligned}
P(X=6)&=C(6,6)(0.7)^6(0.3)^0\\
&=\frac{6!}{6!0!}(0.7)^6\\
&\approx 0.12
\end{aligned}$$

■

EXAMPLE 9.28 The P.A.R. Bearings Company manufactures ball bearings, which are packaged in lots of a hundred each. The Quality Control Department of the company has determined that 2% of the ball bearings manufactured do not meet the specifications imposed by a buyer. Find the average number of ball bearings per package that fail to meet with the specifications imposed by the buyer.

SOLUTION The experiment under consideration is binomial. The average number of ball bearings per package that fail to meet with the specifications is therefore given by the expected value of the associated binomial random variable. Using Formula 9.15 we find that the required number is given by

$$\begin{aligned}
\mu&=E(X)=np\\
&=(100)(0.02)\\
&=2
\end{aligned}$$

or 2 substandard ball bearings in a package of 100. ■

9.4 EXERCISES

1. A binomial experiment consists of 5 independent trials. The probability of success in each trial is 0.4.

(***a***) Find the probability of obtaining exactly 0, 1, 2, 3, 4, and 5 successes, respectively, in this experiment.

(*b*) Construct the binomial distribution and draw the histogram associated with this experiment.

(*c*) Compute the mean and the standard deviation of the random variable associated with this experiment.

2. Let the random variable X denote the number of girls in a 5-child family. If the probability of a female birth is 0.5,

(*a*) find the probability of 0, 1, 2, 3, 4, and 5 girls in a 5-child family.

(*b*) construct the binomial distribution and draw the histogram associated with this experiment.

(*c*) compute the mean and the standard deviation of the random variable X.

3. The probability that a fuse produced by a certain manufacturing process will be defective is $\frac{1}{50}$. Is it correct to infer from this statement that there is at most 1 defective fuse in each lot of 50 produced by this process? Justify your answer.

4. Let X be the number of successes in 5 independent trials of a binomial experiment in which the probability of success is $p = \frac{2}{5}$. Find

(*a*) $P(X = 4)$ (*b*) $P(2 \leq X \leq 4)$

5. A fair die is cast 4 times. Calculate the probability of obtaining exactly 2 sixes.

6. If the probability that a certain tennis player will serve an ace is $\frac{1}{4}$, what is the probability that he will serve exactly 2 aces out of 5 services?

7. Mayco, a mail order department store, has 6 telephone lines available for customers who wish to place their orders. If the probability that during business hours any one of the 6 telephone lines is engaged is $\frac{1}{4}$, find the probability that when a customer calls to place an order all 6 lines will be in use.

8. From experience, the manager of Kramer's Book Mart knows that 40% of the people who are browsing in the store will make a purchase. What is the probability that among 10 people who are browsing in the store, at least 3 will make a purchase?

9. An advertisement for Brand A chicken noodle soup claims that 60% of all consumers prefer Brand A over Brand B, the chief competitor's product. To test this claim, Mr. Alan Horowitz, the host of *The Consumer Advocate*, selected 10 people at random from the audience. After tasting both soups, each person was asked to state his preference. Find the probability that

(*a*) the company's claim was supported by the experiment; that is, 6 or more people stated a preference for Brand A.

(*b*) the company's claim was not supported by the experiment; that is, less than 6 people stated a preference for Brand A.

10. It is estimated that 1/3 of the general population has blood type A^+. If a sample of 9 people are selected at random, what is the probability that

(*a*) exactly 3 of these people have blood type A^+?

(*b*) at most 3 of these people have blood type A^+?

11. A biology quiz consists of 8 multiple-choice questions. Five must be answered correctly to receive a passing grade. If each question has 5 possible answers of which only 1 is correct, what is the probability that a student who guesses at random on each question will pass the examination?

12. A psychology quiz consists of 10 true or false questions. If a student knows the correct answer to 6 of the questions but determines the answer to the remaining questions by flipping a coin, what is the probability that she will obtain a score of at least 90%?

13. The probability that a video-disc player produced by the V.C.A. Television Company is defective is estimated to be 0.02. If a sample of 10 sets is selected at random, what is the probability that the sample contains

(*a*) no defectives?

(*b*) at most 2 defective sets?

14. As part of its quality control program, the video-cartridges produced by the Starr Communications Company are subjected to a final inspection before shipment. A sample of 6 cartridges is selected at random from each lot of cartridges produced and the lot is rejected if the sample contains 1 or more defective cartridges. If 1.5% of the cartridges produced by the company are defective, find the probability that a shipment will be accepted.

15. An automobile manufacturing company utilizes 10 industrial robots as welders on its assembly line. On a given working day, the probability that a robot will be inoperative is .05. What is the probability that on a given working day

(*a*) exactly 2 robots are inoperative?

(*b*) more than 2 robots are inoperative?

16. The probability that an airplane engine will fail in a transcontinental flight is 0.001. Assuming that engine failures are independent of each other, what is the probability that, on a certain transcontinental flight, a 4-engine plane will experience

(*a*) exactly 1 engine failure?

(*b*) exactly 2 engine failures?

(*c*) more than 2 engine failures? *Note*: in this event, the airplane will crash!

17. The manager of Toy World has decided to accept a shipment of electronic games if none of a random sample of 20 is found to be defective.

(*a*) What is the probability that he will accept the shipment if 10% of the electronic games are defective?

(*b*) What is the probability that he will accept the shipment if 5% of the electronic games are defective?

18. Refer to problem 17. If the manager's criterion for accepting shipment is that there be no more than 1 defective electronic game in a random sample of 20, what is the probability that he will accept the shipment if 10% of the electronic games are defective?

19. Refer to problem 17. If the manager of the store changes his sample size to 10, and decides to accept shipment if none of the games are defective, what is the probability that he will accept the shipment if 10% of the games are defective?

20. How many times must a person toss a coin if the chances of obtaining at least 1 head are to be 99% or better?

21. A new drug has been found to be effective in treating 75% of the people afflicted by a certain disease. If the drug is administered to 500 people who have this disease, what are the mean and the standard deviation of the number of people for whom the drug can be expected to be effective?

22. At a certain university the probability that an entering freshman will graduate within 4 years is 0.6. From an incoming class of 2000 freshmen, find

(***a***) the expected number of students who will graduate within 4 years.

(***b***) the standard deviation of the number of students who will graduate within 4 years.

9.5 The Normal Distribution

finite and continuous probability distributions

The probability distributions discussed in the preceding sections were all associated with finite random variables; that is, random variables that take on finitely many values. Such probability distributions are referred to as *finite probability distributions.* In this section, we shall consider probability distributions associated with a continuous random variable; that is, a random variable that may take on any value lying in an interval of real numbers. Such probability distributions are called *continuous probability distributions.*

probability density function

Unlike a finite probability distribution, which may be exhibited in the form of a table, a continuous probability distribution is defined by a function f whose domain coincides with the interval of values taken on by the random variable associated with the experiment. Such a function f is called the *probability density function* associated with the probability distribution and has the following properties:

1. $f(x)$ is nonnegative for all values of x.

2. The area of the region between the graph of f and the x-axis is equal to 1. (See Figure 9.9.)

Now suppose we are given a continuous probability distribution defined by some probability density function f (see Figure 9.10). Then the probability that the random variable X assumes a value in an interval $a<x<b$ is given by the area of the region between the graph of f and the x-axis from $x=a$ to $x=b$. We denote the value of this probability by $P(a<X<b)$. Because the area under one point of the graph of f is equal to zero, we see immediately that, in fact, $P(a<X<b)=P(a<X\leq b)=P(a\leq X<b)=P(a\leq X\leq b)$. Observe that

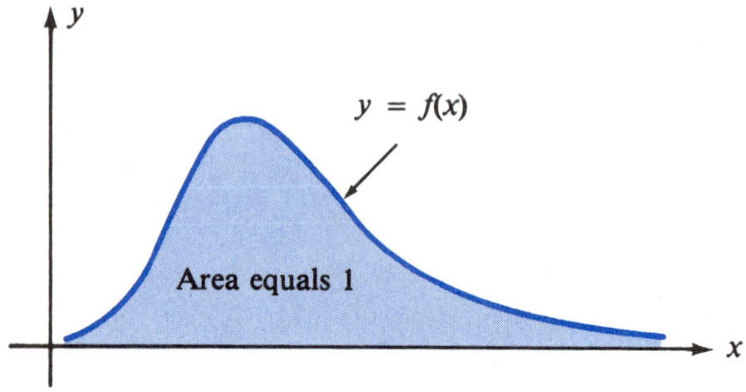

Figure 9.9

Property 2 of the probability density function states that the probability that a continuous random variable takes on a value lying in its range is 1, a certainty, which is expected. The reader should note the analogy between the areas under the probability density curves and the histograms associated with finite probability distributions (see Section 9.1).

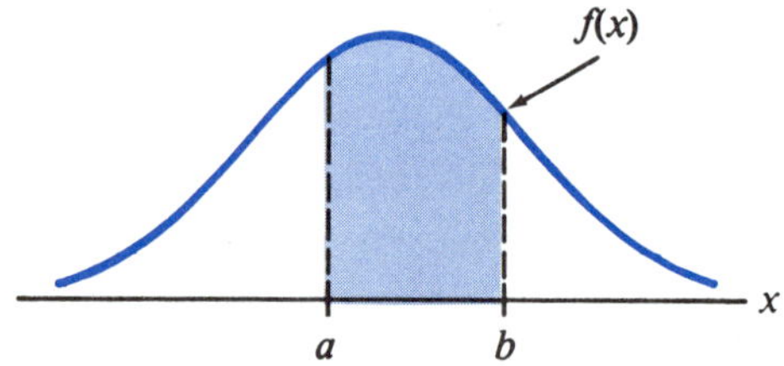

Figure 9.10

The mean μ and the standard deviation σ of a continuous probability distribution have roughly the same meanings as the mean and standard deviation of a finite probability distribution. Thus, the mean of a continuous probability distribution is a measure of central tendency of the probability distribution, while the standard deviation of the probability distribution measures its spread about its mean. Both these numbers will play an important role in the following discussion.

normal distribution

For the remainder of the section we shall discuss a special class of continuous probability distributions known as *normal distributions*. The normal distribution is without doubt the most important of all the probability distributions. Many phenomena such as the heights of people in a given population, the weights of newborn infants, the IQ of college students, the actual weights of 16 ounce packages of cereals, and so on, have probability distributions, which are normal. The normal distribution also provides us with an accurate approximation to the distributions of many random variables associated with random-sampling problems. In fact, in the next section we shall see how a normal distribution may be used to approximate a binomial distribution under certain conditions.

normal curve

The graph of a normal distribution, which is bell-shaped, is called a *normal curve* (see Figure 9.11).

The normal curve (and therefore the corresponding normal distribution) is completely determined by its mean μ and standard deviation σ. In fact, the normal

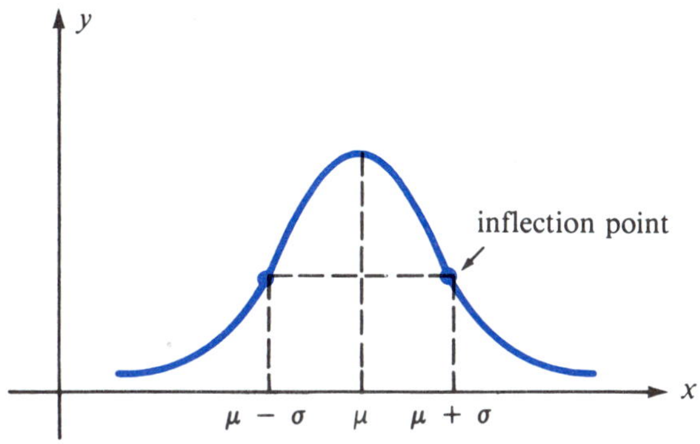

Figure 9.11

curve has the following characteristics described in terms of these two parameters:*

1. The curve has a peak at $x = \mu$.

2. The curve is symmetrical with respect to the vertical line $x = \mu$.

3. The curve is *concave downward* (it bends downward) between $x = \mu - \sigma$ and $x = \mu + \sigma$ and *concave upward* (it bends upward) for $x < \mu - \sigma$ and for $x > \mu + \sigma$.

4. The curve has two *inflection points* (points where its concavity changes—see Property 3) located a distance of σ units on either side of its mean.

5. The curve is *asymptotic* to the x-axis; that is, as $|x|$ grows without bound the curve gets closer and closer to the x-axis but always stays above it.

Figure 9.12 shows two normal distributions with different means μ_1 and μ_2 but the same standard deviation. Next, Figure 9.13 shows two normal distributions with the same mean but different standard deviations σ_1 and σ_2. (Which number is smaller?)

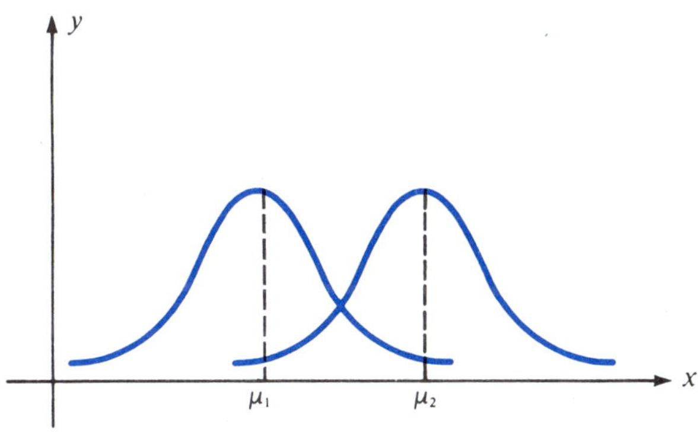

Figure 9.12

* The probability density function associated with this normal curve is given by

$$y = \frac{1}{\sigma\sqrt{2\pi}} e^{-(\frac{1}{2})[(x-\mu)/\sigma]^2}$$

but its direct usage will not be required in our discussion of the normal distribution.

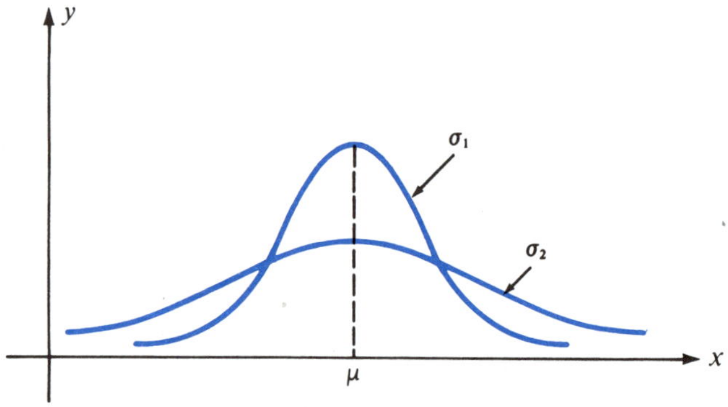

Figure 9.13

In general, the mean μ of a normal distribution determines where the center of the curve is located while the standard deviation σ of a normal distribution determines the sharpness (or flatness) of the curve.

As the above discussion reveals, there are infinitely many normal curves corresponding to different choices of the parameters μ and σ, which characterize such curves. Fortunately, any normal curve may be easily transformed into any other normal curve (as we shall see later on) so that in the study of normal curves (and their corresponding normal distributions) it suffices to single out one such particular curve for special attention. Such a normal curve is chosen to have mean $\mu = 0$ and standard deviation $\sigma = 1$ and is called the *standard normal curve*. The corresponding distribution is called the *standard normal distribution*. The random variable itself is called the *standard normal variable* and commonly denoted by Z.

standard normal curve, distribution, and variable

Areas under the standard normal curve have been extensively computed and tabulated. Table VI in Appendix II gives the areas of the regions under the standard normal curve to the left of the number z; these areas correspond, of course, to probabilities of the form $P(Z < z)$ or $P(Z \leq z)$. The next several examples illustrate the use of this table in computations involving the probabilities associated with the standard normal variable.

EXAMPLE 9.29 Let Z be the standard normal variable. By first making a sketch of the appropriate region under the standard normal curve, find the values of

(a) $P(Z < 1.24)$

(b) $P(Z > 0.5)$

(c) $P(0.24 < Z < 1.48)$

(d) $P(-1.65 < Z < 2.02)$

SOLUTION **(a)** The region under the standard normal curve associated with the probability $P(Z < 1.24)$ is shown in Figure 9.14. To find the area of the required region using Table VI in Appendix II, we first locate the number 1.2 in the column and the number 0.04 in the row, both headed by z, and read off the number 0.8925 appearing in the body of the table. Thus,

$$P(Z < 1.24) = 0.8925$$

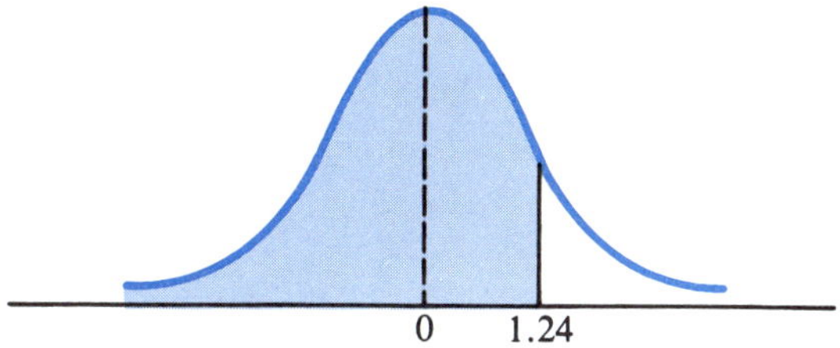

Figure 9.14

(**b**) The region under the standard normal curve associated with the probability $P(Z > 0.5)$ is shown in Figure 9.15 (**a**). Observe, however, that the required area is, by virtue of the symmetry of the standard normal curve, equal to the shaded area shown in Figure 9.15 (**b**).

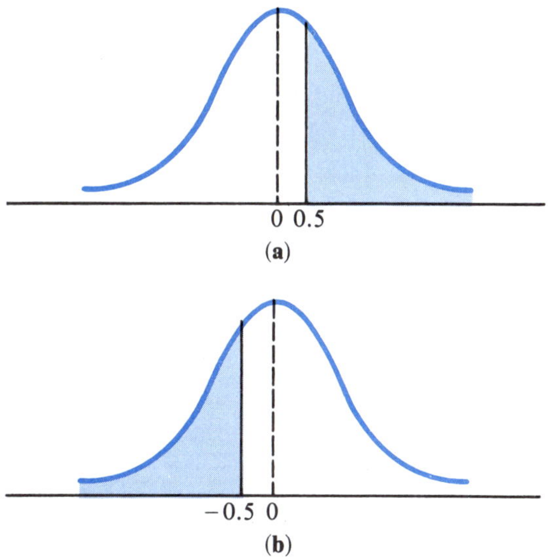

Figure 9.15

Thus,

$$P(Z > 0.5) = P(Z < -0.5)$$
$$= 0.3085$$

(**c**) The probability $P(0.24 < Z < 1.48)$ is equal to the shaded area shown in Figure 9.16. But this area is obtained by subtracting the area under the curve to the left of $z = 0.24$ from the area under the curve to the left of $z = 1.48$; that is,

$$P(0.24 < Z < 1.48) = P(Z < 1.48) - P(Z < 0.24)$$
$$= 0.9306 - 0.5948$$
$$= 0.3358$$

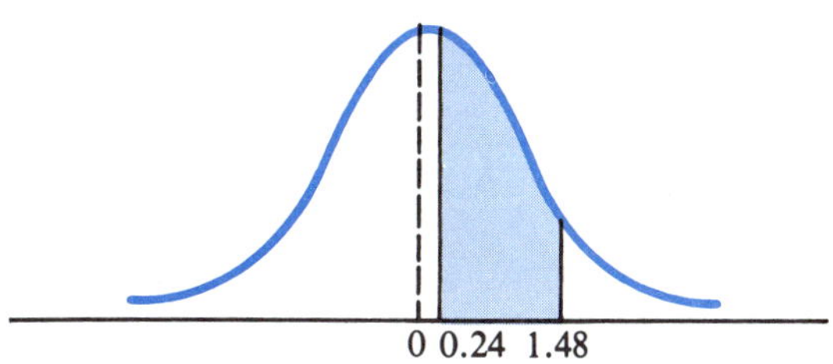

Figure 9.16

(d) The probability $P(-1.65 < Z < 2.02)$ is given by the shaded area shown in Figure 9.17. We have

$$\begin{aligned} P(-1.65 < Z < 2.02) &= P(Z < 2.02) - P(Z < -1.65) \\ &= 0.9783 - 0.0495 \\ &= 0.9288 \end{aligned}$$

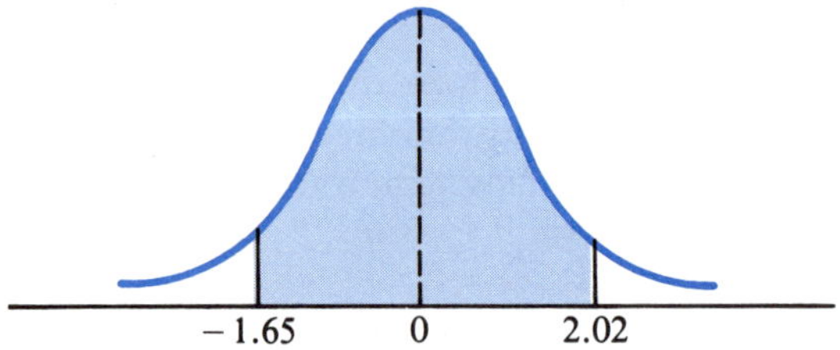

Figure 9.17

■

EXAMPLE 9.30 Let Z be the standard normal variable. Find the value of z if z satisfies

(a) $P(Z < z) = 0.9474$

(b) $P(Z > z) = 0.9115$

(c) $P(-z < Z < z) = 0.7888$

SOLUTION **(a)** Refer to Figure 9.18. We want the value of Z such that the area of the region under the standard normal curve and to the left of $Z = z$ is 0.9474. Locating the number 0.9474 in Table VI, in Appendix II and reading back we find that $z = 1.62$.

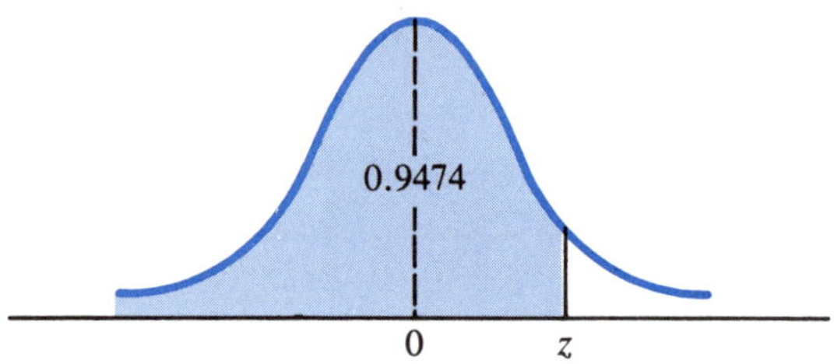

Figure 9.18

(b) Since $P(Z > z)$, or equivalently, the area of the region to the right of z is greater than 0.5, z must be negative (see Figure 9.19). Therefore $-z$ is positive. Furthermore, the area of the region to the right of z is the same as the area of the region to the left of $-z$. Therefore

$$\begin{aligned} P(Z > z) &= P(Z < -z) \\ &= 0.9115 \end{aligned}$$

Looking up the table, we find $-z = 1.35$ and so $z = -1.35$.

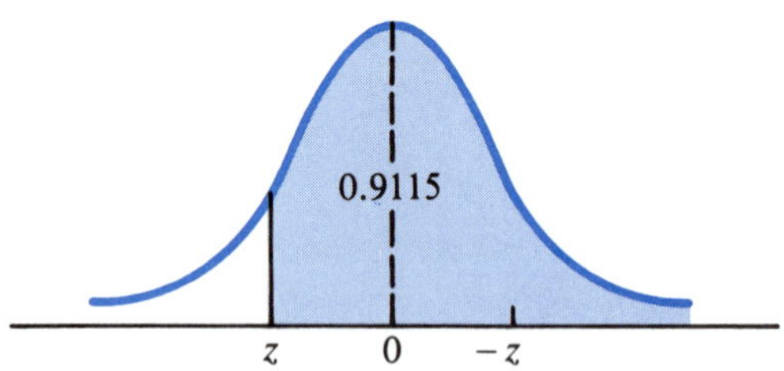

Figure 9.19

(c) The region associated with $P(-z<Z<z)$ is shown in Figure 9.20. Observe that the area of the region to the left of z is equal to the area to the left of $-z$ plus the area of the region between $-z$ and z. Thus,

$$\begin{aligned} P(Z<z) &= P(Z<-z)+P(-z<Z<z) \\ &= [1-P(Z<z)]+P(-z<Z<z) \qquad \text{Why?} \end{aligned}$$

Therefore, $2P(Z<z)=1+P(-z<Z<z)$

and
$$\begin{aligned} P(Z<z) &= \frac{1}{2}[1+P(-z<Z<z)] \\ &= \frac{1}{2}(1+0.7888) \\ &= 0.8944 \end{aligned}$$

Consulting the table, we find $z=1.25$.

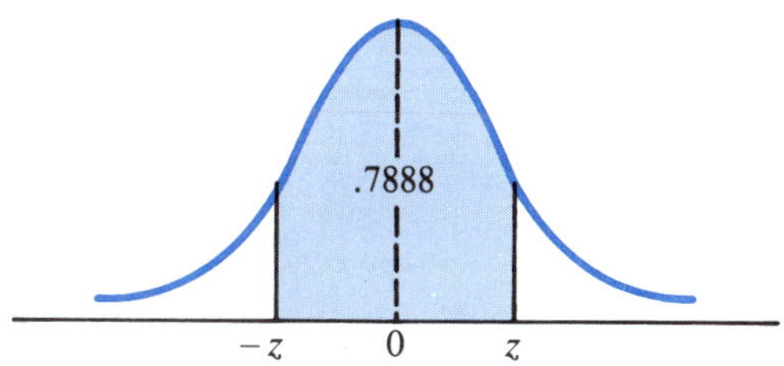

Figure 9.20

We now turn our attention to the computation of probabilities associated with normal distributions whose means and standard deviations are not necessarily equal to 0 and 1, respectively. As mentioned earlier any normal curve may be transformed into the standard normal curve by means of a suitable transformation. In particular, it may be shown that if X is a normal random variable with mean μ and standard deviation σ, then it can be transformed into the standard normal random variable Z by means of the transformation

(9.18)
$$Z=\frac{X-\mu}{\sigma}$$

Under the transformation (9.18) the numbers a and b are mapped onto the numbers $(a-\mu)/\sigma$ and $(b-\mu)/\sigma$, respectively. (See Figure 9.21.) Moreover, the transformation (9.18) has the important property of being area-preserving. The area of the region under the normal curve (with random variable X) between $x=a$ and $x=b$ is *equal* to the area of the region under the standard normal curve between $z=(a-\mu)/\sigma$ and $z=(b-\mu)/\sigma$. In terms of probabilities associated with these distributions, we have

$$P(a<X<b)=P\left(\frac{a-\mu}{\sigma}<Z<\frac{b-\mu}{\sigma}\right)$$

Thus, with the help of the transformation (9.18) computations of probabilities associated with any normal distribution may be reduced to the computations of areas of regions under the standard normal curve.

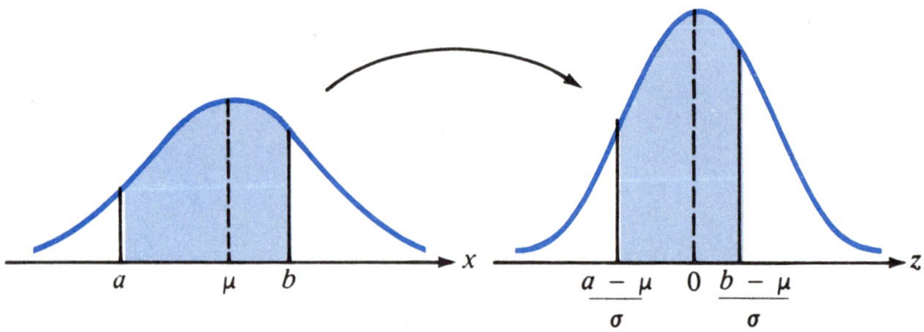

Figure 9.21

EXAMPLE 9.31 Suppose X is a normal random variable with $\mu = 100$ and $\sigma = 20$. Find the values of

(a) $P(X<120)$ **(b)** $P(X>70)$ **(c)** $P(75<X<110)$

SOLUTION Using the transformation (9.18) and the table of values of Z, we have

(a)
$$\begin{aligned} P(X<120) &= P\left(Z<\frac{120-100}{20}\right) \\ &= P(Z<1) \\ &= 0.8413 \end{aligned}$$

(b)
$$\begin{aligned} P(X>70) &= P\left(Z>\frac{70-100}{20}\right) \\ &= P(Z>-1.5) \\ &= P(Z<1.5) \\ &= 0.9332 \end{aligned}$$

(c)
$$\begin{aligned} P(75<X<110) &= P\left(\frac{75-100}{20}<Z<\frac{110-100}{20}\right) \\ &= P(-1.25<Z<0.5) \\ &= P(Z<0.5)-P(Z<-1.25) \qquad \text{(See Figure 9.22)} \\ &= 0.6915-0.1056 \\ &= 0.5859 \end{aligned}$$

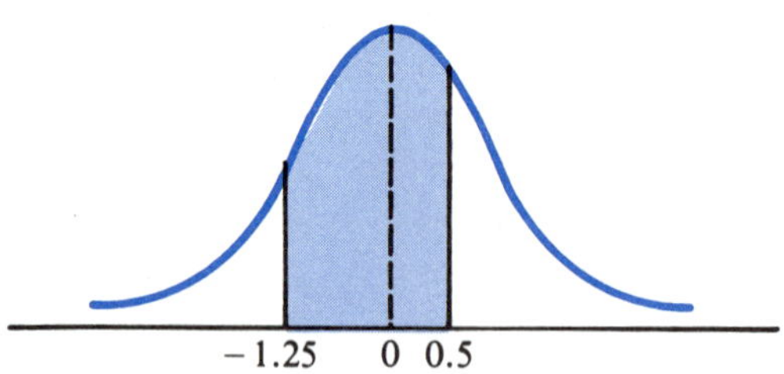

Figure 9.22

9.5 EXERCISES

In problems 1–6, find the value of the probability of the standard normal variable Z corresponding to the shaded area under the standard normal curve.

1. $P(Z<1.45)$

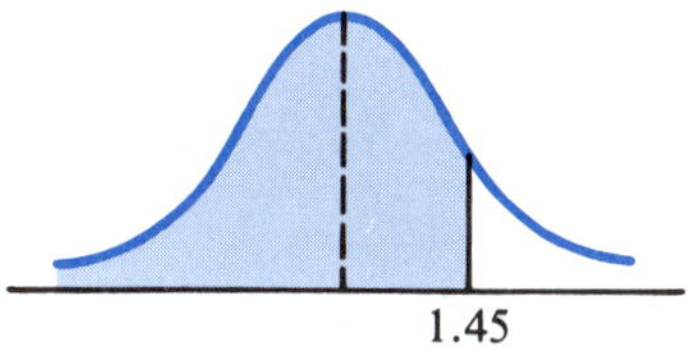

2. $P(Z>1.11)$

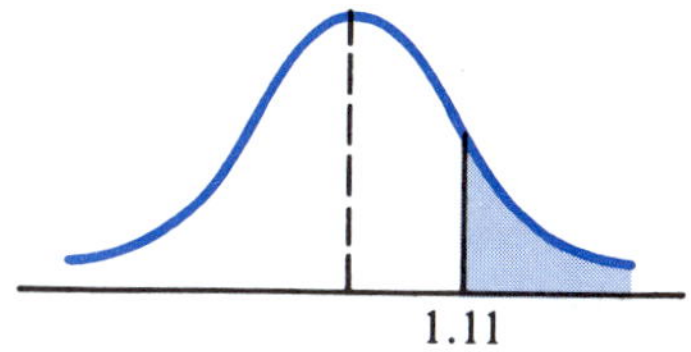

3. $P(Z<-1.75)$

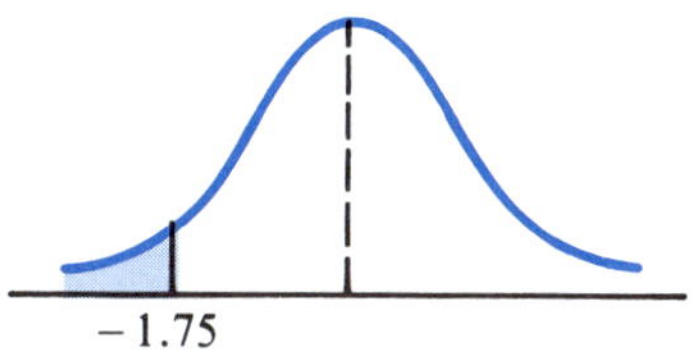

4. $P(0.3<Z<1.83)$

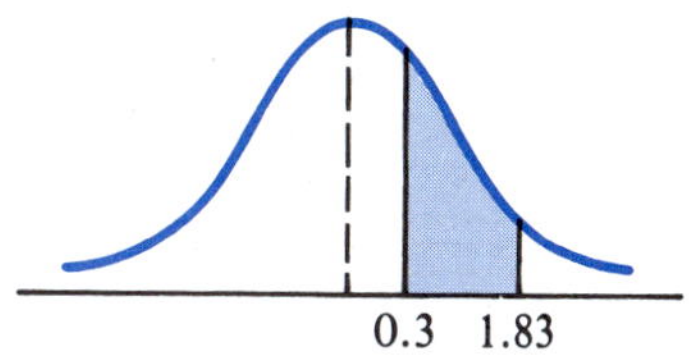

5. $P(-1.32<Z<1.74)$

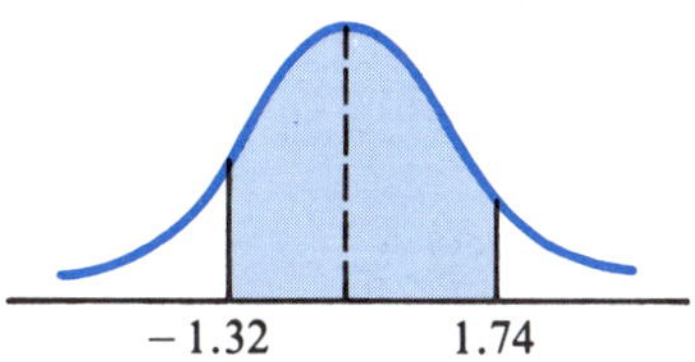

6. $P(-2.35<Z<-0.51)$

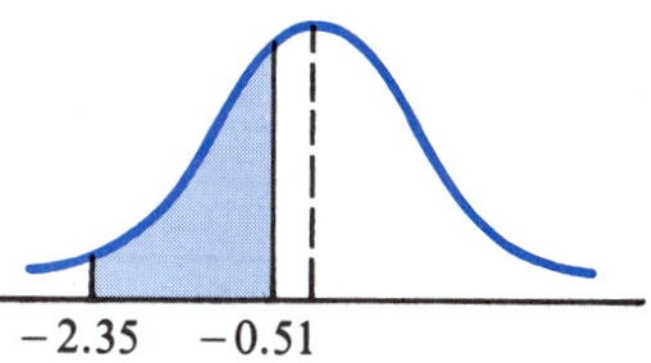

In problems 7–14, (a) make a sketch of the area under the standard normal curve corresponding to the given probability and (b) find the value of the probability of the standard normal variable Z corresponding to this area.

7. $P(Z<1.37)$

8. $P(Z>2.24)$

9. $P(Z<-0.65)$

10. $P(0.45<Z<1.75)$

11. $P(Z>-1.25)$

12. $P(-1.48<Z<1.54)$

13. $P(0.68<Z<2.02)$

14. $P(-1.41<Z<-0.24)$

15. Let Z be the standard normal variable. Find the values of z if z satisfies

(***a***) $P(Z<z)=0.8907$ (***b***) $P(Z<z)=0.2090$

16. Let Z be the standard normal variable. Find the values of z if z satisfies

(***a***) $P(Z>z)=0.9678$ (***b***) $P(-z<Z<z)=0.8354$

17. Suppose X is a normal random variable with $\mu = 380$ and $\sigma = 20$. Find the value of

(*a*) $P(X < 405)$ (*b*) $P(400 < X < 430)$ (*c*) $P(X > 400)$

18. Suppose X is a normal random variable with $\mu = 50$ and $\sigma = 5$. Find the value of

(*a*) $P(X < 60)$ (*b*) $P(X > 43)$ (*c*) $P(46 < X < 58)$

9.6

Applications of the Normal Distribution

In this section we shall look at some applications involving the normal distribution.

EXAMPLE 9.32 The medical records of infants delivered at the Kaiser Memorial Hospital show that the infants' birth weights in pounds are normally distributed with a mean of 7.4 and a standard deviation of 1.2. Find the probability that an infant selected at random from among those delivered at the hospital weighed more than 9.2 pounds at birth.

SOLUTION Let X be the normal random variable denoting the birth weights of infants delivered at the hospital. Then the probability that an infant selected at random has a birth weight of more than 9.2 pounds is given by $P(X > 9.2)$. To compute $P(X > 9.2)$ we use the transformation (9.18) keeping in mind that, in this case, $\mu = 7.4$ and $\sigma = 1.2$. We find

$$\begin{aligned} P(X > 9.2) &= P\left(Z > \frac{9.2 - 7.4}{1.2}\right) \\ &= P(Z > 1.5) \\ &= P(Z < -1.5) \\ &= 0.0668 \end{aligned}$$

Thus, the probability that an infant delivered at the hospital weighs more than 9.2 pounds is 0.0668. ■

EXAMPLE 9.33 The Idaho Natural Produce Corporation ships potatoes to its distributors in bags with a mean weight of 50 pounds and standard deviation of 0.5 pounds. If a bag of potatoes is selected at random from a shipment, what is the probability that it weighs

(a) more than 51 pounds?

(b) less than 48 pounds?

(c) between 49 and 51 pounds?

SOLUTION Let X denote the weight of potatoes packed by the company. Then the mean and standard deviation of X are $\mu = 50$ and $\sigma = 0.5$, respectively.

(**a**) The probability that a bag selected at random weighs more than 51 pounds is given by

$$\begin{aligned} P(X>51) &= P\left(Z>\frac{51-50}{0.5}\right) \\ &= P(Z>2) \\ &= P(Z<-2) \\ &= 0.0228 \end{aligned}$$

(**b**) The probability that a bag selected at random weighs less than 48 pounds is given by

$$\begin{aligned} P(X<48) &= P\left(Z<\frac{48-50}{0.5}\right) \\ &= P(Z<-4) \\ &= 0 \end{aligned}$$

(**c**) The probability that a bag selected at random weighs between 49 and 51 pounds is given by

$$\begin{aligned} P(49<X<51) &= P\left(\frac{49-50}{0.5}<Z<\frac{51-50}{0.5}\right) \\ &= P(-2<Z<2) \\ &= P(Z<2)-P(Z<-2) \\ &= 0.9772-0.0228 \\ &= 0.9544 \end{aligned}$$

■

EXAMPLE 9.34 The grade-point average of the Senior Class of Jefferson High School is normally distributed with a mean of 2.7 and a standard deviation of 0.4 points. If a senior in the top 10% of his or her class is eligible for admission to any of the 9 campuses of the State University system, what is the minimum grade-point average that a senior should have to ensure eligibility for admission to the State University system?

SOLUTION Let X denote the grade-point average of a randomly selected senior at the Jefferson High School and let x denote the minimum gradepoint average to ensure his or her eligibility for admission to the University. Since only the top 10% are eligible for admission, x must satisfy the equation

$$P(X \geq x) = 0.1$$

Using transformation (9.18) with $\mu = 2.7$ and $\sigma = 0.4$, we find

$$P(X \geq x) = P\left(Z \geq \frac{x-2.7}{0.4}\right) = 0.1$$

But, this is equivalent to the equation

$$P\left(Z \le \frac{x - 2.7}{0.4}\right) = 0.9 \qquad \text{Why?}$$

Consulting Table VI in Appendix II, we find,

$$\frac{x - 2.7}{0.4} = 1.28$$

(Compare results with Example 9.30.) Upon solving for x, we obtain

$$\begin{aligned} x &= (1.28)(0.4) + 2.7 \\ &\approx 3.2 \end{aligned}$$

Thus, to ensure eligibility for admission to one of the 9 campuses of the State University system a senior at Jefferson High School should have a minimum 3.2 grade-point average. ■

As mentioned in the last section one important application of the normal distribution is that, under certain conditions, it provides us with an accurate approximation to other continuous probability distributions. We shall now show how a binomial distribution may be approximated by a suitable normal distribution. This technique leads to a convenient and simple solution to certain problems involving binomial probabilities.

Recall that a binomial distribution is a probability distribution of the form

(9.19) $$P(X = x) = C(n, x)p^x q^{n-x} \qquad (x = 0, 1, 2, \ldots, n)$$

(See Section 9.4.) For small values of n, the arithmetic computations of the binomial probabilities may be done with relative ease. However, if n is large, then the work involved becomes prodigious even when tables of $P(X = x)$ are available. For example, if $n = 50$, $p = 0.3$, then the probability of 10 or more successes is given by

$$\begin{aligned} P(X \ge 10) &= P(X = 10) + P(X = 11) + \cdots + P(X = 50) \\ &= \frac{50!}{10!40!}(0.3)^{10}(0.7)^{40} + \frac{50!}{11!39!}(0.3)^{11}(0.7)^{39} + \cdots \\ &\quad + \frac{50!}{50!0!}(0.3)^{50}(0.7)^{0} \end{aligned}$$

To see how the normal distribution helps us in such situations, let us consider the coin-tossing experiment. Suppose a fair coin is tossed 20 times and we wish to compute the probability of obtaining 10 or more heads. The solution to this problem may be obtained, of course, by computing

$$P(X \ge 10) = P(X = 10) + P(X = 11) + \cdots + P(X = 20)$$

The inconvenience of this approach for solving the problems at hand has already been pointed out. As an alternative solution, let us begin by interpreting the solution in terms of finding the area of suitable rectangles of the histogram for the distribution associated with the problem. Using Formula (9.19) we compute the probability of obtaining exactly x heads in 20 tosses of the coin. The results lead to the binomial distribution displayed in Table 9.10.

Table 9.10

x	$P(X=x)$
0	0.0000
1	0.0000
2	0.0002
3	0.0011
4	0.0046
5	0.0148
6	0.0370
7	0.0739
8	0.1201
9	0.1602
10	0.1762
11	0.1602
12	0.1201
⋮	⋮
20	0.0000

Using the data from Table 9.10, we next construct the histogram for the distribution (see Figure 9.23). The probability of obtaining 10 or more heads in 20 tosses of the coin is equal to the sum of the areas of the shaded rectangles of the histogram of the binomial distribution shown in Figure 9.24.

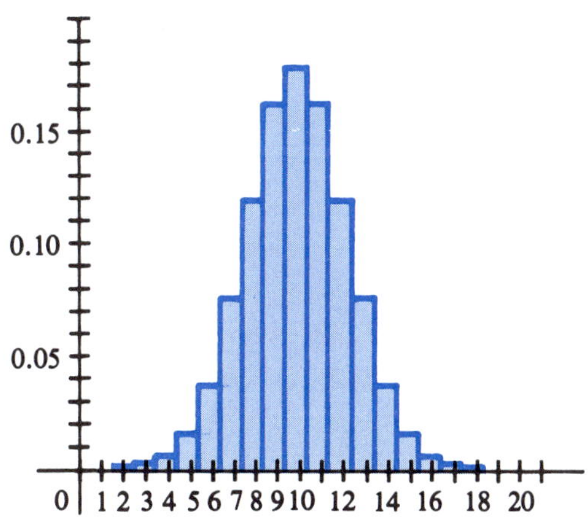

Figure 9.23

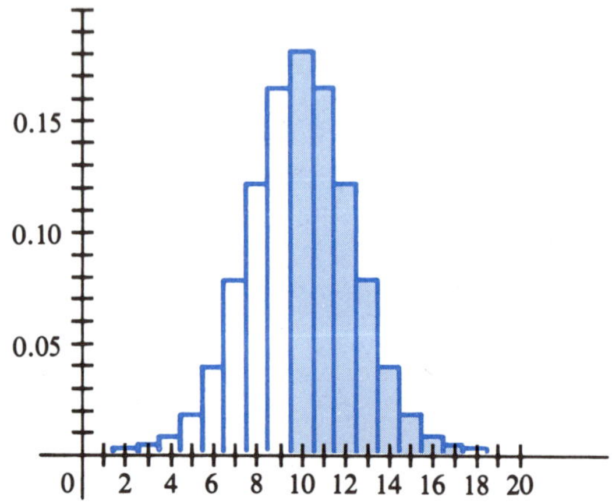

Figure 9.24

Next, let us observe that the shape of the histogram suggests that the binomial distribution under consideration may be approximated by a suitable normal distribution. Since the mean and standard deviation of the binomial distribution are given by

$$\begin{aligned} \mu &= np \\ &= (20)(0.5) \\ &= 10 \end{aligned}$$

and

$$\begin{aligned} \sigma &= \sqrt{npq} \\ &= \sqrt{(20)(0.5)(0.5)} \\ &= 2.24 \end{aligned}$$

respectively (see Section 9.4), the natural choice of a normal curve for this purpose is one with a mean of 10 and standard deviation of 2.24. Figure 9.25 shows such a normal curve superimposed on the histogram of the binomial distribution. The good fit suggests that the sum of the areas of the rectangles representing $P(X \geq 10)$, the probability of obtaining 10 or more heads in 20 tosses of the coin, may be approximated by the area of an appropriate region under the normal curve. To determine this region let us note that the base of the portion of the histogram representing the required probability extends from $x = 9.5$ on. (See Figure 9.26.) Therefore the required region under the normal curve should also have $x \geq 9.5$. Letting Y denote the continuous normal variable, we have

$$\begin{aligned} P(X \geq 10) &\approx P(Y \geq 9.5) \\ &= P(Y > 9.5) \\ &= P\left(Z > \frac{9.5 - 10}{2.24}\right) \\ &= P(Z > -0.22) \\ &= P(Z < 0.22) \\ &= 0.5871 \end{aligned}$$

The exact value of $P(X \geq 10)$ may be found by computing

$$P(X = 10) + P(X = 11) + \cdots + P(X = 20)$$

in the usual fashion and is equal to 0.5881. Thus, the normal distribution with suitably chosen mean and standard deviation does provide us with a good approximation to the binomial distribution.

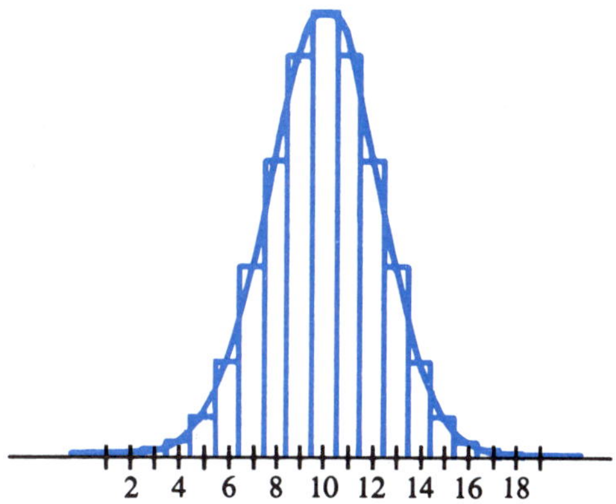

Figure 9.25

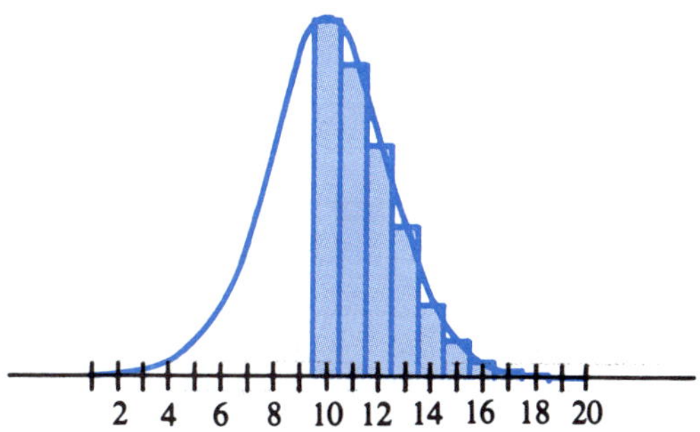

Figure 9.26

central limit theorem

In the general case, the following result, which is a special case of the *central limit theorem*, guarantees the accuracy of the approximation of a binomial distribution by a normal distribution under certain conditions.

THEOREM

Suppose we are given a binomial distribution associated with a (binomial) experiment involving n trials each with a probability of success p and probability of failure q. Then if n is large and p is not close to 0 or 1, the binomial distribution may be approximated by a normal distribution with

$$\mu = np \quad \text{and} \quad \sigma = \sqrt{npq}$$

In fact, it can be shown that if both np and nq are greater than 5, then the error resulting from this approximation is negligible.

EXAMPLE 9.35 An automobile manufacturer receives the microprocessors used to regulate fuel consumption in its automobiles in shipments of a 1000 each from a certain supplier. It has been estimated that, on the average, 1% of the microprocessors manufactured by the supplier are defective. Determine the probability that more than 20 of the microprocessors in a single shipment are defective.

SOLUTION Let X denote the number of defective microprocessors in a single shipment. Then X has a binomial distribution with $n = 1000$, $p = 0.01$, and $q = 0.99$, so that

$$\mu = (1000)(0.01) = 10$$

and

$$\sigma = \sqrt{(1000)(0.01)(0.99)} \approx 3.15$$

Approximating the binomial distribution by a normal distribution with a mean of 10 and a standard deviation of 3.15, we find that the probability that more than 20 of the microprocessors in a shipment are defective is given by

$$\begin{aligned} P(X > 20) &\approx P(Y > 20.5) \qquad \text{(where } Y \text{ denotes the normal random variable)} \\ &= P\left(Z > \frac{20.5 - 10}{3.15}\right) \\ &= P(Z > 3.33) \\ &= P(Z < -3.33) \\ &= 0.0004 \end{aligned}$$

In other words, approximately 0.04% of the shipments containing 1000 microprocessors each will contain 20 or more defective units. ■

EXAMPLE 9.36 The probability that a heart-transplant operation performed at the Medical Center is successful (that is, the patient survives a year or more after undergoing such an operation) is 0.7. Of 100 patients who had undergone such an operation what is the probability that

(**a**) less than 75 of them would survive a year or more after the operation?

(**b**) between 80 and 90 of them, inclusive, would survive a year or more after the operation?

SOLUTION Let X denote the number of patients who survive a year or more after undergoing a heart-transplant operation at the Medical Center. Then X is a binomial random variable. Also, $n = 100$, $p = 0.7$, and $q = 0.3$ so that

$$\mu = (100)(0.7) = 70$$

and

$$\sigma = \sqrt{(100)(0.7)(0.3)} \approx 4.58$$

Approximating the binomial distribution by a normal distribution with a mean of

70 and a standard deviation of 4.58, we find upon letting Y denote the associated normal random variable:

(**a**) The probability that less than 75 of the patients would survive a year or more is given by

$$\begin{aligned} P(X<75) &\approx P(Y<74.5) \qquad \text{Why?} \\ &= P\left(Z<\frac{74.5-70}{4.58}\right) \\ &= P(Z<0.98) \\ &= 0.8365 \end{aligned}$$

(**b**) The probability that between 80 and 90, inclusive, of the patients would survive a year or more is given by

$$\begin{aligned} P(80 \le X \le 90) &\approx P(79.5<Y<90.5) \\ &= P\left(\frac{79.5-70}{4.58}<Z<\frac{90.5-70}{4.58}\right) \\ &= P(2.07<Z<4.48) \\ &= P(Z<4.48)-P(Z<2.07) \\ &= 1-0.9808 \qquad \textit{Note}: P(Z<4.48)\approx 1 \\ &= 0.0192 \end{aligned}$$

■

9.6 EXERCISES

1. The medical records of infants delivered at the Kaiser Memorial Hospital show that the infants' lengths at birth in inches are normally distributed with a mean of 20 and a standard deviation of 2.6. Find the probability that an infant selected at random from among those delivered at the hospital measured

(*a*) longer than 22 inches.

(*b*) less than 18 inches.

(*c*) between 19 and 21 inches long.

2. According to the data released by the Chamber of Commerce of a certain city, the weekly wages of factory workers are normally distributed with a mean of \$300 and a standard deviation of \$50. Find the probability that a worker selected at random from the city makes a weekly wage of

(*a*) less than \$200 a week.

(*b*) more than \$360 a week.

(*c*) between \$250 and \$350 a week.

3. The TKK Products Corporation manufactures electric light bulbs in the 50, 60, 75, and 100 watt range. Laboratory tests show that the lives of these light bulbs are normally distributed with a mean of 750 hours and a standard deviation of 75 hours. What is the probability that a TKK light bulb selected at random will burn

(*a*) for more than 900 hours?

(*b*) for less than 600 hours?

(*c*) between 750 and 900 hours?

(*d*) between 600 and 800 hours?

4. On the average a student takes 100 words per minute midway through an advanced shorthand course at the American Institute of Stenography. Assuming that the dictation speeds of the students are normally distributed and that the standard deviation is 20 words per minute, find the probability that a student randomly selected from the course could take dictation at a speed of

(*a*) more than 120 words per minute.

(*b*) between 80 and 120 words per minute.

(*c*) less than 80 words per minute.

5. The IQ's of students at the Wilson Elementary School were measured recently and found to be normally distributed with a mean of 100 and a standard deviation of 15. What is the probability that a student selected at random will have an IQ of

(*a*) 140 or higher?

(*b*) 120 or higher?

(*c*) between 100 and 120?

(*d*) 90 or less?

6. The tread lives under normal driving conditions of the Super Titan radial tires are normally distributed with a mean of 40,000 miles and a standard deviation of 2000 miles. What is the probability that a tire selected at random will have a tread life of more than 35,000 miles? If 4 new tires are installed in a car and they experience even wear, determine the probability that all 4 tires still have useful tread lives after 35,000 miles of driving.

7. To be eligible for further consideration, applicants for certain positions with the Civil Service must first pass a written qualifying examination. To qualify, a test score of 70 or more must be obtained. In a recent examination given to a group of applicants, it was found that the scores on the examination were normally distributed with a mean of 60 points and a standard deviation of 10 points. Determine the percentage of applicants who passed the written qualifying examination.

8. The General Manager of the Service Department of the MCA Television Company has estimated that the time that elapses between the dates of purchase and the dates on which the 19-inch sets manufactured by the company first require service is normally distributed with a mean of 22 months and a standard deviation of 4 months. If the company gives a 1-year warranty on parts and labor for these sets, determine the percentage of sets manufactured and sold by the company that may require service before the warranty period runs out.

9. The scores on an economics examination are normally distributed with a mean of 72 and a standard deviation of 16. If the instructor assigns a grade of A to 10% of the class, what is the lowest score a student may have and still obtain an A?

10. The scores on a sociology examination are normally distributed with a mean of 70 and a standard deviation of 10. If the instructor assigns A's to 15%, B's to 25%, C's to 40%, D's to 15%, and F's to 5% of the class, find the cut-off points for these grades.

In Problems 11–20, use the appropriate normal distributions to approximate the resulting binomial distributions.

11. A fair coin is tossed 20 times. Find the probability of obtaining

(*a*) less than 8 heads.

(*b*) more than 6 heads.

(*c*) between 6 and 10 heads inclusive.

12. A coin is weighted so that the probability of obtaining a head in a single toss is 0.4. If the coin is tossed 25 times, determine the probability of obtaining

(*a*) less than 10 heads.

(*b*) between 10 and 12 heads inclusive.

(*c*) more than 15 heads.

13. A basketball player has a 75% chance of making a free throw. What is the probability of his making 100 or more free throws in 120 trials?

14. A marksman's chance of hitting a target with each of his shots is 60%. If he fires 30 shots, what is the probability of his hitting the target

(*a*) at least 20 times?

(*b*) less than 10 times?

(*c*) between 15 and 20 times, inclusive?

15. The P.A.R. Bearings Company is the principal supplier of ball bearings for the Sperry Gyroscope Company. It has been determined that 6% of the ball bearings shipped are rejected because they fail to meet tolerance requirements. What is the probability that a shipment of 200 ball bearings contains more than 10 rejects?

16. The manager of C & R Clothiers, a major manufacturer of men's shirts, has determined that 3% of the shirts made by the company do not meet with the standards set by the company and are sold as "seconds" to discount and outlet stores. What is the probability that in a day's production of 200 dozen shirts, less than 10 dozen will be classified as "seconds"?

17. The Colorado Mining and Mineral Company has 800 employees engaged in its mining operations. It has been estimated that the probability of a worker meeting with an accident during a one-year period is 0.1. What is the probability that more than 70 workers will meet with an accident during the one-year period?

18. An experiment was conducted to test the effectiveness of a new drug in treating a certain disease. The drug was administered to 50 mice that had been previously exposed to the disease. It was found that 35 mice subsequently recovered from the disease. It was determined that the natural recovery rate from the disease is 0.5.

(*a*) Determine the probability that 35 or more of the mice not treated with the drug would recover from the disease.

(*b*) Using the results obtained in part (*a*), comment on the effectiveness of the drug in the treatment of the disease.

19. The Manager of the Madison Finance Company has estimated that, because of a recession year, 5% of its 400 loan accounts will be delinquent. If the manager's estimate is correct, what is the probability that 25 or more of the accounts will be delinquent?

*****20.*** Because of late cancellations, Neptune Lines, an operator of cruise ships, has a policy of accepting more reservations than there are accommodations available. From experience, 8% of the bookings for the 90-day around-the-world cruise on the S.S. Drion, which has accommodations for 2000 passengers, are subsequently cancelled. If the management of Neptune Lines has decided, for public relations reasons, that a person who has made a reservation should have a probability of 0.99 of obtaining accommodation on the ship, determine the largest number of reservations that should be taken for a cruise on the S.S. Drion.

9 Chapter Review

EXERCISES

1. A man purchased a $25,000 1-year term life insurance policy for $375. Assuming that the probability that he will live for another year is 0.989, find the company's expected gain.

2. The probability distribution of a random variable X is shown in the following table.

x	$P(X=x)$
0	0.1
1	0.1
2	0.2
3	0.3
4	0.2
5	0.1

(*a*) Compute $P(1 \leq X \leq 4)$.

(*b*) Compute the mean and standard deviation of X.

3. A binomial experiment consists of four trials in which the probability of success in any one trial is $\frac{2}{5}$.

(*a*) Construct the probability distribution for the experiment.

(*b*) Compute the mean and standard deviation of the probability distribution.

4. Let Z be the standard normal variable. Make a rough sketch of the appropriate region under the standard normal curve and find

(*a*) $P(Z<0.5)$ (*b*) $P(Z<-0.75)$ (*c*) $P(-0.75<Z<0.5)$

5. Let Z be the standard normal variable. Find z if z satisfies

(*a*) $P(Z<z)=0.9922$ (*b*) $P(Z<z)=0.1469$

(*c*) $P(Z>z)=0.9788$ (*d*) $P(-z<Z<z)=0.8444$

6. Let X be a normal random variable with $\mu=10$ and $\sigma=2$. Find the values of

(*a*) $P(X<11)$ (*b*) $P(X>8)$ (*c*) $P(7<X<9)$

7. If the probability that a bowler will bowl a strike is 0.7, what is the probability that he will get exactly two strikes in four attempts? at least two strikes in four attempts?

8. The heights of 4000 women who participated in a recent survey were found to be normally distributed with a mean of 64.5 inches and a standard deviation of 2.5 inches. What percentage of these women have heights of 67 inches or greater?

9. Refer to problem 8. Use the Chebychev inequality to estimate the probability that the height of a woman who participated in the survey will fall within two standard deviations of the mean; that is, that her height will be between 59.5 and 69.5 inches.

10. The proprietor of a hardware store will accept a shipment of ceramic wall tiles if no more than 2 of a random sample of 20 is found to be defective. What is the probability that he will accept shipment if 10% of the tiles in a certain shipment are defective?

11. The Dayton Iron Works Company manufactures steel rods to a specification of 1 inch diameter. These rods are accepted by the buyer if they fall within the tolerance limits of 0.995 and 1.005. Assuming that the diameter of the rods are normally distributed about a mean of 1 inch and a standard deviation of 0.002 inches. Estimate the percentage of rods that will be rejected by the buyer.

12. A coin is biased so that the probability of it landing heads is 0.6. If the coin is tossed 100 times, what is the probability that heads will appear more than 50 times in the 100 tosses?

13. A division of the Soloron Corporation manufactures photo-voltaic cells for use in the company's solar energy converters. It is estimated that 5% of the cells manufactured are defective. In a batch of 200 cells manufactured by the company, what is the probability that it will contain at most 20 defective units?

10

THE DERIVATIVE

Historically, the development of calculus by Isaac Newton (1642–1727) and Gottfried Wilhelm von Leibniz (1646–1716) resulted from investigations into solving certain classes of mathematical problems such as (a) *finding the tangent to a curve at a given point,* (b) *finding the rates of change of certain physical quantities, and* (c) *finding the areas of planar regions bounded by arbitrary curves (see Figure 10.1).*

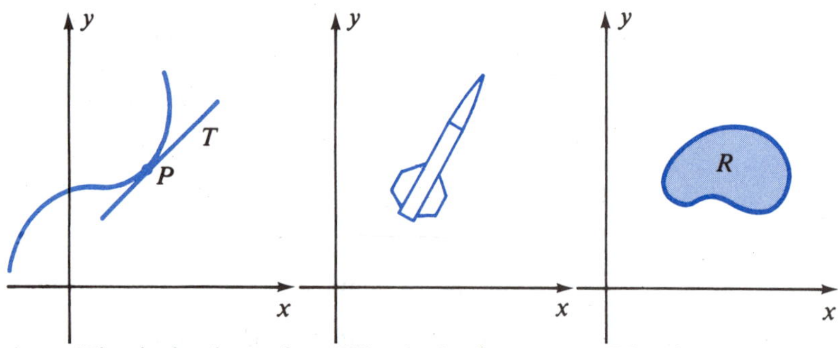

What is the slope of the tangent line T at the point P?

What is the (instantaneous) velocity of the rocket at some time T?

What is the area of the region R?

Figure 10.1

The study of the first two classes of problems mentioned above led to the creation of differential calculus, which relies on the concept of the derivative of a function. The study of the third class of problems led to the creation of integral calculus, which relies on the concept of the integral of a function. Both the derivative of a function and the integral of a function are defined in terms of a more fundamental concept—the limit of a function. Incidentally, the derivative and the integral of a function are related as we will see in section 13.2.

10.1 Limits and Continuity

In much of mathematical work we are required to determine the value (if one exists) that a function $f(x)$ approaches as x approaches some fixed number a. For example, suppose we are given the function

$$f(x)=\frac{x^2-4}{x-2}$$

and we wish to see if $f(x)$ approaches some number L as x approaches the number $x=2$.

Since x may approach the number 2 from either the left or the right of the point $x=2$, let us pick a sequence of numbers such as 1.5, 1.9, 1.99 and 1.999 that approaches the number 2 from the left, and the sequence 2.5, 2.1, 2.01 and 2.001 that approaches the number 2 from the right. The values of $f(x)$ corresponding to these sequences of numbers are given in the following table:

x	1.5	1.9	1.99	1.999	2.001	2.01	2.1	2.5
$f(x)$	3.5	3.9	3.99	3.999	4.001	4.01	4.1	4.5

From the table we see that as x gets closer and closer to 2, $f(x)$ gets closer and closer to 4. The graph of the function f shown in Figure 10.2 confirms this observation. In this situation we say that the *limit of the function*

$$f(x)=\frac{x^2-4}{x-2}$$

at the point x = 2 is 4, written

$$\lim_{x\to 2}\frac{x^2-4}{x-2}=4$$

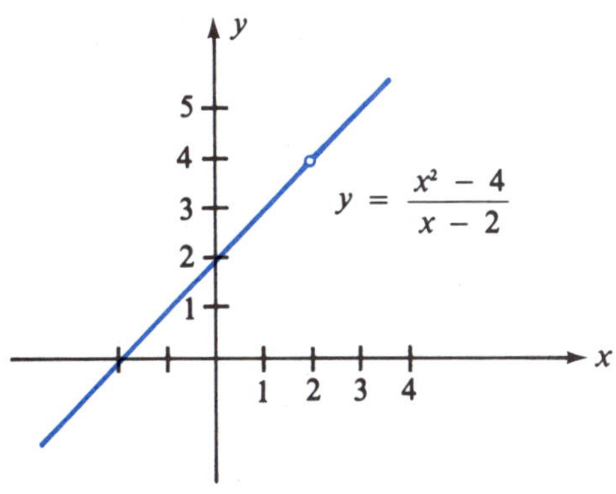

Figure 10.2

Observe that the point $x = 2$ is not in the domain of the function f (for this reason, the point (2, 4) is missing from the graph of f). This, however, is inconsequential since the existence or nonexistence of $f(x)$ at $x = 2$ plays no role in our computation of the limit. This example motivates the following definition.

DEFINITION Let $f(x)$ be a function that is defined for all values of x close to $x = a$ with the possible exception of a itself. Then $f(x)$ has the *limit* L at the point $x = a$, written

$$\lim_{x \to a} f(x) = L$$

if the values of $f(x)$ can be made arbitrarily close to L by restricting x to be sufficiently close to a.

Let us consider some examples involving the computation of limits.

EXAMPLE 10.1 Let

$$g(x) = \begin{cases} x + 2 & \text{if } x \neq 1 \\ 1 & \text{if } x = 1 \end{cases}$$

Evaluate $\lim_{x \to 1} g(x)$.

SOLUTION The domain of $g(x)$ is the set of all real numbers. The graph of the function is shown in Figure 10.3. From the graph of $g(x)$ we see that

$$\lim_{x \to 1} g(x) = 3$$

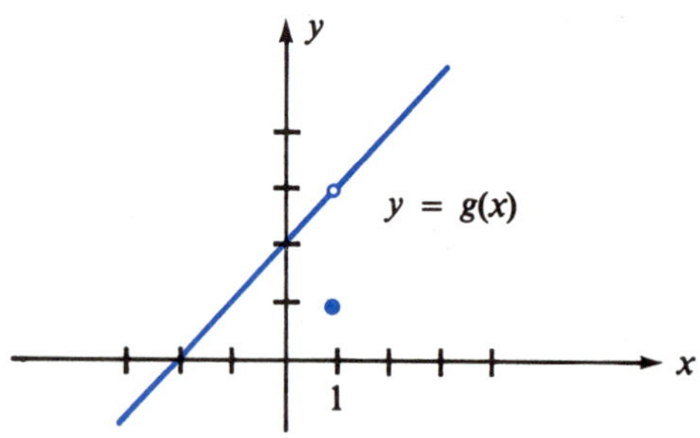

Figure 10.3

■

Observe that in the last example $g(1) = 1$, which is not equal to the limit of the function $g(x)$ at $x = 1$.

EXAMPLE 10.2 Evaluate the limit of each of the following functions at the point indicated.

(a) $f(x) = \begin{cases} -1 & \text{if } x < 0 \\ 1 & \text{if } x \geq 0 \end{cases}$; $x = 0$

(**b**) $g(x)=\frac{1}{x^2}; \quad x=0$

SOLUTION The graphs of the functions $f(x)$ and $g(x)$ are shown in Figure 10.4.

(**a**) Referring to Figure 10.4(a) we see that no matter how close x is to $x=0, f(x)$ takes on the values 1 and -1 depending on whether x is positive or negative. Thus $f(x)$ does not approach any *specific* real number L as x approaches 0. We conclude that the limit of $f(x)$ does *not* exist at $x=0$.

(**b**) Referring to Figure 10.4(b) we see that as x approaches $x=0$ (from either side) $g(x)$ increases without bound and thus does not approach any specific real number. We conclude, accordingly, that the limit of $g(x)$ does not exist at $x=0$.

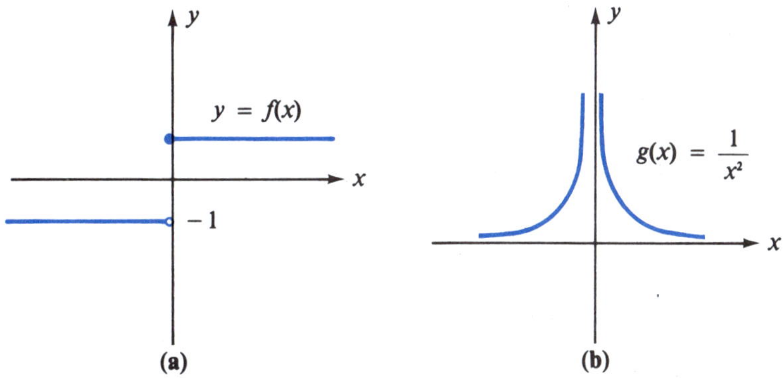

Figure 10.4 ■

Until now, we have relied on knowing the actual values of a function or the graph of a function to help us evaluate the limit of the function $f(x)$ at the point $x=a$. The following properties of limits, which we list without proof, enable us to evaluate limits of functions algebraically.

Property 1 If $f(x)=c$, where c is a constant, the $\lim_{x\to a} f(x)=c$

Property 1 states that the limit of the constant function $f(x)=c$ at any point $x=a$ is equal to the value of the (constant) function, namely, c.

EXAMPLE 10.3 If $f(x)=3$, then $\lim_{x\to 2} f(x)=\lim_{x\to 2} 3=3$ and $\lim_{x\to -4} f(x)=\lim_{x\to -4} 3=3$. ■

Property 2 If $f(x)=x$, then $\lim_{x\to a} f(x)=\lim_{x\to a} x=a$

Property 2 states that the limit of the identity function $f(x)=x$ at any point $x=a$ is equal to the number a.

EXAMPLE 10.4 If $f(x)=x$, then $\lim_{x\to 3} f(x)=\lim_{x\to 3} x=3$ and $\lim_{x\to -2} f(x)=\lim_{x\to -2} x=-2$. ■

Property 3 If $\lim_{x\to a} f(x)=L$ and $[f(x)]^n$ is defined, where n is a real number, then

$$\lim_{x\to a} [f(x)]^n = \left[\lim_{x\to a} f(x)\right]^n = L^n$$

Property 3 states that the limit of the nth power of a function is equal to the nth power of the limit of the function. For this result to be true we must assume that x is chosen so that the nth power of $f(x)$ is defined for x close to $x = a$. For example, if $n = 1/2$ then $f(x)$ cannot be negative (see Chapter 5).

EXAMPLE 10.5 If $f(x) = x^3$ and $g(x) = x^{3/2}$, then $\lim_{x\to 2} f(x) = \lim_{x\to 2} x^3 = [\lim_{x\to 2} x]^3 = 2^3 = 8$ and $\lim_{x\to 4} g(x) = \lim_{x\to 4} x^{3/2} = [\lim_{x\to 4} x]^{3/2} = 4^{3/2} = 8$. ■

Property 4 If $\lim_{x\to a} f(x) = L$ and k is a constant, then

$$\lim_{x\to a} kf(x) = k[\lim_{x\to a} f(x)] = kL$$

Property 4 states that the limit of a constant times a function is equal to the constant times the limit of the function.

EXAMPLE 10.6 If $f(x) = 5x^4$, then $\lim_{x\to 2} 5x^4 = 5[\lim_{x\to 2} x^4] = 5(2)^4 = 80$. ■

Observe that we have used Property 3 of limits in obtaining the second of the chain of equalities above.

Property 5 If $\lim_{x\to a} f(x) = L$ and $\lim_{x\to a} g(x) = M$, then

$$\lim_{x\to a} [f(x) \pm g(x)] = \lim_{x\to a} f(x) \pm \lim_{x\to a} g(x) = L \pm M$$

Property 5 states that the limit of the sum (difference) of two functions is equal to the sum (difference) of their limits. This result is easily extended to the case involving the sum and/or difference of any finite number of functions.

EXAMPLE 10.7 **(a)** $\lim_{x\to 2} (3x^3 - 4) = \lim_{x\to 2} 3x^3 - \lim_{x\to 2} 4 = 3(2)^3 - 4 = 20$

(b) $\lim_{x\to 1} (5x^4 - 2x^3 + 1) = \lim_{x\to 1} 5x^4 - \lim_{x\to 1} 2x^3 + \lim_{x\to 1} 1$

$= 5(1)^4 - 2(1)^3 + 1 = 4$ ■

Property 6 If $\lim_{x\to a} f(x) = L$ and $\lim_{x\to a} g(x) = M$, then

$$\lim_{x\to a} f(x)g(x) = [\lim_{x\to a} f(x)][\lim_{x\to a} g(x)] = LM$$

Property 6 states that the limit of the product of two functions is equal to the product of their limits. This result is also easily extended to the case involving the product of any finite number of functions.

EXAMPLE 10.8

$$\lim_{x\to 3} 2x^3\sqrt{x^2+7} = [\lim_{x\to 3} 2]\,[\lim_{x\to 3} x^3]\,[\lim_{x\to 3} (x^2+7)^{1/2}]$$
$$= 2(3)^3(3^2+7)^{1/2} = 216$$ ■

Property 7 If $\lim_{x\to a} f(x) = L$ and $\lim_{x\to a} g(x) = M$ and $M \neq 0$, then

$$\lim_{x\to a} \frac{f(x)}{g(x)} = \frac{\lim_{x\to a} f(x)}{\lim_{x\to a} g(x)} = \frac{L}{M}$$

Property 7 states that the limit of the quotient of two functions is equal to the quotient of their limits provided the denominator is not equal to zero.

EXAMPLE 10.9

$$\lim_{x\to 2} \frac{2x^2+1}{x+1} = \frac{\lim_{x\to 2}(2x^2+1)}{\lim_{x\to 2}(x+1)} = \frac{2(2)^2+1}{2+1} = 3$$ ■

We emphasize once again that Property 7 of limits is valid only when the limit of the function appearing in the denominator is not equal to zero at the point in question. In the case where the numerator has a limit different from zero while the denominator has a limit equal to zero, the limit of the quotient does not exist at the point in question (see Example 10.2 part b).

In certain situations, the application of Property 7 to the evaluation of the limit of a quotient leads to the expression "0/0" (that is, both the numerator and the denominator have limit zero at $x = a$). In this event, we say that the quotient $f(x)/g(x)$ has the *indeterminate form* 0/0 at $x = a$. This case occurs in the study of the derivative of a function which we shall cover in the next two sections. As the name suggests, the form "0/0" does not provide a solution to our problem. To solve the problem, one normally finds an equivalent expression for the quotient and then evaluates it. The next several examples illustrate this process.

EXAMPLE 10.10 (See the example on page 413). Evaluate

$$\lim_{x\to 2} \frac{x^2-4}{x-2}$$

SOLUTION Since both the numerator and the denominator of the expression approach zero as x approaches 2, the quotient

$$\frac{x^2-4}{x-2}$$

has the indeterminate form 0/0. We rewrite

$$\frac{x^2-4}{x-2} = \frac{(x-2)(x+2)}{(x-2)}$$

which, upon cancelling the common factors, is equivalent to $x+2$. Thus,

$$\lim_{x\to 2} \frac{x^2-4}{x-2} = \lim_{x\to 2}(x+2) = 4$$

as concluded earlier. ■

EXAMPLE 10.11 Evaluate

$$\lim_{x\to-3}\frac{x^2+2x-3}{x^2+4x+3}$$

SOLUTION

$$\lim_{x\to-3}\frac{x^2+2x-3}{x^2+4x+3}=\frac{\text{“}0\text{”}}{0} \qquad \text{(an indeterminate form)}$$

We rewrite

$$\frac{x^2+2x-3}{x^2+4x+3}=\frac{(x+3)(x-1)}{(x+3)(x+1)}=\frac{x-1}{x+1}$$

upon cancelling the common factor $(x+3)$. Therefore,

$$\lim_{x\to-3}\frac{x^2+2x-3}{x^2+4x+3}=\lim_{x\to-3}\frac{x-1}{x+1}=\frac{-3-1}{-3+1}=2$$

■

EXAMPLE 10.12 Evaluate

$$\lim_{h\to0}\frac{\sqrt{1+h}-1}{h}$$

SOLUTION Letting h approach zero, we obtain the expression "0/0". Let us rationalize the numerator of the quotient (see Appendix I) by multiplying both the numerator and the denominator by the expression $(\sqrt{1+h}+1)$. We obtain

$$\frac{\sqrt{1+h}-1}{h}=\frac{(\sqrt{1+h}-1)(\sqrt{1+h}+1)}{h(\sqrt{1+h}+1)}=\frac{1+h-1}{h(\sqrt{1+h}+1)}=\frac{h}{h(\sqrt{1+h}+1)}$$

$$=\frac{1}{\sqrt{1+h}+1}$$

Therefore,

$$\lim_{h\to0}\frac{\sqrt{1+h}-1}{h}=\lim_{h\to0}\frac{1}{\sqrt{1+h}+1}=\frac{1}{\sqrt{1}+1}=\frac{1}{2}$$

■

The concept of a limit is related to the concept of continuity which is our next topic.

A function f is continuous at the point $x=a$ if the following conditions are satisfied:

1. $f(a)$ is defined

2. $\lim_{x\to a}f(x)=f(a)$

continuous function Thus, a function f *is continuous at the point* $x=a$ provided that the limit of f at the point $x=a$ exists and has the value $f(a)$. Geometrically, f is continuous at the point $x=a$ if proximity of x to a implies proximity of $f(x)$ to $f(a)$.

discontinuous function If f is not continuous at $x=a$ then f *is said to be discontinuous at* a. Also, f *is continuous on an interval* if f is continuous at every point in the interval.

EXAMPLE 10.13 Discuss the continuity of the functions defined by the following rules:

(a) $f(x)=x+2$

(b) $g(x)=\dfrac{x^2-4}{x-2} \quad (x \neq 2)$

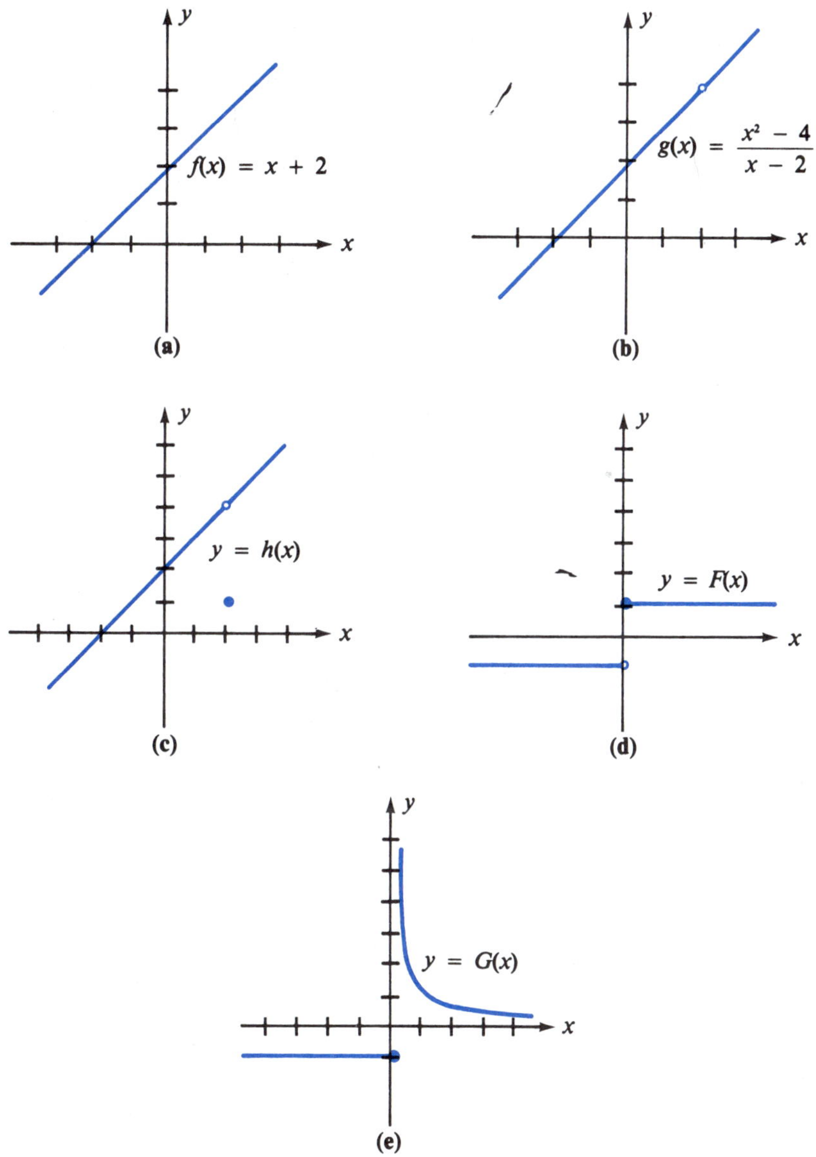

Figure 10.5

(c) $h(x)=\begin{cases} x+2 & \text{if } x \neq 2 \\ 1 & \text{if } x=2 \end{cases}$

(d) $F(x)=\begin{cases} -1 & \text{if } x<0 \\ 1 & \text{if } x \geq 0 \end{cases}$

(e) $G(x)=\begin{cases} 1/x & \text{if } x>0 \\ -1 & \text{if } x \leq 0 \end{cases}$ (See Figure 10.5.)

SOLUTION (a) The function f is continuous for all values of x since the two conditions for continuity for each x are satisfied.

(b) The function g fails to be continuous at the point $x=2$ since g is not defined at that point. It is continuous everywhere else.

(c) The function h is discontinuous at $x=2$ because the second condition for continuity is violated; the limit as x approaches 2 of $h(x)$ exists and has the value 4 but this limit is not equal to $h(2)=1$. It is continuous for all other values of x.

(d) The function F is continuous everywhere except at the point $x=0$ where the limit of $F(x)$ fails to exist as x approaches 0 (see Example 10.2 part a).

(e) Since the right-hand limit of $G(x)$ does not exist as x approaches zero, we conclude that G fails to be continuous at $x=0$. The function G is continuous at all other points. ■

The above example clearly illustrates the following geometrical property of a continuous function: a function f is continuous over an interval if it is possible to trace the graph of f over this interval without lifting one's pencil from the paper.

The following properties of continuous functions (which we state without proof) follow directly from the definition of continuity and the corresponding properties of limits:

Property 1 The constant function $f(x)=c$ is continuous everywhere.

Property 2 The identity function $f(x)=x$ is continuous everywhere.

If $f(x)$ and $g(x)$ are continuous at $x=a$, then

Property 3 $[f(x)]^n$, where n is a real number, is continuous at $x=a$ whenever it is defined at that point.

Property 4 $f(x) \pm g(x)$ is continuous at $x=a$.

Property 5 $f(x)g(x)$ is continuous at $x=a$.

Property 6 $\dfrac{f(x)}{g(x)}$ is continuous at $x=a$ provided $g(a) \neq 0$.

EXAMPLE 10.14 Property 2 states the function $f(x)=x$ is continuous everywhere. Therefore the function $g(x)=x^n$, where n is a positive integer, is continuous everywhere by

Property 3 since it is defined for all values of x. Property 1 and Property 5 may now be used to show that the function $h(x)=cx^n$, where c is a constant and n is a positive integer, is also continuous. Finally, repeated applications of Property 4 imply that a polynomial P of degree n defined by

$$P(x)=a_0x^n+a_1x^{n-1}+a_2x^{n-2}+\cdots+a_n,$$

where $a_0, a_1, \ldots, a_n$ are constants with $a_0 \neq 0$ is continuous everywhere. For example, the trinomial $P(x)=3x^3+2x^2-x+10$ is continuous everywhere. ■

EXAMPLE 10.15 Discuss the continuity of the rational function R defined by

$$R(x)=\frac{p(x)}{q(x)} \qquad (q(x)\neq 0)$$

where p and q are polynomial functions.

SOLUTION Since the polynomial functions p and q are continuous (Example 10.14) we may use Property 6 of continuous functions to conclude that the rational function R is continuous whenever it is defined. In other words, it is continuous everywhere except for values of x where $q(x)=0$. For example, the function F defined by

$$F(x)=\frac{8x^{10}-4x+1}{x^2+1}$$

is continuous everywhere since the denominator never equals zero. On the other hand, the function $G(x)$ defined by

$$G(x)=\frac{4x^3-3x^2+1}{x^2-3x+2}$$

is discontinuous at $x=1$ and $x=2$ since $x^2-3x+2=(x-2)(x-1)$ equals zero at precisely these points. ■

Finally, we wish to remark that Property 2 for the continuity of a function f at the point $x=a$, namely,

$$\lim_{x\to a} f(x)=f(a)$$

tells us that for a continuous function f, the limit of $f(x)$ at $x=a$ may be found by evaluating the function f at $x=a$.

EXAMPLE 10.16 Refer to Example 10.10. Find the limit of the function h defined by

$$h(x)=\frac{x^2-4}{x-2} \qquad (x\neq 2)$$

as x approaches 2.

SOLUTION As in Example 10.10, we observe that the function h is equivalent to the function f defined by $f(x)=x+2$ except for $x=2$. But f is a continuous function everywhere, so that

$$\lim_{x\to 2} f(x)=\lim_{x\to 2}(x+2)=f(2)=2+2=4$$

This result agrees with the limit of $h(x)$ as x approaches 2 found earlier. ■

10.1 EXERCISES

In problems 1 through 10, complete the table by computing f(x) *at the given values of* x *and use the results thus obtained to guess at the indicated limit if it exists.*

1. $f(x)=x+2;\quad \lim_{x\to 1} f(x)$

x	0.9	0.99	0.999	1.001	1.01	1.1
$f(x)$						

2. $f(x)=5x-2;\quad \lim_{x\to -1} f(x)$

x	−1.1	−1.01	−1.001	−0.999	−0.99	−0.9
$f(x)$						

3. $f(x)=x^2+1;\quad \lim_{x\to 2} f(x)$

x	1.9	1.99	1.999	2.001	2.01	2.1
$f(x)$						

4. $f(x)=2x^2-1;\quad \lim_{x\to 1} f(x)$

x	0.9	0.99	0.999	1.001	1.01	1.1
$f(x)$						

5. $f(x)=\dfrac{|x|}{x}\quad (x\neq 0);\quad \lim_{x\to 0} f(x)$

x	−0.1	−0.01	−0.001	0.001	0.01	0.1
$f(x)$						

6. $f(x)=\dfrac{1}{(x-1)^2}$ $(x \neq 1)$; $\lim_{x\to 1} f(x)$

x	0.9	0.99	0.999	1.001	1.01	1.1
$f(x)$						

7. $f(x)=\dfrac{1}{x-2}$ $(x \neq 2)$; $\lim_{x\to 2} f(x)$

x	1.9	1.99	1.999	2.001	2.01	2.1
$f(x)$						

8. $f(x)=\dfrac{x^2+x-2}{x-1}$ $(x \neq 1)$; $\lim_{x\to 1} f(x)$

x	0.9	0.99	0.999	1.001	1.01	1.1
$f(x)$						

****9.*** $f(x)=\dfrac{e^x-1}{x}$ $(x \neq 0)$; $\lim_{x\to 0} f(x)$

x	−0.1	−0.01	−0.001	0.001	0.01	0.1
$f(x)$						

10. $f(x)=\dfrac{x-1}{x-1}$ $(x \neq 1)$; $\lim_{x\to 1} f(x)$

x	0.9	0.99	0.999	1.001	1.01	1.1
$f(x)$						

In problems 11 through 16, use the graph of the function f *to determine if* $\lim_{x\to a} f(x)$ *exists. Justify your answers.*

11.

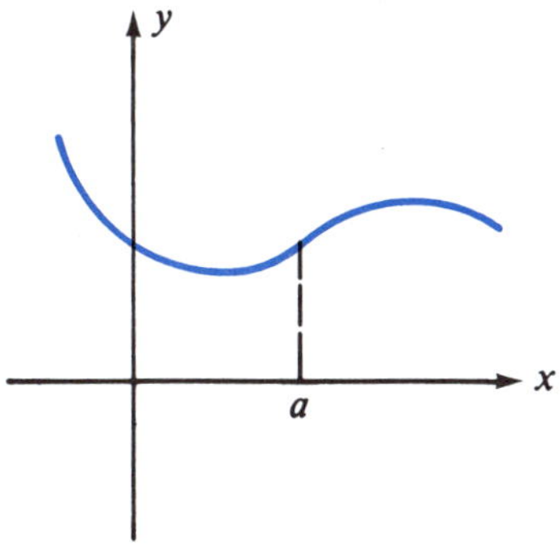

12.

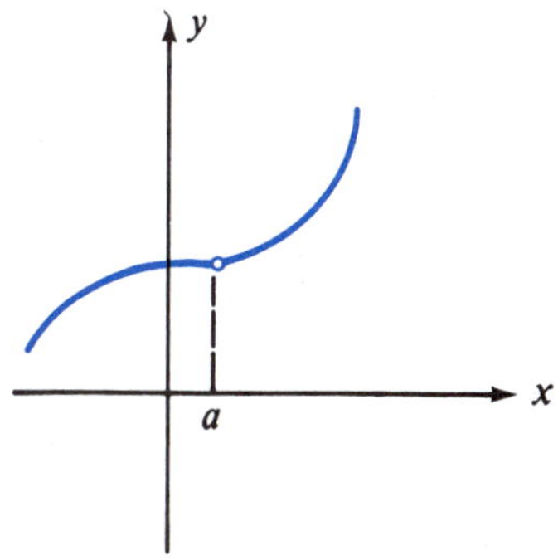

13.

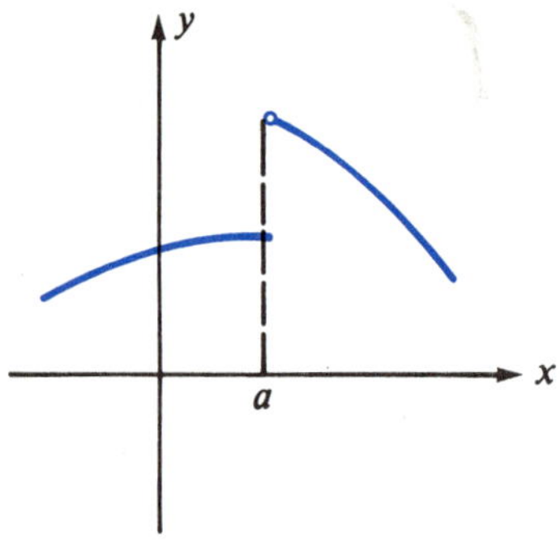

14.

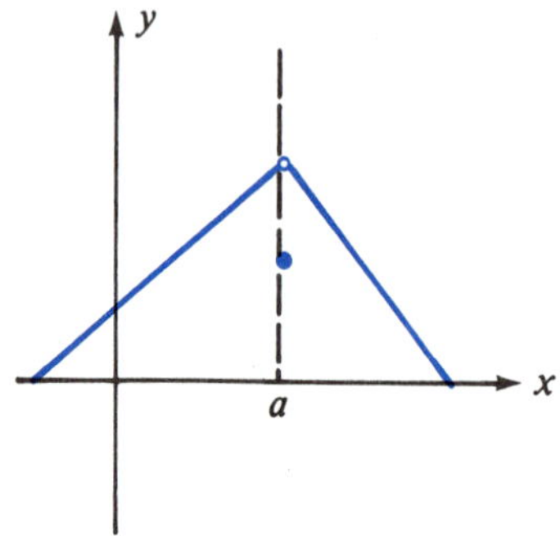

15.

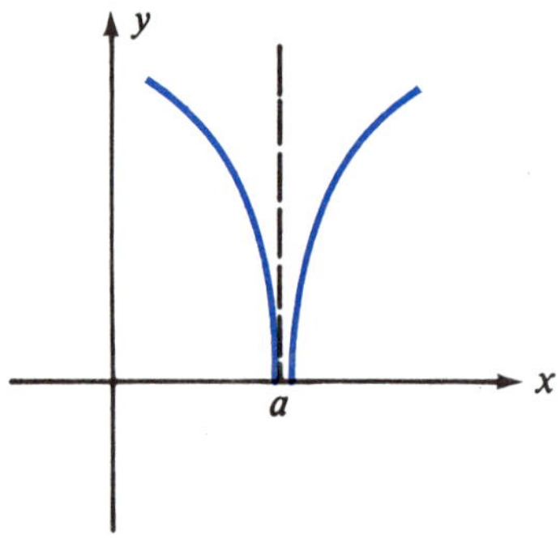

16.

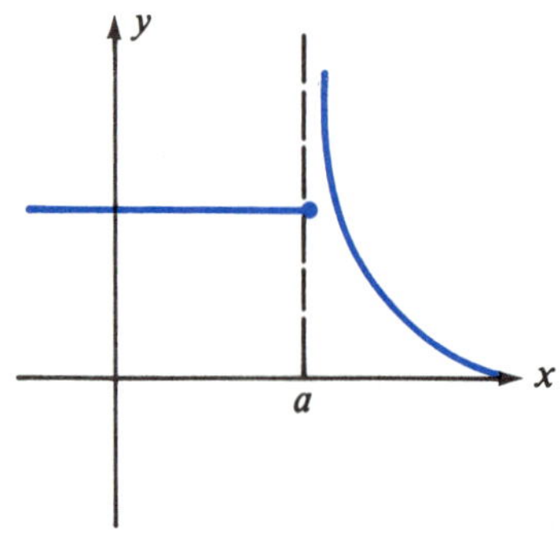

In problems 17 through 21, make a sketch of the graph of the function f *and evaluate* $\lim_{x \to a} f(x)$ *for the given value of* a, *if it exists.*

17. $f(x)=\begin{cases} x-1 & \text{if } x \le 3 \\ -2x+8 & \text{if } x>3 \end{cases}$ $\quad a=3$

18. $f(x)=\begin{cases} x & \text{if } x<1 \\ 0 & \text{if } x=1 \\ -x+2 & \text{if } x>1 \end{cases}$ $\quad a=1$

19. $f(x)=\begin{cases} 2x-4 & \text{if } x \le 4 \\ x-2 & \text{if } x>4 \end{cases}$ $\quad a=4$

20. $f(x)=\begin{cases} -2x+4 & \text{if } x<1 \\ 4 & \text{if } x=1 \\ x^2+1 & \text{if } x>1 \end{cases}$ $\quad a=1$

21. $f(x)=\begin{cases} |x| & \text{if } x \ne 0 \\ 1 & \text{if } x=0 \end{cases}$ $\quad a=0$

In problems 22 through 43, find the indicated limits if they exist.

22. $\lim_{x \to 2} 3$

23. $\lim_{x \to 3} x$

24. $\lim_{x \to -2} -3x$

25. $\lim_{x \to 3} (4x^2-2x+1)$

26. $\lim_{x \to 0} (4x^5-20x^2+2x+1)$

27. $\lim_{x \to 2} (x^3+1)(x^2+1)$

28. $\lim_{x\to 0}(2x^2-1)(2x+4)$

29. $\lim_{x\to 2}(x^2+1)(x^2-4)$

30. $\lim_{x\to 2}\dfrac{2x+1}{x+2}\quad (x\neq -2)$

31. $\lim_{x\to -3}\dfrac{x+1}{x+3}\quad (x\neq -3)$

32. $\lim_{x\to -3}\dfrac{x+3}{|x+3|}\quad (x\neq -3)$

33. $\lim_{x\to 2}\dfrac{x^3-8}{x-2}\quad (x\neq 2)$

34. $\lim_{x\to -5}\dfrac{x^2-25}{x+5}\quad (x\neq -5)$

35. $\lim_{x\to 0}\dfrac{2x^2-3x}{x}\quad (x\neq 0)$

36. $\lim_{x\to -2}\dfrac{x^2-4}{x+2}\quad (x\neq -2)$

37. $\lim_{x\to -2}\dfrac{x^2-x-6}{x^2+x-2}\quad (x\neq -2)$

38. $\lim_{x\to -3}\sqrt{2x^4+x^2}$

39. $\lim_{x\to 2}\sqrt{\dfrac{2x^3+4}{x^2+1}}$

40. $\lim_{x\to 1}\dfrac{\sqrt{x}-1}{x-1}\quad (x\neq 1)$ *Hint*: Multiply by $\dfrac{\sqrt{x}+1}{\sqrt{x}+1}$.

41. $\lim_{x\to 4}\dfrac{x-4}{\sqrt{x}-2}\quad (x\neq 4)$ *Hint*: See Problem 40.

42. $\lim_{x\to -1}\dfrac{3x^3+x^2+1}{x^3+1}\quad (x\neq -1)$

***43.** $\lim_{x\to 1}\dfrac{x^4-1}{x^3-1}\quad (x\neq 1)$

44. For the function f whose graph appears below, explain why f is not continuous at the points x_0, x_1, x_2, x_3, x_4 and x_5.

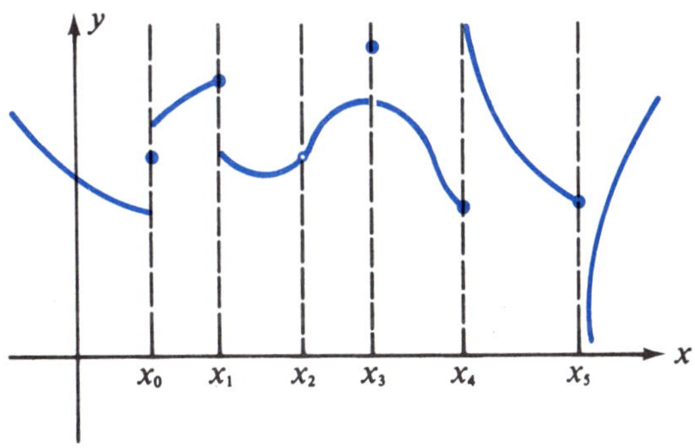

In problems 45 through 52, discuss the continuity of each of the following functions. At each point of discontinuity of the function indicate which of the condition(s) for continuity is (are) violated. Make a sketch of the function.

45. $f(x)=\begin{cases}2x-4 & \text{if } x\leq 0\\ 1 & \text{if } x>0\end{cases}$

46. $f(x)=\begin{cases}x^2+1 & \text{if } x\neq 0\\ 0 & \text{if } x=0\end{cases}$

47. $f(x)=\begin{cases} x+5 & \text{if } x\le 0 \\ -x^2+5 & \text{if } x>0 \end{cases}$

48. $f(x)=|x-1|$

49. $f(x)=\begin{cases} x+5 & \text{if } x<0 \\ 2 & \text{if } x=0 \\ -x^2+5 & \text{if } x>0 \end{cases}$

50. $f(x)=\begin{cases} \dfrac{x^2-1}{x+1} & \text{if } x\ne -1 \\ 1 & \text{if } x=-1 \end{cases}$

51. $f(x)=\begin{cases} -|x|+1 & \text{if } x\ne 0 \\ 0 & \text{if } x=0 \end{cases}$

52. $f(x)=\begin{cases} 1/x^2 & \text{if } x\ne 0 \\ 1 & \text{if } x=0 \end{cases}$

In problems 53 through 56, determine all values of x *for which the function is discontinuous.*

53. $f(x)=\dfrac{2x}{x^2-1}$

54. $f(x)=\dfrac{1}{(x-1)(x-2)}$

55. $f(x)=\dfrac{x^2-2x}{x^2-3x+2}$

56. $f(x)=\dfrac{x^2-3x+2}{x^2-2x}$

57. Discuss the continuity of the "postage function" of problem 28, Exercise set 2.1.

58. The base salary of a salesman working on commission is \$12,000. For each \$50,000 of sales beyond \$100,000 he is paid a \$1,000 commission. Sketch a graph showing his earnings as a function of the level of his sales. Discuss the continuity of the function.

59. The fee charged per car in a downtown parking lot is \$1.00 for the first half-hour and \$0.50 for each additional half-hour or part thereof subject to a maximum of \$5.00. Derive a function f relating the parking fee to the length of time a car is left in the lot. Sketch the graph of f and discuss the continuity of the function f.

60. The function giving the cost of a certain commodity is defined by

$$C(x)=\begin{cases} 5x & \text{if } 0<x<10 \\ 4x & \text{if } 10\le x<30 \\ 3.5x & \text{if } 30\le x<60 \\ 3.25x & \text{if } x\ge 60 \end{cases}$$

where x is the number of pounds of a certain commodity sold and $C(x)$ is measured in dollars. Sketch the graph of the function C and discuss its continuity.

10.2

More on Limits

In the last section we studied the limit of a function f at a point $x=a$, where a is a real number. In certain applications of mathematics we are required to study the behavior of $f(x)$ as x increases or decreases without bound. As an example let us suppose we are given the function

$$f(x)=\frac{2x^2}{1+x^2}$$

and wish to determine what happens to $f(x)$ as x gets larger and larger. Picking the sequence of numbers 1, 2, 5, 10, 100 and 1000 for the successive values of x and computing the corresponding values of $f(x)$, we obtain the following table of values:

x	1	2	5	10	100	1000
$f(x)$	1	1.6	1.92	1.98	1.9998	1.999998

From the table we see that as x gets larger and larger, $f(x)$ gets closer and closer to 2. The graph of the function f, shown in Figure 10.6, confirms this observation.

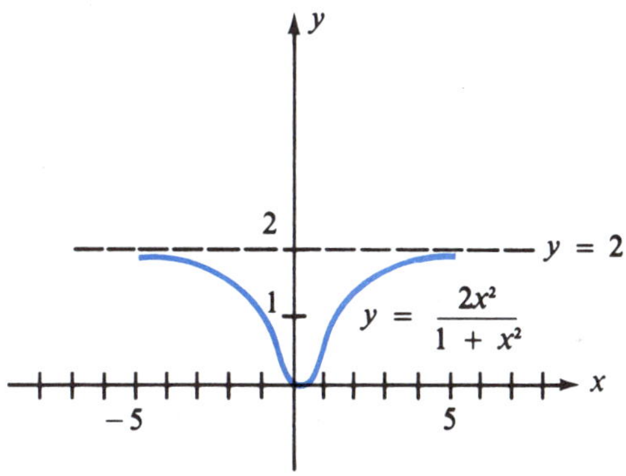

Figure 10.6

In this situation we say that the *limit of the function*

$$f(x)=\frac{2x^2}{1+x^2}$$

as x increases without bound is 2, written

$$\lim_{x\to\infty}\frac{2x^2}{1+x^2}=2$$

In general, we define the limit of a function at infinity as follows:

DEFINITION

The function $f(x)$ has the limit L as x increases without bound (approaches infinity), written

$$\lim_{x\to\infty} f(x)=L$$

if the values of $f(x)$ can be made arbitrarily close to L by taking x large enough. Similarly, the function $f(x)$ has the limit L as x decreases without bound (approaches minus infinity), written

$$\lim_{x \to -\infty} f(x) = L$$

if the values of $f(x)$ can be made arbitrarily close to L by taking x to be negative and sufficiently large in absolute value.

EXAMPLE 10.17 Let f and g be the functions defined in Example 10.2, that is,

$$f(x) = \begin{cases} -1 & \text{if } x < 0 \\ 1 & \text{if } x \geq 0 \end{cases} \quad \text{and} \quad g(x) = \frac{1}{x^2}$$

Evaluate

(a) $\lim_{x \to \infty} f(x)$ and $\lim_{x \to -\infty} f(x)$

(b) $\lim_{x \to \infty} g(x)$ and $\lim_{x \to -\infty} g(x)$

SOLUTION Referring to the graphs of the respective functions (see Figure 10.4), we see that

(a) $\lim_{x \to \infty} f(x) = 1$ and $\lim_{x \to -\infty} f(x) = -1$

(b) $\lim_{x \to \infty} \frac{1}{x^2} = 0$ and $\lim_{x \to -\infty} \frac{1}{x^2} = 0$ ■

The properties of limits listed earlier except for Property 2 are valid when a is replaced by ∞. Instead of Property 2 we have the following properties for the limit at infinity:

Property 2′

$$\lim_{x \to \infty} \frac{1}{x^n} = 0 \quad \text{for all } n > 0$$

and

$$\lim_{x \to -\infty} \frac{1}{x^n} = 0 \quad \text{for all } n > 0\text{, provided that } \frac{1}{x^n} \text{ is defined}$$

EXAMPLE 10.18 Let

$$f(x) = \frac{3x^2 + 8x - 4}{2x^2 + 4x - 5}$$

Compute $\lim_{x \to \infty} f(x)$ if it exists.

SOLUTION Since both the limits of the numerator and the denominator do not exist as x approaches infinity the property pertaining to the limit of a quotient (Property 7) is not applicable. Let us put the function in a form in which we can find the required limit. By dividing both the numerator and the denominator by x^2, the highest power in x appearing in the denominator (so that we obtain an equivalent expression valid for $x \neq 0$), we obtain

$$\lim_{x\to\infty} \frac{3x^2+8x-4}{2x^2+4x-5} = \lim_{x\to\infty} \frac{3+8/x-4/x^2}{2+4/x-5/x^2}$$

$$= \frac{\lim_{x\to\infty} 3+\lim_{x\to\infty} 8/x - \lim_{x\to\infty} 4/x^2}{\lim_{x\to\infty} 2+\lim_{x\to\infty} 4/x - \lim_{x\to\infty} 5/x^2}$$

$$= \frac{3+0-0}{2+0-0} = \frac{3}{2}$$

Observe that we have used Property 2′ in evaluating the second and third terms of both the numerator and the denominator. ■

Following is an application of the limit concept to the mathematics of finance. Recall from Section 6.2 that the compound interest formula states that if P dollars are invested at a nominal interest rate of r per year, compounded m times a year, then at the end of n conversion periods the accumulated amount is given by

(10.1) $$A_n = P\left(1+\frac{r}{m}\right)^n$$

(see Formula 6.10). Now intuition suggests that, all other terms being equal, the more often the interest is compounded (that is, the larger m is), the larger the accumulated amount will be. This is confirmed by the results of Example 6.10, where we calculated the accumulated amounts after 3 years on an initial investment of \$1000 invested at 8% per year compounded (a) annually $(m=1)$ (b) semiannually $(m=2)$, (c) quarterly $(m=4)$ and (d) monthly $(m=12)$. The results are reproduced in Table 10.1.

Table 10.1

Number of conversion periods (m)	Accumulated amount (\$)
1	1259.71
2	1265.32
4	1268.24
12	1271.75

An interesting question is what happens to the accumulated amount when the number of conversions per year becomes arbitrarily large? To answer this question let us rewrite Formula (10.1) in a slightly different form. Observe that, if t denotes the life of the investment in years then we have the relationship

$$mt = n$$

so that Formula (10.1) may be rewritten in the form

(10.2)
$$A = P\left(1+\frac{r}{m}\right)^{mt} = P\left[\left(1+\frac{r}{m}\right)^{m}\right]^{t}$$

Now, letting $m \to \infty$ we find that

$$\lim_{m\to\infty}\left[P\left(1+\frac{r}{m}\right)^{m}\right]^{t} = P\left[\lim_{m\to\infty}\left(1+\frac{r}{m}\right)^{m}\right]^{t} \qquad \text{Why?}$$

Next, upon making the substitution $u = m/r$ and observing that $u \to \infty$ as $m \to \infty$, the above expression reduces to

$$P\left[\lim_{u\to\infty}\left(1+\frac{1}{u}\right)^{ur}\right]^{t} = P\left[\lim_{u\to\infty}\left(1+\frac{1}{u}\right)^{u}\right]^{rt}$$

But

$$\lim_{u\to\infty}\left(1+\frac{1}{u}\right)^{u} = e \qquad \text{(See problem 12 in Exercise set 10.2.)}$$

so that

$$\lim_{m\to\infty} P\left[\left(1+\frac{r}{m}\right)^{m}\right]^{t} = Pe^{rt}$$

The formula

(10.3)
$$A(t) = Pe^{rt}$$

gives the accumulated amount when interest is compounded "infinitely" often per year and Formula (10.3) is called the *continuous compound interest formula.*

EXAMPLE 10.19 Find the accumulated amount after 3 years if $1000 is invested at 8% per year compounded

(**a**) daily (take the number of days in a year to be 360) and

(**b**) continuously.

SOLUTION (**a**) Using Formula (10.1) with $P = 1000$, $r = 0.08$, $m = 360$ and $n = (360)(3) = 1080$, we find using a pocket calculator,

$$A_{1080} = 1000\left(1+\frac{0.08}{360}\right)^{1080}$$
$$\approx 1271.20$$

or $1271.20.

(b) Here we use Formula (10.3) with $P = 1000$, $r = 0.08$ and $t = 3$, obtaining

$$\begin{aligned} A(3) &= 1000\, e^{(0.08)(3)} \\ &\approx 1271.25 \qquad \text{(using the “}e^x\text{” key)} \end{aligned}$$

or \$1271.25. ■

Observe that the accumulated amounts corresponding to interest compounded daily and interest compounded continuously differ by very little. The continuous compound interest formula is a very important tool in theoretical work in financial analysis.

Finally, solving Equation (10.3) for P we obtain

(10.4) $$P(t) = A(t)\, e^{-rt}$$

which gives the present value in terms of the future (accumulated) value for the case of continuous compounding.

EXAMPLE 10.20 The Blakely Investment Company owns an office building located in the commercial district of a city. Due to the continued success of an urban-renewal program, local business is enjoying a mini-boom. The market value of the property is $V(t) = 300{,}000\, e^{\sqrt{t}/2}$, where $V(t)$ is measured in dollars and t is the time in years from the present. If the expected rate of inflation is 9% compounded continuously for the next ten years, find an expression for the present value $P(t)$ of the market price of the property valid for the next 10 years. Compute $P(7)$, $P(8)$ and $P(9)$ and interpret your results.

SOLUTION Using Formula (10.4) with $A(t) = V(t)$, and $r = 0.09$, we find that the present value of the market price of the property t years from now $(0 \le t \le 10)$ is given by

$$\begin{aligned} P(t) &= V(t)\, e^{-0.09t} \\ &= 300{,}000\, e^{-0.09t + \sqrt{t}/2} \end{aligned}$$

Letting $t = 7$, 8, and 9, respectively, we find using a pocket calculator that

$$\begin{aligned} P(7) &= 300{,}000\, e^{-0.09(7) + \sqrt{7}/2} = 599{,}837 \text{ or } \$599{,}837 \\ P(8) &= 300{,}000\, e^{-0.09(8) + \sqrt{8}/2} = 600{,}640 \text{ or } \$600{,}640 \\ P(9) &= 300{,}000\, e^{-0.09(9) + \sqrt{9}/2} = 598{,}115 \text{ or } \$598{,}115 \end{aligned}$$

From the results of the above computations, we see that the present value of the market price of the property seems to decrease after a certain period of growth. This suggests that there is an optimal time for the owners to sell the property. Later (see Problem 8, Exercise set 11.7) we will show that the highest present value of the market price of the property is \$600,778 which occurs at time $t = 7.7$ years. ■

10.2 EXERCISES

In problems 1 through 6, complete the table by computing f(x) *at the given values of* x *and use the results to guess at the indicated limits if they exist.*

1. $f(x)=\dfrac{1}{x^2+1}$; $\lim_{x\to\infty} f(x)$ and $\lim_{x\to-\infty} f(x)$

x	1	10	100	1000	−1	−10	−100	−1000
$f(x)$								

2. $f(x)=\dfrac{2x}{x+1}\ (x\neq -1)$; $\lim_{x\to\infty} f(x)$ and $\lim_{x\to-\infty} f(x)$

x	1	10	100	1000	−5	−10	−100	−1000
$f(x)$								

3. $f(x)=3x^3-x^2+10$; $\lim_{x\to\infty} f(x)$ and $\lim_{x\to-\infty} f(x)$

x	1	5	10	100	1000	−1	−5	−10	−100	−1000
$f(x)$										

4. $f(x)=\dfrac{|x|}{x}\ (x\neq 0)$; $\lim_{x\to\infty} f(x)$ and $\lim_{x\to-\infty} f(x)$

x	1	10	100	−1	−10	−100
$f(x)$						

5. $f(x)=\dfrac{\sqrt{x}-1}{\sqrt{x}+1}$; $\lim_{x\to\infty} f(x)$

x	1	9	16	25	100	10,000	1,000,000
$f(x)$							

6. $f(x)=e^{-x^2}$; $\lim_{x\to\infty} f(x)$ and $\lim_{x\to-\infty} f(x)$

x	1	2	3	4	5	10	−1	−2	−3	−4	−5	−10
$f(x)$												

In problems 7 through 11, make a sketch of the function f *and evaluate* $\lim_{x\to\infty} f(x)$ *and* $\lim_{x\to-\infty} f(x)$ *if they exist.*

7. $f(x) = 2x^2 - 10$

8. $f(x) = x^3 - x$

9. $f(x) = \dfrac{1}{x^2}$

10. $f(x) = \dfrac{x^2}{x^2+1}$

11. $f(x) = 2 - |x|$

12. Let $f(n) = (1 + 1/n)^n$. Compute $f(n)$ for $n = 10$, 100, 1000, 10,000, 100,000, and 1,000,000 to five significant figures. (Use a pocket calculator with a "y^x" function.) The limit,

$$\lim_{n\to\infty}\left(1+\frac{1}{n}\right)^n$$

can be shown to exist and is denoted by the irrational number $e = 2.71828\ldots$.

In problems 13 through 22, find the indicated limits if they exist.

13. $\lim_{x\to\infty} \dfrac{3x+2}{x-5}$

14. $\lim_{x\to-\infty} \dfrac{4x^2-1}{x+2}$

15. $\lim_{x\to-\infty} \dfrac{3x^3+x^2+1}{x^3+1}$

16. $\lim_{x\to-\infty} \dfrac{x^4+1}{x^3-1}$

17. $\lim_{x\to\infty} \dfrac{4x^4-3x^2+1}{2x^4+x^3+x^2+x+1}$

18. $\lim_{x\to\infty} \dfrac{x^5-x^3+x-1}{x^6+2x^2+1}$

19. $\lim_{x\to\infty} \sqrt{\dfrac{4x^2+2x-1}{x^2+2}}$

20. $\lim_{x\to-\infty} \sqrt{\dfrac{16x^4-1}{2x^4-3x^2+8}}$

21. $\lim_{x\to\infty} \dfrac{4x+5}{\sqrt{2x^2+1}}$

22. $\lim_{x\to\infty} \dfrac{\sqrt{9x^4+2x^2+1}}{2x^2-1}$

23. Find the accumulated amount after 4 years if \$5000 is invested at 10% per year compounded continuously.

24. What is the total deposit at the end of 5 years if an amount of \$10,000 is deposited in a bank that pays interest at the rate of 8% per annum compounded annually? semiannually? quarterly? continuously?

25. Investment A offers a 10% return compounded semiannually, while Investment B offers a $9\frac{3}{4}$% return compounded continuously. Which investment has a higher rate of return over a 4-year period?

26. Find the present value of \$59,673 due in 5 years at an interest rate of 8% per annum compounded continuously.

27. A condominium complex was purchased by a group of private investors for \$1.4 million and sold 6 years later for \$3.6 million. Find the annual rate of return (compounded continuously) on their investment.

28. Having received a large inheritance, a child's parents wish to establish a trust for their child's college education. If they will need an estimated \$50,000 in 8 years, how much should they set aside in trust now, if they can invest the money at $10\frac{1}{2}\%$ compounded (**a**) quarterly? (**b**) continuously?

29. An investor purchased a piece of waterfront property. Because of the development of a marina in the vicinity, the market value of the property is expected to increase according to the rule $V(t)=80{,}000\,e^{\sqrt{t}/2}$, where $V(t)$ is measured in dollars and t is the time in years from the present. If the rate of inflation is expected to be 9% compounded continuously for the next 8 years, find an expression for the present value $P(t)$ of the market price of the property valid for the next 8 years. What is the market value of the property expected to be in 4 years?

30. Show that the effective rate of interest R corresponding to a nominal interest rate r per year compounded continuously is given by:

$$R=e^r-1$$

Hint: From Equation (6.11) we see that the effective rate $\bar{R}$ corresponding to a nominal interest rate r per year compounded m times a year is given by

$$\bar{R}=\left(1+\frac{r}{m}\right)^m-1$$

Let m tend to infinity in the above expression.

31. Refer to problem 30. Find the effective rate of interest corresponding to a nominal rate of 10% per year compounded (***a***) quarterly, (***b***) monthly and (***c***) continuously.

32. Refer to problem 30. Bank A pays interest on deposits at a 7% annual rate compounded quarterly, while Bank B pays interest on deposits at a $7\frac{1}{8}\%$ annual rate compounded continuously. Which bank has the higher effective rate of interest?

10.3

Rate of Change

In Chapter 2, we saw that a linear function f defined by $y=f(x)=mx+b$ (m, b, constants) has a graph that is a straight line L lying in the plane. Furthermore, the rate at which such a function is changing with respect to x is constant everywhere. It is given by the slope m of the line L.

In contrast, the graph of a nonlinear function f is not a straight line (although parts of it may be comprised of straight line segments) and the rate at which the function changes may vary from point to point. To discover a yardstick which will measure how fast f is changing for any value of x, consider the graph of a function f in Figure 10.7.

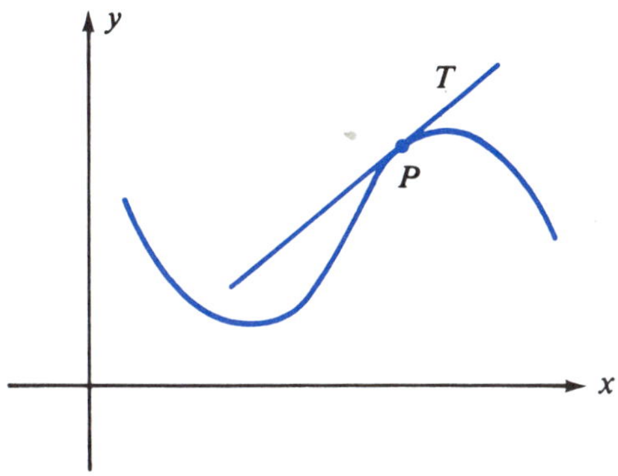

Figure 10.7

For a concrete interpretation of the following, think of the curve as representing a stretch of roller-coaster track. When the car is at the point P on the curve, a passenger sitting erect in the car and looking straight ahead will have a line of sight that is parallel to the line T, the tangent to the curve at P.

It should be evident that the rate at which the car is climbing or descending at any point on the curve is reflected by the slope of the tangent line to the curve at the point in question. These observations lead to the following definition:

DEFINITION The rate of change of the function f when $x = a$ is given by the slope of the tangent line to the graph of f at the point $(a, f(a))$.

To complete this definition, we must compute the slope of the tangent line T to the graph of the function f at any point $(x, f(x))$ lying on the graph. Since we must have two distinct points on a line to determine the slope of the line, an indirect approach is necessary. Observe that the tangent line T may be approximated by a sequence of secant lines, each secant line passing through the point $P(x, f(x))$ and a neighboring point on the graph of f. The approximation improves as the neighboring point is chosen closer and closer to the point P (Figure 10.8).

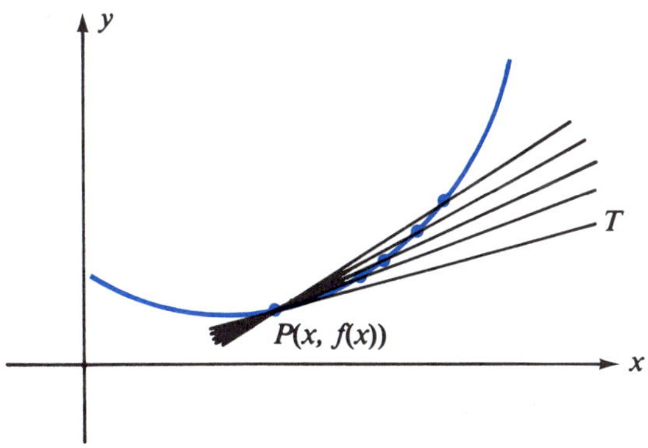

Figure 10.8

Now, each secant line passes through two distinct points—the point $P(x, f(x))$ and a point on the graph close to P—so that the slope of each secant line may be determined. These observations suggest that the slope of a tangent line T to the graph of f at the point P may be found by studying the limiting behavior of the slopes corresponding to a sequence of secant lines that approximate T.

EXAMPLE 10.21 Let f be a function defined by the rule $f(x)=(1/4)x^2$. The points $Q_1(5, 6.25)$, $Q_2(4, 4)$, $Q_3(3, 2.25)$, $Q_4(2.5, 1.5625)$, $Q_5(2.1, 1.1025)$ and $Q_6(2.01, 1.010025)$ lie on the graph of f. This may be verified by direct substitution. Observe that this sequence of points $Q_1, Q_2, Q_3, \ldots, Q_6$ approaches the point $P(2, 1)$ and that the corresponding sequence of secant lines through P and $Q_1, Q_2, \ldots, Q_6$, respectively, gives a better and better approximation of the tangent line T to the graph at P (see Figure 10.9). For clarity, we show only the four points Q_1, Q_2, Q_3 and Q_4 and the corresponding secant lines S_1, S_2, S_3, S_4. If $m_{S_1}, m_{S_2}, \ldots, m_{S_6}$ denote the slopes of the secant lines $S_1, S_2, \ldots, S_6$, respectively, then Equation 1.4 gives

$$m_{S_1}=\frac{6.25-1}{5-2}=1.75$$

and similarly, $m_{S_2}=1.5$, $m_{S_3}=1.25$, $m_{S_4}=1.125$, $m_{S_5}=1.025$, and $m_{S_6}=1.0025$. Observe that these slopes approach the number 1, which will be shown later to be the slope of the tangent line T to the graph of f, at the point $P(2, 1)$ (see Example 10.24).

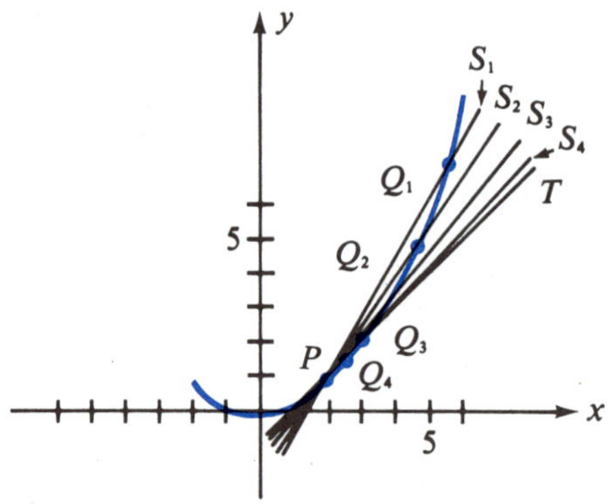

Figure 10.9

It is possible to find a general expression involving the function $f(x)$ that describes the slopes of the approximating sequence of secant lines. To accomplish this, consider a member of the family that passes through the point $P(x, f(x))$ and a neighboring point Q. Note that the x-coordinate of Q has the form $x+\Delta x$ where Δx (read "delta x") is some appropriate nonzero number and the corresponding y-coordinate of Q is $f(x+\Delta x)$ (Figure 10.10). Using Formula (1.4), the slope of the secant line S is given by

(10.5)
$$m_S=\frac{f(x+\Delta x)-f(x)}{\Delta x}$$

Since any member of the approximating family of secant lines may be obtained by specifying an appropriate number Δx, Equation (10.5) does give a general expression for the slopes of the approximating secant lines.

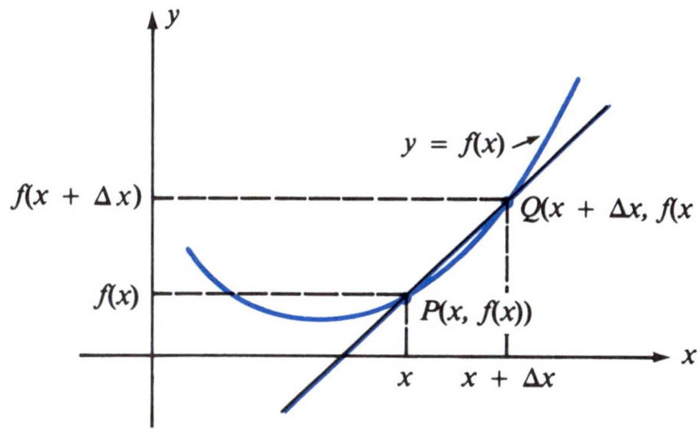

Figure 10.10

EXAMPLE 10.22 Refer to Example 10.21. Observe that the x-coordinates of the points $Q_1(5, 6.25)$, $Q_2(4, 4)$, $Q_3(3, 2.25)$, $Q_4(2.5, 1.5625)$, $Q_5(2.1, 1.1025)$ and $Q_6(2.01, 1.010025)$ are $x_1 = 5$, $x_2 = 4$, $x_3 = 3$, $x_4 = 2.5$, $x_5 = 2.1$ and $x_6 = 2.01$, respectively. The point $P(2, 1)$ has x-coordinate 2. Thus, the sequence x_1, x_2, x_3, x_4, x_5 and x_6 may be generated by taking $\Delta x = 3$, 2, 1, 0.5, 0.1 and 0.01, respectively. Note that by taking Δx sufficiently small, the point $Q(2 + \Delta x, f(2 + \Delta x))$ may be made as close to the point $P(2, f(2))$ as we please. Finally, observe that the slope of the secant line S_1 is found using Equation (10.5) with $x = 2$ and $\Delta x = 3$. Thus

$$
\begin{aligned}
m_{S_1} &= \frac{f(x+\Delta x) - f(x)}{\Delta x} \\
&= \frac{f(2+3) - f(2)}{3} = \frac{f(5) - f(2)}{3} \\
&= \frac{6.25 - 1}{3} = 1.75
\end{aligned}
$$

as obtained before. ■

Finally we are in the position to define the slope of the tangent line T to the graph of f at the point $P(x, f(x))$ and hence the rate of change of the function f at x. Observe that as the number Δx approaches zero, the point $Q(x + \Delta x, f(x + \Delta x))$ approaches the point $P(x, f(x))$ along the graph of f so that the sequence of secant lines through the points P and Q will approach the tangent line through $P(x, f(x))$. (See Figures 10.8 and 10.9). Thus, as Δx approaches zero the expression for the slope of the family of secant lines given in Equation (10.5) may be expected to approach the slope of the tangent line T at $P(x, f(x))$. This motivates the following definition:

DEFINITION The slope of the tangent line to the graph of f at the point $P(x, f(x))$ is given by

(10.6)
$$\lim_{\Delta x \to 0} \frac{f(x+\Delta x)-f(x)}{\Delta x}$$

(if it exists) and measures the rate of change of the function f at x.

EXAMPLE 10.23 Use Formula (10.6) to find the slope of the linear function $f(x)=mx+b$ where m and b are constants.

SOLUTION We have

$$\begin{aligned}\lim_{\Delta x \to 0} \frac{f(x+\Delta x)-f(x)}{\Delta x} &= \lim_{\Delta x \to 0} \frac{[m(x+\Delta x)+b]-[mx+b]}{\Delta x} \\ &= \lim_{\Delta x \to 0} \frac{m(\Delta x)}{\Delta x} \\ &= \lim_{\Delta x \to 0} m \qquad (\text{since } \Delta x \neq 0) \\ &= m\end{aligned}$$

This result is expected since the graph of f is a straight line. Therefore the tangent line to the graph of f at any point on the graph coincides with the line itself and thus must have the same slope m as the straight line. ■

EXAMPLE 10.24 Use Formula 10.6 to find the slope of the tangent line to the graph of $y=f(x)=(1/4)x^2$ at any point (x, y). What is the slope of the tangent line T to the graph of f at the point (2, 1) (see Example 10.21)? What is the equation of T?

SOLUTION The slope of the tangent line to the graph of f at any point (x, y) on the graph is given by

$$\begin{aligned}&\lim_{\Delta x \to 0} \frac{f(x+\Delta x)-f(x)}{\Delta x} \\ &\quad= \lim_{\Delta x \to 0} \frac{(1/4)(x+\Delta x)^2-(1/4)x^2}{\Delta x} \\ &\quad= \lim_{\Delta x \to 0} \frac{(1/4)x^2+(1/2)x(\Delta x)+1/4(\Delta x)^2-(1/4)x^2}{\Delta x} \\ &\quad= \lim_{\Delta x \to 0} \frac{\Delta x[(1/2)x+(1/4)\Delta x]}{\Delta x} \\ &\quad= \lim_{\Delta x \to 0} \left(\frac{1}{2}x+\frac{1}{4}\Delta x\right) \qquad (\text{since } \Delta x \neq 0) \\ &\quad= \frac{1}{2}x\end{aligned}$$

To find the slope of the tangent line T at the point (2, 1) we substitute $x = 2$ in the expression $(1/2)x$ getting $(1/2)(2) = 1$ as the required slope. Finally, knowing the point (2, 1) through which T passes and the slope of T found earlier, we may use the point-slope form of the equation of a line to write down the equation of T. We have

$$y - 1 = 1(x - 2)$$

or

$$y = x - 1$$

We conclude with an alternative approach for determining the rate of change of a function f when $x = a$ and show that this approach yields the same results obtained earlier. Let us denote the rule for the function f by $y = f(x)$. The number

difference quotient

$\Delta y = f(x + \Delta x) - f(x)$ measures the net change Δy in y corresponding to a net change Δx in x (Figure 10.11). Thus, the *difference quotient*

(10.7)
$$\frac{\Delta y}{\Delta x} = \frac{f(x + \Delta x) - f(x)}{\Delta x}$$

measures the *average rate of change of y with respect to x* over the interval $[x, x + \Delta x]$, and provides us with an approximation to the rate of change of the function f at x. The approximations become better and better as the intervals over which the averaging is done become shorter and shorter. This leads to the definition of the *rate of change of f at x*:

(10.8)
$$\lim_{\Delta x \to 0} \frac{\Delta y}{\Delta x} = \lim_{\Delta x \to 0} \frac{f(x + \Delta x) - f(x)}{\Delta x}$$

instantaneous rate of change

For emphasis, the rate of change of a function f at x is often called the *instantaneous rate of change of f at x*. This distinguishes it from the average rate of change of f which is computed over an *interval* $[x, x + \Delta x]$ rather than at a *point x*.

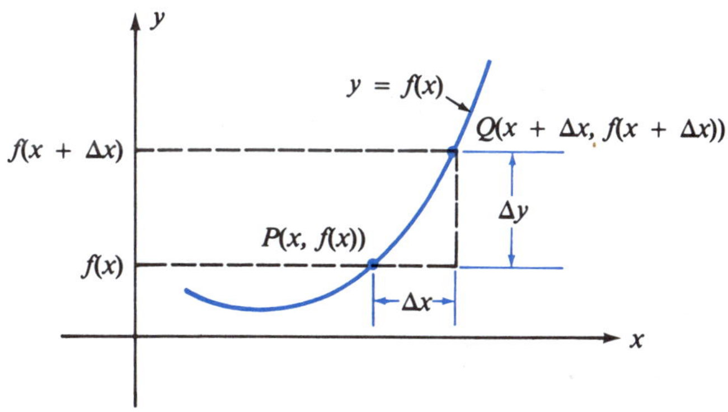

Figure 10.11

Now, observe that the expression on the right of Equation (10.8) is identical to that on the right of Equation (10.6). This means that the difference quotient simultaneously measures the slope of the secant line through the points $P(x, f(x))$ and $Q(x+\Delta x, f(x+\Delta x))$ and the average rate of change of $f(x)$ over the interval $[x, x+\Delta x]$. Thus, the limit of the right-hand side of Equation (10.8) measures both the slope of the tangent line to the graph of f at the point $P(x, f(x))$ and the (instantaneous) rate of change of the function f at x.

The following example illustrates how the average rate of change of a function and its limit are used to compute some familiar quantities.

EXAMPLE 10.25 Suppose the distance s (in feet) covered by a car, t seconds after starting from rest, is given by the function $f(t)=2t^2$ $(0 \le t \le 30)$ so that $s=f(t)=2t^2$.

(a) Calculate the average velocity of the car over the time interval [22, 23], [22, 22.1], and [22, 22.01].

(b) Calculate the (instantaneous) velocity of the car when $t=22$.

(c) Compare the results obtained in part (**a**) with the result obtained in part (**b**).

SOLUTION **(a)** The average velocity of the car over the time interval [22, 23] is given by the ratio

$$\frac{\text{distance traveled}}{\text{time elapsed}}=\frac{\Delta s}{\Delta t}=\frac{f(23)-f(22)}{1}=1058-968=90$$

or 90 feet per second. Similarly, we find that the average velocity of the car over the time interval [22, 22.1] is 88.2 feet per second and its average velocity over the time interval [22, 22.01] is 88.02 feet per second.

(b) It is intuitively clear that the instantaneous velocity of the car at any time t may be approximated more and more accurately by computing its average velocity over smaller and smaller intervals of time. Since the average velocity of the car over the time interval $[t, t+\Delta t]$ is

$$\frac{f(t+\Delta t)-f(t)}{\Delta t}$$

we are led to define the instantaneous velocity of the car at time t to be the limit

$$\lim_{\Delta t \to 0} \frac{f(t+\Delta t)-f(t)}{\Delta t}$$

Thus, the velocity of the car at any time t is given by

$$\begin{aligned} v &= \lim_{\Delta t \to 0} \frac{2(t+\Delta t)^2-2t^2}{\Delta t} \\ &= \lim_{\Delta t \to 0} \frac{2t^2+4t(\Delta t)+2(\Delta t)^2-2t^2}{\Delta t} \\ &= \lim_{\Delta t \to 0} (4t+2\Delta t) \\ &= 4t \end{aligned}$$

In particular, the velocity of the car 22 seconds from rest ($t=22$) is given by

$$v = 4(22)$$

or 88 feet/second (60 miles per hour).

(c) The computations performed in part (**a**) show that as the time intervals, over which the average velocity of the car are computed, become smaller and smaller, the average velocities over these intervals do approach 88 ft./sec., the instantaneous velocity of the car at $t=22$. ■

10.3 EXERCISES

1. Let f be the function defined by $f(x)=x^2$.

(***a***) Verify by direct substitution that the points $Q_1(3, 9)$, $Q_2(2, 4)$, $Q_3(1.5, 2.25)$, $Q_4(1.1, 1.21)$ and $Q_5(1.01, 1.0201)$ lie on the graph of f.

(***b***) ***1*** Compute the slopes of the secant lines S_1, S_2, S_3, S_4 and S_5 through the point $P(1, 1)$ and Q_1, Q_2, Q_3, Q_4 and Q_5, respectively.

2 Use these values to guess at the slope of the tangent line T to the graph of f at the point $P(1, 1)$.

(***c***) Let $P(x, x^2)$ be a point that lies on the graph of f and Q be a neighboring point on the graph, which has the x-coordinate $x+\Delta x$.

1 Find the y-coordinate of the point Q by evaluating $f(x+\Delta x)$.

2 Use Equation (10.5) to show that the slope of the secant line through P and Q is $2x+\Delta x$.

3 Find the slope of the tangent line T at P by evaluating $\lim_{\Delta x \to 0} (2x+\Delta x)$.

4 Use this result to find the slope of the tangent line at the point $P(1, 1)$. How does this compare with the result obtained in part (2) of ***b***?

2. Let f be the function defined by $f(x)=(1/2)x^2+1$.

(***a***) Verify by direct substitution that the points $Q_1(4, 9)$, $Q_2(3, 5.5)$, $Q_3(2, 3)$, $Q_4(1.5, 2.125)$ and $Q_5(1.1, 1.605)$ lie on the graph of f.

(***b***) ***1*** Compute the slopes of the secant lines S_1, S_2, S_3, S_4 and S_5 through the point $P(1, 1.5)$ and Q_1, Q_2, Q_3, Q_4 and Q_5, respectively.

2 Use these values to guess at the slope of the tangent line T at the point $P(1, 1.5)$.

(***c***) Let $P(x, (1/2)x^2+1)$ be a point that lies on the graph of f and Q be a neighboring point on the graph with an x-coordinate of $x+\Delta x$.

1 Find the y-coordinate of the point Q by evaluating $f(x+\Delta x)$.

2 Use equation (10.5) to show that the slope of the secant line through P and Q is $x+(1/2)\Delta x$.

3 Find the slope of the tangent line T at P by evaluating $\lim_{\Delta x \to 0} (x+(1/2)\Delta x)$.

4 Use this result to find the slope of the tangent line at the point $P(1, 1.5)$. How does this compare with the result obtained in part (2) of ***b***?

In problems 3 through 8, use Formula (10.6) to find the slope of the tangent line to the graph of each of the given functions.

3. $f(x)=13$ ***4.*** $f(x)=2x+7$ ***5.*** $f(x)=8-4x$

6. $f(x)=3x^2$ ***7.*** $f(x)=-\frac{1}{2}x^2$ ***8.*** $f(x)=2x^2+5x$

In problems 9 through 12, find the slope of the tangent line to the graph of each function at the given point and determine the equation of the tangent line.

9. $f(x)=2x+7$ at $(2, 11)$ ***10.*** $f(x)=-3x+4$ at $(-1, 7)$

11. $f(x)=3x^2$ at $(1, 3)$ ***12.*** $f(x)=3x-x^2$ at $(-2, -10)$

13. Let $y=f(x)=x^2+x$.

(***a***) Find the average rate of change of y with respect to x in the interval from $x=2$ to $x=3$, in the interval from $x=2$ to $x=2.5$, and in the interval from $x=2$ to $x=2.1$.

(***b***) Find the (instantaneous) rate of change of y at $x=2$.

(***c***) Compare the results obtained in part (***a***) with the result of part (***b***).

14. Suppose the distance s (in feet) covered by a car starting from rest in t seconds is given by the function $s(t)=t^2+48t$.

(***a***) Calculate the average velocity of the car over the time intervals [20, 21], [20, 20.1] and [20, 20.01].

(***b***) Calculate the (instantaneous) velocity of the car when $t=20$.

(***c***) Compare part (***a***) results with the result of part (***b***).

15. A ball is thrown straight up with an initial velocity of 128 feet/second, so that its height (in feet) after t seconds is given by $s(t)=128t-16t^2$.

(***a***) What is the average velocity of the ball over the time intervals [2, 3], [2, 2.5] and [2, 2.1]?

(***b***) What is the instantaneous velocity at time $t=2$?

(***c***) What is the instantaneous velocity at time $t=5$? Is the ball rising or falling at this time?

(***d***) When will the ball hit the ground?

10.4 The Derivative

In Section 10.3 we saw that given a function f defined by the rule $y=f(x)$, the limit

(10.9)
$$f'(x)=\lim_{\Delta x\to 0}\frac{f(x+\Delta x)-f(x)}{\Delta x}$$

if it exists, measures both the slope of the tangent line to the graph of f at the point $P(x, f(x))$ and the rate of change of the function f at x.

derivative of a function

The function f' given by the rule $f'(x)$ (read "f prime of x") is defined at each point x where the limit exists and is called the *derivative of f with respect to x* since it is derived from the function f. Thus, the derivative of a function f is a function, f', which gives the slope of the tangent line to the graph of f at any point $(x, f(x))$ (and thus the rate of change of f at x). Other notations for the derivative of f include $D_x f(x)$, read "the derivative of f with respect to x" and dy/dx (read "dee y dee x") or y' (read "y prime"). The last two are used when the rule for f is written in the form $y = f(x)$. A word of caution, dy/dx is *not* a fraction!

EXAMPLE 10.26 Let f be a function defined by $f(x) = x^2 - 4x$.

(a) Compute the derivative f' of f.

(b) Find the point on the graph of f where the tangent line to the curve is horizontal.

(c) Sketch the graph of f and the tangent line to the curve at the point found in part **(b)**.

(d) What is the rate of change of f at this point?

SOLUTION **(a)**

$$\begin{aligned} f'(x) &= \lim_{\Delta x \to 0} \frac{f(x+\Delta x) - f(x)}{\Delta x} \\ &= \lim_{\Delta x \to 0} \frac{[(x+\Delta x)^2 - 4(x+\Delta x)] - [x^2 - 4x]}{\Delta x} \\ &= \lim_{\Delta x \to 0} \frac{x^2 + 2x(\Delta x) + (\Delta x)^2 - 4x - 4(\Delta x) - x^2 + 4x}{\Delta x} \\ &= \lim_{\Delta x \to 0} \frac{\Delta x(2x - 4 + \Delta x)}{\Delta x} \\ &= \lim_{\Delta x \to 0} (2x - 4 + \Delta x) \\ &= 2x - 4 \end{aligned}$$

Thus, the derivative f' of the function f is defined by the rule $f'(x) = 2x - 4$.

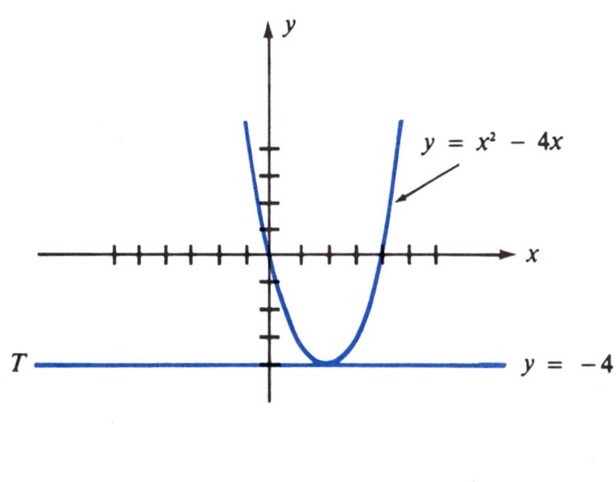

Figure 10.12

(**b**) At a point on the graph of f where the tangent line to the curve is horizontal and hence has slope zero, the derivative f' of f is zero. Accordingly, to find such point(s) we set $f'(x)=0$, which gives $2x-4=0$ or $x=2$. The corresponding value of y is given by $y=f(2)=-4$ and the required point is $(2, -4)$.

(**c**) The graph of f and the tangent line are shown in Figure 10.12.

(**d**) The rate of change of f at $x=2$ is zero. ■

EXAMPLE 10.27 Let f be a function defined by $f(x)=1/x$.

(**a**) Compute the derivative f' of f.

(**b**) Find the slope of the tangent line T to the graph of f when $x=1$.

(**c**) Find the equation of the tangent line T in part (**b**).

SOLUTION (**a**)

$$\begin{aligned} f'(x) &= \lim_{\Delta x \to 0} \frac{f(x+\Delta x)-f(x)}{\Delta x} \\ &= \lim_{\Delta x \to 0} \frac{\dfrac{1}{x+\Delta x}-\dfrac{1}{x}}{\Delta x} \\ &= \lim_{\Delta x \to 0} \frac{\dfrac{x-(x+\Delta x)}{x(x+\Delta x)}}{\Delta x} \\ &= \lim_{\Delta x \to 0} \frac{-\Delta x}{(\Delta x)x(x+\Delta x)} \\ &= \lim_{\Delta x \to 0} \frac{-1}{x(x+\Delta x)} \\ &= -\frac{1}{x^2} \end{aligned}$$

Thus the derivative f' of the function f is defined by the rule $f'(x)=-1/x^2$.

(**b**) The slope of the tangent line T to the graph of f when $x=1$ is given by $f'(1)=-1$.

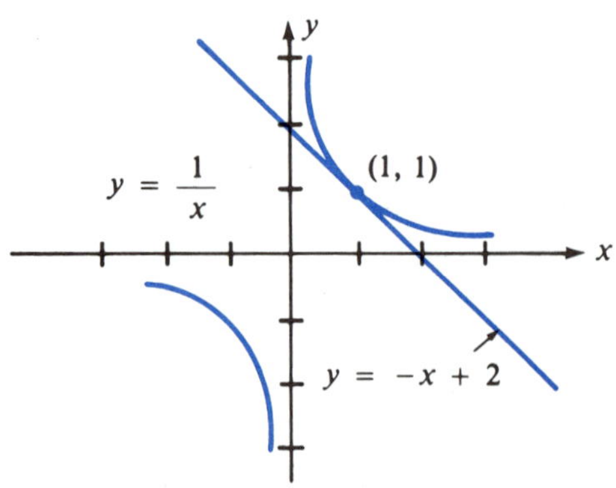

Figure 10.13

(c) When $x = 1$, $y = f(1) = 1$ and T is tangent to the graph of f at the point $(1, 1)$. The slope of T is -1, from part **(b)**. Thus, the equation of T is

$$y - 1 = -1(x - 1)$$

or

$$y = -x + 2 \qquad \text{(See Figure 10.13.)}$$

■

EXAMPLE 10.28 Let f be a function defined by $f(x) = \sqrt{x}$.

(a) Find the derivative f' of f.

(b) At which of the two points $x = 1$ or $x = 4$ is the function increasing at a faster rate?

(c) Find the equation of the tangent lines to the graph of f when $x = 1$ and $x = 4$, respectively.

SOLUTION **(a)**

$$\begin{aligned} f'(x) &= \lim_{\Delta x \to 0} \frac{f(x + \Delta x) - f(x)}{\Delta x} \\ &= \lim_{\Delta x \to 0} \frac{\sqrt{x + \Delta x} - \sqrt{x}}{\Delta x} \qquad \left(\text{form } \frac{0}{0}!\right) \\ &= \lim_{\Delta x \to 0} \frac{(\sqrt{x + \Delta x} - \sqrt{x})(\sqrt{x + \Delta x} + \sqrt{x})}{\Delta x(\sqrt{x + \Delta x} + \sqrt{x})} \qquad \text{(Rationalize the numerator!)} \\ &= \lim_{\Delta x \to 0} \frac{(x + \Delta x) - x}{\Delta x(\sqrt{x + \Delta x} + \sqrt{x})} \\ &= \lim_{\Delta x \to 0} \frac{\Delta x}{\Delta x(\sqrt{x + \Delta x} + \sqrt{x})} \\ &= \lim_{\Delta x \to 0} \frac{1}{\sqrt{x + \Delta x} + \sqrt{x}} \qquad \left(\text{no longer in indeterminate form } \frac{0}{0}.\right) \\ &= \frac{1}{2\sqrt{x}} \end{aligned}$$

(b) The rates at which the function f is changing at $x = 1$ and $x = 4$ are given by $f'(1) = 1/2$ and $f'(4) = 1/4$, respectively. Therefore, we conclude that f is increasing at a faster rate at $x = 1$ than at $x = 4$.

(c) The slopes of the tangent lines at $x = 1$ and $x = 4$ are given by $f'(1) = 1/2$ and $f'(4) = 1/4$, respectively. Since these lines pass through the points $(1, 1)$ and $(4, 2)$, respectively, the required equations are

$$y - 1 = \frac{1}{2}(x - 1)$$

or

$$y = \frac{1}{2}x + \frac{1}{2}$$

and $$y-2=\frac{1}{4}(x-4)$$

or $$y=\frac{1}{4}x+1 \qquad \text{(See Figure 10.14.)}$$

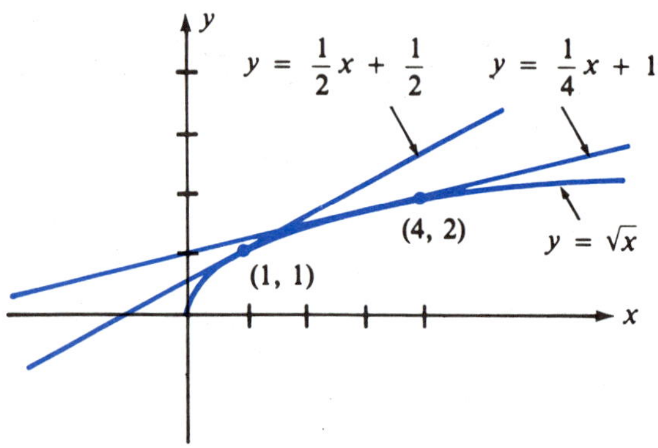

Figure 10.14 ■

In practical applications, one encounters functions that fail to be differentiable (that is, do not possess derivatives) at certain values of x. The next example illustrates a function which has a derivative that does not exist at the origin.

EXAMPLE 10.29 Show that the function $f(x)=|x|$ whose graph is shown in Figure 10.15 is not differentiable at $x=0$.

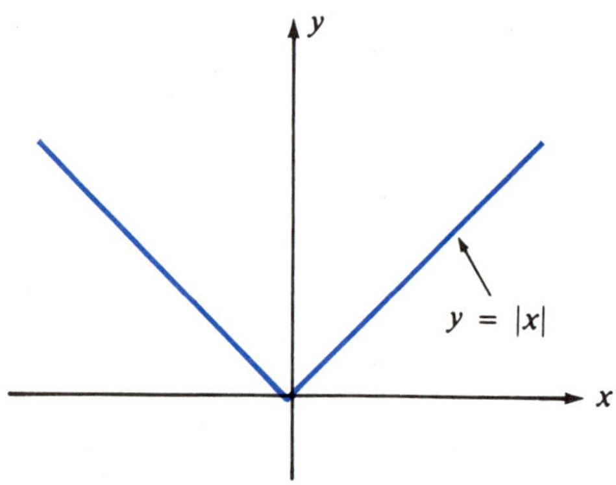

Figure 10.15

SOLUTION The derivative of the function $f(x)$ at $x=0$ is obtained by evaluating the limit (10.9) when $x=0$. Thus,

$$f'(0)=\lim_{\Delta x\to 0}\frac{f(0+\Delta x)-f(0)}{\Delta x}$$

$$=\lim_{\Delta x\to 0}\frac{f(\Delta x)-f(0)}{\Delta x}$$

if it exists. To show that $f'(0)$ does not exist, which will prove our assertion, it suffices to show that the limit of the quotient

$$\frac{f(\Delta x)-f(0)}{\Delta x}=\frac{|\Delta x|}{\Delta x}$$

does not exist as $\Delta x \to 0$. To do this, observe that if $\Delta x > 0$, then $|\Delta x| = \Delta x$ and

$$\frac{f(\Delta x)-f(0)}{\Delta x}=\frac{\Delta x}{\Delta x}=1$$

while if $\Delta x < 0$, then $|\Delta x| = -\Delta x$ so that

$$\frac{f(\Delta x)-f(0)}{\Delta x}=\frac{-\Delta x}{\Delta x}=-1$$

Thus, no matter how small Δx is in absolute value, the quotient

$$\frac{f(\Delta x)-f(0)}{\Delta x}$$

takes on the value 1 or -1 according to whether $\Delta x > 0$ or $\Delta x < 0$. We conclude that

$$f'(0)=\lim_{\Delta x\to 0}\frac{f(\Delta x)-f(0)}{\Delta x}$$

does not exist. The function is differentiable everywhere else. You should have no difficulty showing that the derivative of f is given by

$$f'(x)=\begin{cases} 1 & \text{if } x>0 \\ -1 & \text{if } x<0 \end{cases}$$ (See Exercise Set 10.4, problem 31.) ■

To conclude this section we will show the connection between continuity and differentiability of a function at a given value $x = a$ in the domain of f. By re-examining the function of Example 10.29, it is clear that $f(x) = |x|$ is continuous everywhere and, in particular, when $x = 0$. But, as demonstrated in Example 10.29, it fails to possess a derivative at $x = 0$. This shows that, in general, the continuity of a function at a point $x = a$ does *not* necessarily imply the differentiability of the function at that point. The converse, however, is true. Thus, *if a function f is differentiable at a point $x = a$ then it is continuous there.* To see this, suppose that f is differentiable at $x = a$ so that the limit

$$f'(a)=\lim_{\Delta x\to 0}\frac{f(a+\Delta x)-f(a)}{\Delta x}$$

exists. We must show that (refer to the definition of continuity in Section 10.1)

$$\lim_{x \to a} f(x) = f(a)$$

or, equivalently,

$$\lim_{x \to a} [f(x) - f(a)] = 0$$

But $x = a + \Delta x$ for some suitable number Δx. Furthermore, $x \to a$ if $\Delta x \to 0$ so that we could prove our result if we could show that

$$\lim_{\Delta x \to 0} [f(a + \Delta x) - f(a)] = 0$$

To do this, let us write the expression $[f(a + \Delta x) - f(a)]$ as

$$f(a + \Delta x) - f(a) = \left[\frac{f(a + \Delta x) - f(a)}{\Delta x}\right] \cdot \Delta x \quad (\Delta x \neq 0)$$

Taking the limit as $\Delta x \to 0$, we obtain

$$\begin{aligned}\lim_{\Delta x \to 0} [f(a + \Delta x) - f(a)] &= \lim_{\Delta x \to 0} \left[\frac{f(a + \Delta x) - f(a)}{\Delta x}\right] \cdot \Delta x \\ &= \left[\lim_{\Delta x \to 0} \frac{f(a + \Delta x) - f(a)}{\Delta x}\right]\left[\lim_{\Delta x \to 0} \Delta x\right] \\ &= f'(a) \cdot 0 \\ &= 0\end{aligned}$$

and our assertion is proved.

The above results show that the requirement that a function be differentiable at a point $x = a$ is more stringent than the mere requirement that it be continuous at that point. In fact, a function f is differentiable at a point $x = a$ provided it is sufficiently "smooth" in a neighborhood of that point. Thus, the failure of the function $f(x) = |x|$ of Example 10.29 to possess a derivative at the point $x = 0$ is due to an abrupt change of direction of the graph of f at that point. The slope changes from -1 to $+1$ as it passes through the origin, which results in a kink there.

EXAMPLE 10.30 Figure 10.16 depicts a portion of the graph of a function. Explain why the function fails to be differentiable at each of the points $x = a, b, c, d, e, f$.

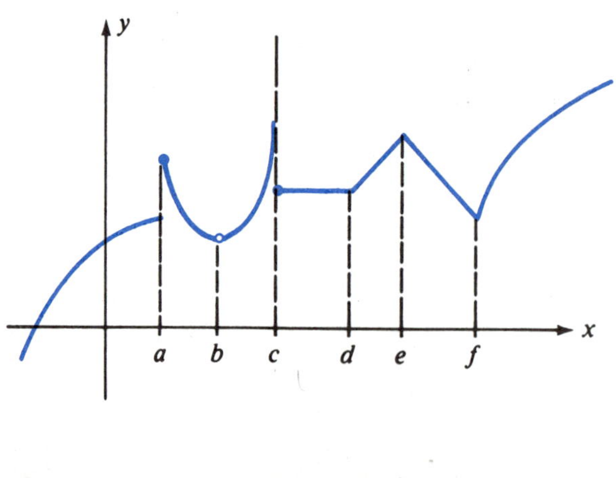

Figure 10.16

SOLUTION The function fails to be differentiable at the points $x = a$, b, and c because it is discontinuous at each of these points (see Section 10.1). The derivative of the function does not exist at $x = d$, e and f because it has a kink at each of these points. For example, the slope of the tangent line to the graph of the function is negative (in fact, -1) if $e < x < f$ and is positive when $x > f$. This results in a kink as shown in Figure 10.16. ■

10.4 EXERCISES

In problems 1 through 10, use Formula (10.9) to find the derivative of each of the following functions.

1. $f(x) = 4x^2 - 3$

2. $f(x) = 3x^2 - 4x + 7$

3. $f(x) = 10 - 4x - 4x^2$

4. $f(x) = -\dfrac{1}{x}$

5. $f(x) = \dfrac{1}{x+2}$

6. $f(x) = x^3 + 2x^2$

7. $f(x) = 3x^3 - 4$

8. $f(x) = 2\sqrt{x}$

9. $f(x) = \sqrt{x+1}$

10. $f(x) = -\dfrac{2}{\sqrt{x}}$

In problems 11 through 16 find the slope of the tangent line to the graph of each function at the given point and determine the equation of the tangent line.

11. $f(x) = 3x^2 - 4x + 7$ at $(2, 11)$

12. $f(x) = 6 - 2x + 4x^2$ at $(3, 36)$

13. $f(x) = -\dfrac{1}{x}$ at $(3, -1/3)$

14. $f(x) = \dfrac{3}{2x}$ at $(1, 3/2)$

15. $f(x) = 2\sqrt{x}$ at $(4, 4)$

16. $f(x) = \sqrt{x-1}$ at $(5, 2)$

17. Let $f(x) = x^3$

(***a***) Find the derivative f' of f.

(***b***) Sketch the graph of f and the tangent line to the curve at the point $(2, 8)$.

(***c***) Write the equation of this tangent line.

18. Let $f(x) = -\sqrt{x}$

(***a***) Find the derivative f' of f.

(***b***) Sketch the graph of f and the tangent line to the curve at the point $(4, -2)$.

(***c***) Write the equation of this tangent line.

19. Let $f(x) = x^2 + 6x$

(***a***) Find the derivative f' of f.

(***b***) Find the point on the graph of f where the tangent line to the curve is horizontal. *Hint*: find the value of x for which $f'(x) = 0$.

(*c*) Sketch the graph of f and the tangent line to the curve at the point found in part (*b*).

20. Let $f(x) = x^2 - 2x + 1$

(*a*) Find the derivative f' of f.

(*b*) Find the point on the graph of f where the tangent line to the curve is horizontal.

(*c*) Sketch the graph of f and the tangent line to the curve at the point found in part (*b*).

(*d*) What is the rate of change of f at this point?

21. Under a set of controlled laboratory conditions the size of the population of a certain bacteria culture at time t (in minutes) is described by the function $P = f(t) = 3t^2 + 2t + 1$. Find the rate of population growth at $t = 10$ minutes.

In problems 22 through 27, the graph of a function is shown. For each function state whether or not (a) f(x) *has a limit at* x = a, *(b)* f(x) *is continuous at* x = a, *and (c)* f(x) *is differentiable at* x = a.

22.

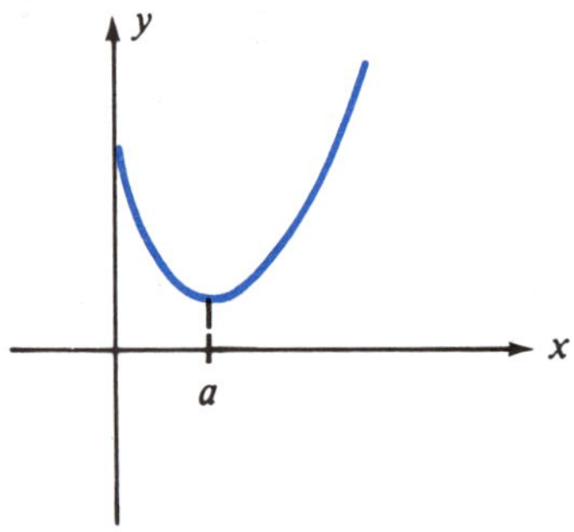

23.

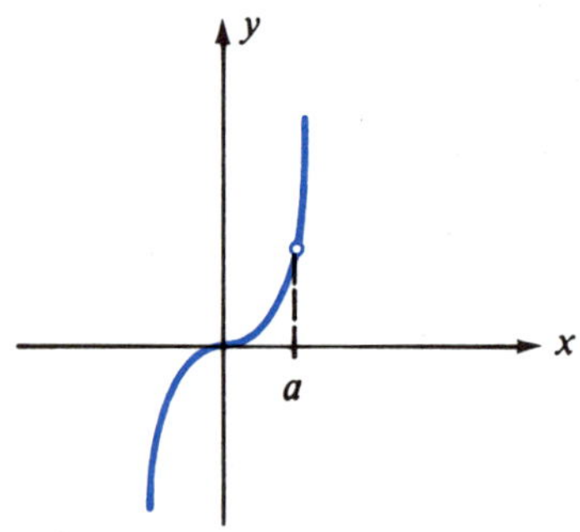

24.

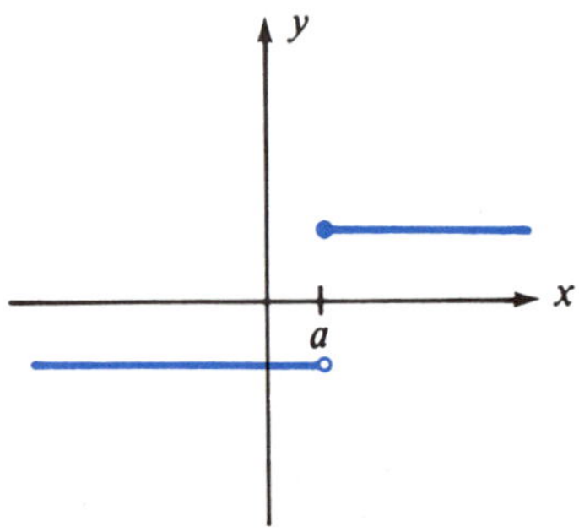

25.

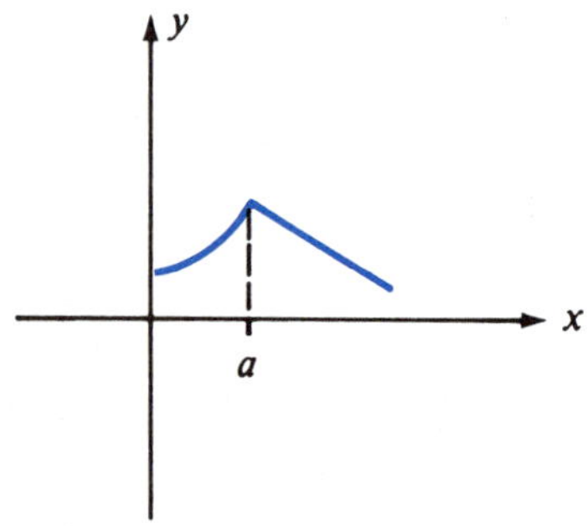

26.

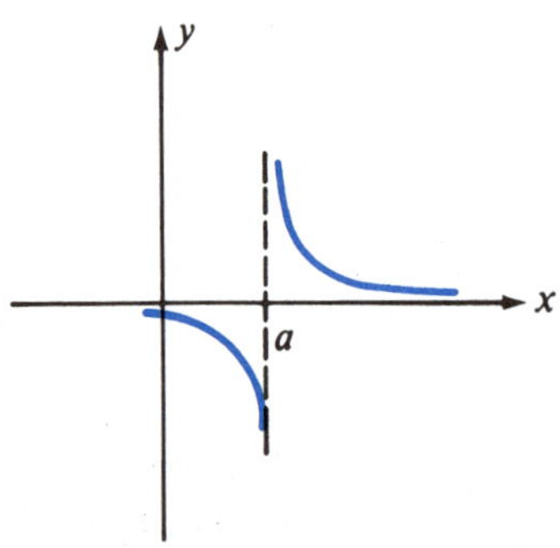

27.

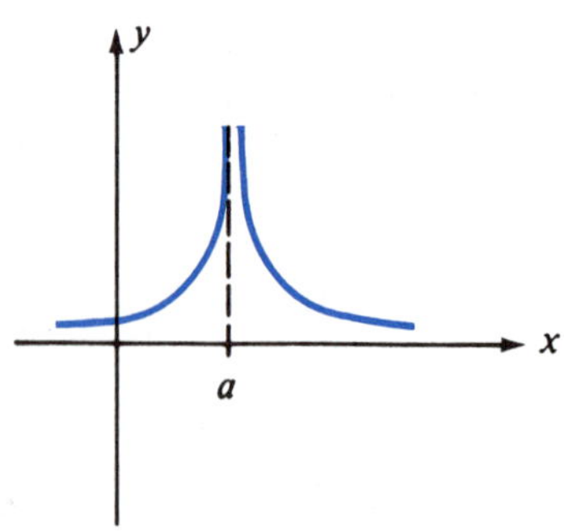

28. Sketch the graph of the function $f(x)=|x+1|$ and show that the function has no derivative at $x=-1$.

29. Sketch the graph of the function $f(x)=1/(x-1)$ and show that the function has no derivative at $x=1$.

***30.** Sketch the graph of the function $f(x)=x^{2/3}$. Is the function continuous at $x=0$? Does $f'(0)$ exist? Why or why not?

***31.** Prove that the derivative of the function $f(x)=|x|$ for $x \neq 0$ is given by

$$f'(x)=\begin{cases} 1 & \text{if } x>0 \\ -1 & \text{if } x<0 \end{cases}$$

Hint: recall the definition of the absolute value of a number.

10.5
Rules of Differentiation

The method used in the last section for computing the derivative of a function is based on a faithful interpretation of the definition of the derivative as the limit of a certain quotient. Thus, to compute the derivative f' of a function f (a process known as differentiation), we first computed the difference quotient

$$\frac{f(x+\Delta x)-f(x)}{\Delta x}$$

and then evaluated its limit as Δx approached zero. As you have probably observed, this process is tedious even for relatively simple functions.

In this section our main purpose is to derive certain rules of differentiation that will simplify the process. In what follows we shall use the expression $(d/dx)fx$ (read "dee, dee x of f of x") to mean "the derivative of f with respect to x at x", that is to say, $(d/dx)fx=f'(x)$.

RULE 1 *Derivative of a constant*
If $f(x)=c$, where c is a constant, then $f'(x)=0$.

Thus the derivative of a constant function is equal to zero. This is intuitively clear since the graph of the constant function is a straight line parallel to the x-axis, and hence has slope zero. To prove the result, we compute,

$$f'(x)=\lim_{\Delta x\to 0}\frac{f(x+\Delta x)-f(x)}{\Delta x}=\lim_{\Delta x\to 0}\frac{c-c}{\Delta x}=\lim_{\Delta x\to 0} 0=0$$

EXAMPLE 10.31 **(a)** If $f(x)=28$, then $f'(x)=\dfrac{d}{dx}(28)=0$.

(b) If $f(x) = -2$, then $f'(x) = \frac{d}{dx}(-2) = 0$. ■

RULE 2

The Power Rule
If $f(x) = x^n$, where n is a real number, then $f'(x) = nx^{n-1}$.

For a proof of this result for the special case $n = 2$ see Exercise Set 10.5, problem 59.

EXAMPLE 10.32 (a) If $f(x) = x$, then $f'(x) = \frac{d}{dx}(x) = 1 \cdot x^{1-1} = x^0 = 1$.

(b) If $f(x) = x^8$, then $f'(x) = \frac{d}{dx}(x^8) = 8x^7$.

(c) If $f(x) = x^{5/2}$, then $f'(x) = \frac{d}{dx}(x^{5/2}) = \frac{5}{2}x^{3/2}$.

(d) If $f(x) = \sqrt{x}$, then $f'(x) = \frac{d}{dx}(x^{1/2}) = \frac{1}{2}x^{-1/2} = \frac{1}{2\sqrt{x}}$ (Compare with Example 10.28.)

(e) If $f(x) = \frac{1}{\sqrt[3]{x}}$, then $f'(x) = \frac{d}{dx}\left(\frac{1}{\sqrt[3]{x}}\right) = \frac{d}{dx}(x^{-1/3}) = -\frac{1}{3}x^{-4/3} = -\frac{1}{3\sqrt[3]{x^4}}$ ■

RULE 3

Derivative of a constant multiple of a function
If $g(x) = cf(x)$, where c is a constant, then $g'(x) = cf'(x)$.

Thus the derivative of a constant times a differentiable function is equal to the constant times the derivative of the function. This result follows from the following computations.

$$\begin{aligned} g'(x) &= \lim_{\Delta x \to 0} \frac{g(x+\Delta x) - g(x)}{\Delta x} = \lim_{\Delta x \to 0} \frac{cf(x+\Delta x) - cf(x)}{\Delta x} \\ &= c \lim_{\Delta x \to 0} \frac{f(x+\Delta x) - f(x)}{\Delta x} \\ &= cf'(x) \end{aligned}$$

EXAMPLE 10.33 (a) If $f(x) = 5x^3$, then $f'(x) = \frac{d}{dx}(5x^3) = 5\frac{d}{dx}(x^3) = 15x^2$.

(b) If $f(x) = \frac{3}{\sqrt{x}}$, then $f'(x) = \frac{d}{dx}(3x^{-1/2}) = 3\left(-\frac{1}{2}x^{-3/2}\right) = -\frac{3}{2x^{3/2}}$. ■

RULE 4

The Sum Rule
If $h(x) = f(x) + g(x)$, then $h'(x) = f'(x) + g'(x)$. If $h(x) = f(x) - g(x)$, then $h'(x) = f'(x) - g'(x)$.

Thus, the derivative of the sum (difference) of two differentiable functions is equal to the sum (difference) of their derivatives. This result is easily extended to the case involving the sum and difference of any finite number of functions. To verify the rule for a sum of two functions, we compute

$$\begin{aligned} h'(x) &= \lim_{\Delta x \to 0} \frac{h(x+\Delta x)-h(x)}{\Delta x} \\ &= \lim_{\Delta x \to 0} \frac{[f(x+\Delta x)+g(x+\Delta x)]-[f(x)+g(x)]}{\Delta x} \\ &= \lim_{\Delta x \to 0} \frac{[f(x+\Delta x)-f(x)]+[g(x+\Delta x)-g(x)]}{\Delta x} \\ &= \lim_{\Delta x \to 0} \frac{f(x+\Delta x)-f(x)}{\Delta x} + \lim_{\Delta x \to 0} \frac{g(x+\Delta x)-g(x)}{\Delta x} \\ &= f'(x)+g'(x) \end{aligned}$$

EXAMPLE 10.34 Find the derivative of the function

$$f(x)=4x^5+3x^4-8x^2+x+3$$

SOLUTION

$$\begin{aligned} f'(x) &= \frac{d}{dx}(4x^5+3x^4-8x^2+x+3) \\ &= \frac{d}{dx}(4x^5)+\frac{d}{dx}(3x^4)-\frac{d}{dx}(8x^2)+\frac{d}{dx}(x)+\frac{d}{dx}(3) \\ &= 20x^4+12x^3-16x+1 \end{aligned}$$

■

RULE 5 *The Product Rule*

If $h(x)=f(x)g(x)$, then

$$h'(x)=f(x)g'(x)+f'(x)g(x)$$

Thus, the derivative of a product of two differentiable functions is given by a sum of two terms, each term being given by the product of one of the functions and the derivative of the other. *It is not given by the product of the derivatives.* This result may be extended to the case involving the product of any finite number of functions (see Exercise set 10.5, problem 60).

EXAMPLE 10.35 Find the derivative of the function

$$f(x)=(x^2+1)(x^3+5x^2+3x+2)$$

SOLUTION By the product rule

$$\begin{aligned} f'(x) &= (x^2+1)\frac{d}{dx}(x^3+5x^2+3x+2)+(x^3+5x^2+3x+2)\frac{d}{dx}(x^2+1) \\ &= (x^2+1)(3x^2+10x+3)+(x^3+5x^2+3x+2)(2x) \\ &= 5x^4+20x^3+12x^2+14x+3 \end{aligned}$$

■

EXAMPLE 10.36 Differentiate (that is, find the derivative of) the function

$$f(x)=x^3(\sqrt{x}+1)$$

SOLUTION By the product rule,

$$\begin{aligned}
f'(x)&=x^3\frac{d}{dx}(x^{1/2}+1)+(x^{1/2}+1)\frac{d}{dx}x^3\\
&=x^3\left(\frac{1}{2}x^{-1/2}\right)+(x^{1/2}+1)(3x^2)\\
&=\frac{1}{2}x^{5/2}+3x^{5/2}+3x^2\\
&=\frac{1}{2}x(7x^{3/2}+6x)
\end{aligned}$$

■

RULE 6 *The Quotient Rule*

If $h(x)=f(x)/g(x)$ and $g(x)\neq 0$, then

$$h'(x)=\frac{g(x)f'(x)-f(x)g'(x)}{g(x)^2}$$

For a proof of this result, see Exercise set 10.5, problem 61. As an aid to remembering the expression for $h'(x)$, observe that it has the following form

$$h'(x)=\frac{\text{(denominator)(derivative of numerator)}-\text{(numerator)(derivative of denominator)}}{\text{(square of denominator)}}$$

EXAMPLE 10.37 If

$$h(x)=\frac{x^2+3x+1}{x^3+2}$$

find the derivative h' of h.

SOLUTION By the quotient rule,

$$\begin{aligned}
h'(x)&=\frac{(x^3+2)\dfrac{d}{dx}(x^2+3x+1)-(x^2+3x+1)\dfrac{d}{dx}(x^3+2)}{(x^3+2)^2}\\
&=\frac{(x^3+2)(2x+3)-(x^2+3x+1)(3x^2)}{(x^3+2)^2}\\
&=\frac{-x^4-6x^3-3x^2+4x+6}{(x^3+2)^2}
\end{aligned}$$

■

EXAMPLE 10.38 Find the derivative h' of the function

$$h(x)=\frac{\sqrt{x}-1}{\sqrt{x}+1}$$

SOLUTION By the quotient rule, we find

$$\begin{aligned}
h'(x)&=\frac{(\sqrt{x}+1)\dfrac{d}{dx}(\sqrt{x}-1)-(\sqrt{x}-1)\dfrac{d}{dx}(\sqrt{x}+1)}{(\sqrt{x}+1)^2}\\
&=\frac{(x^{1/2}+1)\left(\dfrac{1}{2}x^{-1/2}\right)-(x^{1/2}-1)\left(\dfrac{1}{2}x^{-1/2}\right)}{(\sqrt{x}+1)^2}\\
&=\frac{1/2+(1/2)x^{-1/2}-1/2+(1/2)x^{-1/2}}{(\sqrt{x}+1)^2}\\
&=\frac{1}{\sqrt{x}(\sqrt{x}+1)^2}
\end{aligned}$$

■

EXAMPLE 10.39 Find the derivative h' of the function

$$h(t)=\frac{(t^2+1)(t^3-1)}{2t^2+1}$$

SOLUTION Using the quotient rule, we find

$$\begin{aligned}
h'(t)&=\frac{(2t^2+1)\dfrac{d}{dt}(t^2+1)(t^3-1)-(t^2+1)(t^3-1)\dfrac{d}{dt}(2t^2+1)}{(2t^2+1)^2}\\
&=\frac{(2t^2+1)[(t^2+1)(3t^2)+(2t)(t^3-1)]-(t^2+1)(t^3-1)(4t)}{(2t^2+1)^2}\\
&=\frac{(2t^2+1)t(5t^3+3t-2)-4t(t^5+t^3-t^2-1)}{(2t^2+1)^2}\\
&=\frac{t(6t^5+7t^3+3t+2)}{(2t^2+1)^2}
\end{aligned}$$

■

RULE 7 *Derivative of the exponential function*

(a) If $f(x)=e^x$, then $f'(x)=e^x$.

(b) If $f(x)=b^x$, where b is a positive constant, then $f'(x)=b^x(\ln b)$.

Thus the derivative of the exponential function with base e is equal to the function itself. The derivative of the exponential function with base other than e differs from the function by a constant factor, namely, the natural logarithm of the base b. Observe that Rule 7(b) reduces to Rule 7(a) when $b=e$ (since $\ln e=1$) as expected.

EXAMPLE 10.40 Compute the derivative of each of the following functions:

(a) $f(x)=x^2 e^x$

(b) $g(x)=3^x$

SOLUTION **(a)** The product rule gives

$$\begin{aligned} f'(x) &= \frac{d}{dx}(x^2 e^x) \\ &= x^2 \frac{d}{dx}(e^x) + e^x \frac{d}{dx}(x^2) \\ &= x^2 e^x + e^x(2x) \\ &= x e^x (x+2) \end{aligned}$$

(b) An application of Rule 7(b) immediately yields the result

$$g'(x)=3^x(\ln 3)$$ ■

RULE 8

Derivative of the logarithmic function

(a) If $f(x)=\ln x$, then $f'(x)=1/x \quad (x>0)$

(b) If $f(x)=\log_b x$, where $b>0$ and $b\neq 1$, then $f'(x)=1/x \ln b \quad (x>0)$

Thus, as in the case of the derivative of the exponential function involving a base other than the base e, the derivative of the logarithmic function with base b differs from the derivative of the natural logarithmic function by a constant factor; in this case the factor is $1/\ln b$. Observe that Rule 8(b) reduces to Rule 8(a) when $b=e$.

EXAMPLE 10.41 Compute the derivative of each of the following functions:

(a) $f(x)=\dfrac{\ln x}{x} \quad (x>0)$

(b) $g(x)=x \log_3 x \quad (x>0)$

SOLUTION **(a)** Using the quotient rule, we obtain

$$\begin{aligned} f'(x) &= \frac{x \cdot \frac{d}{dx}(\ln x) - (\ln x) \cdot \frac{d}{dx}(x)}{x^2} \\ &= \frac{x(1/x) - \ln x}{x^2} \\ &= \frac{1-\ln x}{x^2} \quad (x>0) \end{aligned}$$

(**b**) Using the product rule, we obtain

$$\begin{aligned} g'(x) &= \frac{d}{dx}(x \log_3 x) \\ &= x\frac{d}{dx}(\log_3 x) + (\log_3 x)\frac{d}{dx}(x) \\ &= x\left(\frac{1}{x \ln 3}\right) + \log_3 x \\ &= \frac{1}{\ln 3} + \log_3 x \quad (x > 0) \end{aligned}$$

■

EXAMPLE 10.42 A group of marine biologists at the Neptune Institute of Oceanography recommended a series of conservation measures over the next decade in order to save a certain species of whales from extinction. According to the experts, after implementing the conservation measures, the population of this species of whales will grow according to the rule $N(t) = 3t^3 + 2t^2 - 10t + 600$ $(0 \leq t \leq 10)$ where $N(t)$ denotes the population at the end of year t. Find the rate of growth of the whale population when $t = 2$ and $t = 6$. What would the population of the whales be eight years after implementing the conservation measures?

SOLUTION The rate of growth of the whale population at any time t is given by

$$N'(t) = 9t^2 + 4t - 10$$

In particular, when $t = 2$ and $t = 6$, we have

$$\begin{aligned} N'(2) &= 9(2)^2 + 4(2) - 10 \\ &= 34 \\ N'(6) &= 9(6)^2 + 4(6) - 10 \\ &= 338 \end{aligned}$$

so that the whale population's rate of growth after one year is 34 per year and after six years it is 338 per year.

The whale population at the end of the eighth year is given by

$$\begin{aligned} N(8) &= 3(8)^3 + 2(8)^2 - 10(8) + 600 \\ &= 2184 \end{aligned}$$

or 2,184 whales. The graph of the function N appears in Figure 10.17. Note the rapid growth of the population in the later years as the conservation measures begin to pay off compared to the growth in the early years.

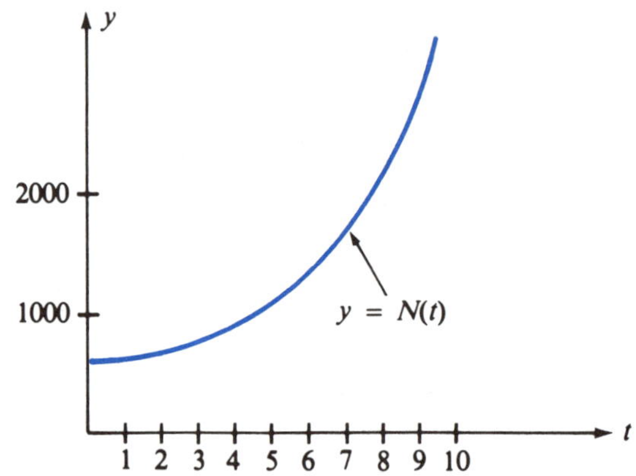

Figure 10.17

EXAMPLE 10.43 The altitude (in feet) of a rocket t seconds into flight is given by $s=f(t)=-t^3+96t^2+195t+5$ $(t\geq 0)$.

(a) Find an expression v for the velocity of the rocket at any time t.

(b) Compute the velocity of the rocket when $t=0$, 30, 50, 65 and 70. Interpret the results.

(c) Using the results from the solution to part **(b)** and the observation that at the highest point in its trajectory the velocity of the rocket is zero, find the maximum altitude attained by the rocket.

SOLUTION **(a)** The velocity of the rocket at any time t is given by

$$v=f'(t)=-3t^2+192t+195$$

(b) The velocity of the rocket when $t=0$, 30, 50, 65 and 70 is given by

$$\begin{aligned}
f'(0) &= -3(0)^2+192(0)+195=195\\
f'(30) &= -3(30)^2+192(30)+195=3255\\
f'(50) &= -3(50)^2+192(50)+195=2295\\
f'(65) &= -3(65)^2+192(65)+195=0\\
f'(70) &= -3(70)^2+192(70)+195=-1065
\end{aligned}$$

or 195, 3255, 2295, 0, and -1065 feet per second. Thus, the rocket has an initial velocity of 195 feet/second $(t=0)$ and begins to accelerate to at least a velocity of 3255 feet/second $(t=30)$. Fifty seconds into the flight, the velocity of the rocket is 2295 feet/second, which is less than that when $t=30$, meaning that the rocket begins to decelerate after an initial period of acceleration. (We shall learn how to determine its maximum velocity and when it is attained later on—see Example 11.32 in Chapter 11.) The deceleration continues, the velocity is 0 feet/second at $t=65$, and -1065 feet/second when $t=70$. The latter figure tells us that 70 seconds into the flight the rocket is heading back to earth with a speed of 1065 feet/second.

(c) The results of part (b) show that the velocity of the rocket is zero when $t = 65$. At this instant of time, its (maximum) altitude is given by

$$\begin{aligned} s = f(65) &= -(65)^3 + 96(65)^2 + 195(65) + 5 \\ &= 143{,}655 \end{aligned}$$

or 143,655 feet. This result will be established again in Chapter 11 (see Example 11.32). A sketch of the graph of the function f appears in Figure 10.18.

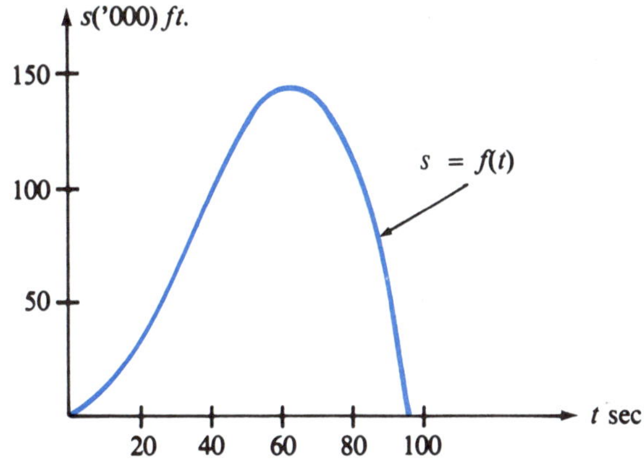

Figure 10.18

10.5 EXERCISES

In problems 1 through 50, find the derivative of the function f by using the rules of differentiation.

1. $f(x) = -3$

2. $f(x) = \pi$

3. $f(x) = x^5$

4. $f(x) = -2x^3$

5. $f(r) = 2\pi r$

6. $f(r) = \pi r^2$

7. $f(x) = \frac{3}{2}x^{30}$

8. $f(x) = 7x^{-12}$

9. $f(x) = 9x^{1/3}$

10. $f(x) = \frac{5}{4}x^{4/5}$

11. $f(x) = 3\sqrt{x}$

12. $f(x) = \frac{2}{\sqrt{x}}$

13. $f(x) = 5x^2 - 3x + 7$

14. $f(x) = x^4 - 2x^2 + 5$

15. $f(x) = 3x^{-1} + 4x^{-2} \quad (x \neq 0)$

16. $f(x) = -\frac{1}{3}(x^{-3} - x^6) \quad (x \neq 0)$

17. $f(x) = 5x^4 - \frac{2}{3}x^3 + x^2 - 3x + 1$

18. $f(t) = t^{-5} - 3t^{-3} + 2t^{-1} + 20 \quad (t \neq 0)$

19. $f(x)=\dfrac{x^3+2x^2+x-1}{3}$

20. $f(x)=(x^3-1)(x^2+1)$

21. $f(w)=(w^3-w^2+w-1)(w^2+2)$

22. $f(x)=(5x^{-1/2})(4x^{3/2}-3x)$

23. $f(x)=\dfrac{1}{5}x^5+(x^2+1)(x^2-x-1)+28$

24. $f(x)=\dfrac{3}{x^3}+\dfrac{4}{\sqrt{x}}+1 \quad (x\neq 0)$

25. $f(x)=\dfrac{1}{x^2+1}$

26. $f(x)=\dfrac{x}{x^2+1}$

27. $f(x)=\dfrac{x^2+1}{x} \quad (x\neq 0)$

28. $f(s)=\dfrac{s^2-4}{s+1} \quad (s\neq -1)$

29. $f(x)=\dfrac{x^3-2}{x^2+1}$

30. $f(x)=\dfrac{x-1}{2x+1} \quad \left(x\neq -\dfrac{1}{2}\right)$

31. $f(x)=\dfrac{x^2+2}{x^2+x+1}$

32. $f(t)=\dfrac{5}{(t+1)(t+2)} \quad (t\neq -1,-2)$

33. $f(x)=\dfrac{(x+1)(x^2+1)}{x-2}$

34. $f(x)=\dfrac{(x^2+1)(x^2+2)}{(x-1)(x-2)} \quad (x\neq 1, 2)$

35. $f(x)=e^{\pi}$

36. $f(x)=3e^x$

37. $f(x)=e^x+x$

38. $f(x)=2e^x-x^2$

39. $f(x)=e^x+x^e$

40. $f(x)=x^3e^x$

41. $f(x)=5^x$

42. $f(x)=\left(\dfrac{1}{2}\right)^x$

43. $f(x)=3\ln x$

44. $f(x)=-\dfrac{1}{2}\ln x$

45. $f(x)=\log_2 x$

46. $f(x)=2\log_{10} x$

47. $f(x)=\dfrac{2\ln x}{x} \quad (x\neq 0)$

48. $f(x)=x\ln x$

49. $f(x)=\dfrac{(e^x)(\ln x)}{x^2-1} \quad (x\neq -1, 1)$

50. $f(x)=\dfrac{3\log_{10} x}{x^3-1} \quad (x\neq 1)$

In problems 51 through 55 find the slope and the equation of the tangent line to the graph of the function f *at the specified point.*

51. $f(x)=x^4-3x^3+2x^2-x+1;\quad (1, 0)$

52. $f(x)=(x^3+1)(x^2-2);\quad (2, 18)$

53. $f(x)=\sqrt{x}+\dfrac{1}{\sqrt{x}};\quad (4, 5/2)$

54. $f(x)=\dfrac{x^2}{x+1};\quad (2, 4/3)$

55. $f(x)=\dfrac{x+1}{x^2+1}$; (1, 1)

56. Let $f(x)=x^3$.

(*a*) Find the point on the graph of f at which the tangent line is horizontal.

(*b*) Sketch the graph of f and exhibit the horizontal tangent line(s).

57. Let $f(x)=x^3+1$.

(*a*) Find the point(s) on the graph of f at which the slope of the tangent line(s) is equal to 12.

(*b*) Find the equation(s) of the tangent line(s) of part (*a*). Sketch the graph of f showing the tangent line(s).

58. Find the equation of the tangent line to the graph of the function $y=3e^x$ at the point (0, 3). Sketch the curve and the tangent line to the curve at that point.

59. Prove the *Power Rule* (Rule 2) for the special case $n=2$. *Hint*: Compute

$$\lim_{\Delta x\to 0}\frac{(x+\Delta x)^2-x^2}{\Delta x}$$

***60.** Extend the *Product Rule* for differentiation to the case involving the product of three differentiable functions: Let $h(x)=u(x)v(x)w(x)$ and show that $h'(x)=u(x)v(x)w'(x)+u(x)v'(x)w(x)+u'(x)v(x)w(x)$. *Hint*: Put $f(x)=u(x)v(x)$, $g(x)=w(x)$ and $h(x)=f(x)g(x)$ and apply the *Product Rule* to the function h.

***61.** Prove the *Quotient Rule* for differentiation (Rule 6). *Hint*: Verify the following steps:

1. $$\frac{h(x+\Delta x)-h(x)}{\Delta x}=\frac{f(x+\Delta x)g(x)-f(x)g(x+\Delta x)}{\Delta x\, g(x+\Delta x)g(x)}$$

2. By adding $[-f(x)g(x)+f(x)g(x)]$ to the numerator and simplifying,

$$\frac{h(x+\Delta x)-h(x)}{\Delta x}=\frac{1}{g(x+\Delta x)g(x)}\times\left\{\left[\frac{f(x+\Delta x)-f(x)}{\Delta x}\right]\cdot g(x)-\left[\frac{g(x+\Delta x)-g(x)}{\Delta x}\right]\cdot f(x)\right\}$$

3. $$h'(x)=\lim_{\Delta x\to 0}\frac{h(x+\Delta x)-h(x)}{\Delta x}=\frac{g(x)f'(x)-f(x)g'(x)}{[g(x)]^2}$$

62. A study, of a certain town in the Sun-belt prepared for the Chamber of Commerce, projected that the population of the town in the next 3 years will grow according to the rule $P(x)=50{,}000+30x^{3/2}+20x$ where $P(x)$ denotes the population x months from now. How fast will the population be increasing 9 months from now? 16 months from now?

63. Five years ago, the government of an island state in the Pacific launched an extensive propaganda campaign toward curbing the population growth in that country. According to the Department of Census, the population for the following four years was $P(x) = -(1/3)x^3 + 64x + 3000$ (measured in thousands of people) where x is measured in years and $x = 0$ at the start of the campaign. Find the rate of change of the population at the end of year one, two, three and four. Was the plan working?

64. The number of bacteria $N(t)$ in a certain culture t minutes after the introduction of an experimental bactericide obeys the rule $N(t) = 10{,}000/(1+t^2) + 2000$. Find the rate of change of the number of bacteria in the culture 1 minute after and 2 minutes after the introduction of the bactericide. What is the population of the bacteria in the culture 1 minute after the introduction of the bactericide? 2 minutes later?

65. From experience the Emory Secretarial School knows that the average student taking Advanced Typing will make progress according to the rule $N(t) = (60t + 180)/(t+6)$ $(t \geq 0)$ where $N(t)$ measures the number of words per minute the student can type after t weeks in the course.

(***a***) Find an expression for $N'(t)$.

(***b***) Compute $N'(t)$ for $t = 1$, 3, 4, and 7 and interpret your results.

(***c***) Sketch the graph of the function N. Does it confirm the results obtained in part (***b***)?

(***d***) What may the average student expect his or her typing speed to be at the end of the 12-week course?

66. A certain species of turtle faces extinction because truckloads of their eggs are collected by dealers to sell as aphrodisiacs. After implementing severe conservation measures, it is hoped that the turtle population will grow according to the rule $N(t) = 2t^3 + 3t^2 - 4t + 1000$ $(0 \leq t \leq 10)$ where $N(t)$ denotes the population at the end of year t. Find the rate of growth of the turtle population when $t = 2$ and $t = 8$. What will the population be ten years after the conservation measures are implemented?

67. The altitude (in feet) of a rocket t seconds into flight is given by $s = f(t) = -2t^3 + 114t^2 + 480t + 1$ $(t \geq 0)$

(***a***) Find an expression v for the velocity of the rocket at any time t.

(***b***) Compute the velocity of the rocket when $t = 0$, 20, 40 and 60. Interpret your results.

(***c***) Using the results from the solution to part (***b***), find the maximum altitude attained by the rocket.

68. During a test by the editors of an auto magazine, the stopping distance s (in feet) of the MacPherson X-2 racing car obeyed the rule $s = f(t) = 120t - 15t^2$ $(t \geq 0)$ where t is the time (in seconds) after the brakes had been applied.

(***a***) Find an expression for the velocity v of the car at any time t.

(*b*) What was the velocity of the car when the brakes were first applied?

(*c*) What was the stopping distance of the car for that particular test? *Hint*: the stopping time is found by setting $v = 0$.

10.6 The Chain Rule

In this section we introduce another rule of differentiation called the *Chain Rule.* When used in conjunction with the rules of differentiation developed in the last section, the Chain Rule enables us to enlarge the class of functions we are able to differentiate.

Consider the function $h(x) = (x^2 + x + 1)^2$. If we computed $h'(x)$ using only the rules of differentiation of the last section, then our approach might be to expand $h(x)$. Thus,

$$\begin{aligned} h(x) &= (x^2 + x + 1)^2 = (x^2 + x + 1)(x^2 + x + 1) \\ &= x^4 + 2x^3 + 3x^2 + 2x + 1 \end{aligned}$$

from which we find

$$\begin{aligned} h'(x) &= 4x^3 + 6x^2 + 6x + 2 \\ &= 2(x^2 + x + 1)(2x + 1) \end{aligned}$$

How about the function $H(x) = (x^2 + x + 1)^{100}$? This same technique may be used to find the derivative of the function H, but the amount of work involved in this case would be prodigious! Consider, also, the function $G(x) = \sqrt{x^2 + 1}$. For each of the two functions H and G, the rules of differentiation of the last section cannot be applied directly to compute the derivatives H' and G'.

Observe that both H and G are composite functions; that is, each is composed of or built up with simpler functions. For example, the function H is composed of two simpler functions $f(x) = x^2 + x + 1$ and $g(x) = x^{100}$ as follows:

$$\begin{aligned} H(x) &= g[f(x)] = f(x)^{100} \\ &= (x^2 + x + 1)^{100} \end{aligned}$$

In a similar manner, we see that the function G is composed of the two simpler functions $f(x) = x^2 + 1$ and $g(x) = \sqrt{x}$. Thus,

$$\begin{aligned} G(x) &= g[f(x)] = \sqrt{f(x)} \\ &= \sqrt{x^2 + 1} \end{aligned}$$

An approach to computing the derivative h' of a composite function $h(x) = g[f(x)]$ is based on the following observation: For each point x in the domain of $h(x)$, put $u = f(x)$ and $y = g[f(x)] = g(u)$ (see Figure 10.19).

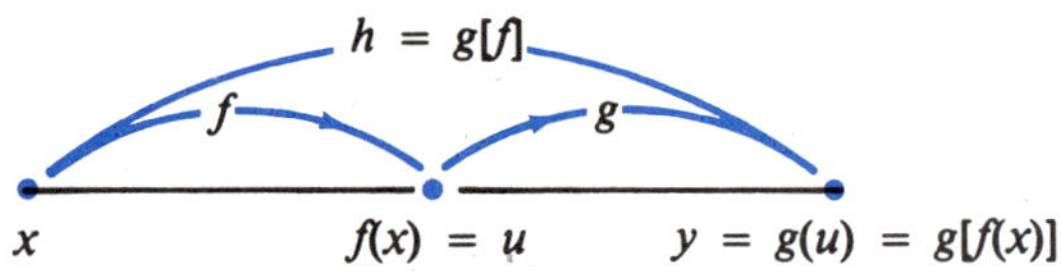

Figure 10.19

Since u is a function of x we may compute the derivative of u with respect to x, if f is a differentiable function, obtaining $du/dx = f'(x)$. Next, g is a function of u and, if g is a differentiable function, we may compute the derivative of g with respect to u, obtaining $dy/du = g'(u)$. Now, since the function h is the composition of the function g with the function f we suspect that the rule $h'(x)$ for the derivative h' of h will be given by an expression that involves the rules for the derivatives of f and g. That this is in fact the case is a consequence of the *Chain Rule* which we now state.

RULE 9

The Chain Rule

Let f and g be differentiable functions with rules given by $u = f(x)$ and $y = g(u)$. Then the composite function $y = h(x) = g(u) = g(f(x))$ is also differentiable and the rule for the derivative h' of h is given by

(10.10)
$$\frac{dy}{dx} = \frac{dy}{du} \cdot \frac{du}{dx}$$

or equivalently,

(10.11)
$$h'(x) = g'(f(x))f'(x)$$

Thus, the Chain Rule enables us to compute the derivative h' of the composite function $h(x) = g[f(x)]$ indirectly by computing separately the derivatives f' and g' of the "component functions" f and g (which are normally relatively simple processes) and then combining them according to Equation (10.10) or Equation (10.11) to obtain the required result.

EXAMPLE 10.44 Find the derivative of the composite function $h(x) = (x^2 + x + 1)^2$ of page 463, using the Chain Rule.

SOLUTION Put $u = f(x) = x^2 + x + 1$ so that $y = g(u) = u^2$. Then,

$$\frac{du}{dx} = f'(x) = 2x + 1 \quad \text{and} \quad \frac{dy}{du} = g'(u) = 2u.$$

Applying the Chain Rule, we obtain

$$h'(x)=\frac{dy}{dx}=\frac{dy}{du}\cdot\frac{du}{dx}=2u(2x+1)=2(x^2+x+1)(2x+1)$$

which agrees with the previous result. ■

Before proceeding further, let us look at a very useful corollary of the Chain Rule. It turns out that many of the composite functions, which have derivatives we wish to find, have the special form $h(x)=g[f(x)]$ where g is defined by the rule $g(x)=x^n$ (n, a real number); that is, $h(x)=[f(x)]^n$. In other words the function h is given by the power of some function f. The function h in Example 10.44 is this type, as are the functions H and G mentioned earlier. For such functions the following corollary of the Chain Rule will yield the respective derivatives with much less work than using the Chain Rule directly.

Corollary 1

The Chain Rule for Powers of Functions

If the function f is differentiable and h is the function defined by $h(x)=[f(x)]^n$ (n, a real number), then the derivative h' of h exists and is given by

(10.12) $$h'(x)=n[f(x)]^{n-1}f'(x)$$

To see this, we observe that $h(x)=g(f(x))$ where $g(x)=x^n$ so that, by virtue of the Chain Rule, we have

$$\begin{aligned}h'(x)&=g'(f(x))f'(x)\\&=n[f(x)]^{n-1}f'(x)\end{aligned}$$

since $g'(x)=nx^{n-1}$.

EXAMPLE 10.45 (Refer to Example 10.44.) Find the derivative h' of the function $h(x)=(x^2+x+1)^2$ using Corollary 1 of the Chain Rule.

SOLUTION A direct application of Corollary 1 immediately yields the result

$$\begin{aligned}h'(x)&=2(x^2+x+1)\frac{d}{dx}(x^2+x+1)\\&=2(x^2+x+1)(2x+1)\end{aligned}$$ ■

EXAMPLE 10.46 Find the derivative H' of the function $H(x)=(x^2+x+1)^{100}$.

SOLUTION Using Corollary 1 of the Chain Rule, we obtain

$$\begin{aligned}H'(x)&=100(x^2+x+1)^{99}\frac{d}{dx}(x^2+x+1)\\&=100(x^2+x+1)^{99}(2x+1)\end{aligned}$$ ■

EXAMPLE 10.47 Differentiate the function $G(x)=\sqrt{x^2+1}$.

SOLUTION We rewrite the function $G(x)$ as

$$G(x)=(x^2+1)^{1/2}$$

and apply Corollary 1 of the Chain Rule, obtaining

$$\begin{aligned} G'(x) &= \frac{1}{2}(x^2+1)^{-1/2}\frac{d}{dx}(x^2+1) \\ &= \frac{1}{2}(x^2+1)^{-1/2}\cdot 2x \\ &= \frac{x}{\sqrt{x^2+1}} \end{aligned}$$

■

EXAMPLE 10.48 Find the derivative of each of the following functions

(a) $y=(e^t+2)^{3/2}$

(b) $y=\sqrt{1+\ln x} \quad (x\geq 1)$

SOLUTION **(a)** Using Corollary 1 of the Chain Rule and Rule 7(a), we find

$$\begin{aligned} \frac{dy}{dt} &= \frac{3}{2}(e^t+2)^{1/2}\frac{d}{dt}(e^t+2) \\ &= \frac{3}{2}(e^t+2)^{1/2}e^t \\ &= \frac{3}{2}e^t(e^t+2)^{1/2} \end{aligned}$$

(b) Using Corollary 1 of the Chain Rule and Rule 8(a), we obtain

$$\begin{aligned} \frac{dy}{dx} &= \frac{1}{2}(1+\ln x)^{-1/2}\frac{d}{dx}(1+\ln x) \\ &= \frac{1}{2}(1+\ln x)^{-1/2}\left(\frac{1}{x}\right) \\ &= \frac{1}{2x\sqrt{1+\ln x}} \end{aligned}$$

■

Another type of composite function, often encountered in practice, has the form $h=g[f(x)]$ where $g(x)=e^x$, that is, $h(x)=g[f(x)]=e^{f(x)}$, and f is a differentiable function of x. In the special case where f is the identity function $f(x)=x$, $h(x)=e^x$, so that the derivative of h is, using Rule 7(a) (Section 10.5), given by $h'(x)=e^x$. In general, to find the derivative of the composite function $h(x)=e^{f(x)}$, we appeal to the following corollary of the Chain Rule.

Corollary 2 *The Chain Rule for exponential functions*
If the function f is differentiable and h is the function defined by $h(x)=e^{f(x)}$, then the derivative h' of h exists and is given by

$$h'(x)=e^{f(x)}\cdot f'(x) \tag{10.13}$$

To see this, observe that $h(x)=g[f(x)]$ where $g(x)=e^x$, so that by virtue of the Chain Rule, we have

$$\begin{aligned} h'(x) &= g'(f(x))f'(x) \\ &= e^{f(x)}f'(x) \end{aligned}$$

since $g'(x)=e^x$.

EXAMPLE 10.49 Find the derivative of the function $f(x)=e^{x^2}$.

SOLUTION Using (10.13) we see immediately that

$$\begin{aligned} f'(x) &= e^{x2}\frac{d}{dx}(x^2) \\ &= 2x\,e^{x2} \end{aligned}$$

■

EXAMPLE 10.50 Differentiate the function $y=e^{-x2+x-1}$.

SOLUTION Using (10.13) we find

$$\begin{aligned} \frac{dy}{dx} &= e^{-x2+x-1}\frac{d}{dx}(-x^2+x-1) \\ &= (-2x+1)\,e^{-x2+x-1} \end{aligned}$$

■

EXAMPLE 10.51 In Section 5.4, we discussed some practical applications of the exponential function $Q(t)=Q_0\,e^{kt}$ where Q_0 and k are positive constants and $t\in[0,\infty)$. A quantity $Q(t)$ growing according to this law experiences *exponential growth*. Show that for a quantity $Q(t)$ experiencing exponential growth, the rate of growth of the quantity, $Q'(t)$, at any time t is directly proportional to the amount of the quantity present.

SOLUTION Using Corollary 2 of the Chain Rule we compute the derivative Q' of the function Q. Thus,

$$\begin{aligned} Q'(t) &= Q_0\,e^{kt}\frac{d}{dt}(kt) \\ &= Q_0\,e^{kt}(k) \\ &= kQ_0\,e^{kt} \\ &= kQ(t) \end{aligned}$$

which is the desired conclusion. ■

We shall now consider the differentiation of composite functions of the form $h = g[f(x)]$ where $g(x) = \ln x\,(x > 0)$. Besides being differentiable, we also require that the function f have a range consisting of positive numbers so that $h(x) = g[f(x)] = \ln f(x)$ is defined. Observe that, in the special case $f(x) = x$, $h(x) = \ln x$ so that the derivative of h, is, by Rule 8(a) (Section 10.5), given by $h'(x) = 1/x$. In the general case, to find the derivative of the composite function $h(x) = \ln f(x)$ we appeal to the following corollary of the Chain Rule.

Corollary 3

The Chain Rule for logarithmic functions

If the function f is differentiable and h is the function defined by $h(x) = \ln f(x)$, then the derivative h' of h exists and is given by

(10.14) $$h'(x) = \frac{f'(x)}{f(x)} \quad (f(x) > 0)$$

To see this, observe that $h(x) = g[f(x)]$ where $g(x) = \ln x$ $(x > 0)$. Since $g'(x) = 1/x$ we have, using the Chain Rule,

$$\begin{aligned} h'(x) &= g'(f(x))f'(x) \\ &= \frac{1}{f(x)} f'(x) \\ &= \frac{f'(x)}{f(x)} \end{aligned}$$

EXAMPLE 10.52 Find the derivative of the function $f(x) = \ln (x^2 + 1)$.

SOLUTION Using (10.14) we see immediately that

$$f'(x) = \frac{\frac{d}{dx}(x^2+1)}{x^2+1} = \frac{2x}{x^2+1}$$ ■

EXAMPLE 10.53 Differentiate the function $y = \ln [(x^2+1)(x^3+2)^6]$.

SOLUTION Using (10.14) and the Product Rule, we have

$$\begin{aligned} y' = \frac{dy}{dx} &= \frac{\frac{d}{dx}[(x^2+1)(x^3+2)^6]}{(x^2+1)(x^3+2)^6} \\ &= \frac{(x^2+1)\cdot\frac{d}{dx}(x^3+2)^6 + (x^3+2)^6\cdot\frac{d}{dx}(x^2+1)}{(x^2+1)(x^3+2)^6} \\ &= \frac{(x^2+1)6(x^3+2)^5(3x^2) + (x^3+2)^6(2x)}{(x^2+1)(x^3+2)^6} \\ &= \frac{2x(10x^3+9x+2)}{(x^2+1)(x^3+2)} \end{aligned}$$

Note: We have used Corollary 1 here.

ALTERNATE SOLUTION We first rewrite the given function using the following properties of logarithms.

$$\begin{aligned} y &= \ln [(x^2+1)(x^3+2)^6] \\ &= \ln (x^2+1) + \ln (x^3+2)^6 \\ &= \ln (x^2+1) + 6 \ln (x^3+2) \end{aligned}$$

Therefore, differentiating and using (10.14), we obtain

$$\begin{aligned} y' &= \frac{\frac{d}{dx}(x^2+1)}{x^2+1} + \frac{6\frac{d}{dx}(x^3+2)}{x^3+2} \\ &= \frac{2x}{x^2+1} + \frac{6(3x^2)}{x^3+2} \\ &= \frac{2x^4+4x+18x^4+18x^2}{(x^2+1)(x^3+2)} \\ &= \frac{2x(10x^3+9x+2)}{(x^2+1)(x^3+2)} \quad \text{as before.} \end{aligned}$$

■

EXAMPLE 10.54 Find the derivative of the function $g(t) = \ln (t^2 e^{-t^2})$.

SOLUTION Here, again to save a lot of work, we simplify the given expression first using the properties of logarithms. We have

$$\begin{aligned} g(t) &= \ln (t^2 e^{-t^2}) \\ &= \ln t^2 + \ln e^{-t^2} \\ &= 2 \ln t - t^2 \qquad \text{(since } \ln e = 1!\text{)} \end{aligned}$$

Therefore,

$$\begin{aligned} g'(t) &= \frac{2}{t} - 2t \\ &= \frac{2(1-t^2)}{t} \end{aligned}$$

■

10.6 EXERCISES

In problems 1 through 5, find the derivative dy/dx *(a) by finding the composite function* y = g(f(x)) *and then differentiating it, and (b) by computing* dy/du *and* du/dx *and then applying the Chain Rule.*

1. $y = g(u) = u^2$ and $u = f(x) = x^3 + 1$
2. $y = g(u) = u^3$ and $u = f(x) = x^2 + 1$
3. $y = g(u) = u^3 + u^2 + 1$ and $u = f(x) = x^2 + x + 1$

4. $y = g(u) = u^3(u^2 - 1)$ and $u = f(x) = x^2 + 2$

5. $y = g(u) = \dfrac{u}{u^2 + 1}$ and $u = f(x) = x^2 - 1$

In problems 6 through 14, find dy/dx *by computing* dy/du *and* du/dx *and then applying the Chain Rule.*

6. $y = g(u) = u^{4/3}$ and $u = f(x) = 3x^2 - 1$

7. $y = g(u) = \sqrt{u}$ and $u = f(x) = 7x - 2x^2$

8. $y = g(u) = 2u^2 + 4u + 1$ and $u = f(x) = 1/(x^2 + 2)$

9. $y = g(u) = u^{-2/3}$ and $u = f(x) = 2x^3 - x^2 + 1$

10. $y = g(u) = 1/u$ and $u = f(x) = 2x^2 - 1$

11. $y = g(u) = \ln u$ and $u = f(x) = 3x^2 + 2x$

12. $y = g(u) = e^u$ and $u = f(x) = x^2 + 2x$

13. $y = g(u) = u^2 e^u$ and $u = f(x) = (x^2 + 1)^5$

14. $y = g(u) = u \ln u$ and $u = f(x) = (x^2 + 1)^4$

In problems 15 through 39, find the derivative of the given function using an appropriate corollary of the Chain Rule.

15. $f(x) = (x^2 + 2)^5$

16. $f(x) = (4x^3 - 3x^2 + 2x - 1)^{10}$

17. $g(t) = \sqrt{3t^2 - t}$

18. $y = \dfrac{1}{(4x^4 + x)^{3/2}}$

19. $y = (4t^3 - 3t^2 + 1)^3$

20. $y = (5t^3 + 2t^2 - t + 4)^{-3}$

21. $f(x) = x^2(3x^2 + 1)^5$

22. $f(x) = \sqrt[3]{1 - x^2}$

23. $g(u) = (1 + u^2)^5(1 - 2u^2)^8$

24. $f(v) = 4v^4 + (4v)^4$

25. $f(x) = (x^2 - x + 1)^8\sqrt{x^4 - 1}$

26. $s = (2t^2 + 1)^4(t^3 - t - 1)^{3/2}$

27. $f(u) = \dfrac{(u^2 + u - 1)^3}{u^3 - 1}$

28. $h(x) = \dfrac{(3x^2 + 1)^3}{(x^2 - 1)^4}$

*29. $y = \sqrt{x + \sqrt{x^2 - 1}}$

*30. $y = [(x^2 + x - 1)^5 - 1]^{3/2}$

31. $f(x) = (e^x + 1)^{25}$

32. $g(t) = (e^t + 1)^{10}(e^t - 2)^5$

33. $y = \dfrac{e^x}{(e^x + 1)^2}$

34. $y = \dfrac{e^x + 1}{\sqrt{2e^x - 1}}$

35. $f(x) = (1 + 2 \ln x)^{5/2}$

36. $g(x) = \ln x\sqrt{1 + \ln x}$

37. $y = e^{x^2} \ln x$

38. $y = \dfrac{(1 + 2e^x)^3}{(1 + \ln x)^2}$

*39. $f(x) = \sqrt{(1 + \ln x)^4 + e^x}$

40. Find thc equation of the tangent line to the graph of $y=(1-x)(x^2-1)^2$ at the point (2, −9).

41. Find the equation of the tangent line to the graph of $y=8/\sqrt{x^2+6x}$ at the point (2, 2).

42. Find the equation of the tangent line to the graph of $y=e^{-x2}$ at the point $(1, 1/e)$.

43. Find the equation of the tangent line to the graph of $y=\ln x^2$ at the point (2, ln 4).

44. Derive Rule 7(b) (Section 10.5) from Rule 7(a). *Hint*: Show that $y=f(x)=b^x$ may be written as $y=f(x)=e^{(\ln b)x}$.

45. The number of viewers of a television series introduced several years ago is approximated by the function

$$N(x)=(60+2x)^{2/3} \quad (1\leq x\leq 26)$$

where $N(x)$ (measured in millions) denotes the number of weekly viewers of the series in the xth week. Find the rate of increase of the weekly audience at the end of the second week; the twelfth week. How many viewers were there in the second week? in the twenty-fourth week?

46. The pulse-rate (the number of beats per minute) of a long distance runner t seconds after leaving the starting line is given by

$$P(t)=\frac{300\sqrt{(1/2)t^2+2t+25}}{t+25} \quad (t\geq 0)$$

Compute $P'(t)$. How fast is the athlete's pulse-rate increasing 10 seconds into the run? 60 seconds into the run? 2 minutes into the run? What is his pulse rate 2 minutes into the run?

47. Government economists of a developing country determined that the purchase of imported perfume is related to a proposed "luxury tax" by the formula

$$N(x)=\sqrt{10{,}000-40x-0.02x^2} \quad (0\leq x\leq 200)$$

where $N(x)$ measures the percentage of normal consumption of perfume when a "luxury tax" of x per cent is imposed on the product. Find the rate of change of $N(x)$ for a tax of 10%, 100% and 150%.

48. The Lady Bug, a woman's apparel chain store, found that t days, $(0\leq t\leq 5)$, after the end of a sales promotion the volume of sales was given by

$$S(t)=20{,}000(1+e^{-0.5t}) \quad (0\leq t\leq 5)$$

dollars. Find the rate of change of the company's sales volume when $t=1$, $t=2$, $t=3$, and $t=4$.

10.7

Marginal Functions in Economics

The derivative is an indispensable tool in marginal analysis, the study of the rate of change of economic quantities. For example, an economist is not merely concerned with the value of the gross national product of an economy at a given time but is equally concerned with the rate at which it is growing or declining. In the same vein, a manufacturer is not only interested in the total cost corresponding to a certain level of production of a commodity, but is also interested in the rate of change of the total cost with respect to the level of production, and so on. Let us begin with an example to explain the meaning of the adjective *marginal* as used by economists.

EXAMPLE 10.55 Suppose the total cost in dollars incurred per week by the Polaraire Company for manufacturing x units of refrigerators is given by the total cost function $C(x) = 8000 + 200x - 0.2x^2$ $(0 \leq x \leq 400)$.

(**a**) What is the actual cost incurred for manufacturing the 251st unit?

(**b**) Find the rate of change of the total cost with respect to x when $x = 250$.

(**c**) Compare the results obtained in parts (**a**) and (**b**).

SOLUTION (**a**) The actual cost incurred in producing the 251st refrigerator is the difference between the total cost incurred in producing the first 251 units and the total cost for producing the first 250 units. Thus, the actual cost is given by

$$\begin{aligned} C(251) - C(250) &= [8000 + 200(251) - 0.2(251)^2] - [8000 + 200(250) - 0.2(250)^2] \\ &= 45599.8 - 45500 \\ &= 99.80 \quad \text{or} \quad \$99.80 \end{aligned}$$

(**b**) The rate of change of the total cost function C with respect to x is given by the derivative of C, that is, $C'(x) = 200 - 0.4x$. Thus, when the level of production is 250 units, the rate of change of the total cost with respect to x is given by

$$\begin{aligned} C'(250) &= 200 - 0.4(250) \\ &= 100 \quad \text{or} \quad \$100 \end{aligned}$$

(**c**) From the solution to part (**a**), we know that the actual cost for producing the 251st refrigerator is \$99.80. This answer is very closely approximated by the answer, \$100, which is the solution to part (**b**). To see why this is so, observe that the difference $C(251) - C(250)$ may be written in the form

$$\frac{C(251) - C(250)}{1} = \frac{C(250+1) - C(250)}{1} = \frac{C(250+\Delta x) - C(250)}{\Delta x}$$

where $\Delta x = 1$. In other words, the difference $C(251) - C(250)$ is precisely the average rate of change of the total cost function C over the interval [250, 251] or, equivalently, the slope of the secant line through the points (250, 45,500) and (251,

45,599.8). On the other hand, the number $C'(250)=100$ is the (instantaneous) rate of change of the total cost function C at $x=250$ or, equivalently, the slope of the tangent line to the graph of C at $x=250$. Now, (see Section 10.3) when Δx is small, the average rate of change of the function C is a good approximation to the (instantaneous) rate of change of the function C, or, equivalently, the slope of the secant line through the points in question is a good approximation to the slope of the tangent line through the point in question. Thus, we may expect

$$C(251)-C(250)=\frac{C(251)-C(250)}{1}=\frac{C(250+\Delta x)-C(250)}{\Delta x}$$

$$\approx \lim_{\Delta x\to 0}\frac{C(250+\Delta x)-C(250)}{\Delta x}=C'(250)$$

which is precisely the case in this example. ■

marginal cost

marginal cost function

Knowing the actual cost incurred producing an additional unit of a certain commodity given that the plant is already at a certain level of operation is very important in business applications. This cost is called the *marginal cost.* But, as we saw in the preceding example, this quantity is suitably approximated by the rate of change of the relevant total cost function evaluated at the appropriate point. For this reason, economists have defined the *marginal cost function* to be the derivative of the corresponding total cost function. In other words, if C is a total cost function then the marginal cost function is defined to be its derivative C'. Thus, the adjective "marginal" is synonymous with "derivative of".

EXAMPLE 10.56 A subsidiary of the Elektra Electronics Company manufactures a programmable electronic pocket calculator. The management of the company determined that the daily total cost of production of these calculators (in dollars) obeys the rule $C(x)=0.0001x^3-0.08x^2+40x+5000$, where x stands for the number of calculators produced.

(**a**) Find the marginal cost function.

(**b**) What is the marginal cost when $x=200$, 300, 400 and 600?

(**c**) Discuss the results obtained in part (**b**).

SOLUTION (**a**) The marginal cost function C' is given by the derivative of the total cost function C. Thus,

$$C'(x)=0.0003x^2-0.16x+40$$

(**b**) The marginal cost when $x=200$, 300, 400 and 600 is given by

$$C'(200)=0.0003(200)^2-0.16(200)+40=20$$
$$C'(300)=0.0003(300)^2-0.16(300)+40=19$$
$$C'(400)=0.0003(400)^2-0.16(400)+40=24$$
$$C'(600)=0.0003(600)^2-0.16(600)+40=52$$

or \$20, \$19, \$24 and \$52, respectively.

(**c**) From the results of part (**b**) we see that the actual cost incurred by the company for producing the 201st calculator (assuming the first two hundred had already been produced) is approximately \$20. The actual cost incurred for producing one additional unit when the level of production is already 300 calculators is approximately \$19, and so on. Observe that when the level of production is already 600 units, the actual cost of producing one additional unit is approximately \$52. The higher cost for producing this additional unit when the level of production is 600 units may be due to several factors. Among them are excessive costs incurred because of overtime or higher maintenance, or production breakdown because of greater stress and strains placed upon the equipment, and so on. The graph of the total cost function appears in Figure 10.20.

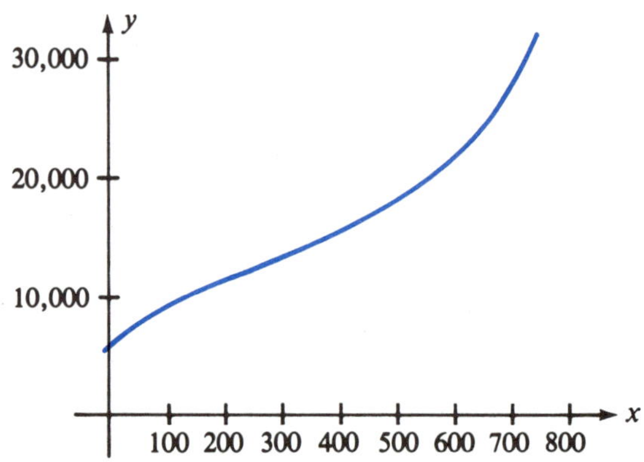

Figure 10.20

average cost

We now introduce another marginal concept closely related to the marginal cost. To this end, let $C(x)$ denote the total cost incurred in the production of x units of a certain commodity. Then the *average cost* of producing x units of the commodity is obtained by dividing the total cost incurred in the production by the number of units produced. Thus, if we let $A(x)$ denote the average cost of producing x units of the commodity, then

$$A(x) = \frac{C(x)}{x}$$

average and marginal average cost functions

The function A is called the *average cost function*. The derivative A' of the average cost function A is called the *marginal average cost function*. It measures the rate of change of the average cost function with respect to the number of units of the commodity produced.

EXAMPLE 10.57 The total cost for producing x units of a certain commodity is given by $C(x) = 400 + 20x$ dollars.

(**a**) Find the average cost function A.

(**b**) Find the marginal average cost function A'.

(**c**) Interpret the results obtained in parts (**a**) and (**b**).

SOLUTION (a) The average cost function is given by

$$A(x)=\frac{C(x)}{x}=\frac{400+20x}{x}$$
$$=20+\frac{400}{x}$$

(b) The marginal average cost function is

$$A'(x)=-\frac{400}{x^2}$$

(c) Since the marginal average cost function is negative for all admissible values of x, the rate of change of the average cost function A is negative for all $x>0$; that is, $A(x)$ decreases as x increases. However, the graph of A always lies above the horizontal line $y=20$ but it approaches it since

$$\lim_{x\to\infty} A(x)=\lim_{x\to\infty}\left(20+\frac{400}{x}\right)$$
$$=20$$

A sketch of the graph of the function $A(x)$ appears in Figure 10.21. The above result is fully expected if we consider its economic implications. Note that as the level of production increases, the fixed cost per unit of production, represented by the term $(400/x)$, drops steadily. The average cost should approach the constant unit cost of production, which is \$20 in this case.

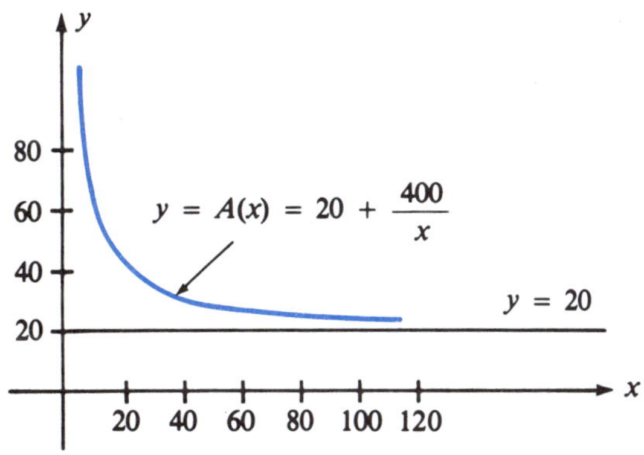

Figure 10.21

EXAMPLE 10.58 Once again consider the subsidiary of the Elektra Electronics Company whose daily total cost for producing their programmable electronic calculators is given by $C(x)=0.0001x^3-0.08x^2+40x+5000$ dollars where x stands for the number of calculators produced (see Example 10.56).

(a) Find the average cost function A.

(b) Find the marginal average cost function A'. Compute $A'(500)$.

(c) Sketch the graph of the function A and discuss the results obtained in parts **(a)** and **(b)**.

SOLUTION **(a)** The average cost function is given by

$$A(x) = \frac{C(x)}{x} = 0.0001x^2 - 0.08x + 40 + \frac{5000}{x}$$

(b) The marginal average cost function is given by

$$A'(x) = 0.0002x - 0.08 - \frac{5000}{x^2}$$

Also,
$$A'(500) = 0.0002(500) - 0.08 - \frac{5000}{(500)^2}$$
$$= 0$$

(c) To sketch the graph of the function A, observe that if x is a small positive number, then $A(x) > 0$. Furthermore, $A(x)$ becomes arbitrarily large as x approaches 0 from the right since the term $(5000/x)$ becomes arbitrarily large as x approaches zero. Next, the result $A'(500) = 0$ obtained in part **(b)** tells us that the tangent line to the graph of the function A is horizontal at the point (500, 35) on the graph. Finally, plotting the points on the graph corresponding to, say, $x = 100, 200, 300, \ldots, 900$, we obtain the sketch in Figure 10.22. As expected, the average cost drops as the level of production increases. But in this case, as opposed to Example 10.57, it reaches a minimum value of \$35 corresponding to a production level of 500 and increases thereafter (see Example 11.33, Chapter 11). This phenomenon is typical in situations where the marginal cost increases from some point on as production increases (see Example 10.56). Note that in Example 10.57, the marginal cost remains constant at any level of production.

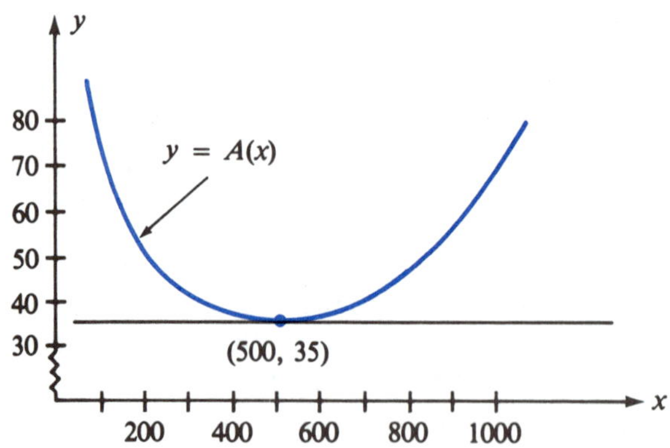

Figure 10.22

Another marginal concept is associated with the total revenue function. Recall that in Section 2.2 we considered total revenue functions that have the form $R(x)=px$ where x is the number of units of a certain commodity sold and where p, the unit selling price, was assumed to be a constant. In general, however, the unit selling price p of a commodity is related to the quantity x of the commodity demanded (see Section 2.5). Solving the demand equation for p in terms of x we obtain the unit price function f given by

$$p=f(x)$$

Thus, in general, the total revenue function R is given by

$$R(x)=px=xf(x)$$

marginal revenue function

where f is the unit price function. Now, given a total revenue function R, the *marginal revenue function* is defined to be the derivative R' of the function R and it measures the rate of change of the total revenue function.

EXAMPLE 10.59 Suppose the relationship between the unit price p in dollars and the quantity demanded, x, of the Acrosonic Model F loudspeaker systems is given by the equation $p=-0.02x+400$ $(0 \leq x \leq 20{,}000)$.

(a) Find the total revenue function R.

(b) Find the marginal revenue function R'.

(c) Compute $R'(2000)$ and interpret the result obtained.

SOLUTION **(a)** The total revenue function R is given by

$$\begin{aligned} R(x) &= px \\ &= x(-0.02x+400) \\ &= -0.02x^2+400x \quad (0 \leq x \leq 20{,}000) \end{aligned}$$

(b) The marginal revenue function R' is given by

$$R'(x)=-0.04x+400$$

(c)

$$\begin{aligned} R'(2000) &= -0.04(2000)+400 \\ &= 320 \end{aligned}$$

Thus, the actual revenue to be realized from the sale of the 2001st loudspeaker system is approximately \$320. ■

marginal profit function

Our final example of a marginal function involves the total profit function. Recall that the total profit function P is given by $P(x)=R(x)-C(x)$ where R and C are the total revenue and total cost functions and x is the number of units of a commodity produced and sold. The *marginal profit function* measures the rate of change of the total profit function P and $P'(x)$ provides us with a good approximation to the actual profit (loss) to be realized from the sale of the $(x+1)$st unit of the commodity (assuming the xth unit has been sold).

EXAMPLE 10.60 (Refer to Example 10.59.) Suppose the total cost for producing x units of the Acrosonic Model F loudspeaker system is $C(x)=100x+200{,}000$ dollars.

(a) Find the total profit function P.

(b) Find the marginal profit function P'.

(c) Compute $P'(2000)$ and interpret your result.

(d) Sketch the graph of the total profit function P.

SOLUTION **(a)** From the solution to part (**a**) of Example 10.59, we have $R(x)=-0.02x^2+400x$. Thus the required total profit function P is given by

$$\begin{aligned}P(x)&=R(x)-C(x)\\&=(-0.02x^2+400x)-(100x+200{,}000)\\&=-0.02x^2+300x-200{,}000\end{aligned}$$

(b) The marginal profit function P' is given by

$$P'(x)=-0.04x+300$$

(c)

$$\begin{aligned}P'(2000)&=-0.04(2000)+300\\&=220\end{aligned}$$

Thus the actual profit realized from the sale of the 2001st loudspeaker system is approximately \$220.

(d) The graph of the profit function P appears in Figure 10.23.

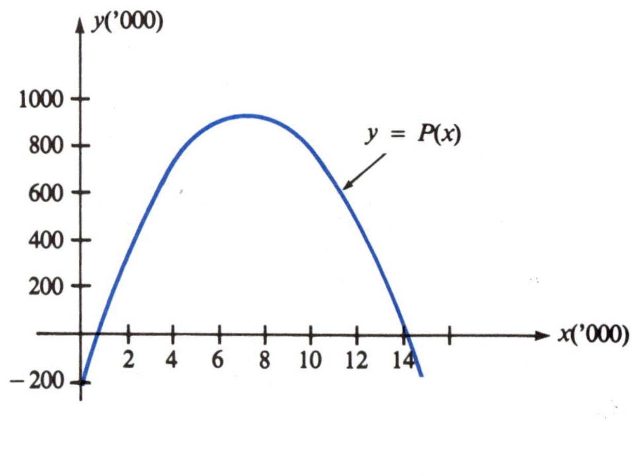

Figure 10.23

10.7 EXERCISES

1. The total cost in dollars incurred by the Lincoln Record Company per week in pressing x long playing records is given by the total cost function $C(x) = 2000 + 2x - 0.0001x^2$ $(0 \leq x \leq 6000)$.

(***a***) What is the actual cost incurred in the production of the 1001st record? the 2001st record?

(***b***) What is the marginal cost when $x = 1000$; when $x = 2000$?

2. A division of Ditton Industries manufactures the "Futura" model micro-wave oven. Given that the daily cost of producing these micro-wave ovens (in dollars) obeys the rule $C(x) = 0.0002x^3 - 0.06x^2 + 120x + 5000$ where x stands for the number of units produced,

(***a***) What is the actual cost incurred in manufacturing the 101st oven? the 201st oven? the 301st oven?

(***b***) What is the marginal cost when $x = 100$; when $x = 200$; when $x = 300$?

3. The management of the Thermo-Master Company, which manufactures an indoor-outdoor thermometer in its Mexico subsidiary, has estimated that the total weekly cost for producing x units of thermometers is given by $C(x) = 5000 + 2x$ dollars.

(***a***) Find the average cost function A.

(***b***) Find the marginal average cost function A'.

(***c***) Interpret your results.

4. Find the average cost function A and the marginal average cost function A' associated with the total cost function C of problem 1.

5. Find the average cost function A and the marginal average cost function A' associated with the total cost function C of problem 2.

6. The management of the Acrosonic Company plans to market the "Electro-Stat", an electro-static speaker system. The marketing department has determined that the demand for these speakers will obey the relationship $p = -0.04x + 800$ $(0 \leq x \leq 20{,}000)$ where p denotes the unit price (in dollars) of the speakers and x denotes the quantity demanded.

(***a***) Find the total revenue function R.

(***b***) Find the marginal revenue function R'.

(***c***) Compute $R'(5000)$ and interpret your result.

7. Refer to problem 6. The production department of the Acrosonic Company estimates that the total cost incurred by the company in manufacturing x units of the "Electro-Stat" speaker systems in the first year of production will be $C(x) = 200x + 300{,}000$ dollars.

(***a***) Find the total profit function P.

(***b***) Find the marginal profit function P'.

(*c*) Compute $P'(5000)$ and $P'(8000)$.

(*d*) Sketch the graph of the total profit function and interpret your solution of parts (*b*) and (*c*) using the graph of P.

8. The weekly demand for the "Pulsar 25" color console television is given by the demand equation $p = 600 - 0.05x$ $(0 \leq x \leq 12{,}000)$, where p denotes the wholesale unit price in dollars and x denotes the quantity demanded. The weekly total cost function associated with manufacturing these sets is given by $C(x) = 0.000002x^3 - 0.03x^2 + 400x + 80{,}000$ where $C(x)$ denotes the total cost incurred in the production of x sets.

(*a*) Find the total revenue function R and the total profit function P.

(*b*) Find the marginal cost function C', the marginal revenue function R' and the marginal profit function P'.

(*c*) Compute $C'(2000)$, $R'(2000)$ and $P'(2000)$. Interpret your results.

(*d*) Sketch the graphs of the functions C, R and P and interpret parts (*b*) and (*c*) using the graphs obtained.

9. Find the average cost function A associated with the total cost function C of problem 8.

(*a*) What is the marginal average cost function A' of A?

(*b*) Compute $A'(5000)$ and $A'(10{,}000)$ and interpret your results.

(*c*) Sketch the graph of A. *Note*: A pocket calculator is helpful here.

10. The Pulsar Corporation also manufactures a series of 19″ color television sets. The quantity x of these sets demanded each week is related to the wholesale unit price p by the relation $p = -0.006x + 180$. The weekly total cost incurred by the company for producing x sets is:

$$C(x) = 0.000002x^3 - 0.02x^2 + 120x + 60{,}000 \text{ dollars}$$

Answer the questions in problem 8 for the above data.

11. Find the average cost function A associated with the total cost function C of problem 10.

(*a*) What is the marginal average cost function A' of A?

(*b*) Compute $A'(5000)$ and $A'(10{,}000)$ and interpret your results.

12. The quantity demanded for the "Sicard" wristwatches per month is related to the unit price by the equation

$$p = \frac{50}{0.01x^2 + 1} \quad (0 \leq x \leq 20)$$

where p is measured in dollars and x is measured in units of a thousand.

(*a*) Find the total revenue function R.

(*b*) Find the marginal revenue function R'.

(*c*) Compute $R'(2)$ and interpret your result.

10.8

Higher Order Derivatives

The derivative f' of a function f is another function that has a domain that is a subset of the domain of f. As such, we may consider the differentiability of the function f' itself. Thus, the function f' has a derivative f'' at a point x in the domain of f' if the limit of the quotient

$$\frac{f'(x+\Delta x)-f'(x)}{\Delta x}$$

exists as $\Delta x \to 0$. Therefore,

(10.15)
$$f''(x)=\lim_{\Delta x\to 0}\frac{f'(x+\Delta x)-f'(x)}{\Delta x}$$

second derivative

provided the limit exists. The function f'' obtained in this manner is called the *second derivative* of the function f just as the derivative f' of f is often called the first derivative of f. Continuing in this fashion, we are led to the consideration of the third, fourth, and higher order derivatives of f whenever they exist. Notations for the first, second, third, and, in general, the nth derivative of a function f at a point x are

$$f'(x), f''(x), f'''(x), \ldots, f^{(n)}(x)$$

or

$$D^1f(x), D^2f(x), D^3f(x), \ldots, D^nf(x)$$

and, in the case f is written in the form $y=f(x)$

$$y', y'', y''', \ldots, y^{(n)}$$

$$\frac{dy}{dx}, \frac{d^2y}{dx^2}, \frac{d^3y}{dx^3}, \ldots, \frac{d^ny}{dx^n}$$

or

$$D^1y, D^2y, D^3y, \ldots, D^ny,$$

respectively.

EXAMPLE 10.61 Find the derivatives of all orders of the polynomial function $f(x)=x^5-3x^4+4x^3-2x^2+x-8$.

SOLUTION We have

$$f'(x)=5x^4-12x^3+12x^2-4x+1$$

$$f''(x)=\frac{d}{dx}f'(x)=20x^3-36x^2+24x-4$$

$$f'''(x)=\frac{d}{dx}f''(x)=60x^2-72x+24$$

$$f^{(\text{iv})}(x) = \frac{d}{dx}f'''(x) = 120x - 72$$

$$f^{(\text{v})}(x) = \frac{d}{dx}f^{(\text{iv})}(x) = 120$$

and, in general,

$$f^{(n)}(x) = 0 \quad \text{for } n \geq 6.$$

Recalling the remark made towards the end of Section 10.4 on the connection between continuity and differentiability, we conclude that the function of Example 10.61 is very "smooth". In fact, every polynomial function has derivatives of all order (see Exercise set 10.8, problem 23) and, consequently, such functions have very smooth graphs.

EXAMPLE 10.62 Find the third derivative of the function $y = x^{2/3}$. What is its domain?

SOLUTION We have

$$y' = \frac{2}{3}x^{-1/3}$$

$$y'' = \left(\frac{2}{3}\right)\left(-\frac{1}{3}\right)x^{-4/3} = -\frac{2}{9}x^{-4/3}$$

so that the required derivative y''' is given by

$$y''' = \left(-\frac{2}{9}\right)\left(-\frac{4}{3}\right)x^{-7/3} = \frac{8}{27}x^{-7/3} = \frac{8}{27x^{7/3}}$$

The (common) domain of the function y', y'' and y''' is the set of all real numbers except $x = 0$. The domain of $y = x^{2/3}$ is the set of all real numbers. The graph of the function $y = x^{2/3}$ appears in Figure 11.5, on page 493.

EXAMPLE 10.63 Find the first four derivatives of the function $y = \ln(1 + x)$.

SOLUTION We have

$$y' = \frac{d}{dx}\ln(1+x) = \frac{1}{1+x} = (1+x)^{-1}$$

$$y'' = \frac{d}{dx}(1+x)^{-1} = (-1)(1+x)^{-2} = -(1+x)^{-2}$$

$$y''' = \frac{d}{dx}[-(1+x)^{-2}] = 2(1+x)^{-3}$$

$$y^{(\text{iv})} = \frac{d}{dx}[2(1+x)^{-3}] = (2)(-3)(1+x)^{-4} = -6(1+x)^{-4}$$

EXAMPLE 10.64 Find the second derivative of the function $y=(2x^2+3)^{3/2}$.

SOLUTION We have, using Corollary 1 of the Chain Rule,

$$y'=\frac{3}{2}(2x^2+3)^{1/2}(4x)=6x(2x^2+3)^{1/2}$$

Next, using the Product Rule and then the Chain Rule, we find

$$\begin{aligned} y''&=(6x)\cdot\frac{d}{dx}(2x^2+3)^{1/2}+\left[\frac{d}{dx}(6x)\right](2x^2+3)^{1/2} \\ &=(6x)\left(\frac{1}{2}\right)(2x^2+3)^{-1/2}(4x)+6(2x^2+3)^{1/2} \\ &=12x^2(2x^2+3)^{-1/2}+6(2x^2+3)^{1/2} \\ &=6(2x^2+3)^{-1/2}[2x^2+(2x^2+3)] \\ &=\frac{6(4x^2+3)}{\sqrt{2x^2+3}} \end{aligned}$$

■

EXAMPLE 10.65 Find the derivatives of all orders of the function $f(x)=x\,e^x$.

SOLUTION We have

$$f'(x)=\frac{d}{dx}(x\,e^x)=x\cdot\frac{d}{dx}e^x+\left[\frac{d}{dx}(x)\right]e^x=x\,e^x+e^x=(x+1)\,e^x$$

$$\begin{aligned} f''(x)&=\frac{d}{dx}(x+1)\,e^x=(x+1)\cdot\frac{d}{dx}e^x+\left[\frac{d}{dx}(x+1)\right]e^x \\ &=(x+1)\,e^x+e^x=(x+2)\,e^x \end{aligned}$$

$$f'''(x)=\frac{d}{dx}[(x+2)\,e^x]=(x+2)\,e^x+e^x=(x+3)\,e^x$$

In general, if n is a positive integer, the nth derivative of f is

$$f^{(n)}(x)=(x+n)\,e^x$$

■

Just as the derivative of a function f at a point x measures the rate of change of the function f at that point, the second derivative of f, the derivative of f', measures the rate of change of the derivative f' of the function f. The third derivative f''' of the function f measures the rate of change of f'', and so on.

Geometrically, the first derivative $f'(x)$ of a function f at a point x measures the slope of the tangent line to the graph of f at the point $(x, f(x))$ on the graph so that the second derivative $f''(x)$ of f at the point x measures the rate of change of the slope of the tangent line at that point. In other words, the second derivative

$f''(x)$ at the point x measures the rate at which the tangent line to the graph of f is *turning* at this particular point. The tangent line turns counter-clockwise if $f''(x)$ is positive at this point and clockwise if $f''(x)$ is negative at the point. The third derivative f''' measures the rate of the tangent line's rate of turning and so on. We shall return to applications involving the geometrical interpretation of higher derivatives of a function in Chapter 11.

The following example gives an interpretation of the second derivative in a familiar role.

EXAMPLE 10.66 (See Example 10.25.) The distance s (in feet) covered by a car in t seconds starting from rest is given by $s = 2t^2$ $(0 \le t \le 30)$. What is the car's acceleration at the end of 30 seconds?

SOLUTION The velocity of the car t seconds from rest is given by

$$v = \frac{ds}{dt} = \frac{d}{dt}(2t^2) = 4t$$

Now, the acceleration of the car t seconds from rest is given by the rate of change of the velocity of t; that is,

$$a = \frac{d}{dt}v = \frac{d}{dt}\left(\frac{ds}{dt}\right) = \frac{d^2s}{dt^2} = \frac{d}{dt}(4t) = 4$$

or 4 feet per second per second, normally abbreviated, 4 ft/sec^2. ■

10.8 EXERCISES

In problems 1 through 20 find the first and second derivatives of the given functions.

1. $f(x) = 4x^2 - 2x + 1$
2. $g(x) = -3x^3 + 24x^2 + 6x - 64$
3. $h(t) = t^4 - 2t^3 + 6t^2 - 3t + 10$
4. $f(x) = x^5 - x^4 + x^3 - x^2 + x - 1$
5. $f(x) = (x^2 + 2)^{10}$
6. $g(t) = (2t^2 - 1)^6(3t^2 + 1)^8$
7. $f(x) = x^{7/2}$
8. $h(w) = (w^2 + 2w + 4)^{5/2}$
9. $f(u) = \dfrac{u}{u^2 + 1}$
10. $F(u) = \dfrac{u^2 - 1}{u^2 + 1}$
11. $f(x) = x^2 e^x$
12. $g(x) = x^2 \ln x$
13. $h(x) = \dfrac{e^x}{1 + e^x}$
14. $f(x) = \ln x^2$
15. $f(x) = \sqrt{2x - 1}$
16. $h(s) = \sqrt[3]{s^2 + 4}$
17. $f(x) = \dfrac{x^2}{\sqrt{x^2 - 1}}$
18. $f(x) = x^2\sqrt{2x^2 - 4}$

19. $h(r) = e^{-r^2}$

20. $f(x) = \ln \sqrt{x^4 + x^2}$

21. Let f be the function defined by the rule $f(x) = x^{5/2}$. Show that f has derivatives of the first and second order at all points x and therefore, in particular, at $x = 0$. Show further that the third derivative of f does not exist at $x = 0$.

****22.*** Construct a function f that has derivatives of order up through and including the nth derivative at a point a but fails to have the $(n+1)$st derivative there. *Hint*: See problem 21.

23. Show that a polynomial function has derivatives of all orders. *Hint*: Let $P(x) = a_0x^n + a_1x^{n-1} + a_2x^{n-2} + \cdots + a_n$, where n is a positive integer and $a_0, a_1, \ldots, a_n$ are constants with $a_0 \neq 0$, be a polynomial of degree n. Compute $P'(x), P''(x), \ldots$.

24. The distance s (in feet) covered by a car in t seconds starting from rest is given by $s = 20t + 8t^2 - t^3$ $(0 \leq t \leq 6)$. Find a general expression for the acceleration of the car at any time t $(0 \leq t \leq 6)$. Show that the car is decelerating $2\frac{2}{3}$ seconds after starting from rest.

25. In a test flight of the McCord Terrier, McCord Aviation's experimental VTOL (vertical take-off and landing) aircraft, it was determined that t seconds after lift-off when operated in the vertical take-off mode the altitude of the aircraft was $h(t) = (1/16)t^4 - t^3 + 4t^2$ feet $(0 \leq t \leq 8)$.

(***a***) Find an expression for the velocity of the aircraft at time t.

(***b***) Find the velocity of the aircraft when $t = 0$ (the initial velocity), $t = 4$ and $t = 8$.

(***c***) Find an expression for the acceleration of the aircraft at time t.

(***d***) Find the acceleration of the aircraft when $t = 0$, $t = 4$, and $t = 8$.

(***e***) Find the height of the aircraft when $t = 0$, $t = 4$, and $t = 8$.

10

Chapter Review

FORMULAS

1 $\dfrac{d}{dx}c = 0$ c, a constant

2 **Power Rule:** $\dfrac{d}{dx}x^n = nx^{n-1}$

3 **Constant Multiple Rule:** $\dfrac{d}{dx}[cf(x)] = c\dfrac{d}{dx}[f(x)]$ c, a constant

4 **Sum Rule:** $\dfrac{d}{dx}[f(x) + g(x)] = \dfrac{d}{dx}[f(x)] + \dfrac{d}{dx}[g(x)]$

5 **Product Rule:** $\frac{d}{dx}[f(x)\cdot g(x)]=f(x)g'(x)+g(x)f'(x)$

6 **Quotient Rule:** $\frac{d}{dx}\left[\frac{f(x)}{g(x)}\right]=\frac{g(x)f'(x)-f(x)g'(x)}{g(x)^2}$

7 $$\frac{d}{dx}e^x=e^x$$

8 $$\frac{d}{dx}b^x=b^x(\ln b)$$

9 $$\frac{d}{dx}(\ln x)=\frac{1}{x}$$

10 $$\frac{d}{dx}(\log_b x)=\frac{1}{x(\ln b)}$$

11 **Chain Rule:** $\frac{d}{dx}f(g(x))=f'(g(x))g'(x)$

12 **Chain Rule for Powers of Functions:** $\frac{d}{dx}[f(x)]^n=n[f(x)]^{n-1}f'(x)$

13 **Chain Rule for Exponential Functions:** $\frac{d}{dx}e^{f(x)}=e^{f(x)}f'(x)$

14 **Chain Rule for Logarithmic Functions:** $\frac{d}{dx}\ln f(x)=\frac{f'(x)}{f(x)}$

EXERCISES

In problems 1 through 10, find the indicated limits, if they exist.

1. $\lim_{x\to 0}(5x-3)$

2. $\lim_{x\to 1}(x^2+1)$

3. $\lim_{x\to -1}(3x^2+4)(2x-1)$

4. $\lim_{x\to 3}\frac{x-3}{x+4}\quad(x\neq -4)$

5. $\lim_{x\to 2}\frac{x+3}{x^2-9}\quad(x\neq\pm 3)$

6. $\lim_{x\to -2}\frac{x^2-2x-3}{x^2+5x+6}\quad(x\neq -2,-3)$

7. $\lim_{x\to 3}\sqrt{2x^3-5}$

8. $\lim_{x\to 3}\frac{4x-3}{\sqrt{x+1}}$

9. $\lim_{x\to\infty}\frac{3x^2+2x+4}{2x^2-3x+1}$

10. $\lim_{x\to -\infty}\frac{x^2}{x+1}$

11. Sketch the graph of the function

$$f(x)=\begin{cases}2x-3 & \text{if } x\leq 2\\ -x+3 & \text{if } x>2\end{cases}$$

and evaluate $\lim_{x\to a}f(x)$ at the point $a=2$, if the limit exists.

12. Sketch the graph of the function

$$f(x)=\begin{cases}4-x & \text{if } x\le 2\\ x+2 & \text{if } x>2\end{cases}$$

and evaluate $\lim_{x\to a} f(x)$ at the point $a=2$, if the limit exists.

In problems 13 through 16, determine all values of x *for which the given functions are discontinuous.*

13. $g(x)=\begin{cases}x+3 & \text{if } x\ne 2\\ 0 & \text{if } x=2\end{cases}$

14. $f(x)=\dfrac{3x+4}{4x^2-2x-2}$

15. $f(x)=\begin{cases}1/(x+1)^2 & \text{if } x\ne -1\\ 2 & \text{if } x=-1\end{cases}$

16. $f(x)=\dfrac{|2x|}{x}$

17. A hotel was purchased by a conglomerate for \$4.5 million and sold 5 years later for \$8.2 million. Find the annual rate of return (compounded continuously).

18. Find the present value of \$119,346 due in 4 years at an interest rate of 10% per annum compounded continuously.

19. Let $y=f(x)=x^2+2$.

(***a***) Find the average rate of change of y with respect to x in the interval [1, 2], in [1, 1.5], and in [1, 1.1].
(***b***) Find the (instantaneous) rate of change of y at $x=1$.

20. Use the definition of the derivative to find the slope of the tangent line to the graph of the function $f(x)=3x+5$ at any point $P(x, f(x))$ on the graph.

21. Use the definition of the derivative to find the slope of the tangent line to the graph of the function $f(x)=-x^2$ at the point $(2, -4)$ and determine an equation of the tangent line.

22. The Photo-Mart transfers movie films to video-cassettes. The fees charged for this service are given by the following schedule. Find a function C relating the cost $C(x)$ to the number of feet x of film transferred. Sketch the graph of the function C and discuss its continuity.

Length of film in feet (x)	$1\le x\le 100$	$100<x\le 200$	$200<x\le 300$	$300<x\le 400$	$x>400$
Price (\$) for conversion	5.00	9.00	12.50	15.00	$(7+.02x)$

In problems 23 through 42, find the derivative of the given function.

23. $f(x)=4x^6$

24. $g(x)=-2x^{-3}$

25. $f(t)=2t^2-3t^3$

26. $h(x)=x^2+\dfrac{2}{x}$

27. $f(x)=\dfrac{\sqrt{x}-1}{\sqrt{x}+1}$

28. $f(t)=\dfrac{t}{2t^2+1}$

29. $h(x)=\dfrac{x^2(x^2+1)}{x^2-1}$

30. $f(x)=\dfrac{x+1}{2x-1}$

31. $f(t)=\sqrt{t}\,e^t+t$

32. $g(x)=e^x\sqrt{1+x^2}$

33. $f(x)=\dfrac{\ln x}{1+e^x}$

34. $g(t)=t\ln t$

35. $f(x)=(3x^3-2)^8$

36. $f(t)=\sqrt{2t^2+1}$

37. $g(t)=\sqrt[3]{1-2t^2}$

38. $h(x)=\dfrac{1+x}{(2x^2+1)^2}$

39. $f(x)=e^{2x2-1}$

40. $g(x)=(1+e^{2x})^{3/2}$

41. $f(r)=\dfrac{re^r}{1+r^2}$

42. $g(x)=\dfrac{e^{x2}}{1+\ln x}$

43. Let $f(x)=2x^3-3x^2-16x+3$

(***a***) Find the point(s) on the graph of f at which the slope of the tangent line is equal to -4.

(***b***) Find the equation(s) of the tangent line(s) of part (***a***).

44. Find the equation of the tangent line to the graph of $y=\sqrt{4-x^2}$ at the point $(1,\sqrt{3})$.

45. Find $h'(0)$ if $h(x)=g(f(x))$ and $g(x)=x+1/x$ and $f(x)=e^x$.

46. Find the equation of the tangent line to the graph of $y=e^{-2x}$ at the point $(1,e^{-2})$.

47. The number of subscribers to CNC Cable Television in the town of Randolph is approximated by the function

$$N(x)=1000(1+2x)^{1/2} \quad (1\le x\le 30)$$

where $N(x)$ denotes the number of subscribers to the service in the xth week. Find the rate of increase of the number of subscribers at the end of the twelfth week.

48. The total cost in dollars incurred by the Herald Record Company per week in pressing x videodiscs is given by the total cost function

$$C(x)=2500+2.2x \quad (0\le x\le 8000)$$

(***a***) What is the marginal cost when $x=1000$? when $x=2000$?

(***b***) Find the average cost function A and the marginal average cost function A'.

(*c*) Using the results from part (*b*) show that the average cost incurred by the company in pressing a videodisc approaches \$2.20 per disc when the level of production is high enough. *Hint*: See Example 10.57, page 474.

49. The marketing department of Telecon Corporation has determined the demand for their cordless phones obeys the relationship $p = -0.02x + 600$ $(0 \leq x \leq 30{,}000)$, where p denotes the unit price (in dollars) of the phones and x denotes the quantity demanded.

(*a*) Find the total revenue function R.

(*b*) Find the total marginal revenue function R'.

(*c*) Compute $R'(10{,}000)$ and interpret your result.

50. The weekly demand for the "Lektro-Copy" photocopying machine is given by the demand equation $p = 2000 - 0.04x$ $(0 \leq x \leq 50{,}000)$ where p denotes the wholesale unit price in dollars and x denotes the quantity demanded. The weekly total cost function for manufacturing these copiers is given by

$$C(x) = 0.000002x^3 - 0.02x^2 + 1000x + 120{,}000$$

where $C(x)$ denotes the total cost incurred in the production of x units.

(*a*) Find the total revenue function R, the total profit function P, and the average cost function A.

(*b*) Find the marginal cost function C', the marginal revenue function R', the marginal profit function P' and the marginal average cost function A'.

(*c*) Compute $C'(3000)$, $R'(3000)$ and $P'(3000)$ and interpret your results.

(*d*) Compute $A'(5000)$ and $A'(8000)$ and interpret your results.

11

APPLICATIONS OF THE DERIVATIVE

11.1 Increasing and Decreasing Functions

Consider the graph of some function f shown in Figure 11.1(a). Once again, think of the curve as representing a stretch of roller-coaster track. We see that as x increases from a to b, the car climbs on that stretch of track corresponding to the portion of the graph of f for $a<x<b$. Geometrically, the graph of f rises as x increases from a to b, and, in this case, f is increasing on the interval (a, b). More specifically, a function f is *increasing on an interval* (a, b) if and only if for any x_1 and x_2 in (a, b) with $x_1<x_2$ then $f(x_1)<f(x_2)$ (see Figure 11.1, part a). We also say that f is *increasing at a point c* if there exists an interval (a, b) containing c and such that f is increasing on (a, b).

increasing function

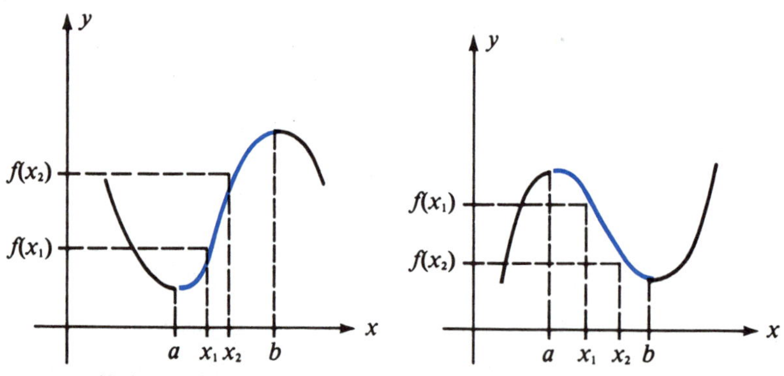

Figure 11.1

f is increasing on (a, b)
(a)

f is decreasing on (a, b)
(b)

decreasing function

Similarly, a function is *decreasing on an interval* (a, b) if and only if whenever x_1 and x_2 are in (a, b) with $x_1 < x_2$ then $f(x_1) > f(x_2)$. Geometrically, a function f is decreasing on (a, b) if the graph of f falls as x increases from a to b (see Figure 11.1, part b). In terms of the roller-coaster analogy, our car will be descending along that stretch of track corresponding to the graph of f for x between a and b. We also say that f is *decreasing at a point* c if there exists an interval (a, b) containing c and such that f is decreasing on (a, b).

Since the rate of change of a function at a point $x = c$ is given by the derivative of the function at that point, the derivative is the natural choice for determining the intervals where a differentiable function is increasing and where it is decreasing. Indeed, as we saw in Chapter 10, the derivative of a function at a point measures both the slope of the tangent line to the graph of the function at that point and the rate of change of the function at the same point. In fact, at a point where the derivative is positive, the slope of the tangent line to the graph is positive and the function is increasing. While at a point where the derivative is negative, the slope of the tangent line to the graph is negative and the function is decreasing (see Figure 11.2).

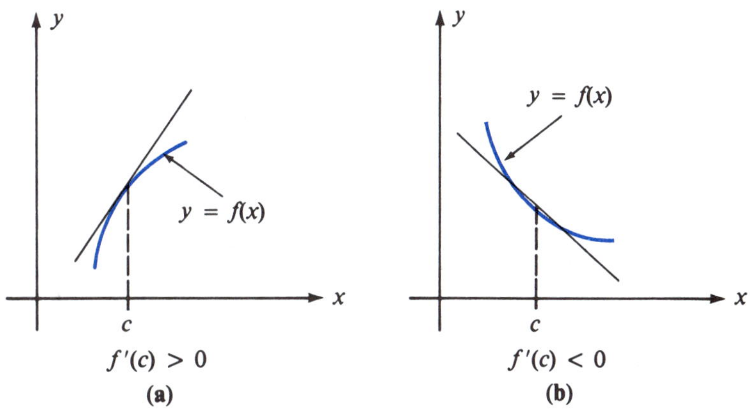

Figure 11.2

The above observation leads to the following important result:

THEOREM 11.1 Suppose a function is differentiable on the interval (a, b):

(a) If $f'(x) > 0$ for each value of x in (a, b), then f is increasing on (a, b).

(b) If $f'(x) < 0$ for each value of x in (a, b), then f is decreasing on (a, b).

(c) If $f'(x) = 0$ for each value of x in (a, b), then f is constant on (a, b).

EXAMPLE 11.1 Find the intervals where the function $f(x) = x^2$ is increasing and where it is decreasing.

SOLUTION The derivative of $f(x) = x^2$ is $f'(x) = 2x$. Since $f'(x) = 2x > 0$ when $x > 0$ and $f'(x) = 2x < 0$ when $x < 0$, f is increasing in the interval $(0, \infty)$ and decreasing in the interval $(-\infty, 0)$ (see Figure 11.3).

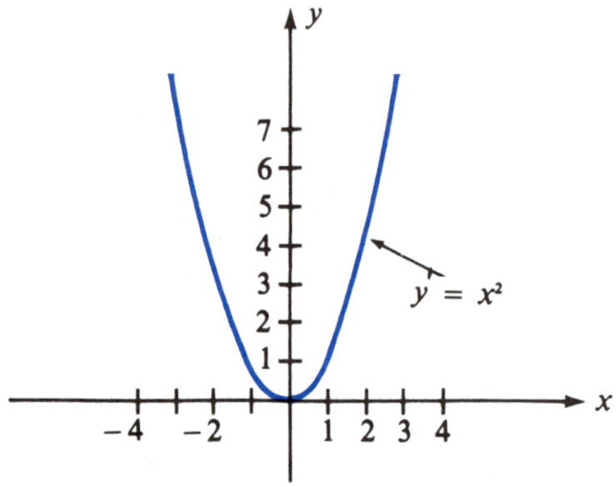

Figure 11.3

Before proceeding further with the applications of Theorem 11.1, let us recall that the graph of a continuous function cannot have any "breaks." One implication of this property is that a continuous function cannot change sign without attaining the value zero for some value of x. This observation suggests the following procedure for determining the sign of the derivative f' of a function f and hence the intervals where the function f is increasing and where it is decreasing.

1. Find all values of x for which the derivative f' of the function f is discontinuous as well as all values of x for which f' is zero. These values of x partition the domain of f into open intervals which have (finite) end-points that are precisely determined by these values of x.

2. On each of the intervals found in Step 1, f' is continuous and does not change sign. To determine the sign of f' in such an interval it suffices to compute $f'(c)$ where c is any conveniently chosen point (called a ***test point***) in the interval. The sign of f' in the interval coincides with the sign of $f'(c)$. Thus, by Theorem 11.1, f is increasing, is constant, or is decreasing on the interval according to whether $f'(c)>0$, $f'(c)=0$, or $f'(c)<0$.

EXAMPLE 11.2 Find the intervals where the function $f(x)=x^{2/3}$ is increasing and where it is decreasing.

SOLUTION The derivative of f is $f'(x)=(2/3)x^{-1/3}=2/(3x^{1/3})$. The function f' is not defined at $x=0$, so that f' is discontinuous there. It is continuous everywhere else. Furthermore, f' is not equal to zero anywhere. The point $x=0$ divides the real line (the domain of f) into the intervals $(-\infty, 0)$ and $(0, \infty)$. Picking $x=-1$ as the test point in the interval $(-\infty, 0)$, we find that $f'(-1)=-(2/3)$, and so $f'(x)<0$ on $(-\infty, 0)$.

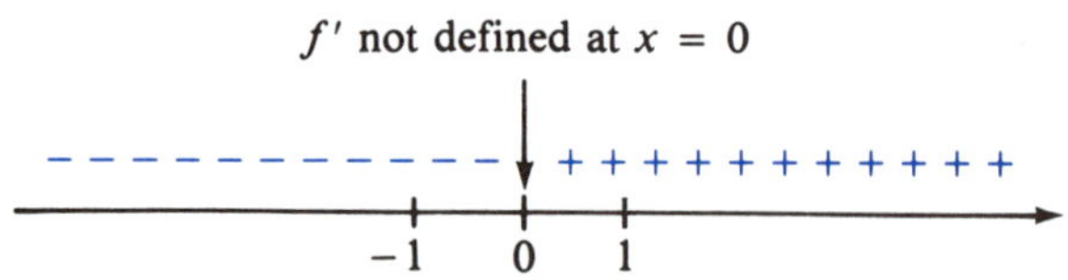

Figure 11.4 Sign diagram for f'.

Similarly, $f'(1)>0$ implies $f'(x)>0$ on $(0, \infty)$. Figure 11.4 exhibits these results in a sign diagram. We conclude that f is decreasing on the interval $(-\infty, 0)$ and increasing on the interval $(0, \infty)$.

The graph of f, shown in Figure 11.5, confirms the results obtained earlier.

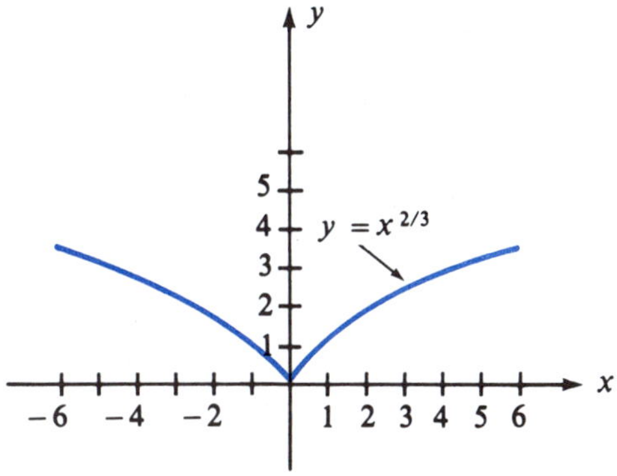

Figure 11.5

EXAMPLE 11.3 Determine the intervals where the function $f(x)=x^3-3x^2-24x+32$ is increasing and where it is decreasing.

SOLUTION The derivative of f is $f'(x)=3x^2-6x-24=3(x+2)(x-4)$ and is continuous everywhere. The zeros of $f'(x)$ are $x=-2$ and $x=4$. To determine the sign of $f'(x)$ in the intervals $(-\infty, -2)$, $(-2, 4)$ and $(4, \infty)$, we compute $f'(x)$ at the test points $x=-3$, $x=0$, and $x=5$, obtaining $f'(-3)=21$, $f'(0)=-24$ and $f'(5)=21$, respectively. Thus $f'(x)$ is positive on the intervals $(-\infty, -2)$ and $(4, \infty)$, and negative on the interval $(-2, 4)$ (see Figure 11.6).

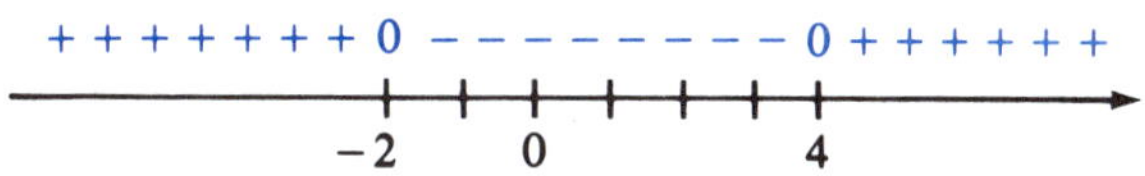

Figure 11.6

With these results we conclude that f is increasing on the intervals $(-\infty, -2)$ and $(4, \infty)$ and is decreasing on the interval $(-2, 4)$. Figure 11.7 shows the graph of f.

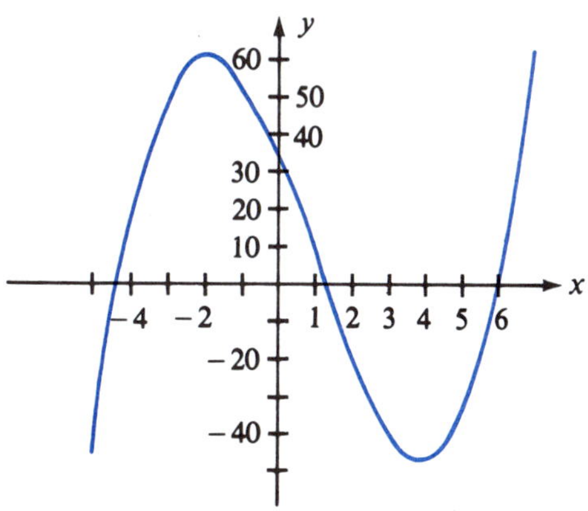

Figure 11.7

EXAMPLE 11.4 Find the intervals where the function $f(x)=x+1/x$ is increasing and where it is decreasing.

SOLUTION The derivative of f is

$$f'(x)=1-\frac{1}{x^2}=\frac{x^2-1}{x^2}$$

Since f' is not defined at $x=0$, it is discontinuous there. Furthermore, $f'(x)$ is equal to zero when $x^2-1=0$ or $x=\pm 1$. These values of x partition the domain of f' into the open intervals $(-\infty,-1)$, $(-1,0)$, $(0,1)$ and $(1,\infty)$, where the sign of f' is different from zero. To determine the signs of f' in each of these intervals, we compute $f'(x)$ at the test points $x=-2$, $-1/2$, $1/2$, and 2, respectively, obtaining $f'(-2)=3/4$, $f'(-1/2)=-3$, $f'(1/2)=-3$, and $f'(2)=3/4$. The sign diagram for f' is shown in Figure 11.8.

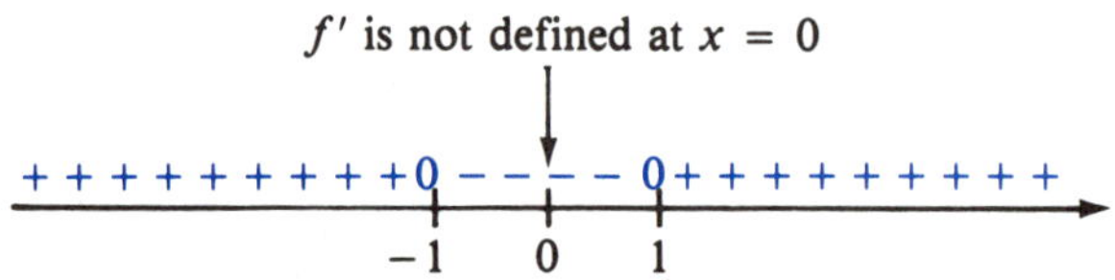

Figure 11.8

The graph of f appears in Figure 11.9. Note that f' does not change sign as we move across the point of discontinuity, $x=0$. (Compare this with Example 11.2.)

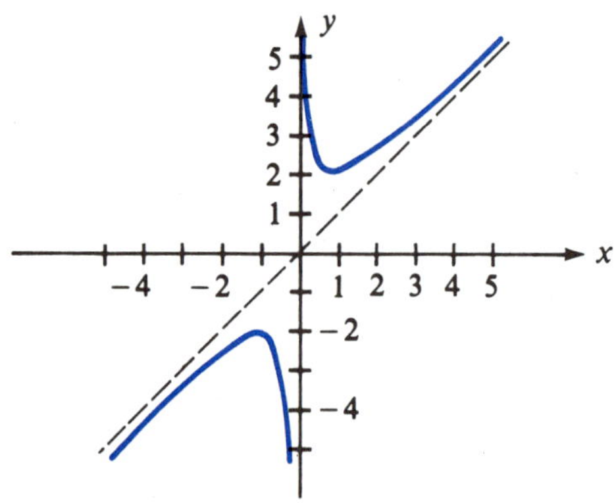

Figure 11.9

■

The last example reminds us that we may not automatically conclude that the derivative f' must change sign when we move across a point of discontinuity of f' or a zero of f'.

EXAMPLE 11.5 (Refer to Example 10.43, page 458). The altitude (in feet) of a rocket, t seconds into flight, is given by $s=f(t)=-t^3+96t^2+195t+5$ $(t\geq 0)$.

(a) Find the intervals where the function f is increasing and where it is decreasing.

(b) Interpret the results obtained in part **(a)**.

SOLUTION (**a**) The derivative of f is

$$\begin{aligned} v = f'(t) &= -3t^2 + 192t + 195 \\ &= -3(t-65)(t+1) \end{aligned}$$

and is equal to zero at $t=-1$ and $t=65$. Since t must be nonnegative, we disregard the root $t=-1$. To determine the signs of $f'(t)$ in the intervals $(0, 65)$ and $(65, \infty)$, let us pick the test points $t=1$ and $t=70$. Since $f'(1)>0$ and $f'(70)<0$, we conclude that f is increasing on the interval $(0, 65)$ and decreasing on the interval $(65, \infty)$. Figure 11.10 shows the sign diagram for f'. The graph of the function f is sketched in Figure 10.18, on page 459.

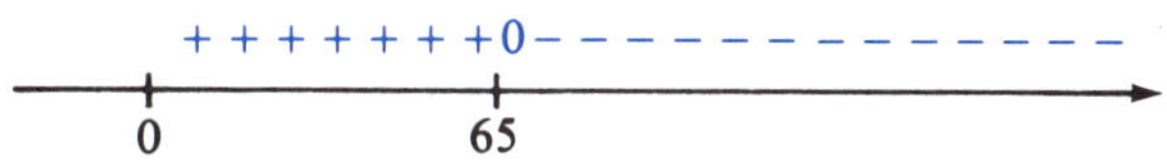

Figure 11.10

(**b**) The derivative of the function f gives the velocity v of the rocket at any time $t \geq 0$. On the interval $(0, 65)$ the derivative of f is positive. Thus, the velocity of the rocket is positive and the rocket is ascending. The result of part (a) shows that $s=f(t)$ is increasing on the interval $(0, 65)$. For $t>65$, $v=f'(t)$ is negative and the rocket is descending. Equivalently, f is decreasing on the interval $(65, T)$, where T denotes the time the rocket impacts the earth. The value of T may be found by solving the equation $s=f(t)=0$. The velocity curve is shown in Figure 11.11. Later (see Example 11.32, page 533) we will show that the maximum velocity of the rocket is 3267 feet/second, attained 32 seconds into flight.

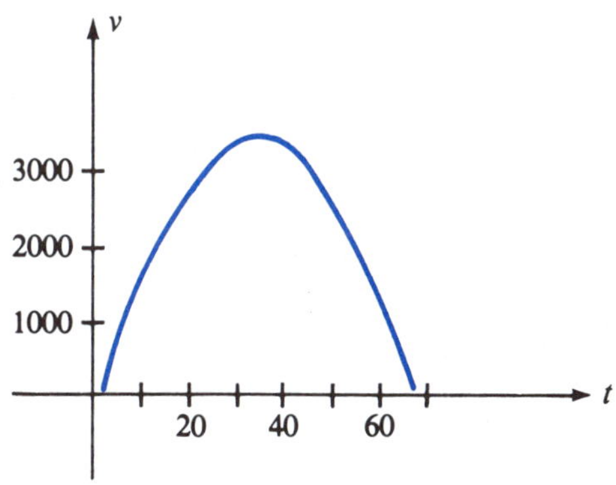

Figure 11.11

■

EXAMPLE 11.6 (Refer to Example 10.60, page 478). The profit function of the Acrosonic Company is given by $P(x) = -0.02x^2 + 300x - 200{,}000$ dollars, where x is the number of Acrosonic Model F loudspeaker systems produced. Find where the function P is increasing and where it is decreasing.

SOLUTION The derivative P' of the function P is

$$P'(x) = -0.04x + 300 = -0.04(x - 7500)$$

Thus, $P'(x)=0$ when $x=7500$. Furthermore, $P'(x)>0$ for x in the interval $(0, 7500)$ and $P'(x)<0$ for $x \in (7500, \infty)$ so that the profit function P is increasing on $(0, 7500)$ and decreasing on $(7500, \infty)$ (see Figure 10.23, page 478). ■

11.1 EXERCISES

In problems 1 through 28 find the intervals where each of the given functions is increasing and where it is decreasing.

1. $f(x)=32$

2. $f(x)=3x+5$

3. $f(x)=2x^2+x+1$

4. $g(x)=x^3+3x^2+1$

5. $h(x)=x^3+3x^2-9x+8$

6. $f(x)=\frac{1}{3}x^3-3x^2+9x+20$

***7.** $f(t)=3t^4-2t^3-9t^2+5$

8. $f(x)=\frac{2}{3}x^3-3x^2+6x-2$

9. $g(x)=(x^2-1)^5$

10. $h(t)=\frac{t}{t-1}$

11. $f(x)=x^{3/5}$

12. $f(x)=\frac{x^2-1}{x}$

13. $h(x)=\frac{x^2}{x-1}$

14. $g(t)=t+\frac{1}{t}$

15. $f(s)=\sqrt{s}+s^{3/2}$

16. $f(x)=\frac{1}{(x-1)^2}$

17. $f(x)=\frac{3x+1}{4x-1}$

18. $g(x)=\frac{x^2+9}{x^2-9}$

19. $h(x)=x+\frac{16}{x}-208$

20. $F(s)=3s^2-\frac{384}{s}-2$

21. $f(x)=\sqrt{x^2-4x+10}$

22. $H(x)=e^{-2x}$

23. $f(x)=e^{-x^2/2}$

24. $g(x)=\frac{1}{2}(e^x+e^{-x})$

25. $E(x)=x^2e^{-x}$

26. $f(x)=\ln x^2 \quad (|x|>0)$

27. $g(x)=\ln\left(\frac{1}{x}\right) \quad (x>0)$

28. $f(x)=x-\ln x \quad (x>0)$

29. Using Theorem 11.1 verify that the linear function $f(x)=mx+b$ is (***a***) increasing everywhere if $m>0$, (***b***) decreasing everywhere if $m<0$ and (***c***) is a constant if $m=0$.

***30.** In what interval is the quadratic function $f(x)=ax^2+bx+c$ $(a\neq 0)$ increasing? In what interval is f decreasing?

31. A stone is thrown straight up from the roof of an 80 foot building. The height of the stone at any time t (in seconds) measured from the ground is given by $h(t) = -16t^2 + 64t + 80$ feet. When is the stone rising and when is it falling? If the stone misses the building, when will it hit the ground? *Hint*: The stone is on the ground when $h(t) = 0$. Sketch the graph of h.

32. The height (in feet) attained by a rocket t seconds into flight is given by the function $h(t) = -(1/3)t^3 + 16t^2 + 33t + 10$. When is the rocket rising and when is it descending? To return the rocket safely back to earth a parachute is deployed when the rocket is at its highest trajectory point. After liftoff, when is the parachute released?

33. The Mexico subsidiary of the Thermo-Master Company manufactures an indoor-outdoor thermometer. The company management estimated that the profit realizable by the company for the manufacture and sale of x units of thermometers per week is $P(x) = -0.001x^2 + 8x - 5000$ dollars. Find the intervals where the profit function P is increasing and the intervals where P is decreasing. Sketch the graph of the function P. What level of production will yield the maximum weekly profit for the company?

34. The Emory Secretarial School finds from experience that the average student taking Advanced Typing will progress according to the rule

$$N(t) = \frac{60t + 180}{t + 6} \quad (t \geq 0)$$

where $N(t)$ measures the number of words per minute the student can type after t weeks in the course. Compute $N'(t)$ and use this result to show that the function N is increasing on the interval $(0, \infty)$.

35. During a flu epidemic, the total number of students on a State University campus who had contracted influenza by the xth day was given by

$$N(x) = \frac{3000}{1 + 99\,e^{-x}} \quad (x \geq 0)$$

(***a***) How many students had influenza initially?

(***b***) Derive an expression for the rate at which the disease was being spread and prove that the function N is increasing on the interval $(0, \infty)$.

(***c***) Sketch the graph of N. What was the total number of students who contracted influenza in that particular epidemic?

36. (***a***) Show that the function $Q(t) = Q_0\,e^{kt}$ $(t \geq 0)$, where Q_0 and k are positive constants, describing a quantity $Q(t)$ exhibiting exponential growth, is increasing on the interval $(0, \infty)$.

(***b***) Show that the function $Q(t) = Q_0\,e^{-kt}$ $(t \geq 0)$, where Q_0 and k are positive constants, describing a quantity exhibiting exponential decay, is decreasing on the interval $(0, \infty)$.

37. Show that the function $Q(t) = C - A\,e^{-kt}$ $(t \geq 0)$, where C, A and k are positive constants, describing a learning curve (see Chapter 5), is increasing on the interval $(0, \infty)$.

**38.* Prove that the logistic function

$$f(t) = \frac{A}{1 + B\,e^{-kt}} \quad (t \geq 0)$$

where A, B and k are positive constants (see Chapter 5) is increasing on $(0, \infty)$.

11.2
Relative Maxima and Relative Minima

In the last section, we saw how the derivative of a function helps us determine where the graph of the function is increasing and where it is decreasing. In this section, we shall see how the first derivative of a function may be used to help us locate certain "high points" and "low points" on the graph of f. Knowing such points is invaluable in curve sketching (Section 11.5) and is very important in solving optimization problems (Section 11.7).

relative maximum

The special kinds of "high points" and "low points" are called the relative maxima and relative minima of a function. More specifically, a function f has a *relative maximum* (also called a *local maximum*) at $x = c$ if there exists an open interval (a, b) containing c such that $f(x) \leq f(c)$ for all x in (a, b). Geometrically, this means that no point on the graph of f with its x-coordinate sufficiently close to $x = c$ can lie above the point $(c, f(c))$. Figure 11.12 depicts the graph of a function f, which has a relative maximum at $x = x_1$ and another at $x = x_3$.

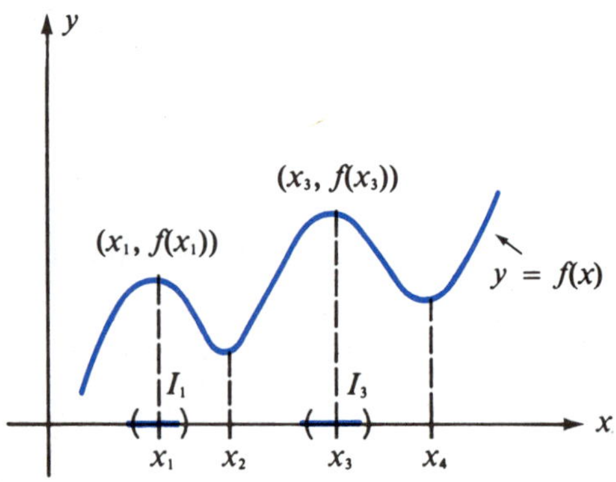

Figure 11.12

Observe that all the points on the graph of f with x-coordinates in the interval I_1 containing x_1 (shown in color) lie on or below the point $(x_1, f(x_1))$. This is also true for the point $(x_3, f(x_3))$ and the interval I_3. Thus, even though there are points on the graph of f that are "higher" than the points $(x_1, f(x_1))$ and $(x_3, f(x_3))$, the latter points are "highest" *relative* to points in their respective neighborhoods. Points on the graph of a function f, which are "highest" and "lowest" with respect to *all* points in the domain of f, will be studied in Section 11.6.

relative minimum

The definition of the relative minimum of a function parallels that of the relative maximum of a function. Thus, a function f has a *relative minimum* (*local minimum*) at $x = c$ if there exists an open interval (a, b) containing c such that $f(x) \geq f(c)$ for all x in (a, b). The graph of the function f, depicted in Figure 11.12, has a relative minimum at $x = x_2$ and another at $x = x_4$.

The first step in our quest for the relative extrema (relative maxima or relative minima) of a function is to consider functions that have derivatives at such points. Suppose that f is a function that is differentiable in some interval (a, b) which contains a point $x = c$, and that the point $(c, f(c))$ is a relative maximum of f (see Figure 11.13 part a).

Observe that this function is nondecreasing for all points x sufficiently close to but lying to the left of the point $x = c$. For all such x, we must have $f'(x) \geq 0$. On the other hand, the function must be nonincreasing for all points x sufficiently close to but lying to the right of the point $x = c$ so that for all such points x, $f'(x) \leq 0$. Thus, at the point $x = c$ itself, the derivative f' of f must equal zero, that is, $f'(c) = 0$. We reach the same conclusion by observing that the slope of the tangent line to the graph of f must change from nonnegative to nonpositive as we move across the point $x = c$ from left to right. Therefore, the tangent line to the graph of f at the relative extrema $(c, f(c))$ must be horizontal; that is, $f'(c) = 0$ (see Figure 11.13 part a). Using a similar argument, you may convince yourself that the derivative f' of a differentiable function f must also be equal to zero, that is, $f'(c) = 0$, at a relative minimum $(c, f(c))$ of f (see Figure 11.13 part b).

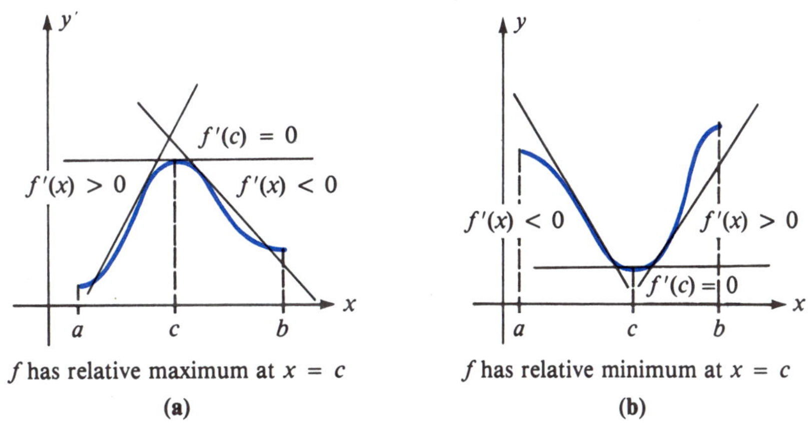

Figure 11.13

The above analysis reveals an important characteristic of the relative extrema of a differentiable function f: $f'(x) = 0$ *at each value of x which gives rise to a relative extremum of f*. Before we develop a procedure for finding such points, a few words of caution are in order.

First, the above result states that if a differentiable function f has a relative extremum at a point $x=c$, then $f'(c)=0$. The converse, if $f'(c)=0$ at some point $x=c$ then f must have a relative extremum at that point was not implied by our analysis and is, in general, false. Consider, for example, the function $f(x)=x^3$. Here $f'(x)=3x^2$ so that $f'(0)=0$, yet f has neither a relative maximum nor a relative minimum at $x=0$ (see Figure 11.14).

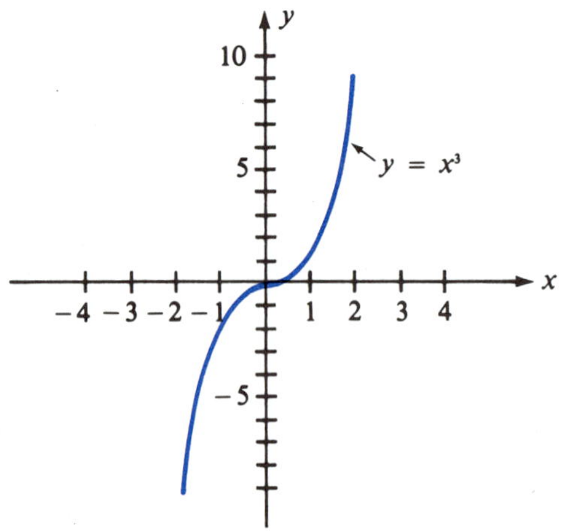

Figure 11.14

Second, our result assumes that the function was differentiable and thus had a derivative at a relative extremum. The functions $f(x)=|x|$ and $g(x)=x^{2/3}$ demonstrate that a relative extremum of a function may exist at a point at which the function does not possess a derivative. Both these functions fail to be differentiable at $x=0$ (see Examples 10.29 and 11.2) but each has a relative minimum there. Figure 11.15 shows the graphs of these functions. Note that the slopes of the tangent lines change from negative to positive as we move across $x=0$, just as in the case of a function that is differentiable at a value of x which gives rise to a relative extremum.

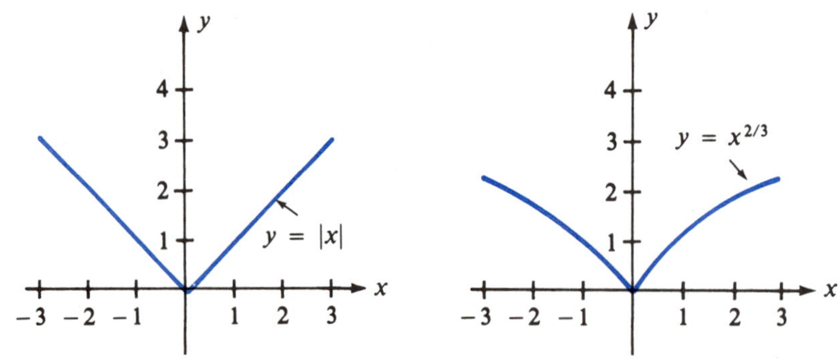

Figure 11.15

We now state a formal procedure for finding the relative extrema of a continuous function, which is differentiable everywhere except at isolated values of x.

Incorporated in the procedure is the so-called First Derivative Test. This test enables us to determine if a point is indeed a relative maximum or a relative minimum or neither a relative maximum nor a relative minimum of the function f. The procedure follows:

1. Compute $f'(x)$.

critical point

2. Determine the points in the domain of f for which $f'(x)=0$ and also those for which $f'(x)$ is discontinuous. These points are called the *critical points* of f and are candidates for the values of x which give rise to the relative extrema of f.

The First Derivative Test

3. (*The First Derivative Test*): Determine the sign of $f'(x)$ to the left and right of each critical point. There are three possibilities:

(*a*) If $f'(x)$ changes sign from positive to negative as we move across a critical point $x=c$ (that is, $f'(x)>0$ for $x<c$ and $f'(x)<0$ for $x>c$), then the point $(c, f(x))$ is a relative maximum of f.

(*b*) If $f'(x)$ changes sign from negative to positive as we move across a critical point $x=c$ (that is, $f'(x)<0$ for $x<c$ and $f'(x)>0$ for $x>c$), then the point $(c, f(x))$ is a relative minimum of f.

(*c*) If $f'(x)$ does not change sign as we move across a critical point $x=c$, then the point $(c, f(x))$ is neither a relative maximum nor a relative minimum of f.

EXAMPLE 11.7 Find the relative maxima and relative minima of the function $f(x)=x^2$.

SOLUTION The derivative of $f(x)=x^2$ is given by $f'(x)=2x$. Setting $f'(x)=0$ yields $x=0$ as the only critical point of f. Since $f'(x)<0$ if $x<0$ and $f'(x)>0$ if $x>0$, we see that $f'(x)$ changes sign from negative to positive as we move across the critical point $x=0$. We conclude that the point $(0, 0)$ is a relative minimum of f (see Figure 11.3, page 492). ■

EXAMPLE 11.8 Find the relative maxima and relative minima of the function $f(x)=x^{2/3}$ (see Example 11.2, page 492).

SOLUTION The derivative of f is $f'(x)=2/(3x^{1/3})$. As noted in Example 11.2, f' is not defined at $x=0$, is continuous everywhere else, and is not equal to zero in its domain. Thus, $x=0$ is the only critical point of the function f. Also from previous results, we have the sign diagram for f' as reproduced in Figure 11.16.

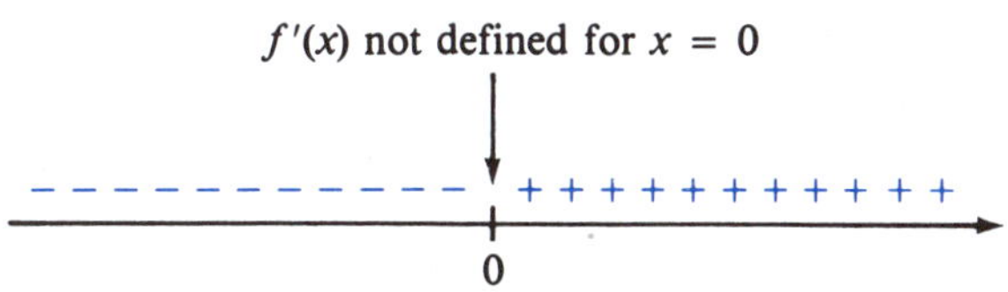

Figure 11.16

Figure 11.16 shows that the sign of $f'(x)$ changes from negative to positive as we move across $x=0$ from left to right. Thus, an application of the First Derivative

Test tells us that $x=0$ gives rise to a relative minimum of f. The value of f at $x=0$ is $f(0)=0$ (see Figure 11.5). ■

EXAMPLE 11.9 Find the relative maxima and relative minima of the function $f(x)=x^3-3x^2-24x+32$ (see Example 11.3, page 493).

SOLUTION The derivative of f is $f'(x)=3x^2-6x-24=3(x+2)(x-4)$ and is continuous everywhere. The zeros of $f'(x)$ are $x=-2$ and $x=4$. They are the only critical points of the function f. The sign diagram for f' is reproduced in Figure 11.17. Examine the two critical points $x=-2$ and $x=4$ for a relative extremum using the First Derivative Test and the sign diagram for f':

1. The critical point $x=-2$: Since the function $f'(x)$ changes sign from positive to negative as we move across $x=-2$ from left to right, we conclude that the point $x=-2$ gives rise to a relative maximum for the function f. The value of $f(x)$ when $x=-2$ is $f(-2)=(-2)^3-3(-2)^2-24(-2)+32=60$, so that the point $(-2, 60)$ is a relative maximum of f.

2. The critical point $x=4$: $f'(x)$ changes sign from negative to positive as we move across $x=4$ from left to right so that the point $(4, -48)$ is a relative minimum of f.

The graph of f appears in Figure 11.7, page 493.

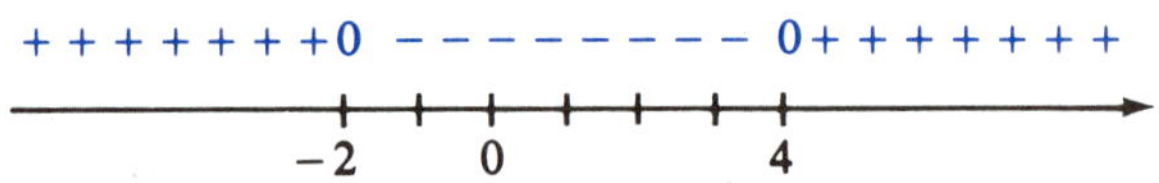

Figure 11.17 ■

EXAMPLE 11.10 Find the relative maxima and the relative minima of the function $f(x)=x+1/x$ (see Example11.4, page 494).

SOLUTION The derivative of f is

$$f'(x)=1-\frac{1}{x^2}$$

$$=\frac{x^2-1}{x^2}$$

$$=\frac{(x+1)(x-1)}{x^2}$$

Since f' is equal to zero at $x=-1$ and $x=1$, these are critical points for the function f. Next, observe that f' is discontinuous at $x=0$. However, because f is not defined at that point, the point $x=0$ does not qualify as a critical point of f. Figure 11.18 shows the sign diagram for f'. Since $f'(x)$ changes sign from positive to negative as we move across $x=-1$ from left to right, the First Derivative Test implies that the point $(-1, -2)$ is a relative maximum for the function f. Next, $f'(x)$ changes sign from negative to positive as we move across $x=1$, from left to right, so that the point (1, 2) is a relative minimum for the function f. The graph of f appears in Figure 11.9, page 494. Note that this function has a relative maximum that lies below the relative minimum.

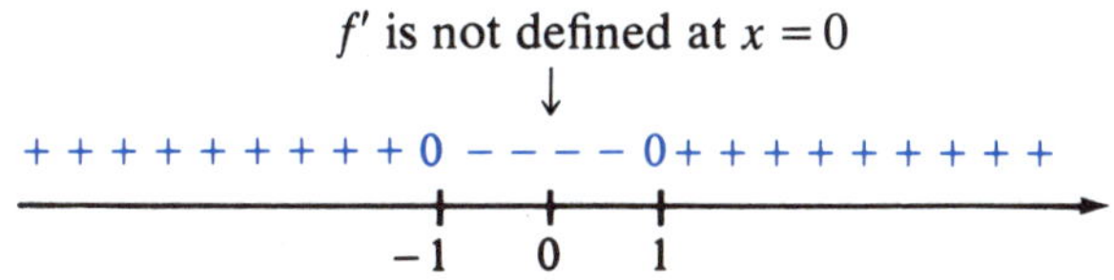

Figure 11.18. ■

11.2 EXERCISES

In problems 1 through 26 find the relative extrema (relative maxima and relative minima) of each of the given functions.

1. $f(x)=x^{2/3}+2$

2. $f(x)=x^{5/3}$

3. $g(x)=\frac{1}{2}x^2-2x+4$

4. $h(t)=-t^2+6t+6$

5. $f(x)=x^3-3x+6$

6. $F(x)=2x^3-9x^2+2x+6$

7. $g(x)=2x^3-\frac{1}{2}x^2-2x+4$

8. $f(x)=x^3-3x^2+2x+1$

9. $f(x)=\frac{1}{2}x^4-x^2$

10. $g(x)=x^4-4x^3+8$

11. $h(x)=\frac{1}{2}x^4-3x^2+4x+8$

12. $f(x)=\frac{1}{4}x^4-\frac{2}{3}x^3-\frac{1}{2}x^2+2x+2$

13. $F(t)=3t^5-20t^3+20$

14. $f(x)=\dfrac{x}{1+x^2}$

15. $f(x)=x+\dfrac{9}{x}+2 \quad (x\neq 0)$

16. $g(x)=2x^2+\dfrac{4000}{x}+10 \quad (x\neq 0)$

17. $f(x)=\dfrac{x^2+4}{x^2-4} \quad (x\neq -2, 2)$

18. $g(t)=\dfrac{t^2}{1+t^2}$

19. $f(x)=x^2e^x$

20. $g(t)=e^{t^2-2t}$

21. $h(x)=x^2e^{-x}$

22. $f(t)=\dfrac{e^t+e^{-t}}{2}$

23. $f(x)=\ln(x^2+1)$

24. $g(t)=\ln(t^2+2t+5)$

25. $g(x)=x-\ln x \quad (x>0)$

26. $f(x)=\ln x-x^2 \quad (x\neq 0)$

****27.*** Show that the quadratic function $f(x)=ax^2+bx+c$ $(a\neq 0)$ has a relative extremum when $x=-b/(2a)$. Show further that the relative extremum is a relative maximum if $a<0$ and is a relative minimum if $a>0$.

***28.** Show that the cubic function $f(x)=ax^3+bx^2+cx+d$ $(a \neq 0)$ has no relative extremum if and only if $b^2-3ac<0$.

11.3

Concavity and Points of Inflection

In the last two sections we saw how the first derivative of a function f is used to help identify certain properties of the function. In this section the second derivative f'' of a function f will be employed to help us identify other properties of f. They will be equally useful as aids in sketching the graph of f and in solving optimization problems. Recall the observation made earlier (Section 10.8) that the second derivative of a function f at a point x measures both the rate of the rate of change of f and the rate of the turning of the tangent line of the graph of f at the point $(x, f(x))$. Thus, it may be expected that the behavior of the second derivative f'' of a function f is intrinsically tied to the "curvature" of the graph of f. The graph of the function f is *concave upward on an interval* (a, b) if the slope of the tangent line to the graph of f at the point $(x, f(x))$ is increasing as x increases from a to b (see Figure 11.19, part a). Observe that when a function is concave upward on an interval (a, b) the tangent line to the graph of f turns counterclockwise as x increases from a to b. We shall also say that f is *concave upward at a point* $x=c$ if there exists an interval (a, b) containing c in which f is concave upward.

concave upward on an interval

concave upward at a point

Similarly, we say that a function f is *concave downward on an interval* (a, b) if the slope of the tangent line to the graph of f at the point $(x, f(x))$ is decreasing as x increases from a to b (see Figure 11.19, part b). Notice that when a function is concave downward on an interval (a, b), the tangent line to the graph of f turns clockwise as x increases from a to b. We shall also say that f is *concave downward at a point* $x=c$, if there exists an interval (a, b) containing c in which f is concave downward.

concave downward on an interval

concave downward at a point

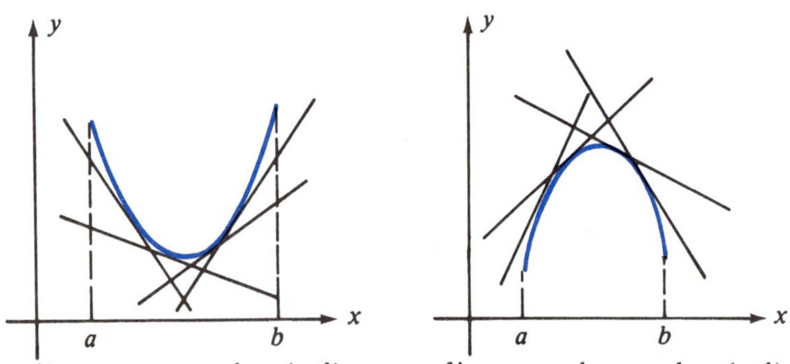

f is concave upward on (a, b)
(a)

f is concave downward on (a, b)
(b)

Figure 11.19

Thus, roughly speaking, a function is concave upward on an interval (a, b) if that portion of the graph of f for $a<x<b$ "holds water," whereas a function is

concave downward on an interval (a, b) if that portion of the graph of f corresponding to the values of x between a and b "spills water."

intervals of concavity

A simple characterization of the *intervals of concavity* of functions that possess derivatives of the second order is easily derived. The second derivative f'' of a function at a point x measures the rate of change of the slope of the tangent line to the graph of the function f at the point $(x, f(x))$. Thus, if $f''(x)$ is positive, then the slope of the tangent line, $f'(x)$, is increasing at that point. Equivalently, the tangent line is turning in a counterclockwise direction at that point, and f is concave upward. Similarly, if f'' is negative at a point x, then the graph of f is concave downward at that point. These observations lead to the following theorem.

THEOREM 11.2 Suppose a function f is twice differentiable on an interval (a, b).

(a) If $f''(x) > 0$ for each value of x in (a, b), then f is concave upward on (a, b).

(b) If $f''(x) < 0$ for each value of x in (a, b), then f is concave downward on (a, b).

The following procedure, based on the conclusion of Theorem 11.2, may be adopted to determine the intervals of concavity of a twice differentiable function:

1. Find all values of x for which the second derivative f'' of the function f is discontinuous as well as all values x for which f'' is zero. These values of x partition the domain of f into open intervals which have (finite) endpoints that are precisely determined by these values of x.

2. On each of these intervals found in Step 1, f'' is continuous and does not change sign, so that in order to determine the sign of f'' in such an interval, it suffices to compute $f''(c)$, where c is any conveniently chosen test point in the interval. The sign of f'' in the interval coincides with the sign of $f''(c)$. By Theorem 11.2, f is concave upward or concave downward in the interval according to whether $f''(c) > 0$ or $f''(c) < 0$.

EXAMPLE 11.11 Determine where the function $f(x) = x^{2/3}$ is concave upward and where it is concave downward.

SOLUTION First, compute the second derivative of f. Since

$$f'(x) = \frac{2}{3}x^{-1/3}$$

we find

$$f''(x) = \frac{2}{3}\left(-\frac{1}{3}\right)x^{-4/3} = -\frac{2}{9x^{4/3}}$$

We see at once that f'' is discontinuous at $x = 0$. Furthermore, f'' is not equal to zero anywhere. The point $x = 0$ divides the real line (the domain of f) into the intervals $(-\infty, 0)$ and $(0, \infty)$. Picking the test point $x = -1$ in the interval $(-\infty, 0)$, we find that $f''(-1) = -2/(9(-1)^{4/3}) = -(2/9) < 0$ and so $f''(x) < 0$ on $(-\infty, 0)$.

Next, picking $x=1$ as the test point in the interval $(0, \infty)$, we find $f''(1) = -(2/9) < 0$, so that $f''(x) < 0$ on $(0, \infty)$ as well. We conclude that f is concave downward on the intervals $(-\infty, 0)$ and $(0, \infty)$. The graph of f is sketched in Figure 11.20.

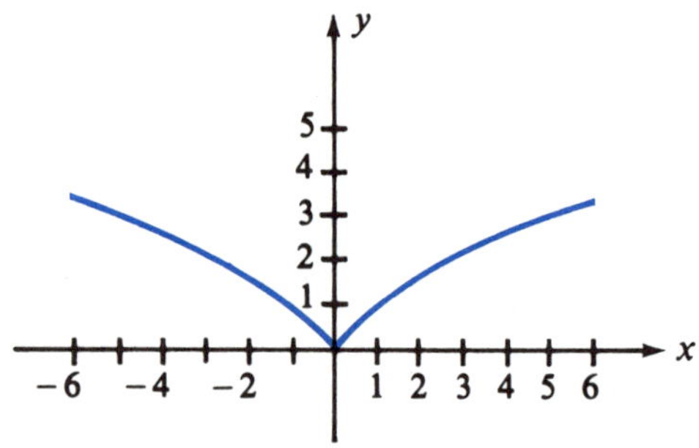

Figure 11.20

EXAMPLE 11.12 Determine where the function $f(x) = x^3 - 3x^2 - 24x + 32$ is concave upward and where it is concave downward.

SOLUTION Here

$$f'(x) = 3x^2 - 6x - 24$$

so that

$$\begin{aligned} f''(x) &= 6x - 6 \\ &= 6(x-1) \end{aligned}$$

and is continuous everywhere. Setting $f''(x) = 0$ gives $x = 1$. The sign diagram of f'' appears in Figure 11.21. We conclude that f is concave downward on the interval $(-\infty, 1)$ and is concave upward on the interval $(1, \infty)$. Figure 11.22 shows the graph of f.

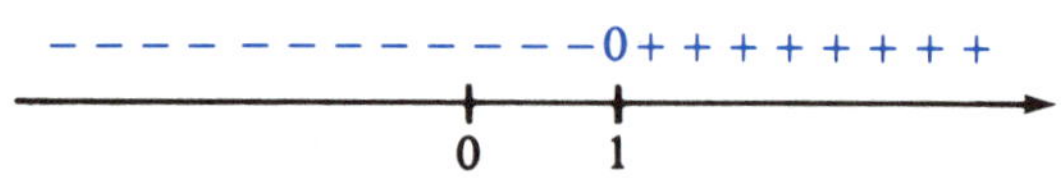

Figure 11.21

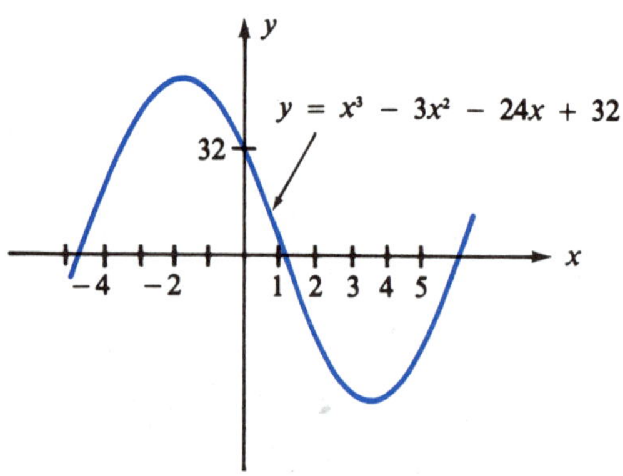

Figure 11.22

EXAMPLE 11.13 Determine the intervals where the function $f(x)=x+1/x$ is concave upward and where it is concave downward.

SOLUTION We have

$$f'(x)=1-\frac{1}{x^2}$$

and

$$f''(x)=\frac{2}{x^3}$$

The sign diagram for f'' appears in Figure 11.23. We deduce from the sign diagram that the function f is concave downward on the interval $(-\infty, 0)$ and concave upward on the interval $(0, \infty)$. The graph of f is sketched in Figure 11.24.

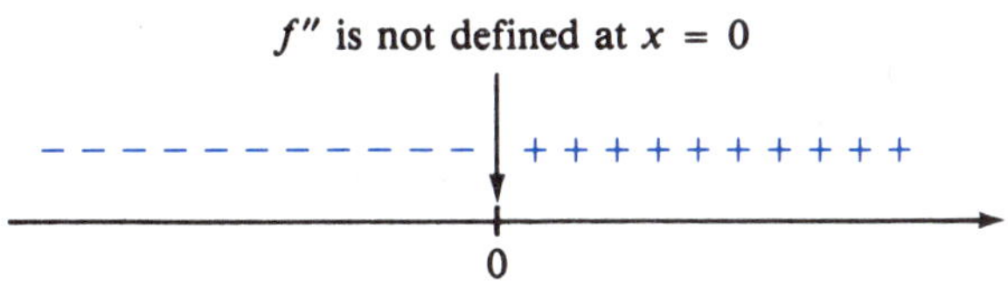

Figure 11.23

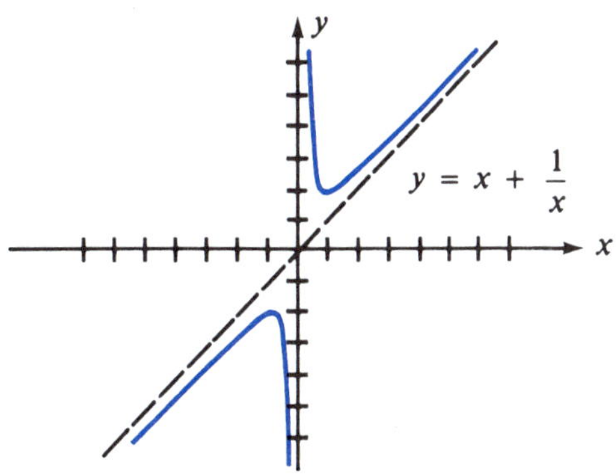

Figure 11.24

As the last example shows, a function may change concavity at one or more points. We call a point at which the concavity of a continuous function changes an *inflection point*. The following procedure may be used to find inflection points:

inflection point

1. Compute $f''(x)$.

2. Determine the points in the domain of f for which $f''(x)=0$ and also those for which $f''(x)$ is discontinuous. Such points are called the *hypercritical points* of f and are candidates for the values of x which give rise to the inflection points of f.

hypercritical points

3. *The Test for Inflection Points:* Determine the sign of $f''(x)$ to the left and right of each *hypercritical point*. If there is a change in the sign of $f''(x)$ as we move across a hypercritical point $x=c$, then $(c, f(c))$ is an inflection point of f. If there is no

The Test for Inflection Points

change in the sign of $f''(x)$ as we move across the hypercritical point $x=c$, then $(c, f(c))$ is not an inflection point of f.

EXAMPLE 11.14 Find the points of inflection of the function $f(x)=x^3$.

SOLUTION

$$f'(x)=3x^2$$

and so

$$f''(x)=6x$$

Now $f''(x)=0$ implies that $x=0$ is the only hypercritical point of f. Since $f''(x)<0$ when $x<0$ and $f''(x)>0$ when $x>0$, we see that f'' changes sign as we move across $x=0$ and so the point (0, 0) is an inflection point of the function f (see Figure 11.25).

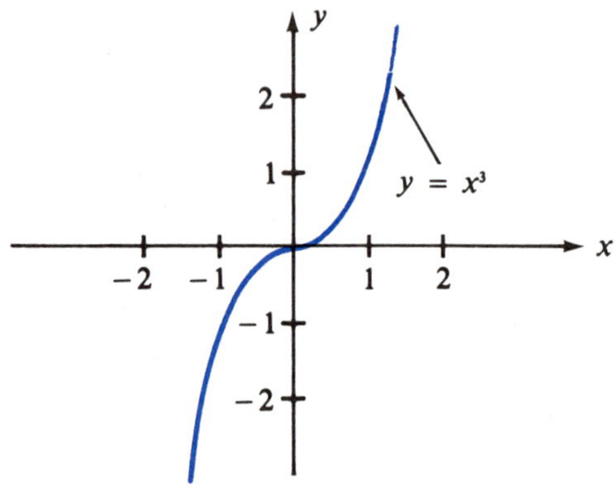

Figure 11.25

■

EXAMPLE 11.15 Find the points of inflection of the function $f(x)=(x-1)^{5/3}$.

SOLUTION The first derivative of f is

$$f'(x)=\frac{5}{3}(x-1)^{2/3}$$

so that the second derivative of f is

$$f''(x)=\frac{10}{9}(x-1)^{-1/3}$$

$$=\frac{10}{9(x-1)^{1/3}}$$

Now, f'' is not defined at $x=1$ and since it is not equal to zero at any point x, $x=1$ is the only hypercritical point of f. Next, since $f''(x)<0$ for $x<1$ and $f''(x)>0$ for $x>1$, the point (1, 0) is an inflection point of f (see Figure 11.26).

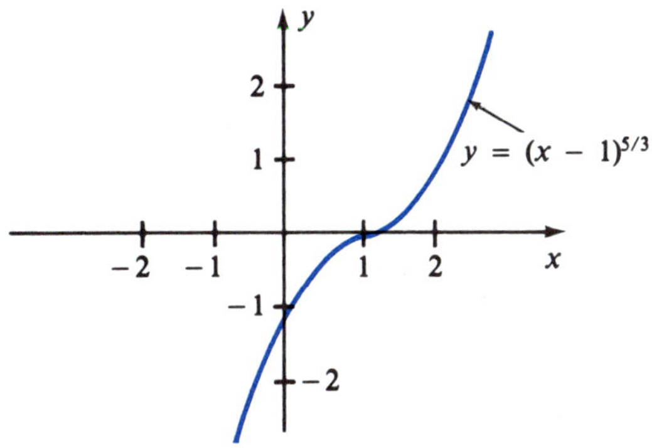

Figure 11.26 ■

EXAMPLE 11.16 Find the points of inflection of the function $f(x)=e^{-x^2}$.

SOLUTION The first derivative of f is

$$f'(x)=-2x\,e^{-x^2}$$

Differentiating $f'(x)$ with respect to x yields

$$\begin{aligned} f''(x)&=(-2x)(-2x\,e^{-x^2})-2\,e^{-x^2}\\ &=2\,e^{-x^2}(2x^2-1)\end{aligned}$$

Setting $f''(x)=0$ gives

$$2\,e^{-x^2}(2x^2-1)=0$$

Since e^{-x^2} never equals zero for any real value of x, we see that $x=\pm 1/\sqrt{2}$ are the only hypercritical points of f. The sign diagram of f'', Figure 11.27, tells us that both $x=-1/\sqrt{2}$ and $x=1/\sqrt{2}$ give rise to inflection points of f. Next,

$$f\left(-\frac{1}{\sqrt{2}}\right)=f\left(\frac{1}{\sqrt{2}}\right)=e^{-1/2}$$

and the inflection points of f are $(-1/\sqrt{2}, e^{-1/2})$ and $(1/\sqrt{2}, e^{-1/2})$. The graph of f appears in Figure 11.28.

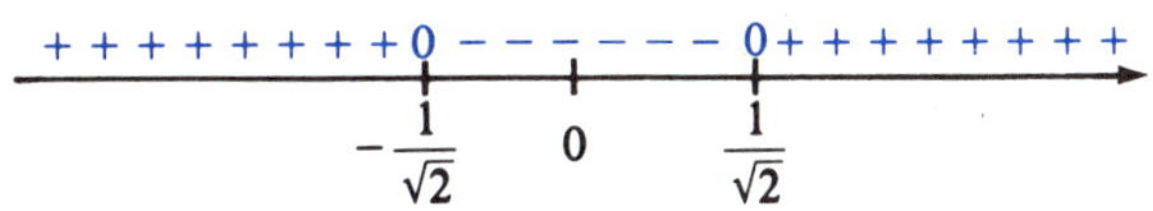

Figure 11.27

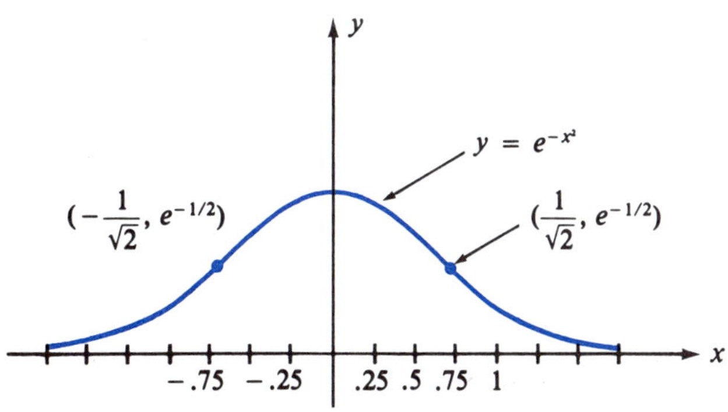

Figure 11.28 ■

The next two examples illustrate familiar interpretations of the significance of the inflection point of a function.

EXAMPLE 11.17 The total sales S, in thousands of dollars, of the Arctic Air Corporation, a manufacturer of automobile air conditioners, is related to the amount of money, x, the company spends on advertising its products by the formula $S = -0.01x^3 + 1.5x^2 + 200$ $(0 \le x \le 100)$ where x is measured in thousands of dollars. Find the inflection point of the function S and discuss its significance.

SOLUTION The first two derivatives of S are given by

$$S' = -0.03x^2 + 3x$$

and

$$S'' = -0.06x + 3$$

Setting $S'' = 0$ gives $x = 50$ as the only hypercritical point of the function S. Moreover, since $S'' > 0$ for $x < 50$ and $S'' < 0$ for $x > 50$, the point (50, 2700) is an inflection point of the function S. The graph of S appears in Figure 11.29. Observe that the total sales of the company increase rather slowly at first, but as more money is spent on advertising its products, the total sales increase rapidly. This rapid increase reflects the effectiveness of its advertisements. However, a point is soon reached after which any additional expenditure in advertising results in increased sales but at a slower rate of increase. This point is commonly known as the *point of diminishing returns*. It is just the point of inflection of the function S.

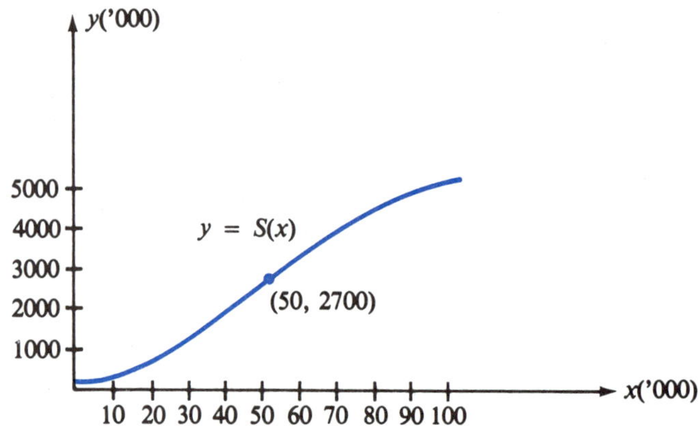

Figure 11.29

■

EXAMPLE 11.18 (Refer to Example 11.5, page 494). The altitude (in feet) of a rocket t seconds into flight is given by $s = f(t) = -t^3 + 96t^2 + 195t + 5$. Find the point of inflection of the function f and give it a physical interpretation.

SOLUTION We have

$$f'(t) = v = -3t^2 + 192t + 195$$

and

$$f''(t) = a = -6t + 192$$

Setting $f''(t)=0$ gives $t=32$. Moreover, we have $f''(t)>0$ for $t<32$ and $f''(t)<0$ for $t>32$, so that the point $(32, 71781)$ is an inflection point of the function f. Since the second derivative f'' of f measures the acceleration of the rocket at any time t, the point of inflection of the function f corresponds to the point at which the acceleration of the rocket changes sign. In this instance the change is from positive to negative or from acceleration to deceleration. This also implies that the velocity of the rocket is greatest when $t=32$ or 32 seconds into flight. The maximum velocity attained is given by $f'(32)=3267$ or 3,267 feet per second. ■

We close this section by summarizing the different roles played by the first derivative f' and the second derivative f'' of a function f in determining the properties of the graph of f. The first derivative f' of f tells us where f is increasing and where f is decreasing while the second derivative f'' of f tells us where f is concave upward and where f is concave downward. These different properties of f are reflected by the signs of f' and f'' in the interval of interest. The following table shows the general characteristics of the function f for various possible combinations of the signs of f' and f'' in the interval (a, b).

Signs of f' and f''	Properties of the graph of f	General shape of the graph of f
1. $f'(x)>0$ $f''(x)>0$	f increasing f concave upward	
2. $f'(x)>0$ $f''(x)<0$	f increasing f concave downward	
3. $f'(x)<0$ $f''(x)>0$	f decreasing f concave upward	
4. $f'(x)<0$ $f''(x)<0$	f decreasing f concave downward	

11.3 EXERCISES

In problems 1 through 6 show that the given function is concave upward everywhere.

1. $f(x)=4x^2-12x+7$

2. $g(x)=x^4+\frac{1}{2}x^2+6x+10$

3. $h(x)=\sqrt{x^2+4}$

4. $f(x)=\frac{1}{x^4}\quad (x\neq 0)$

5. $f(x)=e^x+e^{-x}$

6. $g(x)=\ln\left(\frac{1}{x^2}\right)\quad (x\neq 0)$

In problems 7 through 28 determine where the given function is concave upward and where it is concave downward.

7. $f(x)=x^{4/7}$

8. $f(x)=x^3-6x^2+2x+1$

9. $g(t)=-5t^3+15t^2+24t-192$

10. $f(x)=\frac{1}{3}x^3-5x^2+10x-2$

11. $f(x)=x^4-6x^3+2x+8$

12. $f(x)=3x^4-6x^3+x-8$

13. $h(t)=3t^5-5t^4+t-2$

14. $g(x)=3x^5-15x^4+20x^3+12x-4$

15. $f(x)=\frac{1}{1+x^2}$

16. $g(x)=\frac{x}{1+x^2}$

17. $h(t)=\frac{t^2}{t-1} \quad (t\neq 1)$

***18.** $h(x)=\sqrt{x^2+2x+5}$

19. $f(x)=\frac{x+1}{x-1} \quad (x\neq 1)$

20. $g(x)=x+\frac{1}{x^2} \quad (x\neq 0)$

21. $h(r)=-\frac{1}{(r-2)^2} \quad (r\neq 2)$

22. $f(x)=\frac{x^2}{x^2-1} \quad (x\neq -1, 1)$

23. $g(x)=e^{x2}$

24. $g(x)=x^2e^{-x}$

***25.** $f(x)=\frac{1}{1+e^{-x}}$

26. $f(t)=t\ln t \quad (t>0)$

27. $g(t)=t^2+\ln t^2 \quad (t\neq 0)$

***28.** $f(x)=\frac{\ln x}{x} \quad (x>0)$

29. Show that the quadratic function $f(x)=ax^2+bx+c$ $(a\neq 0)$ is concave upward if $a>0$ and is concave downward if $a<0$. Thus, by examining the sign of the coefficient of x^2 one can tell immediately whether the parabola opens upward or downward.

In problems 30 through 37 find the inflection points, if any, of each of the given functions.

30. $f(x)=6x^3-18x^2+12x-15$

31. $f(t)=\frac{1}{4}t^4-\frac{1}{3}t^3-\frac{1}{2}t^2+5t+10$

32. $g(x)=2x^5-10x^4+8x-400$

33. $h(x)=x^6-5x^4+12$

34. $f(x)=\frac{e^x-e^{-x}}{2}$

35. $g(x)=e^{-x2}$

36. $g(x)=x-\ln x \quad (x>0)$

37. $f(t)=\ln(1+t^2)$

38. Show that both the exponential growth function $f(t)=Q_0e^{kt}$ $(t\geq 0)$ and the exponential decay function $f(t)=Q_0e^{-kt}$ $(t\geq 0)$, where Q_0 and k are positive constants, are concave upward everywhere.

39. Show that the learning curve described by the function $f(x) = C - Ae^{-kx}$ $(x \geq 0)$, where C, A and k are positive constants and $C > A$ (see Section 5.4) is concave downward everywhere.

40. Show that the cubic function $f(x) = ax^3 + bx^2 + cx + d$ $(a \neq 0)$ has one and only one inflection point. Find the coordinates of this point.

***41.** Find the inflection point of the logistic function

$$f(t) = \frac{A}{1 + Be^{-kt}} \quad (t \geq 0)$$

where A, B and k are positive constants (see Section 5.4).

42. The total sales S, in thousands of dollars, of the Cannon Precision Instruments Corporation, is related to the amount of money, x, the company spends on advertising its products by the formula $S = -0.002x^3 + 0.6x^2 + x + 500$ $(0 \leq x \leq 200)$ where x is measured in thousands of dollars. Find the inflection point of the function S and discuss its significance.

43. Faced by increasing energy costs the rate of growth of the profit of the four-year old Venice Glassblowing Company has begun to decline. The management of the company, after consultation with energy experts, decided to implement certain energy conservation measures aimed at cutting energy bills. The general manager reports that, according to his calculations, the rate of growth of the company's profit should once again be on the increase within four year's time. If the profit of the company (in hundreds of dollars) x years from now is given by $P = x^3 - 9x^2 + 40x + 50$ $(0 \leq x \leq 8)$, determine if the general manager's forecast will be accurate. *Hint:* Find the inflection point of the function P and study the concavity of P.

44. An efficiency study conducted for the Elektra Electronics Company showed that the number of "Space Commander" walkie-talkies assembled by the average worker t hours after starting work at 8 A.M. is given by $N(t) = -t^3 + 6t^2 + 15t$ $(0 \leq t \leq 4)$. At what time during the morning shift is the average worker performing at peak efficiency?

45. A subsidiary of the Elektra Electronics Company manufactures a programmable electronic pocket calculator. The management of the company determined that the daily cost of producing these calculators (in dollars) obeys the rule $C(x) = 0.0001x^3 - 0.08x^2 + 40x + 5000$ where x stands for the number of calculators produced. Find the inflection point of the function C and interpret your result.

46. The altitude (in feet) of a rocket t seconds into flight is given by $s = f(t) = -t^3 + 54t^2 + 480t + 6$. Find the point of inflection of the function f and interpret your result. What is the maximum velocity attained by the rocket?

11.4

The Second Derivative Test

In this section we show how the second derivative f'' of a function f is used to locate the relative extrema of the function. Observe that at a local extremum $(c, f(c))$ of a differentiable function not only must $f'(c)=0$, but the graph of f must also be "locally" concave—downward if the point is a relative maximum and upward if it is a relative minimum (see Figure 11.30).

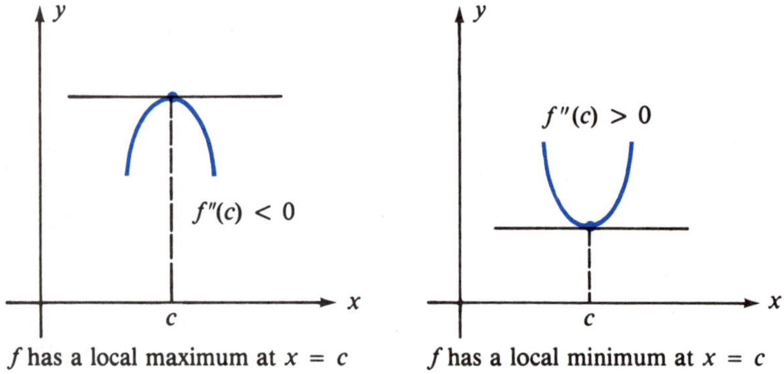

Figure 11.30

From our previous work, we know that if $f''(c)<0$, then f is "locally" concave downward, while if $f''(c)>0$, then f is "locally" concave upward. This suggests that for a twice differentiable function f, a critical point $x=c$ is, in fact, a relative maximum if the further condition $f''(c)<0$ holds and is a relative minimum if the condition $f''(c)>0$ holds. Before stating these results formally, let us look at the case where $x=c$ is a critical point of a function f but $f''(c)=0$.

EXAMPLE 11.19 Consider the functions $f(x)=x^3$, $g(x)=x^4$ and $h(x)=-x^4$.

(a) Show that $x=0$ is a critical point of each of the functions f, g and h.

(b) Show that the second derivative of each of the functions, f, g and h equals zero at $x=0$.

(c) Show that f has neither a relative maximum nor a relative minimum at $x=0$, that g has a relative minimum at $x=0$ and that h has a relative maximum at $x=0$.

SOLUTION **(a)** We have

$$f'(x)=3x^2, \quad g'(x)=4x^3 \quad \text{and} \quad h'(x)=-4x^3$$

so that

$$f'(0)=0, \quad g'(0)=0 \quad \text{and} \quad h'(0)=0$$

showing that $x=0$ is a critical point of each of the functions f, g and h.

(**b**) We have

$$f''(x)=6x, \quad g''(x)=12x^2 \quad \text{and} \quad h''(x)=-12x^2$$

so that

$$f''(0)=0, \quad g''(0)=0 \quad \text{and} \quad h''(0)=0$$

as was to be shown.

(**c**) Since $f'(x)>0$ for both $x>0$ and $x<0$, $f'(x)$ does not change sign as we move across the critical point $x=0$ of f. So, by the First Derivative Test, f does not possess a relative extremum at $x=0$. Next, observe that $g'(x)$ changes sign from negative to positive as we move across $x=0$ implying that the point $(0, 0)$ is a relative minimum for the function g. Finally, we see that $h'(x)>0$ for $x<0$ and $h'(x)<0$ for $x>0$, so that the function h has a relative maximum at the point $(0, 0)$ (see Figure 11.31).

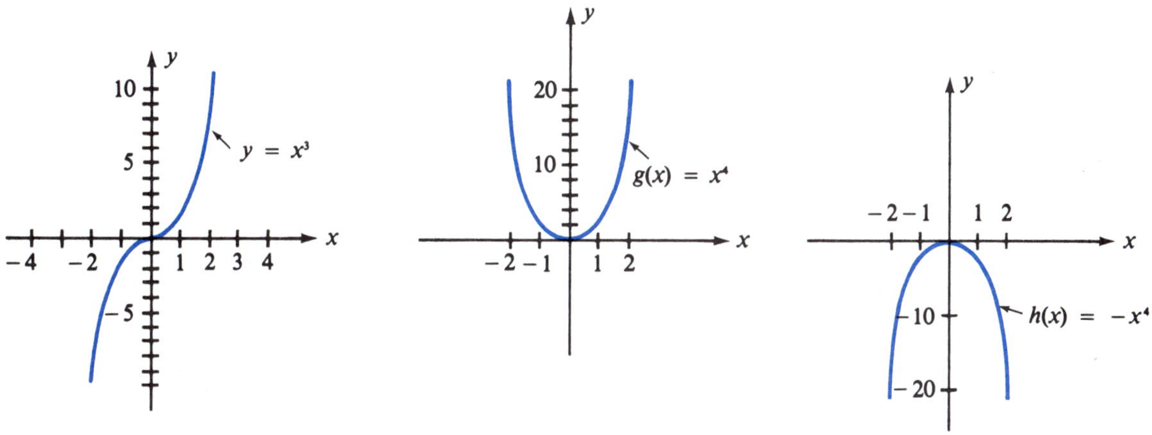

Figure 11.31 ■

The above results lead to an alternative procedure for determining whether a critical point of a twice differentiable function f is in fact a relative extremum of f. This test uses the second derivative of f and is accordingly called the Second Derivative Test. The procedure follows:

1. Compute $f'(x)$ and $f''(x)$.

2. Find all the critical points of f by solving the equation $f'(x)=0$.

The Second Derivative Test

3. *The Second Derivative Test*: Suppose $x=c$ is a critical point of f found in Step 2. Compute $f''(c)$. Three cases result:

- (*a*) If $f''(c)<0$, then f has a relative maximum at $x=c$.
- (*b*) If $f''(c)>0$, then f has a relative minimum at $x=c$.
- (*c*) If $f''(c)=0$, the test fails; that is, it is inconclusive.

Notice that both the First Derivative Test and the Second Derivative Test are used to classify critical points of f as the relative maxima or relative minima of f. What are the pros and cons of the two tests? Since the Second Derivative

Test is applicable only to twice differentiable functions, it is less versatile than the First Derivative Test. For example, it cannot be used to locate the relative minimum (0, 0) of the function $f(x)=x^{2/3}$ (see Example 11.8). Furthermore, the Second Derivative Test is inconclusive when f'' is equal to zero at a critical point of f, whereas the First Derivative Test always yields positive conclusions (see Example 11.19). The Second Derivative Test is also inconvenient to use if the second derivative f'' of the given function f is difficult to compute. On the plus side, the conclusions of the Second Derivative Test are important in theoretical work (see problem 11, in Exercise set 11.7). Also, if the second derivative f'' of a function f is not too difficult to compute (for example, if f is a polynomial function) then the Second Derivative Test is easy to apply since it involves just the evaluation of f'' at the critical point $x=c$ of the function f.

EXAMPLE 11.20 Determine the relative extrema of the function $f(x)=x^3-3x^2-24x+32$ using the Second Derivative Test. (See Example 11.9, page 502).

SOLUTION We have

$$\begin{aligned} f'(x) &= 3x^2-6x-24 \\ &= 3(x+2)(x-4) \end{aligned}$$

so that $f'(x)=0$ gives $x=-2$ and $x=4$, the critical points of f, as in Example 11.9. Next, we compute

$$\begin{aligned} f''(x) &= 6x-6 \\ &= 6(x-1) \end{aligned}$$

Since $f''(-2)=6(-2-1)=-18<0$, the Second Derivative Test implies that the point $(-2, 60)$ is a relative maximum of f. Also, $f''(4)=6(4-1)=18>0$ and the Second Derivative Test implies that the point $(4, -48)$ is a relative minimum of f, which confirms the results obtained in Example 11.9. ■

11.4 EXERCISES

In problems 1 through 8, find the relative extrema of each of the given functions using the Second Derivative Test.

1. $f(x)=\frac{1}{3}x^3-2x^2-5x-10$

2. $g(x)=3x^4+4x^3-24x^2-48x+12$

3. $f(t)=t^4-4t^3$

4. $f(x)=\dfrac{x^2+9}{x^2-9}$

5. $f(x)=x+\dfrac{1}{x} \quad (x\neq 0)$

6. $h(x)=x^2e^{-x}$

7. $f(x)=\ln(x^2+2x+5)$

8. $g(t)=t^2-\frac{1}{2}\ln t \quad (t>0)$

11.5

Curve Sketching

In the last several sections, we saw how the first and second derivatives of a function are used to reveal various properties of the function. These techniques, combined with those developed in Section 2.3, give us a powerful method for sketching the graphs of most types of functions encountered in practical applications. Before proceeding you may wish to review Section 2.3 on the techniques of graphing.

A summary of the information about a function f that may be obtained using the techniques we have developed so far follows. This information can then be used to sketch its graph.

1. The domain of f

2. The x- and y-intercepts of f

3. The symmetry of f about the y-axis and the origin

4. The intervals where f is increasing and where f is decreasing

5. The relative extrema of f

6. The concavity of f

7. The inflection points of f

8. The behavior of f for large absolute values of x

9. The horizontal and vertical asymptotes of f

Items 1 through 8 concerning a function f are review. To introduce the notion of an *asymptote* of the graph of a function, consider the function

$$f(x) = \frac{x+1}{x-1}$$

Its graph is shown in Figure 11.32.

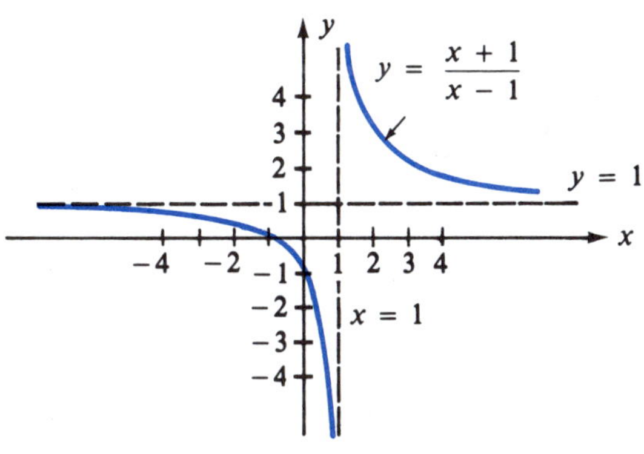

Figure 11.32

horizontal asymptote

vertical asymptote

Observe that the graph of f approaches the horizontal line $y=1$ as x becomes arbitrarily large (and, in this case, as x tends to minus infinity as well). The line $y=1$ is called a *horizontal asymptote* of the graph of f. Observe, also, that the graph of f approaches the vertical line $x=1$ as x approaches the point $x=1$ from the right (and, in this case, from the left as well). The line $x=1$ is called a *vertical asymptote* of the graph of f. In general, to find the horizontal asymptotes of the graph of a function f, we evaluate

$$\lim_{x\to\infty} f(x) \quad \text{and} \quad \lim_{x\to-\infty} f(x)$$

If either limit exists, for example, if

$$\lim_{x\to\infty} f(x)=b$$

then the line $y=b$ is a horizontal asymptote of the graph of f. For the function we are considering we find that

$$\begin{aligned}\lim_{x\to\infty} f(x) &= \lim_{x\to\infty}\frac{x+1}{x-1}=\lim_{x\to\infty}\frac{1+1/x}{1-1/x}\\ &=1\end{aligned}$$

so that the line $y=1$ is a horizontal asymptote of the graph of f as observed earlier. Note that

$$\lim_{x\to-\infty} f(x)=1$$

as well, as may be verified by the reader.

Next, to find the vertical asymptotes of the graph of a function f, we normally find the point(s) where the denominator of $f(x)$ is equal to zero. Such values of x are candidates for the vertical asymptotes of the graph of f. Suppose, for example, that the denominator of $f(x)$ is equal to zero at $x=a$. We then evaluate

$$\lim_{x\to a^+} f(x) \quad \text{and} \quad \lim_{x\to a^-} f(x)$$

called, respectively, the *right-hand limit* and *left-hand limit* of $f(x)$ at $x=a$. These limits are evaluated as described in Chapter 10 but restricting x to lie to the right of $x=a$ (that is, $x>a$) in the former and restricting x to lie to the left of $x=a$ $(x<a)$ in the latter. If either limit approaches plus or minus infinity, the line $x=a$ is a vertical asymptote of the graph of f. For the function

$$f(x)=\frac{x+1}{x-1}$$

the denominator is equal to zero when $x = 1$. Next, we find

$$\lim_{x \to 1^+} f(x) = \lim_{x \to 1^+} \frac{x+1}{x-1} = \infty$$

and

$$\lim_{x \to 1^-} f(x) = \lim_{x \to 1^-} \frac{x+1}{x-1} = -\infty$$

which confirms that the vertical line $x = 1$ is in fact a vertical asymptote of the graph of f as observed earlier.

EXAMPLE 11.21 Sketch the graph of the function $y = f(x) = x^3 - 4x^2 - 3x + 18$.

SOLUTION We obtain the following information on the graph of f.

1. The domain of f is the interval $(-\infty, \infty)$.

2. Setting $y = 0$ gives

$$x^3 - 4x^2 - 3x + 18 = 0$$

By trial and error we find that the number $x = -2$ is a root and therefore $(x+2)$ is a factor of the above equation. Dividing $f(x)$ by $(x+2)$ we obtain

$$(x+2)(x^2 - 6x + 9) = 0$$

or

$$(x+2)(x-3)^2 = 0$$

which gives $x = -2$ and $x = 3$ as the x-intercepts of f. The y-intercept is $y = 18$.

3. There is no symmetry of f with respect to the y-axis or the origin.

4.

$$f'(x) = 3x^2 - 8x - 3 = (3x+1)(x-3)$$

Setting $f'(x) = 0$ gives $x = -1/3$ or $x = 3$. The sign diagram for f' shows that f is increasing on the intervals $(-\infty, -1/3)$ and $(3, \infty)$, and decreasing on the interval $(-1/3, 3)$.

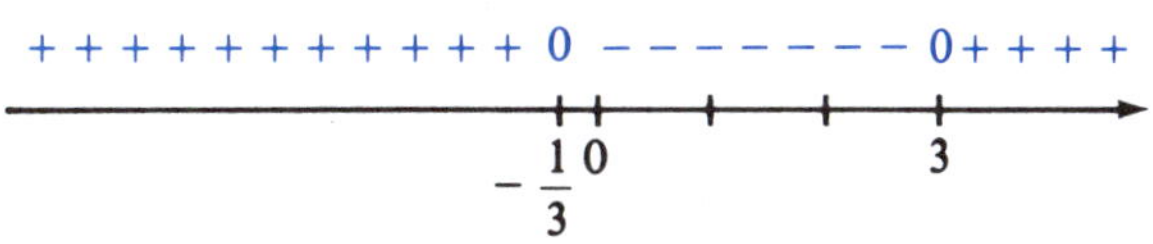

5. From the results of (*4*) we see that $x = -1/3$ and $x = 3$ are critical points of f. Furthermore f' changes sign from positive to negative as we move across $x = -1/3$, so that the point $x = -1/3$ gives rise to a relative maximum of f. Similarly, we see that $x = 3$ gives rise to a relative minimum of f. Now,

$$f\left(-\frac{1}{3}\right)=\left(-\frac{1}{3}\right)^3-4\left(-\frac{1}{3}\right)^2-3\left(-\frac{1}{3}\right)+18=\frac{500}{27}$$

and
$$f(3)=3^3-4(3)^2-3(3)+18=0$$

so that the point $(-1/3, 500/27)$ is a relative maximum of f and the point $(3, 0)$ is a relative minimum of f.

6.
$$\begin{aligned} f''(x)&=6x-8\\ &=2(3x-4)\end{aligned}$$

and is equal to zero when $x = 4/3$. The sign diagram of f'' shows that f is concave downward on the interval $(-\infty, 4/3)$ and concave upward on the interval $(4/3, \infty)$.

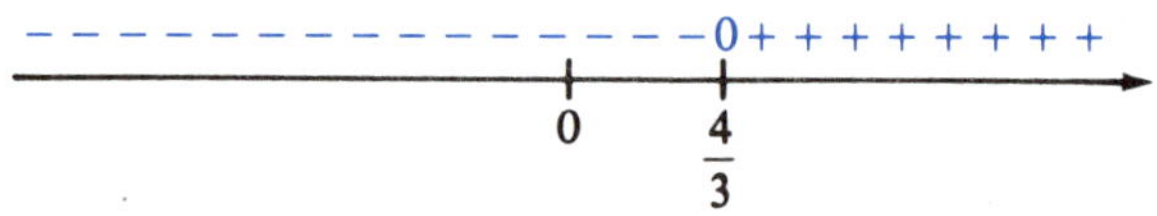

7. From the results of (*6*) we see that $x = 4/3$ is a hypercritical point of f and since f'' changes sign as we move across it, the point $x = 4/3$ in fact gives rise to an inflection point of f. Since

$$f\left(\frac{4}{3}\right)=\left(\frac{4}{3}\right)^3-4\left(\frac{4}{3}\right)^2-3\left(\frac{4}{3}\right)+18=\frac{250}{27}$$

the required inflection point of f is $(4/3, 250/27)$.

8. Since

$$\lim_{x\to-\infty} f(x)=\lim_{x\to-\infty}(x^3-4x^2-3x+18)=-\infty$$

and
$$\lim_{x\to\infty} f(x)=\lim_{x\to\infty}(x^3-4x^2-3x+18)=\infty$$

we see that f decreases without bound as x decreases without bound and increases without bound as x increases without bound.

9. There are no horizontal or vertical asymptotes.

The graph of f is sketched in Figure 11.33.

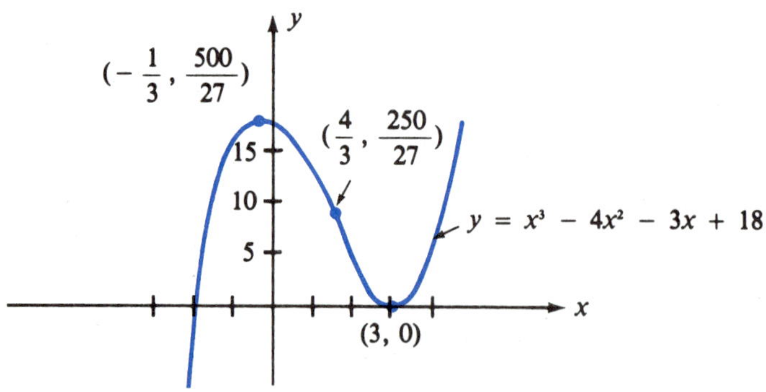

Figure 11.33

■

EXAMPLE 11.22 Sketch the graph of the function $y = f(x) = (x+1)/(x-1)$.

SOLUTION Here, we have

1. f is undefined when $x = 1$ so that the domain of f is the set of all real numbers other than $x = 1$.

2. Setting $y = 0$ gives $x = -1$, the x-intercept of f. Next, setting $x = 0$ gives $y = -1$ as the y-intercept of f.

3. y is not symmetric with respect to the y-axis or the origin.

4.
$$f'(x) = \frac{(x-1)(1)-(x+1)(1)}{(x-1)^2} = -\frac{2}{(x-1)^2}$$

and is discontinuous at $x = 1$. The sign diagram of f' shows that $f'(x) < 0$ whenever it is defined. Thus, f is decreasing on the intervals $(-\infty, 1)$ and $(1, \infty)$.

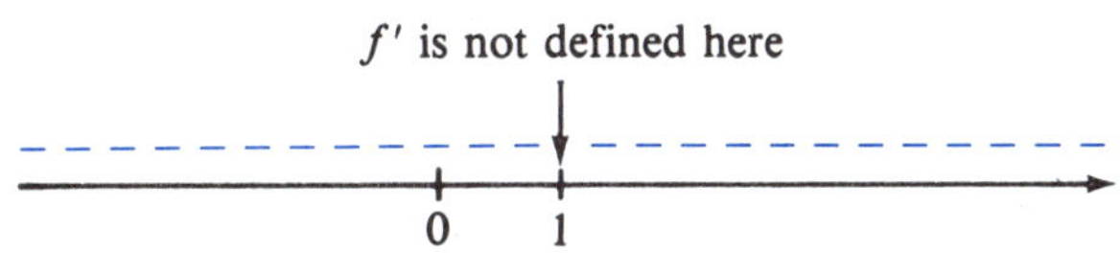

5. From the results of (*4*) we see that there are no critical points of f since $f'(x)$ is never equal to zero for any value of x in the domain of f.

6.
$$f''(x) = \frac{d}{dx}[-2(x-1)^{-2}] = 4(x-1)^{-3}$$
$$= \frac{4}{(x-1)^3}$$

The sign diagram of f'' shows immediately that f is concave downward on the interval $(-\infty, 1)$ and concave upward on the interval $(1, \infty)$.

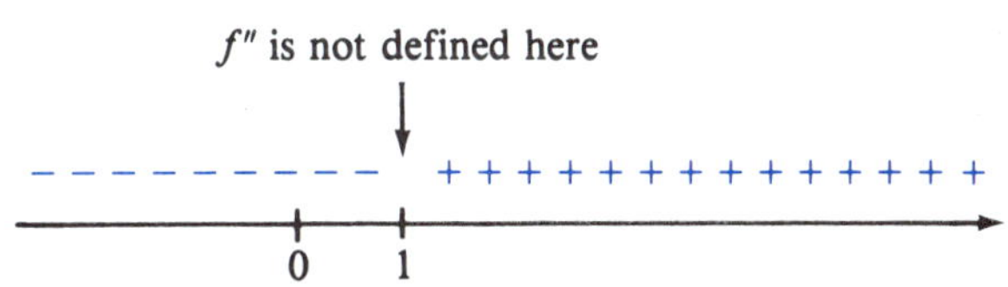

7. From the results of (*6*) we see that there are no hypercritical points of f since $f''(x)$ is never equal to zero for any value of x in the domain of f. Hence, f has no inflection points.

8. Since

$$\lim_{x\to\infty} \frac{x+1}{x-1} = 1 \qquad \text{and} \qquad \lim_{x\to\infty} \frac{x+1}{x-1}$$

(see page 518), we see that $f(x)$ approaches the line $y = 1$ as x becomes arbitrarily large. For $x > 1$, $f(x) > 1$ and $f(x)$ approaches $y = 1$ from above. For $x < 1$, $f(x) < 1$ so $f(x)$ approaches $y = 1$ from below.

9. The straight line $x = 1$ is a vertical asymptote of the graph of f (see page 518). Also, from the results of (*8*) we conclude that $y = 1$ is a horizontal asymptote of the graph of f.

The graph of f was sketched earlier (see Figure 11.32). ■

EXAMPLE 11.23 Sketch the graph of the function $f(x) = x/(1+x^2)$.

SOLUTION First we obtain the following data on f:

1. Since $1+x^2 \geq 1$ for all real values of x, the denominator of f is not equal to zero for any real value of x. Therefore, the domain of f is the set of all real numbers.

2. Setting $y = f(x) = 0$ gives $x = 0$ as the x-intercept of f. Setting $x = 0$ gives $y = 0$ as the y-intercept of f.

3. Since $f(-x) = -f(x)$ we see that f is symmetric with respect to the origin.

4.
$$f'(x) = \frac{(1+x^2)(1) - x(2x)}{(1+x^2)^2} = \frac{1-x^2}{(1+x^2)^2}$$

Setting $f'(x) = 0$ gives $x = \pm 1$. The sign diagram of f' shows that f is decreasing on the intervals $(-\infty, -1)$ and $(1, \infty)$ and increasing on the interval $(-1, 1)$.

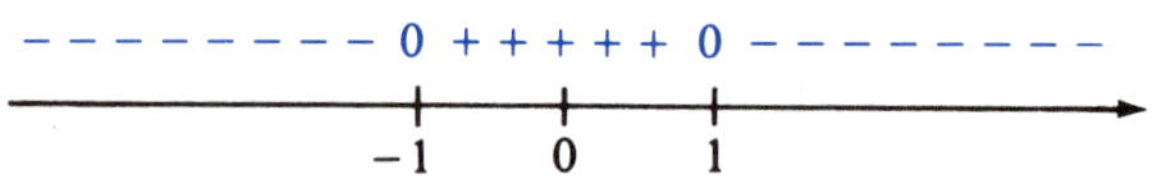

5. From the results of (*4*) we see that f has critical points at $x = -1$ and $x = 1$. The First Derivative Test confirms that the point $(-1, -1/2)$ is a relative minimum of f while the point $(1, 1/2)$ is a relative maximum of f.

6.
$$f''(x) = \frac{(1+x^2)^2(-2x) - (1-x^2)2(1+x^2)(2x)}{(1+x^2)^4} = \frac{(1+x^2)[-2x - 2x^3 - 4x + 4x^3]}{(1+x^2)^4} = \frac{2x(x^2-3)}{(1+x^2)^3}$$

Setting $f''(x) = 0$ gives $x = 0$, $-\sqrt{3}$ or $\sqrt{3}$. The sign diagram of f'' shows that f is concave downward on the intervals $(-\infty, -\sqrt{3})$ and $(0, \sqrt{3})$, and concave upward on the intervals $(-\sqrt{3}, 0)$ and $(\sqrt{3}, \infty)$.

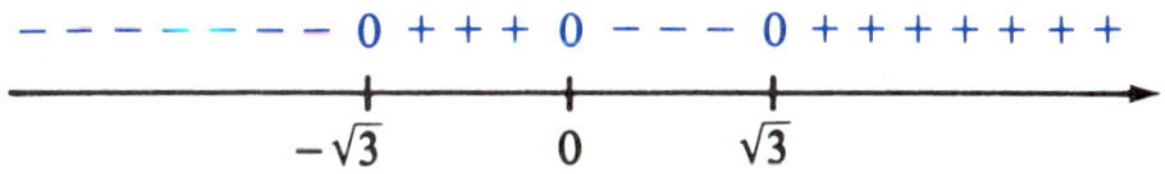

7. From the results of (*6*) we see that $x=\pm\sqrt{3}$ and $x=0$ are hypercritical points of f and the sign diagram of f'' further verifies that the points $(-\sqrt{3}, -\sqrt{3}/4)$, $(0, 0)$ and $(\sqrt{3}, \sqrt{3}/4)$ are, in fact, inflection points of f.

8. Since

$$\lim_{x\to\infty} \frac{x}{1+x^2}=0$$

and

$$\lim_{x\to-\infty} \frac{x}{1+x^2}=0$$

we see that $f(x)$ approaches 0 as x becomes arbitrarily large in absolute value.

9. There are no vertical asymptotes of f. However, $y=0$ is a horizontal asymptote of f (see step *8*).

The graph of f is sketched in Figure 11.34.

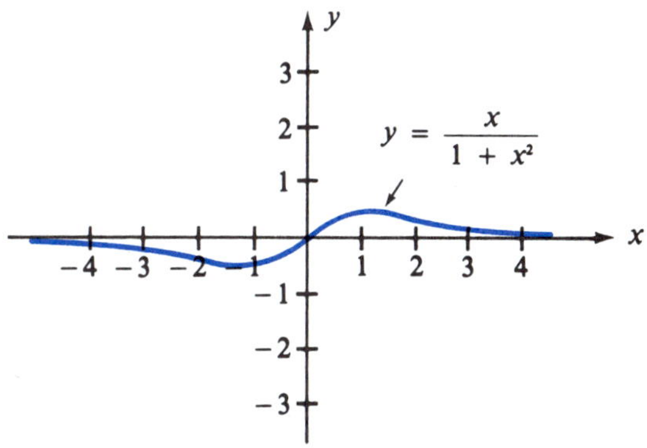

Figure 11.34

■

EXAMPLE 11.24 Sketch the graph of the function $f(x)=x\,e^{-x}$.

SOLUTION First we gather the following information on f:

1. The domain of f is the set of all real numbers.

2. Setting $y=0$ gives $x=0$ as the x-intercept of f (note that e^{-x} is never zero for any real value of x). Next, setting $x=0$ gives $y=0$ as the y-intercept of f.

3. There is no symmetry of f with respect to the y-axis or the origin.

4.

$$\begin{aligned} f'(x) &= -x\,e^{-x}+e^{-x} \\ &= e^{-x}(1-x) \end{aligned}$$

Since e^{-x} is not equal to zero for any real value of x, we see that $f'(x)=0$ gives

$x = 1$ which results in the following sign diagram for f'. Thus, f is increasing on the interval $(-\infty, 1)$ and decreasing on the interval $(1, \infty)$.

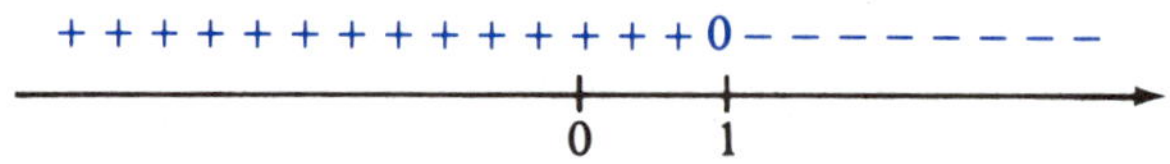

5. The results of (*4*) show that the critical point $x = 1$ of f gives a relative maximum $(1, e^{-1})$ of f.

6.

$$\begin{aligned} f''(x) &= -e^{-x} - e^{-x}(1-x) \\ &= e^{-x}(x-2) \end{aligned}$$

Setting $f''(x) = 0$ gives $x = 2$. From the following sign diagram for f'', we see that f is concave downward on the interval $(-\infty, 2)$ and concave upward on the interval $(2, \infty)$.

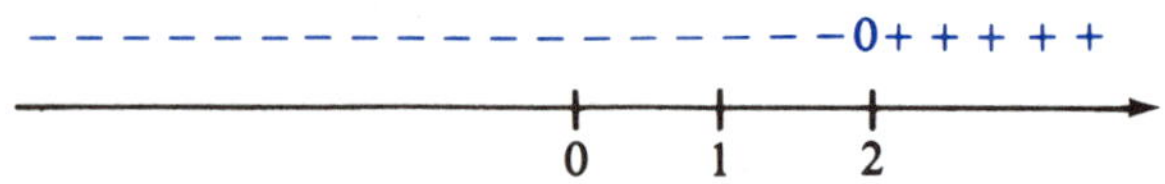

7. The result of (*6*) confirms that $x = 2$ is a hypercritical point of f. Furthermore, the sign diagram for f'' shows that the point $(2, 2e^{-2})$ is, in fact, an inflection point of f.

8. You may convince yourself by evaluating $f(x)$ at x for increasing values of x that

$$\lim_{x\to\infty} f(x) = \lim_{x\to\infty} x\,e^{-x} = \lim_{x\to\infty} \frac{x}{e^{x}} = 0$$

and similarly, by evaluating $f(x)$ at x for decreasing values of x that

$$\lim_{x\to-\infty} f(x) = \lim_{x\to-\infty} x\,e^{-x} = -\infty$$

9. There are no vertical asymptotes of f. The x-axis is a horizontal asymptote of f (see step (*8*)).

The graph of f is sketched in Figure 11.35.

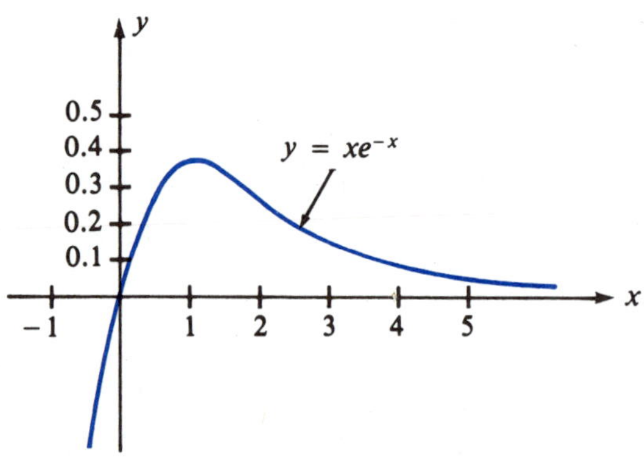

Figure 11.35

■

11.5 EXERCISES

In problems 1 through 26 obtain as much information as possible on each of the given functions. Then use this information to sketch the graph of the function.

1. $f(x)=x^2-2x+3$

2. $g(x)=4-3x-2x^2$

3. $h(x)=\frac{1}{2}(x-2)^2+1$

4. $f(x)=2x^3+1$

5. $f(x)=x^3-3x+1$

6. $h(t)=2t^3-15t^2+36t-20$

7. $f(x)=-2x^3+3x^2+12x+2$

***8.** $g(x)=\frac{1}{3}x^3-2x^2+2x+1$

9. $f(t)=3t^4+4t^3$

10. $h(x)=\frac{3}{2}x^4-2x^3-6x^2+8$

11. $f(x)=\sqrt{x^2+5}$

12. $f(t)=\sqrt{t^2-4}$

13. $g(x)=\frac{1}{2}x-\sqrt{x}$

14. $f(x)=\frac{1}{x+1}$

15. $g(x)=\frac{x}{x-1}$

16. $h(x)=\frac{x+2}{x-2}$

17. $f(x)=\frac{x}{x^2-4}$

18. $f(t)=\frac{t^2}{1+t^2}$

19. $f(x)=xe^x$

20. $g(t)=t^2e^{-t}$

21. $f(t)=e^t-t$

22. $h(x)=\frac{e^x+e^{-x}}{2}$

23. $f(x)=\ln(x^2+1)$

24. $g(t)=t-\ln t$

25. $f(x)=\ln(x^2+2x+5)$

***26.** $f(x)=\frac{\ln x}{x}$

11.6

Absolute Maxima and Absolute Minima

We mentioned the notion of the *absolute extrema* (absolute maxima or absolute minima) of a function f in Section 11.2. Recall that a point $(c, f(c))$ on the graph of the function f is an *absolute maximum* of f if $f(x)\leq f(c)$ for all points x in the domain of f. Similarly, a point $(c, f(c))$ on the graph of the function f is an *absolute minimum* of f if $f(x)\geq f(c)$ for all points x in the domain of f. Geometrically, the absolute maximum and the absolute minimum of a function are, respectively, the highest and lowest points on the graph of f. Figure 11.36 depicts the graph of a function f defined on the closed interval $[a, b]$ which has an absolute maximum at the point $(b, f(b))$ and an absolute minimum at the point $(x_3, f(x_3))$.

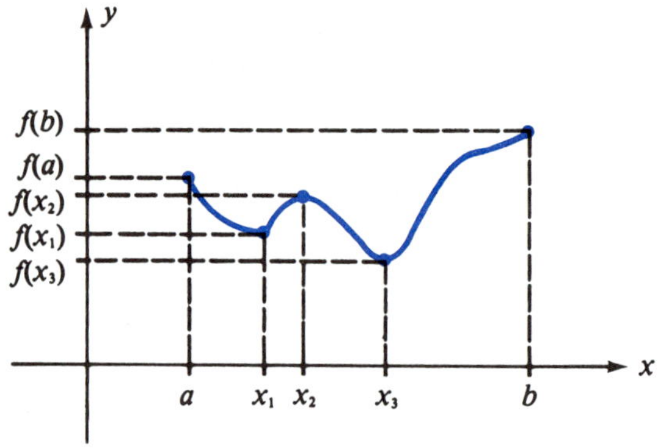

Figure 11.36

Observe that every absolute extremum is, *a fortiori*, a relative extremum. The converse is false. For example, at each of the points $x = a$, $x = x_1$, $x = x_2$, $x = x_3$, and $x = b$ a relative extremum of f occurs but only at $x = x_3$ and $x = b$ does an absolute extremum (absolute minimum and the absolute maximum, respectively) of f occur. Observe too, that $f(x_3)$ and $f(b)$ are, respectively, the smallest and the largest values of $f(x)$ (see Figure 11.36).

A general method for finding the absolute extrema of a function f follows:

1. Sketch the graph of f.

2. Locate the highest point, if one exists, on the graph. This point will be the absolute maximum of f. Similarly, the absolute minimum of f is found by locating the lowest point on the graph of f.

EXAMPLE 11.25 Find the absolute extrema of the following functions:

(a) $f(x) = x^2$

(b) $g(x) = -x^2$

SOLUTION **(a)** The graph of f appears in Figure 11.37 (a). As seen earlier, the point (0, 0) is a relative minimum of f. Clearly, this point is also the absolute minimum of f.

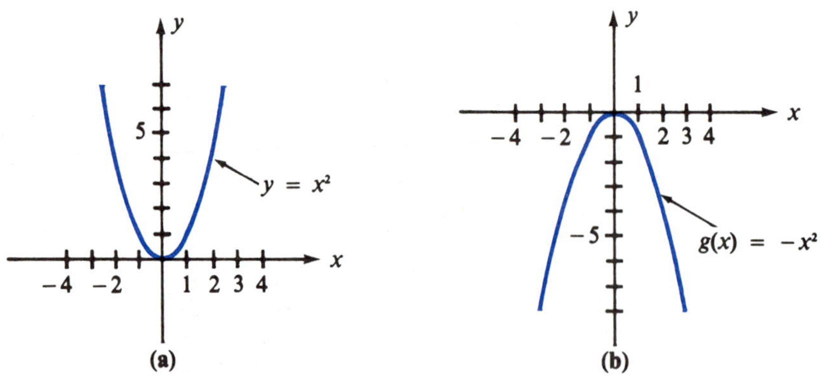

Figure 11.37

On the other hand, it is easy to see that $f(x)$ may be made as large as we please by taking x sufficiently large so that f has no absolute maximum.

(b) The graph of g appears in Figure 11.37 (b). From the graph of g, we see that the point $(0, 0)$ is the absolute maximum of g. Also, it is clear that the function g has no absolute minimum since $g(x)$ decreases without bound as x increases without bound. ■

EXAMPLE 11.26 Find the absolute extrema of the function $f(x) = x^3$.

SOLUTION The graph of f appears in Figure 11.38. Since $f(x)$ may be made as large as we please by taking x sufficiently large, we conclude that the function f has no absolute maximum. Also, we see that f has no absolute minimum.

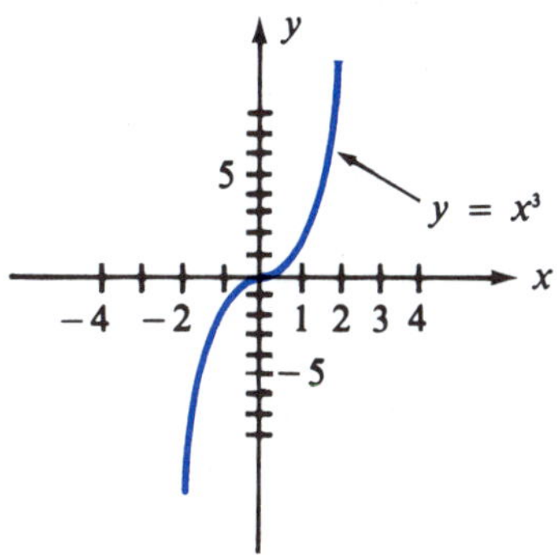

Figure 11.38 ■

EXAMPLE 11.27 Find the absolute extrema of the function $h(x) = x^2$ defined on the interval $(-1, 2)$.

SOLUTION The function h has the same rule of definition as that of the function f in Example 11.25, but the domain of h is the open interval $(-1, 2)$. The graph of h appears in Figure 11.39.

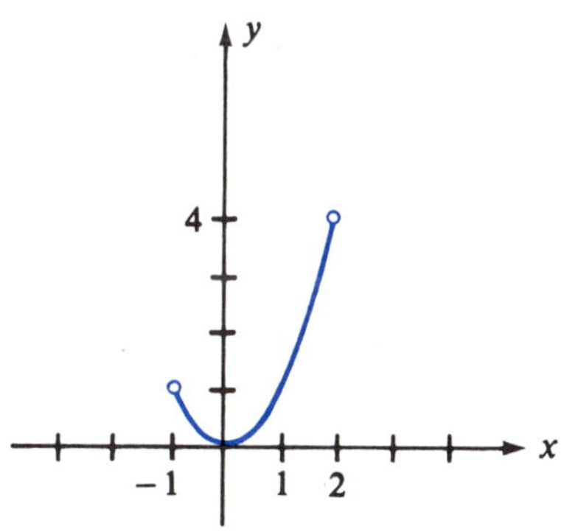

Figure 11.39

The graph of h shows that the point $(0, 0)$ is the absolute minimum of the function h. However, there is no absolute maximum for h. Observe that the function h is increasing on the interval $(0, 2)$ so that the closer x gets to the number 2 (from the left), the larger $h(x)$ gets. Furthermore, $h(x)$ approaches the number 4 as x

approaches 2. But since the number 2 does *not* lie in the domain of h, the value of $h(x)$ is always strictly less than 4. In other words, $h(x)$ does not attain a largest value for some point x in the domain of h. Thus, the function h has no absolute maximum. ■

The above examples demonstrate that a continuous function defined on an arbitrary interval may or may not have an absolute maximum (absolute minimum). However, in practical applications (see the next section) involving continuous functions there is an important case in which the relative extrema always exist for the function. More specifically, if a function f is continuous and is defined on a closed, bounded interval, that is, an interval $[a, b]$ where a and b are both real numbers that also belong to the domain of f, then the following theorem guarantees that both the absolute maximum and the absolute minimum of f exist.

THEOREM 11.3 Let f be a continuous function on a closed, bounded interval $[a, b]$, then f attains both its absolute maximum and its absolute minimum on $[a, b]$. In other words, there exist points $x = x_1$ and $x = x_2$ lying in $[a, b]$ such that the point $(x_1, f(x_1))$ is the absolute maximum of f and the point $(x_2, f(x_2))$ is the absolute minimum of f on $[a, b]$.

In many practical applications, the function involved is not only continuous on a closed, bounded interval $[a, b]$ but is also differentiable in the open interval (a, b). To locate the absolute maximum as well as the absolute minimum for such functions use the following procedure, which is based on the results of the last few sections.

1. Find the critical points of f.

2. Compute the value of f at each of the critical points of f found in Step 1; also compute $f(a)$ and $f(b)$.

3. The absolute maximum (absolute minimum) of f will correspond to the largest (smallest) number found in Step 2.

The above procedure is justified as follows: If the absolute extremum of f occurs at an interior point; that is, a point in the open interval (a, b) then it must be a relative extremum of f and hence its x-coordinate must be a critical point of f. Otherwise, the absolute extremum of f must occur at one or the other (or both) of the endpoints of the interval $[a, b]$.

EXAMPLE 11.28 Find the absolute extrema of the function $F(x) = x^2$ defined on the interval $[-1, 2]$.

SOLUTION The derivative of F is

$$F'(x) = 2x$$

so that $x = 0$ is the only critical point of F. Next, we evaluate $F(x)$ at $x = -1$, $x = 0$ and $x = 2$. Thus,

$$F(-1) = 1, \qquad F(0) = 0 \quad \text{and} \quad F(2) = 4$$

It follows that the point $(0, 0)$ is the absolute minimum of F and the point $(2, 4)$ is the absolute maximum of F. The graph of F, which appears in Figure 11.40, confirms our results. (Compare results with Examples 11.25 (a) and 11.27.)

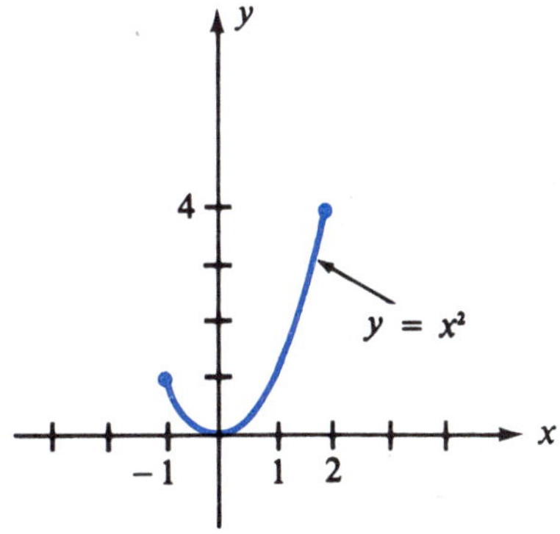

Figure 11.40

EXAMPLE 11.29 Find the absolute extrema of the function $f(x) = x^3 - 2x^2 - 4x + 4$ defined on the interval $[0, 3]$.

SOLUTION The function f is defined on the closed, bounded interval $[0, 3]$, where it is continuous. It is also differentiable on the open interval $(0, 3)$. The derivative of f is

$$\begin{aligned} f'(x) &= 3x^2 - 4x - 4 \\ &= (3x + 2)(x - 2) \end{aligned}$$

and is equal to zero when $x = -2/3$ and $x = 2$. Since the point $x = -2/3$ lies outside the domain of f it is dropped from further consideration and $x = 2$ is seen to be the sole critical point of f. Next, we evaluate $f(x)$ at the critical point of f as well as at the endpoints of f obtaining

$$f(0) = 4, \qquad f(2) = -4 \quad \text{and} \quad f(3) = 1$$

From these results, we conclude that the point $(2, -4)$ is the absolute minimum of f and the point $(0, 4)$ is the absolute maximum of f. The graph of f, which appears in Figure 11.41, confirms our results. Observe that the absolute maximum of f

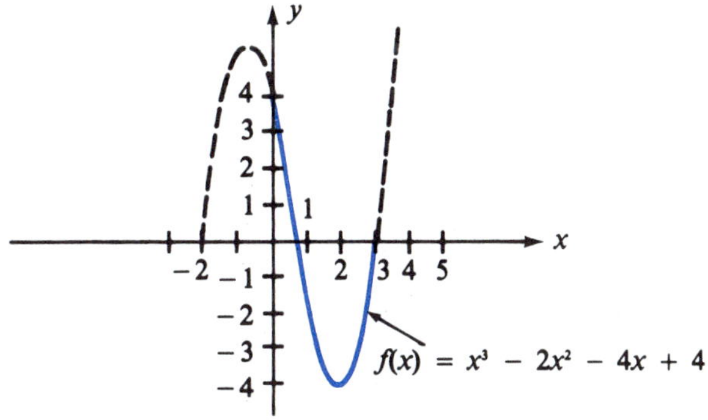

Figure 11.41

occurs at an endpoint, $x=0$, of the interval $[0, 3]$, while the absolute minimum of f occurs at an interior point, $x=2$. ■

EXAMPLE 11.30 Find the absolute extrema of the function $f(x)=-2x^3+9x^2-12x+6$ defined on the interval $[0, \infty)$.

SOLUTION The function f is continuous in its domain and differentiable in the interval $(0, \infty)$. However, since the domain of f is not a bounded, closed interval, Theorem 11.3 is not applicable. There is no guarantee that the absolute maximum and/or absolute minimum of f exists. Furthermore, we cannot use the procedure for locating the absolute extrema of f by evaluating f at the critical points of f and the endpoints of the domain of f in this case. Therefore, we resort to the graphical method. Using the techniques of graphing, we sketch the graph of f depicted in Figure 11.42. The graph of the function f shows that the absolute maximum of f is given by the point $(0, 6)$. There is no absolute minimum for f since $f(x)$ is unbounded below.

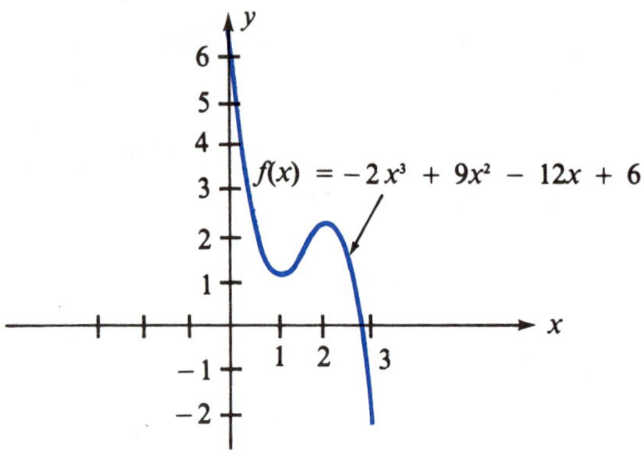

Figure 11.42

■

11.6 EXERCISES

In Problems 1 through 28 find the absolute maximum and the absolute minimum, if any, of each of the given functions.

1. $f(x)=2x^2+3x-4$

2. $g(x)=-x^2+4x+3$

3. $h(x)=x^{1/3}$

4. $f(x)=\dfrac{1}{1+x^2}$

5. $f(x)=x^2-2x-3$ on $(0, 4)$

6. $g(x)=x^2-2x-3$ on $[0, 4)$

7. $h(x)=x^2-2x-3$ on $(0, 4]$

8. $F(x)=x^2-2x-3$ on $[0, 4]$

9. $f(x)=x^3+3x^2-1$ on $[-3, 2]$

10. $g(x)=x^3+3x^2-1$ on $[-3, 1]$

11. $f(x)=-\frac{1}{3}x^3+\frac{1}{2}x^2+2x+1$ on $[-2, 3]$

12. $g(x)=3x^4+4x^3$ on $[-2, 1]$

13. $f(x)=\frac{1}{2}x^4-\frac{2}{3}x^3-2x^2+3$ on $[-2, 3]$

14. $f(x)=\frac{x+1}{x-1}$ on $[1, 3]$

15. $g(t)=\frac{t}{t-1}$ on $[2, 4]$

16. $f(x)=4x+\frac{1}{x}$ on $[1, 3]$

17. $f(t)=\frac{1}{(t-1)^2}$ on $[2, 3]$

18. $g(x)=\frac{1}{8}x^2-4\sqrt{x}$ on $[0, 9]$

19. $f(x)=\frac{1}{x}$ on $(0, \infty)$

20. $g(x)=\frac{1}{x}$ on $(0, 2]$

21. $f(x)=\frac{1}{x^2+2x+5}$ on $[-2, 1]$

22. $f(x)=e^{-x^2}$ on $[-1, 1]$

23. $g(x)=(2x-1)\,e^{-x}$ on $[0, \infty)$

24. $h(x)=e^{x^2-4}$ on $[-2, 2]$

****25.*** $f(x)=\ln x^2$ on $(0, 2]$

26. $f(x)=x-\ln x$ on $\left[\frac{1}{2}, 3\right]$

27. $f(x)=\frac{\ln x}{x}$ on $[1, \infty)$

28. $g(x)=\frac{x}{\ln x}$ on $[2, \infty)$

29. Let f be a constant function; that is, $f(x)=c$ where c is some real number. Show that every point, $x=a$, is an absolute maximum and, at the same time, an absolute minimum of f.

30. Show that a polynomial function, unless it is a constant function, defined on the interval $(-\infty, \infty)$ cannot have both an absolute maximum and an absolute minimum (see Chapter 10, page 421).

****31.*** One condition that must be satisfied before Theorem 11.3 is applicable is that the function f must be *continuous* on the closed, bounded interval $[a, b]$. Define a function f on the closed, bounded interval $[-1, 1]$ using the rule

$$f(x)=\begin{cases} 1/x & \text{if } x\in[-1, 1],\ x\neq 0 \\ 0 & \text{if } x=0 \end{cases}$$

(***a***) Show that f is not continuous at $x=0$.

(***b***) Show that $f(x)$ does not attain an absolute maximum or absolute minimum on the interval $[-1, 1]$.

(***c***) Confirm your results by sketching the function f.

11.7

Optimization Problems

In this section we shall see how the techniques of the differential calculus are used to solve a large class of optimization problems. As an example, suppose the profit of a certain manufacturer is given by $P(x)$ dollars where x is the number of units of the commodity produced. Suppose that the management of the company decides that the output should be no less than a units and no more than b units. Then the problem of determining the level of production that will yield the largest profit to the manufacturer is equivalent to the following: Find the point x_0 belonging to the interval $[a, b]$ such that the point $(x_0, P(x_0))$ is the absolute maximum of the profit function P on $[a, b]$. The value $P(x_0)$ is then the maximum profit realizable by the manufacturer corresponding to the optimal level of production of x_0 units of the commodity.

EXAMPLE 11.31 (Refer to Examples 10.59 and 10.60.) The total profit of the Acrosonic Company from the manufacture and sale of x units of their Acrosonic Model F loudspeaker systems is given by $P(x) = -0.02x^2 + 300x - 200{,}000$ dollars $(0 \le x \le 20{,}000)$. How many units of the loudspeaker systems should be produced in order to maximize the company's profits?

SOLUTION The profit function P is continuous on the closed, bounded interval $[0, 20{,}000]$ and differentiable in the open interval $(0, 20{,}000)$. To find the absolute maximum of P on $[0, 20{,}000]$, first we find the critical points of P in the interval $(0, 20{,}000)$. To accomplish this, we compute

$$P'(x) = -0.04x + 300$$

Solving the equation $P'(x) = 0$ gives $x = 7500$. Next, we evaluate $P(x)$ at $x = 7500$ as well as at the end points $x = 0$ and $x = 20{,}000$ of the interval $[0, 20{,}000]$ obtaining

$$P(0) = -200{,}000$$

$$P(7500) = 925{,}000$$

and

$$P(20{,}000) = -2{,}200{,}000$$

From the above computations it is clear that the absolute maximum of the function P is the point $(7500, 925{,}000)$. Thus, by producing 7500 units of the Acrosonic Model F loudspeaker systems, the company will realize a maximum profit of \$925,000. See Figure 10.23, on page 478 for a sketch of the graph of the function P. ■

The last example represents the type of optimization problems we shall encounter in this section. First, the problem should be formulated in terms of a function f which involves some appropriate variable x. Second, the primary objective of the problem involves the optimization (maximization or minimization) of the objective function f with respect to x.

EXAMPLE 11.32 (Refer to Example 11.5 on page 494 and Example 10.43 on page 458.) The altitude (in feet) of a rocket t seconds into flight is given by $s=f(t)=-t^3+96t^2+195t+5$ $(t \geq 0)$.

(a) Find the maximum altitude attained by the rocket.

(b) Find the maximum velocity attained by the rocket.

SOLUTION **(a)** The maximum altitude attained by the rocket is given by the largest value of the function f in the closed, bounded interval $[0, T]$ where T denotes the time the rocket impacts the earth. We know that such a number exists since the dominant term in the expression for the continuous function f is $-t^3$, so that for t large enough the value of $f(t)$ must change from positive to negative and, in particular, it must attain the value 0 for some T. To find the absolute maximum of f we compute

$$\begin{aligned} f'(t) &= -3t^2+192t+195 \\ &= -3(t-65)(t+1) \end{aligned}$$

and solve the equation $f'(t)=0$ obtaining $t=-1$ and $t=65$. We ignore $t=-1$ since it lies outside the interval $[0, T]$. This leaves the critical point $t=65$ of f. Continuing, we next compute

$$f(0)=5, \qquad f(65)=143{,}655 \quad \text{and} \quad f(T)=0$$

and conclude, accordingly, that the absolute maximum of f is the point (65, 143,655). Thus, the maximum altitude of the rocket is 143,655 feet attained 65 seconds into flight. The graph of f is sketched in Figure 10.18 on page 459.

(b) To find the maximum velocity attained by the rocket, we find the largest value of the function which describes the velocity of the rocket at any time t, namely,

$$v=f'(t)=-3t^2+192t+195 \quad (t \geq 0)$$

We find the critical point of v by setting $v'=0$. But

$$v'=-6t+192$$

and the critical point of v is $t=32$. Since

$$v''=-6<0$$

the Second Derivative Test implies that $t=32$ gives rise to a relative maximum of v. Our computation has in fact clarified the property of the "velocity curve." Since $v''<0$ everywhere, the velocity curve is concave downwards everywhere. With this observation, we assert that the relative maximum must, in fact, be the absolute maximum of v. The maximum velocity of the rocket is given by evaluating v at

$t = 32$, or

$$f'(32) = -3(32)^2 + 192(32) + 195$$
$$= 3267$$

or 3267 feet/second. The graph of the velocity function v is sketched in Figure 11.11 on page 495. ■

EXAMPLE 11.33 (Refer to Example 10.58 on page 475). The daily average cost function (in dollars per unit) of the Elektra Electronics Company is given by

$$A(x) = 0.0001x^2 - 0.08x + 40 + \frac{5000}{x} \quad (x > 0)$$

where x stands for the number of programmable electronic calculators produced by the company. Show that a level of production of 500 units per day results in a minimum average cost for the company.

SOLUTION The function A is differentiable and therefore continuous in the interval $(0, \infty)$ which is not a closed, bounded interval. In order to solve the problem we resort to the graphical method. Using the techniques of graphing from the last section, we sketch the graph of A (see Figure 10.22, page 476). Now,

$$A'(x) = 0.0002x - 0.08 - \frac{5000}{x^2}$$

Substituting the (given) value of $x = 500$ into $A'(x)$ gives $A'(500) = 0$ so that $x = 500$ is a critical point of A. Next,

$$A''(x) = 0.0002 + \frac{10{,}000}{x^3}$$

Thus,

$$A''(500) = 0.0002 + \frac{10{,}000}{(500)^3} > 0$$

and by the Second Derivative Test, at the point $x = 500$ a relative minimum of the function A occurs. Furthermore, $A''(x) > 0$ for all $x > 0$. This implies that the graph of A is concave upward everywhere, so the relative minimum of A must be the absolute minimum of A. The minimum average cost is given by

$$A(500) = 0.0001(500)^2 - 0.08(500) + 40 + \frac{5000}{500}$$
$$= 35$$

or \$35 per unit. ■

EXAMPLE 11.34 A man wishes to have an enclosed vegetable garden in his backyard. He has 50 feet of fencing material to use to enclose his garden which will be rectangular in shape. Find the dimensions for a garden of maximum area that he can have if all of the fencing material is used.

SOLUTION Let x and y (in feet) denote the dimensions of two adjacent sides of the garden (see Figure 11.43). The perimeter of the rectangle is $(2x+2y)$ feet and this must be equal to 50 feet. Thus, we have the equation

$$2x+2y=50 \tag{11.1}$$

The area of the rectangle is given by

$$A=xy \tag{11.2}$$

Solving (11.1) for y in terms of x, we obtain

$$y=25-x \tag{11.3}$$

Substituting this value of y into (11.2), we have

$$\begin{aligned} A &= x(25-x) \\ &= -x^2+25x \end{aligned} \tag{11.4}$$

(Remember that the function to be optimized must involve just one variable!)

Since the area A of the rectangle must be nonnegative, x must satisfy the inequality $0 \le x \le 25$.

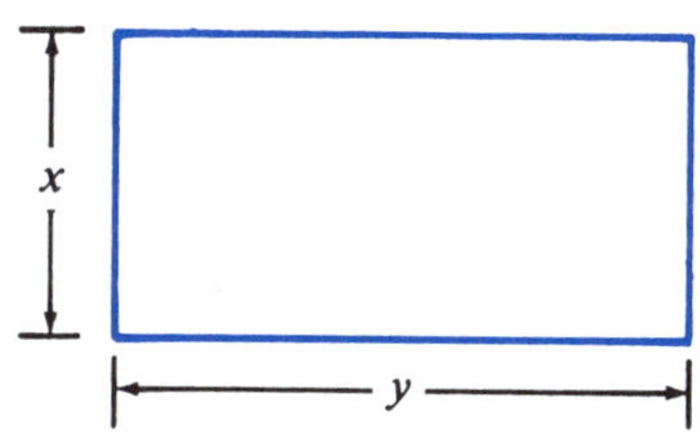

Figure 11.43

The problem reduces to the following: Find the absolute maximum of the objective function $A=f(x)=-x^2+25x$ on the closed, bounded interval $[0, 25]$. The derivative of the function A is given by

$$A'=f'(x)=-2x+25$$

Setting $A'=0$ gives

$$-2x+25=0$$

or $x=12.5$ as the critical point of A. Next, we evaluate the function $A=f(x)$ at

$x = 12.5$ and the end points $x = 0$ and $x = 25$ of the interval $[0, 25]$ obtaining

$$f(0) = 0, \qquad f(12.5) = 156.25 \quad \text{and} \quad f(25) = 0$$

We see that the absolute maximum of the function f is the point (12.5, 156.25). From (11.3) we see that when $x = 12.5$, the value of y is given by $y = 12.5$. Thus, the man would have a garden of maximum area (156.25 square feet) if it took the form of a square with sides 12.5 feet long. ■

EXAMPLE 11.35 By cutting away identical squares from each corner and folding up the resulting flaps, a rectangular piece of cardboard is turned into an open box. If the piece of cardboard is 16 inches long and 10 inches wide, find the dimensions of the box that will yield the maximum volume.

SOLUTION Let x denote the length (in inches) of one side of each of the identical squares that will be cut away from the cardboard (see Figure 11.44). The dimensions of the resulting box are $(16-2x)$ inches long, $(10-2x)$ inches wide and x inches high. Its volume is

$$\begin{aligned} V(x) &= (16-2x)(10-2x)x \\ &= 4(8-x)(5-x)x \\ &= 4(x^3 - 13x^2 + 40x) \end{aligned}$$

cubic inches. Since each of the sides must be non negative, x must satisfy the inequality $0 \le x \le 5$. This problem is equivalent to the problem of finding the absolute maximum of the function V on the closed, bounded interval [0, 5]. Differentiating $V(x)$ we obtain

$$\begin{aligned} V'(x) &= 4(3x^2 - 26x + 40) \\ &= 4(3x - 20)(x - 2) \end{aligned}$$

Upon setting $V'(x) = 0$ and solving the resulting equation for x, we obtain $x = 20/3$ and $x = 2$. Since $20/3$ lies outside the interval $[0, 5]$ it is no longer considered and we are interested only in the critical point $x = 2$ of V. Next, evaluating $V(x)$ at $x = 0$, $x = 5$ (the end points of the interval $[0, 5]$) and $x = 2$, we obtain

$$V(0) = 0, \qquad V(2) = 144 \quad \text{and} \quad V(5) = 0$$

Thus, the volume of the box is maximized by taking $x = 2$. The dimensions of the box are $12'' \times 6'' \times 2''$, and the volume is 144 cubic inches.

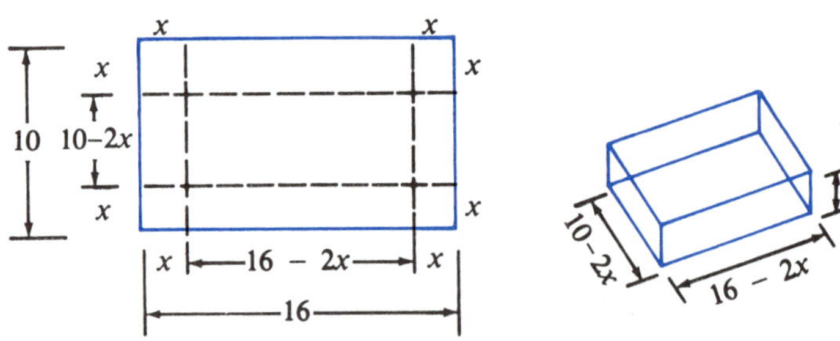

Figure 11.44 ■

EXAMPLE 11.36 The Betty Moore Company requires that its corned beef hash containers have a capacity of 36 cubic inches. The containers must have the form of right-circular cylinders and be made of tin. Determine the radius and height of the container that requires the least amount of metal.

SOLUTION Let the radius and height of a container be r inches and h inches, respectively (see Figure 11.45). The amount of tin used to construct such a container is given by the total surface area of the cylinder. Now, the area of the base (and top) of the cylinder is given by πr^2 square inches while the area of its side is given by $2\pi rh$. So, if S denotes the total surface area of the cylinder, we have

$$S = 2\pi r^2 + 2\pi rh \tag{11.5}$$

Next, the requirement that the volume of a container be 36 cubic inches implies that

$$\pi r^2 h = 36 \tag{11.6}$$

Solving (11.6) for h, we obtain

$$h = \frac{36}{\pi r^2} \tag{11.7}$$

which, when substituted into (11.5), yields

$$\begin{aligned} S &= 2\pi r^2 + 2\pi r\left(\frac{36}{\pi r^2}\right) \\ &= 2\pi r^2 + \frac{72}{r} \end{aligned} \tag{11.8}$$

Clearly, the radius r of the container must satisfy the inequality $r > 0$. The problem now reduces to the following: Find the absolute minimum of the objective function $S = f(r)$ on the interval $(0, \infty)$.

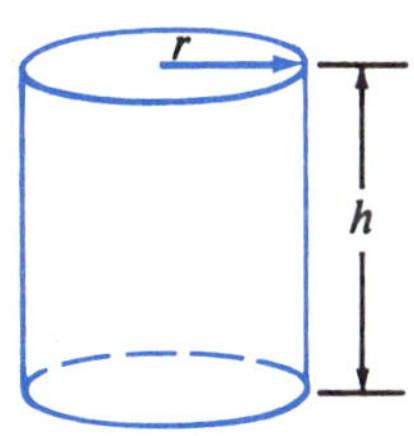

Figure 11.45

Using the curve sketching techniques of the last section, we obtain the graph of f depicted in Figure 11.46. To find the critical point of f we compute

$$S' = 4\pi r - \frac{72}{r^2}$$

and solve the equation $S' = 0$ for r:

$$4\pi r - \frac{72}{r^2} = 0,$$

$$4\pi r^3 - 72 = 0$$

$$r^3 = \frac{18}{\pi}$$

(11.9) or

$$r = \sqrt[3]{\frac{18}{\pi}} \approx 1.8$$

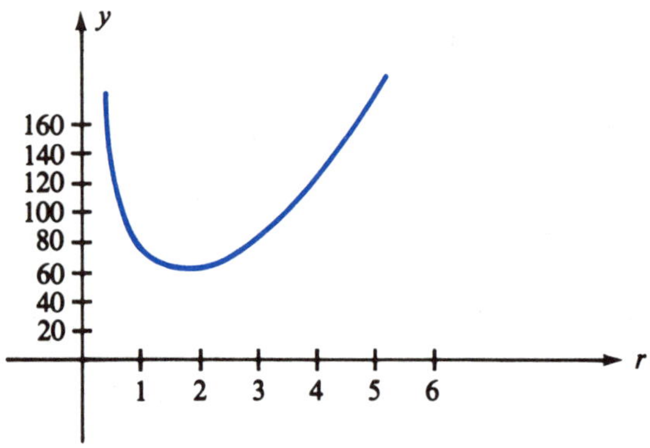

Figure 11.46

Next, let us show that this value of r gives rise to the absolute minimum of f. To show this, let us first compute

$$S'' = 4\pi + \frac{144}{r^3}$$

The Second Derivative Test implies that the value of r given in (11.9) gives rise to a relative minimum of f. Finally, the fact that this relative minimum of f is also the absolute minimum of f follows from the concavity upward of f everywhere, the latter property being a consequence of the fact that $S'' > 0$ for all $r > 0$. To find the height of the required container, we substitute the value of r given in (11.9) into (11.7) yielding

$$\begin{aligned} h &= \frac{36}{\pi \sqrt[3]{(18/\pi)^2}} \\ &= \frac{36}{\sqrt[3]{18^2 \pi}} \\ &= \sqrt[3]{36^3/(18^2 \pi)} \\ &= 2\sqrt[3]{18/\pi} \\ &= 2r \end{aligned}$$

Thus, the required container has a radius of approximately 1.8 inches and a height, which is twice the size of the radius, or approximately 3.6 inches. ■

Our last example shows how optimization techniques are applied in order to keep the order and storage costs of a firm's inventory of products to a minimum.

EXAMPLE 11.37 The Dixie Import–Export Company is the sole agent for the Excalibur 250 c.c. motorcycle. Management estimates that the demand for these motorcycles is 10,000 per year and that they will sell at a uniform rate throughout the year. The cost incurred in ordering each shipment of motorcycles is \$10,000 while the cost of storing each motorcycle for a year is \$200.

The management of the Dixie Import–Export faces the following problem: Ordering too many motorcycles at one time ties up valuable storage space and increases the storage cost. On the other hand, placing orders too frequently increases the ordering costs. What should the size of each order be, and how often should the order be placed so that ordering and storage costs are kept at a minimum?

SOLUTION Let x denote the number of motorcycles in each order. Then, assuming that each shipment arrives just as the previous shipment has been sold, the average number of motorcycles in storage during the year is $x/2$. Why? Thus, the storage cost incurred by the company in the year is given by $200(x/2)$ or $100x$ dollars. Next, since the company requires 10,000 motorcycles for the year and since each order is for x motorcycles, the number of orders required is $10{,}000/x$. This gives an ordering cost of $10{,}000\ (10{,}000/x) = 100{,}000{,}000/x$ dollars for the year. Thus, the total yearly cost incurred by the company, which includes the ordering and storage costs attributed to the sale of these motorcycles, is given by

$$C(x) = 100x + \frac{100{,}000{,}000}{x}$$

The problem reduces to finding the absolute minimum of the function C in the interval $(0, 10{,}000]$. To accomplish this, we compute

$$C'(x) = 100 - \frac{100{,}000{,}000}{x^2}$$

Setting $C'(x) = 0$ and solving the resulting equation, we obtain $x = \pm 1000$. Since the number -1000 is outside the domain of the function C, it is rejected and $x = 1000$ is the only critical point of C. Next, we find

$$C''(x) = \frac{200{,}000{,}000}{x^3}$$

Since $C''(1000) > 0$, the Second Derivative Test implies that the critical point $x = 1000$ is in fact a relative minimum of the function C. Also, since $C''(x) > 0$ for all x in $(0, 10{,}000]$, the function C is concave upward everywhere so that the point $x = 1000$ is also the absolute minimum of C. Thus, in order to keep the ordering and storage costs to a minimum the company should place 10,000/1000 or 10 orders a year, each for a shipment of 1000 motorcycles. ■

11.7 EXERCISES

1. The estimated monthly profit realizable by the Cannon Precision Instruments Corporation for the manufacture and sale of x units of its Model M1 camera is $P(x) = -0.04x^2 + 240x - 10{,}000$ dollars. Determine the number of cameras the company should produce per month in order to maximize its profits.

2. The quantity demanded per month of the Walter Serkin recording of Beethoven's "Moonlight" Sonata manufactured by the Phonola Record Industries is related to the price per record. The equation $p = -0.00042x + 6$ $(0 \leq x \leq 12{,}000)$, where p denotes the unit price in dollars and x is the number of records demanded, relates the demand to the price. The total monthly cost for pressing and packaging x copies of this classical recording is given by $C = 600 + 2x - 0.00002x^2$ $(0 \leq x \leq 20{,}000)$ dollars. Determine the number of copies the company should produce per month in order to maximize its profits.

3. The management of Trappee and Sons, Incorporated, producers of the famous "Texa-Pep" hot sauce estimated that their profit from the daily production and sale of x cases (each case consists of 24 bottles) of the hot sauce is given by $P = -0.000002x^3 + 6x - 400$ dollars. What is the largest possible profit the company can make in one day?

4. The quantity demanded per month of the "Sicard" wrist watch is related to the unit price by the equation

$$p = \frac{50}{0.01x^2 + 1} \quad (0 \leq x \leq 20)$$

where p is measured in dollars and x is measured in units of a thousand. How many watches must be sold to yield a maximum revenue?

5. The weekly demand for the Pulsar 25" color console television is given by the demand equation $p = -0.05x + 600$ $(0 \leq x \leq 12{,}000)$ where p denotes the wholesale unit price in dollars and x denotes the quantity demanded. The weekly total cost function associated with the manufacture of these sets is given by $C = 0.000002x^3 - 0.03x^2 + 400x + 80{,}000$ where $C(x)$ denotes the total cost incurred in the production of x sets. Find the level of production that will yield a maximum profit for the manufacturer. *Hint*: Use the quadratic formula.

6. The altitude (in feet) attained by a model rocket t seconds into flight is given by the function $h(t) = -(1/3)t^3 + 4t^2 + 20t + 2$. Find the maximum altitude attained by the rocket.

7. A stone is thrown straight up from the roof of an 80 foot building. The height of the stone at any time t (in seconds) measured from the ground is given by $h(t) = -16t^2 + 64t + 80$ feet. What is the maximum height the stone reaches?

8. Refer to Example 10.20 (page 431). Verify that the optimal present value of the office building is \$600,778 and occurs at time $t = 7.7$ years.

9. The total monthly cost in dollars incurred by the Cannon Precision Instruments Corporation for manufacturing x units of the Model M1 cameras is given by the function $C = 0.0025x^2 + 80x + 10{,}000$.

(***a***) Find the average cost function A.

(***b***) Find the level of production that results in the smallest average production cost.

(***c***) Find the level of production for which the average cost is equal to the marginal cost.

(***d***) Compare the result obtained in part (***c***) with that of part (***b***). Also, see problem 11.

10. The daily total cost in dollars incurred by Trappee and Sons, Incorporated for producing x cases of the "Texa-Pep" hot sauce is given by the function $C = 0.000002x^3 + 5x + 400$. Using this function, answer the questions posed in problem 9.

****11.*** Prove that if a cost function $C(x)$ is concave upward, $(C''(x) > 0)$, then the level of production which will result in the smallest average production cost occurs when

$$A(x) = C'(x)$$

that is, when the average cost $A(x)$ is equal to the marginal cost $C'(x)$. *Hint*: *1.* Show that

$$A'(x) = \frac{xC'(x) - C(x)}{x^2}$$

so that the critical point of the function A occurs when $xC'(x) - C(x) = 0$.
2. Show that

$$A''(x) = \frac{C''(x)}{x}$$

Use the Second Derivative Test to reach the desired conclusion.

****12.*** Prove that if a revenue function $R(x)$ is concave downward $(R''(x) < 0)$, then the level of sales that will result in the largest average revenue (the average revenue is defined as the function $\bar{R}(x) = R(x)/x$, $x > 0$) occurs when $\bar{R}(x) = R'(x)$. *Hint*: Use an approach similar to the one given in the hint for problem 11.

13. The owner of the Rancho Los Feliz has 3000 yards of fencing material available to enclose a rectangular piece of grazing land along the straight portion of a river. If fencing is not required along the river, what are the dimensions of the pasture of maximum area? What is this area?

14. As an alternative plan (see problem 13), the owner of the Rancho Los Feliz might use the 3000 yards of fencing material to enclose a rectangular piece of grazing land along the straight portion of a river and then subdivide it by means of a fence running parallel to the sides. Again, no fencing is required along the river. What are the dimensions of the pasture of maximum area? What is this area? (See diagram.)

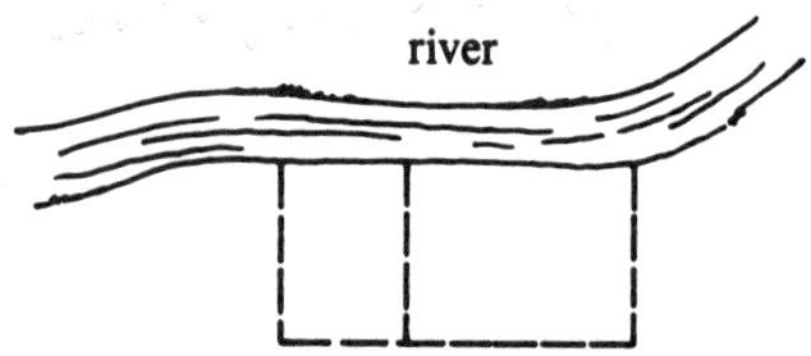

15. The management of the UNICO Department Store decided to enclose an 800 square foot area outside the building. This rectangular space will display potted plants and flowers. One side is provided by the external wall of the store. Pine board will be used for two sides of the enclosure while the fourth side is made of galvanized steel fencing material. If the pine board fencing costs \$6 per running foot and the steel fencing costs \$3 per running foot, determine the dimensions of the enclosure, which can be erected at the lowest cost in materials.

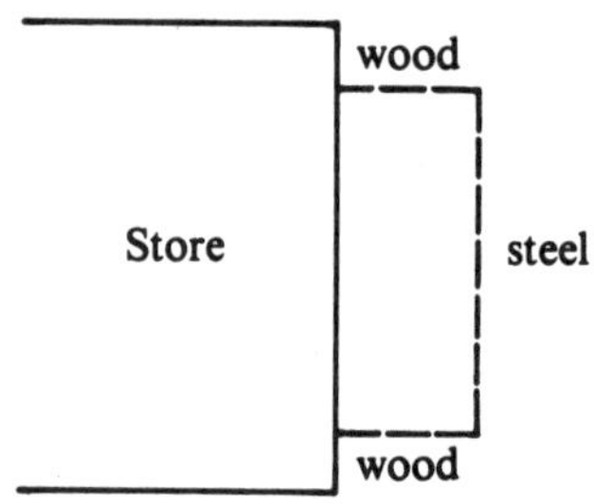

16. By cutting away identical squares from each corner and folding up the resulting flaps an open box is made from a rectangular piece of cardboard. If the piece of cardboard is 15 inches long and 8 inches wide, find the dimensions of the box that will yield the maximum volume.

17. If an open box is made from a tin sheet 8 inches square by cutting out identical squares from each corner and bending up the resulting flaps, determine the dimensions of the box with the largest volume that can be made.

18. If an open box has a square base, a volume of 108 cubic inches, and is constructed from a tin sheet, find the dimensions of such a box if a minimal amount of material is used in its construction.

19. What are the dimensions of a closed rectangular box with a square cross-section and a capacity of 128 cubic inches that is constructed using the least amount of material?

20. Postal regulations specify that a parcel sent by parcel post may have a combined length and girth that does not exceed 100 inches. Find the dimensions of a rectangular package that has a square cross-section and largest volume that may be sent through the mail. *Hint*: The length plus girth is $4x+h$—see illustration. What is the volume of such a package?

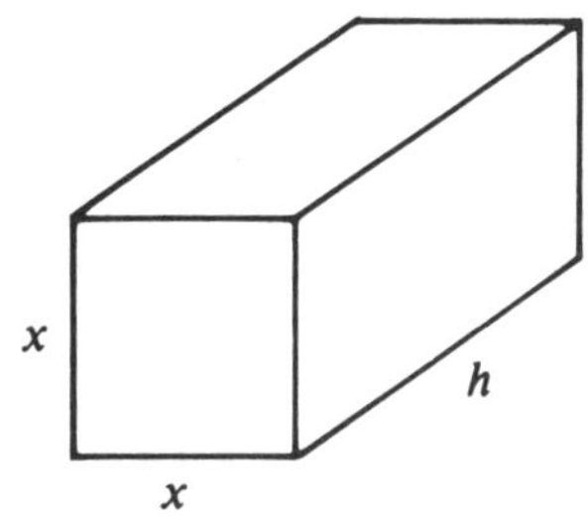

21. The enclosure of the Acrosonic Model D loudspeaker system will have a rectangular shape and an internal volume of 2.4 cubic feet. For esthetic reasons, it has been decided that the height of the enclosure is to be 1.5 times its width. If the top, bottom, and sides of the enclosure are constructed of veneer costing 40 cents per square foot and the front (ignore the cut-outs in the baffle) and rear are constructed of particle-board costing 20 cents per square foot, what are the dimensions of the enclosure, which can be constructed at a minimum cost?

22. Postal regulations specify that a parcel sent by parcel post may have a combined length and girth that does not exceed 100 inches. Find the dimensions of a cylindrical package having the greatest volume that may be sent through the mail. What is the volume of such a package? Compare with problem 20. *Hint*: The length plus girth is $2\pi r+l$.

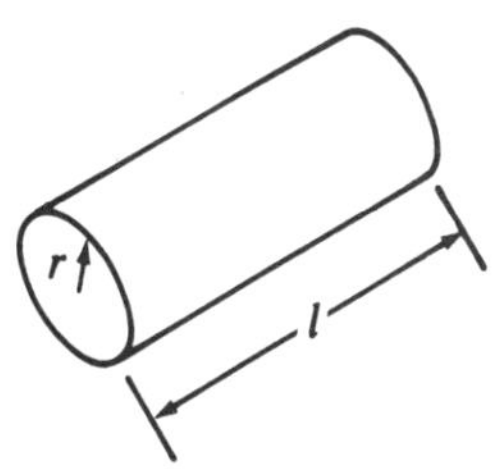

23. The Betty Moore Company requires its corned beef hash containers to have a capacity of 64 cubic inches. The containers, to be made of a tin alloy, are in the form of right-circular cylinders. Find the radius and height of the container that can be made at a minimum cost, if the metal for the side and bottom costs 4 cents per square inch and the metal for the pull-off lid costs 2 cents per square inch.

24. The Production Editor of the Saunders–Roe Publishing House decided that the pages of a book should have one-inch margins at the top and bottom and half-inch margins on the sides. The editor has further stipulated that each page of the book should have an area of 50 square inches (see following figure). Determine the page dimensions that will result in a maximum printed area for the page.

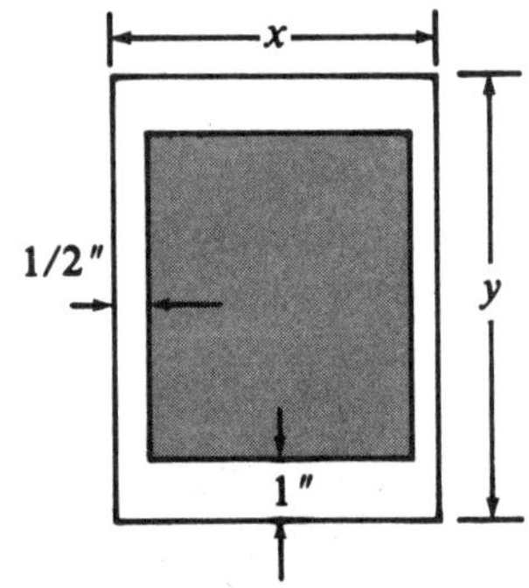

25. If exactly 200 people sign up for a charter flight, the Leisure World Travel Agency charges \$300 per person. However, if more than 200 people sign up for the flight (assume this is the case) then each fare is reduced by \$1 for each additional person beyond 200. Determine the number of passengers that will result in a maximum revenue for the travel agency. What is the maximum revenue? What would be the fare charged per passenger in this case? *Hint*: Let x denote the number of passengers beyond 200. Show that the revenue function R is given by $R(x)=(200+x)(300-x)$.

26. The demand for motorcycle tires imported by the Dixie Import–Export Company is 40,000 per year and may be assumed to be uniform. The cost of ordering a shipment of tires is \$400, while the cost of storing each tire for a year is \$2.00. Determine the number of tires in each shipment, if the ordering and storage costs are to be kept to a minimum. (Assume that each shipment of tires arrives just as the previous one has been sold.)

27. The McDuff Preserves Company expects to bottle and sell 2,000,000 jars of their 32-ounce jars of jams. The company orders its containers from the Consolidated Bottle Company. The cost of ordering a shipment of bottles is \$200 while the cost of storing each empty bottle for a year is \$0.40. Determine the number of orders the company should place per year and the number of bottles in each shipment, if the ordering and storage costs are to be kept to a minimum. (Assume that each shipment of bottles is used up before the next shipment arrives.)

28. The Neilsen Cookie Company sells its assorted butter cookies in containers that have a net content of 1 pound. The estimated demand for the cookies is 1,000,000 units. The set-up cost for each production run is \$500 and the manufacturing cost is \$0.50 for each container of cookies. The cost of storing each container of cookies over the year is \$0.40. Assuming uniformity of demand throughout the year and instantaneous production, determine the number of containers of cookies to be produced per production run in order to keep the production cost at a minimum. *Hint*: Show, following the method of Example 11.37, that the total production cost is given by the function $C(x)=500{,}000{,}000/x+0.2x+500{,}000$. Then minimize the function C on the interval $(0, 1{,}000{,}000]$.

11

Chapter Review

EXERCISES

In problems 1 through 10, (a) find the intervals where the given function f is increasing and where it is decreasing, (b) find the relative extrema of f, (c) find the intervals where f is concave upward and where it is concave downward and (d) find the inflection points, if any, of f.

1. $f(x)=\frac{1}{3}x^3-x^2+x-6$

2. $f(x)=x^4-2x^2$

3. $f(x)=\sqrt{x-1}$

4. $f(x)=x\sqrt{x-1}$

5. $f(x)=\frac{2x}{x+1}$

6. $f(x)=\frac{-1}{1+x^2}$

7. $f(x)=e^{2x}$

8. $f(x)=x\,e^{-2x}$

9. $f(x)=x+\ln x \quad (x>0)$

10. $f(x)=(\ln x)^2 \quad (x>0)$

In problems 11 through 24 obtain as much information as possible on each of the given functions. Then use this information to sketch the graph of the function.

11. $f(x)=x^2-5x+5$

12. $f(x)=-2x^2-x+1$

13. $g(x)=2x^3-6x^2+6x+1$

14. $g(x)=\frac{1}{3}x^3-x^2+x-3$

15. $h(x)=x\sqrt{x-2}$

16. $h(x)=\frac{x}{1+x^2}$

17. $f(x)=\frac{x-2}{x+2}$

18. $f(x)=x-\frac{1}{x}$

19. $f(x)=x\,e^{-2x}$

20. $f(x)=\frac{e^x-e^{-x}}{2}$

21. $f(x)=x\,e^{-x^2}$

22. $g(x)=(\ln x)^2$

23. $f(x)=\ln(x^2+1)$

24. $f(x)=x^2-\ln x \quad (x>0)$

In problems 25 through 36 find the absolute maximum and the absolute minimum, if any, of each of the given functions.

25. $f(x)=2x^2+3x-2$

26. $g(x)=x^{2/3}$

27. $f(t)=t\,e^{-t}$

28. $g(t)=\sqrt{25-t^2}$

29. $f(x)=\frac{1}{3}x^3-x^2+x+1 \quad \text{on } [0, 2]$

30. $h(t)=t^3-6t^2 \quad \text{on } [2, 5]$

31. $g(x)=\frac{x}{x^2+1} \quad \text{on } [0, 5]$

32. $f(x)=x-\frac{1}{x} \quad \text{on } [1, 3]$

33. $h(t)=t-\frac{1}{t}$ on $[1, 3]$

34. $f(s)=s\sqrt{1-s^2}$ on $[-1, 1]$

35. $f(x)=x e^{-x^2}$ on $[0, 2]$

36. $g(t)=\frac{\ln t}{t}$ on $[1, 2]$

37. The monthly profit (measured in thousands of dollars) of the Odyssey Travel Agency depends on the amount of money x spent on advertising per month according to the rule

$$P(x)=-x^2+8x+20$$

where x is also measured in thousands of dollars. What should the monthly advertising budget of the company be in order to maximize its monthly profits?

38. The weekly demand for the videodiscs manufactured by the Herald Record Company is given by $p=-0.0021x^2+10$ $(0 \leq x \leq 4000)$ where p denotes the unit price in dollars and x denotes the quantity demanded in units of a thousand. The weekly total cost function associated with producing these discs is given by $C(x)=-0.0001x^2+2.2x+2500$ where $C(x)$ denotes the total cost incurred in pressing x discs. Find the level of production that will yield a maximum profit for the manufacturer. *Hint*: Use the quadratic equation.

39. The total monthly cost in dollars incurred by the Carlota Music Company for manufacturing x units of its Professional Series guitars is given by the function $C(x)=0.001x^2+100x+4000$.

(***a***) Find the average cost function A.

(***b***) Determine the level of production that will result in the smallest average production cost.

40. The average worker at Wakefield Avionics Inc. can assemble $N(t)=-2t^3+12t^2+2t$ $(0 \leq t \leq 4)$ ready-to-fly radio-controlled model airplanes t hours into the 8 A.M. to 12 noon morning shift. At what time during this shift is the average worker performing at peak efficiency?

41. It has been estimated that the total production of oil from a certain oil well is given by

$$T(t)=-1000(t+10)\,e^{-0.1t}+10{,}000$$

thousand barrels t years after production has begun. Determine the year at which the oil well is producing at maximum capacity.

42. We wish to construct a closed rectangular box that has a volume of 4 cubic feet. The length of the base of the box will be twice as long as its width. The material for the top and bottom of the box costs 30 cents per square foot. The material for the sides of the box costs 20 cents per square foot. Find the dimensions of the box that can be constructed at a minimum cost.

43. The Lehen Vinters Company imports a certain brand of beer. The demand, which may be assumed to be uniform, is 800,000 cases per year. The cost of ordering a shipment of beer is \$500, while the cost of storing each case of beer for a year is \$2.00. Determine the number of cases of beer in each shipment, if the ordering and storage costs are to be kept to a minimum. (Assume that each shipment of beer arrives just as the previous one has been sold.)

12

THE INDEFINITE INTEGRAL

12.1 Antiderivatives

As discussed earlier, the derivative of a (differentiable) function is another function f' that is derived from the function f through a process we call differentiation. In many applications, one is interested in precisely the opposite process; that is, given the derivative f' of a differentiable function f, one wishes to recapture f from one's knowledge of f'.

anti-differentiation The solution to the above problem depends on a process called *antidifferentiation*, which is the main topic of this chapter. Briefly, antidifferentiation is to differentiation what subtraction of real numbers is to addition of real numbers. To put it another way, antidifferentiation and differentiation are inverse operations in the sense that one undoes what the other does.

antiderivative A function F is an *antiderivative* of the function f if it has the function f as its derivative; that is, if $F' = f$.

EXAMPLE 12.1 Show that $F(x) = (1/3)x^3 - 2x^2 + x - 1$ is an antiderivative of $f(x) = x^2 - 4x + 1$.

SOLUTION Differentiating the function F, we obtain

$$F'(x) = x^2 - 4x + 1 = f(x)$$

and the desired result follows. ■

EXAMPLE 12.2 (**a**) Show that $G(x) = x$ is an antiderivative of $f(x) = 1$.

(**b**) Show that $F(x) = x + C$, where C is a constant, is also an antiderivative of $f(x) = 1$.

SOLUTION (**a**) Since $G'(x)=1=f(x)$ we see that $G(x)=x$ is in fact an antiderivative of $f(x)=1$.

(**b**) The derivative of the function F is given by $F'(x)=1$ (since the derivative of a constant is equal to 0). It is equal to $f(x)$ so that F is also an antiderivative of f, as we wanted to show. ■

Example 12.2 suggests that once an antiderivative G of a function f is known, then another antiderivative of f may be found by adding an arbitrary constant to the function G. The following theorem concludes that no function, other than those obtained in this manner, can be an antiderivative of f. Its proof is sketched in problem 19, in Exercise set 12.1.

THEOREM 12.1 Let G be an antiderivative of a function f. Then any other antiderivative F of f must be of the form $F(x)=G(x)+C$, where C is a constant.

Returning to Example 12.2 we see that there are infinitely many antiderivatives of the function $f(x)=1$. We obtain each one by specializing the constant C in the function $F(x)=x+C$. Figure 12.1 shows the graphs of some of these antiderivatives for selected values of C. These graphs constitute part of a family of infinitely many parallel straight lines. Each line has a slope equal to 1. This result is expected since there are infinitely many curves, namely, straight lines with a given slope equal to 1. The antiderivatives $F(x)=x+C$ (C, a constant) are precisely the functions representing this family of straight lines.

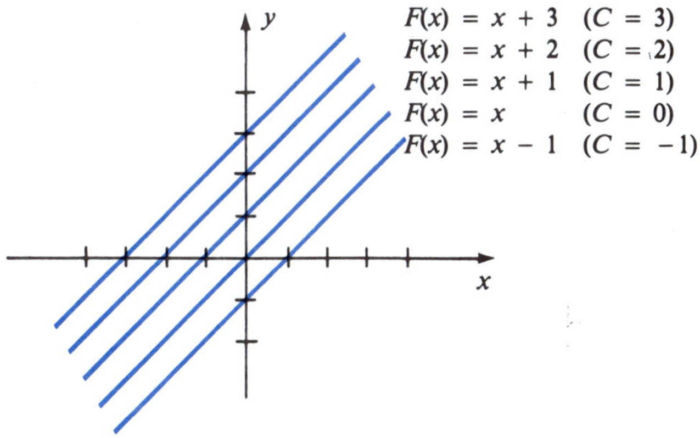

Figure 12.1

EXAMPLE 12.3 Prove that the function $G(x)=x^2$ is an antiderivative of the function $f(x)=2x$. Write a general expression for the antiderivative of f.

SOLUTION Since $G'(x)=2x=f(x)$, we have shown that $G(x)=x^2$ is in fact an antiderivative of $f(x)=2x$. By Theorem 12.1, every antiderivative of the function $f(x)=2x$ has the form $F(x)=x^2+C$, where C is some constant. The graphs of a few of the antiderivatives of f are shown in Figure 12.2.

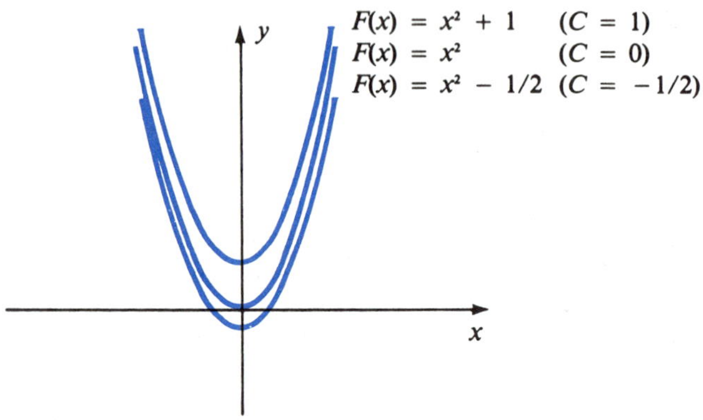

Figure 12.2

The next example involves a familiar interpretation of the antiderivative.

EXAMPLE 12.4 The velocity of a car (measured in feet/second) t seconds after starting from rest is given by the function $f(t)=2t$ $(0 \leq t \leq 20)$. Find the displacement of the car at any time t.

SOLUTION Let $s=F(t)$ be a function describing the position of the car at any time t $(0 \leq t \leq 20)$. Then the velocity of the car at time t is given by

$$v=\frac{ds}{dt}=F'(t)$$

But the velocity of the car at time t is given by $f(t)=2t$ $(0 \leq t \leq 20)$. Therefore, we have

$$F'(t)=f(t)$$

and this problem is equivalent to one of finding an antiderivative F of the function $f(t)=2t$. Using the result of Example 12.3, we have

$$s=F(t)=t^2+C \quad (C\text{, a constant})$$

Next, observe that when $t=0$, the displacement $s=0$, so that we have

$$0=0^2+C$$

or $C=0$ and thus the required expression for the displacement of the car at any time t is given by

$$s=F(t)=t^2$$

Notice that the "initial condition" helped us select the required function from the infinitely many antiderivatives of the function f. This situation is typical of problems involving antidifferentiation.

constant of integration

Before proceeding further, let us introduce the following notation: If $f(x)$ is a function with antiderivatives of the form $F(x)+C$ (C, an arbitrary constant called the *constant of integration*), then we write

$$\int f(x)\,dx = F(x)+C$$

and read "the indefinite integral of $f(x)$ dee x is equal to $F(x)+C$". The symbol

$$\int$$

is called an *integral sign* and indicates that the operation of antidifferentiation will be performed on some function $f(x)$, called the *integrand*. The expression dx following the integrand $f(x)$ reminds us that the operation is performed with respect to x. Thus the expression "the indefinite integral of ..." is synonymous with the expression "the antiderivative of ...". Using this notation, the results of Examples 12.2, and 12.3 may be written

$$\int 1\,dx = x+C \quad \text{and} \quad \int 2x\,dx = x^2+K$$

where C and K are arbitrary constants.

12.1 EXERCISES

In problems 1 through 10 verify directly that the function F *is an antiderivative of the function* f.

1. $F(x)=\frac{1}{3}x^3+2x^2-x+2, \quad f(x)=x^2+4x-1$

2. $F(x)=\frac{x}{x^2+1}, \quad f(x)=\frac{1-x^2}{(x^2+1)^2}$

3. $F(x)=x\,e^x+\pi, \quad f(x)=e^x(1+x)$

4. $F(x)=\ln x+x^2+10, \quad f(x)=\frac{1}{x}+2x$

5. $F(x)=\sqrt{x}+e^x-8, \quad f(x)=\frac{1}{2\sqrt{x}}+e^x$

6. $F(x)=(2x^2+1)^5, \quad f(x)=20x(2x^2+1)^4$

7. $F(x)=e^{3x^2-2x+1}, \quad f(x)=2(3x-1)\,e^{3x^2-2x+1}$

8. $F(x)=\ln(5x^4+2x+1), \quad f(x)=\frac{2(10x^3+1)}{5x^4+2x+1}$

9. $F(x)=\ln(e^x+e^{-x}),\quad f(x)=\dfrac{e^x-e^{-x}}{e^x+e^{-x}}$

*****10.*** $F(x)=(e^x+\ln x^2)^3,\quad f(x)=\dfrac{3(x\,e^x+2)(e^x+\ln x^2)^2}{x}$

In problems 11 through 17 (a) verify that the function G *is an antiderivative of* f, *(b) find all antiderivatives of* f *and (c) sketch the graphs of a few members of the family of antiderivatives found in part (b).*

11. $G(x)=2x,\quad f(x)=2$

12. $G(x)=2x^2,\quad f(x)=4x$

13. $G(x)=\dfrac{1}{3}x^3,\quad f(x)=x^2$

14. $G(x)=e^x,\quad f(x)=e^x$

15. $G(x)=\ln x,\quad f(x)=\dfrac{1}{x}$

16. $G(x)=\sqrt{x+1},\quad f(x)=\dfrac{1}{2\sqrt{x+1}}$

17. $G(x)=\dfrac{1}{x^2+1},\quad f(x)=-\dfrac{2x}{(x^2+1)^2}$

18. The velocity of a car (measured in feet/second) t seconds after starting from rest is given by the function $f(t)=2\sqrt{t}$ $(0\le t\le 30)$. Verify that the function $F(t)=(4/3)t^{3/2}$ is an antiderivative of f. Use this result to find the displacement of the car at any time t.

*****19.*** Prove Theorem 12.1. *Hint*: Verify the following results.

(***a***) If $H'(x)=0$ for all x, then $H(x)=C$, where C is a constant.

(***b***) If $F(x)$ and $G(x)$ are any two antiderivatives of $f(x)$, then the function $H(x)=F(x)-G(x)$ satisfies $H'(x)=0$ for all x.

(***c***) Thus, from the result of part (a), $H(x)=F(x)-G(x)=C$ for some constant C and so $F(x)=G(x)+C$, as we wished to show.

12.2 Rules of Integration

integrating

In this section we shall develop some of the rules for finding the antiderivatives (indefinite integral) of a given function f. This process of antidifferentiation is also called *integration*. We speak of *integrating* the function f when we wish to find the indefinite integral of f.

Because integration and differentiation are inverse operations, we discover many of the rules of integration by first making an "educated guess" at the antiderivative F of the function f to be integrated. Then, this result is verified by demonstrating that $F' = f$.

RULE 1

Indefinite integral of a constant
If $f(x) = k$, where k is a constant, then f has an antiderivative given by

$$\int k\,dx = kx + C$$

To prove this result, observe that $F'(x) = \frac{d}{dx}(kx + C) = k = f(x)$.

EXAMPLE 12.5 Evaluate each of the following indefinite integrals.

(a) $\int 2\,dx$ **(b)** $\int -4\,dx$ **(c)** $\int \pi^2\,dx$ **(d)** $\int (e-1)\,dx$

SOLUTION Each of the integrands above has the form $f(x) = k$ where k is a constant. Thus Rule 1 is applicable in each case and yields the following results:

(a) $\int 2\,dx = 2x + C$ **(b)** $\int -4\,dx = -4x + C$

(c) $\int \pi^2\,dx = \pi^2 x + C$ **(d)** $\int (e-1)\,dx = (e-1)x + C$ ■

RULE 2

The Power Rule
If $f(x) = x^n$ where n is a real number with $n \neq -1$, then

$$\int x^n\,dx = \frac{1}{n+1}x^{n+1} + C$$

Thus, the antiderivative of a power function is another power function obtained from the integrand by increasing its power by 1 and dividing by the new power. To prove this result observe that

$$\begin{aligned} F'(x) &= \frac{d}{dx}\left[\frac{1}{n+1}x^{n+1} + C\right] \\ &= \frac{n+1}{n+1}x^n \\ &= x^n = f(x) \end{aligned}$$

EXAMPLE 12.6 Evaluate each of the following indefinite integrals:

(a) $\int x^3\,dx$ **(b)** $\int x^{3/2}\,dx$ **(c)** $\int x^{-1/2}\,dx$ **(d)** $\int \frac{1}{x^{3/2}}\,dx$

SOLUTION Each of the integrands above is a power function with exponent $n \neq -1$. Applying Rule 2 in each case yields the following results:

(a) $\int x^3\,dx = \frac{1}{4}x^4 + C$

(b) $\int x^{3/2}\,dx = \frac{1}{5/2}x^{5/2} + C = \frac{2}{5}x^{5/2} + C$

(c) $\int x^{-1/2}\,dx = \frac{1}{1/2}x^{1/2} + C = 2x^{1/2} + C$

(d) $\int \frac{1}{x^{3/2}}\,dx = \int x^{-3/2}\,dx = \frac{1}{-1/2}x^{-1/2} + C = -2x^{-1/2} + C$ ■

The above results may be verified by differentiating each of the antiderivatives and showing that each is equal to the corresponding integrand.

RULE 3 *Indefinite integral of a constant multiple of a function*
If c is a constant and f has an antiderivative, then

$$\int cf(x)\,dx = c\int f(x)\,dx$$

Thus, the indefinite integral of a constant multiple of a function is equal to the constant multiple of the indefinite integral of the function. This result follows from the corresponding rule of differentiation (see Rule 3 in Section 10.5).

EXAMPLE 12.7 Evaluate each of the following indefinite integrals:

(a) $\int 2x^3\,dx$ (b) $\int 2\pi r\,dr$ (c) $\int -3x^{-2}\,dx$

SOLUTION Each of the integrands above has the form $cf(x)$ where c is a constant. Applying Rule 3 we obtain

(a) $\int 2x^3\,dx = 2\int x^3\,dx = 2\left[\frac{1}{4}x^4 + K\right] = \frac{1}{2}x^4 + 2K = \frac{1}{2}x^4 + C,$

where $C = 2K$. From now on we shall write the constant of integration as C, since any multiple of an arbitrary constant is an arbitrary constant.

(b) $\int 2\pi r\,dr = 2\pi\int r\,dr = (2\pi)\left(\frac{1}{2}\right)r^2 + C = \pi r^2 + C$

(c) $\int -3x^{-2}\,dx = -3\int x^{-2}\,dx = (-3)(-1)x^{-1} + C = \frac{3}{x} + C$ ■

RULE 4

The Sum Rule
If f and g are functions that have antiderivatives, (that is, are *integrable*), then

$$\int [f(x)+g(x)]\,dx = \int f(x)\,dx + \int g(x)\,dx$$

and

$$\int [f(x)-g(x)]\,dx = \int f(x)\,dx - \int g(x)\,dx$$

Thus, the indefinite integral of a sum (difference) of two integrable functions is equal to the sum (difference) of their indefinite integrals. This result is easily extended to the case involving the sum and difference of any finite number of functions. As in Rule 3, the proof of Rule 4 follows from the corresponding rule of differentiation (see Rule 4 in Section 10.5).

EXAMPLE 12.8 Evaluate the indefinite integral

$$\int (3x^5+4x^{3/2}-2x^{-1/2})\,dx$$

SOLUTION Applying the extended version of Rule 4, we find that

$$\begin{aligned}\int (3x^5+4x^{3/2}-2x^{-1/2})\,dx \\ &= \int 3x^5\,dx + \int 4x^{3/2}\,dx - \int 2x^{-1/2}\,dx \\ &= 3\int x^5\,dx + 4\int x^{3/2}\,dx - 2\int x^{-1/2}\,dx \\ &= (3)\left(\frac{1}{6}\right)x^6 + (4)\left(\frac{2}{5}\right)x^{5/2} - (2)(2)x^{1/2} + C \\ &= \frac{1}{2}x^6 + \frac{8}{5}x^{5/2} - 4x^{1/2} + C\end{aligned}$$

■

Observe that we have combined the three constants of integration, which are the results of evaluating the three indefinite integrals, together to obtain one constant C. After all, the sum of three arbitrary constants is just an arbitrary constant.

RULE 5

The indefinite integral of the exponential function

(a) $\int e^x\,dx = e^x + C$

(b) $$\int b^x\,dx = \frac{b^x}{\ln b} + C \quad (b\text{, a positive constant})$$

Thus, the indefinite integral of the exponential function with base e is just equal to the function itself (except, of course, for the constant of integration). The indefinite integral of the exponential function with base other than e differs from the function by a constant factor, namely, the reciprocal of the natural logarithm of b. Observe that Rule 5(b) reduces to Rule 5(a) when $b = e$ (since $\ln e = 1$). The proofs of these rules follow from the corresponding rules for differentiating exponential functions (see Rule 7 in Section 10.5).

EXAMPLE 12.9 Evaluate the indefinite integral

$$\int (2e^x + 3^x - x^3)\,dx$$

SOLUTION We have

$$\begin{aligned}\int (2e^x + 3^x - x^3)\,dx \\ &= \int 2e^x\,dx + \int 3^x\,dx - \int x^3\,dx \\ &= 2\int e^x\,dx + \int 3^x\,dx - \int x^3\,dx\end{aligned}$$

which, upon applying Rule 5(a) and Rule 5(b) to the evaluation of the first and second indefinite integrals,

$$= 2e^x + \frac{3^x}{\ln 3} - \frac{1}{4}x^4 + C$$

■

The last rule of integration in this section covers the integration of the function $f(x) = x^{-1}$. Remember that this function constituted the only exceptional case in the integration of the power function $f(x) = x^n$ (see Rule 2), which has an antiderivative that was, accordingly, not found by using that rule.

RULE 6 *The indefinite integral of the function $f(x) = x^{-1}$*

$$\int x^{-1}\,dx = \int \frac{1}{x}\,dx = \ln x + C$$

To prove Rule 6 observe that

$$\frac{d}{dx}\ln x = \frac{1}{x} \qquad \text{(See Rule 8(a) in Section 10.5.)}$$

EXAMPLE 12.10 Evaluate the indefinite integral

$$\int \left(2x+\frac{3}{x}+\frac{4}{x^2}\right) dx$$

SOLUTION

$$\begin{aligned}\int \left(2x+\frac{3}{x}+\frac{4}{x^2}\right) dx &= \int 2x\,dx+\int \frac{3}{x}\,dx+\int \frac{4}{x^2}\,dx\\ &= 2\int x\,dx+3\int \frac{1}{x}\,dx+4\int x^{-2}\,dx\\ &= 2\left(\frac{1}{2}\right)x^2+3\ln x+4(-1)x^{-1}+C\\ &= x^2+3\ln x-\frac{4}{x}+C\end{aligned}$$

■

Many applications require that a *specific* antiderivative f be found, given that we know its derivative f'. In such instances, some condition on f must be specified. We illustrate this in the next several examples.

EXAMPLE 12.11 Find the function f if it is known that $f'(x)=3x^2-4x+8$ and $f(1)=9$.

SOLUTION Integrating the function f', we find

$$\begin{aligned}f(x) &= \int f'(x)\,dx\\ &= \int (3x^2-4x+8)\,dx\\ &= x^3-2x^2+8x+C\end{aligned}$$

Using the condition $f(1)=9$, we have

$$9=f(1)=1^3-2(1)^2+8(1)+C$$

or

$$C=2$$

Therefore, the required function f is given by $f(x)=x^3-2x^2+8x+2$. ■

EXAMPLE 12.12 Find the rule for the function f given that (1) the slope of the tangent line to the graph of f at any point $P(x,f(x))$ is given by the expression $3x^2-6x+3$ and (2) the graph of f passes through the point $(2, 9)$.

SOLUTION The slope of the tangent line to the graph of the function f at any point $P(x,f(x))$

is given by the derivative f' of f. Thus, the first condition implies that

$$f'(x) = 3x^2 - 6x + 3$$

which, upon integration, yields

$$\begin{aligned} f(x) &= \int (3x^2 - 6x + 3)\,dx \\ &= x^3 - 3x^2 + 3x + k \end{aligned}$$

where k is the constant of integration.

To evaluate k, we use condition (2) which implies that $f(2) = 9$, or

$$9 = f(2) = 2^3 - 3(2)^2 + 3(2) + k$$

or $k = 7$. Hence, the required rule of definition of the function f is

$$f(x) = x^3 - 3x^2 + 3x + 7$$

■

EXAMPLE 12.13 The management of the Staedtler Office Equipment Company determined that the daily marginal cost function associated with the production of their battery-operated pencil sharpeners is given by $C'(x) = 0.000006x^2 - 0.006x + 4$, where $C'(x)$ is measured in dollars per unit and x denotes the number of units produced. Management has also determined that the daily fixed cost incurred in the production of these pencil sharpeners is \$100. Find the total cost incurred by the company for producing the first 500 pencil sharpeners per day.

SOLUTION We find the daily total cost function C associated with producing the pencil sharpeners by integrating the marginal cost function $C'(x)$. Thus,

$$\begin{aligned} C(x) &= \int C'(x)\,dx \\ &= \int (0.000006x^2 - 0.006x + 4)\,dx \\ &= 0.000002x^3 - 0.003x^2 + 4x + k \end{aligned}$$

where k is a constant. To determine the value of k, we use the knowledge that the daily fixed cost incurred by the company for producing the pencil sharpeners is \$100; that is $C(0) = 100$, obtaining

$$100 = C(0) = k$$

Thus, the required total cost function is given by

$$C(x) = 0.000002x^3 - 0.003x^2 + 4x + 100$$

In particular, the total cost incurred by the company for producing the first 500 units of pencil sharpeners is given by

$$\begin{aligned} C(500) &= 0.000002(500)^3 - 0.003(500)^2 + 4(500) + 100 \\ &= 1600 \quad \text{or} \quad \$1600 \end{aligned}$$

■

EXAMPLE 12.14 The management of the Staedtler Office Equipment Company determined that the daily marginal revenue function associated with the production and sale of their battery-operated pencil sharpeners is given by $R'(x) = -0.0006x + 6$ where x denotes the number of units produced and sold and $R'(x)$ is measured in dollars per unit.

(a) Determine the revenue function $R(x)$ associated with the production and sale of these pencil sharpeners.

(b) What is the demand equation that relates the wholesale unit price of the pencil sharpeners to the quantity demanded?

SOLUTION **(a)** The total revenue function R is found by integrating the marginal revenue function $R'(x)$. Thus,

$$\begin{aligned} R(x) &= \int R'(x)\,dx \\ &= \int (-0.0006x + 6)\,dx \\ &= -0.0003x^2 + 6x + C \end{aligned}$$

where C is a constant. To determine the value of C, observe that the total revenue realized by the company is nil when the production and sales level is zero, that is, $R(0) = 0$. This condition implies that

$$R(0) = -0.0003(0)^2 + 6(0) + C = 0$$

or $C = 0$. Thus, the required total revenue function is given by

$$R(x) = -0.0003x^2 + 6x$$

(b) Let p denote the unit wholesale price of the pencil sharpeners. Then $R(x) = px$. Thus

$$p = \frac{R(x)}{x} = -0.0003x + 6$$

and so the required demand equation is

$$p = -0.0003x + 6$$

■

EXAMPLE 12.15 The current circulation of the *Investor's Digest* is 2000 copies per week. Circulation is expected to grow at the rate of $5+2t^{2/3}$ copies per week, t weeks from now, for the next 3 years. Determine the circulation of the digest 125 weeks from now.

SOLUTION Let $S(t)$ denote the circulation of the digest t weeks from now. Then $S'(t)$, the rate of change of the circulation, is given by

$$S'(t) = 5 + 2t^{2/3}$$

Therefore,

$$\begin{aligned} S(t) &= \int (5 + 2t^{2/3})\, dt \\ &= 5t + (2)\left(\frac{3}{5}\right)t^{5/3} + C \\ &= 5t + \frac{6}{5}t^{5/3} + C \end{aligned}$$

To determine the value of C, observe that the circulation at $t = 0$ is 2000. Therefore,

$$S(0) = 2000 = 5(0) + \frac{6}{5}(0) + C$$

and $C = 2000$, so that

$$S(t) = 5t + \frac{6}{5}t^{5/3} + 2000$$

After 125 weeks the circulation will be

$$\begin{aligned} S(125) &= 5(125) + \frac{6}{5}(125)^{5/3} + 2000 \\ &= 6375 \end{aligned}$$

or 6375 copies per week. ■

12.2 EXERCISES

In problems 1 through 24, evaluate each of the indefinite integrals.

1. $\int \sqrt{2}\, dx$

2. $\int x^3\, dx$

3. $\int x^{2/3}\, dx$

4. $\int x^{-4}\, dx$

5. $\int \frac{2}{x^2}\,dx$

6. $\int \frac{3}{\sqrt{t}}\,dt$

7. $\int \pi\sqrt{t}\,dt$

8. $\int (1+u+u^2)\,du$

9. $\int (x^2+x+x^{-3})\,dx$

10. $\int (t^{3/2}+2t^{1/2}-4t^{-1/2})\,dt$

11. $\int \left(\sqrt{x}+\frac{3}{\sqrt{x}}\right)dx$

12. $\int \left(\frac{u^3+2u^2-u}{3u}\right)du$

13. $\int \left(\frac{1}{x^2}-\frac{1}{\sqrt[3]{x^2}}+\frac{1}{\sqrt{x}}\right)dx$

14. $\int \sqrt{t}\,(t^2+t-1)\,dt$

15. $\int \frac{1}{x^2}(x^4-2x^2+1)\,dx$

16. $\int u^{-2}(1-u^2+u^4)\,du$

17. $\int 4\,e^x\,dx$

18. $\int (1+x+e^x)\,dx$

19. $\int (1+3^x)\,dx$

20. $\int (2+x+2^x+3^x)\,dx$

21. $\int \left(\frac{x^3+x^2-x+1}{x^2}\right)dx$

22. $\int \left(\sqrt{x}+\frac{3}{x}-2\,e^x\right)dx$

23. $\int (x+1)^2\left(1-\frac{1}{x}\right)dx$

***24.** $\int (e^t+t^e-3\pi^t)\,dt$

From the given information in problems 25 through 28, find the function f.

25. $f'(x)=3x^2+4x-1;\quad f(2)=9$

26. $f'(x)=e^x-2x;\quad f(0)=2$

27. $f'(x)=\frac{x+1}{x};\quad f(1)=1$

28. $f'(x)=1+e^x+\frac{1}{x};\quad f(1)=3+e$

In problems 29 through 31, find the function f, *given that the slope of the tangent line to the graph of* f *at any point* (x, f(x)) *is* f'(x) *and that the graph of* f *passes through the point* $P_0(x_0, y_0)$.

29. $f'(x)=\frac{1}{2}x^{-1/2};\quad P_0(2, \sqrt{2})$

30. $f'(t)=t^2-2t+3;\quad P_0(1, 2)$

31. $f'(x)=e^x+x;\quad P_0(0, 3)$

32. The Staedtler Office Equipment Company produces an electric pencil sharpener. The daily marginal cost function associated with producing these pencil sharpeners is $C'(x) = 0.000009x^2 - 0.009x + 8$, where $C'(x)$ is measured in dollars per unit and x denotes the number of units produced. Management determined that the daily fixed cost incurred producing these pencil sharpeners is \$120. Find the total cost incurred by the company for producing the first 500 pencil sharpeners per day.

33. The management of the Staedtler Office Equipment Company determined that the daily marginal revenue function associated with the production and sale of their electric pencil sharpeners is given by $R'(x) = -0.009x + 12$, where x denotes the number of units produced and sold and $R'(x)$ is measured in dollars per unit.

(***a***) Determine the revenue function $R(x)$ associated with producing and selling these pencil sharpeners.

(***b***) What is the demand equation which relates the wholesale unit price with the quantity demanded of the pencil sharpeners manufactured by the company?

34. Refer to problems 32 and 33. Determine the level of production of electric pencil sharpeners, so that the daily profit is maximized. *Hint*: Set $P'(x) = R'(x) - C'(x) = 0$.

35. The Cannon Precision Instruments Corporation makes an automatic electronic flash with Thyrister circuitry. The estimated marginal profit associated with the production and sale of these electronic flashes is $(-0.004x + 20)$ dollars per unit per month, when the production level is x units per month. The company's fixed cost for producing and selling these electronic flashes is \$16,000 per month. At what level of production does the company realize a maximum profit? What is the maximum monthly profit?

36. A study conducted by Tele-Cable Incorporated estimates that the number of subscribers to the cable television service will grow at the rate of $100 + 210t^{3/4}$ new subscribers per month, t months from the starting date of the service. If 5000 subscribers signed up for the service prior to this starting date, how many subscribers will there be 16 months from this date?

37. On an average summer day in a city the level of carbon monoxide in the air is 2 parts per million. An environmental protection group's study predicts that, unless more stringent measures are taken to protect the atmosphere in the city, the concentration of carbon monoxide present in the air will increase at the rate of $0.003t^2 + 0.06t + 0.1$ parts per million per year t years from now. If no further pollution control efforts are made to protect the atmosphere, what will the concentration of carbon monoxide be on an average summer day 5 years from now?

38. The development of Astro World ("The Amusement Park of the Future") in the outskirts of a city, will increase the city population at the rate of $4500\sqrt{t} + 1000$ people per year, t years from the start of construction. The population prior to the beginning of construction is 30,000. Determine the projected population 9 years after construction of the park has begun.

39. As part of their quality control program, the chess sets manufactured by the Jones Brothers Company are subjected to a final inspection before packing. The rate of increase of the number of sets checked by an inspector per hour, t hours into the 8 A.M. to 12 noon morning shift, is approximately $N'(t) = -3t^2 + 12t + 45$ $(0 \leq t \leq 4)$. Find an expression $N(t)$ that approximates the number of sets inspected at the end of t hours. *Hint*: $N(0) = 0$. Determine the number of sets that would have been inspected by the average inspector in a morning shift.

40. The velocity (in feet per second) of a rocket t seconds into vertical flight is given by $v(t) = -3t^2 + 192t + 120$. Find an expression $h(t)$ that gives the altitude of the rocket (in feet) t seconds after liftoff. What is the altitude of the rocket 30 seconds after liftoff? *Hint*: $h'(t) = v(t)$; $h(0) = 0$.

12.3 Integration by Substitution

In the preceding section we developed certain rules of integration which are closely related to the corresponding rules of differentiation in Section 10.5. In this section we introduce a method of integration, called the *method of substitution* which is related to the Chain Rule (see Section 10.6) for the differentiation of functions. When used in conjunction with the rules of integration developed earlier, the method of substitution is a powerful tool for the integration of a large class of functions.

Recall that if F is the composition of two differentiable functions f and g, with a rule of definition given by $F(x) = f(g(x))$, then the Chain Rule states that

$$F'(x) = f'(g(x))g'(x)$$

Referring to the definition of the antiderivative of a function, we conclude, accordingly, that

(12.1)
$$F(x) = \int F'(x)\,dx = \int f'(g(x))g'(x)\,dx = f(g(x)) + C$$

is an antiderivative of $F'(x)$. The special relationships in (12.1) form the basis of integration by the method of substitution.

EXAMPLE 12.16 Using the relation in (12.1), evaluate

$$\int (x^2+3)^4(2x)\,dx$$

SOLUTION Let $g(x) = x^2 + 3$ so that

$$g'(x) = 2x$$

If we define the function f' by

$$f'(u) = u^4$$

then the integrand of the indefinite integral we are considering has the form

$$(x^2+3)^4(2x) = [g(x)]^4 g'(x) = f'(g(x))g'(x)$$

From the last equality of (12.1), namely,

$$\int f'(g(x))g'(x)\,dx = f(g(x)) + C$$

we conclude that the required antiderivative is found if we know the antiderivative of the function f'. But

$$f'(u) = u^4$$

so that

$$f(u) = \frac{1}{5}u^5 + C$$

Thus

$$\begin{aligned}\int (x^2+3)^4(2x)\,dx &= \int f'(g(x))g'(x)\,dx\\ &= f(g(x)) + C\\ &= \frac{1}{5}(x^2+3)^5 + C\end{aligned}$$

■

The notations involved in solving Example 12.16 are cumbersome. In practice, one usually performs a little notational sleight of hand to rewrite the integral in a more recognizable form. Then the rules of integration (see Section 12.2), are used to complete the solution of the problem. This formal procedure is justified since it leads to the correct solution of the problem. Consider, once again, the indefinite integral

(12.2) $$\int f'(g(x))g'(x)\,dx$$

Putting $u = g(x)$, so that

$$\frac{du}{dx} = g'(x)$$

we find that

(12.3) $$\int f'(g(x))g'(x)\,dx = \int f'(u)\frac{du}{dx}\,dx$$

If we write

$$\frac{du}{dx}\,dx = du$$

that is, if the "dx"s are cancelled then (12.3) reads

(12.4) $$\int f'(g(x))g'(x)\,dx = \int f'(u)\frac{du}{dx}\,dx = \int f'(u)\,du$$

Thus, formally, we find the antiderivative $F(x) = f(g(x))$ by making the substitution $u = g(x)$ in (12.2) and evaluating

$$\int f'(u)\,du$$

using one of the integration formulas developed earlier.

EXAMPLE 12.17 Rework Example 12.16 using the relationships in (12.4).

SOLUTION We want to evaluate the indefinite integral

(12.5) $$I = \int (x^2+3)^4(2x)\,dx$$

Put $u = x^2 + 3$ so that

$$\begin{aligned} du &= \frac{du}{dx}\,dx \\ &= \frac{d}{dx}(x^2+3)\,dx \\ &= 2x\,dx \end{aligned}$$

Making this substitution into the expression for I yields

(12.6) $$\begin{aligned} I &= \int u^4 du \\ &= \frac{1}{5}u^5 + C \\ &= \frac{1}{5}(x^2+3)^5 + C \end{aligned}$$

which agrees with the results of Example 12.16. Observe how the proper substitution reduces the integral in (12.5) to that in (12.6). The integral in (12.6) is easily integrated using Rule 2 of Section 12.2. ■

EXAMPLE 12.18 Evaluate $\int 3\sqrt{3x+1}\,dx$.

SOLUTION Put $u = 3x+1$. Then $du = 3\,dx$. The given indefinite integral becomes

$$\begin{aligned}\int 3\sqrt{3x+1}\,dx &= \int \sqrt{3x+1}\cdot 3\,dx\\ &= \int \sqrt{u}\,du\\ &= \int u^{1/2}\,du\\ &= \frac{2}{3}u^{3/2}+C\\ &= \frac{2}{3}(3x+1)^{3/2}+C\end{aligned}$$

EXAMPLE 12.19 Evaluate $\int x^2\sqrt{x^3+1}\,dx$.

SOLUTION Put $u = x^3+1$. Then $du = 3x^2\,dx$ or $x^2\,dx = 1/3\,du$. Making the appropriate substitutions we have

$$\begin{aligned}\int x^2\sqrt{x^3+1}\,dx &= \int \sqrt{x^3+1}\cdot x^2\,dx\\ &= \int u^{1/2}\cdot\frac{1}{3}\,du\\ &= \frac{1}{3}\int u^{1/2}\,du\\ &= \frac{1}{3}\left(\frac{2}{3}\right)u^{3/2}+C\\ &= \frac{2}{9}(x^3+1)^{3/2}+C\end{aligned}$$

Note that we have used Rule 1 of integration to move the constant 1/3 out of the integral sign.

EXAMPLE 12.20 Evaluate $\int x/(3x^2+1)\,dx$.

SOLUTION Put $u = 3x^2+1$. Then $du = 6x\,dx$ or $x\,dx = 1/6\,du$. Making the appropriate substitutions we have

$$\int \frac{x}{3x^2+1}\,dx = \int \frac{1/6}{u}\,du$$
$$= \frac{1}{6}\int \frac{1}{u}\,du$$
$$= \frac{1}{6}\ln u + C$$
$$= \frac{1}{6}\ln(3x^2+1) + C$$

EXAMPLE 12.21 Evaluate $\int (x^2+1/3)\,e^{x3+x}\,dx$.

SOLUTION You may convince yourself that the substitution $u = x^2+1/3$ does not simplify the given integral. Let us therefore, try the substitution $u = x^3+x$. This implies that $du = (3x^2+1)\,dx = 3(x^2+1/3)\,dx$ or $(x^2+1/3)\,dx = (1/3)\,du$. Making these substitutions, we have

$$\int \left(x^2+\frac{1}{3}\right) e^{x3+x}\,dx = \int \frac{1}{3}e^u\,du$$
$$= \frac{1}{3}\int e^u\,du$$
$$= \frac{1}{3}e^u + C$$
$$= \frac{1}{3}e^{x3+x} + C$$

At this point we wish to remind the reader that the success of the substitution method for evaluating the indefinite integrals in the last several examples was due to lucky coincidence. Each substitution $u = g(x)$ transformed the given indefinite integral into an equivalent indefinite integral having the form, $\int f'(u)\,du$, which is easily integrated using a familiar rule of integration. As useful as it is as a tool for evaluating integrals, this technique of integration has its limitations as the following example shows. Consider

$$I = \int (x^2+1)\,e^{x3+x}\,dx$$

Putting $u = x^3+x$ as in the last example, we find that $du = (3x^2+1)\,dx = 3(x^2+1/3)\,dx$. If we attempt to make a "change of variable" as before, we see that

$$e^{x3+x} = e^u$$

which is in line with our goal. But the other "factor"

$$(x^2+1)\,dx$$

cannot be expressed as a constant multiple of "du". Our attempt to write the indefinite integral I in the form

$$I = \int f'(u)\,du$$

is unsuccessful. Hence, the method of substitution fails to work in this case and some other technique of integration must be used. Note how closely the integrand in this example resembles the integrand of Example 12.21, but, as is often the case using this method of integration, a miss is as good as a mile!

Since the method of substitution is essentially a "trial and error" method, one should exhaust all possible substitutions before concluding that the method is not applicable. We continue our explanation of how this method is used.

EXAMPLE 12.22 Evaluate

$$\int \frac{e^x}{1+e^x}\,dx$$

SOLUTION Put $u = 1+e^x$ so that $du = (d/dx)(1+e^x)\,dx = e^x\,dx$. Thus

$$\int \frac{e^x}{1+e^x}\,dx = \int \frac{du}{u}$$
$$= \ln u + C$$
$$= \ln(1+e^x) + C$$

■

EXAMPLE 12.23 Evaluate

$$\int \frac{(\ln x)^2}{2x}\,dx$$

SOLUTION Put $u = \ln x$. Then $du = (d/dx)(\ln x)\,dx = (1/x)\,dx$. Thus,

$$\int \frac{(\ln x)^2}{2x}\,dx = \frac{1}{2}\int \frac{(\ln x)^2}{x}\,dx$$
$$= \frac{1}{2}\int u^2\,du$$
$$= \frac{1}{6}u^3 + C$$
$$= \frac{1}{6}(\ln x)^3 + C$$

■

Our next example illustrates how the method of substitution works in situations where the substitutions are not immediately obvious.

EXAMPLE 12.24 Evaluate

$$\int \frac{x^3}{\sqrt{1+x^2}}\, dx$$

SOLUTION Let us put $u = 1 + x^2$ so that $du = (d/dx)(1+x^2)\, dx = 2x\, dx$ and $x\, dx = (1/2)\, du$. Now, turning our attention to the integrand we see immediately that the denominator $\sqrt{1+x^2}$ may be written as $\sqrt{u}$. But the numerator presents us with a slightly more difficult problem of how to replace the variable x by the variable u. Granted we can write x^3 as $x^2 \cdot x$ so that

$$\begin{aligned} x^3\, dx &= x^2 \cdot x\, dx \\ &= x^2\left(\frac{1}{2}\, du\right) \end{aligned}$$

How do we replace the factor x^2 in terms of u? Well, in this case we are lucky. From the original substitution $u = 1 + x^2$, we find that $x^2 = u - 1$. Thus, we may write

$$x^3\, dx = (u-1)\left(\frac{1}{2}\, du\right)$$

and so

$$\begin{aligned} \int \frac{x^3}{\sqrt{1+x^2}}\, dx &= \int \frac{x^2}{\sqrt{1+x^2}}(x\, dx) \\ &= \int \frac{(u-1)}{\sqrt{u}}\left(\frac{1}{2}\, du\right) \\ &= \frac{1}{2}\int \left(\sqrt{u} - \frac{1}{\sqrt{u}}\right) du \\ &= \frac{1}{2}\int (u^{1/2} - u^{-1/2})\, du \\ &= \frac{1}{2}\left[\frac{2}{3}u^{3/2} - 2u^{1/2}\right] + C \\ &= \left[\frac{1}{3}u^{3/2} - u^{1/2}\right] + C \\ &= \frac{1}{3}u^{1/2}(u-3) + C \\ &= \frac{1}{3}\sqrt{1+x^2}(x^2-2) + C \end{aligned}$$

■

EXAMPLE 12.25 A study prepared by the Marketing Department of the Universal Instruments Company forecasts that, after introduction into the market, sales of its new line of Galaxy Home Computers will grow at the rate of $2000-1500\,e^{-0.05t}$ units per month ($0 \le t \le 60$). Find an expression that gives the total number of computers that will sell t months after they are made available in the market. How many computers will the company sell in the first year they appear on the market?

SOLUTION Let $N(t)$ denote the total number of computers that may be expected to be sold t months after their introduction in the market. Then, the rate of growth of sales of the computers is given by $N'(t)$ units per month. Thus,

$$N'(t) = 2000 - 1500\,e^{-0.05t}$$

so that

$$N(t) = \int (2000 - 1500\,e^{-0.05t})\,dt$$

$$= \int 2000\,dt - 1500 \int e^{-0.05t}\,dt$$

Upon integrating the second integral by the method of substitution (put $u = -0.05t$), we obtain

$$N(t) = 2000t + \frac{1500}{0.05}e^{-0.05t} + C$$

$$= 2000t + 30{,}000\,e^{-0.05t} + C$$

To determine the value of C, note that the number of computers sold at the end of month 0 is nil, so that $N(0) = 0$. This gives

$$N(0) = 30{,}000 + C = 0 \qquad (\text{since } e^0 = 1)$$

or $C = -30{,}000$. Therefore, the required expression is given by

$$N(t) = 2000t + 30{,}000\,e^{-0.05t} - 30{,}000$$

$$= 2000t + 30{,}000(e^{-0.05t} - 1)$$

The number of computers that the company may expect to sell in the first year they appear on the market is given by

$$N(12) = 2000(12) + 30{,}000(e^{-0.05(12)} - 1)$$

$$= 10{,}464$$

or 10,464 units. ■

12.3 EXERCISES

In problems 1 through 30 evaluate each of the indefinite integrals.

1. $\int 4(4x+3)^4\,dx$

2. $\int 4x(2x^2+1)^7\,dx$

3. $\int (x^3-2x)^2(3x^2-2)\,dx$

4. $\int (3x^2-2x+1)(x^3-x^2+x)^4\,dx$

5. $\int \frac{4x}{(2x^2+3)^3}\,dx$

6. $\int \frac{3x^2+2}{(x^3+2x)^2}\,dx$

7. $\int 3t^2\sqrt{t^3+2}\,dt$

8. $\int t^2(t^3+2)^{3/2}\,dt$

9. $\int (x^2-1)^9 x\,dx$

10. $\int \frac{\sqrt{1+u^{-1}}}{u^2}\,du$

11. $\int (x^{2/3}-1)^5 x^{-1/3}\,dx$

12. $\int \frac{\sqrt{x^{1/3}-1}}{x^{2/3}}\,dx$

13. $\int \frac{x^2}{\sqrt{x^3-1}}\,dx$

14. $\int \frac{2}{x-2}\,dx$

15. $\int \frac{x}{3x^2-1}\,dx$

16. $\int \frac{x^2-1}{x^3-3x+1}\,dx$

17. $\int e^{2t+3}\,dt$

18. $\int x e^{-x^2}\,dx$

19. $\int x^2 e^{x^3-1}\,dx$

20. $\int (e^x-e^{-x})\,dx$

21. $\int \frac{e^{\sqrt{x}}}{\sqrt{x}}\,dx$

22. $\int \frac{e^{2x}}{1+e^{2x}}\,dx$

23. $\int \frac{e^{3x}+x^2}{(e^{3x}+x^3)^3}\,dx$

24. $\int \frac{e^{-u}-1}{e^{-u}+u}\,du$

***25.** $\int \left(x e^{x^2}-\frac{x}{x^2+2}\right)dx$

26. $\int \frac{\ln 5x}{x}\,dx$

27. $\int \frac{(\ln u)^3}{u}\,du$

28. $\int x(x-1)^5\,dx$

***29.** $\int v^2(1-v)^6\,dv$

30. $\int x^3(x^2+1)^{3/2}\,dx$

In problems 31 through 34 find the function f *given that the slope of the tangent line to the graph of* f *at any point* (x, f(x)) *is* f′(x) *and that the graph of* f *passes through the point* $P_0(x_0, y_0)$.

31. $f'(x)=5(2x-1)^4$; $P_0(1,3)$

32. $f'(x)=\dfrac{3x^2}{2\sqrt{x^3-1}}$; $P_0(1,1)$

33. $f'(x)=-2x\,e^{-x^2+1}$; $P_0(1,0)$

34. $f'(x)=1-\dfrac{2x}{x^2+1}$; $P_0(0,2)$

35. The registrar of Kellogg University estimates that the total student enrollment in the University's Division of Continuing Education will grow at the rate of $N'(t)=2000(1+0.2t)^{-3/2}$ students per year, t years from now. If the current student enrollment is 1000, find an expression giving the total student enrollment t years from now. What will the student enrollment be 5 years from now?

36. The number of viewers of a weekly TV news-magazine show, introduced in the 1980 season, has been increasing at the rate of $3(2+(1/2)x)^{-1/3}$ million viewers per year in its xth year on the air, $(1\le x\le 5)$. The number of viewers in its first year on the air is given by $9(5/2)^{2/3}$ million. Find the number of viewers of the TV news-magazine show in the 1985 season.

37. The average student enrolled in the 20-week Advanced Shorthand course at the American Institute of Stenography progresses according to the rule $N'(t)=6\,e^{-0.05t}$ $(0\le t\le 20)$, where $N'(t)$ measures the rate of change of the number of words per minute of dictation the student takes in shorthand after t weeks in the course. Assuming the average student enrolled in this course begins with a dictation speed of 60 words per minute, find an expression $N(t)$ that gives the dictation speed of the student after t weeks in the course.

38. Two thousand pairs of Acrosonic Model F loudspeaker systems sold in the first year they appeared in the market. Since then, the sales of these loudspeaker systems have been growing at the rate of $f'(t)=2000(3-2\,e^{-t})$ units per year, where t denotes the number of years these systems have been in the market. Determine the number of systems that were sold in the first five years after their introduction.

39. Suppose a patient is given a continuous intravenous infusion of glucose at a constant rate of r milligrams per minute. Then, the rate at which the amount of glucose in the bloodstream is changing at time t due to this infusion is given by $A'(t)=r\,e^{-at}$ milligrams per minute, where a is a positive constant associated with the rate at which excess glucose is eliminated from the bloodstream and is dependent on the patient's rate of metabolism. Derive an expression for the amount of glucose in the bloodstream at time t. *Hint*: $A(0)=0$.

12.4

Integration by Parts

Integration by parts, a technique of integration like the method of substitution discussed in the last section, is based on a corresponding rule of differentiation. In this case, the rule of differentiation is the product rule that asserts that if f and g are differentiable functions, then

(12.7) $$\frac{d}{dx}[f(x)g(x)]=f(x)g'(x)+g(x)f'(x)$$

If we integrate both sides of (12.7) with respect to x, we obtain

$$\int \frac{d}{dx}[f(x)g(x)]\,dx=\int f(x)g'(x)\,dx+\int g(x)f'(x)\,dx$$

or,
$$f(x)g(x)=\int f(x)g'(x)\,dx+\int g(x)f'(x)\,dx$$

The last equation may be written in the form

(12.8) $$\int f(x)g'(x)\,dx=f(x)g(x)-\int g(x)f'(x)\,dx$$

and is called the formula for *integration by parts.* The integration by parts formula (12.8) is useful since it enables us to express one indefinite integral in terms of another. Thus, if a given indefinite integral is difficult (or impossible) to evaluate in its present form, by using formula (12.8) the given indefinite integral is expressed in terms of another, which may be evaluated more conveniently.

EXAMPLE 12.26 Evaluate $\int x\,e^x\,dx$.

SOLUTION You may convince yourself that none of the methods of integration developed so far will enable us to evaluate the given indefinite integral in its present form. Therefore we will attempt to rewrite it in terms of an indefinite integral, which, hopefully will be easier to evaluate. To this end, we use the integration by parts formula (12.8) by putting

$$f(x)=x \quad \text{and} \quad g'(x)=e^x$$

so that
$$f'(x)=1 \quad \text{and} \quad g(x)=e^x$$

and thus

$$\begin{aligned}\int x e^x \, dx &= \int f(x)g'(x)\, dx \\ &= f(x)g(x) - \int g(x)f'(x)\, dx \\ &= x e^x - \int e^x \, dx \\ &= x e^x - e^x + C \\ &= (x-1)e^x + C\end{aligned}$$

■

The method of integration by parts, like the method of substitution, is one of "trial and error". Therefore, the success of the method depends on the proper choice of the functions $f(x)$ and $g'(x)$. For example, if we chose

$$f(x) = e^x \quad \text{and} \quad g'(x) = x$$

in the last example, then

$$f'(x) = e^x \quad \text{and} \quad g(x) = \frac{1}{2}x^2$$

so that formula (12.8) would have yielded

$$\begin{aligned}\int x e^x \, dx &= \int f(x)g'(x)\, dx \\ &= f(x)g(x) - \int g(x)f'(x)\, dx \\ &= \frac{1}{2}x^2 e^x - \int \frac{1}{2}x^2 e^x \, dx\end{aligned}$$

Since the indefinite integral on the right-hand side of the above equation is not readily evaluated (it is, in fact, more complicated than the original integral!), choosing the functions $f(x)$ and $g'(x)$ as above has not helped to evaluate the given indefinite integral.

EXAMPLE 12.27 Evaluate

$$\int x\sqrt{x-1}\, dx.$$

SOLUTION Let us put

$$f(x) = x \quad \text{and} \quad g'(x) = \sqrt{x-1} = (x-1)^{1/2}$$

Then,

$$f'(x) = 1 \quad \text{and} \quad g(x) = \frac{2}{3}(x-1)^{3/2}$$

Thus,

$$\begin{aligned}
\int x\sqrt{x-1}\,dx &= \int f(x)g'(x)\,dx \\
&= f(x)g(x) - \int g(x)f'(x)\,dx \\
&= \frac{2}{3}x(x-1)^{3/2} - \int \frac{2}{3}(x-1)^{3/2}\cdot 1\,dx \\
&= \frac{2}{3}x(x-1)^{3/2} - \frac{2}{3}\int (x-1)^{3/2}\,dx \\
&= \frac{2}{3}x(x-1)^{3/2} - \left(\frac{2}{3}\right)\cdot\left(\frac{2}{5}\right)(x-1)^{5/2} + C \\
&= \frac{2}{3}(x-1)^{3/2}\left[x - \frac{2}{5}(x-1)\right] + C \\
&= \frac{2}{3}(x-1)^{3/2}\left(\frac{3}{5}x + \frac{2}{5}\right) + C \\
&= \frac{2}{15}(x-1)^{3/2}(3x+2) + C
\end{aligned}$$

■

EXAMPLE 12.28 Evaluate

$$\int x \ln x\,dx.$$

SOLUTION Putting

$$f(x) = \ln x \quad \text{and} \quad g'(x) = x,$$

we have

$$f'(x) = \frac{1}{x} \quad \text{and} \quad g(x) = \frac{1}{2}x^2$$

Thus

$$\begin{aligned}
\int x \ln x\,dx &= \int f(x)g'(x)\,dx \\
&= f(x)g(x) - \int g(x)f'(x)\,dx \\
&= \frac{1}{2}x^2 \ln x - \int \frac{1}{2}x^2\cdot\left(\frac{1}{x}\right)dx
\end{aligned}$$

$$= \frac{1}{2}x^2 \ln x - \frac{1}{2}\int x\,dx$$

$$= \frac{1}{2}x^2 \ln x - \frac{1}{4}x^2 + C$$

$$= \frac{1}{2}x^2\left(\ln x - \frac{1}{2}\right) + C$$

■

EXAMPLE 12.29 The estimated rate at which oil will be produced from a certain oil well, t years after production has begun, is given by $R(t) = 100te^{-0.1t}$ thousand barrels per year. Find an expression that describes the total production of oil at the end of year t.

SOLUTION Let $T(t)$ denote the total production of oil from the oil well at the end of year t ($t \geq 0$). Then the rate of oil production will be given by $T'(t)$ thousand barrels per year. Thus,

$$T'(t) = R(t) = 100te^{-0.1t}$$

so that

$$T(t) = \int 100te^{-0.1t}\,dt$$

$$= 100\int te^{-0.1t}\,dt$$

We use the technique of integration by parts to evaluate the above integral. Let

$$f(t) = t \quad \text{and} \quad g'(t) = e^{-0.1t}$$

so that

$$f'(t) = 1 \quad \text{and} \quad g(t) = -\frac{1}{0.1}e^{-0.1t} = -10\,e^{-0.1t}$$

Therefore,

$$T(t) = 100\left[-10te^{-0.1t} + 10\int e^{-0.1t}\,dt\right]$$

$$= 100[-10te^{-0.1t} - 100\,e^{-0.1t}] + C$$

$$= -1000\,e^{-0.1t}(t + 10) + C$$

To determine the value of C, note that the total quantity of oil produced at the end of year 0 is nil, so that $T(0) = 0$. This gives

$$T(0) = -1000(10) + C = 0$$

or

$$C = 10{,}000$$

Thus, the required production function is given by

$$T(t) = -1000\,e^{-0.1t}(t + 10) + 10{,}000$$

■

12.4 EXERCISES

In problems 1 through 18 evaluate each of the indefinite integrals.

1. $\int x e^{2x}\, dx$

2. $\int x e^{-x}\, dx$

3. $\int (x+1) e^{x}\, dx$

4. $\int x(x+1)^{-3/2}\, dx$

5. $\int x(x+4)^{-2}\, dx$

6. $\int \frac{x}{\sqrt{2x+3}}\, dx$

7. $\int x \ln 2x\, dx$

8. $\int x^3 \ln x\, dx$

9. $\int x^2 \ln 2x\, dx$

10. $\int \sqrt{x} \ln x\, dx$

11. $\int \sqrt{x} \ln \sqrt{x}\, dx$

12. $\int \frac{\ln x}{\sqrt{x}}\, dx$

13. $\int x^3(x^2+2)^5\, dx$ *Hint*: Put $f(x)=x^2$.

14. $\int \ln x\, dx$ *Hint*: Put $f(x)=\ln x$ and $g'(x)\, dx = 1$.

15. $\int x^2 e^{-x}\, dx$ *Hint*: Integrate by parts twice.

16. $\int x(\ln x)^2\, dx$ *Hint*: Integrate by parts twice.

17. $\int x \ln (x+1)\, dx$ *Hint*: First make the substitution $u = x+1$, then integrate by parts.

***18.** $\int x^3 e^{-x^2+1}\, dx$ *Hint*: First make the substitution $u=-x^2+1$, then integrate by parts.

19. In keeping with the projected increase in worldwide demand for steam coal, the boiler-firing fuel used for electricity generation, the management of the Consolidated Mining Company decided to step up their mining operations. Plans call for increasing the yearly production of steam coal by $2te^{-0.05t}$ million metric tons per year for the next 20 years. Current yearly coal production is 20 million metric tons. Find a function describing the company's total production of steam coal at the end of t years. How much coal would the company have produced over the next 20 years if this plan were carried out?

20. The sales of the latest recording by the "Brittania", a British rock group, are currently at the rate of $2te^{-0.1t}$ units per week (each unit represents 10,000 albums) where t denotes the number of weeks since the release of the recording. Find an expression that gives the total number of units of the record albums sold as a function t. How many record albums will have sold by the end of the twentieth week?

12 Chapter Review

FORMULAS

1. $\int k\,dx = kx + C \quad k$, a constant

2. **Power Rule:** $\int x^n\,dx = \frac{1}{n+1}x^{n+1} + C$

3. **Constant Multiple Rule:** $\int cf(x)\,dx = c\int f(x)\,dx$

4. **Sum Rule:** $\int [f(x) \pm g(x)]\,dx = \int f(x)\,dx \pm \int g(x)\,dx$

5. $\int e^x\,dx = e^x + C$

6. $\int b^x\,dx = \frac{b^x}{\ln b} + C$ (b, a positive constant)

7. $\int x^{-1}\,dx = \int \frac{1}{x}\,dx = \ln x + C$

8. **Method of substitution:** $\int f(g(x))g'(x)\,dx = \int f(u)\,du, \quad u = g(x)$

9. **Integration by parts:** $\int f(x)g'(x)\,dx = f(x)g(x) - \int g(x)f'(x)\,dx$

EXERCISES

In problems 1 though 18 evaluate each of the given indefinite integrals.

1. $\int \left(x^4 - 2x^3 + \frac{1}{x^2}\right) dx$

2. $\int (x^{1/3} - \sqrt{x} + 4)\,dx$

3. $\int (x^2 + 1)(\sqrt{x} - 1)\,dx$

4. $\int \left(x^2 - x + \frac{2}{x} + 5\right) dx$

5. $\int \sqrt{2x + 1}\,dx$

6. $\int (3x - 1)(3x^2 - 2x + 1)^{1/3}\,dx$

7. $\int x^2(x^3+2)^{10}\,dx$

8. $\int \frac{x-1}{x^2-2x+5}\,dx$

9. $\int 2\,e^{-2x}\,dx$

10. $\int \left(x+\frac{1}{2}\right)e^{x^2+x+1}\,dx$

11. $\int \frac{e^{-x}-1}{(e^{-x}+x)^2}\,dx$

12. $\int \frac{(\ln x)^5}{x}\,dx$

13. $\int \frac{\ln x^2}{x}\,dx$

14. $\int x^3(x^2+1)^{10}\,dx$

15. $\int x\sqrt{x+1}\,dx$

16. $\int \frac{x}{\sqrt{x-2}}\,dx$

17. $\int x\,e^{-x}\,dx$

18. $\int \ln 5x\,dx$

In problems 19 through 22 find the function f *given that the slope of the tangent line to the graph at any point* (x, f(x)) *is* f′(x) *and that the graph of* f *passes through the point* $P_0(x_0, y_0)$.

19. $f'(x)=3x^2-4x+1;\quad P_0(1,1)$

20. $f'(x)=\frac{x}{\sqrt{x^2+1}};\quad P_0(0,1)$

21. $f'(x)=1-e^{-x};\quad P_0(0,2)$

22. $f'(x)=\frac{\ln x}{\sqrt{x}};\quad P_0(1,-2)$

23. The management of the National Electric Corporation determined that the daily marginal cost function associated with producing their automatic drip coffeemaker is given by

$$C'(x)=0.00003x^2-0.03x+20$$

where $C'(x)$ is measured in dollars per unit and x denotes the number of units produced. Management has also determined that the daily fixed cost incurred in producing these coffeemakers is \$500. What is the total cost incurred by the company for producing the first 400 coffeemakers per day?

24. Refer to problem 23. Management has also determined that the daily marginal revenue function associated with the production and sale of their coffeemakers is given by $R'(x)=-0.03x+60$, where x denotes the number of units produced and sold and $R'(x)$ is measured in dollars per unit.

(*a*) Determine the revenue function $R(x)$ associated with producing and selling these coffeemakers.

(*b*) What is the demand equation relating the wholesale unit price to the quantity of coffeemakers demanded?

25. The Franklin National Life Insurance Company purchased a new computer for \$200,000. If the rate at which the computer's resale value changes is given by the function $V'(t)=3800(t-10)$ where t is the length of time since the purchase

date and $V'(t)$ is measured in dollars per year, find an expression $V(t)$ that gives the resale value of the computer after t years. How much would the computer cost after 6 years?

26. The Marketing Department of the Vista Vision Corporation forecasts that sales of their new line of projection television systems will grow at the rate of $3000-2000\,e^{-0.04t}$ units per month $(0 \leq t \leq 24)$, once introduced into the market. Find an expression giving the total number of units of the projection television systems that the company may expect to sell t months from the time they are put on the market. How many units of the projection television systems may the company expect to sell during the first year?

27. Due to the increasing cost of fuel, the manager of the City Transit Authority estimates that the number of commuters using the city subway system will increase at the rate of $3000(1+0.4t)^{-1/2}$ $(0 \leq t \leq 36)$ per month, t months from now. If 100,000 commuters are currently using the system, find an expression giving the total number of commuters who will be using the subway t months from now. How many commuters will be using the subway 6 months from now?

28. The sales of the Starr Communication Company's newest video cartridge game, "Laser Beams", are currently at the rate of $t\,e^{-0.05t}$ units per month, (each unit represents 1000 cartridges), where t denotes the number of months since the release of the cartridge. Find an expression giving the total number of units of the video cartridge games sold as a function of t. How many video games will be sold by the end of the first year?

13

THE DEFINITE INTEGRAL

13.1

The Definite Integral

In the last chapter we mainly concerned ourselves with finding the indefinite integral (antiderivative) F of a function f, and we used the notation

$$F(x) = \int f(x)\, dx$$

to denote it. In many practical situations, however, the solution of a problem involves the evaluation of the function $F(x)$ at one or more specific values of x. For example, the solution of Example 12.13 called for the evaluation of $C(x)$ at $x = 0$ and $x = 500$ where $C(x)$, the daily total cost function, was found by integrating the given daily marginal cost function $C'(x)$. In fact, $C(0)$ gives the daily fixed cost of the company, whereas $C(500)$ gives the daily total cost incurred by the company for producing the first 500 units of their battery operated pencil sharpeners. Therefore, the difference

(13.1) $$C(500) - C(0)$$

represents the cost incurred by the company when the level of production is raised from zero to 500 units per day; that is, the difference $C(500) - C(0)$ measures the net change of the total cost function $C(x)$ over the interval [0, 500]. More generally, if F is any function, then the net change of $F(x)$ over the interval $[a, b]$ is the number $F(b) - F(a)$ and is abbreviated by the symbol

(13.2) $$F(x)\Big|_a^b$$

Thus

$$F(x)\Big|_a^b = F(b) - F(a)$$

Using this notation (13.1) may be abbreviated as

$$C(x)\Big|_0^{500}$$

If the function F is an antiderivative of some function f, then Formula 13.2 measures the net change of the function

$$F(x) = \int f(x)\,dx$$

definite integral

over the interval $[a, b]$. This observation motivates the following definition: Let f be a function defined on the interval $[a, b]$. Then the *definite integral of f over the interval* $[a, b]$ measures the net change, $F(b)-F(a)$, of an antiderivative F of f over that interval.

We use the notation

$$\int_a^b f(x)\,dx$$

to denote the definite integral of f over the interval $[a, b]$. Thus,

(13.3)

$$\int_a^b f(x)\,dx = F(x)\Big|_a^b = F(b) - F(a)$$

lower and upper limits of integration

The numbers a and b are called, respectively, the *lower limit* and the *upper limit* of integration and the symbol on the left is read "the integral of f from a to b."

EXAMPLE 13.1 Evaluate

$$\int_1^3 (3x^2+1)\,dx$$

SOLUTION An antiderivative of the function $f(x) = 3x^2 + 1$ is given by $F(x) = x^3 + x + C$, where C is an arbitrary constant. Therefore

$$\begin{aligned}\int_1^3 (3x^2+1)\,dx &= x^3 + x + C\Big|_1^3 \\ &= [(3)^3 + 3 + C] - [(1)^3 + 1 + C] \\ &= 28\end{aligned}$$

■

Observe that in the evaluation of the definite integral in Example 13.1 the constant of integration "dropped out." This is true in general for, if $F(x)+C$ denotes an antiderivative of some function f, then

$$\begin{aligned} F(x)+C\Big|_a^b &= [F(b)+C]-[F(a)+C] \\ &= F(b)+C-F(a)-C \\ &= F(b)-F(a) \end{aligned}$$

With this fact in mind, we may, in all future computations involving the evaluation of a definite integral, drop the constant of integration from our calculations.

EXAMPLE 13.2 Evaluate

$$\int_{-1}^{1} e^{(1/2)x}\,dx$$

SOLUTION An antiderivative of the integrand $f(x)=e^{(1/2)x}$ is given by $F(x)=2e^{(1/2)x}$. Therefore,

$$\begin{aligned} \int_{-1}^{1} e^{(1/2)x}\,dx &= 2\,e^{(1/2)x}\Big|_{-1}^{1} \\ &= 2\,e^{1/2}-2\,e^{-1/2} \\ &= 2(e^{1/2}-e^{-1/2}) \end{aligned}$$

■

EXAMPLE 13.3 The management of the Staedtler Office Equipment Company determined that the daily marginal cost function associated with producing their battery-operated pencil sharpener is given by $C'(x)=0.000006x^2-0.006x+4$, where $C'(x)$ is measured in dollars per unit and x denotes the number of units produced. Management has also determined that the daily fixed cost incurred for producing these pencil sharpeners is \$100. Find the company's daily total cost for producing

(a) the first 500 units and

(b) the 201st through 400th units of their battery-operated pencil sharpeners.

SOLUTION **(a)** We find that the daily manufacturing cost incurred by the company in raising the production level from $x=0$ to $x=500$ is given by

$$\begin{aligned} \int_0^{500} C'(x)\,dx &= \int_0^{500} (0.000006x^2-0.006x+4)\,dx \\ &= 0.000002x^3-0.003x^2+4x\Big|_0^{500} \\ &= [0.000002(500)^3-0.003(500)^2+4(500)] \\ &\quad -[0.000002(0)^3-0.003(0)^2+4(0)] \\ &= 0.000002(500)^3-0.003(500)^2+4(500) \\ &= 1500 \quad \text{or} \quad \$1500 \end{aligned}$$

Since the fixed cost is \$100 per day, the required total cost incurred daily by the company for producing 500 pencil sharpeners is \$1,600.

(b) The daily total cost incurred by the company for producing the 201st through 400th units of battery-operated pencil sharpeners is given by

$$\int_{200}^{400} C'(x)\,dx = \int_{200}^{400} (0.000006x^2 - 0.006x + 4)\,dx$$

$$= 0.000002x^3 - 0.003x^2 + 4x \Big|_{200}^{400}$$

$$= [0.000002(400)^3 - 0.003(400)^2 + 4(400)] - [0.000002(200)^3 - 0.003(200)^2 + 4(200)]$$

$$= 1248 - 696$$

$$= 552 \quad \text{or} \quad \$552$$

■

EXAMPLE 13.4 An efficiency study conducted for the Elektra Electronics Company showed that the rate at which the number of "Space Commander" walkie-talkies are assembled by the average worker, t hours after starting work at 8 A.M., is given by the function $f(t) = -3t^2 + 12t + 15$ $(0 \le t \le 4)$. Determine the number of walkie-talkies assembled by the average worker in the first hour of the morning shift. How many units can the average worker be expected to assemble in the second hour of the morning shift?

SOLUTION Let $N(t)$ denote the number of walkie-talkies assembled by the average worker t hours after starting work in the morning shift. Then, we have $N'(t) = f(t) = -3t^2 + 12t + 15$. Therefore, the number of units assembled by the average worker in the first hour of the morning shift is given by

$$N(1) - N(0) = \int_0^1 N'(t)\,dt$$

$$= \int_0^1 (-3t^2 + 12t + 15)\,dt$$

$$= -t^3 + 6t^2 + 15t \Big|_0^1$$

$$= -1 + 6 + 15$$

$$= 20 \quad \text{or} \quad 20 \text{ units}$$

The number of units the average worker is expected to assemble in the second hour of the morning shift is given by the definite integral

$$\int_1^2 N'(t)\,dt = \int_1^2 (-3t^2+12t+15)\,dt$$

$$= -t^3+6t^2+15t\Big|_1^2$$

$$= [-2^3+6(2)^2+15(2)]-[-1^3+6(1)^2+15(1)]$$

$$= 46-20$$

$$= 26 \quad \text{or} \quad 26 \text{ units}$$

■

EXAMPLE 13.5 The rate of electricity consumption in a certain city is expected to grow exponentially with a growth constant given by $k=0.04$. If the rate of consumption at present is 40 million kilowatt-hours (kwh) per year, what should the total production of electricity be over the next three years in order to meet the projected demand?

SOLUTION If $R(t)$ denotes the expected rate of consumption of electricity t years from now, then

$$R(t) = 40\,e^{0.04t}$$

million kwh per year (see Section 5.4). Next, if $C(t)$ denotes the expected total consumption of electricity over a period of t years, then $C'(t)=R(t)$. Therefore, the total consumption of electricity expected over the next three years is given by

$$\int_0^3 C'(t)\,dt = \int_0^3 40\,e^{0.04t}\,dt$$

$$= \frac{40}{0.04}e^{0.04t}\Big|_0^3$$

$$= 1000(e^{0.12}-1)$$

$$= 127.5 \quad \text{or} \quad 127.5 \text{ million kwh}$$

and this amount must be produced over the next three years in order to meet the demand. ■

The next example shows two approaches generally adopted when evaluating a definite integral using the method of substitution.

EXAMPLE 13.6 Evaluate

$$\int_0^2 x\sqrt{1+x^2}\,dx$$

SOLUTION *First Method* We first evaluate the corresponding indefinite integral

$$I = \int x\sqrt{1+x^2}\,dx$$

Let us make the substitution

$$u = 1 + x^2$$

so that

$$du = \frac{d}{dx}(1+x^2)\,dx$$
$$= 2x\,dx$$

or

$$x\,dx = \frac{1}{2}\,du$$

Then

$$I = \int \frac{1}{2}\sqrt{u}\,du = \frac{1}{2}\int u^{1/2}\,du$$
$$= \frac{1}{3}u^{3/2} + C$$
$$= \frac{1}{3}(1+x^2)^{3/2} + C$$

Using the above result, we now evaluate the given definite integral as follows.

$$\int_0^2 x\sqrt{1+x^2}\,dx = \frac{1}{3}(1+x^2)^{3/2}\Big|_0^2$$
$$= \frac{1}{3}[(1+4)^{3/2} - 1^{3/2}]$$
$$= \frac{1}{3}(\sqrt{125} - 1)$$

Second Method As before, we make the substitution

(13.4) $$u = 1 + x^2$$

so that

$$du = 2x\,dx$$

or

$$x\,dx = \frac{1}{2}\,du$$

Next, we make the following observation: The given definite integral is evaluated *with respect to x* with the range of integration given by the interval $[0, 2]$. If we perform the integration *with respect to u* via the substitution (13.4), then we must adjust the range of integration suitably to agree with the integration performed with respect to the new variable. To determine the proper range of integration, note that when $x = 0$, Equation 13.4 implies that $u = 1 + 0^2 = 1$, which gives the required lower limit of integration with respect to u. Similarly, when $x = 2$, $u = 1 + 2^2 = 5$ is the required upper limit of integration with respect to u. Thus, the range of integration when the integration is performed with respect to u is given by the interval $[1, 5]$. Therefore, we may write

$$\begin{aligned}\int_0^2 x\sqrt{1+x^2}\,dx &= \int_1^5 \frac{1}{2}\sqrt{u}\,du \\ &= \frac{1}{2}\int_1^5 u^{1/2}\,du \\ &= \frac{1}{3}u^{3/2}\Big|_1^5 \\ &= \frac{1}{3}(5^{3/2}-1^{3/2}) \\ &= \frac{1}{3}(\sqrt{125}-1)\end{aligned}$$

which agrees with the result obtained using the first method. ■

EXAMPLE 13.7 Evaluate

$$\int_0^2 x\,e^{2x^2}\,dx$$

SOLUTION Let us put

$$u = 2x^2$$

so that

$$du = 4x\,dx$$

or

$$x\,dx = \frac{1}{4}\,du$$

Furthermore when $x=0$, $u=0$, and when $x=2$, $u=8$. This gives the lower and upper limits of integration for integration with respect to u. Making the indicated substitutions, we find

$$\begin{aligned}\int_0^2 x\,e^{2x^2}\,dx &= \int_0^8 \frac{1}{4}e^u\,du \\ &= \frac{1}{4}e^u\Big|_0^8 \\ &= \frac{1}{4}(e^8-1)\end{aligned}$$

■

We close this section by listing the following useful properties of the definite integral, some of which parallel the rules of integration of Section 12.2. Let f and

g be functions. Then, we have

Property 1
$$\int_a^a f(x)\,dx = 0$$

Property 2
$$\int_a^b f(x)\,dx = -\int_b^a f(x)\,dx$$

Property 3
$$\int_a^b cf(x)\,dx = c\int_a^b f(x)\,dx \qquad (c\text{, a constant})$$

Property 4
$$\int_a^b [f(x)+g(x)]\,dx = \int_a^b f(x)\,dx + \int_a^b g(x)\,dx$$
$$\int_a^b [f(x)-g(x)]\,dx = \int_a^b f(x)\,dx - \int_a^b g(x)\,dx$$

Property 5
$$\text{If } a<c<b\text{, then } \int_a^b f(x)\,dx = \int_a^c f(x)\,dx + \int_c^b f(x)\,dx$$

Property 5 states that if c is a number lying between a and b so that the interval $[a, b]$ is divided into the intervals $[a, c]$ and $[c, b]$, then the integral of f over the interval $[a, b]$ may be expressed as the sum of the integral of f over the interval $[a, c]$ and the integral of f over the interval $[c, b]$. We will give a geometrical interpretation of this property in the next section.

13.1 EXERCISES

In problems 1 through 32, evaluate each of the definite integrals.

1. $\int_2^4 3\,dx$

2. $\int_{-1}^0 (4-x)\,dx$

3. $\int_{-1}^3 2x^2\,dx$

4. $\int_{-2}^2 (x^2-1)\,dx$

5. $\int_1^4 \sqrt{u}\,du$

6. $\int_1^8 4x^{1/3}\,dx$

7. $\int_0^1 (x^3-2x^2+1)\,dx$

8. $\int_1^2 (t^5-t^3+1)\,dt$

9. $\int_1^4 \left(\sqrt{x}-\frac{1}{\sqrt{x}}\right)dx$

10. $\int_2^4 \frac{1}{x}\,dx$

11. $\int_0^4 x(x^2-1)\,dx$

12. $\int_{-3}^{-1} \frac{1}{x^2}\,dx$

13. $\int_0^1 e^{-x}\,dx$

14. $\int_0^1 (e^{2x}+x^2+1)\,dx$

15. $\int_0^2 (e^t-e^{-t})\,dt$

16. $\int_1^2 \left(4e^{2u}-\frac{1}{u}\right)du$

17. $\int_3^6 \frac{2}{x-2}\,dx$

18. $\int_1^2 \left(1+\frac{1}{u}+\frac{1}{u^2}\right)du$

19. $\int_1^5 x\sqrt{x-1}\,dx$

20. $\int_0^{\ln 2} x\,e^x\,dx$
Hint: Integrate by parts.

21. $\int_1^2 x\ln x\,dx$
Hint: Integrate by parts.

22. $\int_1^4 \ln x\,dx$
Hint: Integrate by parts.

23. $\int_0^2 x\,e^{-x}\,dx$
Hint: Integrate by parts.

24. $\int_0^1 x^2 e^{-x}\,dx$
Hint: Integrate by parts.

25. $\int_1^2 (2x-1)^4\,dx$

26. $\int_1^2 (2x+4)(x^2+4x-8)^3\,dx$

27. $\int_{-1}^1 x^2(x^3+1)^4\,dx$

28. $\int_{-1}^1 x\,e^{x^2+1}\,dx$

29. $\int_1^5 \sqrt{2x-1}\,dx$

30. $\int_0^1 \frac{x}{1+2x^2}\,dx$

31. $\int_0^1 \frac{e^x}{1+e^x}\,dx$

32. $\int_1^4 x\sqrt{x+1}\,dx$

33. A division of Ditton Industries manufactures a deluxe toaster-oven. The management of the company has determined that the daily marginal cost function associated with producing these toaster-ovens is given by the rule $C'(x)=0.0003x^2-0.12x+20$, where $C'(x)$ is measured in dollars per unit and x denotes the number of units produced. Management has also determined that the daily fixed cost incurred in the production is \$800.

(*a*) Find the total cost incurred by the company for producing the first 300 units of these toaster-ovens per day.

(*b*) What is the total cost incurred by the company in the production of the 201st through 300th units of the toaster-ovens per day?

34. The management of Ditton Industries determined that the daily marginal revenue function associated with selling x units of their deluxe toaster-ovens is given by $R'(x)=-0.1x+40$, where $R'(x)$ is measured in dollars per unit.

(*a*) Find the daily total revenue realized from the sale of 200 units of the toaster-ovens.

(*b*) Find the additional revenue realized when the production (and sales) level is increased from 200 to 300 units.

35. Refer to problem 33. The daily marginal profit function associated with the production and sales of the deluxe toaster-ovens manufactured by Ditton Industries is known to be given by $P'(x) = -0.0003x^2 + 0.02x + 20$, where x denotes the number of units manufactured and sold daily and $P'(x)$ is measured in dollars per unit.

(*a*) Find the total profit realizable from the manufacture and sale of 200 units of the toaster-ovens per day.

(*b*) What is the additional daily profit realizable if the production and sale of the toaster-ovens is increased from 200 to 220 units per day?

36. Tempco Electronics, a division of Tempco Toys Incorporated, manufactures an electronic football game. An efficiency study showed that the rate at which the games are assembled by the average worker t hours after starting work at 8 A.M., is given by $-(3/2)t^2 + 6t + 20$, $(0 \leq t \leq 4)$ units per hour.

(*a*) Find the total number of games the average worker may be expected to assemble in the 4-hour morning shift.

(*b*) What is the number of units the average worker may be expected to assemble in the first hour of the morning shift? in the second hour of the morning shift?

37. A study, proposed in 1980 by researchers from the major producers and consumers of the world's coal, concluded that coal could and must play an important role in fueling global economic growth over the next twenty years. The world production of coal in 1980 was 3.5 billion metric tons. If output were to increase at the rate of $3.5\,e^{0.05t}$ billion metric tons per year in year t ($t = 0$ corresponding to 1980), determine the amount of coal that would have been produced worldwide between 1980 and the end of the century.

38. In a recent pre-trial run for an attempt at the world water speed record, the velocity of the Sea Falcon II at the time of firing the booster rocket ($t = 0$) was approximately 440 feet per second. The velocity of the boat t seconds later was given by $f(t) = -t^2 + 20t + 440$ feet per second $(0 \leq t \leq 20)$. Find the distance covered by the boat over the 20-second period.

39. A bottle of white wine at room temperature (68°F) is placed in a refrigerator at 4 P.M. Its temperature after t hours is changing at the rate of $-18\,e^{-0.6t}$ degrees Fahrenheit per hour. By how many degrees will the temperature of the bottle of wine have dropped by 7 P.M.? What will the temperature of the wine be at 7 P.M.?

40. The velocity of a dragster t seconds after leaving the starting line is $100t\,e^{-0.2t}$ feet per second. What is the distance covered by the dragster in the first 10 seconds of its run?

41. The *net investment flow*, which is the rate of capital formation, of the giant conglomerate LTF Incorporated is projected to be $t\sqrt{(1/2)t^2 + 1}$ million dollars per year. Find the accruement to the capital stock of the company in the second year. *Hint*: The amount is given by

$$\int_1^2 t\sqrt{\frac{1}{2}t^2+1}\,dt$$

42. Prove Property 1 of the definite integral. *Hint*: Let F be an antiderivative of f, and use the definition of the definite integral.

43. Prove Property 2 of the definite integral. *Hint*: see Problem 42.

44. Verify by direct computation that

$$\int_1^3 x^2\,dx = -\int_3^1 x^2\,dx$$

45. Prove Property 3 of the definite integral. *Hint*: see Problem 42.

46. Verify by direct computation that

$$\int_1^9 2\sqrt{x}\,dx = 2\int_1^9 \sqrt{x}\,dx$$

47. Verify by direct computation that

$$\int_0^1 (1+x-e^x)\,dx = \int_0^1 dx + \int_0^1 x\,dx - \int_0^1 e^x\,dx$$

What properties of the definite integral were demonstrated in this exercise?

48. Verify by direct computation that

$$\int_0^3 (1+x^3)\,dx = \int_0^1 (1+x^3)\,dx + \int_1^3 (1+x^3)\,dx$$

What property of the definite integral was demonstrated here?

49. Verify by direct computation that

$$\int_0^3 (1+x^3)\,dx = \int_0^1 (1+x^3)\,dx + \int_1^2 (1+x^3)\,dx + \int_2^3 (1+x^3)\,dx$$

hence showing that Property 5 may be extended.

13.2 Areas Under a Curve

One of the most important applications of the definite integral lies in the calculation of areas bounded by arbitrary curves. We begin by considering a relatively simple region R in the xy-plane (Figure 13.1), which is bounded above by the graph of a continuous, nonnegative function f, below by the x-axis, and on the left and right by the vertical lines $x=a$ and $x=b$, respectively. For the sake of brevity, we shall also refer to such a region as the region under the curve $y=f(x)$ from $x=a$ to $x=b$. Then, the *Fundamental Theorem of Calculus* tells us that the area of the region R is given by the definite integral

Fundamental Theorem of Calculus

(13.5)
$$\int_a^b f(x)\,dx$$

Before we attempt to justify this very important result, let us convince ourselves of its validity by applying it to compute the areas of some planar regions, which may also be found using more elementary methods.

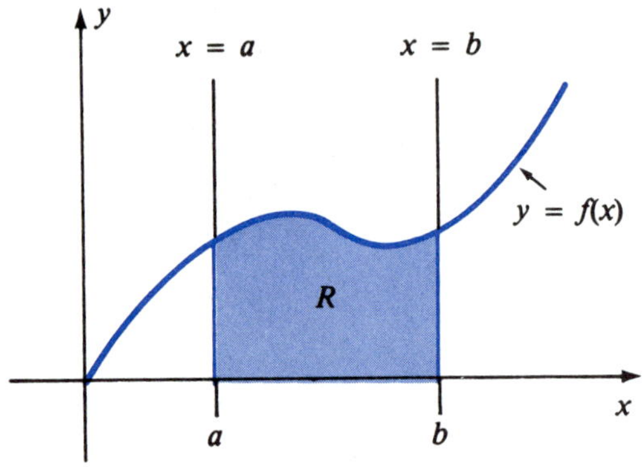

Figure 13.1

EXAMPLE 13.8 Let R be the region that is bounded above by the graph of the function $f(x)=3$, below by the x-axis, and on the left and right by the vertical lines $x=2$ and $x=6$, respectively. Verify, by direct computation, that the Fundamental Theorem of Calculus is true for the region R.

SOLUTION The region R is a rectangle with adjacent sides equal to 3 and 4 units (see Figure 13.2), so that the area of R is given by 3×4 or 12 square units. Next, we find, using Formula 13.5 that

$$\begin{aligned}\int_2^6 3\,dx &= 3\int_2^6 dx\\ &= 3x\Big|_2^6\\ &= 18-6\\ &= 12\end{aligned}$$

and conclude, accordingly, that the Fundamental Theorem of Calculus is true for the case under consideration, as we wished to show.

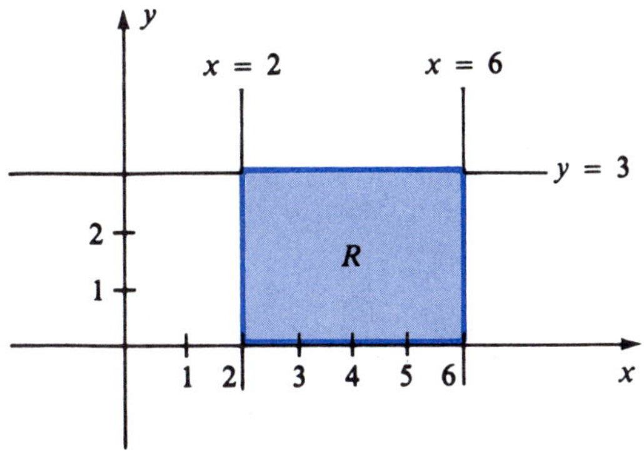

Figure 13.2

EXAMPLE 13.9 Find the area of the region R under the curve $y=x$ from $x=1$ to $x=3$.

SOLUTION The region R is shown in Figure 13.3(a). Using the Fundamental Theorem of Calculus, we conclude that the area of the region R is given by

$$\begin{aligned}\int_1^3 x\,dx &= \frac{1}{2}x^2\Big|_1^3\\ &= \frac{9}{2}-\frac{1}{2}\\ &= 4\end{aligned}$$

or 4 square units. We can verify this result since we may compute the area of R by elementary means. In fact, the required area is given by the area of the rectangle R_1 (width × height) plus the area of the triangle R_2 ($\frac{1}{2}$ base × height) (see Figure 13.3 part b), or,

$$(2)(1)+\frac{1}{2}(2)(2)=2+2=4$$

in agreement with the previous result.

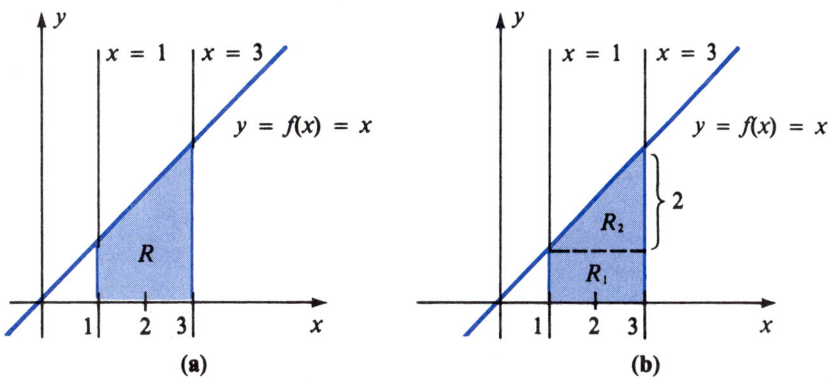

Figure 13.3

Before giving an intuitive "proof" of a version of the Fundamental Theorem of Calculus, let us restate it again more formally.

THEOREM

Let $f(x)$ be a continuous nonnegative function with the domain containing the interval $[a, b]$. Then the area of the region R bounded above by the graph of f, below by the x-axis, and on the left and right by the vertical lines $x = a$ and $x = b$, respectively, is given by the definite integral

$$\int_a^b f(x)\,dx$$

Let us define a function $A(t)$, which measures the area of the region under the curve $y = f(x)$ from $x = a$ to $x = t$ where $a \le t \le b$ (Figure 13.4). If h is a small positive number, then $A(t+h)$ measures the area of the region under the curve $y = f(x)$ from $x = a$ to $x = t + h$. Therefore, the difference

$$A(t+h) - A(t)$$

gives the area of the region under the curve $y = f(x)$ from $x = t$ to $x = t + h$ (Figure 13.5).

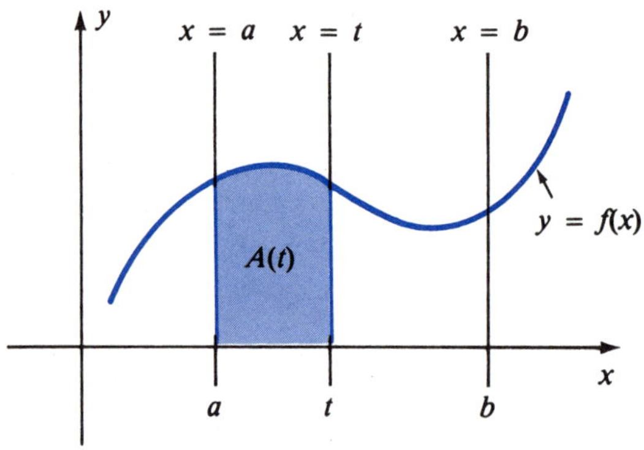

Figure 13.4

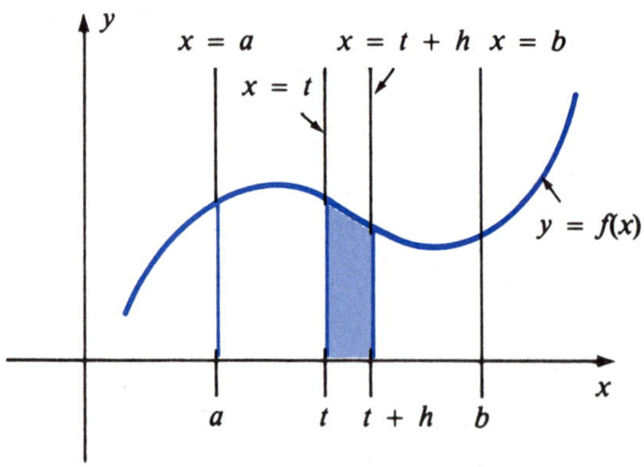

Figure 13.5

However the area of this last region is approximately equal to the area of the rectangle of width h and height $f(t)$, whose area is accordingly given by the expression $h \cdot f(t)$ (see Figure 13.6). Thus,

$$A(t+h)-A(t) \approx h \cdot f(t)$$

where the approximations improve as h is taken to be smaller and smaller.

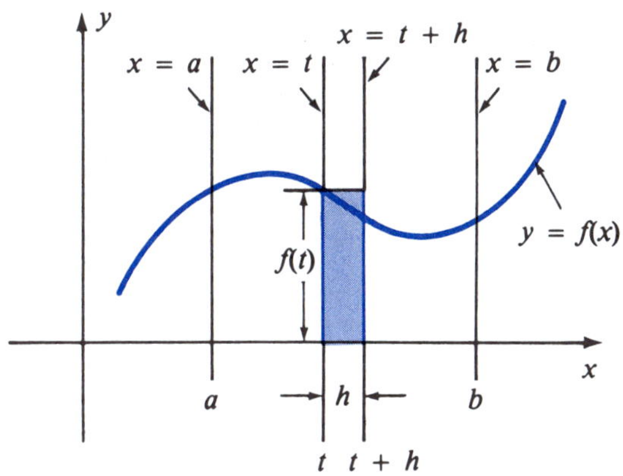

Figure 13.6

Dividing both sides of the above relationship by h, we obtain

$$\frac{A(t+h)-A(t)}{h} \approx f(t)$$

Taking the limit as h approaches zero, we find, by the definition of the derivative, that the left-hand side is

$$\lim_{h \to 0} \frac{A(t+h)-A(t)}{h} = A'(t)$$

The right-hand side, which is independent of h, remains constant throughout the limiting process; because the approximation becomes exact as h approaches zero, we find that

$$A'(t) = f(t)$$

Since the above equation holds for all values of t in the interval $[a, b]$, we have shown that the *area function* $A(x)$ is an antiderivative of the function $f(x)$.

Finally, we observe that $A(a)=0$ and $A(b)=$ area of the region R described in the hypothesis of the theorem. Thus, the area of the region R is

$$\begin{aligned} A(b) &= A(b)-A(a) \qquad (\text{since } A(a)=0) \\ &= \int_a^b A'(x)\,dx \\ &= \int_a^b f(x)\,dx \end{aligned}$$

as we wished to demonstrate.

EXAMPLE 13.10 Find the area of the region bounded above by the graph of the function $f(x)=x^2+1$, below by the x-axis, and by the vertical lines $x=-1$ and $x=2$.

SOLUTION The region R under consideration is shown in Figure 13.7. Using the Fundamental Theorem of Calculus, the area of the region R is given by

$$\begin{aligned} \int_{-1}^{2} (x^2+1)\,dx &= \left(\frac{1}{3}x^3+x\right)\Big|_{-1}^{2} \\ &= \left[\frac{1}{3}(8)+2\right]-\left[\frac{1}{3}(-1)^3+(-1)\right] \\ &= 6 \end{aligned}$$

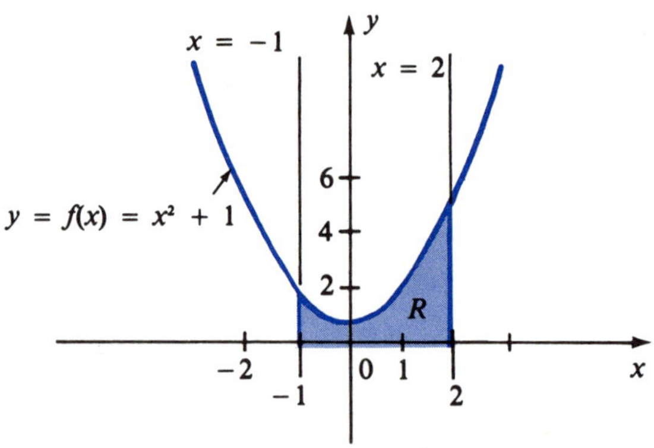

Figure 13.7

EXAMPLE 13.11 Using a geometrical interpretation of the definite integral, show that Property 5 (see Section 13.1), namely,

$$\int_a^b f(x)\,dx = \int_a^c f(x)\,dx + \int_c^b f(x)\,dx \qquad (a \le c \le b)$$

is valid for the case where f is a nonnegative, continuous function.

SOLUTION By the Fundamental Theorem of Calculus, we interpret the integral

$$\int_a^b f(x)\,dx$$

as the area of the region under the curve $y=f(x)$ from $x=a$ to $x=b$ (Figure 13.8). Similarly, we interpret the definite integrals

$$\int_a^c f(x)\,dx \quad \text{and} \quad \int_c^b f(x)\,dx$$

as the areas of the regions under the curve $y=f(x)$ from $x=a$ to $x=c$ and from $x=c$ to $x=b$, respectively. Since the two regions do not overlap, it is clear that

$$\int_a^b f(x)\,dx = \int_a^c f(x)\,dx + \int_c^b f(x)\,dx$$

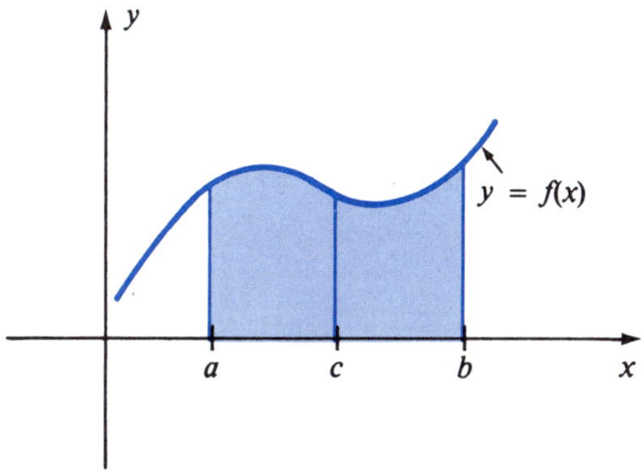

Figure 13.8

We now recall the remark made in the introductory paragraph in Chapter 10, namely, that although the motivations that led to the development of the differential calculus and the integral calculus were seemingly unrelated, the two subjects turned out, in fact, to be very closely related. The Fundamental Theorem of Calculus is so named because of the important role it plays in establishing this connection. To recapitulate, the Fundamental Theorem of Calculus states that the area under the curve of a nonnegative function f from $x=a$ to $x=b$ is given by the definite integral of f over the interval $[a, b]$. Since

$$\int_a^b f(x)\,dx = F(b)-F(a)$$

where F is an antiderivative of f, that is to say $F'=f$, the link is thereby established between differential calculus and integral calculus.

13.2 EXERCISES

In problems 1 through 4, find the area of the region under each of the given curves y = f(x) *from* x = a *to* x = b *using the Fundamental Theorem of Calculus. Then, verify the result obtained using elementary means.*

1. $f(x)=2;\quad a=1, b=4$

2. $f(x)=4;\quad a=-1, b=3$

3. $f(x)=2x;\quad a=1, b=3$

4. $f(x)=-\frac{1}{4}x+1;\quad a=1, b=3$

In problems 5 through 22, find the area of the region under each of the given curves y = f(x) *from* x = a *to* x = b.

5. $f(x)=2x^2+1;\quad a=2, b=4$

6. $f(x)=-x^2+4;\quad a=-1, b=2$

7. $f(x)=4x-x^2;\quad a=0, b=4$

8. $f(x)=\frac{1}{x^2};\quad a=2, b=4$

9. $f(x)=\sqrt{x};\quad a=1, b=9$

10. $f(x)=x^3+x^2+1;\quad a=0, b=2$

11. $f(x)=x^3-4x^2-3x+18;\quad a=-2, b=3.$ *Hint*: See Figure 11.33.

12. $f(x)=\frac{1}{\sqrt{2x+4}};\quad a=0, b=6$

13. $f(x)=x\sqrt{3x^2+1};\quad a=1, b=4$

14. $f(x)=e^{-x};\quad a=-2, b=4$

15. $f(x)=e^x-x;\quad a=1, b=2$

16. $f(x)=xe^{x2+1};\quad a=0, b=2$

17. $f(x)=\frac{1}{x+1};\quad a=0, b=4$

18. $f(x)=\frac{x}{x^2+1};\quad a=1, b=3$

***19.** $f(x)=\ln x;\quad a=1, b=5$ *Hint*: Integrate by parts.

***20.** $f(x)=xe^{-x};\quad a=0, b=3$ *Hint*: See Figure 11.35; integrate by parts.

21. $f(x)=\begin{cases} x^2 & x\leq 2 \\ x+2 & x>2 \end{cases};\quad a=0, b=4$ *Hint*: Use Property 5 of Section 13.1.

***22.** $f(x)=|2x+1|;\quad a=-1, b=1$

13.3 Areas of Planar Regions

In Section 13.2 we found, via the Fundamental Theorem of Calculus, the area of a region under the curve $y=f(x)$ (f, a nonnegative function) from $x=a$ to $x=b$ by evaluating an appropriate definite integral, namely

$$\int_a^b f(x)\,dx$$

In this section, we show how to use the Fundamental Theorem of Calculus to find the areas of more complicated regions in the plane.

Consider, first of all, the region R, which is bounded below by the graph of a nonpositive function f, above by the x-axis, and to the left and right by the vertical lines $x=a$ and $x=b$, respectively (Figure 13.9).

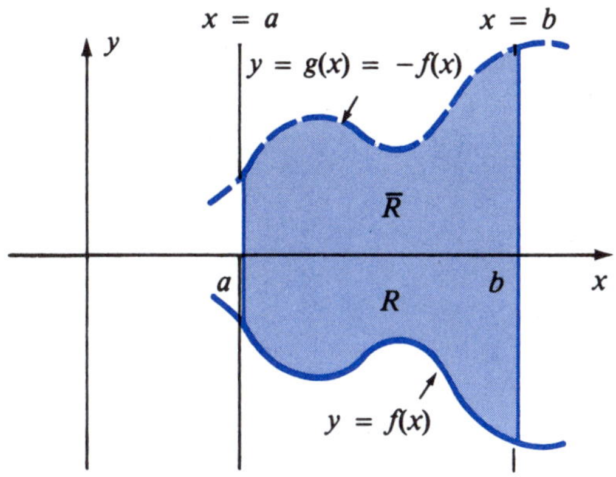

Figure 13.9

To find the area of R we first observe that the function g defined by

$$g(x)=-f(x)$$

has a graph that is symmetrical to the graph of f with respect to the x-axis, so that the region $\bar{R}$, which is a mirror reflection of R, has the same area as that of R. Furthermore, since $f(x)$ is nonpositive, we see that $g(x)=-f(x)$ is nonnegative; so by the Fundamental Theorem of Calculus, the area of the region $\bar{R}$ (and therefore that of R as well) is given by

$$\begin{aligned}\int_a^b g(x)\,dx &= \int_a^b -f(x)\,dx \\ &= -\int_a^b f(x)\,dx\end{aligned}$$

Thus, the area of a region bounded below by the graph of a continuous, nonpositive function f, above by the x-axis from $x=a$ to $x=b$, is given by

$$-\int_a^b f(x)\,dx$$

EXAMPLE 13.12 Find the area of the region bounded by the x-axis, the curve $y=-x^2+4x-8$, and the lines $x=-1$ and $x=4$.

SOLUTION The region R under consideration is shown in Figure 13.10. Since $y=f(x)$ is negative for all x and in particular for x in the interval $[-1, 4]$, we see that the area of R is given by

$$-\int_{-1}^{4} f(x)\,dx = -\int_{-1}^{4} (-x^2+4x-8)\,dx$$

$$= \frac{1}{3}x^3 - 2x^2 + 8x \Big|_{-1}^{4}$$

$$= \left[\frac{1}{3}(64) - 2(16) + 8(4)\right] - \left[\frac{1}{3}(-1) - 2(1) + 8(-1)\right]$$

$$= 31\frac{2}{3} \quad \text{or} \quad 31\frac{2}{3} \text{ square units}$$

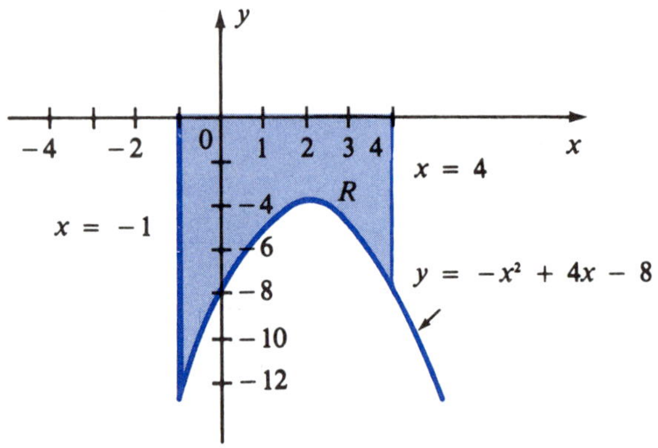

Figure 13.10

Now, suppose f is a continuous function with domain containing the interval $[a, b]$, and suppose $f(x)$ assumes both positive and negative values on $[a, b]$ as shown in Figure 13.11. To find the area of the region R bounded by the graph of f, the x-axis, and the lines $x=a$ and $x=b$ (shown shaded in Figure 13.11), we first determine the subintervals contained in the interval $[a, b]$ for which f is nonnegative and those for which f is nonpositive. For the region R under consideration, we find that $f(x) \geq 0$ on $[a, c]$ and $f(x) \leq 0$ on $[c, b]$. We now use the results obtained earlier to compute the required area. Indeed, the area of R_1 is given by

$$\int_a^c f(x)\,dx$$

whereas, the area of R_2 is given by

$$-\int_c^b f(x)\,dx$$

so that the area of R, which is the sum of the area of R_1 and R_2, is given by

$$\int_a^c f(x)\,dx - \int_c^b f(x)\,dx$$

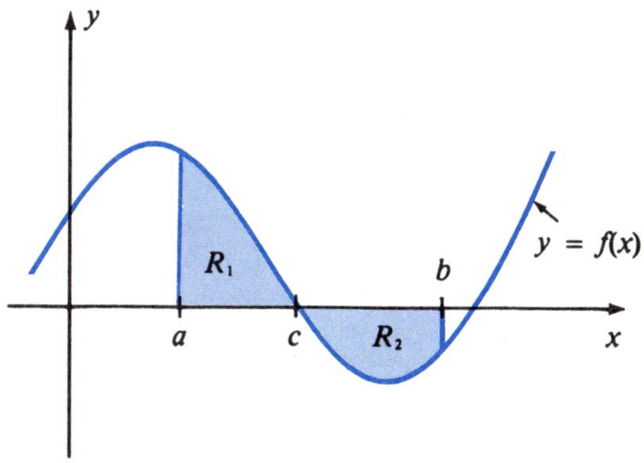

Figure 13.11

EXAMPLE 13.13 Find the area of the region bounded by the graph of the function $f(x)=x^3$, the x-axis, and the lines $x=-1$ and $x=1$.

SOLUTION The region in question is shown in Figure 13.12. Since $f \leq 0$ on the interval $[-1, 0]$ and $f \geq 0$ on the interval $[0, 1]$, the required area is given by

$$-\int_{-1}^{0} x^3\,dx + \int_{0}^{1} x^3\,dx = -\frac{1}{4}x^4\Big|_{-1}^{0} + \frac{1}{4}x^4\Big|_{0}^{1}$$

$$= \frac{1}{4} + \frac{1}{4}$$

$$= \frac{1}{2} \quad \text{or} \quad \frac{1}{2} \text{ square units}$$

The reader may verify that, because of symmetry, we can obtain the required area by computing

$$-2\int_{-1}^{0} x^3\,dx \quad \text{or} \quad 2\int_{0}^{1} x^3\,dx$$

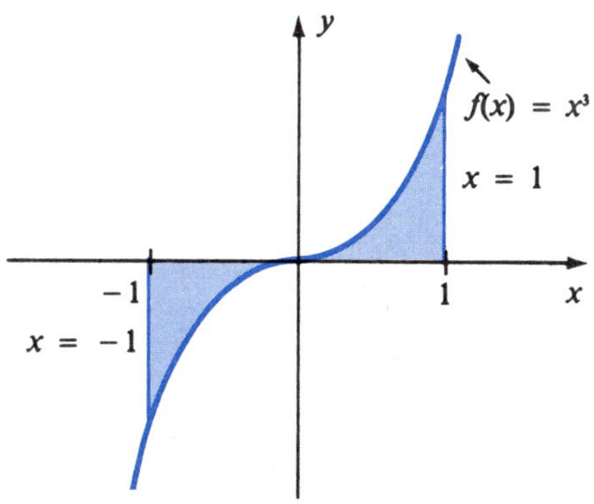

Figure 13.12

■

We now turn our attention to finding the area of a planar region bounded both above and below by the graphs of functions. First, consider the situation when the graph of one function lies above that of another. More specifically, let R be the region in the xy-plane (Figure 13.13), which is bounded above by the graph of a continuous function f, below by a continuous function g where $f(x) \geq g(x)$ $(a \leq x \leq b)$, and to the left and right by the vertical lines $x = a$ and $x = b$, respectively. In Figure 13.13 we see that we can find the area of R by computing the area of the region under the curve $y = f(x)$ from $x = a$ to $x = b$ and then subtracting from it the area of the region under the curve $y = g(x)$ from $x = a$ to $x = b$. Thus, the required area is

$$\int_a^b f(x)\,dx - \int_a^b g(x)\,dx$$

(13.6) or

$$\int_a^b [f(x) - g(x)]\,dx$$

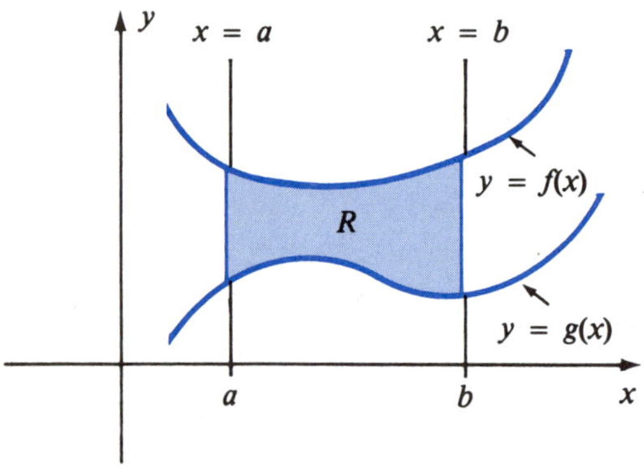

Figure 13.13

upon using Property 4 of the definite integral (see Section 13.1).

Even though we supposed, in the derivation of Formula 13.6 that both f and g are nonnegative (see Figure 13.13), it may be shown that this formula is equally valid even if f and g are not nonnegative (see problem 30 in Exercise Set 13.3). Furthermore when $g(x) = 0$, that is, when the lower boundary of the region R is the x-axis, Formula 13.6 gives the area of the region under the curve $y = f(x)$ from $x = a$ to $x = b$ as we would expect.

EXAMPLE 13.14 Find the area of the region bounded by the graphs of the functions $f(x) = (1/2)x + 3$ and $g(x) = x^2$ and the vertical lines $x = -1$ and $x = 1$.

SOLUTION We first sketch the graphs of the functions $f(x) = (1/2)x + 3$ and $g(x) = x^2$, the vertical lines $x = -1$ and $x = 1$, and identify the region R whose area is to be calculated (Figure 13.14). Since the graph of the function f always lies above that of the function g for values of x satisfying $-1 \leq x \leq 1$, we see, by Formula 13.6, that the area of the region R is given by

$$\int_{-1}^{1}\left[\left(\frac{x}{2}+3\right)-x^2\right]dx=\int_{-1}^{1}\left(-x^2+\frac{x}{2}+3\right)dx$$

$$=-\frac{1}{3}x^3+\frac{1}{4}x^2+3x\Big|_{-1}^{1}$$

$$=\left(-\frac{1}{3}+\frac{1}{4}+3\right)-\left(\frac{1}{3}+\frac{1}{4}-3\right)$$

$$=5\frac{1}{3}\quad\text{or}\quad 5\frac{1}{3}\text{ square units}$$

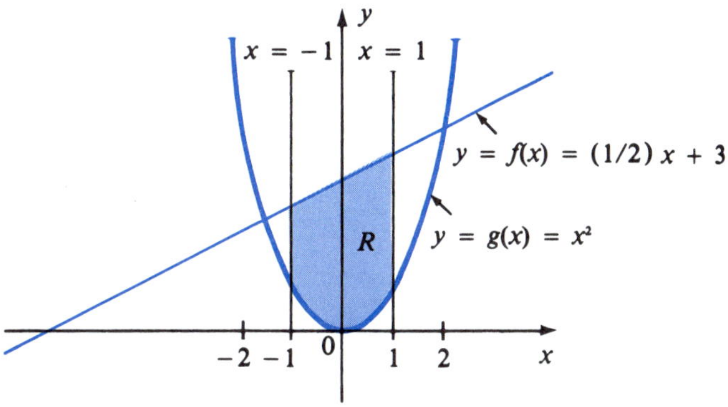

Figure 13.14

EXAMPLE 13.15 Find the area of the region R that is completely enclosed by the graphs of the functions $f(x)=(1/2)x+3$ and $g(x)=x^2$ (compare Example 13.14).

SOLUTION The region R is shown in Figure 13.15. Let us find the points of intersection of the two curves or, more accurately, the points of intersection of the straight line $y=(1/2)x+3$ and the parabola $y=x^2$. To this end, we solve the system comprising these two equations simultaneously. We have, upon equating the two values of y,

$$x^2=\frac{1}{2}x+3\quad\text{or}\quad 2x^2-x-6=0$$

which we factor as

$$(2x+3)(x-2)=0$$

Thus $x=-3/2$ or $x=2$ so that the points of intersection of the two curves are $(-3/2, 9/4)$ and $(2, 4)$.

Thus, we could also view the region R under consideration as bounded above by the graph of the function $f(x)=(1/2)x+3$, below by the graph of the function $g(x)=x^2$, *and* to the left and right by the vertical lines $x=-3/2$ and $x=2$,

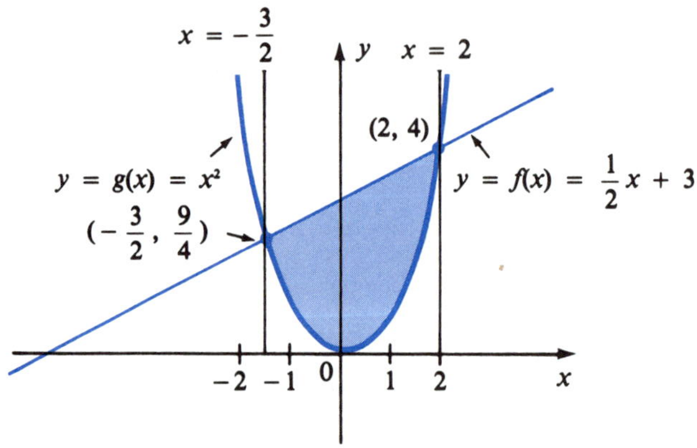

Figure 13.15

respectively. Next, since the graph of the function f always lies above that of the function g for $-3/2 \leq x \leq 2$, we can use Formula 13.6 to compute the desired area:

$$\begin{aligned}\int_{-3/2}^{2}\left[\left(\frac{x}{2}+3\right)-x^2\right]dx &= \int_{-3/2}^{2}\left(-x^2+\frac{x}{2}+3\right)dx \\ &= -\frac{1}{3}x^3+\frac{1}{4}x^2+3x\bigg|_{-3/2}^{2} \\ &= \left[-\frac{8}{3}+1+6\right]-\left[\frac{9}{8}+\frac{9}{16}-\frac{9}{2}\right] \\ &= 7\frac{7}{48} \quad \text{or} \quad 7\frac{7}{48}\text{ square units}\end{aligned}$$

■

EXAMPLE 13.16 Find the area of the region R bounded by the graphs of the functions $f(x)=x^2-2x-1$ and $g(x)=-e^x-1$ and the vertical lines $x=-1$ and $x=1$.

SOLUTION Figure 13.16 shows the region whose area is to be found. Since the graph of the function f always lies above that of the function g, the area of the region R is given by

$$\begin{aligned}\int_{-1}^{1}[(x^2-2x-1)-(-e^x-1)]\,dx &= \int_{-1}^{1}(x^2-2x+e^x)\,dx \\ &= \frac{1}{3}x^3-x^2+e^x\bigg|_{-1}^{1} \\ &= \left(\frac{1}{3}-1+e\right)-\left(-\frac{1}{3}-1+e^{-1}\right) \\ &= \frac{2}{3}+e-\frac{1}{e} \\ &\approx 3.02 \quad \text{or} \quad 3.02\text{ square units}\end{aligned}$$

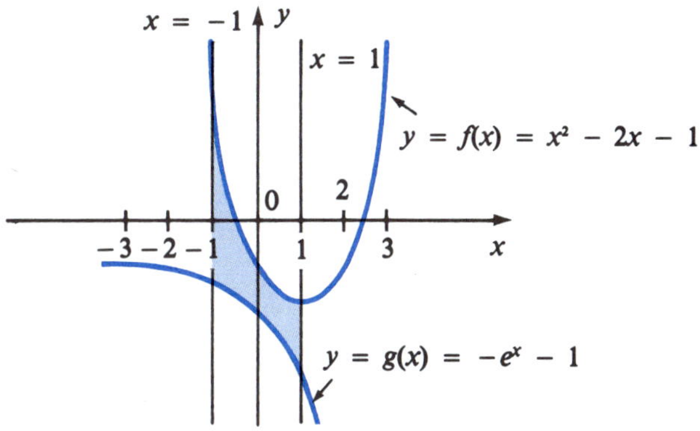

Figure 13.16

Formula 13.6, which gives the area of the region between the curves $y = f(x)$ and $y = g(x)$ for $a \leq x \leq b$, is valid when the graph of the function f lies above that of the function g over the interval $[a, b]$. Example 13.17 shows how to use Formula 13.6 to find the area of a region when the latter condition does not hold.

EXAMPLE 13.17 Find the area of the region that is completely enclosed by the graphs of the functions $f(x) = x^3 - 3x + 3$ and $g(x) = x + 3$.

SOLUTION First sketch the graphs of the functions $y = f(x) = x^3 - 3x + 3$ and $y = g(x) = x + 3$, and identify the required region R. We can view the region R as two subregions R_1 and R_2 shown in Figure 13.17. By solving the equations $y = x + 3$ and $y = x^3 - 3x + 3$ simultaneously, we find the points of intersection of the two curves. Eliminating y from the equations gives

$$x^3 - 3x + 3 = x + 3$$

or

$$x^3 - 4x = 0$$

$$x(x^2 - 4) = 0$$

$$x(x+2)(x-2) = 0 \quad \text{or} \quad x = 0, -2, \text{or } 2$$

Hence the points of intersection of the two curves are $(-2, 1)$, $(0, 3)$ and $(2, 5)$.

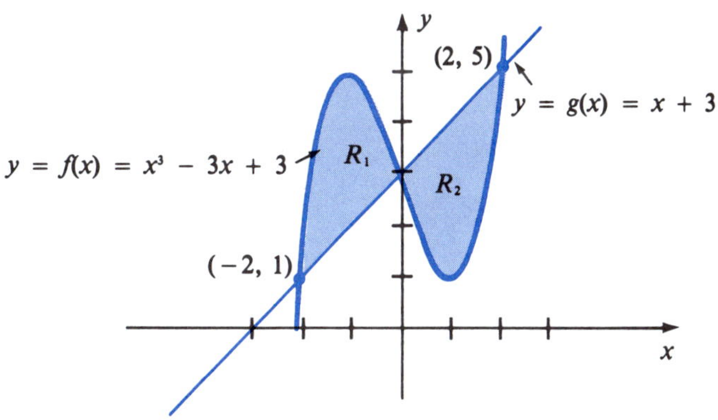

Figure 13.17

For $-2 \le x \le 0$, we see that the graph of the function f lies above that of the function g, so that the area of the region R_1 is, by virtue of Formula 13.6,

$$\begin{aligned}\int_{-2}^{0} [(x^3-3x+3)-(x+3)]\,dx &= \int_{-2}^{0} (x^3-4x)\,dx \\ &= \frac{1}{4}x^4-2x^2\Big|_{-2}^{0} \\ &= -(4-8) \\ &= 4 \quad \text{or} \quad 4 \text{ square units}\end{aligned}$$

For $0 \le x \le 2$, the graph of the function g lies above that of the function f, and the area of R_2 is given by

$$\begin{aligned}\int_{0}^{2} [(x+3)-(x^3-3x+3)]\,dx &= \int_{0}^{2} (-x^3+4x)\,dx \\ &= -\frac{1}{4}x^4+2x^2\Big|_{0}^{2} \\ &= -4+8 \\ &= 4 \quad \text{or} \quad 4 \text{ square units}\end{aligned}$$

Therefore, the required area is $4+4$ or 8 square units. ■

EXAMPLE 13.18 In a 1979 study for the Economic Development Board of a developing country, government economists and energy experts concluded that if the Energy Conservation Bill were implemented in 1980, then the country's oil consumption for the next 5 years could be expected to grow in accordance with the law $R(t)=20\,e^{0.05t}$, where t is measured in years ($t=0$ corresponds to the year 1980) and $R(t)$ is measured in millions of barrels per year. Without the government-imposed conservation measures, however, the expected rate of growth of oil consumption would be given by $R_1(t)=20\,e^{0.08t}$ millions of barrels per year, where t has the same meaning as before. Using the given data, determine how much oil could be saved from 1980–1985 through the implementation of the bill.

SOLUTION Under the Energy Conservation Bill, the total amount of oil that would be consumed between 1980 and 1985 is given by

(13.7)
$$\int_{0}^{5} R(t)\,dt = \int_{0}^{5} 20\,e^{0.05t}\,dt$$

Otherwise, the total amount of oil that would be consumed between 1980 and 1985 is given by

(13.8)
$$\int_{0}^{5} R_1(t)\,dt = \int_{0}^{5} 20\,e^{0.08t}\,dt$$

Now, Equation 13.7 may be interpreted as the area of the region under the curve $y = R(t)$ from $t = 0$ to $t = 5$. Similarly, we interpret Equation 13.8 as the area of the region under the curve $y = R_1(t)$ from $t = 0$ to $t = 5$. Note, further, that the graph of $y = R_1(t) = 20\,e^{0.08t}$ always lies on or above that of the graph of $y = R(t) = 20\,e^{0.05t}$ $(t \geq 0)$. Thus, the area of the (shaded) region S in Figure 13.18 shows the amount of oil that could be saved over the years from 1980 to 1985 with the implementation of the Energy Conservation Bill. But the area of the region S is given by

$$\begin{aligned}\int_0^5 [R_1(t) - R(t)]\,dt &= \int_0^5 [20\,e^{0.08t} - 20\,e^{0.05t}]\,dt \\ &= 20\int_0^5 (e^{0.08t} - e^{0.05t})\,dt \\ &= 20\left(\frac{e^{0.08t}}{0.08} - \frac{e^{0.05t}}{0.05}\right)\Bigg|_0^5 \\ &= 20\left[\left(\frac{e^{0.4}}{0.08} - \frac{e^{0.25}}{0.05}\right) - \left(\frac{1}{0.08} - \frac{1}{0.05}\right)\right] \\ &\approx 9.4 \quad \text{or} \quad 9.4 \text{ square units}\end{aligned}$$

Thus, the amount of oil that would have been saved would be 9.4 million barrels.

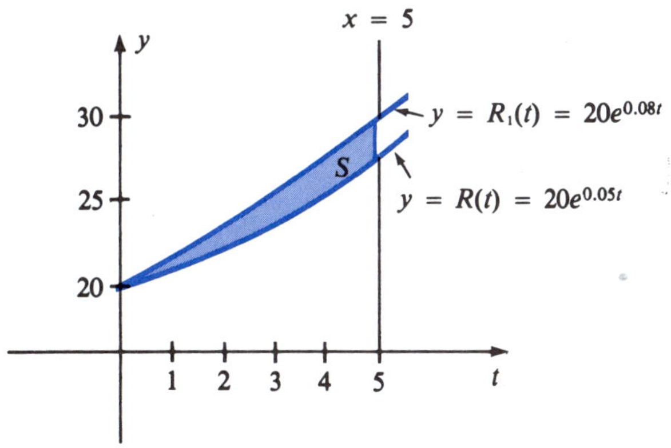

Figure 13.18

13.3 EXERCISES

In problems 1 through 6, find the area of the region bounded below by the graph of each of the given functions and above by the x-axis from x = a to x = b.

1. $f(x) = -x^2$; $a = -1, b = 2$

2. $f(x) = x^2 - 5x + 4$; $a = 1, b = 3$

3. $f(x) = x^3$; $a = -1, b = 0$

4. $f(x) = -1 - \sqrt{x}$; $a = 0, b = 9$

5. $f(x) = -e^{(1/2)x}$; $a = -2, b = 4$

***6.** $f(x) = -\ln x$; $a = 1, b = 4$

In problems 7 through 12, find the area of the region bounded by the graph of each of the given functions, the x*-axis and the lines* x = a *and* x = b.

7. $f(x)=x;\quad a=-1, b=2$

8. $f(x)=x^2-2x;\quad a=-1, b=1$

9. $f(x)=-x^2+4x-3;\quad a=-1, b=2$

10. $f(x)=x^3-4x^2+3x;\quad a=0, b=2$

11. $f(x)=e^x-1;\quad a=-1, b=3$

***12.** $f(x)=\ln x;\quad a=1/2, b=2$

In problems 13 through 20, find the area of the region bounded by the graphs of each of the given pairs of functions f *and* g *and the vertical lines* x = a *and* x = b.

13. $f(x)=x+2, g(x)=x^2-4;$ $a=-1, b=2$

14. $f(x)=-x^2+2x+3,$ $g(x)=-x+3;$ $a=0, b=2$

15. $f(x)=9-x^2, g(x)=2x+3;$ $a=-1, b=1$

16. $f(x)=x^2+1, g(x)=\frac{1}{3}x^3;$ $a=-1, b=2$

17. $f(x)=\sqrt{x}, g(x)=-\frac{1}{2}x-1;$ $a=1, b=4$

18. $f(x)=x^2, g(x)=\frac{1}{x^2};$ $a=1, b=3$

19. $f(x)=e^x, g(x)=\frac{1}{x};\quad a=1, b=2$

***20.** $f(x)=x, g(x)=\ln x;$ $a=1, b=3$

In problems 21 through 25, find the area of the region that is completely enclosed by the graphs of the given pairs of functions f *and* g.

21. $f(x)=x+2$ and $g(x)=x^2-4$

22. $f(x)=-x^2+4x$ and $g(x)=2x-3$

23. $f(x)=x^2$ and $g(x)=x^3$

24. $f(x)=\sqrt{x}$ and $g(x)=x^2$

***25.** $f(x)=2x$ and $g(x)=x\sqrt{x+1}$

26. Tests conducted by Auto Test Magazine on two identical models of the Phoenix Elite, one equipped with a standard engine and the other equipped with a turbo-charger, found that the acceleration of the former is given by $a=f(t)=4+0.8t$ feet per second per second, t seconds after starting from rest at full throttle, while the acceleration of the latter is given by $a=g(t)=4+1.2t+0.03t^2$ feet per second per second $(0\leq t\leq 12)$. How much faster is the model equipped with a turbo-charger than the one with the standard engine moving at the end of a 10-second test run at full throttle?

27. Because of the increasingly important role played by coal as a viable alternative energy source, the production of coal has been growing at the rate of $3.5\,e^{0.05t}$ billion metric tons per year, t years from 1980 (which corresponds to $t=0$). Had it not been for the energy crisis, the rate of production of coal since 1980 might have been $3.5\,e^{0.01t}$ billion metric tons per year, t years from 1980. Determine the additional amount of coal that would be produced between 1980 and the end of the century as an alternate energy source.

28. Carl Williams, the new proprietor of Carl Williams Auto Sales, estimates that with extensive television advertising, car sales over the next several years could be increasing at the rate of $5\,e^{0.3t}$ thousand cars per year, t years from now, instead of at the current rate of $(5+0.5^{3/2})$ thousand cars per year, t years from now. Find the additional number of cars Mr. Williams expects to sell over the next 5 years by implementing his advertising plans.

29. In an endeavor to curb population growth in an island state in Southeast Asia, the government of that country decided to launch an extensive propaganda campaign. As things stand, without curbs, the government expects the rate of population growth to be $60\,e^{0.02t}$ thousand people per year, t years from now, over the next five years. However, successful implementation of the proposed campaign is expected to result in a population growth rate of $-t^2+60$ thousand people per year, t years from now over the next five years. By how much less would the population of the country increase in five years time if the campaign were mounted?

30. Show that the area of a region R bounded above by the graph of a function f and below by the graph of a function g from $x=a$ to $x=b$ is given by

$$\int_a^b [f(x)-g(x)]\,dx$$

Hint: The validity of the formula was verified in the text for the case when both f and g are nonnegative. Now let f and g be two functions such that $f(x)\geq g(x)$ for $a\leq x\leq b$. Then there exists some nonnegative constant c such that the curves

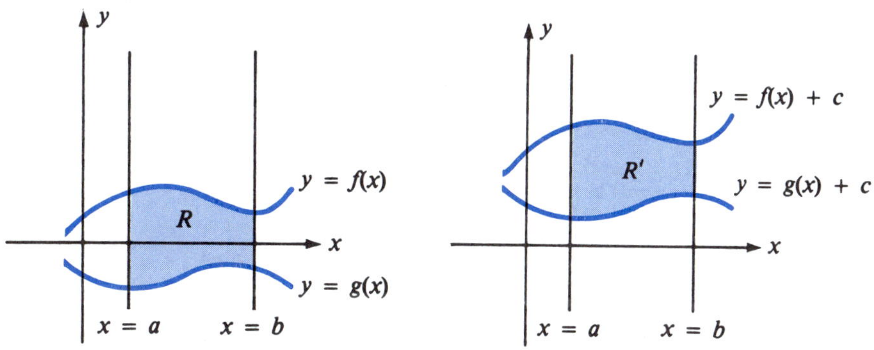

$y=f(x)+c$ and $y=g(x)+c$ are translated in the y-direction in such a way that the region R' has the same area as the region R (see the above figures). Show that the area of R' is given by

$$\int_a^b \{[f(x)+c]-[g(x)+c]\}\,dx = \int_a^b [f(x)-g(x)]\,dx$$

13.4

Riemann Sums

Let us return to the problem of finding the area of a region R under the graph of a continuous, nonnegative function f from $x=a$ to $x=b$ (Figure 13.19).

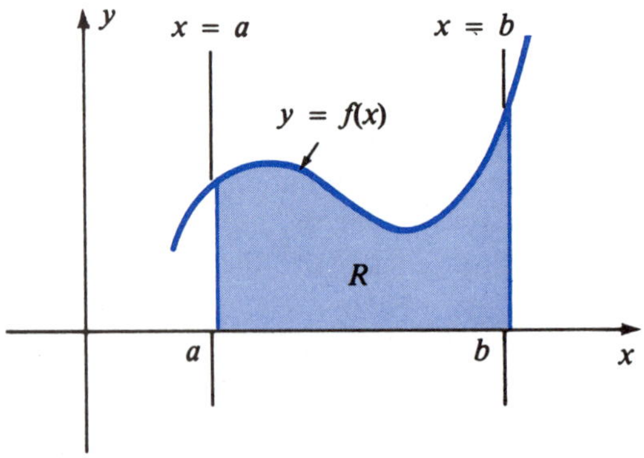

Figure 13.19

It was shown in Section 13.3, thanks to the Fundamental Theorem of Calculus, that the area of such a region R is given by the definite integral of the function f over the interval $[a, b]$, namely,

(13.9)
$$\int_a^b f(x)\,dx = F(b) - F(a)$$

where F is an antiderivative of f. However, this approach is somewhat artificial since the area of the region R is defined in terms of the values of the antiderivative of f. Another disadvantage of this approach is that, in cases where it is difficult or impossible to find the antiderivative of the function f, Formula 13.9 proves to be useless.

In this section we present a more natural and more direct approach to attacking this problem, which is due to the German mathematician Bernhard Riemann (1826–1866).

First, we divide the interval $[a, b]$ into n subintervals, each of equal length, by means of the $(n+1)$ points $x_0 = a, x_1, x_2, \ldots, x_n = b$ where n is a positive integer (Figure 13.20). Since the length of the interval $[a, b]$ is $(b-a)$ units, the length of each subinterval is easily seen to be given by

$$\Delta x = \frac{b-a}{n}$$

Partitioning the interval $[a, b]$ in this manner also leads to the subdivision of the region R into n nonoverlapping subregions $R_1, R_2, \ldots, R_n$, such that R_1 represents the region under the curve $y=f(x)$ from $x=x_0$ to $x=x_1$, R_2 represents the region under the curve $y=f(x)$ from $x=x_1$ to $x=x_2, \ldots$ and R_n represents the

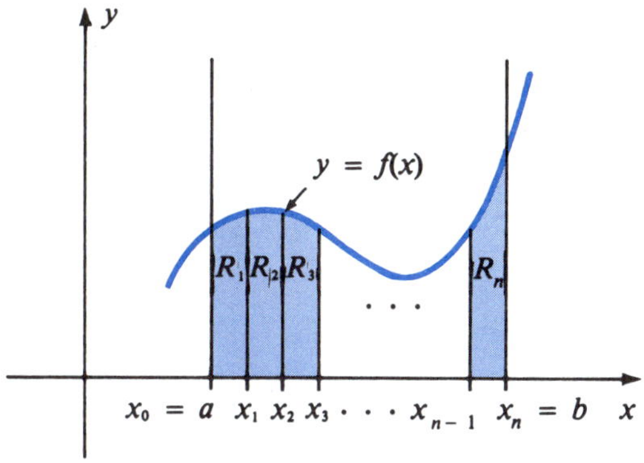

Figure 13.20

region under the curve $y=f(x)$ from $x=x_{n-1}$ to $x=x_n$. Clearly, the area of the region R is equal to the sum of the areas of the subregions $R_1, R_2, \ldots, R_n$.

Our next step involves finding an expression that will give us an approximation to the area of R. To this end, let us consider the subregion R_1, shown magnified for the sake of clarity in Figure 13.21.

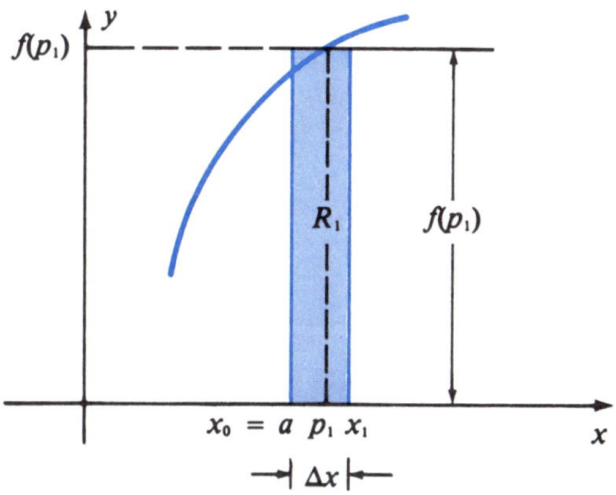

Figure 13.21

Pick *any* point p_1 in the interval $[x_0, x_1]$, and consider the rectangle with base of length Δx and height $f(p_1)$ and, therefore, of area $f(p_1)\Delta x$. From Figure 13.21 we see that the area of this rectangle gives a good approximation to the area of the subregion R_1. In a similar manner, we approximate the areas of the subregions $R_2, R_3, \ldots, R_n$ by the areas of rectangles, each with base of length Δx and height given by $f(p_2), f(p_3), \ldots, f(p_n)$, respectively, where $p_2, p_3, \ldots, p_n$ are points in the respective intervals $[x_1, x_2], [x_2, x_3], \ldots, [x_{n-1}, x_n]$. Then the area of the region R is approximated by the sum

$$\begin{aligned} S_n &= f(p_1)\,\Delta x + f(p_2)\,\Delta x + f(p_3)\,\Delta x + \cdots + f(p_n)\,\Delta x \\ &= [f(p_1)+f(p_2)+f(p_3)+\cdots+f(p_n)]\,\Delta x \\ &= \frac{(b-a)}{n}[f(p_1)+f(p_2)+f(p_3)+\cdots+f(p_n)] \qquad \left(\text{since } \Delta x = \frac{b-a}{n}\right) \end{aligned}$$

Riemann sum

The sum S_n is called the *Riemann sum* of the function f corresponding to the partition of the interval $[a, b]$ into n subintervals of equal length as described earlier.

EXAMPLE 13.19 Let $f(x)=x^2$, and compute the Riemann sum of f over the interval $[0, 1]$ by partitioning the interval into

(a) 2 subintervals of the same length ($n=2$),

(b) 5 subintervals of the same length ($n=5$),

(c) 10 subintervals of the same length ($n=10$),

where in each case the points p_i $(1 \leq i \leq n)$ are taken to be the midpoints of the respective subintervals.

SOLUTION **(a)** Here $a=0$, $b=1$, and $n=2$ so that

$$\Delta x = \frac{b-a}{n} = \frac{1}{2} = 0.5$$

and

$$x_0 = a = 0, \quad x_1 = 0.5, \quad \text{and} \quad x_2 = b = 1$$

The subregions R_1 and R_2 and the corresponding rectangles used in the approximation are shown in Figure 13.22. We also have

$$p_1 = 0.25 \quad \text{and} \quad p_2 = 0.75$$

Therefore,

$$\begin{aligned} S_2 &= \Delta x[f(p_1)+f(p_2)] \\ &= 0.5[(0.25)^2+(0.75)^2] \\ &= 0.5(0.0625+0.5625) \\ &= 0.3125 \end{aligned}$$

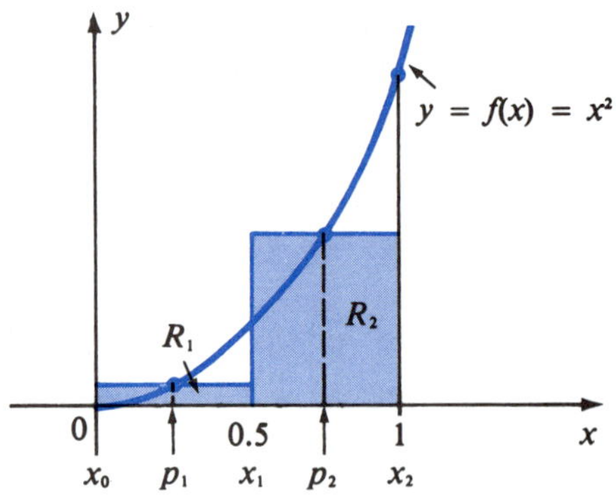

Figure 13.22

(**b**) Here

$$\Delta x = \frac{b-a}{n} = \frac{1}{5} = 0.2$$

and

$$x_0 = 0, \quad x_1 = 0.2, \quad x_2 = 0.4, \quad x_3 = 0.6, \quad x_4 = 0.8, \quad \text{and} \quad x_5 = 1$$

The five subregions with the corresponding rectangles used in the approximation are shown in Figure 13.23. In this case

$$p_1 = 0.1, \quad p_2 = 0.3, \quad p_3 = 0.5, \quad p_4 = 0.7, \quad \text{and} \quad p_5 = 0.9$$

Therefore,

$$\begin{aligned} S_5 &= \Delta x[f(p_1) + f(p_2) + f(p_3) + f(p_4) + f(p_5)] \\ &= 0.2[(0.1)^2 + (0.3)^2 + (0.5)^2 + (0.7)^2 + (0.9)^2] \\ &= 0.2[0.01 + 0.09 + 0.25 + 0.49 + 0.81] \\ &= 0.33 \end{aligned}$$

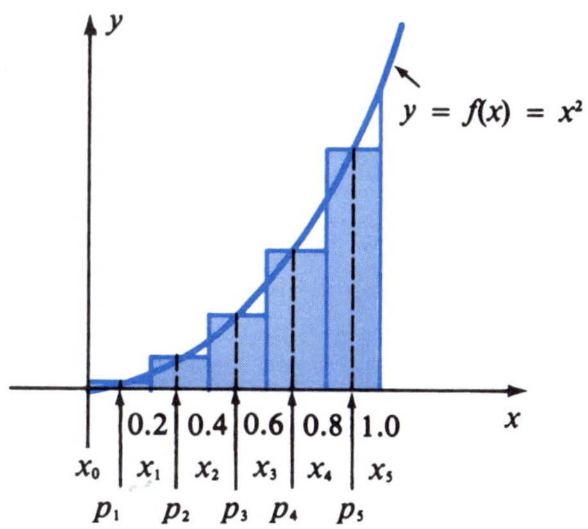

Figure 13.23

(**c**) Here

$$\Delta x = \frac{b-a}{n} = 0.1$$

and

$$x_0 = 0, \quad x_1 = 0.1, \quad x_2 = 0.2, \quad x_3 = 0.3, \quad \ldots, \quad x_{10} = 1$$

The ten subregions, with the corresponding rectangles used in the approximation, are shown in Figure 13.24. The points p_i in this case are

$$p_1 = 0.05, \quad p_2 = 0.15, \quad p_3 = 0.25, \quad p_4 = 0.35, \quad \ldots, \quad p_{10} = 0.95$$

Therefore,

$$\begin{aligned} S_{10} &= \Delta x[f(p_1) + f(p_2) + f(p_3) + \cdots + f(p_{10})] \\ &= 0.1[(0.05)^2 + (0.15)^2 + (0.25)^2 + (0.35)^2 + \cdots + (0.95)^2] \\ &= 0.1(3.325) \\ &= 0.3325 \end{aligned}$$

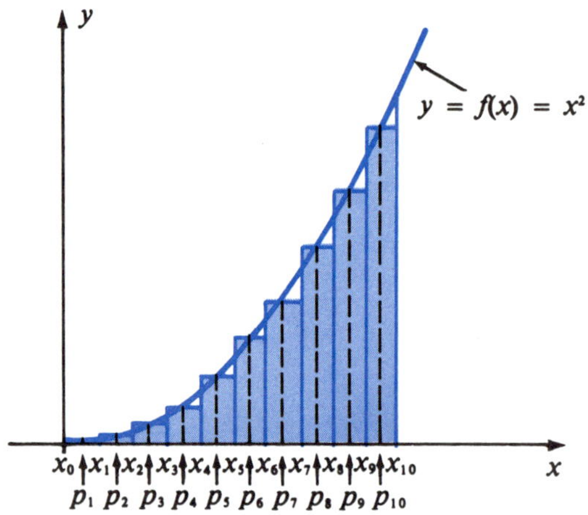

Figure 13.24

The exact area of the region R under the curve $y = x^2$ from $x = 0$ to $x = 1$ may be found using the Fundamental Theorem of Calculus. Indeed, the required area is given by

$$\begin{aligned} \int_0^1 x^2\,dx &= \frac{1}{3}x^3 \Big|_0^1 \\ &= \frac{1}{3} = 0.333\ldots \end{aligned}$$

Compare the results obtained in Example 13.19 with this result, and note that the Riemann sum S_n of f seems to approximate the area of the region R with better and better accuracy as n increases. In fact, we can expect this phenomenon to occur since as n increases, the region R is subdivided into a greater number of nonoverlapping subregions. As a consequence, the width of the rectangle, whose area is used in the approximation of the area of a relevant subregion, shrinks and this leads to an improved approximation. Thus, it is reasonable to expect that as n approaches infinity, the Riemann sum S_n should approach $1/3$, the exact value of the area of the region R.

To prove the last assertion, let us first derive a general expression for the Riemann sum S_n of the function $f(x)=x^2$ corresponding to the partition of the interval $[0, 1]$ into n subintervals of equal length, where the points p_i $(1 \leq i \leq n)$ are taken to be the midpoints of the respective subintervals. Observe that the length of each subinterval is given by

$$\Delta x = \frac{b-a}{n} = \frac{1}{n}$$

so that the points in the partition of the interval $[0, 1]$ (Figure 13.25) in this case are

$$x_0 = 0, \quad x_1 = \frac{1}{n}, \quad x_2 = \frac{2}{n}, \quad x_3 = \frac{3}{n}, \quad \ldots, \quad x_{n-1} = \frac{n-1}{n}, x_n = 1$$

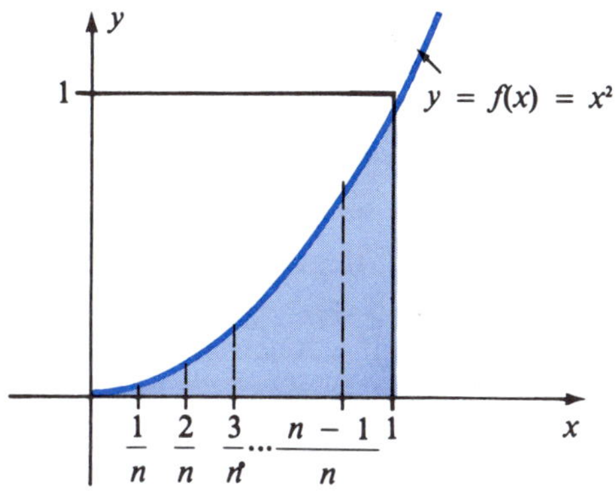

Figure 13.25

The points p_i are given by

$$p_1 = \frac{1}{2}\Delta x = \frac{1}{2n}, \quad p_2 = \frac{1}{n} + \frac{1}{2n} = \frac{3}{2n},$$

$$p_3 = \frac{2}{n} + \frac{1}{2n} = \frac{5}{2n}, \quad \ldots, \quad p_n = \frac{n-1}{n} + \frac{1}{2n} = \frac{2n-1}{2n}$$

Thus, the required Riemann sum is given by

$$\begin{aligned} S_n &= \Delta x[f(p_1)+f(p_2)+f(p_3)+\cdots+f(p_n)] \\ &= \frac{1}{n}\left[\left(\frac{1}{2n}\right)^2 + \left(\frac{3}{2n}\right)^2 + \left(\frac{5}{2n}\right)^2 + \cdots + \left(\frac{2n-1}{2n}\right)^2\right] \\ &= \left(\frac{1}{n}\right)\left(\frac{1}{2n}\right)^2 [1^2+3^2+5^2+\cdots+(2n-1)^2] \\ &= \frac{1}{4n^3}[1^2+3^2+5^2+\cdots+(2n-1)^2] \end{aligned}$$

Now, the sum within the parenthesis, which is just the sum of the squares of the first n odd integers, is equal to

$$\frac{n(2n-1)(2n+1)}{3}$$

Using this fact we write

$$S_n = \frac{1}{4n^3} \cdot \frac{n(2n-1)(2n+1)}{3} = \frac{(2n-1)(2n+1)}{12n^2}$$

Finally, taking the limit as n approaches infinity, we find

$$\begin{aligned}\lim_{n\to\infty} S_n &= \lim_{n\to\infty} \frac{(2n-1)(2n+1)}{12n^2} \\ &= \lim_{n\to\infty} \frac{1}{12}\left(2-\frac{1}{n}\right)\left(2+\frac{1}{n}\right) \\ &= \frac{1}{12}(2)(2) \\ &= \frac{1}{3} \quad \text{or} \quad \frac{1}{3} \text{ square units}\end{aligned}$$

which agrees with the area of the region R obtained earlier using the Fundamental Theorem of Calculus.

In general, if a function f is integrable over an interval $[a, b]$ and if S_n is a Riemann sum of f, then it is true that

(13.10) $$\lim_{n\to\infty} S_n = \int_a^b f(x)\,dx$$

13.4 EXERCISES

1. Find an approximation to the area of the region R under the curve $y = f(x)$ from $x = 1$ to $x = 5$ shown in the following figure by considering the Riemann sum S_n of the function f corresponding to a partition of the interval $[1, 5]$ into 4 subintervals each of equal length ($n = 4$).

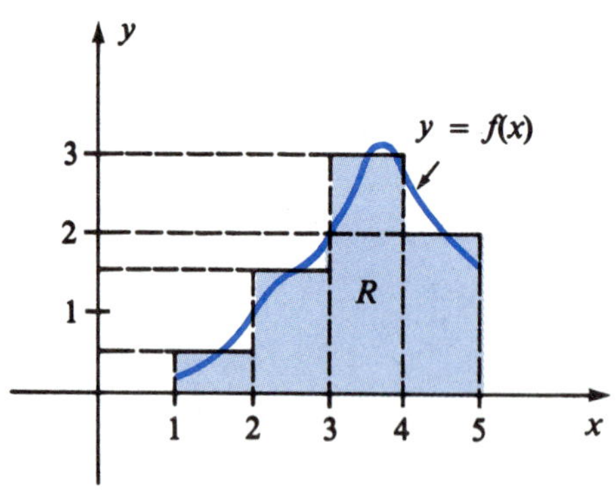

2. Redo problem 1, this time by considering the Riemann sum S_n of the function f corresponding to a partition of the interval $[1, 5]$ into 8 subintervals each of equal length ($n = 8$). *Hint*: Here $x_0 = 1$, $x_1 = 3/2$, $x_2 = 2$, $x_3 = 5/2$, $x_4 = 3, \ldots, x_8 = 5$ and $\Delta x = 1/2$. Furthermore, we may pick $p_1 = 5/4$, $p_2 = 7/4, \ldots, p_8 = 19/4$. Estimate the values of $f(p_1), f(p_2), \ldots, f(p_8)$ from the figure in problem 1.

3. Let $f(x) = x^2$, and compute the Riemann sum of f over the interval $[0, 1]$ by partitioning the interval into

(***a***) 2 subintervals of the same length ($n = 2$),

(***b***) 5 subintervals of the same length ($n = 5$),

(***c***) 10 subintervals of the same length ($n = 10$),

where in each case the points p_i $(1 \leq i \leq n)$ are taken to be the *left* endpoints of the respective subintervals. For example, in the case $n = 2$, $x_0 = 0$, $x_1 = 1/2$ and $x_2 = 1$ so that $p_1 = 0$ and $p_2 = 1/2$. Does the Riemann sum S_n approach $1/3$ as n gets larger?

4. Repeat problem 3 but this time let the points p_i $(1 \leq i \leq n)$ be the *right* endpoints of the respective subintervals.

5. Let $f(x) = x^2$, and compute the Riemann sum of f over the interval $[2, 4]$ by partitioning the interval into

(***a***) 2 subintervals of the same length ($n = 2$),

(***b***) 5 subintervals of the same length ($n = 5$),

(***c***) 10 subintervals of the same length ($n = 10$),

where in each case the points p_i $(1 \leq i \leq n)$ are taken to be the midpoints of the respective subintervals. *Hint*: For the case $n = 2$, $x_0 = 2$, $x_1 = 3$, $x_2 = 4$ and $p_1 = 2.5$, $p_2 = 3.5$.

6. Repeat problem 5 with the points p_i $(1 \leq i \leq n)$ taken to be the left endpoints of the respective subintervals.

7. Repeat problem 5 with the points p_i $(1 \leq i \leq n)$ taken to be the right endpoints of the respective subintervals.

8. Let $f(x) = x^2$, and find an expression for the Riemann sum S_n of f over the interval $[0, 1]$ corresponding to a partition of the interval into n equal subintervals with the points p_i chosen to be the left endpoints of the respective subintervals. Evaluate

$$\lim_{n\to\infty} S_n \quad \text{and} \quad \int_0^1 x^2\,dx$$

and hence prove that

$$\lim_{n\to\infty} S_n = \int_0^1 x^2\,dx$$

Hint: You will need the formula

$$1^2 + 2^2 + 3^2 + \cdots + (n-1)^2 = \frac{(n-1)n(2n-1)}{6}$$

9. Repeat problem 8, this time choosing the points p_i to be the right endpoints of the respective subintervals. *Hint*:

$$1^2+2^2+3^2+\cdots+n^2=\frac{n(n+1)(2n+1)}{6}$$

13.5

Additional Applications of the Definite Integral

By considering the Riemann sums of appropriate functions, we can often derive formulas for computing certain quantities of interest. We begin by deriving a formula for computing the consumers' surplus. To this end, suppose $p=d(x)$ is the demand function that relates the unit price p of a commodity and the quantity x demanded of it. Then, as was explained in Section 2.5, the function d is a decreasing function of x (see Figure 13.26).

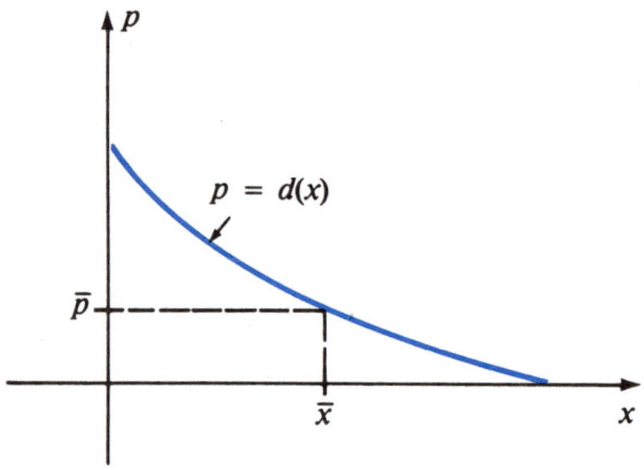

Figure 13.26

Suppose that a fixed unit market price $\bar{p}$ has been established for the commodity using some suitable criterion and that, corresponding to this unit price, the quantity demanded of the commodity is $\bar{x}$ units. Then those consumers who would be willing to pay a unit price higher than $\bar{p}$ for the commodity would in effect experience a savings to themselves. This difference between what the consumers *would* be willing to pay for $\bar{x}$ units of the commodity and what they *actually* pay for them is called the *consumers' surplus*.

consumers' surplus

To derive a formula for computing the consumers' surplus, divide the interval $[0, \bar{x}]$ into n subintervals, each of equal length, by means of the $(n+1)$ points $x_0=0, x_1, x_2, \ldots, x_n=\bar{x}$ (see Figure 13.27). Since the length of the interval $[0, \bar{x}]$ is $\bar{x}$ units, the length of each subinterval is easily seen to be given by

$$\Delta x=\frac{\bar{x}}{n}$$

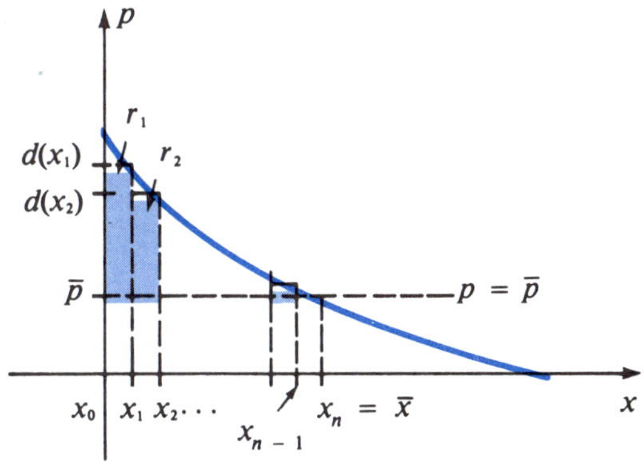

Figure 13.27

Referring again to Figure 13.27, we observe that there are consumers who would pay a unit price of at least $d(x_1)$ dollars for the first Δx units of the commodity instead of the market price of $\bar{p}$ dollars per unit. The savings to these consumers is approximately given by

$$d(x_1)\,\Delta x - \bar{p}\,\Delta x = [d(x_1) - \bar{p}]\,\Delta x$$

which is just the area of the rectangle r_1. Pursuing the same line of reasoning, we find that the savings to the consumers who would be willing to pay a unit price of at least $d(x_2)$ dollars for the next Δx units (from x_1 through x_2) of the commodity, instead of the market price of $\bar{p}$ dollars per unit, is approximately given by

$$d(x_2)\,\Delta x - \bar{p}\,\Delta x = [d(x_2) - \bar{p}]\,\Delta x$$

Continuing, we approximate the total savings to the consumers in purchasing $\bar{x}$ units of the commodity by the sum

$$\begin{aligned}
&[d(x_1) - \bar{p}]\,\Delta x + [d(x_2) - \bar{p}]\,\Delta x + \cdots + [d(x_n) - \bar{p}]\,\Delta x \\
&\quad = [d(x_1) + d(x_2) + \cdots + d(x_n)]\,\Delta x - \underbrace{[\bar{p}\,\Delta x + \bar{p}\,\Delta x + \cdots + \bar{p}\,\Delta x]}_{n \text{ terms}} \\
&\quad = [d(x_1) + d(x_2) + \cdots + d(x_n)]\,\Delta x - n\bar{p}\,\Delta x \\
&\quad = [d(x_1) + d(x_2) + \cdots + d(x_n)]\,\Delta x - \bar{p}\bar{x}
\end{aligned}$$

Now, the first term in the last expression is just the Riemann sum of the demand function $p = d(x)$ over the interval $[0, \bar{x}]$. Letting n approach infinity and using Equation 13.10, we obtain the desired formula for the consumers' surplus. Thus, the consumers' surplus, or CS for short, is given by

(13.11) $$\text{CS} = \int_0^{\bar{x}} d(x)\,dx - \bar{p}\bar{x}$$

It is just the area of the region bounded above by the demand curve $p = d(x)$ and below by the straight line $p = \bar{p}$ from $x = 0$ to $x = \bar{x}$ (Figure 13.28). The last statement also follows immediately if we rewrite Formula 13.11 in the form

$$\int_0^{\bar{x}} [d(x) - \bar{p}]\, dx$$

and interpret the result geometrically.

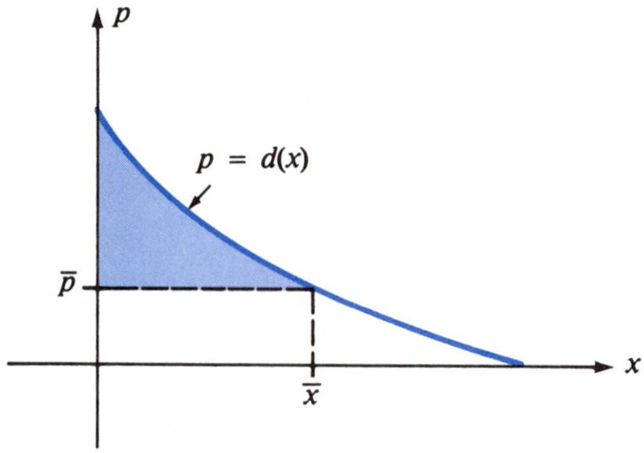

Figure 13.28

EXAMPLE 13.20 The demand function for a certain make of cartridge typewriter ribbons is given by $p = d(x) = -0.01x^2 - 0.1x + 6$, where p is the unit price in dollars and x is the quantity demanded each week, measured in units of a thousand. Determine the consumers' surplus if the market price is set at \$4 per cartridge.

SOLUTION When $p = 4$, we have

$$\begin{aligned} -0.01x^2 - 0.1x + 6 &= 4 \\ x^2 + 10x - 200 &= 0 \\ (x + 20)(x - 10) &= 0 \end{aligned}$$

Hence $x = -20$ or $x = 10$. Since x must be nonnegative, we reject the first root. Next, using Equation 13.11 with $\bar{p} = 4$ and $\bar{x} = 10$, we find that the consumers' surplus is given by

$$\begin{aligned} \text{CS} &= \int_0^{10} (-0.01x^2 - 0.1x + 6)\, dx - (4)(10) \\ &= \left(-\frac{1}{300}x^3 - \frac{1}{20}x^2 + 6x\right)\Big|_0^{10} - 40 \\ &= -\frac{1000}{300} - \frac{100}{20} + 60 - 40 \\ &= 11\frac{2}{3} \quad \text{or} \quad \$11{,}666.67 \end{aligned}$$

(Recall that x is measured in units of a thousand). ■

Proceeding in an analogous manner, we can derive a formula for computing the producers' surplus. To this end, suppose $p = s(x)$ is the supply equation that relates the unit price p of a certain commodity to the quantity x that the supplier will make available in the market at that price. Then, the function s is an increasing function of x as shown in Figure 13.29.

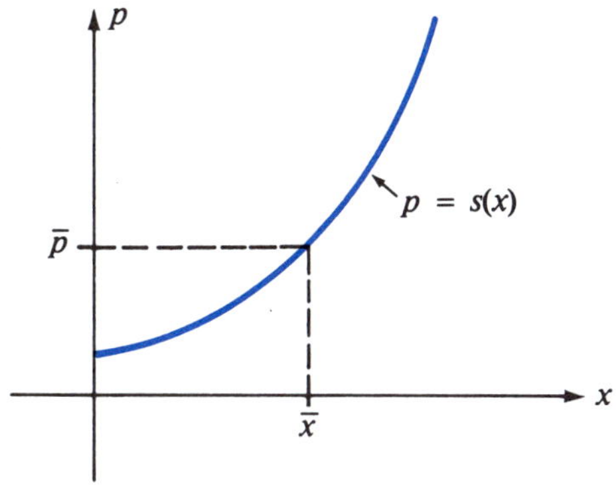

Figure 13.29

Again, suppose that a fixed market price $\bar{p}$ has been established for the commodity and that, corresponding to this unit price, a quantity of $\bar{x}$ units will be made available in the market by the supplier. Then, the suppliers who would be willing to make the commodity available at a lower price stand to gain from the fact that the market price is set as such. The difference between what the suppliers actually receive and what they would be willing to receive is called the *producers' surplus*. We proceed as in the derivation of the equation for computing the consumers' surplus, and we find that the producers' surplus, PS, is given by

producers' surplus

(13.12)
$$\text{PS} = \bar{p}\bar{x} - \int_0^{\bar{x}} s(x)\, dx$$

Geometrically, the producers' surplus is given by the area of the region bounded above by the straight line $p = \bar{p}$ and below by the supply curve $p = s(x)$ (Figure 13.30). We can also show that the last statement is true by casting Formula 13.12

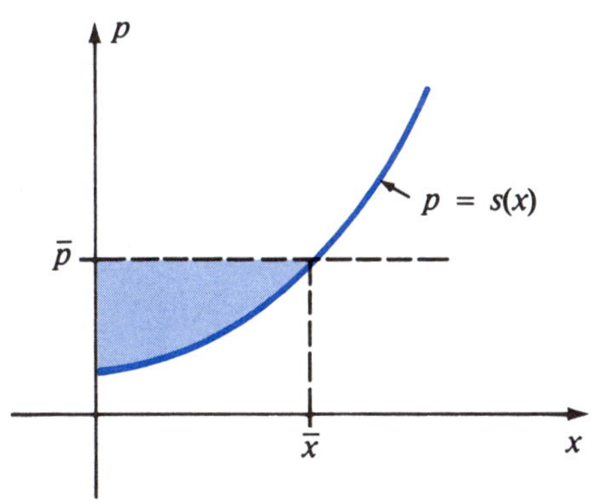

Figure 13.30

in the form

$$\int_0^{\bar{x}} [\bar{p} - s(x)]\,dx$$

and interpreting the definite integral geometrically.

EXAMPLE 13.21 The demand function for a certain make of 10-speed bicycle is given by $p = d(x) = -0.001x^2 + 250$, where p is the unit price in dollars and x is the quantity demanded, measured in units of a thousand. It is also known that the supply function for these bicycles is given by $p = s(x) = 0.0006x^2 + 0.02x + 100$, where p stands for the unit price in dollars and x stands for the number of bicycles that suppliers will put on the market, measured in units of a thousand. Determine the consumers' surplus and the producers' surplus, if the market price of a bicycle is set at the equilibrium price.

SOLUTION Recall that the equilibrium price is the unit price of the commodity when market equilibrium occurs. We determine the equilibrium price by solving for the point of intersection of the demand curve and the supply curve (see Figure 13.31).

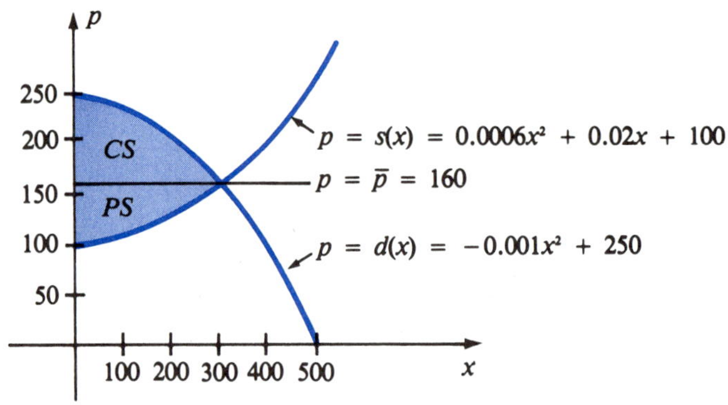

Figure 13.31

To solve the system of equations comprising

$$p = -0.001x^2 + 250$$

and

$$p = 0.0006x^2 + 0.02x + 100$$

we simply substitute the first equation into the second, thereby obtaining

$$\begin{aligned} 0.0006x^2 + 0.02x + 100 &= -0.001x^2 + 250 \\ 0.0016x^2 + 0.02x - 150 &= 0 \\ 16x^2 + 200x - 1{,}500{,}000 &= 0 \\ 2x^2 + 25x - 187{,}500 &= 0 \end{aligned}$$

The last equation may be factored as follows:

$$(2x+625)(x-300)=0$$

Thus, $x=-625/2$ or $x=300$. The first number lies outside the interval of interest, and we are left with the solution $x=300$ with a corresponding value of

$$\begin{aligned} p &= -0.001\,(300)^2+250 \\ &= 160. \end{aligned}$$

Thus, the equilibrium point is (300, 160), that is, the equilibrium quantity is 300,000 and the equilibrium price is \$160. Setting the market price at \$160 per unit and using Equation 13.11 with $\bar{p}=160$ and $\bar{x}=300$, we find that the consumers' surplus is given by

$$\begin{aligned} \text{CS} &= \int_0^{300} (-0.001x^2+250)\,dx-(160)(300) \\ &= \left(-\frac{1}{3{,}000}x^3+250x\right)\Bigg|_0^{300} -48{,}000 \\ &= -\frac{300^3}{3000}+(250)(300)-48{,}000 \\ &= 18{,}000 \quad \text{or} \quad \$18{,}000{,}000 \end{aligned}$$

(Recall that x is measured in units of a thousand). Next, using Equation 13.12 we find the producer's surplus is given by

$$\begin{aligned} \text{PS} &= (160)(300)-\int_0^{300} (0.0006x^2+0.02x+100)\,dx \\ &= 48{,}000-(0.0002x^3+0.01x^2+100x)\Big|_0^{300} \\ &= 48{,}000-[(0.0002)(300)^3+(0.01)(300)^2+100(300)] \\ &= 11{,}700 \quad \text{or} \quad \$11{,}700{,}000 \end{aligned}$$

■

To further illustrate the Riemann sum as an aid in deriving useful formulas for computing quantities of interest, we consider the definition of the *average value of a function* $f(x)$ over an interval $[a, b]$. Recall that the average value of a set of n numbers $y_1, y_2, \ldots, y_n$ is the number

$$\frac{y_1+y_2+\cdots+y_n}{n}$$

Now let us divide the interval $[a, b]$ into n subintervals each of equal length by means of the points $x_0=a, x_1, x_2, \ldots, x_n=b$, so that the length of each of the subintervals is given by $\Delta x = (b-a)/n$. If $p_1, p_2, \ldots, p_n$ are points in the subintervals $[x_0, x_1], [x_1, x_2], \ldots, [x_{n-1}, x_n]$, respectively, then the average value of the numbers $f(p_1), f(p_2), \ldots, f(p_n)$ is given by

(13.13)
$$\frac{f(p_1)+f(p_2)+\cdots+f(p_n)}{n}$$

which we can write as

$$\begin{aligned}
&\frac{b-a}{b-a}\left[\frac{f(p_1)}{n}+\frac{f(p_2)}{n}+\cdots+\frac{f(p_n)}{n}\right]\\
&=\frac{1}{b-a}\left[f(p_1)\left(\frac{b-a}{n}\right)+f(p_2)\left(\frac{b-a}{n}\right)+\cdots+f(p_n)\left(\frac{b-a}{n}\right)\right]\\
&=\frac{1}{b-a}[f(p_1)\,\Delta x+f(p_2)\,\Delta x+\cdots+f(p_n)\,\Delta x]\\
&=\frac{1}{b-a}[f(p_1)+f(p_2)+\cdots+f(p_n)]\,\Delta x
\end{aligned}$$

average value of a function over an interval

As n becomes larger and larger, the expression 13.13 approximates with increasing accuracy the average value of the function f over the interval $[a, b]$; we therefore define the *average value of* $f(x)$ *over* $[a, b]$ to be

$$\begin{aligned}
\lim_{n\to\infty}\left[\frac{f(p_1)+f(p_2)+\cdots+f(p_n)}{n}\right] &= \lim_{n\to\infty}\frac{1}{b-a}[f(p_1)+f(p_2)+\cdots+f(p_n)]\,\Delta x\\
&=\frac{1}{b-a}\lim_{n\to\infty}[f(p_1)+f(p_2)+\cdots+f(p_n)]\,\Delta x\\
&=\frac{1}{b-a}\int_a^b f(x)\,dx
\end{aligned}$$

by Equation 13.10.

EXAMPLE 13.22 The Dixie Import–Export Company places an order for 400 Excalibur 500 c.c. motorcycles every two months. Assuming that the motorcycles are sold at a uniform rate throughout the year and that each shipment arrives just as the previous shipment has been sold, determine the average number of motorcycles in storage during the year (see Example 11.37).

SOLUTION The inventory of Excalibur 500 c.c. motorcycles on hand at any time t during the year may be represented graphically as shown in Figure 13.32, where y represents the level of inventory on hand and t is measured in months.

Now let f denote the inventory function. Note that f is not continuous at the points $x = 2, 4, 6, \ldots, 10$. This observation suggests that f may be represented piecemeal over the interval $[0, 12]$ by the rules $f_1, f_2, \ldots, f_6$ with subdomains $[0, 2]$,

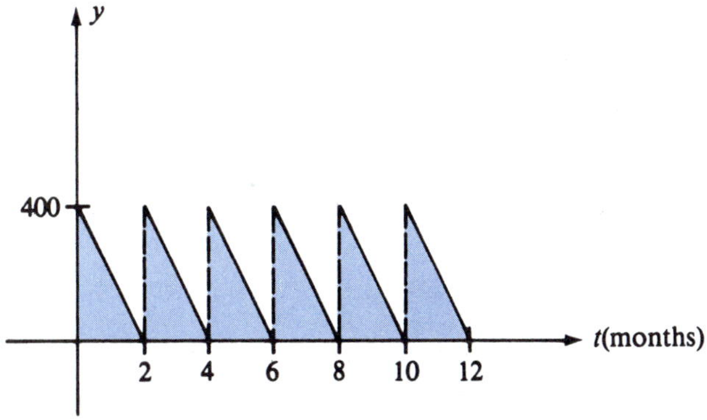

Figure 13.32

(2, 4], . . . , (10, 12], respectively. However, for the present purpose, it is not necessary for us to know all these rules precisely, as we shall see momentarily. Using Property 5 of the definite integral, we find that the average value of f over the interval [0, 12] is given by

$$A = \frac{1}{12}\int_0^{12} f(t)\,dt = \frac{1}{12}\left[\int_0^2 f_1(t)\,dt + \int_2^4 f_2(t)\,dt + \cdots + \int_0^{12} f_6(t)\,dt\right]$$

Interpreting each of the definite integrals inside the square brackets as the area under a curve, we see that

$$\int_0^2 f_1(t)\,dt = \int_2^4 f_2(t)\,dt = \cdots = \int_{10}^{12} f_6(t)\,dt$$

so that

$$\begin{aligned} A &= \frac{1}{12}\int_0^{12} f(t)\,dt \\ &= \frac{1}{12}(6)\int_0^2 f_1(t)\,dt \\ &= \frac{1}{2}\int_0^2 f_1(t)\,dt \end{aligned}$$

But $f_1(t) = -200t + 400$. (This is just the equation of a straight line through the points (0, 400) and (2, 0).) Therefore,

$$\begin{aligned} A &= \frac{1}{2}\int_0^2 (-200t + 400)\,dt \\ &= \frac{1}{2}(-100t^2 + 400t)\Big|_0^2 \\ &= \frac{1}{2}(-400 + 800) \\ &= 200 \end{aligned}$$

That is, the average number of Excalibur 500 c.c. motorcycles in storage during the year is 200 or exactly one-half of the size of each order, a fact we accepted intuitively in Example 11.37. ■

13.5 EXERCISES

1. The demand function for a certain brand of long-playing records is given by $p=d(x)=-0.01x^2-0.2x+8$, where p is the wholesale unit price in dollars and x is the quantity demanded each week, measured in units of a thousand. Determine the consumers' surplus if the wholesale market price is set at \$5 per disc.

2. It is known that the quantity demanded of a certain make of portable hair dryers is x hundred units per week when the corresponding wholesale unit price is $p=d(x)=\sqrt{225-5x}$ dollars. Determine the consumers' surplus if the wholesale market price is set at \$10 per unit.

3. The supplier of the portable hair dryers of problem 2 will make x hundred units of the hair dryers available in the market when the wholesale unit price is $p=s(x)=\sqrt{36+1.8x}$ dollars. Determine the producers' surplus if the wholesale market price is set at \$9 per unit.

4. The supply function for the long-playing records of problem 1 is given by $p=s(x)=0.01x^2+0.1x+3$, where p is the unit wholesale price in dollars and x stands for the quantity that will be made available in the market by the supplier measured in units of a thousand. Determine the producers' surplus if the wholesale market price is set at the equilibrium price.

5. The management of the Titan Tire Company has determined that the quantity demanded, x, of their Super Titan tires per week is related to the unit price, p, by the relation $p=d(x)=144-x^2$, where p is measured in dollars and x is measured in units of a thousand. The company will make x units of the tires available in the market if the unit price is $p=s(x)=48+(1/2)x^2$ dollars. Determine the consumers' surplus and the producers' surplus when the market unit price is set at the equilibrium price.

6. The quantity demanded x (in units of a hundred) of the Mikado miniature cameras per week is related to the unit price p (in dollars) by $p=d(x)=-0.2x^2+80$, while the quantity x (in units of a hundred) that the supplier is willing to make available in the market is related to the unit price p (in dollars) by $p=s(x)=0.1x^2+x+40$. If the market price is set at the equilibrium price, find the consumers' surplus and the producers' surplus.

In problems 7 through 14, find the average value of each function f *over the indicated interval* [a, b].

7. $f(x)=8-x;\quad [1,4]$

8. $f(x)=\frac{1}{2}x^2;\quad [0,9]$

9. $f(x)=\sqrt{x};\quad [0,4]$

10. $f(x)=x^3;\quad [-1,1]$

11. $f(x)=\frac{1}{x^2}$; $[2, 4]$

12. $f(x)=e^{-x}$; $[0, 4]$

13. $f(x)=x^2\sqrt{x^3+1}$; $[0, 2]$

14. $f(x)=x \ln x$; $\left[\frac{1}{2}, 2\right]$

15. Refer to Example 11.37. Show that the average number of motorcycles in storage during the year is $x/2$. *Hint*: See Example 13.22.

16. The number of integrated circuits used to manufacture the Galaxy Home Computers that are on hand at a division of the Universal Instruments Company over a twelve-week period as a function f of time is shown in the following figure.

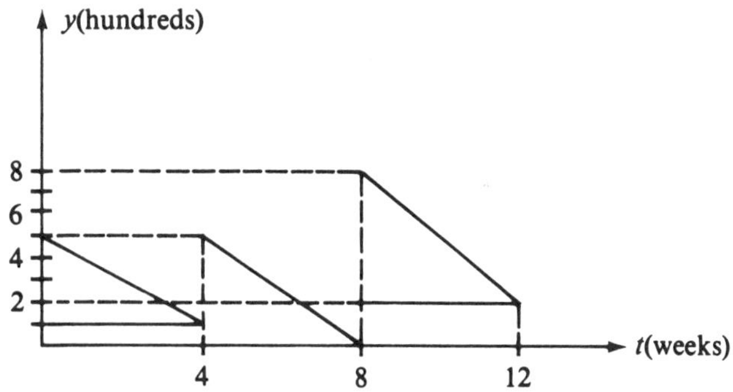

(***a***) Show that the function f is described by the rule

$$f(t)=\begin{cases} -t+5 & 0 \le t < 4 \\ -\frac{5}{4}t+10 & 4 \le t < 8 \\ -\frac{3}{2}t+20 & 8 \le t < 12 \end{cases}$$

(***b***) Find the average number of integrated circuits on hand over the 12-week period.

17. The temperature at 6 A.M. on a certain day in December was measured at 5.6°F. In the next t hours $(0 \le t \le 12)$, the temperature was given by the function $T=-0.05t^3+0.4t^2+3.8t+5.6$°F. Determine the average temperature on that day over the 12-hr. period from 6 A.M. to 6 P.M.

18. The rate of climb of a sounding rocket t seconds into flight is given by $-3t^2+192t+120$ feet per second. Find the average rate of climb of the rocket in the first 30 seconds of its flight.

19. The population of a Southwest city, which is currently 200,000, is expected to grow exponentially in the next 10 years with a growth constant of 0.04. If the prediction holds true, what would the average population of the city be over the next 10 years?

20. Suppose worldwide coal production grows at the rate of $3.5\,e^{0.05t}$ billion metric tons per year in year t ($t=0$ corresponding to 1980) for the rest of the century. Determine the average rate of growth of coal production over the twenty-year period from 1980 to the year 2000.

21. The sales of the Universal Instruments Company in the first t years of its operation was approximated by the function $S(t)=t\sqrt{0.2t^2+4}$, where $S(t)$ is measured in millions of dollars. What was the average yearly sales of the company over its first five years of operation?

22. The concentration of a certain drug in a patient's bloodstream t hours after injection is $C(t)=0.2t/(t^2+1)$ milligrams per cubic centimeter. Determine the average concentration of the drug in the patient's bloodstream over the first four hours after the drug was injected.

13.6 Improper Integrals (Optional)

improper integrals

Up to now, all the definite integrals we have encountered have had finite intervals of integration. In many applications, however, one is concerned with integrals that have unbounded intervals of integration. Such integrals are called *improper integrals*.

To motivate the definition of an improper integral of a function f over an infinite interval, consider the problem of finding the area of the region R under the curve $y=f(x)=1/x^2$ and to the right of the vertical line $x=1$, as shown in Figure 13.33.

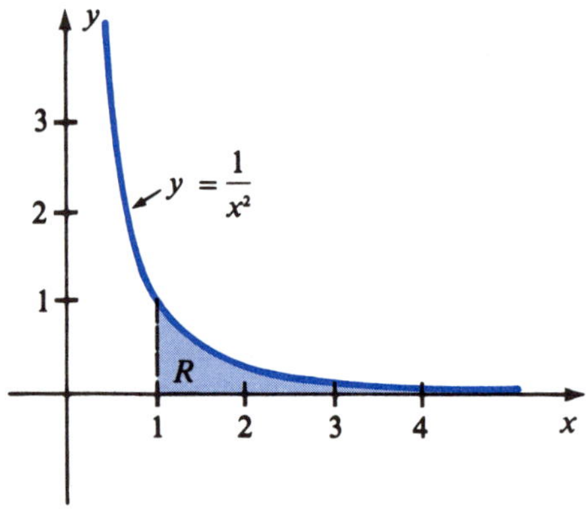

Figure 13.33

Because the interval over which the integration must be performed is unbounded, the method of the last section may not be applied directly towards the solution of the problem at hand. However, all is not lost, for we can approximate the region R by the definite integral

$$\int_1^b \frac{1}{x^2}\,dx \tag{13.14}$$

which gives the area of the region under the curve $y = f(x) = 1/x^2$ from $x = 1$ to $x = b$ (see Figure 13.34). Clearly, the approximation to the area of the region R by the definite integral (13.14) improves as the upper limit of integration b is taken to be larger. This observation suggests that if we define an area function $I(b)$ by

(13.15) $$I(b) = \int_1^b \frac{1}{x^2}\,dx$$

then we can find the area of the required region R by evaluating the limit of $I(b)$ as b tends to infinity; that is, the area of R is given by

(13.16) $$\lim_{b\to\infty} I(b) = \lim_{b\to\infty} \int_1^b \frac{1}{x^2}\,dx$$

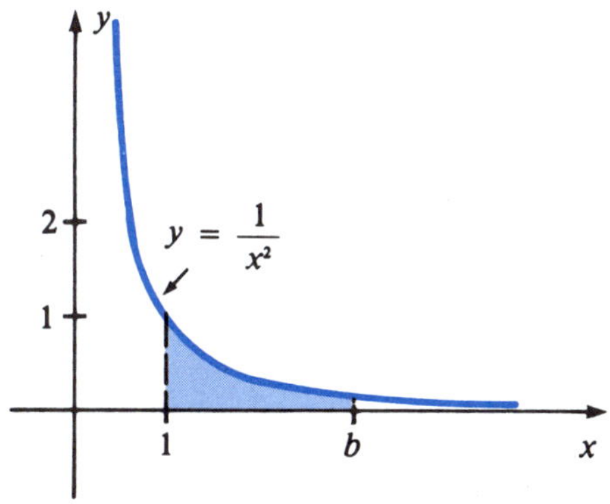

Figure 13.34

EXAMPLE 13.23

(a) Evaluate the definite integral $I(b)$ of Equation 13.15.

(b) Compute $I(b)$ for $b = 10, 100, 1000, 10{,}000$.

(c) Evaluate the limit in Equation 13.16.

(d) Interpret the results of parts **(b)** and **(c)**.

SOLUTION **(a)**

$$\begin{aligned} I(b) &= \int_1^b \frac{1}{x^2}\,dx \\ &= -\frac{1}{x}\bigg|_1^b \\ &= -\frac{1}{b} + 1 \end{aligned}$$

(b) From the result of part **(a)**,

$$\begin{aligned} I(b) &= 1 - \frac{1}{b} \\ &= \frac{b-1}{b} \end{aligned}$$

Therefore,

$$I(10)=\frac{10-1}{10}=0.9$$

$$I(100)=\frac{100-1}{100}=0.99$$

$$I(1000)=\frac{1000-1}{1000}=0.999$$

$$I(10{,}000)=\frac{10{,}000-1}{10{,}000}=0.9999$$

(c) Once again, using the result of part (**a**), we find

$$\begin{aligned}\lim_{b\to\infty} I(b) &= \lim_{b\to\infty}\int_1^b \frac{1}{x^2}\,dx\\ &= \lim_{b\to\infty}\left(1-\frac{1}{b}\right)\\ &= 1\end{aligned}$$

(d) The result of part (**c**) tells us that the area of the region R is 1 square unit. The results of the computations performed in part (**b**) reinforce our expectation that $I(b)$ should approach 1, the area of the region R, as b approaches infinity. ■

The above discussion, together with the results of Example 13.23, suggests that we define the (improper) integral of a continuous function f over the infinite interval $[a, \infty)$, written

$$\int_a^\infty f(x)\,dx$$

by

(13.17)
$$\begin{aligned}\int_a^\infty f(x)\,dx &= \lim_{b\to\infty} I(b)\\ &= \lim_{b\to\infty}\int_a^b f(x)\,dx\end{aligned}$$

if the limit exists. In this case, the improper integral is said to be *convergent*. An improper integral for which the limit in Equation 13.17 fails to exist is said to be *divergent* (see problem 8, Exercise Set 13.6).

EXAMPLE 13.24 Find the area of the region R under the curve $y=e^{-(1/2)x}$ for $x\geq 0$.

SOLUTION The region R under consideration is shown in Figure 13.35. Taking $b>0$, compute the area of the region under the curve $y = e^{-(1/2)x}$ from $x = 0$ to $x = b$, namely,

$$I(b) = \int_0^b e^{-(1/2)x}\,dx$$

$$= -2\,e^{-(1/2)x}\Big|_0^b$$

$$= -2\,e^{-(1/2)b} + 2$$

Then the area of the required region R is given by

$$\lim_{b\to\infty} I(b) = \lim_{b\to\infty} (2 - 2\,e^{-(1/2)b})$$

$$= 2 - 2\lim_{b\to\infty} \frac{1}{e^{(1/2)b}}$$

$$= 2 \quad \text{or} \quad 2 \text{ square units}$$

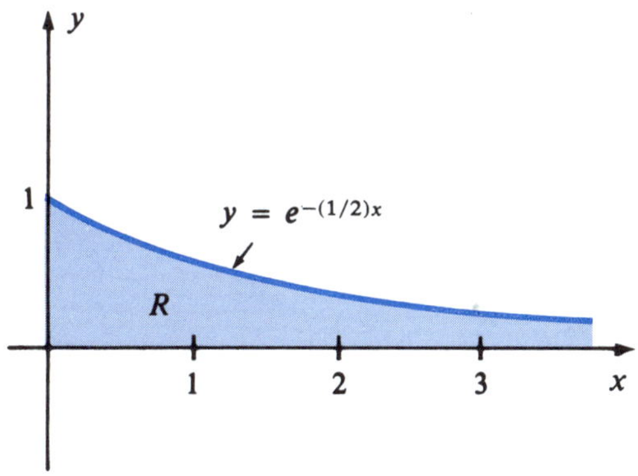

Figure 13.35

■

The improper integral (13.17) has an interval of integration that is unbounded on the right. Improper integrals with intervals of integration that are unbounded on the left also arise in practice. An improper integral in which the interval of integration is unbounded on the left is defined in a manner analogous to one whose interval of integration is unbounded on the right. Thus, we define the improper integral of a continuous function f over the infinite interval $(-\infty, b]$ by

(13.18)
$$\int_{-\infty}^b f(x)\,dx = \lim_{a\to-\infty} \int_a^b f(x)\,dx$$

if the limit exists. In this case, the improper integral is said to be *convergent*. Otherwise, the improper integral is said to be *divergent*.

EXAMPLE 13.25 Find the area of the region R bounded above by the x-axis, below by the curve $y = -e^{2x}$, and on the right by the vertical line $x = 1$.

SOLUTION The region R under consideration is shown in Figure 13.36. Taking $a<1$, compute the area of the region bounded above by the x-axis, below by the curve $y=-e^{2x}$ from $x=a$ to $x=1$, namely,

$$\begin{aligned} I(a) &= -\int_a^1 -e^{2x}\,dx \\ &= \int_a^1 e^{2x}\,dx \\ &= \frac{1}{2}e^{2x}\Big|_a^1 \\ &= \frac{1}{2}e^2 - \frac{1}{2}e^{2a} \end{aligned}$$

Then, the area of the required region is given by

$$\begin{aligned} \lim_{a\to-\infty} I(a) &= \lim_{a\to-\infty}\left(\frac{1}{2}e^2-\frac{1}{2}e^{2a}\right) \\ &= \frac{1}{2}e^2 - \frac{1}{2}\lim_{a\to-\infty} e^{2a} \\ &= \frac{1}{2}e^2 \quad \text{or} \quad \approx 3.70 \text{ square inches} \end{aligned}$$

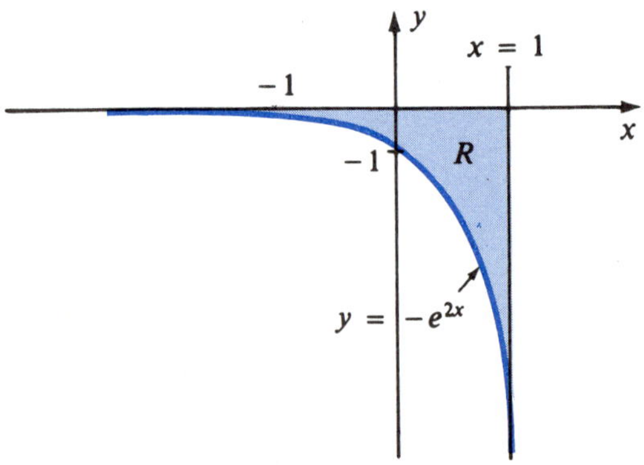

Figure 13.36

Another kind of improper integral, found in practical applications, involves the integration of a function f over the infinite interval $(-\infty, \infty)$. In fact, if f is a continuous function defined on the infinite interval $(-\infty, \infty)$, then the improper integral of f over the interval $(-\infty, \infty)$ is defined as follows: Pick *any* real number c, and consider the improper integrals

(13.19) $$\int_{-\infty}^{c} f(x)\,dx \quad \text{and} \quad \int_{c}^{\infty} f(x)\,dx$$

If both of the above improper integrals are convergent, then we define

(13.20) $$\int_{-\infty}^{\infty} f(x)\,dx = \int_{-\infty}^{c} f(x)\,dx + \int_{c}^{\infty} f(x)\,dx$$

and say that the improper integral on the left of Equation 13.20 is convergent. If at least one of the two improper integrals in Equation 13.20 is divergent, then the improper integral of f on $(-\infty, \infty)$ is *not* defined.

EXAMPLE 13.26 Evaluate the improper integral

$$\int_{-\infty}^{\infty} x\,e^{-x^2}\,dx$$

and give a geometrical interpretation of the results obtained.

SOLUTION Take the point c in definition 13.20 to be $c = 0$. Let us first evaluate

$$\begin{aligned}\int_{-\infty}^{0} x\,e^{-x^2}\,dx &= \lim_{a\to-\infty} \int_{a}^{0} x\,e^{-x^2}\,dx \\ &= \lim_{a\to-\infty} -\frac{1}{2}e^{-x^2}\Big|_{a}^{0} \\ &= \lim_{a\to-\infty}\left[-\frac{1}{2}+\frac{1}{2}e^{-a^2}\right] \\ &= -\frac{1}{2}\end{aligned}$$

Next, we evaluate

$$\begin{aligned}\int_{0}^{\infty} x\,e^{-x^2}\,dx &= \lim_{b\to\infty} \int_{0}^{b} x\,e^{-x^2}\,dx \\ &= \lim_{b\to\infty} -\frac{1}{2}e^{-x^2}\Big|_{0}^{b} \\ &= \lim_{b\to\infty}\left[-\frac{1}{2}e^{-b^2}+\frac{1}{2}\right] \\ &= \frac{1}{2}\end{aligned}$$

Therefore,

$$\begin{aligned}\int_{-\infty}^{\infty} x\,e^{-x^2}\,dx &= \int_{-\infty}^{0} x\,e^{-x^2}\,dx + \int_{0}^{\infty} x\,e^{-x^2}\,dx \\ &= -\frac{1}{2}+\frac{1}{2} \\ &= 0\end{aligned}$$

The graph of $y = x\,e^{-x^2}$ is sketched in Figure 13.37. A glance at Figure 13.37 tells us that the improper integral,

$$\int_{-\infty}^{0} x\,e^{-x^2}\,dx$$

gives the *negative* of the area of the region R_1, bounded above by the x-axis and below by the curve $y = x\,e^{-x^2}$, and bounded on the right by the y-axis ($x = 0$). On the other hand, the improper integral,

$$\int_{0}^{\infty} x\,e^{-x^2}\,dx$$

gives the area of the region R_2 under the curve $y = x\,e^{-x^2}$ for $x \geq 0$. Since the graph of f is symmetrical with respect to the origin, the area of R_1 is equal to the area of R_2. In other words,

$$\int_{-\infty}^{0} x\,e^{-x^2}\,dx = -\int_{0}^{\infty} x\,e^{-x^2}\,dx$$

Therefore,

$$\begin{aligned}\int_{-\infty}^{\infty} x\,e^{-x^2}\,dx &= \int_{-\infty}^{0} x\,e^{-x^2}\,dx + \int_{0}^{\infty} x\,e^{-x^2}\,dx \\ &= -\int_{0}^{\infty} x\,e^{-x^2}\,dx + \int_{0}^{\infty} x\,e^{-x^2}\,dx \\ &= 0\end{aligned}$$

as was shown earlier.

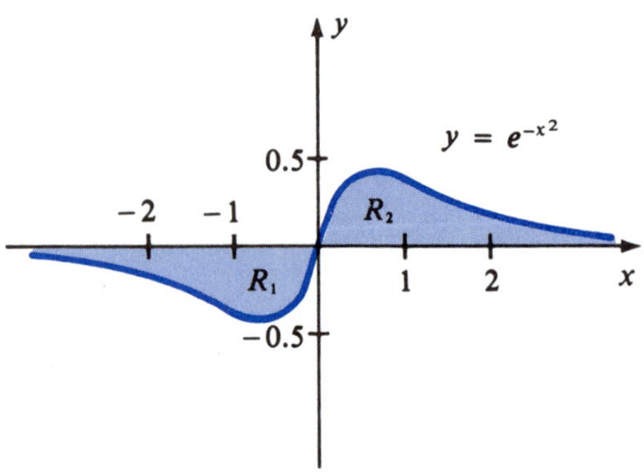

Figure 13.37

■

We close this section by looking at an application of the definite integral to the computation of probabilities associated with a continuous random variable. Recall (see Section 9.5) that a probability density function f associated with a continuous probability distribution has the following properties:

1. $f(x)$ is nonnegative for all values of x.
2. The area of the region under the graph of f is equal to 1.

Also, recall that the probability that the random variable X assumes a value in an interval $a < x < b$, $P(a < X < b)$, is given by the area of the region under the graph of f from $x = a$ and $x = b$; that is,

$$P(a < X < b) = \int_a^b f(x)\,dx$$

EXAMPLE 13.27 The TKK Products Corporation manufactures a 200 watt electric light bulb. Laboratory tests show that the life spans of these light bulbs have a distribution described by the probability density function

$$f(x) = 0.001\,e^{-0.001x}$$

Determine:

(a) the probability that a light bulb will have a life span of 500 hours or less;

(b) the probability that a light bulb will have a life span of more than 500 hours;

(c) the probability that a light bulb will have a life span of more than 1000 hours but less than 1500 hours.

SOLUTION Let X denote the life span of a light bulb.

(a) The probability that a light bulb will have a life span of 500 hours or less is given by

$$\begin{aligned} P(0 \le X \le 500) &= \int_0^{500} 0.001\,e^{-0.001x}\,dx \\ &= -e^{-0.001x}\Big|_0^{500} \\ &= -e^{-0.5} + 1 \\ &\approx 0.3935 \end{aligned}$$

(b) The probability that a light bulb will have a life span of more than 500 hours is given by

$$\begin{aligned}
P(X>500) &= \int_{500}^{\infty} 0.001\, e^{-0.001x}\, dx \\
&= \lim_{b\to\infty} \int_{500}^{b} 0.001\, e^{-0.001x}\, dx \\
&= \lim_{b\to\infty} -e^{-0.001x}\Big|_{500}^{b} \\
&= \lim_{b\to\infty} (-e^{-0.001b}+e^{-0.5}) \\
&= e^{-0.5} \\
&\approx 0.6065
\end{aligned}$$

This result may also be obtained by observing that

$$\begin{aligned}
P(X>500) &= 1-P(X\le 500) \\
&= 1-0.3935 \qquad \text{(using the result from part (a))} \\
&= 0.6065
\end{aligned}$$

(**c**) The probability that a light bulb will have a life span of more than 1000 hours but less than 1500 hours is given by

$$\begin{aligned}
P(1000<X<1500) &= \int_{1000}^{1500} 0.001\, e^{-0.001x}\, dx \\
&= -e^{-0.001x}\Big|_{1000}^{1500} \\
&= -e^{-1.5}+e^{-1} \\
&\approx -0.2231+0.3679 \\
&= 0.1448
\end{aligned}$$

■

The probability density function of Example 13.27 has the form

$$f(x)=k\,e^{-kx}$$

exponentially distributed

where $x\ge 0$ and k is a positive constant (see Figure 13.38). A random variable with such a probability density function is *exponentially distributed.* It may be shown that the reciprocal $(1/k)$ of the constant k in the probability density function is equal to the average value of X, that is

$$\mu(X)=\frac{1}{k}$$

Thus, the average life span of the TKK 200-watt light bulbs of Example 13.27 is (1/0.001) or 1000 hours.

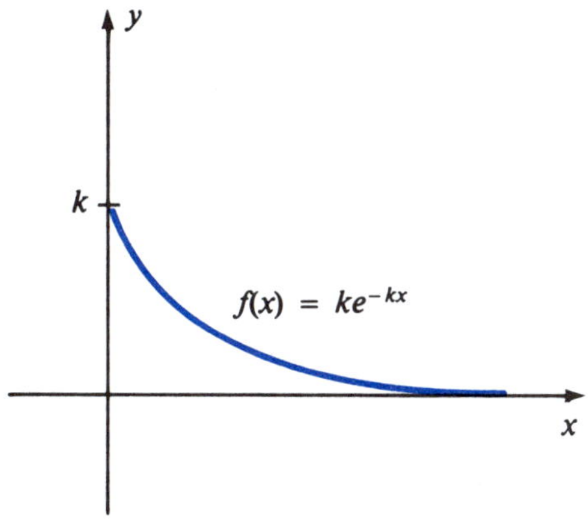

Figure 13.38

13.6 EXERCISES

In problems 1 through 6, find the area of the region under each of the curves y = f(x) *over the indicated interval.*

1. $f(x) = \frac{2}{x^2}$; $x \geq 3$

2. $f(x) = \frac{1}{(x-2)^2}$; $x \geq 3$

3. $f(x) = \frac{1}{x^{3/2}}$; $x \geq 1$

4. $f(x) = \frac{1}{(x+1)^{5/2}}$; $x \geq 0$

5. $f(x) = e^{2x}$; $x \leq 2$

6. $f(x) = \frac{1}{(1-x)^{3/2}}$; $x \leq 0$

7. Find the area of the region bounded by the graph of the function

$$f(x) = \frac{x}{(1+x^2)^2}$$

and the x-axis.

8. Consider the improper integral

$$\int_0^\infty \sqrt{x}\,dx$$

(***a***) Evaluate $I(b) = \int_0^b \sqrt{x}\,dx$.

(***b***) Show that

$$\lim_{b\to\infty} I(b) = \infty$$

thus proving that the given improper integral is *divergent.*

In problems 9 through 18, evaluate each improper integral whenever it is convergent.

9. $\int_1^\infty \frac{1}{x^3}\,dx$

10. $\int_1^\infty \frac{1}{x^{3/2}}\,dx$

11. $\int_1^\infty \frac{1}{x}\,dx$

12. $\int_1^\infty \frac{1}{\sqrt{x}}\,dx$

13. $\int_1^\infty \frac{1}{(2x-1)^{3/2}}\,dx$

14. $\int_{-\infty}^0 e^{3x}\,dx$

15. $\int_{-\infty}^\infty x\,dx$

16. $\int_{-\infty}^\infty \frac{x^2}{(x^3+1)^3}\,dx$

17. $\int_{-\infty}^\infty \left(x-\frac{1}{2}\right)e^{-x^2+x-1}\,dx$

18. $\int_{-\infty}^\infty \frac{x e^{-x^2}}{1+e^{-x^2}}\,dx$

19. The National Welding Company utilizes industrial robots in some of its assembly line operations. Management determined that on the average a robot breaks down after 1000 hours of usage and that the lengths of time between breakdowns is exponentially distributed.

(***a***) What is the probability that a robot selected at random will break down between 600 and 800 hours of usage?

(***b***) What is the probability that a robot will break down after 1200 hours of usage?

20. Suppose that the time intervals between the arrival of successive cars at an expressway toll booth during rush hours are exponentially distributed and that the average time interval between arrivals is 8 seconds. Find the probability that the average time interval between the arrival of successive cars at the toll booth is more than 8 seconds.

21. A study conducted by Uni-Mart, a mail-order department store, revealed that the time intervals between incoming telephone calls on its toll free 800 line between 10 A.M. and 2 P.M. were exponentially distributed and that the average time interval was 30 seconds. What is the probability that the time interval between successive calls is more than 2 minutes?

22. The micro-processors manufactured by the United Motor Works Company, which are used in automobiles to regulate fuel consumption, are guaranteed against defects for 20,000 miles of usage. Tests conducted in the laboratory under simulated driving conditions reveal that the distances driven before these micro-processors break down are exponentially distributed and that the average distance driven before the micro-processors fail is 50,000 miles. What is the probability that a micro-processor selected at random will fail during the warranty period?

13

Chapter Review

EXERCISES *In problems 1 through 8 evaluate each of the definite integrals.*

1. $\int_0^2 (4x^3-9x^2+2x-1)\,dx$

2. $\int_1^4 (\sqrt{x}+x^{-3/2})\,dx$

3. $\int_0^1 20x(2x^2+1)^4\,dx$

4. $\int_{-1}^0 12(x^2-2x)(x^3-3x^2+1)^3\,dx$

5. $\int_0^2 \frac{x}{x^2+1}\,dx$

6. $\int_0^2 x\,e^{-(1/2)x^2}\,dx$

7. $\int_0^2 xe^{2x}\,dx$

8. $\int_{-1}^0 \frac{e^{-x}}{(1+e^{-x})^2}\,dx$

9. The management of a Ditton Industries division determined that the daily marginal cost function associated with producing their standard toaster-ovens is given by $C'(x)=0.00003x^2-0.03x+10$ where $C'(x)$ is measured in dollars per unit and x denotes the number of units manufactured. Management has also determined that the daily fixed cost incurred in the production of these toaster-ovens is \$600. Find the total cost incurred by the company in producing the first 500 units of toaster-ovens.

10. The 1980 world production of coal was 3.5 billion metric tons. If output were to increase at the rate of $3.5\,e^{0.04t}$ billion metric tons per year in year t ($t=0$ corresponding to 1980), determine the amount of coal that would be produced worldwide between 1980 and the end of 1985.

11. Find the area of the region under the curve $y=3x^2+2x+1$ from $x=-1$ to $x=2$.

12. Find the area of the region under the curve $y=e^{2x}$ from $x=0$ to $x=2$.

13. Find the area of the region bounded by the graph of the function $y=1/x^2$, the x-axis, and the lines $x=1$ and $x=3$.

14. Find the area of the region bounded by the curve $y=-x^2-x+2$ and the x-axis.

15. Find the area of the region bounded by the graphs of the functions $f(x)=e^x$ and $g(x)=x$ and the vertical lines $x=0$ and $x=2$.

16. Find the area of the region that is completely enclosed by the graphs of $f(x)=x^4$ and $g(x)=x$.

17. Find the area of the region between the curve $y=x(x-1)(x-2)$ and the x-axis.

18. Using current production techniques, the rate of oil production from a certain oil well t years from now is estimated by $R_1(t)=100\,e^{0.05t}$ thousand barrels per year. Using a new production technique, however, it is estimated that the rate of oil production from that oil well t years from now will be given by $R_2(t) = 100\,e^{0.08t}$ thousand barrels per year. Determine the additional amount of oil that would be produced over the next ten years if the new technique is adopted.

19. The demand function for a brand of blank video cassettes is given by $p = d(x) = -0.01x^2 - 0.2x + 23$, where p is the wholesale unit price in dollars and x is the quantity demanded each week, measured in units of a thousand. Determine the consumers' surplus if the wholesale unit price is set at \$8 per cassette.

20. The quantity demanded x (in units of a hundred) of the Field and Stream 5×7 sport tents per week is related to the unit price p (in dollars) by the relation $p = d(x) = -0.1x^2 - x + 40$; the quantity x (in units of a hundred) that the supplier is willing to make available in the market is related to the unit price by the relation $p = s(x) = 0.1x^2 + 2x + 20$. If the market price is set at the equilibrium price, find the consumers' surplus and the producers' surplus.

21. Find the average value of the function $f(x) = x/(x^2 + 1)$ over the interval $[0, 2]$.

22. The population of a Sunbelt city, currently 80,000, is expected to grow exponentially in the next 5 years with a growth constant of 0.05. If the prediction comes true, what would the average population of the city be over the next five years?

14

CALCULUS OF SEVERAL VARIABLES

14.1

Functions of Several Variables

Up to now, our study of calculus has been restricted to that of a function of one variable. In many practical situations, however, the formulation of a problem results in a mathematical model that involves a function of two or more variables. For example, the profit of the Ace Novelty Company of Example 4.16, Chapter 4, depends on the number of each of the three types of souvenirs it plans to produce; letting x, y, and z denote the number of Type A, Type B, and Type C souvenirs to be made, we found that the company's profit was given by $P = 6x + 5y + 4z$, which is a function of the three variables x, y, and z.

Although this chapter deals with real-valued functions of several variables, we state most of our definitions and results for the case of a function of two variables. One reason for adopting this approach is that, as we will see presently, there is a geometrical interpretation for this special case, which serves as an important visual aid. Then we can draw upon the experience gained from studying the two-variable case to understand the concepts and results connected with the more general case, which, by and large, is just a simple extension of the lower-dimensional case.

real-valued function of two variables

A *real-valued function of two variables f* consists of

1. a set A of ordered pairs of real numbers (x, y) called the *domain* of the function and

2. a rule that associates with each ordered pair in the domain of f one and only one real number, normally denoted by $z = f(x, y)$.

independent and dependent variables

The variables x and y are called *independent variables*, while the variable z, which is dependent on the values of x and y, is referred to accordingly as the *dependent variable.*

range of a function

As in the case of a real-valued function of one real variable, the set of all real numbers $z = f(x, y)$ that are images of the ordered pairs (x, y) of A is called the *range* of the function f. And, unless specified, the domain of the function f will be taken to be the largest possible set for which the rule defining f is meaningful. We shall also, in keeping with common practice, often refer to the rule defining the function as the function itself.

EXAMPLE 14.1 Let f be the function defined by the rule $f(x, y) = x + xy + y^2 + 2$. Compute $f(0, 0)$, $f(1, 2)$ and $f(2, 1)$.

SOLUTION We have

$$f(0, 0) = 0 + (0)(0) + 0^2 + 2 = 2$$
$$f(1, 2) = 1 + (1)(2) + 2^2 + 2 = 9$$

and

$$f(2, 1) = 2 + (2)(1) + 1^2 + 2 = 7$$

■

The domain of a function of two variables $f(x, y)$ is a set of ordered pairs of real numbers and may therefore be viewed as a subset of the xy-plane.

EXAMPLE 14.2 Find the domain of each of the following functions.

(a) $f(x, y) = x^2 + y^2$

(b) $g(x, y) = \dfrac{2}{x - y}$

(c) $h(x, y) = \sqrt{1 - x^2 - y^2}$

SOLUTION **(a)** $f(x, y)$ is defined for all real values of x and y, so that the domain of the function f is the set of all points (x, y) in the xy-plane.

(b) Here, $g(x, y)$ is defined for all $x \neq y$, and so the domain of the function g is the set of all points in the xy-plane except those lying on the line $y = x$ (see Figure 14.1 part a).

(c) We require that $1 - x^2 - y^2 \geq 0$ or $x^2 + y^2 \leq 1$, which is just the set of all points (x, y) lying on and inside the circle of radius 1 with center at the origin (see Figure 14.1 part b).

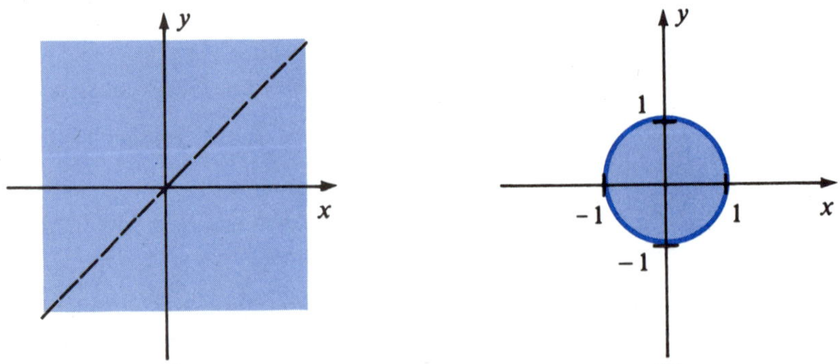

Figure 14.1 **(a)** Domain of g **(b)** Domain of h

■

EXAMPLE 14.3 The Acrosonic Company manufactures a bookshelf loudspeaker system, which may be bought fully assembled or in kit form. The demand equations that relate the unit prices, p and q, to the quantities demanded weekly, x and y, of the assembled and kit versions of the loudspeaker systems are given by

$$p = 300 - \frac{1}{4}x - \frac{1}{8}y \quad \text{and} \quad q = 240 - \frac{1}{8}x - \frac{3}{8}y$$

(a) What is the weekly total revenue function $R(x, y)$?

(b) Discuss the domain of the function R.

SOLUTION **(a)** The weekly revenue realizable from the sale of x units of the assembled speaker systems at p dollars per unit is given by xp dollars. Similarly, the weekly revenue realizable from the sale of y units of the kits at q dollars per unit is given by yq dollars. Therefore the weekly total revenue function R is given by

$$\begin{aligned} R(x, y) &= xp + yq \\ &= x\left(300 - \frac{1}{4}x - \frac{1}{8}y\right) + y\left(240 - \frac{1}{8}x - \frac{3}{8}y\right) \\ &= -\frac{1}{4}x^2 - \frac{3}{8}y^2 - \frac{1}{4}xy + 300x + 240y \end{aligned}$$

(b) To find the domain of the function R, let us observe that the quantities x, y, p, and q must be nonnegative. This observation leads to the following system of linear inequalities.

$$\begin{aligned} 300 - \frac{1}{4}x - \frac{1}{8}y &\geq 0 \\ 240 - \frac{1}{8}x - \frac{3}{8}y &\geq 0 \\ x &\geq 0 \\ y &\geq 0 \end{aligned}$$

Using the techniques developed in Section 4.1, we sketch the domain D of the function R (see Figure 14.2).

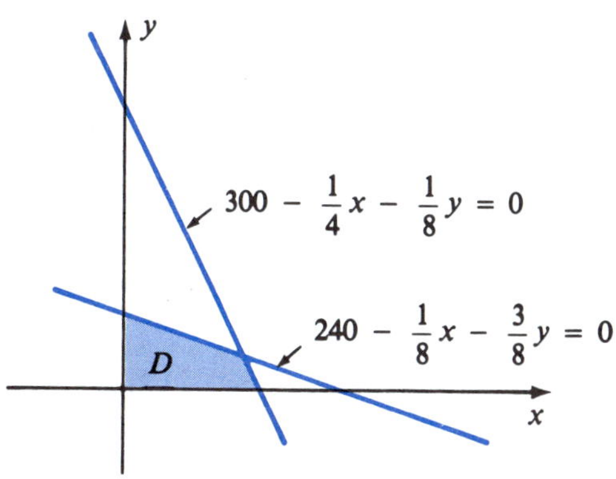

Figure 14.2

■

To exhibit a function of two variables graphically, let us recall that an ordered triple of real numbers (x, y, z) represents a point in 3-dimensional space, and that, conversely, we can represent every point P in 3-dimensional space by an ordered triple (x, y, z) with the numbers x, y, and z representing its x-, y- and z-coordinates, respectively (see Figure 14.3).

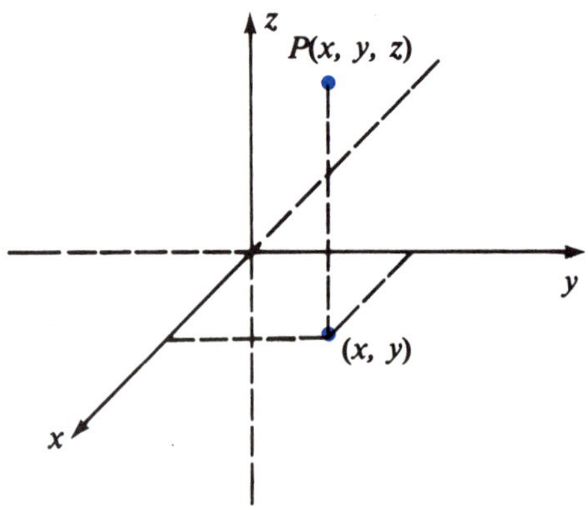

Figure 14.3

Now, if $f(x, y)$ is a function of two variables x and y, we have seen earlier that the domain of f is a subset of the xy-plane. Put $z = f(x, y)$ so that associated with each point (x, y) there is one and only one point $(x, y, z) \equiv (x, y, f(x, y))$ in 3-dimensional space. The totality of all such points comprises the *graph* of the function f and is, except for certain degenerate cases, a surface in 3-dimensional space (Figure 14.4).

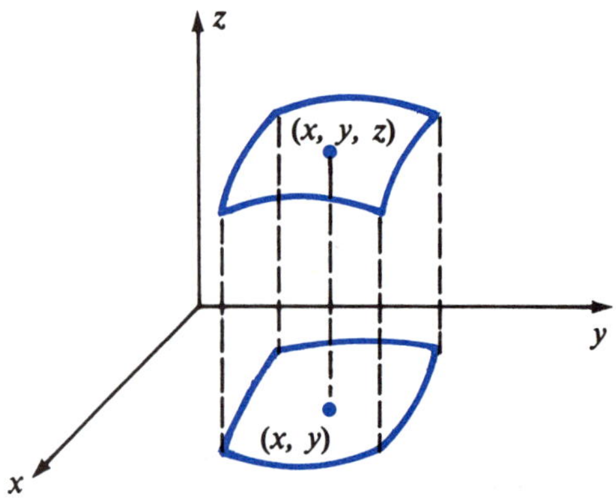

Figure 14.4

In interpreting the graph of a function $f(x, y)$ one often thinks of the value $z = f(x, y)$ of the function at the point (x, y) as the "height" of the point (x, y, z) on the graph of f. If $f(x, y) > 0$, then the point (x, y, z) is $f(x, y)$ units above the xy-plane; if $f(x, y) < 0$, then the point (x, y, z) is $|f(x, y)|$ units below the xy-plane.

The graph of a function of two variables is, in general, difficult to sketch, and we shall not develop a systematic procedure for sketching the graphs of such functions.

14.1 EXERCISES

1. Let $f(x, y) = x^2 + 2xy - x + 3$. Compute $f(1, 2)$, $f(2, 1)$, $f(-1, 2)$, and $f(2, -1)$.

2. Let $h(x, y) = (x + y)/(x - y)$. Compute $f(0, 1)$, $f(-1, 1)$, $f(2, 1)$, and $f(\pi, -\pi)$.

3. Let $g(s, t) = 3s\sqrt{t} + t\sqrt{s} + 2$. Compute $g(1, 2)$, $g(2, 1)$, $g(0, 4)$, and $g(4, 9)$.

4. Let $f(x, y) = xy\, e^{x^2+y^2}$. Compute $f(0, 0)$, $f(0, 1)$, $f(1, 1)$, and $f(-1, -1)$.

5. Let $g(r, s, t) = r\, e^{s/t}$. Compute $g(1, 1, 1)$, $g(1, 0, 1)$, and $g(-1, -1, -1)$.

6. Let $f(u, v) = (u^2 + v^2)\, e^{uv^2}$. Compute $f(0, 1)$, $f(-1, -1)$, $f(a, b)$, and $f(b, a)$.

7. Let $h(s, t) = s \ln t - t \ln s$. Compute $h(1, e)$, $h(e, 1)$ and $h(e, e)$.

8. Let $g(u, v, w) = (u\, e^{vw} + v\, e^{uw} + w\, e^{uv})/(u^2 + v^2 + w^2)$. Compute $g(1, 2, 3)$ and $g(3, 2, 1)$.

In problems 9 through 16, find the domain of each of the functions whose rule is given.

9. $f(x, y) = 2x + 3y$

10. $g(x, y, z) = x^2 + y^2 + z^2$

11. $h(u, v) = \dfrac{uv}{u - v}$

12. $f(s, t) = \sqrt{s^2 + t^2}$

13. $f(x, y, z) = \sqrt{x^2 + 2y^2 + 3z^2}$

14. $g(r, s) = \sqrt{rs}$

15. $h(u, v) = \sqrt{4 - u^2 - v^2}$

**16.* $f(x, y, z) = \sqrt{4 - x^2 - y^2 - z^2}$

17. The Country Workshop manufactures both finished and unfinished furniture for the home. The estimated quantities demanded each week of its roll-top desks in the finished and unfinished version are x and y units when the corresponding unit prices are

$$p = 200 - \frac{1}{5}x - \frac{1}{10}y$$

$$q = 160 - \frac{1}{10}x - \frac{1}{4}y$$

dollars, respectively.

(*a*) What is the weekly total revenue function $R(x, y)$?

(*b*) Find the domain of the function R.

18. For the total revenue function $R(x, y)$ of problem 17, compute $R(100, 60)$ and $R(60, 100)$. Interpret your results.

19. The Weston Publishing Company publishes a deluxe edition and a standard edition of its English language dictionary. The management of the company estimates that the number of deluxe edition copies demanded is x copies per day, while the number of standard edition copies demanded is y copies per day when the unit prices are

$$p = 20 - 0.005x - 0.001y$$
$$q = 15 - 0.001x - 0.003y$$

dollars, respectively.

(***a***) Find the daily total revenue function $R(x, y)$.

(***b***) Find the domain of the function R.

20. For the total revenue function $R(x, y)$ of problem 19, compute $R(300, 200)$ and $R(200, 300)$. Interpret your results.

21. The volume of a certain mass of gas is related to its pressure and temperature by the formula

$$V = \frac{30.9T}{P}$$

where the volume V is measured in liters, the temperature T is measured in degrees Kelvin (obtained by adding 273° to the Centigrade temperature), and the pressure P is measured in millimeters of mercury pressure.

(***a***) Find the domain of the function V.

(***b***) Calculate the volume of the gas at standard temperature and pressure, that is, when $T = 273°\text{K}$ and $P = 760$ mm. of mercury.

22. An empirical formula by E. F. Dubois relates the surface area A of a human body (in square meters) to its weight W in kilograms and its height H in centimeters. The formula is given by

$$S = 0.007184\,W^{0.425}H^{0.725}$$

and is used by physiologists in metabolism studies.

(***a***) Find the domain of the function S.

(***b***) What is the surface area of a human body weighing 70 kilograms and having a height of 178 centimeters. (The use of a pocket calculator is recommended.)

14.2 Partial Derivatives

For a function $f(x)$ of one variable x, there is no ambiguity when we speak about the rate of change of $f(x)$ with respect to x since x must be constrained to move along the x-axis. The situation becomes more complicated, however, when we study the rate of change of a function of two or more variables. For example, the domain D of a function of two variables $f(x, y)$ is a subset of the plane (see Figure 14.5), so that if $P_0(x_0, y_0)$ is any point in the domain of f, there are infinitely many directions in which one can approach the point P_0. We may therefore ask for the rate of change of f at P_0 along any of these directions.

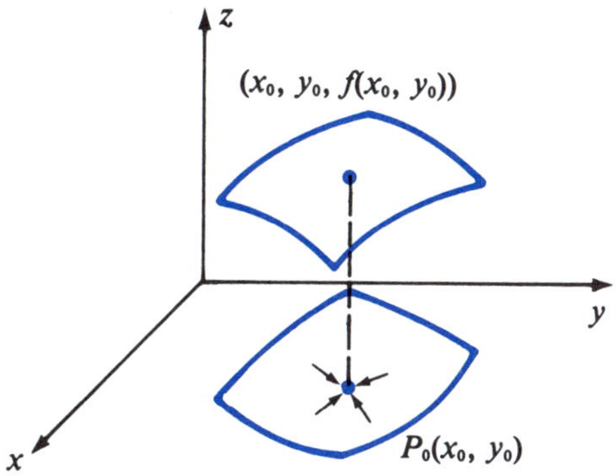

Figure 14.5

We shall not deal with the general problem posed above. Instead, we shall restrict ourselves to studying the rate of change of the function $f(x, y)$ at a point $P_0(x_0, y_0)$ in each of two *preferred directions*, namely, in the direction parallel to the x-axis and the direction parallel to the y-axis. To this end, put $y = y_0$, where y_0 is a constant, so that $f(x, y_0)$ is a function of the one variable x. Since the equation $z = f(x, y)$ is the equation of a surface, the equation $z = f(x, y_0)$ is the equation of the curve C on the surface formed by the intersection of the surface and the plane $y = y_0$ (see Figure 14.6).

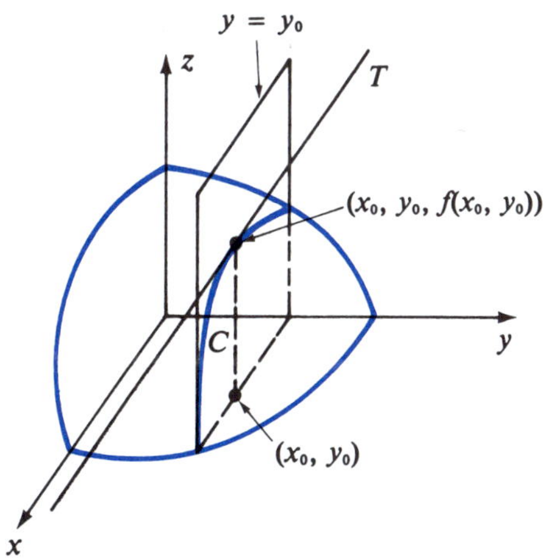

Figure 14.6

first partial derivative with respect to x

Because $f(x, y_0)$ is a function of one variable x, we may compute the derivative of f with respect to x. This derivative, obtained by keeping the variable y fixed, and differentiating the function $f(x, y)$ with respect to x, is called the *first partial derivative of f with respect to x* and is written

$$\frac{\partial z}{\partial x} \quad \text{or} \quad \frac{\partial f}{\partial x} \quad \text{or} \quad f_x$$

It measures both the slope of the tangent line T to the curve C and the rate of change of the function f in the x-direction when $y = y_0$. In particular, the slope of the tangent line T, as well as the rate of change of the function $f(x, y)$ at the point $P_0(x_0, y_0, z_0)$ in the x-direction, is given by $\partial f/\partial x$ evaluated at (x_0, y_0), namely,

$$\left.\frac{\partial f}{\partial x}\right|_{(x_0,y_0)} \equiv f_x(x_0, y_0)$$

first partial derivative with respect to y

In a similar manner, we define the *first partial derivative of f with respect to y*, written

$$\frac{\partial z}{\partial y} \quad \text{or} \quad \frac{\partial f}{\partial y} \quad \text{or} \quad f_y$$

as the derivative obtained by keeping the variable x fixed and differentiating the resulting function $f(x, y)$ with respect to y. It measures both the slope of the tangent line T to the curve C, obtained by holding x constant (see Figure 14.7), and the rate of change of the function f in the y-direction when $x = x_0$. In particular, the slope of the tangent line T as well as the rate of change of the function $f(x, y)$ at the point $P_0(x_0, y_0, z_0)$ in the y-direction is given by

$$\left.\frac{\partial f}{\partial y}\right|_{(x_0,y_0)} \equiv f_y(x_0, y_0)$$

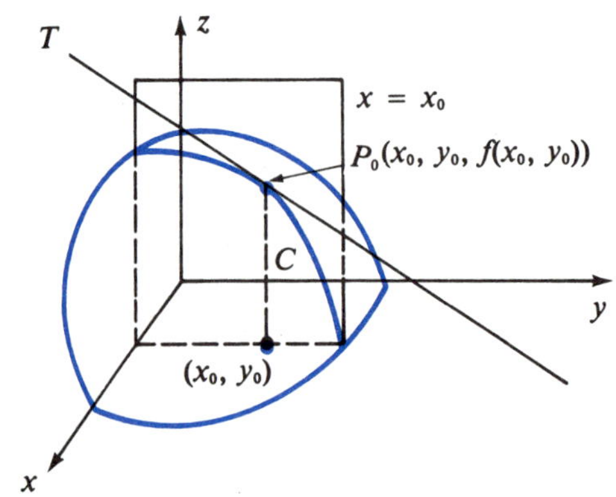

Figure 14.7

EXAMPLE 14.4 Find the partial derivatives $\partial f/\partial x$ and $\partial f/\partial y$ of the function $f(x, y) = x^2 - xy^2 + y^3$. What is the rate of change of the function f in the x-direction at the point $(1, 2, 5)$? What is the rate of change of the function f in the y-direction at the point $(1, 2, 5)$?

SOLUTION To compute $\partial f/\partial x$, we think of the variable y as a constant and differentiate the resulting function of x with respect to x. Let us write

$$f(x, y) = x^2 - xy^2 + y^3$$

where the variable y to be treated as a constant is shown in color. Then,

$$\frac{\partial f}{\partial x} = 2x - y^2$$

To compute $\partial f/\partial y$, we think of the variable x as being fixed, that is, as a constant, and differentiate the resulting function of y with respect to y. In this case,

$$f(x, y) = x^2 - xy^2 + y^3$$

so that

$$\frac{\partial f}{\partial y} = -2xy + 3y^2$$

The rate of change of the function f in the x-direction at the point (1, 2, 5) is given by

$$f_x(1, 2) = \left.\frac{\partial f}{\partial x}\right|_{(1,2)} = 2(1) - 2^2 = -2$$

or a decrease of 2 units for each unit increase in the x-direction, y being kept constant ($y = 2$). The rate of change of the function f in the y-direction at the point (1, 2, 5) is given by

$$f_y(1, 2) = \left.\frac{\partial f}{\partial y}\right|_{(1,2)} = -2(1)(2) + 3(2)^2 = 8$$

or an increase of 8 units for each unit increase in the y-direction, x being kept constant ($x = 1$). ■

EXAMPLE 14.5 Compute the first partial derivatives of each of the following functions:

(a) $f(x, y) = \dfrac{xy}{x^2 + y^2}$

(b) $g(s, t) = (s^2 - st + t^2)^5$

(c) $h(u, v) = e^{u^2 - v^2}$

(d) $f(x, y) = \ln(x^2 + 2y^2)$

SOLUTION **(a)** To compute $\partial f/\partial x$, we think of the variable y as a constant. Thus,

$$f(x, y) = \frac{xy}{x^2 + y^2}$$

so that upon using the quotient rule, we have

$$\frac{\partial f}{\partial x}=\frac{(x^2+y^2)y-xy(2x)}{(x^2+y^2)^2}$$
$$=\frac{y(y^2-x^2)}{(x^2+y^2)^2}$$

upon simplification and factorization. To compute $\partial f/\partial y$, we think of the variable x as a constant. Thus,

$$f(x, y)=\frac{xy}{x^2+y^2}$$

so that upon using the quotient rule once again, we obtain

$$\frac{\partial f}{\partial y}=\frac{(x^2+y^2)x-xy(2y)}{(x^2+y^2)^2}$$
$$=\frac{x(x^2-y^2)}{(x^2+y^2)^2}$$

(b) To compute $\partial g/\partial s$, we treat the variable t as if it were a constant. Thus,

$$g(s, t)=(s^2-st+t^2)^5$$

Using the corollary to the chain rule for power functions, we find

$$\frac{\partial g}{\partial s}=5(s^2-st+t^2)^4\cdot(2s-t)$$
$$=5(2s-t)(s^2-st+t^2)^4$$

To compute $\partial g/\partial t$, we treat the variable s as if it were a constant. Thus,

$$g(s, t)=(s^2-st+t^2)^5$$
$$\frac{\partial g}{\partial t}=5(s^2-st+t^2)^4(-s+2t)$$
$$=5(2t-s)(s^2-st+t^2)^4$$

(c) To compute $\partial h/\partial u$, we think of the variable v as a constant. Thus,

$$h(u, v)=e^{u2-v2}$$

Using the corollary to the chain rule for exponential functions, we have

$$\frac{\partial h}{\partial u}=e^{u2-v2}\cdot 2u$$
$$=2u\,e^{u2-v2}$$

Next, we treat the variable u as if it were a constant,

$$h(u, v) = e^{u^2 - v^2}$$

and obtain

$$\frac{\partial h}{\partial v} = e^{u^2 - v^2} \cdot (-2v)$$

$$= -2v\, e^{u^2 - v^2}$$

(**d**) To compute $\partial f / \partial x$, we think of the variable y as a constant. Thus,

$$f(x, y) = \ln (x^2 + 2y^2)$$

so that the corollary to the chain rule for logarithmic functions gives

$$\frac{\partial f}{\partial x} = \frac{2x}{x^2 + 2y^2}$$

Next, we treat the variable x as if it were a constant, and find

$$f(x, y) = \ln (x^2 + 2y^2)$$

$$\frac{\partial f}{\partial y} = \frac{4y}{x^2 + 2y^2}$$

For an economic interpretation of the first partial derivatives of a function of two variables, we turn our attention to the function

(14.1) $$f(x, y) = ax^b y^{1-b}$$

where a and b are positive constants with $0 < b < 1$. The function of Equation 14.1 is called the *Cobb-Douglas production function*. Here x stands for the amount of money expended for labor, y stands for the cost of capital equipment (buildings, machineries, and other tools of production), and the function f measures the output of the finished product (in suitable units) and is called, accordingly, the *production function*. The partial derivative f_x is called the *marginal productivity of labor*. It measures the rate of change of production with respect to the amount of money expended for labor with the level of capital expenditure held constant. Similarly, the partial derivative f_y is called the *marginal productivity of capital* and measures the rate of change of production with respect to the amount expended on capital with the level of labor expenditure held fixed.

marginal productivity of labor and capital

EXAMPLE 14.6 The production for a certain country in the early years following World War II is described by the function $f(x, y) = 30x^{2/3}y^{1/3}$ units, when x units of labor and y units of capital were utilized.

(**a**) Compute f_x and f_y.

(b) What is the marginal productivity of labor and the marginal productivity of capital when the amounts expended on labor and capital are 125 units and 27 units, respectively?

(c) Should the government have encouraged capital investment rather than increased expenditure on labor to increase the productivity of that country?

SOLUTION **(a)**

$$f_x = 30 \cdot \frac{2}{3}x^{-1/3}y^{1/3}$$

$$= 20\left(\frac{y}{x}\right)^{1/3}$$

$$f_y = 30x^{2/3} \cdot \frac{1}{3}y^{-2/3}$$

$$= 10\left(\frac{x}{y}\right)^{2/3}$$

(b) The required marginal productivity of labor is given by

$$f_x(125, 27) = 20\left(\frac{27}{125}\right)^{1/3} = 20\left(\frac{3}{5}\right)$$

or 12 units per unit increase in labor expenditure (capital expenditure being held constant at 27 units). The required marginal productivity of capital is given by

$$f_y(125, 27) = 10\left(\frac{125}{27}\right)^{2/3} = 10\left(\frac{25}{9}\right)$$

or $27\frac{7}{9}$ units per unit increase in capital expenditure (labor outlay being held constant at 125 units).

(c) From the results of part (b), we see that a unit increase in capital expenditure resulted in a much faster increase in the productivity than a unit increase in labor expenditure would have. Therefore, the government should have encouraged increased spending on capital rather than on labor, at least during the early years of reconstruction. ■

In general, to compute the partial derivative of a function f of several variables with respect to one variable, say x, we think of the other variables as if they were constants and differentiate the resulting function with respect to x.

EXAMPLE 14.7 Compute the first partial derivatives of the function

$$w = f(x, y, z) = xyz - x e^{yz} + x \ln y$$

SOLUTION Here we have a function of three variables x, y, and z, and we are required to compute

$$\frac{\partial f}{\partial x}, \quad \frac{\partial f}{\partial y}, \quad \text{and} \quad \frac{\partial f}{\partial z}$$

To compute f_x, we think of the other two variables, y and z, as fixed, and we differentiate the resulting function of x with respect to x, thereby obtaining

$$f_x = yz - e^{yz} + \ln y$$

To compute f_y, we think of the other two variables, x and z, as constants and differentiate the resulting function of y with respect to y. We then obtain

$$f_y = xz - xz\, e^{yz} + \frac{x}{y}$$

Finally, to compute f_z, we treat the variables x and y as constants and differentiate the function f with respect to x getting

$$f_z = xy - xy\, e^{yz}$$

■

second-order partial derivative

The first partial derivatives $f_x(x, y)$ and $f_y(x, y)$ of a function $f(x, y)$ of the two variables x and y are also functions of x and y. As such, we may differentiate each of the functions f_x and f_y to obtain the *second-order partial derivatives of f*. Thus, differentiating the function f_x with respect to x leads to the second partial derivative

$$f_{xx} \equiv \frac{\partial^2 f}{\partial x^2} = \frac{\partial}{\partial x}(f_x)$$

On the other hand, differentiation of f_x with respect to y leads to the second partial derivative

$$f_{xy} \equiv \frac{\partial^2 f}{\partial y\, \partial x} = \frac{\partial}{\partial y}(f_x)$$

Similarly, differentiation of the function f_y with respect to x and with respect to y leads to

$$f_{yx} \equiv \frac{\partial^2 f}{\partial x\, \partial y} = \frac{\partial}{\partial x}(f_y)$$

and

$$f_{yy} \equiv \frac{\partial^2 f}{\partial y^2} = \frac{\partial}{\partial y}(f_y)$$

respectively. Note that it is not true in general that $f_{xy} = f_{yx}$. However, in most practical applications f_{xy} and f_{yx} are equal, and we shall assume this to be the case in what follows.

EXAMPLE 14.8 Find the second-order partial derivatives of the function

$$f(x, y) = x^3 - 3x^2y + 3xy^2 + y^2$$

SOLUTION The first partial derivatives of f are

$$f_x = \frac{\partial}{\partial x}(x^3 - 3x^2y + 3xy^2 + y^2)$$
$$= 3x^2 - 6xy + 3y^2$$
$$f_y = \frac{\partial}{\partial y}(x^3 - 3x^2y + 3xy^2 + y^2)$$
$$= -3x^2 + 6xy + 2y$$

Therefore,

$$f_{xx} = \frac{\partial}{\partial x}(f_x) = \frac{\partial}{\partial x}(3x^2 - 6xy + 3y^2)$$
$$= 6x - 6y = 6(x - y)$$
$$f_{xy} = \frac{\partial}{\partial y}(f_x) = \frac{\partial}{\partial y}(3x^2 - 6xy + 3y^2)$$
$$= -6x + 6y = 6(y - x)$$
$$f_{yx} = \frac{\partial}{\partial x}(f_y) = \frac{\partial}{\partial x}(-3x^2 + 6xy + 2y)$$
$$= -6x + 6y = 6(y - x)$$
$$f_{yy} = \frac{\partial}{\partial y}(f_y) = \frac{\partial}{\partial y}(-3x^2 + 6xy + 2y)$$
$$= 6x + 2$$

■

EXAMPLE 14.9 Find the second-order partial derivatives of the function

$$f(x, y) = e^{xy^2}$$

SOLUTION We have

$$f_x = \frac{\partial}{\partial x}(e^{xy^2})$$
$$= y^2 e^{xy^2}$$

and

$$f_y = \frac{\partial}{\partial y}(e^{xy^2})$$
$$= 2xy\, e^{xy^2}$$

so that the required second-order partial derivatives of f are

$$f_{xx} = \frac{\partial}{\partial x}(f_x) = \frac{\partial}{\partial x}(y^2 e^{xy^2})$$
$$= y^4 e^{xy^2}$$

$$f_{xy} = \frac{\partial}{\partial y}(f_x) = \frac{\partial}{\partial y}(y^2 e^{xy^2})$$
$$= 2y e^{xy^2} + 2xy^3 e^{xy^2}$$
$$= 2y e^{xy^2}(1 + xy^2)$$

$$f_{yx} = \frac{\partial}{\partial x}(f_y) = \frac{\partial}{\partial x}(2xy e^{xy^2})$$
$$= 2y e^{xy^2} + 2xy^3 e^{xy^2}$$
$$= 2y e^{xy^2}(1 + xy^2)$$

$$f_{yy} = \frac{\partial}{\partial y}(f_y) = \frac{\partial}{\partial y}(2xy e^{xy^2})$$
$$= 2x e^{xy^2} + (2xy)(2xy) e^{xy^2}$$
$$= 2x e^{xy^2}(1 + 2xy^2)$$

■

14.2 EXERCISES

In problems 1 through 28, compute the first-order partial derivatives of each of the following functions.

1. $f(x, y) = 1 + x^2 + y^2$

2. $g(x, y) = 4x^3 - 5y^4$

3. $h(u, v) = \sqrt{uv}$

4. $f(x, y) = x\sqrt{1 + y^2}$

5. $f(s, t) = (s^2 - st + t^2)^3$

6. $g(u, v) = \dfrac{u - v}{u + v}$

7. $f(x, y) = \dfrac{x^2 - y^2}{x^2 + y^2}$

8. $g(s, t) = s^2 t + st^{-3}$

9. $f(x, y) = e^{xy+1}$

10. $g(x, y) = (x^2 + y^2)e^{xy}$

11. $h(u, v) = e^{u+v}$

12. $f(x, y) = (e^x + e^y)^5$

13. $f(x, y) = x \ln y + y \ln x$

14. $g(u, v) = \ln\left(\dfrac{u}{v}\right)$

15. $h(u, v) = \ln(u + 2v)$

16. $f(x, y) = x^2 e^{y^2}$

17. $g(u, v) = e^u \ln v$

18. $f(x, y) = \dfrac{e^{xy}}{x + y}$

19. $f(s, t)=\ln(e^s+e^t)$

*****20.*** $g(x, y)=x^2e^{xy}\ln(1+x^2y^2)$

21. $f(x, y, z)=xyz+xy^2+yz^2+zx^2$

22. $g(u, v, w)=\dfrac{2uvw}{u^2+v^2+w^2}$

23. $h(r, s, t)=e^{rst}$

24. $f(x, y, z)=x\,e^{y/z}$

25. $g(u, v, w)=\ln(u^2+v^2+w^2)$

26. $h(u, v, w)=uvw\ln(1+uvw)$

27. $f(x, y, z)=\sqrt{xyz}+e^{xyz}+\ln xyz$

*****28.*** $g(x, y, z)=e^{x+\ln yz+\sqrt{z}}$

29. Let $f(x, y)=x^2+xy+y^2+2x-y$. Compute $f_x(-1, 2)$ and $f_y(-1, 2)$. Interpret your results.

30. Let $f(x, y)=e^{xy}$. Compute $f_x(1, 1)$ and $f_y(1, 1)$. Interpret your results.

31. Let $f(x, y, z)=x^2y^2+z^2$. Compute $f_x(1, 1, 2)$, $f_y(1, 1, 2)$, and $f_z(1, 1, 2)$. Interpret your results.

32. Let $f(u, v, w)=ue^{v2+w2}+\ln(1+u^2+v^2+w^2)$. Compute $f_u(1, 0, 2)$, $f_v(1, 0, 2)$, and $f_w(1, 0, 2)$. Interpret your results.

In problems 33 through 42, compute the second-order partial derivatives of each of the following functions. In each case, verify that the mixed derivatives f_{xy} *and* f_{yx} *are equal.*

33. $f(x, y)=x^2-2xy+2y^2+x-2y$

34. $f(x, y)=x^3+x^2y^2+y^3+x+y$

35. $f(x, y)=\sqrt{x^2+y^2}$

36. $f(x, y)=x\sqrt{y}+y\sqrt{x}$

37. $f(x, y)=\dfrac{x+y}{x-y}$

38. $f(x, y)=xy\,e^{xy}+1$

39. $f(x, y)=e^{-x/y}$

40. $f(x, y)=\ln(1+x^2y^2)$

*****41.*** $f(x, y)=1+\sqrt{xy}+e^{x/y}+\ln\left(\dfrac{x}{y}\right)$

*****42.*** $f(x, y)=1+x^2y^3+e^{x2+y2}+\ln(1+x^3y)$

43. The productivity of a South American country is given by the function $f(x, y)=20x^{3/4}y^{1/4}$ (in suitable units) when x units of labor and y units of capital are utilized.

(***a***) What is the marginal productivity of labor and the marginal productivity of capital when the amounts expended on labor and capital are 256 and 16 units, respectively?

(***b***) Should the government encourage capital investment rather than increased expenditure on labor at this time to increase the productivity of the country?

44. The productivity of a country in Western Europe is given by the function $f(x, y)=40x^{4/5}y^{1/5}$ (in suitable units) when x units of labor and y units of capital are utilized.

(***a***) What is the marginal productivity of labor and the marginal productivity of capital when the amounts expended on labor and capital are 32 and 243 units, respectively?

(*b*) Should the government encourage capital investment rather than increased expenditure on labor at this time to increase productivity?

45. The weekly total revenue (in dollars) of the Country Workshop associated with the manufacture and sale of their roll-top desks is given by the function

$$R(x, y) = -0.2x^2 - 0.25y^2 - 0.2xy + 200x + 160y$$

where x denotes the number of finished units and y denotes the number of unfinished units manufactured and sold per week. Compute $\partial R/\partial x$ and $\partial R/\partial y$ when $x = 300$ and $y = 250$. Interpret your results.

46. The monthly profit (in dollars) of the Bond and Barker Department Store depends on the level of inventory x (in thousands of dollars) and the floor space y (in thousands of square feet) available for display of the merchandise as given by the relation

$$P(x, y) = -0.02x^2 - 15y^2 + xy + 39x + 25y - 20{,}000$$

Compute $\partial P/\partial x$ and $\partial P/\partial y$ when $x = 4000$ and $y = 150$. Interpret your results. Repeat with $x = 5000$ and $y = 150$.

47. The volume V (in liters) of a certain mass of gas is related to its pressure (in millimeters of mercury) and its temperature T (in degrees Kelvin) by the law

$$V = \frac{30.9T}{P}$$

Compute $\partial V/\partial T$ and $\partial V/\partial P$ when $T = 300$ and $P = 800$. Interpret your results.

48. The formula

$$S = 0.007184W^{0.425}H^{0.725}$$

gives the surface area S of a human body (in square meters) in terms of its weight W in kilograms and its height H in centimeters. Compute $\partial S/\partial W$ and $\partial S/\partial H$ when $W = 70$ kg. and $H = 180$ cm. Interpret your results.

14.3

Maxima and Minima of Functions of Several Variables

We saw in Chapter 11, how the solution to a practical problem formulated in terms of a function f of one variable often centers around the determination of an extreme value of f with respect to that variable. For example, we can solve the problem of finding the production level x of a firm that will yield a maximum profit by finding the absolute maximum of the profit function $P(x)$ with respect to x. On the other hand, to find the production level, x, of a manufacturer that will result in a minimal cost of operation, we find the absolute minimum of the cost function $C(x)$ with respect to x.

The notion of an extreme value of a function plays an equally important role in the case of a function of several variables. As in the case of a function of one variable, it is important to distinguish between the concept of a relative maximum (relative minimum) of f and that of an absolute maximum (absolute minimum) of f. More specifically, a function $f(x, y)$ of two variables has a *relative maximum* (*relative minimum*) at a point (a, b) belonging to the domain of f, if for all points (x, y) that are sufficiently close to the point (a, b), we have $f(x, y) \leq f(a, b)((f(x, y) \geq f(a, b))$. Geometrically, this means that no point on the graph of f corresponding to points (x, y) lying sufficiently close to the point (a, b) can be above (or below) the point $(a, b, f(a, b))$. Figure 14.8 depicts the graph of a function f of two variables that has a relative maximum at the point (a, b) and another at the point (c, d).

relative maximum and minimum at a point

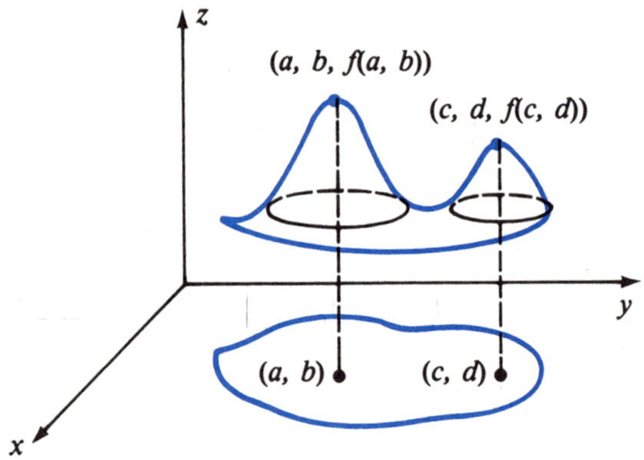

Figure 14.8

absolute maximum and minimum at a point

On the other hand, a function $f(x, y)$ of two variables has an *absolute maximum* (*absolute minimum*) at a point (a, b) if $f(x, y) \leq f(a, b)(f(x, y) \geq f(a, b))$ for *all* points (x, y) in the domain of f. Geometrically, the absolute maximum and the absolute minimum of a function f are, respectively, the highest and the lowest points on the graph of f. Figure 14.9 depicts the graph of a function f of two

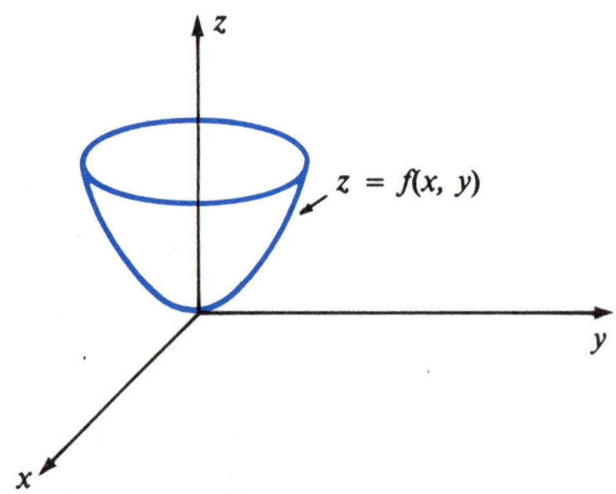

Figure 14.9

variables that has an absolute minimum at the origin. Clearly the function f has no absolute maximum since it is unbounded above.

Just as the first and second derivatives play an important role in determining the relative extrema of a function of one variable, the first and second partial derivatives are powerful tools for locating and classifying the relative extrema of functions of several variables.

Suppose now that the differentiable function $f(x, y)$ of two variables has a relative maximum (relative minimum) at a point (a, b) in the domain of f. From Figure 14.10 it is clear that at the point (a, b) the slope of the "tangent lines" to the surface in *any* direction must be zero. In particular, this implies that both

$$\frac{\partial f}{\partial x}(a, b) \quad \text{and} \quad \frac{\partial f}{\partial y}(a, b)$$

must be zero.

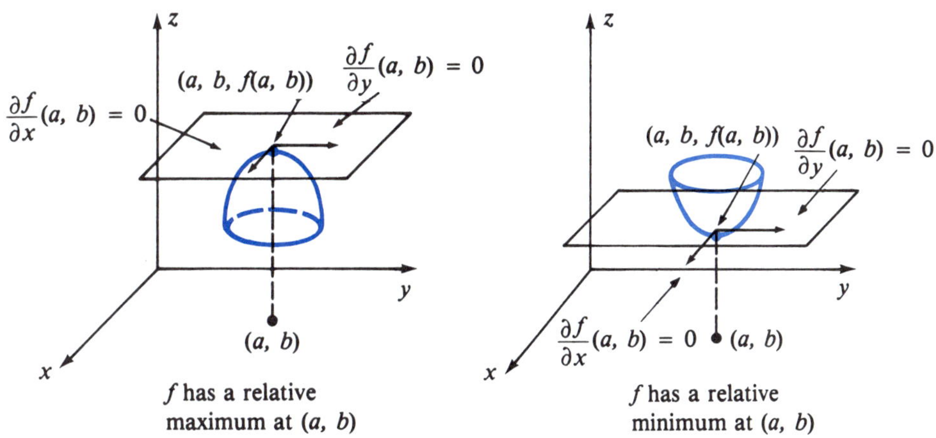

Figure 14.10

critical point

The point (a, b) is called a *critical point* of the function f. Lest we are tempted to conclude that a critical point of a function f must automatically be a relative extremum of f, let us consider the graph of the function f in Figure 14.11. Here we have both

$$\frac{\partial f}{\partial x}(a, b)=0 \quad \text{and} \quad \frac{\partial f}{\partial y}(a, b)=0$$

Clearly, the point $(a, b, f(a, b))$, called a *saddle point*, is neither a relative maximum nor a relative minimum of the function f since there are points near by that are higher and also those near by that are lower than the point $(a, b, f(a, b))$. Thus, as in the case of a function of one variable, we may only conclude that a critical point of a function of two (or more) variables is just a candidate for a relative extremum of f.

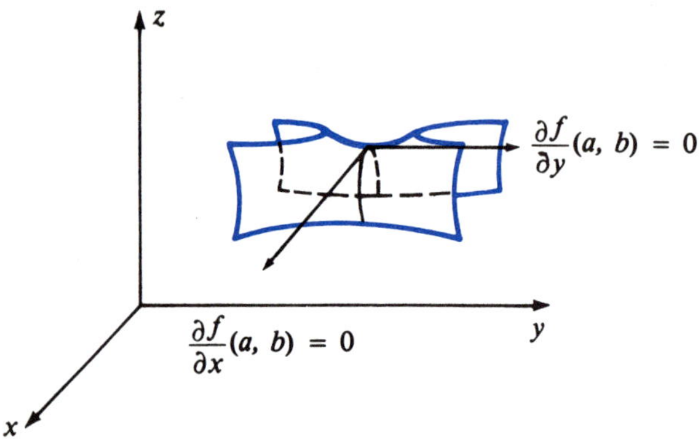

Figure 14.11

Second Derivative Test

To determine the nature of a critical point of a function $f(x, y)$ of two variables, we make use of the second partial derivatives of f. The resulting test, which aids us in classifying these points, is called the *Second Derivative Test* and is incorporated in the following procedure for finding and classifying the relative extrema of f:

1. Find the critical points of $f(x, y)$ by solving the system of simultaneous equations

$$f_x = 0$$
$$f_y = 0$$

2. *The Second Derivative Test* Suppose the point (a, b) is a critical point of $f(x, y)$ found in Step 1. Compute

$$f_{xx}(a, b), \quad f_{xy}(a, b), \quad f_{yy}(a, b)$$

and put

$$\Delta = f_{xx}(a, b)f_{yy}(a, b) - f_{xy}^2(a, b)$$

Then

(*a*) $\Delta > 0$ and $f_{xx}(a, b) < 0$ implies that $f(x, y)$ has a relative maximum at the point (a, b).

(*b*) $\Delta > 0$ and $f_{xx}(a, b) > 0$ implies that $f(x, y)$ has a relative minimum at the point (a, b).

(*c*) $\Delta < 0$ implies that $f(x, y)$ has neither a relative maximum nor a relative minimum at the point (a, b).

(*d*) $\Delta = 0$ implies that the test is inconclusive, and some other technique must be used to solve the problem.

EXAMPLE 14.10 Find the relative extrema of the function $f(x, y) = x^2 + y^2$.

SOLUTION We have

$$f_x = 2x$$

and

$$f_y = 2y$$

To find the critical point(s) of f, we set $f_x = 0$ and $f_y = 0$ and solve the resulting system of simultaneous equations

$$2x = 0$$
$$2y = 0$$

obtaining $x = 0$, $y = 0$ or $(0, 0)$ as the sole critical point of f. Next, we apply the Second Derivative Test to determine the nature of the critical point $(0, 0)$. We compute

$$f_{xx} = 2, \quad f_{xy} = 0, \quad f_{yy} = 2$$

so that, in particular,

$$f_{xx}(0, 0) = 2, \quad f_{xy}(0, 0) = 0, \quad \text{and} \quad f_{yy}(0, 0) = 2$$

Therefore,

$$\begin{aligned}\Delta &= f_{xx}(0, 0)f_{yy}(0, 0) - f_{xy}^2(0, 0)\\ &= (2)(2) - 0\\ &= 4 > 0\end{aligned}$$

Since $\Delta > 0$ and $f_{xx}(0, 0) = 2 > 0$, we conclude that $f(x, y)$ has a relative minimum at the point $(0, 0)$. The relative minimum $(0, 0, 0)$ in this case also happens to be the absolute minimum of f. The graph of the function f is easily sketched in this case (Figure 14.12) and confirms the results obtained earlier.

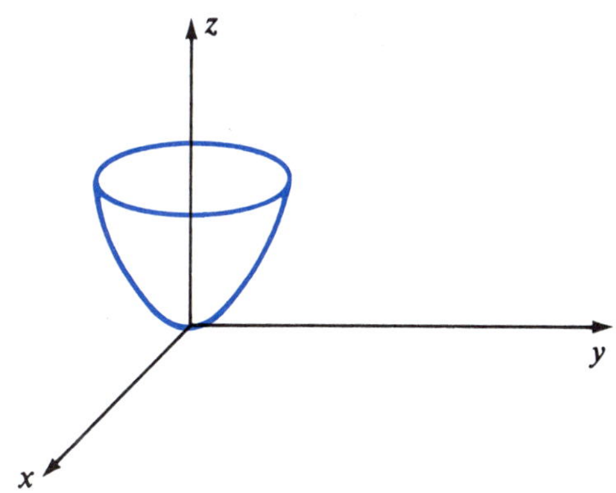

Figure 14.12

■

EXAMPLE 14.11 Find the relative extrema of the function

$$f(x, y) = 3x^2 - 4xy + 4y^2 - 4x + 8y + 4$$

SOLUTION We have

$$f_x = 6x - 4y - 4$$

and

$$f_y = -4x + 8y + 8$$

To find the critical points of f, we set $f_x = 0$ and $f_y = 0$ and solve the resulting system of simultaneous equations

$$6x - 4y = 4$$
$$-4x + 8y = -8$$

Multiplying the first equation by 2 and the second equation by 3, we obtain the equivalent system

$$12x - 8y = 8$$
$$-12x + 24y = -24$$

Adding the two equations gives $16y = -16$, or $y = -1$. We substitute this value for y into either equation in the system to get $x = 0$. Thus, the only critical point of f is the point $(0, -1)$. Next, we apply the Second Derivative Test to determine if the point $(0, -1)$ gives rise to a relative extremum of f:

$$f_{xx} = 6, \quad f_{xy} = -4, \quad f_{yy} = 8$$

so that, in particular,

$$f_{xx}(0, -1) = 6, \quad f_{xy}(0, -1) = -4, \quad \text{and} \quad f_{yy}(0, -1) = 8$$

Therefore,

$$\begin{aligned}\Delta &= f_{xx}(0, -1)f_{yy}(0, -1) - f_{xy}^2(0, -1)\\ &= (6)(8) - (-4)^2\\ &= 32 > 0\end{aligned}$$

Since $\Delta > 0$ and $f_{xx}(0, -1) = 6 > 0$, we conclude that $f(x, y)$ has a relative minimum at the point $(0, -1)$. The value of $f(x, y)$ at the point $(0, -1)$ is given by

$$\begin{aligned}f(0, -1) &= 3(0)^2 - 4(0)(-1) + 4(-1)^2 - 4(0) + 8(-1) + 4\\ &= 0\end{aligned}$$

■

EXAMPLE 14.12 Find the relative extrema of the function

$$f(x, y) = 4y^3 + x^2 - 12y^2 - 36y + 2$$

SOLUTION To find the critical points of f, we set $f_x = 0$ and $f_y = 0$ simultaneously, obtaining

$$f_x = 2x = 0$$
$$f_y = 12y^2 - 24y - 36 = 0$$

The first equation implies that $x = 0$. The second equation implies that

$$y^2 - 2y - 3 = 0$$
$$(y + 1)(y - 3) = 0$$

that is, $y=-1$ or 3. Therefore, there are two critical points of the function f, namely, $(0, -1)$ and $(0, 3)$. We next apply the Second Derivative Test to determine the nature of each of the two critical points. To this end, we compute

$$f_{xx}=2, \quad f_{xy}=0, \quad f_{yy}=24y-24=24(y-1)$$

For the point $(0, -1)$:

$$f_{xx}(0,-1)=2, \quad f_{xy}(0,-1)=0, \quad \text{and} \quad f_{yy}(0,-1)=-48$$

$$\begin{aligned}\Delta &= f_{xx}(0,-1)f_{yy}(0,-1)-f_{xy}^2(0,-1)\\ &=(2)(-48)-0\\ &=-96<0\end{aligned}$$

Since $\Delta<0$, we conclude that the critical point $(0, -1)$ of f does not give rise to either a relative maximum or a relative minimum of f.

For the point $(0, 3)$:

$$f_{xx}(0,3)=2, \quad f_{xy}(0,3)=0, \quad f_{yy}(0,3)=48$$

$$\begin{aligned}\Delta &= f_{xx}(0,3)f_{yy}(0,3)-f_{xy}^2(0,3)\\ &=(2)(48)-0\\ &=96>0\end{aligned}$$

Since $\Delta>0$ and $f_{xx}(0,3)>0$, we conclude that the function f has a relative minimum at the point $(0, 3)$. Furthermore, since

$$\begin{aligned}f(0,3) &= 4(3)^3+(0)^2-12(3)^2-36(3)+2\\ &=-106\end{aligned}$$

we see that the relative minimum of f is the point $(0, 3, -106)$. ■

As in the case of a practical optimization problem involving a function of one variable, the solution to an optimization problem involving a function of several variables calls for finding the *absolute* extremum of the objective function. Determining the absolute extremum of a function of several variables is more difficult than that of merely finding the relative extrema of the function. However, in many situations, the absolute extremum of a function actually coincides with the largest of the relative extrema of the function. We will assume that the problems considered here belong to this category.

EXAMPLE 14.13 The total weekly revenue (in dollars) that the Acrosonic Company realizes in producing and selling its bookshelf loudspeaker systems is given by

$$R(x,y)=-\frac{1}{4}x^2-\frac{3}{8}y^2-\frac{1}{4}xy+300x+240y$$

where x denotes the number of fully assembled units and y denotes the number of kits produced and sold per week (see Example 14.3). The total weekly cost attributable to the production of these loudspeakers is $C(x, y) = 180x + 140y + 5000$ dollars, where x and y have the same meaning as before. Determine the number of assembled units and the number of kits the company should produce per week to maximize the company's profit.

SOLUTION The contribution to the weekly profit of the company stemming from the production and sale of the bookshelf loudspeaker systems is given by

$$\begin{aligned} P(x, y) &= R(x, y) - C(x, y) \\ &= \left(-\frac{1}{4}x^2 - \frac{3}{8}y^2 - \frac{1}{4}xy + 300x + 240y\right) - (180x + 140y + 5{,}000) \\ &= -\frac{1}{4}x^2 - \frac{3}{8}y^2 - \frac{1}{4}xy + 120x + 100y - 5{,}000 \end{aligned}$$

To find the relative maximum of the profit function $P(x, y)$, we first locate the critical point(s) of P. Setting $P_x(x, y)$ and $P_y(x, y)$ equal to zero, we obtain

$$P_x = -\frac{1}{2}x - \frac{1}{4}y + 120 = 0$$

$$P_y = -\frac{3}{4}y - \frac{1}{4}x + 100 = 0$$

Solving the first of the above equations for y yields

$$y = -2x + 480$$

which, upon substitution into the second equation, yields

$$-\frac{3}{4}(-2x + 480) - \frac{1}{4}x + 100 = 0$$

$$6x - 1440 - x + 400 = 0$$

or

$$x = 208$$

We substitute this value of x into the equation $y = -2x + 480$ to get

$$y = 64$$

Therefore, the function P has the sole critical point (208, 64). To show that the point (208, 64) affords a solution to our problem, we use the Second Derivative Test:

$$P_{xx} = -\frac{1}{2}, \quad P_{xy} = -\frac{1}{4}, \quad P_{yy} = -\frac{3}{4}$$

In particular, at the point (208, 64), we have

$$P_{xx}(208, 64) = -\frac{1}{2}, \quad P_{xy}(208, 64) = -\frac{1}{4}, \quad \text{and} \quad P_{yy}(208, 64) = -\frac{3}{4}$$

Therefore,

$$\begin{aligned}\Delta &= P_{xx}(208, 64)P_{yy}(208, 64) - P_{xy}^2(208, 64)\\ &= \left(-\frac{1}{2}\right)\left(-\frac{3}{4}\right) - \left(-\frac{1}{4}\right)^2\\ &= \frac{3}{8} - \frac{1}{16}\\ &= \frac{5}{16} > 0\end{aligned}$$

Since $\Delta > 0$ and $P_{xx}(208, 64) < 0$, the point (208, 64) yields a relative maximum of P. In view of the remark made prior to this example, we conclude that the company can maximize its weekly profit by manufacturing 208 assembled units and 64 kits of their bookshelf loudspeaker systems. The maximum weekly profit realizable from the production and sale of these loudspeaker systems is given by

$$\begin{aligned}P(208, 64) &= -\frac{1}{4}(208)^2 - \frac{3}{8}(64)^2 - \frac{1}{4}(208)(64) + 120(208) + 100(64) - 5000\\ &= 10{,}680 \quad \text{or} \quad \$10{,}680.\end{aligned}$$

■

14.3 EXERCISES

In problems 1 through 16, find the critical point(s) of each of the given functions. Then use the Second Derivative Test to classify the nature of each of these point(s), if possible. Finally, determine the relative extrema of each function.

1. $f(x, y) = 1 - 2x^2 - 3y^2$
2. $f(x, y) = x^2 - xy + y^2 + 1$
3. $f(x, y) = x^2 - y^2 - 2x + 4y + 1$
4. $f(x, y) = 2x^2 + y^2 - 4x + 6y + 3$
5. $f(x, y) = x^2 + 2xy + 2y^2 - 4x + 8y - 1$
6. $f(x, y) = x^2 - 4xy + 2y^2 + 4x + 8y - 1$
7. $f(x, y) = 2x^3 + y^2 - 9x^2 - 4y + 12x - 2$
8. $f(x, y) = 2x^3 + y^2 - 6x^2 - 4y + 12x - 2$
9. $f(x, y) = x^3 + y^2 - 2xy + 7x - 8y + 4$
10. $f(x, y) = 2y^3 - 3y^2 - 12y + 2x^2 - 6x + 2$
11. $f(x, y) = x^3 - 3xy + y^3 - 2$
12. $f(x, y) = e^{x^2 - y^2}$

13. $f(x, y) = e^{x^2+y^2}$ **14.** $f(x, y) = e^{xy}$

15. $f(x, y) = \ln(1 + x^2 + y^2)$ **16.** $f(x, y) = \ln xy - 2x - 4y + 1$

17. The total weekly revenue (in dollars) of the Country Workshop realized in the manufacture and sale of its roll-top desks is given by

$$R(x, y) = -0.2x^2 - 0.25y^2 - 0.2xy + 200x + 160y$$

where x denotes the number of finished units and y denotes the number of unfinished units manufactured and sold per week (see problem 17, Exercise Set 14.1). The total weekly cost attributable to the manufacture of these desks is given by

$$C(x, y) = 100x + 70y + 4000$$

dollars. Determine the number of finished units and the number of unfinished units the company should manufacture per week in order to maximize its profit. What is the maximum profit realizable?

18. The total daily revenue (in dollars) of the Weston Publishing Company realized in the publication and sale of its English language dictionaries is given by

$$R(x, y) = -0.005x^2 - 0.003y^2 - 0.002xy + 20x + 15y$$

where x denotes the number of deluxe copies and y denotes the number of standard copies published and sold daily (see problem 19, Exercise Set 14.1). The total daily cost of publishing these dictionaries is given by $C(x, y) = 6x + 3y + 200$ dollars. Determine how many deluxe copies and how many standard copies the company should publish per day to maximize its profits. What is the maximum profit realizable?

19. An open rectangular box having a volume of 108 cubic inches is to be constructed from a tin sheet. Find the dimensions of such a box if the amount of material used in its construction is to be minimal. *Hint*: Let the dimensions of the box be x'' by y'' by z''. Then $xyz = 108$ and the amount of material used is given by $S = xy + 2yz + 2xz$. Show that $S = f(x, y) = xy + (216/x) + (216/y)$. Minimize $f(x, y)$.

20. Postal regulations specify that a parcel sent by parcel post may have a length and girth combined not exceeding 100 inches. Find the dimensions of a rectangular package having the greatest possible volume under these regulations. *Hint*: Let the dimensions of the box be x'' by y'' by z'' (see the following illustration). Then, $2x + 2z + y = 100$, and the volume $V = xyz$. Show that $V = f(x, z) = 100xz - 2x^2z - 2xz^2$. Maximize $f(x, z)$.

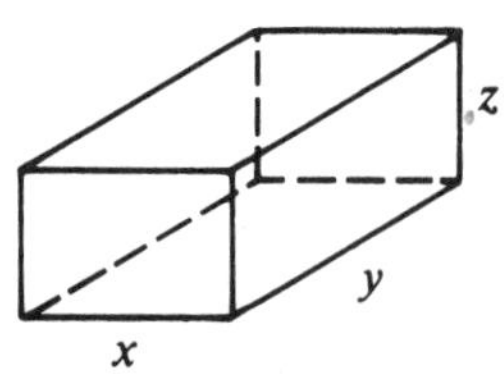

14.4

Constrained Maxima and Minima and the Method of Lagrange Multipliers

unconstrained relative extremum

In Section 14.3 we studied the problem of determining the relative extrema of a function $f(x, y)$ without any restrictions placed on the independent variables x and y, save, of course, the requirement that the point (x, y) lies in the domain of f. Such a relative extremum of a function f is accordingly referred to as an *unconstrained relative extremum* of f. However, in many practical optimization problems, we must maximize or minimize an objective function in which the independent variables are subjected to certain further constraints. In fact, a typical linear programming problem, as shown in Chapter 4, involves the optimization of a (linear) objective function in which the independent variables are subjected to constraints that take the form of (linear) inequalities and sometimes (linear) equations.

constrained relative extremum

In this section we discuss a powerful method for determining the relative extrema of a function $f(x, y)$ whose independent variables x and y are required to satisfy one or more constraints of the form $g(x, y) = 0$. Such a relative extremum of a function f is called a *constrained relative extremum* of f. We can see the difference between an unconstrained extremum of a function $f(x, y)$ of two variables and a constrained extremum of f, where the independent variables x and y are subjected to a constraint of the form $g(x, y) = 0$, by considering the geometry of the two cases. Figure 14.13(a) depicts the graph of a function $f(x, y)$, which has an unconstrained relative minimum at the point $(0, 0, 0)$. However, when the independent variables x and y are subjected to an equality constraint of the form $g(x, y) = 0$, the points (x, y, z) that satisfy both $z = f(x, y)$ and the constraint equation $g(x, y) = 0$ lie on a curve C. Therefore the constrained relative minimum of f must also lie on C (see Figure 14.13 part b).

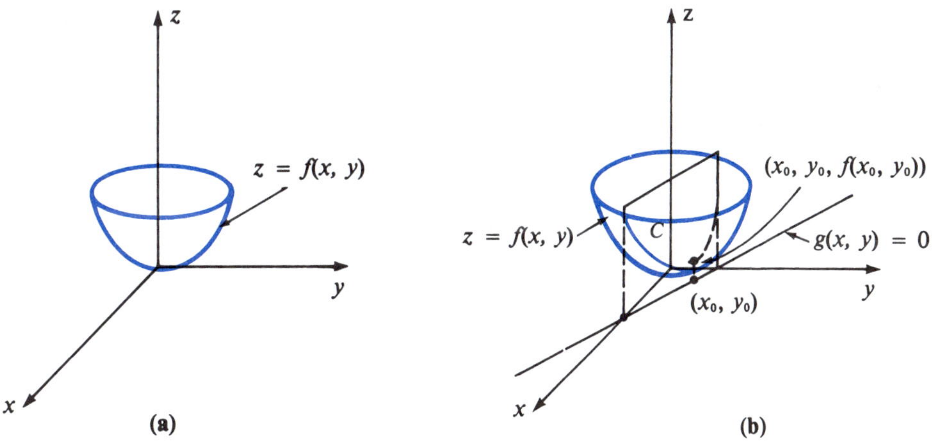

Figure 14.13

Our first example on the determination of the constrained extremum of a function $f(x, y)$ involves an equality constraint $g(x, y) = 0$ in which we easily solve for the variable y explicitly in terms of x. In this case, we may apply the technique used in the solution of Example 11.34, Section 11.7, to solve the problem.

EXAMPLE 14.14 Find the relative minimum of the function $f(x, y) = 2x^2 + y^2$ subject to the constraint $g(x, y) = x + y - 1 = 0$.

SOLUTION Solving the constraint equation for y explicitly in terms of x, we obtain $y = -x + 1$. Substituting this value of y into the objective function $f(x, y) = 2x^2 + y^2$ results in a function of x,

$$\begin{aligned} h(x) &= 2x^2 + (-x+1)^2 \\ &= 3x^2 - 2x + 1 \end{aligned}$$

The function h describes the curve C lying on the graph of f on which the (constrained) relative minimum of f occurs. To find this point, use the technique developed in Chapter 11 to determine the relative extrema of a function of one variable:

$$\begin{aligned} h'(x) &= 6x - 2 \\ &= 2(3x - 1) \end{aligned}$$

Setting $h'(x) = 0$ gives $x = 1/3$ as the sole critical point of the function h. Next, we find

$$h''(x) = 6$$

and, in particular,

$$h''\left(\frac{1}{3}\right) = 6 > 0$$

so that, by the Second Derivative Test, the point $x = 1/3$ gives rise to a relative minimum of h. Substitute this value of x into the constraint equation $x + y - 1 = 0$ to get $y = 2/3$. Thus, the point $(1/3, 2/3)$ gives rise to the required (constrained) relative minimum of f. Since

$$\begin{aligned} f\left(\frac{1}{3}, \frac{2}{3}\right) &= 2\left(\frac{1}{3}\right)^2 + \left(\frac{2}{3}\right)^2 \\ &= \frac{2}{3} \end{aligned}$$

the required constrained relative minimum of f is the point $(1/3, 2/3, 2/3)$. It may be shown that the point $(1/3, 2/3, 2/3)$ is in fact a constrained absolute minimum of f (see Figure 14.14).

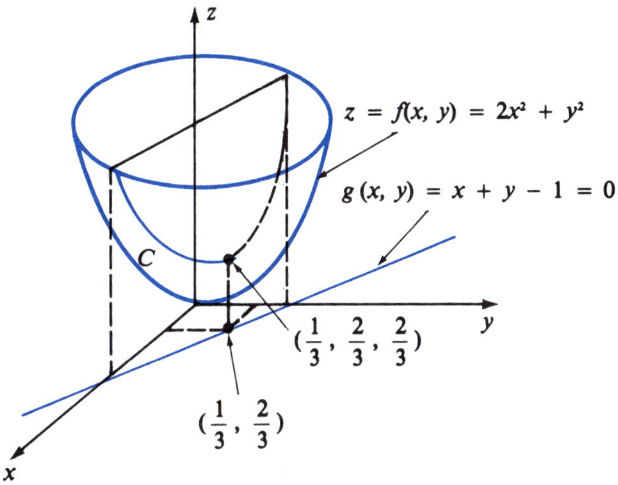

Figure 14.14

The major drawback of the technique used in Example 14.14 is that it relies on our ability to solve the constraint equation $g(x, y)=0$ for y explicitly in terms of x. This, of course, is not always an easy task. Moreover, even in the case where we can solve the constraint equation $g(x, y)=0$ for y explicitly in terms of x, the resulting function of one variable that is to be optimized may turn out to be unnecessarily complicated. Fortunately, an easier method of solution exists. This method, called the Method of Lagrange Multipliers (Joseph Lagrange, 1736–1813), is as follows:

The Method of Lagrange Multipliers

To find the relative extremum of the objective function $f(x, y)$ subject to the constraint $g(x, y)=0$

1. form an auxiliary function

$$F(x, y, \lambda)=f(x, y)+\lambda g(x, y)$$

Lagrangian function

called the *Lagrangian function* (the variable λ is called the *Lagrange multiplier*), and

2. determine the critical points of F; that is, solve the system comprising the equations

$$F_x=0$$
$$F_y=0$$
and
$$F_\lambda=0$$

Then each critical point (x, y) of F found in Step 2 is a candidate for a (constrained) relative maximum or relative minimum of f.

Let us resolve Example 14.14 using the Method of Lagrange Multipliers.

EXAMPLE 14.15 Find the relative minimum of the function $f(x, y)=2x^2+y^2$ subject to the constraint $x+y=1$ using the Method of Lagrange Multipliers.

SOLUTION Write the constraint equation $x+y=1$ in the form $g(x, y)=x+y-1=0$. Then form the Lagrangian function

$$\begin{aligned} F(x, y, \lambda) &= f(x, y)+\lambda g(x, y) \\ &= 2x^2+y^2+\lambda(x+y-1) \end{aligned}$$

To find the critical point(s) of the function F, solve the system comprising the equations

$$\begin{aligned} F_x &= 4x+\lambda=0 \\ F_y &= 2y+\lambda=0 \\ F_\lambda &= x+y-1=0 \end{aligned}$$

Solving the first and the second of the above system of equations for x and y in terms of λ, we obtain

$$x=-\frac{1}{4}\lambda, \qquad y=-\frac{1}{2}\lambda$$

which, upon substitution into the third equation, yields

$$-\frac{1}{4}\lambda-\frac{1}{2}\lambda-1=0 \quad \text{or} \quad \lambda=-\frac{4}{3}$$

Therefore, $x=1/3$ and $y=2/3$ which gives the point $(1/3, 2/3)$ as the sole critical point of F. Using the Second Derivative Test we can show that the point $(1/3, 2/3)$ affords a relative minimum to the function F and therefore also affords a constrained relative minimum to the function f, in agreement with the result obtained earlier. ■

EXAMPLE 14.16 (Refer to Example 14.3.) The total weekly profit (in dollars) of the Acrosonic Company realized in producing and selling its bookshelf loudspeaker systems is given by the profit function

$$P(x, y)=-\frac{1}{4}x^2-\frac{3}{8}y^2-\frac{1}{4}xy+120x+100y-5000$$

where x denotes the number of fully assembled units and y denotes the number of kits produced and sold per week. The company's management decided that production of these loudspeaker systems should be restricted to a total of exactly 230 units per week. Under this condition, how many fully assembled units and how many kits should be produced per week to maximize the weekly profit of the company?

SOLUTION The problem is equivalent to the problem of maximizing the function

$$P(x, y) = -\frac{1}{4}x^2 - \frac{3}{8}y^2 - \frac{1}{4}xy + 120x + 100y - 5000$$

subject to the constraint

$$g(x, y) = x + y - 230 = 0$$

The Lagrangian function is

$$\begin{aligned} F(x, y, \lambda) &= P(x, y) + \lambda g(x, y) \\ &= -\frac{1}{4}x^2 - \frac{3}{8}y^2 - \frac{1}{4}xy + 120x + 100y - 5000 + \lambda(x + y - 230) \end{aligned}$$

To find the critical point(s) of F, solve the following system of equations:

$$F_x = -\frac{1}{2}x - \frac{1}{4}y + 120 + \lambda = 0$$

$$F_y = -\frac{3}{4}y - \frac{1}{4}x + 100 + \lambda = 0$$

$$F_\lambda = x + y - 230 = 0$$

Solving the first of the above system of equations for λ, we obtain

$$\lambda = \frac{1}{2}x + \frac{1}{4}y - 120$$

which, upon substitution into the second equation, yields

$$-\frac{3}{4}y - \frac{1}{4}x + 100 + \frac{1}{2}x + \frac{1}{4}y - 120 = 0$$

or

$$-\frac{1}{2}y + \frac{1}{4}x - 20 = 0$$

Solving the last equation for y gives

$$y = \frac{1}{2}x - 40$$

When we substitute this value of y into the third equation of the system, we have

$$x + \frac{1}{2}x - 40 - 230 = 0$$

or

$$x = 180$$

The corresponding value of y is $(1/2)(180)-40$ or 50. Thus, the required constrained relative minimum of P occurs at the point (180, 50). Again, we can show that the point (180, 50) in fact yields a constrained absolute maximum for P. Thus, the weekly profit of the company is maximized by producing 180 assembled and 50 kit versions of their bookshelf loudspeaker systems. The maximum weekly profit realizable is given by

$$P(180, 50) = -\frac{1}{4}(180)^2 - \frac{3}{8}(50)^2 - \frac{1}{4}(180)(50) + 120(180) + 100(50) - 5000$$

$$= 10{,}312.5 \quad \text{or} \quad \$10{,}312.50$$

14.4 EXERCISES

In problems 1 through 8, use the Method of Lagrange Multipliers to optimize each of the given functions subject to a given constraint.

1. Minimize the function $f(x, y) = x^2 + 3y^2$ subject to the constraint $x + y - 1 = 0$.

2. Maximize the function $f(x, y) = 2x + 3y - x^2 - y^2$ subject to the constraint $x + 2y = 9$.

3. Minimize the function $f(x, y) = x^2 + y^2 - xy$ subject to the constraint $x + 2y - 14 = 0$.

4. Maximize the function $f(x, y) = x + 5y - 2xy - x^2 - 2y^2$ subject to the constraint $2x + y = 4$.

5. Minimize the function $f(x, y) = x^2 + 4y^2$ subject to the constraint $xy = 1$.

6. Maximize the function $f(x, y) = xy$ subject to the constraint $2x + 3y - 6 = 0$.

****7.*** Find the maximum and minimum values of the function $f(x, y) = xy$ subject to the constraint $x^2 + y^2 = 16$.

****8.*** Find the maximum and minimum values of the function $f(x, y) = e^{xy}$ subject to the constraint $x^2 + y^2 = 8$.

9. The Country Workshop's total weekly profit (in dollars) realized for manufacturing and selling its roll-top desks is given by the profit function

$$P(x, y) = -0.2x^2 - 0.25y^2 - 0.2xy + 100x + 90y - 4000$$

where x stands for the number of finished units and y denotes the number of unfinished units manufactured and sold per week. The company's management decided to restrict the manufacture of these desks to a total of exactly 200 units per week. How many finished and how many unfinished units should be manufactured per week to maximize the company's weekly profit?

10. The Weston Publishing Company's total daily profit (in dollars) realized in the publication and sale of its dictionaries is given by the profit function

$$P(x, y) = -0.005x^2 - 0.003y^2 - 0.002xy + 14x + 12y - 200$$

where x stands for the number of deluxe edition copies and y denotes the number of standard edition copies sold daily. The management decided that publication of these dictionaries should be restricted to a total of exactly 400 copies per day. How many deluxe copies and how many standard copies should be published per day to maximize the daily profit of the company?

11. The Ross–Simons Company has a monthly advertising budget of \$60,000. Their marketing department estimates that if they spend x dollars on advertising in newspapers and y dollars on television advertising, then the monthly sales will be given by $z = f(x, y) = 90x^{1/4}y^{3/4}$ dollars. Determine how much money the company should spend on newspaper advertisements and on television advertisements per month to maximize its monthly sales.

12. The management of UNICO Department Store decided to enclose an 800-ft.^{2} area outside their building to display potted plants. The enclosed area will be a rectangle, a side of which is provided by the external wall of the store. Two sides of the enclosure will be erected from pine board while the fourth side will be made from galvanized steel fencing material. If the pine board fencing costs \$6 per running foot and the steel fencing costs \$3 per running foot, determine the dimensions of the enclosure that can be erected at the lowest cost in materials.

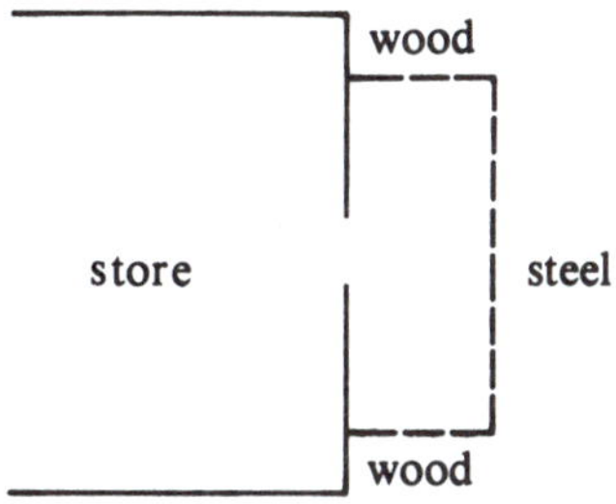

13. The Betty Moore Company requires containers with a capacity of 64 cubic inches for its corned beef hash. The containers are right-circular cylinders to be made of a tin alloy. Find the radius and height of the container that can be made at a minimum cost if the metal for the side and bottom costs 4 cents per square inch and the metal for the pull-off lid costs 2 cents per square inch. *Hint*: Let the radius and height of the container be r and h inches, respectively. Then, the volume of the container is $\pi r^2 h = 64$, and the cost is given by $C(r, h) = 8\pi rh + 6\pi r^2$.

14 Chapter Review

EXERCISES

1. Let $f(x, y) = xy/(x^2 + y^2)$. Compute $f(0, 1)$, $f(1, 0)$, and $f(1, 1)$. Does $f(0, 0)$ exist?

2. Let $h(x, y, z) = xy\,e^z + (x/y)$. Compute $h(1, 1, 0)$, $h(-1, 1, 1)$, and $h(1, -1, 1)$.

3. Find the domain of the function

$$f(u, v) = \frac{\sqrt{u}}{u - v}$$

4. Find the domain of the function

$$f(x, y, z) = \frac{xy\sqrt{z}}{(1-x)(1-y)(1-z)}$$

In problems 5 through 10 compute the first partial derivatives of each of the following functions.

5. $f(x, y) = x^2y^3 + 3xy^2 + \dfrac{x}{y}$

6. $f(u, v) = \sqrt{uv^2 - 2u}$

7. $g(x, y) = \dfrac{xy}{x^2 + y^2}$

8. $h(x, y) = (2xy + 3y^2)^5$

9. $f(x, y) = (x^2 + y^2)\, e^{x^2+y^2}$

10. $f(x, y) = \ln\left(1 + \dfrac{x^2}{y^2}\right)$

In problems 11 through 15, compute the second-order partial derivatives of each of the following functions.

11. $f(x, y) = x^3 - 2x^2y + y^2 + x - 2y$

12. $f(x, y) = (2x^2 + 3y^2)^3$

13. $g(x, y) = e^{x^2+y^2}$

14. $h(s, t) = \ln\left(\dfrac{s}{t}\right)$

15. Let $f(x, y, z) = x^3y^2z + xy^2z + 3xy - 4z$. Compute $f_x(1, 1, 0)$, $f_y(1, 1, 0)$, and $f_z(1, 1, 0)$, and interpret your results.

In problems 16 through 20, find the critical point(s) of each of the given functions. Then use the Second Derivative Test to classify the nature of each of these points, if possible. Finally, determine the relative extrema of each function.

16. $f(x, y) = 2x^2 + y^2 - 8x - 6y + 4$

17. $f(x, y) = x^2 + 3xy + y^2 - 10x - 20y + 12$

18. $f(x, y) = x^3 + y^2 - 4xy + 17x - 10y + 8$

19. $f(x, y) = e^{2x^2+y^2}$

20. $f(x, y) = \ln(x^2 + y^2 - 2x - 2y + 4)$

In problems 21 through 24 use the Method of Lagrange Multipliers to optimize each of the given functions subject to a given constraint.

21. Maximize the function $f(x, y) = -3x^2 - y^2 + 2xy$ subject to the constraint $2x + y = 4$.

22. Minimize the function $f(x, y) = 2x^2 + 3y^2 - 6xy + 4x - 9y + 10$ subject to the constraint $x + y = 1$.

23. Find the maximum and minimum of the function $f(x, y) = 2x - 3y + 1$ subject to the constraint $2x^2 + 3y^2 - 125 = 0$.

24. Find the maximum and minimum of the function $f(x, y) = e^{x-y}$ subject to the constraint $x^2 + y^2 = 1$.

25. A division of Ditton Industries makes a 16-speed and a 10-speed electric blender. The company's management estimates that x units of the 16-speed model are demanded daily and y units of the 10-speed model are demanded daily when the unit prices are

$$p = 80 - 0.02x - 0.1y$$

and

$$q = 60 - 0.1x - 0.05y$$

dollars, respectively.

(***a***) Find the daily total revenue function $R(x, y)$.

(***b***) Find the domain of the function R.

(***c***) Compute $R(100, 300)$, and interpret your result.

26. The Odyssey Travel Agency's monthly revenue (in thousands of dollars) depends on the amount of money x spent on advertising per month and the number of agents y in its employ in accordance with the rule

$$R(x, y) = -x^2 - 0.5y^2 + xy + 8x + 3y + 20$$

Determine the amount of money the agency should spend per month and the number of agents it should have in its employ in order to maximize its monthly revenue.

27. The owner of the Rancho Grande wants to enclose a rectangular piece of grazing land along the straight portion of a river and then subdivide it using a fence running parallel to the sides. No fencing is required along the river. If the material for the sides cost \$3 per running yard and the material for the divider costs \$2 per running yard, what will the dimensions of a 303,750-yard pasture be if the cost of fencing material is kept to a minimum?

28. The production of Q units of a commodity is related to the amount of labor x and the amount of capital y (in suitable units) expended by the equation

$$Q = f(x, y) = x^{3/4}y^{1/4}$$

If an expenditure of 100 units is available for production, how should it be apportioned between labor and capital so that Q is maximized? *Hint*: Use the Method of Lagrange Multipliers to maximize the function Q subject to the constraint $x + y + 100$.

I

REVIEW OF ALGEBRA

In this appendix, we first recall the definition and properties of the real number system. Then we review the techniques of algebra, which are normally covered in an elementary algebra course. The topics covered in this review were chosen because of their relevance to the study of calculus.

We suggest that the reader make a cursory examination of each of the topics and only study those with which he or she does not feel completely at ease.

A.1

The System of Real Numbers

In this appendix we shall briefly review the *system of real numbers*. The system comprises a set of objects called real numbers together with two operations, called addition and multiplication, which enable us to combine two or more real numbers to obtain other real numbers. These operations are subjected to certain rules which we shall state after first recalling the set of real numbers.

The set of real numbers may be constructed from the set of *natural* (also called *counting*) *numbers*

$$N = \{1, 2, 3, \ldots\}$$

by adjoining other objects (numbers) to it. Thus, the set

$$W = \{0, 1, 2, 3, \ldots\}$$

obtained by adjoining the single number 0 to N is called the set of *whole numbers*. By adjoining the *negatives* of the numbers 1, 2, 3, . . . to the set W of whole numbers we obtain the set of *integers*

$$I = \{\ldots, -3, -2, -1, 0, 1, 2, 3, \ldots\}$$

Next, consider the set

$$Ra = \left\{ \frac{a}{b} \middle| a \text{ and } b \text{ are integers with } b \neq 0 \right\}$$

Now, the set I of integers is contained in the set Ra of *rational numbers*. To see this, observe that each integer may be written in the form a/b with $b = 1$ and thus qualifies as a member of the set Ra. The converse, however, is false for the rational numbers (fractions) such as

$$\frac{1}{2}, \frac{23}{25}, \text{ and so on}$$

are clearly not integers.

The sets N, W, I, and Ra constructed thus far have

$$N \subset W \subset I \subset Ra$$

that is, N is a proper subset of W; W is a proper subset of I, and so on.

Finally, consider the set Ir of all numbers that cannot be expressed in the form a/b where a, b are integers ($b \neq 0$). The members of this set, called the set of *irrational numbers*, include $\sqrt{2}$, $\sqrt{3}$, π, and so on. The set

$$R = Ra \cup Ir$$

that is, the set comprising all rational numbers as well as irrational numbers, is called the set of *real numbers* (see Figure A.1).

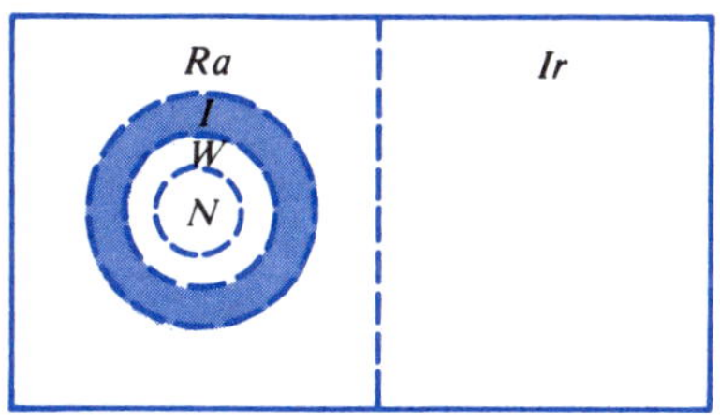

Figure A.1

We recall the following important representation of real numbers: Every real number has a decimal representation; a rational number has a representation in terms of a repeated decimal. For example,

$$\frac{1}{7} = 0.142857142857142857\ldots$$ (Note that the block of integers 142857 repeats.)

On the other hand, the irrational number $\sqrt{2}$ has a representation in terms of a nonrepeating decimal, thus

$$\sqrt{2} = 1.41428\ldots$$

As mentioned earlier, any two real numbers may be combined to obtain another real number. The operation of *addition*, written +, enables us to combine any two numbers a and b to obtain their sum, denoted by $a+b$. Another operation, called *multiplication*, and written $\cdot$, enables us to combine any two real numbers a and b to form their product, the number $a \cdot b$ or written more simply ab. These two operations are subjected to the following rules of operation: Given any three real numbers a, b, and c, we have

I Under Addition

1.	$a+b=b+a$	(Commutative Law of Addition)
2.	$a+(b+c)=(a+b)+c$	(Associative Law of Addition)
3.	$a+0=a$	(Identity Law of Addition)
4.	$a+(-a)=0$	(Inverse Law of Addition)

II Under Multiplication

1.	$ab=ba$	(Commutative Law of Multiplication)
2.	$a(bc)=(ab)c$	(Associative Law of Multiplication)
3.	$a\cdot 1=a$	(Identity Law of Multiplication)
4.	$a(1/a)=1 \quad (a\neq 0)$	(Inverse Law of Multiplication)

III Under Addition and Multiplication

1.	$a(b+c)=ab+ac$	(Distributive Law for Addition and Multiplication)

A.2

Exponents and Radicals

The rules defining the exponential expression a^n when $a>0$ for all rational values of n are given in Table 1.

The first three definitions are also valid for negative values of a, whereas the fourth definition is only valid for negative values of a when n is odd. Thus,

$$(-8)^{1/3} = \sqrt[3]{-8} = -2 \qquad (n \text{ is odd})$$

$$(-8)^{1/2} \text{ has no real root} \qquad (n \text{ is even})$$

The five laws of exponents are listed in Table 2. These laws are valid for any real numbers a and b and for all rational as well as integral values of m and n. The use of these laws in algebraic computations is illustrated in the following examples.

Definition of a^n $(a>0)$	Example
1. **Integer Exponent:** If n is a positive integer, then $a^n = a \cdot a \cdot a \ldots a$, n factors of a	$2^5 = 2 \cdot 2 \cdot 2 \cdot 2 \cdot 2 = 32$, 5 factors
2. **Zero Exponent:** If n is equal to zero, then $a^0 = 1$; 0^0 is not defined	$7^0 = 1$
3. **Negative Exponent:** If n is a positive integer, then $a^{-n} = \dfrac{1}{a^n}$ $(a \neq 0)$	$6^{-2} = \dfrac{1}{6^2} = \dfrac{1}{36}$
4. **Fractional Exponent:** (a) If n is a positive integer, then $a^{1/n}$ or $\sqrt[n]{a}$ denotes the **nth root** of a	$16^{1/2} = \sqrt{16} = 4$; $27^{1/3} = \sqrt[3]{27} = 3$
(b) If m and n are positive integers then $a^{m/n} = \sqrt[n]{a^m} = (\sqrt[n]{a})^m$	$8^{2/3} = (\sqrt[3]{8})^2 = 4$
(c) If m and n are positive integers, then $a^{-m/n} = \dfrac{1}{a^{m/n}}$ $(a \neq 0)$	$9^{-3/2} = \dfrac{1}{9^{3/2}} = \dfrac{1}{27}$

Table 1

Law	Example
1. $a^m \cdot a^n = a^{m+n}$	$x^2 \cdot x^3 = x^{2+3} = x^5$
2. $\dfrac{a^m}{a^n} = a^{m-n}$ $(a \neq 0)$	$\dfrac{x^7}{x^4} = x^{7-4} = x^3$
3. $(a^m)^n = a^{m \cdot n}$	$(x^4)^3 = x^{4 \cdot 3} = x^{12}$
4. $(ab)^n = a^n \cdot b^n$	$(2x)^4 = 2^4 \cdot x^4 = 16x^4$
5. $\left(\dfrac{a}{b}\right)^n = \dfrac{a^n}{b^n}$ $(a \neq 0)$	$\left(\dfrac{x}{2}\right)^3 = \dfrac{x^3}{2^3} = \dfrac{x^3}{8}$

Table 2

EXAMPLE 1 Simplify the given expression:

(a) $(3x^2)(4x^3)$ **(b)** $\dfrac{16^{5/4}}{16^{1/2}}$ **(c)** $(6^{2/3})^3$ **(d)** $(x^3y^{-2})^{-2}$ **(e)** $\left(\dfrac{y^{3/2}}{x^{1/4}}\right)^{-2}$

SOLUTION **(a)** $(3x^2)(4x^3) = 12x^{2+3} = 12x^5$

(b) $\dfrac{16^{5/4}}{16^{1/2}} = 16^{5/4-1/2} = 16^{3/4} = (\sqrt[4]{16})^3 = 8$

(c) $(6^{2/3})^3 = 6^{2/3\cdot 3} = 6^{6/3} = 6^2 = 36$

(d) $(x^3y^{-2})^{-2} = (x^3)^{-2}(y^{-2})^{-2} = x^{(3)(-2)}y^{((-2)(-2)} = x^{-6}y^4 = \dfrac{y^4}{x^6}$

(e) $\left(\dfrac{y^{3/2}}{x^{1/4}}\right)^{-2} = \dfrac{y^{(3/2)(-2)}}{x^{(1/4)(-2)}} = \dfrac{y^{-3}}{x^{-1/2}} = \dfrac{\sqrt{x}}{y^3}$ ■

EXAMPLE 2 Simplify the given expression:

(a) $\sqrt[4]{16x^4y^8}$ **(b)** $\sqrt{12m^3n}\cdot\sqrt{3m^5n}$ **(c)** $\dfrac{\sqrt[3]{-27x^6}}{\sqrt[3]{8y^3}}$ **(d)** $\sqrt[3]{24x^5y^4}$

SOLUTION **(a)** $\sqrt[4]{16x^4y^8} = (16x^4y^8)^{1/4} = 16^{1/4}\cdot x^{4/4}\cdot y^{8/4} = 2xy^2$

(b) $\sqrt{12m^3n}\cdot\sqrt{3m^5n} = \sqrt{36m^8n^2} = (36m^8n^2)^{1/2} = 36^{1/2}\cdot m^{8/2}\cdot n^{2/2} = 6m^4n$

(c) $\dfrac{\sqrt[3]{-27x^6}}{\sqrt[3]{8y^3}} = \dfrac{(-27x^6)^{1/3}}{(8y^3)^{1/3}} = \dfrac{-27^{1/3}x^{6/3}}{8^{1/3}y^{3/3}} = -\dfrac{3x^2}{2y}$

(d) $\sqrt[3]{24x^5y^4} = (24x^5y^4)^{1/3} = (2^3)^{1/3}\cdot 3^{1/3}\cdot x^{5/3}\cdot y^{4/3} = 2\cdot 3^{1/3}\cdot x\cdot x^{2/3}\cdot y\cdot y^{1/3}$
$= 2xy\sqrt[3]{3x^2y}$ ■

When simplifying radicals it is sometimes necessary to rationalize the denominator, a process in which radicals are eliminated from the denominator of an algebraic expression. This process is illustrated in the next example.

EXAMPLE 3 Rationalize the denominator:

(a) $\dfrac{3x}{2\sqrt{x}}$ **(b)** $\sqrt[3]{\dfrac{x}{y}}$

SOLUTION **(a)** $\dfrac{3x}{2\sqrt{x}} = \dfrac{3x}{2\sqrt{x}}\cdot\dfrac{\sqrt{x}}{\sqrt{x}} = \dfrac{3x\sqrt{x}}{2\sqrt{x^2}} = \dfrac{3x\sqrt{x}}{2x} = \dfrac{3}{2}\sqrt{x}$

(b) $\sqrt[3]{\dfrac{x}{y}} = \sqrt[3]{\dfrac{x}{y}}\cdot\sqrt[3]{\dfrac{y^2}{y^2}} = \dfrac{\sqrt[3]{xy^2}}{\sqrt[3]{y^3}} = \dfrac{\sqrt[3]{xy^2}}{y}$ ■

A.2 EXERCISES

In problems 1 through 6, evaluate each of the given expressions.

1. $27^{2/3}$ **2.** $8^{-4/3}$ **3.** $\left(\dfrac{9}{4}\right)^{3/2}$ **4.** $(7^{1/2})^4$

5. $9^{2/3}\div 9^{1/6}$ **6.** $\left(\left(\dfrac{1}{8}\right)^{1/3}\right)^{-2}$ **7.** $\dfrac{\sqrt{32}}{\sqrt{8}}$ **8.** $\sqrt[3]{\dfrac{-8}{27}}$

In problems 9 through 22, simplify each of the given expressions using positive exponents only.

9. $(2x^3)(-4x^{-2})$ **10.** $(x^2y^{-3})(x^{-5}y^3)$ **11.** $\dfrac{6a^{-5}}{3a^{-3}}$

12. $\dfrac{5x^6y^3}{2x^2y^7}$ *13.* $y^{-3/2}y^{5/3}$ *14.* $(2x^3y^2)^3$

15. $(a^3b^{-2}c^2)^{-2}$ *16.* $\dfrac{x^{3/4}}{x^{-1/4}}$ *17.* $\left(\dfrac{x^3y^2}{z^2}\right)^2$

18. $\left(\dfrac{3x^5}{2x^2}\right)^3$ *19.* $\left(\dfrac{y^{4/3}}{x^{-1/2}}\right)^{-3}$ *20.* $\dfrac{a^6b^{-5}}{(a^3b^{-2})^{-3}}$

21. $\dfrac{5^0}{(2^{-3}x^{-3}y^2)^2}$ *22.* $\left[\left(\dfrac{x}{y}\right)^{-1}\right]^{-3}$

In problems 21 through 26, simplify each of the given expressions.

23. $\sqrt[3]{8x^6y^3}$ *24.* $\dfrac{3\sqrt{x}}{2x^{5/2}}$ *25.* $\sqrt{8x^2y^3}\cdot\sqrt{18x^4y^5}$

26. $\dfrac{\sqrt{36x^8}}{\sqrt{25y^6}}$ *27.* $\sqrt[6]{64x^8y^3}$ *28.* $\sqrt[3]{-32x^6y^4}$

In problems 29 through 32, rationalize the denominators of each of the given expressions.

29. $\dfrac{3}{2\sqrt{x}}$ *30.* $\dfrac{5x^2}{\sqrt{3x}}$ *31.* $\sqrt{\dfrac{2x}{y}}$ *32.* $\sqrt[3]{\dfrac{5x}{2y}}$

A.3

Addition, Subtraction and Multiplication of Polynomials

An algebraic expression involving one term is called a *monomial.* For example,

$$5,\ x,\ 8y,\ 7x^2,\ 6x^3y \quad \text{and} \quad 3x^2y^3z$$

are all monomials. The monomial $8y$ is the product of two factors, the constant 8 and the *variable* y. The numerical factor of a monomial such as the number 8 in the monomial $8y$, is called the *coefficient* of the variable y. The *degree of a monomial* is the sum of the exponents of the variables. Thus, the degree of 5 is 0 (no variable), the degree of $4x^2$ in the variable x is 2, and the degree of $6x^2yz$ *in the variables* x, y *and* z is 4. The degree of the monomial $6x^2yz$ *in the variable* x alone is 2.

A *polynomial* is a monomial or the sum of two or more monomials. For example,

$$x^2+4x+4,\ x^3+5,\ x^4+3x^2+3,\ x^2y+xy+y$$

are all polynomials. A polynomial consisting of 2 terms is called a *binomial* and a polynomial consisting of 3 terms is called a *trinomial.* The *degree of a polynomial* is the degree of the term of the highest degree without a zero coefficient. For example the polynomial x^4-3x^3+2x+1 is of degree 4 in x and the polynomial $3x^2+3xy+2y^2$ is of degree 2 in x.

Addition and Subtraction of Polynomials

Constant terms and terms having the same variable factor are called *like* or *similar* terms. Like terms involving variables may be combined by adding or subtracting their numerical coefficients. For example,

$$3x + 7x = 10x \quad \text{and} \quad \frac{1}{2}xy + 3xy = \frac{7}{2}xy$$

To add or subtract two or more polynomials, first remove the parenthesis and then combine like terms. The resulting expression is written in order of decreasing degree from left to right. The justification for this procedure is based on the properties of real numbers discussed earlier.

EXAMPLE 4 (**a**) $(4x^2+3x-5)+(3x^2-2x+6) = 4x^2+3x-5+3x^2-2x+6$
$= 7x^2+x+1$

(**b**) $(5x^2+5x-8)-(3x^2-4x-6) = 5x^2+5x-8-3x^2+4x+6$
$= 2x^2+9x-2$

(**c**) $2t^3-\{t^2-[t-(2t-1)]+4\} = 2t^3-\{t^2-[t-2t+1]+4\}$
$= 2t^3-\{t^2-[-t+1]+4\}$
$= 2t^3-\{t^2+t-1+4\}$
$= 2t^3-\{t^2+t+3\}$
$= 2t^3-t^2-t-3$ ■

A polynomial is said to be *simplified* if none of its terms are similar. Observe that when the polynomial in part (**c**) of the preceding example was simplified the innermost grouping symbols were removed first; that is, the parenthesis ( ) were removed first, the brackets [ ] second, and then the braces { }.

Multiplication of Polynomials

When two polynomials are multiplied, each term of one polynomial is multiplied by each term of the other. The resulting product is then expressed in simplified form.

EXAMPLE 5 Expand the expression: $(x+3)(x-2)$

SOLUTION

$$\begin{aligned}(x+3)(x-2) &= x(x-2)+3(x-2)\\ &= x^2-2x+3x-6\\ &= x^2+x-6\end{aligned}$$ ■

The above procedure is based on the properties of the real number system. In particular, the Distributive Property

$$a \cdot (b+c) = ab+ac$$

is used to justify the step

$$x \cdot (x-2) = x^2-2x$$

EXAMPLE 6 Perform the indicated multiplication:

(**a**) $(3x-4)(3x^2-2x+3)$ (**b**) $(2x-y)(x+y^2)$ (**c**) $(t-1)(t+2)(t+3)$

SOLUTION (a)
$$\begin{aligned}(3x-4)(3x^2-2x+3) &= 3x(3x^2-2x+3)-4(3x^2-2x+3)\\ &= 9x^3-6x^2+9x-12x^2+8x-12\\ &= 9x^3-18x^2+17x-12\end{aligned}$$

(b)
$$\begin{aligned}(2x-y)(x+y^2) &= 2x(x+y^2)-y(x+y^2)\\ &= 2x^2+2xy^2-yx-y^3\\ &= 2x^2+2xy^2-xy-y^3\end{aligned}$$

(c)
$$\begin{aligned}(t-1)(t+2)(t+3) &= (t-1)[(t+2)(t+3)]\\ &= (t-1)[t(t+3)+2(t+3)]\\ &= (t-1)[t^2+3t+2t+6]\\ &= (t-1)(t^2+5t+6)\\ &= t(t^2+5t+6)+(-1)(t^2+5t+6)\\ &= t^3+5t^2+6t-t^2-5t-6\\ &= t^3+4t^2+t-6\end{aligned}$$

■

Certain product formulas that are frequently used in algebraic computations are given in Table 3.

Formula	Example
1. $(a+b)^2=a^2+2ab+b^2$	$(2x+3y)^2=(2x)^2+2(2x)(3y)+(3y)^2$ $=4x^2+12xy+9y^2$
2. $(a-b)^2=a^2-2ab+b^2$	$(4x-2y)^2=(4x)^2-2(4x)(2y)+(2y)^2$ $=16x^2-16xy+4y^2$
3. $(a+b)(a-b)=a^2-b^2$	$(2x+y)(2x-y)=(2x)^2-(y)^2$ $=4x^2-y^2$

Table 3

A.3 EXERCISES

In problems 1 through 20, perform the indicated operation and simplify each of the given expressions.

1. $(7x^2-2x+5)+(2x^2+5x-4)$

2. $(3x^2+5xy+2y)+(4-3xy-2x^2)$

3. $(5y^2-2y+1)-(y^2-3y-7)$

4. $3(2a-b)-4(b-2a)$

5. $x-\{2x-[-x-(1-x)]\}$

6. $3x^2-\{x^2+1-x[x-(2x-1)]\}+2$

7. $(x+8)(x-2)$

8. $(5x+2)(3x-4)$

9. $(3x+5y)(4x-5y)$

10. $(a+5)^2$

11. $(x+2y)^2$

12. $(3a-4b)^2$

13. $(6-3x)^2$

14. $(2x+y)(2x-y)$

15. $(3x+2)(2-3x)$

16. $(2x^2+ay)(3x-ay)$

17. $(3x+2)(4x^2+3x+4)$

18. $(4x-3)(x^3-2x^2+x-3)$

19. $(x+1)(x-1)(x+3)$

20. $(t-1)(t-2)(t-3)$

A.4 Factoring

Factoring is the process of expressing a polynomial as a product of other polynomials. For example, by applying the distributive property we may write

$$3x^2-x=x(3x-1)$$

The first step in factoring a polynomial is to check to see if the polynomial contains any common monomial factor. If it does, the greatest common factor is then factored out. For example, the common factor of the algebraic expression $2a^2x+4ax+6a$ is $2a$ since

$$2a^2x+4ax+6a=\mathbf{2a}\cdot ax+\mathbf{2a}\cdot 2x+\mathbf{2a}\cdot 3=\mathbf{2a}(ax+2x+3)$$

EXAMPLE 7 Factor out the greatest monomial factor in each of the following expressions:

(a) $4x^2-6xy+2x$ **(b)** $6a^4b^4c-3a^3b^2c-9a^2b^2$ **(c)** $2x^{3/2}-3x^{1/2}$

SOLUTION **(a)** $4x^2-6xy+2x=2x(2x-3y+1)$

(b) $6a^4b^4c-3a^3b^2c-9a^2b^2=3a^2b^2(2a^2b^2c-ac-3)$

(c) $2x^{3/2}-3x^{1/2}=x^{1/2}(2x-3)$ ■

Sometimes a polynomial may be factored by regrouping and rearranging the terms of the polynomial and then factoring out a common term. This technique is illustrated in the following example.

EXAMPLE 8 Factorize the following:

(a) $2ax+2ay+bx+by$ **(b)** $3xy-4-2y+6x$

SOLUTION **(a)** We begin by factoring the common term $2a$ from the first two terms and the common term b from the last two terms. Thus,

$$2ax+2ay+bx+by=2a(x+y)+b(x+y)$$

Since $(x+y)$ is common to both terms of the polynomial we may factor out this term. Hence,

$$2a(x+y)+b(x+y)=(x+y)(2a+b)$$

(b)
$$\begin{aligned}3xy-4-2y+6x&=3xy+6x-2y-4\\&=3x(y+2)-2(y+2)\\&=(3x-2)(y+2)\end{aligned}$$
■

A polynomial is *prime* or *irreducible* over a given set of numbers if it cannot be expressed as a product of two polynomials of positive degree with coefficients belonging to that set. For example, x^2+2x+2 is prime over the set of polynomials with *integral coefficients* since it cannot be expressed as the product of two polynomials of positive degree which have *integral coefficients.*

Having first taken out the common factors, one may then continue with the factorization process until the polynomial has been *completely factored*; that is, until the polynomial has been expressed as the product of a constant and/or one or more prime polynomials.

Certain product formulas that are useful in factoring binomials and trinomials are summarized in Table 4.

Table 4

Formula	Example
1. **Difference of Two Squares**	
$x^2-y^2=(x+y)(x-y)$	$x^2-36=(x+6)(x-6)$
	$8x^2-2y^2=2(4x^2-y^2)$
	$=2(2x+y)(2x-y)$
	$9-a^6=(3+a^3)(3-a^3)$
2. **Perfect-Square Trinomial**	
$x^2+2xy+y^2=(x+y)^2$	$x^2+8x+16=(x+4)^2$
$x^2-2xy+y^2=(x-y)^2$	$4x^2-4xy+y^2=(2x-y)^2$
3. **Sum of Two Cubes**	
$x^3+y^3=(x+y)(x^2-xy+y^2)$	$z^3+27=z^3+(3)^3$
	$=(z+3)(z^2-3z+9)$
4. **Difference of Two Cubes**	
$x^3-y^3=(x-y)(x^2+xy+y^2)$	$8x^3-y^6=(2x)^3-(y^2)^3$
	$=(2x-y^2)(4x^2+2xy^2+y^4)$

If the polynomial is a second-degree polynomial of the form

$$px^2+qx+r$$

with integral coefficients, then its factors must be of the form $(ax+b)(cx+d)$ where $ac=p$, $ad+bc=q$ and $bd=r$. The procedure used to find the coefficients a, b, c and d, which satisfy the given conditions, when factorizing a polynomial of this form, is illustrated in the next several examples.

EXAMPLE 9 Factorize: $x^2-7x+12$

SOLUTION We observe that the given polynomial is of the form px^2+qx+r, where $p=1$, $q=-7$ and $r=12$. We wish to find the factors $(ax+b)(cx+d)$ of this polynomial such that $ac=1$, $ad+bc=-7$ and $bd=12$.

1. Find the possible coefficients of the first degree terms and the possible coefficients of the constant terms.

(*a*) Since $ac = 1$, the only possible first degree terms are

$$(x \quad)(x \quad)$$

(*b*) The product of the constant terms is positive (+12) and their sum is negative (−7). Therefore, both of the constant terms must be negative. The only negative integers satisfying these conditions are (−4) and (−3).

2. *Determine which of the possibilities yield the desired factorization.*

The only possibility in this case is $(x-4)(x-3)$ which is the correct factorization since

$$(x-4)(x-3) = x^2 - 7x + 12$$

■

EXAMPLE 10 Factorize: (**a**) $6x^2 - 13x - 8$ (**b**) $12x^2 + 12x - 9$

SOLUTION (**a**) Since $ac = 6$, the possible first degree terms are

$$(6x \quad)(x \quad) \quad \text{and} \quad (3x \quad)(2x \quad)$$

The product of the constant terms bd is (−8). Thus, the possible constant terms are:

$$\begin{matrix} (1)(-8), (8)(-1), (2)(-4), \\ (-1)(8), (-8)(1), (-2)(4), \end{matrix} \quad \text{and} \quad \begin{matrix} (4)(-2) \\ (-4)(2) \end{matrix}$$

We must find the coefficients that satisfy the additional condition that $ad + bc = 8$. From the various possibilities

$$\begin{matrix} (6x+1)(x-8) & & (3x+1)(2x-8) \\ (6x-1)(x+8) & & (3x-1)(2x+8) \\ \vdots & \text{and} & \vdots \\ (6x-4)(x+2) & & (3x-4)(2x+2) \end{matrix}$$

we find by trial and error that the correct factorization is

$$6x^2 - 13x - 8 = (3x-8)(2x+1)$$

(**b**) Since each term has the common factor 3, we have

$$12x^2 + 12x - 9 = 3(4x^2 + 4x - 3)$$

Using the trial and error method of factorization, we find that

$$4x^2 + 4x - 3 = (2x+3)(2x-1)$$

Thus, we have

$$12x^2 + 12x - 9 = 3(2x+3)(2x-1)$$

■

We may also use this method to factorize polynomials of the form $px^2 + qxy + ry^2$ as illustrated in the next example.

EXAMPLE 11 Factorize: $3x^2-4xy-4y^2$

SOLUTION If the given polynomial may be factorized then its factors must be of the form $(ax+by)\cdot(cx+dy)$ where $ac=3$, $ad+bc=-4$ and $bd=-4$. By trial and error we obtain the factorization

$$3x^2-4xy-4y^2=(3x+2y)(x-2y)$$ ■

A.4 EXERCISES

In problems 1 through 4, factor out the greatest common monomial from each of the given expressions.

1. $4x^5-12x^4-6x^3$

2. $4x^2y^2z-2x^5y^2+6x^3y^2z^2$

3. $7a^4-42a^2b^2+49a^3b$

4. $3x^{2/3}-2x^{1/3}$

In problems 5 through 26, factorize each of the given expressions.

5. $6ac+3bc-4ad-2bd$

6. $3x^3-x^2+3x-1$

7. $xyz+z-2xy-2$

8. $4a^2-b^2$

9. $12x^2-3y^2$

10. $16-a^4$

11. $4x^2+4x+1$

12. $9a^2x^2+6ax+1$

13. $9a^2-12ab+4b^2$

14. $10-14x-12x^2$

15. $x^2-2x-15$

16. $12x^2-x-6$

17. $18x^2+3x-6$

18. $12x^2-2x-30$

19. $9x^2-16y^2$

20. $(x+y)^2-1$

21. $8a^2-2ab-6b^2$

22. $2y^6-xy^3-3x^2$

23. $27x^3+64y^3$

24. x^6+125

25. x^3-27

26. $16a^3-2b^6$

A.5 Operations with Algebraic Fractions

Rational Expressions

Quotients of polynomials are called *rational expressions*. Examples of rational expressions are

$$\frac{6x-1}{2x+3},\quad \frac{3x^2y^3-2xy}{4x}\quad \text{and}\quad \frac{2}{5ab},$$

Since rational expressions are quotients in which the variables represent real numbers, the properties of the real numbers apply to rational expressions as well and operations with rational fractions are performed in the same manner as operations with arithmetic fractions. For example, using the properties of the real number system, we write

$$\frac{ac}{bc}=\frac{a}{b}$$

where a, b and c are any real numbers and b and c are different from zero.

Similarly, using the same properties of real numbers, we write

$$\frac{(x+2)(x-3)}{(x-2)(x-3)}=\frac{x+2}{x-2} \qquad (x \neq 2, 3)$$

after "cancelling" the common factors.

A rational expression is *simplified* or in lowest terms when the numerator and denominator have no common factors other than 1 and -1.

EXAMPLE 12 Simplify the given expressions:

(a) $\dfrac{3x^2+7x-6}{x^2-9}$ (b) $\dfrac{3-4x-4x^2}{2x-1}$

SOLUTION (a) $\dfrac{3x^2+7x-6}{x^2-9}=\dfrac{(3x-2)(x+3)}{(x+3)(x-3)}=\dfrac{3x-2}{x-3}$

(b) $\dfrac{3-4x-4x^2}{2x-1}=\dfrac{(1-2x)(3+2x)}{2x-1}=\dfrac{-(2x-1)(2x+3)}{2x-1}=-(2x+3)$ ■

The operations of multiplication and division are performed with algebraic fractions in the same manner as with arithmetic fractions (see Table 5). When rational expressions are multiplied and divided the resulting expressions should be simplified.

Operation	Example
If P, Q, R and S are polynomials, then	
1. **Multiplication**	
$\dfrac{P}{Q}\cdot\dfrac{R}{S}=\dfrac{PR}{QS}$ $(Q, S \neq 0)$	$\dfrac{2x}{y}\cdot\dfrac{(x+1)}{y-1)}=\dfrac{2x(x+1)}{y(y-1)}=\dfrac{2x^2+2x}{y^2-y}$
2. **Division**	
$\dfrac{P}{Q}\div\dfrac{R}{S}=\dfrac{P}{Q}\cdot\dfrac{S}{R}=\dfrac{PS}{QR}$ $(Q, R, S \neq 0)$	$\dfrac{x^2+3}{y}\div\dfrac{y^2+1}{x}=\dfrac{x^2+3}{y}\cdot\dfrac{x}{y^2+1}=\dfrac{x^3+3x}{y^3+y}$

Table 5

EXAMPLE 13 Perform the indicated operations and simplify:

(a) $\dfrac{2x-8}{x+2}\cdot\dfrac{x^2+4x+4}{x^2-16}$ (b) $\dfrac{x^2-6x+9}{3x+12}\div\dfrac{x^2-9}{6x^2+18x}$

SOLUTION

(a)
$$\frac{2x-8}{x+2}\cdot\frac{x^2+4x+4}{x^2-16}=\frac{2(x-4)}{x+2}\cdot\frac{(x+2)^2}{(x+4)(x-4)}$$
$$=\frac{2(x-4)(x+2)(x+2)}{(x+2)(x+4)(x-4)}$$
$$=\frac{2(x+2)}{x+4}$$

(b)
$$\frac{x^2-6x+9}{3x+12}\div\frac{x^2-9}{6x^2+18x}=\frac{x^2-6x+9}{3x+12}\cdot\frac{6x^2+18x}{x^2-9}$$
$$=\frac{(x-3)^2}{3(x+4)}\cdot\frac{6x(x+3)}{(x+3)(x-3)}$$
$$=\frac{(x-3)(x-3)(6x)(x+3)}{3(x+4)(x+3)(x-3)}$$
$$=\frac{2x(x-3)}{x+4}$$

■

The operations of addition and subtraction are performed with rational expressions by finding a common denominator of the fractions and then adding or subtracting the fractions. In Table 6, for fractions with equal denominators, we have the following:

Table 6

Operation	Example
If P, Q and R are polynomials then,	
1. **Addition**	
$\frac{P}{R}+\frac{Q}{R}=\frac{P+Q}{R}$ $(R\neq 0)$	$\frac{2x}{x+2}+\frac{6x}{x+2}=\frac{2x+6x}{x+2}=\frac{8x}{x+2}$
2. **Subtraction**	
$\frac{P}{R}-\frac{Q}{R}=\frac{P-Q}{R}$ $(R\neq 0)$	$\frac{3y}{y-x}-\frac{y}{y-x}=\frac{3y-y}{y-x}=\frac{2y}{y-x}$

To add or subtract fractions that have different denominators, we first find a common denominator, preferably the least common denominator (LCD), and the indicated operations are then carried out following the procedure described above.

To find the least common denominator (LCD) of two or more rational expressions

1. *Find the prime factors of each denominator.*

2. *Form the product of the different prime factors which occur in the denominators.* Each prime factor in this product should be raised to the highest power of that factor appearing in the denominators.

The same procedure is used when arithmetic fractions are added and subtracted as the following example shows.

EXAMPLE 14 Express as a rational number in lowest terms:

$$\frac{3}{18}+\frac{5}{24}$$

SOLUTION Using the procedure outlined above to find the LCD, we have

1. $18=2\cdot 3^2$ and $24=2^3\cdot 3$ (prime factors of each denominator)
2. $\text{LCD}=2^3\cdot 3^2=72$ (product of prime factors, in which each factor is raised to the highest power of that factor appearing in the denominators)

Next, each fraction is expressed as an equivalent fraction having 72 as a denominator and the resulting fractions are then combined. Thus,

$$\begin{aligned}\frac{3}{18}\cdot\frac{4}{4}+\frac{5}{24}\cdot\frac{3}{3}&=\frac{12}{72}+\frac{15}{72}\\&=\frac{27}{72}\\&=\frac{3}{8}\qquad\text{(reduced to lowest terms)}\end{aligned}$$

■

An analogous procedure is used to find the LCD for rational expressions as the next example illustrates.

EXAMPLE 15 Simplify:

(a) $\dfrac{3x+4}{4x}+\dfrac{4y-2}{3y}$ **(b)** $\dfrac{3}{x^2-16}-\dfrac{4}{x^2-8x+16}$ **(c)** $\dfrac{1}{x+h}-\dfrac{1}{x}$

SOLUTION **(a)**

$$\begin{aligned}\frac{3x+4}{4x}+\frac{4y-2}{3y}&=\frac{3x+4}{4x}\cdot\frac{3y}{3y}+\frac{4y-2}{3y}\cdot\frac{4x}{4x}\qquad(\text{LCD}=(4x)(3y)=12xy)\\&=\frac{9xy+12y}{12xy}+\frac{16xy-8x}{12xy}\\&=\frac{25xy-8x+12y}{12xy}\end{aligned}$$

(b)

$$\begin{aligned}\frac{3}{x^2-16}-\frac{4}{x^2-8x+16}&=\frac{3}{(x+4)(x-4)}-\frac{4}{(x-4)(x-4)}\qquad(\text{LCD}=(x+4)(x-4)^2)\\&=\frac{3}{(x+4)(x-4)}\cdot\frac{x-4}{x-4}-\frac{4}{(x-4)^2}\cdot\frac{x+4}{x+4}\\&=\frac{3x-12}{(x+4)(x-4)^2}-\frac{4x+16}{(x+4)(x-4)^2}\\&=\frac{-x-28}{(x+4)(x-4)^2}\\&=\frac{-(x+28)}{(x+4)(x-4)^2}\end{aligned}$$

(c) $$\frac{1}{x+h}-\frac{1}{x}=\frac{1}{x+h}\cdot\frac{x}{x}-\frac{1}{x}\cdot\frac{x+h}{x+h} \qquad (\text{LCD}=(x)(x+h))$$

$$=\frac{x}{x(x+h)}-\frac{x+h}{x(x+h)}$$

$$=\frac{x-x-h}{x(x+h)}$$

$$=\frac{-h}{x(x+h)}$$

■

Other Algebraic Fractions

The techniques used to simplify rational expressions may also be used to simplify algebraic fractions in which the numerator and denominator are not polynomials as illustrated in the next example.

EXAMPLE 16 Simplify:

(a) $\dfrac{1+1/(x+1)}{x-4/x}$ **(b)** $\dfrac{x^{-1}+y^{-1}}{x^{-2}-y^{-2}}$

SOLUTION **(a)** $$\frac{1+\dfrac{1}{x+1}}{x-\dfrac{4}{x}}=\frac{1\cdot\dfrac{x+1}{x+1}+\dfrac{1}{x+1}}{x\cdot\dfrac{x}{x}-\dfrac{4}{x}}=\frac{\dfrac{x+1+1}{x+1}}{\dfrac{x^2-4}{x}}$$

$$=\frac{x+2}{x+1}\cdot\frac{x}{x^2-4}=\frac{x+2}{x+1}\cdot\frac{x}{(x+2)(x-2)}$$

$$=\frac{x}{(x+1)(x-2)}$$

(b) $$\frac{x^{-1}+y^{-1}}{x^{-2}-y^{-2}}=\frac{\dfrac{1}{x}+\dfrac{1}{y}}{\dfrac{1}{x^2}-\dfrac{1}{y^2}}=\frac{\dfrac{y+x}{xy}}{\dfrac{y^2-x^2}{x^2y^2}}$$

$$=\frac{y+x}{xy}\cdot\frac{x^2y^2}{y^2-x^2}=\frac{y+x}{xy}\cdot\frac{(xy)^2}{(y+x)(y-x)}$$

$$=\frac{xy}{y-x}$$

■

When the denominator of an algebraic fraction contains sums or differences involving radicals, we may transform the fraction into an equivalent one with a denominator that does not contain radicals by *rationalizing the denominator.* In doing so, we make use of the fact that

$$(\sqrt{a}+\sqrt{b})(\sqrt{a}-\sqrt{b})=(\sqrt{a})^2-(\sqrt{b})^2=a-b$$

This procedure is illustrated in the following example.

EXAMPLE 17 Simplify: $\dfrac{1}{1+\sqrt{x}}$

SOLUTION Upon multiplying the numerator and the denominator by $(1-\sqrt{x})$, we obtain

$$\begin{aligned}\frac{1}{1+\sqrt{x}} &= \frac{1}{1+\sqrt{x}}\cdot\frac{1-\sqrt{x}}{1-\sqrt{x}}\\ &= \frac{1-\sqrt{x}}{1-(\sqrt{x})^2}\\ &= \frac{1-\sqrt{x}}{1-x}\end{aligned}$$

■

In other situations, it may be necessary to rationalize the numerator of an algebraic expression. In differential calculus, for example, one encounters the following problem.

EXAMPLE 18 Rationalize the numerator: $\sqrt{x+h}-\sqrt{x}$

SOLUTION

$$\begin{aligned}\sqrt{x+h}-\sqrt{x} &= (\sqrt{x+h}-\sqrt{x})\cdot\frac{\sqrt{x+h}+\sqrt{x}}{\sqrt{x+h}+\sqrt{x}}\\ &= \frac{(\sqrt{x+h})^2-(\sqrt{x})^2}{\sqrt{x+h}+\sqrt{x}}\\ &= \frac{(x+h)-x}{\sqrt{x+h}+\sqrt{x}}\\ &= \frac{h}{\sqrt{x+h}+\sqrt{x}}\end{aligned}$$

■

A.5 EXERCISES

In problems 1 through 4, simplify each of the given expressions.

1. $\dfrac{x^2+x-2}{x^2-4}$

2. $\dfrac{2a^2-3ab-9b^2}{2ab^2+3b^3}$

3. $\dfrac{12t^2+12t+3}{4t^2-1}$

4. $\dfrac{x^3+2x^2-3x}{-2x^2-x+3}$

In problems 5 through 20, perform the indicated operation and simplify each of the given expressions.

5. $\dfrac{2a^2-2b^2}{b-a}\cdot\dfrac{4a+4b}{a^2+2ab+b^2}$

6. $\dfrac{x^2-6x+9}{x^2-x-6}\cdot\dfrac{3x+6}{2x^2-7x+3}$

7. $\dfrac{3x^2+2x-1}{2x+6}\div\dfrac{x^2-1}{x^2+2x-3}$

8. $\dfrac{3x^2-4xy-4y^2}{x^2y}\div\dfrac{(2y-x)^2}{x^3y}$

9. $\frac{a+1}{3a}+\frac{b-2}{5b}$

10. $\frac{2x}{2x-1}-\frac{3x}{2x+5}$

11. $\frac{4}{x^2-9}-\frac{5}{x^2-6x+9}$

12. $\frac{x}{1-x}+\frac{2x+3}{x^2-1}$

13. $\frac{x}{2x^2+11x+15}-\frac{2x}{2x^2+5x-3}$

14. $2+\frac{1}{a+2}-\frac{2a}{a-2}$

15. $x-\frac{x^2}{x+2}+\frac{2}{x-2}$

16. $\frac{6}{x}-\frac{4}{3x+6}+\frac{3x}{x^2-4}$

17. $\frac{1+1/x}{1-1/x}$

18. $\frac{1/x+1/y}{1-1/(xy)}$

19. $\frac{x^{-2}-y^{-2}}{x+y}$

20. $\frac{x^{-3}-y^{-3}}{x^{-1}-y^{-1}}$

In problems 21 through 24, rationalize the denominator of each of the given expressions.

21. $\frac{\sqrt{a}+\sqrt{b}}{\sqrt{a}-\sqrt{b}}$

22. $\frac{1}{\sqrt{x}+5}$

23. $\frac{a}{1-\sqrt{a}}$

24. $\frac{1}{\sqrt{x}-\sqrt{y}}$

In problems 25 through 26, rationalize the numerator of each of the given expressions.

25. $\frac{\sqrt{x}-1}{x}$

26. $\frac{\sqrt{x+3}-\sqrt{x}}{3}$

A.6

Solving Equations

The *solution* or *root* of an equation involving one variable is a number which when substituted for the variable makes the equation true. For example, the solution of the equation

$$2x-8=0$$

is 4 since $2(4)-8=0$. In order *to solve an equation*, we must find the value(s) of the variable(s) that satisfy the given equation. The set of all solutions of an equation is called the *solution set*. Two equations are *equivalent* if they have the same solution set.

In the process of solving equations, one or more of the following properties of real numbers is applied until an equivalent equation is obtained for which the solution set is evident.

For any real numbers a, b and c

1. Addition Property — If $a=b$, then $a+c=b+c$
2. Subtraction Property — If $a=b$, then $a-c=b-c$
3. Multiplication Property — If $a=b$, then $ac=bc$

4. Division Property If $a = b$ and $c \neq 0$, then $\frac{a}{c} = \frac{b}{c}$

The next several examples are given in order that the reader may review the process of solving an equation.

EXAMPLE 19 Solve the equation: $5x + 6 = 3x - 4$

SOLUTION We first try to isolate the variable x on the left side of the equation. Thus, we have

$$
\begin{aligned}
5x + 6 &= 3x - 4 \\
5x + 6 - 3x &= 3x - 4 - 3x && \text{Subtraction Property} \\
2x + 6 &= -4 && \text{Simplification} \\
2x + 6 - 6 &= -4 - 6 && \text{Subtraction Property} \\
2x &= -10 && \text{Simplification} \\
\frac{2x}{2} &= \frac{-10}{2} && \text{Division Property} \\
x &= -5
\end{aligned}
$$

To verify that $x = -5$ is a solution, we substitute this value of x in the original equation and check to see if the equality holds.

$$
\begin{aligned}
5(-5) + 6 &\stackrel{?}{=} 3(-5) - 4 \\
-19 &= -19 \qquad (\checkmark)
\end{aligned}
$$

■

EXAMPLE 20 Solve the equations:

(**a**) $\frac{x+2}{3} + \frac{x-5}{2} = 4$ (**b**) $\frac{3}{x-2} = \frac{4}{x-3}$

SOLUTION (**a**) We first clear the equations of all fractions by multiplying both sides of the equation by the least common denominator (6).

$$
\begin{aligned}
6 \cdot \frac{x+2}{3} + 6 \cdot \frac{x-5}{2} &= 6(4) \\
2(x + 2) + 3(x - 5) &= 24 \\
2x + 4 + 3x - 15 &= 24 \\
5x &= 35 \\
x &= 7
\end{aligned}
$$

(**b**) We first clear the equation of all fractions by multiplying by the LCD, $(x - 2)(x - 3)$:

$$
\begin{aligned}
(x - 2)(x - 3) \cdot \frac{3}{x-2} &= (x - 2)(x - 3) \cdot \frac{4}{x-3} \\
3(x - 3) &= 4(x - 2) \\
3x - 9 &= 4x - 8 \\
-x &= 1 \\
x &= -1
\end{aligned}
$$

■

Some equations may be solved by the method of factoring. This method of solution is based on the following property of real numbers:

Property If a and b are real numbers and $ab = 0$, then either $a = 0$, $b = 0$ or both a and b are equal to 0.

The use of this method is illustrated in the next two examples.

EXAMPLE 21 Solve the equations:

(a) $x^2 - 6x + 9 = 0$ **(b)** $6x^2 + 5x - 6 = 0$ **(c)** $5x^3 - 5x = 0$

SOLUTION **(a)** We begin by factoring the left side of the equation

$$(x-3)^2 = 0$$

Setting each factor equal to zero, we have

$$x - 3 = 0$$

and

$$x = 3$$

(b) Factoring the left side of the equation, we have

$$(2x+3)(3x-2) = 0$$

Setting each factor equal to zero gives

$$2x + 3 = 0 \quad \text{or} \quad 3x - 2 = 0$$

$$x = -\frac{3}{2} \qquad x = \frac{2}{3}$$

Thus, $x = 2/3, -3/2$.

(c) Factoring the left side of the equation, we have

$$5x(x^2 - 1) = 0$$

and

$$5x = 0 \quad \text{or} \quad x^2 = 1$$

$$x = 0 \qquad x = \pm 1$$

■

EXAMPLE 22 Solve the equation: $x = 4 + \sqrt{4x + 16}$

SOLUTION We begin by isolating the radical to one side of the equation:

$$x - 4 = \sqrt{4x + 16}$$

In order to eliminate the radical, we square both sides of the equation:

$$(x-4)^2 = (\sqrt{4x+16})^2$$

$$x^2 - 8x + 16 = 4x + 16$$

$$x^2 - 12x = 0$$

$$x(x - 12) = 0$$

$$x = 0 \quad \text{or} \quad x = 12$$

Check:

$$0 \stackrel{?}{=} 4+\sqrt{4(0)+16}=4+4=8 \quad (\surd)$$
$$12 \stackrel{?}{=} 4+\sqrt{4(12)+16}=4+8=12 \quad (\surd)$$

We refer to the value 0 in the preceding example as an *extraneous* solution. It is a solution of the equation $x^2-8x+16=4x+16$ but it is *not* a solution of the original equation $x=4+\sqrt{4x+16}$. Thus, whenever an equation is raised to some power, care should be taken to check that no extraneous solutions have been introduced.

A.6 EXERCISES

In problems 1 through 20, solve each of the given equations.

1. $5a-4=10-2a$

2. $3x-4=6x+5$

3. $\dfrac{x}{5}-3=-2$

4. $\dfrac{2x-1}{3}+\dfrac{x-5}{4}=14$

5. $\dfrac{11-2a}{4a-3}=\dfrac{5}{9}$

6. $\dfrac{-3}{2-x}=\dfrac{5}{x+5}$

7. $\dfrac{3}{x}+6=5-\dfrac{2}{x}$

8. $\dfrac{4x+5}{2x-2}=\dfrac{2x+1}{x-2}$

9. $\dfrac{3x-7}{6x+1}=\dfrac{2x-3}{4x+1}$

10. $\dfrac{4}{6x+10}-\dfrac{1}{3x+5}=-1$

11. $x^2-x-12=0$

12. $8x^2+10x+3=0$

13. $z^3-16z=0$

14. $2y^2-32y-72=0$

15. $\dfrac{2a}{a+2}=\dfrac{3a+1}{2a+3}$

16. $\dfrac{2x-1}{x+7}=\dfrac{5x-4}{3x+13}$

17. $x=\sqrt{3x+4}$

18. $\sqrt{2x-4}=x-6$

19. $\sqrt{3x+7}=2x-7$

20. $2\sqrt{2x-1}-\sqrt{2x+6}=2$

II

TABLES

TABLE I Exponential Functions

x	e^x	e^{-x}	x	e^x	e^{-x}
0.00	1.0000	1.0000	1.5	4.4817	0.2231
0.01	1.0101	0.9901	1.6	4.9530	0.2019
0.02	1.0202	0.9802	1.7	5.4739	0.1827
0.03	1.0305	0.9705	1.8	6.0496	0.1653
0.04	1.0408	0.9608	1.9	6.6859	0.1496
0.05	1.0513	0.9512	2.0	7.3891	0.1353
0.06	1.0618	0.9418	2.1	8.1662	0.1225
0.07	1.0725	0.9324	2.2	9.0250	0.1108
0.08	1.0833	0.9331	2.3	9.9742	0.1003
0.09	1.0942	0.9139	2.4	11.023	0.0907
0.10	1.1052	0.9048	2.5	12.182	0.0821
0.11	1.1163	0.8958	2.6	13.464	0.0743
0.12	1.1275	0.8869	2.7	14.880	0.0672
0.13	1.1388	0.8781	2.8	16.445	0.0608
0.14	1.1503	0.8694	2.9	18.174	0.0550
0.15	1.1618	0.8607	3.0	20.086	0.0498
0.16	1.1735	0.8521	3.1	22.198	0.0450
0.17	1.1853	0.8437	3.2	24.533	0.0408
0.18	1.1972	0.8353	3.3	27.113	0.0369
0.19	1.2092	0.8270	3.4	29.964	0.0334
0.20	1.2214	0.8187	3.5	33.115	0.0302
0.21	1.2337	0.8106	3.6	36.598	0.0273
0.22	1.2161	0.8025	3.7	40.447	0.0247
0.23	1.2586	0.7945	3.8	44.701	0.0224
0.24	1.2712	0.7866	3.9	49.402	0.0202
0.25	1.2840	0.7788	4.0	54.598	0.0183
0.30	1.3499	0.7408	4.1	60.340	0.0166
0.35	1.4191	0.7047	4.2	66.686	0.0150
0.40	1.4918	0.6703	4.3	73.700	0.0136
0.45	1.5683	0.6376	4.4	81.451	0.0123
0.50	1.6487	0.6065	4.5	90.017	0.0111
0.55	1.7333	0.5769	4.6	99.484	0.0101
0.60	1.8221	0.5488	4.7	109.95	0.0091
0.65	1.9155	0.5220	4.8	121.51	0.0082
0.70	2.0138	0.4966	4.9	134.29	0.0074
0.75	2.1170	0.4724	5.0	148.41	0.0067
0.80	2.2255	0.4493	5.5	244.69	0.0041
0.85	2.3396	0.4274	6.0	403.43	0.0025
0.90	2.4596	0.4066	6.5	665.14	0.0015
0.95	2.5857	0.3867	7.0	1096.6	0.0009
1.0	2.7183	0.3679	7.5	1808.0	0.0006
1.1	3.0042	0.3329	8.0	2981.0	0.0003
1.2	3.3201	0.3012	8.5	4914.8	0.0002
1.3	3.6693	0.2725	9.0	8103.1	0.0001
1.4	4.0552	0.2466	10.0	22026	0.00005

TABLE II Common Logarithms

x	0	1	2	3	4	5	6	7	8	9
1.0	.0000	.0043	.0086	.0128	.0170	.0212	.0253	.0294	.0334	.0374
1.1	.0414	.0453	.0492	.0531	.0569	.0607	.0645	.0682	.0719	.0755
1.2	.0792	.0828	.0864	.0899	.0934	.0969	.1004	.1038	.1072	.1106
1.3	.1139	.1173	.1206	.1239	.1271	.1303	.1335	.1367	.1399	.1430
1.4	.1461	.1492	.1523	.1553	.1584	.1614	.1644	.1673	.1703	.1732
1.5	.1761	.1790	.1818	.1847	.1875	.1903	.1931	.1959	.1987	.2014
1.6	.2041	.2068	.2095	.2122	.2148	.2175	.2201	.2227	.2253	.2279
1.7	.2304	.2330	.2355	.2380	.2405	.2430	.2455	.2480	.2504	.2529
1.8	.2553	.2577	.2601	.2625	.2648	.2672	.2695	.2718	.2742	.2765
1.9	.2788	.2810	.2833	.2856	.2878	.2900	.2923	.2945	.2967	.2989
2.0	.3010	.3032	.3054	.3075	.3096	.3118	.3139	.3160	.3181	.3201
2.1	.3222	.3243	.3263	.3284	.3304	.3324	.3345	.3365	.3385	.3404
2.2	.3424	.3444	.3464	.3483	.3502	.3522	.3541	.3560	.3579	.3598
2.3	.3617	.3636	.3655	.3674	.3692	.3711	.3729	.3747	.3766	.3784
2.4	.3802	.3820	.3838	.3856	.3874	.3892	.3909	.3927	.3945	.3962
2.5	.3979	.3997	.4014	.4031	.4048	.4065	.4082	.4099	.4116	.4133
2.6	.4150	.4166	.4183	.4200	.4216	.4232	.4249	.4265	.4281	.4298
2.7	.4314	.4330	.4346	.4362	.4378	.4393	.4409	.4425	.4440	.4456
2.8	.4472	.4487	.4502	.4518	.4533	.4548	.4564	.4579	.4594	.4609
2.9	.4624	.4639	.4654	.4669	.4683	.4698	.4713	.4728	.4742	.4757
3.0	.4771	.4786	.4800	.4814	.4829	.4843	.4857	.4871	.4886	.4900
3.1	.4914	.4928	.4942	.4955	.4969	.4983	.4997	.5011	.5024	.5038
3.2	.5051	.5065	.5079	.5092	.5105	.5119	.5132	.5145	.5159	.5172
3.3	.5185	.5198	.5211	.5224	.5237	.5250	.5263	.5276	.5289	.5302
3.4	.5315	.5328	.5340	.5353	.5366	.5378	.5391	.5403	.5416	.5428
3.5	.5441	.5453	.5465	.5478	.5490	.5502	.5514	.5527	.5539	.5551
3.6	.5563	.5575	.5587	.5599	.5611	.5623	.5635	.5647	.5658	.5670
3.7	.5682	.5694	.5705	.5717	.5729	.5740	.5752	.5763	.5775	.5786
3.8	.5798	.5809	.5821	.5832	.5843	.5855	.5866	.5877	.5888	.5899
3.9	.5911	.5922	.5933	.5944	.5955	.5966	.5977	.5988	.5999	.6010
4.0	.6021	.6031	.6042	.6053	.6064	.6075	.6085	.6096	.6107	.6117
4.1	.6128	.6138	.6149	.6160	.6170	.6180	.6191	.6201	.6212	.6222
4.2	.6232	.6243	.6253	.6263	.6274	.6284	.6294	.6304	.6314	.6325
4.3	.6335	.6345	.6355	.6365	.6375	.6385	.6395	.6405	.6415	.6425
4.4	.6435	.6444	.6454	.6464	.6474	.6484	.6493	.6503	.6513	.6522
4.5	.6532	.6542	.6551	.6561	.6571	.6580	.6590	.6599	.6609	.6618
4.6	.6628	.6637	.6646	.6656	.6665	.6675	.6684	.6693	.6702	.6712
4.7	.6721	.6730	.6739	.6749	.6758	.6767	.6776	.6785	.6794	.6803
4.8	.6812	.6821	.6830	.6839	.6848	.6857	.6866	.6875	.6884	.6893
4.9	.6902	.6911	.6920	.6928	.6937	.6946	.6955	.6964	.6972	.6981
5.0	.6990	.6998	.7007	.7016	.7024	.7033	.7042	.7050	.7059	.7067
5.1	.7076	.7084	.7093	.7101	.7110	.7118	.7126	.7135	.7143	.7152
5.2	.7160	.7168	.7177	.7185	.7193	.7202	.7210	.7218	.7226	.7235
5.3	.7243	.7251	.7259	.7267	.7275	.7284	.7292	.7300	.7308	.7316
5.4	.7324	.7332	.7340	.7348	.7356	.7364	.7372	.7380	.7388	.7396
x	0	1	2	3	4	5	6	7	8	9

TABLE II (continued)

x	0	1	2	3	4	5	6	7	8	9
5.5	.7404	.7412	.7419	.7427	.7435	.7443	.7451	.7459	.7466	.7474
5.6	.7482	.7490	.7497	.7505	.7513	.7520	.7528	.7536	.7543	.7551
5.7	.7559	.7566	.7574	.7582	.7589	.7597	.7604	.7612	.7619	.7627
5.8	.7634	.7642	.7649	.7657	.7664	.7672	.7679	.7686	.7694	.7701
5.9	.7709	.7716	.7723	.7731	.7738	.7745	.7752	.7760	.7767	.7774
6.0	.7782	.7789	.7796	.7803	.7810	.7818	.7825	.7832	.7839	.7846
6.1	.7853	.7860	.7868	.7875	.7882	.7889	.7896	.7903	.7910	.7917
6.2	.7924	.7931	.7938	.7945	.7952	.7959	.7966	.7973	.7980	.7987
6.3	.7993	.8000	.8007	.8014	.8021	.8028	.8035	.8041	.8048	.8055
6.4	.8062	.8069	.8075	.8082	.8089	.8096	.8102	.8109	.8116	.8122
6.5	.8129	.8136	.8142	.8149	.8156	.8162	.8169	.8176	.8182	.8189
6.6	.8195	.8202	.8209	.8215	.8222	.8228	.8235	.8241	.8248	.8254
6.7	.8261	.8267	.8274	.8280	.8287	.8293	.8299	.8306	.8312	.8319
6.8	.8325	.8331	.8338	.8344	.8351	.8357	.8363	.8370	.8376	.8382
6.9	.8388	.8395	.8401	.8407	.8414	.8420	.8426	.8432	.8439	.8445
7.0	.8451	.8457	.8463	.8470	.8476	.8482	.8488	.8494	.8500	.8506
7.1	.8513	.8519	.8525	.8531	.8537	.8543	.8549	.8555	.8561	.8567
7.2	.8573	.8579	.8585	.8591	.8597	.8603	.8609	.8615	.8621	.8627
7.3	.8633	.8639	.8645	.8651	.8657	.8663	.8669	.8675	.8681	.8686
7.4	.8692	.8698	.8704	.8710	.8716	.8722	.8727	.8733	.8739	.8745
7.5	.8751	.8756	.8762	.8768	.8774	.8779	.8785	.8791	.8797	.8802
7.6	.8808	.8814	.8820	.8825	.8831	.8837	.8842	.8848	.8854	.8859
7.7	.8865	.8871	.8876	.8882	.8887	.8893	.8899	.8904	.8910	.8915
7.8	.8921	.8927	.8932	.8938	.8943	.8949	.8954	.8960	.8965	.8971
7.9	.8976	.8982	.8987	.8993	.8998	.9004	.9009	.9015	.9020	.9025
8.0	.9031	.9036	.9042	.9047	.9053	.9058	.9063	.9069	.9074	.9079
8.1	.9085	.9090	.9096	.9101	.9106	.9112	.9117	.9122	.9128	.9133
8.2	.9138	.9143	.9149	.9154	.9159	.9165	.9170	.9175	.9180	.9186
8.3	.9191	.9196	.9201	.9206	.9212	.9217	.9222	.9227	.9232	.9238
8.4	.9243	.9248	.9253	.9258	.9263	.9269	.9274	.9279	.9284	.9289
8.5	.9294	.9299	.9304	.9309	.9315	.9320	.9325	.9330	.9335	.9340
8.6	.9345	.9350	.9355	.9360	.9365	.9370	.9375	.9380	.9385	.9390
8.7	.9395	.9400	.9405	.9410	.9415	.9420	.9425	.9430	.9435	.9440
8.8	.9445	.9450	.9455	.9460	.9465	.9469	.9474	.9479	.9484	.9489
8.9	.9494	.9499	.9504	.9509	.9513	.9518	.9523	.9528	.9533	.9538
9.0	.9542	.9547	.9552	.9557	.9562	.9566	.9571	.9576	.9581	.9586
9.1	.9590	.9595	.9600	.9605	.9609	.9614	.9619	.9624	.9628	.9633
9.2	.9638	.9643	.9647	.9652	.9657	.9661	.9666	.9671	.9675	.9680
9.3	.9685	.9689	.9694	.9699	.9703	.9708	.9713	.9717	.9722	.9727
9.4	.9731	.9736	.9741	.9745	.9750	.9754	.9759	.9763	.9768	.9773
9.5	.9777	.9782	.9786	.9791	.9795	.9800	.9805	.9809	.9814	.9818
9.6	.9823	.9827	.9832	.9836	.9841	.9845	.9850	.9854	.9859	.9863
9.7	.9868	.9872	.9877	.9881	.9886	.9890	.9894	.9899	.9903	.9908
9.8	.9912	.9917	.9921	.9926	.9930	.9934	.9939	.9943	.9948	.9952
9.9	.9956	.9961	.9965	.9969	.9974	.9978	.9983	.9987	.9991	.9996
x	0	1	2	3	4	5	6	7	8	9

TABLE III Natural Logarithms

n	$\log_e n$	n	$\log_e n$	n	$\log_e n$
0.1	7.6974*	4.5	1.5041	9.0	2.1972
0.2	8.3906	4.6	1.5261	9.1	2.2083
0.3	8.7960	4.7	1.5476	9.2	2.2192
0.4	9.0837	4.8	1.5686	9.3	2.2300
		4.9	1.5892	9.4	2.2407
0.5	9.3069	5.0	1.6094	9.5	2.2513
0.6	9.4892	5.1	1.6292	9.6	2.2618
0.7	9.6433	5.2	1.6487	9.7	2.2721
0.8	9.7769	5.3	1.6677	9.8	2.2824
0.9	9.8946	5.4	1.6864	9.9	2.2925
1.0	0.0000	5.5	1.7047	10	2.3026
1.1	0.0953	5.6	1.7228	11	2.3979
1.2	0.1823	5.7	1.7405	12	2.4849
1.3	0.2624	5.8	1.7579	13	2.5649
1.4	0.3365	5.9	1.7750	14	2.6391
1.5	0.4055	6.0	1.7918	15	2.7081
1.6	0.4700	6.1	1.8083	16	2.7726
1.7	0.5306	6.2	1.8245	17	2.8332
1.8	0.5878	6.3	1.8405	18	2.8904
1.9	0.6419	6.4	1.8563	19	2.9444
2.0	0.6931	6.5	1.8718	20	2.9957
2.1	0.7419	6.6	1.8871	25	3.2189
2.2	0.7885	6.7	1.9021	30	3.4012
2.3	0.8329	6.8	1.9169	35	3.5553
2.4	0.8755	6.9	1.9315	40	3.6889
2.5	0.9163	7.0	1.9459	45	3.8067
2.6	0.9555	7.1	1.9601	50	3.9120
2.7	0.9933	7.2	1.9741	55	4.0073
2.8	1.0296	7.3	1.9879	60	4.0943
2.9	1.0647	7.4	2.0015	65	4.1744
3.0	1.0986	7.5	2.0149	70	4.2485
3.1	1.1314	7.6	2.0281	75	4.3175
3.2	1.1632	7.7	2.0412	80	4.3820
3.3	1.1939	7.8	2.0541	85	4.4427
3.4	1.2238	7.9	2.0669	90	4.4998
3.5	1.2528	8.0	2.0794	100	4.6052
3.6	1.2809	8.1	2.0919	110	4.7005
3.7	1.3083	8.2	2.1041	120	4.7875
3.8	1.3350	8.3	2.1163	130	4.8676
3.9	1.3610	8.4	2.1282	140	4.9416
4.0	1.3863	8.5	2.1401	150	5.0106
4.1	1.4110	8.6	2.1518	160	5.0752
4.2	1.4351	8.7	2.1633	170	5.1358
4.3	1.4586	8.8	2.1748	180	5.1930
4.4	1.4816	8.9	2.1861	190	5.2470

* Subtract 10 for $n < 1$. Thus $\log_e 0.1 = 7.6974 - 10 = -2.3026$.

TABLE IV Compound Amount, Present Value, Annuity

$i = \frac{1}{4}\%$

n	$(1+i)^n$	$(1+i)^{-n}$	$s_{\overline{n}\rceil i}$	$a_{\overline{n}\rceil i}$	$s^{-1}_{\overline{n}\rceil i}$
1	1.0025 0000	0.9975 0623	1.0000 0000	0.9975 0623	1.0000 0000
2	1.0050 0625	0.9950 1869	2.0025 0000	1.9925 2492	0.4993 7578
3	1.0075 1877	0.9925 3734	3.0075 0625	2.9850 6227	0.3325 0139
4	1.0100 3756	0.9900 6219	4.0150 2502	3.9751 2446	0.2490 6445
5	1.0125 6266	0.9875 9321	5.0250 6258	4.9627 1766	0.1990 0250
6	1.0150 9406	0.9851 3038	6.0376 2523	5.9478 4804	0.1656 2803
7	1.0176 3180	0.9826 7370	7.0527 1930	6.9305 2174	0.1417 8928
8	1.0201 7588	0.9802 2314	8.0703 5110	7.9107 4487	0.1239 1035
9	1.0227 2632	0.9777 7869	9.0905 2697	8.8885 2357	0.1100 0462
10	1.0252 8313	0.9753 4034	10.1132 5329	9.8638 6391	0.0988 8015
11	1.0278 4634	0.9729 0807	11.1385 3642	10.8367 7198	0.0897 7840
12	1.0304 1596	0.9704 8187	12.1663 8277	11.8072 5384	0.0821 9370
13	1.0329 9200	0.9680 6171	13.1967 9872	12.7753 1555	0.0757 7595
14	1.0355 7448	0.9656 4759	14.2297 9072	13.7409 6314	0.0702 7510
15	1.0381 6341	0.9632 3949	15.2653 6520	14.7042 0264	0.0655 0777
16	1.0407 5882	0.9608 3740	16.3035 2861	15.6650 4004	0.0613 3642
17	1.0433 6072	0.9584 4130	17.3442 8743	16.6234 8133	0.0576 5587
18	1.0459 6912	0.9560 5117	18.3876 4815	17.5795 3250	0.0543 8433
19	1.0485 8404	0.9536 6700	19.4336 1727	18.5331 9950	0.0514 5722
20	1.0512 0550	0.9512 8878	20.4822 0131	19.4844 8828	0.0488 2288
21	1.0538 3352	0.9489 1649	21.5334 0682	20.4334 0477	0.0464 3947
22	1.0564 6810	0.9465 5011	22.5872 4033	21.3799 5488	0.0442 7278
23	1.0591 0927	0.9441 8964	23.6437 0843	22.3241 4452	0.0422 9455
24	1.0617 5704	0.9418 3505	24.7028 1770	23.2659 7957	0.0404 8121
25	1.0644 1144	0.9394 8634	25.7645 7475	24.2054 6591	0.0388 1298
26	1.0670 7247	0.9371 4348	26.8289 8619	25.1426 0939	0.0372 7312
27	1.0697 4015	0.9348 0646	27.8960 5865	26.0774 1585	0.0358 4736
28	1.0724 1450	0.9324 7527	28.9657 9880	27.0098 9112	0.0345 2347
29	1.0750 9553	0.9301 4990	30.0382 1330	27.9400 4102	0.0332 9093
30	1.0777 8327	0.9278 3032	31.1133 0883	28.8678 7134	0.0321 4059
31	1.0804 7773	0.9255 1653	32.1910 9210	29.7933 8787	0.0310 6449
32	1.0831 7892	0.9232 0851	33.2715 6983	30.7165 9638	0.0300 5569
33	1.0858 8687	0.9209 0624	34.3547 4876	31.6375 0262	0.0291 0806
34	1.0886 0159	0.9186 0972	35.4406 3563	32.5561 1234	0.0282 1620
35	1.0913 2309	0.9163 1892	36.5292 3722	33.4724 3126	0.0273 7533
36	1.0940 5140	0.9140 3384	37.6205 6031	34.3864 6510	0.0265 8121
37	1.0967 8653	0.9117 5445	38.7146 1171	35.2982 1955	0.0258 3004
38	1.0995 2850	0.9094 8075	39.8113 9824	36.2077 0030	0.0251 1843
39	1.1022 7732	0.9072 1272	40.9109 2673	37.1149 1302	0.0244 4335
40	1.1050 3301	0.9049 5034	42.0132 0405	38.0198 6336	0.0238 0204
41	1.1077 9559	0.9026 9361	43.1182 3706	38.9225 5697	0.0231 9204
42	1.1105 6508	0.9004 4250	44.2260 3265	39.8229 9947	0.0226 1112
43	1.1133 4149	0.8981 9701	45.3365 9774	40.7211 9648	0.0220 5724
44	1.1161 2485	0.8959 5712	46.4499 3923	41.6171 5359	0.0215 2855
45	1.1189 1516	0.8937 2281	47.5660 6408	42.5108 7640	0.0210 2339
46	1.1217 1245	0.8914 9407	48.6849 7924	43.4023 7047	0.0205 4022
47	1.1245 1673	0.8892 7090	49.8066 9169	44.2916 4137	0.0200 7762
48	1.1273 2802	0.8870 5326	50.9312 0842	45.1786 9463	0.0196 3433
49	1.1301 4634	0.8848 4116	52.0585 3644	46.0635 3580	0.0192 0915
50	1.1329 7171	0.8826 3457	53.1886 8278	46.9461 7037	0.0188 0099

* An abbreviated version of Table II, from MATHEMATICS OF INVESTMENT by Paul R. Rider and Carl H. Fischer.

TABLE IV (continued)

$i = \frac{1}{4}\%$

n	$(1+i)^n$	$(1+i)^{-n}$	$s_{\overline{n}\mid i}$	$a_{\overline{n}\mid i}$	$s_{\overline{n}\mid i}^{-1}$
51	1.1358 0414	0.8804 3349	54.3216 5449	47.8266 0386	0.0184 0886
52	1.1386 4365	0.8782 3790	55.4574 5862	48.7048 4176	0.0180 3184
53	1.1414 9026	0.8760 4778	56.5961 0227	49.5808 8953	0.0176 6906
54	1.1443 4398	0.8738 6312	57.7375 9252	50.4547 5265	0.0173 1974
55	1.1472 0484	0.8716 8391	58.8819 3650	51.3264 3656	0.0169 8314
56	1.1500 7285	0.8695 1013	60.0291 4135	52.1959 4669	0.0166 5858
57	1.1529 4804	0.8673 4178	61.1792 1420	53.0632 8847	0.0163 4542
58	1.1558 3041	0.8651 7883	62.3321 6223	53.9284 6730	0.0160 4308
59	1.1587 1998	0.8630 2128	63.4879 9264	54.7914 8858	0.0157 5101
60	1.1616 1678	0.8608 6911	64.6467 1262	55.6523 5769	0.0154 6869
61	1.1645 2082	0.8587 2230	65.8083 2940	56.5110 7999	0.0151 9564
62	1.1674 3213	0.8565 8085	66.9728 5023	57.3676 6083	0.0149 3142
63	1.1703 5071	0.8544 4474	68.1402 8235	58.2221 0557	0.0146 7561
64	1.1732 7658	0.8523 1395	69.3106 3306	59.0744 1952	0.0144 2780
65	1.1762 0977	0.8501 8848	70.4839 0964	59.9246 0800	0.0141 8764
66	1.1791 5030	0.8480 6831	71.6601 1942	60.7726 7631	0.0139 5476
67	1.1820 9817	0.8459 5343	72.8392 6971	61.6186 2974	0.0137 2886
68	1.1850 5342	0.8438 4382	74.0213 6789	62.4624 7355	0.0135 0961
69	1.1880 1605	0.8417 3947	75.2064 2131	63.3042 1302	0.0132 9674
70	1.1909 8609	0.8396 4037	76.3944 3736	64.1438 5339	0.0130 8996
71	1.1939 6356	0.8375 4650	77.5854 2345	64.9813 9989	0.0128 8902
72	1.1969 4847	0.8354 5786	78.7793 8701	65.8168 5774	0.0126 9368
73	1.1999 4084	0.8333 7442	79.9763 3548	66.6502 3216	0.0125 0370
74	1.2029 4069	0.8312 9618	81.1762 7632	67.4815 2834	0.0123 1887
75	1.2059 4804	0.8292 2312	82.3792 1701	68.3107 5146	0.0121 3898
76	1.2089 6291	0.8271 5523	83.5851 6505	69.1379 0670	0.0119 6385
77	1.2119 8532	0.8250 9250	84.7941 2797	69.9629 9920	0.0117 9327
78	1.2150 1528	0.8230 3491	86.0061 1329	70.7860 3411	0.0116 2708
79	1.2180 5282	0.8209 8246	87.2211 2857	71.6070 1657	0.0114 6511
80	1.2210 9795	0.8189 3512	88.4391 8139	72.4259 5169	0.0113 0721
81	1.2241 5070	0.8168 9289	89.6602 7934	73.2428 4458	0.0111 5321
82	1.2272 1108	0.8148 5575	90.8844 3004	74.0577 0033	0.0110 0298
83	1.2302 7910	0.8128 2369	92.1116 4112	74.8705 2402	0.0108 5639
84	1.2333 5480	0.8107 9670	93.3419 2022	75.6813 2072	0.0107 1330
85	1.2364 3819	0.8087 7476	94.5752 7502	76.4900 9548	0.0105 7359
86	1.2395 2928	0.8067 5787	95.8117 1321	77.2968 5335	0.0104 3714
87	1.2426 2811	0.8047 4600	97.0512 4249	78.1015 9935	0.0103 0384
88	1.2457 3468	0.8027 3915	98.2938 7060	78.9043 3850	0.0101 7357
89	1.2488 4901	0.8007 3731	99.5396 0527	79.7050 7581	0.0100 4625
90	1.2519 7114	0.7987 4046	100.7884 5429	80.5038 1627	0.0099 2177
91	1.2551 0106	0.7967 4859	102.0404 2542	81.3005 6486	0.0098 0004
92	1.2582 3882	0.7947 6168	103.2955 2649	82.0953 2654	0.0096 8096
93	1.2613 8441	0.7927 7973	104.5537 6530	82.8881 0628	0.0095 6446
94	1.2645 3787	0.7908 0273	105.8151 4972	83.6789 0900	0.0094 5044
95	1.2676 9922	0.7888 3065	107.0796 8759	84.4677 3966	0.0093 3884
96	1.2708 6847	0.7868 6349	108.3473 8681	85.2546 0315	0.0092 2957
97	1.2740 4564	0.7849 0124	109.6182 5528	86.0395 0439	0.0091 2257
98	1.2772 3075	0.7829 4388	110.8923 0091	86.8224 4827	0.0090 1776
99	1.2804 2383	0.7809 9140	112.1695 3167	87.6034 3967	0.0089 1508
100	1.2836 2489	0.7790 4379	113.4499 5550	88.3824 8346	0.0088 1446

TABLE IV (continued)

$i = \frac{1}{2}\%$

n	$(1+i)^n$	$(1+i)^{-n}$	$s_{\overline{n}\rceil i}$	$a_{\overline{n}\rceil i}$	$s^{-1}_{\overline{n}\rceil i}$
1	1.0050 0000	0.9950 2488	1.0000 0000	0.9950 2488	1.0000 0000
2	1.0100 2500	0.9900 7450	2.0050 0000	1.9850 9938	0.4987 5312
3	1.0150 7513	0.9851 4876	3.0150 2500	2.9702 4814	0.3316 7221
4	1.0201 5050	0.9802 4752	4.0301 0013	3.9504 9566	0.2481 3279
5	1.0252 5125	0.9753 7067	5.0502 5063	4.9258 6633	0.1980 0997
6	1.0303 7751	0.9705 1808	6.0755 0188	5.8963 8441	0.1645 9546
7	1.0355 2940	0.9656 8963	7.1058 7939	6.8620 7404	0.1407 2854
8	1.0407 0704	0.9608 8520	8.1414 0879	7.8229 5924	0.1228 2886
9	1.0459 1058	0.9561 0468	9.1821 1583	8.7790 6392	0.1089 0736
10	1.0511 4013	0.9513 4794	10.2280 2641	9.7304 1186	0.0977 7057
11	1.0563 9583	0.9466 1489	11.2791 6654	10.6770 2673	0.0886 5903
12	1.0616 7781	0.9419 0534	12.3355 6237	11.6189 3207	0.0810 6643
13	1.0669 8620	0.9372 1924	13.3972 4018	12.5561 5131	0.0746 4224
14	1.0723 2113	0.9325 5646	14.4642 2639	13.4887 0777	0.0691 3609
15	1.0776 8274	0.9279 1688	15.5365 4752	14.4166 2465	0.0643 6436
16	1.0830 7115	0.9233 0037	16.6142 3026	15.3399 2502	0.0601 8937
17	1.0884 8651	0.9187 0684	17.6973 0141	16.2586 3186	0.0565 0579
18	1.0939 2894	0.9141 3616	18.7857 8791	17.1727 6802	0.0532 3173
19	1.0993 9858	0.9095 8822	19.8797 1685	18.0823 5624	0.0503 0253
20	1.1048 9558	0.9050 6290	20.9791 1544	18.9874 1915	0.0476 6645
21	1.1104 2006	0.9005 6010	22.0840 1101	19.8879 7925	0.0452 8163
22	1.1159 7216	0.8960 7971	23.1944 3107	20.7840 5896	0.0431 1380
23	1.1215 5202	0.8916 2160	24.3104 0322	21.6756 8055	0.0411 3465
24	1.1271 5978	0.8871 8567	25.4319 5524	22.5628 6622	0.0393 2061
25	1.1327 9558	0.8827 7181	26.5591 1502	23.4456 3803	0.0376 5186
26	1.1384 5955	0.8783 7991	27.6919 1059	24.3240 1794	0.0361 1163
27	1.1441 5185	0.8740 0986	28.8303 7015	25.1980 2780	0.0346 8565
28	1.1498 7261	0.8696 6155	29.9745 2200	26.0676 8936	0.0333 6167
29	1.1556 2197	0.8653 3488	31.1243 9461	26.9330 2423	0.0321 2914
30	1.1614 0008	0.8610 2973	32.2800 1658	27.7940 5397	0.0309 7892
31	1.1672 0708	0.8567 4600	33.4414 1666	28.6507 9997	0.0299 0304
32	1.1730 4312	0.8524 8358	34.6086 2375	29.5032 8355	0.0288 9453
33	1.1789 0833	0.8482 4237	35.7816 6686	30.3515 2592	0.0279 4727
34	1.1848 0288	0.8440 2226	36.9605 7520	31.1955 4818	0.0270 5586
35	1.1907 2689	0.8398 2314	38.1453 7807	32.0353 7132	0.0262 1550
36	1.1966 8052	0.8356 4492	39.3361 0496	32.8710 1624	0.0254 2194
37	1.2026 6393	0.8314 8748	40.5327 8549	33.7025 0372	0.0246 7139
38	1.2086 7725	0.8273 5073	41.7354 4942	34.5298 5445	0.0239 6045
39	1.2147 2063	0.8232 3455	42.9441 2666	35.3530 8900	0.0232 8607
40	1.2207 9424	0.8191 3886	44.1588 4730	36.1722 2786	0.0226 4552
41	1.2268 9821	0.8150 6354	45.3796 4153	36.9872 9141	0.0220 3631
42	1.2330 3270	0.8110 0850	46.6065 3974	37.7982 9991	0.0214 5622
43	1.2391 9786	0.8069 7363	47.8395 7244	38.6052 7354	0.0209 0320
44	1.2453 9385	0.8029 5884	49.0787 7030	39.4082 3238	0.0203 7541
45	1.2516 2082	0.7989 6402	50.3241 6415	40.2071 9640	0.0198 7117
46	1.2578 7892	0.7949 8907	51.5757 8497	41.0021 8547	0.0193 8894
47	1.2641 6832	0.7910 3390	52.8336 6390	41.7932 1937	0.0189 2733
48	1.2704 8916	0.7870 9841	54.0978 3222	42.5803 1778	0.0184 8503
49	1.2768 4161	0.7831 8250	55.3683 2138	43.3635 0028	0.0180 6087
50	1.2832 2581	0.7792 8607	56.6451 6299	44.1427 8635	0.0176 5376

TABLE IV (continued)

$i = \frac{1}{2}\%$

n	$(1+i)^n$	$(1+i)^{-n}$	$s_{\overline{n}\rceil i}$	$a_{\overline{n}\rceil i}$	$s_{\overline{n}\rceil i}^{-1}$
51	1.2896 4194	0.7754 0902	57.9283 8880	44.9181 9537	0.0172 6269
52	1.2960 9015	0.7715 5127	59.2180 3075	45.6897 4664	0.0168 8675
53	1.3025 7060	0.7677 1270	60.5141 2090	46.4574 5934	0.0165 2507
54	1.3090 8346	0.7638 9324	61.8166 9150	47.2213 5258	0.0161 7686
55	1.3156 2887	0.7600 9277	63.1257 7496	47.9814 4535	0.0158 4139
56	1.3222 0702	0.7563 1122	64.4414 0384	48.7377 5657	0.0155 1797
57	1.3288 1805	0.7525 4847	65.7636 1086	49.4903 0505	0.0152 0598
58	1.3354 6214	0.7488 0445	67.0924 2891	50.2391 0950	0.0149 0481
59	1.3421 3946	0.7450 7906	68.4278 9105	50.9841 8855	0.0146 1392
60	1.3488 5015	0.7413 7220	69.7700 3051	51.7255 6075	0.0143 3280
61	1.3555 9440	0.7376 8378	71.1188 8066	52.4632 4453	0.0140 6096
62	1.3623 7238	0.7340 1371	72.4744 7507	53.1972 5824	0.0137 9796
63	1.3691 8424	0.7303 6190	73.8368 4744	53.9276 2014	0.0135 4337
64	1.3760 3016	0.7267 2826	75.2060 3168	54.6543 4839	0.0132 9681
65	1.3829 1031	0.7231 1269	76.5820 6184	55.3774 6109	0.0130 5789
66	1.3898 2486	0.7195 1512	77.9649 7215	56.0969 7621	0.0128 2627
67	1.3967 7399	0.7159 3544	79.3547 9701	56.8129 1165	0.0126 0163
68	1.4037 5785	0.7123 7357	80.7515 7099	57.5252 8522	0.0123 8366
69	1.4107 7664	0.7088 2943	82.1553 2885	58.2341 1465	0.0121 7206
70	1.4178 3053	0.7053 0291	83.5661 0549	58.9394 1756	0.0119 6657
71	1.4249 1968	0.7017 9394	84.9839 3602	59.6412 1151	0.0117 6693
72	1.4320 4428	0.6983 0243	86.4088 5570	60.3395 1394	0.0115 7289
73	1.4392 0450	0.6948 2829	87.8408 9998	61.0343 4222	0.0113 8422
74	1.4464 0052	0.6913 7143	89.2801 0448	61.7257 1366	0.0112 0070
75	1.4536 3252	0.6879 3177	90.7265 0500	62.4136 4543	0.0110 2214
76	1.4609 0069	0.6845 0923	92.1801 3752	63.0981 5466	0.0108 4832
77	1.4682 0519	0.6811 0371	93.6410 3821	63.7792 5836	0.0106 7908
78	1.4755 4622	0.6777 1513	95.1092 4340	64.4569 7350	0.0105 1423
79	1.4829 2395	0.6743 4342	96.5847 8962	65.1313 1691	0.0103 5360
80	1.4903 3857	0.6709 8847	98.0677 1357	65.8023 0538	0.0101 9704
81	1.4977 9026	0.6676 5022	99.5580 5214	66.4699 5561	0.0100 4439
82	1.5052 7921	0.6643 2858	101.0558 4240	67.1342 8419	0.0098 9552
83	1.5128 0561	0.6610 2346	102.5611 2161	67.7953 0765	0.0097 5028
84	1.5203 6964	0.6577 3479	104.0739 2722	68.4530 4244	0.0096 0855
85	1.5279 7148	0.6544 6248	105.5942 9685	69.1075 0491	0.0094 7021
86	1.5356 1134	0.6512 0644	107.1222 6834	69.7587 1135	0.0093 3513
87	1.5432 8940	0.6479 6661	108.6578 7968	70.4066 7796	0.0092 0320
88	1.5510 0585	0.6447 4290	110.2011 6908	71.0514 2086	0.0090 7431
89	1.5587 6087	0.6415 3522	111.7521 7492	71.6929 5608	0.0089 4837
90	1.5665 5468	0.6383 4350	113.3109 3580	72.3312 9958	0.0088 2527
91	1.5743 8745	0.6351 6766	114.8774 9048	72.9664 6725	0.0087 0493
92	1.5822 5939	0.6320 0763	116.4518 7793	73.5984 7487	0.0085 8724
93	1.5901 7069	0.6288 6331	118.0341 3732	74.2273 3818	0.0084 7213
94	1.5981 2154	0.6257 3464	119.6243 0800	74.8530 7282	0.0083 5950
95	1.6061 1215	0.6226 2153	121.2224 2954	75.4756 9434	0.0082 4930
96	1.6141 4271	0.6195 2391	122.8285 4169	76.0952 1825	0.0081 4143
97	1.6222 1342	0.6164 4170	124.4426 8440	76.7116 5995	0.0080 3583
98	1.6303 2449	0.6133 7483	126.0648 9782	77.3250 3478	0.0079 3242
99	1.6384 7611	0.6103 2321	127.6952 2231	77.9353 5799	0.0078 3115
100	1.6466 6849	0.6072 8678	129.3336 9842	78.5426 4477	0.0077 3194

TABLE IV (continued)

$i = \frac{3}{4}\%$

n	$(1+i)^n$	$(1+i)^{-n}$	$s_{\overline{n}\rvert i}$	$a_{\overline{n}\rvert i}$	$s_{\overline{n}\rvert i}^{-1}$
1	1.0075 0000	0.9925 5583	1.0000 0000	0.9925 5583	1.0000 0000
2	1.0150 5625	0.9851 6708	2.0075 0000	1.9777 2291	0.4981 3200
3	1.0226 6917	0.9778 3333	3.0225 5625	2.9555 5624	0.3308 4579
4	1.0303 3919	0.9705 5417	4.0452 2542	3.9261 1041	0.2472 0501
5	1.0380 6673	0.9633 2920	5.0755 6461	4.8894 3961	0.1970 2242
6	1.0458 5224	0.9561 5802	6.1136 3135	5.8455 9763	0.1635 6891
7	1.0536 9613	0.9490 4022	7.1594 8358	6.7946 3785	0.1396 7488
8	1.0615 9885	0.9419 7540	8.2131 7971	7.7366 1325	0.1217 5552
9	1.0695 6084	0.9349 6318	9.2747 7856	8.6715 7642	0.1078 1929
10	1.0775 8255	0.9280 0315	10.3443 3940	9.5995 7958	0.0966 7123
11	1.0856 6441	0.9210 9494	11.4219 2194	10.5206 7452	0.0875 5094
12	1.0938 0690	0.9142 3815	12.5075 8636	11.4349 1267	0.0799 5148
13	1.1020 1045	0.9074 3241	13.6013 9325	12.3423 4508	0.0735 2188
14	1.1102 7553	0.9006 7733	14.7034 0370	13.2430 2242	0.0680 1146
15	1.1186 0259	0.8939 7254	15.8136 7923	14.1369 9395	0.0632 3639
16	1.1269 9211	0.8873 1766	16.9322 8183	15.0243 1261	0.0590 5879
17	1.1354 4455	0.8807 1231	18.0592 7394	15.9050 2492	0.0553 7321
18	1.1439 6039	0.8741 5614	19.1947 1849	16.7791 8107	0.0520 9766
19	1.1525 4009	0.8676 4878	20.3386 7888	17.6468 2984	0.0491 6740
20	1.1611 8414	0.8611 8985	21.4912 1897	18.5080 1969	0.0465 3063
21	1.1698 9302	0.8547 7901	22.6524 0312	19.3627 9870	0.0441 4543
22	1.1786 6722	0.8484 1589	23.8222 9614	20.2112 1459	0.0419 7748
23	1.1875 0723	0.8421 0014	25.0009 6336	21.0533 1473	0.0399 9846
24	1.1964 1353	0.8358 3140	26.1884 7059	21.8891 4614	0.0381 8474
25	1.2053 8663	0.8296 0933	27.3848 8412	22.7187 5547	0.0365 1650
26	1.2144 2703	0.8234 3358	28.5902 7075	23.5421 8905	0.0349 7693
27	1.2235 3523	0.8173 0380	29.8046 9778	24.3594 9286	0.0335 5176
28	1.2327 1175	0.8112 1966	31.0282 3301	25.1707 1251	0.0322 2871
29	1.2419 5709	0.8051 8080	32.2609 4476	25.9758 9331	0.0309 9723
30	1.2512 7176	0.7991 8690	33.5029 0184	26.7750 8021	0.0298 4816
31	1.2606 5630	0.7932 3762	34.7541 7361	27.5683 1783	0.0287 7452
32	1.2701 1122	0.7873 3262	36.0148 2991	28.3556 5045	0.0277 6634
33	1.2796 3706	0.7814 7158	37.2849 4113	29.1371 2203	0.0268 2048
34	1.2892 3434	0.7756 5418	38.5645 7819	29.9127 7621	0.0259 3053
35	1.2989 0359	0.7698 8008	39.8538 1253	30.6826 5629	0.0250 9170
36	1.3086 4537	0.7641 4896	41.1527 1612	31.4468 0525	0.0242 9973
37	1.3184 6021	0.7584 6051	42.4613 6149	32.2052 6576	0.0235 5082
38	1.3283 4866	0.7528 1440	43.7798 2170	32.9580 8016	0.0228 4157
39	1.3383 1128	0.7472 1032	45.1081 7037	33.7052 9048	0.0221 6893
40	1.3483 4861	0.7416 4796	46.4464 8164	34.4469 3844	0.0215 3016
41	1.3584 6123	0.7361 2701	47.7948 3026	35.1830 6545	0.0209 2276
42	1.3686 4969	0.7306 4716	49.1532 9148	35.9137 1260	0.0203 4452
43	1.3789 1456	0.7252 0809	50.5219 4117	36.6389 2070	0.0197 9338
44	1.3892 5642	0.7198 0952	51.9008 5573	37.3587 3022	0.0192 6751
45	1.3996 7584	0.7144 5114	53.2901 1215	38.0731 8136	0.0187 6521
46	1.4101 7341	0.7091 3264	54.6897 8799	38.7823 1401	0.0182 8495
47	1.4207 4971	0.7038 5374	56.0999 6140	39.4861 6774	0.0178 2532
48	1.4314 0533	0.6986 1414	57.5207 1111	40.1847 8189	0.0173 8504
49	1.4421 4087	0.6934 1353	58.9521 1644	40.8781 9542	0.0169 6292
50	1.4529 5693	0.6882 5165	60.3942 5732	41.5664 4707	0.0165 5787

TABLE IV (continued)

$i = \frac{3}{4}\%$

n	$(1+i)^n$	$(1+i)^{-n}$	$s_{\overline{n}\mid i}$	$a_{\overline{n}\mid i}$	$s_{\overline{n}\mid i}^{-1}$
51	1.4638 5411	0.6831 2819	61.8472 1424	42.2495 7525	0.0161 6888
52	1.4748 3301	0.6780 4286	63.3110 6835	42.9276 1812	0.0157 9503
53	1.4858 9426	0.6729 9540	64.7859 0136	43.6006 1351	0.0154 3546
54	1.4970 3847	0.6679 8551	66.2717 9562	44.2685 9902	0.0150 8938
55	1.5082 6626	0.6630 1291	67.7688 3409	44.9316 1193	0.0147 5605
56	1.5195 7825	0.6580 7733	69.2771 0035	45.5896 8926	0.0144 3478
57	1.5309 7509	0.6531 7849	70.7966 7860	46.2428 6776	0.0141 2496
58	1.5424 5740	0.6483 1612	72.3276 5369	46.8911 8388	0.0138 2597
59	1.5540 2583	0.6434 8995	73.8701 1109	47.5346 7382	0.0135 3727
60	1.5656 8103	0.6386 9970	75.4241 3693	48.1733 7352	0.0132 5836
61	1.5774 2363	0.6339 4511	76.9898 1795	48.8073 1863	0.0129 8873
62	1.5892 5431	0.6292 2592	78.5672 4159	49.4365 4455	0.0127 2795
63	1.6011 7372	0.6245 4185	80.1564 9590	50.0610 8640	0.0124 7560
64	1.6131 8252	0.6198 9266	81.7576 6962	50.6809 7906	0.0122 3127
65	1.6252 8139	0.6152 7807	83.3708 5214	51.2962 5713	0.0119 9460
66	1.6374 7100	0.6106 9784	84.9961 3353	51.9069 5497	0.0117 6524
67	1.6497 5203	0.6061 5170	86.6336 0453	52.5131 0667	0.0115 4286
68	1.6621 2517	0.6016 3940	88.2833 5657	53.1147 4607	0.0113 2716
69	1.6745 9111	0.5971 6070	89.9454 8174	53.7119 0677	0.0111 1785
70	1.6871 5055	0.5927 1533	91.6200 7285	54.3046 2210	0.0109 1464
71	1.6998 0418	0.5883 0306	93.3072 2340	54.8929 2516	0.0107 1728
72	1.7125 5271	0.5839 2363	95.0070 2758	55.4768 4880	0.0105 2554
73	1.7253 9685	0.5795 7681	96.7195 8028	56.0564 2561	0.0103 3917
74	1.7383 3733	0.5752 6234	98.4449 7714	56.6316 8795	0.0101 5796
75	1.7513 7486	0.5709 7999	100.1833 1446	57.2026 6794	0.0099 8170
76	1.7645 1017	0.5667 2952	101.9346 8932	57.7693 9746	0.0098 1020
77	1.7777 4400	0.5625 1069	103.6991 9949	58.3319 0815	0.0096 4328
78	1.7910 7708	0.5583 2326	105.4769 4349	58.8902 3141	0.0094 8074
79	1.8045 1015	0.5541 6701	107.2680 2056	59.4443 9842	0.0093 2244
80	1.8180 4398	0.5500 4170	109.0725 3072	59.9944 4012	0.0091 6821
81	1.8316 7931	0.5459 4710	110.8905 7470	60.5403 8722	0.0090 1790
82	1.8454 1691	0.5418 8297	112.7222 5401	61.0822 7019	0.0088 7136
83	1.8592 5753	0.5378 4911	114.5676 7091	61.6201 1930	0.0087 2847
84	1.8732 0196	0.5338 4527	116.4269 2845	62.1539 6456	0.0085 8908
85	1.8872 5098	0.5298 7123	118.3001 3041	62.6838 3579	0.0084 5308
86	1.9014 0536	0.5259 2678	120.1873 8139	63.2097 6257	0.0083 2034
87	1.9156 6590	0.5220 1169	122.0887 8675	63.7317 7427	0.0081 9076
88	1.9300 3339	0.5181 2575	124.0044 5265	64.2499 0002	0.0080 6423
89	1.9445 0865	0.5142 6873	125.9344 8604	64.7641 6875	0.0079 4064
90	1.9590 9246	0.5104 4043	127.8789 9469	65.2746 0918	0.0078 1989
91	1.9737 8565	0.5066 4063	129.8380 8715	65.7812 4981	0.0077 0190
92	1.9885 8905	0.5028 6911	131.8118 7280	66.2841 1892	0.0075 8657
93	2.0035 0346	0.4991 2567	133.8004 6185	66.7832 4458	0.0074 7382
94	2.0185 2974	0.4954 1009	135.8039 6531	67.2786 5467	0.0073 6356
95	2.0336 6871	0.4917 2217	137.8224 9505	67.7703 7685	0.0072 5571
96	2.0489 2123	0.4880 6171	139.8561 6377	68.2584 3856	0.0071 5020
97	2.0642 8814	0.4844 2850	141.9050 8499	68.7428 6705	0.0070 4696
98	2.0797 7030	0.4808 2233	143.9693 7313	69.2236 8938	0.0069 4592
99	2.0953 6858	0.4772 4301	146.0491 4343	69.7009 3239	0.0068 4701
100	2.1110 8384	0.4736 9033	148.1445 1201	70.1746 2272	0.0067 5017

TABLE IV (continued)

$i = 1\%$

n	$(1+i)^n$	$(1+i)^{-n}$	$s_{\overline{n}\mid i}$	$a_{\overline{n}\mid i}$	$s^{-1}_{\overline{n}\mid i}$
1	1.0100 0000	0.9900 9901	1.0000 0000	0.9900 9901	1.0000 0000
2	1.0201 0000	0.9802 9605	2.0100 0000	1.9703 9506	0.4975 1244
3	1.0303 0100	0.9705 9015	3.0301 0000	2.9409 8521	0.3300 2211
4	1.0406 0401	0.9609 8034	4.0604 0100	3.9019 6555	0.2462 8109
5	1.0510 1005	0.9514 6569	5.1010 0501	4.8534 3124	0.1960 3980
6	1.0615 2015	0.9420 4524	6.1520 1506	5.7954 7647	0.1625 4837
7	1.0721 3535	0.9327 1805	7.2135 3521	6.7281 9453	0.1386 2828
8	1.0828 5671	0.9234 8322	8.2856 7056	7.6516 7775	0.1206 9029
9	1.0936 8527	0.9143 3982	9.3685 2727	8.5660 1758	0.1067 4036
10	1.1046 2213	0.9052 8695	10.4622 1254	9.4713 0453	0.0955 8208
11	1.1156 6835	0.8963 2372	11.5668 3467	10.3676 2825	0.0864 5408
12	1.1268 2503	0.8874 4923	12.6825 0301	11.2550 7747	0.0788 4879
13	1.1380 9328	0.8786 6260	13.8093 2804	12.1337 4007	0.0724 1482
14	1.1494 7421	0.8699 6297	14.9474 2132	13.0037 0304	0.0669 0117
15	1.1609 6896	0.8613 4947	16.0968 9554	13.8650 5252	0.0621 2378
16	1.1725 7864	0.8528 2126	17.2578 6449	14.7178 7378	0.0579 4460
17	1.1843 0443	0.8443 7749	18.4304 4314	15.5622 5127	0.0542 5806
18	1.1961 4748	0.8360 1731	19.6147 4757	16.3982 6858	0.0509 8205
19	1.2081 0895	0.8277 3992	20.8108 9504	17.2260 0850	0.0480 5175
20	1.2201 9004	0.8195 4447	22.0190 0399	18.0455 5297	0.0454 1531
21	1.2323 9194	0.8114 3017	23.2391 9403	18.8569 8313	0.0430 3075
22	1.2447 1586	0.8033 9621	24.4715 8598	19.6603 7934	0.0408 6372
23	1.2571 6302	0.7954 4179	25.7163 0183	20.4558 2113	0.0388 8584
24	1.2697 3465	0.7875 6613	26.9734 6485	21.2433 8726	0.0370 7347
25	1.2824 3200	0.7797 6844	28.2431 9950	22.0231 5570	0.0354 0675
26	1.2952 5631	0.7720 4796	29.5256 3150	22.7952 0366	0.0338 6888
27	1.3082 0888	0.7644 0392	30.8208 8781	23.5596 0759	0.0324 4553
28	1.3212 9097	0.7568 3557	32.1290 9669	24.3164 4316	0.0311 2444
29	1.3345 0388	0.7493 4215	33.4503 8766	25.0657 8530	0.0298 9502
30	1.3478 4892	0.7419 2292	34.7848 9153	25.8077 0822	0.0287 4811
31	1.3613 2740	0.7345 7715	36.1327 4045	26.5422 8537	0.0276 7573
32	1.3749 4068	0.7273 0411	37.4940 6785	27.2695 8947	0.0266 7089
33	1.3886 9009	0.7201 0307	38.8690 0853	27.9896 9255	0.0257 2744
34	1.4025 7699	0.7129 7334	40.2576 9862	28.7026 6589	0.0248 3997
35	1.4166 0276	0.7059 1420	41.6602 7560	29.4085 8009	0.0240 0368
36	1.4307 6878	0.6989 2495	43.0768 7836	30.1075 0504	0.0232 1431
37	1.4450 7647	0.6920 0490	44.5076 4714	30.7995 0994	0.0224 6805
38	1.4595 2724	0.6851 5337	45.9527 2361	31.4846 6330	0.0217 6150
39	1.4741 2251	0.6783 6967	47.4122 5085	32.1630 3298	0.0210 9160
40	1.4888 6373	0.6716 5314	48.8863 7336	32.8346 8611	0.0204 5560
41	1.5037 5237	0.6650 0311	50.3752 3709	33.4996 8922	0.0198 5102
42	1.5187 8989	0.6584 1892	51.8789 8946	34.1581 0814	0.0192 7563
43	1.5339 7779	0.6518 9992	53.3977 7936	34.8100 0806	0.0187 2737
44	1.5493 1757	0.6454 4546	54.9317 5715	35.4554 5352	0.0182 0441
45	1.5648 1075	0.6390 5492	56.4810 7472	36.0945 0844	0.0177 0505
46	1.5804 5885	0.6327 2764	58.0458 8547	36.7272 3608	0.0172 2775
47	1.5962 6344	0.6264 6301	59.6263 4432	37.3536 9909	0.0167 7111
48	1.6122 2608	0.6202 6041	61.2226 0777	37.9739 5949	0.0163 3384
49	1.6283 4834	0.6141 1921	62.8348 3385	38.5880 7871	0.0159 1474
50	1.6446 3182	0.6080 3882	64.4631 8218	39.1961 1753	0.0155 1273

TABLE IV (continued)

$i = 1\%$

n	$(1+i)^n$	$(1+i)^{-n}$	$s_{\overline{n}\rvert i}$	$a_{\overline{n}\rvert i}$	$s^{-1}_{\overline{n}\rvert i}$
51	1.6610 7814	0.6020 1864	66.1078 1401	39.7981 3617	0.0151 2680
52	1.6776 8892	0.5960 5806	67.7688 9215	40.3941 9423	0.0147 5603
53	1.6944 6581	0.5901 5649	69.4465 8107	40.9843 5072	0.0143 9956
54	1.7114 1047	0.5843 1336	71.1410 4688	41.5686 6408	0.0140 5658
55	1.7285 2457	0.5785 2808	72.8524 5735	42.1471 9216	0.0137 2637
56	1.7458 0982	0.5728 0008	74.5809 8192	42.7199 9224	0.0134 0824
57	1.7632 6792	0.5671 2879	76.3267 9174	43.2871 2102	0.0131 0156
58	1.7809 0060	0.5615 1365	78.0900 5966	43.8486 3468	0.0128 0573
59	1.7987 0960	0.5559 5411	79.8709 6025	44.4045 8879	0.0125 2020
60	1.8166 9670	0.5504 4962	81.6696 6986	44.9550 3841	0.0122 4445
61	1.8348 6367	0.5449 9962	83.4863 6655	45.5000 3803	0.0119 7800
62	1.8532 1230	0.5396 0358	85.3212 3022	46.0396 4161	0.0117 2041
63	1.8717 4443	0.5342 6097	87.1744 4252	46.5739 0258	0.0114 7125
64	1.8904 6187	0.5289 7126	89.0461 8695	47.1028 7385	0.0112 3013
65	1.9093 6649	0.5237 3392	90.9366 4882	47.6266 0777	0.0109 9667
66	1.9284 6015	0.5185 4844	92.8460 1531	48.1451 5621	0.0107 7052
67	1.9477 4475	0.5134 1429	94.7744 7546	48.6585 7050	0.0105 5136
68	1.9672 2220	0.5083 3099	96.7222 2021	49.1669 0149	0.0103 3889
69	1.9868 9442	0.5032 9801	98.6894 4242	49.6701 9949	0.0101 3280
70	2.0067 6337	0.4983 1486	100.6763 3684	50.1685 1435	0.0099 3282
71	2.0268 3100	0.4933 8105	102.6831 0021	50.6618 9539	0.0097 3870
72	2.0470 9931	0.4884 9609	104.7099 3121	51.1503 9148	0.0095 5019
73	2.0675 7031	0.4836 5949	106.7570 3052	51.6340 5097	0.0093 6706
74	2.0882 4601	0.4788 7078	108.8246 0083	52.1129 2175	0.0091 8910
75	2.1091 2847	0.4741 2949	110.9128 4684	52.5870 5124	0.0090 1609
76	2.1302 1975	0.4694 3514	113.0219 7530	53.0564 8637	0.0088 4784
77	2.1515 2195	0.4647 8726	115.1521 9506	53.5212 7364	0.0086 8416
78	2.1730 3717	0.4601 8541	117.3037 1701	53.9814 5905	0.0085 2488
79	2.1947 6754	0.4556 2912	119.4767 5418	54.4370 8817	0.0083 6983
80	2.2167 1522	0.4511 1794	121.6715 2172	54.8882 0611	0.0082 1885
81	2.2388 8237	0.4466 5142	123.8882 3694	55.3348 5753	0.0080 7179
82	2.2612 7119	0.4422 2913	126.1271 1931	55.7770 8666	0.0079 2851
83	2.2838 8390	0.4378 5063	128.3883 9050	56.2149 3729	0.0077 8887
84	2.3067 2274	0.4335 1547	130.6722 7440	56.6484 5276	0.0076 5273
85	2.3297 8997	0.4292 2324	132.9789 9715	57.0776 7600	0.0075 1998
86	2.3530 8787	0.4249 7350	135.3087 8712	57.5026 4951	0.0073 9050
87	2.3766 1875	0.4207 6585	137.6618 7499	57.9234 1535	0.0072 6417
88	2.4003 8494	0.4165 9985	140.0384 9374	58.3400 1520	0.0071 4089
89	2.4243 8879	0.4124 7510	142.4388 7868	58.7524 9030	0.0070 2056
90	2.4486 3267	0.4083 9119	144.8632 6746	59.1608 8148	0.0069 0306
91	2.4731 1900	0.4043 4771	147.3119 0014	59.5652 2919	0.0067 8832
92	2.4978 5019	0.4003 4427	149.7850 1914	59.9655 7346	0.0066 7624
93	2.5228 2869	0.3963 8046	152.2828 6933	60.3619 5392	0.0065 6673
94	2.5480 5698	0.3924 5590	154.8056 9803	60.7544 0982	0.0064 5971
95	2.5735 3755	0.3885 7020	157.3537 5501	61.1429 8002	0.0063 5511
96	2.5992 7293	0.3847 2297	159.9272 9256	61.5277 0299	0.0062 5284
97	2.6252 6565	0.3809 1383	162.5265 6548	61.9086 1682	0.0061 5284
98	2.6515 1831	0.3771 4241	165.1518 3114	62.2857 5923	0.0060 5503
99	2.6780 3349	0.3734 0832	167.8033 4945	62.6591 6755	0.0059 5936
100	2.7048 1383	0.3697 1121	170.4813 8294	63.0288 7877	0.0058 6574

TABLE IV (continued)

$i = 1\frac{1}{4}\%$

n	$(1+i)^n$	$(1+i)^{-n}$	$s_{\overline{n}\rceil i}$	$a_{\overline{n}\rceil i}$	$s_{\overline{n}\rceil i}^{-1}$
1	1.0125 0000	0.9876 5432	1.0000 0000	0.9876 5432	1.0000 0000
2	1.0251 5625	0.9754 6106	2.0125 0000	1.9631 1538	0.4968 9441
3	1.0379 7070	0.9634 1833	3.0376 5625	2.9265 3371	0.3292 0117
4	1.0509 4534	0.9515 2428	4.0756 2695	3.8780 5798	0.2453 6102
5	1.0640 8215	0.9397 7706	5.1265 7229	4.8178 3504	0.1950 6211
6	1.0773 8318	0.9281 7488	6.1906 5444	5.7460 0992	0.1615 3381
7	1.0908 5047	0.9167 1593	7.2680 3762	6.6627 2585	0.1375 8872
8	1.1044 8610	0.9053 9845	8.3588 8809	7.5681 2429	0.1196 3314
9	1.1182 9218	0.8942 2069	9.4633 7420	8.4623 4498	0.1056 7055
10	1.1322 7083	0.8831 8093	10.5816 6637	9.3455 2591	0.0945 0307
11	1.1464 2422	0.8722 7746	11.7139 3720	10.2178 0337	0.0853 6839
12	1.1607 5452	0.8615 0860	12.8603 6142	11.0793 1197	0.0777 5831
13	1.1752 6395	0.8508 7269	14.0211 1594	11.9301 8466	0.0713 2100
14	1.1899 5475	0.8403 6809	15.1963 7988	12.7705 5275	0.0658 0515
15	1.2048 2918	0.8299 9318	16.3863 3463	13.6005 4592	0.0610 2646
16	1.2198 8955	0.8197 4635	17.5911 6382	14.4202 9227	0.0568 4672
17	1.2351 3817	0.8096 2602	18.8110 5336	15.2299 1829	0.0531 6023
18	1.2505 7739	0.7996 3064	20.0461 9153	16.0295 4893	0.0498 8479
19	1.2662 0961	0.7897 5866	21.2967 6893	16.8193 0759	0.0469 5548
20	1.2820 3723	0.7800 0855	22.5629 7854	17.5993 1613	0.0443 2039
21	1.2980 6270	0.7703 7881	23.8450 1577	18.3696 9495	0.0419 3748
22	1.3142 8848	0.7608 6796	25.1430 7847	19.1305 6291	0.0397 7238
23	1.3307 1709	0.7514 7453	26.4573 6695	19.8820 3744	0.0377 9666
24	1.3473 5105	0.7421 9707	27.7880 8403	20.6242 3451	0.0359 8665
25	1.3641 9294	0.7330 3414	29.1354 3508	21.3572 6865	0.0343 2247
26	1.3812 4535	0.7239 8434	30.4996 2802	22.0812 5299	0.0327 8729
27	1.3985 1092	0.7150 4626	31.8808 7337	22.7962 9925	0.0313 6677
28	1.4159 9230	0.7062 1853	33.2793 8429	23.5025 1778	0.0300 4863
29	1.4336 9221	0.6974 9978	34.6953 7659	24.2000 1756	0.0288 2228
30	1.4516 1336	0.6888 8867	36.1290 6880	24.8889 0623	0.0276 7854
31	1.4697 5853	0.6803 8387	37.5806 8216	25.5692 9010	0.0266 0942
32	1.4881 3051	0.6719 8407	39.0504 4069	26.2412 7418	0.0256 0791
33	1.5067 3214	0.6636 8797	40.5385 7120	26.9049 6215	0.0246 6786
34	1.5255 6629	0.6554 9429	42.0453 0334	27.5604 5644	0.0237 8387
35	1.5446 3587	0.6474 0177	43.5708 6983	28.2078 5822	0.0229 5111
36	1.5639 4382	0.6394 0916	45.1155 0550	28.8472 6737	0.0221 6533
37	1.5834 9312	0.6315 1522	46.6794 4932	29.4787 8259	0.0214 2270
38	1.6032 8678	0.6237 1873	48.2926 4243	30.1025 0133	0.0207 1983
39	1.6233 2787	0.6160 1850	49.8862 2921	30.7185 1983	0.0200 5365
40	1.6436 1946	0.6084 1334	51.4895 5708	31.3269 3316	0.0194 2141
41	1.6641 6471	0.6009 0206	53.1331 7654	31.9278 3522	0.0188 2063
42	1.6849 6677	0.5934 8352	54.7973 4125	32.5213 1874	0.0182 4906
43	1.7060 2885	0.5861 5656	56.4823 0801	33.1074 7530	0.0177 0466
44	1.7273 5421	0.5789 2006	58.1883 3687	33.6863 9536	0.0171 8557
45	1.7489 4614	0.5717 7290	59.9156 9108	34.2581 6825	0.0166 9012
46	1.7708 0797	0.5647 1397	61.6646 3721	34.8228 8222	0.0162 1675
47	1.7929 4306	0.5577 4219	63.4354 4518	35.3806 2442	0.0157 6406
48	1.8153 5485	0.5508 5649	65.2283 8824	35.9314 8091	0.0153 3075
49	1.8380 4679	0.5440 5579	67.0437 4310	36.4755 3670	0.0149 1563
50	1.8610 2237	0.5373 3905	68.8817 8989	37.0128 7574	0.0145 1763

TABLE IV (continued)

$i = 1\frac{1}{4}\%$

n	$(1+i)^n$	$(1+i)^{-n}$	$s_{\overline{n}\vert i}$	$a_{\overline{n}\vert i}$	$s^{-1}_{\overline{n}\vert i}$
51	1.8842 8515	0.5307 0524	70.7428 1226	37.5435 8099	0.0141 3571
52	1.9078 3872	0.5241 5332	72.6270 9741	38.0677 3431	0.0137 6897
53	1.9316 8670	0.5176 8229	74.5349 3613	38.5854 1660	0.0134 1653
54	1.9558 3279	0.5112 9115	76.4666 2283	39.0967 0776	0.0130 7760
55	1.9802 8070	0.5049 7892	78.4224 5562	39.6016 8667	0.0127 5145
56	2.0050 3420	0.4987 4461	80.4027 3631	40.1004 3128	0.0124 3739
57	2.0300 9713	0.4925 8727	82.4077 7052	40.5930 1855	0.0121 3478
58	2.0554 7335	0.4865 0594	84.4378 6765	41.0795 2449	0.0118 4303
59	2.0811 6676	0.4804 9970	86.4933 4099	41.5600 2419	0.0115 6158
60	2.1071 8135	0.4745 6760	88.5745 0776	42.0345 9179	0.0112 8993
61	2.1335 2111	0.4687 0874	90.6816 8910	42.5033 0054	0.0110 2758
62	2.1601 9013	0.4629 2222	92.8152 1022	42.9662 2275	0.0107 7410
63	2.1871 9250	0.4572 0713	94.9754 0034	43.4234 2988	0.0105 2904
64	2.2145 3241	0.4515 6259	97.1625 9285	43.8749 9247	0.0102 9203
65	2.2422 1407	0.4459 8775	99.3771 2526	44.3209 8022	0.0100 6268
66	2.2702 4174	0.4404 8173	101.6193 3933	44.7614 6195	0.0098 4065
67	2.2986 1976	0.4350 4368	103.8895 8107	45.1965 0563	0.0096 2560
68	2.3273 5251	0.4296 7277	106.1882 0083	45.6261 7840	0.0094 1724
69	2.3564 4442	0.4243 6817	108.5155 5334	46.0505 4656	0.0092 1527
70	2.3858 9997	0.4191 2905	110.8719 9776	46.4696 7562	0.0090 1941
71	2.4157 2372	0.4139 5462	113.2578 9773	46.8836 3024	0.0088 2941
72	2.4459 2027	0.4088 4407	115.6736 2145	47.2924 7431	0.0086 4501
73	2.4764 9427	0.4037 9661	118.1195 4172	47.6962 7093	0.0084 6600
74	2.5074 5045	0.3988 1147	120.5960 3599	48.0950 8240	0.0082 9215
75	2.5387 9358	0.3938 8787	123.1034 8644	48.4889 7027	0.0081 2325
76	2.5705 2850	0.3890 2506	125.6422 8002	48.8779 9533	0.0079 5910
77	2.6026 6011	0.3842 2228	128.2128 0852	49.2622 1761	0.0077 9953
78	2.6351 9336	0.3794 7879	130.8154 6863	49.6416 9640	0.0076 4435
79	2.6681 3327	0.3747 9387	133.4506 6199	50.0164 9027	0.0074 9341
80	2.7014 8494	0.3701 6679	136.1187 9526	50.3866 5706	0.0073 4652
81	2.7352 5350	0.3655 9683	138.8202 8020	50.7522 5389	0.0072 0356
82	2.7694 4417	0.3610 8329	141.5555 3370	51.1133 3717	0.0070 6437
83	2.8040 6222	0.3566 2547	144.3249 7787	51.4699 6264	0.0069 2881
84	2.8391 1300	0.3522 2268	147.1290 4010	51.8221 8532	0.0067 9675
85	2.8746 0191	0.3478 7426	149.9681 5310	52.1700 5958	0.0066 6808
86	2.9105 3444	0.3435 7951	152.8427 5501	52.5136 3909	0.0065 4267
87	2.9469 1612	0.3393 3779	155.7532 8945	52.8529 7688	0.0064 2041
88	2.9837 5257	0.3351 4843	158.7002 0557	53.1881 2531	0.0063 0119
89	3.0210 4948	0.3310 1080	161.6839 5814	53.5191 3611	0.0061 8490
90	3.0588 1260	0.3269 2425	164.7050 0762	53.8460 6035	0.0060 7146
91	3.0970 4775	0.3228 8814	167.7638 2021	54.1689 4850	0.0059 6076
92	3.1357 6085	0.3189 0187	170.8608 6796	54.4878 5037	0.0058 5271
93	3.1749 5786	0.3149 6481	173.9966 2881	54.8028 1518	0.0057 4724
94	3.2146 4483	0.3110 7636	177.1715 8667	55.1138 9154	0.0056 4425
95	3.2548 2789	0.3072 3591	180.3862 3151	55.4211 2744	0.0055 4366
96	3.2955 1324	0.3034 4287	183.6410 5940	55.7245 7031	0.0054 4540
97	3.3367 0716	0.2996 9666	186.9365 7264	56.0242 6698	0.0053 4941
98	3.3784 1600	0.2959 9670	190 2732 7980	56.3202 6368	0.0052 5560
99	3.4206 4620	0.2923 4242	193.6516 9580	56.6126 0610	0.0051 6391
100	3.4634 0427	0.2887 3326	197.0723 4200	56.9013 3936	0.0050 7428

TABLE IV (continued)

$i = 1\frac{1}{2}\%$

n	$(1+i)^n$	$(1+i)^{-n}$	$s_{\overline{n}\mid i}$	$a_{\overline{n}\mid i}$	$s_{\overline{n}\mid i}^{-1}$
1	1.0150 0000	0.9852 2167	1.0000 0000	0.9852 2167	1.0000 0000
2	1.0302 2500	0.9706 6175	2.0150 0000	1.9558 8342	0.4962 7792
3	1.0456 7838	0.9563 1699	3.0452 2500	2.9122 0042	0.3283 8296
4	1.0613 6355	0.9421 8423	4.0909 0338	3.8543 8465	0.2444 4478
5	1.0772 8400	0.9282 6033	5.1522 6693	4.7826 4497	0.1940 8932
6	1.0934 4326	0.9145 4219	6.2295 5093	5.6971 8717	0.1605 2521
7	1.1098 4491	0.9010 2679	7.3229 9419	6.5982 1396	0.1365 5616
8	1.1264 9259	0.8877 1112	8.4328 3911	7.4859 2508	0.1185 8402
9	1.1433 8998	0.8745 9224	9.5593 3169	8.3605 1732	0.1046 0982
10	1.1605 4083	0.8616 6723	10.7027 2167	9.2221 8455	0.0934 3418
11	1.1779 4894	0.8489 3323	11.8632 6249	10.0711 1779	0.0842 9384
12	1.1956 1817	0.8363 8742	13.0412 1143	10.9075 0521	0.0766 7999
13	1.2135 5244	0.8240 2702	14.2368 2960	11.7315 3222	0.0702 4036
14	1.2317 5573	0.8118 4928	15.4503 8205	12.5433 8150	0.0647 2332
15	1.2502 3207	0.7998 5150	16.6821 3778	13.3432 3301	0.0599 4436
16	1.2689 8555	0.7880 3104	17.9323 6984	14.1312 6405	0.0557 6508
17	1.2880 2033	0.7763 8526	19.2013 5539	14.9076 4931	0.0520 7966
18	1.3073 4064	0.7649 1159	20.4893 7572	15.6725 6089	0.0488 0578
19	1.3269 5075	0.7536 0747	21.7967 1636	16.4261 6837	0.0458 7847
20	1.3468 5501	0.7424 7042	23.1236 6710	17.1686 3879	0.0432 4574
21	1.3670 5783	0.7314 9795	24.4705 2211	17.9001 3673	0.0408 6550
22	1.3875 6370	0.7206 8763	25.8375 7994	18.6208 2437	0.0387 0331
23	1.4083 7715	0.7100 3708	27.2251 4364	19.3308 6145	0.0367 3075
24	1.4295 0281	0.6995 4392	28.6335 2080	20.0304 0537	0.0349 2410
25	1.4509 4535	0.6892 0583	30.0630 2361	20.7196 1120	0.0332 6345
26	1.4727 0953	0.6790 2052	31.5139 6896	21.3986 3172	0.0317 3196
27	1.4948 0018	0.6689 8574	32.9866 7850	22.0676 1746	0.0303 1527
28	1.5172 2218	0.6590 9925	34.4814 7867	22.7267 1671	0.0290 0108
29	1.5399 8051	0.6493 5887	35.9987 0085	23.3760 7558	0.0277 7878
30	1.5630 8022	0.6397 6243	37.5386 8137	24.0158 3801	0.0266 3919
31	1.5865 2642	0.6303 0781	39.1017 6159	24.6461 4582	0.0255 7430
32	1.6103 2432	0.6209 9292	40.6882 8801	25.2671 3874	0.0245 7710
33	1.6344 7918	0.6118 1568	42.2986 1233	25.8789 5442	0.0236 4144
34	1.6589 9637	0.6027 7407	43.9330 9152	26.4817 2849	0.0227 6189
35	1.6838 8132	0.5938 6608	45.5920 8789	27.0755 9458	0.0219 3363
36	1.7091 3954	0.5850 8974	47.2759 6921	27.6606 8431	0.0211 5240
37	1.7347 7663	0.5764 4309	48.9851 0874	28.2371 2740	0.0204 1437
38	1.7607 9828	0.5679 2423	50.7198 8538	28.8050 5163	0.0197 1613
39	1.7872 1025	0.5595 3126	52.4806 8366	29.3645 8288	0.0190 5463
40	1.8140 1841	0.5512 6232	54.2678 9391	29.9158 4250	0.0184 2710
41	1.8412 2868	0.5431 1559	56.0819 1232	30.4589 6079	0.0178 3106
42	1.8688 4712	0.5350 8925	57.9231 4100	30.9940 5004	0.0172 6426
43	1.8968 7982	0.5271 8153	59.7919 8812	31.5212 3157	0.0167 2465
44	1.9253 3302	0.5193 9067	61.6888 6794	32.0406 2223	0.0162 1038
45	1.9542 1301	0.5117 1494	63.6142 0096	32.5523 3718	0.0157 1976
46	1.9835 2621	0.5041 5265	65.5684 1398	33.0564 8983	0.0152 5125
47	2.0132 7910	0.4967 0212	67.5519 4018	33.5531 9195	0.0148 0342
48	2.0434 7829	0.4893 6170	69.5652 1929	34.0425 5365	0.0143 7500
49	2.0741 3046	0.4821 2975	71.6086 9758	34.5246 8339	0.0139 6478
50	2.1052 4242	0.4750 0468	73.6828 2804	34.9996 8807	0.0135 7168

TABLE IV (continued)

$i = 1\frac{1}{2}\%$

n	$(1+i)^n$	$(1+i)^{-n}$	$s_{\overline{n}\vert i}$	$a_{\overline{n}\vert i}$	$s_{\overline{n}\vert i}^{-1}$
51	2.1368 2106	0.4679 8491	75.7880 7046	35.4676 7298	0.0131 9469
52	2.1688 7337	0.4610 6887	77.9248 9152	35.9287 4185	0.0128 3287
53	2.2014 0647	0.4542 5505	80.0937 6489	36.3829 9690	0.0124 8537
54	2.2344 2757	0.4475 4192	82.2951 7136	36.8305 3882	0.0121 5138
55	2.2679 4398	0.4409 2800	84.5295 9893	37.2714 6681	0.0118 3018
56	2.3019 6314	0.4344 1182	86.7975 4292	37.7058 7863	0.0115 2106
57	2.3364 9259	0.4279 9194	89.0995 0606	38.1338 7058	0.0112 2341
58	2.3175 3998	0.4216 6694	91.4359 9865	38.5555 3751	0.0109 3661
59	2.4071 1308	0.4154 3541	93.8075 3863	38.9709 7292	0.0106 6012
60	2.4432 1978	0.4092 9597	96.2146 5171	39.3802 6889	0.0103 9343
61	2.4798 6807	0.4032 4726	98.6578 7149	39.7835 1614	0.0101 3604
62	2.5170 6609	0.3972 8794	101.1377 3956	40.1808 0408	0.0098 8751
63	2.5548 2208	0.3914 1669	103.6548 0565	40.5722 2077	0.0096 4741
64	2.5931 4442	0.3856 3221	106.2096 2774	40.9578 5298	0.0094 1534
65	2.6320 4158	0.3799 3321	108.8027 7215	41.3377 8618	0.0091 9094
66	2.6715 2221	0.3743 1843	111.4348 1374	41.7121 0461	0.0089 7386
67	2.7115 9504	0.3687 8663	114.1063 3594	42.0808 9125	0.0087 6376
68	2.7522 6896	0.3633 3658	116.8179 3098	42.4442 2783	0.0085 6033
69	2.7935 5300	0.3579 6708	119.5701 9995	42.8021 9490	0.0083 6329
70	2.8354 5629	0.3526 7692	122.3637 5295	43.1548 7183	0.0081 7235
71	2.8779 8814	0.3474 6495	125.1992 0924	43.5023 3678	0.0079 8727
72	2.9211 5796	0.3423 3000	128.0771 9738	43.8446 6677	0.0078 0779
73	2.9649 7533	0.3372 7093	130.9983 5534	44.1819 3771	0.0076 3368
74	3.0094 4996	0.3322 8663	133.9633 3067	44.5142 2434	0.0074 6473
75	3.0545 9171	0.3273 7599	136.9727 8063	44.8416 0034	0.0073 0072
76	3.1004 1059	0.3225 3793	140.0273 7234	45.1641 3826	0.0071 4146
77	3.1469 1674	0.3177 7136	143.1277 8292	45.4819 0962	0.0069 8676
78	3.1941 2050	0.3130 7523	146.2746 9967	45.7949 8485	0.0068 3645
79	3.2420 3230	0.3084 4850	149.4688 2016	46.1034 3335	0.0066 9036
80	3.2906 6279	0.3038 9015	152.7108 5247	46.4073 2349	0.0065 4832
81	3.3400 2273	0.2993 9916	156.0015 1525	46.7067 2265	0.0064 1019
82	3.3901 2307	0.2949 7454	159.3415 3798	47.0016 9720	0.0062 7583
83	3.4409 7492	0.2906 1531	162.7316 6105	47.2923 1251	0.0061 4509
84	3.4925 8954	0.2863 2050	166.1726 3597	47.5786 3301	0.0060 1784
85	3.5449 7838	0.2820 8917	169.6652 2551	47.8607 2218	0.0058 9396
86	3.5981 5306	0.2779 2036	173.2102 0389	48.1386 4254	0.0057 7333
87	3.6521 2535	0.2738 1316	176.8083 5695	48.4124 5571	0.0056 5584
88	3.7069 0723	0.2697 6666	180.4604 8230	48.6822 2237	0.0055 4138
89	3.7625 1084	0.2657 7997	184.1673 8954	48.9480 0234	0.0054 2984
90	3.8189 4851	0.2618 5218	187.9299 0038	49.2098 5452	0.0053 2113
91	3.8762 3273	0.2579 8245	191.7488 4889	49.4678 3696	0.0052 1516
92	3.9343 7622	0.2541 6990	195.6250 8162	49.7220 0686	0.0051 1182
93	3.9933 9187	0.2504 1369	199.5594 5784	49.9724 2055	0.0050 1104
94	4.0532 9275	0.2467 1300	203.5528 4971	50.2191 3355	0.0049 1273
95	4.1140 9214	0.2430 6699	207.6061 4246	50.4622 0054	0.0048 1681
96	4.1758 0352	0.2394 7487	211.7202 3459	50.7016 7541	0.0047 2321
97	4.2384 4057	0.2359 3583	215.8960 3811	50.9376 1124	0.0046 3186
98	4.3020 1718	0.2324 4909	220.1344 7868	51.1700 6034	0.0045 4268
99	4.3665 4744	0.2290 1389	224.4364 9586	51.3990 7422	0.0044 5560
100	4.4320 4565	0.2256 2944	228.8030 4330	51.6247 0367	0.0043 7057

TABLE IV (continued)

$i = 1\frac{3}{4}\%$

n	$(1+i)^n$	$(1+i)^{-n}$	$s_{\overline{n}\rceil i}$	$a_{\overline{n}\rceil i}$	$s^{-1}_{\overline{n}\rceil i}$
1	1.0175 0000	0.9828 0098	1.0000 0000	0.9828 0098	1.0000 0000
2	1.0353 0625	0.9658 9777	2.0175 0000	1.9486 9875	0.4956 6295
3	1.0534 2411	0.9492 8528	3.0528 0625	2.8979 8403	0.3275 6746
4	1.0718 5903	0.9329 5851	4.1062 3036	3.8309 4254	0.2435 3237
5	1.0906 1656	0.9169 1254	5.1780 8938	4.7478 5508	0.1931 2142
6	1.1097 0235	0.9011 4254	6.2687 0596	5.6489 9762	0.1595 2256
7	1.1291 2215	0.8856 4378	7.3784 0831	6.5346 4139	0.1355 3059
8	1.1488 8178	0.8704 1157	8.5075 3045	7.4050 5297	0.1175 4292
9	1.1689 8721	0.8554 4135	9.6564 1224	8.2604 9432	0.1035 5813
10	1.1894 4449	0.8407 2860	10.8253 9945	9.1012 2291	0.0923 7534
11	1.2102 5977	0.8262 6889	12.0148 4394	9.9274 9181	0.0832 3038
12	1.2314 3931	0.8120 5788	13.2251 0371	10.7395 4969	0.0756 1377
13	1.2529 8950	0.7980 9128	14.4565 4303	11.5376 4097	0.0691 7283
14	1.2749 1682	0.7843 6490	15.7095 3253	12.3220 0587	0.0636 5562
15	1.2972 2786	0.7708 7459	16.9844 4935	13.0928 8046	0.0588 7739
16	1.3199 2935	0.7576 1631	18.2816 7721	13.8504 9677	0.0546 9958
17	1.3430 2811	0.7445 8605	19.6016 0656	14.5950 8282	0.0510 1623
18	1.3665 3111	0.7317 7990	20.9446 3468	15.3268 6272	0.0477 4492
19	1.3904 4540	0.7191 9401	22.3111 6578	16.0460 5673	0.0448 2061
20	1.4147 7820	0.7068 2458	23.7016 1119	16.7528 8130	0.0421 9122
21	1.4395 3681	0.6946 6789	25.1163 8938	17.4475 4919	0.0398 1464
22	1.4647 2871	0.6827 2028	26.5559 2620	18.1302 6948	0.0376 5638
23	1.4903 6146	0.6709 7817	28.0206 5490	18.8012 4764	0.0356 8796
24	1.5164 4279	0.6594 3800	29.5110 1637	19.4606 8565	0.0338 8565
25	1.5429 8054	0.6480 9632	31.0274 5915	20.1087 8196	0.0322 2952
26	1.5699 8269	0.6369 4970	32.5704 3969	20.7457 3166	0.0307 0269
27	1.5974 5739	0.6259 9479	34.1404 2238	21.3717 2644	0.0292 9079
28	1.6254 1290	0.6152 2829	35.7378 7977	21.9869 5474	0.0279 8151
29	1.6538 5762	0.6046 4697	37.3632 9267	22.5916 0171	0.0267 6424
30	1.6828 0013	0.5942 4764	39.0171 5029	23.1858 4934	0.0256 2975
31	1.7122 4913	0.5840 2716	40.6999 5042	23.7698 7650	0.0245 7005
32	1.7422 1349	0.5739 8247	42.4121 9955	24.3438 5897	0.0235 7812
33	1.7727 0223	0.5641 1053	44.1544 1305	24.9079 6951	0.0226 4779
34	1.8037 2452	0.5544 0839	45.9271 1527	25.4623 7789	0.0217 7363
35	1.8352 8970	0.5448 7311	47.7308 3979	26.0072 5100	0.0209 5082
36	1.8674 0727	0.5355 0183	49.5661 2949	26.5427 5283	0.0201 7507
37	1.9000 8689	0.5262 9172	51.4335 3675	27.0690 4455	0.0194 4257
38	1.9333 3841	0.5172 4002	53.3336 2365	27.5862 8457	0.0187 4990
39	1.9671 7184	0.5083 4400	55.2669 6206	28.0946 2857	0.0180 9399
40	2.0015 9734	0.4996 0098	57.2341 3390	28.5942 2955	0.0174 7209
41	2.0366 2530	0.4910 0834	59.2357 3124	29.0852 3789	0.0168 8170
42	2.0722 6624	0.4825 6348	61.2723 5654	29.5678 0135	0.0163 2057
43	2.1085 3090	0.4742 6386	63.3446 2278	30.0420 6522	0.0157 8666
44	2.1454 3019	0.4661 0699	65.4531 5367	30.5081 7221	0.0152 7810
45	2.1829 7522	0.4580 9040	67.5985 8386	30.9662 6261	0.0147 9321
46	2.2211 7728	0.4502 1170	69.7815 5908	31.4164 7431	0.0143 3043
47	2.2600 4789	0.4424 6850	72.0027 3637	31.8589 4281	0.0138 8836
48	2.2995 9872	0.4348 5848	74.2627 8425	32.2938 0129	0.0134 6569
49	2.3398 4170	0.4273 7934	76.5623 8298	32.7211 8063	0.0130 6124
50	2.3807 8893	0.4200 2883	78.9022 2468	33.1412 0946	0.0126 7391

TABLE IV (continued)

$i = 1\frac{3}{4}\%$

n	$(1+i)^n$	$(1+i)^{-n}$	$s_{\overline{n}\rceil i}$	$a_{\overline{n}\rceil i}$	$s^{-1}_{\overline{n}\rceil i}$
51	2.4224 5274	0.4128 0475	81.2830 1361	33.5540 1421	0.0123 0269
52	2.4648 4566	0.4057 0492	83.7054 6635	33.9597 1913	0.0119 4665
53	2.5079 8046	0.3987 2719	86.1703 1201	34.3584 4633	0.0116 0492
54	2.5518 7012	0.3918 6947	88.6782 9247	34.7503 1579	0.0112 7672
55	2.5965 2785	0.3851 2970	91.2301 6259	35.1354 4550	0.0109 6129
56	2.6419 6708	0.3785 0585	93.8266 9043	35.5139 5135	0.0106 5795
57	2.6882 0151	0.3719 9592	96.4686 5752	35.8859 4727	0.0103 6606
58	2.7352 4503	0.3655 9796	99.1568 5902	36.2515 4523	0.0100 8503
59	2.7831 1182	0.3593 1003	101.8921 0405	36.6108 5526	0.0098 1430
60	2.8318 1628	0.3531 3025	104.6752 1588	36.9639 8552	0.0095 5336
61	2.8813 7306	0.3470 5676	107.5070 3215	37.3110 4228	0.0093 0172
62	2.9317 9709	0.3410 8772	110.3884 0522	37.6521 3000	0.0090 5892
63	2.9831 0354	0.3352 2135	113.3202 0231	37.9873 5135	0.0088 2455
64	3.0343 0785	0.3294 5587	116.3033 0585	38.3168 0723	0.0085 9821
65	3.0884 2574	0.3237 8956	119.3386 1370	38.6405 9878	0.0083 7952
66	3.1424 7319	0.3182 2069	122.4270 3944	38.9588 1748	0.0081 6813
67	3.1974 6647	0.3127 4761	125.5695 1263	39.2715 6509	0.0079 6372
68	3.2534 2213	0.3073 6866	128.7669 7910	39.5789 3375	0.0077 6596
69	3.3103 5702	0.3020 8222	132.0204 0124	39.8810 1597	0.0075 7459
70	3.3682 8827	0.2968 8670	135.3307 5826	40.1779 0267	0.0073 8930
71	3.4272 3331	0.2917 8054	138.6990 4653	40.4696 8321	0.0072 0985
72	3.4872 0990	0.2867 6221	142.1262 7984	40.7564 4542	0.0070 3600
73	3.5482 3607	0.2818 3018	145.6134 8974	41.0382 7560	0.0068 6750
74	3.6103 3020	0.2769 8298	149.1617 2581	41.3152 5857	0.0067 0413
75	3.6735 1098	0.2722 1914	152.7720 5601	41.5874 7771	0.0065 4570
76	3.7377 9742	0.2675 3724	156.4455 6699	41.8550 1495	0.0063 9200
77	3.8032 0888	0.2629 3586	160.1833 6441	42.1179 5081	0.0062 4284
78	3.8697 6503	0.2584 1362	163.9865 7329	42.3763 6443	0.0060 9806
79	3.9374 8592	0.2539 6916	167.8563 3832	42.6303 3359	0.0059 5748
80	4.0063 9192	0.2496 0114	171.7938 2424	42.8799 3474	0.0058 2093
81	4.0765 0378	0.2453 0825	175.8002 1617	43.1252 4298	0.0056 8828
82	4.1478 4260	0.2410 8919	179.8767 1995	43.3663 3217	0.0055 5936
83	4.2204 2984	0.2369 4269	184.0245 6255	43.6032 7486	0.0054 3406
84	4.2942 8737	0.2328 6751	188.2449 9239	43.8361 4237	0.0053 1223
85	4.3694 3740	0.2288 6242	192.5392 7976	44.0650 0479	0.0051 9375
86	4.4459 0255	0.2249 2621	196.9087 1716	44.2899 3099	0.0050 7850
87	4.5237 0584	0.2210 5770	201.3546 1971	44.5109 8869	0.0049 6636
88	4.6028 7070	0.2172 5572	205.8783 2555	44.7282 4441	0.0048 5724
89	4.6834 2093	0.2135 1914	210.4811 9625	44.9417 6355	0.0047 5102
90	4.7653 8080	0.2098 4682	215.1646 1718	45.1516 1037	0.0046 4760
91	4.8487 7496	0.2062 3766	219.9299 9798	45.3578 4803	0.0045 4690
92	4.9336 2853	0.2026 9057	224.7787 7295	45.5605 3860	0.0044 4882
93	5.0199 6703	0.1992 0450	229.7124 0148	45.7597 4310	0.0043 5327
94	5.1078 1645	0.1957 7837	234.7323 6850	45.9555 2147	0.0042 6017
95	5.1972 0324	0.1924 1118	239.8401 8495	46.1479 3265	0.0041 6944
96	5.2881 5429	0.1891 0190	245.0373 8819	46.3370 3455	0.0040 8101
97	5.3806 9699	0.1858 4953	250.3255 4248	46.5228 8408	0.0039 9480
98	5.4748 5919	0.1826 5310	255.7062 3947	46.7055 3718	0.0039 1074
99	5.5706 6923	0.1795 1165	261.1810 9866	46.8850 4882	0.0038 2876
100	5.6681 5594	0.1764 2422	266.7517 6789	47.0614 7304	0.0037 4880

TABLE IV (continued)

$i = 2\%$

n	$(1+i)^n$	$(1+i)^{-n}$	$s_{\overline{n}\|i}$	$a_{\overline{n}\|i}$	$s^{-1}_{\overline{n}\|i}$
1	1.0200 0000	0.9803 9216	1.0000 0000	0.9803 9216	1.0000 0000
2	1.0404 0000	0.9611 6878	2.0200 0000	1.9415 6094	0.4950 4950
3	1.0612 0800	0.9423 2233	3.0604 0000	2.8838 8327	0.3267 5467
4	1.0824 3216	0.9238 4543	4.1216 0800	3.8077 2870	0.2426 2375
5	1.1040 8080	0.9057 3081	5.2040 4016	4.7134 5951	0.1921 5839
6	1.1261 6242	0.8879 7138	6.3081 2096	5.6014 3089	0.1585 2581
7	1.1486 8567	0.8705 6018	7.4342 8338	6.4719 9107	0.1345 1196
8	1.1716 5938	0.8534 9037	8.5829 6905	7.3254 8144	0.1165 0980
9	1.1950 9257	0.8367 5527	9.7546 2843	8.1622 3671	0.1025 1544
10	1.2189 9442	0.8203 4830	10.9497 2100	8.9825 8501	0.0913 2653
11	1.2433 7431	0.8042 6304	12.1687 1542	9.7868 4805	0.0821 7794
12	1.2682 4179	0.7884 9318	13.4120 8973	10.5733 4122	0.0745 5960
13	1.2936 0663	0.7730 3253	14.6803 3152	11.3483 7375	0.0681 1835
14	1.3194 7876	0.7578 7502	15.9739 3815	12.1062 4877	0.0626 0197
15	1.3458 6834	0.7430 1473	17.2934 1692	12.8492 6350	0.0578 2547
16	1.3727 8571	0.7284 4581	18.6392 8525	13.5777 0931	0.0536 5013
17	1.4002 4142	0.7141 6256	20.0120 7096	14.2918 7188	0.0499 6984
18	1.4282 4625	0.7001 5937	21.4123 1238	14.9920 3125	0.0467 0210
19	1.4568 1117	0.6864 3076	22.8405 5863	15.6784 6201	0.0437 8177
20	1.4859 4740	0.6729 7133	24.2973 6980	16.3514 3334	0.0411 5672
21	1.5156 6634	0.6597 7582	25.7833 1719	17.0112 0916	0.0387 8477
22	1.5459 7967	0.6468 3904	27.2989 8354	17.6580 4820	0.0366 3140
23	1.5768 9926	0.6341 5592	28.8449 6321	18.2922 0412	0.0346 6810
24	1.6084 3725	0.6217 2149	30.4218 6247	18.9139 2560	0.0328 7110
25	1.6406 0599	0.6095 3087	32.0302 9972	19.5234 5647	0.0312 2044
26	1.6734 1811	0.5975 7928	33.6709 0572	20.1210 3576	0.0296 9923
27	1.7068 8648	0.5858 6204	35.3443 2383	20.7068 9780	0.0282 9309
28	1.7410 2421	0.5743 7455	37.0512 1031	21.2812 7236	0.0269 8967
29	1.7758 4469	0.5631 1231	38.7922 3451	21.8443 8466	0.0257 7836
30	1.8113 6158	0.5520 7089	40.5680 7921	22.3964 5555	0.0246 4992
31	1.8475 8882	0.5412 4597	42.3794 4079	22.9377 0152	0 0235 9635
32	1.8845 4059	0.5306 3330	44.2270 2961	23.4683 3482	0.0226 1061
33	1.9222 3140	0.5202 2873	46.1115 7020	23.9885 6355	0.0216 8653
34	1.9606 7603	0.5100 2817	48.0338 0160	24.4985 9172	0.0208 1867
35	1.9998 8955	0.5000 2761	49.9944 7763	24.9986 1933	0.0200 0221
36	2.0398 8734	0.4902 2315	51.9943 6719	25.4888 4248	0.0192 3285
37	2.0806 8509	0.4806 1093	54.0342 5453	25.9694 5341	0.0185 0678
38	2.1222 9879	0.4711 8719	56.1149 3962	26.4406 4060	0.0178 2057
39	2.1647 4477	0.4619 4822	58.2372 3841	26.9025 8883	0.0171 7114
40	2.2080 3966	0.4528 9042	60.4019 8318	27.3554 7924	0.0165 5575
41	2.2522 0046	0.4440 1021	62.6100 2284	27.7994 8945	0.0159 7188
42	2.2972 4447	0.4353 0413	64.8622 2330	28.2347 9358	0.0154 1729
43	2.3431 8936	0.4267 6875	67.1594 6777	28.6615 6233	0.0148 8993
44	2.3900 5314	0.4184 0074	69.5026 5712	29.0799 6307	0.0143 8794
45	2.4378 5421	0.4101 9680	71.8927 1027	29.4901 5987	0.0139 0962
46	2.4866 1129	0.4021 5373	74.3305 6447	29.8923 1360	0.0134 5342
47	2.5363 4351	0.3942 6836	76.8171 7576	30.2865 8196	0.0130 1792
48	2.5870 7039	0.3865 3761	79.3535 1927	30.6731 1957	0.0126 0184
49	2.6388 1179	0.3789 5844	81.9405 8966	31.0520 7801	0.0122 0396
50	2.6915 8803	0.3715 2788	84.5794 0145	31.4236 0589	0.0118 2321

TABLE IV (continued)

$i = 2\%$

n	$(1+i)^n$	$(1+i)^{-n}$	$s_{\overline{n}\mid i}$	$a_{\overline{n}\mid i}$	$s_{\overline{n}\mid i}^{-1}$
51	2.7454 1979	0.3642 4302	87.2709 8948	31.7878 4892	0.0114 5856
52	2.8003 2819	0.3571 0100	90.0164 0927	32.1449 4992	0.0111 0909
53	2.8563 3475	0.3500 9902	92.8167 3746	32.4950 4894	0.0107 7392
54	2.9134 6144	0.3432 3433	95.6730 7221	32.8382 8327	0.0104 5226
55	2.9717 3067	0.3365 0425	98.5865 3365	33.1747 8752	0.0101 4337
56	3.0311 6529	0.3299 0613	101.5582 6432	33.5046 9365	0.0098 4656
57	3.0917 8859	0.3234 3738	104.5894 2961	33.8281 3103	0.0095 6120
58	3.1536 2436	0.3170 9547	107.6812 1820	34.1452 2650	0.0092 8667
59	3.2166 9685	0.3108 7791	110.8348 4257	34.4561 0441	0.0090 2243
60	3.2810 3079	0.3047 8227	114.0515 3942	34.7608 8668	0.0087 6797
61	3.3466 5140	0.2988 0614	117.3325 7021	35.0596 9282	0.0085 2278
62	3.4135 8443	0.2929 4720	120.6792 2161	35.3526 4002	0.0082 8643
63	3.4818 5612	0.2872 0314	124.0928 0604	35.6398 4316	0.0080 5848
64	3.5514 9324	0.2815 7170	127.5746 6216	35.9214 1486	0.0078 3855
65	3.6225 2311	0.2760 5069	131.1261 5541	36.1974 6555	0.0076 2624
66	3.6949 7357	0.2706 3793	134.7486 7852	36.4681 0348	0.0074 2122
67	3.7688 7304	0.2653 3130	138.4436 5209	36.7334 3478	0.0072 2316
68	3.8442 5050	0.2601 2873	142.2125 2513	36.9935 6351	0.0070 3173
69	3.9211 3551	0.2550 2817	146.0567 7563	37.2485 9168	0.0068 4665
70	3.9995 5822	0.2500 2761	149.9779 1114	37.4986 1929	0.0066 6765
71	4.0795 4939	0.2451 2511	153.9774 6937	37.7437 4441	0.0064 9446
72	4.1611 4038	0.2403 1874	158.0570 1875	37.9840 6314	0.0063 2683
73	4.2443 6318	0.2356 0661	162.2181 5913	38.2196 6975	0.0061 6454
74	4.3292 5045	0.2309 8687	166.4625 2231	38.4506 5662	0.0060 0736
75	4.4158 3546	0.2264 5771	170.7917 7276	38.6771 1433	0.0058 5508
76	4.5041 5216	0.2220 1737	175.2076 0821	38.8991 3170	0.0057 0751
77	4.5942 3521	0.2176 6408	179.7117 6038	39.1167 9578	0.0055 6447
78	4.6861 1991	0.2133 9616	184.3059 9558	39.3301 9194	0.0054 2576
79	4.7798 4231	0.2092 1192	188.9921 1549	39.5394 0386	0.0052 9123
80	4.8754 3916	0.2051 0973	193.7719 5780	39.7445 1359	0.0051 6071
81	4.9729 4794	0.2010 8797	198.6473 9696	39.9456 0156	0.0050 3405
82	5.0724 0690	0.1971 4507	203.6203 4490	40.1427 4663	0.0049 1110
83	5.1738 5504	0.1932 7948	208.6927 5180	40.3360 2611	0.0047 9173
84	5.2773 3214	0.1894 8968	213.8666 0683	40.5255 1579	0.0046 7581
85	5.3828 7878	0.1857 7420	219.1439 3897	40.7112 8999	0.0045 6321
86	5.4905 3636	0.1821 3157	224.5268 1775	40.8934 2156	0.0044 5381
87	5.6003 4708	0.1785 6036	230.0173 5411	41.0719 8192	0.0043 4750
88	5.7123 5402	0.1750 5918	235.6177 0119	41.2470 4110	0.0042 4416
89	5.8266 0110	0.1716 2665	241.3300 5521	41.4186 6774	0.0041 4370
90	5.9431 3313	0.1682 6142	247.1566 5632	41.5869 2916	0.0040 4602
91	6.0619 9579	0.1649 6217	253.0997 8944	41.7518 9133	0.0039 5101
92	6.1832 3570	0.1617 2762	259.1617 8523	41.9136 1895	0.0038 5859
93	6.3069 0042	0.1585 5649	265.3450 2094	42.0721 7545	0.0037 6868
94	6.4330 3843	0.1554 4754	271.6519 2135	42.2276 2299	0.0036 8118
95	6.5616 9920	0.1523 9955	278.0849 5978	42.3800 2254	0.0035 9602
96	6.6929 3318	0.1494 1132	284.6466 5898	42.5294 3386	0.0035 1313
97	6.8267 9184	0.1464 8169	291.3395 9216	42.6759 1555	0.0034 3242
98	6.9633 2768	0.1436 0950	298.1663 8400	42.8195 2505	0.0033 5383
99	7.1025 9423	0.1407 9363	305.1297 1168	42.9603 1867	0.0032 7729
100	7.2446 4612	0.1380 3297	312.2323 0591	43.0983 5164	0.0032 0274

TABLE IV (continued)

$i = 2\frac{1}{4}\%$

n	$(1+i)^n$	$(1+i)^{-n}$	$s_{\overline{n}\mid i}$	$a_{\overline{n}\mid i}$	$s_{\overline{n}\mid i}^{-1}$
1	1.0225 0000	0.9779 9511	1.0000 0000	0.9779 9511	1.0000 0000
2	1.0455 0625	0.9564 7444	2.0225 0000	1.9344 6955	0.4944 3758
3	1.0690 3014	0.9354 2732	3.0680 0625	2.8698 9687	0.3259 4458
4	1.0930 8332	0.9148 4335	4.1370 3639	3.7847 4021	0.2417 1893
5	1.1176 7769	0.8947 1232	5.2301 1971	4.6794 5253	0.1912 0021
6	1.1428 2544	0.8750 2427	6.3477 9740	5.5544 7680	0.1575 3496
7	1.1685 3901	0.8557 6946	7.4906 2284	6.4102 4626	0.1335 0025
8	1.1948 3114	0.8369 3835	8.6591 6186	7.2471 8461	0.1154 8462
9	1.2217 1484	0.8185 2161	9.8539 9300	8.0657 0622	0.1014 8170
10	1.2492 0343	0.8005 1013	11.0757 0784	8.8662 1635	0.0902 8768
11	1.2773 1050	0.7828 9499	12.3249 1127	9.6491 1134	0.0811 3649
12	1.3060 4999	0.7656 6748	13.6022 2177	10.4147 7882	0.0735 1740
13	1.3354 3611	0.7488 1905	14.9082 7176	11.1635 9787	0.0670 7686
14	1.3654 8343	0.7323 4137	16.2437 0788	11.8959 3924	0.0615 6230
15	1.3962 0680	0.7162 2628	17.6091 9130	12.6121 6551	0.0567 8852
16	1.4276 2146	0.7004 6580	19.0053 9811	13.3126 3131	0.0526 1663
17	1.4597 4294	0.6850 5212	20.4330 1957	13.9976 8343	0.0489 4039
18	1.4925 8716	0.6699 7763	21.8927 6251	14.6676 6106	0.0456 7720
19	1.5261 7037	0.6552 3484	23.3853 4966	15.3228 9590	0.0427 6182
20	1.5605 0920	0.6408 1647	24.9115 2003	15.9637 1237	0.0401 4207
21	1.5956 2066	0.6267 1538	26.4720 2923	16.5904 2775	0.0377 7572
22	1.6315 2212	0.6129 2457	28.0676 4989	17.2033 5232	0.0356 2821
23	1.6682 3137	0.5994 3724	29.6991 7201	17.8027 8955	0.0336 7097
24	1.7057 6658	0.5862 4668	31.3674 0338	18.3890 3624	0.0318 8023
25	1.7441 4632	0.5733 4639	33.0731 6996	18.9623 8263	0.0302 3599
26	1.7833 8962	0.5607 2997	34.8173 1628	19.5231 1260	0.0287 2134
27	1.8235 1588	0.5483 9117	36.6007 0590	20.0715 0376	0.0273 2188
28	1.8645 4499	0.5363 2388	38.4242 2178	20.6078 2764	0.0260 2525
29	1.9064 9725	0.5245 2213	40.2887 6677	21.1323 4977	0.0248 2081
30	1.9493 9344	0.5129 8008	42.1952 6402	21.6453 2985	0.0236 9934
31	1.9932 5479	0.5016 9201	44.1446 5746	22.1470 2186	0.0226 5280
32	2.0381 0303	0.4906 5233	46.1379 1226	22.6376 7419	0.0216 7415
33	2.0839 6034	0.4798 5558	48.1760 1528	23.1175 2977	0.0207 5722
34	2.1308 4945	0.4692 9641	50.2599 7563	23.5868 2618	0.0198 9655
35	2.1787 9356	0.4589 6960	52.3908 2508	24.0457 9577	0.0190 8731
36	2.2278 1642	0.4488 7002	54.5696 1864	24.4946 6579	0.0183 2522
37	2.2779 4229	0.4389 9268	56.7974 3506	24.9336 5848	0.0176 0643
38	2.3291 9599	0.4293 3270	59.0753 7735	25.3629 9118	0.0169 2753
39	2.3816 0290	0.4198 8528	61.4045 7334	25.7828 7646	0.0162 8543
40	2.4351 8897	0.4106 4575	63.7861 7624	26.1935 2221	0.0156 7738
41	2.4899 8072	0.4016 0954	66.2213 6521	26.5951 3174	0.0151 0087
42	2.5460 0528	0.3927 7216	68.7113 4592	26.9879 0390	0.0145 5364
43	2.6032 9040	0.3841 2925	71.2573 5121	27.3720 3316	0.0140 3364
44	2.6618 6444	0.3756 7653	73.8606 4161	27.7477 0969	0.0135 3901
45	2.7217 5639	0.3674 0981	76.5225 0605	28.1151 1950	0.0130 6805
46	2.7829 9590	0.3593 2500	79.2442 6243	28.4744 4450	0.0126 1921
47	2.8456 1331	0.3514 1809	82.0272 5834	28.8258 6259	0.0121 9107
48	2.9096 3961	0.3436 8518	84.8728 7165	29.1695 4777	0.0117 8233
49	2.9751 0650	0.3361 2242	87.7825 1126	29.5056 7019	0.0113 9179
50	3.0420 4640	0.3287 2608	90.7576 1776	29.8343 9627	0.0110 1836

TABLE IV (continued)

$i = 2\frac{1}{4}\%$

n	$(1+i)^n$	$(1+i)^{-n}$	$s_{\overline{n}\rvert i}$	$a_{\overline{n}\rvert i}$	$s_{\overline{n}\rvert i}^{-1}$
51	3.1104 9244	0.3214 9250	93.7996 6416	30.1558 8877	0.0106 6102
52	3.1804 7852	0.3144 1810	96.9101 5661	30.4703 0687	0.0103 1884
53	3.2520 3929	0.3074 9936	100.0906 3513	30.7778 0623	0.0099 9094
54	3.3252 1017	0.3007 3287	103.3426 7442	31.0785 3910	0.0096 7654
55	3.4000 2740	0.2941 1528	106.6678 8460	31.3726 5438	0.0093 7489
56	3.4765 2802	0.2876 4330	110.0679 1200	31.6602 9768	0.0090 8530
57	3.5547 4990	0.2813 1374	113.5444 4002	31.9416 1142	0.0088 0712
58	3.6347 3177	0.2751 2347	117.0991 8992	32.2167 3489	0.0085 3977
59	3.7165 1324	0.2690 6940	120.7339 2169	32.4858 0429	0.0082 8268
60	3.8001 3479	0.2631 4856	124.4504 3493	32.7489 5285	0.0080 3533
61	3.8856 3782	0.2573 5801	128.2505 6972	33.0063 1086	0.0077 9724
62	3.9730 6467	0.2516 9487	132.1362 0754	33.2580 0573	0.0075 6795
63	4.0624 5862	0.2461 5635	136.1092 7221	33.5041 6208	0.0073 4704
64	4.1538 6394	0.2407 3971	140.1717 3083	33.7449 0179	0.0071 3411
65	4.2473 2588	0.2354 4226	144.3255 9477	33.9803 4405	0.0069 2878
66	4.3428 9071	0.2302 6138	148.5729 2066	34.2106 0543	0.0067 3070
67	4.4406 0576	0.2251 9450	152.9158 1137	34.4357 9993	0.0065 3955
68	4.5405 1939	0.2202 3912	157.3564 1713	34.6560 3905	0.0063 5500
69	4.6426 8107	0.2153 9278	161.8969 3651	34.8714 3183	0.0061 7677
70	4.7471 4140	0.2106 5309	166.5396 1758	35.0820 8492	0.0060 0458
71	4.8539 5208	0.2060 1769	171.2867 5898	35.2881 0261	0.0058 3816
72	4.9631 6600	0.2014 8429	176.1407 1106	35.4895 8691	0.0056 7728
73	5.0748 3723	0.1970 5065	181.1038 7705	35.6866 3756	0.0055 2169
74	5.1890 2107	0.1927 1458	186.1787 1429	35.8793 5214	0.0053 7118
75	5.3057 7405	0.1884 7391	191.3677 3536	36.0678 2605	0.0052 2554
76	5.4251 5396	0.1843 2657	196.6735 0941	36.2521 5262	0.0050 8457
77	5.5472 1993	0.1802 7048	202.0986 6337	36.4324 2310	0.0049 4808
78	5.6720 3237	0.1763 0365	207.6458 8329	36.6087 2675	0.0048 1589
79	5.7996 5310	0.1724 2411	213.3179 1567	36.7811 5085	0.0046 8784
80	5.9301 4530	0.1686 2993	219.1175 6877	36.9497 8079	0.0045 6376
81	6.0635 7357	0.1649 1925	225.0477 1407	37.1147 0004	0.0044 4350
82	6.2000 0397	0.1612 9022	231.1112 8763	37.2759 9026	0.0043 2692
83	6.3395 0406	0.1577 4105	237.3112 9160	37.4337 3130	0.0042 1387
84	6.4821 4290	0.1542 6997	243.6507 9567	37.5880 0127	0.0041 0423
85	6.6279 9112	0.1508 7528	250.1329 3857	37.7388 7655	0.0039 9787
86	6.7771 2092	0.1475 5528	256.7609 2969	37.8864 3183	0.0038 9467
87	6.9296 0614	0.1443 0835	263.5380 5060	38.0307 4018	0.0037 9452
88	7.0855 2228	0.1411 3286	270.4676 5674	38.1718 7304	0.0036 9730
89	7.2449 4653	0.1380 2724	277.5531 7902	38.3099 0028	0.0036 0291
90	7.4079 5782	0.1349 8997	284.7981 2555	38.4448 9025	0.0035 1126
91	7.5746 3688	0.1320 1953	292.2060 8337	38.5769 0978	0.0034 2224
92	7.7450 6621	0.1291 1445	299.7807 2025	38.7060 2423	0.0033 3577
93	7.9193 3020	0.1262 7331	307.5257 8645	38.8322 9754	0.0032 5176
94	8.0975 1512	0.1234 9468	315.4451 1665	38.9557 9221	0.0031 7012
95	8.2797 0921	0.1207 7719	323.5426 3177	39.0765 6940	0.0030 9078
96	8.4660 0267	0.1181 1950	331.8223 4099	39.1946 8890	0.0030 1366
97	8.6564 8773	0.1155 2029	340.2883 4366	39.3102 0920	0.0029 3868
98	8.8512 5871	0.1129 7828	348.9448 3139	39.4231 8748	0.0028 6578
99	9.0504 1203	0.1104 9221	357.7960 9010	39.5336 7968	0.0027 9489
100	9.2540 4630	0.1080 6084	366.8465 0213	39.6417 4052	0.0027 2594

TABLE IV (continued)

$i = 2\frac{1}{2}\%$

n	$(1+i)^n$	$(1+i)^{-n}$	$s_{\overline{n}\rvert i}$	$a_{\overline{n}\rvert i}$	$s^{-1}_{\overline{n}\rvert i}$
1	1.0250 0000	0.9756 0976	1.0000 0000	0.9756 0976	1.0000 0000
2	1.0506 2500	0.9518 1440	2.0250 0000	1.9274 2415	0.4938 2716
3	1.0768 9063	0.9285 9941	3.0756 2500	2.8560 2356	0.3251 3717
4	1.1038 1289	0.9059 5064	4.1525 1563	3.7619 7421	0.2408 1788
5	1.1314 0821	0.8838 5429	5.2563 2852	4.6458 2850	0.1902 4686
6	1.1596 9342	0.8622 9687	6.3877 3673	5.5081 2536	0.1565 4997
7	1.1886 8575	0.8412 6524	7.5474 3015	6.3493 9060	0.1324 9543
8	1.2184 0290	0.8207 4657	8.7361 1590	7.1701 3717	0.1144 6735
9	1.2488 6297	0.8007 2836	9.9545 1880	7.9708 6553	0.1004 5689
10	1.2800 8454	0.7811 9840	11.2033 8177	8.7520 6393	0.0892 5876
11	1.3120 8666	0.7621 4478	12.4834 6631	9.5142 0871	0.0801 0596
12	1.3448 8882	0.7435 5589	13.7955 5297	10.2577 6460	0.0724 8713
13	1.3785 1104	0.7254 2038	15.1404 4179	10.9831 8497	0.0660 4827
14	1.4129 7382	0.7077 2720	16.5189 5284	11.6909 1217	0.0605 3653
15	1.4482 9817	0.6904 6556	17.9319 2666	12.3813 7773	0.0557 6646
16	1.4845 0562	0.6736 2493	19.3802 2483	13.0550 0266	0.0515 9899
17	1.5216 1826	0.6571 9506	20.8647 3045	13.7121 9772	0.0479 2777
18	1.5596 5872	0.6411 6591	22.3863 4871	14.3533 6363	0.0446 7008
19	1.5986 5019	0.6255 2772	23.9460 0743	14.9788 9134	0.0417 6062
20	1.6386 1644	0.6102 7094	25.5446 5761	15.5891 6229	0.0391 4713
21	1.6795 8185	0.5953 8629	27.1832 7405	16.1845 4857	0.0367 8733
22	1.7215 7140	0.5808 6467	28.8628 5590	16.7654 1324	0.0346 4661
23	1.7646 1068	0.5666 9724	30.5844 2730	17.3321 1048	0.0326 9638
24	1.8087 2595	0.5528 7535	32.3490 3798	17.8849 8583	0.0309 1282
25	1.8539 4410	0.5393 9059	34.1577 6393	18.4243 7642	0.0292 7592
26	1.9002 9270	0.5262 3472	36.0117 0803	18.9506 1114	0.0277 6875
27	1.9478 0002	0.5133 9973	37.9120 0073	19.4640 1087	0.0263 7687
28	1.9964 9502	0.5008 7778	39.8598 0075	19.9648 8866	0.0250 8793
29	2.0464 0739	0.4886 6125	41.8562 9577	20.4535 4991	0.0238 9127
30	2.0975 6758	0.4767 4269	43.9027 0316	20.9302 9259	0.0227 7764
31	2.1500 0677	0.4651 1481	46.0002 7074	21.3954 0741	0.0217 3900
32	2.2037 5694	0.4537 7055	48.1502 7751	21.8491 7796	0.0207 6831
33	2.2588 5086	0.4427 0298	50.3540 3445	22.2918 8094	0.0198 5938
34	2.3153 2213	0.4319 0534	52.6128 8531	22.7237 8628	0.0190 0675
35	2.3732 0519	0.4213 7107	54.9282 0744	23.1451 5734	0.0182 0558
36	2.4325 3532	0.4110 9372	57.3014 1263	23.5562 5107	0.0174 5158
37	2.4933 4870	0.4010 6705	59.7339 4794	23.9573 1812	0.0167 4090
38	2.5556 8242	0.3912 8492	62.2272 9664	24.3486 0304	0.0160 7012
39	2.6195 7448	0.3817 4139	64.7829 7906	24.7303 4443	0.0154 3615
40	2.6850 6384	0.3724 3062	67.4025 5354	25.1027 7505	0.0148 3623
41	2.7521 9043	0.3633 4695	70.0876 1737	25.4661 2200	0.0142 6786
42	2.8209 9520	0.3544 8483	72.8398 0781	25.8206 0683	0.0137 2876
43	2.8915 2008	0.3458 3886	75.6608 0300	26.1664 4569	0.0132 1688
44	2.9638 0808	0.3374 0376	78.5523 2308	26.5038 4945	0.0127 3037
45	3.0379 0328	0.3291 7440	81.5161 3116	26.8330 2386	0.0122 6752
46	3.1138 5086	0.3211 4576	84.5540 3443	27.1541 6962	0.0118 2676
47	3.1916 9713	0.3133 1294	87.6678 8530	27.4674 8255	0.0114 0669
48	3.2714 8956	0.3056 7116	90.8595 8243	27.7731 5371	0.0110 0599
49	3.3532 7680	0.2982 1576	94.1310 7199	28.0713 6947	0.0106 2348
50	3.4371 0872	0.2909 4221	97.4843 4879	28.3623 1168	0.0102 5806

TABLE IV (continued)

$i = 2\frac{1}{2}\%$

n	$(1+i)^n$	$(1+i)^{-n}$	$s_{\overline{n}\mid i}$	$a_{\overline{n}\mid i}$	$s_{\overline{n}\mid i}^{-1}$
51	3.5230 3644	0.2838 4606	100.9214 5751	28.6461 5774	0.0099 0870
52	3.6111 1235	0.2769 2298	104.4444 9395	28.9230 8072	0.0095 7446
53	3.7013 9016	0.2701 6876	108.0556 0629	29.1932 4948	0.0092 5449
54	3.7939 2491	0.2635 7928	111.7569 9645	29.4568 2876	0.0089 4799
55	3.8887 7303	0.2571 5052	115.5509 2136	29.7139 7928	0.0086 5419
56	3.9859 9236	0.2508 7855	119.4396 9440	29.9648 5784	0.0083 7243
57	4.0856 4217	0.2447 5956	123.4256 8676	30.2096 1740	0.0081 0204
58	4.1877 8322	0.2387 8982	127.5113 2893	30.4484 0722	0.0078 4244
59	4.2924 7780	0.2329 6568	131.6991 1215	30.6813 7290	0.0075 9307
60	4.3997 8975	0.2272 8359	135.9915 8995	30.9086 5649	0.0073 5340
61	4.5097 8449	0.2217 4009	140.3913 7970	31.1303 9657	0.0071 2294
62	4.6225 2910	0.2163 3179	144.9011 6419	31.3467 2836	0.0069 0126
63	4.7380 9233	0.2110 5541	149.5236 9330	31.5577 8377	0.0066 8790
64	4.8565 4464	0.2059 0771	154.2617 8563	31.7636 9148	0.0064 8249
65	4.9779 5826	0.2008 8557	159.1183 3027	31.9645 7705	0.0062 8463
66	5.1024 0721	0.1959 8593	164.0962 8853	32.1605 6298	0.0060 9398
67	5.2299 6739	0.1912 0578	169.1986 9574	32.3517 6876	0.0059 1021
68	5.3607 1658	0.1865 4223	174.4286 6314	32.5383 1099	0.0057 3300
69	5.4947 3449	0.1819 9241	179.7893 7971	32.7203 0340	0.0055 6206
70	5.6321 0286	0.1775 5358	185.2841 1421	32.8978 5698	0.0053 9712
71	5.7729 0543	0.1732 2300	190.9162 1706	33.0710 7998	0.0052 3790
72	5.9172 2806	0.1689 9805	196.6891 2249	33.2400 7803	0.0050 8417
73	6.0651 5876	0.1648 7615	202.6063 5055	33.4049 5417	0.0049 3568
74	6.2167 8773	0.1608 5478	208.6715 0931	33.5658 0895	0.0047 9222
75	6.3722 0743	0.1569 3149	214.8882 9705	33.7227 4044	0.0046 5358
76	6.5315 1261	0.1531 0389	221.2605 0447	33.8758 4433	0.0045 1956
77	6.6948 0043	0.1493 6965	227.7920 1709	34.0252 1398	0.0043 8997
78	6.8621 7044	0.1457 2649	234.4868 1751	34.1709 4047	0.0042 6463
79	7.0337 2470	0.1421 7218	241.3489 8795	34.3131 1265	0.0041 4338
80	7.2095 6782	0.1387 0457	248.3827 1265	34.4518 1722	0.0040 2605
81	7.3898 0701	0.1353 2153	255.5922 8047	34.5871 3875	0.0039 1248
82	7.5745 5219	0.1320 2101	262.9820 8748	34.7191 5976	0.0038 0254
83	7.7639 1599	0.1288 0098	270.5566 3966	34.8479 6074	0.0036 9608
84	7.9580 1389	0.1256 5949	278.3205 5566	34.9736 2023	0.0035 9298
85	8.1569 6424	0.1225 9463	286.2785 6955	35.0962 1486	0.0034 9310
86	8.3608 8834	0.1196 0452	294.4355 3379	35.2158 1938	0.0033 9633
87	8.5699 1055	0.1166 8733	302.7964 2213	35.3325 0671	0.0033 0255
88	8.7841 5832	0.1138 4130	311.3663 3268	35.4463 4801	0.0032 1165
89	9.0037 6228	0.1110 6468	320.1504 9100	35.5574 1269	0.0031 2353
90	9.2288 5633	0.1083 5579	329.1542 5328	35.6657 6848	0.0030 3809
91	9.4595 7774	0.1057 1296	338.3831 0961	35.7714 8144	0.0029 5523
92	9.6960 6718	0.1031 3460	347.8426 8735	35.8746 1604	0.0028 7486
93	9.9384 6886	0.1006 1912	357.5387 5453	35.9752 3516	0.0027 9690
94	10.1869 3058	0.0981 6500	367.4772 2339	36.0734 0016	0.0027 2126
95	10.4416 0385	0.0957 7073	377.6641 5398	36.1691 7089	0.0026 4786
96	10.7026 4395	0.0934 3486	388.1057 5783	36.2626 0574	0.0025 7662
97	10.9702 1004	0.0911 5596	398.8084 0177	36.3537 6170	0.0025 0747
98	11.2444 6530	0.0889 3264	409.7786 1182	36.4426 9434	0.0024 4034
99	11.5255 7693	0.0867 6355	421.0230 7711	36.5294 5790	0.0023 7517
100	11.8137 1635	0.0846 4737	432.5486 5404	36.6141 0526	0.0023 1188

TABLE IV (continued)

$i = 2\frac{3}{4}\%$

n	$(1+i)^n$	$(1+i)^{-n}$	$s_{\overline{n}\rceil i}$	$a_{\overline{n}\rceil i}$	$s^{-1}_{\overline{n}\rceil i}$
1	1.0275 0000	0.9732 3601	1.0000 0000	0.9732 3601	1.0000 0000
2	1.0557 5625	0.9471 8833	2.0275 0000	1.9204 2434	0.4932 1825
3	1.0847 8955	0.9218 3779	3.0832 5625	2.8422 6213	0.3243 3243
4	1.1146 2126	0.8971 6573	4.1680 4580	3.7394 2787	0.2399 2059
5	1.1452 7334	0.8731 5400	5.2826 6706	4.6125 8186	0.1892 9832
6	1.1767 6836	0.8497 8491	6.4279 4040	5.4623 6678	0.1555 7083
7	1.2091 2949	0.8270 4128	7.6047 0876	6.2894 0806	0.1314 9747
8	1.2423 8055	0.8049 0635	8.8138 3825	7.0943 1441	0.1134 5795
9	1.2765 4602	0.7833 6385	10.0562 1880	7.8776 7826	0.0994 4095
10	1.3116 5103	0.7623 9791	11.3327 6482	8.6400 7616	0.0882 3972
11	1.3477 2144	0.7419 9310	12.6444 1585	9.3820 6926	0.0790 8629
12	1.3847 8378	0.7221 3440	13.9921 3729	10.1042 0366	0.0714 6871
13	1.4228 6533	0.7028 0720	15.3769 2107	10.8070 1086	0.0650 3252
14	1.4619 9413	0.6839 9728	16.7997 8639	11.4910 0814	0.0595 2457
15	1.5021 9896	0.6656 9078	18.2617 8052	12.1566 9892	0.0547 5917
16	1.5435 0944	0.6478 7424	19.7639 7948	12.8045 7315	0.0505 9710
17	1.5859 5595	0.6305 3454	21.3074 8892	13.4351 0769	0.0469 3186
18	1.6295 6973	0.6136 5892	22.8934 4487	14.0487 6661	0.0436 8063
19	1.6743 8290	0.5972 3496	24.5230 1460	14.6460 0157	0.0407 7802
20	1.7204 2843	0.5812 5057	26.1973 9750	15.2272 5213	0.0381 7173
21	1.7677 4021	0.5656 9398	27.9178 2593	15.7929 4612	0.0358 1941
22	1.8163 5307	0.5505 5375	29.6855 6615	16.3434 9987	0.0036 8640
23	1.8663 0278	0.5358 1874	31.5019 1921	16.8793 1861	0.0317 4410
24	1.9176 2610	0.5214 7809	33.3682 2199	17.4007 9670	0.0299 6863
25	1.9703 6082	0.5075 2126	35.2858 4810	17.9083 1795	0.0283 3997
26	2.0245 4575	0.4939 3796	37.2562 0892	18.4022 5592	0.0268 4116
27	2.0802 2075	0.4807 1821	39.2807 5467	18.8829 7413	0.0254 5776
28	2.1374 2682	0.4678 5227	41.3609 7542	19.3508 2640	0.0241 7738
29	2.1962 0606	0.4553 3068	43.4984 0224	19.8061 5708	0.0229 8935
30	2.2566 0173	0.4431 4421	45.6946 0830	20.2493 0130	0.0218 8442
31	2.3186 5828	0.4312 8391	47.9512 1003	20.6805 8520	0.0208 5453
32	2.3824 2138	0.4197 4103	50.2698 6831	21.1003 2623	0.0198 9263
33	2.4479 3797	0.4085 0708	52.6522 8969	21.5088 3332	0.0189 9253
34	2.5152 5626	0.3975 7380	55.1002 2765	21.9064 0712	0.0181 4875
35	2.5844 2581	0.3869 3314	57.6154 8391	22.2933 4026	0.0173 5645
36	2.6554 9752	0.3765 7727	60.1999 0972	22.6699 1753	0.0166 1132
37	2.7285 2370	0.3664 9856	62.8554 0724	23.0364 1609	0.0159 0953
38	2.8035 5810	0.3566 8959	65.5839 3094	23.3931 0568	0.0152 4764
39	2.8806 5595	0.3471 4316	68.3874 8904	23.7402 4884	0.0146 2256
40	2.9598 7399	0.3378 5222	71.2681 4499	24.0781 0106	0.0140 3151
41	3.0412 7052	0.3288 0995	74.2280 1898	24.4069 1101	0.0134 7200
42	3.1249 0546	0.3200 0968	77.2692 8950	24.7269 2069	0.0129 4175
43	3.2108 4036	0.3114 4495	80.3941 9496	25.0383 6563	0.0124 3871
44	3.2991 3847	0.3031 0944	83.6050 3532	25.3414 7507	0.0119 6100
45	3.3898 6478	0.2949 9702	86.9041 7379	25.6364 7209	0.0115 0693
46	3.4830 8606	0.2871 0172	90.2940 3857	25.9235 7381	0.0110 7493
47	3.5788 7093	0.2794 1773	93.7771 2463	26.2029 9154	0.0106 6358
48	3.6772 8988	0.2719 3940	97.3559 9556	26.4749 3094	0.0102 7158
49	3.7784 1535	0.2646 6122	101.0332 8544	26.7395 9215	0.0098 9773
50	3.8823 2177	0.2575 7783	104.8117 0079	26.9971 6998	0.0095 4092

TABLE IV (continued)

$i = 2\frac{3}{4}\%$

n	$(1+i)^n$	$(1+i)^{-n}$	$s_{\overline{n}\mid i}$	$a_{\overline{n}\mid i}$	$s_{\overline{n}\mid i}^{-1}$
51	3.9890 8562	0.2506 8402	108.6940 2256	27.2478 5400	0.0092 0014
52	4.0987 8547	0.2439 7471	112.6831 0818	27.4918 2871	0.0088 7444
53	4.2115 0208	0.2374 4497	116.7818 9365	27.7292 7368	0.0085 6297
54	4.3273 1838	0.2310 9000	120.9933 9573	27.9603 6368	0.0082 6491
55	4.4463 1964	0.2249 0511	125.3207 1411	28.1852 6879	0.0079 7953
56	4.5685 9343	0.2188 8575	129.7670 3375	28.4041 5454	0.0077 0612
57	4.6942 2975	0.2130 2749	134.3356 2718	28.6171 8203	0.0074 4404
58	4.8233 2107	0.2073 2603	139.0298 5692	28.8245 0806	0.0071 9270
59	4.9559 6239	0.2017 7716	143.8531 7799	29.0262 8522	0.0069 5153
60	5.0922 5136	0.1963 7679	148.8091 4038	29.2226 6201	0.0067 2002
61	5.2322 8827	0.1911 2097	153.9013 9174	29.4137 8298	0.0064 9767
62	5.3761 7620	0.1860 0581	159.1336 8002	29.5997 8879	0.0062 8402
63	5.5240 2105	0.1810 2755	164.5098 5622	29.7808 1634	0.0060 7866
64	5.6759 3162	0.1761 8253	170.0338 7726	29.9569 9887	0.0058 8118
65	5.8320 1974	0.1714 6718	175.7098 0889	30.1284 6605	0.0056 9120
66	5.9924 0029	0.1668 7804	181.5418 2863	30.2953 4409	0.0055 0837
67	6.1571 9130	0.1624 1172	187.5342 2892	30.4577 5581	0.0053 3236
68	6.3265 1406	0.1580 6493	193.6914 2021	30.6158 2074	0.0051 6285
69	6.5004 9319	0.1538 3448	200.0179 3427	30.7696 5522	0.0049 9955
70	6.6792 5676	0.1497 1726	206.5184 2746	30.9193 7247	0.0048 4218
71	6.8629 3632	0.1457 1023	213.1976 8422	31.0650 8270	0.0046 9048
72	7.0516 6706	0.1418 1044	220.0606 2054	31.2068 9314	0.0045 4420
73	7.2455 8791	0.1380 1503	227.1122 8760	31.3449 0816	0.0044 0311
74	7.4448 4158	0.1343 2119	234.3578 7551	31.4792 2936	0.0042 6698
75	7.6495 7472	0.1307 2622	241.8027 1709	31.6099 5558	0.0041 3560
76	7.8599 3802	0.1272 2747	249.4522 9181	31.7371 8304	0.0040 0878
77	8.0760 8632	0.1238 2235	257.3122 2983	31.8610 0540	0.0038 8633
78	8.2981 7869	0.1205 0837	265.3883 1615	31.9815 1377	0.0037 6806
79	8.5263 7861	0.1172 8309	273.6864 9485	32.0987 9685	0.0036 5382
80	8.7608 5402	0.1141 4412	282.2128 7345	32.2129 4098	0.0035 4342
81	9.0017 7751	0.1110 8917	290.9737 2747	32.3240 3015	0.0034 3674
82	9.2493 2639	0.1081 1598	299.9755 0498	32.4321 4613	0.0033 3361
83	9.5036 8286	0.1052 2237	309.2248 3137	32.5373 6850	0.0032 3389
84	9.7650 3414	0.1024 0620	318.7285 1423	32.6397 7469	0.0031 3747
85	10.0335 7258	0.0996 6540	328.4935 4837	32.7394 4009	0.0030 4420
86	10.3094 9583	0.0969 9795	338.5271 2095	32.8364 3804	0.0029 5397
87	10.5930 0696	0.0944 0190	348.8366 1678	32.9308 3994	0.0028 6667
88	10.8843 1465	0.0918 7533	359.4296 2374	33.0227 1527	0.0027 8219
89	11.1836 3331	0.0894 1638	370.3139 3839	33.1121 3165	0.0027 0041
90	11.4911 8322	0.0870 2324	381.4975 7170	33.1991 5489	0.0026 2125
91	11.8071 9076	0.0846 9415	392.9887 5492	33.2838 4905	0.0025 4460
92	12.1318 8851	0.0824 2740	404.7959 4568	33.3662 7644	0.0024 7038
93	12.4655 1544	0.0802 2131	416.9278 3418	33.4464 9776	0.0023 9850
94	12.8083 1711	0.0780 7427	429.3933 4962	33.5245 7202	0.0023 2887
95	13.1605 4584	0.0759 8469	442.2016 6674	33.6005 5671	0.0022 6141
96	13.5224 6085	0.0739 5104	455.3622 1257	33.6745 0775	0.0021 9605
97	13.8943 2852	0.0719 7181	468.8846 7342	33.7464 7956	0.0021 3272
98	14.2764 2255	0.0700 4556	482.7790 0194	33.8165 2512	0.0020 7134
99	14.6690 2417	0.0681 7086	497.0554 2449	33.8846 9598	0.0020 1185
100	15.0724 2234	0.0663 4634	511.7244 4867	33.9510 4232	0.0019 5418

TABLE IV (continued)

$i = 3\%$

n	$(1+i)^n$	$(1+i)^{-n}$	$s_{\overline{n}\rceil i}$	$a_{\overline{n}\rceil i}$	$s^{-1}_{\overline{n}\rceil i}$
1	1.0300 0000	0.9708 7379	1.0000 0000	0.9708 7379	1.0000 0000
2	1.0609 0000	0.9425 9591	2.0300 0000	1.9134 6970	0.4926 1084
3	1.0927 2700	0.9151 4166	3.0909 0000	2.8286 1135	0.3235 3036
4	1.1255 0881	0.8884 8705	4.1836 2700	3.7170 9840	0.2390 2705
5	1.1592 7407	0.8626 0878	5.3091 3581	4.5797 0719	0.1883 5457
6	1.1940 5230	0.8374 8426	6.4684 0988	5.4171 9144	0.1545 9750
7	1.2298 7387	0.8130 9151	7.6624 6218	6.2302 8296	0.1305 0635
8	1.2667 7008	0.7894 0923	8.8923 3605	7.0196 9219	0.1124 5639
9	1.3047 7318	0.7664 1673	10.1591 0613	7.7861 0892	0.0984 3386
10	1.3439 1638	0.7440 9391	11.4638 7931	8.5302 0284	0.0872 3051
11	1.3842 3387	0.7224 2128	12.8077 9569	9.2526 2411	0.0780 7745
12	1.4257 6089	0.7013 7988	14.1920 2956	9.9540 0399	0.0704 6209
13	1.4685 3371	0.6809 5134	15.6177 9045	10.6349 5533	0.0640 2954
14	1.5125 8972	0.6611 1781	17.0863 2416	11.2960 7314	0.0585 2634
15	1.5579 6742	0.6418 6195	18.5989 1389	11.9379 3509	0.0537 6658
16	1.6047 0644	0.6231 6694	20.1568 8130	12.5611 0203	0.0496 1085
17	1.6528 4763	0.6050 1645	21.7615 8774	13.1661 1847	0.0459 5253
18	1.7024 3306	0.5873 9461	23.4144 3537	13.7535 1308	0.0427 0870
19	1.7535 0605	0.5702 8603	25.1168 6844	14.3237 9911	0.0398 1388
20	1.8061 1123	0.5536 7575	26.8703 7449	14.8774 7486	0.0372 1571
21	1.8602 9457	0.5375 4928	28.6764 8572	15.4150 2414	0.0348 7178
22	1.9161 0341	0.5218 9250	30.5367 8030	15.9369 1664	0.0327 4739
23	1.9735 8651	0.5066 9175	32.4528 8370	16.4436 0839	0.0308 1390
24	2.0327 9411	0.4919 3374	34.4264 7022	16.9355 4212	0.0290 4742
25	2.0937 7793	0.4776 0557	36.4592 6432	17.4131 4769	0.0274 2787
26	2.1565 9127	0.4636 9473	38.5530 4225	17.8768 4242	0.0259 3829
27	2.2212 8901	0.4501 8906	40.7096 3352	18.3270 3147	0.0245 6421
28	2.2879 2768	0.4370 7675	42.9309 2252	18.7641 0823	0.0232 9323
29	2.3565 6551	0.4243 4636	45.2188 5020	19.1884 5459	0.0221 1467
30	2.4272 6247	0.4119 8676	47.5754 1571	19.6004 4135	0.0210 1926
31	2.5000 8035	0.3999 8715	50.0026 7818	20.0004 2849	0.0199 9893
32	2.5750 8276	0.3883 3703	52.5027 5852	20.3887 6553	0.0190 4662
33	2.6523 3524	0.3770 2625	55.0778 4128	20.7657 9178	0.0181 5612
34	2.7319 0530	0.3660 4490	57.7301 7652	21.1318 3668	0.0173 2196
35	2.8138 6245	0.3553 8340	60.4620 8181	21.4872 2007	0.0165 3929
36	2.8982 7833	0.3450 3243	63.2759 4427	21.8322 5250	0.0158 0379
37	2.9852 2668	0.3349 8294	66.1742 2259	22.1672 3544	0.0151 1162
38	3.0747 8348	0.3252 2615	69.1594 4927	22.4924 6159	0.0144 5934
39	3.1670 2698	0.3157 5355	72.2342 3275	22.8082 1513	0.0138 4385
40	3.2620 3779	0.3065 5684	75.4012 5973	23.1147 7197	0.0132 6238
41	3.3598 9893	0.2976 2800	78.6632 9753	23.4123 9997	0.0127 1241
42	3.4606 9589	0.2889 5922	82.0231 9645	23.7013 5920	0.0121 9167
43	3.5645 1677	0.2805 4294	85.4838 9234	23.9819 0213	0.0116 9811
44	3.6714 5227	0.2723 7178	89.0484 0911	24.2542 7392	0.0112 2985
45	3.7815 9584	0.2644 3862	92.7198 6139	24.5187 1254	0.0107 8518
46	3.8950 4372	0.2567 3653	96.5014 5723	24.7754 4907	0.0103 6254
47	4.0118 9503	0.2492 5876	100.3965 0095	25.0247 0783	0.0099 6051
48	4.1322 5188	0.2419 9880	104.4083 9598	25.2667 0664	0.0095 7777
49	4.2562 1944	0.2349 5029	108.5406 4785	25.5016 5693	0.0092 1314
50	4.3839 0602	0.2281 0708	112.7968 6729	25.7297 6401	0.0088 6550

TABLE IV (continued)

$i = 3\%$

n	$(1+i)^n$	$(1+i)^{-n}$	$s_{\overline{n}\vert i}$	$a_{\overline{n}\vert i}$	$s^{-1}_{\overline{n}\vert i}$
51	4.5154 2320	0.2214 6318	117.1807 7331	25.9512 2719	0.0085 3382
52	4.6508 8590	0.2150 1280	121.6961 9651	26.1662 3999	0.0082 1718
53	4.7904 1247	0.2087 5029	126.3470 8240	26.3749 9028	0.0079 1471
54	4.9341 2485	0.2026 7019	131.1374 9488	26.5776 6047	0.0076 2558
55	5.0821 4859	0.1967 6717	136.0716 1972	26.7744 2764	0.0073 4907
56	5.2346 1305	0.1910 3609	141.1537 6831	26.9654 6373	0.0070 8447
57	5.3916 5144	0.1854 7193	146.3883 8136	27.1509 3566	0.0068 3114
58	5.5534 0098	0.1800 6984	151.7800 3280	27.3310 0549	0.0065 8848
59	5.7200 0301	0.1748 2508	157.3334 3379	27.5058 3058	0.0063 5593
60	5.8916 0310	0.1697 3309	163.0534 3680	27.6755 6367	0.0061 3296
61	6.0683 5120	0.1647 8941	168.9450 3991	27.8403 5307	0.0059 1908
62	6.2504 0173	0.1599 8972	175.0133 9110	28.0003 4279	0.0057 1385
63	6.4379 1379	0.1553 2982	181.2637 9284	28.1556 7261	0.0055 1682
64	6.6310 5120	0.1508 0565	187.7017 0662	28.3064 7826	0.0053 2760
65	6.8299 8273	0.1464 1325	194.3327 5782	28.4528 9152	0.0051 4581
66	7.0348 8222	0.1421 4879	201.1627 4055	28.5950 4031	0.0049 7110
67	7.2459 2868	0.1380 0853	208.1976 2277	28.7330 4884	0.0048 0313
68	7.4633 0654	0.1339 8887	215.4435 5145	28.8670 3771	0.0046 4159
69	7.6872 0574	0.1300 8628	222.9068 5800	28.9971 2399	0.0044 8618
70	7.9178 2191	0.1262 9736	230.5940 6374	29.1234 2135	0.0043 3663
71	8.1553 5657	0.1226 1880	238.5118 8565	29.2460 4015	0.0041 9266
72	8.4000 1727	0.1190 4737	246.6672 4222	29.3650 8752	0.0040 5405
73	8.6520 1778	0.1155 7998	255.0672 5949	29.4806 6750	0.0039 2053
74	8.9115 7832	0.1122 1357	263.7192 7727	29.5928 8106	0.0037 9191
75	9.1789 2567	0.1089 4521	272.6308 5559	29.7018 2628	0.0036 6796
76	9.4542 9344	0.1057 7205	281.8097 8126	29.8075 9833	0.0035 4849
77	9.7379 2224	0.1026 9131	291.2640 7469	29.9102 8964	0.0034 3331
78	10.0300 5991	0.0997 0030	301.0019 9693	30.0099 8994	0.0033 2224
79	10.3309 6171	0.0967 9641	311.0320 5684	30.1067 8635	0.0032 1510
80	10.6408 9056	0.0939 7710	321.3630 1855	30.2007 6345	0.0031 1175
81	10.9601 1727	0.0912 3990	332.0039 0910	30.2920 0335	0.0030 1201
82	11.2889 2079	0.0885 8243	342.9640 2638	30.3805 8577	0.0029 1576
83	11.6275 8842	0.0860 0236	354.2529 4717	30.4665 8813	0.0028 2284
84	11.9764 1607	0.0834 9743	365.8805 3558	30.5500 8556	0.0027 3313
85	12.3357 0855	0.0810 6547	377.8569 5165	30.6311 5103	0.0026 4650
86	12.7057 7981	0.0787 0434	390.1926 6020	30.7098 5537	0.0025 6284
87	13.0869 5320	0.0764 1198	402.8984 4001	30.7862 6735	0.0024 8202
88	13.4795 6180	0.0741 8639	415.9853 9321	30.8604 5374	0.0024 0393
89	13.8839 4865	0.0720 2562	429.4649 5500	30.9324 7936	0.0023 2848
90	14.3004 6711	0.0699 2779	443.3489 0365	31.0024 0714	0.0022 5556
91	14.7294 8112	0.0678 9105	457.6493 7076	31.0702 9820	0.0021 8508
92	15.1713 6556	0.0659 1364	472.3788 5189	31.1362 1184	0.0021 1694
93	15.6265 0652	0.0639 9383	487.5502 1744	31.2002 0567	0.0020 5107
94	16.0953 0172	0.0621 2993	503.1767 2397	21.2623 3560	0.0019 8737
95	16.5781 6077	0.0603 2032	519.2720 2569	31.3226 5592	0.0019 2577
96	17.0755 0559	0.0585 6342	535 8501 8645	31.3812 1934	0.0018 6619
97	17.5877 7076	0.0568 5769	552.9256 9205	31.4380 7703	0.0018 0856
98	18.1154 0388	0.0552 0164	570.5134 6281	31.4932 7867	0.0017 5281
99	18.6588 6600	0.0535 9383	588.6288 6669	31.5468 7250	0.0016 9886
100	19.2186 3198	0.0520 3284	607.2877 3270	31.5989 0534	0.0016 4667

TABLE IV (continued)

$i = 3\frac{1}{2}\%$

n	$(1+i)^n$	$(1+i)^{-n}$	$s_{\overline{n}\rceil i}$	$a_{\overline{n}\rceil i}$	$s_{\overline{n}\rceil i}^{-1}$
1	1.0350 0000	0.9661 8357	1.0000 0000	0.9661 8357	1.0000 0000
2	1.0712 2500	0.9335 1070	2.0350 0000	1.8996 9428	0.4914 0049
3	1.1087 1788	0.9019 4271	3.1062 2500	2.8016 3698	0.3219 3418
4	1.1475 2300	0.8714 4223	4.2149 4288	3.6730 7921	0.2372 5114
5	1.1876 8631	0.8419 7317	5.3624 6588	4.5150 5238	0.1864 8137
6	1.2292 5533	0.8135 0064	6.5501 5218	5.3285 5302	0.1526 6821
7	1.2722 7926	0.7859 9096	7.7794 0751	6.1145 4398	0.1285 4449
8	1.3168 0904	0.7594 1156	9.0516 8677	6.8739 5554	0.1104 7665
9	1.3628 9735	0.7337 3097	10.3684 9581	7.6076 8651	0.0964 4601
10	1.4105 9876	0.7089 1881	11.7313 9316	8.3166 0532	0.0852 4137
11	1.4599 6972	0.6849 4571	13.1419 9192	9.0015 5104	0.0760 9197
12	1.5110 6866	0.6617 8330	14.6019 6164	9.6633 3433	0.0684 8395
13	1.5639 5606	0.6394 0415	16.1130 3030	10.3027 3849	0.0620 6157
14	1.6186 9452	0.6177 8179	17.6769 8636	10.9205 2028	0.0565 7073
15	1.6753 4883	0.5968 9062	19.2956 8088	11.5174 1090	0.0518 2507
16	1.7339 8604	0.5767 0591	20.9710 2971	12.0941 1681	0.0476 8483
17	1.7946 7555	0.5572 0378	22.7050 1575	12.6513 2059	0.0440 4313
18	1.8574 8920	0.5383 6114	24.4996 9130	13.1896 8173	0.0408 1684
19	1.9225 0132	0.5201 5569	26.3571 8050	13.7098 3742	0.0379 4033
20	1.9897 8886	0.5025 6588	28.2796 8181	14.2124 0330	0.0353 6108
21	2.0594 3147	0.4855 7090	30.2694 7068	14.6979 7420	0.0330 3659
22	2.1315 1158	0.4691 5063	32.3289 0215	15.1671 2484	0.0309 3207
23	2.2061 1448	0.4532 8563	34.4604 1373	15.6204 1047	0.0290 1880
24	2.2833 2849	0.4379 5713	36.6665 2821	16.0583 6760	0.0272 7283
25	2.3632 4498	0.4231 4699	38.9498 5669	16.4815 1459	0.0256 7404
26	2.4459 5856	0.4088 3767	41.3131 0168	16.8903 5226	0.0242 0540
27	2.5315 6711	0.3950 1224	43.7590 6024	17.2853 6451	0.0228 5241
28	2.6201 7196	0.3816 5434	46.2906 2734	17.6670 1885	0.0216 0265
29	2.7118 7798	0.3687 4815	48.9107 9930	18.0357 6700	0.0204 4538
30	2.8067 9370	0.3562 7841	51.6226 7728	18.3920 4541	0.0193 7133
31	2.9050 3148	0.3442 3035	54.4294 7098	18.7362 7576	0.0183 7240
32	3.0067 0759	0.3325 8971	57.3345 0247	19.0688 6547	0.0174 4150
33	3.1119 4235	0.3213 4271	60.3412 1005	19.3902 0818	0.0165 7242
34	3.2208 6033	0.3104 7605	63.4531 5240	19.7006 8423	0.0157 5966
35	3.3335 9045	0.2999 7686	66.6740 1274	20.0006 6110	0.0149 9835
36	3.4502 6611	0.2898 3272	70.0076 0318	20.2904 9381	0.0142 8416
37	3.5710 2543	0.2800 3161	73.4578 6930	20.5705 2542	0.0136 1325
38	3.6960 1132	0.2705 6194	77.0288 9472	20.8410 8736	0.0129 8214
39	3.8253 7171	0.2614 1250	80.7249 0604	21.1024 9987	0.0123 8775
40	3.9592 5972	0.2525 7247	84.5502 7775	21.3550 7234	0.0118 2728
41	4.0978 3381	0.2440 3137	88.5095 3747	21.5991 0371	0.0112 9822
42	4.2412 5799	0.2357 7910	92.6073 7128	21.8348 8281	0.0107 9828
43	4.3897 0202	0.2278 0590	96.8486 2928	22.0626 8870	0.0103 2539
44	4.5433 4160	0.2201 0231	101.2383 3130	22.2827 9102	0.0098 7768
45	4.7023 5855	0.2126 5924	105.7816 7290	22.4954 5026	0.0094 5343
46	4.8669 4110	0.2054 6787	110.4840 3145	22.7009 1813	0.0090 5108
47	5.0372 8404	0.1985 1968	115.3509 7255	22.8994 3780	0.0086 6919
48	5.2135 8898	0.1918 0645	120.3882 5659	23.0912 4425	0.0083 0646
49	5.3960 6459	0.1853 2024	125.6018 4557	23.2765 6450	0.0079 6167
50	5.5849 2686	0.1790 5337	130.9979 1016	23.4556 1787	0.0076 3371

TABLE IV (continued)

$i = 3\frac{1}{2}\%$

n	$(1+i)^n$	$(1+i)^{-n}$	$s_{\overline{n}\rceil i}$	$a_{\overline{n}\rceil i}$	$s^{-1}_{\overline{n}\rceil i}$
51	5.7803 9930	0.1729 9843	136.5828 3702	23.6286 1630	0.0073 2156
52	5.9827 1327	0.1671 4824	142.3632 3631	23.7957 6454	0.0070 2429
53	6.1921 0824	0.1614 9589	148.3459 4958	23.9572 6043	0.0067 4100
54	6.4088 3202	0.1560 3467	154.5380 5782	24.1132 9510	0.0064 7090
55	6.6331 4114	0.1507 5814	160.9468 8984	24.2640 5323	0.0062 1323
56	6.8653 0108	0.1456 6004	167.5800 3099	24.4097 1327	0.0059 6730
57	7.1055 8662	0.1407 3433	174.4453 3207	24.5504 4760	0.0057 3245
58	7.3542 8215	0.1359 7520	181.5509 1869	24.6864 2281	0.0055 0810
59	7.6116 8203	0.1313 7701	188.9052 0085	24.8177 9981	0.0052 9366
60	7.8780 9090	0.1269 3431	196.5168 8288	24.9447 3412	0.0050 8862
61	8.1538 2408	0.1226 4184	204.3949 7378	25.0673 7596	0.0048 9249
62	8.4392 0793	0.1184 9453	212.5487 9786	25.1858 7049	0.0047 0480
63	8.7345 8020	0.1144 8747	220.9880 0579	25.3003 5796	0.0045 2513
64	9.0402 9051	0.1106 1591	229.7225 8599	25.4109 7388	0.0043 5308
65	9.3567 0068	0.1068 7528	238.7628 7650	25.5178 4916	0.0041 8826
66	9.6841 8520	0.1032 6114	248.1195 7718	25.6211 1030	0.0040 3031
67	10.0231 3168	0.0997 6922	257.8037 6238	25.7208 7951	0.0038 7892
68	10.3739 4129	0.0963 9538	267.8268 9406	25.8172 7489	0.0037 3375
69	10.7370 2924	0.0931 3563	278.2008 3535	25.9104 1052	0.0035 9453
70	11.1128 2526	0.0899 8612	288.9378 6459	26.0003 9664	0.0034 6095
71	11.5017 7414	0.0869 4311	300.0506 8985	26.0873 3975	0.0033 3277
72	11.9043 3624	0.0840 0300	311.5524 6400	26.1713 4275	0.0032 0973
73	12.3209 8801	0.0811 6232	323.4568 0024	26.2525 0508	0.0030 9160
64	12.7522 2259	0.0784 1770	335.7777 8824	26.3309 2278	0.0029 7816
75	13.1985 5038	0.0757 6590	348.5300 1083	26.4066 8868	0.0028 6919
76	13.6604 9964	0.0732 0376	361.7285 6121	26.4798 9244	0.0027 6450
77	14.1386 1713	0.0707 2827	375.3890 6085	26.5506 2072	0.0026 6390
78	14.6334 6873	0.0683 3650	389.5276 7798	26.6189 5721	0.0025 6721
79	15.1456 4013	0.0660 2560	404.1611 4671	26.6849 8281	0 0024 7426
80	15.6757 3754	0.0637 9285	419.3067 8685	26.7487 7567	0.0023 8489
81	16.2243 8835	0.0616 3561	434.9825 2439	26.8104 1127	0.0022 9894
82	16.7922 4195	0.0595 5131	451.2069 1274	26.8699 6258	0.0022 1628
83	17.3799 7041	0.0575 3750	467.9991 5469	26.9275 0008	0.0021 3676
84	17.9882 6938	0.0555 9178	485.3791 2510	26.9830 9186	0.0020 6025
85	18.6178 5881	0.0537 1187	503.3673 9448	27.0368 0373	0.0019 8662
86	19.2694 8387	0.0518 9553	521.9852 5329	27.0886 9926	0.0019 1576
87	19.9439 1580	0.0501 4060	541.2547 3715	27.1388 3986	0.0018 4756
88	20.6419 5285	0.0484 4503	561.1986 5295	27.1872 8489	0.0017 8190
89	21.3644 2120	0.0468 0679	581.8406 0581	27.2340 9168	0.0017 1868
90	22.1121 7595	0.0452 2395	603.2050 2701	27.2793 1564	0.0016 5781
91	22.8861 0210	0.0436 9464	625.3172 0295	27.3230 1028	0.0015 9919
92	23.6871 1568	0.0422 1704	648.2033 0506	27.3652 2732	0.0015 4273
93	24.5161 6473	0.0407 8941	671.8904 2073	27.4060 1673	0.0014 8834
94	25.3742 3049	0.0394 1006	696.4065 8546	27.4454 2680	0.0014 3594
95	26.2623 2856	0.0380 7735	721.7808 1595	27.4835 0415	0.0013 8546
96	27.1815 1006	0.0367 8971	748.0431 4451	27.5202 9387	0.0013 3682
97	28.1328 6291	0.0355 4562	775.2246 5457	27.5558 3948	0.0012 8995
98	29.1175 1311	0.0343 4359	803.3575 1748	27.5901 8308	0.0012 4478
99	30.1366 2607	0.0331 8221	832.4750 3059	27.6233 6529	0.0012 0124
100	31.1914 0798	0.0320 6011	862.6116 5666	27.6554 2540	0.0011 5927

TABLE IV (continued)

$i = 4\%$

n	$(1+i)^n$	$(1+i)^{-n}$	$s_{\overline{n}\rceil i}$	$a_{\overline{n}\rceil i}$	$s_{\overline{n}\rceil i}^{-1}$
1	1.0400 0000	0.9615 3846	1.0000 0000	0.9615 3846	1.0000 0000
2	1.0816 0000	0.9245 5621	2.0400 0000	1.8860 9467	0.4901 9608
3	1.1248 6400	0.8889 9636	3.1216 0000	2.7750 9103	0.3203 4854
4	1.1698 5856	0.8548 0419	4.2464 6400	3.6298 9522	0.2354 9005
5	1.2166 5290	0.8219 2711	5.4163 2256	4.4518 2233	0.1846 2711
6	1.2653 1902	0.7903 1453	6.6329 7546	5.2421 3686	0.1507 6190
7	1.3159 3178	0.7599 1781	7.8982 9448	6.0020 5467	0.1266 0961
8	1.3685 6905	0.7306 9021	9.2142 2626	6.7327 4487	0.1085 2783
9	1.4233 1181	0.7025 8674	10.5827 9531	7.4353 3161	0.0944 9299
10	1.4802 4428	0.6755 6417	12.0061 0712	8.1108 9578	0.0832 9094
11	1.5394 5406	0.6495 8093	13.4863 5141	8.7604 7671	0.0741 4904
12	1.6010 3222	0.6245 9705	15.0258 0546	9.3850 7376	0.0665 5217
13	1.6650 7351	0.6005 7409	16.6268 3768	9.9856 4785	0.0601 4373
14	1.7316 7645	0.5774 7508	18.2919 1119	10.5631 2293	0.0546 6897
15	1.8009 4351	0.5552 6450	20.0235 8764	11.1183 8743	0.0499 4110
16	1.8729 8125	0.5339 0818	21.8245 3114	11.6522 9561	0.0458 2000
17	1.9479 0050	0.5133 7325	23.6975 1239	12.1656 6885	0.0421 9852
18	2.0258 1652	0.4936 2812	25.6454 1288	12.6592 9697	0.0389 9333
19	2.1068 4918	0.4746 4242	27.6712 2940	13.1339 3940	0.0361 3862
20	2.1911 2314	0.4563 8695	29.7780 7858	13.5903 2634	0.0335 8175
21	2.2787 6807	0.4388 3360	31.9692 0172	14.0291 5995	0.0312 8011
22	2.3699 1879	0.4219 5539	34.2479 6979	14.4511 1533	0.0291 9881
23	2.4647 1554	0.4057 2633	36.6178 8858	14.8568 4167	0.0273 0906
24	2.5633 0416	0.3901 2147	39.0826 0412	15.2469 6314	0.0255 8683
25	2.6658 3633	0.3751 1680	41.6459 0829	15.6220 7994	0.0240 1196
26	2.7724 6978	0.3606 8923	44.3117 4462	15.9827 6918	0.0225 6738
27	2.8833 6858	0.3468 1657	47.0842 1440	16.3295 8575	0.0212 3854
28	2.9987 0332	0.3334 7747	49.9675 8298	16.6630 6322	0.0200 1298
29	3.1186 5145	0.3206 5141	52.9662 8630	16.9837 1463	0.0188 7993
30	3.2433 9751	0.3083 1867	56.0849 3775	17.2920 3330	0.0178 3010
31	3.3731 3341	0.2964 6026	59.3283 3526	17.5884 9356	0.0168 5535
32	3.5080 5875	0.2850 5794	62.7014 6867	17.8735 5150	0.0159 4859
33	3.6483 8110	0.2740 9417	66.2095 2742	18.1476 4567	0.0151 0357
34	3.7943 1634	0.2635 5209	69.8579 0851	18.4111 9776	0.0143 1477
35	3.9460 8899	0.2534 1547	73.6522 2486	18.6646 1323	0.0135 7732
36	4.1039 3255	0.2436 6872	77.5983 1385	18.9082 8195	0.0128 8688
37	4.2680 8986	0.2342 9685	81.7022 4640	19.1425 7880	0.0122 3957
38	4.4388 1345	0.2252 8543	85.9703 3626	19.3678 6423	0.0116 3192
39	4.6163 6599	0.2166 2061	90.4091 4971	19.5844 8484	0.0110 6083
40	4.8010 2063	0.2082 8904	95.0255 1570	19.7927 7388	0.0105 2349
41	4.9930 6145	0.2002 7793	99.8265 3633	19.9930 5181	0.0100 1738
42	5.1927 8391	0.1925 7493	104.8195 9778	20.1856 2674	0.0095 4020
43	5.4004 9527	0.1851 6820	110.0123 8169	20.3707 9494	0.0090 8989
44	5.6165 1508	0.1780 4635	115.4128 7696	20.5488 4129	0.0086 6454
45	5.8411 7568	0.1711 9841	121.0293 9204	20.7200 3970	0.0082 6246
46	6.0748 2271	0.1646 1386	126.8705 6772	20.8846 5356	0.0078 8205
47	6.3178 1562	0.1582 8256	132.9453 9043	21.0429 3612	0.0075 2189
48	6.5705 2824	0.1521 9476	139.2632 0604	21.1951 3088	0.0071 8065
49	6.8333 4937	0.1463 4112	145.8337 3429	21.3414 7200	0.0068 5712
50	7.1066 8335	0.1407 1262	152.6670 8366	21.4821 8462	0.0065 5020

TABLE IV (continued)

$i = 4\%$

n	$(1+i)^n$	$(1+i)^{-n}$	$s_{\overline{n}\vert i}$	$a_{\overline{n}\vert i}$	$s_{\overline{n}\vert i}^{-1}$
51	7.3909 5068	0.1353 0059	159.7737 6700	21.6174 8521	0.0062 5885
52	7.6865 8871	0.1300 9672	167.1647 1768	21.7475 8193	0.0059 8212
53	7.9940 5226	0.1250 9300	174.8513 0639	21.8726 7493	0.0057 1915
54	8.3138 1435	0.1202 8173	182.8453 5865	21.9929 5667	0.0054 6910
55	8.6463 6692	0.1156 5551	191.1591 7299	22.1086 1218	0.0052 3124
56	8.9922 2160	0.1112 0722	199.8055 3991	22.2198 1940	0.0050 0487
57	9.3519 1046	0.1069 3002	208.7977 6151	22.3267 4943	0.0047 8932
58	9.7259 8688	0.1028 1733	218.1496 7197	22.4295 6676	0.0045 8401
59	10.1150 2635	0.0988 6282	227.8756 5885	22.5284 2957	0.0043 8836
60	10.5196 2741	0.0950 6040	237.9906 8520	22.6234 8997	0.0042 0185
61	10.9404 1250	0.0914 0423	248.5103 1261	22.7148 9421	0.0040 2398
62	11.3780 2900	0.0878 8868	259.4507 2511	22.8027 8289	0.0038 5430
63	11.8331 5016	0.0845 0835	270.8287 5412	22.8872 9124	0.0036 9237
64	12.3064 7617	0.0812 5803	282.6619 0428	22.9685 4927	0.0035 3780
65	12.7987 3522	0.0781 3272	294.9683 8045	23.0466 8199	0.0033 9019
66	13.3106 8463	0.0751 2762	307.7671 1567	23.1218 0961	0.0032 4921
67	13.8431 1201	0.0722 3809	321.0778 0030	23.1940 4770	0.0031 1451
68	14.3968 3649	0.0694 5970	334.9209 1231	23.2635 0740	0.0029 8578
69	14.9727 0995	0.0667 8818	349.3177 4880	23.3302 9558	0.0028 6272
70	15.5716 1835	0.0642 1940	364.2904 5876	23.3945 1498	0.0027 4506
71	16.1944 8308	0.0617 4942	379.8620 7711	23.4562 6440	0.0026 3253
72	16.8422 6241	0.0593 7445	396.0565 6019	23.5156 3885	0.0025 2489
73	17.5159 5290	0.0570 9081	412.8988 2260	23.5727 2966	0.0024 2190
74	18.2165 9102	0.0548 9501	430.4147 7550	23.6276 2468	0.0023 2334
75	18.9452 5466	0.0527 8367	448.6313 6652	23.6804 0834	0.0022 2900
76	19.7030 6485	0.0507 5353	467.5766 2118	23.7311 6187	0.0021 2869
77	20.4911 8744	0.0488 0147	487.2796 8603	23.7799 6333	0.0020 5221
78	21.3108 3494	0.0469 2449	507.7708 7347	23.8268 8782	0.0019 6939
79	22.1632 6834	0.0451 1970	529.0817 0841	23.8720 0752	0.0018 9007
80	23.0497 9907	0.0433 8433	551.2449 7675	23.9153 9185	0.0018 1408
81	23.9717 9103	0.0417 1570	574.2947 7582	23.9571 0754	0.0017 4127
82	24.9306 6267	0.0401 1125	598.2665 6685	23.9972 1879	0.0016 7150
83	25.9278 8918	0.0385 6851	623.1972 2952	24.0357 8730	0.0016 0463
84	26.9650 0475	0.0370 8510	649.1251 1870	24.0728 7240	0.0015 4054
85	28.0436 0494	0.0356 5875	676.0901 2345	24.1085 3116	0.0014 7909
86	29.1653 4914	0.0342 8726	704.1337 2839	24.1428 1842	0.0014 2018
87	30.3319 6310	0.0329 6852	733.2990 7753	24.1757 8694	0.0013 6370
88	31.5452 4163	0.0317 0050	763.6310 4063	24.2074 8745	0.0013 0953
89	32.8070 5129	0.0304 8125	795.1762 8225	24.2379 6870	0.0012 5758
90	34.1193 3334	0.0293 0890	827.9833 3354	24.2672 7759	0.0012 0775
91	35.4841 0668	0.0281 8163	862.1026 6688	24.2954 5923	0.0011 5995
92	36.9034 7094	0.0270 9772	897.5867 7356	24.3225 5695	0.0011 1410
93	38.3796 0978	0.0260 5550	934.4902 4450	24.3486 1245	0.0010 7010
94	39.9147 9417	0.0250 5337	972.8698 5428	24.3736 6582	0.0010 2789
95	41.5113 8594	0.0240 8978	1012.7846 4845	24.3977 5559	0.0009 8738
96	43.1718 4138	0.0231 6325	1054.2960 3439	24.4209 1884	0.0009 4850
97	44.8987 1503	0.0222 7235	1097.4678 7577	24.4431 9119	0.0009 1119
98	46.6946 6363	0.0214 1572	1142.3665 9080	24.4646 0692	0.0008 7538
99	48.5624 5018	0.0205 9204	1189.0612 5443	24.4851 9896	0.0008 4100
100	50.5049 4818	0.0198 0004	1237.6237 0461	24.5049 9900	0.0008 0800

TABLE IV (continued)

$i = 4\frac{1}{2}\%$

n	$(1+i)^n$	$(1+i)^{-n}$	$s_{\overline{n}\vert i}$	$a_{\overline{n}\vert i}$	$s_{\overline{n}\vert i}^{-1}$
1	1.0450 0000	0.9569 3780	1.0000 0000	0.9569 3780	1.0000 0000
2	1.0920 2500	0.9157 2995	2.0450 0000	1.8726 6775	0.4889 9756
3	1.1411 6613	0.8762 9660	3.1370 2500	2.7489 6435	0.3187 7336
4	1.1925 1860	0.8385 6134	4.2781 9113	3.5875 2570	0.2337 4365
5	1.2461 8194	0.8024 5105	5.4707 0973	4.3899 7674	0.1827 9164
6	1.3022 6012	0.7678 9574	6.7168 9166	5.1578 7248	0.1488 7839
7	1.3608 6183	0.7348 2846	8.0191 5179	5.8927 0094	0.1247 0147
8	1.4221 0061	0.7031 8513	9.3800 1362	6.5958 8607	0.1066 0965
9	1.4860 9514	0.6729 0443	10.8021 1423	7.2687 9050	0.0925 7447
10	1.5529 6942	0.6439 2768	12.2882 0937	7.9127 1818	0.0813 7882
11	1.6228 5305	0.6161 9874	13.8411 7879	8.5289 1692	0.0722 4818
12	1.6958 8143	0.5896 6386	15.4640 3184	9.1185 8078	0.0646 6619
13	1.7721 9610	0.5642 7164	17.1599 1327	9.6828 5242	0.0582 7535
14	1.8519 4492	0.5399 7286	18.9321 0937	10.2228 2528	0.0528 2032
15	1.9352 8244	0.5167 2044	20.7840 5429	10.7395 4573	0.0481 1381
16	2.0223 7015	0.4944 6932	22.7193 3673	11.2340 1505	0.0440 1537
17	2.1133 7681	0.4731 7639	24.7417 0689	11.7071 9143	0.0404 1758
18	2.2084 7877	0.4528 0037	26.8550 8370	12.1599 9180	0.0372 3690
19	2.3078 6031	0.4333 0179	29.0635 6246	12.5932 9359	0.0344 0734
20	2.4117 1402	0.4146 4286	31.3714 2277	13.0079 3645	0.0318 7614
21	2.5202 4116	0.3967 8743	33.7831 3680	13.4047 2388	0.0296 0057
22	2.6336 5201	0.3797 0089	36.3033 7795	13.7844 2476	0.0275 4565
23	2.7521 6635	0.3633 5013	38.9370 2996	14.1477 7489	0.0256 8249
24	2.8760 1383	0.3477 0347	41.6891 9631	14.4954 7837	0.0239 8703
25	3.0054 3446	0.3327 3060	44.5652 1015	14.8282 0896	0.0224 3903
26	3.1406 7901	0.3184 0248	47.5706 4460	15.1466 1145	0.0210 2137
27	3.2820 0956	0.3046 9137	50.7113 2361	15.4513 0282	0.0197 1946
28	3.4296 9999	0.2915 7069	53.9933 3317	15.7428 7351	0.0185 2081
29	3.5840 3649	0.2790 1502	57.4230 3316	16.0218 8853	0.0174 1461
30	3.7453 1813	0.2670 0002	61.0070 6966	16.2888 8854	0.0163 9154
31	3.9138 5745	0.2555 0241	64.7523 8779	16.5443 9095	0.0154 4345
32	4.0899 8104	0.2444 9991	68.6662 4524	16.7888 9086	0.0145 6320
33	4.2740 3018	0.2339 7121	72.7562 2628	17.0228 6207	0.0137 4453
34	4.4663 6154	0.2238 9589	77.0302 5646	17.2467 5796	0.0129 8191
35	4.6673 4781	0.2142 5444	81.4966 1800	17.4610 1240	0.0122 7045
36	4.8773 7846	0.2050 2817	86.1639 6581	17.6660 4058	0.0116 0578
37	5.0968 6049	0.1961 9921	91.0413 4427	17.8622 3979	0.0109 8402
38	5.3262 1921	0.1877 5044	96.1382 0476	18.0499 9023	0.0104 0169
39	5.5658 9908	0.1796 6549	101.4644 2398	18.2296 5572	0.0098 5567
40	5.8163 6454	0.1719 2870	107.0303 2306	18.4015 8442	0.0093 4315
41	6.0781 0094	0.1645 2507	112.8466 8760	18.5661 0949	0.0088 6158
42	6.3516 1548	0.1574 4026	118.9247 8854	18.7235 4975	0.0084 0868
43	6.6374 3818	0.1506 6054	125.2764 0402	18.8742 1029	0.0079 8235
44	6.9361 2290	0.1441 7276	131.9138 4220	19.0183 8305	0.0075 8071
45	7.2482 4843	0.1379 6437	138.8499 6510	19.1563 4742	0.0072 0202
46	7.5744 1961	0.1320 2332	146.0982 1353	19.2883 7074	0.0068 4471
47	7.9152 6849	0.1263 3810	153.6726 3314	19.4147 0884	0.0065 0734
48	8.2714 5557	0.1208 9771	161.5879 0163	19.5356 0654	0.0061 8858
49	8.6436 7107	0.1156 9158	169.8593 5720	19.6512 9813	0.0058 8722
50	9.0326 3627	0.1107 0965	178.5030 2828	19.7620 0778	0.0056 0215

TABLE IV (continued)

$i = 4\frac{1}{2}\%$

n	$(1+i)^n$	$(1+i)^{-n}$	$s_{\overline{n}\|i}$	$a_{\overline{n}\|i}$	$s^{-1}_{\overline{n}\|i}$
51	9.4391 0490	0.1059 4225	187.5356 6455	19.8679 5003	0.0053 3232
52	9.8638 6463	0.1013 8014	196.9747 6946	19.9693 3017	0.0050 7679
53	10.3077 3853	0.0970 1449	206.8386 3408	20.0663 4466	0.0048 3469
54	10.7715 8677	0.0928 3683	217.1463 7262	20.1591 8149	0.0046 0519
55	11.2563 0817	0.0888 3907	227.9179 5938	20.2480 2057	0.0043 8754
56	11.7628 4204	0.0850 1347	239.1742 6756	20.3330 3404	0.0041 8105
57	12.2921 6993	0.0813 5260	250.9371 0960	20.4143 8664	0.0039 8506
58	12.8453 1758	0.0778 4938	263.2292 7953	20.4922 3602	0.0037 9897
59	13.4233 5687	0.0744 9701	276.0745 9711	20.5667 3303	0.0036 2221
60	14.0274 0793	0.0712 8901	289.4979 5398	20.6380 2204	0.0034 5426
61	14.6586 4129	0.0682 1915	303.5253 6190	20.7062 4118	0.0032 9462
62	15.3182 8014	0.0652 8148	318.1840 0319	20.7715 2266	0.0031 4284
63	16.0076 0275	0.0624 7032	333.5022 8333	20.8339 9298	0.0029 9848
64	16.7279 4487	0.0597 8021	349.5098 8608	20.8937 7319	0.0028 6115
65	17.4807 0239	0.0572 0594	366.2378 3096	20.9509 7913	0.0027 3047
66	18.2673 3400	0.0547 4253	383.7185 3335	21.0057 2165	0.0026 0608
67	19.0893 6403	0.0523 8519	401.9858 6735	21.0581 0684	0.0024 8765
68	19.9483 8541	0.0501 2937	421.0752 3138	21.1082 3621	0.0023 7487
69	20.8460 6276	0.0479 7069	441.0236 1679	21.1562 0690	0.0022 6745
70	21.7841 3558	0.0459 0497	461.8696 7955	21.2021 1187	0.0021 6511
71	22.7644 2168	0.0439 2820	483.6538 1513	21.2460 4007	0.0020 6759
72	23.7888 2066	0.0420 3655	506.4182 3681	21.2880 7662	0.0019 7465
73	24.8593 1759	0.0402 2637	530.2070 5747	21.3283 0298	0.0018 8606
74	25.9779 8688	0.0384 9413	555.0663 7505	21.3667 9711	0.0018 0159
75	27.1469 9629	0.0368 3649	581.0443 6193	21.4036 3360	0.0017 2104
76	28.3686 1112	0.0352 5023	608.1913 5822	21.4388 8383	0.0016 4422
77	29.6451 9862	0.0337 3228	636.5599 6934	21.4726 1611	0.0015 7094
78	30.9792 3256	0.0322 7969	666.2051 6796	21.5048 9579	0.0015 0104
79	32.3732 9802	0.0308 8965	697.1844 0052	21.5357 8545	0.0014 3434
80	33.8300 9643	0.0295 5948	729.5576 9854	21.5653 4493	0.0013 7069
81	35.3524 5077	0.0282 8658	763.3877 9497	21.5936 3151	0.0013 0995
82	36.9433 1106	0.0270 6850	798.7402 4575	21.6207 0001	0.0012 5197
83	38.6057 6006	0.0259 0287	835.6835 5680	21.6466 0288	0.0011 9663
84	40.3430 1926	0.0247 8744	874.2893 1686	21.6713 9032	0.0011 4379
85	42.1584 5513	0.0237 2003	914 6323 3612	21.6951 1035	0.0010 9334
86	44.0555 8561	0.0226 9860	956.7907 9125	21.7178 0895	0.0010 4516
87	46.0380 8696	0.0217 2115	1000.8463 7685	21.7395 3009	0.0009 9915
88	48.1098 0087	0.0207 8579	1046.8844 6381	21.7603 1588	0.0009 5522
89	50.2747 4191	0.0198 9070	1094.9942 6468	21.7802 0658	0.0009 1325
90	52.5371 0530	0.0190 3417	1145.2690 0659	21.7992 4075	0.0008 7316
91	54.9012 7503	0.0182 1451	1197.8061 1189	21.8174 5526	0.0008 3486
92	57.3718 3241	0.0174 3016	1252.7073 8692	21.8348 8542	0.0007 9827
93	59.9535 6487	0.0166 7958	1310.0792 1933	21.8515 6499	0.0007 6331
94	62.6514 7529	0.0159 6132	1370.0327 8420	21.8675 2631	0.0007 2991
95	65.4707 9168	0.0152 7399	1432.6842 5949	21.8828 0030	0.0006 9799
96	68.4169 7730	0.0146 1626	1498.1550 5117	21.8974 1655	0.0006 6749
97	71.4957 4128	0.0139 8685	1566.5720 2847	21.9114 0340	0.0006 3834
98	74.7130 4964	0.0133 8454	1638 0677 6976	21.9247 8794	0.0006 1048
99	78.0751 3687	0.0128 0817	1712.7808 1939	21.9375 9612	0.0005 8385
100	81.5885 1803	0.0122 5663	1790.8559 5627	21.9498 5274	0.0005 5839

TABLE IV (continued)

$i = 5\%$

n	$(1+i)^n$	$(1+i)^{-n}$	$s_{\overline{n}\mid i}$	$a_{\overline{n}\mid i}$	$s_{\overline{n}\mid i}^{-1}$
1	1.0500 0000	0.9523 8095	1.0000 0000	0.9523 8095	1.0000 0000
2	1.1025 0000	0.9070 2948	2.0500 0000	1.8594 1043	0.4878 0488
3	1.1576 2500	0.8638 3760	2.1525 0000	2.7232 4803	0.3172 0856
4	1.2155 0625	0.8227 0247	4.3101 2500	3.5459 5050	0.2320 1183
5	1.2762 8156	0.7835 2617	5.5256 3125	4.3294 7667	0.1809 7480
6	1.3400 9564	0.7462 1540	6.8019 1281	5.0756 9206	0.1470 1747
7	1.4071 0042	0.7106 8133	8.1420 0845	5.7863 7340	0.1228 1982
8	1.4774 5544	0.6768 3936	9.5491 0888	6.4632 1276	0.1047 2181
9	1.5513 2822	0.6446 0892	11.0265 6432	7.1078 2168	0.0906 9008
10	1.6288 9463	0.6139 1325	12.5778 9254	7.7217 3493	0.0795 0458
11	1.7103 3936	0.5846 7929	14.2067 8716	8.3064 1422	0.0703 8889
12	1.7958 5633	0.5568 3742	15.9171 2652	8.8632 5164	0.0628 2541
13	1.8856 4914	0.5303 2135	17.7129 8285	9.3935 7299	0.0564 5577
14	1.9799 3160	0.5050 6795	19.5986 3199	9.8986 4094	0.0510 2397
15	2.0789 2818	0.4810 1710	21.5785 6359	10.3796 5804	0.0463 4229
16	2.1828 7459	0.4581 1152	23.6574 9177	10.8377 6956	0.0422 6991
17	2.2920 1832	0.4362 9669	25.8403 6636	11.2740 6625	0.0386 9914
18	2.4066 1923	0.4155 2065	28.1323 8467	11.6895 8690	0.0355 4622
19	2.5269 5020	0.3957 3396	30.5390 0391	12.0853 2086	0.0327 4501
20	2.6532 9771	0.3768 8948	33.0659 5410	12.4622 1034	0.0302 4259
21	2.7859 6259	0.3589 4236	35.7192 5181	12.8211 5271	0.0279 9611
22	2.9252 6072	0.3418 4987	38.5052 1440	13.1630 0258	0.0259 7051
23	3.0715 2376	0.3255 7131	41.4304 7512	13.4885 7388	0.0241 3682
24	3.2250 9994	0.3100 6791	44.5019 9887	13.7986 4179	0.0224 7090
25	3.3863 5494	0.2953 0277	47.7270 9882	14.0939 4457	0.0209 5246
26	3.5556 7269	0.2812 4073	51.1134 5376	14.3751 8530	0.0195 6432
27	3.7334 5632	0.2678 4832	54.6691 2645	14.6430 3362	0.0182 9186
28	3.9201 2914	0.2550 9364	58.4025 8277	14.8981 2726	0.0171 2253
29	4.1161 3560	0.2429 4632	62.3227 1191	15.1410 7358	0.0160 4551
30	4.3219 4238	0.2313 7745	66.4388 4750	15.3724 5103	0.0150 5144
31	4.5380 3949	0.2203 5947	70.7607 8988	15.5928 1050	0.0141 3212
32	4.7649 4147	0.2098 6617	75.2988 2937	15.8026 7667	0.0132 8042
33	5.0031 8854	0.1998 7254	80.0637 7084	16.0025 4921	0.0124 9004
34	5.2533 4797	0.1903 5480	85.0669 5938	16.1929 0401	0.0117 5545
35	5.5160 1537	0.1812 9029	90.3203 0735	16.3741 9429	0.0110 7171
36	5.7918 1614	0.1726 5741	95.8363 2272	16.5468 5171	0.0104 3446
37	6.0814 0694	0.1644 3563	101.6281 3886	16.7112 8734	0.0098 3979
38	6.3854 7729	0.1566 0536	107.7095 4580	16.8678 9271	0.0092 8423
39	6.7047 5115	0.1491 4797	114.0950 2309	17.0170 4067	0.0087 6462
40	7.0399 8871	0.1420 4568	120.7997 7424	17.1590 8635	0.0082 7816
41	7.3919 8815	0.1352 8160	127.8397 6295	17.2943 6796	0.0078 2229
42	7.7615 8756	0.1288 3962	135.2317 5110	17.4232 0758	0.0073 9471
43	8.1496 6693	0.1227 0440	142.9933 3866	17.5459 1198	0.0069 9333
44	8.5571 5028	0.1168 6133	151.1430 0559	17.6627 7331	0.0066 1625
45	8.9850 0779	0.1112 9651	159.7001 5587	17.7740 6982	0.0062 6173
46	9.4342 5818	0.1059 9668	168.6851 6366	17.8800 6650	0.0059 2820
47	9.9059 7109	0.1009 4921	178.1194 2185	17.9810 1571	0.0056 1421
48	10.4012 6965	0.0961 4211	188.0253 9294	18.0771 5782	0.0053 1843
49	10.9213 3313	0.0915 6391	198.4266 6259	18.1697 2173	0.0050 3965
50	11.4673 9979	0.0872 0373	209.3479 9572	18.2559 2546	0.0047 7674

TABLE IV (continued)

$i = 6\%$

n	$(1+i)^n$	$(1+i)^{-n}$	$s_{\overline{n}\rvert i}$	$a_{n\rvert i}$	$s^{-1}_{\overline{n}\rvert i}$
1	1.0600 0000	0.9433 9623	1.0000 0000	0.9433 9623	1.0000 0000
2	1.1236 0000	0.8899 9644	2.0600 0000	1.8333 9267	0.4854 3689
3	1.1910 1600	0.8396 1928	3.1836 0000	2.6730 1195	0.3141 0981
4	1.2624 7696	0.7920 9366	4.3746 1600	3.4651 0561	0.2285 9149
5	1.3382 2558	0.7472 5817	5.6370 9296	4.2123 6379	0.1773 9640
6	1.4185 1911	0.7049 6054	6.9753 1854	4.9173 2433	0.1433 6263
7	1.5036 3026	0.6650 5711	8.3938 3765	5.5823 8144	0.1191 3502
8	1.5938 4807	0.6274 1237	9.8974 6791	6.2097 9381	0.1010 3594
9	1.6894 7896	0.5918 9846	11.4913 1598	6.8016 9227	0.0870 2224
10	1 7908 4770	0.5583 9478	13.1807 9494	7.3600 8705	0.0758 6796
11	1.8982 9856	0.5267 8753	14.9716 4264	7.8868 7458	0.0667 9294
12	2.0121 9647	0.4969 6936	16.8699 4120	8.3838 4394	0.0592 7703
13	2.1329 2826	0.4688 3902	18.8821 3767	8.8526 8296	0.0529 6011
14	2.2609 0396	0.4423 0096	21.0150 6593	9.2949 8393	0.0475 8491
15	2.3965 5819	0.4172 6506	23.2759 6988	9.7122 4899	0.0429 6276
16	2.5403 5168	0.3936 4628	25.6725 2808	10.1058 9527	0.0389 5214
17	2.6927 7279	0.3713 6442	28.2128 7976	10.4772 5969	0.0354 4480
18	2.8543 3915	0.3503 4379	30.9056 5255	10.8276 0348	0.0323 5654
19	3.0255 9950	0.3305 1301	33.7599 9170	11.1581 1649	0.0296 2086
20	3.2071 3547	0.3118 0473	36.7855 9120	11.4699 2122	0.0271 8456
21	3.3995 6360	0.2941 5540	39.9927 2668	11.7640 7662	0.0250 0455
22	3.6035 3742	0.2775 0510	43.3922 9028	12.0415 8172	0.0230 4557
23	3.8197 4966	0.2617 9726	46.9958 2769	12.3033 7898	0.0212 7848
24	4.0489 3464	0.2469 7855	50.8155 7735	12.5503 5753	0.0196 7900
25	4.2918 7072	0.2329 9863	54.8645 1200	12.7833 5616	0.0182 2672
26	4.5493 8296	0.2198 1003	59.1563 8272	13.0031 6619	0.0169 0435
27	4.8223 4594	0.2073 6795	63.7057 6568	13.2105 3414	0.0156 9717
28	5.1116 8670	0.1956 3014	68.5281 1162	13.4061 6428	0.0145 9255
29	5.4183 8790	0.1845 5674	73.6397 9832	13.5907 2102	0.0135 7961
30	5.7434 9117	0.1741 1013	79.0581 8622	13.7648 3115	0.0126 4891
31	6.0881 0064	0.1642 5484	84.8016 7739	13.9290 8599	0.0117 9222
32	6.4533 8668	0.1549 5740	90.8897 7803	14.0840 4339	0.0110 0234
33	6.8405 8988	0.1461 8622	97.3431 6471	14.2302 2961	0.0102 7293
34	7.2510 2528	0.1379 1153	104.1837 5460	14.3681 4114	0.0095 9843
35	7.6860 8679	0.1301 0522	111.4347 7987	14.4982 4636	0.0089 7386
36	8.1472 5200	0.1227 4077	119.1208 6666	14.6209 8713	0.0083 9483
37	8.6360 8712	0.1157 9318	127.2681 1866	14.7367 8031	0.0078 5743
38	9.1542 5235	0.1092 3885	135.9042 0578	14.8460 1916	0.0073 5812
39	9.7035 0749	0.1030 5552	145.0584 5813	14.9490 7468	0.0068 9377
40	10.2857 1794	0.0972 2219	154.7619 6562	15.0462 9687	0.0064 6154
41	10.9028 6101	0.0917 1905	165.0476 8356	15.1380 1592	0.0060 5886
42	11.5570 3267	0.0865 2740	175.9505 4457	15.2245 4332	0.0056 8342
43	12.2504 5463	0.0816 2962	187.5075 7724	15.3061 7294	0.0053 3312
44	12.9854 8191	0.0770 0908	199.7580 3188	15.3831 8202	0.0050 0606
45	13.7546 1083	0.0726 5007	212.7435 1379	15.4558 3209	0.0047 0050
46	14.5904 8748	0.0685 3781	226.5081 2462	15.5243 6990	0.0044 1485
47	15.4659 1673	0.0646 5831	241.0986 1210	15.5890 2821	0.0041 4768
48	16.3938 7173	0.0609 9840	256.5645 2882	15.6500 2661	0.0038 9766
49	17.3775 0403	0.0575 4566	272.9584 0055	15.7075 7227	0.0036 6356
50	18.4201 5427	0.0542 8836	290.3359 0458	15.7618 6064	0.0034 4429

TABLE IV (continued)

$i = 7\%$

n	$(1+i)^n$	$(1+i)^{-n}$	$s_{\overline{n}\rceil i}$	$a_{\overline{n}\rceil i}$	$s^{-1}_{\overline{n}\rceil i}$
1	1.0700 0000	0.9345 7944	1.0000 0000	0.9345 7944	1.0000 0000
2	1.1449 0000	0.8734 3873	2.0700 0000	1.8080 1817	0.4830 9179
3	1.2250 4300	0.8162 9788	2.2149 0000	2.6243 1604	0.3110 5166
4	1.3107 9601	0.7628 9521	4.4399 4300	3.3872 1126	0.2252 2812
5	1.4025 5173	0.7129 8618	5.7507 3901	4.1001 9744	0.1738 9069
6	1.5007 3035	0.6663 4222	7.1532 9074	4.7665 3966	0.1397 9580
7	1.6057 8148	0.6227 4974	8.6540 2109	5.3892 8940	0.1155 5322
8	1.7181 8618	0.5820 0910	10.2598 0257	5.9712 9851	0.0974 6776
9	1.8384 5921	0.5439 3374	11.9779 8875	6.5152 3225	0.0834 8647
10	1.9671 5136	0.5083 4929	13.8164 4796	7.0235 8154	0.0723 7750
11	2.1048 5195	0.4750 9280	15.7835 9932	7.4986 7434	0.0633 5690
12	2.2521 9159	0.4440 1196	17.8884 5127	7.9426 8630	0.0559 0199
13	2.4098 4500	0.4149 6445	20.1406 4286	8.3576 5074	0.0496 5085
14	2.5785 3415	0.3878 1724	22.5504 8786	8.7454 6799	0.0443 4494
15	2.7590 3154	0.3624 4602	25.1290 2201	9.1079 1401	0.0397 9462
16	2.9521 6375	0.3387 3460	27.8880 5355	9.4466 4860	0.0358 5765
17	3.1588 1521	0.3165 7439	20.8402 1730	9.7632 2299	0.0324 2519
18	3.3799 3228	0.2958 6392	33.9990 3251	10.0590 8691	0.0294 1260
19	3.6165 2754	0.2765 0832	37.3789 6479	10.3355 9524	0.0267 5301
20	3.8696 8446	0.2584 1900	40.9954 9232	10.5940 1425	0.0243 9293
21	4.1405 6237	0.2415 1309	44.8651 7678	10.8355 2733	0.0222 8900
22	4.4304 0174	0.2257 1317	49.0057 3916	11.0612 4050	0.0204 0577
23	4.7405 2986	0.2109 4688	53.4361 4090	11.2721 8738	0.0187 1393
24	5.0723 6695	0.1971 4662	58.1766 7076	11.4693 3400	0.0171 8902
25	5.4274 3264	0.1842 4918	63.2490 3772	11.6535 8318	0.0158 1052
26	5.8073 5292	0.1721 9549	68.6764 7036	11.8257 7867	0.0145 6103
27	6.2138 6763	0.1609 3037	74.4838 2328	11.9867 0904	0.0134 2573
28	6.6488 3836	0.1504 0221	80.6976 9091	12.1371 1125	0.0123 9193
29	7.1142 5705	0.1405 6282	87.3465 2927	12.2776 7407	0.0114 4865
30	7.6122 5504	0.1313 6712	94.4607 8632	12.4090 4118	0.0105 8640
31	8.1451 1290	0.1227 7301	102.0730 4137	12.5318 1419	0.0097 9691
32	8.7152 7080	0.1147 4113	110.2181 5426	12.6465 5532	0.0090 7292
33	9.3253 3975	0.1072 3470	118.9334 2506	12.7537 9002	0.0084 0807
34	9.9781 1354	0.1002 1934	128.2587 6481	12.8540 0936	0.0077 9674
35	10.6765 8148	0.0936 6294	138.2368 7835	12.9476 7230	0.0072 3396
36	11.4239 4219	0.0875 3546	148.9134 5984	13.0352 0776	0.0067 1531
37	12.2236 1814	0.0818 0884	160.3374 0202	13.1170 1660	0.0062 3685
38	13.0792 7141	0.0764 5686	172.5610 2017	13.1934 7345	0.0057 9505
39	13.9948 2041	0.0714 5501	185.6402 9158	13.2649 2846	0.0053 8676
40	14.9744 5784	0.0667 8038	199.6351 1199	13.3317 0884	0.0050 0914
41	16.0226 6989	0.0624 1157	214.6095 6983	13.3941 2041	0.0046 5962
42	17.1442 5678	0.0583 2857	230.6322 3972	13.4524 4898	0.0043 3591
43	18.3443 5475	0.0545 1268	247.7764 9650	13.5069 6167	0.0040 3590
44	19.6284 5959	0.0509 4643	266.1208 5125	13.5579 0810	0.0037 5769
45	21.0024 5176	0.0476 1349	285.7493 1084	13.6055 2159	0.0034 9957
46	22.4726 2338	0.0444 9859	306.7517 6260	13.6500 2018	0.0032 5996
47	24.0457 0702	0.0415 8747	329.2243 8598	13.6916 0764	0.0030 3744
48	25.7289 0651	0.0388 6679	353.2700 9300	13.7304 7443	0.0028 3070
49	27.5299 2997	0.0363 2410	378.9989 9951	13.7667 9853	0.0026 3853
50	29.4570 2506	0.0339 4776	406.5289 2947	13.8007 4629	0.0024 5985

TABLE IV (continued)

$i = 8\%$

n	$(1+i)^n$	$(1+i)^{-n}$	$s_{\overline{n}\mid i}$	$a_{\overline{n}\mid i}$	$s^{-1}_{\overline{n}\mid i}$
1	1.0800 0000	0.9259 2593	1.0000 0000	0.9259 2593	1.0000 0000
2	1.1664 0000	0.8573 3882	2.0800 0000	1.7832 6475	0.4807 6923
3	1.2597 1200	0.7938 3224	3.2464 0000	2.5770 9699	0.3080 3351
4	1.3604 8896	0.7350 2985	4.5061 1200	3.3121 2684	0.2219 2080
5	1.4693 2808	0.6805 8320	5.8666 0096	3.9927 1004	0.1704 5645
6	1.5868 7432	0.6301 6963	7.3359 2904	4.6228 7966	0.1363 1539
7	1.7138 2427	0.5834 9040	8.9228 0336	5.2063 7006	0.1120 7240
8	1.8509 3021	0.5402 6888	10.6366 2763	5.7466 3894	0.0940 1476
9	1.9990 0463	0.5002 4897	12.4875 5784	6.2468 8791	0.0800 7971
10	2.1589 2500	0.4631 9349	14.4865 6247	6.7100 8140	0.0690 2949
11	2.3316 3900	0.4288 8286	16.6454 8746	7.1389 6426	0.0600 7634
12	2.5181 7012	0.3971 1376	18.9771 2646	7.5360 7802	0.0526 9502
13	2.7196 2373	0.3676 9792	21.4952 9658	7.9037 7594	0.0465 2181
14	2.9371 9362	0.3404 6104	24.2149 2030	8.2442 3698	0.0412 9685
15	3.1721 6911	0.3152 4170	27.1521 1393	8.5594 7869	0.0368 2954
16	3.4259 4264	0.2918 9047	30.3242 8304	8.8513 6916	0.0329 7687
17	3.7000 1805	0.2702 6895	33.7502 2569	9.1216 3811	0.0296 2943
18	3.9960 1950	0.2502 4903	37.4502 4374	9.3718 8714	0.0267 0210
19	4.3157 0106	0.2317 1206	41.4462 6324	9.6035 9920	0.0241 2763
20	4.6609 5714	0.2145 4821	45.7619 6430	9.8181 4741	0.0218 5221
21	5.0338 3372	0.1986 5575	50.4229 2144	10.0168 0316	0.0198 3225
22	5.4365 4041	0.1839 4051	55.4567 5516	10.2007 4366	0.0180 3207
23	5.8714 6365	0.1703 1528	60.8932 9557	10.3710 5895	0.0164 2217
24	6.3411 8074	0.1576 9934	66.7647 5922	10.5287 5828	0.0149 7796
25	6.8484 7520	0.1460 1790	73.1059 3995	10.6747 7619	0.0136 7878
26	7.3963 5321	0.1352 0176	79.9544 1515	10.8099 7795	0.0125 0713
27	7.9880 6147	0.1251 8682	87.3507 6836	10.9351 6477	0.0114 4809
28	8.6271 0639	0.1159 1372	95.3388 2983	11.0510 7849	0.0104 8891
29	9.3172 7490	0.1073 2752	103.9659 3622	11.1584 0601	0.0096 1854
30	10.0626 5689	0.0993 7733	113.2832 1111	11.2577 8334	0.0088 2743
31	10.8676 6944	0.0920 1605	123.3458 6800	11.3497 9939	0.0081 0728
32	11.7370 8300	0.0852 0005	134.2135 3744	11.4349 9944	0.0074 5081
33	12.6760 4964	0.0788 8893	145.9506 2044	11.5138 8837	0.0068 5163
34	13.6901 3361	0.0730 4531	158.6266 7007	11.5869 3367	0.0063 0411
35	14.7853 4429	0.0676 3454	172.3168 0368	11.6545 6822	0.0058 0326
36	15.9681 7184	0.0626 2458	187.1021 4797	11.7171 9279	0.0053 4467
37	17.2456 2558	0.0579 8572	203.0703 1981	11.7751 7851	0.0049 2440
38	18.6252 7563	0.0536 9048	220.3159 4540	11.8288 6899	0.0045 3894
39	20.1152 9768	0.0497 1341	238.9412 2103	11.8785 8240	0.0041 8513
40	21.7245 2150	0.0460 3093	259.0565 1871	11.9246 1333	0.0038 6016
41	23.4624 8322	0.0426 2123	280.7810 4021	11.9672 3457	0.0035 6149
42	25.3394 8187	0.0394 6411	304.2435 2342	12.0066 9867	0.0032 8684
43	27.3666 4042	0.0365 4084	329.5830 0530	12.0432 3951	0.0030 3414
44	29.5559 7166	0.0338 3411	356.9496 4572	12.0770 7362	0.0028 0152
45	31.9204 4939	0.0313 2788	386.5056 1738	12.1084 0150	0.0025 8728
46	34.4740 8534	0.0290 0730	418.4260 6677	12.1374 0880	0.0023 8991
47	37.2320 1217	0.0268 5861	452.9001 5211	12.1642 6741	0.0022 0799
48	40.2105 7314	0.0248 6908	490.1321 6428	12.1891 3649	0.0020 4027
49	32.4274 1899	0.0230 2693	530.3427 3742	12.2121 6341	0.0018 8557
50	46.9016 1251	0.0213 2123	573.7701 5642	12.2334 8464	0.0017 4286

TABLE V Binomial Probabilities

n	x	p = 0.05	0.1	0.2	0.3	0.4	0.5	0.6	0.7	0.8	0.9	0.95
2	0	0.902	0.810	0.640	0.490	0.360	0.250	0.160	0.090	0.040	0.010	0.002
	1	0.095	0.180	0.320	0.420	0.480	0.500	0.480	0.420	0.320	0.180	0.095
	2	0.002	0.010	0.040	0.090	0.160	0.250	0.360	0.490	0.640	0.810	0.902
3	0	0.857	0.729	0.512	0.343	0.216	0.125	0.064	0.027	0.008	0.001	
	1	0.135	0.243	0.384	0.441	0.432	0.375	0.288	0.189	0.096	0.027	0.007
	2	0.007	0.027	0.096	0.189	0.288	0.375	0.432	0.441	0.384	0.243	0.135
	3		0.001	0.008	0.027	0.064	0.125	0.216	0.343	0.512	0.729	0.857
4	0	0.815	0.656	0.410	0.240	0.130	0.062	0.026	0.008	0.002		
	1	0.171	0.292	0.410	0.412	0.346	0.250	0.154	0.076	0.026	0.004	
	2	0.014	0.049	0.154	0.265	0.346	0.375	0.346	0.265	0.154	0.049	0.014
	3		0.004	0.026	0.076	0.154	0.250	0.346	0.412	0.410	0.292	0.171
	4			0.002	0.008	0.026	0.062	0.130	0.240	0.410	0.656	0.815
5	0	0.774	0.590	0.328	0.168	0.078	0.031	0.010	0.002			
	1	0.204	0.328	0.410	0.360	0.259	0.156	0.077	0.028	0.006		
	2	0.021	0.073	0.205	0.309	0.346	0.312	0.230	0.132	0.051	0.008	0.001
	3	0.001	0.008	0.051	0.132	0.230	0.312	0.346	0.309	0.205	0.073	0.021
	4			0.006	0.028	0.077	0.156	0.259	0.360	0.410	0.328	0.204
	5				0.002	0.010	0.031	0.078	0.168	0.328	0.590	0.774
6	0	0.735	0.531	0.262	0.118	0.047	0.016	0.004	0.001			
	1	0.232	0.354	0.393	0.303	0.187	0.094	0.037	0.010	0.002		
	2	0.031	0.098	0.246	0.324	0.311	0.234	0.138	0.060	0.015	0.001	
	3	0.002	0.015	0.082	0.185	0.276	0.312	0.276	0.185	0.082	0.015	0.002
	4		0.001	0.015	0.060	0.138	0.234	0.311	0.324	0.246	0.098	0.031
	5			0.002	0.010	0.037	0.094	0.187	0.303	0.393	0.354	0.232
	6				0.001	0.004	0.016	0.047	0.118	0.262	0.531	0.735
7	0	0.698	0.478	0.210	0.082	0.028	0.008	0.002				
	1	0.257	0.372	0.367	0.247	0.131	0.055	0.017	0.004			
	2	0.041	0.124	0.275	0.318	0.261	0.164	0.077	0.025	0.004		
	3	0.004	0.023	0.115	0.227	0.290	0.273	0.194	0.097	0.029	0.003	
	4		0.003	0.029	0.097	0.194	0.273	0.290	0.227	0.115	0.023	0.004
	5			0.004	0.025	0.077	0.164	0.261	0.318	0.275	0.124	0.041
	6				0.004	0.017	0.055	0.131	0.247	0.367	0.372	0.257
	7					0.002	0.008	0.028	0.082	0.210	0.478	0.698
8	0	0.663	0.430	0.168	0.058	0.017	0.004	0.001				
	1	0.279	0.383	0.336	0.198	0.090	0.031	0.008	0.001			
	2	0.051	0.149	0.294	0.296	0.209	0.109	0.041	0.010	0.001		
	3	0.005	0.033	0.147	0.254	0.279	0.219	0.124	0.047	0.009		
	4		0.005	0.046	0.136	0.232	0.273	0.232	0.136	0.046	0.005	
	5			0.009	0.047	0.124	0.219	0.279	0.254	0.147	0.033	0.005
	6			0.001	0.010	0.041	0.109	0.209	0.296	0.294	0.149	0.051
	7				0.001	0.008	0.031	0.090	0.198	0.336	0.383	0.279
	8					0.001	0.004	0.017	0.058	0.168	0.430	0.663

TABLE V (continued)

		p										
n	*x*	0.05	0.1	0.2	0.3	0.4	0.5	0.6	0.7	0.8	0.9	0.95
9	0	0.630	0.387	0.134	0.040	0.010	0.002					
	1	0.299	0.387	0.302	0.156	0.060	0.018	0.004				
	2	0.063	0.172	0.302	0.267	0.161	0.070	0.021	0.004			
	3	0.008	0.045	0.176	0.267	0.251	0.164	0.074	0.021	0.003		
	4	0.001	0.007	0.066	0.172	0.251	0.246	0.167	0.074	0.017	0.001	
	5		0.001	0.017	0.074	0.167	0.246	0.251	0.172	0.066	0.007	0.001
	6			0.003	0.021	0.074	0.164	0.251	0.267	0.176	0.045	0.008
	7				0.004	0.021	0.070	0.161	0.267	0.302	0.172	0.063
	8					0.004	0.018	0.060	0.156	0.302	0.387	0.299
	9						0.002	0.010	0.040	0.134	0.387	0.630
10	0	0.599	0.349	0.107	0.028	0.006	0.001					
	1	0.315	0.387	0.268	0.121	0.040	0.010	0.002				
	2	0.075	0.194	0.302	0.233	0.121	0.044	0.011	0.001			
	3	0.010	0.057	0.201	0.267	0.215	0.117	0.042	0.009	0.001		
	4	0.001	0.011	0.088	0.200	0.251	0.205	0.111	0.037	0.006		
	5		0.001	0.026	0.103	0.201	0.246	0.201	0.103	0.026	0.001	
	6			0.006	0.037	0.111	0.205	0.251	0.200	0.088	0.011	0.001
	7			0.001	0.009	0.042	0.117	0.215	0.267	0.201	0.057	0.010
	8				0.001	0.011	0.044	0.121	0.233	0.302	0.194	0.075
	9					0.002	0.010	0.040	0.121	0.268	0.387	0.315
	10						0.001	0.006	0.028	0.107	0.349	0.599
11	0	0.569	0.314	0.086	0.020	0.004						
	1	0.329	0.384	0.236	0.093	0.027	0.005	0.001				
	2	0.087	0.213	0.295	0.200	0.089	0.027	0.005	0.001			
	3	0.014	0.071	0.221	0.257	0.177	0.081	0.023	0.004			
	4	0.001	0.016	0.111	0.220	0.236	0.161	0.070	0.017	0.002		
	5		0.002	0.039	0.132	0.221	0.226	0.147	0.057	0.010		
	6			0.010	0.057	0.147	0.226	0.221	0.132	0.039	0.002	
	7			0.002	0.017	0.070	0.161	0.236	0.220	0.111	0.016	0.001
	8				0.004	0.023	0.081	0.177	0.257	0.221	0.071	0.014
	9				0.001	0.005	0.027	0.089	0.200	0.295	0.213	0.087
	10					0.001	0.005	0.027	0.093	0.236	0.384	0.329
	11							0.004	0.020	0.086	0.314	0.569
12	0	0.540	0.282	0.069	0.014	0.002						
	1	0.341	0.377	0.206	0.071	0.017	0.003					
	2	0.099	0.230	0.283	0.168	0.064	0.016	0.002				
	3	0.017	0.085	0.236	0.240	0.142	0.054	0.012	0.001			
	4	0.002	0.021	0.133	0.231	0.213	0.121	0.042	0.008	0.001		
	5		0.004	0.053	0.158	0.227	0.193	0.101	0.029	0.003		
	6			0.016	0.079	0.177	0.226	0.177	0.079	0.016		
	7			0.003	0.029	0.101	0.193	0.227	0.158	0.053	0.004	
	8			0.001	0.008	0.042	0.121	0.213	0.231	0.133	0.021	0.002
	9				0.001	0.012	0.054	0.142	0.240	0.236	0.085	0.017
	10					0.002	0.016	0.064	0.168	0.283	0.230	0.099
	11						0.003	0.017	0.071	0.206	0.377	0.341
	12							0.002	0.014	0.069	0.282	0.540

TABLE V (continued)

		p										
n	*x*	0.05	0.1	0.2	0.3	0.4	0.5	0.6	0.7	0.8	0.9	0.95
13	0	0.513	0.254	0.055	0.010	0.001						
	1	0.351	0.367	0.179	0.054	0.011	0.002					
	2	0.111	0.245	0.268	0.139	0.045	0.010	0.001				
	3	0.021	0.100	0.246	0.218	0.111	0.035	0.006	0.001			
	4	0.003	0.028	0.154	0.234	0.184	0.087	0.024	0.003			
	5		0.006	0.069	0.180	0.221	0.157	0.066	0.014	0.001		
	6		0.001	0.023	0.103	0.197	0.209	0.131	0.044	0.006		
	7			0.006	0.044	0.131	0.209	0.197	0.103	0.023	0.001	
	8			0.001	0.014	0.066	0.157	0.221	0.180	0.069	0.006	
	9				0.003	0.024	0.087	0.184	0.234	0.154	0.028	0.003
	10				0.001	0.006	0.035	0.111	0.218	0.246	0.100	0.021
	11					0.001	0.010	0.045	0.139	0.268	0.245	0.111
	12						0.002	0.011	0.054	0.179	0.367	0.351
	13							0.001	0.010	0.055	0.254	0.513
14	0	0.488	0.229	0.044	0.007	0.001						
	1	0.359	0.356	0.154	0.041	0.007	0.001					
	2	0.123	0.257	0.250	0.113	0.032	0.006	0.001				
	3	0.026	0.114	0.250	0.194	0.085	0.022	0.003				
	4	0.004	0.035	0.172	0.229	0.155	0.061	0.014	0.001			
	5		0.008	0.086	0.196	0.207	0.122	0.041	0.007			
	6		0.001	0.032	0.126	0.207	0.183	0.092	0.023	0.002		
	7			0.009	0.062	0.157	0.209	0.157	0.062	0.009		
	8			0.002	0.023	0.092	0.183	0.207	0.126	0.032	0.001	
	9				0.007	0.041	0.122	0.207	0.196	0.086	0.008	
	10				0.001	0.014	0.061	0.155	0.229	0.172	0.035	0.004
	11					0.003	0.022	0.085	0.194	0.250	0.114	0.026
	12					0.001	0.006	0.032	0.113	0.250	0.257	0.123
	13						0.001	0.007	0.041	0.154	0.356	0.359
	14							0.001	0.007	0.044	0.229	0.488
15	0	0.463	0.206	0.035	0.005							
	1	0.366	0.343	0.132	0.031	0.005						
	2	0.135	0.267	0.231	0.092	0.022	0.003					
	3	0.031	0.129	0.250	0.170	0.063	0.014	0.002				
	4	0.005	0.043	0.188	0219	0.127	0.042	0.007	0.001			
	5	0.001	0.010	0.103	0.206	0.186	0.092	0.024	0.003			
	6		0.002	0.043	0.147	0.207	0.153	0.061	0.012	0.001		
	7			0.014	0.081	0.177	0.196	0.118	0.035	0.003		
	8			0.003	0.035	0.118	0.196	0.177	0.081	0.014		
	9			0.001	0.012	0.061	0.153	0.207	0.147	0.043	0.002	
	10				0.003	0.024	0.092	0.186	0.206	0.103	0.010	0.001
	11				0.001	0.007	0.042	0.127	0.219	0.188	0.043	0.005
	12					0.002	0.014	0.063	0.170	0.250	0.129	0.031
	13						0.003	0.022	0.092	0.231	0.267	0.135
	14							0.005	0.031	0.132	0.343	0.366
	15								0.005	0.035	0.206	0.463

TABLE VI **The Standard** Normal Distribution

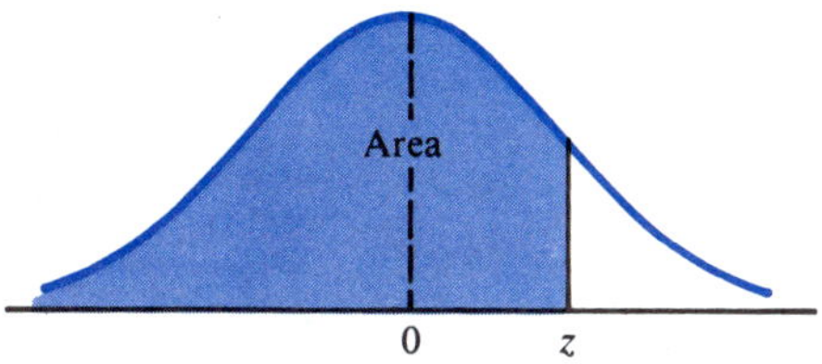

$F_Z(z) = P[Z \leq z]$

z	0.00	0.01	0.02	0.03	0.04	0.05	0.06	0.07	0.08	0.09
−3.4	0.0003	0.0003	0.0003	0.0003	0.0003	0.0003	0.0003	0.0003	0.0003	0.0002
−3.3	0.0005	0.0005	0.0005	0.0004	0.0004	0.0004	0.0004	0.0004	0.0004	0.0003
−3.2	0.0007	0.0007	0.0006	0.0006	0.0006	0.0006	0.0006	0.0005	0.0005	0.0005
−3.1	0.0010	0.0009	0.0009	0.0009	0.0008	0.0008	0.0008	0.0008	0.0007	0.0007
−3.0	0.0013	0.0013	0.0013	0.0012	0.0012	0.0011	0.0011	0.0011	0.0010	0.0010
−2.9	0.0019	0.0018	0.0017	0.0017	0.0016	0.0016	0.0015	0.0015	0.0014	0.0014
−2.8	0.0026	0.0025	0.0024	0.0023	0.0023	0.0022	0.0021	0.0021	0.0020	0.0019
−2.7	0.0035	0.0034	0.0033	0.0032	0.0031	0.0030	0.0029	0.0028	0.0027	0.0026
−2.6	0.0047	0.0045	0.0044	0.0043	0.0041	0.0040	0.0039	0.0038	0.0037	0.0036
−2.5	0.0062	0.0060	0.0059	0.0057	0.0055	0.0054	0.0052	0.0051	0.0049	0.0048
−2.4	0.0082	0.0080	0.0078	0.0075	0.0073	0.0071	0.0069	0.0068	0.0066	0.0064
−2.3	0.0107	0.0104	0.0102	0.0099	0.0096	0.0094	0.0091	0.0089	0.0087	0.0084
−2.2	0.0139	0.0136	0.0132	0.0129	0.0125	0.0122	0.0119	0.0116	0.0113	0.0110
−2.1	0.0179	0.0174	0.0170	0.0166	0.0162	0.0158	0.0154	0.0150	0.0146	0.0143
−2.0	0.0228	0.0222	0.0217	0.0212	0.0207	0.0202	0.0197	0.0192	0.0188	0.0183
−1.9	0.0287	0.0281	0.0274	0.0268	0.0262	0.0256	0.0250	0.0244	0.0239	0.0233
−1.8	0.0359	0.0352	0.0344	0.0336	0.0329	0.0322	0.0314	0.0307	0.0301	0.0294
−1.7	0.0446	0.0436	0.0427	0.0418	0.0409	0.0401	0.0392	0.0384	0.0375	0.0367
−1.6	0.0548	0.0537	0.0526	0.0516	0.0505	0.0495	0.0485	0.0475	0.0465	0.0455
−1.5	0.0668	0.0655	0.0643	0.0630	0.0618	0.0606	0.0594	0.0582	0.0571	0.0559
−1.4	0.0808	0.0793	0.0778	0.0764	0.0749	0.0735	0.0722	0.0708	0.0694	0.0681
−1.3	0.0968	0.0951	0.0934	0.0918	0.0901	0.0885	0.0869	0.0853	0.0838	0.0823
−1.2	0.1151	0.1131	0.1112	0.1093	0.1075	0.1056	0.1038	0.1020	0.1003	0.0985
−1.1	0.1357	0.1335	0.1314	0.1292	0.1271	0.1251	0.1230	0.1210	0.1190	0.1170
−1.0	0.1587	0.1562	0.1539	0.1515	0.1492	0.1469	0.1446	0.1423	0.1401	0.1379
−0.9	0.1841	0.1814	0.1788	0.1762	0.1736	0.1711	0.1685	0.1660	0.1635	0.1611
−0.8	0.2119	0.2090	0.2061	0.2033	0.2005	0.1977	0.1949	0.1922	0.1894	0.1867
−0.7	0.2420	0.2389	0.2358	0.2327	0.2296	0.2266	0.2236	0.2206	0.2177	0.2148
−0.6	0.2743	0.2709	0.2676	0.2643	0.2611	0.2578	0.2546	0.2514	0.2483	0.2451
−0.5	0.3085	0.3050	0.3015	0.2981	0.2946	0.2912	0.2877	0.2843	0.2810	0.2776

TABLE VI (continued)

$$F_z(z) = P[Z \leq z]$$

z	0.00	0.01	0.02	0.03	0.04	0.05	0.06	0.07	0.08	0.09
−0.4	0.3446	0.3409	0.3372	0.3336	0.3300	0.3264	0.3228	0.3192	0.3156	0.3121
−0.3	0.3821	0.3783	0.3745	0.3707	0.3669	0.3632	0.3594	0.3557	0.3520	0.3483
−0.2	0.4207	0.4168	0.4129	0.4090	0.4052	0.4013	0.3974	0.3936	0.3897	0.3859
−0.1	0.4602	0.4562	0.4522	0.4483	0.4443	0.4404	0.4364	0.4325	0.4286	0.4247
−0.0	0.5000	0.4960	0.4920	0.4880	0.4840	0.4801	0.4761	0.4721	0.4681	0.4641
0.0	0.5000	0.5040	0.5080	0.5120	0.5160	0.5199	0.5239	0.5279	0.5319	0.5359
0.1	0.5398	0.5438	0.5478	0.5517	0.5557	0.5596	0.5636	0.5675	0.5714	0.5753
0.2	0.5793	0.5832	0.5871	0.5910	0.5948	0.5987	0.6026	0.6064	0.6103	0.6141
0.3	0.6179	0.6217	0.6255	0.6293	0.6331	0.6368	0.6406	0.6443	0.6480	0.6517
0.4	0.6554	0.6591	0.6628	0.6664	0.6700	0.6736	0.6772	0.6808	0.6844	0.6879
0.5	0.6915	0.6950	0.6985	0.7019	0.7054	0.7088	0.7123	0.7157	0.7190	0.7224
0.6	0.7257	0.7291	0.7324	0.7357	0.7389	0.7422	0.7454	0.7486	0.7517	0.7549
0.7	0.7580	0.7611	0.7642	0.7673	0.7704	0.7734	0.7764	0.7794	0.7823	0.7852
0.8	0.7881	0.7910	0.7939	0.7967	0.7995	0.8023	0.8051	0.8078	0.8106	0.8133
0.9	0.8159	0.8186	0.8212	0.8238	0.8264	0.8289	0.8315	0.8340	0.8365	0.8389
1.0	0.8413	0.8438	0.8461	0.8485	0.8508	0.8531	0.8554	0.8577	0.8599	0.8621
1.1	0.8643	0.8665	0.8686	0.8708	0.8729	0.8749	0.8770	0.8790	0.8810	0.8830
1.2	0.8849	0.8869	0.8888	0.8907	0.8925	0.8944	0.8962	0.8980	0.8997	0.9015
1.3	0.9032	0.9049	0.9066	0.9082	0.9099	0.9115	0.9131	0.9147	0.9162	0.9177
1.4	0.9192	0.9207	0.9222	0.9236	0.9251	0.9265	0.9278	0.9292	0.9306	0.9319
1.5	0.9332	0.9345	0.9357	0.9370	0.9382	0.9394	0.9406	0.9418	0.9429	0.9441
1.6	0.9452	0.9463	0.9474	0.9484	0.9495	0.9505	0.9515	0.9525	0.9535	0.9545
1.7	0.9554	0.9564	0.9573	0.9582	0.9591	0.9599	0.9608	0.9616	0.9625	0.9633
1.8	0.9641	0.9649	0.9656	0.9664	0.9671	0.9678	0.9686	0.9693	0.9699	0.9706
1.9	0.9713	0.9719	0.9726	0.9732	0.9738	0.9744	0.9750	0.9756	0.9761	0.9767
2.0	0.9772	0.9778	0.9783	0.9788	0.9793	0.9798	0.9803	0.9808	0.9812	0.9817
2.1	0.9821	0.9826	0.9830	0.9834	0.9838	0.9842	0.9846	0.9850	0.9854	0.9857
2.2	0.9861	0.9864	0.9868	0.9871	0.9875	0.9878	0.9881	0.9884	0.9887	0.9890
2.3	0.9893	0.9896	0.9898	0.9901	0.9904	0.9906	0.9909	0.9911	0.9913	0.9916
2.4	0.9918	0.9920	0.9922	0.9925	0.9927	0.9929	0.9931	0.9932	0.9934	0.9936
2.5	0.9938	0.9940	0.9941	0.9943	0.9945	0.9946	0.9948	0.9949	0.9951	0.9952
2.6	0.9953	0.9955	0.9956	0.9957	0.9959	0.9960	0.9961	0.9962	0.9963	0.9964
2.7	0.9965	0.9966	0.9967	0.9968	0.9969	0.9970	0.9971	0.9972	0.9973	0.9974
2.8	0.9974	0.9975	0.9976	0.9977	0.9977	0.9978	0.9979	0.9979	0.9980	0.9981
2.9	0.9981	0.9982	0.9982	0.9983	0.9984	0.9984	0.9985	0.9985	0.9986	0.9986
3.0	0.9987	0.9987	0.9987	0.9988	0.9988	0.9989	0.9989	0.9989	0.9990	0.9990
3.1	0.9990	0.9991	0.9991	0.9991	0.9992	0.9992	0.9992	0.9992	0.9993	0.9993
3.2	0.9993	0.9993	0.9994	0.9994	0.9994	0.9994	0.9994	0.9995	0.9995	0.9995
3.3	0.9995	0.9995	0.9995	0.9996	0.9996	0.9996	0.9996	0.9996	0.9996	0.9997
3.4	0.9997	0.9997	0.9997	0.9997	0.9997	0.9997	0.9997	0.9997	0.9997	0.9998

1-14

ANSWERS TO ODD-NUMBERED EXERCISES

Chapter 1

EXERCISES 1.1
page 5

1. (a), (b), (d), (g), (h)

3. (***a***) {2, 3, 4, 5, 6} (***b***) {A, H, I, M, O, P, S, T, U}
(***c***) {−2} (***d***) {−2}
(***e***) ∅ (***f***) $\{-\sqrt{2}, \sqrt{2}\}$
(***g***) {−2, 3} (***h***) {−1}

5. (***a***) T (***b***) F (***c***) F
(***d***) F (***e***) T (***f***) F

7. (a), (b), (c)

9. (***a***) ∅ (***b***) ∅, {1} (***c***) ∅, {1}, {2}, {1, 2}
(***d***) ∅, {1}, {2}, {3}, {1, 2}, {1, 3}, {2, 3}, {1, 2, 3}
(***e***) ∅, {1}, {2}, {3}, {4}, {1, 2}, {1, 3}, {1, 4}, {2, 3}, {2, 4}, {3, 4}, {1, 2, 3}, {1, 2, 4}, {1, 3, 4}, {2, 3, 4}, {1, 2, 3, 4}

11. (***a***) ∅, {IBM}, {U.S. Steel}, {Union Carbide}, {Boeing}, {IBM, U.S. Steel}, {IBM, Union Carbide}, {IBM, Boeing}, {U.S. Steel, Union Carbide}, {U.S. Steel, Boeing}, {Union Carbide, Boeing}, {IBM, U.S. Steel, Union Carbide}, {IBM, U.S. Steel, Boeing}, {IBM, Union Carbide, Boeing}, {U.S. Steel, Union Carbide, Boeing}, {IBM, U.S. Steel, Union Carbide, Boeing}
All except the last subset listed above are proper subsets of A.

13. $A \subset C$

15. (***a***)
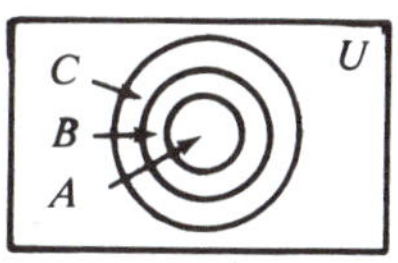

(***b***)
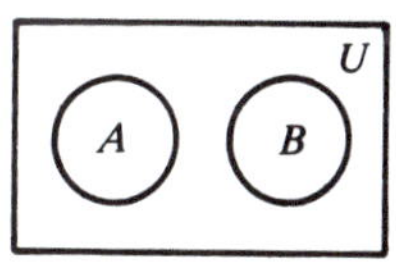

(***c***)
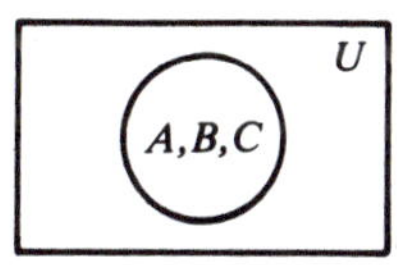

EXERCISES 1.2
page 11

1. (***a***)
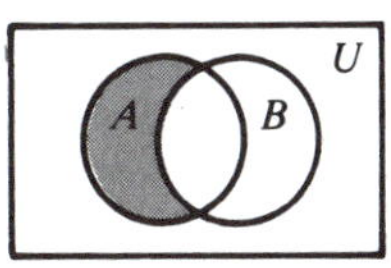

(***b***)
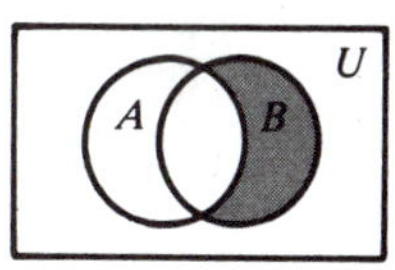

(***c***)
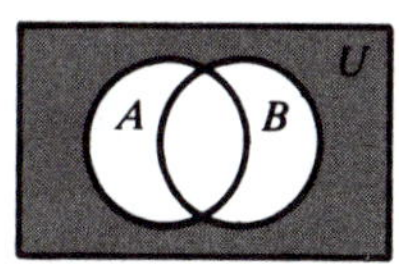

(*d*) 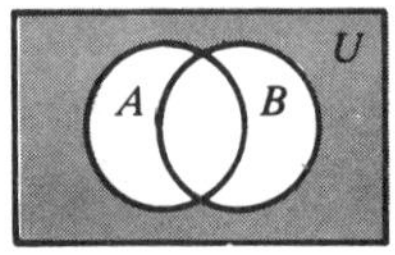

(*e*) 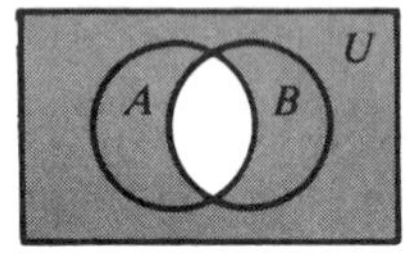

(*f*) 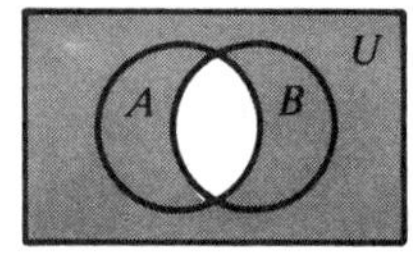

3. (*a*) {2, 4, 6, 8, 10} (*b*) {1, 2, 4, 5, 6, 8, 9, 10} (*c*) U
(*d*) ∅ (*e*) {1, 2, 3, 4, 5, 7, 8, 9} (*f*) {2, 3, 4, 6, 7, 8, 10}
(*g*) C (*h*) U (*i*) ∅
(*j*) {6, 10} (*k*) {1, 3, 5, 6, 7, 9, 10} (*l*) ∅

5. The set of employees at the Universal Life Insurance Company
(*a*) who do not drink tea (*b*) who do not drink coffee
(*c*) who drink tea and/or coffee (*d*) who drink both tea and coffee
(*e*) who drink tea but not coffee (*f*) who drink coffee but not tea
(*g*) who drink neither tea nor coffee (*h*) who drink neither tea nor coffee
(*i*) who do not drink both tea and coffee

7. The set of employees at a hospital
(*a*) who are not doctors (*b*) who are not nurses
(*c*) who are doctors and/or nurses (*d*) who are both doctors and administrators
(*e*) who are male nurses (*f*) who are female doctors
(*g*) who are female nurses (*h*) who are females but not doctors
(*i*) who are neither doctors nor nurses

9. (*a*) 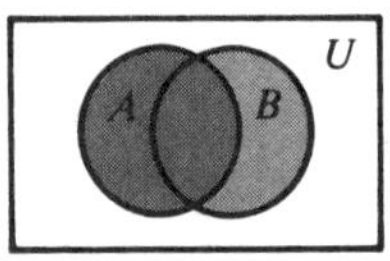

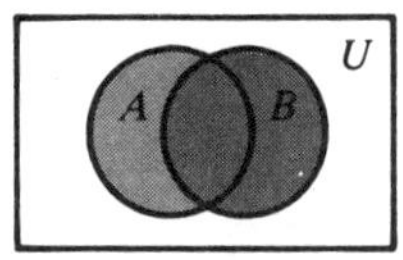

(*b*) 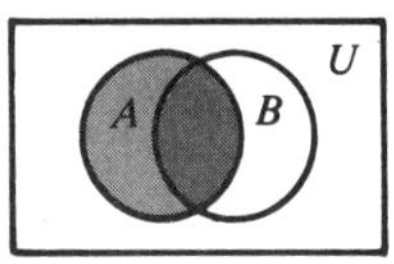

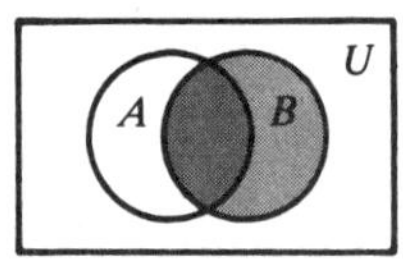

EXERCISES 1.3
page 18

1. $(-\infty, 2)$ ***3.*** $(-\infty, -5]$ ***5.*** $[-1, 3]$
7. $(-\infty, -3)$ or $(3, \infty)$ ***9.*** $(-1, 5]$ ***11.*** $[-3, 5]$
13. $[-5/2, 1]$ ***15.*** ∅ ***17.*** $(-\infty, 3]$ or $[5, \infty)$
19. $(-1, 1)$ or $(1, 3/2]$ ***21.*** $x = \pm 5$ ***23.*** $x = -1$ or $x = 7/3$
25. $x = -2$ and $x = -1/2$ ***27.*** $(-3/2, 3/2)$
29. (*a*) F (*b*) F (*c*) F (*d*) F (*e*) T (*f*) T (*g*) T (*h*) F
31. $\$600 \leq R \leq \$1000$ ***33.*** $C \geq \$50.70$
35. (*a*) $5° < F° < 23°$ (*b*) $17.2° < C° < 26.7°$ ***37.*** \$18,666.67

EXERCISES 1.4
page 24

1. 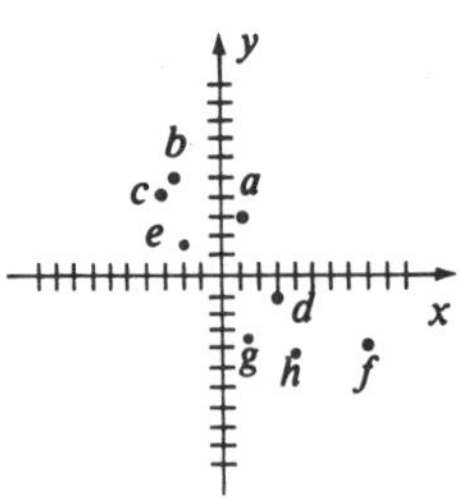

3. (*a*) I (*b*) II (*c*) IV (*d*) II (*e*) III (*f*) IV

5. 5 **7.** 13 **9.** 9.06 **11.** (3, 4)

13. $r=\sqrt{(x-h)^2+(y-k)^2}$ **17.** No

19. Model C **21.** freight train; \$1100

EXERCISES 1.5
page 37

1. 5 **3.** $\frac{5}{6}$ **5.** $\frac{d-b}{c-a}(a \neq c)$

7. Parallel **9.** Parallel

11. Not perpendicular (3, −4) **15.** No

17. (*a*) $2x-y-10=0$ (*b*) $x+y-6=0$ (*c*) $y-2=0$

19. (*a*) $y=3x+4$ (*b*) $y=-2x-1$ (*c*) $y=5$

21. $x-2y+6=0$

23. (*a*) $y=-6$ (*b*) $3x-2y=0$ (*c*) $y=b$

25. $k=8$

27. (*a*) $4x+3y-12=0$ (*b*) $2x+y+4=0$
(*c*) $6x-4y+3=0$ (*d*) $x-8y-4=0$

29. (*a*)

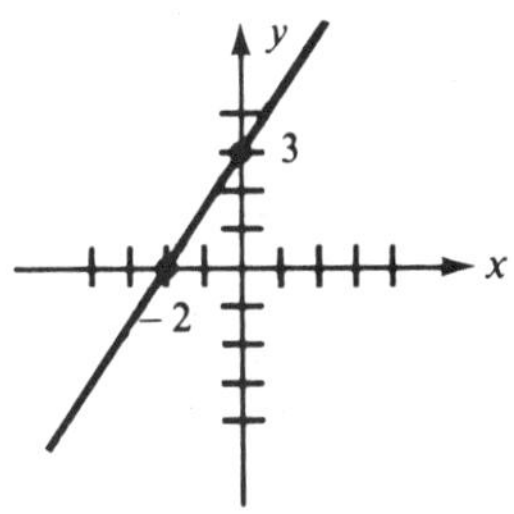

(*b*)

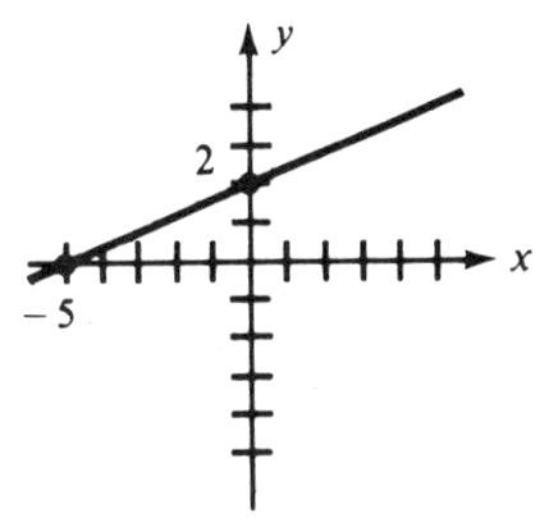

(*c*)

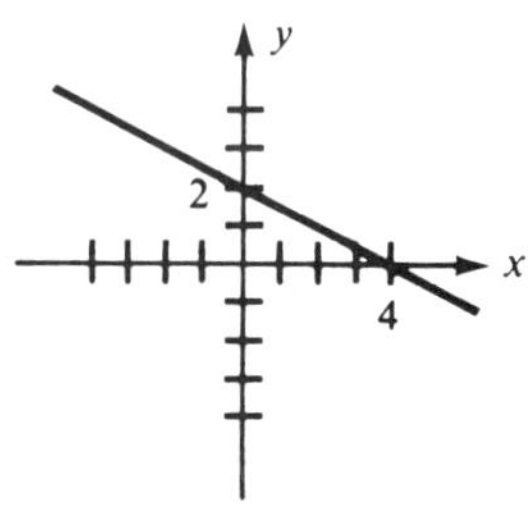

(*d*)

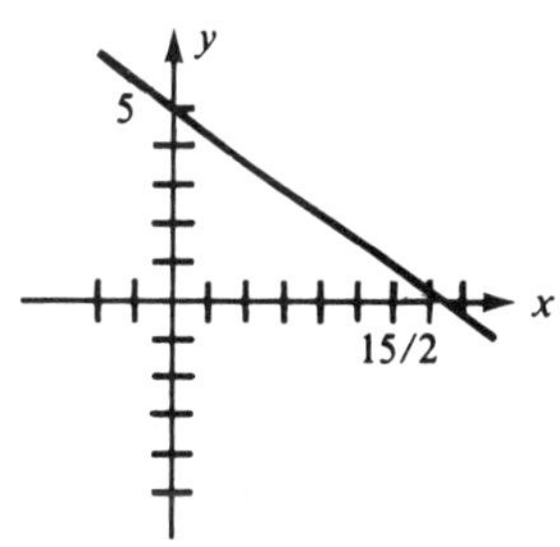

(*e*)

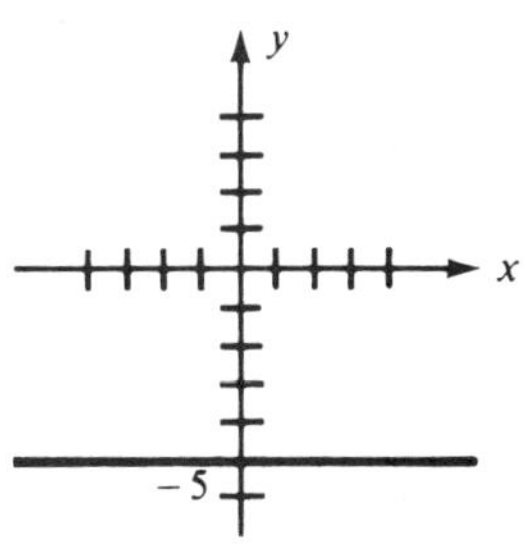

(*f*)

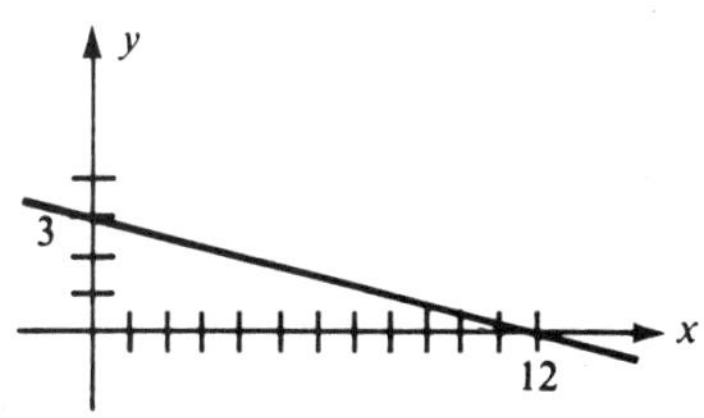

31. (*a*)

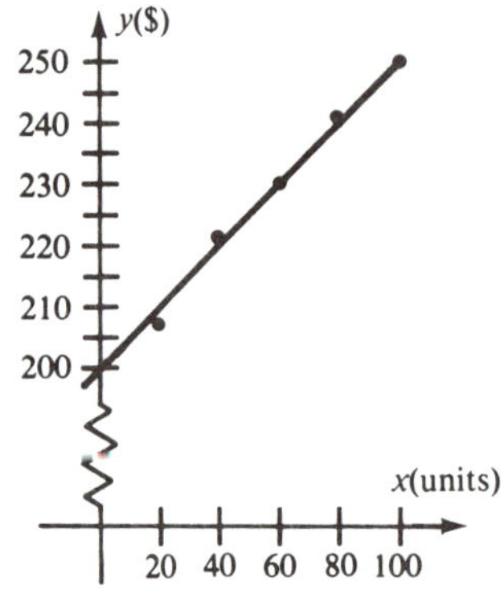

(*c*) $x-2y+400=0$ (*d*) $227

Ch. 1 REVIEW EXERCISES page 40

1. (*a*) {3} (*b*) {A, E, H, L, S, T} (*c*) {4, 6, 8, 10} (*d*) {−4}

3. $\varnothing, \{g\}, \{f\}, \{e\}, \{e, g\}, \{f, g\}, \{e, f\}, \{e, f, g\}$ all except the last are proper subsets of A.

5. (*a*) $(A \cup B \cup C)^c$ (*b*) $A \cup B$ (*c*) $(A \cap B \cap C^c)$

7. (*a*) 5 (*b*) 2 **9.** $(-1, 4)$

11. $x=\frac{2}{3}$ and $x=\frac{3}{2}$ **13.** $5y+3x=-29$ **15.**

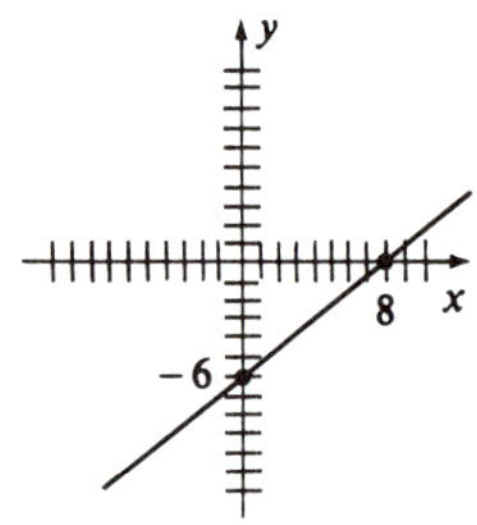

Chapter 2

EXERCISES 2.1 page 48

1. $21, -9, 5a+6, -5a+6, 5a+21$ **3.** $-4, 1, -|a|+1, -|a|+1, -|a-1|+1$

5. 5, 1, 1 **7.** 6 billion dollars, 43.5 billion dollars, 81 billion dollars

9. $S=4\pi r^2$ **11.** All real numbers except 0 **13.** $(-\infty, -5] \cup [5, \infty)$

15. All real numbers except 2 **17.** All real numbers except −2 and 1

19. $(-\infty, -1] \cup [3, \infty)$

21.

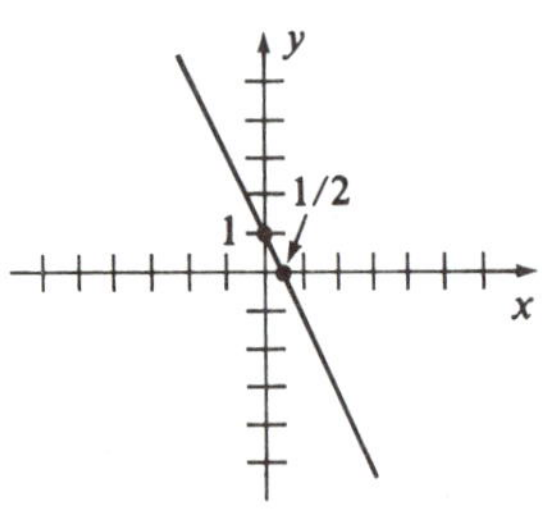

23.

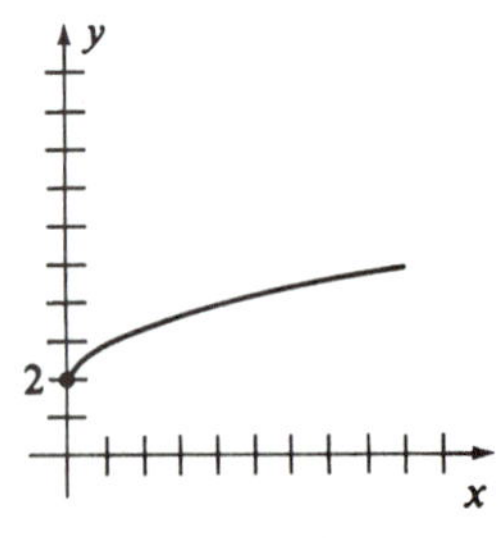

25.

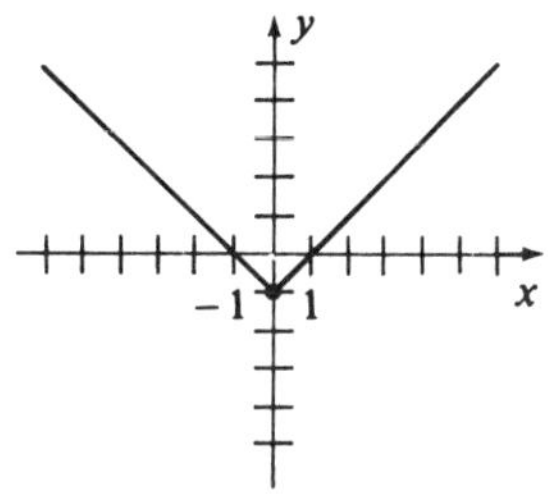

27.

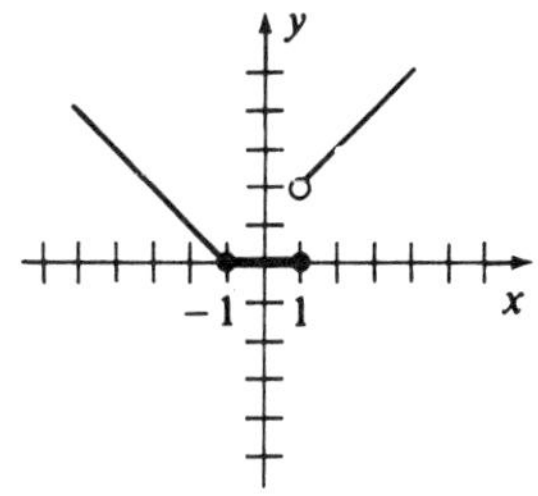

29. (***a***)

$$f(x)=\begin{cases} \ldots \\ 2178.04+39.51\,(x-40) & \text{if } 40<x\le 100 \\ 4548.64+32.67\,(x-100) & \text{if } 100<x\le 300 \\ 11{,}082.64+31.53\,(x-300) & \text{if } 300<x\le 500 \\ 17{,}388.64+29.25\,(x-500) & \text{if } 500>x \end{cases}$$

(***b***) $(0, \infty)$

(***c***)

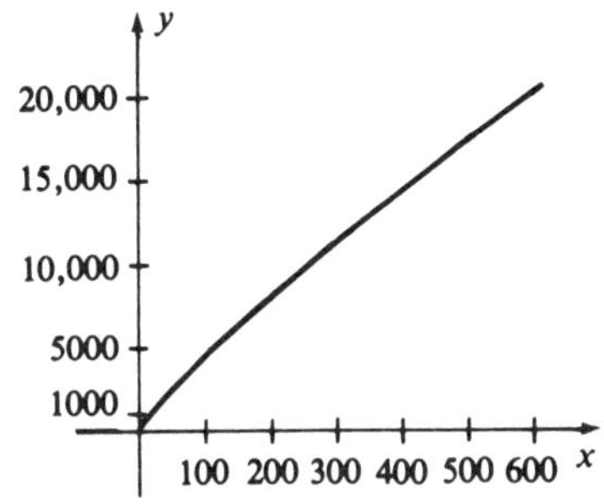

(***d***) $41.93

31.

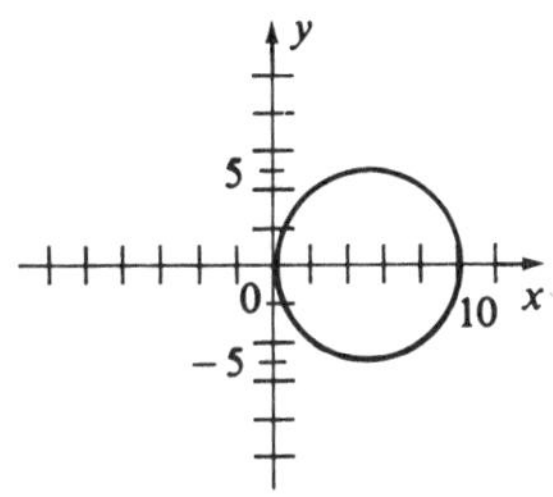

y is not a function of x

33.

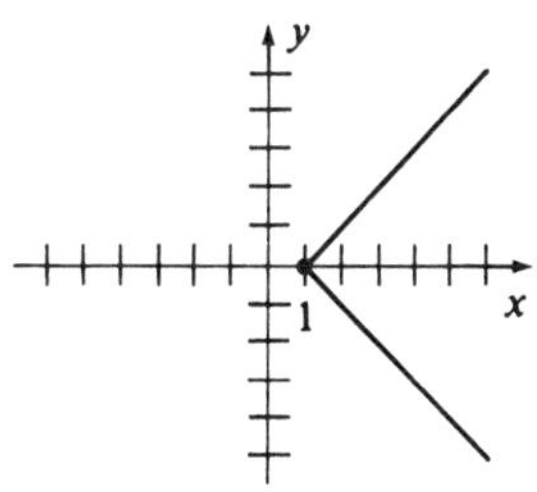

y is not a function of x

35. No ***37.*** No ***39.*** Yes ***41.*** No

EXERCISES 2.2 page 61

1. $80; $580 ***3.*** $836 ***5.*** 108 days
7. 24% per annum ***9.*** $172.22 per month ***11.*** 10% per annum
13. $9850 ***15.*** $800,000; $700,000
17. (***a***) $V = 250{,}000 - 24{,}000n$ (***b***)

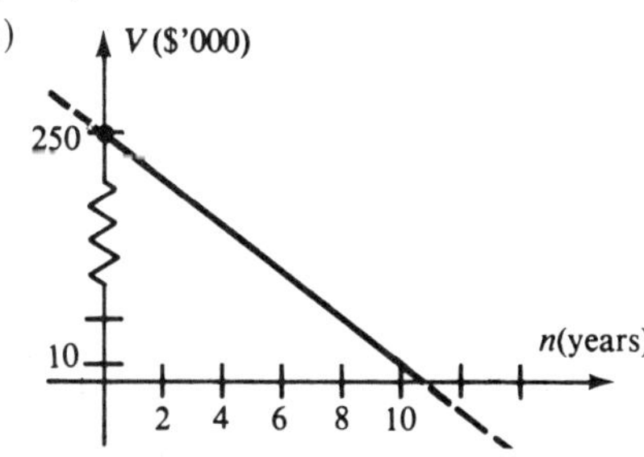

(***c***) $154,000

(***d***) $24,000 per year

19. $V = -\left(\dfrac{C-S}{N}\right)n + C$ **21.** $(-3, 5)$ **23.** $\left(\dfrac{1}{2}, \dfrac{5}{2}\right)$ **25.** $(3, -2)$

27. (*a*)

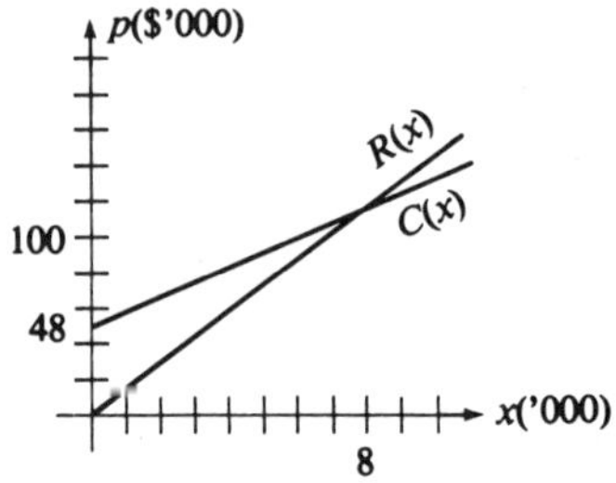

(*b*) 8000 units; $112,000

(*c*)

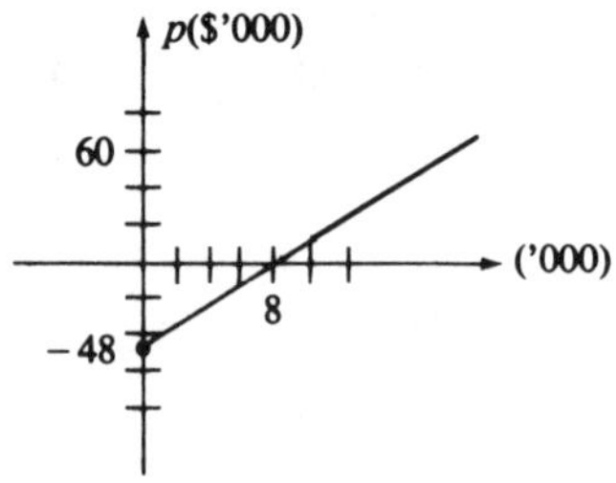

(*d*) $x = 8000$

29. 2000 units; $42,000 **31.** 167 units; $45,090

33. (*a*) 5000 units; $40,000 (*b*) 6579 units

35. (*a*) $C_1(x) = .15x + 30$
$C_2(x) = .20x + 25$

(*b*)

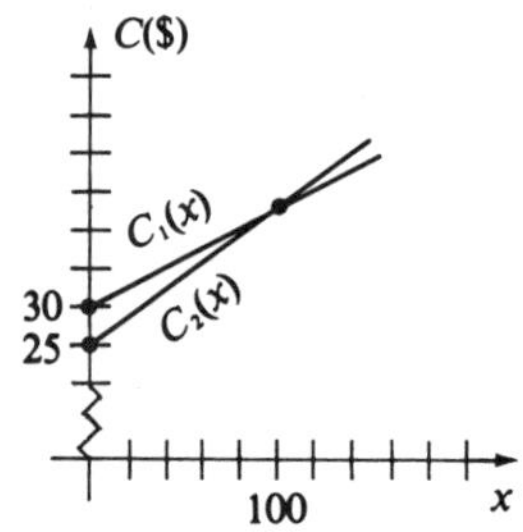

(*c*) Acme Truck Leasing Company
(*d*) (100, 45)

EXERCISES 2.3 page 67

1. (*a*) all real numbers
(*b*) all real numbers
(*c*) $(-2, 0)$; $(0, 4)$
(*d*) no symmetry
(*e*) as x increases (decreases) without bound y increases (decreases) without bound

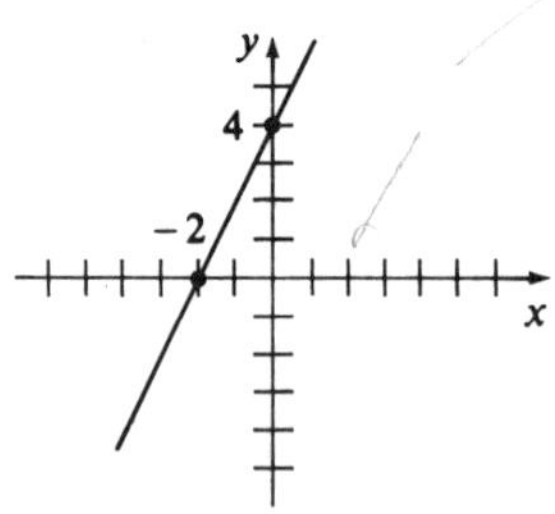

3. (*a*) all real numbers except 0
(*b*) −1 and 1
(*c*) no intercepts
(*d*) symmetric about the origin
(*e*) as x increases (decreases) without bound, y remains constant

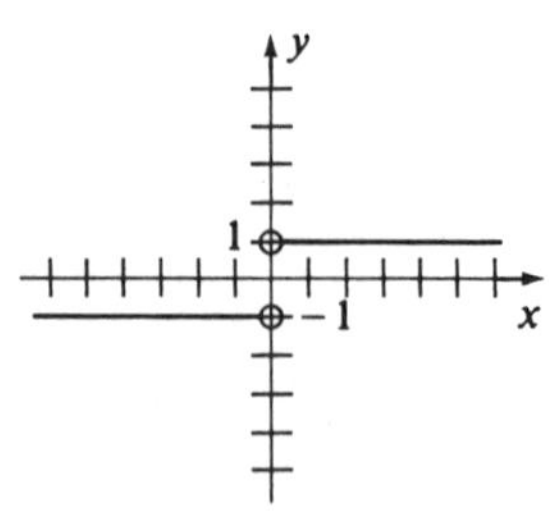

5. (*a*) all real numbers
(*b*) $[0, \infty)$
(*c*) $(0, 0)$
(*d*) symmetric about the y-axis
(*e*) as x increases (decreases) without bound, y increases without bound

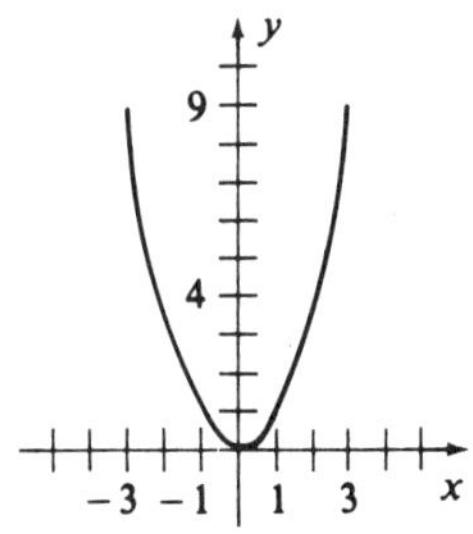

7. (*a*) all real numbers
(*b*) $[0, \infty)$
(*c*) $(0, 0)$
(*d*) symmetric about the y-axis
(*e*) as x increases (decreases) without bound y increases without bound

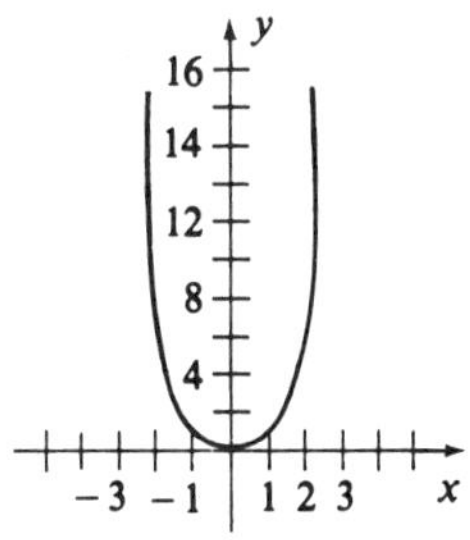

9. (*a*) all real numbers
(*b*) all real numbers
(*c*) $(-1, 0)$; $(0, 0)$; $(1, 0)$
(*d*) symmetric about the origin
(*e*) as x increases (decreases) without bound y increases (decreases) without bound

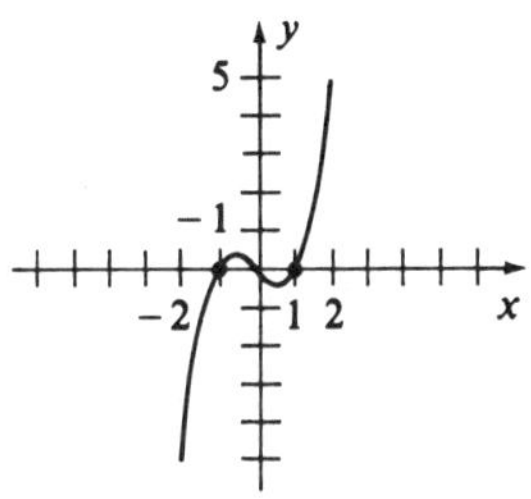

11. (*a*) all real numbers
(*b*) $[0, \infty)$
(*c*) $(0, 0)$
(*d*) symmetric about the y-axis
(*e*) as x increases or decreases without bound y increases without bound

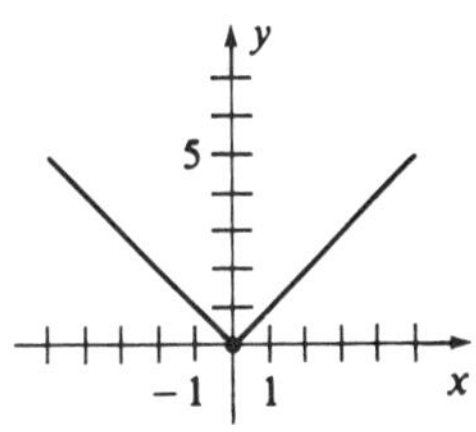

13. (*a*) all real numbers
(*b*) $[0, \infty)$
(*c*) $(1, 0)$; $(0, 1)$
(*d*) no symmetry
(*e*) as x increases or decreases without bound y increases without bound

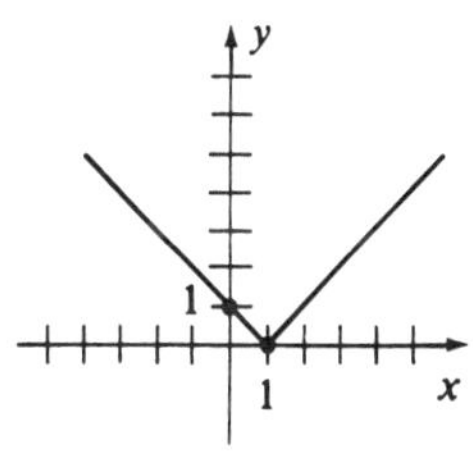

15. (*a*) all real numbers
(*b*) $(0, 1/4]$
(*c*) $(0, 1/4)$
(*d*) symmetric about the y-axis
(*e*) as x increases or decreases without bound, y approaches zero

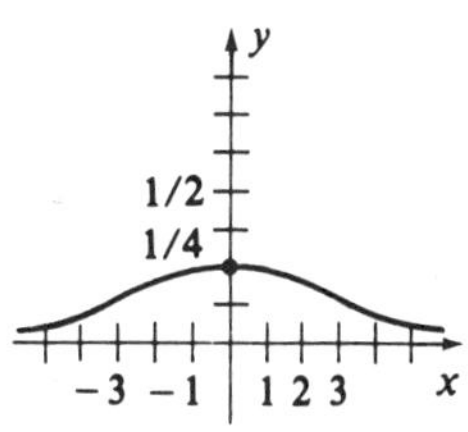

17. (***a***) all real numbers
(***b***) [0, 1)
(***c***) (0, 0)
(***d***) symmetric about the y-axis
(***e***) as x increases or decreases without bound, y approaches 1

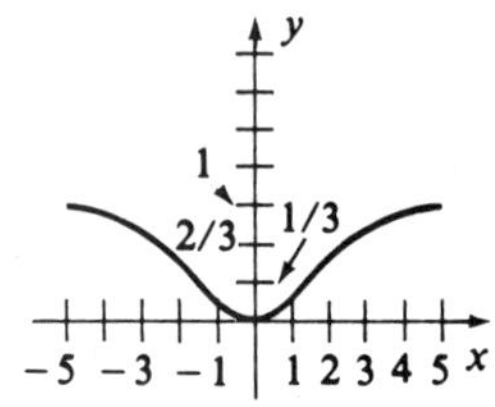

19. (***a***) all real numbers except 1
(***b***) all real numbers except 0
(***c***) (0, −1)
(***d***) no symmetry
(***e***) as x increases or decreases without bound, y approaches 0

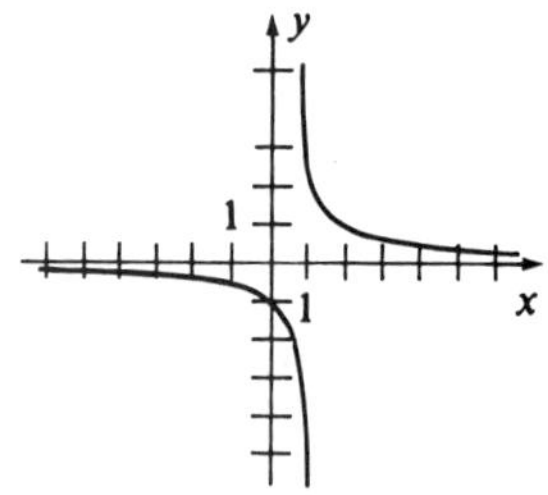

EXERCISES 2.4
page 72

1. Yes
3. Yes
5. 2 real roots; $x = -4$ or $x = 3$
7. no real solution

9. (***a***) $\left(\frac{5}{2}, \frac{1}{4}\right)$ (***b***) (3, 0); (2, 0) (***c***)

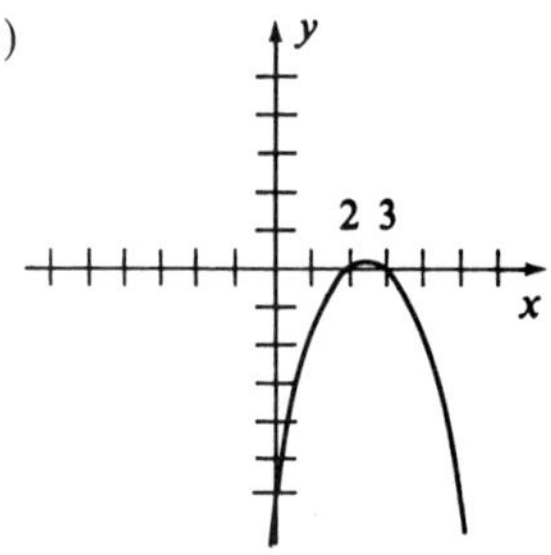

11. (***a***) $\left(\frac{1}{3}, \frac{2}{3}\right)$ (***b***) none (***c***)

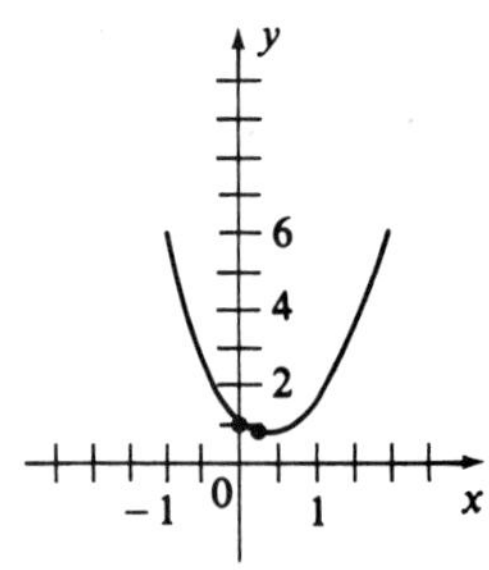

EXERCISES 2.5
page 79

1. (***a***)

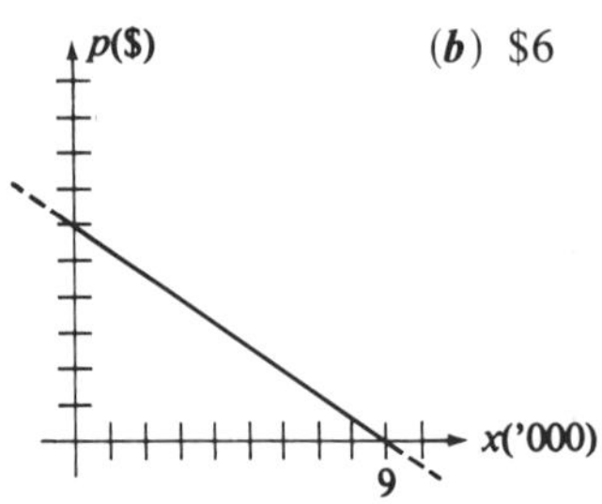

(***b***) $6 (***c***) 9000 units

3. (*a*)

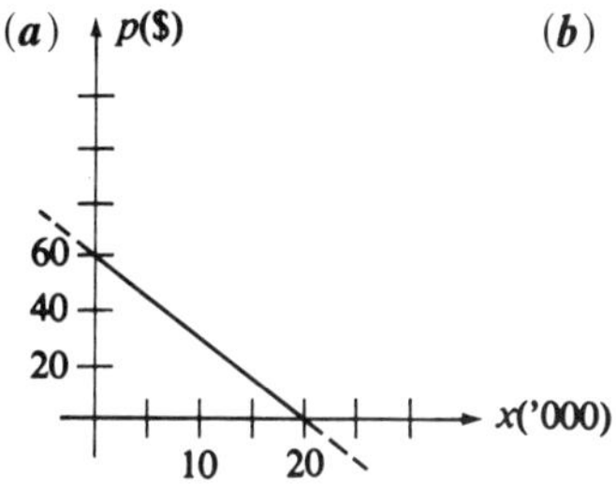

(*b*) \$60 (*c*) 20,000 units

5. (*a*)

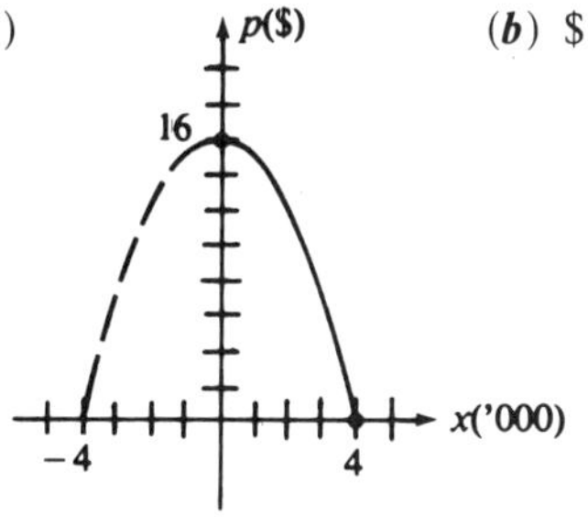

(*b*) \$16 (*c*) 4000 units

7. $p=(-3/40)x+130$; \$130; 1733

9. $p=-(1/10)x^2+10$; 5000 units

11. (*a*)

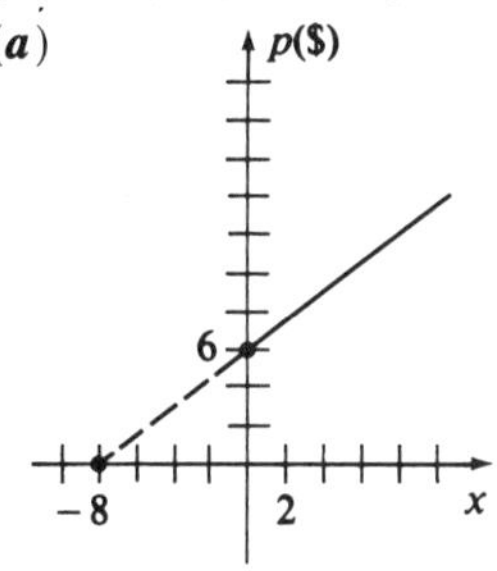

(*b*) \$6

13. (*a*)

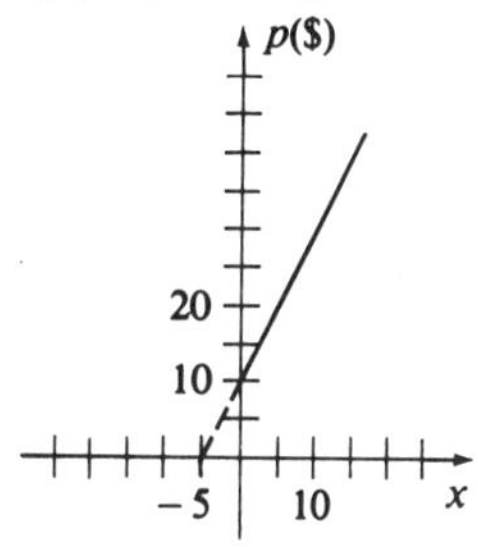

(*b*) \$10

15. (*a*)

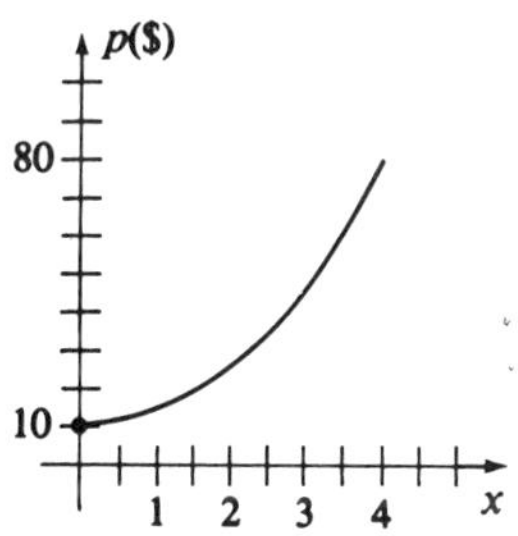

(*b*) \$10

17. $p=(1/2)x+40$ (x in units of a thousand); 60,000 units

19.

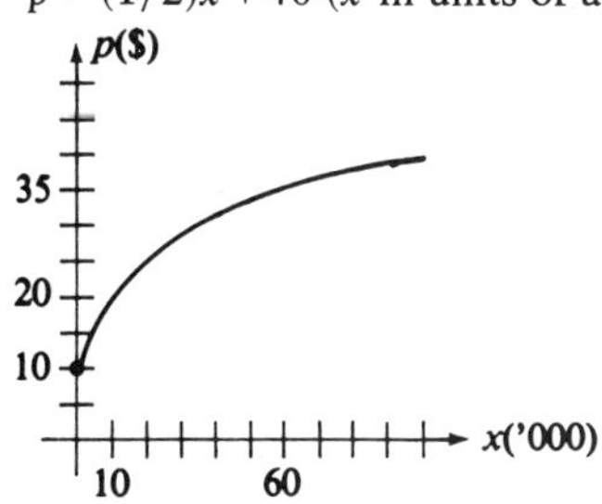

$p=(1/10)\sqrt{x}+10$; \$10

21. 2000 units; \$18

23. 11,000 units; \$3

25. (*a*) $p = (-1/2)x + 2000$ (*b*) $p = .09x + 600$ (*c*) 2373; \$813.50

Ch. 2 REVIEW EXERCISES page 81

1. (*a*) domain: $[-1/2, \infty)$; range: $(-\infty, \infty)$
(*b*) No
(*c*) Yes

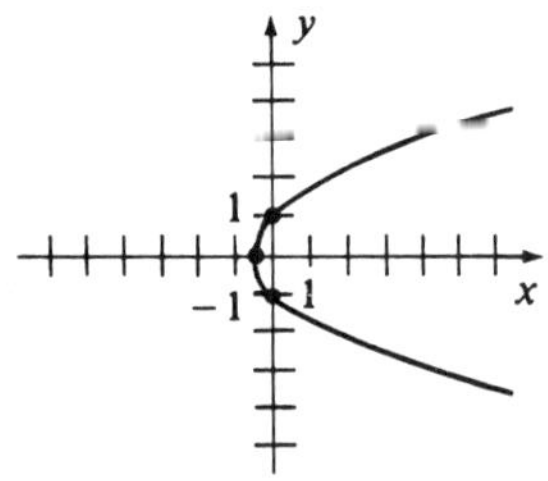

3.

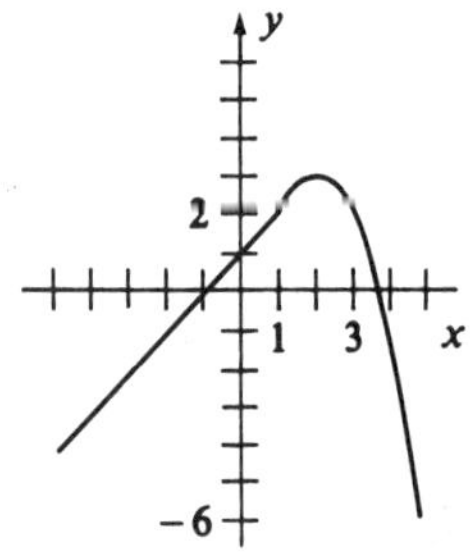

5. (*a*) $V = 300{,}000 - 22500n$ (*b*) \$22,500 per year

7. (*a*) all real numbers
(*b*) $[-1, \infty)$
(*c*) (1, 0), (3, 0); (0, 3)
(*d*) none
(*e*) as x increases or decreases without bound y increases without bound

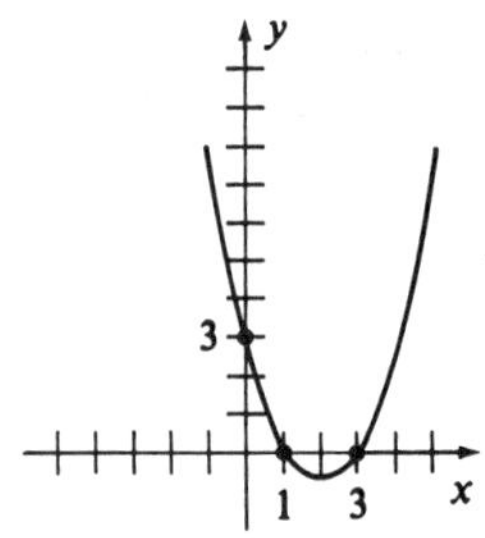

9. (*a*) all real numbers
(*b*) all real numbers
(*c*) (−1, 0); (0, 1)
(*d*) none
(*e*) as x increases (decreases) without bound, y increases (decreases) without bound

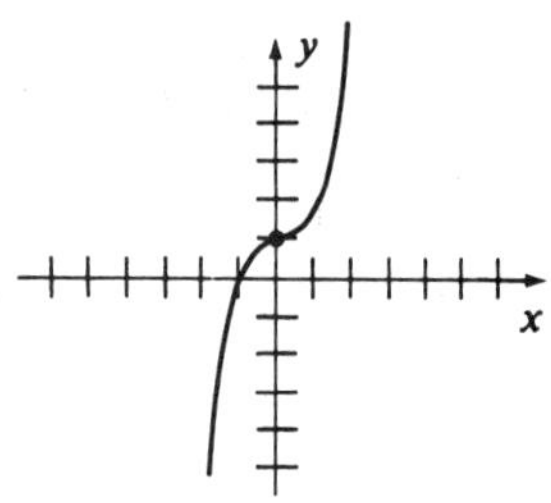

11. $p = -.05x + 200$

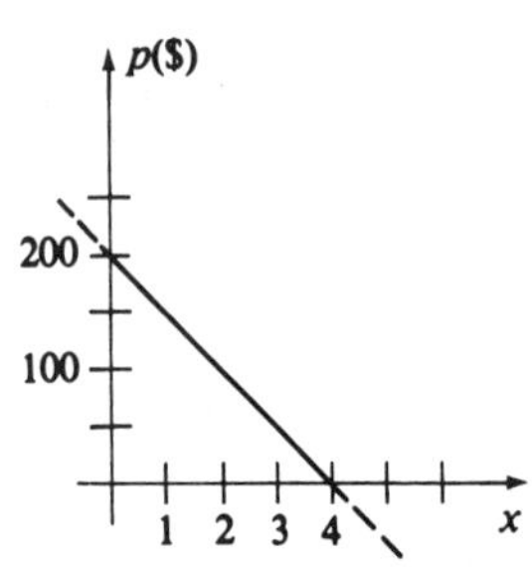

13. 6000 units; \$22

Chapter 3

EXERCISES 3.1 page 89

1. (*a*) 4×4 (*b*) $a_{14}=-4;\ a_{21}=-11;\ a_{31}=6;\ a_{43}=5$

3. $\begin{bmatrix} -5 & -1 & 23 \\ 25 & 14 & 17 \\ 33 & 21 & 30 \end{bmatrix}$

5. (*a*) $\begin{bmatrix} 1 & 6 \\ 6 & -1 \\ 2 & 2 \end{bmatrix}$ (*b*) $\begin{bmatrix} -8 & -8 \\ -3 & -7 \\ 14 & -6 \end{bmatrix}$ (*c*) $\begin{bmatrix} 1 & 1 & -4 \\ -1 & -8 & 1 \\ 6 & 3 & 1 \end{bmatrix}$ (*d*) $\begin{bmatrix} 2 & -6 & 16 \\ 8 & 28 & 2 \\ -16 & 0 & 0 \end{bmatrix}$

7. $x=6,\ y=2,\ u=1,\ z=0$ **9.** $x=20,\ y=4,\ z=-2,\ u=2$

13. $\begin{bmatrix} 4 & 3 \\ 2 & 4 \\ 0 & -1 \\ -1 & 5 \end{bmatrix}$ **15.** $\begin{bmatrix} 1 & 2 & 6 & 4 \\ 2 & 3 & 2 & 5 \\ 6 & 2 & 3 & 0 \\ 4 & 5 & 0 & 2 \end{bmatrix}$

17. (*a*)

$A =$

	Text	Fict.	Non-Fict.	Ref.
Hard.	5280	1680	2320	1890
Paper.	1940	2810	1490	2070

(*b*)

$B =$

	Text	Fict.	Non-Fict.	Ref.
Hard.	6340	2220	1790	1980
Paper.	2050	3100	1720	2710

(*c*)

$C =$

	Text	Fict.	Non-Fict.	Ref.
Hard.	11,620	3900	4110	3870
Paper.	3990	5910	3210	4780

EXERCISES 3.2 page 98

1. (*a*) 2×5; not defined (*b*) $3\times 3;\ 4\times 4$
(*c*) $1\times 1;\ 7\times 7$ (*d*) $4\times 4;\ 4\times 4$

3. A must be a square matrix

5. $\begin{bmatrix} 6 & -3 & 0 \\ -2 & 1 & -8 \\ 4 & -4 & 9 \end{bmatrix}$ **7.** $\begin{bmatrix} -4 & -20 & 4 \\ 4 & 12 & 0 \\ 12 & 32 & 20 \end{bmatrix}$ **9.** $\begin{bmatrix} 4 & 2 & -10 \\ 6 & 16 & 2 \\ 10 & 26 & 6 \end{bmatrix}$

13. (*a*) $\begin{bmatrix} 9 & -3 & -18 \\ 6 & 7 & 9 \\ 6 & -2 & -12 \end{bmatrix}$ (*b*) $\begin{bmatrix} 9 & -3 & -18 \\ 6 & 7 & 9 \\ 6 & -2 & -12 \end{bmatrix}$

17. (*a*) $\begin{bmatrix} 47 & -10 \\ 20 & 7 \end{bmatrix}$ (*b*) $\begin{bmatrix} 49 & -15 \\ 18 & 5 \end{bmatrix}$

19. $\begin{bmatrix} 2 \\ 3 \\ 4 \end{bmatrix}$; $\begin{bmatrix} 980 \\ 1590 \\ 1255 \\ 1650 \end{bmatrix}$; \$5475

21. (*a*)
$$\begin{array}{l} \\ \text{L.A.} \\ \text{Seattle} \end{array} \begin{array}{c} \begin{array}{ccc} \text{Plush} & \text{S. Mat.} & \text{Trim} \end{array} \\ \begin{bmatrix} 4410 & 64{,}000 & 25{,}400 \\ 3350 & 49{,}000 & 19{,}000 \end{bmatrix} \end{array}$$

(*b*)
$$\begin{array}{l} \text{L.A.} \\ \text{Seattle} \end{array} \begin{bmatrix} 32{,}595 \\ 24{,}725 \end{bmatrix}$$

(*c*) \$57,320

23. (*a*)
$$A = \begin{array}{r} \\ \text{Mad.} \\ \text{Chi.} \\ \text{Bos.} \\ \text{N.Y.C.} \\ \text{Phil.} \end{array} \begin{array}{c} \begin{array}{ccccc} \text{Mad.} & \text{Chi.} & \text{Bos.} & \text{N.Y.C.} & \text{Phil.} \end{array} \\ \begin{bmatrix} 0 & 1 & 0 & 0 & 0 \\ 1 & 0 & 1 & 1 & 1 \\ 0 & 1 & 0 & 1 & 0 \\ 0 & 1 & 1 & 0 & 1 \\ 0 & 1 & 0 & 1 & 0 \end{bmatrix} \end{array}$$

(*b*)
$$B = \begin{array}{r} \\ \text{Mad.} \\ \text{Chi.} \\ \text{Bos.} \\ \text{N.Y.C.} \\ \text{Phil.} \end{array} \begin{array}{c} \begin{array}{ccccc} \text{Mad.} & \text{Chi.} & \text{Bos.} & \text{N.Y.C.} & \text{Phil.} \end{array} \\ \begin{bmatrix} 1 & 0 & 1 & 1 & 1 \\ 0 & 4 & 1 & 2 & 1 \\ 1 & 1 & 2 & 1 & 2 \\ 1 & 2 & 1 & 3 & 1 \\ 1 & 1 & 2 & 1 & 2 \end{bmatrix} \end{array}$$

EXERCISES 3.3
page 107

1. Unique solution; (2, 1)
3. Infinitely many solutions; $(t, (2/5)t-2)$, t a parameter
5. No solution

EXERCISES 3.4
page 117

1.
$$\left[\begin{array}{ccc|c} 1 & 3 & 1 & 3 \\ 3 & 8 & 3 & 7 \\ 2 & -3 & 1 & -10 \end{array}\right] \xrightarrow[R_3-2R_1]{R_2-3R_1} \left[\begin{array}{ccc|c} 1 & 3 & 1 & 3 \\ 0 & -1 & 0 & -2 \\ 0 & -9 & -1 & -16 \end{array}\right] \xrightarrow{-R_2} \left[\begin{array}{ccc|c} 1 & 3 & 1 & 3 \\ 0 & 1 & 0 & 2 \\ 0 & -9 & -1 & -16 \end{array}\right]$$
$$\xrightarrow[R_3+9R_2]{R_1-3R_2} \left[\begin{array}{ccc|c} 1 & 0 & 1 & -3 \\ 0 & 1 & 0 & 2 \\ 0 & 0 & -1 & 2 \end{array}\right] \xrightarrow[-R_3]{R_1+R_3} \left[\begin{array}{ccc|c} 1 & 0 & 0 & -1 \\ 0 & 1 & 0 & 2 \\ 0 & 0 & 1 & -2 \end{array}\right]$$

3.
$$\begin{aligned} x+3y+\ z &= \ \ 3 \\ 3x+8y+3z &= \ \ 7; \quad x = -1,\ y=2,\ z=-2 \\ 2x-3y+\ z &= -10 \end{aligned}$$

5. (*a*) Yes (*b*) $(3, -1, 2)$
7. (*a*) Yes (*b*) $(1, 2, t)$ t, a parameter
9. (*a*) Yes (*b*) $(3, -2, 1, 2)$
11. (*a*) Yes (*b*) $(2, -1, 2-t, t)$ t, a parameter
13. $(2, s, t, u)$ s, t, u parameters
15. $(22/5, -9/5)$
17. $(7/9, -1/9, -2/3)$
19. $(19, -7, -15)$
21. $(2, 0, -3)$
23. No solution
25. $(\frac{3}{5}t+\frac{1}{5}, \frac{4}{5}t+\frac{8}{5}, t)$ t, a parameter
27. $(1, 0, -2, -1)$
29. No solution
31. $(-256, -33, -12{,}167)$
33. \$40,000 in a savings account, \$120,000 in mutual funds, \$80,000 in money market certificates
35. 60 compact, 30 intermediate and 10 full-sized cars

37. (*a*)
$$\begin{aligned} x_1 - x_2 \quad\quad\quad\quad &= 200 \\ x_1 \quad\quad - x_5 \quad &= 100 \\ -x_2 + x_3 \quad\quad + x_6 &= 600 \\ -x_3 + x_4 \quad\quad &= 200 \\ x_4 - x_5 + x_6 &= 700 \end{aligned}$$

(*b*) $x_1 = s + 100$, $x_2 = s - 100$, $x_3 = s - t + 500$, $x_4 = s - t + 700$, $x_5 = s$, $x_6 = t$

(250, 50, 600, 800, 150, 50)
(300, 100, 600, 800, 200, 100)

(*c*) (300, 100, 700, 900, 200, 0)

EXERCISES 3.5 page 126

5. $\begin{bmatrix} 1/7 & -2/7 \\ 1/7 & 3/14 \end{bmatrix}$ **7.** $\begin{bmatrix} 2 & -11 & -3 \\ 1 & -6 & -2 \\ 0 & -1 & 0 \end{bmatrix}$ **9.** does not exist

11. $\begin{bmatrix} -13/10 & 7/5 & 1/2 \\ 2/5 & -1/5 & 0 \\ -7/10 & 3/5 & 1/2 \end{bmatrix}$ **13.** $\begin{bmatrix} 3 & 4 & -6 & 1 \\ -2 & -3 & 5 & -1 \\ -4 & -4 & 7 & -1 \\ -4 & -5 & 8 & -1 \end{bmatrix}$ **15.** $x = 24/5$, $y = 23/5$

17. $x = -1$, $y = 3$, $z = 2$ **19.** $x = -2/17$, $y = -10/17$, $z = -60/17$

21. $x_1 = 1$, $x_2 = -4$, $x_3 = 5$, $x_4 = -1$ **23.** (*a*) $A^{-1} = \begin{bmatrix} -5/2 & -3/2 \\ 2 & 1 \end{bmatrix}$

25. (*a*) $ABC = \begin{bmatrix} 4 & 10 \\ 2 & 3 \end{bmatrix}$, $A^{-1} = \begin{bmatrix} 3 & -5 \\ 1 & -2 \end{bmatrix}$, $B^{-1} = \begin{bmatrix} 1 & -3 \\ -1 & 4 \end{bmatrix}$,
$C^{-1} = \begin{bmatrix} 1/8 & -3/8 \\ 1/4 & 1/4 \end{bmatrix}$

EXERCISES 3.6 page 132

1. (*a*) \$10 million (*b*) \$160 million (*c*) agricultural; manufacturing and transportation

3. (*a*) 443.75 million, 381.25 million, and 281.25 million dollar's worth of agricultural products, manufactured goods, and transportation, respectively.
(*b*) 243.75 million, 281.25 million, and 221.25 million dollar's worth of agricultural products, manufactured goods, and transportation, respectively.

5. \$13.3 million and \$17.5 million **7.** \$20, \$20 and \$20 million

Ch. 3 REVIEW EXERCISES page 133

1. $\begin{bmatrix} 2 & 2 \\ -1 & 4 \\ 3 & 3 \end{bmatrix}$ **3.** $\begin{bmatrix} -6 & -2 \end{bmatrix}$ **5.** $\begin{bmatrix} 8 & 9 & 11 \\ -10 & -1 & 3 \\ 11 & 12 & 10 \end{bmatrix}$

7. $\begin{bmatrix} 6 & 18 & 6 \\ -12 & 6 & 18 \\ 24 & 0 & 12 \end{bmatrix}$ **9.** $\begin{bmatrix} -11 & -16 & -15 \\ -4 & -2 & -10 \\ -6 & 14 & 2 \end{bmatrix}$ **11.** $\begin{bmatrix} -3 & 17 & 8 \\ -2 & 56 & 27 \\ 74 & 78 & 116 \end{bmatrix}$

13. \$2,300,000; \$2,450,000 **15.** $x = 1$, $y = -1$

17. $x = 2$, $y = 2t - 5$, $z = t$; t, a parameter **19.** $x = 1$, $y = -1$, $z = 2$, $w = 2$

21. $\begin{bmatrix} 3/4 & -1/2 \\ -1/8 & 1/4 \end{bmatrix}$

23. $\begin{bmatrix} 0 & -1/5 & 2/5 \\ -2 & 1 & 1 \\ -1 & 1/5 & 3/5 \end{bmatrix}$

25. $A^{-1} = \begin{bmatrix} 0 & 1/7 & 2/7 \\ -1 & -4/7 & 6/7 \\ -1/2 & -1/2 & 1/2 \end{bmatrix}$; $x = 3$, $y = -1$, $z = 2$

27. 30 of each type

Chapter 4

EXERCISES 4.1 page 140

1.

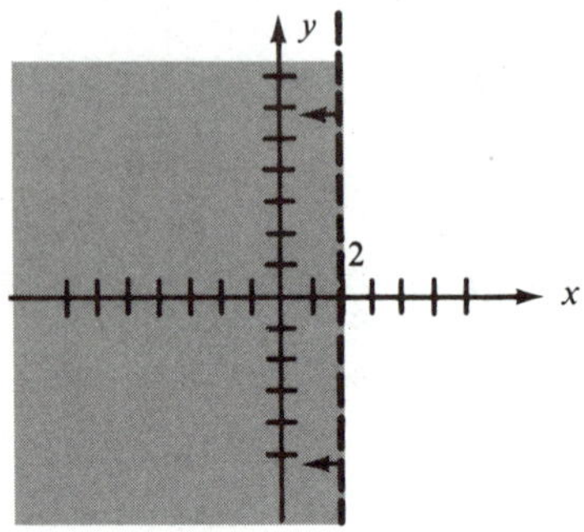

3.

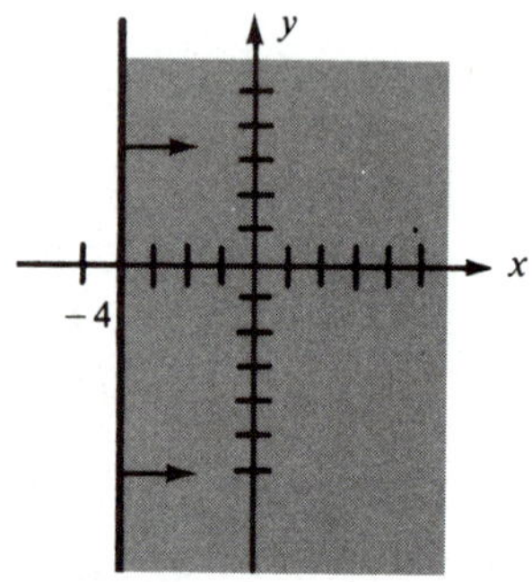

5.

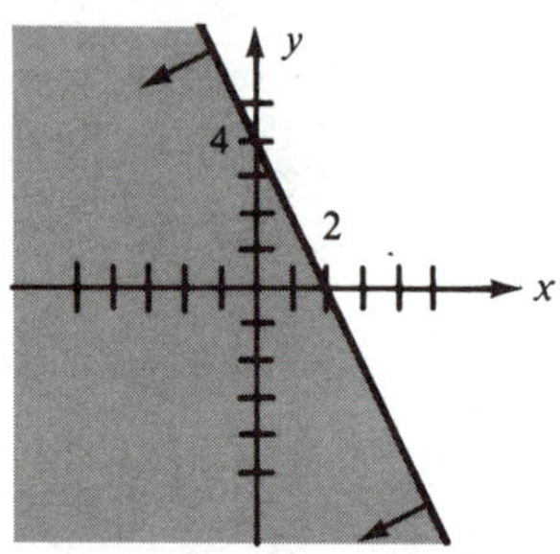

7.

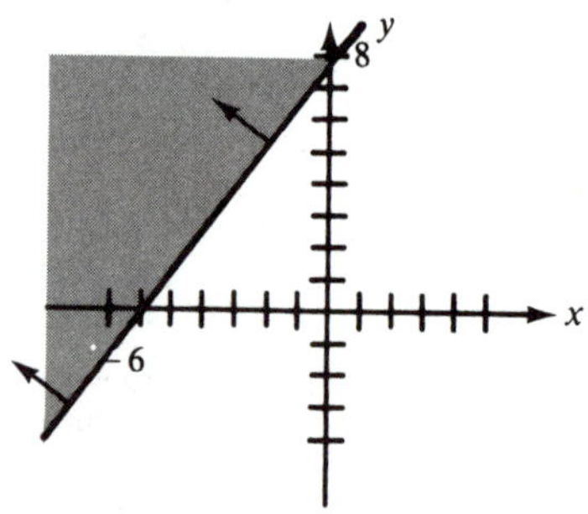

9.

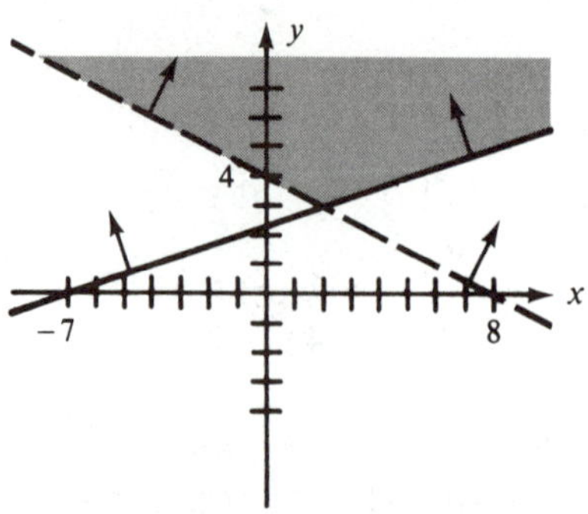

11.

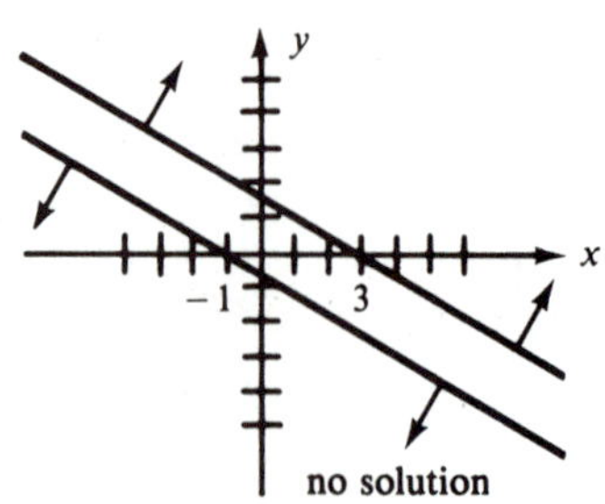

13.

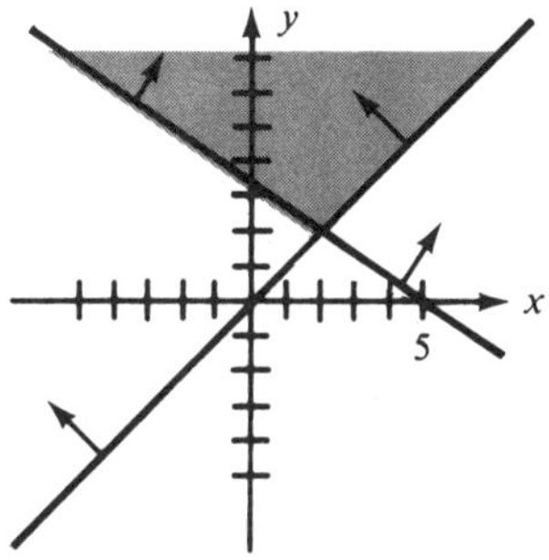

15.

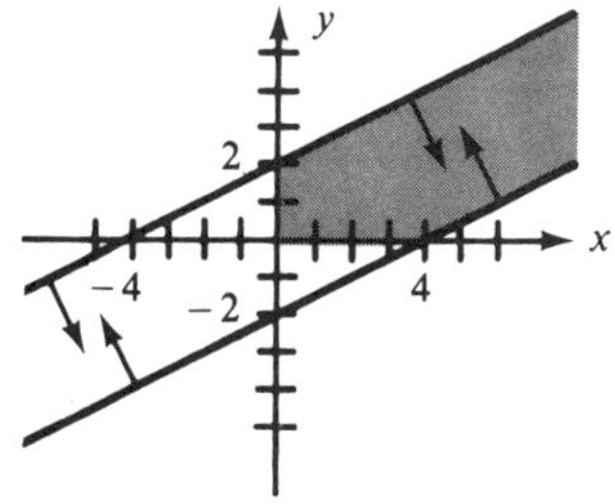

17.

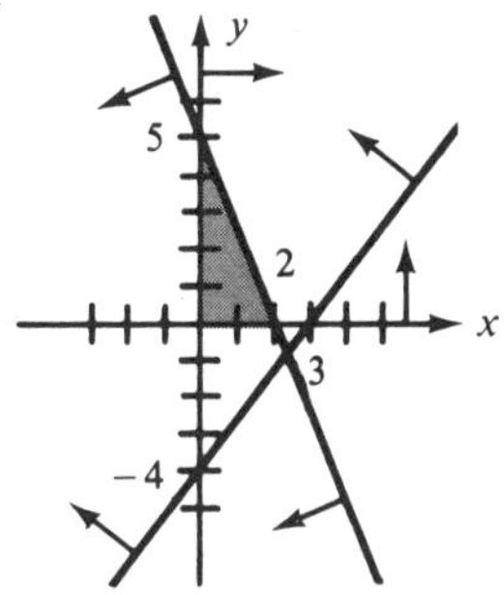

19.

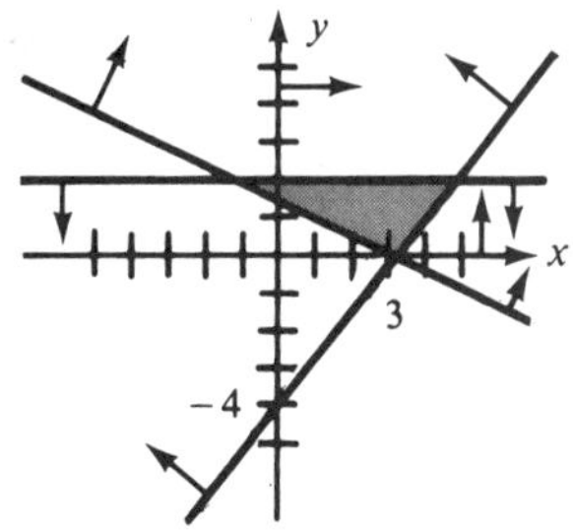

21.

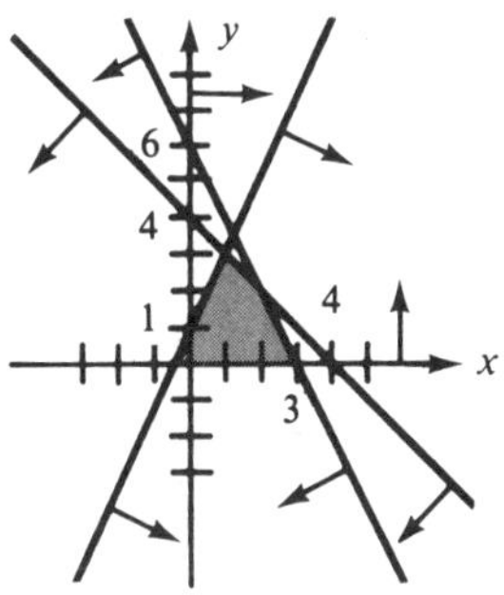

23.

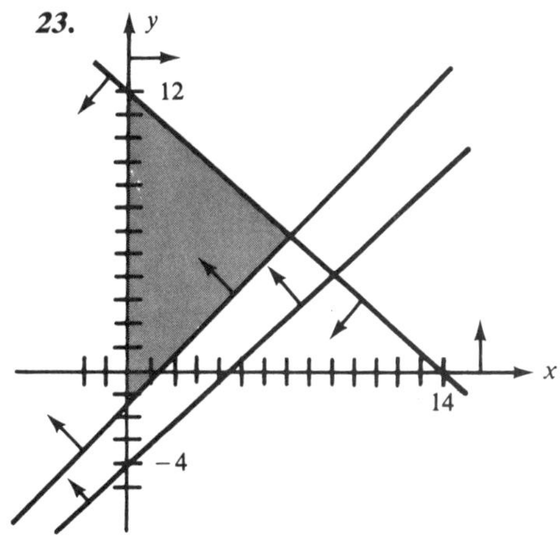

25.

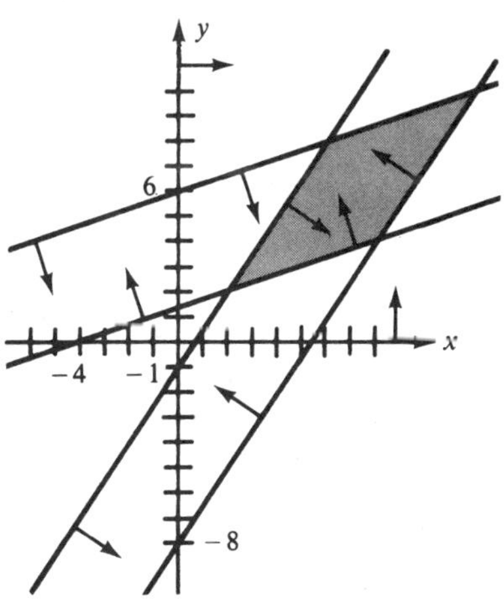

EXERCISES 4.2
page 146

1. Maximize $P = 3x + 4y$ subject to
$$\begin{aligned} 6x + 9y &\le 300 \\ 5x + 4y &\le 180 \\ x \ge 0,\ y &\ge 0 \end{aligned}$$

3. Maximize $P = 2x + (3/2)y$ subject to
$$\begin{aligned} 3x + 4y &\le 1000 \\ 6x + 3y &\le 1200 \\ x \ge 150,\ y &\ge 0 \end{aligned}$$

5. Minimize $C = 2x + 5y$ subject to
$$\begin{aligned} 30x + 25y &\ge 400 \\ x + 0.5y &\ge 10 \\ 2x + 5y &\ge 40 \\ x \ge 0,\ y &\ge 0 \end{aligned}$$

7. Maximize $P = 18x + 12y + 15z$ subject to
$$\begin{aligned} 2x + y + 2z &\le 900 \\ 3x + y + 2z &\le 1080 \\ 2x + 2y + z &\le 840 \\ x \ge 0,\ y \ge 0,\ z &\ge 0 \end{aligned}$$

9. Maximize $P = 26x + 28y + 24z$ subject to
$$\begin{aligned} (5/4)x + (3/2)y + (3/2)z &\le 310 \\ x + y + (3/4)z &\le 205 \\ x + y + (1/2)z &\le 190 \\ x \ge 0,\ y \ge 0,\ z &\ge 0 \end{aligned}$$

11. Minimize $C = 60x_1 + 60x_2 + 80x_3 + 80x_4 + 70x_5 + 50x_6$ subject to
$$\begin{aligned} x_1 + x_2 + x_3 &\le 300 \\ x_4 + x_5 + x_6 &\le 250 \\ x_1 + x_4 &\ge 200 \\ x_2 + x_5 &\ge 150 \\ x_3 + x_6 &\ge 200 \\ x_1 \ge 0,\ x_2 \ge 0,\ \ldots,\ x_6 &\ge 0 \end{aligned}$$

13. Maximize $P = 180x + 200y + 300z$ subject to
$$\begin{aligned} 2.5x + 3y + 4z &\le 70 \\ x &\le 9 \\ y &\le 12 \\ z &\le 6 \\ x \ge 0,\ y \ge 0,\ z &\ge 0 \end{aligned}$$

EXERCISES 4.3
page 155

1. $x = 0,\ y = 6,\ P = 18$

3. $x = 14,\ y = 3,\ C = 58$

5. Any point (x, y) lying on the line segment joining (5, 20) to (12, 6), $C = 90$.

7. $x = 3,\ y = 3,\ C = 75$

9. $x = 15,\ y = 17.5,\ P = 115$

11. $x = 10,\ y = 38,\ P = 134$

13. max: $x = 6,\ y = 33/2,\ P = 258$
min: $x = 15,\ y = 3,\ P = 186$

15. max: $x = 5,\ y = 15,\ P = 70$
min: $x = 0,\ y = 5,\ P = 20$

17. 120 Model A, 160 Model B, $P = \$480$

19. \$16 million in Home Owner loans, \$4 million in Automobile loans; $P = \$2.08$ million

21. 65 acres of Crop A, 80 acres of Crop B, $P = \$25{,}750$

23. 3 oz. of Brand A, 4 oz. of Brand B; $C = 25¢$

25. 750 urban and 750 suburban families; $P = \$2{,}737.50$

EXERCISES 4.4
page 174

1. $x = 30,\ y = 50,\ u = 0,\ v = 0,\ P = 300$

3. $x = 6,\ y = 12,\ u = 0,\ v = 0,\ P = 78$

5. $x = 0,\ y = 10,\ u = 2,\ v = 20,\ P = 120$

7. $x = 15,\ y = 0,\ z = 0,\ u = 0,\ v = 5,\ P = 45$
or $x = 0,\ y = 15,\ z = 0,\ u = 0,\ v = 5,\ P = 45$

9. $x = 5,\ y = 4,\ z = 0,\ u = 0,\ v = 0,\ w = 0,\ P = 13$

11. $x = 0,\ y = 60,\ z = 20,\ u = 40,\ v = 0,\ w = 0,\ P = 200$

13. $x = 0,\ y = 10,\ z = 0,\ t = 0,\ u = 46,\ v = 86,\ w = 22,\ P = 60$

15. 180 units of Product A, 140 units of Product B and 200 units of Product C; maximum profit of \$7920

17. 80 units of Model A, 80 units of Model B and 60 units of Model C; maximum profit of \$5760

19. **9000 bottles Formula I, 7833 bottles Formula II, 6000 bottles Formula III; maximum profit \$4986.67**

EXERCISES 4.5 page 185

1. $x = 4,\ y = 0,\ C = -8$

3. $x = 4,\ y = 3,\ C = -18$

5. $x = 0,\ y = 13,\ z = 18,\ w = 14,\ C = -111$

7. Maximize $P = 4u + 6v$ subject to; $x = 4,\ y = 0,\ C = 8$

$$\begin{aligned} u + 3v &\le 2 \\ 2u + 2v &\le 5 \\ u \ge 0,\ v &\ge 0 \end{aligned}$$

9. Maximize $P = 60u + 40v + 30w$ subject to; $x = 10,\ y = 20,\ C = 140$

$$\begin{aligned} 6u + 2v + w &\le 6 \\ u + v + w &\le 4 \\ u \ge 0,\ v \ge 0,\ w &\ge 0 \end{aligned}$$

11. Maximize $P = 10u + 20v$ subject to; $x = 0,\ y = 0,\ z = 10, C = 1200$

$$\begin{aligned} 20u + v &\le 200 \\ 10u + v &\le 150 \\ u + 2v &\le 120 \\ u \ge 0,\ v &\ge 0 \end{aligned}$$

13. Maximize $P = 10u + 24v + 16w$ subject to; $x = 8,\ y = 0,\ z = 8,\ C = 80$

$$\begin{aligned} u + 2v + w &\le 6 \\ 2u + v + w &\le 8 \\ 2u + v + w &\le 4 \\ u \ge 0,\ v \ge 0,\ w &\ge 0 \end{aligned}$$

15. Maximize $P = 6u + 2v + 4w$ subject to; $x = \frac{1}{3},\ y = \frac{4}{3},\ z = 0,\ C = 26$

$$\begin{aligned} 2u + 6v \qquad &\le 30 \\ 4u \qquad + 6w &\le 12 \\ 3u + v + 2w &\le 20 \\ u \ge 0,\ v \ge 0,\ w &\ge 0 \end{aligned}$$

17. Loc. I: 500 to Warehouse A, 200 to Warehouse B
Loc. II: 200 to Warehouse B, 400 to Warehouse C
Shipping Cost: \$20,800

19. 8 oz. orange juice; 6 oz. pink grapefruit juice; 178 calories.

Ch. 4 REVIEW EXERCISES page 188

1. $x = 0,\ y = 4,\ P = 20$

3. $x = 3,\ y = 10,\ P = 29$

5. $x = 20,\ y = 0,\ C = 40$

7. max: $x = 22,\ y = 0,\ Q = 22$
min: $x = 3,\ y = 5/2,\ Q = 11/2$

9. $x = \dfrac{56}{5},\ y = \dfrac{2}{5},\ z = 0,\ u = 0,\ v = 0,\ P = 23\dfrac{3}{5}$

11. $x = \dfrac{3}{4},\ y = 0,\ z = \dfrac{7}{4},\ C = 60$

13. \$40,000 in each company, $P = \$13{,}600$

15. \$70,000 in blue chip stocks; \$30,000 in speculative stocks

Chapter 5

EXERCISES 5.1 page 195

1. (*a*) 16 (*b*) $\frac{9}{64}$ (*c*) 1

3. (*a*) $\frac{1}{144}$ (*b*) $-\frac{1}{3}$ (*c*) 729

5. (*a*) 27 (*b*) −32 (*c*) 7

7. (*a*) $\frac{1}{12}$ (*b*) 0.3 (*c*) 2

9. (*a*) 64 (*b*) 2 (*c*) $\frac{1}{9}$

11. (*a*) T (*b*) T (*c*) F (*d*) F (*e*) F (*f*) T

13. (*a*) $\frac{1}{x^2y^2}$ (*b*) $\frac{3}{s^2}$ (*c*) $\frac{1}{x^{5/6}}$ (*d*) $\frac{a}{4b^2}$ (*e*) $\frac{3}{x^2}$ (*f*) $\frac{1}{2y^{1/3}}$

15. (*a*) $\frac{1}{7}x$ (*b*) $2x^{11/6}$ (*c*) x

17. (*a*) x^{-3} (*b*) x^{-1} (*c*) a^{-4m}

19. (*a*) 2.828 (*b*) 2.828 (*c*) 5.196 (*d*) 2.449

21. 4.729 *23.* $x=3$ *25.* $x=2$

27. $x=\frac{5}{4}$ *29.* $x=1, 2$

EXERCISES 5.2 page 201

1.

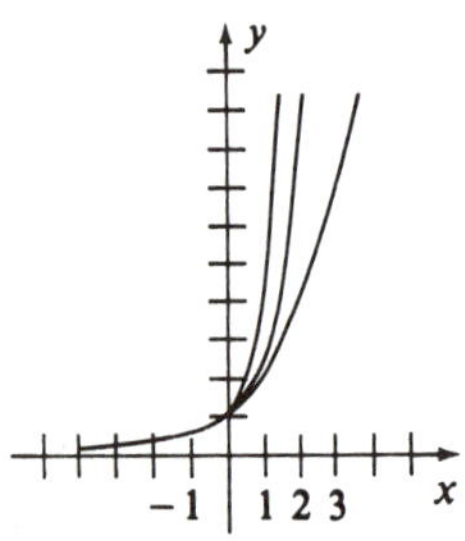

3.

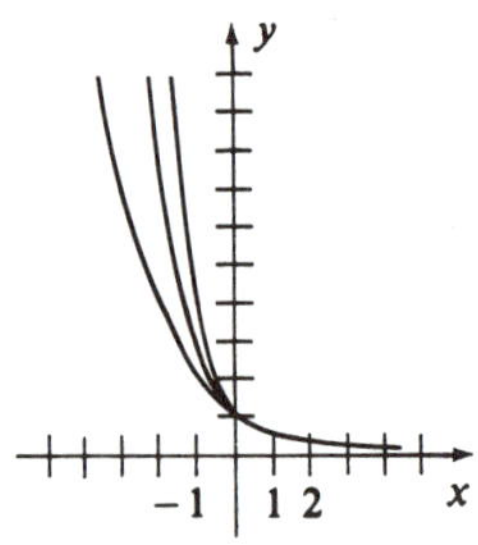

5.

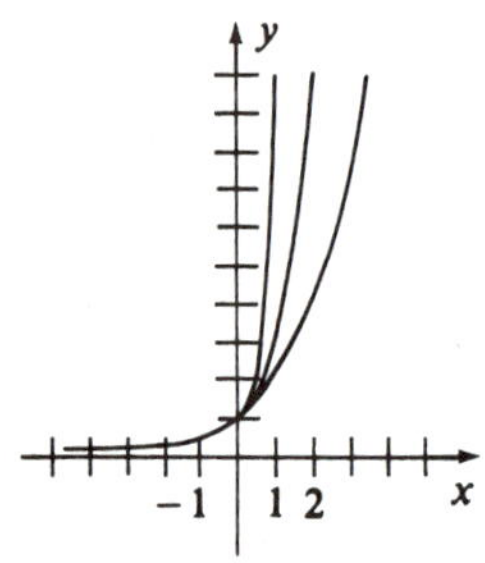

7.

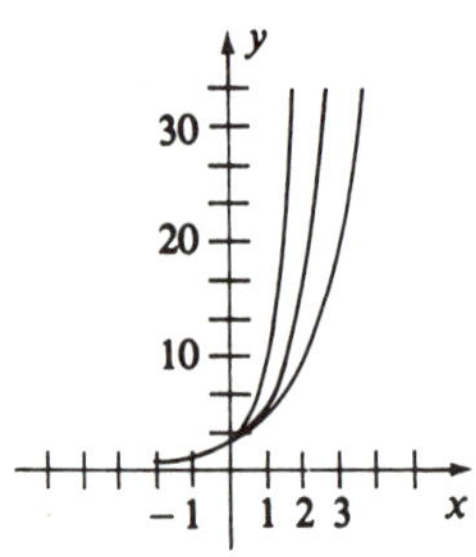

9.

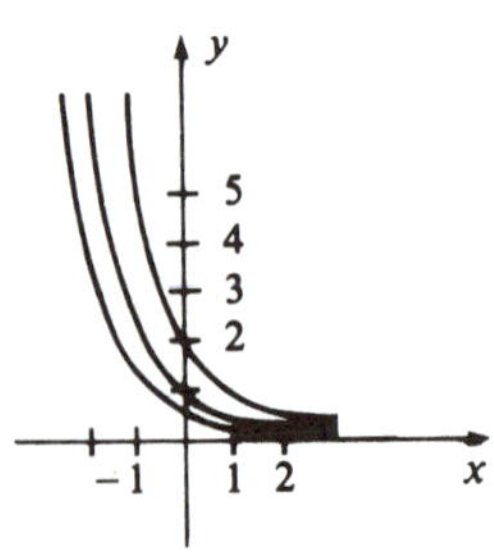

11.

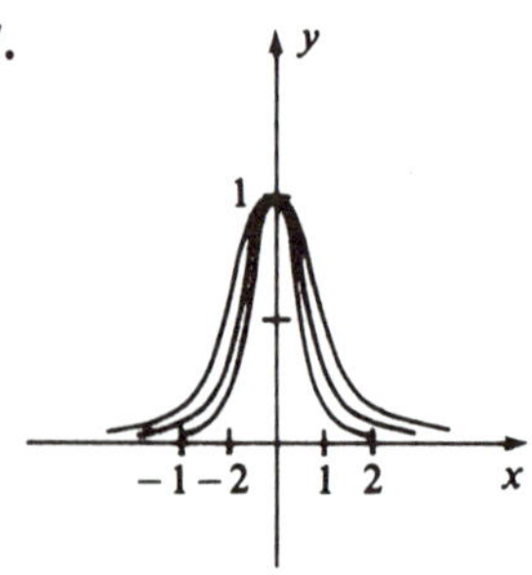

EXERCISES 5.3 page 207

1. (*a*) $\log_2 64=6$ (*b*) $\log_7 1=0$ *3.* (*a*) $\log_5 \frac{1}{125}=-3$ (*b*) $\log_{1/3} \frac{1}{3}=1$

5. (*a*) $\log_b c=2a$ (*b*) $\log_{10}(.001)=-3$ *7.* (*a*) $x=-4$ (*b*) $x=\frac{2}{3}$

9. (*a*) $x = 3$ (*b*) $x = 8$ **11.** (*a*) $x = \frac{7}{4}$ (*b*) $x = 1$

13. (*a*) 9 (*b*) -1 (*c*) 2

15. (*a*) 1.0792 (*b*) -0.125 (*c*) 1.2042 (*d*) 0.2386 (*e*) 1.6813 (*f*) -2.4771

17. $t = -0.331$ **19.** $t = 0.251$ **21.** $t = 2(\ln B - \ln A)$

23.

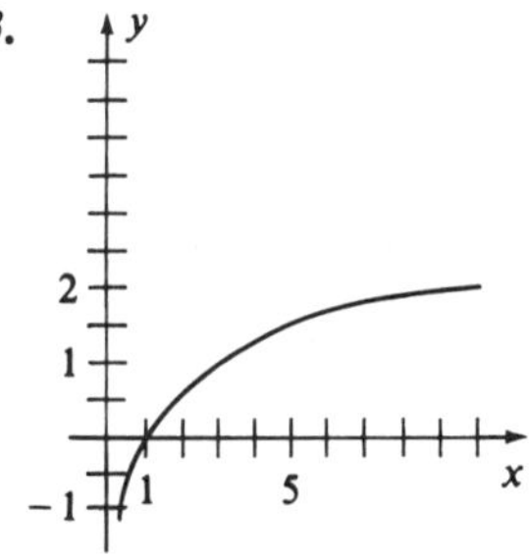

25.

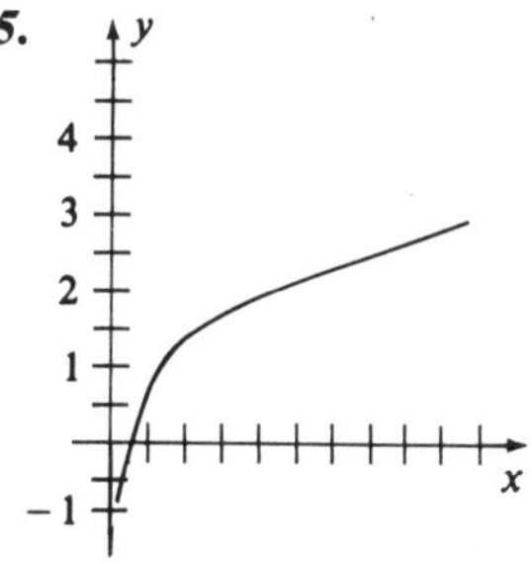

27.

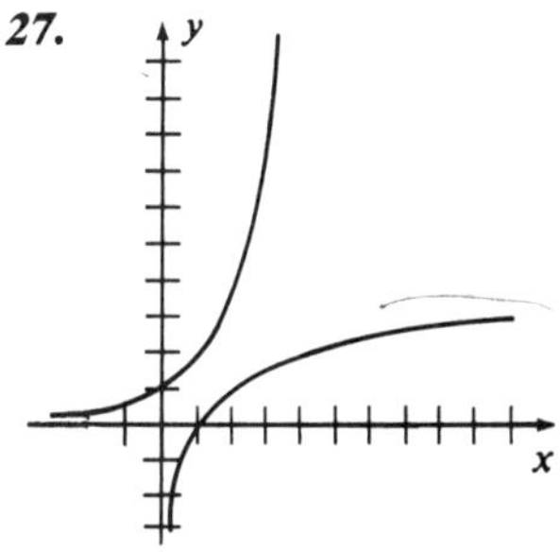

29. (*a*) $I = 10^5 I_0$ (*b*) $I = 10^8 I_0$; 1000 times (*c*) 1585 times

31. (*a*) $k = 0.6931$

EXERCISES 5.4 page 216

1. (*a*) .05 (*b*) 400

(*c*)

t	0	10	20	100	1000
Q	400	660	1087	59365	2.07×10^{24}

(*d*) 13.86 min.

3. $Q(t) = 100e^{.035t}$; 263 min: $Q(t) = 1000e^{.035t}$

5. (*a*) 54.93 years (*b*) 1.21×10^{10} **7.** \$176,198

9. $Q(t) = 100e^{-.049t}$; 70.6 grams **11.** 13,412 years

13.

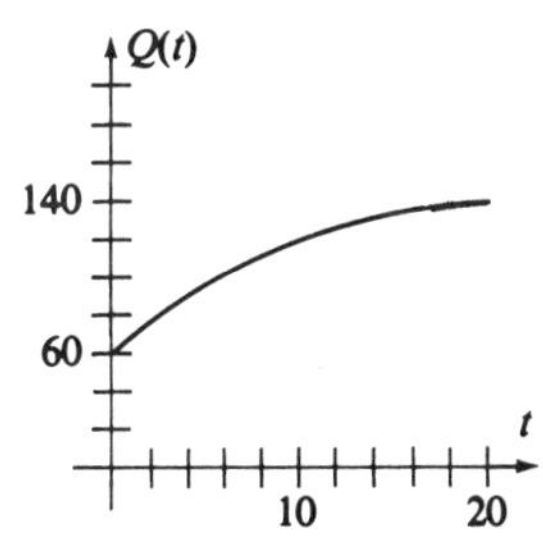

(*a*) 60 w.p.m.
(*b*) 107 w.p.m.
(*c*) 136 w.p.m.

15.

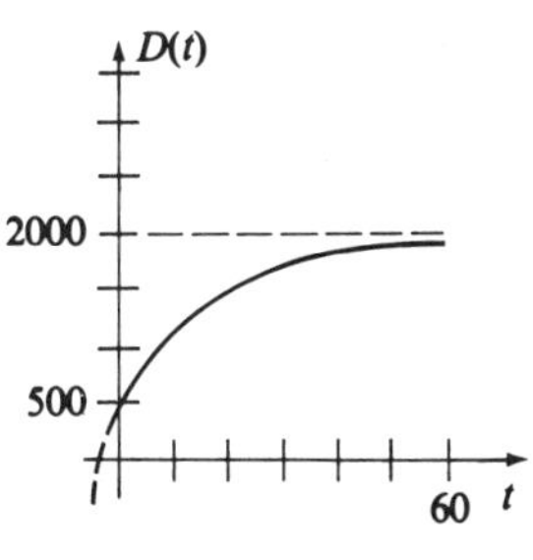

(*a*) 573 computers; 1177 computers; 1548 computers; 1925 computers
(*b*) 2000 computers

17. (*a*) 2 (*b*) 749 (*c*) 1000 **19.** 1080

Ch. 5 REVIEW EXERCISES page 220

1. (*a*) $\frac{1}{12}$ (*b*) $\frac{1}{243}$ (*c*) $\frac{1}{4}$

3. (*a*) $x=3$ (*b*) $x=-1.1552$

5. (*a*) $\log_{2/3}\frac{27}{8}=-3$ (*b*) $\log_{16}(0.125)=-\frac{1}{4}$

7. (*a*) $x+y+z$ (*b*) $2y+x-z$ (*c*) $2z+y$

9. (*a*) $Q(t)=2000e^{1.1t}$ (*b*) 162,902

11.

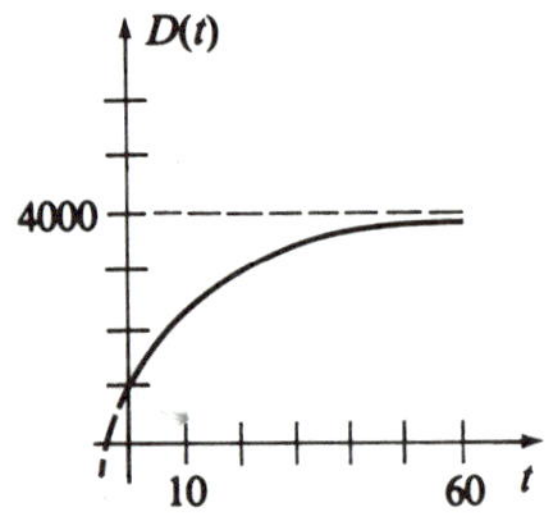

(*a*) 1175 players; 2540 players; 3289 players
(*b*) 4000 players

Chapter 6

EXERCISES 6.1 page 228

1. 30 ***3.*** −4.5 ***5.*** −3, 8, 19, 30, 41

7. $x+6y$ ***9.*** 795 ***11.*** 792

13. 550 ***15.*** (*a*) 275 (*b*) −280

17. 76 days ***19.*** $7.90 ***21.*** (*b*) $800

23. G.P.; 256; 508 ***25.*** not a G.P. ***27.*** G.P.; $\frac{1}{3}$; $364^{1/3}$

29. 3; 0 ***31.*** 293,866 ***33.*** $33,667.38

35. annual raise of 8% per year

37. (*a*) $20,113.60 (*b*) $87,537.33

EXERCISES 6.2 page 237

1. $1718.19 ***3.*** $4974.48 ***5.*** $27,566.88

7. $261,751.50 ***9.*** $214,983 ***11.*** $10\frac{1}{4}$%

13. 8.3% ***15.*** $29,227.60 ***17.*** $30,255.96

19. $25,165.80 ***21.*** (*a*) $37,518.25 (*b*) $12,518.25

23. $670.84 ***25.*** 116% ***27.*** $3.795 million

29. 11.72% ***31.*** $26,267.58 ***33.*** $7167.89 ***35.*** $15,000

37. (*a*) 9% (*b*) 9.202% (*c*) 9.308% (*d*) 9.381%

39. $40,000; double-declining balance method

EXERCISES 6.3 page 244

1. $15,937.40 ***3.*** $54,759.60 ***5.*** $37,965.60

7. $28,733.19 ***9.*** $15,558.62 ***11.*** $15,011.28

13. $109,658.81 ***15.*** $453.05 ***17.*** $6080.40

19. $490,907.50

EXERCISES 6.4 page 249

1. \$16,274.53 *3.* (*a*) \$295 (*b*) \$1580; \$527
5. (*a*) \$193.60; \$152.18 (*b*) \$969.60; \$1304.64
7. \$658.31; \$17,495.74; \$20,212.67; \$34,115.46
9. \$3135.47 *11.* \$14,497.38

Ch. 6 REVIEW EXERCISES page 251

1. (*a*) 49 (*b*) 397.5
3. (*a*) \$7320.50 (*b*) \$7387.30 (*c*) \$7422.55 (*d*) \$7446.75
5. \$40,000 *7.* \$5557.65
9. \$2,592,695; \$8,612,000 *11.* \$218.64
13. (*a*) \$1011.10 (*b*) \$207,330 (*c*) \$35,753.43

Chapter 7

EXERCISES 7.1 page 258

1. (*a*) $n(A)=4$ (*b*) $n(B)=5$ (*c*) $n(A\cup B)=7$ (*d*) $n(A\cap B)=2$
3. $n(B)=20$
5. (*a*) 140 (*b*) 100 (*c*) 120 (*d*) 40 (*e*) 60 (*f*) 60
7. 60, 10, 30
9. (*a*) 106 (*b*) 64 (*c*) 38 (*d*) 14
11. (*a*) 64 (*b*) 72 (*c*) 10
(*d*) 13 (*e*) 38 (*f*) 36
(*g*) 36 (*h*) 15 (*i*) 64
13. (*a*) 373 (*b*) 219 (*c*) 131 (*d*) 96

EXERCISES 7.2 page 263

1. 12 *3.* 64 *5.* 24
7. 24 *9.* 108 *11.* 4096
13. 17,576,000 *15.* 2,340,000 *17.* 217

EXERCISES 7.3 page 272

1. (*a*) 20 (*b*) 720 (*c*) 60
3. (*a*) 35 (*b*) 1 (*c*) 1
5. 120 *7.* 5040 *9.* 45 *11.* 665,280
13. (*a*) 3,628,800 (*b*) 5184 *15.* (*a*) 120 (*b*) 36
17. 369,600 *19.* (*a*) 848 (*b*) 37
21. (*a*) 220 (*b*) 55 (*c*) 185
23. 336 *25.* 1575 *27.* 56 *29.* 15

Ch. 7 REVIEW EXERCISES page 276

1. (*a*) 150 (*b*) 230 (*c*) 270
(*d*) 30 (*e*) 70 (*f*) 200
3. (*a*) 60 (*b*) 125 *5.* (*a*) 446 (*b*) 377 (*c*) 34
7. (*a*) 1287 (*b*) 288 *9.* 1050
11. (*a*) 487,635 (*b*) 550 (*c*) 341,055

Chapter 8

EXERCISES 8.1 page 281

1. $S=\{(n,n,n),(n,n,d),(n,d,n),(n,d,d),(d,n,n),(d,n,d),(d,d,n),(d,d,d)\}$

3. (*a*) {1, 2, 3, 4, 5} (*b*) {2} (*c*) {1, 3, 5)}

5. (*a*) {(H, 1), (H, 2), (H, 3), (H, 4), (H, 5), (H, 6), (T, 1), (T, 2), (T, 3), (T, 4), (T, 5), (T, 6)}
(*b*) {(H, 2), (H, 4), (H, 6)}

7. (*a*) ∅, {1}, {2}, {3}, {1, 2}, {1, 3}, {2, 3}, {1, 2, 3} (*b*) 4 (*c*) 4

9. (*a*) $\{x|x>0\}$ (*b*) $\{x|0<x\leq 2\}$ (*c*) $\{x|x>2\}$

11. {(A, E), (A, F), (A, G), (A, H), (B, E), (B, F), (B, G), (B, H), (C, E), (C, F), (C, G), (C, H), (D, E), (D, F), (D, G), (D, H)}

EXERCISES 8.2 page 290

1.

Grade	A	B	C	D	F
Probability	.10	.25	.45	.15	.05

3.

Number of calls received/minute	10	11	12	13	14	15	16	17	18	19
Probability	.05	.125	.1	.025	.1	.3	.2	0	.05	.05

5. (*a*) 1/4 (*b*) 1/2 (*c*) 1/13 ***7.*** (*a*) 1/6 (*b*) 11/36

9. 3/8 ***11.*** .65 ***13.*** (*a*) .00001 (*b*) .00531

15. (*a*) 1/6 (*b*) 5/6 (*c*) 1

EXERCISES 8.3 page 297

1. 12/13 ***3.*** $P(S)\neq 1$

5. Since the 5 events are not mutually exclusive property 3 cannot be used; that is, he or she could win more than one purse.

7. Since the 4 events are not mutually exclusive, property 3 cannot be used; that is, he or she could be admitted to more than one school.

9. $P(G\cup C)^c\neq 1-P(G)-P(C)$; he has not considered the case where customers buy both glasses and contact lenses.

11. (*a*) 1/52 (*b*) 4/13 (*c*) 9/13

13. (*a*) 1/2, 3/8 (*b*) 1/2, 5/8 (*c*) 1/8 (*d*) 3/4

15. (*a*) .5 (*b*) .5 (*c*) .1

17. (*a*) .81 (*b*) .53 (*c*) .19

19. (*a*) .90 (*b*) .40 (*c*) .40

EXERCISES 8.4 page 304

1. (*a*) 1/32 (*b*) 5/32 (*c*) 31/32 ***3.*** (*a*) .042 (*b*) .420 (*c*) .659

5. (*a*) 1/4 (*b*) 3/8 (*c*) 7/8 ***7.*** (*a*) .022 (*b*) .312

9. (*a*) .005 (*b*) .145 ***11.*** (*a*) .120; .013 (*b*) .15; .015

13. 1/729 ***15.*** (*a*) .0001 (*b*) .0018 (*c*) .0504 (*d*) .2916

17. (*a*) .0000154 (*b*) .00392 (*c*) .00197

19. (*a*) .618 (*b*) .059 ***21.*** .03

EXERCISES 8.5 page 319

1. (*a*) .4 (*b*) .33 ***3.*** (*a*) .8 (*b*) .75

5. (*a*) .24 (*b*) .76 ***7.*** (*a*) 1/4 (*b*) 13/51 (*c*) 12/51

9. (*a*) .5 (*b*) .4 (*c*) .2 (*d*) .35 (*e*) No (*f*) No

11. (*a*) 5/12 (*b*) 5/8 *13.* .012 *15.* .1875

17. (*a*) (*1*) .28 (*2*) .39 (*3*) .18 (*4*) .643 (*5*) .292 (*b*) No

19. not independent *21.* (*a*) .0000001 (*b*) .927 (*c*) .071

23. .0000068

EXERCISES 8.6 page 327

1. (*a*) 1/12 (*b*) 1/4 (*c*) 1/18 (*d*) 3/14

3. (*a*) .025 (*b*) .24 (*c*) .24

5. (*a*) .497 (*b*) .959

7. .407 *9.* (*a*) .4906 (*b*) .62 (*c*) .186

11. (*a*) .543 (*b*) .545 (*c*) .456

EXERCISES 8.7 page 342

1. Yes *3.* No *5.* $X_0T = [.4\ \ .6]$

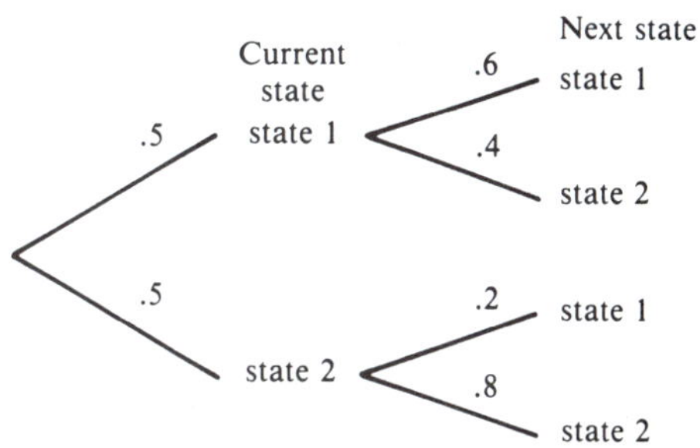

7. (*a*) Vote is evenly split (*b*) Republican

9. 37% Univ. Bookstore; 35% Campus Bookstore; 28% Book-Mart;
34.5% Univ. Bookstore; 31.35% Campus Bookstore; 34.15% Book-Mart.

11. 14% elec., 42.75% gas, 31.7% oil, 11.55% solar

13. not regular *15.* not regular

17. [10/11 1/11] *19.* [3/13 3/13 7/13]

21. (*a*) 40.8% 1-wage earner; 59.2% 2-wage earners
(*b*) 30% 1-wage earner; 70% 2-wage earners

23. (*a*) 31.7% ABC, 37.35% CBS, 30.95% NBC
(*b*) $33\frac{1}{3}$% ABC, $33\frac{1}{3}$% CBS, $33\frac{1}{3}$% NBC

Ch. 8 REVIEW EXERCISES page 346

1. (*a*) 0 (*b*) .6 (*c*) .6 (*d*) .4 (*e*) 1

3. (*a*) .49 (*b*) .39 (*c*) .48 *5.* (*a*) .019 (*b*) .981

7. (*a*) .284 (*b*) .984 *9.* 2/15 *11.* .457 *13.* .368

Chapter 9

EXERCISES 9.1 page 356

1. any positive integer

3. (*a*) See (b).

(*b*)

Outcome	GGG	GGR	GRG	RGG	GRR	RGR	RRG	RRR
Value	3	2	2	2	1	1	1	0

(*c*) GGG

5. any positive integer; infinite discrete

7. $0 \le x \le \infty$; continuous

9. any positive integer; infinite discrete

11. (a) .20 (b) .60 (c) .30 (d) 1

13. .35

15. (a)

x	2	3	4	5	6	7	8
$P(X=x)$	.35	.20	.245	.125	.066	.01	.004

(b)

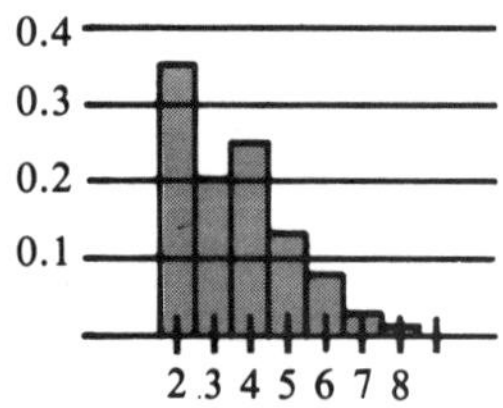

EXERCISES 9.2 page 366

1. (a) 2.6 (b)

x	0	1	2	3	4
$P(X=x)$	0	.1	.4	.3	.2

; 2.6

3. .86 5. $78.50 7. .91 9. .12 11. −49¢ 13. $48.96

15. (a) Dahl: 8.52; Farthington: 7.25 (b) Farthington Auto Sales

17. (a) 7:3 (b) 3:7

19. .43

21. −10.5¢

23. (b) −$15.79

25. mean: $5.94; mode: $6.00; median: $5.95

EXERCISES 9.3 page 377

1. $\mu = 2$, $V(x) = 1$, $\sigma = 1$

3. $\mu = 0$, $V(x) = 1$, $\sigma = 1$

5. (a)

7. (a) Venture A: $\mu = \$25{,}000$; $V(x) = 8.85 \times 10^8$;
Venture B: $\mu = \$24{,}000$; $V(x) = 3.99 \times 10^8$
(b) Venture A (c) Venture B

9. 1

11. $\mu = \$98{,}200$; $V(x) = 7.75 \times 10^8$, $\sigma = \$27{,}800$

13. (a) at least .75 (b) at least .96

15. at least 75%

17. at least 7/16

19. $c = .1$

EXERCISES 9.4 page 388

1. (a) $P(X=0) \approx .08$, $P(X=1) \approx .26$, $P(X=2) \approx .35$, $P(X=3) \approx .23$, $P(X=4) \approx .08$ $P(X=5) \approx .01$

(b)

x	0	1	2	3	4	5
$P(X=x)$	.08	.26	.35	.23	.08	.01

(c) $\mu = 2$, $\sigma = 1.1$

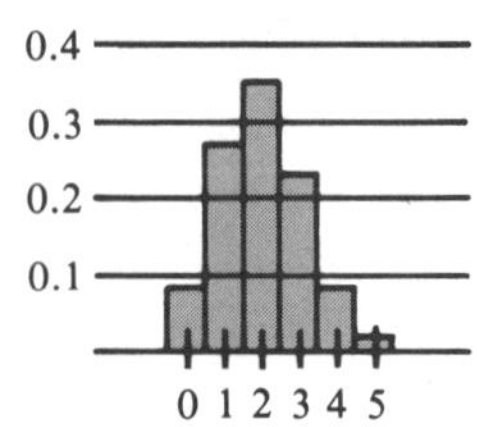

3. No; probability that at most 1 is defective is .74

5. $\approx .116$

7. $\approx .0002$

9. (a) $\approx .633$ (b) $\approx .367$

11. ≈.010 ***13.*** (***a***) ≈.817 (***b***) ≈.999 ***15.*** (***a***) ≈.075 (***b***) ≈.012

17. (***a***) ≈.122 (***b***) ≈.359 ***19.*** ≈.349 ***21.*** $\mu = 375; \sigma \approx 9.68$

EXERCISES 9.5
page 399

1. .9265 ***3.*** .0401 ***5.*** .8657

7. (***a***)

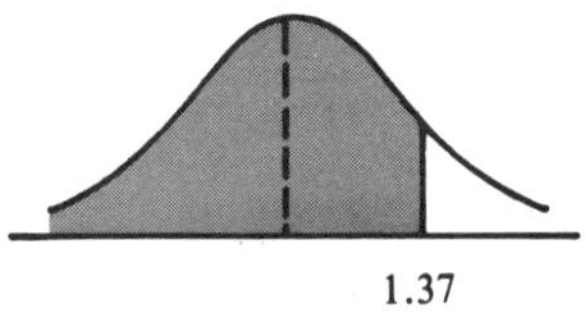

(***b***) .9147

9. (***a***)

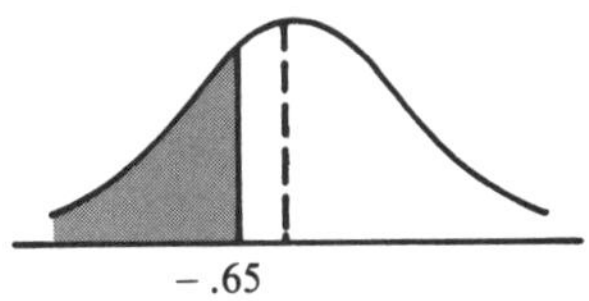

(***b***) .2578

11. (***a***)

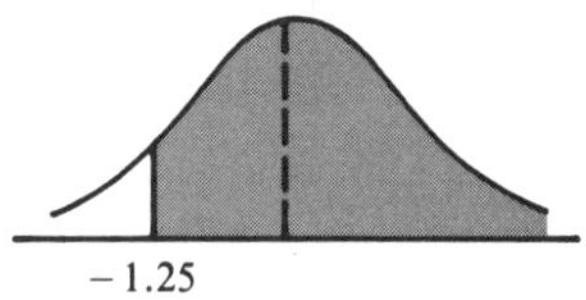

(***b***) .8944

13. (***a***)

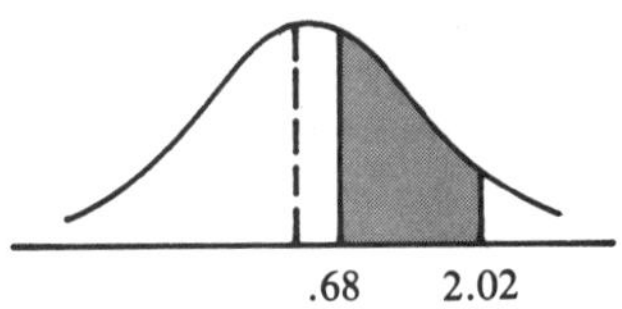

(***b***) .2266

15. (***a***) 1.23 (***b***) −.81 ***17.*** (***a***) .8944 (***b***) .1525 (***c***) .1587

EXERCISES 9.6
page 407

1. (***a***) .2206 (***b***) .2206 (***c***) .3034

3. (***a***) .0228 (***b***) .0228 (***c***) .4772 (***d***) .7258

5. (***a***) .0038 (***b***) .0918 (***c***) .4082 (***d***) .2514 ***7.*** 15.87%

9. 92.5 ***11.*** (***a***) .1314 (***b***) .9406 (***c***) .5649

13. .0228 ***15.*** .6736 ***17.*** .8686 ***19.*** .1515

Ch. 9 REVIEW EXERCISES
page 410

1. \$95.88

3. (***a***)

x	0	1	2	3	4
$P(X = x)$	.1296	.3456	.3456	.1536	.0256

(***b***) $\mu = 1.6, \sigma = .98$

5. (***a***) 2.42 (***b***) −1.05 (***c***) −2.03 (***d***) 1.42

7. .2646; .9163 ***9.*** at least .75 ***11.*** 0.6% ***13.*** .9997

Chapter 10

EXERCISES 10.1 page 422

1.

x	0.9	0.99	0.999	1.001	1.01	1.1
$f(x)$	2.9	2.99	2.999	3.001	3.01	3.1

; $\lim_{x\to 1}(x+2)=3$

3.

x	1.9	1.99	1.999	2.001	2.01	2.1
$f(x)$	4.61	4.960	4.996	5.004	5.04	5.41

; $\lim_{x\to 2}(x^2+1)=5$

5.

x	−0.1	−0.01	−0.001	0.001	0.01	0.1
$f(x)$	−1	−1	−1	1	1	1

; $\lim_{x\to 0}\frac{|x|}{x}$ does not exist

7.

x	1.9	1.99	1.999	2.001	2.01	2.1
$f(x)$	−10	−100	−1000	1000	100	10

; $\lim_{x\to 2}\frac{1}{x-2}$ does not exist

9.

x	−0.1	−0.01	−0.001	0.001	0.01	0.1
$f(x)$	0.952	0.995	0.9995	1.0005	1.005	1.052

; $\lim_{x\to 0}\frac{e^x-1}{x}=1$

11. The limit exists ***13.*** does not exist ***15.*** does not exist

17.

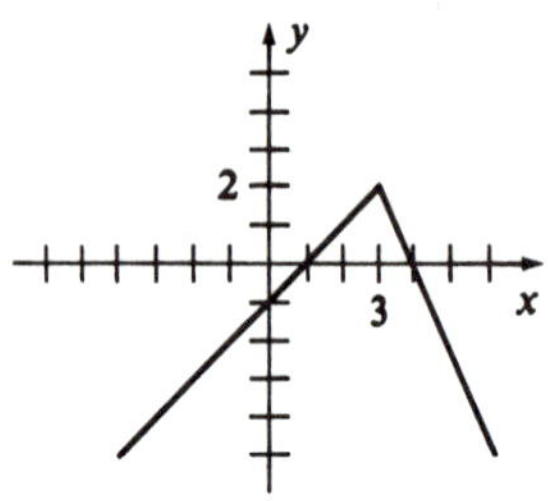

$\lim_{x\to 3} f(x) = 2$

19.

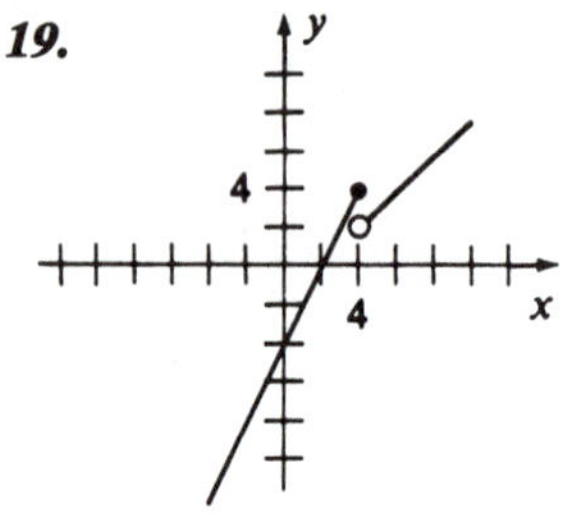

$\lim_{x\to 4} f(x)$ does not exist

21.

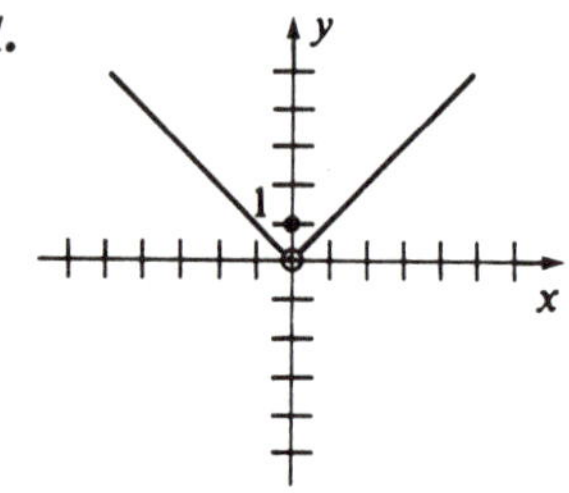

$\lim_{x\to 0} f(x) = 0$

23. 3 ***25.*** 31 ***27.*** 45 ***29.*** 0 ***31.*** does not exist

33. 12 ***35.*** −3 ***37.*** 5/3

39. 2 ***41.*** 4 ***43.*** 4/3

45.

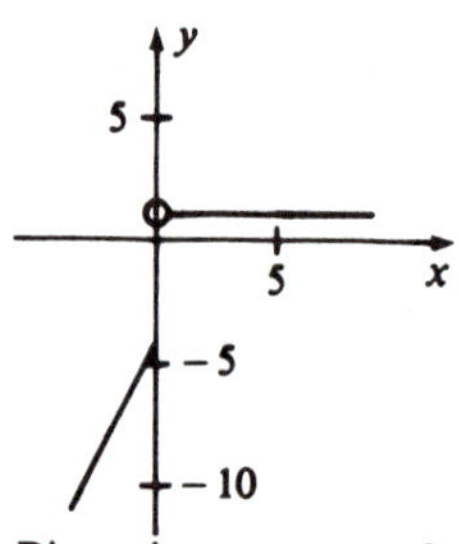

Discontinuous at $x = 0$; condition 2 is violated

47.

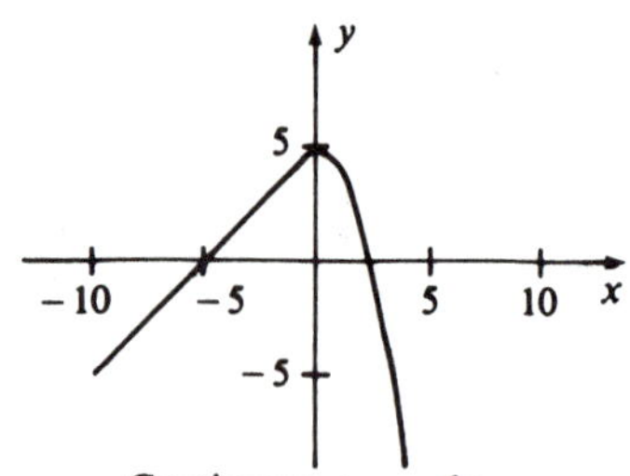

Continuous everywhere

49.

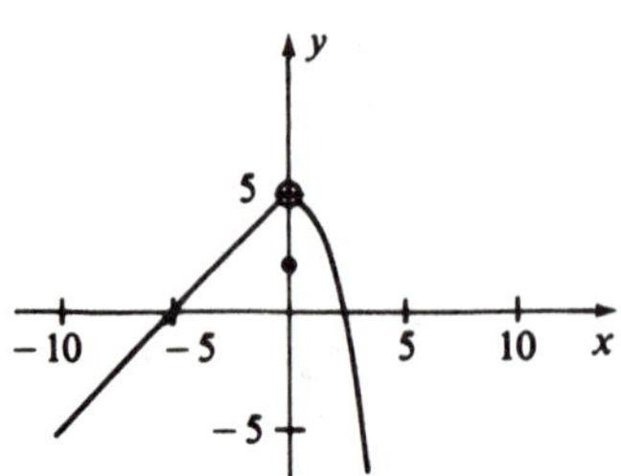

Discontinuous at $x = 0$; condition 2 is violated

51.

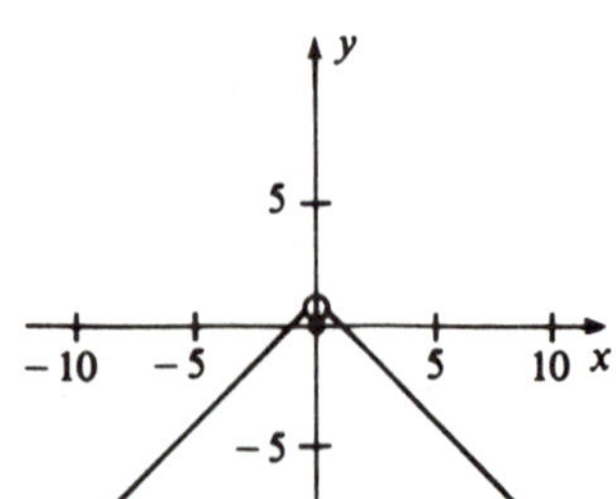

Discontinuous at $x = 0$; condition 2 is violated

53. −1 and 1 ***55.*** 1 and 2 ***57.*** Discontinuous at $x = 1, 2, 3, \ldots, 11$.

59.
$$f(t)=\begin{cases}1 & \text{if } 0<t\le 1/2\\ 1.5 & \text{if } 1/2<t\le 1\\ 2.0 & \text{if } 1<t\le (3/2)\\ \ldots & \\ 5 & \text{if } t>4\end{cases}$$

f is discontinuous at $t = 1/2, 1, 3/2, \ldots, 4$

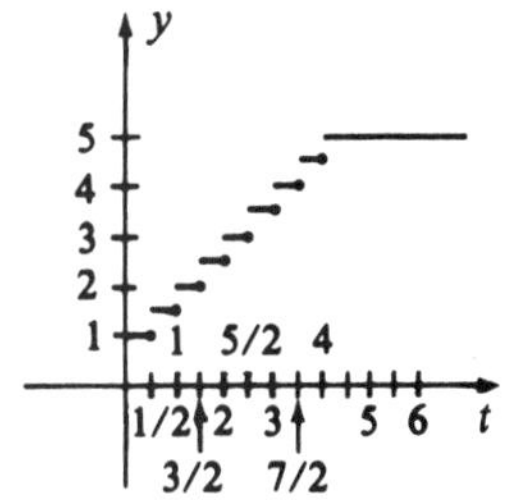

EXERCISES 10.2 page 432

1.

x	1	10	100	1000	−1	−10	−100	−1000
$f(x)$	0.5	0.0099	0.0001	0.0000	0.5	0.0099	0.0001	0.0000

$$\lim_{x\to\infty}\frac{1}{x^2+1}=\lim_{x\to-\infty}\frac{1}{x^2+1}=0$$

3.

x	1	5	10	100	1000	−1	−5	−10	−100	−1000
$f(x)$	12	360	2910	2,990,010	2.999×10^9	6	−390	−3090	−3,009,990	-3.001×10^9

$\lim_{x\to\infty}(3x^3-x^2+10)=\infty$, $\lim_{x\to-\infty}(3x^3-x^2+10)=-\infty$

5.

x	1	9	16	25	100	10,000	1,000,000
$f(x)$	0	0.5	0.6	0.6667	0.8182	0.9802	0.9980

$$\lim_{x\to\infty}\frac{\sqrt{x}-1}{\sqrt{x}+1}=1$$

7.

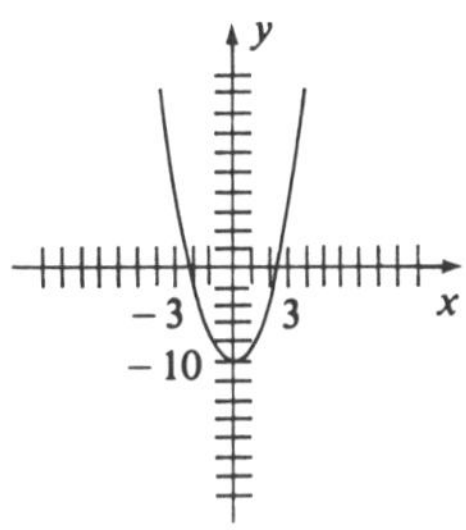

$\lim_{x\to\infty}(2x^2-10)=$

$\lim_{x\to-\infty}(2x^2-10)=\infty$

9.

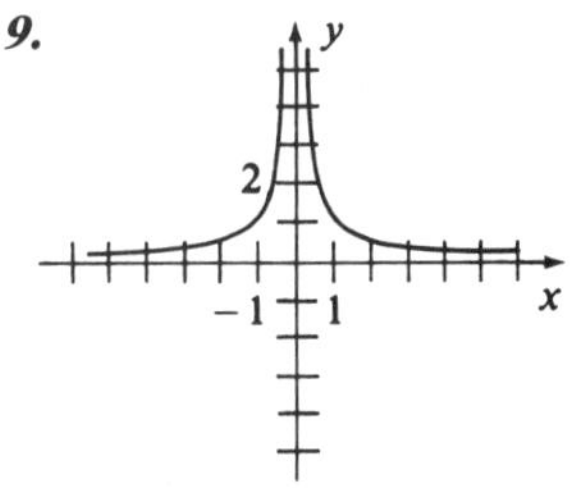

$$\lim_{x\to\infty}\frac{1}{x^2}=\lim_{x\to-\infty}\frac{1}{x^2}=0$$

11.

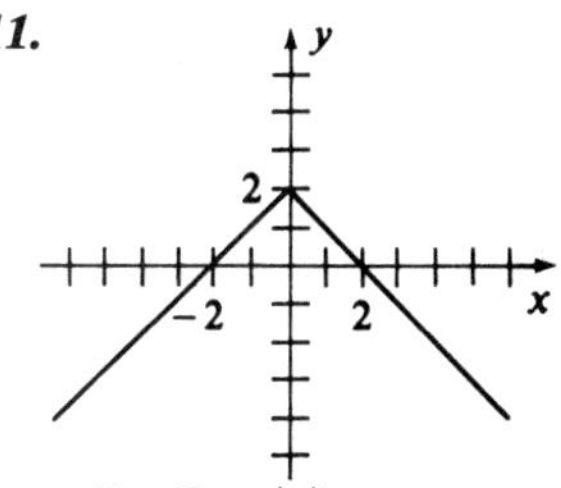

$\lim_{x\to\infty}(2-|x|)=$

$\lim_{x\to-\infty}(2-|x|)=-\infty$

13. 3 ***15.*** 3 ***17.*** 2 ***19.*** 2 ***21.*** $2\sqrt{2}$ ***23.*** \$7459.12

25. Investment A ***27.*** 15.74% per annum

29. $80{,}000\,e^{\sqrt{t/2}-0.09t}$; \$151,719

31. (***a***) 10.381% (***b***) 10.471% (***c***) 10.517%

EXERCISES 10.3 page 441

1. (***b***) (*1*) 4; 3; 2.5; 2.1; 2.01 (*2*) 2
(***c***) (*1*) $x^2+2x\,\Delta x+(\Delta x)^2$ (*3*) $2x$ (*4*) 2

3. 0 ***5.*** −4 ***7.*** $-x$ ***9.*** 2; $y=2x+7$

11. 6; $y = 6x - 3$ ***13.*** (***a***) 6; 5.5; 5.1 (***b***) 5

15. (***a***) 48 ft/sec; 56 ft/sec; 62.4 ft/sec (***b***) 64 ft/sec
(***c***) −32 ft/sec; falling (***d***) t = 8 secs.

EXERCISES 10.4 page 449

1. $8x$ ***3.*** $-4-8x$ ***5.*** $-\dfrac{1}{(x+2)^2}$ ***7.*** $9x^2$ ***9.*** $\dfrac{1}{2\sqrt{x+1}}$

11. 8; $y = 8x - 5$ ***13.*** $\dfrac{1}{9}$; $y = \dfrac{1}{9}x - \dfrac{2}{3}$ ***15.*** $\dfrac{1}{2}$; $y = \dfrac{1}{2}x + 2$

17. (***a***) $3x^2$
(***b***)

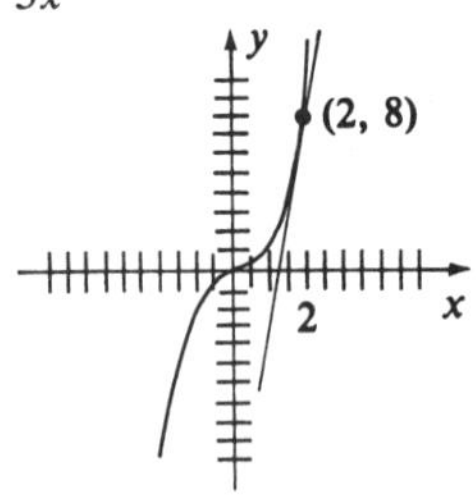

(***c***) $y = 12x - 16$

19. (***a***) $2x + 6$
(***b***) $(-3, -9)$
(***c***)

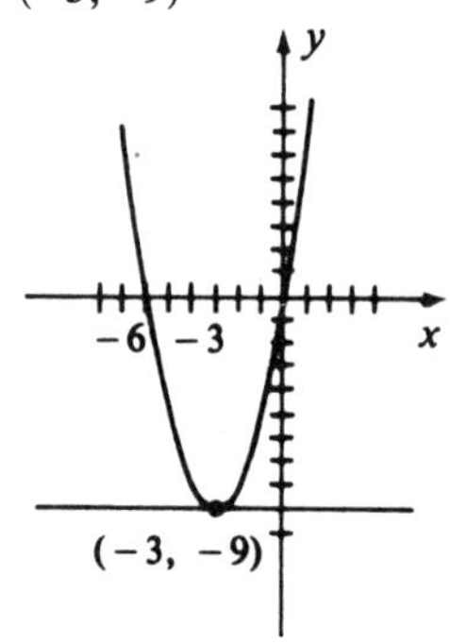

21. 62 bacteria per minute ***23.*** (***a***) Yes (***b***) No (***c***) No

25. (***a***) Yes (***b***) Yes (***c***) No

27. (***a***) No (***b***) No (***c***) No

29.

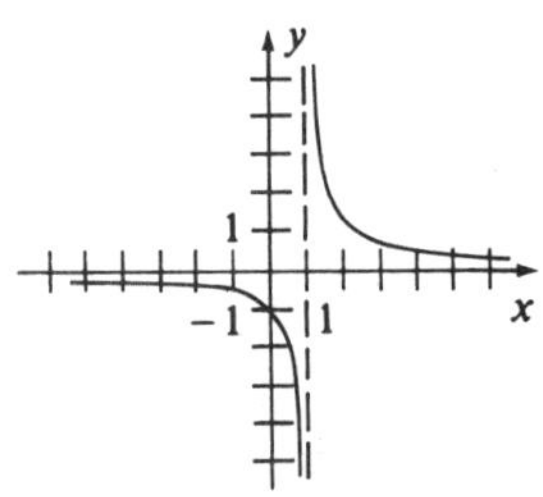

EXERCISES 10.5 page 459

1. 0 ***3.*** $5x^4$ ***5.*** 2π ***7.*** $45x^{29}$

9. $\dfrac{3}{x^{2/3}}$ ***11.*** $\dfrac{3}{2\sqrt{x}}$ ***13.*** $10x - 3$ ***15.*** $\dfrac{-(3x+8)}{x^3}$

17. $20x^3 - 2x^2 + 2x - 3$ ***19.*** $x^2 + \dfrac{4}{3}x + \dfrac{1}{3}$

21. $5w^4 - 4w^3 + 9w^2 - 6w + 2$ ***23.*** $x^4 + 4x^3 - 3x^2 - 1$

25. $\dfrac{-2x}{(x^2+1)^2}$ ***27.*** $\dfrac{x^2-1}{x^2}$ ***29.*** $\dfrac{x(x^3+3x+4)}{(x^2+1)^2}$

31. $\dfrac{x^2-2x-2}{(x^2+x+1)^2}$ ***33.*** $\dfrac{2x^3-5x^2-4x-3}{(x-2)^2}$ ***35.*** 0

37. $e^x + 1$

39. $e^x + ex^{e-1}$

41. $(\ln 5)5^x$

43. $\dfrac{3}{x}$

45. $\dfrac{1}{(\ln 2)x}$

47. $\dfrac{2(1-\ln x)}{x^2}$

49. $\dfrac{e^x(x^3 \ln x - 2x^2 \ln x - x \ln x + x^2 - 1)}{x(x^2-1)^2}$

51. $-2;\ y = -2x + 2$

53. $\dfrac{3}{16};\ y = \dfrac{3}{16}x + \dfrac{7}{4}$

55. $-\dfrac{1}{2};\ y = -\dfrac{1}{2}x + \dfrac{3}{2}$

57. (***a***) $(-2, -7), (2, 9)$

(***b***) $y = 12x + 17$ and $y = 12x - 15$

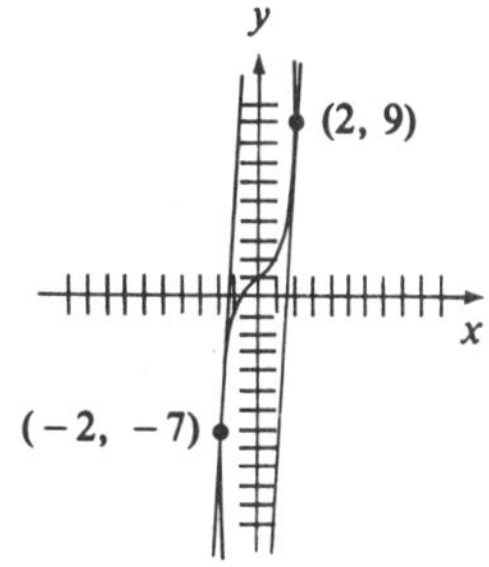

63. 63,000; 60,000; 55,000; 48,000; Yes

65. (***a***) $N'(t) = \dfrac{180}{(t+6)^2}$

(***b***) 3.67, 2.22, 1.80, 1.07

(***c***)

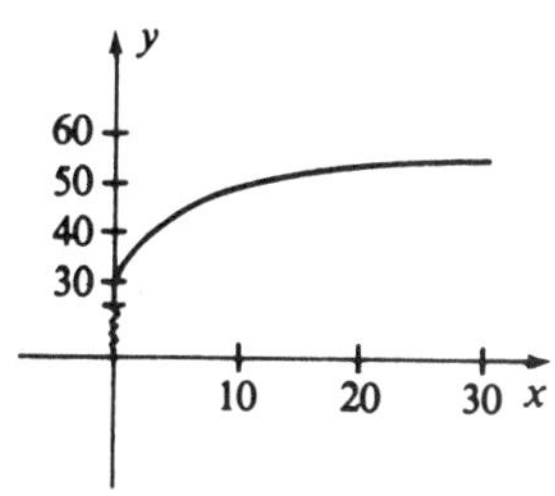

(***d***) 50 words per minute

67. (***a***) $v = f'(t) = -6t^2 + 228t + 480$

(***b***) 480 ft/sec, 2640 ft/sec, 0 ft/sec, −7440 ft/sec

(***c***) 73,601 feet

EXERCISES 10.6 page 469

1. $6x^2(x^3+1)$

3. $(x^2+x+1)(6x^3+9x^2+13x+5)$

5. $\dfrac{-2x^3(x^2-2)}{(x^4-2x^2+2)^2}$

7. $\dfrac{7-4x}{2\sqrt{7x-2x^2}}$

9. $\dfrac{4x(1-3x)}{3\sqrt[3]{(2x^3-x^2+1)^5}}$

11. $\dfrac{2(3x+1)}{3x^2+2x}$

13. $10x(x^2+1)^9[2+(x^2+1)^5]\,e^{(x^2+1)^5}$

15. $10x(x^2+2)^4$

17. $\dfrac{6t-1}{2\sqrt{3t^2-t}}$

19. $18t(2t-1)(4t^3-3t^2+1)^2$

21. $2x(18x^2+1)(3x^2+1)^4$

23. $-2u(1+u^2)^4(1-2u^2)^7(26u^2+11)$

25. $\dfrac{2(x^2-x+1)^7(9x^5-5x^4+x^3-8x+4)}{\sqrt{x^4-1}}$

27. $\dfrac{3(u^2+u-1)^2(u^4+u^2-2u-1)}{(u^3-1)^2}$

29. $\dfrac{x+\sqrt{x^2-1}}{2\sqrt{x^2-1}\sqrt{x+\sqrt{x^2-1}}}$

31. $25\,e^x(e^x+1)^{24}$ **33.** $\dfrac{e^x(1-e^x)}{(e^x+1)^3}$ **35.** $\dfrac{5(1+2\ln x)^{3/2}}{x}$

37. $e^{x^2}\left(\dfrac{1}{x}+2x(\ln x)\right)$ **39.** $\dfrac{4(1+\ln x)^3+x\,e^x}{2x\sqrt{(1+\ln x)^4+e^x}}$

41. $5x+8y=26$ **43.** $x-y=2-\ln 4$

45. .333 million/week; .304 million/week; 16 million; 22.7 million

47. 20.6% drop in consumption/% increase in tax;
28.9% drop in consumption/% increase in tax;
38.6% drop in consumption/% increase in tax

EXERCISES 10.7
page 479

1. (*a*) \$1.80/record; \$1.60/record (*b*) \$1.80/record; \$1.60/record

3. (*a*) $A(x)=2+\dfrac{5000}{x}$ (*b*) $A'(x)=-\dfrac{5000}{x^2}$

5. $A(x)=0.0002x^2-0.06x+120+\dfrac{5000}{x}$; $A'(x)=0.0004x-0.06-\dfrac{5000}{x^2}$

7. (*a*) $P(x)=-0.04x^2+600x-300{,}000$
(*b*) $P'(x)=-0.08x+600$
(*c*) 200; −40
(*d*)

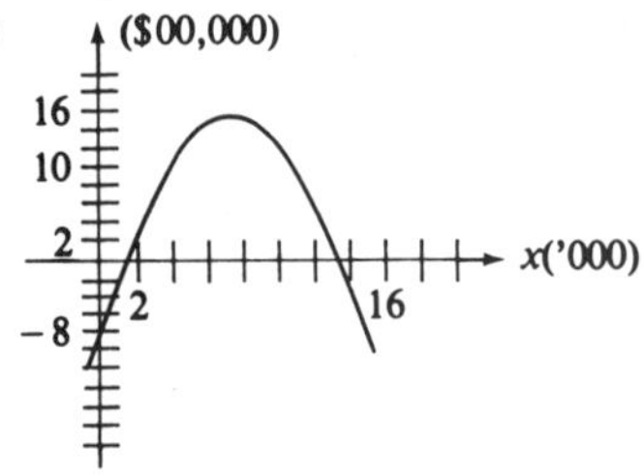

9. $A(x)=0.000002x^2-0.03x+400+\dfrac{80{,}000}{x}$

(*a*) $A'(x)=0.000004x-0.03-\dfrac{80{,}000}{x^2}$

(*b*) −0.0132; 0.0092

(*c*)

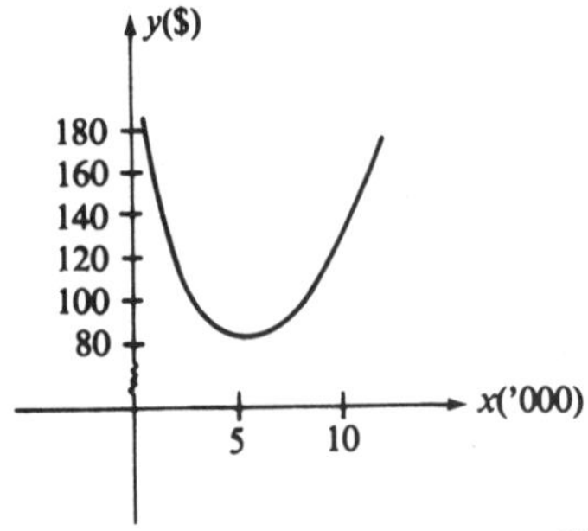

11. $A(x)=0.000002x^2-0.02x+120+\dfrac{60{,}000}{x}$

(*a*) $A'(x)=0.000004x-0.02-\dfrac{60{,}000}{x^2}$

(*b*) −0.0024, 0.0194

EXERCISES 10.8 page 484

1. $f'(x)=8x-2;\ f''(x)=8$

3. $h'(t)=4t^3-6t^2+12t-3;$ $h''(t)=12t^2-12t+12$

5. $f'(x)=20x(x^2+2)^9;\ f''(x)=20(19x^2+2)(x^2+2)^8$

7. $f'(x)=\frac{7}{2}x^{5/2};\ f''(x)=\frac{35}{4}x^{3/2}$

9. $f'(u)=\frac{1-u^2}{(u^2+1)^2};\ f''(u)=\frac{2u(u^2-3)}{(u^2+1)^3}$

11. $f'(x)=x(2+x)e^x;\ f''(x)=(2+4x+x^2)e^x$

13. $h'(x)=\frac{e^x}{(1+e^x)^2};\ h''(x)=\frac{e^x(1-e^x)}{(1+e^x)^3}$

15. $f'(x)=\frac{1}{\sqrt{2x-1}};\ f''(x)=\frac{-1}{\sqrt{(2x-1)^3}}$

17. $f'(x)=\frac{x(x^2-2)}{\sqrt{(x^2-1)^3}};\ f''(x)=\frac{x^2+2}{\sqrt{(x^2-1)^5}}$

19. $h'(r)=-2re^{-r^2};\ h''(r)=2(2r^2-1)\,e^{-r^2}$

25. (*a*) $v=t(t^2/4-3t+8)$ (*b*) 0 ft/sec; 0 ft/sec; 0 ft/sec
(*c*) $a=(3/4)t^2-6t+8$ (*d*) 8 ft/sec^2; -4 ft/sec^2; 8 ft/sec^2
(*e*) 0 ft; 16 ft; 0 ft

Ch. 10 REVIEW EXERCISES page 486

1. -3 *3.* -21 *5.* -1 *7.* 7

9. 3/2 *11.* 1 *13.* $x=2$ *15.* $x=-1$

17. 12% per year *19.* (*a*) 3, 2.5, 2.1 (*b*) 2

21. -4; $y=-4x+4$ *23.* $24x^5$ *25.* $4t-9t^2$

27. $\frac{1}{\sqrt{x}(\sqrt{x}+1)^2}$ *29.* $\frac{2x(x^4-2x^2-1)}{(x^2-1)^2}$ *31.* $\frac{(1+2t)\,e^t}{2\sqrt{t}}+1$

33. $\frac{1+e^x-x\,e^x\ln x}{x(1+e^x)^2}$ *35.* $72x^2(3x^3-2)^7$

37. $\frac{-4t}{3(1-2t^2)^{2/3}}$ *39.* $4x\,e^{2x^2-1}$

41. $\frac{e^r(1+r-r^2+r^3)}{(1+r^2)^2}$ *43.* (*a*) $(-1, 14)$; $(2, -25)$ (*b*) $y=-4x+10$ and $y=-4x-17$

45. 0 *47.* 200

49. (*a*) $-0.02x^2+600x$ (*b*) $-0.04x+600$ (*c*) 200

Chapter 11

EXERCISES 11.1 page 496

1. f is constant on $(-\infty, \infty)$

3. increasing on $(-1/4, \infty)$; decreasing on $(-\infty, -1/4)$

5. increasing on $(-\infty, -3)\cup(1, \infty)$; decreasing on $(-3, 1)$

7. increasing on $(-1, 0)\cup(3/2, \infty)$; decreasing on $(-\infty, -1)\cup(0, 3/2)$

9. increasing on $(0, 1)\cup(1, \infty)$; decreasing on $(-\infty, -1)\cup(-1, 0)$

11. increasing on $(-\infty, 0)\cup(0, \infty)$

13. increasing on $(-\infty, 0) \cup (2, \infty)$; decreasing on $(0, 1) \cup (1, 2)$

15. increasing on $(0, \infty)$

17. decreasing on $(-\infty, 1/4) \cup (1/4, \infty)$

19. increasing on $(-\infty, -4) \cup (4, \infty)$; decreasing on $(-4, 0) \cup (0, 4)$

21. increasing on $(2, \infty)$; decreasing on $(-\infty, 2)$

23. increasing on $(-\infty, 0)$; decreasing on $(0, \infty)$

25. increasing on $(0, 2)$; decreasing on $(-\infty, 0) \cup (2, \infty)$

27. decreasing on $(0, \infty)$

31. rising in the time interval $(0, 2)$; falling in the time interval $(2, 5)$; when $t = 5$

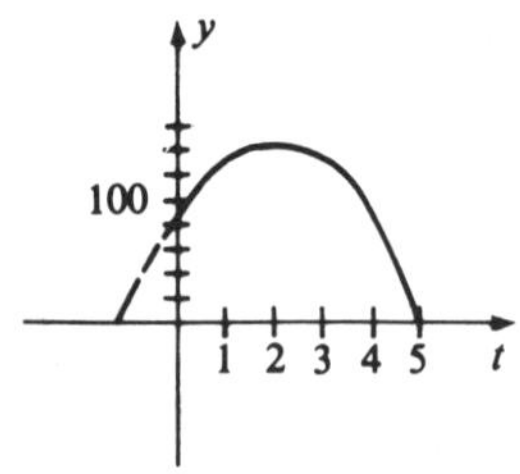

33. increasing on $(0, 4000)$; decreasing on $(4000, \infty)$

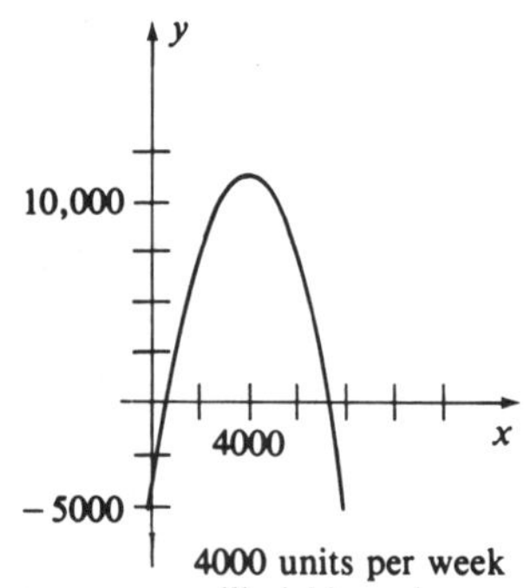

35. (*a*) 30

(*b*) $N'(x) = \dfrac{297{,}000\, e^{-x}}{(1 + 99e^{-x})^2}$

(*c*) 3000

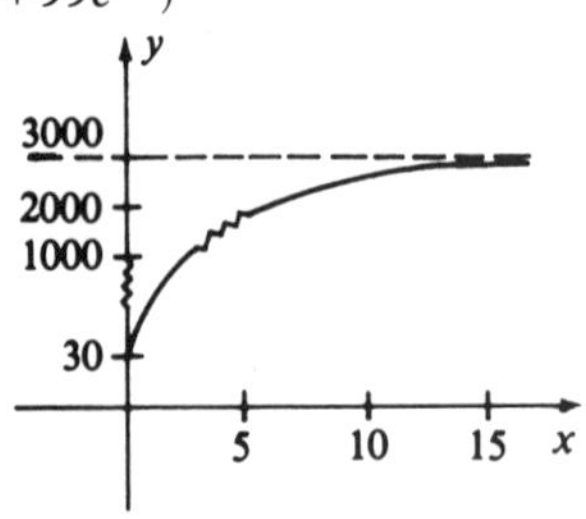

EXERCISES 11.2
page 503

1. rel. min $(0, 2)$

3. rel. min $(2, 2)$

5. rel. max $(-1, 8)$; rel. min $(1, 4)$

7. rel. max $(-1/2, 37/8)$; rel. min $(2/3, 82/27)$
9. rel. max $(0, 0)$; rel. min $(-1, -1/2)$ and $(1, -1/2)$
11. rel. min $(-2, -4)$
13. rel. max $(-2, 84)$; rel. min $(2, -44)$
15. rel. max $(-3, -4)$; rel. min $(3, 8)$
17. rel. max $(0, -1)$
19. rel. max $(-2, 4e^{-2})$; rel. min $(0, 0)$
21. rel. max $(2, 4e^{-2})$; rel. min $(0, 0)$
23. rel. min $(0, 0)$
25. rel. min $(1, 1)$

EXERCISES 11.3 page 511

7. f is concave down on $(-\infty, 0) \cup (0, \infty)$
9. g is concave up on $(-\infty, 1)$ and concave down on $(1, \infty)$
11. f is concave up on $(-\infty, 0) \cup (3, \infty)$ and concave down on $(0, 3)$
13. h is concave up on $(1, \infty)$ and concave down on $(-\infty, 0) \cup (0, 1)$
15. f is concave up on $(-\infty, -1/\sqrt{3}) \cup (1/\sqrt{3}, \infty)$ and concave down on $(-1/\sqrt{3}, 1/\sqrt{3})$
17. h is concave up on $(1, \infty)$ and concave down on $(-\infty, 1)$
19. f is concave up on $(1, \infty)$ and concave down on $(-\infty, 1)$
21. h is concave down on $(-\infty, 2) \cup (2, \infty)$
23. g is concave upward everywhere
25. f is concave up on $(-\infty, 0)$ and concave down on $(0, \infty)$
27. g is concave up on $(-\infty, -1) \cup (1, \infty)$ and concave down on $(-1, 0) \cup (0, 1)$
31. $(-1/3, 2687/324)$ and $(1, 173/12)$
33. $(-\sqrt{2}, 0)$ and $(\sqrt{2}, 0)$
35. $(-\sqrt{2}/2, e^{-1/2})$ and $(\sqrt{2}/2, e^{-1/2})$
37. $(-1, \ln 2)$ and $(1, \ln 2)$
41. $(\ln \sqrt[k]{B}, A/2)$
43. yes
45. $(266.67, 11{,}874.08)$

EXERCISES 11.4 page 516

1. rel. max $(-1, -\frac{22}{3})$; rel. min $(5, -\frac{130}{3})$
3. rel. min $(3, -27)$
5. rel. max $(-1, -2)$; rel. min $(1, 2)$
7. rel. min $(-1, \ln 4)$

EXERCISES 11.5 page 525

1.
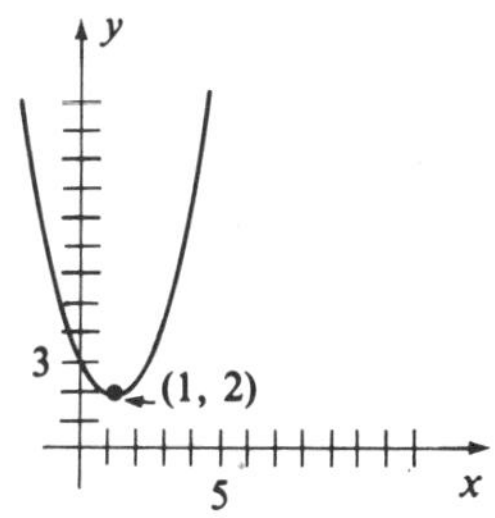

3.
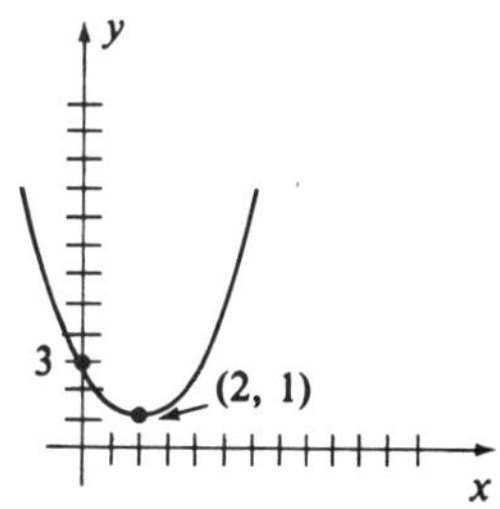

5.
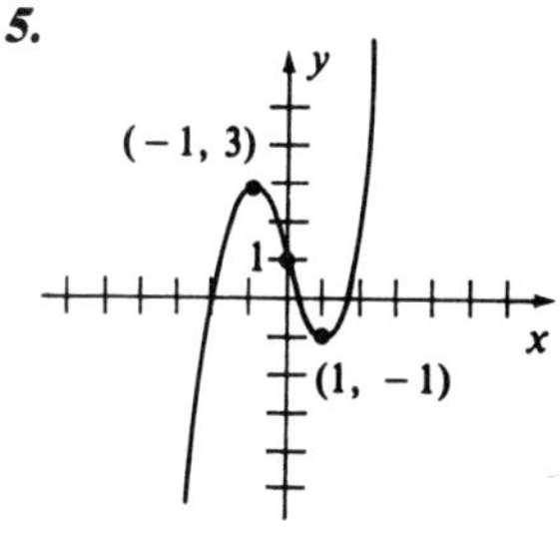

7.

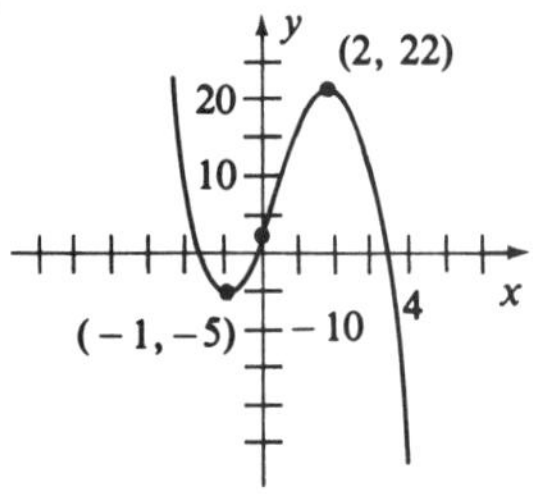

9.

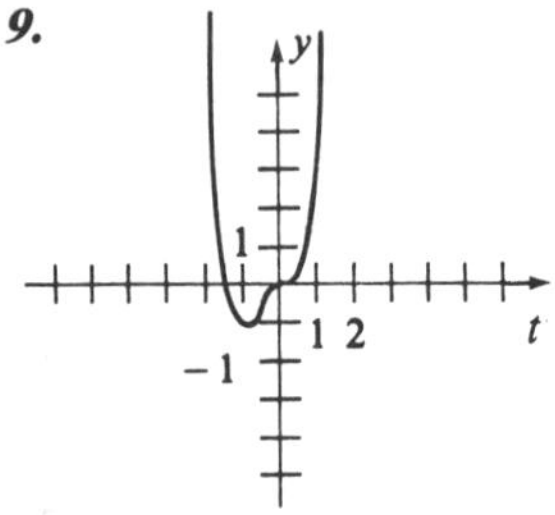

11.

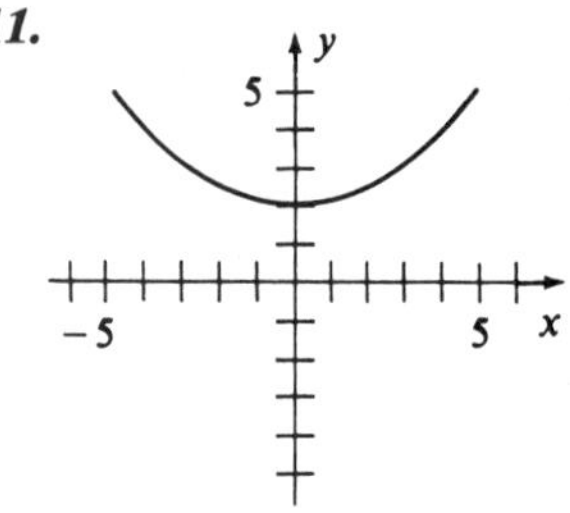

13.

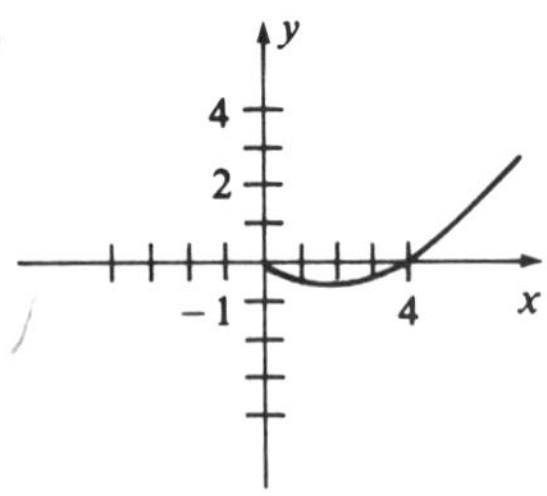

15.

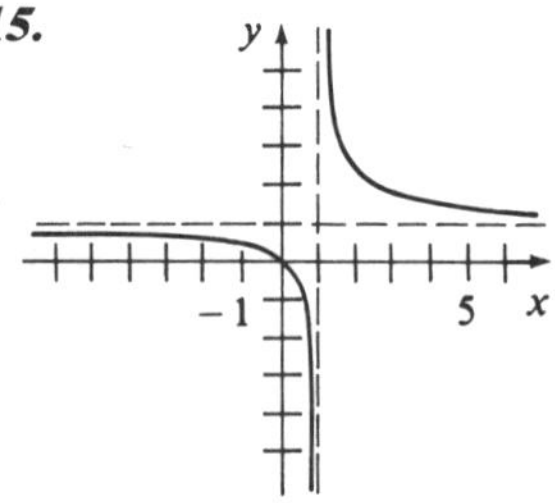

17.

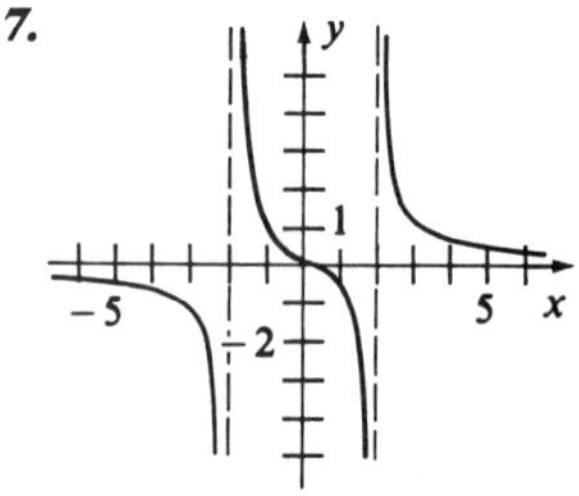

19.

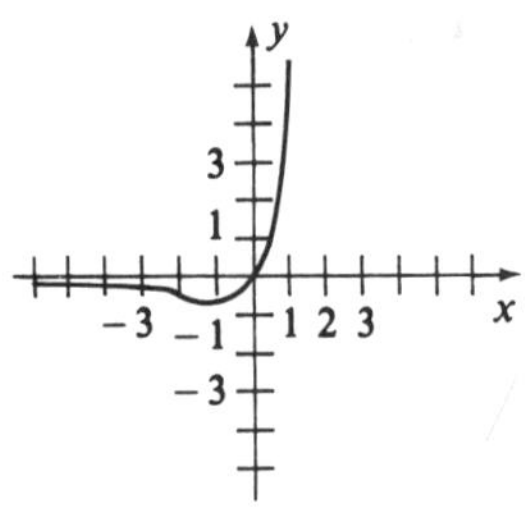

21.

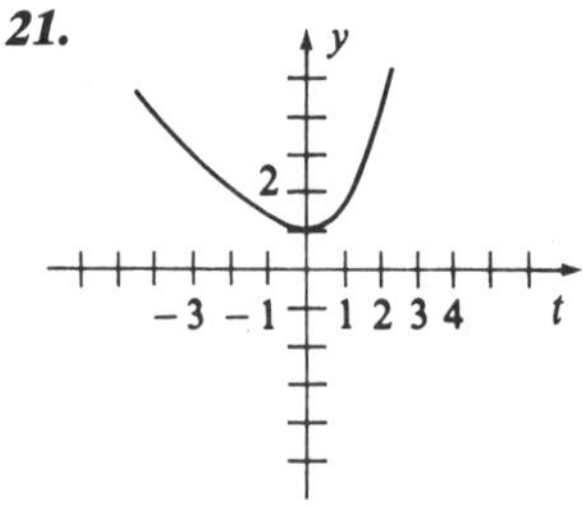

23.

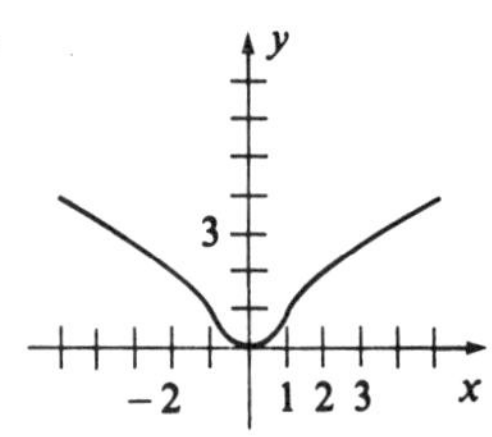

25.

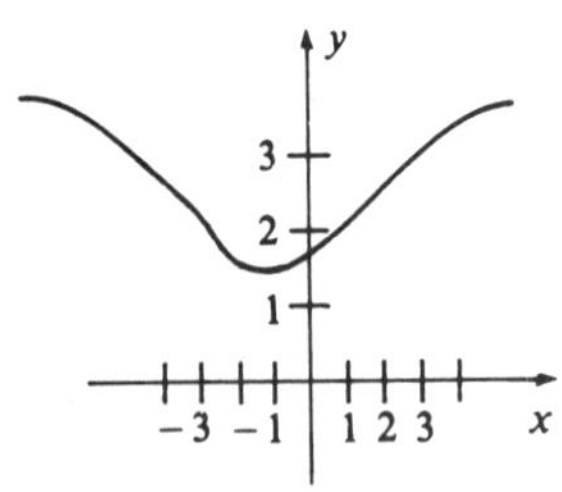

EXERCISES 11.6
page 530

1. abs. min $(-3/4, -41/8)$

3. no abs. extremum

5. abs. min $(1, -4)$

7. abs. max $(4, 5)$; abs. min $(1, -4)$

9. abs. max $(2, 19)$; abs. min $(-3, -1)$ and $(0, -1)$

11. abs. max $(2, 13/3)$; abs. min $(-1, -1/6)$

13. abs. max $(-2, 25/3)$; abs. min $(2, -7/3)$

15. abs. max $(2, 2)$; abs. min $(4, 4/3)$

17. abs. max $(2, 1)$; abs. min $(3, 1/4)$

19. no abs. extremum

21. abs. max $(-1, 1/4)$; abs. min $(1, 1/8)$

23. abs. max $(3/2, 2e^{-3/2})$; abs. min $(0, -1)$

25. abs. max $(2, \ln 4)$

27. abs. max $(e, 1/e)$; abs. min $(1, 0)$

31. (*c*)

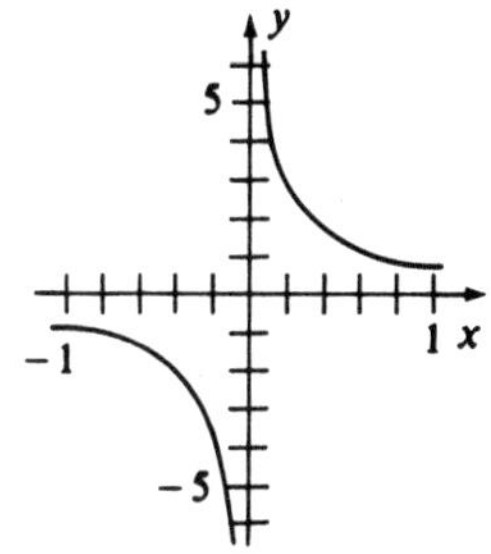

EXERCISES 11.7 page 540

1. 3000

3. \$3600

5. 3333

7. 144 ft

9. (*a*) $A(x) = 0.0025x + 80 + \dfrac{10{,}000}{x}$
(*b*) $x = 2000$
(*c*) $x = 2000$
(*d*) same result

13. 750 yds × 1500 yds; 1,125,000 sq. yds

15. $10\sqrt{2}$ ft × $40\sqrt{2}$ ft

17. 16/3 in × 16/3 in × 4/3 in

19. ≈5.04 in × 5.04 in × 5.04 in

21. $\frac{2}{3}\sqrt[3]{9}$ ft. × $\sqrt[3]{9}$ ft. × $\frac{2}{5}\sqrt[3]{9}$ ft.

23. $r = 4\sqrt[3]{\dfrac{2}{3\pi}}$ in; $h = 4\sqrt[3]{\dfrac{9}{4\pi}}$ in.

25. 250; \$62,500; \$250

27. 141; 14,142

Ch. 11 REVIEW EXERCISES page 545

1. (*a*) f increasing on $(-\infty, 1) \cup (1, \infty)$
(*b*) no relative extrema
(*c*) concave up on $(1, \infty)$
concave down on $(-\infty, 1)$
(*d*) $(1, -17/3)$

3. (*a*) f increasing on $(1, \infty)$
(*b*) rel. min at $(1, 0)$
(*c*) concave down on $(1, \infty)$
(*d*) no inflection point

5. (*a*) f increasing on $(-\infty, -1) \cup (-1, \infty)$
(*b*) no relative extrema
(*c*) concave up on $(-\infty, -1)$
concave down on $(-1, \infty)$
(*d*) no inflection point

7. (*a*) f increasing on $(-\infty, \infty)$
(*b*) no relative extrema
(*c*) concave up on $(-\infty, \infty)$
(*d*) no inflection point

9. (*a*) f increasing on $(0, \infty)$
(*b*) no relative extrema
(*c*) concave down on $(0, \infty)$
(*d*) no inflection point

11.

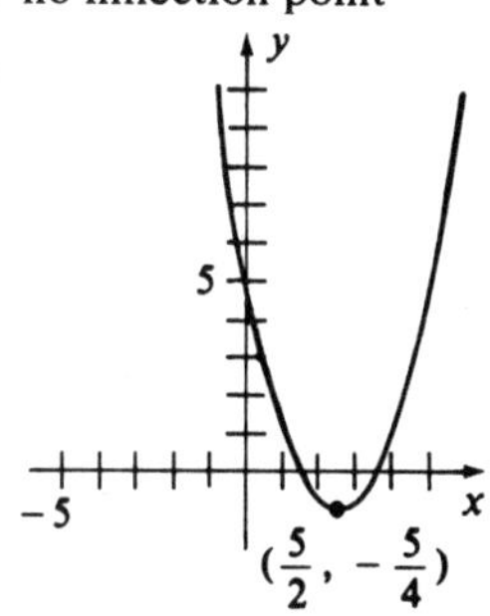

13.

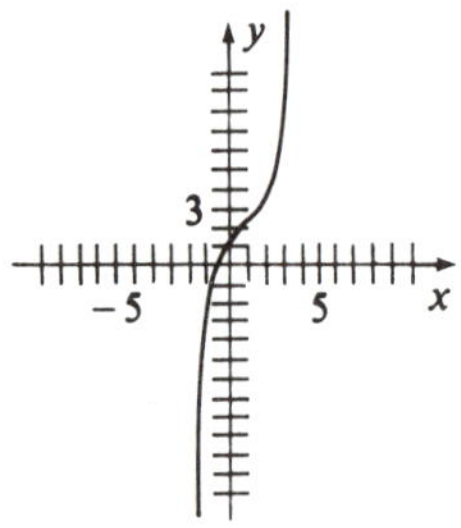

15.

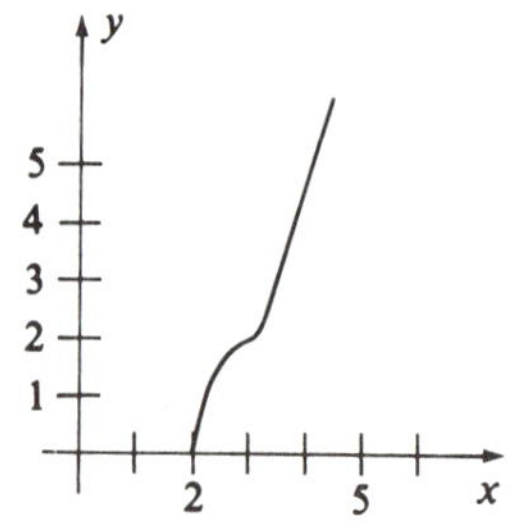

17.

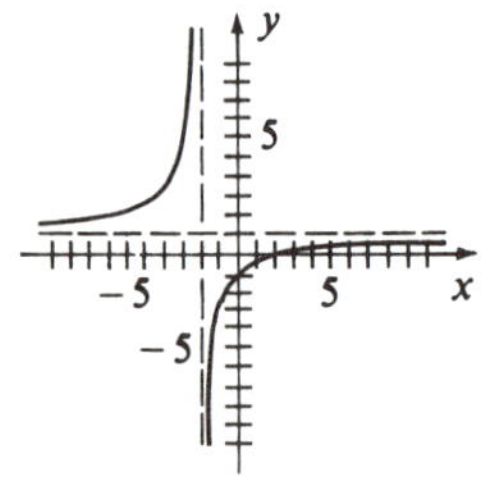

19.

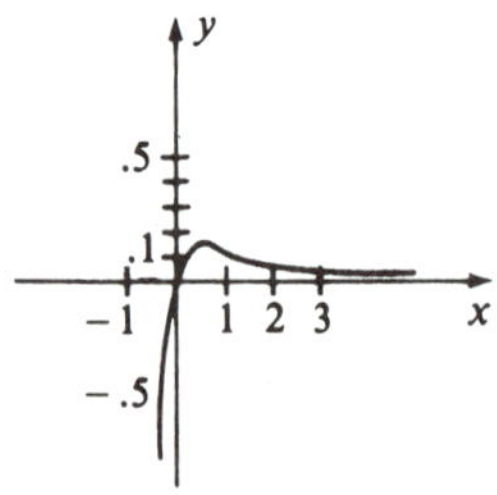

21.

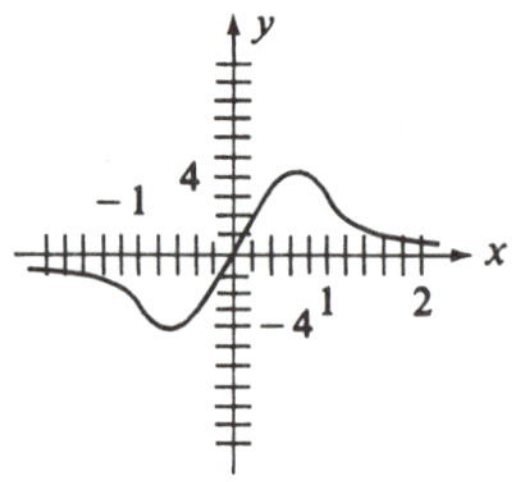

23.

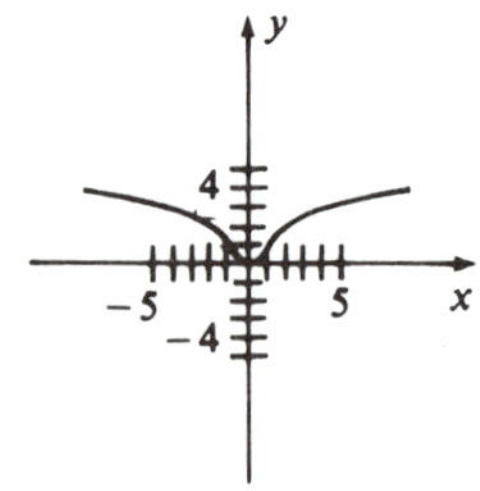

25. abs. min $\left(-\frac{3}{4}, -\frac{25}{8}\right)$

27. abs. max $(1, e^{-1})$

29. abs. max $\left(2, \frac{5}{3}\right)$; abs. min $(0, 1)$

31. abs. max $\left(1, \frac{1}{2}\right)$; abs. min $(0, 0)$

33. abs. max $\left(3, \frac{8}{3}\right)$; abs. min $(1, 0)$

35. abs. max $\left(\frac{1}{\sqrt{2}}, \frac{1}{\sqrt{2}} e^{-1/2}\right)$; abs. min $(0, 0)$

37. \$4000

39. (*a*) $A(x) = 0.001x + 100 + \dfrac{4000}{x}$ (*b*) 2000 units

41. year 10

43. 20,000 cases

Chapter 12

EXERCISES 12.1 page 551

11. (*b*) $G(x) = 2x + C$

(*c*)

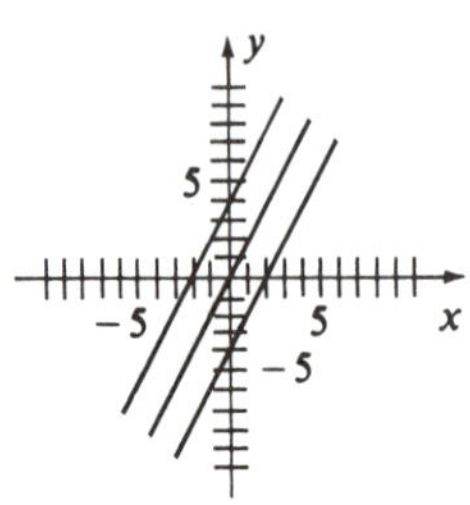

13. (*b*) $G(x) = \frac{1}{3}x^3 + C$

(*c*)

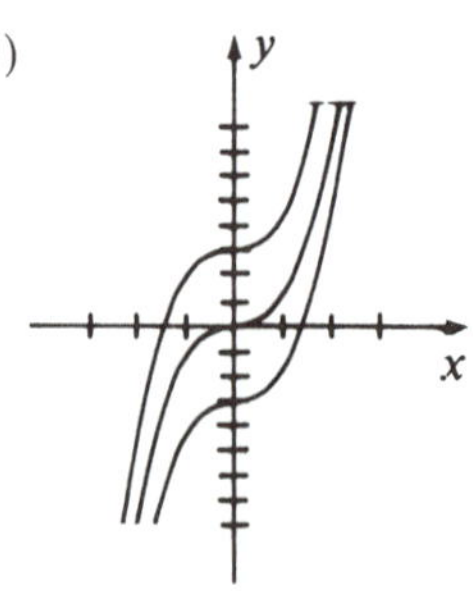

15. (*b*) $G(x) = \ln x + C$

(*c*)

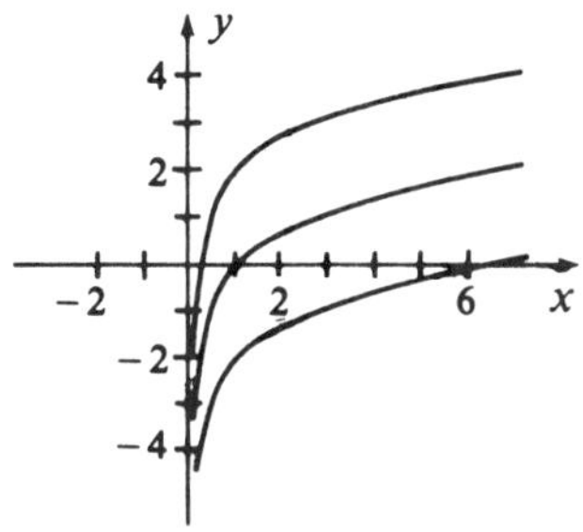

17. (*b*) $G(x) = \dfrac{1}{x^2+1} + C$

(*c*)

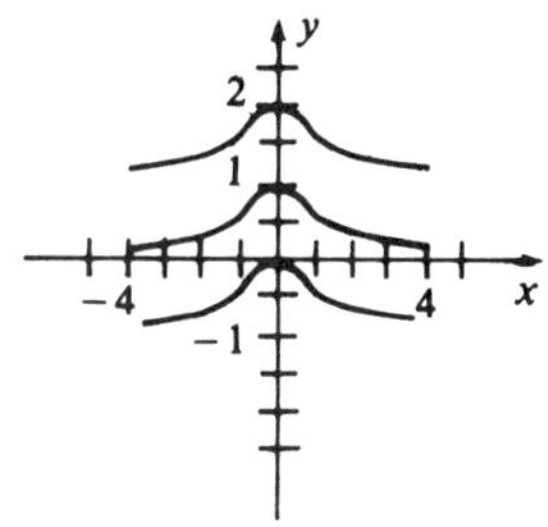

EXERCISES 12.2
page 560

1. $\sqrt{2}x + C$ **3.** $\frac{3}{5}x^{5/3} + C$ **5.** $-\frac{2}{x} + C$ **7.** $\frac{2\pi}{3}t^{3/2} + C$

9. $\frac{1}{3}x^3 + \frac{1}{2}x^2 - \frac{1}{2}x^{-2} + C$ **11.** $\frac{2}{3}x^{3/2} + 6x^{1/2} + C$ **13.** $-\frac{1}{x} - 3x^{1/3} + 2x^{1/2} + C$

15. $\frac{1}{3}x^3 - 2x - \frac{1}{x} + C$ **17.** $4e^x + C$ **19.** $x + \frac{3^x}{\ln 3} + C$

21. $\frac{1}{2}x^2 + x - \ln x - \frac{1}{x} + C$ **23.** $\frac{1}{3}x^3 + \frac{1}{2}x^2 - x - \ln x + C$

25. $f(x) = x^3 + 2x^2 - x - 5$ **27.** $f(x) = x + \ln x$

29. $f(x) = \sqrt{x}$ **31.** $f(x) = e^x + \frac{1}{2}x^2 + 2$

33. (*a*) $R(x) = -0.0045x^2 + 12x$ (*b*) $p = d(x) = -0.0045x + 12$

35. 5000 units per month; \$34,000 per month

37. 3.375 parts per million

39. $N(t) = -t^3 + 6t^2 + 45t$; 212 sets

EXERCISES 12.3
page 571

1. $\frac{1}{5}(4x+3)^5 + C$ **3.** $\frac{1}{3}(x^3 - 2x)^3 + C$ **5.** $-\frac{1}{2(2x^2+3)^2} + C$

7. $\frac{2}{3}(t^3+2)^{3/2} + C$ **9.** $\frac{1}{20}(x^2-1)^{10} + C$ **11.** $\frac{1}{4}(x^{2/3}-1)^6 + C$

13. $\frac{2}{3}(x^3-1)^{1/2} + C$ **15.** $\frac{1}{6}\ln(3x^2-1) + C$ **17.** $\frac{1}{2}e^{2t+3} + C$

19. $\frac{1}{3}e^{x^3-1} + C$ **21.** $2e^{\sqrt{x}} + C$ **23.** $-\frac{1}{6(e^{3x}+x^3)^2} + C$

25. $\frac{1}{2}e^{x^2} - \frac{1}{2}\ln(x^2+2) + C$ **27.** $\frac{1}{4}(\ln u)^4 + C$

29. $-\frac{1}{252}(1-v)^7(28v^2 + 7v + 1) + C$ **31.** $f(x) = \frac{1}{2}[(2x-1)^5 + 5]$

33. $f(x)=e^{-x^2+1}-1$

35. $N(t)=21{,}000-\dfrac{20{,}000}{\sqrt{1+0.2t}}$; 6,858

37. $N(t)=60(3-2e^{-0.05t})$

39. $A(t)=\dfrac{r}{a}(1-e^{-at})$

EXERCISES 12.4 page 577

1. $\frac{1}{4}e^{2x}(2x-1)+C$

3. xe^x+C

5. $-\frac{x}{x+4}+\ln(x+4)+C$

7. $\frac{x^2}{4}(2\ln 2x-1)+C$

9. $\frac{x^3}{9}(3\ln 2x-1)+C$

11. $\frac{2}{9}x^{3/2}(3\ln\sqrt{x}-1)+C$

13. $\frac{(x^2+2)^6(3x^2-1)}{42}+C$

15. $-(x^2+2x+2)e^{-x}+C$

17. $\frac{1}{2}(x^2-1)\ln(x+1)-\frac{1}{4}(x+1)(x-3)+C$

19. $-40(t+20)e^{-0.05t}+820$; 231.39 million metric tons

Ch. 12 REVIEW EXERCISES page 578

1. $\frac{1}{5}x^5-\frac{1}{2}x^4-\frac{1}{x}+C$

3. $\frac{2}{7}x^{7/2}-\frac{1}{3}x^3+\frac{2}{3}x^{3/2}-x+C$

5. $\frac{1}{3}(2x+1)^{3/2}+C$

7. $\frac{1}{33}(x^3+2)^{11}+C$

9. $-e^{-2x}+C$

11. $\frac{1}{e^{-x}+x}+C$

13. $(\ln x)^2+C$

15. $\frac{2}{15}(x+1)^{3/2}(3x-2)+C$

17. $-(1+x)e^{-x}+C$

19. $f(x)=x^3-2x^2+x+1$

21. $f(x)=x+e^{-x}+1$

23. \$6,740

25. $V(t)=1900(t-10)^2+10{,}000$; \$40,400

27. $N(t)=15{,}000\sqrt{1+0.4t}+85{,}000$; 112,659

Chapter 13

EXERCISES 13.1 page 588

1. 6

3. $18\frac{2}{3}$

5. $4\frac{2}{3}$

7. $\frac{7}{12}$

9. $2\frac{2}{3}$

11. 56

13. $1-\frac{1}{e}$

15. $e^2+e^{-2}-2$

17. $2\ln 4$

19. $18\frac{2}{15}$

21. $2\ln 2-\frac{3}{4}$

23. $1-3e^{-2}$

25. $24\frac{1}{5}$

27. $2\frac{2}{15}$

29. $8\frac{2}{3}$

31. $\ln(1+e)-\ln 2$

33. (*a*) \$4100 (*b*) \$900

35. (*a*) \$2800 (*b*) \$219.20

37. 120.3 billion metric tons

39. (*a*) 25°F (*b*) 43°F

41. 2.24 million dollars

EXERCISES 13.2 page 598

1. 6 *3.* 8 *5.* $39\frac{1}{3}$ *7.* $10\frac{2}{3}$

9. $17\frac{1}{3}$ *11.* $52\frac{1}{12}$ *13.* $37\frac{2}{9}$ *15.* $e^2-e-\frac{3}{2}$

17. $\ln 5$ *19.* $5\ln 5-4$ *21.* $12\frac{2}{3}$

EXERCISES 13.3 page 607

1. 3 *3.* $\frac{1}{4}$ *5.* $2(e^2-e^{-1})$ *7.* $2\frac{1}{2}$

9. $7\frac{1}{3}$ *11.* e^3-4+e^{-1} *13.* $16\frac{1}{2}$ *15.* $11\frac{1}{3}$

17. $11\frac{5}{12}$ *19.* $e^2-e-\ln 2$ *21.* $20\frac{5}{6}$ *23.* $\frac{1}{12}$

25. $1\frac{4}{15}$ *27.* 42.8 billion metric tons *29.* 57,179 people

EXERCISES 13.4 page 616

1. 7 *3.* (*a*) 0.125 (*b*) 0.24 (*c*) 0.29

5. (*a*) 18.5 (*b*) 18.64 (*c*) 18.66

7. (*a*) 25 (*b*) 21.12 (*c*) 19.88

9. $S_n=\frac{(n+1)(2n+1)}{6n^2}$; $\lim_{n\to\infty} S_n=\int_0^1 x^2\,dx=\frac{1}{3}$

EXERCISES 13.5 page 626

1. \$16,667 *3.* \$3500 *5.* \$341,333, \$170,667 *7.* $5\frac{1}{2}$

9. $1\frac{1}{3}$ *11.* $\frac{1}{8}$ *13.* $2\frac{8}{9}$ *17.* 26°F *19.* 245,912

21. \$$6\frac{1}{3}$ million

EXERCISES 13.6 page 637

1. $\frac{2}{3}$ *3.* 2 *5.* $\frac{1}{2}e^4$ *7.* 1 *9.* $\frac{1}{2}$ *11.* divergent

13. 1 *15.* divergent *17.* 0 *19.* (*a*) 0.0995 (*b*) 0.3012 *21.* 0.0183

Ch. 13 REVIEW EXERCISES page 639

1. −6 *3.* 242 *5.* $\frac{1}{2}\ln 5$ *7.* $\frac{1}{4}(3e^4+1)$ *9.* \$14,350 *11.* 15

13. $\frac{2}{3}$ *15.* e^2-3 *17.* $\frac{1}{2}$ *19.* \$270,000 *21.* $\frac{1}{4}\ln 5$

Chapter 14

EXERCISES 14.1 page 645

1. $f(1,2)=7, f(2,1)=9, f(-1,2)=1, f(2,-1)=1$
3. $g(1,2)=4+3\sqrt{2}$, $g(2,1)=8+\sqrt{2}$, $g(0,4)=2$, $g(4,9)=56$
5. $g(1,1,1)=e$, $g(1,0,1)=1$, $g(-1,-1,-1)=-e$
7. $h(1,e)=1$, $h(e,1)=-1$, $h(e,e)=0$
9. All real values of x and y
11. All real values of u and v with $u \neq v$
13. All real values of x, y and z
15. All real values of u and v satisfying $u^2+v^2 \leq 4$
17. (a) $R(x,y)=-\frac{1}{5}x^2-\frac{1}{4}y^2-\frac{1}{5}xy+200x+160y$
    (b) The set of points (x,y) satisfying $(1/5)x+(1/10)y \leq 200$, $(1/10)x+(1/4)y \leq 160$, $x \geq 0, y \geq 0$
19. (a) $R(x,y)=-0.005x^2-0.003y^2-0.002xy+20x+15y$
    (b) The set of points (x,y) satisfying $0.005x+0.001y \leq 20$, $0.001x+0.003y \leq 15$, $x \geq 0, y \geq 0$
21. All values of P and T with $P \neq 0$ (b) $V=11.10$ liters

EXERCISES 14.2 page 655

1. $2x, 2y$
3. $\frac{1}{2}\sqrt{\frac{v}{u}}, \frac{1}{2}\sqrt{\frac{u}{v}}$
5. $3(2s-t)(s^2-st+t^2)^2, 3(2t-s)(s^2-st+t^2)^2$
7. $\frac{4xy^2}{(x^2+y^2)^2}, \frac{-4x^2y}{(x^2+y^2)^2}$
9. $y\,e^{xy+1}, x\,e^{xy+1}$
11. e^{u+v}, e^{u+v}
13. $\ln y+\frac{y}{x}, \ln x+\frac{x}{y}$
15. $\frac{1}{u+2v}, \frac{2}{u+2v}$
17. $e^u \ln v, \frac{e^u}{v}$
19. $\frac{e^s}{e^s+e^t}, \frac{e^t}{e^s+e^t}$
21. $yz+y^2+2xz, xz+2xy+z^2, xy+2yz+x^2$
23. $st\,e^{rst}, rt\,e^{rst}, rs\,e^{rst}$
25. $\frac{2u}{u^2+v^2+w^2}, \frac{2v}{u^2+v^2+w^2}, \frac{2w}{u^2+v^2+w^2}$
27. $\frac{1}{2}\sqrt{\frac{yz}{x}}+yz\,e^{xyz}+\frac{1}{x}, \frac{1}{2}\sqrt{\frac{xz}{y}}+xz\,e^{xyz}+\frac{1}{y}, \frac{1}{2}\sqrt{\frac{xy}{z}}+xy\,e^{xyz}+\frac{1}{z}$
29. $f_x(-1,2)=2, f_y(-1,2)=2$
31. $f_x(1,1,2)=2, f_y(1,1,2)=2, f_z(1,1,2)=4$
33. $f_{xx}=2, f_{yy}=4, f_{xy}=f_{yx}=-2$

35. $f_{xx}=\dfrac{y^2}{(x^2+y^2)^{3/2}}$, $f_{yy}=\dfrac{x^2}{(x^2+y^2)^{3/2}}$, $f_{xy}=f_{yx}=\dfrac{-xy}{(x^2+y^2)^{3/2}}$

37. $f_{xx}=\dfrac{4y}{(x-y)^3}$, $f_{yy}=\dfrac{4x}{(x-y)^3}$, $f_{xy}=f_{yx}=\dfrac{-2(x+y)}{(x-y)^3}$

39. $f_{xx}=\dfrac{e^{-x/y}}{y^2}$, $f_{yy}=\dfrac{x(x-2y)\,e^{-x/y}}{y^4}$, $f_{xy}=f_{yx}=\dfrac{(y-x)\,e^{-x/y}}{y^3}$

41. $f_{xx}=-\dfrac{1}{4x}\sqrt{\dfrac{y}{x}}+\dfrac{1}{y^2}e^{x/y}-\dfrac{1}{x^2}$, $f_{yy}=-\dfrac{1}{4y}\sqrt{\dfrac{x}{y}}+\dfrac{x(x+2y)}{y^4}e^{x/y}+\dfrac{1}{y^2}$

$f_{xy}=f_{yx}=\dfrac{1}{4\sqrt{xy}}-\dfrac{(x+y)}{y^3}e^{x/y}$

43. (*a*) $7\frac{1}{2}$ units/unit change in labor, 40 units/unit change in capital
(*b*) Yes

45. \$30/unit change in finished products, −\$25/unit change in unfinished products

47. 0.039 liters/degree, −0.015 liters/millimeter of mercury

EXERCISES 14.3 page 665

1. (0, 0); (0, 0) max; $f(0, 0)=1$ **3.** (1, 2); (1, 2) saddle point

5. (8, −6); (8, −6) min; $f(8, -6)=-41$

7. (1, 2) and (2, 2); (1, 2) saddle point, (2, 2) min; $f(2, 2)=-2$

9. $\left(-\frac{1}{3}, \frac{11}{3}\right)$ and (1, 5); $\left(-\frac{1}{3}, \frac{11}{3}\right)$ saddle point, (1, 5) min; $f(1, 5)=-13$

11. (0, 0) and (1, 1); (0, 0) saddle point, (1, 1) min; $f(1, 1)=-3$

13. (0, 0); (0, 0) min; $f(0, 0)=1$ **15.** (0, 0); (0, 0) min; $f(0, 0)=0$

17. 200 finished units and 100 unfinished units; \$10,500

19. 6 in × 6 in × 3 in

EXERCISES 14.4 page 672

1. $\frac{3}{4}$ at $\left(\frac{3}{4}, \frac{1}{4}\right)$ **3.** 21 at (4, 5)

5. 4 at $\left(\sqrt{2}, \frac{\sqrt{2}}{2}\right)$ and $\left(-\sqrt{2}, -\frac{\sqrt{2}}{2}\right)$

7. max of 8 at $(2\sqrt{2}, 2\sqrt{2})$ and $(-2\sqrt{2}, -2\sqrt{2})$, min of −8 at $(2\sqrt{2}, -2\sqrt{2})$ and $(-2\sqrt{2}, 2\sqrt{2})$

9. 140 finished and 60 unfinished units

11. \$15,000 on newspaper and \$45,000 on TV

13. $\frac{4}{3}\sqrt[3]{\frac{18}{\pi}}$ in radius and $2\sqrt[3]{\frac{18}{\pi}}$ in height

Ch. 14 REVIEW EXERCISES page 673

1. $f(0, 1)=0$, $f(1, 0)=0$, $f(1, 1)=1/2$; No

3. The set of all ordered pairs of real numbers (u, v) such that $u \geq 0$ and $u \neq v$

5. $2xy^3+3y^2+\dfrac{1}{y}$, $3x^2y^2+6xy-\dfrac{x}{y^2}$

7. $\dfrac{y(y-x)(y+x)}{(x^2+y^2)^2}, \dfrac{x(x-y)(x+y)}{(x^2+y^2)^2}$

9. $2x(1+x^2+y^2)\,e^{x^2+y^2}, 2y(1+x^2+y^2)\,e^{x^2+y^2}$

11. $f_{xx}=6x-4y, f_{xy}=f_{yx}=-4x, f_{yy}=2$

13. $g_{xx}=2(1+2x^2)\,e^{x^2+y^2}, g_{xy}=g_{yx}=4xy\,e^{x^2+y^2}, g_{yy}=2(1+2y^2)\,e^{x^2+y^2}$

15. $f_x(1,1,0)=3, f_y(1,1,0)=3, f_z(1,1,0)=-2$

17. $(8,-2)$; $(8,-2)$ saddle point

19. $(0,0)$; $(0,0)$ min; $f(0,0)=1$

21. $-\dfrac{352}{121}$ at $\left(\dfrac{12}{11}, \dfrac{20}{11}\right)$

23. max of 26 at $(5,-5)$ and min of -24 at $(-5,5)$

25. (*a*) $R(x,y)=-0.02x^2-0.05y^2-0.2xy+80x+60y$
(*b*) The set of all points (x, y) satisfying

$$0.02x+0.1y \le 80$$
$$0.1x+0.05y \le 60$$
$$x \ge 0, y \ge 0$$

(*c*) 15,300

27. 337.5 yd × 900 yd

Algebra Review

EXERCISES A.2 page A4

1. 9 **3.** $\dfrac{27}{8}$ **5.** 3 **7.** 2 **9.** $-8x$

11. $\dfrac{2}{a^2}$ **13.** $y^{1/6}$ **15.** $\dfrac{b^4}{a^6c^4}$ **17.** $\dfrac{x^6y^4}{z^4}$

19. $\dfrac{1}{x^{3/2}y^4}$ **21.** $\dfrac{64x^6}{y^4}$ **23.** $2x^2y$ **25.** $12x^3y^4$

27. $2x^{4/3}y^{1/2}$ **29.** $\dfrac{3\sqrt{x}}{2x}$ **31.** $\dfrac{\sqrt{2xy}}{y}$

EXERCISES A.3 page A7

1. $9x^2+3x+1$ **3.** $4y^2+y+8$ **5.** $-x-1$ **7.** $x^2+6x-16$

9. $12x^2+5xy-25y^2$ **11.** $x^2+4xy+4y^2$ **13.** $9x^2-36x+36$

15. $-9x^2+4$ **17.** $12x^3+17x^2+18x+8$ **19.** x^3+3x^2-x-3

EXERCISES A.4 page A11

1. $2x^3(2x^2-6x-3)$ **3.** $7a^2(a^2+7ab-6b^2)$ **5.** $(3c-2d)(2a+b)$

7. $(z-2)(xy+1)$ **9.** $3(2x-y)(2x+y)$ **11.** $(2x+1)^2$

13. $(3a-2b)^2$ **15.** $(x-5)(x+3)$ **17.** $3(3x+2)(2x-1)$

19. $(3x-4y)(3x+4y)$ **21.** $2(4a+3b)(a-b)$

23. $(3x+4y)(9x^2-12xy+16y^2)$ **25.** $(x-3)(x^2+3x+9)$

EXERCISES A.5 page A16

1. $\dfrac{x-1}{x-2}$ *3.* $\dfrac{3(2t+1)}{2t-1}$ *5.* -8 *7.* $\dfrac{1}{2}(3x-1)$

9. $\dfrac{8ab-6a+5b}{15ab}$ *11.* $\dfrac{-(x+27)}{(x+3)(x-3)^2}$

13. $\dfrac{-x(2x+11)}{(2x+5)(2x-1)(x+3)}$ *15.* $\dfrac{2(x+1)}{x+2}$ *17.* $\dfrac{x+1}{x-1}$

19. $\dfrac{y-x}{(xy)^2}$ *21.* $\dfrac{a+2\sqrt{ab}+b}{a-b}$

23. $\dfrac{a+a\sqrt{a}}{1-a}$ *25.* $\dfrac{x-1}{x\sqrt{x}+x}$

EXERCISES A.6 page A20

1. $a=2$ *3.* $x=5$ *5.* $a=3$ *7.* $x=-5$

9. $x=-\dfrac{4}{9}$ *11.* $x=4$ or $x=-3$ *13.* $z=0$ or $z=4$ or $z=-4$

15. $a=2$ or $a=-1$ *17.* $x=4$ *19.* $x=6$

INDEX